COMPENDIUM OF INTERNATIONAL MIGRATION LAW INSTRUMENTS

COMPENDIUM OF INTERNATIONAL MIGRATION LAW INSTRUMENTS

compiled and edited by

Richard Perruchoud

and

Katarína Tömölová

IOM International Organization for Migration

T•M•C•ASSER PRESS

Published by T·M·C·ASSER PRESS
P.O. Box 16163, 2500 BD The Hague, The Netherlands
<www.asserpress.nl>

T·M·C·ASSER PRESS' English language books are distributed exclusively by:

Cambridge University Press, The Edinburgh Building, Shaftesbury Road,
Cambridge CB2 2RU, UK,
or
for customers in the USA, Canada and Mexico:
Cambridge University Press, 100 Brook Hill Drive, West Nyack, NY 10994-2133, USA
<www.cambridge.org>

INTERNATIONAL ORGANIZATION FOR MIGRATION

17 route des Morillons, 1211 Geneva 19, Switzerland
Tel: +41.22.717 91 11; Fax: +41.22.798 61 50;
E-mail: hq@iom.int; Internet: http://www.iom.int

IOM is committed to the principle that humane and orderly migration benefits migrants and society. As an intergovernmental body, IOM acts with its partners in the international community to: assist in meeting the operational challenges of migration; advance understanding of migration issues; encourage social and economic development through migration; and uphold the human dignity and well-being of migrants.

ISBN 978-90-6704-248-2 (hardback)
ISBN 978-90-6704-249-9 (paperback)

PRINTED IN THE NETHERLANDS

INTRODUCTION

Traditionally, the regulation of migratory movements was left to individual State sovereignty, where States had the sole authority over their territory and population. With the increase in global movements, States came to recognise the need for regional and international cooperation in this field; thus, the number of norms of global scope has increased over time.

There is, however, no worldwide legislation establishing an exact legal framework for the movement of persons with which States must comply. Currently, "international migration law" is an umbrella term for the complex web of legal relationships among persons, groups and States that together regulate the movements of individuals. It is a branch of law that has developed over time and, indeed, continues to develop with the ever-increasing need for international cooperation and regulation involving States, migrants and international civil society in general.

This publication seeks to assist readers, be they students, academics, practitioners or migrants themselves, to better orientate themselves in the web of norms and principles existing at the international level. The focus of the compendium is on bringing together a comprehensive compilation of universal instruments with varying degrees of legal force – from authoritative international treaties, through customary international law, to the sets of principles and guidelines which, although non-binding, are nonetheless of clear contemporary relevance and can contribute to the progressive development of law in areas not yet covered by "hard" obligations. To further this end, this volume is being released as a companion to *International Migration Law: Developing Paradigms and Key Challenges*,* in order that the readers have access not merely to a comprehensive compilation of the relevant norms in abstract, but also to how these norms have been applied and are developing in various concrete contexts.

The instruments listed in this compendium are grouped in fourteen thematic sections, each including both "hard law" and selected "soft law" standards. The structure follows a general legal outline, by introducing first the common human rights standards (Section 1), followed by the more specific "migrant"-related conventions and recommendations of the United Nations and the International Labour Organization (Section 2). The subsequent sections then present core documents regulating specific migration-related issues, such as nationality and statelessness (Section 3), trafficking and smuggling (Section 4), international maritime law (Section 5), State security (Section 6) and detention (Section 7). The legal sources covering diplomatic and consular protection, the movement of service providers under GATS, migration and development, and the rights of

* R. Cholewinsky, R. Perruchoud and E. MacDonald, eds., *International Migration Law – Developing Paradigms and Key Challenges* (The Hague, T.M.C. Asser Press 2007).

minorities can be found in Sections 8, 9, 10 and 11. Finally, the reader will find fundamental instruments regulating forced migration, in terms mainly of the protection of refugees (Section 12), internally displaced persons (Section 13) and civilian population under international humanitarian law (Section 14).

All documents are published in their official English version, with the original source cited in each. Additionally, the text of each convention or agreement is accompanied by a list of State parties who have signed or ratified it; as relevant, it also indicates in brackets with an asterisk any reservations made to specific provisions of the instrument in question. The editors, however, encourage readers to consult the original sources for any details on declarations or for updates on the status of each treaty.

Most of the core instruments have been reproduced in full. Others, however, represent only those selected parts of the original document that relate directly to migrants, their rights, or the migration process itself. Of course, any act of selection is by definition subjective and, in particular in the context of a field as vast and complex as that of international migration law, it is impossible to be absolutely comprehensive. However, the editors hope that, by providing a wide degree of relevant excerpts of migration-related laws alongside the full versions of all of the central instruments in the field, the readers, if they do not find precisely what they are looking for in these pages, will at the very least find precisely where to look.

Geneva, June 2007

Richard PERRUCHOUD
Katarína TÖMÖLOVÁ

TABLE OF CONTENTS

ABBREVIATIONS

CAT	Convention against Torture and Other Cruel, Inhuman or Degrading Treatment or Punishment / Committee against Torture
CCPR	International Covenant on Civil and Political Rights
CEDAW	Convention on the Elimination of All Forms of Discrimination against Women / Committee on the Elimination of Discrimination Against Women
CERD	Committee on the Elimination of Racial Discrimination
CESCR	Committee on Economic, Social and Cultural Rights
CRC	Convention on the Rights of the Child / Committee on the Rights of the Child
GATS	General Agreement on Trade in Services
HRC	Human Rights Committee
ICRC	International Committee of the Red Cross
ILO	International Labour Organization
IMO	International Maritime Organization
IOM	International Organization for Migration
L.N.T.S.	League of Nations Treaty Series
UN	United Nations
U.N. Doc.	United Nations Document
UNESCO	United Nations Educational, Scientific and Cultural Organization
U.N.G.A. Res.	United Nations General Assembly Resolution
UNHCR	United Nations High Commissioner for Refugees
U.N.T.S.	United Nations Treaty Series
WTO	World Trade Organization

SOURCE DATABASES AND USEFUL WEBSITES

ICRC	*International Committee of the Red Cross Database on International Humaniarian Law* Contains around 100 IHL treaties, commentaries on the Geneva Conventions and their Additional Protocols and an up-to-date list of the signatories as well as an implementation database. http://www.icrc.org/web/eng/siteeng0.nsf/iwpList2/Info_resources:IHL_databases
ILOLEX	*Database on International Labour Standards* ILOLEX is a trilingual database containing ILO Conventions and Recommendations, ratification information, comments of the Committee of Experts and the Committee on Freedom of Association, representations, complaints, interpretations, General Surveys, and numerous related documents. http://www.ilo.org/ilolex/index.htm
IMO	*International Maritime Organization* www.imo.org
IOM	*International Migration Law Database* Draws together relevant international conventions, regional and bilateral treaties, international and regional resolutions and declarations, and national legislation. www.iml.iom.int
UNESCO	*United Nations Educational, Scientific and Cultural Organization* www.unesco.org
UNHCHR	*United Nations High Commissioner for Human Rights* www.ohchr.org
UNHCR	*United Nations High Commissioner for Refugees* *Refworld* Is an information tool containing over 75,000 full-text searchable documents, including comprehensive in-depth reports, hundreds of detailed country maps, and recent UNHCR statistics. www.unhcr.org
UNTREATY	*United Nations Treaty Collection* Prepared and updated regularly by the Treaty Section of the Office of Legal Affairs of the United Nations, this on-line service offers access to over 158,000 records of treaties and related subsequent treaty actions. Please note that subscription to the database is necessary. http://untreaty.un.org/English/treaty.asp
WTO	*World Trade Organization* www.wto.org

Admiralty Law Guide	*Admiralty and Maritime Law Guide* Includes over 1,500 annotated links to admiralty law resources on the Internet and a growing database of admiralty case digests, opinions and international maritime conventions. http://www.admiraltylawguide.com/

1. HUMAN RIGHTS LAW

1.1 Treaties

Convention on the Political Rights of Women, 1952*

Adoption: 20 December 1952**
Entry into force: 7 July 1954
Parties: 120 (Status as of 1 April 2007)

AFGHANISTAN 16 Nov 1966 a, ALBANIA 12 May 1955 a (*VII, IX), ALGERIA 5 Aug 2004 a, ANGOLA 17 Sep 1986 a, ANTIGUA AND BARBUDA 25 Oct 1988 d, ARGENTINA 27 Feb 1961(*IX), AUSTRALIA 10 Dec 1974 a (*III), AUSTRIA 18 Apr 1969, BAHAMAS 16 Aug 1977 d, BANGLADESH 5 Oct 1998 a, BARBADOS 12 Jan 1973 a, BELARUS 11 Aug 1954, BELGIUM 20 May 1964 a, BOLIVIA 22 Sep 1970, BOSNIA AND HERZEGOVINA 1 Sep 1993 d, BRAZIL 13 Aug 1963, BULGARIA 17 Mar 1954 a (*VII), BURKINA FASO 9 Dec 1998 a, BURUNDI 18 Feb 1993 a, CANADA 30 Jan 1957 a, CENTRAL AFRICAN REPUBLIC 4 Sep 1962 d, CHILE 18 Oct 1967, COLOMBIA 5 Aug 1986 a, CONGO 15 Oct 1962 d, COSTA RICA 25 Jul 1967, CÔTE D'IVOIRE 18 Dec 1995 a, CROATIA 12 Oct 1992 d, CUBA 8 Apr 1954, CYPRUS 12 Nov 1968, CZECH REPUBLIC 22 Feb 1993 d, DEMOCRATIC REPUBLIC OF THE CONGO 12 Oct 1977 a, DENMARK 7 Jul 1954 (*III), DOMINICAN REPUBLIC 11 Dec 1953, ECUADOR 23 Apr 1954 (*I), EGYPT 8 Sep 1981 a, ETHIOPIA 21 Jan 1969, FIJI 12 Jun 1972 d (*III), FINLAND 6 Oct 1958 a (*III), FRANCE 22 Apr 1957, GABON 19 Apr 1967, GEORGIA 6 Jul 2005 a, GERMANY 4 Nov 1970 a (*III), GHANA 28 Dec 1965 a, GREECE 29 Dec 1953, GUATEMALA 7 Oct 1959 (*I, II, III, IX), GUINEA 24 Jan 1978, HAITI 12 Feb 1958, HUNGARY 20 Jan 1955 (*VII), ICELAND 30 Jun 1954, INDIA 1 Nov 1961 (*III), INDONESIA 16 Dec 1958 (*VII, IX), IRELAND 14 Nov 1968 a (*III), ISRAEL 6 Jul 1954, ITALY 6 Mar 1968 a (*III), JAMAICA 14 Aug 1966 a, JAPAN 13 Jul 1955, JORDAN 1 Jul 1992 a, KAZAKHSTAN 28 Mar 2000 a, KYRGYZSTAN 10 Feb 1997 a, LAO PEOPLE'S DEMOCRATIC REPUBLIC 28 Jan 1969 a, LATVIA 14 Apr 1992 a, LEBANON 5 Jun 1956, LESOTHO 4 Nov 1974 a (*III), LIBYAN ARAB JAMAHIRIYA 16 May 1989 a, LUXEMBOURG 1 Nov 1976, MADAGASCAR 12 Feb 1964 a, MALAWI 29 Jun 1966 a, MALI 16 Jul 1974 a, MALTA 9 Jul 1968 a (*III), MAURITANIA 4 May 1976 a, MAURITIUS 18 Jul 1969 d (*III), MEXICO 23 Mar 1981, MOLDOVA 26 Jan 1993 a, MONGOLIA 18 Aug 1965 a (*IV, V), MONTENEGRO 23 Oct 2006 d, MOROCCO 22 Nov 1976 a, NEPAL 26 Apr 1966 a (*IX), NETHERLANDS 30 Jul 1971, NEW ZEALAND 22 May 1968 a (*III), NICARAGUA 17 Jan 1957 a, NIGER 7 Dec 1964 d, NIGERIA 17 Nov 1980, NORWAY 24 Aug 1956, PAKISTAN 7 Dec 1954 (*III), PAPUA NEW GUINEA 27 Jan 1982 a, PARAGUAY 22 Feb 1990, PERU 1 Jul 1975 a, PHILIPPINES 12 Sep 1957, POLAND 11 Aug 1954 (*VII), REPUBLIC OF KOREA 23 Jun 1959 a, ROMANIA 6 Aug 1954, RUSSIAN FEDERATION 3 May 1954 (*VII), RWANDA 26 Sep 2003 a, SAINT VINCENT AND THE GRENADINES 27 Apr 1999 d (*III), SENEGAL 2 May 1963 d, SERBIA 12 Mar 2001 d, SIERRA LEONE 25 Jul 1962 a (*III), SLOVAKIA 28 May 1993 d, SLOVENIA 6 Jul 1992 d, SOLOMON ISLANDS 3 Sep 1981 a, SPAIN 14 Jan 1974 a (*I, II, III), SWAZILAND 20 Jul 1970 a (*III), SWEDEN 31 Mar 1954, TAJIKISTAN 7 Jun 1999 a, THAILAND 30 Nov 1954, THE FORMER YUGOSLAV REPUBLIC OF MACEDONIA 18 Jan 1994 d, TRINIDAD AND TOBAGO 24 Jun 1966 a, TUNISIA 24 Jan 1968 a (*IX), TURKEY 26 Jan 1960, TURKMENISTAN 11 OCT 1999 A, UGANDA 21 Jun

* Source: U.N.G.A. Res. 640 (VII), 193 U.N.T.S. 135.

** The Convention was opened for signature on 31 March 1953.

1995 a, UKRAINE 15 Nov 1954 (*VII), UNITED KINGDOM OF GREAT BRITAIN AND NORTHERN IRELAND 24 Feb 1967 a (*III, VII), UNITED REPUBLIC OF TANZANIA 19 Jun 1975 a, UNITED STATES OF AMERICA 8 Apr 1976 a, UZBEKISTAN 29 Sep 1997 a, VENEZUELA (BOLIVARIAN REPUBLIC OF) 31 May 1983 a (*IX), YEMEN 9 Feb 1987 a (*VII, IX), ZAMBIA 4 Feb 1972 a, ZIMBABWE 5 Jun 1995 a.

The Contracting Parties,

Desiring to implement the principle of equality of rights for men and women contained in the Charter of the United Nations,

Recognizing that everyone has the right to take part in the government of his country directly or indirectly through freely chosen representatives, and has the right to equal access to public service in his country, and desiring to equalize the status of men and women in the enjoyment and exercise of political rights, in accordance with the provisions of the Charter of the United Nations and of the Universal Declaration of Human Rights,

Having resolved to conclude a Convention for this purpose,

Hereby agree as hereinafter provided:

Article I

Women shall be entitled to vote in all elections on equal terms with men, without any discrimination.

Article II

Women shall be eligible for election to all publicly elected bodies, established by national law, on equal terms with men, without any discrimination.

Article III

Women shall be entitled to hold public office and to exercise all public functions, established by national law, on equal terms with men, without any discrimination.

Article IV

1. This Convention shall be open for signature on behalf of any Member of the United Nations and also on behalf of any other State to which an invitation has been addressed by the General Assembly.

2. This Convention shall be ratified and the instruments of ratification shall be deposited with the Secretary-General of the United Nations.

Article V

1. This Convention shall be open for accession to all States referred to in paragraph 1 of article IV.

2. Accession shall be effected by the deposit of an instrument of accession with the Secretary-General of the United Nations.

Article VI

1. This Convention shall come into force on the ninetieth day following the date of deposit of the sixth instrument of ratification or accession.

2. For each State ratifying or acceding to the Convention after the deposit of the sixth instrument of ratification or accession the Convention shall enter into force on the ninetieth day after deposit by such State of its instrument of ratification or accession.

Article VII

In the event that any State submits a reservation to any of the articles of this Convention at the time of signature, ratification or accession, the Secretary-General shall communicate the text of the reservation to all States which are or may become Parties to this Convention. Any State which objects to the reservation may, within a period of ninety days from the date of the said communication (or upon the date of its becoming a Party to the Convention), notify the Secretary-General that it does not accept it. In such case, the Convention shall not enter into force as between such State and the State making the reservation.

Article VIII

1. Any State may denounce this Convention by written notification to the Secretary-General of the United Nations. Denunciation shall take effect one year after the date of receipt of the notification by the Secretary-General.

2. This Convention shall cease to be in force as from the date when the denunciation which reduces the number of Parties to less than six becomes effective.

Article IX

Any dispute which may arise between any two or more Contracting States concerning the interpretation or application of this Convention, which is not settled by negotiation, shall at the request of any one of the parties to the dispute be referred to the International Court of Justice for decision, unless they agree to another mode of settlement.

Article X

The Secretary-General of the United Nations shall notify all Members of the United Nations and the non-member States contemplated in paragraph 1 of article IV of this Convention of the following:

(a) Signatures and instruments of ratification received in accordance with article IV;

(b) Instruments of accession received in accordance with article V;

(c) The date upon which this Convention enters into force in accordance with article VI;

(d) Communications and notifications received in accordance with article VII;

(e) Notifications of denunciation received in accordance with paragraph 1 of article VIII;

(f) Abrogation in accordance with paragraph 2 of article VIII.

Article XI

1. This Convention, of which the Chinese, English, French, Russian and Spanish texts shall be equally authentic, shall be deposited in the archives of the United Nations.

2. The Secretary-General of the United Nations shall transmit a certified copy to all Members of the United Nations and to the non-member States contemplated in paragraph 1 of article IV.

Convention against Discrimination in Education, 1960*

Adoption: 14 December 1960
Entry into force: 22 May 1962
Parties: 93 (Status as of 1 April 2007)

ALBANIA 21 Nov 1963, ALGERIA 24 Dec 1968, ARGENTINA 30 Oct 1963, ARMENIA 5 Sep 1993, AUSTRALIA 29 Nov 1966, BARBADOS 24 Jun 1975, BELARUS 12 Dec 1962, BELIZE 1 Dec 1982, BOSNIA AND HERZEGOVINA 12 Jul 1993, BRAZIL 19 Apr 1968, BRUNEI DARUSSALAM 25 Jan 1985, BULGARIA 4 Dec 1962, CENTRAL AFRICAN REPUBLIC 22 Feb 1962, CHILE 26 Oct 1971, CHINA 12 Feb 1965, CONGO 16 Sep 1968, COSTA RICA 10 Sep 1963, COTE D'IVOIRE 24 Nov 1999, CROATIA 6 Jul 1992, CUBA 2 Nov 1962, CYPRUS 9 Jun 1970, CZECH REPUBLIC 26 Mar 1993, DENMARK 4 Oct 1963, DOMINICA 14 Mar 1993, DOMINICAN REPUBLIC 30 Aug 1977, ECUADOR 5 Mar 1979, EGYPT 28 Mar 1962, FINLAND 10 Oct 1971, FRANCE 11 Sep 1961, GEORGIA 4 Nov 1992, GERMANY 17 Jul 1968, GUATEMALA 4 Feb 1983, GUINEA 11 Dec 1964, HUNGARY 16 Jan 1964, INDONESIA 10 Jan 1967, IRAN (ISLAMIC REPUBLIC OF) 17 Jul 1968, IRAQ 28 Jun 1977, ISRAEL 22 Sep 1961, ITALY 6 Oct 1966, JAMAICA 16 Mar 2006, JORDAN 6 Apr 1976, KUWAIT 15 Jan 1963, KYRGYZSTAN 3 Jul 1995, LEBANON 27 Oct 1964, LIBERIA 17 May 1962, LIBYAN ARAB JAMAHIRIYA 9 Jan 1973, LUXEMBOURG 20 Jan 1964, MADAGASCAR 21 Dec 1964, MALTA 5 Jan 1966, MAURITIUS 20 Aug 1970, MONGOLIA 4 Nov 1964, MOROCCO 30 Aug 1968, NETHERLANDS 25 Mar 1966, NEW ZEALAND 12 Feb 1963, NICARAGUA 28 Sep 1981, NIGER 16 Jul 1968, NIGERIA 18 Nov 1969, NORWAY 8 Jan, 1963, PANAMA10 Aug 1967, PERU 19 Dec 1966, PHILIPPINES 19 Nov 1964, POLAND 15 Sep 1964, PORTUGAL 8 Jan 1981, REPUBLIC OF MOLDOVA 17 Mar 1993, ROMANIA 9 Jul 1964, RUSSIAN FEDERATION 1 Aug 1962, RWANDA 28 Dec 2000, SAINT VINCENT AND THE GRENADINES 22 Jan 1985, SAUDI ARABIA 17 Aug 1973, SENEGAL 25 Sep 1967, SERBIA 11 Sep 2001, SIERRA LEONE 2 Jun 1967, SLOVAKIA 31 Mar 1993, SLOVENIA 5 Nov 1992, SOLOMON ISLANDS 19 Mar 1982, SOUTH AFRICA 9 Mar 2000, SPAIN 20 Aug 1969, SRI LANKA 11 Aug 1983, SWAZILAND 8 Oct 1970, SWEDEN 21 Mar 1968, TAJIKISTAN 28 Aug 1992, THE FORMER YUGOSLAV REPUBLIC OF MACEDONIA 30 Apr 1997, TUNISIA 29 Aug 1969, UGANDA 9 Sep 1968, UKRAINE 19 Dec 1962, UNITED REPUBLIC OF GREAT BRITAIN AND NORTHERN IRELAND 14 Mar 1962, UNITED REPUBLIC OF TANZANIA 3 Jan 1979, URUGUAY 3 May 2004, UZBEKISTAN 8 Dec 1997, VENEZUELA 16 Dec 1997, VIET NAM 12 Jun 1968, ZIMBABWE 30 May 2006.

The General Conference of the United Nations Educational, Scientific and Cultural Organization, meeting in Paris from 14 November to 15 December 1960, at its eleventh session,

Recalling that the Universal Declaration of Human Rights asserts the principle of non-discrimination and proclaims that every person has the right to education,

Considering that discrimination in education is a violation of rights enunciated in that Declaration,

Considering that, under the terms of its Constitution, the United Nations Educational, Scientific and Cultural Organization has the purpose of instituting collaboration among the nations with

* Source: 429 U.N.T.S. 93, www.unesco.org.

a view to furthering for all universal respect for human rights and equality of educational opportunity,

Recognizing that, consequently, the United Nations Educational, Scientific and Cultural Organization, while respecting the diversity of national educational systems, has the duty not only to proscribe any form of discrimination in education but also to promote equality of opportunity and treatment for all in education,

Having before it proposals concerning the different aspects of discrimination in education, constituting item 17.1.4 of the agenda of the session,

Having decided at its tenth session that this question should be made the subject of an international convention as well as of recommendations to Member States,

Adopts this Convention on the fourteenth day of December 1960.

Article 1

1. For the purpose of this Convention, the term "discrimination" includes any distinction, exclusion, limitation or preference which, being based on race, colour, sex, language, religion, political or other opinion, national or social origin, economic condition or birth, has the purpose or effect of nullifying or impairing equality of treatment in education and in particular:

(a) Of depriving any person or group of persons of access to education of any type or at any level;

(b) Of limiting any person or group of persons to education of an inferior standard;

(c) Subject to the provisions of article 2 of this Convention, of establishing or maintaining separate educational systems or institutions for persons or groups of persons; or

(d) Of inflicting on any person or group of persons conditions which are incompatible with the dignity of man.

2. For the purposes of this Convention, the term "education" refers to all types and levels of education, and includes access to education, the standard and quality of education, and the conditions under which it is given.

Article 2

When permitted in a State, the following situations shall not be deemed to constitute discrimination, within the meaning of article 1 of this Convention:

(a) The establishment or maintenance of separate educational systems or institutions for pupils of the two sexes, if these systems or institutions offer equivalent access to education, provide a teaching staff with qualifications of the same standard as well as school premises and equipment of the same quality, and afford the opportunity to take the same or equivalent courses of study;

(b) The establishment or maintenance, for religious or linguistic reasons, of separate educational systems or institutions offering an education which is in keeping with the wishes of the pupil's parents or legal guardians, if participation in such systems or attendance at such institutions is optional and if the education provided conforms to such standards as may be laid down or approved by the competent authorities, in particular for education of the same level;

(c) The establishment or maintenance of private educational institutions, if the object of the institutions is not to secure the exclusion of any group but to provide educational facilities in addition to those provided by the public authorities, if the institutions are conducted in accordance with that object, and if the education provided conforms with such standards as may be laid down or approved by the competent authorities, in particular for education of the same level.

Article 3

In order to eliminate and prevent discrimination within the meaning of this Convention, the States Parties thereto undertake:

(a) To abrogate any statutory provisions and any administrative instructions and to discontinue any administrative practices which involve discrimination in education;

(b) To ensure, by legislation where necessary, that there is no discrimination in the admission of pupils to educational institutions;

(c) Not to allow any differences of treatment by the public authorities between nationals, except on the basis of merit or need, in the matter of school fees and the grant of scholarships or other forms of assistance to pupils and necessary permits and facilities for the pursuit of studies in foreign countries;

(d) Not to allow, in any form of assistance granted by the public authorities to educational institutions, any restrictions or preference based solely on the ground that pupils belong to a particular group;

(e) To give foreign nationals resident within their territory the same access to education as that given to their own nationals.

Article 4

The States Parties to this Convention undertake furthermore to formulate, develop and apply a national policy which, by methods appropriate to the circumstances and to national usage, will tend to promote equality of opportunity and of treatment in the matter of education and in particular:

(a) To make primary education free and compulsory; make secondary education in its different forms generally available and accessible to all; make higher education equally accessible to all on the basis of individual capacity; assure compliance by all with the obligation to attend school prescribed by law;

(b) To ensure that the standards of education are equivalent in all public education institutions of the same level, and that the conditions relating to the quality of education provided are also equivalent;

(c) To encourage and intensify by appropriate methods the education of persons who have not received any primary education or who have not completed the entire primary education course and the continuation of their education on the basis of individual capacity;

(d) To provide training for the teaching profession without discrimination.

Article 5

1. The States Parties to this Convention agree that:

(a) Education shall be directed to the full development of the human personality and to the strengthening of respect for human rights and fundamental freedoms; it shall promote understanding, tolerance and friendship among all nations, racial or religious groups, and shall further the activities of the United Nations for the maintenance of peace;

(b) It is essential to respect the liberty of parents and, where applicable, of legal guardians, firstly to choose for their children institutions other than those maintained by the public authorities but conforming to such minimum educational standards as may be laid down or approved by the competent authorities and, secondly, to ensure in a manner consistent with the procedures followed in the State for the application of its legislation, the religious and moral education of the children in conformity with their own convictions; and no person or group of persons should be compelled to receive religious instruction inconsistent with his or their conviction;

(c) It is essential to recognize the right of members of national minorities to carry on their own educational activities, including the maintenance of schools and, depending on the educational policy of each State, the use or the teaching of their own language, provided however:

(i) That this right is not exercised in a manner which prevents the members of these minorities from understanding the culture and language of the community as a whole and from participating in its - activities, or which prejudices national sovereignty;

(ii) That the standard of education is not lower than the general standard laid down or approved by the competent authorities; and

(iii) That attendance at such schools is optional.

2. The States Parties to this Convention undertake to take all necessary measures to ensure the application of the principles enunciated in paragraph 1 of this article.

Article 6

In the application of this Convention, the States Parties to it undertake to pay the greatest attention to any recommendations hereafter adopted by the General Conference of the United Nations Educational, Scientific and Cultural Organization defining the measures to be taken against the different forms of discrimination in education and for the purpose of ensuring equality of opportunity and treatment in education.

Article 7

The States Parties to this Convention shall in their periodic reports submitted to the General Conference of the United Nations Educational, Scientific and Cultural Organization on dates and in a manner to be determined by it, give information on the legislative and administrative provisions which they have adopted and other action which they have taken for the application of this Convention, including that taken for the formulation and the development of the national policy defined in article 4 as well as the results achieved and the obstacles encountered in the application of that policy.

Article 8

Any dispute which may arise between any two or more States Parties to this Convention concerning the interpretation or application of this Convention which is not settled by negotiations shall at the request of the parties to the dispute be referred, failing other means of settling the dispute, to the International Court of Justice for decision.

Article 9

Reservations to this Convention shall not be permitted.

Article 10

This Convention shall not have the effect of diminishing the rights which individuals or groups may enjoy by virtue of agreements concluded between two or more States, where such rights are not contrary to the letter or spirit of this Convention.

Article 11

This Convention is drawn up in English, French, Russian and Spanish, the four texts being equally authoritative.

Article 12

1. This Convention shall be subject to ratification or acceptance by States Members of the United Nations Educational, Scientific and Cultural Organization in accordance with their respective constitutional procedures.

2. The instruments of ratification or acceptance shall be deposited with the Director-General of the United Nations Educational, Scientific and Cultural Organization.

Article 13

1. This Convention shall be open to accession by all States not Members of the United Nations Educational, Scientific and Cultural Organization which are invited to do so by the Executive Board of the Organization.

2. Accession shall be effected by the deposit of an instrument of accession with the Director-General of the United Nations Educational, Scientific and Cultural Organization.

Article 14

This Convention shall enter into force three months after the date of the deposit of the third instrument of ratification, acceptance or accession, but only with respect to those States which have deposited their respective instruments on or before that date. It shall enter into force with respect to any other State three months after the deposit of its instrument of ratification, acceptance or accession.

Article 15

The States Parties to this Convention recognize that the Convention is applicable not only to their metropolitan territory but also to all non-self-governing, trust, colonial and other territories for the international relations of which they are responsible; they undertake to consult, if necessary, the governments or other competent authorities of these territories on or before ratification, acceptance or accession with a view to securing the application of the Convention to those territories, and to notify the Director-General of the United Nations Educational, Scientific and Cultural Organization of the territories to which it is accordingly applied, the notification to take effect three months after the date of its receipt.

Article 16

1. Each State Party to this Convention may denounce the Convention on its own behalf or on behalf of any territory for whose international relations it is responsible.

2. The denunciation shall be notified by an instrument in writing, deposited with the Director-General of the United Nations Educational, Scientific and Cultural Organization.

3. The denunciation shall take effect twelve months after the receipt of the instrument of denunciation.

Article 17

The Director-General of the United Nations Educational, Scientific and Cultural Organization shall inform the States Members of the Organization, the States not members of the Organization which are referred to in article 13, as well as the United Nations, of the deposit of all the instruments of ratification, acceptance and accession provided for in articles 12 and 13, and of notifications and denunciations provided for in articles 15 and 16 respectively.

Article 18

1. This Convention may be revised by the General Conference of the United Nations Educational, Scientific and Cultural Organization. Any such revision shall, however, bind only the States which shall become Parties to the revising convention.

2. If the General Conference should adopt a new convention revising this Convention in whole or in part, then, unless the new convention otherwise provides, this Convention shall cease to be open to ratification, acceptance or accession as from the date on which the new revising convention enters into force.

Article 19

In conformity with Article 102 of the Charter of the United Nations, this Convention shall be registered with the Secretariat of the United Nations at the request of the Director-General of the United Nations Educational, Scientific and Cultural Organization.

DONE in Paris, this fifteenth day of December 1960, in two authentic copies bearing the signatures of the President of the eleventh session of the General Conference and of the Director-General of the United Nations Educational, Scientific and Cultural Organization, which shall be deposited in the archives of the United Nations Educational, Scientific and Cultural Organization, and certified true copies of which shall be delivered to all the States referred to in articles 12 and 13 as well as to the United Nations.

The foregoing is the authentic text of the Convention duly adopted by the General Conference of the United Nations Educational, Scientific and Cultural Organization during its eleventh session, which was held in Paris and declared closed the fifteenth day of December 1960.

IN FAITH WHEREOF we have appended our signatures this fifteenth day of December 1960.

International Convention on the Elimination of All Forms of Racial Discrimination, 1965*

Adoption: 21 December 1965**
Entry into force: 4 January 1969
Parties: 173 (Status as of 1 April 2007)

AFGHANISTAN 6 Jul 1983 a (*22), ALBANIA 11 May 1983, ALGERIA 14 Feb 1972, ANDORRA 22 Sep 2006, ANTIGUA AND BARBUDA 25 Oct 1988 d, ARGENTINA 2 Oct 1968, ARMENIA 23 Jul 1993 a, AUSTRALIA 30 Sep 1975, AUSTRIA 9 May 1972, AZERBAIJAN 16 Aug 1996 a, BAHAMAS 5 Aug 1975 d, BAHRAIN 27 Mar 1990 a (*22), BANGLADESH 11 June 1979 a, BARBADOS 8 Nov 1972 a, BELARUS 8 Apr 1969, BELGIUM 7 Aug 1975, BELIZE 14 Nov 2001, BENIN 30 Nov 2001, BHUTAN signed 26 Mar 1973, BOLIVIA 22 Sep 1970, BOSNIA AND HERZEGOVINA 16 Jul 1993 d, BOTSWANA 20 Feb 1974 a, BRAZIL 27 Mar 1968, BULGARIA 8 Aug 1966, BURKINA FASO 18 Jul 1974 a, BURUNDI 27 Oct 1977, CAMBODIA 28 Nov 1983, CAMEROON 24 Jun 1971, CANADA 14 Oct 1970, CAPE VERDE 3 Oct 1979 a, CENTRAL AFRICAN REPUBLIC 16 Mar 1971, CHAD 17 Aug 1977 a, CHILE 20 Oct 1971, CHINA 29 Dec 1981 a (*22), COLOMBIA 2 Sep 1981, COMOROS 27 Sep 2004, CONGO 11 Jul 1988 a, COSTA RICA 16 Jan 1967, CÔTE D'IVOIRE 4 Jan 1973 a, CROATIA 12 Oct 1992 d, CUBA 15 Feb 1972 (*22), CYPRUS 21 Apr 1967, CZECH REPUBLIC 22 Feb 1993 d, DEMOCRATIC REPUBLIC OF CONGO 21 Apr 1967, DENMARK 9 Dec 1971, DJIBOUTI signed 14 June 2006, DOMINICAN REPUBLIC 25 May 1983 a, ECUADOR 22 May 1966 a, EGYPT 1 May 1967 (*22), EL SALVADOR 30 Nov 1979 a, EQUATORIAL GUINEA 8 Oct 2002 a (*22), ERITREA 31 Jul 2001 a, ESTONIA 21 Oct 1991 a, ETHIOPIA 23 Jun 1976 a, FIJI 11 Jan 1973 d (*2, 3, 5c, 5d, 5e, 5v, 6, 15, 20), FINLAND 14 Jul 1970, FRANCE 14 Jul 1971 a, GABON 29 Feb 1980, GAMBIA 29 Dec 1978 a, GEORGIA 2 Jun 1999 a, GERMANY 16 May 1969, GHANA 8 Sep 1966, GREECE 18 Jun 1970, GRENADA signed 17 Dec 1981, GUATEMALA 18 Jan 1983, GUINEA 14 Mar 1977, GUINEA-BISSAU signed 12 Sep 2000, GUYANA 15 Feb 1977, HAITI 19 Dec 1972, HOLY SEE 1 May 1969, HONDURAS 10 Oct 2002 a, HUNGARY 4 May 1967, ICELAND 13 Mar 1967, INDIA 3 Dec 1968, INDONESIA 25 Jun 1999 a (*22), IRAN 29 Aug 1968, IRAQ 14 Jan 1970 (*22), IRELAND 29 Dec 2000, ISRAEL 3 Jan 1979 (*22), ITALY 5 Jan 1976, JAMAICA 4 June 1971, JAPAN 15 Dec 1995 a (*4a-b), JORDAN 30 May 1974 a, KAZAKHSTAN 26 Aug 1998 a, KENYA 13 Sep 2001 a, KUWAIT 15 Oct 1968 a (*22), KYRGYZSTAN 5 Sep 1997 a, LAO PEOPLE'S DEMOCRATIC REPUBLC 22 Feb 1974 a, LATVIA 14 Apr 1992 a, LEBANON 12 Nov 1971 a (*22), LESOTHO 4 Nov 1971 a, LIBERIA 5 Nov 1976 a, LIBYAN ARAB JAMAHIRIYA 3 Jul 1968 a (*22), LIECHTENSTEIN 1 Mar 2000 a, LITHUANIA 10 Dec 1998, LUXEMBOURG 1 May 1978, MADAGASCAR 7 Feb 1969 (*22), MALAWI 11 Jun 1996 a, MALDIVES 24 Apr 1984 a, MALI 16 Jul 1974 a, MALTA 27 May 1971, MAURITIUS 30 May 1972 a, MEXICO 20 FEB 1975, MONACO 27 Sep 1995 a (2.1, 4), MONGOLIA 6 AUG 1969, MONTENEGRO 23 Oct 2006 d, MOROCCO 18 Dec 1970 (*22), MOZAMBIQUE 18 Apr 1983 a (*22), NAMIBIA 11 Nov 1982 a, NAURU signed 12 Nov 2001, NEPAL 30 Jan 1971 a (*22), NETHERLANDS 10 Dec 1971, NEW ZEALAND 22 Nov 1972, NICARAGUA 15 Feb 1978 a, NIGER 27 Apr 1967, NIGERIA 16 Oct 1967 a, NORWAY 6 Aug 1970, OMAN 2 Jan 2003 a, PAKISTAN 21 Sep 1966, PANAMA 16 Aug 1967, PAPUA NEW GUINEA 27 Jan 1982 a (*4a-c), PARAGUAY signed 13 Sep 2000, PERU 29 Sep 1971, PHILIPPINES 15 Sep 1967, POLAND

* Source: U.N.G.A. Res. 2105 A (XX), 660 U.N.T.S. 195.

** The Convention was open for signature on 7 March 1966.

5 Dec 1968, PORTUGAL 24 Aug 1982 a, QATAR 22 Jul 1976 a, REPUBLIC OF KOREA 5 Dec 1978, REPUBLIC OF MOLDOVA 26 Jan 1993 a, REPUBLIC OF SERBIA 12 Mar 2001 d, ROMANIA 15 Sep 1970 a, RUSSIAN FEDERATION 4 Feb 1969, RWANDA 16 Apr 1975 a (*22), SAINT KITTS AND NEVIS 13 Oct 2006 a, SAINT LUCIA 14 Feb 1990 d, SAINT VINCENT AND THE GRENADINES 9 NOV 1981 a, SAN MARINO 12 Mar 2002, SAO TOME AND PRINCIPE signed on 6 Sep 2000, SAUDI ARABIA 23 Sep 1997 a (*22), SENEGAL 19 Apr 1972, SEYCHELLES 7 Mar 1978 a, SIERRA LEONE 2 Aug 1967, SLOVAKIA 28 May 1993 d, SLOVENIA 6 Jul 1992 d, SOLOMON ISLANDS 17 Mar 1982 d, SOMALIA 26 Aug 1975, SOUTH AFRICA 10 Dec 1998, SPAIN 13 Sep 1968 a, SRI LANKA 18 Feb 1982 a, SUDAN 21 Mar 1977 a, SURINAME 15 Mar 1984 d, SWAZILAND 7 Apr 1969 a, SWEDEN 6 Dec 1971, SWITZERLAND 29 Nov 1994 a (*2.1, 4), SYRIAN ARAB REUPUBLIC 21 Apr 1969 a (*22), TAJIKSTAN 1 Jan 1995 a, THAILAND 28 Jan 2003 a (*4a-c, 22), THE FORMER YUGOSLAV REPUBLIC OF MACEDONIA 18 Jan 1994 d, TIMOR-LESTE 16 Apr 2003 a, TOGO 1 Sep 1972 a, TONGA 16 Feb 1972 a (*5d, 5v), TRINIDAD AND TOBAGO 4 Oct 1973, TUNISIA 13 Jan 1967, TURKEY 16 Sep 2002 (*22), TURKMENISTAN 29 Sep 1994 a, UGANDA 21 Nov 1980 a, UKRAINE 7 Mar 1969, UNITED ARAB EMIRATES 7 Mar 1969, UNITED KINGDOM OF GREAT BRITAIN AND NORTHERN IRELAND 7 Mar 1969 (*territorial regarding Rhodesia), UNITED REPUBLIC OF TANZANIA 27 Oct 1972 a, UNITED STATES OF AMERICA 21 Oct 1994 (*2, 3, 5), URUGUAY 30 Aug 1968, UZBEKISTAN 28 Sep 1995 a, VENEZUELA 10 Oct 1967, VIET NAM 9 Jun 1982 a (*22), YEMEN 18 Oct 1972 a (*22), ZAMBIA 4 Feb 1972, ZIMBABWE 13 May 1991.

The States Parties to this Convention,

Considering that the Charter of the United Nations is based on the principles of the dignity and equality inherent in all human beings, and that all Member States have pledged themselves to take joint and separate action, in co-operation with the Organization, for the achievement of one of the purposes of the United Nations which is to promote and encourage universal respect for and observance of human rights and fundamental freedoms for all, without distinction as to race, sex, language or religion,

Considering that the Universal Declaration of Human Rights proclaims that all human beings are born free and equal in dignity and rights and that everyone is entitled to all the rights and freedoms set out therein, without distinction of any kind, in particular as to race, colour or national origin,

Considering that all human beings are equal before the law and are entitled to equal protection of the law against any discrimination and against any incitement to discrimination,

Considering that the United Nations has condemned colonialism and all practices of segregation and discrimination associated therewith, in whatever form and wherever they exist, and that the Declaration on the Granting of Independence to Colonial Countries and Peoples of 14 December 1960 (General Assembly resolution 1514 (XV)) has affirmed and solemnly proclaimed the necessity of bringing them to a speedy and unconditional end,

Considering that the United Nations Declaration on the Elimination of All Forms of Racial Discrimination of 20 November 1963 (General Assembly resolution 1904 (XVIII)) solemnly affirms the necessity of speedily eliminating racial discrimination throughout the world in all its forms and manifestations and of securing understanding of and respect for the dignity of the human person,

Convinced that any doctrine of superiority based on racial differentiation is scientifically false, morally condemnable, socially unjust and dangerous, and that there is no justification for racial discrimination, in theory or in practice, anywhere,

Reaffirming that discrimination between human beings on the grounds of race, colour or ethnic origin is an obstacle to friendly and peaceful relations among nations and is capable of disturbing peace and security among peoples and the harmony of persons living side by side even within one and the same State,

Convinced that the existence of racial barriers is repugnant to the ideals of any human society,

Alarmed by manifestations of racial discrimination still in evidence in some areas of the world and by governmental policies based on racial superiority or hatred, such as policies of apartheid, segregation or separation,

Resolved to adopt all necessary measures for speedily eliminating racial discrimination in all its forms and manifestations, and to prevent and combat racist doctrines and practices in order to promote understanding between races and to build an international community free from all forms of racial segregation and racial discrimination,

Bearing in mind the Convention concerning Discrimination in respect of Employment and Occupation adopted by the International Labour Organization in 1958, and the Convention against Discrimination in Education adopted by the United Nations Educational, Scientific and Cultural Organization in 1960,

Desiring to implement the principles embodied in the United Nations Declaration on the Elimination of Al l Forms of Racial Discrimination and to secure the earliest adoption of practical measures to that end,

Have agreed as follows:

PART I

Article I

1. In this Convention, the term "racial discrimination" shall mean any distinction, exclusion, restriction or preference based on race, colour, descent, or national or ethnic origin which has the purpose or effect of nullifying or impairing the recognition, enjoyment or exercise, on an equal footing, of human rights and fundamental freedoms in the political, economic, social, cultural or any other field of public life.

2. This Convention shall not apply to distinctions, exclusions, restrictions or preferences made by a State Party to this Convention between citizens and non-citizens.

3. Nothing in this Convention may be interpreted as affecting in any way the legal provisions of States Parties concerning nationality, citizenship or naturalization, provided that such provisions do not discriminate against any particular nationality.

4. Special measures taken for the sole purpose of securing adequate advancement of certain racial or ethnic groups or individuals requiring such protection as may be necessary in order to ensure such groups or individuals equal enjoyment or exercise of human rights and fundamental freedoms shall not be deemed racial discrimination, provided, however, that such measures do not, as a consequence, lead to the maintenance of separate rights for different racial groups and that they shall not be continued after the objectives for which they were taken have been achieved.

Article 2

1. States Parties condemn racial discrimination and undertake to pursue by all appropriate means and without delay a policy of eliminating racial discrimination in all its forms and promoting understanding among all races, and, to this end:

(a) Each State Party undertakes to engage in no act or practice of racial discrimination against persons, groups of persons or institutions and to en sure that all public authorities and public institutions, national and local, shall act in conformity with this obligation;

(b) Each State Party undertakes not to sponsor, defend or support racial discrimination by any persons or organizations;

(c) Each State Party shall take effective measures to review governmental, national and local policies, and to amend, rescind or nullify any laws and regulations which have the effect of creating or perpetuating racial discrimination wherever it exists;

(d) Each State Party shall prohibit and bring to an end, by all appropriate means, including legislation as required by circumstances, racial discrimination by any persons, group or organization;

(e) Each State Party undertakes to encourage, where appropriate, integrationist multiracial organizations and movements and other means of eliminating barriers between races, and to discourage anything which tends to strengthen racial division.

2. States Parties shall, when the circumstances so warrant, take, in the social, economic, cultural and other fields, special and concrete measures to ensure the adequate development and protection of certain racial groups or individuals belonging to them, for the purpose of guaranteeing them the full and equal enjoyment of human rights and fundamental freedoms. These measures shall in no case en tail as a con sequence the maintenance of unequal or separate rights for different racial groups after the objectives for which they were taken have been achieved.

Article 3

States Parties particularly condemn racial segregation and apartheid and undertake to prevent, prohibit and eradicate all practices of this nature in territories under their jurisdiction.

Article 4

States Parties condemn all propaganda and all organizations which are based on ideas or theories of superiority of one race or group of persons of one colour or ethnic origin, or which attempt to justify or promote racial hatred and discrimination in any form, and undertake to adopt immediate and positive measures designed to eradicate all incitement to, or acts of, such discrimination and, to this end, with due regard to the principles embodied in the Universal Declaration of Human Rights and the rights expressly set forth in article 5 of this Convention, inter alia:

(a) Shall declare an offence punishable by law all dissemination of ideas based on racial superiority or hatred, incitement to racial discrimination, as well as all acts of violence or incitement to such acts against any race or group of persons of another colour or ethnic origin, and also the provision of any assistance to racist activities, including the financing thereof;

(b) Shall declare illegal and prohibit organizations, and also organized and all other propaganda activities, which promote and incite racial discrimination, and shall recognize participation in such organizations or activities as an offence punishable by law;

(c) Shall not permit public authorities or public institutions, national or local, to promote or incite racial discrimination.

Article 5

In compliance with the fundamental obligations laid down in article 2 of this Convention, States Parties undertake to prohibit and to eliminate racial discrimination in all its forms and to guarantee the right of everyone, without distinction as to race, colour, or national or ethnic origin, to equality before the law, notably in the enjoyment of the following rights:

(a) The right to equal treatment before the tribunals and all other organs administering justice;

(b) The right to security of person and protection by the State against violence or bodily harm, whether inflicted by government officials or by any individual group or institution;

(c) Political rights, in particular the right to participate in elections-to vote and to stand for election-on the basis of universal and equal suffrage, to take part in the Government as well as in the conduct of public affairs at any level and to have equal access to public service;

(d) Other civil rights, in particular:

(i) The right to freedom of movement and residence within the border of the State;

(ii) The right to leave any country, including one's own, and to return to one's country;

(iii) The right to nationality;

(iv) The right to marriage and choice of spouse;

(v) The right to own property alone as well as in association with others;

(vi) The right to inherit;

(vii) The right to freedom of thought, conscience and religion;

(viii) The right to freedom of opinion and expression;

(ix) The right to freedom of peaceful assembly and association;

(e) Economic, social and cultural rights, in particular:

(i) The rights to work, to free choice of employment, to just and favourable conditions of work, to protection against unemployment, to equal pay for equal work, to just and favourable remuneration;

(ii) The right to form and join trade unions;

(iii) The right to housing;

(iv) The right to public health, medical care, social security and social services;

(v) The right to education and training;

(vi) The right to equal participation in cultural activities;

(f) The right of access to any place or service intended for use by the general public, such as transport hotels, restaurants, cafes, theatres and parks.

Article 6

States Parties shall assure to everyone within their jurisdiction effective protection and remedies, through the competent national tribunals and other State institutions, against any acts of racial discrimination which violate his human rights and fundamental freedoms contrary to this Convention, as well as the right to seek from such tribunals just and adequate reparation or satisfaction for any damage suffered as a result of such discrimination.

Article 7

States Parties undertake to adopt immediate and effective measures, particularly in the fields of teaching, education, culture and information, with a view to combating prejudices which lead to racial discrimination and to promoting understanding, tolerance and friendship among nations and racial or ethnical groups, as well as to propagating the purposes and principles of the Charter of the United Nations, the Universal Declaration of Human Rights, the United Nations Declaration on the Elimination of All Forms of Racial Discrimination, and this Convention.

PART II

Article 8

1. There shall be established a Committee on the Elimination of Racial Discrimination (hereinafter referred to as the Committee) consisting of eighteen experts of high moral standing and acknowledged impartiality elected by States Parties from among their nationals, who shall serve in their personal capacity, consideration being given to equitable geographical distribution and to the representation of the different forms of civilization as well as of the principal legal systems.

2. The members of the Committee shall be elected by secret ballot from a list of persons nominated by the States Parties. Each State Party may nominate one person from among its own nationals.

3. The initial election shall be held six months after the date of the entry into force of this Convention. At least three months before the date of each election the Secretary-General of the United Nations shall address a letter to the States Parties inviting them to submit their nominations within two months. The Secretary-General shall prepare a list in alphabetical order of all persons thus nominated, indicating the States Parties which have nominated them, and shall submit it to the States Parties.

4. Elections of the members of the Committee shall be held at a meeting of States Parties convened by the Secretary-General at United Nations Headquarters. At that meeting, for which two thirds of the States Parties shall constitute a quorum, the persons elected to the Committee shall be nominees who obtain the largest number of votes and an absolute majority of the votes of the representatives of States Parties present and voting.

5. (a) The members of the Committee shall be elected for a term of four years. However, the terms of nine of the members elected at the first election shall expire at the end of two years; immediately after the first election the names of these nine members shall be chosen by lot by the Chairman of the Committee;

(b) For the filling of casual vacancies, the State Party whose expert has ceased to function as a member of the Committee shall appoint another expert from among its nationals, subject to the approval of the Committee.

6. States Parties shall be responsible for the expenses of the members of the Committee while they are in performance of Committee duties.

Article 9

1. States Parties undertake to submit to the Secretary-General of the United Nations, for consideration by the Committee, a report on the legislative, judicial, administrative or other measures which they have adopted and which give effect to the provisions of this Convention:

(a) within one year after the entry into force of the Convention for the State concerned; and

(b) Thereafter every two years and whenever the Committee so requests. The Committee may request further information from the States Parties.

2. The Committee shall report annually, through the Secretary General, to the General Assembly of the United Nations on its activities and may make suggestions and general recommendations based on the examination of the reports and information received from the States Parties. Such suggestions and general recommendations shall be reported to the General Assembly together with comments, if any, from States Parties.

Article 10

1. The Committee shall adopt its own rules of procedure.

2. The Committee shall elect its officers for a term of two years.

3. The secretariat of the Committee shall be provided by the Secretary General of the United Nations.

4. The meetings of the Committee shall normally be held at United Nations Headquarters.

Article 11

1. If a State Party considers that another State Party is not giving effect to the provisions of this Convention, it may bring the matter to the attention of the Committee. The Committee shall then transmit the communication to the State Party concerned. Within three months, the receiving State shall submit to the Committee written explanations or statements clarifying the matter and the remedy, if any, that may have been taken by that State.

2. If the matter is not adjusted to the satisfaction of both parties, either by bilateral negotiations or by any other procedure open to them, within six months after the receipt by the receiving State of the initial communication, either State shall have the right to refer the matter again to the Committee by notifying the Committee and also the other State.

3. The Committee shall deal with a matter referred to it in accordance with paragraph 2 of this article after it has ascertained that all available domestic remedies have been invoked and exhausted in the case, in conformity with the generally recognized principles of international law. This shall not be the rule where the application of the remedies is unreasonably prolonged.

4. In any matter referred to it, the Committee may call upon the States Parties concerned to supply any other relevant information.

5. When any matter arising out of this article is being considered by the Committee, the States Parties concerned shall be entitled to send a representative to take part in the proceedings of the Committee, without voting rights, while the matter is under consideration.

Article 12

1. (a) After the Committee has obtained and collated all the information it deems necessary, the Chairman shall appoint an ad hoc Conciliation Commission (hereinafter referred to as the

Commission) comprising five persons who may or may not be members of the Committee. The members of the Commission shall be appointed with the unanimous consent of the parties to the dispute, and its good offices shall be made available to the States concerned with a view to an amicable solution of the matter on the basis of respect for this Convention;

(b) If the States parties to the dispute fail to reach agreement within three months on all or part of the composition of the Commission, the members of the Commission not agreed upon by the States parties to the dispute shall be elected by secret ballot by a two-thirds majority vote of the Committee from among its own members.

2. The members of the Commission shall serve in their personal capacity. They shall not be nationals of the States parties to the dispute or of a State not Party to this Convention.

3. The Commission shall elect its own Chairman and adopt its own rules of procedure.

4. The meetings of the Commission shall normally be held at United Nations Headquarters or at any other convenient place as determined by the Commission.

5. The secretariat provided in accordance with article 10, paragraph 3, of this Convention shall also service the Commission whenever a dispute among States Parties brings the Commission into being.

6. The States parties to the dispute shall share equally all the expenses of the members of the Commission in accordance with estimates to be provided by the Secretary-General of the United Nations.

7. The Secretary-General shall be empowered to pay the expenses of the members of the Commission, if necessary, before reimbursement by the States parties to the dispute in accordance with paragraph 6 of this article.

8. The information obtained and collated by the Committee shall be made available to the Commission, and the Commission may call upon the States concerned to supply any other relevant information.

Article 13

1. When the Commission has fully considered the matter, it shall prepare and submit to the Chairman of the Committee a report embodying its findings on all questions of fact relevant to the issue between the parties and containing such recommendations as it may think proper for the amicable solution of the dispute.

2. The Chairman of the Committee shall communicate the report of the Commission to each of the States parties to the dispute. These States shall, within three months, inform the Chairman of the Committee whether or not they accept the recommendations contained in the report of the Commission.

3. After the period provided for in paragraph 2 of this article, the Chairman of the Committee shall communicate the report of the Commission and the declarations of the States Parties concerned to the other States Parties to this Convention.

Article 14

1. A State Party may at any time declare that it recognizes the competence of the Committee to receive and consider communications from individuals or groups of individuals within its jurisdiction claiming to be victims of a violation by that State Party of any of the rights set forth in this Convention. No communication shall be received by the Committee if it concerns a State Party which has not made such a declaration.

2. Any State Party which makes a declaration as provided for in paragraph I of this article may establish or indicate a body within its national legal order which shall be competent to receive and consider petitions from individuals and groups of individuals within its jurisdiction who claim to be victims of a violation of any of the rights set forth in this Convention and who have exhausted other available local remedies.

3. A declaration made in accordance with paragraph 1 of this article and the name of any body established or indicated in accordance with paragraph 2 of this article shall be deposited by the State Party concerned with the Secretary-General of the United Nations, who shall transmit copies thereof to the other States Parties. A declaration may be withdrawn at any time by notification to the Secretary-General, but such a withdrawal shall not affect communications pending before the Committee.

4. A register of petitions shall be kept by the body established or indicated in accordance with paragraph 2 of this article, and certified copies of the register shall be filed annually through appropriate channels with the Secretary-General on the understanding that the contents shall not be publicly disclosed.

5. In the event of failure to obtain satisfaction from the body established or indicated in accordance with paragraph 2 of this article, the petitioner shall have the right to communicate the matter to the Committee within six months.

6. (a) The Committee shall confidentially bring any communication referred to it to the attention of the State Party alleged to be violating any provision of this Convention, but the identity of the individual or groups of individuals concerned shall not be revealed without his or their express consent. The Committee shall not receive anonymous communications;

(b) Within three months, the receiving State shall submit to the Committee written explanations or statements clarifying the matter and the remedy, if any, that may have been taken by that State.

7. (a) The Committee shall consider communications in the light of all information made available to it by the State Party concerned and by the petitioner. The Committee shall not consider any communication from a petitioner unless it has ascertained that the petitioner has exhausted all available domestic remedies. However, this shall not be the rule where the application of the remedies is unreasonably prolonged;

(b) The Committee shall forward its suggestions and recommendations, if any, to the State Party concerned and to the petitioner.

8. The Committee shall include in its annual report a summary of such communications and, where appropriate, a summary of the explanations and statements of the States Parties concerned and of its own suggestions and recommendations.

9. The Committee shall be competent to exercise the functions provided for in this article only when at least ten States Parties to this Convention are bound by declarations in accordance with paragraph I of this article.

Article 15

1. Pending the achievement of the objectives of the Declaration on the Granting of Independence to Colonial Countries and Peoples, contained in General Assembly resolution 1514 (XV) of 14 December 1960, the provisions of this Convention shall in no way limit the right of petition granted to these peoples by other international instruments or by the United Nations and its specialized agencies.

2. (a) The Committee established under article 8, paragraph 1, of this Convention shall receive copies of the petitions from, and submit expressions of opinion and recommendations on these petitions to, the bodies of the United Nations which deal with matters directly related to the principles and objectives of this Convention in their consideration of petitions from the inhabitants of Trust and Non-Self-Governing Territories and all other territories to which General Assembly resolution 1514 (XV) applies, relating to matters covered by this Convention which are before these bodies;

(b) The Committee shall receive from the competent bodies of the United Nations copies of the reports concerning the legislative, judicial, administrative or other measures directly related to the principles and objectives of this Convention applied by the administering Powers within the Territories mentioned in subparagraph (a) of this paragraph, and shall express opinions and make recommendations to these bodies.

3. The Committee shall include in its report to the General Assembly a summary of the petitions and reports it has received from United Nations bodies, and the expressions of opinion and recommendations of the Committee relating to the said petitions and reports.

4. The Committee shall request from the Secretary-General of the United Nations all information relevant to the objectives of this Convention and available to him regarding the Territories mentioned in paragraph 2 (a) of this article.

Article 16

The provisions of this Convention concerning the settlement of disputes or complaints shall be applied without prejudice to other procedures for settling disputes or complaints in the field of discrimination laid down in the constituent instruments of, or conventions adopted by, the United Nations and its specialized agencies, and shall not prevent the States Parties from having recourse to other procedures for settling a dispute in accordance with general or special international agreements in force between them.

PART III

Article 17

1. This Convention is open for signature by any State Member of the United Nations or member of any of its specialized agencies, by any State Party to the Statute of the International Court of Justice, and by any other State which has been invited by the General Assembly of the United Nations to become a Party to this Convention.

2. This Convention is subject to ratification. Instruments of ratification shall be deposited with the Secretary-General of the United Nations.

Article 18

1. This Convention shall be open to accession by any State referred to in article 17, paragraph 1, of the Convention. 2. Accession shall be effected by the deposit of an instrument of accession with the Secretary-General of the United Nations.

Article 19

1. This Convention shall enter into force on the thirtieth day after the date of the deposit with the Secretary-General of the United Nations of the twenty-seventh instrument of ratification or instrument of accession.

2. For each State ratifying this Convention or acceding to it after the deposit of the twenty-seventh instrument of ratification or instrument of accession, the Convention shall enter into force on the thirtieth day after the date of the deposit of its own instrument of ratification or instrument of accession.

Article 20

1. The Secretary-General of the United Nations shall receive and circulate to all States which are or may become Parties to this Convention reservations made by States at the time of ratification or accession. Any State which objects to the reservation shall, within a period of ninety days from the date of the said communication, notify the Secretary-General that it does not accept it.

2. A reservation incompatible with the object and purpose of this Convention shall not be permitted, nor shall a reservation the effect of which would inhibit the operation of any of the bodies established by this Convention be allowed. A reservation shall be considered incompatible or inhibitive if at least two thirds of the States Parties to this Convention object to it.

3. Reservations may be withdrawn at any time by notification to this effect addressed to the Secretary-General. Such notification shall take effect on the date on which it is received.

Article 21

A State Party may denounce this Convention by written notification to the Secretary-General of the United Nations. Denunciation shall take effect one year after the date of receipt of the notification by the Secretary General.

Article 22

Any dispute between two or more States Parties with respect to the interpretation or application of this Convention, which is not settled by negotiation or by the procedures expressly provided for in this Convention, shall, at the request of any of the parties to the dispute, be referred to the International Court of Justice for decision, unless the disputants agree to another mode of settlement.

Article 23

1. A request for the revision of this Convention may be made at any time by any State Party by means of a notification in writing addressed to the Secretary-General of the United Nations.

2. The General Assembly of the United Nations shall decide upon the steps, if any, to be taken in respect of such a request.

Article 24

The Secretary-General of the United Nations shall inform all States referred to in article 17, paragraph 1, of this Convention of the following particulars:

(a) Signatures, ratifications and accessions under articles 17 and 18;

(b) The date of entry into force of this Convention under article 19;

(c) Communications and declarations received under articles 14, 20 and 23;

(d) Denunciations under article 21.

Article 25

1. This Convention, of which the Chinese, English, French, Russian and Spanish texts are equally authentic, shall be deposited in the archives of the United Nations.

2. The Secretary-General of the United Nations shall transmit certified copies of this Convention to all States belonging to any of the categories mentioned in article 17, paragraph 1, of the Convention.

International Covenant on Economic, Social and Cultural Rights, 1966*

Adoption: 16 December 1966
Entry into force: 3 January 1976
Parties: 156 (Status as of 1 April 2007)

AFGHANISTAN 24 Jan 1983 a, ALBANIA 4 Oct 1991 a, ALGERIA 12 Sep 1989, ANDORRA signed 5 Aug 2002, ANGOLA 10 Jan 1992 a, ARGENTINA 8 Aug 1986 (*15), ARMENIA 23 Jun 1993 a, AUSTRALIA 13 Aug 1980 (*10.2a-b, 10.3, 14, 20), AUSTRIA 10 Sep 1978 (*9, 10.3, 12.4, 14, 26), AZERBAIJAN 13 Aug 1992 a, BANGLADESH 6 Sep 2000 a (*10, 11, 14), BARBADOS 5 Jan 1973 a (*14.3d), BELARUS 12 Nov 1973, BELGIUM 21 Apr 1983 (*10.2a, 10.3, 14.1,19-23), BELIZE 10 Jun 1996 a (*12.2, 14.3d, 14.6), BENIN 12 Mar 1992 a, BOLIVIA 12 Aug 1982 a, BOSNIA AND HERZEGOVINA 1 Sep 1993 d, BOTSWANA 8 Sep 2000 (*7, 12.3), BRAZIL 24 Jan 1992 a, BULGARIA 21 Sep 1970, BURKINA FASO 4 Jan 1999 a, BURINDI 9 May 1990 a, CAMBODIA 26 May 1992 a, CAMEROON 27 Jun 1984 a, CANADA 19 May 1976 a, CAPE VERDE 6 Aug 1993 a, CENTRAL AFRICAN REPUBLIC 8 May 1981 a, CHAD 9 Jun 1995 a, CHILE 10 Feb 1972, CHINA signed 5 Oct 1998, COLOMBIA 20 Oct 1969, CONGO 5 Oct 1983 a (*11), COSTA RICA 29 Nov 1968, CÔTE D'IVOIRE 26 Mar 1992 a, CROATIA 12 Oct 1992 d, CYPRUS 2 Apr 1969, CZECH REPUBLIC 22 Feb 1993 d, DEMOCRATIC PEOPLE'S REPUBLIC OF KOREA 14 Sep 1981 a, DEMOCRATIC REPUBLIC OF THE CONGO 1 Nov 1976 a, DENMARK 6 Jan 1972 (*10.3, 14.1, 14.5, 14.7, 20.1), DJIBOUTI 5 Nov 2002 a, DOMINICA 17 Jun 1993 a, DOMINICAN REPUBLIC 4 Jan 1978, ECUADOR 6 Mar 1969, EGYPT 14 Jan 1982, EL SALVADOR 30 Nov 1979, EQUATORIAL GUINEA 25 Sep 1987 a, ERITREA 22 Jan 2002 a, ESTONIA 21 Oct 1991 a, ETHIOPIA 11 Jun 1993 a, FINLAND 19 Aug 1975 (*10.2b, 10.3, 14.7, 20.1), FRANCE 4 Nov 1980 a (*4.1, 9, 13, 14, 20.1, 27), GABON 21 Jan 1983 a, GAMBIA 22 Mar 1979 a (14.3d), GEORGIA 3 May 1994 a, GERMANY 17 Dec 1973 (*14.3d, 14.5, 15), GHANA 7 Sep 2000, GREECE 5 May 1997 a, GRENADA 6 Sep 1991 a, GUATEMALA 5 May 1992 a, GUINEA 24 Jan 1978, GUINEA-BISSAU signed 12 Sep 2000, GUYUNA 15 Feb 1977 (*14.3d, 14.6), HAITI 6 Feb 1991 a, HONDURAS 25 Aug 1997, HUNGARY 17 Jan 1974, ICELAND 22 Aug 1979 (*10.2b, 10.3, 13, 14.7, 20.1), INDIA 10 Apr 1979 a, INDONESIA 23 Feb 2006 a, IRAN (ISLAMIC REPUBLIC OF) 24 Jun 1975, IRAQ 25 Jan 1971, IRELAND 8 Dec 1989 (*10.2, 14, 19.2, 20.1), ISRAEL 3 Oct 1991 (*23), ITALY 15 Sep 1978 (*15.1, 19.3), JAMAICA 3 Oct 1975, JAPAN 21 Jun 1979, JORDAN 28 May 1975, KAZAKHSTAN 24 Jan 2006, KENYA 1 May 1972 a, KUWAIT 21 May 1996 a (*25b), KYRGYZTAN 7 Oct 1994 a, LAO PEOPLE'S DEMOCRATIC REPUBLIC 13 Feb 2007, LATVIA 14 Apr 1992 a, LEBANON 3 Nov 1972 a, LESOTHO 9 Sep 1992 a, LIBERIA 22 Sep 2004, LIBYA ARAB JAMARHIRIYA 15 May 1970 a, LIECHTENSTEIN 10 Dec 1998 a (*14.1, 17.1, 24.3, 26), LITHUANIA 20 Nov 1991 a, LUXEMBOURG 18 Aug 1983 (*10.3, 14.5, 20.1), MADAGASCAR 21 Jun 1971, MALAWI 22 Dec 1993 a, MALDIVES 19 Sep 2006 a, MALI 16 Jul 1974 a, MALTA 13 Sep 1990 a (*13, 14.2, 14.6, 19, 20, 22), MAURITANIA 17 Nov 2004 a (*18, 23.4), MAURITIUS 12 Dec 1973 a, MEXICO 23 Mar 1981 a (*13, 25b, MONACO 28 Aug 1997 (*2, 3, 13, 14.5, 19, 25, 26), MONGOLIA 18 Nov 1974, MONTENEGRO 23 Oct 2006 d, MOROCCO 3 May 1979, MOZAMBIQUE 21 Jul 1993 a, NAMIBIA 28 Nov 1994 a, NAURU signed 12 Nov 2001, NEPAL 14 May 1991 a, NETHERLANDS 11 Dec 1978 (*10, 12.1, 12.2, 12.4, 14.3d, 14.5, 14.7, 19.2, 20.1, 25c), NEW ZEALAND 28 Dec 1978 (*10.2b, 10.3, 14.6, 20, 22) NICARAGUA 12 Mar 1980 a, NIGER 7 Mar 1986 a, NIGERIA 29 Jul 1993 a, NORWAY 13 Sep 1972 (*10.2b, 10.3, 14.5, 14.7, 20.1),

* Source: U.N.G.A. Res. 2200 A (XXI), 993 U.N.T.S. 3.

PANAMA 8 Mar 1977, PARAGUAY 10 Jun 1992 a, PERU 28 Apr 1978, PHILIPPINES 23 Oct 1986, POLAND 18 Mar 1977, PORTUGAL 15 Jun 1978, REPUBLIC OF KOREA 10 Apr 1990 a (*14.5, 22), REPUBLIC OF MOLDOVA 26 Jan 1993 a, REPUBLIC OF SERBIA 12 Mar 2001 d, ROMANIA 9 Dec 1974, RUSSIAN FEDERATION 16 Oct 1973, RWANDA 16 Apr 1975 a, SAINT VINCENT AND THE GRENADINES 9 Nov 1981 a, SAN MARINO 18 Oct 1985 a, SAO TOME AND PRINCIPE signed 31 Oct 1995, SENEGAL 13 Feb 1978, SEYCHELLES 5 May 1992 a, SIERRA LEONE 23 Aug 1996 a, SLOVAKIA 28 May 1993 d, SLOVENIA 6 Jul 1992 d, SOMALIA 24 Jan 1990 a, SOUTH AFRICA 10 Dec 1998, SPAIN 27 Apr 1977, SRI LANKA 11 Jun 1980 a, SUDAN 18 Mar 1986 a, SURINAME 28 Dec 1976 a, SWAZILAND 26 Mar 2004 a, SWEDEN 6 Dec 1971 (*10.3, 14.7, 20.1), SWITZERLAND 18 Jun 1992 a (*10.2b, 12.1, 14.1, 14.5, 20, 25b, 26), SYRIAN ARAB REPUBLIC 21 Apr 1969 a, TAJIKISTAN 4 Jan 1999 a, THAILAND 29 Oct 1996 a, THE FORMER YUGOSLAV REPUBLIC OF MACEDONIA 18 Jan 1994 d, TIMOR-LESTE 18 Sep 2003 a, TOGO 24 May 1984 a, TRINIDAD AND TOBAGO 21 Dec 1978 a (*4.2, 10.2b, 10.3, 12.2, 14.5, 14.6, 21, 26) TUNISIA 18 Mar 1969, TURKEY 23 Sep 2003 (*27), TURKMENISTAN 1 May 1997 a, UGANDA 21 Jun 1995 a, UKRAINE 12 Nov 1973, UNITED KINGDOM OF GREAT BRITAIN AND NORTHERN IRELAND 20 May 1976 (*10.2a, 10.2b, 10.3, 11, 12.1, 12.4, 13, 14.3d, 20, 23, 24, 25b), UNITED REPUBLIC OF TANZANIA 11 Jun 1976 a, UNITED STATES OF AMERICA 8 Jun 1992 (*6.5, 7, 10.2b, 10.3, 20, 14.4, 15.1c,), URUGUAY 1 Apr 1970, UZBEKISTAN 28 Sep 1995 a, VENEZUELA (BOLIVARIAN REPUBLIC OF) 10 May 1978 (*14.3d), Viet Nam 24 Sep 1982 a, YEMEN 9 Feb 1987 a, ZAMBIA 10 Apr 1984 a, ZIMBABWE 13 May 1991 a.

Preamble

The States Parties to the present Covenant,

Considering that, in accordance with the principles proclaimed in the Charter of the United Nations, recognition of the inherent dignity and of the equal and inalienable rights of all members of the human family is the foundation of freedom, justice and peace in the world,

Recognizing that these rights derive from the inherent dignity of the human person,

Recognizing that, in accordance with the Universal Declaration of Human Rights, the ideal of free human beings enjoying freedom from fear and want can only be achieved if conditions are created whereby everyone may enjoy his economic, social and cultural rights, as well as his civil and political rights,

Considering the obligation of States under the Charter of the United Nations to promote universal respect for, and observance of, human rights and freedoms,

Realizing that the individual, having duties to other individuals and to the community to which he belongs, is under a responsibility to strive for the promotion and observance of the rights recognized in the present Covenant,

Agree upon the following articles:

PART I

Article 1

1. All peoples have the right of self-determination. By virtue of that right they freely determine their political status and freely pursue their economic, social and cultural development.

2. All peoples may, for their own ends, freely dispose of their natural wealth and resources without prejudice to any obligations arising out of international economic co-operation, based

upon the principle of mutual benefit, and international law. In no case may a people be deprived of its own means of subsistence.

3. The States Parties to the present Covenant, including those having responsibility for the administration of Non-Self-Governing and Trust Territories, shall promote the realization of the right of self-determination, and shall respect that right, in conformity with the provisions of the Charter of the United Nations.

PART II

Article 2

1. Each State Party to the present Covenant undertakes to take steps, individually and through international assistance and co-operation, especially economic and technical, to the maximum of its available resources, with a view to achieving progressively the full realization of the rights recognized in the present Covenant by all appropriate means, including particularly the adoption of legislative measures.

2. The States Parties to the present Covenant undertake to guarantee that the rights enunciated in the present Covenant will be exercised without discrimination of any kind as to race, colour, sex, language, religion, political or other opinion, national or social origin, property, birth or other status.

3. Developing countries, with due regard to human rights and their national economy, may determine to what extent they would guarantee the economic rights recognized in the present Covenant to non-nationals.

Article 3

The States Parties to the present Covenant undertake to ensure the equal right of men and women to the enjoyment of all economic, social and cultural rights set forth in the present Covenant.

Article 4

The States Parties to the present Covenant recognize that, in the enjoyment of those rights provided by the State in conformity with the present Covenant, the State may subject such rights only to such limitations as are determined by law only in so far as this may be compatible with the nature of these rights and solely for the purpose of promoting the general welfare in a democratic society.

Article 5

1. Nothing in the present Covenant may be interpreted as implying for any State, group or person any right to engage in any activity or to perform any act aimed at the destruction of any of the rights or freedoms recognized herein, or at their limitation to a greater extent than is provided for in the present Covenant.

2. No restriction upon or derogation from any of the fundamental human rights recognized or existing in any country in virtue of law, conventions, regulations or custom shall be admitted on the pretext that the present Covenant does not recognize such rights or that it recognizes them to a lesser extent.

PART III

Article 6

1. The States Parties to the present Covenant recognize the right to work, which includes the right of everyone to the opportunity to gain his living by work which he freely chooses or accepts, and will take appropriate steps to safeguard this right.

2. The steps to be taken by a State Party to the present Covenant to achieve the full realization of this right shall include technical and vocational guidance and training programmes, policies and techniques to achieve steady economic, social and cultural development and full and productive employment under conditions safeguarding fundamental political and economic freedoms to the individual.

Article 7

The States Parties to the present Covenant recognize the right of everyone to the enjoyment of just and favourable conditions of work which ensure, in particular:

(a) Remuneration which provides all workers, as a minimum, with:

(i) Fair wages and equal remuneration for work of equal value without distinction of any kind, in particular women being guaranteed conditions of work not inferior to those enjoyed by men, with equal pay for equal work;

(ii) A decent living for themselves and their families in accordance with the provisions of the present Covenant;

(b) Safe and healthy working conditions;

(c) Equal opportunity for everyone to be promoted in his employment to an appropriate higher level, subject to no considerations other than those of seniority and competence;

(d) Rest, leisure and reasonable limitation of working hours and periodic holidays with pay, as well as remuneration for public holidays

Article 8

1. The States Parties to the present Covenant undertake to ensure:

(a) The right of everyone to form trade unions and join the trade union of his choice, subject only to the rules of the organization concerned, for the promotion and protection of his economic and social interests. No restrictions may be placed on the exercise of this right other than those prescribed by law and which are necessary in a democratic society in the interests of national security or public order or for the protection of the rights and freedoms of others;

(b) The right of trade unions to establish national federations or confederations and the right of the latter to form or join international trade-union organizations;

(c) The right of trade unions to function freely subject to no limitations other than those prescribed by law and which are necessary in a democratic society in the interests of national security or public order or for the protection of the rights and freedoms of others;

(d) The right to strike, provided that it is exercised in conformity with the laws of the particular country.

2. This article shall not prevent the imposition of lawful restrictions on the exercise of these rights by members of the armed forces or of the police or of the administration of the State.

3. Nothing in this article shall authorize States Parties to the International Labour Organization Convention of 1948 concerning Freedom of Association and Protection of the Right to Organize to take legislative measures which would prejudice, or apply the law in such a manner as would prejudice, the guarantees provided for in that Convention.

Article 9

The States Parties to the present Covenant recognize the right of everyone to social security, including social insurance.

Article 10

The States Parties to the present Covenant recognize that:

1. The widest possible protection and assistance should be accorded to the family, which is the natural and fundamental group unit of society, particularly for its establishment and while it is responsible for the care and education of dependent children. Marriage must be entered into with the free consent of the intending spouses.

2. Special protection should be accorded to mothers during a reasonable period before and after childbirth. During such period working mothers should be accorded paid leave or leave with adequate social security benefits.

3. Special measures of protection and assistance should be taken on behalf of all children and young persons without any discrimination for reasons of parentage or other conditions. Children and young persons should be protected from economic and social exploitation. Their employment in work harmful to their morals or health or dangerous to life or likely to hamper their normal development should be punishable by law. States should also set age limits below which the paid employment of child labour should be prohibited and punishable by law.

Article 11

1. The States Parties to the present Covenant recognize the right of everyone to an adequate standard of living for himself and his family, including adequate food, clothing and housing, and to the continuous improvement of living conditions. The States Parties will take appropriate steps to ensure the realization of this right, recognizing to this effect the essential importance of international co-operation based on free consent.

2. The States Parties to the present Covenant, recognizing the fundamental right of everyone to be free from hunger, shall take, individually and through international co-operation, the measures, including specific programmes, which are needed:

(a) To improve methods of production, conservation and distribution of food by making full use of technical and scientific knowledge, by disseminating knowledge of the principles of nutrition and by developing or reforming agrarian systems in such a way as to achieve the most efficient development and utilization of natural resources;

(b) Taking into account the problems of both food-importing and food-exporting countries, to ensure an equitable distribution of world food supplies in relation to need.

Article 12

1. The States Parties to the present Covenant recognize the right of everyone to the enjoyment of the highest attainable standard of physical and mental health.

2. The steps to be taken by the States Parties to the present Covenant to achieve the full realization of this right shall include those necessary for:

(a) The provision for the reduction of the stillbirth-rate and of infant mortality and for the healthy development of the child;

(b) The improvement of all aspects of environmental and industrial hygiene;

(c) The prevention, treatment and control of epidemic, endemic, occupational and other diseases;

(d) The creation of conditions which would assure to all medical service and medical attention in the event of sickness.

Article 13

1. The States Parties to the present Covenant recognize the right of everyone to education. They agree that education shall be directed to the full development of the human personality and the sense of its dignity, and shall strengthen the respect for human rights and fundamental freedoms. They further agree that education shall enable all persons to participate effectively in a free society, promote understanding, tolerance and friendship among all nations and all racial, ethnic or religious groups, and further the activities of the United Nations for the maintenance of peace.

2. The States Parties to the present Covenant recognize that, with a view to achieving the full realization of this right:

(a) Primary education shall be compulsory and available free to all;

(b) Secondary education in its different forms, including technical and vocational secondary education, shall be made generally available and accessible to all by every appropriate means, and in particular by the progressive introduction of free education;

(c) Higher education shall be made equally accessible to all, on the basis of capacity, by every appropriate means, and in particular by the progressive introduction of free education;

(d) Fundamental education shall be encouraged or intensified as far as possible for those persons who have not received or completed the whole period of their primary education;

(e) The development of a system of schools at all levels shall be actively pursued, an adequate fellowship system shall be established, and the material conditions of teaching staff shall be continuously improved.

3. The States Parties to the present Covenant undertake to have respect for the liberty of parents and, when applicable, legal guardians to choose for their children schools, other than those established by the public authorities, which conform to such minimum educational standards as may be laid down or approved by the State and to ensure the religious and moral education of their children in conformity with their own convictions.

4. No part of this article shall be construed so as to interfere with the liberty of individuals and bodies to establish and direct educational institutions, subject always to the observance of the principles set forth in paragraph I of this article and to the requirement that the education given in such institutions shall conform to such minimum standards as may be laid down by the State.

Article 14

Each State Party to the present Covenant which, at the time of becoming a Party, has not been able to secure in its metropolitan territory or other territories under its jurisdiction compulsory primary education, free of charge, undertakes, within two years, to work out and adopt a detailed plan of action for the progressive implementation, within a reasonable number of years, to be fixed in the plan, of the principle of compulsory education free of charge for all.

Article 15

1. The States Parties to the present Covenant recognize the right of everyone:

(a) To take part in cultural life;

(b) To enjoy the benefits of scientific progress and its applications;

(c) To benefit from the protection of the moral and material interests resulting from any scientific, literary or artistic production of which he is the author.

2. The steps to be taken by the States Parties to the present Covenant to achieve the full realization of this right shall include those necessary for the conservation, the development and the diffusion of science and culture.

3. The States Parties to the present Covenant undertake to respect the freedom indispensable for scientific research and creative activity.

4. The States Parties to the present Covenant recognize the benefits to be derived from the encouragement and development of international contacts and co-operation in the scientific and cultural fields.

PART IV

Article 16

1. The States Parties to the present Covenant undertake to submit in conformity with this part of the Covenant reports on the measures which they have adopted and the progress made in achieving the observance of the rights recognized herein.

2. (a) All reports shall be submitted to the Secretary-General of the United Nations, who shall transmit copies to the Economic and Social Council for consideration in accordance with the provisions of the present Covenant;

(b) The Secretary-General of the United Nations shall also transmit to the specialized agencies copies of the reports, or any relevant parts therefrom, from States Parties to the present Covenant which are also members of these specialized agencies in so far as these reports, or parts therefrom, relate to any matters which fall within the responsibilities of the said agencies in accordance with their constitutional instruments.

Article 17

1. The States Parties to the present Covenant shall furnish their reports in stages, in accordance with a programme to be established by the Economic and Social Council within one year of the entry into force of the present Covenant after consultation with the States Parties and the specialized agencies concerned.

2. Reports may indicate factors and difficulties affecting the degree of fulfilment of obligations under the present Covenant.

3. Where relevant information has previously been furnished to the United Nations or to any specialized agency by any State Party to the present Covenant, it will not be necessary to reproduce that information, but a precise reference to the information so furnished will suffice.

Article 18

Pursuant to its responsibilities under the Charter of the United Nations in the field of human rights and fundamental freedoms, the Economic and Social Council may make arrangements with the specialized agencies in respect of their reporting to it on the progress made in achieving the observance of the provisions of the present Covenant falling within the scope of their activities. These reports may include particulars of decisions and recommendations on such implementation adopted by their competent organs.

Article 19

The Economic and Social Council may transmit to the Commission on Human Rights for study and general recommendation or, as appropriate, for information the reports concerning human rights submitted by States in accordance with articles 16 and 17, and those concerning human rights submitted by the specialized agencies in accordance with article 18.

Article 20

The States Parties to the present Covenant and the specialized agencies concerned may submit comments to the Economic and Social Council on any general recommendation under article 19 or reference to such general recommendation in any report of the Commission on Human Rights or any documentation referred to therein.

Article 21

The Economic and Social Council may submit from time to time to the General Assembly reports with recommendations of a general nature and a summary of the information received from the States Parties to the present Covenant and the specialized agencies on the measures taken and the progress made in achieving general observance of the rights recognized in the present Covenant.

Article 22

The Economic and Social Council may bring to the attention of other organs of the United Nations, their subsidiary organs and specialized agencies concerned with furnishing technical assistance any matters arising out of the reports referred to in this part of the present Covenant which may assist such bodies in deciding, each within its field of competence, on the advisability of international measures likely to contribute to the effective progressive implementation of the present Covenant.

Article 23

The States Parties to the present Covenant agree that international action for the achievement of the rights recognized in the present Covenant includes such methods as the conclusion of conventions, the adoption of recommendations, the furnishing of technical assistance and the holding of regional meetings and technical meetings for the purpose of consultation and study organized in conjunction with the Governments concerned.

Article 24

Nothing in the present Covenant shall be interpreted as impairing the provisions of the Charter of the United Nations and of the constitutions of the specialized agencies which define the respective responsibilities of the various organs of the United Nations and of the specialized agencies in regard to the matters dealt with in the present Covenant.

Article 25

Nothing in the present Covenant shall be interpreted as impairing the inherent right of all peoples to enjoy and utilize fully and freely their natural wealth and resources.

PART V

Article 26

1. The present Covenant is open for signature by any State Member of the United Nations or member of any of its specialized agencies, by any State Party to the Statute of the International Court of Justice, and by any other State which has been invited by the General Assembly of the United Nations to become a party to the present Covenant.

2. The present Covenant is subject to ratification. Instruments of ratification shall be deposited with the Secretary-General of the United Nations.

3. The present Covenant shall be open to accession by any State referred to in paragraph 1 of this article.

4. Accession shall be effected by the deposit of an instrument of accession with the Secretary-General of the United Nations.

5. The Secretary-General of the United Nations shall inform all States which have signed the present Covenant or acceded to it of the deposit of each instrument of ratification or accession.

Article 27

1. The present Covenant shall enter into force three months after the date of the deposit with the Secretary-General of the United Nations of the thirty-fifth instrument of ratification or instrument of accession.

2. For each State ratifying the present Covenant or acceding to it after the deposit of the thirty-fifth instrument of ratification or instrument of accession, the present Covenant shall enter into force three months after the date of the deposit of its own instrument of ratification or instrument of accession.

Article 28

The provisions of the present Covenant shall extend to all parts of federal States without any limitations or exceptions.

Article 29

1. Any State Party to the present Covenant may propose an amendment and file it with the Secretary-General of the United Nations. The Secretary-General shall thereupon communicate any proposed amendments to the States Parties to the present Covenant with a request that they notify him whether they favour a conference of States Parties for the purpose of considering and voting upon the proposals. In the event that at least one third of the States Parties favours such a conference, the Secretary-General shall convene the conference under the auspices of the United Nations. Any amendment adopted by a majority of the States Parties present and voting at the conference shall be submitted to the General Assembly of the United Nations for approval.

2. Amendments shall come into force when they have been approved by the General Assembly of the United Nations and accepted by a two-thirds majority of the States Parties to the present Covenant in accordance with their respective constitutional processes.

3. When amendments come into force they shall be binding on those States Parties which have accepted them, other States Parties still being bound by the provisions of the present Covenant and any earlier amendment which they have accepted.

Article 30

Irrespective of the notifications made under article 26, paragraph 5, the Secretary-General of the United Nations shall inform all States referred to in paragraph I of the same article of the following particulars:

(a) Signatures, ratifications and accessions under article 26;

(b) The date of the entry into force of the present Covenant under article 27 and the date of the entry into force of any amendments under article 29.

Article 31

1. The present Covenant, of which the Chinese, English, French, Russian and Spanish texts are equally authentic, shall be deposited in the archives of the United Nations.

2. The Secretary-General of the United Nations shall transmit certified copies of the present Covenant to all States referred to in article 26.

International Covenant on Civil and Political Rights, 1966*

Adoption: 16 December 1966
Entry into force: 23 March 1976**
Parties: 160 (Status as of 1 April 2007)

AFGHANISTAN 24 Jan 1983 a, ALBANIA 4 Oct 1991 a, ALGERIA 12 Sep 1989, ANDORRA 22 Sep 2006, ANGOLA 10 Jan 1992 a, ARGENTINA 8 Aug 1986, ARMENIA 23 Jun 1993 a, AUSTRALIA 13 Aug 1980 (*10.2a-b, 10.3, 14, 20), AUSTRIA 10 Sep 1978, AZERBAIJAN 13 Aug 1992 a, BAHRAIN 20 Sep 2006 a, BANGLADESH 6 Sep 2000 a (*14.3d), BARBADOS 5 Jan 1973 a (*14.3d), BELARUS 12 Nov 1973, BELGIUM 21 Apr 1983 (*10.2a, 10.3, 14.1,19, 21, 22), BELIZE 10 Jun 1996 a (*12.2, 14.3d, 14.6), BENIN 12 Mar 1992 a, BOLIVIA 12 Aug 1982 a, BOSNIA AND HERZEGOVINA 1 Sep 1993 d, BOTSWANA 8 Sep 2000 (*7, 12.3), BRAZIL 24 Jan 1992 a, BULGARIA 21 Sep 1970, BURKINA FASO 4 Jan 1999 a, BURINDI 9 May 1990 a, CAMBODIA 26 May 1992 a, CAMEROON 27 Jun 1984 a, CANADA 19 May 1976 a, CAPE VERDE 6 Aug 1993 a, CENTRAL AFRICAN REPUBLIC 8 May 1981 a, CHAD 9 Jun 1995 a, CHILE 10 Feb 1972, CHINA signed 5 Oct 1998, COLOMBIA 20 Oct 1969, CONGO 5 Oct 1983 a (*11), COSTA RICA 29 Nov 1968, COTE D'IVOIRE 26 Mar 1992 a, CROATIA 12 Oct 1992 d, CYPRUS 2 Apr 1969, CZECH REPUBLIC 22 Feb 1993 d, DEMOCRATIC PEOPLE'S REPUBLIC OF KOREA 14 Sep 1981 a, DEMOCRATIC REPUBLIC OF THE CONGO 1 Nov 1976 a, DENMARK 6 Jan 1972 (*10.3, 14.1, 14.5, 14.7, 20.1), DJIBOUTI 5 Nov 2002 a, DOMINICA 17 Jun 1993 a, DOMINICAN REPUBLIC 4 Jan 1978, ECUADOR 6 Mar 1969, EGYPT 14 Jan 1982, EL SALVADOR 30 Nov 1979, EQUATORIAL GUINEA 25 Sep 1987 a, ERITREA 22 Jan 2002 a, ESTONIA 21 Oct 1991 a, ETHIOPIA 11 Jun 1993 a, FINLAND 19 Aug 1975 (*10.2b, 10.3, 14.7, 20.1), FRANCE 4 Nov 1980 a (*4.1, 9, 14, 20.1, 27) GABON 21 Jan 1983 a, GAMBIA 22 Mar 1979 a (14.3d), GEORGIA 3 May 1994 a, GERMANY 17 Dec 1973, GHANA 7 Sep 2000, GREECE 5 May 1997 a, GRENADA 6 Sep 1991 a, GUATEMALA 5 May 1992 a, GUINEA 24 Jan 1978, GUINEA-BISSAU signed 12 Sep 2000, GUYUNA 15 Feb 1977 (*14.3d, 14.6), HAITI 6 Feb 1991 a, HONDURAS 25 Aug 1997, HUNGARY 17 Jan 1974, ICELAND 22 Aug 1979 (*10.2b, 10.3, 13, 14.7, 20.1), INDIA 10 Apr 1979 a, INDONESIA 23 Feb 2006 a, IRAN (ISLAMIC REPUBLIC OF) 24 Jun 1975, IRAQ 25 Jan 1971, IRELAND 8 Dec 1989 (*10.2, 14, 19.2, 20.1), ISRAEL 3 Oct 1991 (*23), ITALY 15 Sep 1978 (*15.1, 19.3), JAMAICA 3 Oct 1975, JAPAN 21 Jun 1979, JORDAN 28 May 1975, KAZAKHSTAN 24 Jan 2006, KENYA 1 May 1972 a, KUWAIT 21 May 1996 a (*25b), KYRGYZTAN 7 Oct 1994 a, LAO PEOPLE'S DEMOCRATIC REPUBLIC signed 7 Dec 2000, LATVIA 14 Apr 1992 a, LEBANON 3 Nov 1972 a, LESOTHO 9 Sep 1992 a, LIBERIA 22 Sep 2004, LIBYA ARAB JAMARHIRIYA 15 May 1970 a, LIECHTENSTEIN 10 Dec 1998 a (*14.1, 17.1, 24.3, 26), LITHUANIA 20 Nov 1991 a, LUXEMBOURG 18 Aug 1983 (*10.3, 20.1), MADAGASCAR 21 Jun 1971, MALAWI 22 Dec 1993 a, MALDIVES 19 Sep 2006 a, MALI 16 Jul 1974 a, MALTA 13 Sep 1990 a (*13, 14.2, 14.6, 19, 20, 22), MAURITANIA 17 Nov 2004 a (*18, 23.4), MAURITIUS 12 Dec 1973 a, MEXICO 23 Mar 1981 a (*13, 25b, MONACO 28 Aug 1997 (*25), MONGOLIA 18 Nov 1974, MONTENEGRO 23 Oct 2006 d, MOROCCO 3 May 1979, MOZAMBIQUE 21 Jul 1993 a, NAMIBIA 28 Nov 1994 a, NAURU signed 12 Nov 2001, NEPAL 14 May 1991 a, NETHERLANDS 11 Dec 1978 (*10, 12.1, 12.2, 12.4, 14.3d, 14.5, 14.7, 19.2, 20.1), NEW ZEALAND 28 Dec 1978 (*10.2b, 10.3, 14.6, 20, 22) NICARAGUA 12 Mar 1980 a, NIGER 7

* Source: U.N.G.A. Res. 2200 A (XXI), 999 U.N.T.S. 171.

** The quoted date of entry into force is for all provisions except those of article 41; 28 March 1979 for provisions of article 41.

Mar 1986 a, NIGERIA 29 Jul 1993 a, NORWAY 13 Sep 1972 (*10.2b, 10.3, 14.5, 14.7, 20.1), PANAMA 8 Mar 1977, PARAGUAY 10 Jun 1992 a, PERU 28 Apr 1978, PHILIPPINES 23 Oct 1986, POLAND 18 Mar 1977, PORTUGAL 15 Jun 1978, REPUBLIC OF KOREA 10 Apr 1990 a (*14.5, 22), REPUBLIC OF MOLDOVA 26 Jan 1993 a, REPUBLIC OF SERBIA 12 Mar 2001 d, ROMANIA 9 Dec 1974, RUSSIAN FEDERATION 16 Oct 1973, RWANDA 16 Apr 1975 a, SAINT VINCENT AND THE GRENADINES 9 Nov 1981 a, SAN MARINO 18 Oct 1985 a, SAO TOME AND PRINCIPE signed 31 Oct 1995, SENEGAL 13 Feb 1978, SEYCHELLES 5 May 1992 a, SIERRA LEONE 23 Aug 1996 a, SLOVAKIA 28 May 1993 d, SLOVENIA 6 Jul 1992 d, SOMALIA 24 Jan 1990 a, SOUTH AFRICA 10 Dec 1998, SPAIN 27 Apr 1977, SRI LANKA 11 Jun 1980 a, SUDAN 18 Mar 1986 a, SURINAME 28 Dec 1976 a, SWAZILAND 26 Mar 2004 a, SWEDEN 6 Dec 1971 (*10.3, 14.7, 20.1), SWITZERLAND 18 Jun 1992 a (*10.2b, 12.1, 14.1, 14.5, 20, 25b, 26), SYRIAN ARAB REPUBLIC 21 Apr 1969 a, TAJIKISTAN 4 Jan 1999 a, THAILAND 29 Oct 1996 a, THE FORMER YUGOSLAV REPUBLIC OF MACEDONIA 18 Jan 1994 d, TIMOR-LESTE 18 Sep 2003 a, TOGO 24 May 1984 a, TRINIDAD AND TOBAGO 21 Dec 1978 a (*4.2, 10.2b, 10.3, 12.2, 14.5, 14.6, 21, 26) TUNISIA 18 Mar 1969, TURKEY 23 Sep 2003 (*27), TURKMENISTAN 1 May 1997 a, UGANDA 21 Jun 1995 a, UKRAINE 12 Nov 1973, UNITED KINGDOM OF GREAT BRITAIN AND NORTHERN IRELAND 20 May 1976 (*10.2a, 10.2b, 10.3, 11, 12.1, 12.4, 13, 14.3d, 20, 23.3, 24.3, 25b), UNITED REPUBLIC OF TANZANIA 11 Jun 1976 a, UNITED STATES OF AMERICA 8 Jun 1992 (*7, 20, 15.1c, 10.2b, 10.3, 14.4), URUGUAY 1 Apr 1970, UZBEKISTAN 28 Sep 1995 a, VENEZUELA (BOLIVARIAN REPUBLIC OF) 10 May 1978 (*14.3d), Viet Nam 24 Sep 1982 a, YEMEN 9 Feb 1987 a, ZAMBIA 10 Apr 1984 a, ZIMBABWE 13 May 1991 a

Preamble

The States Parties to the present Covenant,

Considering that, in accordance with the principles proclaimed in the Charter of the United Nations, recognition of the inherent dignity and of the equal and inalienable rights of all members of the human family is the foundation of freedom, justice and peace in the world,

Recognizing that these rights derive from the inherent dignity of the human person,

Recognizing that, in accordance with the Universal Declaration of Human Rights, the ideal of free human beings enjoying civil and political freedom and freedom from fear and want can only be achieved if conditions are created whereby everyone may enjoy his civil and political rights, as well as his economic, social and cultural rights,

Considering the obligation of States under the Charter of the United Nations to promote universal respect for, and observance of, human rights and freedoms,

Realizing that the individual, having duties to other individuals and to the community to which he belongs, is under a responsibility to strive for the promotion and observance of the rights recognized in the present Covenant,

Agree upon the following articles:

PART I

Article 1

1. All peoples have the right of self-determination. By virtue of that right they freely determine their political status and freely pursue their economic, social and cultural development.

2. All peoples may, for their own ends, freely dispose of their natural wealth and resources without prejudice to any obligations arising out of international economic co-operation, based upon the principle of mutual benefit, and international law. In no case may a people be deprived of its own means of subsistence.

3. The States Parties to the present Covenant, including those having responsibility for the administration of Non-Self-Governing and Trust Territories, shall promote the realization of the right of self-determination, and shall respect that right, in conformity with the provisions of the Charter of the United Nations.

PART II

Article 2

1. Each State Party to the present Covenant undertakes to respect and to ensure to all individuals within its territory and subject to its jurisdiction the rights recognized in the present Covenant, without distinction of any kind, such as race, colour, sex, language, religion, political or other opinion, national or social origin, property, birth or other status.

2. Where not already provided for by existing legislative or other measures, each State Party to the present Covenant undertakes to take the necessary steps, in accordance with its constitutional processes and with the provisions of the present Covenant, to adopt such laws or other measures as may be necessary to give effect to the rights recognized in the present Covenant.

3. Each State Party to the present Covenant undertakes:

(a) To ensure that any person whose rights or freedoms as herein recognized are violated shall have an effective remedy, notwithstanding that the violation has been committed by persons acting in an official capacity;

(b) To ensure that any person claiming such a remedy shall have his right thereto determined by competent judicial, administrative or legislative authorities, or by any other competent authority provided for by the legal system of the State, and to develop the possibilities of judicial remedy;

(c) To ensure that the competent authorities shall enforce such remedies when granted.

Article 3

The States Parties to the present Covenant undertake to ensure the equal right of men and women to the enjoyment of all civil and political rights set forth in the present Covenant.

Article 4

1. In time of public emergency which threatens the life of the nation and the existence of which is officially proclaimed, the States Parties to the present Covenant may take measures derogating from their obligations under the present Covenant to the extent strictly required by the exigencies of the situation, provided that such measures are not inconsistent with their other obligations under international law and do not involve discrimination solely on the ground of race, colour, sex, language, religion or social origin.

2. No derogation from articles 6, 7, 8 (paragraphs I and 2), 11, 15, 16 and 18 may be made under this provision.

3. Any State Party to the present Covenant availing itself of the right of derogation shall immediately inform the other States Parties to the present Covenant, through the intermediary

of the Secretary-General of the United Nations, of the provisions from which it has derogated and of the reasons by which it was actuated. A further communication shall be made, through the same intermediary, on the date on which it terminates such derogation.

Article 5

1. Nothing in the present Covenant may be interpreted as implying for any State, group or person any right to engage in any activity or perform any act aimed at the destruction of any of the rights and freedoms recognized herein or at their limitation to a greater extent than is provided for in the present Covenant.

2. There shall be no restriction upon or derogation from any of the fundamental human rights recognized or existing in any State Party to the present Covenant pursuant to law, conventions, regulations or custom on the pretext that the present Covenant does not recognize such rights or that it recognizes them to a lesser extent.

PART III

Article 6

1. Every human being has the inherent right to life. This right shall be protected by law. No one shall be arbitrarily deprived of his life.

2. In countries which have not abolished the death penalty, sentence of death may be imposed only for the most serious crimes in accordance with the law in force at the time of the commission of the crime and not contrary to the provisions of the present Covenant and to the Convention on the Prevention and Punishment of the Crime of Genocide. This penalty can only be carried out pursuant to a final judgement rendered by a competent court.

3. When deprivation of life constitutes the crime of genocide, it is understood that nothing in this article shall authorize any State Party to the present Covenant to derogate in any way from any obligation assumed under the provisions of the Convention on the Prevention and Punishment of the Crime of Genocide.

4. Anyone sentenced to death shall have the right to seek pardon or commutation of the sentence. Amnesty, pardon or commutation of the sentence of death may be granted in all cases.

5. Sentence of death shall not be imposed for crimes committed by persons below eighteen years of age and shall not be carried out on pregnant women.

6. Nothing in this article shall be invoked to delay or to prevent the abolition of capital punishment by any State Party to the present Covenant.

Article 7

No one shall be subjected to torture or to cruel, inhuman or degrading treatment or punishment. In particular, no one shall be subjected without his free consent to medical or scientific experimentation.

Article 8

1. No one shall be held in slavery; slavery and the slave-trade in all their forms shall be prohibited.

2. No one shall be held in servitude.

3. (a) No one shall be required to perform forced or compulsory labour;

(b) Paragraph 3 (a) shall not be held to preclude, in countries where imprisonment with hard labour may be imposed as a punishment for a crime, the performance of hard labour in pursuance of a sentence to such punishment by a competent court;

(c) For the purpose of this paragraph the term "forced or compulsory labour" shall not include:

(i) Any work or service, not referred to in subparagraph (b), normally required of a person who is under detention in consequence of a lawful order of a court, or of a person during conditional release from such detention;

(ii) Any service of a military character and, in countries where conscientious objection is recognized, any national service required by law of conscientious objectors;

(iii) Any service exacted in cases of emergency or calamity threatening the life or well-being of the community;

(iv) Any work or service which forms part of normal civil obligations.

Article 9

1. Everyone has the right to liberty and security of person. No one shall be subjected to arbitrary arrest or detention. No one shall be deprived of his liberty except on such grounds and in accordance with such procedure as are established by law.

2. Anyone who is arrested shall be informed, at the time of arrest, of the reasons for his arrest and shall be promptly informed of any charges against him.

3. Anyone arrested or detained on a criminal charge shall be brought promptly before a judge or other officer authorized by law to exercise judicial power and shall be entitled to trial within a reasonable time or to release. It shall not be the general rule that persons awaiting trial shall be detained in custody, but release may be subject to guarantees to appear for trial, at any other stage of the judicial proceedings, and, should occasion arise, for execution of the judgement.

4. Anyone who is deprived of his liberty by arrest or detention shall be entitled to take proceedings before a court, in order that court may decide without delay on the lawfulness of his detention and order his release if the detention is not lawful.

5. Anyone who has been the victim of unlawful arrest or detention shall have an enforceable right to compensation.

Article 10

1. All persons deprived of their liberty shall be treated with humanity and with respect for the inherent dignity of the human person.

2. (a) Accused persons shall, save in exceptional circumstances, be segregated from convicted persons and shall be subject to separate treatment appropriate to their status as unconvicted persons;

(b) Accused juvenile persons shall be separated from adults and brought as speedily as possible for adjudication. 3. The penitentiary system shall comprise treatment of prisoners the essential aim of which shall be their reformation and social rehabilitation. Juvenile offenders shall be segregated from adults and be accorded treatment appropriate to their age and legal status.

Article 11

No one shall be imprisoned merely on the ground of inability to fulfil a contractual obligation.

Article 12

1. Everyone lawfully within the territory of a State shall, within that territory, have the right to liberty of movement and freedom to choose his residence.

2. Everyone shall be free to leave any country, including his own.

3. The above-mentioned rights shall not be subject to any restrictions except those which are provided by law, are necessary to protect national security, public order (ordre public), public health or morals or the rights and freedoms of others, and are consistent with the other rights recognized in the present Covenant.

4. No one shall be arbitrarily deprived of the right to enter his own country.

Article 13

An alien lawfully in the territory of a State Party to the present Covenant may be expelled therefrom only in pursuance of a decision reached in accordance with law and shall, except where compelling reasons of national security otherwise require, be allowed to submit the reasons against his expulsion and to have his case reviewed by, and be represented for the purpose before, the competent authority or a person or persons especially designated by the competent authority.

Article 14

1. All persons shall be equal before the courts and tribunals. In the determination of any criminal charge against him, or of his rights and obligations in a suit at law, everyone shall be entitled to a fair and public hearing by a competent, independent and impartial tribunal established by law. The press and the public may be excluded from all or part of a trial for reasons of morals, public order (ordre public) or national security in a democratic society, or when the interest of the private lives of the parties so requires, or to the extent strictly necessary in the opinion of the court in special circumstances where publicity would prejudice the interests of justice; but any judgement rendered in a criminal case or in a suit at law shall be made public except where the interest of juvenile persons otherwise requires or the proceedings concern matrimonial disputes or the guardianship of children.

2. Everyone charged with a criminal offence shall have the right to be presumed innocent until proved guilty according to law.

3. In the determination of any criminal charge against him, everyone shall be entitled to the following minimum guarantees, in full equality:

(a) To be informed promptly and in detail in a language which he understands of the nature and cause of the charge against him;

(b) To have adequate time and facilities for the preparation of his defence and to communicate with counsel of his own choosing;

(c) To be tried without undue delay;

(d) To be tried in his presence, and to defend himself in person or through legal assistance of his own choosing; to be informed, if he does not have legal assistance, of this right; and to have legal assistance assigned to him, in any case where the interests of justice so require, and without payment by him in any such case if he does not have sufficient means to pay for it;

(e) To examine, or have examined, the witnesses against him and to obtain the attendance and examination of witnesses on his behalf under the same conditions as witnesses against him;

(f) To have the free assistance of an interpreter if he cannot understand or speak the language used in court;

(g) Not to be compelled to testify against himself or to confess guilt.

4. In the case of juvenile persons, the procedure shall be such as will take account of their age and the desirability of promoting their rehabilitation.

5. Everyone convicted of a crime shall have the right to his conviction and sentence being reviewed by a higher tribunal according to law.

6. When a person has by a final decision been convicted of a criminal offence and when subsequently his conviction has been reversed or he has been pardoned on the ground that a new or newly discovered fact shows conclusively that there has been a miscarriage of justice, the person who has suffered punishment as a result of such conviction shall be compensated according to law, unless it is proved that the non-disclosure of the unknown fact in time is wholly or partly attributable to him.

7. No one shall be liable to be tried or punished again for an offence for which he has already been finally convicted or acquitted in accordance with the law and penal procedure of each country.

Article 15

1. No one shall be held guilty of any criminal offence on account of any act or omission which did not constitute a criminal offence, under national or international law, at the time when it was committed. Nor shall a heavier penalty be imposed than the one that was applicable at the time when the criminal offence was committed. If, subsequent to the commission of the offence, provision is made by law for the imposition of the lighter penalty, the offender shall benefit thereby.

2. Nothing in this article shall prejudice the trial and punishment of any person for any act or omission which, at the time when it was committed, was criminal according to the general principles of law recognized by the community of nations.

Article 16

Everyone shall have the right to recognition everywhere as a person before the law.

Article 17

1. No one shall be subjected to arbitrary or unlawful interference with his privacy, family, home or correspondence, nor to unlawful attacks on his honour and reputation.

2. Everyone has the right to the protection of the law against such interference or attacks.

Article 18

1. Everyone shall have the right to freedom of thought, conscience and religion. This right shall include freedom to have or to adopt a religion or belief of his choice, and freedom, either individually or in community with others and in public or private, to manifest his religion or belief in worship, observance, practice and teaching.

2. No one shall be subject to coercion which would impair his freedom to have or to adopt a religion or belief of his choice.

3. Freedom to manifest one's religion or beliefs may be subject only to such limitations as are prescribed by law and are necessary to protect public safety, order, health, or morals or the fundamental rights and freedoms of others.

4. The States Parties to the present Covenant undertake to have respect for the liberty of parents and, when applicable, legal guardians to ensure the religious and moral education of their children in conformity with their own convictions.

Article 19

1. Everyone shall have the right to hold opinions without interference.

2. Everyone shall have the right to freedom of expression; this right shall include freedom to seek, receive and impart information and ideas of all kinds, regardless of frontiers, either orally, in writing or in print, in the form of art, or through any other media of his choice.

3. The exercise of the rights provided for in paragraph 2 of this article carries with it special duties and responsibilities. It may therefore be subject to certain restrictions, but these shall only be such as are provided by law and are necessary:

(a) For respect of the rights or reputations of others;

(b) For the protection of national security or of public order (ordre public), or of public health or morals.

Article 20

1. Any propaganda for war shall be prohibited by law.

2. Any advocacy of national, racial or religious hatred that constitutes incitement to discrimination, hostility or violence shall be prohibited by law.

Article 21

The right of peaceful assembly shall be recognized. No restrictions may be placed on the exercise of this right other than those imposed in conformity with the law and which are necessary in a democratic society in the interests of national security or public safety, public order (ordre public), the protection of public health or morals or the protection of the rights and freedoms of others.

Article 22

1. Everyone shall have the right to freedom of association with others, including the right to form and join trade unions for the protection of his interests.

2. No restrictions may be placed on the exercise of this right other than those which are prescribed by law and which are necessary in a democratic society in the interests of national security or public safety, public order (ordre public), the protection of public health or morals or the protection of the rights and freedoms of others. This article shall not prevent the imposition of lawful restrictions on members of the armed forces and of the police in their exercise of this right.

3. Nothing in this article shall authorize States Parties to the International Labour Organization Convention of 1948 concerning Freedom of Association and Protection of the Right to Organize to take legislative measures which would prejudice, or to apply the law in such a manner as to prejudice, the guarantees provided for in that Convention.

Article 23

1. The family is the natural and fundamental group unit of society and is entitled to protection by society and the State.

2. The right of men and women of marriageable age to marry and to found a family shall be recognized.

3. No marriage shall be entered into without the free and full consent of the intending spouses.

4. States Parties to the present Covenant shall take appropriate steps to ensure equality of rights and responsibilities of spouses as to marriage, during marriage and at its dissolution. In the case of dissolution, provision shall be made for the necessary protection of any children.

Article 24

1. Every child shall have, without any discrimination as to race, colour, sex, language, religion, national or social origin, property or birth, the right to such measures of protection as are required by his status as a minor, on the part of his family, society and the State.

2. Every child shall be registered immediately after birth and shall have a name.

3. Every child has the right to acquire a nationality.

Article 25

Every citizen shall have the right and the opportunity, without any of the distinctions mentioned in article 2 and without unreasonable restrictions:

(a) To take part in the conduct of public affairs, directly or through freely chosen representatives;

(b) To vote and to be elected at genuine periodic elections which shall be by universal and equal suffrage and shall be held by secret ballot, guaranteeing the free expression of the will of the electors;

(c) To have access, on general terms of equality, to public service in his country.

Article 26

All persons are equal before the law and are entitled without any discrimination to the equal protection of the law. In this respect, the law shall prohibit any discrimination and guarantee to all persons equal and effective protection against discrimination on any ground such as race, colour, sex, language, religion, political or other opinion, national or social origin, property, birth or other status.

Article 27

In those States in which ethnic, religious or linguistic minorities exist, persons belonging to such minorities shall not be denied the right, in community with the other members of their group, to enjoy their own culture, to profess and practise their own religion, or to use their own language.

PART IV

Article 28

1. There shall be established a Human Rights Committee (hereafter referred to in the present Covenant as the Committee). It shall consist of eighteen members and shall carry out the functions hereinafter provided.

2. The Committee shall be composed of nationals of the States Parties to the present Covenant who shall be persons of high moral character and recognized competence in the field of human rights, consideration being given to the usefulness of the participation of some persons having legal experience.

3. The members of the Committee shall be elected and shall serve in their personal capacity.

Article 29

1. The members of the Committee shall be elected by secret ballot from a list of persons possessing the qualifications prescribed in article 28 and nominated for the purpose by the States Parties to the present Covenant.

2. Each State Party to the present Covenant may nominate not more than two persons. These persons shall be nationals of the nominating State.

3. A person shall be eligible for renomination.

Article 30

1. The initial election shall be held no later than six months after the date of the entry into force of the present Covenant.

2. At least four months before the date of each election to the Committee, other than an election to fill a vacancy declared in accordance with article 34, the Secretary-General of the United Nations shall address a written invitation to the States Parties to the present Covenant to submit their nominations for membership of the Committee within three months.

3. The Secretary-General of the United Nations shall prepare a list in alphabetical order of all the persons thus nominated, with an indication of the States Parties which have nominated them, and shall submit it to the States Parties to the present Covenant no later than one month before the date of each election.

4. Elections of the members of the Committee shall be held at a meeting of the States Parties to the present Covenant convened by the Secretary General of the United Nations at the Headquarters of the United Nations. At that meeting, for which two thirds of the States Parties to the present Covenant shall constitute a quorum, the persons elected to the Committee shall be those nominees who obtain the largest number of votes and an absolute majority of the votes of the representatives of States Parties present and voting.

Article 31

1. The Committee may not include more than one national of the same State.

2. In the election of the Committee, consideration shall be given to equitable geographical distribution of membership and to the representation of the different forms of civilization and of the principal legal systems.

Article 32

1. The members of the Committee shall be elected for a term of four years. They shall be eligible for re-election if renominated. However, the terms of nine of the members elected at the first election shall expire at the end of two years; immediately after the first election, the names of these nine members shall be chosen by lot by the Chairman of the meeting referred to in article 30, paragraph 4.

2. Elections at the expiry of office shall be held in accordance with the preceding articles of this part of the present Covenant.

Article 33

1. If, in the unanimous opinion of the other members, a member of the Committee has ceased to carry out his functions for any cause other than absence of a temporary character, the Chairman of the Committee shall notify the Secretary-General of the United Nations, who shall then declare the seat of that member to be vacant.

2. In the event of the death or the resignation of a member of the Committee, the Chairman shall immediately notify the Secretary-General of the United Nations, who shall declare the seat vacant from the date of death or the date on which the resignation takes effect.

Article 34

1. When a vacancy is declared in accordance with article 33 and if the term of office of the member to be replaced does not expire within six months of the declaration of the vacancy, the Secretary-General of the United Nations shall notify each of the States Parties to the present Covenant, which may within two months submit nominations in accordance with article 29 for the purpose of filling the vacancy.

2. The Secretary-General of the United Nations shall prepare a list in alphabetical order of the persons thus nominated and shall submit it to the States Parties to the present Covenant. The election to fill the vacancy shall then take place in accordance with the relevant provisions of this part of the present Covenant.

3. A member of the Committee elected to fill a vacancy declared in accordance with article 33 shall hold office for the remainder of the term of the member who vacated the seat on the Committee under the provisions of that article.

Article 35

The members of the Committee shall, with the approval of the General Assembly of the United Nations, receive emoluments from United Nations resources on such terms and conditions as the General Assembly may decide, having regard to the importance of the Committee's responsibilities.

Article 36

The Secretary-General of the United Nations shall provide the necessary staff and facilities for the effective performance of the functions of the Committee under the present Covenant.

Article 37

1. The Secretary-General of the United Nations shall convene the initial meeting of the Committee at the Headquarters of the United Nations.

2. After its initial meeting, the Committee shall meet at such times as shall be provided in its rules of procedure.

3. The Committee shall normally meet at the Headquarters of the United Nations or at the United Nations Office at Geneva.

Article 38

Every member of the Committee shall, before taking up his duties, make a solemn declaration in open committee that he will perform his functions impartially and conscientiously.

Article 39

1. The Committee shall elect its officers for a term of two years. They may be re-elected.

2. The Committee shall establish its own rules of procedure, but these rules shall provide, inter alia, that:

(a) Twelve members shall constitute a quorum;

(b) Decisions of the Committee shall be made by a majority vote of the members present.

Article 40

1. The States Parties to the present Covenant undertake to submit reports on the measures they have adopted which give effect to the rights recognized herein and on the progress made in the enjoyment of those rights: (a) Within one year of the entry into force of the present Covenant for the States Parties concerned;

(b) Thereafter whenever the Committee so requests.

2. All reports shall be submitted to the Secretary-General of the United Nations, who shall transmit them to the Committee for consideration. Reports shall indicate the factors and difficulties, if any, affecting the implementation of the present Covenant.

3. The Secretary-General of the United Nations may, after consultation with the Committee, transmit to the specialized agencies concerned copies of such parts of the reports as may fall within their field of competence.

4. The Committee shall study the reports submitted by the States Parties to the present Covenant. It shall transmit its reports, and such general comments as it may consider appropriate, to the States Parties. The Committee may also transmit to the Economic and Social Council these comments along with the copies of the reports it has received from States Parties to the present Covenant.

5. The States Parties to the present Covenant may submit to the Committee observations on any comments that may be made in accordance with paragraph 4 of this article.

Article 41

1. A State Party to the present Covenant may at any time declare under this article that it recognizes the competence of the Committee to receive and consider communications to the effect that a State Party claims that another State Party is not fulfilling its obligations under the present Covenant. Communications under this article may be received and considered only if submitted by a State Party which has made a declaration recognizing in regard to itself the competence of the Committee. No communication shall be received by the Committee if it concerns a State Party which has not made such a declaration. Communications received under this article shall be dealt with in accordance with the following procedure:

(a) If a State Party to the present Covenant considers that another State Party is not giving effect to the provisions of the present Covenant, it may, by written communication, bring the matter to the attention of that State Party. Within three months after the receipt of the communication the receiving State shall afford the State which sent the communication an explanation, or any other statement in writing clarifying the matter which should include, to the extent possible and pertinent, reference to domestic procedures and remedies taken, pending, or available in the matter;

(b) If the matter is not adjusted to the satisfaction of both States Parties concerned within six months after the receipt by the receiving State of the initial communication, either State shall have the right to refer the matter to the Committee, by notice given to the Committee and to the other State;

(c) The Committee shall deal with a matter referred to it only after it has ascertained that all available domestic remedies have been invoked and exhausted in the matter, in conformity with the generally recognized principles of international law. This shall not be the rule where the application of the remedies is unreasonably prolonged;

(d) The Committee shall hold closed meetings when examining communications under this article;

(e) Subject to the provisions of subparagraph (c), the Committee shall make available its good offices to the States Parties concerned with a view to a friendly solution of the matter on the basis of respect for human rights and fundamental freedoms as recognized in the present Covenant;

(f) In any matter referred to it, the Committee may call upon the States Parties concerned, referred to in subparagraph (b), to supply any relevant information;

(g) The States Parties concerned, referred to in subparagraph (b), shall have the right to be represented when the matter is being considered in the Committee and to make submissions orally and/or in writing;

(h) The Committee shall, within twelve months after the date of receipt of notice under subparagraph (b), submit a report:

(i) If a solution within the terms of subparagraph (e) is reached, the Committee shall confine its report to a brief statement of the facts and of the solution reached;

(ii) If a solution within the terms of subparagraph (e) is not reached, the Committee shall confine its report to a brief statement of the facts; the written submissions and record of the oral submissions made by the States Parties concerned shall be attached to the report. In every matter, the report shall be communicated to the States Parties concerned.

2. The provisions of this article shall come into force when ten States Parties to the present Covenant have made declarations under paragraph I of this article. Such declarations shall be deposited by the States Parties with the Secretary-General of the United Nations, who shall transmit copies thereof to the other States Parties. A declaration may be withdrawn at any time by notification to the Secretary-General. Such a withdrawal shall not prejudice the consideration of any matter which is the subject of a communication already transmitted under this article; no further communication by any State Party shall be received after the notification of withdrawal of the declaration has been received by the Secretary-General, unless the State Party concerned has made a new declaration.

Article 42

1. (a) If a matter referred to the Committee in accordance with article 41 is not resolved to the satisfaction of the States Parties concerned, the Committee may, with the prior consent of the States Parties concerned, appoint an ad hoc Conciliation Commission (hereinafter referred to as the Commission). The good offices of the Commission shall be made available to the States Parties concerned with a view to an amicable solution of the matter on the basis of respect for the present Covenant;

(b) The Commission shall consist of five persons acceptable to the States Parties concerned. If the States Parties concerned fail to reach agreement within three months on all or part of the composition of the Commission, the members of the Commission concerning whom no agreement has been reached shall be elected by secret ballot by a two-thirds majority vote of the Committee from among its members.

2. The members of the Commission shall serve in their personal capacity. They shall not be nationals of the States Parties concerned, or of a State not Party to the present Covenant, or of a State Party which has not made a declaration under article 41.

3. The Commission shall elect its own Chairman and adopt its own rules of procedure.

4. The meetings of the Commission shall normally be held at the Headquarters of the United Nations or at the United Nations Office at Geneva. However, they may be held at such other convenient places as the Commission may determine in consultation with the Secretary-General of the United Nations and the States Parties concerned.

5. The secretariat provided in accordance with article 36 shall also service the commissions appointed under this article.

6. The information received and collated by the Committee shall be made available to the Commission and the Commission may call upon the States Parties concerned to supply any other relevant information.

7. When the Commission has fully considered the matter, but in any event not later than twelve months after having been seized of the matter, it shall submit to the Chairman of the Committee a report for communication to the States Parties concerned:

(a) If the Commission is unable to complete its consideration of the matter within twelve months, it shall confine its report to a brief statement of the status of its consideration of the matter;

(b) If an amicable solution to the matter on tie basis of respect for human rights as recognized in the present Covenant is reached, the Commission shall confine its report to a brief statement of the facts and of the solution reached;

(c) If a solution within the terms of subparagraph (b) is not reached, the Commission's report shall embody its findings on all questions of fact relevant to the issues between the States Parties concerned, and its views on the possibilities of an amicable solution of the matter. This report shall also contain the written submissions and a record of the oral submissions made by the States Parties concerned;

(d) If the Commission's report is submitted under subparagraph (c), the States Parties concerned shall, within three months of the receipt of the report, notify the Chairman of the Committee whether or not they accept the contents of the report of the Commission.

8. The provisions of this article are without prejudice to the responsibilities of the Committee under article 41.

9. The States Parties concerned shall share equally all the expenses of the members of the Commission in accordance with estimates to be provided by the Secretary-General of the United Nations.

10. The Secretary-General of the United Nations shall be empowered to pay the expenses of the members of the Commission, if necessary, before reimbursement by the States Parties concerned, in accordance with paragraph 9 of this article.

Article 43

The members of the Committee, and of the ad hoc conciliation commissions which may be appointed under article 42, shall be entitled to the facilities, privileges and immunities of experts on mission for the United Nations as laid down in the relevant sections of the Convention on the Privileges and Immunities of the United Nations.

Article 44

The provisions for the implementation of the present Covenant shall apply without prejudice to the procedures prescribed in the field of human rights by or under the constituent instruments and the conventions of the United Nations and of the specialized agencies and shall not prevent the States Parties to the present Covenant from having recourse to other procedures for settling a dispute in accordance with general or special international agreements in force between them.

Article 45

The Committee shall submit to the General Assembly of the United Nations, through the Economic and Social Council, an annual report on its activities.

PART V

Article 46

Nothing in the present Covenant shall be interpreted as impairing the provisions of the Charter of the United Nations and of the constitutions of the specialized agencies which define the respective responsibilities of the various organs of the United Nations and of the specialized agencies in regard to the matters dealt with in the present Covenant.

Article 47

Nothing in the present Covenant shall be interpreted as impairing the inherent right of all peoples to enjoy and utilize fully and freely their natural wealth and resources.

PART VI

Article 48

1. The present Covenant is open for signature by any State Member of the United Nations or member of any of its specialized agencies, by any State Party to the Statute of the International Court of Justice, and by any other State which has been invited by the General Assembly of the United Nations to become a Party to the present Covenant.

2. The present Covenant is subject to ratification. Instruments of ratification shall be deposited with the Secretary-General of the United Nations.

3. The present Covenant shall be open to accession by any State referred to in paragraph 1 of this article.

4. Accession shall be effected by the deposit of an instrument of accession with the Secretary-General of the United Nations.

5. The Secretary-General of the United Nations shall inform all States which have signed this Covenant or acceded to it of the deposit of each instrument of ratification or accession.

Article 49

1. The present Covenant shall enter into force three months after the date of the deposit with the Secretary-General of the United Nations of the thirty-fifth instrument of ratification or instrument of accession.

2. For each State ratifying the present Covenant or acceding to it after the deposit of the thirty-fifth instrument of ratification or instrument of accession, the present Covenant shall enter into force three months after the date of the deposit of its own instrument of ratification or instrument of accession.

Article 50

The provisions of the present Covenant shall extend to all parts of federal States without any limitations or exceptions.

Article 51

1. Any State Party to the present Covenant may propose an amendment and file it with the Secretary-General of the United Nations. The Secretary-General of the United Nations shall thereupon communicate any proposed amendments to the States Parties to the present Covenant with a request that they notify him whether they favour a conference of States Parties for the purpose of considering and voting upon the proposals. In the event that at least one third of the States Parties favours such a conference, the Secretary-General shall convene the conference under the auspices of the United Nations. Any amendment adopted by a majority of the States Parties present and voting at the conference shall be submitted to the General Assembly of the United Nations for approval.

2. Amendments shall come into force when they have been approved by the General Assembly of the United Nations and accepted by a two-thirds majority of the States Parties to the present Covenant in accordance with their respective constitutional processes. 3. When amendments come into force, they shall be binding on those States Parties which have accepted them, other States Parties still being bound by the provisions of the present Covenant and any earlier amendment which they have accepted.

Article 52

1. Irrespective of the notifications made under article 48, paragraph 5, the Secretary-General of the United Nations shall inform all States referred to in paragraph I of the same article of the following particulars:

(a) Signatures, ratifications and accessions under article 48;

(b) The date of the entry into force of the present Covenant under article 49 and the date of the entry into force of any amendments under article 51.

Article 53

1. The present Covenant, of which the Chinese, English, French, Russian and Spanish texts are equally authentic, shall be deposited in the archives of the United Nations.

2. The Secretary-General of the United Nations shall transmit certified copies of the present Covenant to all States referred to in article 48.

Convention on the Elimination of All Forms of Discrimination against Women, 1979*

Adoption: 18 December 1979
Entry into force: 3 September 1981
Parties: 185 (Status as of 1 April 2007)

AFGHANISTAN 5 Mar 2003, ALBANIA 11 May 1994 a, ALGERIA 22 May 1996 a (*2, 9.2, 15.4, 16, 29.1, 41, 43), ANDORRA 15 Jan 1997 a, ANGOLA 17 Sep 1986 a, ANTIGUA AND BARBUDA 1 Aug 1989 a, ARGENTINA 15 Jul 1985 (*29.1), ARMENIA 13 Sep 1993 a, AUSTRALIA 28 Jul 1983 (*11.2), AUSTRIA 31 Mar 1982 (*11), AZERBAIJAN 10 Jul 1995 a, BAHAMAS 6 Oct 1993 a (*2a, 9.2, 16h, 29.1), BAHRAIN 18 Jun 2002 a (*2, 9.2, 15.4, 16, 29.1), BANGLADESH 6 Nov 1984 a (*2), BARBADOS 16 Oct 1980, BELARUS 4 Feb 1981, BELGIUM 10 Jul 1985, BELIZE 16 May 1990, BENIN 12 Mar 1992, BHUTAN 31 Aug 1981, BOLIVIA 8 Jun 1990, BOSNIA AND HERZEGOVINA 1 Sep 1993 d, BOTSWANA 13 Aug 1996 a, BRAZIL 1 Feb 1984 (*29.1), BRUNEI DARUSSALAM 24 May 2006 a (*9.2, 29.1), BULGARIA 8 Feb 1982, BURKINA FASO 14 Oct 1987 a, BURUNDI 8 Jan 1992, CAMBODIA 15 Oct 1992 a, CAMEROON 23 Aug 1994, CANADA 10 Dec 1981, CAPE VERDE 5 Dec 1980 a, CENTRAL AFRICAN REPUBLIC 21 Jun 1991 a, CHAD 9 Jun 1995 a, CHILE 7 Dec 1989, CHINA 4 Nov 1980 a (*29.1), COLOMBIA 19 Jan 1992, COMOROS 31 Oct 1994 a, CONGO 26 Jul 1982, COOK ISLANDS 11 Aug 2006 a, COSTA RICA 4 Apr 1986, COTE D'IVOIRE 18 Dec 1995, CROATIA 9 Sep 1992 d, CUBA 17 Jul 1980 (*29), CYPRUS 23 1985 a, CZECH REPUBLIC 22 Feb 1993 d, DEMOCRATIC PEOPLE'S REPUBLIC OF KOREA 27 Feb 2001 a (*2f, 9.2, 29.1), DEMOCRATIC REPUBLIC OF THE CONGO 17 Oct 1986, DENMARK 21 Apr 1983, DJIBOUTI 2 Dec 1998 a, DOMINICA 15 Sep 1980, DOMINICAN REPUBLIC 2 Sep 1982, ECUADOR 2 Sep 1982, EGYPT 9 Nov 1981 (*2, 9.2, 16, 29), EL SALVADOR 19 Aug 1981 (*29), EQUATORIAL GUINEA 23 Oct 1984 a, ERITREA 5 Sep 1995 a, ESTONIA 21 Oct 1991 a, ETHIOPIA 10 Sep 1981 (*29.1), FIJI 28 Aug 1995 a, FINLAND 4 Sep 1986, FRANCE 14 Dec 1983 (*14.2c, 14.2h, 16.1g, 29.1), GABON 21 Jan 1983, GAMBIA 16 Apr 1993, GEORGIA 26 Oct 1994 a, GERMANY 10 Jul 1985 (*29), GHANA 2 Jan 1986, GREECE 7 Jun 1983, GRENADA 30 Aug 1990, GUATEMALA 12 Aug 1982, GUINEA 9 Aug 1982, GUINEA-BISSAU 23 Aug 1985, GUYANA 17 Jul 1980, HAITI 20 Jul 1981, HONDURAS 3 Mar 1983, HUNGARY 22 Dec 1980, ICELAND 18 Jun 1985, INDIA 9 Jul 1993 (*29.1), INDONESIA 13 Sep 1984 (*29.1), IRAQ 13 Aug 1986 a (*2f, 2g, 9.1, 9.2, 16, 29.1), IRELAND 23 Dec 1985 a (*16.1d, 16.1f, 11.1, 13a), ISRAEL 3 Oct 1991 (*7b, 16), ITALY 3 10 Jun 1985, JAMAICA 19 Oct 1984 (*29.1), JAPAN 25 Jun 1985, JORDAN 1 Jul 1992 (*9.2, 15.4, 16.1c, 16.1d, 16.1g), KAZAKHSTAN 26 Aug 1998 a, KENYA 9 Mar 1984 a, KIRIBATI 17 Mar 2004 a, KUWAIT 2 Sep 1994 a (*9.2, 16f, 29.1), KYRGYZSTAN 10 Feb 1997 a, LAO PEOPLE'S DEMOCRATIC REPUBLIC 14 Aug 1981, LATVIA 14 Apr 1992, LEBANON 16 Apr 1997 a (*9.2, 16.1c, 16.1d, 16.1f, 16.1g, 29.1), LESOTHO 22 Aug 1995 (*2, general), LIBERIA 17 Jul 1984 a, LIBYAN ARAB JAMAHIRIYA 16 May 1989 a (*2, 16c, 16d, general), LIECHTENSTEIN 22 Dec 1995 a (*1), LITHUANIA 18 Jan 1994 a, LUXEMBOURG 2 Feb 1989 (*7, 16.1g), MADAGASCAR 17 Mar 1989, MALAWI 12 Mar 1987 a, MALAYSIA 5 Jul 1995 a (*5a, 7b, 9, 16, general), MALDIVES 1 Jul 1993 a (*7a, 16), MALI 10 Sep 1985, MALTA 8 Mar 1991 a (*11, 13, 15, 16), MARSHALL ISLANDS 2 Mar 2006 a, MAURITANIA 10 May 2001 a (*general), MAURITIUS 9 Jul 1984 a (*29.1), MEXICO 23 Mar 1981, MICRONESIA (FEDERATED STATES) 1 Sep 2004 a (*2f, 5, 11.1d, 11.2b, 16, 29.1), MONACO 18 Mar 2005 a (*7b, 9, 16.1g, 16.1e, 29.2), MONGOLIA 20 Jul

* Source: U.N.G.A. Res. 34/180, 1249 U.N.T.S. 13.

1981, MONTENEGRO 23 Oct 2006 d, MOROCCO 21 Jun 1993 a (*2, 9.2, 15.4, 16, 29), MOZAMBIQUE 21 Apr 1997 a, MYANMAR 22 Jul 1997 a (*29), NAMIBIA 23 Nov 1992 a, NEPAL 22 Apr 1991, NETHERLANDS 23 Jul 1991, NEW ZEALAND 10 Jan 1985 (*2f, 5a, general), NICARAGUA 27 Oct 1981, NIGER 8 Oct 1999 a (*2d, 2f, 5a, 15.4, 16.1c, 16.1e, 16.1g, 29.1), NIGERIA 13 Jun 1985, NORWAY 21 May 1981, OMAN 7 Feb 2006 a (*9.2, 15.4, 16, 29.1), PAKISTAN 12 Mar 1991 a (*29.1, general), PANAMA 29 Oct 1981, PAPUA NEW GUINEA 12 Jan 1995 a, PARAGUAY 6 Apr 1987 a, PERU 13 Sep 1982, PHILIPPINES 5 Aug 1981, Poland 30 Jul 1980, PORTUGAL 30 Jul 1980, REPUBLIC OF KOREA 27 Dec 1984 (*16.1g), REPUBLIC OF MOLDOVA 1 Jul 1994 a, REPUBLIC OF SERBIA 12 Mar 2001 d, ROMANIA 7 Jan 1982, RUSSIAN FEDERATION 23 Jan 1981, RWANDA 2 Mar 1981, SAINT KITTS AND NEVIS 25 Apr 1985 a, SAINT LUCIA 8 Oct 1982 a, SAINT VINCENT AND THE GRENADINES 4 Aug 1981 a, SAMOA 25 Sep 1992 a, SAN MARINO 10 Dec 2003, SAO TOME AND PRINCIPE 3 Jun 2003, SAUDI ARABIA 7 Sep 2000 (*2.9, 29.1), SENEGAL 5 Feb 1985, SEYCHELLES 5 May 1992 a, SIERRA LEONE 11 Nov 1988, SINGAPORE 5 Oct 1995 a (*2, 11.1, 16, 29.1), SLOVAKIA 28 May 1993 d, SLOVENIA 6 Jul 1992 d, SOLOMON ISLANDS 6 May 2002, SOUTH AFRICA 15 Dec 1995, SPAIN 5 Jan 1984 (*general), SRI LANKA 5 Oct 1981, SURINAME 1 Mar 1993 a, SWAZILAND 26 Mar 2004 a, SWEDEN 2 Jul 1980, SWITZERLAND 27 Mar 1997 (*15.2, 16.1g, 16.1h), SYRIAN ARAB REPUBLIC 28 Mar 2003 a (*2, 9.2, 15.4, 16.1c, 16.1d, 16.1f, 16.1g, 16.2, 29.1), TAJIKISTAN 26 Oct 1993 a, THAILAND 9 Aug 1985 a (*7, 10), THE FORMER YUGOSLAV REPUBLIC OF MACEDONIA 18 Jan 1994 d, TIMOR-LESTE 16 Apr 2003 a, TOGO 26 Sep 1983 a, TRINIDAD AND TOBAGO 12 Jan 1990 (*29.1), TUNISIA 20 Sep 1985 (*9.2, 16.1c-d, 16.1f-g, 29.1, general), TURKEY 20 Dec 1985 a (*29.1), TURKMENISTAN 1 May 1997 a, TUVALU 6 Oct 1999 a, UGANDA 22 Jul 1985, UKRAINE 12 Mar 1981, UNITED ARAB EMIRATES 6 Oct 2004 a (*2f, 9, 15.2, 16, 29.1), UNITED KINGDOM OF GREAT BRITAIN AND NORTHERN IRELAND 7 Apr 1986 (*10), UNITED REPUBLIC OF TANZANIA 20 Aug 1985, UNITED STATES OF AMERICA signed 17 Jul 1980, URUGUAY 9 Oct 1981, UZBEKISTAN 19 Jul 1995 a, VANUATU 8 Sept 1995 a, VENEZUELA (BOLIVARIAN REPUBLIC OF) 2 May 1983 (*29.1), VIET NAM 17 Feb 1982 (*29.1), YEMEN 30 May 1984 a (*29.1), ZAMBIA 21 Jun 1985, ZIMBABWE 13 May 1991 a.

The States Parties to the present Convention,

Noting that the Charter of the United Nations reaffirms faith in fundamental human rights, in the dignity and worth of the human person and in the equal rights of men and women,

Noting that the Universal Declaration of Human Rights affirms the principle of the inadmissibility of discrimination and proclaims that all human beings are born free and equal in dignity and rights and that everyone is entitled to all the rights and freedoms set forth therein, without distinction of any kind, including distinction based on sex,

Noting that the States Parties to the International Covenants on Human Rights have the obligation to ensure the equal rights of men and women to enjoy all economic, social, cultural, civil and political rights,

Considering the international conventions concluded under the auspices of the United Nations and the specialized agencies promoting equality of rights of men and women,

Noting also the resolutions, declarations and recommendations adopted by the United Nations and the specialized agencies promoting equality of rights of men and women,

Concerned, however, that despite these various instruments extensive discrimination against women continues to exist,

Recalling that discrimination against women violates the principles of equality of rights and respect for human dignity, is an obstacle to the participation of women, on equal terms with men, in the political, social, economic and cultural life of their countries, hampers the growth of the prosperity of society and the family and makes more difficult the full development of the potentialities of women in the service of their countries and of humanity,

Concerned that in situations of poverty women have the least access to food, health, education, training and opportunities for employment and other needs,

Convinced that the establishment of the new international economic order based on equity and justice will contribute significantly towards the promotion of equality between men and women,

Emphasizing that the eradication of apartheid, all forms of racism, racial discrimination, colonialism, neo-colonialism, aggression, foreign occupation and domination and interference in the internal affairs of States is essential to the full enjoyment of the rights of men and women,

Affirming that the strengthening of international peace and security, the relaxation of international tension, mutual co-operation among all States irrespective of their social and economic systems, general and complete disarmament, in particular nuclear disarmament under strict and effective international control, the affirmation of the principles of justice, equality and mutual benefit in relations among countries and the realization of the right of peoples under alien and colonial domination and foreign occupation to self-determination and independence, as well as respect for national sovereignty and territorial integrity, will promote social progress and development and as a consequence will contribute to the attainment of full equality between men and women,

Convinced that the full and complete development of a country, the welfare of the world and the cause of peace require the maximum participation of women on equal terms with men in all fields,

Bearing in mind the great contribution of women to the welfare of the family and to the development of society, so far not fully recognized, the social significance of maternity and the role of both parents in the family and in the upbringing of children, and aware that the role of women in procreation should not be a basis for discrimination but that the upbringing of children requires a sharing of responsibility between men and women and society as a whole,

Aware that a change in the traditional role of men as well as the role of women in society and in the family is needed to achieve full equality between men and women,

Determined to implement the principles set forth in the Declaration on the Elimination of Discrimination against Women and, for that purpose, to adopt the measures required for the elimination of such discrimination in all its forms and manifestations,

Have agreed on the following:

PART I

Article 1

For the purposes of the present Convention, the term "discrimination against women" shall mean any distinction, exclusion or restriction made on the basis of sex which has the effect or purpose of impairing or nullifying the recognition, enjoyment or exercise by women, irrespective of their marital status, on a basis of equality of men and women, of human rights and fundamental freedoms in the political, economic, social, cultural, civil or any other field.

Article 2

States Parties condemn discrimination against women in all its forms, agree to pursue by all appropriate means and without delay a policy of eliminating discrimination against women and, to this end, undertake:

(a) To embody the principle of the equality of men and women in their national constitutions or other appropriate legislation if not yet incorporated therein and to ensure, through law and other appropriate means, the practical realization of this principle;

(b) To adopt appropriate legislative and other measures, including sanctions where appropriate, prohibiting all discrimination against women;

(c) To establish legal protection of the rights of women on an equal basis with men and to ensure through competent national tribunals and other public institutions the effective protection of women against any act of discrimination;

(d) To refrain from engaging in any act or practice of discrimination against women and to ensure that public authorities and institutions shall act in conformity with this obligation;

(e) To take all appropriate measures to eliminate discrimination against women by any person, organization or enterprise;

(f) To take all appropriate measures, including legislation, to modify or abolish existing laws, regulations, customs and practices which constitute discrimination against women;

(g) To repeal all national penal provisions which constitute discrimination against women.

Article 3

States Parties shall take in all fields, in particular in the political, social, economic and cultural fields, all appropriate measures, including legislation, to en sure the full development and advancement of women, for the purpose of guaranteeing them the exercise and enjoyment of human rights and fundamental freedoms on a basis of equality with men.

Article 4

1. Adoption by States Parties of temporary special measures aimed at accelerating de facto equality between men and women shall not be considered discrimination as defined in the present Convention, but shall in no way entail as a consequence the maintenance of unequal or separate standards; these measures shall be discontinued when the objectives of equality of opportunity and treatment have been achieved.

2. Adoption by States Parties of special measures, including those measures contained in the present Convention, aimed at protecting maternity shall not be considered discriminatory.

Article 5

States Parties shall take all appropriate measures:

(a) To modify the social and cultural patterns of conduct of men and women, with a view to achieving the elimination of prejudices and customary and all other practices which are based on the idea of the inferiority or the superiority of either of the sexes or on stereotyped roles for men and women;

(b) To ensure that family education includes a proper understanding of maternity as a social function and the recognition of the common responsibility of men and women in the upbringing and development of their children, it being understood that the interest of the children is the primordial consideration in all cases.

Article 6

States Parties shall take all appropriate measures, including legislation, to suppress all forms of traffic in women and exploitation of prostitution of women.

PART II

Article 7

States Parties shall take all appropriate measures to eliminate discrimination against women in the political and public life of the country and, in particular, shall ensure to women, on equal terms with men, the right:

(a) To vote in all elections and public referenda and to be eligible for election to all publicly elected bodies;

(b) To participate in the formulation of government policy and the implementation thereof and to hold public office and perform all public functions at all levels of government;

(c) To participate in non-governmental organizations and associations concerned with the public and political life of the country.

Article 8

States Parties shall take all appropriate measures to ensure to women, on equal terms with men and without any discrimination, the opportunity to represent their Governments at the international level and to participate in the work of international organizations.

Article 9

1. States Parties shall grant women equal rights with men to acquire, change or retain their nationality. They shall ensure in particular that neither marriage to an alien nor change of nationality by the husband during marriage shall automatically change the nationality of the wife, render her stateless or force upon her the nationality of the husband.

2. States Parties shall grant women equal rights with men with respect to the nationality of their children.

PART III

Article 10

States Parties shall take all appropriate measures to eliminate discrimination against women in order to ensure to them equal rights with men in the field of education and in particular to ensure, on a basis of equality of men and women:

(a) The same conditions for career and vocational guidance, for access to studies and for the achievement of diplomas in educational establishments of all categories in rural as well as in urban areas; this equality shall be ensured in pre-school, general, technical, professional and higher technical education, as well as in all types of vocational training;

(b) Access to the same curricula, the same examinations, teaching staff with qualifications of the same standard and school premises and equipment of the same quality;

(c) The elimination of any stereotyped concept of the roles of men and women at all levels and in all forms of education by encouraging coeducation and other types of education which will help to achieve this aim and, in particular, by the revision of textbooks and school programmes and the adaptation of teaching methods;

(d) The same opportunities to benefit from scholarships and other study grants;

(e) The same opportunities for access to programmes of continuing education, including adult and functional literacy programmes, particularly those aimed at reducing, at the earliest possible time, any gap in education existing between men and women;

(f) The reduction of female student drop-out rates and the organization of programmes for girls and women who have left school prematurely;

(g) The same Opportunities to participate actively in sports and physical education;

(h) Access to specific educational information to help to ensure the health and well-being of families, including information and advice on family planning.

Article 11

1. States Parties shall take all appropriate measures to eliminate discrimination against women in the field of employment in order to ensure, on a basis of equality of men and women, the same rights, in particular:

(a) The right to work as an inalienable right of all human beings;

(b) The right to the same employment opportunities, including the application of the same criteria for selection in matters of employment;

(c) The right to free choice of profession and employment, the right to promotion, job security and all benefits and conditions of service and the right to receive vocational training and retraining, including apprenticeships, advanced vocational training and recurrent training;

(d) The right to equal remuneration, including benefits, and to equal treatment in respect of work of equal value, as well as equality of treatment in the evaluation of the quality of work;

(e) The right to social security, particularly in cases of retirement, unemployment, sickness, invalidity and old age and other incapacity to work, as well as the right to paid leave;

(f) The right to protection of health and to safety in working conditions, including the safeguarding of the function of reproduction.

2. In order to prevent discrimination against women on the grounds of marriage or maternity and to ensure their effective right to work, States Parties shall take appropriate measures:

(a) To prohibit, subject to the imposition of sanctions, dismissal on the grounds of pregnancy or of maternity leave and discrimination in dismissals on the basis of marital status;

(b) To introduce maternity leave with pay or with comparable social benefits without loss of former employment, seniority or social allowances;

(c) To encourage the provision of the necessary supporting social services to enable parents to combine family obligations with work responsibilities and participation in public life, in particular through promoting the establishment and development of a network of child-care facilities;

(d) To provide special protection to women during pregnancy in types of work proved to be harmful to them.

3. Protective legislation relating to matters covered in this article shall be reviewed periodically in the light of scientific and technological knowledge and shall be revised, repealed or extended as necessary

Article 12

1. States Parties shall take all appropriate measures to eliminate discrimination against women in the field of health care in order to ensure, on a basis of equality of men and women, access to health care services, including those related to family planning.

2. Notwithstanding the provisions of paragraph I of this article, States Parties shall ensure to women appropriate services in connection with pregnancy, confinement and the post-natal period, granting free services where necessary, as well as adequate nutrition during pregnancy and lactation.

Article 13

States Parties shall take all appropriate measures to eliminate discrimination against women in other areas of economic and social life in order to ensure, on a basis of equality of men and women, the same rights, in particular:

(a) The right to family benefits;

(b) The right to bank loans, mortgages and other forms of financial credit;

(c) The right to participate in recreational activities, sports and all aspects of cultural life.

Article 14

1. States Parties shall take into account the particular problems faced by rural women and the significant roles which rural women play in the economic survival of their families, including their work in the non-monetized sectors of the economy, and shall take all appropriate measures to ensure the application of the provisions of the present Convention to women in rural areas.

2. States Parties shall take all appropriate measures to eliminate discrimination against women in rural areas in order to ensure, on a basis of equality of men and women, that they participate in and benefit from rural development and, in particular, shall ensure to such women the right:

(a) To participate in the elaboration and implementation of development planning at all levels;

(b) To have access to adequate health care facilities, including information, counselling and services in family planning;

(c) To benefit directly from social security programmes;

(d) To obtain all types of training and education, formal and non-formal, including that relating to functional literacy, as well as, inter alia, the benefit of all community and extension services, in order to increase their technical proficiency;

(e) To organize self-help groups and co-operatives in order to obtain equal access to economic opportunities through employment or self employment;

(f) To participate in all community activities;

(g) To have access to agricultural credit and loans, marketing facilities, appropriate technology and equal treatment in land and agrarian reform as well as in land resettlement schemes;

(h) To enjoy adequate living conditions, particularly in relation to housing, sanitation, electricity and water supply, transport and communications.

PART IV

Article 15

1. States Parties shall accord to women equality with men before the law.

2. States Parties shall accord to women, in civil matters, a legal capacity identical to that of men and the same opportunities to exercise that capacity. In particular, they shall give women equal rights to conclude contracts and to administer property and shall treat them equally in all stages of procedure in courts and tribunals.

3. States Parties agree that all contracts and all other private instruments of any kind with a legal effect which is directed at restricting the legal capacity of women shall be deemed null and void.

4. States Parties shall accord to men and women the same rights with regard to the law relating to the movement of persons and the freedom to choose their residence and domicile.

Article 16

1. States Parties shall take all appropriate measures to eliminate discrimination against women in all matters relating to marriage and family relations and in particular shall ensure, on a basis of equality of men and women:

(a) The same right to enter into marriage;

(b) The same right freely to choose a spouse and to enter into marriage only with their free and full consent;

(c) The same rights and responsibilities during marriage and at its dissolution;

(d) The same rights and responsibilities as parents, irrespective of their marital status, in matters relating to their children; in all cases the interests of the children shall be paramount;

(e) The same rights to decide freely and responsibly on the number and spacing of their children and to have access to the information, education and means to enable them to exercise these rights;

(f) The same rights and responsibilities with regard to guardianship, wardship, trusteeship and adoption of children, or similar institutions where these concepts exist in national legislation; in all cases the interests of the children shall be paramount;

(g) The same personal rights as husband and wife, including the right to choose a family name, a profession and an occupation;

(h) The same rights for both spouses in respect of the ownership, acquisition, management, administration, enjoyment and disposition of property, whether free of charge or for a valuable consideration.

2. The betrothal and the marriage of a child shall have no legal effect, and all necessary action, including legislation, shall be taken to specify a minimum age for marriage and to make the registration of marriages in an official registry compulsory.

PART V

Article 17

1. For the purpose of considering the progress made in the implementation of the present Convention, there shall be established a Committee on the Elimination of Discrimination

against Women (hereinafter referred to as the Committee) consisting, at the time of entry into force of the Convention, of eighteen and, after ratification of or accession to the Convention by the thirty-fifth State Party, of twenty-three experts of high moral standing and competence in the field covered by the Convention. The experts shall be elected by States Parties from among their nationals and shall serve in their personal capacity, consideration being given to equitable geographical distribution and to the representation of the different forms of civilization as well as the principal legal systems.

2. The members of the Committee shall be elected by secret ballot from a list of persons nominated by States Parties. Each State Party may nominate one person from among its own nationals.

3. The initial election shall be held six months after the date of the entry into force of the present Convention. At least three months before the date of each election the Secretary-General of the United Nations shall address a letter to the States Parties inviting them to submit their nominations within two months. The Secretary-General shall prepare a list in alphabetical order of all persons thus nominated, indicating the States Parties which have nominated them, and shall submit it to the States Parties.

4. Elections of the members of the Committee shall be held at a meeting of States Parties convened by the Secretary-General at United Nations Headquarters. At that meeting, for which two thirds of the States Parties shall constitute a quorum, the persons elected to the Committee shall be those nominees who obtain the largest number of votes and an absolute majority of the votes of the representatives of States Parties present and voting.

5. The members of the Committee shall be elected for a term of four years. However, the terms of nine of the members elected at the first election shall expire at the end of two years; immediately after the first election the names of these nine members shall be chosen by lot by the Chairman of the Committee.

6. The election of the five additional members of the Committee shall be held in accordance with the provisions of paragraphs 2, 3 and 4 of this article, following the thirty-fifth ratification or accession. The terms of two of the additional members elected on this occasion shall expire at the end of two years, the names of these two members having been chosen by lot by the Chairman of the Committee.

7. For the filling of casual vacancies, the State Party whose expert has ceased to function as a member of the Committee shall appoint another expert from among its nationals, subject to the approval of the Committee.

8. The members of the Committee shall, with the approval of the General Assembly, receive emoluments from United Nations resources on such terms and conditions as the Assembly may decide, having regard to the importance of the Committee's responsibilities.

9. The Secretary-General of the United Nations shall provide the necessary staff and facilities for the effective performance of the functions of the Committee under the present Convention.

Article 18

1. States Parties undertake to submit to the Secretary-General of the United Nations, for consideration by the Committee, a report on the legislative, judicial, administrative or other measures which they have adopted to give effect to the provisions of the present Convention and on the progress made in this respect:

(a) Within one year after the entry into force for the State concerned;

(b) Thereafter at least every four years and further whenever the Committee so requests.

2. Reports may indicate factors and difficulties affecting the degree of fulfilment of obligations under the present Convention.

Article 19

1. The Committee shall adopt its own rules of procedure.

2. The Committee shall elect its officers for a term of two years.

Article 20

1. The Committee shall normally meet for a period of not more than two weeks annually in order to consider the reports submitted in accordance with article 18 of the present Convention.

2. The meetings of the Committee shall normally be held at United Nations Headquarters or at any other convenient place as determined by the Committee.

Article 21

1. The Committee shall, through the Economic and Social Council, report annually to the General Assembly of the United Nations on its activities and may make suggestions and general recommendations based on the examination of reports and information received from the States Parties. Such suggestions and general recommendations shall be included in the report of the Committee together with comments, if any, from States Parties.

2. The Secretary-General of the United Nations shall transmit the reports of the Committee to the Commission on the Status of Women for its information.

Article 22

The specialized agencies shall be entitled to be represented at the consideration of the implementation of such provisions of the present Convention as fall within the scope of their activities. The Committee may invite the specialized agencies to submit reports on the implementation of the Convention in areas falling within the scope of their activities.

PART VI

Article 23

Nothing in the present Convention shall affect any provisions that are more conducive to the achievement of equality between men and women which may be contained:

(a) In the legislation of a State Party; or

(b) In any other international convention, treaty or agreement in force for that State.

Article 24

States Parties undertake to adopt all necessary measures at the national level aimed at achieving the full realization of the rights recognized in the present Convention.

Article 25

1. The present Convention shall be open for signature by all States.

2. The Secretary-General of the United Nations is designated as the depositary of the present Convention.

3. The present Convention is subject to ratification. Instruments of ratification shall be deposited with the Secretary-General of the United Nations.

4. The present Convention shall be open to accession by all States. Accession shall be effected by the deposit of an instrument of accession with the Secretary-General of the United Nations.

Article 26

1. A request for the revision of the present Convention may be made at any time by any State Party by means of a notification in writing addressed to the Secretary-General of the United Nations.

2. The General Assembly of the United Nations shall decide upon the steps, if any, to be taken in respect of such a request.

Article 27

1. The present Convention shall enter into force on the thirtieth day after the date of deposit with the Secretary-General of the United Nations of the twentieth instrument of ratification or accession.

2. For each State ratifying the present Convention or acceding to it after the deposit of the twentieth instrument of ratification or accession, the Convention shall enter into force on the thirtieth day after the date of the deposit of its own instrument of ratification or accession.

Article 28

1. The Secretary-General of the United Nations shall receive and circulate to all States the text of reservations made by States at the time of ratification or accession.

2. A reservation incompatible with the object and purpose of the present Convention shall not be permitted.

3. Reservations may be withdrawn at any time by notification to this effect addressed to the Secretary-General of the United Nations, who shall then inform all States thereof. Such notification shall take effect on the date on which it is received.

Article 29

1. Any dispute between two or more States Parties concerning the interpretation or application of the present Convention which is not settled by negotiation shall, at the request of one of them, be submitted to arbitration. If within six months from the date of the request for arbitration the parties are unable to agree on the organization of the arbitration, any one of those parties may refer the dispute to the International Court of Justice by request in conformity with the Statute of the Court.

2. Each State Party may at the time of signature or ratification of the present Convention or accession thereto declare that it does not consider itself bound by paragraph I of this article. The other States Parties shall not be bound by that paragraph with respect to any State Party which has made such a reservation.

3. Any State Party which has made a reservation in accordance with paragraph 2 of this article may at any time withdraw that reservation by notification to the Secretary-General of the United Nations.

Article 30

The present Convention, the Arabic, Chinese, English, French, Russian and Spanish texts of which are equally authentic, shall be deposited with the Secretary-General of the United Nations. IN WITNESS WHEREOF the undersigned, duly authorized, have signed the present Convention.

Convention on the Civil Aspects of International Child Abduction, 1980 [excerpts]*

Adoption: 25 October 1980
Entry into force: 1 December 1983
Parties: 77 (Status as of 1 April 2007)

ARGENTINA 19 Mar 1991, AUSTRALIA 29 Oct 1986 (*territorial), AUSTRIA 12 May 1987, BAHAMAS 1 Oct 1993 a, BELARUS 12 Jan 1998 a (*26.2), BELGIUM 9 Feb 1999, BELIZE 22 June 1989 a (*24, 26.2), BOSNIA AND HERZEGOVINA 23 Aug 1993 d, BRAZIL 19 Oct 1999 a (*24), BULGARIA 20 May 2003 a (*26.2), BURKINA FASO 25 May 1992 a, CANADA 2 June 1983 (*24, 26.2), CHILE 23 Feb 1994 a (*4), COLOMBIA 13 Dec 1995 a, COSTA RICA 9 Nov 1998 a, CROATIA 5 Apr 1993 d, CYPRUS 4 Nov 1994 a, CZECH REPUBLIC 15 Dec 1997 (*26.2), DENMARK 17 Apr 1991 (*territorial, 24, 26.2), DOMINICAN REPUBLIC 11 Aug 2004 a, ECUADOR 22 Jan 1992 a, EL SALVADOR 5 Feb 2001 a (*24, 26.2), ESTONIA 18 Apr 2001 a (*24, 26.2), FIJI 16 Mar 1999 a, FINLAND 25 May 1994 (*24, 26.2), FRANCE 16 Sep 1982 (*territorial, 24, 26.2), GEORGIA 24 July 1997 a, GERMANY 27 Sep 1990 (*24, 26.2), GREECE 19 Mar 1993 (*24, 26.2), GUATEMALA 6 Feb 2002 a (*24, 26.2), HONDURAS 20 Dec 1993 a, HUNGARY 7 Apr 1986 a, ICELAND 14 Aug 1996 a (* 24, 26.2), IRELAND 16 July 1991, ISRAEL 4 Sep 1991 (*26.2), ITALY 22 Feb 1995, LATVIA 15 Nov 2001 a (*24), LITHUANIA 5 June 2002 a (*24, 26.2), LUXEMBOURG 8 Oct 1986 (*26.2), MACEDONIA (FORMER YOUGOSLAV REPUBLIC OF) 20 Sep 1993 d, MALTA 26 Oct 1999 a, MAURITIUS 23 Mar 1993 a (*26.2), MEXICO 20 June 1991 a, MOLDOVA 10 Apr 1998 a (*26.2), MONACO 12 Nov 1992 a (*26.2), MONTENEGRO 1 Jan 2007 d, NETHERLANDS 12 June 1990 (*26.2), NEW ZEALAND 31 May 1991 a (*24, 26.2), NICARAGUA 14 Dec 2000 a, NORWAY 9 Jan 1989 (*24, 26.2), PANAMA 2 Feb 1994 a (* 24, 26.2), PARAGUAY 13 May 1998 a, PERU 28 May 2001 a, POLAND 10 Aug 1992 a (*26.2), PORTUGAL 29 Sep 1983, ROMANIA 20 Nov 1992 a, SAINT KITTS AND NEVIS 31 May 1994 a (*26.2), SAN MARINO 14 Dec 2006 a (* 26.2), SERBIA 19 Apr 2001 d, SLOVAKIA 7 Nov 2000 (* 26.2), SLOVENIA 22 Mar 1994 a, SOUTH AFRICA 8 July 1997 a (*24, 26.2), SPAIN 16 June 1987, SRI LANKA 28 Sep 2001 a, SWEDEN 22 Mar 1989 (*26.2), SWITZERLAND 11 Oct 1983, THAILAND 14 Aug 2002 a (*24), TRINIDAD AND TOBAGO 7 June 2000 a, TURKEY 31 May 2000 (* 26.2), TURKMENISTAN 29 Dec 1997 a, UKRAINE 2 June 2006 a, UNITED KINGDOM 20 May 1986 (*26.2), UNITED STATES OF AMERICA 29 Apr 1988 (*24, 26.2), URUGUAY 16 Nov 1999 a, UZBEKISTAN 31 May 1999 a (*26.2), VENEZUELA 16 Oct 1996 (*26.2), ZIMBABWE 4 Apr 1995 a (*26.2).

[...]

CHAPTER I – SCOPE OF THE CONVENTION

Article 1

The objects of the present Convention are:

a) to secure the prompt return of children wrongfully removed to or retained in any Contracting State; and

b) to ensure that rights of custody and of access under the law of one Contracting State are effectively respected in other Contracting States.

* Source: 1343 U.N.T.S. 98.

Article 2

Contracting States shall take all appropriate measures to secure within their territories the implementation of the objects of the Convention. For this purpose they shall use the most expeditious procedures available.

Article 3

The removal or the retention of a child is to be considered wrongful where:

a) it is in breach of rights of custody attributed to a person, an institution or any other body, either jointly or alone, under the law of the State in which the child was habitually resident immediately before the removal or retention; and

b) at the time of removal or retention those rights were actually exercised, either jointly or alone, or would have been so exercised but for the removal or retention.

The rights of custody mentioned in sub-paragraph a) above, may arise in particular by operation of law or by reason of a judicial or administrative decision, or by reason of an agreement having legal effect under the law of that State.

Article 4

The Convention shall apply to any child who was habitually resident in a Contracting State immediately before any breach of custody or access rights. The Convention shall cease to apply when the child attaint the age of 16 years.

Article 5

For the purposes of this Convention:

a) "rights of custody" shall include rights relating to the care of the person of the child and, in particular, the right to determine the child's place of residence;

b) "rights of access" shall include the right to take a child for a limited period of time to a place other than the child's habitual residence.

CHAPTER II – CENTRAL AUTHORITIES

Article 6

A Contracting State shall designate a Central Authority to discharge the duties, which are imposed by the Convention upon such authorities.

Federal States, States with more than one system of law or States having autonomous territorial organizations shall be free to appoint more than one Central Authority and to specify the territorial extent of their powers. Where a State has appointed more than one Central Authority, it shall designate the Central Authority to which applications may be addressed for transmission to the appropriate Central Authority within that State.

Article 7

Central Authorities shall co-operate with each other and promote co-operation amongst the competent authorities in their respective States to secure the prompt return of children and to achieve the other objects of this Convention.

In particular, either directly or through any intermediary, they shall take all appropriate measures:

a) to discover the whereabouts of a child who has been wrongfully removed or retained;

b) to prevent further harm to the child or prejudice to interested parties by taking or causing to be taken provisional measures;

c) to secure the voluntary return of the child or to bring about an amicable resolution of the issues;

d) to exchange, where desirable, information relating to the social background of the child;

e) to provide information of a general character as to the law of their State in connection with the application of the Convention;

f) to initiate or facilitate the institution of judicial or administrative proceedings with a view to obtaining the return of the child and, in a proper case, to make arrangements for organizing or securing the effective exercise of rights of access;

g) where the circumstances so require, to provide or facilitate the provision of legal aid and advice, including the participation of legal counsel and advisers;

h) to provide such administrative arrangements as may be necessary and appropriate to secure the safe return of the child;

i) to keep other each other informed with respect to the operation of this Convention and, as far as possible, to eliminate any obstacles to its application.

CHAPTER III – RETURN OF CHILDREN

Article 8

Any person, institution or other body claiming that a child has been removed or retained in breach of custody rights may apply either to the Central Authority of the child's habitual residence or to the Central Authority of any other Contracting State for assistance in securing the return of the child.

The application shall contain:

a) information concerning the identity of the applicant, of the child and of the person alleged to have removed or retained the child;

b) where available, the date of birth of the child;

c) the grounds on which the applicant's claim for return of the child is based;

d) all available information relating to the whereabouts of the child and the identity of the person with whom the child is presumed to be.

The application may be accompanied or supplemented by

e) an authenticated copy of any relevant decision or agreement;

f) a certificate or an affidavit emanating from a Central Authority, or other competent authority of the State of the child's habitual residence, or from a qualified person, concerning the relevant law of that State;

g) any other relevant document.

Article 9

If the Central Authority, which receives an application, referred to in Article 8, has reason to believe that the child is in another Contracting State, it shall directly and without delay transmit the application to the Central Authority of that Contracting State and inform the requesting Central Authority, or the applicant, as the case may be.

Article 10

The Central Authority of the State where the child is shall take or cause to be taken all appropriate measures in order to obtain the voluntary return of the child.

Article 11

The judicial or administrative authorities of Contracting States shall act expeditiously in proceedings for the return of children.

If the judicial or administrative authority concerned has not reached a decision within six weeks from the date of commencement of the proceedings, the applicant or the Central Authority of the requested State, on its own initiative or if asked by the Central Authority of the requesting State, shall have the right to request a statement of the reasons for the delay. If the Central Authority of the requested State receives a reply, that Authority shall transmit the reply to the Central Authority of the requesting State, or to the applicant, as the case may be.

Article 12

Where a child has been wrongfully removed or retained in terms of Article 3 and, at the date of the commencement of the proceedings before the judicial or administrative authority of the Contracting State where the child is, a period of less than one year has elapsed from the date of the wrongful removal or retention, the authority concerned shall order the return of the child forthwith.

The judicial or administrative authority, even where the proceedings have been commenced after the expiration of the period of one year referred to in the preceding paragraph, shall also order the return of the child, unless it is demonstrated that the child is now settled in its new environment.

Where the judicial or administrative authority in the requested State has reason to believe that the child has been taken to another State, it may stay the proceedings or dismiss the application for the return of the child.

Article 13

Notwithstanding the provisions of the preceding Article, the judicial or administrative authority of the requested State is not bound to order the return of the child if the person, institution or other body which opposes its return establishes that:

a) the person, institution or other body having the care of the person of the child was not actually exercising the custody rights at the time of removal or retention, or had consented to or subsequently acquiesced in the removal of retention; or

b) there is a grave risk that his or her return would expose the child to physical or psychological harm or otherwise place the child in an intolerable situation.

The judicial or administrative authority may also refuse to order the return of the child if it finds that the child objects to being returned and has attained an age and degree of maturity at which it is appropriate to take account of its views.

In considering the circumstances referred to in this Article, the judicial and administrative authorites shall take into account the information relating to the social background of the child provided by the Central Authority or other competent authority of the child's habitual residence.

Article 14

In ascertaining whether there has been a wrongful removal of retention within the meaning of Article 3, the judicial or administrative authorities of the requested State may take notice directly of the law of, and of judicial or administrative decisions, formally recognized or not in the State of the habitual residence of the child, without recourse to the specific procedures for the proof of that law or for the recognition of foreign decisions which would otherwise be applicable.

Article 15

The judicial or administrative authorities of a Contracting State may, prior to the making of an order for the return of the child, request that the applicant obtain from the authorities of the State of the habitual residence of the child a decision or other determination that the removal or retention was wrongful within the meaning of Article 3 of the Convention, where such a decision or determination may be obtained in that State. The Central Authorities of the Contracting States shall so far as practicable assist applicants to obtain such a decision or determination.

Article 16

After receiving notice of a wrongful removal or retention of a child in the sense of Article 3, the judicial or administrative authorities of the Contracting State to which the child has been removed or in which it has been retained shall not decide on the merits of rights of custody until it has been determined that the child is not to be returned under this Convention or unless an application under the Convention is not lodged within a reasonable time following receipt of the notice.

Article 17

The sole fact that a decision relating to custody has been given in or is entitled to recognition in the requested State shall not be a ground for refusing to return a child under this Convention, but the judicial or administrative authorities of the requested State may take account of the reasons for that decision in applying this Convention.

Article 18

The provisions of this Chapter do not limit the power of a judicial or administrative authority to order the return of the child at any time.

Article 19

A decision under this Convention concerning the return of the child shall not be taken to be determination on the merits of any custody issue.

Article 20

The return of the child under the provision of Article 12 may be refused if this would not be permitted by the fundamental principles of the requested State relating to the protection of human rights and fundamental freedoms.

[...]

CHAPTER V – GENERAL PROVISIONS

[…]

Article 26

Each Central Authority shall bear its own costs in applying this Convention.

Central Authorities and other public services of Contracting States shall not impose any charges in relation to applications submitted under this Convention. In particular, they may not require any payment from the applicant towards the costs and expenses of the proceedings or, where applicable, those arising from the participation of legal counsel or advisers. However, they may require the payment of the expenses incurred or to be incurred in implementing the return of the child.

However, a Contracting State may, by making a reservation in accordance with Article 42, declare that it shall not be bound to assume any costs referred to in the preceding paragraph resulting from the participation of legal counsel or advisers or from court proceedings, except insofar as those costs may be covered by its system of legal aid and advice.

Upon ordering the return of a child or issuing an order concerning rights of access under this Convention, the judicial or administrative authorities may, where appropriate, direct the person who removed or retained the child, or who prevented the exercise of rights of access, to pay necessary expenses incurred by or on behalf of the applicant, including travel expenses, any costs incurred or payments made for locating the child, the costs of legal representation of the applicant, and those of returning the child.

[…]

Convention against Torture and Other Cruel, Inhuman or Degrading Treatment or Punishment, 1984*

Adoption: 10 December 1984
Entry into force: 26 June 1987
Parties: 144 (Status as of 1 April 2007)

AFGHANISTAN 1 Apr 1987 (*20, 30.1), ALBANIA 11 May 1994 a, ALGERIA 12 Sep 1989, ANDORRA 22 Sep 2006, ANTIGUA AND BARBUDA 19 Jul 1993 a, ARGENTINA 24 Sept 1986, ARMENIA 1993 a, AUSTRALIA 8 Aug 1989, AUSTRIA 29 Jul 1987, AZERBAIJAN 16 Aug 1996 a, BAHRAIN 6 Mar 1998 a (*30.1), BANGLADESH 5 Oct 1998 a, BELARUS 13 Mar 1987, BELGIUM 25 Jun 1990, BELIZE 17 Mar 1986 a, BENIN 12 Mar 1992 a, BOLIVIA 12 Apr 1999, BOSNIA AND HERZEGOVINA 1 Sep 1993 d, BOTSWANA 8 Sep 2000, BRAZIL 28 Sep 1989, BULGARIA 16 Dec 1986, BURKINA FASO 4 Jan 1999 a, BURUNDI 18 Feb 1993 a, CAMBODIA 15 Oct 1992 a, CAMEROON 19 Dec 1986 a, CANADA 24 Jun 1987, CAPE VERDE 4 Jun 1992 a, CHAD 9 Jun 1995 a, CHILE 30 Sep 1988 (*30.1), CHINA 4 Oct 1988 (*20, 30.1), COLOMBIA 8 Dec 1987, COMOROS signed 22 Sep 2000, CONGO 30 Jul 2003 a, COSTA RICA 11 Nov 1993, CÔTE D'IVOIRE 18 Dec 1995 a, CROATIA 12 Oct 1992 d, CUBA 17 May 1995, CYPRUS 18 Jul 1991, CZECH REPUBLIC 22 Feb 1993 d, DEMOCRATIC REPUBLIC OF THE CONGO 18 Mar 1996 a, DENMARK 27 May 1987, DJIBOUTI 5 Nov 2002 a, DOMINICAN REPUBLIC signed 4 Feb 1985, ECUADOR 30 Mar 1988 (*extradition of nationals), EGYPT 25 Jun 1986 a, EL SALVADOR 17 Jun 1996 a, EQUATORIAL GUINEA 8 Oct 2002 a (*20, 30.1), ESTONIA 21 Oct 1991 a, ETHIOPIA 14 Mar 1994 a, FINLAND 30 Aug 1989, FRANCE 18 Feb 1986 (*30.1), GABON 8 Sep 2000, GAMBIA singed 23 Oct 1985, GEORGIA 26 Oct 1990, GERMANY 1 Oct 1990 (*3), GHANA 7 Sep 2000, GREECE 6 Oct 1988, GUATEMALA 5 Jan 1990 a, GUINEA 10 Oct 1989, GUINEA-BISSAU signed 12 Sep 2000, GUYUNA 19 May 1988, HOLY SEE 26 Jun 2002, HONDURAS 5 Dec 1996 a, HUNGARY 5 Dec 1996 a, ICELAND 23 Oct 1996, INDIA signed 14 Oct 1997, INDONESIA 28 Oct 1998 (*30.1), IRELAND 11 Apr 2002, ISRAEL 3 Oct 1991 (*20, 30.1), ITALY 12 Jan 1989, JAPAN 29 Jun 1999 a, JORDAN 13 Nov 1991 a, KAZAKHSTAN 26 Aug 1998 a, KENYA 21 Feb 1997 a, KUWAIT 8 Mar 1996 a (*20, 30.1), KYRGYZSTAN 5 Sep 1997 a, LATVIA 14 Apr 1992 a, LEBANON 5 Oct 2000 a, LESOTHO 12 Nov 2002 a, LIBERIA 22 Sep 2004 a, LIBYAN ARAB JAMAHIRIYA 16 May 1989 a, LIECHTENSTEIN 2 Nov 1990, LITHUANIA 1 Feb 1996 a, LUXEMBOURG 29 Sep 1987, MADAGASCAR 13 Dec 2005, MALAWI 11 Jun 1996 a, MALDIVES 20 Apr 2004 a, MALI 26 Feb 1999 a, MALTA 13 Sep 1990, MAURITANIA 17 Nov 2004 a (*20, 30.1), MAURITIUS 9 Dec 1992 a, MEXICO 23 Jan 1986, MONACO 6 Dec 1991 a (*30.1), MONGOLIA 24 Jan 2002 a, MONTENEGRO 23 Oct 2006 d, MOROCCO 21 Jun 1993 (*20), MOZAMBIQUE 13 Sep 1999 a, NAMIBIA 28 Nov 1994 a, NAURU signed 12 Nov 2001, NEPAL 14 May 1991 a, NETHERLANDS 21 Dec 1988, NEW ZEALAND 10 Dec 1989 (*14), NICARAGUA 5 Jul 2005, NIGER 5 Oct 1998 a, NIGERIA 28 Jun 2001, NORWAY 9 Jul 1986, PANAMA 24 Aug 1987 (30.1), PARAGUAY 12 Mar 1990, PERU 7 Jul 1988, PHILIPPINES 18 Jun 1986 a, POLAND 26 Jul 1989 (*20, 30.1), PORTUGAL 9 Feb 1989, QATAR 11 Jan 2000 a (*21, 22), REPUBLIC OF KOREA 9 Jan 1995 a, REPUBLIC OF MOLDOVA 28 Nov 1995 a, REPUBLIC OF SERBIA 12 Mar 2001 d, ROMANIA 18 Dec 1990 a, RUSSIAN FEDERATION 3 Mar 1987, SAINT VINCENT AND THE GRENADINES 1 Aug 2001 a, SAN MARINO 27 Nov 2006, SAO TOME AND PRINCIPE signed 6 Sep 2000, SAUDI ARABIA 23 Sep 1997 a (*20, 30.1), SENEGAL 21 Aug 1986, SEYCHELLES 5

* Source: U.N.G.A. Res. 39/46, 1465 U.N.T.S. 85.

May 1992 a, SIERRA LEONE 25 Apr 2001, SLOVAKIA 28 May 1993 d, SLOVENIA 16 Jul 1993 a, SOMALIA 24 Jan 1990 a, SOUTH AFRICA 10 Dec 1998, SPAIN 21 Oct 1987, SRI LANKA 3 Jan 1994 a, SUDAN signed 4 Jun 1986, SWAZILAND 26 Mar 2004 a, SWEDEN 8 Jan 1986, SWITZERLAND 2 Dec 1986, SYRIAN ARAB REPUBLIC 19 Aug 2004 a (*20), TAJIKISTAN 11 Jan 1995 a, THE FORMER YUGOSLAV REPUBLIC OF MACEDONIA 12 Dec 1994 d, TIMOR-LESTE 16 Apr 2003 a, TOGO 18 Nov 1987 (*general), TUNISIA 23 Sep 1988, TURKEY 2 Aug 1988 (30.1), TURKMENISTAN 25 Jun 1999 a, UGANDA 3 Nov 1986 a, UKRAINE 24 Feb 1987, UNITED KINGDOM OF GREAT BRITAIN AND NORTHERN IRELAND 8 Dec 1988 (*general), UNITED STATES OF AMERICA 21 Oct 1994 (*1, 3, 10-14, 16, 30), URUGUAY 24 Oct 1986, UZBEKISTAN 28 Sep 1995 a, VENEZUELA (BOLIVERIAN REPUBLIC OF) 29 Jul 1991, YEMEN 5 Nov 1991 a, ZAMBIA 7 Oct 1998 a.

The States Parties to this Convention,

Considering that, in accordance with the principles proclaimed in the Charter of the United Nations, recognition of the equal and inalienable rights of all members of the human family is the foundation of freedom, justice and peace in the world,

Recognizing that those rights derive from the inherent dignity of the human person,

Considering the obligation of States under the Charter, in particular Article 55, to promote universal respect for, and observance of, human rights and fundamental freedoms,

Having regard to article 5 of the Universal Declaration of Human Rights and article 7 of the International Covenant on Civil and Political Rights, both of which provide that no one shall be subjected to torture or to cruel, inhuman or degrading treatment or punishment,

Having regard also to the Declaration on the Protection of All Persons from Being Subjected to Torture and Other Cruel, Inhuman or Degrading Treatment or Punishment, adopted by the General Assembly on 9 December 1975,

Desiring to make more effective the struggle against torture and other cruel, inhuman or degrading treatment or punishment throughout the world,

Have agreed as follows:

PART I

Article 1

1. For the purposes of this Convention, the term "torture" means any act by which severe pain or suffering, whether physical or mental, is intentionally inflicted on a person for such purposes as obtaining from him or a third person information or a confession, punishing him for an act he or a third person has committed or is suspected of having committed, or intimidating or coercing him or a third person, or for any reason based on discrimination of any kind, when such pain or suffering is inflicted by or at the instigation of or with the consent or acquiescence of a public official or other person acting in an official capacity. It does not include pain or suffering arising only from, inherent in or incidental to lawful sanctions.

2. This article is without prejudice to any international instrument or national legislation which does or may contain provisions of wider application.

Article 2

1. Each State Party shall take effective legislative, administrative, judicial or other measures to prevent acts of torture in any territory under its jurisdiction.

2. No exceptional circumstances whatsoever, whether a state of war or a threat of war, internal political in stability or any other public emergency, may be invoked as a justification of torture.

3. An order from a superior officer or a public authority may not be invoked as a justification of torture.

Article 3

1. No State Party shall expel, return ("refouler") or extradite a person to another State where there are substantial grounds for believing that he would be in danger of being subjected to torture.

2. For the purpose of determining whether there are such grounds, the competent authorities shall take into account all relevant considerations including, where applicable, the existence in the State concerned of a consistent pattern of gross, flagrant or mass violations of human rights.

Article 4

1. Each State Party shall ensure that all acts of torture are offences under its criminal law. The same shall apply to an attempt to commit torture and to an act by any person which constitutes complicity or participation in torture. 2. Each State Party shall make these offences punishable by appropriate penalties which take into account their grave nature.

Article 5

1. Each State Party shall take such measures as may be necessary to establish its jurisdiction over the offences referred to in article 4 in the following cases:

(a) When the offences are committed in any territory under its jurisdiction or on board a ship or aircraft registered in that State;

(b) When the alleged offender is a national of that State;

(c) When the victim is a national of that State if that State considers it appropriate.

2. Each State Party shall likewise take such measures as may be necessary to establish its jurisdiction over such offences in cases where the alleged offender is present in any territory under its jurisdiction and it does not extradite him pursuant to article 8 to any of the States mentioned in paragraph I of this article.

3. This Convention does not exclude any criminal jurisdiction exercised in accordance with internal law.

Article 6

1. Upon being satisfied, after an examination of information available to it, that the circumstances so warrant, any State Party in whose territory a person alleged to have committed any offence referred to in article 4 is present shall take him into custody or take other legal measures to ensure his presence. The custody and other legal measures shall be as provided in the law of that State but may be continued only for such time as is necessary to enable any criminal or extradition proceedings to be instituted.

2. Such State shall immediately make a preliminary inquiry into the facts.

3. Any person in custody pursuant to paragraph I of this article shall be assisted in communicating immediately with the nearest appropriate representative of the State of which he is a national, or, if he is a stateless person, with the representative of the State where he usually resides.

4. When a State, pursuant to this article, has taken a person into custody, it shall immediately notify the States referred to in article 5, paragraph 1, of the fact that such person is in custody and of the circumstances which warrant his detention. The State which makes the preliminary inquiry contemplated in paragraph 2 of this article shall promptly report its findings to the said States and shall indicate whether it intends to exercise jurisdiction.

Article 7

1. The State Party in the territory under whose jurisdiction a person alleged to have committed any offence referred to in article 4 is found shall in the cases contemplated in article 5, if it does not extradite him, submit the case to its competent authorities for the purpose of prosecution.

2. These authorities shall take their decision in the same manner as in the case of any ordinary offence of a serious nature under the law of that State. In the cases referred to in article 5, paragraph 2, the standards of evidence required for prosecution and conviction shall in no way be less stringent than those which apply in the cases referred to in article 5, paragraph 1.

3. Any person regarding whom proceedings are brought in connection with any of the offences referred to in article 4 shall be guaranteed fair treatment at all stages of the proceedings.

Article 8

1. The offences referred to in article 4 shall be deemed to be included as extraditable offences in any extradition treaty existing between States Parties. States Parties undertake to include such offences as extraditable offences in every extradition treaty to be concluded between them.

2. If a State Party which makes extradition conditional on the existence of a treaty receives a request for extradition from another State Party with which it has no extradition treaty, it may consider this Convention as the legal basis for extradition in respect of such offences. Extradition shall be subject to the other conditions provided by the law of the requested State.

3. States Parties which do not make extradition conditional on the existence of a treaty shall recognize such offences as extraditable offences between themselves subject to the conditions provided by the law of the requested State.

4. Such offences shall be treated, for the purpose of extradition between States Parties, as if they had been committed not only in the place in which they occurred but also in the territories of the States required to establish their jurisdiction in accordance with article 5, paragraph 1.

Article 9

1. States Parties shall afford one another the greatest measure of assistance in connection with criminal proceedings brought in respect of any of the offences referred to in article 4, including the supply of all evidence at their disposal necessary for the proceedings.

2. States Parties shall carry out their obligations under paragraph I of this article in conformity with any treaties on mutual judicial assistance that may exist between them.

Article 10

1. Each State Party shall ensure that education and information regarding the prohibition against torture are fully included in the training of law enforcement personnel, civil or military, medical personnel, public officials and other persons who may be involved in the custody, interrogation or treatment of any individual subjected to any form of arrest, detention or imprisonment.

2. Each State Party shall include this prohibition in the rules or instructions issued in regard to the duties and functions of any such person.

Article 11

Each State Party shall keep under systematic review interrogation rules, instructions, methods and practices as well as arrangements for the custody and treatment of persons subjected to any form of arrest, detention or imprisonment in any territory under its jurisdiction, with a view to preventing any cases of torture.

Article 12

Each State Party shall ensure that its competent authorities proceed to a prompt and impartial investigation, wherever there is reasonable ground to believe that an act of torture has been committed in any territory under its jurisdiction.

Article 13

Each State Party shall ensure that any individual who alleges he has been subjected to torture in any territory under its jurisdiction has the right to complain to, and to have his case promptly and impartially examined by, its competent authorities. Steps shall be taken to ensure that the complainant and witnesses are protected against all ill-treatment or intimidation as a consequence of his complaint or any evidence given.

Article 14

1. Each State Party shall ensure in its legal system that the victim of an act of torture obtains redress and has an enforceable right to fair and adequate compensation, including the means for as full rehabilitation as possible. In the event of the death of the victim as a result of an act of torture, his dependants shall be entitled to compensation.

2. Nothing in this article shall affect any right of the victim or other persons to compensation which may exist under national law.

Article 15

Each State Party shall ensure that any statement which is established to have been made as a result of torture shall not be invoked as evidence in any proceedings, except against a person accused of torture as evidence that the statement was made.

Article 16

1. Each State Party shall undertake to prevent in any territory under its jurisdiction other acts of cruel, inhuman or degrading treatment or punishment which do not amount to torture as defined in article I, when such acts are committed by or at the instigation of or with the consent or acquiescence of a public official or other person acting in an official capacity. In particular, the obligations contained in articles 10, 11, 12 and 13 shall apply with the substitution for references to torture of references to other forms of cruel, inhuman or degrading treatment or punishment.

2. The provisions of this Convention are without prejudice to the provisions of any other international instrument or national law which prohibits cruel, inhuman or degrading treatment or punishment or which relates to extradition or expulsion.

PART II

Article 17

1. There shall be established a Committee against Torture (hereinafter referred to as the Committee) which shall carry out the functions hereinafter provided. The Committee shall consist of ten experts of high moral standing and recognized competence in the field of human rights, who shall serve in their personal capacity. The experts shall be elected by the States Parties, consideration being given to equitable geographical distribution and to the usefulness of the participation of some persons having legal experience.

2. The members of the Committee shall be elected by secret ballot from a list of persons nominated by States Parties. Each State Party may nominate one person from among its own nationals. States Parties shall bear in mind the usefulness of nominating persons who are also members of the Human Rights Committee established under the International Covenant on Civil and Political Rights and who are willing to serve on the Committee against Torture.

3. Elections of the members of the Committee shall be held at biennial meetings of States Parties convened by the Secretary-General of the United Nations. At those meetings, for which two thirds of the States Parties shall constitute a quorum, the persons elected to the Committee shall be those who obtain the largest number of votes and an absolute majority of the votes of the representatives of States Parties present and voting.

4. The initial election shall be held no later than six months after the date of the entry into force of this Convention. At least four months before the date of each election, the Secretary-General of the United Nations shall address a letter to the States Parties inviting them to submit their nominations within three months. The Secretary-General shall prepare a list in alphabetical order of all persons thus nominated, indicating the States Parties which have nominated them, and shall submit it to the States Parties.

5. The members of the Committee shall be elected for a term of four years. They shall be eligible for re-election if renominated. However, the term of five of the members elected at the first election shall expire at the end of two years; immediately after the first election the names of these five members shall be chosen by lot by the chairman of the meeting referred to in paragraph 3 of this article.

6. If a member of the Committee dies or resigns or for any other cause can no longer perform his Committee duties, the State Party which nominated him shall appoint another expert from among its nationals to serve for the remainder of his term, subject to the approval of the majority of the States Parties. The approval shall be considered given unless half or more of the States Parties respond negatively within six weeks after having been informed by the Secretary-General of the United Nations of the proposed appointment.

7. States Parties shall be responsible for the expenses of the members of the Committee while they are in performance of Committee duties.

Article 18

1. The Committee shall elect its officers for a term of two years. They may be re-elected.

2. The Committee shall establish its own rules of procedure, but these rules shall provide, inter alia, that:

(a) Six members shall constitute a quorum;

(b) Decisions of the Committee shall be made by a majority vote of the members present.

3. The Secretary-General of the United Nations shall provide the necessary staff and facilities for the effective performance of the functions of the Committee under this Convention.

4. The Secretary-General of the United Nations shall convene the initial meeting of the Committee. After its initial meeting, the Committee shall meet at such times as shall be provided in its rules of procedure.

5. The States Parties shall be responsible for expenses incurred in connection with the holding of meetings of the States Parties and of the Committee, including reimbursement to the United Nations for any expenses, such as the cost of staff and facilities, incurred by the United Nations pursuant to paragraph 3 of this article.

Article 19

1. The States Parties shall submit to the Committee, through the Secretary-General of the United Nations, reports on the measures they have taken to give effect to their undertakings under this Convention, within one year after the entry into force of the Convention for the State Party concerned. Thereafter the States Parties shall submit supplementary reports every four years on any new measures taken and such other reports as the Committee may request.

2. The Secretary-General of the United Nations shall transmit the reports to all States Parties.

3. Each report shall be considered by the Committee which may make such general comments on the report as it may consider appropriate and shall forward these to the State Party concerned. That State Party may respond with any observations it chooses to the Committee.

4. The Committee may, at its discretion, decide to include any comments made by it in accordance with paragraph 3 of this article, together with the observations thereon received from the State Party concerned, in its annual report made in accordance with article 24. If so requested by the State Party concerned, the Committee may also include a copy of the report submitted under paragraph I of this article.

Article 20

1. If the Committee receives reliable information which appears to it to contain well-founded indications that torture is being systematically practiced in the territory of a State Party, the Committee shall invite that State Party to co-operate in the examination of the information and to this end to submit observations with regard to the information concerned.

2. Taking into account any observations which may have been submitted by the State Party concerned, as well as any other relevant information available to it, the Committee may, if it decides that this is warranted, designate one or more of its members to make a confidential inquiry and to report to the Committee urgently.

3. If an inquiry is made in accordance with paragraph 2 of this article, the Committee shall seek the co-operation of the State Party concerned. In agreement with that State Party, such an inquiry may include a visit to its territory.

4. After examining the findings of its member or members submitted in accordance with paragraph 2 of this article, the Commission shall transmit these findings to the State Party concerned together with any comments or suggestions which seem appropriate in view of the situation.

5. All the proceedings of the Committee referred to in paragraphs I to 4 of this article s hall be confidential, and at all stages of the proceedings the co-operation of the State Party shall be sought. After such proceedings have been completed with regard to an inquiry made in accordance with paragraph 2, the Committee may, after consultations with the State Party concerned, decide to include a summary account of the results of the proceedings in its annual report made in accordance with article 24.

Article 21

1. A State Party to this Convention may at any time declare under this article that it recognizes the competence of the Committee to receive and consider communications to the effect that a State Party claims that another State Party is not fulfilling its obligations under this Convention. Such communications may be received and considered according to the procedures laid down in this article only if submitted by a State Party which has made a declaration recognizing in regard to itself the competence of the Committee. No communication shall be dealt with by the Committee under this article if it concerns a State Party which has not made such a declaration. Communications received under this article shall be dealt with in accordance with the following procedure;

(a) If a State Party considers that another State Party is not giving effect to the provisions of this Convention, it may, by written communication, bring the matter to the attention of that State Party. Within three months after the receipt of the communication the receiving State shall afford the State which sent the communication an explanation or any other statement in writing clarifying the matter, which should include, to the extent possible and pertinent, reference to domestic procedures and remedies taken, pending or available in the matter;

(b) If the matter is not adjusted to the satisfaction of both States Parties concerned within six months after the receipt by the receiving State of the initial communication, either State shall have the right to refer the matter to the Committee, by notice given to the Committee and to the other State;

(c) The Committee shall deal with a matter referred to it under this article only after it has ascertained that all domestic remedies have been invoked and exhausted in the matter, in conformity with the generally recognized principles of international law. This shall not be the rule where the application of the remedies is unreasonably prolonged or is unlikely to bring effective relief to the person who is the victim of the violation of this Convention;

(d) The Committee shall hold closed meetings when examining communications under this article;

(e) Subject to the provisions of subparagraph (c), the Committee shall make available its good offices to the States Parties concerned with a view to a friendly solution of the matter on the basis of respect for the obligations provided for in this Convention. For this purpose, the Committee may, when appropriate, set up an ad hoc conciliation commission;

(f) In any matter referred to it under this article, the Committee may call upon the States Parties concerned, referred to in subparagraph (b), to supply any relevant information;

(g) The States Parties concerned, referred to in subparagraph (b), shall have the right to be represented when the matter is being considered by the Committee and to make submissions orally and/or in writing;

(h) The Committee shall, within twelve months after the date of receipt of notice under subparagraph (b), submit a report:

(i) If a solution within the terms of subparagraph (e) is reached, the Committee shall confine its report to a brief statement of the facts and of the solution reached;

(ii) If a solution within the terms of subparagraph (e) is not reached, the Committee shall confine its report to a brief statement of the facts; the written submissions and record of the oral submissions made by the States Parties concerned shall be attached to the report.

In every matter, the report shall be communicated to the States Parties concerned.

2. The provisions of this article shall come into force when five States Parties to this Convention have made declarations under paragraph 1 of this article. Such declarations shall be deposited by the States Parties with the Secretary-General of the United Nations, who shall transmit copies thereof to the other States Parties. A declaration may be withdrawn at any time by notification to the Secretary-General. Such a withdrawal shall not prejudice the consideration of any matter which is the subject of a communication already transmitted under this article; no further communication by any State Party shall be received under this article after the notification of withdrawal of the declaration has been received by the Secretary-General, unless the State Party concerned has made a new declaration.

Article 22

1. A State Party to this Convention may at any time declare under this article that it recognizes the competence of the Committee to receive and consider communications from or on behalf of individuals subject to its jurisdiction who claim to be victims of a violation by a State Party of the provisions of the Convention. No communication shall be received by the Committee if it concerns a State Party which has not made such a declaration.

2. The Committee shall consider inadmissible any communication under this article which is anonymous or which it considers to be an abuse of the right of submission of such communications or to be incompatible with the provisions of this Convention.

3. Subject to the provisions of paragraph 2, the Committee shall bring any communications submitted to it under this article to the attention of the State Party to this Convention which has made a declaration under paragraph I and is alleged to be violating any provisions of the Convention. Within six months, the receiving State shall submit to the Committee written explanations or statements clarifying the matter and the remedy, if any, that may have been taken by that State.

4. The Committee shall consider communications received under this article in the light of all information made available to it by or on behalf of the individual and by the State Party concerned. 5. The Committee shall not consider any communications from an individual under this article unless it has ascertained that:

(a) The same matter has not been, and is not being, examined under another procedure of international investigation or settlement;

(b) The individual has exhausted all available domestic remedies; this shall not be the rule where the application of the remedies is unreasonably prolonged or is unlikely to bring effective relief to the person who is the victim of the violation of this Convention.

6. The Committee shall hold closed meetings when examining communications under this article.

7. The Committee shall forward its views to the State Party concerned and to the individual.

8. The provisions of this article shall come into force when five States Parties to this Convention have made declarations under paragraph 1 of this article. Such declarations shall be deposited by the States Parties with the Secretary-General of the United Nations, who shall transmit copies thereof to the other States Parties. A declaration may be withdrawn at any time by notification to the Secretary-General. Such a withdrawal shall not prejudice the consideration

of any matter which is the subject of a communication already transmitted under this article; no further communication by or on behalf of an individual shall be received under this article after the notification of withdrawal of the declaration has been received by the Secretary General, unless the State Party has made a new declaration.

Article 23

The members of the Committee and of the ad hoc conciliation commissions which may be appointed under article 21, paragraph I (e), shall be entitled to the facilities, privileges and immunities of experts on mission for the United Nations as laid down in the relevant sections of the Convention on the Privileges and Immunities of the United Nations.

Article 24

The Committee shall submit an annual report on its activities under this Convention to the States Parties and to the General Assembly of the United Nations.

PART III

Article 25

1. This Convention is open for signature by all States. 2. This Convention is subject to ratification. Instruments of ratification shall be deposited with the Secretary-General of the United Nations.

Article 26

This Convention is open to accession by all States. Accession shall be effected by the deposit of an instrument of accession with the Secretary General of the United Nations.

Article 27

1. This Convention shall enter into force on the thirtieth day after the date of the deposit with the Secretary-General of the United Nations of the twentieth instrument of ratification or accession.

2. For each State ratifying this Convention or acceding to it after the deposit of the twentieth instrument of ratification or accession, the Convention shall enter into force on the thirtieth day after the date of the deposit of its own instrument of ratification or accession.

Article 28

1. Each State may, at the time of signature or ratification of this Convention or accession thereto, declare that it does not recognize the competence of the Committee provided for in article 20.

2. Any State Party having made a reservation in accordance with paragraph I of this article may, at any time, withdraw this reservation by notification to the Secretary-General of the United Nations.

Article 29

1. Any State Party to this Convention may propose an amendment and file it with the Secretary-General of the United Nations. The Secretary General shall thereupon communicate the proposed amendment to the States Parties with a request that they notify him whether

they favour a conference of States Parties for the purpose of considering and voting upon the proposal. In the event that within four months from the date of such communication at least one third of the States Parties favours such a conference, the Secretary General shall convene the conference under the auspices of the United Nations. Any amendment adopted by a majority of the States Parties present and voting at the conference shall be submitted by the Secretary-General to all the States Parties for acceptance.

2. An amendment adopted in accordance with paragraph I of this article shall enter into force when two thirds of the States Parties to this Convention have notified the Secretary-General of the United Nations that they have accepted it in accordance with their respective constitutional processes.

3. When amendments enter into force, they shall be binding on those States Parties which have accepted them, other States Parties still being bound by the provisions of this Convention and any earlier amendments which they have accepted.

Article 30

1. Any dispute between two or more States Parties concerning the interpretation or application of this Convention which cannot be settled through negotiation shall, at the request of one of them, be submitted to arbitration. If within six months from the date of the request for arbitration the Parties are unable to agree on the organization of the arbitration, any one of those Parties may refer the dispute to the International Court of Justice by request in conformity with the Statute of the Court.

2. Each State may, at the time of signature or ratification of this Convention or accession thereto, declare that it does not consider itself bound by paragraph I of this article. The other States Parties shall not be bound by paragraph I of this article with respect to any State Party having made such a reservation.

3. Any State Party having made a reservation in accordance with paragraph 2 of this article may at any time withdraw this reservation by notification to the Secretary-General of the United Nations.

Article 31

1. A State Party may denounce this Convention by written notification to the Secretary-General of the United Nations. Denunciation becomes effective one year after the date of receipt of- the notification by the Secretary-General.

2. Such a denunciation shall not have the effect of releasing the State Party from its obligations under this Convention in regard to any act or omission which occurs prior to the date at which the denunciation becomes effective, nor shall denunciation prejudice in any way the continued consideration of any matter which is already under consideration by the Committee prior to the date at which the denunciation becomes effective.

3. Following the date at which the denunciation of a State Party becomes effective, the Committee shall not commence consideration of any new matter regarding that State.

Article 32

The Secretary-General of the United Nations shall inform all States Members of the United Nations and all States which have signed this Convention or acceded to it of the following:

(a) Signatures, ratifications and accessions under articles 25 and 26;

(b) The date of entry into force of this Convention under article 27 and the date of the entry into force of any amendments under article 29;

(c) Denunciations under article 31.

Article 33

1. This Convention, of which the Arabic, Chinese, English, French, Russian and Spanish texts are equally authentic, shall be deposited with the Secretary-General of the United Nations.

2. The Secretary-General of the United Nations shall transmit certified copies of this Convention to all States.

Convention on the Rights of the Child, 1989*

Adoption: 20 November 1989
Entry into force: 2 September 1990
Parties: 193 (Status as of 1 April 2007)

AFGHANISTAN 28 Mar 1994 (*general), ALBANIA 27 Feb 1992, ALGERIA 16 Apr 1993 (*14.1, 14.2, 13, 16, 17), ANDORRA 2 Jan 1996 (*7, 8), ANGOLA 5 Dec 1990, ANTIGUA AND BARBUDA 5 Oct 1993, ARGENTINA 4 Dec 1990 (*21b-e, 24f), ARMENIA 23 Jun 1993 a, AUSTRALIA 17 Dec 1990 (*37c), AUSTRIA 6 Aug 1992 (*13, 15, 17), AZERBAIJAN 13 Aug 1992 a, BAHAMAS 20 Feb 1991 (*2), BAHRAIN 13 Feb 1992 a, BANGLADESH 3 Aug 1990 (*14.1, 21), BARBADOS 9 Oct 1990, BELARUS 1 Oct 1990, BELGIUM 16 Dec 1991 (*2.1, 13, 15, 40), BELIZE 2 May 1990, BENIN 3 Aug 1990, BHUTAN 1 Aug 1990, BOLIVIA 26 Jun 1990, BOSNIA AND HERZEGOVINA 1 Sep 1993 d (*9.1), BOTSWANA 14 Mar 1995 a (*1, general), BRAZIL 24 Sep 1990, BRUNEI DARUSSALAM 27 Dec 1995 a (*14, 20, 21, general), BULGARIA 3 Jun 1991, BURKINA FASO 31 Aug 1990, BURUNDI 19 Oct 1990, CAMBODIA 15 Oct 1992 a, CAMEROON 11 Jan 1993, CANADA 13 Dec 1991 (*21, 37c), CAPE VERDE 4 Jun 1992 a, CENTRAL AFRICAN REPUBLIC 23 Apr 1992, CHAD 2 Oct 1990, CHINA 2 Mar 1992 (*6), COLOMBIA 28 Jan 1991 (*38), COMOROS 22 Jun 1993, CONGO 14 Oct 1993 a, COOK ISLANDS 6 Jun 1997 a (*2, 10, 37), COSTA RICA 21 Aug 1990, CÔTE D'IVIORE 4 Feb 1991, CROATIA 12 Oct 1992 d (delete this *9.1), CUBA 21 Aug 1991 (*1), CYPRUS 7 Feb 1991, CZECH REPUBLIC 22 Feb 1993 d (*7.1), DEMOCRATIC PEOPLE'S REPUBLIC OF KOREA 21 Sep 1990, DEMOCRATIC REPUBLIC OF THE CONGO 27 Feb 1990, DENMARK 19 Jul 1991 (*40.2b), DJIBOUTI 6 Dec 1990 (general), DOMINICA 13 Mar 1991, DOMINICAN REPUBLIC 11 Jun 1991, ECUADOR 23 Mar 1990, EGYPT 6 Jul 1990, EL SALVADOR 10 Jul 1990, EQUATORIAL GUINEA 15 Jun 1992 a, ERITREA 3 Aug 1994, ESTONIA 21 Oct 1991, ETHIOPIA 14 May 1991 a, FIJI 13 Aug 1993, FINLAND 20 Jun 1991, FRANCE 7 Aug 1990 (*6, 30, 40.2b), GABON 9 Feb 1994, GAMBIA 8 Aug 1990, GEORGIA 2 Jun 1994 a, GERMANY 6 Mar 1992 (*9, 10, 18, 22, 40.2b), GHANA 5 Feb 1990, GREECE 11 May 1993, GRENADA 5 Nov 1990, GUATEMALA 6 Jun 1990, GUINEA 13 Jul 1990 a, GUINEA-BISSAU 20 Aug 1990, GUYUNA 14 Jan 1991, HAITI 8 Jun 1995, HOLY SEE 20 Apr 1990 (*13-16, 24.2f, 28, general), HONDURAS 10 Aug 1990, HUNGARY 7 Oct 1991, ICELAND 28 Oct 1992 (*9, 37), INDIA 11 Dec 1992 a (* 32.2a), INDONESIA 5 Sep 1990, IRAN (ISLAMIC REPUBLIC OF) 13 Jul 1994 (*general), IRAQ 15 Jun 1994 a (*14.1), IRELAND 28 Sept 1992 (*general), ISRAEL 3 Oct 1991, ITALY 5 Sep 1991, JAMAICA 14 May 1991, JAPAN 22 Apr 1994 (*9.1, 10.1 37c), JORDAN 24 May 1991 (*14, 20, 21), KAZAKHSTAN 12 Aug 1994, KENYA 30 Jul 1990, KIRIBATI 11 Dec 1995 a (*12-16, 24, 26, 28), KUWAIT 21 Oct 1991 (*7, 21, general), KYRGYZSTAN 7 Oct 1994 a, LAO PEOPLE'S DEMOCRATIC REPUBLIC 8 May 1991 a, LATVIA 14 Apr 1992 a, LEBANON 14 May 1991, LESOTHO 10 Mar 1992, LIBERIA 4 Jun 1993, LIBYAN ARAB JAMARHIRIYA 15 Apr 1993 a, LIECHTENSTEIN 22 Dec 1995 (*7, 10), LITHUANIA 31 Jan 1992 a, LUXEMBOURG 7 Mar 1994 (*6, 7, 15, general), MADAGASCAR 19 Mar 1991, MALAWI 2 Jan 1991 a, MALAYSIA 17 Feb 1995 a (*1, 2, 7, 13-15, 28, 37), MALDIVES 11 Feb 1991 (*14, 21, general), MALI 20 Sep 1990 (*16), MALTA 30 Sep 1990, MARSHALL ISLANDS 4 Oct 1993, MAURITANIA 16 May 1991 (*general), MAURITIUS 26 Jul 1990 a (*22), MEXICO 21 Sep 1990, MICRONESIA (FEDERATED STATES OF) 5 May 1993 a, MONACO 21 Jun 1993 a (*7, 40.2b), MONGOLIA 5 Jul 1990, MONTENEGRO 23 Oct 2006 d, MOROCCO 21 Jun 1993 (*14), MOZAMBIQUE 26 Apr

* Source: 1577 U.N.T.S. 3.

1994, MYANMAR 15 Jul 1991 a, NAMIBIA 30 Sep 1990, NAURU 27 Jul 1994 a, NEPAL 14 Sep 1990, NETHERLANDS 6 Feb 1995 a (*26, 37c, 40), NEW ZEALAND 6 Apr 1993 (*32, 37c, general), NICARAGUA 5 Oct 1990, NIGER 30 Sep 1990, NIGERIA 19 Apr 1991, NIUE 20 Dec 1995 a, NORWAY 8 Jan 1991, OMAN 9 Dec 1996 a (*7, 9.4, 14, 21), PAKISTAN 12 Nov 1990, PALAU 4 Aug 1995 a, PANAMA 12 Dec 1990, PAPUA NEW GUINEA 2 Mar 1993, PARAGUAY 25 Sep 1990, PERU 4 Sep 1990, PHILIPPINES 21 Aug 1990, POLAND 7 Jun 1991 (*7, 12-16, 24.2f, 38), PORTUGAL 21 Sep 1990, QATAR 3 Apr 1995 (*general), REPUBLIC OF KOREA 20 Nov 1991 (*9.3, 21a, 40.2b), REPUBLIC OF MOLDOVA 26 Jan 1993 a, REPUBLIC OF SERBIA 12 Mar 2001, ROMANIA 28 Sep 1990, RUSSIAN FEDERATION 16 Aug 1990, RWANDA 24 Jan 1991, SAINT KITTS AND NEVIS 24 Jul 1990, SAINT LUCIA 16 Jun 1993, SAINT VINCENT AND THE GRENADINES 26 Oct 1993, SAMOA 29 Nov 1994 (*28.1a), SAN MARINO 25 Nov 1991 a, SAO TOME AND PRINCIPE 14 May 1991 a, SAUDI ARABIA 26 Jan 1996 a (*general), SENEGAL 31 Jul 1990, SEYCHELLES 7 Sep 1990 a, SIERRA LEONE 18 Jun 1990, SINGAPORE 5 Oct 1995 a (*12-17, 19, 28.1a, 32, 37), SLOVAKIA 28 May 1993 d, SLOVENIA 6 Jul 1992 d, SOLOMON ISLANDS 10 Apr 1995 a, SOMALIA signed 9 May 2002, SOUTH AFRICA 16 Jun 1995, SPAIN 6 Dec 1990, SRI LANKA 12 Jul 1991, SUDAN 3 Aug 1990, SURINAME 1 Mar 1993, SWAZILAND 7 Sep 1995, SWEDEN 29 Jun 1990, SWITZERLAND 24 Feb 1997 (*7, 10.1, 37c, 40), SYRIAN ARAB REPUBLIC 15 Jul 1993 (*14, 20, 21), TAJIKISTAN 26 Oct 1993 a, THAILAND 27 Mar 1992 a (*7, 22), THE FORMER YUGOLAVE REPUBLIC OF MACEDONIA 2 Dec 1993 d, TIMOR-LESTE 16 Apr 2003 a, TOGO 1 Aug 2003 a, TONGA 6 Nov 1995 a, TRINIDAD AND TOBAGO 5 Dec 1991, TUNISIA 30 Jan 1992 (*2, 6, 7, general), TURKEY 4 Apr 1995 (*17, 29, 30), TURKMENISTAN 20 Sep 1993 a, TUVALU 22 Sep 1995 a, UGANDA 17 Aug 1990, UKRAINE 28 Aug 1991, UNITED ARAB EMIRATES 3 Jan 1997 a (*7, 14, 17, 21), UNITED KINGDOM OF GREAT BRITAIN AND NORTHERN IRELAND 16 Dec 1991 (*22, 32, 37c, general), UNITED REPUBLIC OF TANZANIA, UNITED STATES OF AMERICA signed 16 Feb 1995, URUGUAY 20 Nov 1990 (*38.2, 38.3), UZBEKISTAN 29 Jun 1994 a, VANUATU 7 Jul 1993, VENEZUELA (BOLIVARIAN REPUBLIC OF) 13 Sep 1990, VIET NAM 28 Feb 1990, YEMEN 1 May 1991, ZAMBIA 6 Dec 1991, ZIMBABWE 11 Sep 1990.

Preamble

The States Parties to the present Convention,

Considering that, in accordance with the principles proclaimed in the Charter of the United Nations, recognition of the inherent dignity and of the equal and inalienable rights of all members of the human family is the foundation of freedom, justice and peace in the world,

Bearing in mind that the peoples of the United Nations have, in the Charter, reaffirmed their faith in fundamental human rights and in the dignity and worth of the human person, and have determined to promote social progress and better standards of life in larger freedom,

Recognizing that the United Nations has, in the Universal Declaration of Human Rights and in the International Covenants on Human Rights, proclaimed and agreed that everyone is entitled to all the rights and freedoms set forth therein, without distinction of any kind, such as race, colour, sex, language, religion, political or other opinion, national or social origin, property, birth or other status,

Recalling that, in the Universal Declaration of Human Rights, the United Nations has proclaimed that childhood is entitled to special care and assistance,

Convinced that the family, as the fundamental group of society and the natural environment for the growth and well being of all its members and particularly children, should be afforded the necessary protection and assistance so that it can fully assume its responsibilities within the community,

Recognizing that the child, for the full and harmonious development of his or her personality, should grow up in a family environment, in an atmosphere of happiness, love and understanding,

Considering that the child should be fully prepared to live an individual life in society, and brought up in the spirit of the ideals proclaimed in the Charter of the United Nations, and in particular in the spirit of peace, dignity, tolerance, freedom, equality and solidarity,

Bearing in mind that the need to extend particular care to the child has been stated in the Geneva Declaration of the Rights of the Child of 1924 and in the Declaration of the Rights of the Child adopted by the General Assembly on 20 November 1959 and recognized in the Universal Declaration of Human Rights, in the International Covenant on Civil and Political Rights (in particular in articles 23 and 24), in the International Covenant on Economic, Social and Cultural Rights (in particular in article 10) and in the statutes and relevant instruments of specialized agencies and international organizations concerned with the welfare of children,

Bearing in mind that, as indicated in the Declaration of the Rights of the Child, "the child, by reason of his physical and mental immaturity, needs special safeguards and care, including appropriate legal protection, before as well as after birth",

Recalling the provisions of the Declaration on Social and Legal Principles relating to the Protection and Welfare of Children, with Special Reference to Foster Placement and Adoption Nationally and Internationally; the United Nations Standard Minimum Rules for the Administration of Juvenile Justice (The Beijing Rules); and the Declaration on the Protection of Women and Children in Emergency and Armed Conflict, Recognizing that, in all countries in the world, there are children living in exceptionally difficult conditions, and that such children need special consideration,

Taking due account of the importance of the traditions and cultural values of each people for the protection and harmonious development of the child, Recognizing the importance of international co-operation for improving the living conditions of children in every country, in particular in the developing countries,

Have agreed as follows:

PART I

Article 1

For the purposes of the present Convention, a child means every human being below the age of eighteen years unless under the law applicable to the child, majority is attained earlier.

Article 2

1. States Parties shall respect and ensure the rights set forth in the present Convention to each child within their jurisdiction without discrimination of any kind, irrespective of the child's or his or her parent's or legal guardian's race, colour, sex, language, religion, political or other opinion, national, ethnic or social origin, property, disability, birth or other status.

2. States Parties shall take all appropriate measures to ensure that the child is protected against all forms of discrimination or punishment on the basis of the status, activities, expressed opinions, or beliefs of the child's parents, legal guardians, or family members.

Article 3

1. In all actions concerning children, whether undertaken by public or private social welfare institutions, courts of law, administrative authorities or legislative bodies, the best interests of the child shall be a primary consideration.

2. States Parties undertake to ensure the child such protection and care as is necessary for his or her well-being, taking into account the rights and duties of his or her parents, legal guardians, or other individuals legally responsible for him or her, and, to this end, shall take all appropriate legislative and administrative measures.

3. States Parties shall ensure that the institutions, services and facilities responsible for the care or protection of children shall conform to the standards established by competent authorities, particularly in the areas of safety, health, in the number and suitability of their staff, as well as competent supervision.

Article 4

States Parties shall undertake all appropriate legislative, administrative, and other measures for the implementation of the rights recognized in the present Convention. With regard to economic, social and cultural rights, States Parties shall undertake such measures to the maximum extent of their available resources and, where needed, within the framework of international co-operation.

Article 5

States Parties shall respect the responsibilities, rights and duties of parents or, where applicable, the members of the extended family or community as provided for by local custom, legal guardians or other persons legally responsible for the child, to provide, in a manner consistent with the evolving capacities of the child, appropriate direction and guidance in the exercise by the child of the rights recognized in the present Convention.

Article 6

1. States Parties recognize that every child has the inherent right to life.

2. States Parties shall ensure to the maximum extent possible the survival and development of the child.

Article 7

1. The child shall be registered immediately after birth and shall have the right from birth to a name, the right to acquire a nationality and. as far as possible, the right to know and be cared for by his or her parents.

2. States Parties shall ensure the implementation of these rights in accordance with their national law and their obligations under the relevant international instruments in this field, in particular where the child would otherwise be stateless.

Article 8

1. States Parties undertake to respect the right of the child to preserve his or her identity, including nationality, name and family relations as recognized by law without unlawful interference.

2. Where a child is illegally deprived of some or all of the elements of his or her identity, States Parties shall provide appropriate assistance and protection, with a view to re-establishing speedily his or her identity.

Article 9

1. States Parties shall ensure that a child shall not be separated from his or her parents against their will, except when competent authorities subject to judicial review determine, in accordance with applicable law and procedures, that such separation is necessary for the best interests of the child. Such determination may be necessary in a particular case such as one involving abuse or neglect of the child by the parents, or one where the parents are living separately and a decision must be made as to the child's place of residence.

2. In any proceedings pursuant to paragraph 1 of the present article, all interested parties shall be given an opportunity to participate in the proceedings and make their views known.

3. States Parties shall respect the right of the child who is separated from one or both parents to maintain personal relations and direct contact with both parents on a regular basis, except if it is contrary to the child's best interests.

4. Where such separation results from any action initiated by a State Party, such as the detention, imprisonment, exile, deportation or death (including death arising from any cause while the person is in the custody of the State) of one or both parents or of the child, that State Party shall, upon request, provide the parents, the child or, if appropriate, another member of the family with the essential information concerning the whereabouts of the absent member(s) of the family unless the provision of the information would be detrimental to the well-being of the child. States Parties shall further ensure that the submission of such a request shall of itself entail no adverse consequences for the person(s) concerned.

Article 10

1. In accordance with the obligation of States Parties under article 9, paragraph 1, applications by a child or his or her parents to enter or leave a State Party for the purpose of family reunification shall be dealt with by States Parties in a positive, humane and expeditious manner. States Parties shall further ensure that the submission of such a request shall entail no adverse consequences for the applicants and for the members of their family.

2. A child whose parents reside in different States shall have the right to maintain on a regular basis, save in exceptional circumstances personal relations and direct contacts with both parents. Towards that end and in accordance with the obligation of States Parties under article 9, paragraph 1, States Parties shall respect the right of the child and his or her parents to leave any country, including their own, and to enter their own country. The right to leave any country shall be subject only to such restrictions as are prescribed by law and which are necessary to protect the national security, public order (ordre public), public health or morals or the rights and freedoms of others and are consistent with the other rights recognized in the present Convention.

Article 11

1. States Parties shall take measures to combat the illicit transfer and non-return of children abroad.

2. To this end, States Parties shall promote the conclusion of bilateral or multilateral agreements or accession to existing agreements.

Article 12

1. States Parties shall assure to the child who is capable of forming his or her own views the right to express those views freely in all matters affecting the child, the views of the child being given due weight in accordance with the age and maturity of the child.

2. For this purpose, the child shall in particular be provided the opportunity to be heard in any judicial and administrative proceedings affecting the child, either directly, or through a representative or an appropriate body, in a manner consistent with the procedural rules of national law.

Article 13

1. The child shall have the right to freedom of expression; this right shall include freedom to seek, receive and impart information and ideas of all kinds, regardless of frontiers, either orally, in writing or in print, in the form of art, or through any other media of the child's choice.

2. The exercise of this right may be subject to certain restrictions, but these shall only be such as are provided by law and are necessary:

(a) For respect of the rights or reputations of others; or

(b) For the protection of national security or of public order (ordre public), or of public health or morals.

Article 14

1. States Parties shall respect the right of the child to freedom of thought, conscience and religion.

2. States Parties shall respect the rights and duties of the parents and, when applicable, legal guardians, to provide direction to the child in the exercise of his or her right in a manner consistent with the evolving capacities of the child.

3. Freedom to manifest one's religion or beliefs may be subject only to such limitations as are prescribed by law and are necessary to protect public safety, order, health or morals, or the fundamental rights and freedoms of others.

Article 15

1. States Parties recognize the rights of the child to freedom of association and to freedom of peaceful assembly.

2. No restrictions may be placed on the exercise of these rights other than those imposed in conformity with the law and which are necessary in a democratic society in the interests of national security or public safety, public order (ordre public), the protection of public health or morals or the protection of the rights and freedoms of others.

Article 16

1. No child shall be subjected to arbitrary or unlawful interference with his or her privacy, family, home or correspondence, nor to unlawful attacks on his or her honour and reputation.

2. The child has the right to the protection of the law against such interference or attacks.

Article 17

States Parties recognize the important function performed by the mass media and shall ensure that the child has access to information and material from a diversity of national and international sources, especially those aimed at the promotion of his or her social, spiritual and moral well-being and physical and mental health.

To this end, States Parties shall:

(a) Encourage the mass media to disseminate information and material of social and cultural benefit to the child and in accordance with the spirit of article 29;

(b) Encourage international co-operation in the production, exchange and dissemination of such information and material from a diversity of cultural, national and international sources;

(c) Encourage the production and dissemination of children's books;

(d) Encourage the mass media to have particular regard to the linguistic needs of the child who belongs to a minority group or who is indigenous;

(e) Encourage the development of appropriate guidelines for the protection of the child from information and material injurious to his or her well-being, bearing in mind the provisions of articles 13 and 18.

Article 18

1. States Parties shall use their best efforts to ensure recognition of the principle that both parents have common responsibilities for the upbringing and development of the child. Parents or, as the case may be, legal guardians, have the primary responsibility for the upbringing and development of the child. The best interests of the child will be their basic concern.

2. For the purpose of guaranteeing and promoting the rights set forth in the present Convention, States Parties shall render appropriate assistance to parents and legal guardians in the performance of their child-rearing responsibilities and shall ensure the development of institutions, facilities and services for the care of children.

3. States Parties shall take all appropriate measures to ensure that children of working parents have the right to benefit from child-care services and facilities for which they are eligible.

Article 19

1. States Parties shall take all appropriate legislative, administrative, social and educational measures to protect the child from all forms of physical or mental violence, injury or abuse, neglect or negligent treatment, maltreatment or exploitation, including sexual abuse, while in the care of parent(s), legal guardian(s) or any other person who has the care of the child.

2. Such protective measures should, as appropriate, include effective procedures for the establishment of social programs to provide necessary support for the child and for those who have the care of the child, as well as for other forms of prevention and for identification, reporting, referral, investigation, treatment and follow-up of instances of child maltreatment described heretofore, and, as appropriate, for judicial involvement.

Article 20

1. A child temporarily or permanently deprived of his or her family environment, or in whose own best interests cannot be allowed to remain in that environment, shall be entitled to special protection and assistance provided by the State.

2. States Parties shall in accordance with their national laws ensure alternative care for such a child.

3. Such care could include, inter alia, foster placement, kafalah of Islamic law, adoption or if necessary placement in suitable institutions for the care of children. When considering solutions, due regard shall be paid to the desirability of continuity in a child's upbringing and to the child's ethnic, religious, cultural and linguistic background.

Article 21

States Parties that recognize and/or permit the system of adoption shall ensure that the best interests of the child shall be the paramount consideration and they shall:

(a) Ensure that the adoption of a child is authorized only by competent authorities who determine, in accordance with applicable law and procedures and on the basis of all pertinent and reliable information, that the adoption is permissible in view of the child's status concerning parents, relatives and legal guardians and that, if required, the persons concerned have given their informed consent to the adoption on the basis of such counseling as may be necessary;

(b) Recognize that inter-country adoption may be considered as an alternative means of child's care, if the child cannot be placed in a foster or an adoptive family or cannot in any suitable manner be cared for in the child's country of origin;

(c) Ensure that the child concerned by inter-country adoption enjoys safeguards and standards equivalent to those existing in the case of national adoption;

(d) Take all appropriate measures to ensure that, in inter-country adoption, the placement does not result in improper financial gain for those involved in it;

(e) Promote, where appropriate, the objectives of the present article by concluding bilateral or multilateral arrangements or agreements, and endeavour, within this framework, to ensure that the placement of the child in another country is carried out by competent authorities or organs.

Article 22

1. States Parties shall take appropriate measures to ensure that a child who is seeking refugee status or who is considered a refugee in accordance with applicable international or domestic law and procedures shall, whether unaccompanied or accompanied by his or her parents or by any other person, receive appropriate protection and humanitarian assistance in the enjoyment of applicable rights set forth in the present Convention and in other international human rights or humanitarian instruments to which the said States are Parties.

2. For this purpose, States Parties shall provide, as they consider appropriate, co-operation in any efforts by the United Nations and other competent intergovernmental organizations or non-governmental organizations co-operating with the United Nations to protect and assist such a child and to trace the parents or other members of the family of any refugee child in order to obtain information necessary for reunification with his or her family. In cases where no parents or other members of the family can be found, the child shall be accorded the same protection as any other child permanently or temporarily deprived of his or her family environment for any reason, as set forth in the present Convention.

Article 23

1. States Parties recognize that a mentally or physically disabled child should enjoy a full and decent life, in conditions which ensure dignity, promote self-reliance and facilitate the child's active participation in the community.

2. States Parties recognize the right of the disabled child to special care and shall encourage and ensure the extension, subject to available resources, to the eligible child and those responsible for his or her care, of assistance for which application is made and which is appropriate to the child's condition and to the circumstances of the parents or others caring for the child.

3. Recognizing the special needs of a disabled child, assistance extended in accordance with paragraph 2 of the present article shall be provided free of charge, whenever possible, taking

into account the financial resources of the parents or others caring for the child, and shall be designed to ensure that the disabled child has effective access to and receives education, training, health care services, rehabilitation services, preparation for employment and recreation opportunities in a manner conducive to the child's achieving the fullest possible social integration and individual development, including his or her cultural and spiritual development

4. States Parties shall promote, in the spirit of international cooperation, the exchange of appropriate information in the field of preventive health care and of medical, psychological and functional treatment of disabled children, including dissemination of and access to information concerning methods of rehabilitation, education and vocational services, with the aim of enabling States Parties to improve their capabilities and skills and to widen their experience in these areas. In this regard, particular account shall be taken of the needs of developing countries.

Article 24

1. States Parties recognize the right of the child to the enjoyment of the highest attainable standard of health and to facilities for the treatment of illness and rehabilitation of health. States Parties shall strive to ensure that no child is deprived of his or her right of access to such health care services.

2. States Parties shall pursue full implementation of this right and, in particular, shall take appropriate measures:

(a) To diminish infant and child mortality;

(b) To ensure the provision of necessary medical assistance and health care to all children with emphasis on the development of primary health care;

(c) To combat disease and malnutrition, including within the framework of primary health care, through, inter alia, the application of readily available technology and through the provision of adequate nutritious foods and clean drinking-water, taking into consideration the dangers and risks of environmental pollution;

(d) To ensure appropriate pre-natal and post-natal health care for mothers;

(e) To ensure that all segments of society, in particular parents and children, are informed, have access to education and are supported in the use of basic knowledge of child health and nutrition, the advantages of breastfeeding, hygiene and environmental sanitation and the prevention of accidents;

(f) To develop preventive health care, guidance for parents and family planning education and services.

3. States Parties shall take all effective and appropriate measures with a view to abolishing traditional practices prejudicial to the health of children.

4. States Parties undertake to promote and encourage international co-operation with a view to achieving progressively the full realization of the right recognized in the present article. In this regard, particular account shall be taken of the needs of developing countries.

Article 25

States Parties recognize the right of a child who has been placed by the competent authorities for the purposes of care, protection or treatment of his or her physical or mental health, to a periodic review of the treatment provided to the child and all other circumstances relevant to his or her placement.

Article 26

1. States Parties shall recognize for every child the right to benefit from social security, including social insurance, and shall take the necessary measures to achieve the full realization of this right in accordance with their national law.

2. The benefits should, where appropriate, be granted, taking into account the resources and the circumstances of the child and persons having responsibility for the maintenance of the child, as well as any other consideration relevant to an application for benefits made by or on behalf of the child.

Article 27

1. States Parties recognize the right of every child to a standard of living adequate for the child's physical, mental, spiritual, moral and social development.

2. The parent(s) or others responsible for the child have the primary responsibility to secure, within their abilities and financial capacities, the conditions of living necessary for the child's development.

3. States Parties, in accordance with national conditions and within their means, shall take appropriate measures to assist parents and others responsible for the child to implement this right and shall in case of need provide material assistance and support programs, particularly with regard to nutrition, clothing and housing.

4. States Parties shall take all appropriate measures to secure the recovery of maintenance for the child from the parents or other persons having financial responsibility for the child, both within the State Party and from abroad. In particular, where the person having financial responsibility for the child lives in a State different from that of the child, States Parties shall promote the accession to international agreements or the conclusion of such agreements, as well as the making of other appropriate arrangements.

Article 28

1. States Parties recognize the right of the child to education and with a view to achieving this right progressively and on the basis of equal opportunity, they shall, in particular:

(a) Make primary education compulsory and available free to all;

(b) Encourage the development of different forms of secondary education, including general and vocational education, make them available and accessible to every child, and take appropriate measures such as the introduction of free education and offering financial assistance in case of need;

(c) Make higher education accessible to all on the basis of capacity by every appropriate means;

(d) Make educational and vocational information and guidance available and accessible to all children;

(e) Take measures to encourage regular attendance at schools and the reduction of drop-out rates.

2. States Parties shall take all appropriate measures to ensure that school discipline is administered in a manner consistent with the child's human dignity and in conformity with the present Convention.

3. States Parties shall promote and encourage international cooperation in matters relating to education, in particular with a view to contributing to the elimination of ignorance and

illiteracy throughout the world and facilitating access to scientific and technical knowledge and modern teaching methods. In this regard, particular account shall be taken of the needs of developing countries.

Article 29

1. States Parties agree that the education of the child shall be directed to:

(a) The development of the child's personality, talents and mental and physical abilities to their fullest potential;

(b) The development of respect for human rights and fundamental freedoms, and for the principles enshrined in the Charter of the United Nations;

(c) The development of respect for the child's parents, his or her own cultural identity, language and values, for the national values of the country in which the child is living, the country from which he or she may originate, and for civilizations different from his or her own;

(d) The preparation of the child for responsible life in a free society, in the spirit of understanding, peace, tolerance, equality of sexes, and friendship among all peoples, ethnic, national and religious groups and persons of indigenous origin;

(e) The development of respect for the natural environment.

2. No part of the present article or article 28 shall be construed so as to interfere with the liberty of individuals and bodies to establish and direct educational institutions, subject always to the observance of the principle set forth in paragraph 1 of the present article and to the requirements that the education given in such institutions shall conform to such minimum standards as may be laid down by the State.

Article 30

In those States in which ethnic, religious or linguistic minorities or persons of indigenous origin exist, a child belonging to such a minority or who is indigenous shall not be denied the right, in community with other members of his or her group, to enjoy his or her own culture, to profess and practice his or her own religion, or to use his or her own language.

Article 31

1. States Parties recognize the right of the child to rest and leisure, to engage in play and recreational activities appropriate to the age of the child and to participate freely in cultural life and the arts.

2. States Parties shall respect and promote the right of the child to participate fully in cultural and artistic life and shall encourage the provision of appropriate and equal opportunities for cultural, artistic, recreational and leisure activity.

Article 32

1. States Parties recognize the right of the child to be protected from economic exploitation and from performing any work that is likely to be hazardous or to interfere with the child's education, or to be harmful to the child's health or physical, mental, spiritual, moral or social development.

2. States Parties shall take legislative, administrative, social and educational measures to ensure the implementation of the present article. To this end, and having regard to the relevant provisions of other international instruments, States Parties shall in particular:

(a) Provide for a minimum age or minimum ages for admission to employment;

(b) Provide for appropriate regulation of the hours and conditions of employment;

(c) Provide for appropriate penalties or other sanctions to ensure the effective enforcement of the present article.

Article 33

States Parties shall take all appropriate measures, including legislative, administrative, social and educational measures, to protect children from the illicit use of narcotic drugs and psychotropic substances as defined in the relevant international treaties, and to prevent the use of children in the illicit production and trafficking of such substances.

Article 34

States Parties undertake to protect the child from all forms of sexual exploitation and sexual abuse. For these purposes, States Parties shall in particular take all appropriate national, bilateral and multilateral measures to prevent:

(a) The inducement or coercion of a child to engage in any unlawful sexual activity;

(b) The exploitative use of children in prostitution or other unlawful sexual practices;

(c) The exploitative use of children in pornographic performances and materials.

Article 35

States Parties shall take all appropriate national, bilateral and multilateral measures to prevent the abduction of, the sale of or traffic in children for any purpose or in any form.

Article 36

States Parties shall protect the child against all other forms of exploitation prejudicial to any aspects of the child's welfare.

Article 37

States Parties shall ensure that:

(a) No child shall be subjected to torture or other cruel, inhuman or degrading treatment or punishment. Neither capital punishment nor life imprisonment without possibility of release shall be imposed for offences committed by persons below eighteen years of age;

(b) No child shall be deprived of his or her liberty unlawfully or arbitrarily. The arrest, detention or imprisonment of a child shall be in conformity with the law and shall be used only as a measure of last resort and for the shortest appropriate period of time;

(c) Every child deprived of liberty shall be treated with humanity and respect for the inherent dignity of the human person, and in a manner which takes into account the needs of persons of his or her age. In particular, every child deprived of liberty shall be separated from adults unless it is considered in the child's best interest not to do so and shall have the right to maintain contact with his or her family through correspondence and visits, save in exceptional circumstances;

(d) Every child deprived of his or her liberty shall have the right to prompt access to legal and other appropriate assistance, as well as the right to challenge the legality of the deprivation of his or her liberty before a court or other competent, independent and impartial authority, and to a prompt decision on any such action.

Article 38

1. States Parties undertake to respect and to ensure respect for rules of international humanitarian law applicable to them in armed conflicts which are relevant to the child.

2. States Parties shall take all feasible measures to ensure that persons who have not attained the age of fifteen years do not take a direct part in hostilities.

3. States Parties shall refrain from recruiting any person who has not attained the age of fifteen years into their armed forces. In recruiting among those persons who have attained the age of fifteen years but who have not attained the age of eighteen years, States Parties shall cndcavour to give priority to those who are oldest.

4. In accordance with their obligations under international humanitarian law to protect the civilian population in armed conflicts, States Parties shall take all feasible measures to ensure protection and care of children who are affected by an armed conflict.

Article 39

States Parties shall take all appropriate measures to promote physical and psychological recovery and social reintegration of a child victim of: any form of neglect, exploitation, or abuse; torture or any other form of cruel, inhuman or degrading treatment or punishment; or armed conflicts. Such recovery and reintegration shall take place in an environment which fosters the health, self-respect and dignity of the child.

Article 40

1. States Parties recognize the right of every child alleged as, accused of, or recognized as having infringed the penal law to be treated in a manner consistent with the promotion of the child's sense of dignity and worth, which reinforces the child's respect for the human rights and fundamental freedoms of others and which takes into account the child's age and the desirability of promoting the child's reintegration and the child's assuming a constructive role in society.

2. To this end, and having regard to the relevant provisions of international instruments, States Parties shall, in particular, ensure that:

(a) No child shall be alleged as, be accused of, or recognized as having infringed the penal law by reason of acts or omissions that were not prohibited by national or international law at the time they were committed;

(b) Every child alleged as or accused of having infringed the penal law has at least the following guarantees:

(i) To be presumed innocent until proven guilty according to law;

(ii) To be informed promptly and directly of the charges against him or her, and, if appropriate, through his or her parents or legal guardians, and to have legal or other appropriate assistance in the preparation and presentation of his or her defence;

(iii) To have the matter determined without delay by a competent, independent and impartial authority or judicial body in a fair hearing according to law, in the presence of legal or other appropriate assistance and, unless it is considered not to be in the best interest of the child, in particular, taking into account his or her age or situation, his or her parents or legal guardians;

(iv) Not to be compelled to give testimony or to confess guilt; to examine or have examined adverse witnesses and to obtain the participation and examination of witnesses on his or her behalf under conditions of equality;

(v) If considered to have infringed the penal law, to have this decision and any measures imposed in consequence thereof reviewed by a higher competent, independent and impartial authority or judicial body according to law;

(vi) To have the free assistance of an interpreter if the child cannot understand or speak the language used;

(vii) To have his or her privacy fully respected at all stages of the proceedings.

3. States Parties shall seek to promote the establishment of laws, procedures, authorities and institutions specifically applicable to children alleged as, accused of, or recognized as having infringed the penal law, and, in particular:

(a) The establishment of a minimum age below which children shall be presumed not to have the capacity to infringe the penal law;

(b) Whenever appropriate and desirable, measures for dealing with such children without resorting to judicial proceedings, providing that human rights and legal safeguards are fully respected. 4. A variety of dispositions, such as care, guidance and supervision orders; counseling; probation; foster care; education and vocational training programs and other alternatives to institutional care shall be available to ensure that children are dealt with in a manner appropriate to their well-being and proportionate both to their circumstances and the offence.

Article 41

Nothing in the present Convention shall affect any provisions which are more conducive to the realization of the rights of the child and which may be contained in:

(a) The law of a State party; or

(b) International law in force for that State.

PART II

Article 42

States Parties undertake to make the principles and provisions of the Convention widely known, by appropriate and active means, to adults and children alike.

Article 43

1. For the purpose of examining the progress made by States Parties in achieving the realization of the obligations undertaken in the present Convention, there shall be established a Committee on the Rights of the Child, which shall carry out the functions hereinafter provided.

2. The Committee shall consist of ten experts of high moral standing and recognized competence in the field covered by this Convention. The members of the Committee shall be elected by States Parties from among their nationals and shall serve in their personal capacity, consideration being given to equitable geographical distribution, as well as to the principal legal systems.

3. The members of the Committee shall be elected by secret ballot from a list of persons nominated by States Parties. Each State Party may nominate one person from among its own nationals.

4. The initial election to the Committee shall be held no later than six months after the date of the entry into force of the present Convention and thereafter every second year. At least four

months before the date of each election, the Secretary-General of the United Nations shall address a letter to States Parties inviting them to submit their nominations within two months. The Secretary-General shall subsequently prepare a list in alphabetical order of all persons thus nominated, indicating States Parties which have nominated them, and shall submit it to the States Parties to the present Convention.

5. The elections shall be held at meetings of States Parties convened by the Secretary-General at United Nations Headquarters. At those meetings, for which two thirds of States Parties shall constitute a quorum, the persons elected to the Committee shall be those who obtain the largest number of votes and an absolute majority of the votes of the representatives of States Parties present and voting.

6. The members of the Committee shall be elected for a term of four years. They shall be eligible for re-election if renominated. The term of five of the members elected at the first election shall expire at the end of two years; immediately after the first election, the names of these five members shall be chosen by lot by the Chairman of the meeting.

7. If a member of the Committee dies or resigns or declares that for any other cause he or she can no longer perform the duties of the Committee, the State Party which nominated the member shall appoint another expert from among its nationals to serve for the remainder of the term, subject to the approval of the Committee.

8. The Committee shall establish its own rules of procedure.

9. The Committee shall elect its officers for a period of two years.

10. The meetings of the Committee shall normally be held at United Nations Headquarters or at any other convenient place as determined by the Committee. The Committee shall normally meet annually. The duration of the meetings of the Committee shall be determined, and reviewed, if necessary, by a meeting of the States Parties to the present Convention, subject to the approval of the General Assembly.

11. The Secretary-General of the United Nations shall provide the necessary staff and facilities for the effective performance of the functions of the Committee under the present Convention.

12. With the approval of the General Assembly, the members of the Committee established under the present Convention shall receive emoluments from United Nations resources on such terms and conditions as the Assembly may decide.

Article 44

1. States Parties undertake to submit to the Committee, through the Secretary-General of the United Nations, reports on the measures they have adopted which give effect to the rights recognized herein and on the progress made on the enjoyment of those rights

(a) Within two years of the entry into force of the Convention for the State Party concerned;

(b) Thereafter every five years.

2. Reports made under the present article shall indicate factors and difficulties, if any, affecting the degree of fulfillment of the obligations under the present Convention. Reports shall also contain sufficient information to provide the Committee with a comprehensive understanding of the implementation of the Convention in the country concerned.

3. A State Party which has submitted a comprehensive initial report to the Committee need not, in its subsequent reports submitted in accordance with paragraph 1 (b) of the present article, repeat basic information previously provided.

4. The Committee may request from States Parties further information relevant to the implementation of the Convention.

5. The Committee shall submit to the General Assembly, through the Economic and Social Council, every two years, reports on its activities.

6. States Parties shall make their reports widely available to the public in their own countries.

Article 45

In order to foster the effective implementation of the Convention and to encourage international co-operation in the field covered by the Convention:

(a) The specialized agencies, the United Nations Children's Fund, and other United Nations organs shall be entitled to be represented at the consideration of the implementation of such provisions of the present Convention as fall within the scope of their mandate. The Committee may invite the specialized agencies, the United Nations Children's Fund and other competent bodies as it may consider appropriate to provide expert advice on the implementation of the Convention in areas falling within the scope of their respective mandates. The Committee may invite the specialized agencies, the United Nations Children's Fund, and other United Nations organs to submit reports on the implementation of the Convention in areas falling within the scope of their activities;

(b) The Committee shall transmit, as it may consider appropriate, to the specialized agencies, the United Nations Children's Fund and other competent bodies, any reports from States Parties that contain a request, or indicate a need, for technical advice or assistance, along with the Committee's observations and suggestions, if any, on these requests or indications;

(c) The Committee may recommend to the General Assembly to request the Secretary-General to undertake on its behalf studies on specific issues relating to the rights of the child;

(d) The Committee may make suggestions and general recommendations based on information received pursuant to articles 44 and 45 of the present Convention. Such suggestions and general recommendations shall be transmitted to any State Party concerned and reported to the General Assembly, together with comments, if any, from States Parties.

PART III

Article 46

The present Convention shall be open for signature by all States.

Article 47

The present Convention is subject to ratification. Instruments of ratification shall be deposited with the Secretary-General of the United Nations.

Article 48

The present Convention shall remain open for accession by any State. The instruments of accession shall be deposited with the Secretary-General of the United Nations.

Article 49

1. The present Convention shall enter into force on the thirtieth day following the date of deposit with the Secretary-General of the United Nations of the twentieth instrument of ratification or accession.

2. For each State ratifying or acceding to the Convention after the deposit of the twentieth instrument of ratification or accession, the Convention shall enter into force on the thirtieth day after the deposit by such State of its instrument of ratification or accession.

Article 50

1. Any State Party may propose an amendment and file it with the Secretary-General of the United Nations. The Secretary-General shall thereupon communicate the proposed amendment to States Parties, with a request that they indicate whether they favour a conference of States Parties for the purpose of considering and voting upon the proposals. In the event that, within four months from the date of such communication, at least one third of the States Parties favour such a conference, the Secretary-General shall convene the conference under the auspices of the United Nations. Any amendment adopted by a majority of States Parties present and voting at the conference shall be submitted to the General Assembly for approval.

2. An amendment adopted in accordance with paragraph 1 of the present article shall enter into force when it has been approved by the General Assembly of the United Nations and accepted by a two-thirds majority of States Parties.

3. When an amendment enters into force, it shall be binding on those States Parties which have accepted it, other States Parties still being bound by the provisions of the present Convention and any earlier amendments which they have accepted.

Article 51

1. The Secretary-General of the United Nations shall receive and circulate to all States the text of reservations made by States at the time of ratification or accession.

2. A reservation incompatible with the object and purpose of the present Convention shall not be permitted.

3. Reservations may be withdrawn at any time by notification to that effect addressed to the Secretary-General of the United Nations, who shall then inform all States. Such notification shall take effect on the date on which it is received by the Secretary-General

Article 52

A State Party may denounce the present Convention by written notification to the Secretary-General of the United Nations. Denunciation becomes effective one year after the date of receipt of the notification by the Secretary-General.

Article 53

The Secretary-General of the United Nations is designated as the depositary of the present Convention.

Article 54

The original of the present Convention, of which the Arabic, Chinese, English, French, Russian and Spanish texts are equally authentic, shall be deposited with the Secretary-General of the United Nations.

IN WITNESS THEREOF the undersigned plenipotentiaries, being duly authorized thereto by their respective governments, have signed the present Convention.

International Convention for the Protection of All Persons from Enforced Disappearance, 2006 [excerpts][*]

Adoption: 20 December 2006[**]
Entry into force: not yet in force
Parties: 57 Signatories (Status as of 1 April 2007)

ALBANIA 6 Feb 2007, ALGERIA 6 Feb 2007, ARGENTINA 6 Feb 2007, AUSTRIA 6 Feb 2007, AZERBAIJAN 6 Feb 2007, BELGIUM 6 Feb 2007, BOLIVIA 6 Feb 2007, BOSNIA AND HERZEGOVINA 6 Feb 2007, BRAZIL 6 Feb 2007, BURKINA FASO 6 Feb 2007, BURUNDI 6 Feb 2007, CAMEROON 6 Feb 2007, CAPE VERDE 6 Feb 2007, CHAD 6 Feb 2007, CHILE 6 Feb 2007, COMOROS 6 Feb 2007, CONGO 6 Feb 2007, COSTA RICA 6 Feb 2007, CROATIA 6 Feb 2007, CUBA 6 Feb 2007, CYPRUS 6 Feb 2007, FINLAND 6 Feb 2007, FRANCE 6 Feb 2007, GHANA 6 Feb 2007, GRENADA 6 Feb 2007, GUATEMALA 6 Feb 2007, HAITI 6 Feb 2007, HONDURAS 6 Feb 2007, INDIA 6 Feb 2007, JAPAN 6 Feb 2007, KENYA 6 Feb 2007, LEBANON 6 Feb 2007, LITHUANIA 6 Feb 2007, LUXEMBOURG 6 Feb 2007, MADAGASCAR 6 Feb 2007, MALDIVES 6 Feb 2007, MALI 6 Feb 2007, MALTA 6 Feb 2007, MEXICO 6 Feb 2007, MOLDOVA 6 Feb 2007, MONACO 6 Feb 2007, MONGOLIA 6 Feb 2007, MONTENEGRO 6 Feb 2007, MOROCCO 6 Feb 2007, NIGER 6 Feb 2007, PARAGUAY 6 Feb 2007, PORTUGAL 6 Feb 2007, SAMOA 6 Feb 2007, SENEGAL 6 Feb 2007, SERBIA 6 Feb 2007, SIERRA LEONE 6 Feb 2007, SWEDEN 6 Feb 2007, THE FORMER YUGOSLAV REPUBLIC OF MACEDONIA 6 Feb 2007, TUNISIA 6 Feb 2007, UGANDA 6 Feb 2007, URUGUAY 6 Feb 2007, VANUATU 6 Feb 2007.

Preamble

The States Parties to this Convention,

Considering the obligation of States under the Charter of the United Nations to promote universal respect for, and observance of, human rights and fundamental freedoms,

Having regard to the Universal Declaration of Human Rights,

Recalling the International Covenant on Economic, Social and Cultural Rights, the International Covenant on Civil and Political Rights and all other relevant international instruments in the fields of human rights, humanitarian law and international criminal law,

Recalling the Declaration on the Protection of All Persons from Enforced Disappearance adopted by the General Assembly of the United Nations in its resolution 47/133 of 18 December 1992,

Aware of the extreme seriousness of enforced disappearance, which constitutes a crime and, in certain circumstances defined in international law, a crime against humanity,

Determined to prevent enforced disappearances and to combat impunity for the crime of enforced disappearance,

Considering the right of any person not to be subjected to enforced disappearance, the right of victims to justice and to reparation,

Affirming the right of any victim to know the truth about the circumstances of an enforced disappearance and the fate of the disappeared person, and the right to freedom to seek, receive and impart information to this end,

* Source: U.N.G.A. Res. A/RES/61/177.

** Convention was opened for signature on 6 February 2007.

Have agreed as follows:

PART I

Article 1

1. No one shall be subjected to enforced disappearance.

2. No exceptional circumstances whatsoever, whether a state of war or a threat of war, internal political instability or any other public emergency, may be invoked as a justification for enforced disappearance.

Article 2

For the purposes of this Convention, enforced disappearance is considered to be the arrest, detention, abduction or any other form of deprivation of liberty committed by agents of the State or by persons or groups of persons acting with the authorization, support or acquiescence of the State, followed by a refusal to acknowledge the deprivation of liberty or by concealment of the fate or whereabouts of the disappeared person, which place such a person outside the protection of the law.

Article 3

Each State Party shall take appropriate measures to investigate acts defined in article 2 committed by persons or groups of persons acting without the authorization, support or acquiescence of the State and to bring those responsible to justice.

Article 4

Each State Party shall take the necessary measures to ensure that enforced disappearance constitutes an offence under its criminal law.

Article 5

The widespread or systematic practice of enforced disappearance constitutes a crime against humanity as defined in applicable international law and shall attract the consequences provided for under such applicable international law.

[…]

Article 9

1. Each State Party shall take the necessary measures to establish its competence to exercise jurisdiction over the offence of enforced disappearance:

(a) When the offence is committed in any territory under its jurisdiction or on board a ship or aircraft registered in that State;

(b) When the alleged offender is one of its nationals;

(c) When the disappeared person is one of its nationals and the State Party considers it appropriate.

2. Each State Party shall likewise take such measures as may be necessary to establish its competence to exercise jurisdiction over the offence of enforced disappearance when the alleged offender is present in any territory under its jurisdiction, unless it extradites or surrenders him or her to another State in accordance with its international obligations or surrenders him or her to an international criminal tribunal whose jurisdiction it has recognized.

3. This Convention does not exclude any additional criminal jurisdiction exercised in accordance with national law.

Article 10

1. Upon being satisfied, after an examination of the information available to it, that the circumstances so warrant, any State Party in whose territory a person suspected of having committed an offence of enforced disappearance is present shall take him or her into custody or take such other legal measures as are necessary to ensure his or her presence. The custody and other legal measures shall be as provided for in the law of that State Party but may be maintained only for such time as is necessary to ensure the person's presence at criminal, surrender or extradition proceedings.

2. A State Party which has taken the measures referred to in paragraph 1 shall immediately carry out a preliminary inquiry or investigations to establish the facts. It shall notify the States Parties referred to in article 9, paragraph 1, of the measures it has taken in pursuance of paragraph 1 of this article, including detention and the circumstances warranting detention, and of the findings of its preliminary inquiry or its investigations, indicating whether it intends to exercise its jurisdiction.

3. Any person in custody pursuant to paragraph 1 may communicate immediately with the nearest appropriate representative of the State of which he or she is a national, or, if he or she is a stateless person, with the representative of the State where he or she usually resides.

Article 11

1. The State Party in the territory under whose jurisdiction a person alleged to have committed an offence of enforced disappearance is found shall, if it does not extradite that person or surrender him or her to another State in accordance with its international obligations or surrender him or her to an international criminal tribunal whose jurisdiction it has recognized, submit the case to its competent authorities for the purpose of prosecution.

2. These authorities shall take their decision in the same manner as in the case of any ordinary offence of a serious nature under the law of that State Party. In the cases referred to in article 9, paragraph 2, the standards of evidence required for prosecution and conviction shall in no way be less stringent than those which apply in the cases referred to in article 9, paragraph 1.

3. Any person against whom proceedings are brought in connection with an offence of enforced disappearance shall be guaranteed fair treatment at all stages of the proceedings. Any person tried for an offence of enforced disappearance shall benefit from a fair trial before a competent, independent and impartial court or tribunal established by law.

[...]

Article 13

1. For the purposes of extradition between States Parties, the offence of enforced disappearance shall not be regarded as a political offence or as an offence connected with a political offence or as an offence inspired by political motives. Accordingly, a request for extradition based on such an offence may not be refused on these grounds alone.

2. The offence of enforced disappearance shall be deemed to be included as an extraditable offence in any extradition treaty existing between States Parties before the entry into force of this convention.

3. States Parties undertake to include the offence of enforced disappearance as an extraditable offence in any extradition treaty subsequently to be concluded between them.

4. If a State Party which makes extradition conditional on the existence of a treaty receives a request for extradition from another State Party with which it has no extradition treaty, it may consider this Convention as the necessary legal basis for extradition in respect of the offence of enforced disappearance.

5. States Parties which do not make extradition conditional on the existence of a treaty shall recognize the offence of enforced disappearance as an extraditable offence between themselves.

6. Extradition shall, in all cases, be subject to the conditions provided for by the law of the requested State Party or by applicable extradition treaties, including, in particular, conditions relating to the minimum penalty requirement for extradition and the grounds upon which the requested State Party may refuse extradition or make it subject to certain conditions.

7. Nothing in this Convention shall be interpreted as imposing an obligation to extradite if the requested State Party has substantial grounds for believing that the request has been made for the purpose of prosecuting or punishing a person on account of that person's sex, race, religion, nationality, ethnic origin, political opinions or membership of a particular social group, or that compliance with the request would cause harm to that person for any one of these reasons.

Article 14

1. States Parties shall afford one another the greatest measure of mutual legal assistance in connection with criminal proceedings brought in respect of an offence of enforced disappearance, including the supply of all evidence at their disposal that is necessary for the proceedings.

2. Such mutual legal assistance shall be subject to the conditions provided for by the domestic law of the requested State Party or by applicable treaties on mutual legal assistance, including, in particular, the conditions in relation to the grounds upon which the requested State Party may refuse to grant mutual legal assistance or may make it subject to conditions.

Article 15

States Parties shall cooperate with each other and shall afford one another the greatest measure of mutual assistance with a view to assisting victims of enforced disappearance, and in searching for, locating and releasing disappeared persons and, in the event of death, in exhuming and identifying them and returning their remains.

Article 16

1. No State Party shall expel, return ("refouler"), surrender or extradite a person to another State where there are substantial grounds for believing that he or she would be in danger of being subjected to enforced disappearance.

2. For the purpose of determining whether there are such grounds, the competent authorities shall take into account all relevant considerations, including, where applicable, the existence in the State concerned of a consistent pattern of gross, flagrant or mass violations of human rights or of serious violations of international humanitarian law.

[...]

Article 24

1. For the purposes of this Convention, "victim" means the disappeared person and any individual who has suffered harm as the direct result of an enforced disappearance.

2. Each victim has the right to know the truth regarding the circumstances of the enforced disappearance, the progress and results of the investigation and the fate of the disappeared person. Each State Party shall take appropriate measures in this regard.

3. Each State Party shall take all appropriate measures to search for, locate and release disappeared persons and, in the event of death, to locate, respect and return their remains.

4. Each State Party shall ensure in its legal system that the victims of enforced disappearance have the right to obtain reparation and prompt, fair and adequate compensation.

5. The right to obtain reparation referred to in paragraph 4 covers material and moral damages and, where appropriate, other forms of reparation such as:

(a) Restitution;

(b) Rehabilitation;

(c) Satisfaction, including restoration of dignity and reputation;

(d) Guarantees of non-repetition.

6. Without prejudice to the obligation to continue the investigation until the fate of the disappeared person has been clarified, each State Party shall take the appropriate steps with regard to the legal situation of disappeared persons whose fate has not been clarified and that of their relatives, in fields such as social welfare, financial matters, family law and property rights.

7. Each State Party shall guarantee the right to form and participate freely in organizations and associations concerned with attempting to establish the circumstances of enforced disappearances and the fate of disappeared persons, and to assist victims of enforced disappearance.

Article 25

1. Each State Party shall take the necessary measures to prevent and punish under its criminal law:

(a) The wrongful removal of children who are subjected to enforced disappearance, children whose father, mother or legal guardian is subjected to enforced disappearance or children born during the captivity of a mother subjected to enforced disappearance;

(b) The falsification, concealment or destruction of documents attesting to the true identity of the children referred to in subparagraph (a).

2. Each State Party shall take the necessary measures to search for and identify the children referred to in paragraph 1 (a) and to return them to their families of origin, in accordance with legal procedures and applicable international agreements.

3. States Parties shall assist one another in searching for, identifying and locating the children referred to in paragraph 1 (a).

4. Given the need to protect the best interests of the children referred to in paragraph 1 (a) and their right to preserve, or to have re-established, their identity, including their nationality, name and family relations as recognized by law, States Parties which recognize a system of adoption or other form of placement of children shall have legal procedures in place to review the adoption or placement procedure, and, where appropriate, to annul any adoption or placement of children that originated in an enforced disappearance.

5. In all cases, and in particular in all matters relating to this article, the best interests of the child shall be a primary consideration, and a child who is capable of forming his or her own views shall have the right to express those views freely, the views of the child being given due weight in accordance with the age and maturity of the child.

[…]

International Convention on the Protection of the Rights of All Migrant Workers and Members of Their Families, 1990 (See section 2.1)

Optional Protocol to the Convention on the Rights of the Child on the Involvement of Children in Armed Conflicts, 2000 (See section 14)

Optional Protocol to the Convention on the Rights of the Child on the Sale of Children, Child Prostitution and Child Pornography, 2000 (See section 4.2)

1.2 Declarations and Other Non-binding Instruments

Universal Declaration of Human Rights, 1948*

Adoption: 10 December 1948

On December 10, 1948 the General Assembly of the United Nations adopted and proclaimed the Universal Declaration of Human Rights the full text of which appears in the following pages. Following this historic act the Assembly called upon all Member countries to publicize the text of the Declaration and "to cause it to be disseminated, displayed, read and expounded principally in schools and other educational institutions, without distinction based on the political status of countries or territories."

PREAMBLE

Whereas recognition of the inherent dignity and of the equal and inalienable rights of all members of the human family is the foundation of freedom, justice and peace in the world,

Whereas disregard and contempt for human rights have resulted in barbarous acts which have outraged the conscience of mankind, and the advent of a world in which human beings shall enjoy freedom of speech and belief and freedom from fear and want has been proclaimed as the highest aspiration of the common people,

Whereas it is essential, if man is not to be compelled to have recourse, as a last resort, to rebellion against tyranny and oppression, that human rights should be protected by the rule of law,

Whereas it is essential to promote the development of friendly relations between nations,

Whereas the peoples of the United Nations have in the Charter reaffirmed their faith in fundamental human rights, in the dignity and worth of the human person and in the equal rights of men and women and have determined to promote social progress and better standards of life in larger freedom,

Whereas Member States have pledged themselves to achieve, in co-operation with the United Nations, the promotion of universal respect for and observance of human rights and fundamental freedoms,

Whereas a common understanding of these rights and freedoms is of the greatest importance for the full realization of this pledge,

Now, Therefore THE GENERAL ASSEMBLY proclaims THIS UNIVERSAL DECLARATION OF HUMAN RIGHTS as a common standard of achievement for all peoples and all nations, to the end that every individual and every organ of society, keeping this Declaration constantly in mind, shall strive by teaching and education to promote respect for these rights and freedoms and by progressive measures, national and international, to secure their universal and effective recognition and observance, both among the peoples of Member States themselves and among the peoples of territories under their jurisdiction.

Article 1

All human beings are born free and equal in dignity and rights. They are endowed with reason and conscience and should act towards one another in a spirit of brotherhood.

* Source: U.N.G.A. Res. 217 A (III).

Article 2

Everyone is entitled to all the rights and freedoms set forth in this Declaration, without distinction of any kind, such as race, colour, sex, language, religion, political or other opinion, national or social origin, property, birth or other status. Furthermore, no distinction shall be made on the basis of the political, jurisdictional or international status of the country or territory to which a person belongs, whether it be independent, trust, non-self-governing or under any other limitation of sovereignty.

Article 3

Everyone has the right to life, liberty and security of person.

Article 4

No one shall be held in slavery or servitude; slavery and the slave trade shall be prohibited in all their forms.

Article 5

No one shall be subjected to torture or to cruel, inhuman or degrading treatment or punishment.

Article 6

Everyone has the right to recognition everywhere as a person before the law.

Article 7

All are equal before the law and are entitled without any discrimination to equal protection of the law. All are entitled to equal protection against any discrimination in violation of this Declaration and against any incitement to such discrimination.

Article 8

Everyone has the right to an effective remedy by the competent national tribunals for acts violating the fundamental rights granted him by the constitution or by law.

Article 9

No one shall be subjected to arbitrary arrest, detention or exile.

Article 10

Everyone is entitled in full equality to a fair and public hearing by an independent and impartial tribunal, in the determination of his rights and obligations and of any criminal charge against him.

Article 11

(1) Everyone charged with a penal offence has the right to be presumed innocent until proved guilty according to law in a public trial at which he has had all the guarantees necessary for his defence.

(2) No one shall be held guilty of any penal offence on account of any act or omission which did not constitute a penal offence, under national or international law, at the time when it was

committed. Nor shall a heavier penalty be imposed than the one that was applicable at the time the penal offence was committed.

Article 12

No one shall be subjected to arbitrary interference with his privacy, family, home or correspondence, nor to attacks upon his honour and reputation. Everyone has the right to the protection of the law against such interference or attacks.

Article 13

(1) Everyone has the right to freedom of movement and residence within the borders of each state.

(2) Everyone has the right to leave any country, including his own, and to return to his country.

Article 14

(1) Everyone has the right to seek and to enjoy in other countries asylum from persecution.

(2) This right may not be invoked in the case of prosecutions genuinely arising from non-political crimes or from acts contrary to the purposes and principles of the United Nations.

Article 15

(1) Everyone has the right to a nationality.

(2) No one shall be arbitrarily deprived of his nationality nor denied the right to change his nationality.

Article 16

(1) Men and women of full age, without any limitation due to race, nationality or religion, have the right to marry and to found a family. They are entitled to equal rights as to marriage, during marriage and at its dissolution.

(2) Marriage shall be entered into only with the free and full consent of the intending spouses.

(3) The family is the natural and fundamental group unit of society and is entitled to protection by society and the State.

Article 17

(1) Everyone has the right to own property alone as well as in association with others.

(2) No one shall be arbitrarily deprived of his property.

Article 18

Everyone has the right to freedom of thought, conscience and religion; this right includes freedom to change his religion or belief, and freedom, either alone or in community with others and in public or private, to manifest his religion or belief in teaching, practice, worship and observance.

Article 19

Everyone has the right to freedom of opinion and expression; this right includes freedom to hold opinions without interference and to seek, receive and impart information and ideas through any media and regardless of frontiers.

Article 20

(1) Everyone has the right to freedom of peaceful assembly and association.

(2) No one may be compelled to belong to an association.

Article 21

(1) Everyone has the right to take part in the government of his country, directly or through freely chosen representatives.

(2) Everyone has the right of equal access to public service in his country.

(3) The will of the people shall be the basis of the authority of government; this will shall be expressed in periodic and genuine elections which shall be by universal and equal suffrage and shall be held by secret vote or by equivalent free voting procedures.

Article 22

Everyone, as a member of society, has the right to social security and is entitled to realization, through national effort and international co-operation and in accordance with the organization and resources of each State, of the economic, social and cultural rights indispensable for his dignity and the free development of his personality.

Article 23

(1) Everyone has the right to work, to free choice of employment, to just and favourable conditions of work and to protection against unemployment.

(2) Everyone, without any discrimination, has the right to equal pay for equal work.

(3) Everyone who works has the right to just and favourable remuneration ensuring for himself and his family an existence worthy of human dignity, and supplemented, if necessary, by other means of social protection.

(4) Everyone has the right to form and to join trade unions for the protection of his interests.

Article 24

Everyone has the right to rest and leisure, including reasonable limitation of working hours and periodic holidays with pay.

Article 25

(1) Everyone has the right to a standard of living adequate for the health and well-being of himself and of his family, including food, clothing, housing and medical care and necessary social services, and the right to security in the event of unemployment, sickness, disability, widowhood, old age or other lack of livelihood in circumstances beyond his control.

(2) Motherhood and childhood are entitled to special care and assistance. All children, whether born in or out of wedlock, shall enjoy the same social protection.

Article 26

(1) Everyone has the right to education. Education shall be free, at least in the elementary and fundamental stages. Elementary education shall be compulsory. Technical and professional education shall be made generally available and higher education shall be equally accessible to all on the basis of merit.

(2) Education shall be directed to the full development of the human personality and to the strengthening of respect for human rights and fundamental freedoms. It shall promote understanding, tolerance and friendship among all nations, racial or religious groups, and shall further the activities of the United Nations for the maintenance of peace.

(3) Parents have a prior right to choose the kind of education that shall be given to their children.

Article 27

(1) Everyone has the right freely to participate in the cultural life of the community, to enjoy the arts and to share in scientific advancement and its benefits.

(2) Everyone has the right to the protection of the moral and material interests resulting from any scientific, literary or artistic production of which he is the author.

Article 28

Everyone is entitled to a social and international order in which the rights and freedoms set forth in this Declaration can be fully realized.

Article 29

(1) Everyone has duties to the community in which alone the free and full development of his personality is possible.

(2) In the exercise of his rights and freedoms, everyone shall be subject only to such limitations as are determined by law solely for the purpose of securing due recognition and respect for the rights and freedoms of others and of meeting the just requirements of morality, public order and the general welfare in a democratic society.

(3) These rights and freedoms may in no case be exercised contrary to the purposes and principles of the United Nations.

Article 30

Nothing in this Declaration may be interpreted as implying for any State, group or person any right to engage in any activity or to perform any act aimed at the destruction of any of the rights and freedoms set forth herein.

Declaration on the Human Rights of Individuals Who are Not Nationals of the Country in which They Live, 1985*

Adoption: 13 December 1985

The General Assembly,

Considering that the Charter of the United Nations encourages universal respect for and observance of the human rights and fundamental freedoms of all human beings, without distinction as to race, sex, language or religion,

Considering that the Universal Declaration of Human Rights proclaims that all human beings are born free and equal in dignity and rights and that everyone is entitled to all the rights and freedoms set forth in that Declaration, without distinction of any kind, such as race, colour, sex, language, religion, political or other opinion, national or social origin, property, birth or other status,

Considering that the Universal Declaration of Human Rights proclaims further that everyone has the right to recognition everywhere as a person before the law, that all are equal before the law and entitled without any discrimination to equal protection of the law, and that all are entitled to equal protection against any discrimination in violation of that Declaration and against any incitement to such discrimination,

Being aware that the States Parties to the International Covenants on Human Rights undertake to guarantee that the rights enunciated in these Covenants will be exercised without discrimination of any kind as to race, colour, sex, language, religion, political or other opinion, national or social origin, property, birth or other status,

Conscious that, with improving communications and the development of peaceful and friendly relations among countries, individuals increasingly live in countries of which they are not nationals,

Reaffirming the purposes and principles of the Charter of the United Nations,

Recognizing that the protection of human rights and fundamental freedoms provided for in international instruments should also be ensured for individuals who are not nationals of the country in which they live,

Proclaims this Declaration:

Article 1

For the purposes of this Declaration, the term "alien" shall apply, with due regard to qualifications made in subsequent articles, to any individual who is not a national of the State in which he or she is present.

Article 2

1. Nothing in this Declaration shall be interpreted as legitimizing the illegal entry into and presence in a State of any alien, nor shall any provision be interpreted as restricting the right of any State to promulgate laws and regulations concerning the entry of aliens and the terms and conditions of their stay or to establish differences between nationals and aliens. However, such

* Source: U.N.G.A. Res. 40/144.

laws and regulations shall not be incompatible with the international legal obligations of that State, including those in the field of human rights.

2. This Declaration shall not prejudice the enjoyment of the rights accorded by domestic law and of the rights which under international law a State is obliged to accord to aliens, even where this Declaration does not recognize such rights or recognizes them to a lesser extent.

Article 3

Every State shall make public its national legislation or regulations affecting aliens.

Article 4

Aliens shall observe the laws of the State in which they reside or are present and regard with respect the customs and traditions of the people of that State.

Article 5

1. Aliens shall enjoy, in accordance with domestic law and subject to the relevant international obligations of the State in which they are present, in particular the following rights:

(a) The right to life and security of person; no alien shall be subjected to arbitrary arrest or detention; no alien shall be deprived of his or her liberty except on such grounds and in accordance with such procedures as are established by law;

(b) The right to protection against arbitrary or unlawful interference with privacy, family, home or correspondence;

(c) The right to be equal before the courts, tribunals and all other organs and authorities administering justice and, when necessary, to free assistance of an interpreter in criminal proceedings and, when prescribed by law, other proceedings;

(d) The right to choose a spouse, to marry, to found a family;

(e) The right to freedom of thought, opinion, conscience and religion; the right to manifest their religion or beliefs, subject only to such limitations as are prescribed by law and are necessary to protect public safety, order, health or morals or the fundamental rights and freedoms of others;

(f) The right to retain their own language, culture and tradition;

(g) The right to transfer abroad earnings, savings or other personal monetary assets, subject to domestic currency regulations.

2. Subject to such restrictions as are prescribed by law and which are necessary in a democratic society to protect national security, public safety, public order, public health or morals or the rights and freedoms of others, and which are consistent with the other rights recognized in the relevant international instruments and those set forth in this Declaration, aliens shall enjoy the following rights:

(a) The right to leave the country;

(b) The right to freedom of expression;

(c) The right to peaceful assembly;

(d) The right to own property alone as well as in association with others, subject to domestic law.

3. Subject to the provisions referred to in paragraph 2, aliens lawfully in the territory of a State shall enjoy the right to liberty of movement and freedom to choose their residence within the borders of the State.

4. Subject to national legislation and due authorization, the spouse and minor or dependent children of an alien lawfully residing in the territory of a State shall be admitted to accompany, join and stay with the alien.

Article 6

No alien shall be subjected to torture or to cruel, inhuman or degrading treatment or punishment and, in particular, no alien shall be subjected without his or her free consent to medical or scientific experimentation.

Article 7

An alien lawfully in the territory of a State may be expelled therefrom only in pursuance of a decision reached in accordance with law and shall, except where compelling reasons of national security otherwise require, be allowed to submit the reasons why he or she should not be expelled and to have the case reviewed by, and be represented for the purpose before, the competent authority or a person or persons specially designated by the competent authority. Individual or collective expulsion of such aliens on grounds of race, colour, religion, culture, descent or national or ethnic origin is prohibited.

Article 8

1. Aliens lawfully residing in the territory of a State shall also enjoy, in accordance with the national laws, the following rights, subject to their obligations under article 4:

(a) The right to safe and healthy working conditions, to fair wages and equal remuneration for work of equal value without distinction of any kind, in particular, women being guaranteed conditions of work not inferior to those enjoyed by men, with equal pay for equal work;

(b) The right to join trade unions and other organizations or associations of their choice and to participate in their activities. No restrictions may be placed on the exercise of this right other than those prescribed by law and which are necessary, in a democratic society, in the interests of national security or public order or for the protection of the rights and freedoms of others;

(c) The right to health protection, medical care, social security, social services, education, rest and leisure, provided that they fulfil the requirements under the relevant regulations for participation and that undue strain is not placed on the resources of the State.

2. With a view to protecting the rights of aliens carrying on lawful paid activities in the country in which they are present, such rights may be specified by the Governments concerned in multilateral or bilateral conventions.

Article 9

No alien shall be arbitrarily deprived of his or her lawfully acquired assets.

Article 10

Any alien shall be free at any time to communicate with the consulate or diplomatic mission of the State of which he or she is a national or, in the absence thereof, with the consulate or diplomatic mission of any other State entrusted with the protection of the interests of the State of which he or she is a national in the State where he or she resides.

Declaration on Social and Legal Principles relating to the Protection and Welfare of Children, with Special Reference to Foster Placement and Adoption Nationally and Internationally, 1986 [excerpts]*

Adoption: 3 December 1986

[...]

C. ADOPTION

Article 13

The primary aim of adoption is to provide the child who cannot be cared for by his or her own parents with a permanent family.

Article 14

In considering possible adoption placements, persons responsible for them should select the most appropriate environment for the child.

Article 15

Sufficient time and adequate counseling should be given to the child's own parents, the prospective adoptive parents and, as appropriate, the child in order to reach a decision on the child's future as early as possible.

Article 16

The relationship between the child to be adopted and the prospective adoptive parents should be observed by child welfare agencies or services prior to the adoption. Legislation should ensure that the child is recognized in law as a member of the adoptive family and enjoys all the rights pertinent thereto.

Article 17

If a child cannot be placed in a foster or an adoptive family or cannot in any suitable manner be cared for in the country of origin, intercountry adoption may be considered as an alternative means of providing the child with a family.

Article 18

Governments should establish policy, legislation and effective supervision for the protection of children involved in intercountry adoption. Intercountry adoption should, wherever possible, only be undertaken when such measures have been established in the States concerned.

Article 19

Policies should be established and laws enacted, where necessary, for the prohibition of abduction and of any other act for illicit placement of children.

* Source: U.N.G.A. Res. 41/85.

Article 20

In intercountry adoption, placements should, as a rule, be made through competent authorities or agencies with application of safeguards and standards equivalent to those existing in respect of national adoption. In no case should the placement result in improper financial gain for those involved in it.

Article 21

In intercountry adoption through persons acting as agents for prospective adoptive parents, special precautions should be taken in order to protect the child's legal and social interests.

Article 22

No intercountry adoption should be considered before it has been established that the child is legally free for adoption and that any pertinent documents necessary to complete the adoption, such as the consent of competent authorities, will become available. It must also be established that the child will be able to migrate and to join the prospective adoptive parents and may obtain their nationality.

Article 23

In intercountry adoption, as a rule, the legal validity of the adoption should be assured in each of the countries involved.

Article 24

Where the nationality of the child differs from that of the prospective adoptive parents, all due weight shall be given to both the law of the State of which the child is a national and the law of the State of which the prospective adoptive parents are nationals. In this connection due regard shall be given to the child's cultural and religious background and interests.

Vienna Declaration and Programme of Action (World Conference on Human Rights, Vienna, 14-25 June 1993) [excerpts]*

Adoption: 25 June 1993

The World Conference on Human Rights,

Considering that the promotion and protection of human rights is a matter of priority for the international community, and that the Conference affords a unique opportunity to carry out a comprehensive analysis of the international human rights system and of the machinery for the protection of human rights, in order to enhance and thus promote a fuller observance of those rights, in a just and balanced manner,

Recognizing and affirming that all human rights derive from the dignity and worth inherent in the human person, and that the human person is the central subject of human rights and fundamental freedoms, and consequently should be the principal beneficiary and should participate actively in the realization of these rights and freedoms,

Reaffirming their commitment to the purposes and principles contained in the Charter of the United Nations and the Universal Declaration of Human Rights,

Reaffirming the commitment contained in Article 56 of the Charter of the United Nations to take joint and separate action, placing proper emphasis on developing effective international cooperation for the realization of the purposes set out in Article 55, including universal respect for, and observance of, human rights and fundamental freedoms for all,

[...]

Solemnly adopts the Vienna Declaration and Programme of Action.

I

1. The World Conference on Human Rights reaffirms the solemn commitment of all States to fulfil their obligations to promote universal respect for, and observance and protection of, all human rights and fundamental freedoms for all in accordance with the Charter of the United Nations, other instruments relating to human rights, and international law. The universal nature of these rights and freedoms is beyond question.

In this framework, enhancement of international cooperation in the field of human rights is essential for the full achievement of the purposes of the United Nations.

Human rights and fundamental freedoms are the birthright of all human beings; their protection and promotion is the first responsibility of Governments.

[...]

14. The existence of widespread extreme poverty inhibits the full and effective enjoyment of human rights; its immediate alleviation and eventual elimination must remain a high priority for the international community.

15. Respect for human rights and for fundamental freedoms without distinction of any kind is a fundamental rule of international human rights law. The speedy and comprehensive elimination of all forms of racism and racial discrimination, xenophobia and related intolerance is a priority

* Source: U.N.Doc. A/CONF.157/23.

task for the international community. Governments should take effective measures to prevent and combat them. Groups, institutions, intergovernmental and non-governmental organizations and individuals are urged to intensify their efforts in cooperating and coordinating their activities against these evils.

[...]

17. The acts, methods and practices of terrorism in all its forms and manifestations as well as linkage in some countries to drug trafficking are activities aimed at the destruction of human rights, fundamental freedoms and democracy, threatening territorial integrity, security of States and destabilizing legitimately constituted Governments. The international community should take the necessary steps to enhance cooperation to prevent and combat terrorism.

18. The human rights of women and of the girl-child are an inalienable, integral and indivisible part of universal human rights. The full and equal participation of women in political, civil, economic, social and cultural life, at the national, regional and international levels, and the eradication of all forms of discrimination on grounds of sex are priority objectives of the international community.

Gender-based violence and all forms of sexual harassment and exploitation, including those resulting from cultural prejudice and international trafficking, are incompatible with the dignity and worth of the human person, and must be eliminated. This can be achieved by legal measures and through national action and international cooperation in such fields as economic and social development, education, safe maternity and health care, and social support.

The human rights of women should form an integral part of the United Nations human rights activities, including the promotion of all human rights instruments relating to women.

The World Conference on Human Rights urges Governments, institutions, intergovernmental and non-governmental organizations to intensify their efforts for the protection and promotion of human rights of women and the girl-child.

19. Considering the importance of the promotion and protection of the rights of persons belonging to minorities and the contribution of such promotion and protection to the political and social stability of the States in which such persons live,

The World Conference on Human Rights reaffirms the obligation of States to ensure that persons belonging to minorities may exercise fully and effectively all human rights and fundamental freedoms without any discrimination and in full equality before the law in accordance with the Declaration on the Rights of Persons Belonging to National or Ethnic, Religious and Linguistic Minorities.

The persons belonging to minorities have the right to enjoy their own culture, to profess and practise their own religion and to use their own language in private and in public, freely and without interference or any form of discrimination.

20. The World Conference on Human Rights recognizes the inherent dignity and the unique contribution of indigenous people to the development and plurality of society and strongly reaffirms the commitment of the international community to their economic, social and cultural well-being and their enjoyment of the fruits of sustainable development. States should ensure the full and free participation of indigenous people in all aspects of society, in particular in matters of concern to them. Considering the importance of the promotion and protection of the rights of indigenous people, and the contribution of such promotion and protection to the political and social stability of the States in which such people live, States should, in accordance with international law, take concerted positive steps to ensure respect for all

human rights and fundamental freedoms of indigenous people, on the basis of equality and non-discrimination, and recognize the value and diversity of their distinct identities, cultures and social organization.

21. The World Conference on Human Rights, welcoming the early ratification of the Convention on the Rights of the Child by a large number of States and noting the recognition of the human rights of children in the World Declaration on the Survival, Protection and Development of Children and Plan of Action adopted by the World Summit for Children, urges universal ratification of the Convention by 1995 and its effective implementation by States parties through the adoption of all the necessary legislative, administrative and other measures and the allocation to the maximum extent of the available resources. In all actions concerning children, non-discrimination and the best interest of the child should be primary considerations and the views of the child given due weight. National and international mechanisms and programmes should be strengthened for the defence and protection of children, in particular, the girl-child, abandoned children, street children, economically and sexually exploited children, including through child pornography, child prostitution or sale of organs, children victims of diseases including acquired immunodeficiency syndrome, refugee and displaced children, children in detention, children in armed conflict, as well as children victims of famine and drought and other emergencies. International cooperation and solidarity should be promoted to support the implementation of the Convention and the rights of the child should be a priority in the United Nations system-wide action on human rights.

The World Conference on Human Rights also stresses that the child for the full and harmonious development of his or her personality should grow up in a family environment which accordingly merits broader protection.

22. Special attention needs to be paid to ensuring non-discrimination, and the equal enjoyment of all human rights and fundamental freedoms by disabled persons, including their active participation in all aspects of society.

23. The World Conference on Human Rights reaffirms that everyone, without distinction of any kind, is entitled to the right to seek and to enjoy in other countries asylum from persecution, as well as the right to return to one's own country. In this respect it stresses the importance of the Universal Declaration of Human Rights, the 1951 Convention relating to the Status of Refugees, its 1967 Protocol and regional instruments. It expresses its appreciation to States that continue to admit and host large numbers of refugees in their territories, and to the Office of the United Nations High Commissioner for Refugees for its dedication to its task. It also expresses its appreciation to the United Nations Relief and Works Agency for Palestine Refugees in the Near East.

The World Conference on Human Rights recognizes that gross violations of human rights, including in armed conflicts, are among the multiple and complex factors leading to displacement of people.

The World Conference on Human Rights recognizes that, in view of the complexities of the global refugee crisis and in accordance with the Charter of the United Nations, relevant international instruments and international solidarity and in the spirit of burden-sharing, a comprehensive approach by the international community is needed in coordination and cooperation with the countries concerned and relevant organizations, bearing in mind the mandate of the United Nations High Commissioner for Refugees. This should include the development of strategies to address the root causes and effects of movements of refugees and other displaced persons, the strengthening of emergency preparedness and response mechanisms, the provision of effective protection and assistance, bearing in mind the special needs of women and children, as well as the achievement of durable solutions, primarily through the preferred solution of dignified and safe voluntary repatriation, including solutions such as those adopted by the international refugee conferences. The World Conference on Human Rights underlines the responsibilities of States, particularly as they relate to the countries of origin.

In the light of the comprehensive approach, the World Conference on Human Rights emphasizes the importance of giving special attention including through intergovernmental and humanitarian organizations and finding lasting solutions to questions related to internally displaced persons including their voluntary and safe return and rehabilitation.

In accordance with the Charter of the United Nations and the principles of humanitarian law, the World Conference on Human Rights further emphasizes the importance of and the need for humanitarian assistance to victims of all natural and man-made disasters.

24. Great importance must be given to the promotion and protection of the human rights of persons belonging to groups which have been rendered vulnerable, including migrant workers, the elimination of all forms of discrimination against them, and the strengthening and more effective implementation of existing human rights instruments. States have an obligation to create and maintain adequate measures at the national level, in particular in the fields of education, health and social support, for the promotion and protection of the rights of persons in vulnerable sectors of their populations and to ensure the participation of those among them who are interested in finding a solution to their own problems.

25. The World Conference on Human Rights affirms that extreme poverty and social exclusion constitute a violation of human dignity and that urgent steps are necessary to achieve better knowledge of extreme poverty and its causes, including those related to the problem of development, in order to promote the human rights of the poorest, and to put an end to extreme poverty and social exclusion and to promote the enjoyment of the fruits of social progress. It is essential for States to foster participation by the poorest people in the decision-making process by the community in which they live, the promotion of human rights and efforts to combat extreme poverty.

[...]

II

[...]

B. Equality, dignity and tolerance

1. Racism, racial discrimination, xenophobia and other forms of intolerance

19. The World Conference on Human Rights considers the elimination of racism and racial discrimination, in particular in their institutionalized forms such as apartheid or resulting from doctrines of racial superiority or exclusivity or contemporary forms and manifestations of racism, as a primary objective for the international community and a worldwide promotion programme in the field of human rights. United Nations organs and agencies should strengthen their efforts to implement such a programme of action related to the third decade to combat racism and racial discrimination as well as subsequent mandates to the same end. The World Conference on Human Rights strongly appeals to the international community to contribute generously to the Trust Fund for the Programme for the Decade for Action to Combat Racism and Racial Discrimination.

[...]

2. Persons belonging to national or ethnic, religious and linguistic minorities

25. The World Conference on Human Rights calls on the Commission on Human Rights to examine ways and means to promote and protect effectively the rights of persons belonging to minorities as set out in the Declaration on the Rights of Persons belonging to National or Ethnic, Religious and Linguistic Minorities. In this context, the World Conference on Human Rights calls upon the Centre for Human Rights to provide, at the request of Governments concerned and as part of its programme of advisory services and technical assistance, qualified expertise on minority issues and human rights, as well as on the prevention and resolution of disputes, to assist in existing or potential situations involving minorities.

26. The World Conference on Human Rights urges States and the international community to promote and protect the rights of persons belonging to national or ethnic, religious and linguistic minorities in accordance with the Declaration on the Rights of Persons belonging to National or Ethnic, Religious and Linguistic Minorities.

27. Measures to be taken, where appropriate, should include facilitation of their full participation in all aspects of the political, economic, social, religious and cultural life of society and in the economic progress and development in their country.

Indigenous people

28. The World Conference on Human Rights calls on the Working Group on Indigenous Populations of the Sub-Commission on Prevention of Discrimination and Protection of Minorities to complete the drafting of a declaration on the rights of indigenous people at its eleventh session.

29. The World Conference on Human Rights recommends that the Commission on Human Rights consider the renewal and updating of the mandate of the Working Group on Indigenous Populations upon completion of the drafting of a declaration on the rights of indigenous people.

30. The World Conference on Human Rights also recommends that advisory services and technical assistance programmes within the United Nations system respond positively to requests by States for assistance which would be of direct benefit to indigenous people. The World Conference on Human Rights further recommends that adequate human and financial resources be made available to the Centre for Human Rights within the overall framework of strengthening the Centre's activities as envisaged by this document.

31. The World Conference on Human Rights urges States to ensure the full and free participation of indigenous people in all aspects of society, in particular in matters of concern to them.

[...]

Migrant workers

33. The World Conference on Human Rights urges all States to guarantee the protection of the human rights of all migrant workers and their families.

34. The World Conference on Human Rights considers that the creation of conditions to foster greater harmony and tolerance between migrant workers and the rest of the society of the State in which they reside is of particular importance.

35. The World Conference on Human Rights invites States to consider the possibility of signing and ratifying, at the earliest possible time, the International Convention on the Rights of All Migrant Workers and Members of Their Families.

3. The equal status and human rights of women

36. The World Conference on Human Rights urges the full and equal enjoyment by women of all human rights and that this be a priority for Governments and for the United Nations. The World Conference on Human Rights also underlines the importance of the integration and full participation of women as both agents and beneficiaries in the development process, and reiterates the objectives established on global action for women towards sustainable and equitable development set forth in the Rio Declaration on Environment and Development and chapter 24 of Agenda 21, adopted by the United Nations Conference on Environment and Development (Rio de Janeiro, Brazil, 3-14 June 1992).

37. The equal status of women and the human rights of women should be integrated into the mainstream of United Nations system-wide activity. These issues should be regularly and systematically addressed throughout relevant United Nations bodies and mechanisms. In particular, steps should be taken to increase cooperation and promote further integration of objectives and goals between the Commission on the Status of Women, the Commission on Human Rights, the Committee for the Elimination of Discrimination against Women, the United Nations Development Fund for Women, the United Nations Development Programme and other United Nations agencies. In this context, cooperation and coordination should be strengthened between the Centre for Human Rights and the Division for the Advancement of Women.

38. In particular, the World Conference on Human Rights stresses the importance of working towards the elimination of violence against women in public and private life, the elimination of all forms of sexual harassment, exploitation and trafficking in women, the elimination of gender bias in the administration of justice and the eradication of any conflicts which may arise between the rights of women and the harmful effects of certain traditional or customary practices, cultural prejudices and religious extremism. The World Conference on Human Rights calls upon the General Assembly to adopt the draft declaration on violence against women and urges States to combat violence against women in accordance with its provisions. Violations of the human rights of women in situations of armed conflict are violations of the fundamental principles of international human rights and humanitarian law. All violations of this kind, including in particular murder, systematic rape, sexual slavery, and forced pregnancy, require a particularly effective response.

[...]

4. The rights of the child

[...]

48. The World Conference on Human Rights urges all States, with the support of international cooperation, to address the acute problem of children under especially difficult circumstances. Exploitation and abuse of children should be actively combated, including by addressing their root causes. Effective measures are required against female infanticide, harmful child labour, sale of children and organs, child prostitution, child pornography, as well as other forms of sexual abuse.

[...]

5. Freedom from torture

[...]

55. The World Conference on Human Rights emphasizes that one of the most atrocious violations against human dignity is the act of torture, the result of which destroys the dignity and impairs the capability of victims to continue their lives and their activities.

56. The World Conference on Human Rights reaffirms that under human rights law and international humanitarian law, freedom from torture is a right which must be protected under all circumstances, including in times of internal or international disturbance or armed conflicts.

[...]

Principles on the Effective Investigation and Documentation of Torture and Other Cruel, Inhuman or Degrading Treatment or Punishment, 2000*

Adoption: 4 December 2000

1. The purposes of effective investigation and documentation of torture and other cruel, inhuman or degrading treatment or punishment (hereinafter "torture or other ill-treatment") include the following:

(a) Clarification of the facts and establishment and acknowledgement of individual and State responsibility for victims and their families;

(b) Identification of measures needed to prevent recurrence;

(c) Facilitation of prosecution and/or, as appropriate, disciplinary sanctions for those indicated by the investigation as being responsible and demonstration of the need for full reparation and redress from the State, including fair and adequate financial compensation and provision of the means for medical care and rehabilitation.

2. States shall ensure that complaints and reports of torture or ill-treatment are promptly and effectively investigated. Even in the absence of an express complaint, an investigation shall be undertaken if there are other indications that torture or ill-treatment might have occurred. The investigators, who shall be independent of the suspected perpetrators and the agency they serve, shall be competent and impartial. They shall have access to, or be empowered to commission investigations by, impartial medical or other experts. The methods used to carry out such investigations shall meet the highest professional standards and the findings shall be made public.

3. (a) The investigative authority shall have the power and obligation to obtain all the information necessary to the inquiry.[1] The persons conducting the investigation shall have at their disposal all the necessary budgetary and technical resources for effective investigation. They shall also have the authority to oblige all those acting in an official capacity allegedly involved in torture or ill-treatment to appear and testify. The same shall apply to any witness. To this end, the investigative authority shall be entitled to issue summonses to witnesses, including any officials allegedly involved, and to demand the production of evidence.

(b) Alleged victims of torture or ill-treatment, witnesses, those conducting the investigation and their families shall be protected from violence, threats of violence or any other form of intimidation that may arise pursuant to the investigation. Those potentially implicated in torture or ill-treatment shall be removed from any position of control or power, whether direct or indirect, over complainants, witnesses and their families, as well as those conducting the investigation.

4. Alleged victims of torture or ill-treatment and their legal representatives shall be informed of, and have access to, any hearing, as well as to all information relevant to the investigation, and shall be entitled to present other evidence.

* Source: U.N.G.A. Res. 55/89. In resolution 55/89, paragraph 3, the General Assembly drew the attention of Governments to the Principles on the Effective Investigation and Documentation of Torture and Other Cruel, Inhuman or Degrading Treatment or Punishment annexed to the resolution and strongly encouraged them to reflect upon the Principles as a useful tool in efforts to combat torture.

[1] Under certain circumstances, professional ethics may require information to be kept confidential. These requirements should be respected.

5. (a) In cases in which the established investigative procedures are inadequate because of insufficient expertise or suspected bias, or because of the apparent existence of a pattern of abuse or for other substantial reasons, States shall ensure that investigations are undertaken through an independent commission of inquiry or similar procedure. Members of such a commission shall be chosen for their recognized impartiality, competence and independence as individuals. In particular, they shall be independent of any suspected perpetrators and the institutions or agencies they may serve. The commission shall have the authority to obtain all information necessary to the inquiry and shall conduct the inquiry as provided for under these Principles.[2]

(b) A written report, made within a reasonable time, shall include the scope of the inquiry, procedures and methods used to evaluate evidence as well as conclusions and recommendations based on findings of fact and on applicable law. Upon completion, the report shall be made public. It shall also describe in detail specific events that were found to have occurred and the evidence upon which such findings were based and list the names of witnesses who testified, with the exception of those whose identities have been withheld for their own protection. The State shall, within a reasonable period of time, reply to the report of the investigation and, as appropriate, indicate steps to be taken in response.

6. (a) Medical experts involved in the investigation of torture or ill-treatment shall behave at all times in conformity with the highest ethical standards and, in particular, shall obtain informed consent before any examination is undertaken. The examination must conform to established standards of medical practice. In particular, examinations shall be conducted in private under the control of the medical expert and outside the presence of security agents and other government officials.

(b) The medical expert shall promptly prepare an accurate written report, which shall include at least the following:

(i) Circumstances of the interview: name of the subject and name and affiliation of those present at the examination; exact time and date; location, nature and address of the institution (including, where appropriate, the room) where the examination is being conducted (e.g., detention centre, clinic or house); circumstances of the subject at the time of the examination (e.g., nature of any restraints on arrival or during the examination, presence of security forces during the examination, demeanour of those accompanying the prisoner or threatening statements to the examiner); and any other relevant factors;

(ii) History: detailed record of the subject's story as given during the interview, including alleged methods of torture or ill-treatment, times when torture or ill-treatment is alleged to have occurred and all complaints of physical and psychological symptoms;

(iii) Physical and psychological examination: record of all physical and psychological findings on clinical examination, including appropriate diagnostic tests and, where possible, colour photographs of all injuries;

(iv) Opinion: interpretation as to the probable relationship of the physical and psychological findings to possible torture or ill-treatment. A recommendation for any necessary medical and psychological treatment and/or further examination shall be given;

(v) Authorship: the report shall clearly identify those carrying out the examination and shall be signed.

(c) The report shall be confidential and communicated to the subject or his or her nominated representative. The views of the subject and his or her representative about the examination

2 See footnote 1 above.

process shall be solicited and recorded in the report. It shall also be provided in writing, where appropriate, to the authority responsible for investigating the allegation of torture or ill-treatment. It is the responsibility of the State to ensure that it is delivered securely to these persons. The report shall not be made available to any other person, except with the consent of the subject or on the authorization of a court empowered to enforce such a transfer.

Declaration and Plan of Action, World Conference against Racism, Racial Discrimination, Xenophobia and Related Intolerance, Durban, 31 August - 7 September 2001 [excerpts]*

Adoption: 8 September 2001

Declaration

Having met in Durban, South Africa, from 31 August to 8 September 2001,

Expressing deep appreciation to the Government of South Africa for hosting this World Conference,

[...]

Affirming that racism, racial discrimination, xenophobia and related intolerance, where they amount to racism and racial discrimination, constitute serious violations of and obstacles to the full enjoyment of all human rights and deny the self-evident truth that all human beings are born free and equal in dignity and rights, are an obstacle to friendly and peaceful relations among peoples and nations, and are among the root causes of many internal and international conflicts, including armed conflicts, and the consequent forced displacement of populations,

[...]

Acknowledging that xenophobia, in its different manifestations, is one of the main contemporary sources and forms of discrimination and conflict, combating which requires urgent attention and prompt action by States, as well as by the international community,

[...]

General Issues

[...]

12. We recognize that interregional and intraregional migration has increased as a result of globalization, in particular from the South to the North, and stress that policies towards migration should not be based on racism, racial discrimination, xenophobia and related intolerance;

Sources, causes, forms and contemporary manifestations of racism, racial discrimination, xenophobia and related intolerance

[...]

16. We recognize that xenophobia against non-nationals, particularly migrants, refugees and asylum-seekers, constitutes one of the main sources of contemporary racism and that human rights violations against members of such groups occur widely in the context of discriminatory, xenophobic and racist practices;

[...]

20. We recognize that racism, racial discrimination, xenophobia and related intolerance are among the root causes of armed conflict and very often one of its consequences and recall that non-discrimination is a fundamental principle of international humanitarian law. We underscore the need for all parties to armed conflicts to abide scrupulously by this principle and for States and the international community to remain especially vigilant during periods of armed conflict and continue to combat all forms of racial discrimination;

[...]

* Source: U.N. Doc. A/Conf.189/12.

30. We affirm the urgent need to prevent, combat and eliminate all forms of trafficking in persons, in particular women and children, and recognize that victims of trafficking are particularly exposed to racism, racial discrimination, xenophobia and related intolerance;

Victims of racism, racial discrimination, xenophobia and related intolerance

[...]

38. We call upon all States to review and, where necessary, revise any immigration policies which are inconsistent with international human rights instruments, with a view to eliminating all discriminatory policies and practices against migrants, including Asians and people of Asian descent;

[...]

46. We recognize the positive economic, social and cultural contributions made by migrants to both countries of origin and destination;

47. We reaffirm the sovereign right of each State to formulate and apply its own legal framework and policies for migration, and further affirm that these policies should be consistent with applicable human rights instruments, norms and standards, and designed to ensure that they are free of racism, racial discrimination, xenophobia and related intolerance;

48. We note with concern and strongly condemn the manifestations and acts of racism, racial discrimination, xenophobia and related intolerance against migrants and the stereotypes often applied to them; reaffirm the responsibility of States to protect the human rights of migrants under their jurisdiction and reaffirm the responsibility of States to safeguard and protect migrants against illegal or violent acts, in particular acts of racial discrimination and crimes perpetrated with racist or xenophobic motivation by individuals or groups? and stress the need for their fair, just and equitable treatment in society and in the workplace;

49. We highlight the importance of creating conditions conducive to greater harmony, tolerance and respect between migrants and the rest of society in the countries in which they find themselves, in order to eliminate manifestations of racism and xenophobia against migrants. We underline that family reunification has a positive effect on integration and emphasize the need for States to facilitate family reunion;

50. We are mindful of the situation of vulnerability in which migrants frequently find themselves, owing, inter alia, to their departure from their countries of origin and to the difficulties they encounter because of differences in language, customs and culture, as well as economic and social difficulties and obstacles to the return of migrants who are undocumented or in an irregular situation;

51. We reaffirm the necessity of eliminating racial discrimination against migrants, including migrant workers, in relation to issues such as employment, social services, including education and health, as well as access to justice, and that their treatment must be in accordance with international human rights instruments, free from racism, racial discrimination, xenophobia and related intolerance;

52. We note with concern that, among other factors, racism, racial discrimination, xenophobia and related intolerance contribute to forced displacement and the movement of people from their countries of origin as refugees and asylum-seekers;

53. We recognize with concern that, despite efforts to combat racism, racial discrimination, xenophobia and related intolerance, instances of various forms of racism, racial discrimination, xenophobia and related intolerance against refugees, asylum-seekers and internally displaced persons, among others, continue;

54. We underline the urgency of addressing the root causes of displacement and of finding durable solutions for refugees and displaced persons, in particular voluntary return in safety and

dignity to the countries of origin, as well as resettlement in third countries and local integration, when and where appropriate and feasible;

55. We affirm our commitment to respect and implement humanitarian obligations relating to the protection of refugees, asylum-seekers, returnees and internally displaced persons, and note in this regard the importance of international solidarity, burden-sharing and international cooperation to share responsibility for the protection of refugees, reaffirming that the 1951 Convention relating to the Status of Refugees and its 1967 Protocol remain the foundation of the international refugee regime and recognizing the importance of their full application by States parties;

[...]

65. We recognize the right of refugees to return voluntarily to their homes and properties in dignity and safety, and urge all States to facilitate such return;

[...]

Measures of prevention, education and protection aimed at the eradication of racism, racial discrimination, xenophobia and related intolerance at the national, regional and international levels

[...]

89. We note with regret that certain media, by promoting false images and negative stereotypes of vulnerable individuals or groups of individuals, particularly of migrants and refugees, have contributed to the spread of xenophobic and racist sentiments among the public and in some cases have encouraged violence by racist individuals and groups;

[...]

Strategies to achieve full and effective equality, including international cooperation and enhancement of the United Nations and other international mechanisms in combating racism, racial discrimination, xenophobia and related intolerance

[...]

111. We reiterate that the international response and policy, including financial assistance, towards refugees and displaced persons in different parts of the world should not be based on discrimination on the grounds of race, colour, descent, or national or ethnic origin of the refugees and displaced persons concerned and, in this context, we urge the international community to provide adequate assistance on an equitable basis to host countries, in particular to host developing countries and countries in transition;

[...]

PROGRAMME OF ACTION

Recognizing the urgent need to translate the objectives of the Declaration into a practical and workable Programme of Action, the World Conference against Racism, Racial Discrimination, Xenophobia and Related Intolerance:

I. Sources, causes, forms and contemporary manifestations of racism, racial discrimination, xenophobia and related intolerance

[...]

II. Victims of racism, racial discrimination, xenophobia and related intolerance

[...]

Migrants

24. Requests all States to combat manifestations of a generalized rejection of migrants and actively to discourage all racist demonstrations and acts that generate xenophobic behaviour and negative sentiments towards, or rejection of, migrants;

25. Invites international and national non-governmental organizations to include monitoring and protection of the human rights of migrants in their programmes and activities and to sensitize Governments and increase public awareness in all States about the need to prevent racist acts and manifestations of discrimination, xenophobia and related intolerance against migrants;

26. Requests States to promote and protect fully and effectively the human rights and fundamental freedoms of all migrants, in conformity with the Universal Declaration of Human Rights and their obligations under international human rights instruments, regardless of the migrants' immigration status;

27. Encourages States to promote education on the human rights of migrants and to engage in information campaigns to ensure that the public receives accurate information regarding migrants and migration issues, including the positive contribution of migrants to the host society and the vulnerability of migrants, particularly those who are in an irregular situation;

28. Calls upon States to facilitate family reunification in an expeditious and effective manner which has a positive effect on integration of migrants, with due regard for the desire of many family members to have an independent status;

29. Urges States to take concrete measures that would eliminate racism, racial discrimination, xenophobia and related intolerance in the workplace against all workers, including migrants, and ensure the full equality of all before the law, including labour law, and further urges States to eliminate barriers, where appropriate, to: participating in vocational training, collective bargaining, employment, contracts and trade union activity; accessing judicial and administrative tribunals dealing with grievances; seeking employment in different parts of their country of residence; and working in safe and healthy conditions;

30. Urges States:

(a) To develop and implement policies and action plans, and to reinforce and implement preventive measures, in order to foster greater harmony and tolerance between migrants and host societies, with the aim of eliminating manifestations of racism, racial discrimination, xenophobia and related intolerance, including acts of violence, perpetrated in many societies by individuals or groups;

(b) To review and revise, where necessary, their immigration laws, policies and practices so that they are free of racial discrimination and compatible with States' obligations under international human rights instruments;

(c) To implement specific measures involving the host community and migrants in order to encourage respect for cultural diversity, to promote the fair treatment of migrants and to develop programmes, where appropriate, that facilitate their integration into social, cultural, political and economic life;

(d) To ensure that migrants, regardless of their immigration status, detained by public authorities are treated with humanity and in a fair manner, and receive effective legal protection and, where appropriate, the assistance of a competent interpreter in accordance with the relevant norms of international law and human rights standards, particularly during interrogation;

(e) To ensure that the police and immigration authorities treat migrants in a dignified and non-discriminatory manner, in accordance with international standards, through, inter alia, organizing specialized training courses for administrators, police officers, immigration officials and other interested groups;

(f) To consider the question of promoting the recognition of the educational, professional and technical credentials of migrants, with a view to maximizing their contribution to their new States of residence;

(g) To take all possible measures to promote the full enjoyment by all migrants of all human rights, including those related to fair wages and equal remuneration for work of equal value without distinction of any kind, and to the right to security in the event of unemployment, sickness, disability, widowhood, old age or other lack of livelihood in circumstances beyond their control, social security, including social insurance, access to education, health care, social services and respect for their cultural identity;

(h) To consider adopting and implementing immigration policies and programmes that would enable immigrants, in particular women and children who are victims of spousal or domestic violence, to free themselves from abusive relationships;

31. Urges States, in the light of the increased proportion of women migrants, to place special focus on gender issues, including gender discrimination, particularly when the multiple barriers faced by migrant women intersect; detailed research should be undertaken not only in respect of human rights violations perpetrated against women migrants, but also on the contribution they make to the economies of their countries of origin and their host countries, and the findings should be included in reports to treaty bodies;

32. Urges States to recognize the same economic opportunities and responsibilities to documented long-term migrants as to other members of society;

33. Recommends that host countries of migrants consider the provision of adequate social services, in particular in the areas of health, education and adequate housing, as a matter of priority, in cooperation with the United Nations agencies, the regional organizations and international financial bodies; also requests that these agencies provide an adequate response to requests for such services;

Refugees

34. Urges States to comply with their obligations under international human rights, refugee and humanitarian law relating to refugees, asylum-seekers and displaced persons, and urges the international community to provide them with protection and assistance in an equitable manner and with due regard to their needs in different parts of the world, in keeping with principles of international solidarity, burden-sharing and international cooperation, to share responsibilities;

35. Calls upon States to recognize the racism, racial discrimination, xenophobia and related intolerance that refugees may face as they endeavour to engage in the life of the societies of their host countries and encourages States, in accordance with their international obligations and commitments, to develop strategies to address this discrimination and to facilitate the full enjoyment of the human rights of refugees. States parties should ensure that all measures relating to refugees must be in full accordance with the 1951 Convention relating to the Status of Refugees and its 1967 Protocol;

36. Urges States to take effective steps to protect refugee and internally displaced women and girls from violence, to investigate any such violations and to bring those responsible to justice, in collaboration, when appropriate, with the relevant and competent organizations;

Other victims

37. Urges States to take all possible measures to ensure that all persons, without any discrimination, are registered and have access to the necessary documentation reflecting their legal identity to enable them to benefit from available legal procedures, remedies and development opportunities, as well as to reduce the incidence of trafficking;

38. Recognizes that victims of trafficking are particularly exposed to racism, racial discrimination, xenophobia and related intolerance. States shall ensure that all measures taken against trafficking

in persons, in particular those that affect the victims of such trafficking, are consistent with internationally recognized principles of non-discrimination, including the prohibition of racial discrimination and the availability of appropriate legal redress;

[...]

56. Urges States, in accordance with their national law and their obligations under the relevant international instruments, to take all measures to the maximum extent of their available resources to guarantee, without any discrimination, the equal right of all children to the immediate registration of birth, in order to enable them to exercise their human rights and fundamental freedoms. States shall grant women equal rights with men with respect to nationality;

[...]

III. Measures of prevention, education and protection aimed at the eradication of racism, racial discrimination, xenophobia and related intolerance at the national, regional and international levels

[...]

63. Encourages the business sector, in particular the tourist industry and Internet providers, to develop codes of conduct, with a view to preventing trafficking in persons and protecting the victims of such traffic, especially those in prostitution, against gender-based and racial discrimination and promoting their rights, dignity and security;

64. Urges States to devise, enforce and strengthen effective measures at the national, regional and international levels to prevent, combat and eliminate all forms of trafficking in women and children, in particular girls, through comprehensive anti-trafficking strategies which include legislative measures, prevention campaigns and information exchange. It also urges States to allocate resources, as appropriate, to provide comprehensive programmes designed to provide assistance to, protection for, healing, reintegration into society and rehabilitation of victims. States shall provide or strengthen training for law enforcement, immigration and other relevant officials who deal with victims of trafficking in this regard;

65. Encourages the bodies, agencies and relevant programmes of the United Nations system and States to promote and to make use of the Guiding Principles on Internal Displacement (E/CN.4/1998/53/Add.2), particularly those provisions relating to non-discrimination,

A. National level

1. Legislative, judicial, regulatory, administrative and other measures to prevent and protect against racism, racial discrimination, xenophobia and related intolerance

[...]

67. Urges States to design or reinforce, promote and implement effective legislative and administrative policies, as well as other preventive measures, against the serious situation experienced by certain groups of workers, including migrant workers, who are victims of racism, racial discrimination, xenophobia and related intolerance. Special attention should be given to protecting people engaged in domestic work and trafficked persons from discrimination and violence, as well as to combating prejudice against them;

[...]

69. Urges States to enact and implement, as appropriate, laws against trafficking in persons, especially women and children, and smuggling of migrants, taking into account practices that endanger human lives or lead to various kinds of servitude and exploitation, such as debt bondage, slavery, sexual exploitation or labour exploitation; also encourages States to create, if they do not already exist, mechanisms to combat such practices and to allocate adequate resources to ensure

law enforcement and the protection of the rights of victims, and to reinforce bilateral, regional and international cooperation, including with non-governmental organizations that assist victims, to combat this trafficking in persons and smuggling of migrants;

[...]

Ratification of and effective implementation of relevant international and regional legal instruments on human rights and non-discrimination

[...]

78. Urges those States that have not yet done so to consider signing and ratifying or acceding to the following instruments:

(a) Convention on the Prevention and Punishment of the Crime of Genocide of 1948;

(b) International Labour Organization Migration for Employment Convention (Revised), 1949 (No.97);

(c) Convention for the Suppression of the Traffic in Persons and of the Exploitation of the Prostitution of Others of 1949;

(d) Convention relating to the Status of Refugees of 1951, and its 1967 Protocol;

(e) International Labour Organization Discrimination (Employment and Occupation) Convention, 1958 (No.111);

(f) Convention against Discrimination in Education, adopted on 14 December 1960 by the General Conference of the United Nations Educational, Scientific and Cultural Organization;

(g) Convention on the Elimination of All Forms of Discrimination against Women of 1979, with a view to achieving universal ratification within five years, and its Optional Protocol of 1999;

(h) Convention on the Rights of the Child of 1989 and its two Optional Protocolsof 2000, and the International Labour Organization Minimum Age Convention, 1973 (No.138) and Worst Forms of Child Labour Convention, 1999 (No.182);

(i) International Labour Organization Migrant Workers (Supplementary Provisions) Convention, 1975 (No.143);

(j) International Labour Organization Indigenous and Tribal Peoples Convention, 1989 (No.169) and the Convention on Biological Diversity of 1992;

(k) International Convention on the Protection of the Rights of All Migrant Workers and Members of Their Families of 1990;

(l) The Rome Statute of the International Criminal Court of 1998;

(m) United Nations Convention against Transnational Organized Crime, the Protocol to Prevent, Suppress and Punish Trafficking in Persons, Especially Women and Children, supplementing the Convention and the Protocol against the Smuggling of Migrants by Land, Sea and Air, supplementing the Convention of 2000;

It further urges States parties to these instruments to implement them fully;

[...]

80. Urges States to seek full respect for, and compliance with, the Vienna Convention on Consular Relations of 1963, especially as it relates to the right of foreign nationals, regardless of their legal and immigration status, to communicate with a consular officer of their own State in the case of arrest or detention;

81. Urges all States to prohibit discriminatory treatment based on race, colour, descent or national or ethnic origin against foreigners and migrant workers, inter alia, where appropriate, concerning the granting of work visas and work permits, housing, health care and access to justice;

[...]

2. Policies and practices

[...]

Employment

[...]

105. Urges States to give special attention, when devising and implementing legislation and policies designed to enhance the protection of workers' rights, to the serious situation of lack of protection, and in some cases exploitation, as in the case of trafficked persons and smuggled migrants, which makes them more vulnerable to ill-treatment such as confinement in the case of domestic workers and also being employed in dangerous and poorly paid jobs;

[...]

3. Education and awareness-raising measures

[...]

Human rights education for public officials and professionals

[...]

133. Urges States to develop and strengthen anti-racist and gender-sensitive human rights training for public officials, including personnel in the administration of justice, particularly in law enforcement, correctional and security services, as well as among health-care, schools and migration authorities;

[...]

138. Urges States to strengthen the human rights training and awareness-raising activities designed for immigration officials, border police and staff of detention centres and prisons, local authorities and other civil servants in charge of enforcing laws, as well as teachers, with particular attention to the human rights of migrants, refugees and asylum-seekers, in order to prevent acts of racial discrimination and xenophobia and to avoid situations where prejudices lead to decisions based on racism, racial discrimination, xenophobia or related intolerance;

139. Urges States to provide or strengthen training for law enforcement, immigration and other relevant officials in the prevention of trafficking in persons. The training should focus on methods used in preventing such trafficking, prosecuting the traffickers and protecting the rights of victims, including protecting the victims from the traffickers. The training should also take into account the need to consider human rights and child- and gender-sensitive issues and it should encourage cooperation with non-governmental organizations, other relevant organizations and other elements of civil society;

[...]

4. Information, communication and the media, including new technologies

[...]

144. Urges States and encourages the private sector to promote the development by the media, including the print and electronic media, including the Internet and advertising, taking into account their independence, through their relevant associations and organizations at the national, regional and international levels, of a voluntary ethical code of conduct and self-regulatory measures, and of policies and practices aimed at:

(a) Combating racism, racial discrimination, xenophobia and related intolerance;

(b) Promoting the fair, balanced and equitable representation of the diversity of their societies, as well as ensuring that this diversity is reflected among their staff;

(c) Combating the proliferation of ideas of racial superiority, justification of racial hatred and discrimination in any form;

(d) Promoting respect, tolerance and understanding among all individuals, peoples, nations and civilizations, for example through assistance in public awareness-raising campaigns;

(e) Avoiding stereotyping in all its forms, and particularly the promotion of false images of migrants, including migrant workers, and refugees, in order to prevent the spread of xenophobic sentiments among the public and to encourage the objective and balanced portrayal of people, events and history;

[...]

B. International level

[...]

IV. Provision of effective remedies, recourse, redress, and other measures at the national, regional and international levels

[...]

V. Strategies to achieve full and effective equality, including international cooperation and enhancement of the United Nations and other international mechanisms in combating racism, racial discrimination, xenophobia and related intolerance and follow-up

[...]

174. Urges States to take or strengthen measures, including through bilateral or multilateral cooperation, to address root causes, such as poverty, underdevelopment and lack of equal opportunity, some of which may be associated with discriminatory practices, that make persons, especially women and children, vulnerable to trafficking, which may give rise to racism, racial discrimination, xenophobia and related intolerance;

[...]

Regional/international cooperation

[...]

182. Encourages States to participate in regional dialogues on problems of migration and invites them to consider negotiating bilateral and regional agreements on migrant workers and designing and implementing programmes with States of other regions to protect the rights of migrants;

183. Urges States, in consultation with civil society, to support or otherwise establish, as appropriate, regional, comprehensive dialogues on the causes and consequences of migration that focus not only on law enforcement and border control, but also on the promotion and protection of the human rights of migrants and on the relationship between migration and development;

184. Encourages international organizations having mandates dealing specifically with migration issues to exchange information and coordinate their activities on matters involving racism, racial discrimination, xenophobia and related intolerance against migrants, including migrant workers, with the support of the Office of the United Nations High Commissioner for Human Rights;

185. Expresses its deep concern over the severity of the humanitarian suffering of affected civilian populations and the burden carried by many receiving countries, particularly developing countries and countries in transition, and requests the relevant international institutions to ensure that urgent adequate financial and humanitarian assistance is maintained for the host countries to enable them to help the victims and to address, on an equitable basis, difficulties of populations

expelled from their homes, and calls for sufficient safeguards to enable refugees to exercise freely their right of return to their countries of origin voluntarily, in safety and dignity;

186. Encourages States to conclude bilateral, subregional, regional and international agreements to address the problem of trafficking in women and children, in particular girls, as well as the smuggling of migrants;

[...]

Office of the High Commissioner for Human Rights

[...]

196. Requests the Office of the High Commissioner for Human Rights to pay special attention to violations of the human rights of victims of racism, racial discrimination, xenophobia and related intolerance, in particular migrants, including migrant workers, to promote international cooperation in combating xenophobia and, to this end, to develop programmes which can be implemented in countries on the basis of appropriate cooperation agreements;

[...]

Decades

[...]

201. Recommends that the General Assembly consider declaring a United Nations year or decade against trafficking in persons, especially in women, youth and children, in order to protect their dignity and human rights;

[...]

Declaration on Territorial Asylum, 1967 ***(See section 12)***

1.3 General Comments

CCPR General Comment No.15: The Position of Aliens under the Covenant, 1986*

Adoption: 11 April 1986

1. Reports from States parties have often failed to take into account that each State party must ensure the rights in the Covenant to "all individuals within its territory and subject to its jurisdiction" (art. 2, para. 1). In general, the rights set forth in the Covenant apply to everyone, irrespective of reciprocity, and irrespective of his or her nationality or statelessness.

2. Thus, the general rule is that each one of the rights of the Covenant must be guaranteed without discrimination between citizens and aliens. Aliens receive the benefit of the general requirement of non-discrimination in respect of the rights guaranteed in the Covenant, as provided for in article 2 thereof. This guarantee applies to aliens and citizens alike. Exceptionally, some of the rights recognized in the Covenant are expressly applicable only to citizens (art. 25), while article 13 applies only to aliens. However, the Committee's experience in examining reports shows that in a number of countries other rights that aliens should enjoy under the Covenant are denied to them or are subject to limitations that cannot always be justified under the Covenant.

3. A few constitutions provide for equality of aliens with citizens. Some constitutions adopted more recently carefully distinguish fundamental rights that apply to all and those granted to citizens only, and deal with each in detail. In many States, however, the constitutions are drafted in terms of citizens only when granting relevant rights. Legislation and case law may also play an important part in providing for the rights of aliens. The Committee has been informed that in some States fundamental rights, though not guaranteed to aliens by the Constitution or other legislation, will also be extended to them as required by the Covenant. In certain cases, however, there has clearly been a failure to implement Covenant rights without discrimination in respect of aliens.

4. The Committee considers that in their reports States parties should give attention to the position of aliens, both under their law and in actual practice. The Covenant gives aliens all the protection regarding rights guaranteed therein, and its requirements should be observed by States parties in their legislation and in practice as appropriate. The position of aliens would thus be considerably improved. States parties should ensure that the provisions of the Covenant and the rights under it are made known to aliens within their jurisdiction.

5. The Covenant does not recognize the right of aliens to enter or reside in the territory of a State party. It is in principle a matter for the State to decide who it will admit to its territory. However, in certain circumstances an alien may enjoy the protection of the Covenant even in relation to entry or residence, for example, when considerations of non-discrimination, prohibition of inhuman treatment and respect for family life arise.

6. Consent for entry may be given subject to conditions relating, for example, to movement, residence and employment. A State may also impose general conditions upon an alien who is in transit. However, once aliens are allowed to enter the territory of a State party they are entitled to the rights set out in the Covenant.

7. Aliens thus have an inherent right to life, protected by law, and may not be arbitrarily deprived of life. They must not be subjected to torture or to cruel, inhuman or degrading

* Source: U.N. Doc. HRI/GEN/1/Rev.7, p. 140.

treatment or punishment; nor may they be held in slavery or servitude. Aliens have the full right to liberty and security of the person. If lawfully deprived of their liberty, they shall be treated with humanity and with respect for the inherent dignity of their person. Aliens may not be imprisoned for failure to fulfil a contractual obligation. They have the right to liberty of movement and free choice of residence; they shall be free to leave the country. Aliens shall be equal before the courts and tribunals, and shall be entitled to a fair and public hearing by a competent, independent and impartial tribunal established by law in the determination of any criminal charge or of rights and obligations in a suit at law. Aliens shall not be subjected to retrospective penal legislation, and are entitled to recognition before the law. They may not be subjected to arbitrary or unlawful interference with their privacy, family, home or correspondence. They have the right to freedom of thought, conscience and religion, and the right to hold opinions and to express them. Aliens receive the benefit of the right of peaceful assembly and of freedom of association. They may marry when at marriageable age. Their children are entitled to those measures of protection required by their status as minors. In those cases where aliens constitute a minority within the meaning of article 27, they shall not be denied the right, in community with other members of their group, to enjoy their own culture, to profess and practise their own religion and to use their own language. Aliens are entitled to equal protection by the law. There shall be no discrimination between aliens and citizens in the application of these rights. These rights of aliens may be qualified only by such limitations as may be lawfully imposed under the Covenant.

8. Once an alien is lawfully within a territory, his freedom of movement within the territory and his right to leave that territory may only be restricted in accordance with article 12, paragraph 3. Differences in treatment in this regard between aliens and nationals, or between different categories of aliens, need to be justified under article 12, paragraph 3. Since such restrictions must, *inter alia*, be consistent with the other rights recognized in the Covenant, a State party cannot, by restraining an alien or deporting him to a third country, arbitrarily prevent his return to his own country (art. 12, para. 4).

9. Many reports have given insufficient information on matters relevant to article 13. That article is applicable to all procedures aimed at the obligatory departure of an alien, whether described in national law as expulsion or otherwise. If such procedures entail arrest, the safeguards of the Covenant relating to deprivation of liberty (arts. 9 and 10) may also be applicable. If the arrest is for the particular purpose of extradition, other provisions of national and international law may apply. Normally an alien who is expelled must be allowed to leave for any country that agrees to take him. The particular rights of article 13 only protect those aliens who are lawfully in the territory of a State party. This means that national law concerning the requirements for entry and stay must be taken into account in determining the scope of that protection, and that illegal entrants and aliens who have stayed longer than the law or their permits allow, in particular, are not covered by its provisions. However, if the legality of an alien's entry or stay is in dispute, any decision on this point leading to his expulsion or deportation ought to be taken in accordance with article 13. It is for the competent authorities of the State party, in good faith and in the exercise of their powers, to apply and interpret the domestic law, observing, however, such requirements under the Covenant as equality before the law (art. 26).

10. Article 13 directly regulates only the procedure and not the substantive grounds for expulsion. However, by allowing only those carried out "in pursuance of a decision reached in accordance with law", its purpose is clearly to prevent arbitrary expulsions. On the other hand, it entitles each alien to a decision in his own case and, hence, article 13 would not be satisfied with laws or decisions providing for collective or mass expulsions. This understanding, in the opinion of the Committee, is confirmed by further provisions concerning the right to submit reasons against expulsion and to have the decision reviewed by and to be represented before

the competent authority or someone designated by it. An alien must be given full facilities for pursuing his remedy against expulsion so that this right will in all the circumstances of his case be an effective one. The principles of article 13 relating to appeal against expulsion and the entitlement to review by a competent authority may only be departed from when "compelling reasons of national security" so require. Discrimination may not be made between different categories of aliens in the application of article 13.

CCPR General Comment No.27*: Article 12 (Freedom of Movement), 1999[1]

Adoption: 1 November 1999

1. Liberty of movement is an indispensable condition for the free development of a person. It interacts with several other rights enshrined in the Covenant, as is often shown in the Committee's practice in considering reports from States parties and communications from individuals. Moreover, the Committee in its General Comment No.15 ("The position of aliens under the Covenant", 1986) referred to the special link between articles 12 and 13.[2]

2. The permissible limitations which may be imposed on the rights protected under article 12 must not nullify the principle of liberty of movement, and are governed by the requirement of necessity provided for in article 12, paragraph 3, and by the need for consistency with the other rights recognized in the Covenant.

3. States parties should provide the Committee in their reports with the relevant domestic legal rules and administrative and judicial practices relating to the rights protected by this article, taking into account the issues discussed in this General Comment. They must also include information on remedies available if these rights are restricted.

Liberty of movement and freedom to choose residence (paragraph 1)

4. Everyone lawfully within the territory of a State enjoys, within that territory, the right to move freely and to choose his or her place of residence. In principle, citizens of a State are always lawfully within the territory of that State. The question whether an alien is "lawfully" within the territory of a State is a matter governed by domestic law, which may subject the entry of an alien to the territory of a State to restrictions, provided they are in compliance with the State's international obligations. In that connection, the Committee has held that an alien who entered the State illegally, but whose status has been regularized, must be considered to be lawfully within the territory for the purposes of art 12.[3] Once a person is lawfully within a State, any restrictions on his or her rights guaranteed by article 12, paragraphs 1 and 2, as well as any treatment different from that accorded to nationals, have to be justified under the rules provided for by article 12, paragraph 3.[4] It is, therefore, important that States parties indicate in their reports the circumstances in which they treat aliens differently from their nationals in this regard, and how they justify this difference in treatment.

5. The right to move freely relates to the whole territory of a State, including all parts of federal States. According to article 12, paragraph 1, persons are entitled to move from one place to another, and to establish themselves in a place of their choice.
The enjoyment of this right must not be made dependent on any particular purpose or reason for the person wanting to move or to stay in a place. Any restrictions must be in conformity with paragraph 3.

6. The State party must ensure that the rights guaranteed in article 12 are protected not only from public but also from private interference. In the case of women, this obligation to protect is particularly pertinent. For example, it is incompatible with article 12, paragraph 1, that

* Source: U.N.Doc. CCPR/C/21/Rev.1/Add.9.

1 Adopted at the 1783rd meeting (sixty-seventh session), held on 18 October 1999.

2 Reissued for technical reasons.

3 Communication No.456/1991, Celepli vs. Sweden, para. 9.2.

4 General Comment No.15, para. 8, in HRI/GEN/1/Rev. 3, 15 August 1997, p. 20.

the right of a woman to move freely and to choose her residence be made subject, by law or practice, to the decision of another person, including a relative.

7. Subject to the provisions of article 12, paragraph 3, the right to reside in a place of one's choice within the territory includes protection against all forms of forced internal displacement. It also precludes preventing the entry or stay of persons in a defined part of the territory. Lawful detention, however, affects more specifically the right to personal liberty and is covered by article 9 of the Covenant. In some circumstances, articles 12 and 9 may come into play together.[5]

Freedom to leave any country, including one's own (paragraph 2)

8. Freedom to leave the territory of a State may not be made dependent on any specific purpose or on the period of time the individual chooses to stay outside the country. Thus travelling abroad is covered as well as departure for permanent emigration. Likewise, the right of the individual to determine the State of destination is part of the legal guarantee. As the scope of article 12, paragraph 2, is not restricted to persons lawfully within the territory of a State, an alien being legally expelled from the country is likewise entitled to elect the State of destination, subject to the agreement of that State.[6]

9. In order to enable the individual to enjoy the rights guaranteed by article 12, paragraph 2, obligations are imposed both on the State of residence and on the State of nationality[7]. Since international travel usually requires appropriate documents, in particular a passport, the right to leave a country must include the right to obtain the necessary travel documents. The issuing of passports is normally incumbent on the State of nationality of the individual. The refusal by a State to issue a passport or prolong its validity for a national residing abroad may deprive this person of the right to leave the country of residence and to travel elsewhere[8]. It is no justification for the State to claim that its national would be able to return to its territory without a passport.

10. The practice of States often shows that legal rules and administrative measures adversely affect the right to leave, in particular, a person's own country. It is therefore of the utmost importance that States parties report on all legal and practical restrictions on the right to leave, which they apply both to nationals and to foreigners, in order to enable the Committee to assess the conformity of these rules and practices with article 12, paragraph 3. States parties should also include information in their reports on measures that impose sanctions on international carriers which bring to their territory persons without required documents, where those measures affect the right to leave another country.

Restrictions (paragraph 3)

11. Article 12, paragraph 3, provides for exceptional circumstances in which rights under paragraphs 1 and 2 may be restricted. This provision authorizes the State to restrict these rights only to protect national security, public order (ordre public), public health or morals and the rights and freedoms of others. To be permissible, restrictions must be provided by law, must be necessary in a democratic society for the protection of these purposes, and must be consistent with all other rights recognized in the Covenant (see para. 18 below).

[5] See e.g Communication No.138/1983, Mpandajila v. Zaire, para. 10; Communication No.157/1983, Mpaka-Nsusu v. Zaire, para. 10; Communication Nos. 241 and 242/1987, Birhashwirwa/Tshisekedi v. Zaire, para. 13.

[6] See General Comment No.15, para. 9, in HRI/GEN/1/Rev. 3, 15 August 1997, p. 21.

[7] See Communication No.106/1981, Montero v. Uruguay, para 9.4; Communication No.57/1979, Vidal Martins v. Uruguay, para. 7; Communication No.77/1980 Lichtensztejn v. Uruguay, para. 6.1.

[8] See Communication No.57/1979, Vidal Martins v. Uruguay, para. 9.

12. The law itself has to establish the conditions under which the rights may be limited. State reports should therefore specify the legal norms upon which restrictions are founded. Restrictions which are not provided for in the law or are not in conformity with the requirements of article 12, paragraph 3, would violate the rights guaranteed by paragraphs 1 and 2.

13. In adopting laws providing for restrictions permitted by article 12, paragraph 3, States should always be guided by the principle that the restrictions must not impair the essence of the right (cf. art 5, para. 1); the relation between right and restriction, between norm and exception, must not be reversed. The laws authorizing the application of restrictions should use precise criteria and may not confer unfettered discretion on those charged with their execution.

14. Article 12, paragraph 3, clearly indicates that it is not sufficient that the restrictions serve the permissible purposes; they must also be necessary to protect them. Restrictive measures must conform to the principle of proportionality; they must be appropriate to achieve their protective function; they must be the least intrusive instrument amongst those which might achieve the desired result; and they must be proportionate to the interest to be protected.

15. The principle of proportionality has to be respected not only in the law that frames the restrictions, but also by the administrative and judicial authorities in applying the law. States should ensure that any proceedings relating to the exercise or restriction of these rights are expeditious and that reasons for the application of restrictive measures are provided.

16. States have often failed to show that the application of their laws restricting the rights enshrined in article 12, paragraphs 1 and 2, are in conformity with all requirements referred to in article 12, paragraph 3. The application of restrictions in any individual case must be based on clear legal grounds and meet the test of necessity and the requirements of proportionality. These conditions would not be met, for example, if an individual were prevented from leaving a country merely on the ground that he or she is the holder of "State secrets", or if an individual were prevented from travelling internally without a specific permit. On the other hand, the conditions could be met by restrictions on access to military zones on national security grounds or limitations on the freedom to settle in areas inhabited by indigenous or minorities communities.[9]

17. A major source of concern are the manifold legal and bureaucratic barriers unnecessarily affecting the full enjoyment of the rights of the individuals to move freely, to leave a country, including their own, and to take up residence. Regarding the right to movement within a country, the Committee has criticized provisions requiring individuals to apply for permission to change their residence or to seek the approval of the local authorities of the place of destination, as well as delays in processing such written applications. States' practice presents an even richer array of obstacles making it more difficult to leave the country, in particular for their own nationals. These rules and practices include, inter alia, lack of access for applicants to the competent authorities and lack of information regarding requirements; the requirement to apply for special forms through which the proper application documents for the issuance of a passport can be obtained; the need for supportive statements from employers or family members; exact description of the travel route; issuance of passports only on payment of high fees substantially exceeding the cost of the service rendered by the administration; unreasonable delays in the issuance of travel documents; restrictions on family members travelling together; requirement of a repatriation deposit or a return ticket; requirement of an invitation from the State of destination or from people living there; harassment of applicants, for example by physical intimidation, arrest, loss of employment or expulsion of their children from school or university; refusal to issue a passport because the applicant is said to harm the good name of

[9] See General Comment No.23, para. 7, in HRI/GEN/1/Rev. 3, 15 August 1997, p. 41.

the country. In the light of these practices, States parties should make sure that all restrictions imposed by them are in full compliance with article 12, paragraph 3.

18. The application of the restrictions permissible under article 12, paragraph 3, needs to be consistent with the other rights guaranteed in the Covenant and with the fundamental principles of equality and non-discrimination. Thus, it would be a clear violation of the Covenant if the rights enshrined in article 12, paragraphs 1 and 2, were restricted by making distinctions of any kind, such as race, colour, sex, language, religion, political or other opinion, national or social origin, property, birth or other status. In examining State reports, the Committee has on several occasions found that measures preventing women from moving freely or leaving the country by requiring them to have the consent or the escort of a male person, constitute a violation of article 12.

The right to enter one's own country (paragraph 4)

19. The right of a person to enter his or her own country recognizes the special relationship of a person to that country. The right has various facets. It implies the right to remain in one's own country. It includes not only the right to return after having left one's own country; it may also entitle a person to come to the country for the first time if he or she was born outside the country (e.g. if that country is the person's state of nationality). The right to return is of the utmost importance for refugees seeking voluntary repatriation. It also implies prohibition of enforced population transfers or mass expulsions to other countries.

20. The wording of article 12, paragraph 4, does not distinguish between nationals and aliens ("no one"). Thus, the persons entitled to exercise this right can be identified only by interpreting the meaning of the phrase "his own country"[10]. The scope of "his own country" is broader than the concept "country of his nationality". It is not limited to nationality in a formal sense, that is, nationality acquired at birth or by conferral; it embraces, at the very least, an individual who, because of his or her special ties to or claims in relation to a given country, cannot be considered to be a mere alien. This would be the case, for example, of nationals of a country who have there been stripped of their nationality in violation of international law and of individuals whose country of nationality has been incorporated into or transferred to another national entity whose nationality is being denied them. The language of article 12, paragraph 4, moreover, permits a broader interpretation that might embrace other categories of long-term residents, including but not limited to stateless persons arbitrarily deprived of the right to acquire the nationality of the country of such residence. Since other factors may in certain circumstances result in the establishment of close and enduring connections between a person and a country, States parties should include in their reports information on the rights of permanent residents to return to their country of residence.

21. In no case may a person be arbitrarily deprived of the right to enter his or her own country. The reference to the concept of arbitrariness in this context is intended to emphasize that it applies to all State action, legislative, administrative, and judicial; it guarantees that even interference provided for by law should be in accordance with the provisions, aims and objectives of the Covenant and should be, in any event, reasonable in the particular circumstances. The Committee considers that there are few, if any, circumstances in which deprivation of the right to enter one's own country could be reasonable. A State party must not, by stripping a person of nationality or by expelling an individual to a third country, arbitrarily prevent this person from returning to his or her own country.

[10] See Communication No.538/1993, Stewart v. Canada.

CERD General Recommendation No.30: Discrimination against Non-citizens, 2005*

Adoption: 4 May 2005

The Committee on the Elimination of Racial Discrimination,

Recalling the Charter of the United Nations and the Universal Declaration of Human Rights, according to which all human beings are born free and equal in dignity and rights and are entitled to the rights and freedoms enshrined therein without distinction of any kind, and the International Covenant on Economic, Social and Cultural Rights, the International Covenant on Civil and Political Rights and the International Convention on the Elimination of All Forms of Racial Discrimination,

Recalling the Durban Declaration in which the World Conference against Racism, Racial Discrimination, Xenophobia and Related Intolerance, recognized that xenophobia against non nationals, particularly migrants, refugees and asylum-seekers, constitutes one of the main sources of contemporary racism and that human rights violations against members of such groups occur widely in the context of discriminatory, xenophobic and racist practices,

Noting that, based on the International Convention on the Elimination of All Forms of Racial Discrimination and general recommendations XI and XX, it has become evident from the examination of the reports of States parties to the Convention that groups other than migrants, refugees and asylum-seekers are also of concern, including undocumented non-citizens and persons who cannot establish the nationality of the State on whose territory they live, even where such persons have lived all their lives on the same territory,

Having organized a thematic discussion on the issue of discrimination against non-citizens and received the contributions of members of the Committee and States parties, as well as contributions from experts of other United Nations organs and specialized agencies and from non-governmental organizations,

Recognizing the need to clarify the responsibilities of States parties to the International Convention on the Elimination of All Forms of Racial Discrimination with regard to non-citizens,

Basing its action on the provisions of the Convention, in particular article 5, which requires States parties to prohibit and eliminate discrimination based on race, colour, descent, and national or ethnic origin in the enjoyment by all persons of civil, political, economic, social and cultural rights and freedoms,

Affirms that:

I. Responsibilities of States Parties to the convention

1. Article 1, paragraph 1, of the Convention defines racial discrimination. Article 1, paragraph 2 provides for the possibility of differentiating between citizens and non-citizens.

Article 1, paragraph 3 declares that, concerning nationality, citizenship or naturalization, the legal provisions of States parties must not discriminate against any particular nationality;

2. Article 1, paragraph 2, must be construed so as to avoid undermining the basic prohibition of discrimination; hence, it should not be interpreted to detract in any way from the rights

* Source: U.N.Doc. HRI/GEN/1/Rev.7/Add.1.

and freedoms recognized and enunciated in particular in the Universal Declaration of Human Rights, the International Covenant on Economic, Social and Cultural Rights and the International Covenant on Civil and Political Rights;

3. Article 5 of the Convention incorporates the obligation of States parties to prohibit and eliminate racial discrimination in the enjoyment of civil, political, economic, social and cultural rights. Although some of these rights, such as the right to participate in elections, to vote and to stand for election, may be confined to citizens, human rights are, in principle, to be enjoyed by all persons. States parties are under an obligation to guarantee equality between citizens and non-citizens in the enjoyment of these rights to the extent recognized under international law;

4. Under the Convention, differential treatment based on citizenship or immigration status will constitute discrimination if the criteria for such differentiation, judged in the light of the objectives and purposes of the Convention, are not applied pursuant to a legitimate aim, and are not proportional to the achievement of this aim. Differentiation within the scope of article 1, paragraph 4, of the Convention relating to special measures is not considered discriminatory;

5. States parties are under an obligation to report fully upon legislation on non-citizens and its implementation. Furthermore, States parties should include in their periodic reports, in an appropriate form, socio-economic data on the non-citizen population within their jurisdiction, including data disaggregated by gender and national or ethnic origin;

Recommends,

Based on these general principles, that the States parties to the Convention, as appropriate to their specific circumstances, adopt the following measures:

II. Measures of a general nature

6. Review and revise legislation, as appropriate, in order to guarantee that such legislation is in full compliance with the Convention, in particular regarding the effective enjoyment of the rights mentioned in article 5, without discrimination;

7. Ensure that legislative guarantees against racial discriminatio n apply to non-citizens regardless of their immigration status, and that the implementation of legislation does not have a discriminatory effect on non-citizens;

8. Pay greater attention to the issue of multiple discrimination faced by non-citizens, in particular concerning the children and spouses of non-citizen workers, to refrain from applying different standards of treatment to female non-citizen spouses of citizens and male non-citizen spouses of citizens, to report on any such practices and to take all necessary steps to address them;

9. Ensure that immigration policies do not have the effect of discriminating against persons on the basis of race, colour, descent, or national or ethnic origin;

10. Ensure that any measures taken in the fight against terrorism do not discriminate, in purpose or effect, on the grounds of race, colour, descent, or national or ethnic origin and that non-citizens are not subjected to racial or ethnic profiling or stereotyping;

III. Protection against hate speech and racial violence

11. Take steps to address xenophobic attitudes and behaviour towards non-citizens, in particular hate speech and racial violence, and to promote a better understanding of the principle of non-discrimination in respect of the situation of non-citizens;

12. Take resolute action to counter any tendency to target, stigmatize, stereotype or profile, on the basis of race, colour, descent, and national or ethnic origin, members of "non-citizen" population groups, especially by politicians, officials, educators and the media, on the Internet and other electronic communications networks and in society at large;

IV. Access to citizenship

13. Ensure that particular groups of non-citizens are not discriminated against with regard to access to citizenship or naturalization, and to pay due attention to possible barriers to naturalization that may exist for long-term or permanent residents;

14. Recognize that deprivation of citizenship on the basis of race, colour, descent, or national or ethnic origin is a breach of States parties' obligations to ensure non-discriminatory enjoyment of the right to nationality;

15. Take into consideration that in some cases denial of citizenship for long-term or permanent residents could result in creating disadvantage for them in access to employment and social benefits, in violation of the Convention's anti-discrimination principles;

16. Reduce statelessness, in particular statelessness among children, by, for example, encouraging their parents to apply for citizenship on their behalf and allowing both parents to transmit their citizenship to their children;

17. Regularize the status of former citizens of predecessor States who now reside within the jurisdiction of the State party;

V. Administration of justice

18. Ensure that non-citizens enjoy equal protection and recognition before the law and in this context, to take action against racially motivated violence and to ensure the access of victims to effective legal remedies and the right to seek just and adequate reparation for any damage suffered as a result of such violence;

19. Ensure the security of non-citizens, in particular with regard to arbitrary detention, as well as ensure that conditions in centres for refugees and asylum-seekers meet international standards;

20. Ensure that non-citizens detained or arrested in the fight against terrorism are properly protected by domestic law that complies with international human rights, refugee and humanitarian law;

21. Combat ill- treatment of and discrimination against non-citizens by police and other law enforcement agencies and civil servants by strictly applying relevant legislation and regulations providing for sanctions and by ensuring that all officials dealing with non-citizens receive special training, including training in human rights;

22. Introduce in criminal law the provision that committing an offence with racist motivation or aim constitutes an aggravating circumstance allowing for a more severe punishment;

23. Ensure that claims of racial discrimination brought by non-citizens are investigated thoroughly and that claims made against officials, notably those concerning discriminatory or racist behaviour, are subject to independent and effective scrutiny;

24. Regulate the burden of proof in civil proceedings involving discrimination based on race, colour, descent, and national or ethnic origin so that once a non-citizen has established a prima

facie case that he or she has been a victim of such discrimination, it shall be for the respondent to provide evidence of an objective and reasonable justification for the differential treatment;

VI. Expulsion and deportation of non-citizens

25. Ensure that laws concerning deportation or other forms of removal of non-citizens from the jur isdiction of the State party do not discriminate in purpose or effect among non-citizens on the basis of race, colour or ethnic or national origin, and that non-citizens have equal access to effective remedies, including the right to challenge expulsion orders, and are allowed effectively to pursue such remedies;

26. Ensure that non-citizens are not subject to collective expulsion, in particular in situations where there are insufficient guarantees that the personal circumstances of each of the persons concerned have been taken into account;

27. Ensure that non-citizens are not returned or removed to a country or territory where they are at risk of being subject to serious human rights abuses, including torture and cruel, inhuman or degrading treatment or punishment;

28. Avoid expulsions of non-citizens, especially of long-term residents, that would result in disproportionate interference with the right to family life;

VII. Economic, social and cultural rights

29. Remove obstacles that prevent the enjoyment of economic, social and cultural rights by non-citizens, notably in the areas of education, housing, employment and health;

30. Ensure that public educational institutions are open to non-citizens and children of undocumented immigrants residing in the territory of a State party;

31. Avoid segregated schooling and different standards of treatment being applied to non-citizens on grounds of race, colour, descent, and national or ethnic origin in elementary and secondary school and with respect to access to higher education;

32. Guarantee the equal enjoyment of the right to adequate housing for citizens and non-citizens, especially by avoiding segregation in housing and ensuring that housing agencies refrain from engaging in discriminatory practices;

33. Take measures to eliminate discrimination against non-citizens in relation to working conditions and work requirements, including employment rules and practices with discriminatory purposes or effects;

34. Take effective measures to prevent and redress the serious problems commonly faced by non-citizen workers, in particular by non-citizen domestic workers, including debt bondage, passport retention, illegal confinement, rape and physical assault;

35. Recognize that, while States parties may refuse to offer jobs to non-citizens without a work permit, all individuals are entitled to the enjoyment of labour and employment rights, including the freedom of assembly and association, once an employment relationship has been initiated until it is terminated;

36. Ensure that States parties respect the right of non-citizens to an adequate standard of physical and mental health by, inter alia, refraining from denying or limiting their access to preventive, curative and palliative health services;

37. Take the necessary measures to prevent practices that deny non-citizens their cultural identity, such as legal or de facto requirements that non-citizens change their name in order to

obtain citizenship, and to take measures to enable non-citizens to preserve and develop their culture;

38. Ensure the right of non-citizens, without discrimination based on race, colour, descent, and national or ethnic origin, to have access to any place or service intended for use by the general public, such as transport, hotels, restaurants, cafés, theatres and parks;

39. The present general recommendation replaces general recommendation XI (1993).

CRC General Comment No.6: Treatment of Unaccompanied and Separated Children Outside their Country of Origin, 2005*

Adoption: 1 September 2005

I. OBJECTIVES OF THE GENERAL COMMENT

1. The objective of this general comment is to draw attention to the particularly vulnerable situation of unaccompanied and separated children; to outline the multifaceted challenges faced by States and other actors in ensuring that such children are able to access and enjoy their rights; and, to provide guidance on the protection, care and proper treatment of unaccompanied and separated children based on the entire legal framework provided by the Convention on the Rights of the Child (the "Convention"), with particular reference to the principles of non-discrimination, the best interests of the child and the right of the child to express his or her views freely.

2. The issuing of this general comment is motivated by the Committee's observation of an increasing number of children in such situations. There are varied and numerous reasons for a child being unaccompanied or separated, including: persecution of the child or the parents; international conflict and civil war; trafficking in various contexts and forms, including sale by parents; and the search for better economic opportunities.

3. The issuing of the general comment is further motivated by the Committee's identification of number of protection gaps in the treatment of such children, including the following: unaccompanied and separated children face greater risks of, inter alia, sexual exploitation and abuse, military recruitment, child labour (including for their foster families) and detention. They are often discriminated against and denied access to food, shelter, housing, health services and education. Unaccompanied and separated girls are at particular risk of gender-based violence, including domestic violence. In some situations, such children have no access to proper and appropriate identification, registration, age assessment, documentation, family tracing, guardianship systems or legal advice. In many countries, unaccompanied and separated children are routinely denied entry to or detained by border or immigration officials. In other cases they are admitted but are denied access to asylum procedures or their asylum claims are not handled in an age and gender-sensitive manner. Some countries prohibit separated children who are recognized as refugees from applying for family reunification; others permit reunification but impose conditions so restrictive as to make it virtually impossible to achieve. Many such children are granted only temporary status, which ends when they turn 18, and there are few effective return programmes.

4. Concerns such as these have led the Committee to frequently raise issues related to unaccompanied and separated children in its concluding observations. This general comment will compile and consolidate standards developed, inter alia, through the Committee's monitoring efforts and shall thereby provide clear guidance to States on the obligations deriving from the Convention with regard to this particular vulnerable group of children. In applying these standards, States parties must be cognizant of their evolutionary character and therefore recognize that their obligations may develop beyond the standards articulated herein. These standards shall in no way impair further-reaching rights and benefits offered to unaccompanied and separated children under regional human rights instruments or national systems, international and regional refugee law or international humanitarian law.

* Source: U.N.Doc. CRC/GC/2005/6.

II. STRUCTURE AND SCOPE OF THE GENERAL COMMENT

5. This general comment applies to unaccompanied and separated children who find themselves outside their country of nationality (consistent with article 7) or, if stateless, outside their country of habitual residence. The general comment applies to all such children irrespective of their residence status and reasons for being abroad, and whether they are unaccompanied or separated. However, it does not apply to children who have not crossed an international border, even though the Committee acknowledges the many similar challenges related to internally displaced unaccompanied and separated children, recognizes that much of the guidance offered below is also valuable in relation to such children, and strongly encourages States to adopt relevant aspects of this general comment in relation to the protection, care and treatment of unaccompanied and separated children who are displaced within their own country.

6. While the mandate of the Committee is confined to its supervisory function in relation to the Convention, its interpretation efforts must be conducted in the context of the entirety of applicable international human rights norms and, therefore, the general comment adopts a holistic approach to the question of the proper treatment of unaccompanied and separated children. This acknowledges that all human rights, including those contained in the Convention, are indivisible and interdependent. The importance of other international human rights instruments to the protection of the child is also recognized in the preamble to the Convention.

III. DEFINITIONS

7. "Unaccompanied children" (also called unaccompanied minors) are children, as defined in article 1 of the Convention, who have been separated from both parents and other relatives and are not being cared for by an adult who, by law or custom, is responsible for doing so.

8. "Separated children" are children, as defined in article 1 of the Convention, who have been separated from both parents, or from their previous legal or customary primary caregiver, but not necessarily from other relatives. These may, therefore, include children accompanied by other adult family members.

9. A "child as defined in article 1 of the Convention", means "every human being below the age of 18 years unless under the law applicable to the child, majority is attained earlier". This means that any instruments governing children in the territory of the State cannot define a child in any way that deviates from the norms determining the age of majority in that State.

10. If not otherwise specified, the guidelines below apply equally to both unaccompanied and separated children.

11. "Country of origin" is the country of nationality or, in the case of a stateless child, the country of habitual residence.

IV. APPLICABLE PRINCIPLES

(a) Legal obligations of States parties for all unaccompanied or separated children in their territory and measures for their implementation

12. State obligations under the Convention apply to each child within the State's territory and to all children subject to its jurisdiction (art. 2). These State obligations cannot be arbitrarily and unilaterally curtailed either by excluding zones or areas from a State's territory or by defining particular zones or areas as not, or only partly, under the jurisdiction of the State. Moreover, State obligations under the Convention apply within the borders of a State, including with respect to those children who come under the State's jurisdiction while attempting to enter the country's

territory. Therefore, the enjoyment of rights stipulated in the Convention is not limited to children who are citizens of a State party and must therefore, if not explicitly stated otherwise in the Convention, also be available to all children - including asylum-seeking, refugee and migrant children - irrespective of their nationality, immigration status or statelessness.

13. Obligations deriving from the Convention vis-à-vis unaccompanied and separated children apply to all branches of government (executive, legislative and judicial). They include the obligation to establish national legislation; administrative structures; and the necessary research, information, data compilation and comprehensive training activities to support such measures. Such legal obligations are both negative and positive in nature, requiring States not only to refrain from measures infringing on such children's rights, but also to take measures to ensure the enjoyment of these rights without discrimination. Such responsibilities are not only limited to the provision of protection and assistance to children who are already unaccompanied or separated, but include measures to prevent separation (including the implementation of safeguards in case of evacuation). The positive aspect of these protection obligations also extends to requiring States to take all necessary measures to identify children as being unaccompanied or separated at the earliest possible stage, including at the border, to carry out tracing activities and, where possible and if in the child's best interest, to reunify separated and unaccompanied children with their families as soon as possible.

14. As reaffirmed in its general comment No.5 (2003) (paras. 18-23), States parties to the Convention have to ensure that the provisions and principles of the treaty are fully reflected and given legal effect in relevant domestic legislation. In case of any conflict in legislation, predominance should always be given to the Convention, in light of article 27 of the Vienna Convention on the Law of Treaties.

15. In order to ensure a conducive legal environment and in light of article 41 (b) of the Convention, States parties are also encouraged to ratify other international instruments that address issues relating to unaccompanied and separated children, including the two Optional Protocols to the Convention on the Rights of the Child (on the involvement of children in armed conflict and on the sale of children, child prostitution and child pornography), the Convention against Torture and Other Cruel, Inhuman or Degrading Treatment or Punishment (the "CAT"), the Convention on the Elimination of All Forms of Discrimination against Women, the Convention relating to the Status of Refugees ("the 1951 Refugee Convention") and the Protocol relating to the Status of Refugees, the Convention on the Reduction of Statelessness, the Convention relating to the Status of Stateless Persons, the Hague Convention on Protection of Children and Cooperation in Respect of Inter-Country Adoption, the Hague Convention on Jurisdiction, Applicable Law, Recognition, Enforcement and Cooperation in Respect of Parental Responsibility and Measures for the Protection of Children, the four Geneva Conventions of 12 August 1949, the Protocol Additional to the Geneva Conventions of 12 August 1949 and relating to the Protection of Victims of International Armed Conflicts (Protocol I) of 8 June 1977, the Protocol Additional to the Geneva Conventions of 12 August 1949, and relating to the Protection of Victims of Non-International Armed Conflicts (Protocol II) of 8 June 1997. The Committee also encourages States parties to the Convention and others concerned to take into account the Office of the United Nations High Commissioner for Refugees (UNHCR)'s Guidelines on Protection and Care (1994) and the Inter-Agency Guiding Principles on Unaccompanied and Separated Children.[1]

[1] These Guiding Principles are jointly endorsed by the International Committee of the Red Cross, the International Rescue Committee, Save the Children/UK, UNICEF, UNHCR, and World Vision International. They are intended to guide the work of all members of the Inter-Agency Standing Committee with respect to unaccompanied and separated children.

16. In view of the absolute nature of obligations deriving from the Convention and their lex specialis character, article 2, paragraph 3, of the International Covenant on Economic, Social and Cultural Rights would not apply with regard to unaccompanied and separated children. In application of article 4 of the Convention, the particular vulnerability of unaccompanied and separated children, explicitly recognized in article 20 of the Convention, must be taken into account and will result in making the assignment of available resources to such children a priority. States are expected to accept and facilitate assistance offered within their respective mandates by the United Nations Children's Fund (UNICEF), UNHCR and other agencies (article 22 (2) of the Convention) in order to meet the needs of unaccompanied and separated children.

17. The Committee believes that reservations made by States parties to the Convention should not in any way limit the rights of unaccompanied and separated children. As is systematically done with States parties during the reporting process, the Committee recommends that, in the light of the Vienna Declaration and Programme of Action adopted at the 1993 World Conference on Human Rights in Vienna,[2] reservations limiting the rights of unaccompanied and separated children be reviewed with the objective of withdrawal.

(b) Non-discrimination (art. 2)

18. The principle of non-discrimination, in all its facets, applies in respect to all dealings with separated and unaccompanied children. In particular, it prohibits any discrimination on the basis of the status of a child as being unaccompanied or separated, or as being a refugee, asylum-seeker or migrant. This principle, when properly understood, does not prevent, but may indeed call for, differentiation on the basis of different protection needs such as those deriving from age and/or gender. Measures should also be taken to address possible misperceptions and stigmatization of unaccompanied or separated children within the society. Policing or other measures concerning unaccompanied or separated children relating to public order are only permissible where such measures are based on the law; entail individual rather than collective assessment; comply with the principle of proportionality; and represent the least intrusive option. In order not to violate the prohibition on non-discrimination, such measures can, therefore, never be applied on a group or collective basis.

(c) Best interests of the child as a primary consideration in the search for short and long-term solutions (art. 3)

19. Article 3 (1) states that "[i]n all actions concerning children, whether undertaken by public or private social welfare institutions, courts of law, administrative authorities or legislative bodies, the best interests of the child shall be a primary consideration". In the case of a displaced child, the principle must be respected during all stages of the displacement cycle. At any of these stages, a best interests determination must be documented in preparation of any decision fundamentally impacting on the unaccompanied or separated child's life.

20. A determination of what is in the best interests of the child requires a clear and comprehensive assessment of the child's identity, including her or his nationality, upbringing, ethnic, cultural and linguistic background, particular vulnerabilities and protection needs. Consequently, allowing the child access to the territory is a prerequisite to this initial assessment process. The assessment process should be carried out in a friendly and safe atmosphere by qualified professionals who are trained in age and gender-sensitive interviewing techniques.

---

[2] Vienna Declaration and Programme of Action (A/CONF.157/23) adopted by the World Conference on Human Rights, held in Vienna, 14-25 June 1993.

21. Subsequent steps, such as the appointment of a competent guardian as expeditiously as possible, serves as a key procedural safeguard to ensure respect for the best interests of an unaccompanied or separated child. Therefore, such a child should only be referred to asylum or other procedures after the appointment of a guardian. In cases where separated or unaccompanied children are referred to asylum procedures or other administrative or judicial proceedings, they should also be provided with a legal representative in addition to a guardian.

22. Respect for best interests also requires that, where competent authorities have placed an unaccompanied or separated child "for the purposes of care, protection or treatment of his or her physical or mental health", the State recognizes the right of that child to a "periodic review" of their treatment and "all other circumstances relevant to his or her placement" (article 25 of the Convention).

(d) The right to life, survival and development (art. 6)

23. The obligation of the State party under article 6 includes protection from violence and exploitation, to the maximum extent possible, which would jeopardize a child's right to life, survival and development. Separated and unaccompanied children are vulnerable to various risks that affect their life, survival and development such as trafficking for purposes of sexual or other exploitation or involvement in criminal activities which could result in harm to the child, or in extreme cases, in death. Accordingly, article 6 necessitates vigilance by States parties in this regard, particularly when organized crime may be involved. While the issue of trafficking of children is beyond the scope of this general comment, the Committee notes that there is often a link between trafficking and the situation of separated and unaccompanied children.

24. The Committee is of the view that practical measures should be taken at all levels to protect children from the risks mentioned above. Such measures could include: priority procedures for child victims of trafficking, the prompt appointment of guardians, the provision of information to children about the risks they may encounter, and establishment of measures to provide follow-up to children particularly at risk. These measures should be regularly evaluated to ensure their effectiveness.

(e) Right of the child to express his or her views freely (art. 12)

25. Pursuant to article 12 of the Convention, in determining the measures to be adopted with regard to unaccompanied or separated children, the child's views and wishes should be elicited and taken into account (art. 12 (1)). To allow for a well-informed expression of such views and wishes, it is imperative that such children are provided with all relevant information concerning, for example, their entitlements, services available including means of communication, the asylum process, family tracing and the situation in their country of origin (arts. 13, 17 and 22 (2)). In guardianship, care and accommodation arrangements, and legal representation, children's views should also be taken into account. Such information must be provided in a manner that is appropriate to the maturity and level of understanding of each child. As participation is dependent on reliable communication, where necessary, interpreters should be made available at all stages of the procedure.

(f) Respect for the principle of non-refoulement

26. In affording proper treatment of unaccompanied or separated children, States must fully respect non-refoulement obligations deriving from international human rights, humanitarian and refugee law and, in particular, must respect obligations codified in article 33 of the 1951 Refugee Convention and in article 3 of CAT.

27. Furthermore, in fulfilling obligations under the Convention, States shall not return a child to a country where there are substantial grounds for believing that there is a real risk of irreparable harm to the child, such as, but by no means limited to, those contemplated under articles 6 and 37 of the Convention, either in the country to which removal is to be effected or in any country to which the child may subsequently be removed. Such non-refoulement obligations apply irrespective of whether serious violations of those rights guaranteed under the Convention originate from non-State actors or whether such violations are directly intended or are the indirect consequence of action or inaction. The assessment of the risk of such serious violations should be conducted in an age and gender-sensitive manner and should, for example, take into account the particularly serious consequences for children of the insufficient provision of food or health services.

28. As underage recruitment and participation in hostilities entails a high risk of irreparable harm involving fundamental human rights, including the right to life, State obligations deriving from article 38 of the Convention, in conjunction with articles 3 and 4 of the Optional Protocol to the Convention on the Rights of the Child on the involvement of children in armed conflict, entail extraterritorial effects and States shall refrain from returning a child in any manner whatsoever to the borders of a State where there is a real risk of underage recruitment, including recruitment not only as a combatant but also to provide sexual services for the military or where there is a real risk of direct or indirect participation in hostilities, either as a combatant or through carrying out other military duties.

(g) Confidentiality

29. States parties must protect the confidentiality of information received in relation to an unaccompanied or separated child, consistent with the obligation to protect the child's rights, including the right to privacy (art. 16). This obligation applies in all settings, including health and social welfare. Care must be taken that information sought and legitimately shared for one purpose is not inappropriately used for that of another.

30. Confidentiality concerns also involve respect for the rights of others. For example, in obtaining, sharing and preserving the information collected in respect of unaccompanied and separated children, particular care must be taken in order not to endanger the well-being of persons still within the child's country of origin, especially the child's family members. Furthermore, information relating to the whereabouts of the child shall only be withheld vis-à-vis the parents where required for the safety of the child or to otherwise secure the "best interests" of the child.

V. RESPONSE TO GENERAL AND SPECIFIC PROTECTION NEEDS

(a) Initial assessment and measures

31. The best interests of the child must also be a guiding principle for determining the priority of protection needs and the chronology of measures to be applied in respect of unaccompanied and separated children. This necessary initial assessment process, in particular, entails the following:

(i) Prioritized identification of a child as separated or unaccompanied immediately upon arrival at ports of entry or as soon as their presence in the country becomes known to the authorities (art. 8). Such identification measures include age assessment and should not only take into account the physical appearance of the individual, but also his or her psychological maturity. Moreover, the assessment must be conducted in a scientific, safe, child and gender-sensitive and fair manner, avoiding any risk of violation of the physical integrity of the child; giving due respect to human dignity; and, in the event of remaining uncertainty, should accord the individual the benefit of the doubt such that if there is a possibility that the individual is a child, she or he should be treated as such;

(ii) Prompt registration by means of an initial interview conducted in an age-appropriate and gender-sensitive manner, in a language the child understands, by professionally qualified persons to collect biodata and social history to ascertain the identity of the child, including, wherever possible, identity of both parents, other siblings, as well as the citizenship of the child, the siblings and the parents;

(iii) In continuation of the registration process, the recording of further information in order to meet the specific needs of the child. This information should include:

– Reasons for being separated or unaccompanied;

– Assessment of particular vulnerabilities, including health, physical, psychosocial, material and other protection needs, including those deriving from domestic violence, trafficking or trauma;

– All available information to determine the potential existence of international protection needs, including those: due to a "well-founded fear of being persecuted for reasons of race, religion, nationality, membership of a particular social group or political opinion" in the child's country of origin (article 1 A (2), 1951 Refugee Convention); deriving from external aggression, occupation, foreign domination or events seriously disturbing public order (article 1 (2), Convention Governing the Specific Aspects of Refugee Problems in Africa); or relating to the indiscriminate effects of generalized violence;

(iv) Unaccompanied and separated children should be provided with their own personal identity documentation as soon as possible;

(v) Tracing of family members to be commenced as early as possible (arts. 22 (2), 9 (3) and 10 (2)).

32. Any further actions relating to the residence and other status of the child in the territory of the State should be based on the findings of an initial protection assessment carried out in accordance with the above procedures. States should refrain from referring unaccompanied and separated children into asylum procedures if their presence in the territory does not raise the question of international refugee protection needs. This is without prejudice to the obligation of States to refer unaccompanied or separated children to relevant procedures serving child protection, such as those foreseen under child welfare legislation.

(b) Appointment of a guardian or adviser and legal representative (arts. 18 (2) and 20 (1))

33. States are required to create the underlying legal framework and to take necessary measures to secure proper representation of an unaccompanied or separated child's best interests. Therefore, States should appoint a guardian or adviser as soon as the unaccompanied or separated child is identified and maintain such guardianship arrangements until the child has either reached the age of majority or has permanently left the territory and/or jurisdiction of the State, in compliance with the Convention and other international obligations. The guardian should be consulted and informed regarding all actions taken in relation to the child. The guardian should have the authority to be present in all planning and decision-making processes, including immigration and appeal hearings, care arrangements and all efforts to search for a durable solution. The guardian or adviser should have the necessary expertise in the field of childcare, so as to ensure that the interests of the child are safeguarded and that the

child's legal, social, health, psychological, material and educational needs are appropriately covered by, inter alia, the guardian acting as a link between the child and existing specialist agencies/individuals who provide the continuum of care required by the child. Agencies or individuals whose interests could potentially be in conflict with those of the child's should not be eligible for guardianship. For example, non-related adults whose primary relationship to the child is that of an employer should be excluded from a guardianship role.

34. In the case of a separated child, guardianship should regularly be assigned to the accompanying adult family member or non-primary family caretaker unless there is an indication that it would not be in the best interests of the child to do so, for example, where the accompanying adult has abused the child. In cases where a child is accompanied by a non-family adult or caretaker, suitability for guardianship must be scrutinized more closely. If such a guardian is able and willing to provide day-to-day care, but unable to adequately represent the child's best interests in all spheres and at all levels of the child's life, supplementary measures (such as the appointment of an adviser or legal representative) must be secured.

35. Review mechanisms shall be introduced and implemented to monitor the quality of the exercise of guardianship in order to ensure the best interests of the child are being represented throughout the decision-making process and, in particular, to prevent abuse.

36. In cases where children are involved in asylum procedures or administrative or judicial proceedings, they should, in addition to the appointment of a guardian, be provided with legal representation.

37. At all times children should be informed of arrangements with respect to guardianship and legal representation and their opinions should be taken into consideration.

38. In large-scale emergencies, where it will be difficult to establish guardianship arrangements on an individual basis, the rights and best interests of separated children should be safeguarded and promoted by States and organizations working on behalf of these children.

(c) Care and accommodation arrangements (arts. 20 and 22)

39. Unaccompanied or separated children are children temporarily or permanently deprived of their family environment and, as such, are beneficiaries of States' obligations under article 20 of the Convention and shall be entitled to special protection and assistance provided by the relevant State.

40. Mechanisms established under national law in order to ensure alternative care for such children in accordance with article 22 of the Convention, shall also cover unaccompanied or separated children outside their country of origin. A wide range of options for care and accommodation arrangements exist and are explicitly acknowledged in article 20 (3) as follows:
"... inter alia, foster placement, *kafalah* of Islamic law, adoption or, if necessary, placement in suitable institutions for the care of children". When selecting from these options, the particular vulnerabilities of such a child, not only having lost connection with his or her family environment, but further finding him or herself outside of his or her country of origin, as well as the child's age and gender, should be taken into account. In particular, due regard ought to be taken of the desirability of continuity in a child's upbringing and to the ethnic, religious, cultural and linguistic background as assessed in the identification, registration and documentation process. Such care and accommodation arrangements should comply with the following parameters:

– Children should not, as a general rule, be deprived of liberty;

– In order to ensure continuity of care and considering the best interests of the child, changes in residence for unaccompanied and separated children should be limited to instances where such change is in the best interests of the child;

– In accordance with the principle of family unity, siblings should be kept together;

– A child who has adult relatives arriving with him or her or already living in the country of asylum should be allowed to stay with them unless such action would be contrary to the best interests of the child. Given the particular vulnerabilities of the child, regular assessments should be conducted by social welfare personnel;

– Irrespective of the care arrangements made for unaccompanied or separated children, regular supervision and assessment ought to be maintained by qualified persons in order to ensure the child's physical and psychosocial health, protection against domestic violence or exploitation, and access to educational and vocational skills and opportunities;

– States and other organizations must take measures to ensure the effective protection of the rights of separated or unaccompanied children living in child-headed households;

– In large-scale emergencies, interim care must be provided for the shortest time appropriate for unaccompanied children. This interim care provides for their security and physical and emotional care in a setting that encourages their general development;

– Children must be kept informed of the care arrangements being made for them, and their opinions must be taken into consideration.

(d) Full access to education (arts. 28, 29 (1) (c), 30 and 32)

41. States should ensure that access to education is maintained during all phases of the displacement cycle. Every unaccompanied and separated child, irrespective of status, shall have full access to education in the country that they have entered in line with articles 28, 29 (1) (c), 30 and 32 of the Convention and the general principles developed by the Committee. Such access should be granted without discrimination and in particular, separated and unaccompanied girls shall have equal access to formal and informal education, including vocational training at all levels. Access to quality education should also be ensured for children with special needs, in particular children with disabilities.

42. The unaccompanied or separated child should be registered with appropriate school authorities as soon as possible and get assistance in maximizing learning opportunities. All unaccompanied and separated children have the right to maintain their cultural identity and values, including the maintenance and development of their native language. All adolescents should be allowed to enrol in vocational/professional training or education, and early learning programmes should be made available to young children. States should ensure that unaccompanied or separated children are provided with school certificates or other documentation indicating their level of education, in particular in preparation of relocation, resettlement or return.

43. States shall, in particular where government capacity is limited, accept and facilitate the assistance offered by UNICEF, the United Nations Educational, Scientific and Cultural Organization (UNESCO), UNHCR and other United Nations agencies within their respective mandates, as well as, where appropriate, other competent intergovernmental organizations or non-governmental organizations (art. 22 (2)) in order to meet the educational needs of unaccompanied and separated children.

(e) Right to an adequate standard of living (art. 27)

44. States should ensure that separated and unaccompanied children have a standard of living adequate for their physical, mental, spiritual and moral development. As provided in article 27 (2) of the Convention, States shall provide material assistance and support programmes, particularly with regard to nutrition, clothing and housing.

45. States shall, in particular where government capacity is limited, accept and facilitate the assistance offered by UNICEF, UNESCO, UNHCR and other United Nations agencies within their respective mandates, as well as, where appropriate, other competent intergovernmental organizations or non-governmental organizations (art. 22 (2)) in order to secure an adequate standard of living for unaccompanied and separated children.

(f) Right to enjoy the highest attainable standard of health and facilities for the treatment of illness and rehabilitation of health (arts. 23, 24 and 39)

46. When implementing the right to enjoy the highest attainable standard of health and facilities for the treatment of illness and rehabilitation of health under article 24 of the Convention, States are obligated to ensure that unaccompanied and separated children have the same access to health care as children who are... nationals....

47. In ensuring their access, States must assess and address the particular plight and vulnerabilities of such children. They should, in particular, take into account the fact that unaccompanied children have undergone separation from family members and have also, to varying degrees, experienced loss, trauma, disruption and violence. Many such children, in particular those who are refugees, have further experienced pervasive violence and the stress associated with a country afflicted by war. This may have created deep-rooted feelings of helplessness and undermined a child's trust in others. Moreover, girls are particularly susceptible to marginalization, poverty and suffering during armed conflict, and many may have experienced gender-based violence in the context of armed conflict. The profound trauma experienced by many affected children calls for special sensitivity and attention in their care and rehabilitation.

48. The obligation under article 39 of the Convention sets out the duty of States to provide rehabilitation services to children who have been victims of any form of abuse, neglect, exploitation, torture, cruel, inhuman and degrading treatment or armed conflicts. In order to facilitate such recovery and reintegration, culturally appropriate and gender-sensitive mental health care should be developed and qualified psychosocial counselling provided.

49. States shall, in particular where government capacity is limited, accept and facilitate assistance offered by UNICEF, the World Health Organization (WHO), United Nations Joint Programme on HIV/AIDS (UNAIDS), UNHCR and other agencies (art. 22 (2)) within their respective mandates, as well as, where appropriate, other competent intergovernmental organizations or non-governmental organizations in order to meet the health and health-care needs of unaccompanied and separated children.

(g) Prevention of trafficking and of sexual and other forms of exploitation, abuse and violence (arts. 34, 35 and 36)

50. Unaccompanied or separated children in a country outside their country of origin are particularly vulnerable to exploitation and abuse. Girls are at particular risk of being trafficked, including for purposes of sexual exploitation.

51. Articles 34 to 36 of the Convention must be read in conjunction with special protection and assistance obligations to be provided according to article 20 of the Convention, in order

to ensure that unaccompanied and separated children are shielded from trafficking, and from sexual and other forms of exploitation, abuse and violence.

52. Trafficking of such a child, or "re-trafficking" in cases where a child was already a victim of trafficking, is one of many dangers faced by unaccompanied or separated children. Trafficking in children is a threat to the fulfilment of their right to life, survival and development (art. 6). In accordance with article 35 of the Convention, States parties should take appropriate measures to prevent such trafficking. Necessary measures include identifying unaccompanied and separated children; regularly inquiring as to their whereabouts; and conducting information campaigns that are age-appropriate, gender-sensitive and in a language and medium that is understandable to the child. Adequate legislation should also be passed and effective mechanisms of enforcement be established with respect to labour regulations and border crossing.

53. Risks are also great for a child who has already been a victim of trafficking, resulting in the status of being unaccompanied or separated. Such children should not be penalized and should receive assistance as victims of a serious human rights violation. Some trafficked children may be eligible for refugee status under the 1951 Convention, and States should ensure that separated and unaccompanied trafficked children who wish to seek asylum or in relation to whom there is otherwise indication that international protection needs exist, have access to asylum procedures. Children who are at risk of being re-trafficked should not be returned to their country of origin unless it is in their best interests and appropriate measures for their protection have been taken. States should consider complementary forms of protection for trafficked children when return is not in their best interests.

(h) Prevention of military recruitment and protection against effects of war (arts. 38 and 39)

Prevention of recruitment

54. State obligations deriving from article 38 of the Convention and from articles 3 and 4 of the Optional Protocol to the Convention on the Rights of the Child on the involvement of children in armed conflict also apply to unaccompanied and separated children. A State must take all necessary measures to prevent recruitment or use of such children by any party to a conflict. This also applies to former child soldiers who have defected from their units and who require protection against re-recruitment.

Care arrangements

55. Care arrangements for unaccompanied and separated children shall be made in a manner which prevents their recruitment, re-recruitment or use by any party to a conflict. Guardianships should not be given to individuals or organizations who are directly or indirectly involved in a conflict.

Former child soldiers

56. Child soldiers should be considered primarily as victims of armed conflict. Former child soldiers, who often find themselves unaccompanied or separated at the cessation of the conflict or following defection, shall be given all the necessary support services to enable reintegration into normal life, including necessary psychosocial counselling. Such children shall be identified and demobilized on a priority basis during any identification and separation operation. Child soldiers, in particular, those who are unaccompanied or separated, should not normally be interned, but rather, benefit from special protection and assistance measures, in particular as regards their demobilization and rehabilitation. Particular efforts must be made to provide

support and facilitate the reintegration of girls who have been associated with the military, either as combatants or in any other capacity.

57. If, under certain circumstances, exceptional internment of a child soldier over the age of 15 years is unavoidable and in compliance with international human rights and humanitarian law, for example, where she or he poses a serious security threat, the conditions of such internment should be in conformity with international standards, including article 37 of the Convention and those pertaining to juvenile justice, and should not preclude any tracing efforts and priority participation in rehabilitation programmes.

Non-refoulement

58. As under-age recruitment and participation in hostilities entails a high risk of irreparable harm involving fundamental human rights, including the right to life, State obligations deriving from article 38 of the Convention, in conjunction with articles 3 and 4 of the Optional Protocol to the Convention on the Rights of the Child on the involvement of children in armed conflict, entail extraterritorial effects and States shall refrain from returning a child in any manner whatsoever to the borders of a State where there is a real risk of under-age recruitment or participation, directly or indirectly, in hostilities.

Child-specific forms and manifestations of persecution[3]

59. Reminding States of the need for age and gender-sensitive asylum procedures and an age and gender-sensitive interpretation of the refugee definition, the Committee highlights that under-age recruitment (including of girls for sexual services or forced marriage with the military) and direct or indirect participation in hostilities constitutes a serious human rights violation and thereby persecution, and should lead to the granting of refugee status where the well-founded fear of such recruitment or participation in hostilities is based on "reasons of race, religion, nationality, membership of a particular social group or political opinion" (article 1A (2), 1951 Refugee Convention).

Rehabilitation and recovery

60. States shall develop, where needed, in cooperation with international agencies and NGOs, a comprehensive age-appropriate and gender-sensitive system of psychological support and assistance for unaccompanied and separated children affected by armed conflict.

(i) Prevention of deprivation of liberty and treatment in cases thereof

61. In application of article 37 of the Convention and the principle of the best interests of the child, unaccompanied or separated children should not, as a general rule, be detained. Detention cannot be justified solely on the basis of the child being unaccompanied or separated, or on their migratory or residence status, or lack thereof. Where detention is exceptionally justified for other reasons, it shall be conducted in accordance with article 37 (b) of the Convention that requires detention to conform to the law of the relevant country and only to be used as a measure of last resort and for the shortest appropriate period of time. In consequence, all efforts, including acceleration of relevant processes, should be made to allow for the immediate release of unaccompanied or separated children from detention and their placement in other forms of appropriate accommodation.

---

[3] On child-specific forms and manifestations of persecution more generally, see section VI (d) below "Child sensitive assessment of protection needs, taking into account persecution of a child-specific nature".

62. In addition to national requirements, international obligations constitute part of the law governing detention. With regard to asylum-seeking, unaccompanied and separated children, States must, in particular, respect their obligations deriving from article 31 (1) of the 1951 Refugee Convention. States should further take into account that illegal entry into or stay in a country by an unaccompanied or separated child may also be justified according to general principles of law, where such entry or stay is the only way of preventing a violation of the fundamental human rights of the child. More generally, in developing policies on unaccompanied or separated children, including those who are victims of trafficking and exploitation, States should ensure that such children are not criminalized solely for reasons of illegal entry or presence in the country.

63. In the exceptional case of detention, conditions of detention must be governed by the best interests of the child and pay full respect to article 37 (a) and (c) of the Convention and other international obligations. Special arrangements must be made for living quarters that are suitable for children and that separate them from adults, unless it is considered in the child's best interests not to do so. Indeed, the underlying approach to such a programme should be "care" and not "detention". Facilities should not be located in isolated areas where culturally appropriate community resources and access to legal aid are unavailable. Children should have the opportunity to make regular contact and receive visits from friends, relatives, religious, social and legal counsel and their guardian. They should also be provided with the opportunity to receive all basic necessities as well as appropriate medical treatment and psychological counselling where necessary. During their period in detention, children have the right to education which ought, ideally, to take place outside the detention premises in order to facilitate the continuance of their education upon release. They also have the right to recreation and play as provided for in article 31 of the Convention. In order to effectively secure the rights provided by article 37 (d) of the Convention, unaccompanied or separated children deprived of their liberty shall be provided with prompt and free access to legal and other appropriate assistance, including the assignment of a legal representative.

VI. ACCESS TO THE ASYLUM PROCEDURE, LEGAL SAFEGUARDS AND RIGHTS IN ASYLUM

(a) General

64. The obligation stemming from article 22 of the Convention to take "appropriate measures" to ensure that a child, whether unaccompanied or accompanied, who is seeking refugee status receives appropriate protection entails, inter alia, the responsibility to set up a functioning asylum system and, in particular, to enact legislation addressing the particular treatment of unaccompanied and separated children and to build capacities necessary to realize this treatment in accordance with applicable rights codified in the Convention and in other international human rights, refugee protection or humanitarian instruments to which the State is a party. States facing resource constraints in staging such capacity-building efforts are strongly encouraged to seek international assistance, including that provided by UNHCR.

65. Taking into account the complementary nature of the obligations under article 22 and those deriving from international refugee law, as well as the desirability of consolidated standards, States should apply international standards relating to refugees as they progressively evolve when implementing article 22 of the Convention.

(b) Access to asylum procedures, regardless of age

66. Asylum-seeking children, including those who are unaccompanied or separated, shall enjoy access to asylum procedures and other complementary mechanisms providing international

protection, irrespective of their age. In the case that facts become known during the identification and registration process which indicate that the child may have a well-founded fear or, even if unable to explicitly articulate a concrete fear, the child may objectively be at risk of persecution for reasons of race, religion, nationality, membership of a particular social group or political opinion, or otherwise be in need of international protection, such a child should be referred to the asylum procedure and/or, where relevant, to mechanisms providing complementary protection under international and domestic law.

67. Unaccompanied or separated children for whom there is no indication of being in need of international protection should not automatically, or otherwise, be referred to asylum procedures, but shall be protected pursuant to other relevant child protection mechanisms such as those provided under youth welfare legislation.

(c) Procedural safeguards and support measures (art. 3 (3))

68. Appropriate measures required under article 22 (1) of the Convention must take into account the particular vulnerabilities of unaccompanied and separated children and the national legal framework and conditions. Such measures should be guided by the considerations set out below.

69. An asylum-seeking child should be represented by an adult who is familiar with the child's background and who is competent and able to represent his or her best interests (see section V (b), "Appointment of a guardian or adviser or legal representative"). The unaccompanied or separated child should also, in all cases, be given access, free of charge, to a qualified legal representative, including where the application for refugee status is processed under the normal procedures for adults.

70. Refugee status applications filed by unaccompanied and separated children shall be given priority and every effort should be made to render a decision promptly and fairly.

71. Minimum procedural guarantees should include that the application will be determined by a competent authority fully qualified in asylum and refugee matters. Where the age and maturity of the child permits, the opportunity for a personal interview with a qualified official should be granted before any final decision is made. Wherever the child is unable to communicate directly with the qualified official in a common language, the assistance of a qualified interpreter should be sought. Moreover, the child should be given the "benefit of the doubt", should there be credibility concerns relating to his or her story as well as a possibility to appeal for a formal review of the decision.

72. The interviews should be conducted by representatives of the refugee determination authority who will take into account the special situation of unaccompanied children in order to carry out the refugee status assessment and apply an understanding of the history, culture and background of the child. The assessment process should comprise a case-by-case examination of the unique combination of factors presented by each child, including the child's personal, family and cultural background. The guardian and the legal representative should be present during all interviews.

73. In cases of large-scale refugee movements where individual refugee status determination is not possible, States may grant refugee status to all members of a group. In such circumstances, all unaccompanied or separated children are entitled to be granted the same status as other members of the particular group.

(d) Child-sensitive assessment of protection needs, taking into account persecution of a child-specific nature

74. When assessing refugee claims of unaccompanied or separated children, States shall take into account the development of, and formative relationship between, international human rights and refugee law, including positions developed by UNHCR in exercising its supervisory functions under the 1951 Refugee Convention. In particular, the refugee definition in that Convention must be interpreted in an age and gender-sensitive manner, taking into account the particular motives for, and forms and manifestations of, persecution experienced by children. Persecution of kin; under-age recruitment; trafficking of children for prostitution; and sexual exploitation or subjection to female genital mutilation, are some of the child-specific forms and manifestations of persecution which may justify the granting of refugee status if such acts are related to one of the 1951 Refugee Convention grounds. States should, therefore, give utmost attention to such child-specific forms and manifestations of persecution as well as gender-based violence in national refugee status-determination procedures.

75. Staff involved in status-determination procedures of children, in particular those who are unaccompanied or separated, should receive training on adopting an application of international and national refugee law that is child, cultural, and gender-sensitive. To properly assess asylum claims of children, information on the situation of children, including those belonging to minorities or marginalized groups, should be included in government efforts to collect country-of-origin information.

(e) Full enjoyment of all international refugee and human rights by children granted refugee status (art. 22)

76. Unaccompanied or separated children recognized as refugees and granted asylum do not only enjoy rights under the 1951 Refugee Convention, but are also entitled to the fullest extent to the enjoyment of all human rights granted to children in the territory or subject to the jurisdiction of the State, including those rights which require a lawful stay in the territory.

(f) Children to benefit from complementary forms of protection

77. In the case that the requirements for granting refugee status under the 1951 Refugee Convention are not met, unaccompanied and separated children shall benefit from available forms of complementary protection to the extent determined by their protection needs. The application of such complementary forms of protection does not obviate States' obligations to address the particular protection needs of the unaccompanied and separated child. Therefore, children granted complementary forms of protection are entitled, to the fullest extent, to the enjoyment of all human rights granted to children in the territory or subject to the jurisdiction of the State, including those rights which require a lawful stay in the territory.

78. In line with the generally applicable principles and, in particular, those relating to the responsibilities of States with regard to unaccompanied or separated children finding themselves in their territory, children who are neither granted refugee status nor benefiting from complementary forms of protection, will still enjoy protection under all norms of the Convention as long as they remain de facto within the States' territories and/or subject to its jurisdiction.

VII. FAMILY REUNIFICATION, RETURN AND OTHER FORMS OF DURABLE SOLUTIONS

(a) General

79. The ultimate aim in addressing the fate of unaccompanied or separated children is to identify a durable solution that addresses all their protection needs, takes into account the child's view and, wherever possible, leads to overcoming the situation of a child being unaccompanied or separated. Efforts to find durable solutions for unaccompanied or separated children should be initiated and implemented without undue delay and, wherever possible, immediately upon the assessment of a child being unaccompanied or separated. Following a rights-based approach, the search for a durable solution commences with analysing the possibility of family reunification.

80. Tracing is an essential component of any search for a durable solution and should be prioritized except where the act of tracing, or the way in which tracing is conducted, would be contrary to the best interests of the child or jeopardize fundamental rights of those being traced. In any case, in conducting tracing activities, no reference should be made to the status of the child as an asylum-seeker or refugee. Subject to all of these conditions, such tracing efforts should also be continued during the asylum procedure. For all children who remain in the territory of the host State, whether on the basis of asylum, complementary forms of protection or due to other legal or factual obstacles to removal, a durable solution must be sought.

(b) Family reunification

81. In order to pay full respect to the obligation of States under article 9 of the Convention to ensure that a child shall not be separated from his or her parents against their will, all efforts should be made to return an unaccompanied or separated child to his or her parents except where further separation is necessary for the best interests of the child, taking full account of the right of the child to express his or her views (art. 12) (see also section IV (e), "Right of the child to express his or her views freely"). While the considerations explicitly listed in article 9, paragraph 1, sentence 2, namely, cases involving abuse or neglect of the child by the parents, may prohibit reunification at any location, other best-interests considerations can provide an obstacle to reunification at specific locations only.

82. Family reunification in the country of origin is not in the best interests of the child and should therefore not be pursued where there is a "reasonable risk" that such a return would lead to the violation of fundamental human rights of the child. Such risk is indisputably documented in the granting of refugee status or in a decision of the competent authorities on the applicability of non-refoulement obligations (including those deriving from article 3 of the Convention against Torture and Other Cruel, Inhuman or Degrading Treatment or Punishment and articles 6 and 7 of the International Covenant on Civil and Political Rights). Accordingly, the granting of refugee status constitutes a legally binding obstacle to return to the country of origin and, consequently, to family reunification therein. Where the circumstances in the country of origin contain lower level risks and there is concern, for example, of the child being affected by the indiscriminate effects of generalized violence, such risks must be given full attention and balanced against other rights-based considerations, including the consequences of further separation. In this context, it must be recalled that the survival of the child is of paramount importance and a precondition for the enjoyment of any other rights.

83. Whenever family reunification in the country of origin is not possible, irrespective of whether this is due to legal obstacles to return or whether the best-interests-based balancing test has decided against return, the obligations under article 9 and 10 of the Convention come

into effect and should govern the host country's decisions on family reunification therein. In this context, States parties are particularly reminded that "applications by a child or his or her parents to enter or leave a State party for the purpose of family reunification shall be dealt with by States parties in a positive, humane and expeditious manner" and "shall entail no adverse consequences for the applicants and for the members of their family" (art. 10 (1)). Countries of origin must respect "the right of the child and his or her parents to leave any country, including their own, and to enter their own country" (art. 10 (2)).

(c) Return to the country of origin

84. Return to the country of origin is not an option if it would lead to a "reasonable risk" that such return would result in the violation of fundamental human rights of the child, and in particular, if the principle of non-refoulement applies. Return to the country of origin shall in principle only be arranged if such return is in the best interests of the child. Such a determination shall, inter alia, take into account:

– The safety, security and other conditions, including socio-economic conditions, awaiting the child upon return, including through home study, where appropriate, conducted by social network organizations;

– The availability of care arrangements for that particular child;

– The views of the child expressed in exercise of his or her right to do so under article 12 and those of the caretakers;

– The child's level of integration in the host country and the duration of absence from the home country;

– The child's right "to preserve his or her identity, including nationality, name and family relations" (art. 8);

– The "desirability of continuity in a child's upbringing and to the child's ethnic, religious, cultural and linguistic background" (art. 20).

85. In the absence of the availability of care provided by parents or members of the extended family, return to the country of origin should, in principle, not take place without advance secure and concrete arrangements of care and custodial responsibilities upon return to the country of origin.

86. Exceptionally, a return to the home country may be arranged, after careful balancing of the child's best interests and other considerations, if the latter are rights-based and override best interests of the child. Such may be the case in situations in which the child constitutes a serious risk to the security of the State or to the society. Non-rights-based arguments such as those relating to general migration control, cannot override best interests considerations.

87. In all cases return measures must be conducted in a safe, child-appropriate and gender-sensitive manner.

88. Countries of origin are also reminded in this context of their obligations pursuant to article 10 of the Convention and, in particular, to respect "the right of the child and his or her parents to leave any country, including their own, and to enter their own country".

(d) Local integration

89. Local integration is the primary option if return to the country of origin is impossible on either legal or factual grounds. Local integration must be based on a secure legal status

(including residence status) and be governed by the Convention rights that are fully applicable to all children who remain in the country, irrespective of whether this is due to their recognition as a refugee, other legal obstacles to return, or whether the best-interests-based balancing test has decided against return.

90. Once it has been determined that a separated or unaccompanied child will remain in the community, the relevant authorities should conduct an assessment of the child's situation and then, in consultation with the child and his or her guardian, determine the appropriate long-term arrangements within the local community and other necessary measures to facilitate such integration. The long-term placement should be decided in the best interests of the child and, at this stage, institutional care should, wherever possible, serve only as a last resort. The separated or unaccompanied child should have the same access to rights (including to education, training, employment and health care) as enjoyed by national children. In ensuring that these rights are fully enjoyed by the unaccompanied or separated child, the host country may need to pay special attention to the extra measures required to address the child's vulnerable status, including, for example, through extra language training.

(e) Intercountry adoption (art. 21)

91. States must have full respect for the preconditions provided under article 21 of the Convention as well as other relevant international instruments, including in particular the Hague Convention on Protection of Children and Cooperation in Respect of Inter-Country Adoption and its 1994 Recommendation Concerning the Application to Refugee and other Internationally Displaced Children when considering the adoption of unaccompanied and separated children. States should, in particular, observe the following:

– Adoption of unaccompanied or separated children should only be considered once it has been established that the child is in a position to be adopted. In practice, this means, inter alia, that efforts with regard to tracing and family reunification have failed, or that the parents have consented to the adoption. The consent of parents and the consent of other persons, institutions and authorities that are necessary for adoption must be free and informed. This supposes notably that such consent has not been induced by payment or compensation of any kind and has not been withdrawn;

– Unaccompanied or separated children must not be adopted in haste at the height of an emergency;

– Any adoption must be determined as being in the child's best interests and carried out in keeping with applicable national, international and customary law;

– The views of the child, depending upon his/her age and degree of maturity, should be sought and taken into account in all adoption procedures. This requirement implies that he/she has been counselled and duly informed of the consequences of adoption and of his/her consent to adoption, where such consent is required. Such consent must have been given freely and not induced by payment or compensation of any kind;

– Priority must be given to adoption by relatives in their country of residence. Where this is not an option, preference will be given to adoption within the community from which the child came or at least within his or her own culture;

– Adoption should not be considered:

– Where there is reasonable hope of successful tracing and family reunification is in the child's best interests;

– If it is contrary to the expressed wishes of the child or the parents;

– Unless a reasonable time has passed during which all feasible steps to trace the parents or other surviving family members has been carried out. This period of time may vary with circumstances, in particular, those relating to the ability to conduct proper tracing; however, the process of tracing must be completed within a reasonable period of time;

– Adoption in a country of asylum should not be taken up when there is the possibility of voluntary repatriation under conditions of safety and dignity in the near future.

(f) Resettlement in a third country

92. Resettlement to a third country may offer a durable solution for an accompanied or separated child who cannot return to the country of origin and for whom no durable solution can be envisaged in the host country. The decision to resettle an unaccompanied or separated child must be based on an updated, comprehensive and thorough best-interests assessment, taking into account, in particular, ongoing international and other protection needs. Resettlement is particularly called for if such is the only means to effectively and sustainably protect a child against refoulement or against persecution or other serious human rights violations in the country of stay. Resettlement is also in the best interests of the unaccompanied or separated child if it serves family reunification in the resettlement country.

93. The best-interests assessment determination, prior to a decision to resettle, needs also to take into account other factors such as: the envisaged duration of legal or other obstacles to a child's return to his or her home country; the child's right to preserve his or her identity, including nationality and name (art. 8); the child's age, sex, emotional state, educational and family background; continuity/discontinuity of care in the host country; the desirability of continuity in a child's upbringing and to the child's ethnic, religious, cultural and linguistic background (art. 20); the right of the child to preserve his or her family relations (art. 8) and related short, medium and long-term possibilities of family reunion either in the home, host, or resettlement country. Unaccompanied or separated children should never be resettled to a third country if this would undermine or seriously hamper future reunion with their family.

94. States are encouraged to provide resettlement opportunities in order to meet all the resettlement needs related to unaccompanied and separated children.

VIII. TRAINING, DATA AND STATISTICS

(a) Training of personnel dealing with unaccompanied and separated children

95. Particular attention should be paid to the training of officials working with separated and unaccompanied children and dealing with their cases. Specialized training is equally important for legal representatives, guardians, interpreters and others dealing with separated and unaccompanied children.

96. Such training should be specifically tailored to the needs and rights of the groups concerned. Nevertheless, certain key elements should be included in all training programmes, including:

– Principles and provisions of the Convention;

– Knowledge of the country of origin of separated and unaccompanied children;

– Appropriate interview techniques;

– Child development and psychology;

– Cultural sensitivity and intercultural communication.

97. Initial training programmes should also be followed up regularly, including through on-the-job learning and professional networks.

(b) Data and statistics on separated and unaccompanied children

98. It is the experience of the Committee that data and statistics collected with regard to unaccompanied and separated children tends to be limited to the number of arrivals and/or number of requests for asylum. This data is insufficient for a detailed analysis of the implementation of the rights of such children. Furthermore, data and statistics are often collected by a variety of different ministries or agencies, which can impede further analysis and presents potential concerns with regard to confidentiality and a child's right to privacy.

99. Accordingly, the development of a detailed and integrated system of data collection on unaccompanied and separated children is a prerequisite for the development of effective policies for the implementation of the rights of such children.

100. Data collected within such a system should ideally include but not be limited to: basic biographical data on each child (including age, sex, country of origin and nationality, ethnic group); total number of unaccompanied and separated children attempting to enter the country and the number that have been refused entry; number of requests for asylum; number of legal representatives and guardians assigned to such children; legal and immigration status (i.e. asylum-seeker, refugee, temporary resident permit); living arrangements (i.e. in institutions, with families or living independently); enrolment in school or vocational training; family reunifications; and, numbers returned to their country of origin. In addition, States parties should consider collecting qualitative data that would allow them to analyse issues that remain insufficiently addressed, such as for instance, disappearances of unaccompanied and separated children and the impact of trafficking.

CEDAW General Recommendation No.24: Article 12 (Women and Health), 1999 [excerpts] *

Adoption: 2 February 1999

[...]

6. While biological differences between women and men may lead to differences in health status, there are societal factors that are determinative of the health status of women and men and can vary among women themselves. For that reason, special attention should be given to the health needs and rights of women belonging to vulnerable and disadvantaged groups, such as migrant women, refugee and internally displaced women, the girl child and older women, women in prostitution, indigenous women and women with physical or mental disabilities.

[...]

16. States parties should ensure that adequate protection and health services, including trauma treatment and counselling, are provided for women in especially difficult circumstances, such as those trapped in situations of armed conflict and women refugees.

[...]

25. Women with disabilities, of all ages, often have difficulty with physical access to health services. Women with mental disabilities are particularly vulnerable, while there is limited understanding, in general, of the broad range of risks to mental health to which women are disproportionately susceptible as a result of gender discrimination, violence, poverty, armed conflict, dislocation and other forms of social deprivation. States parties should take appropriate measures to ensure that health services are sensitive to the needs of women with disabilities and are respectful of their human rights and dignity.

[...]

* Source: U.N.Doc. A/54/38/Rev.1.

CESCR General Comment No.14: Article 12 (The Right to the Highest Attainable Standard of Health), 2000 [excerpts] *

Adoption: 11 August 2000

I. NORMATIVE CONTENT OF ARTICLE 12

[...]

8. The right to health is not to be understood as a right to be healthy. The right to health contains both freedoms and entitlements. The freedoms include the right to control one's health and body, including sexual and reproductive freedom, and the right to be free from interference, such as the right to be free from torture, non-consensual medical treatment and experimentation. By contrast, the entitlements include the right to a system of health protection which provides equality of opportunity for people to enjoy the highest attainable level of health.

9. The notion of "the highest attainable standard of health" in article 12.1 takes into account both the individual's biological and socio-economic preconditions and a State's available resources. There are a number of aspects which cannot be addressed solely within the relationship between States and individuals; in particular, good health cannot be ensured by a State, nor can States provide protection against every possible cause of human ill health. Thus, genetic factors, individual susceptibility to ill health and the adoption of unhealthy or risky lifestyles may play an important role with respect to an individual's health. Consequently, the right to health must be understood as a right to the enjoyment of a variety of facilities, goods, services and conditions necessary for the realization of the highest attainable standard of health.

[...]

12. The right to health in all its forms and at all levels contains the following interrelated and essential elements, the precise application of which will depend on the conditions prevailing in a particular State party:

[...]

(b) Accessibility. Health facilities, goods and services (6) have to be accessible to everyone without discrimination, within the jurisdiction of the State party. Accessibility has four overlapping dimensions:

Non-discrimination: health facilities, goods and services must be accessible to all, especially the most vulnerable or marginalized sections of the population, in law and in fact, without discrimination on any of the prohibited grounds. (7)

Physical accessibility: health facilities, goods and services must be within safe physical reach for all sections of the population, especially vulnerable or marginalized groups, such as ethnic minorities and indigenous populations, women, children, adolescents, older persons, persons with disabilities and persons with HIV/AIDS. Accessibility also implies that medical services and underlying determinants of health, such as safe and potable water and adequate sanitation facilities, are within safe physical reach, including in rural areas. Accessibility further includes adequate access to buildings for persons with disabilities.

[...]

* Source: U.N.Doc. E/C.12/2000/4.

II. STATES PARTIES' OBLIGATIONS

[...]

Specific legal obligations

34. In particular, States are under the obligation to respect the right to health by, inter alia, refraining from denying or limiting equal access for all persons, including prisoners or detainees, minorities, asylum seekers and illegal immigrants, to preventive, curative and palliative health services; abstaining from enforcing discriminatory practices as a State policy; and abstaining from imposing discriminatory practices relating to women's health status and needs. Furthermore, obligations to respect include a State's obligation to refrain from prohibiting or impeding traditional preventive care, healing practices and medicines, from marketing unsafe drugs and from applying coercive medical treatments, unless on an exceptional basis for the treatment of mental illness or the prevention and control of communicable diseases. Such exceptional cases should be subject to specific and restrictive conditions, respecting best practices and applicable international standards, including the Principles for the Protection of Persons with Mental Illness and the Improvement of Mental Health Care.[1]

[...]

[1] General Assembly resolution 46/119 (1991).

CRC General Comment No. 3: HIV/AIDS and the Rights of the Child, 2003 [excerpts] *

Adoption: 17 March 2003

[...]

IV. Prevention, Care, Treatment and Support

[...]

C. Child and adolescent sensitive health services

21. In some countries, even when child- and adolescent-friendly HIV-related services are available, they are not sufficiently accessible to children with disabilities, indigenous children, children belonging to minorities, children living in rural areas, children living in extreme poverty or children who are otherwise marginalized within the society. In others, where the health system's overall capacity is already strained, children with HIV have been routinely denied access to basic health care. States parties must ensure that services are provided to the maximum extent possible to all children living within their borders, without discrimination, and that they sufficiently take into account differences in gender, age and the social, economic, cultural and political context in which children live.

[...]

V. Vulnerability and Children Needing Special Protection

30. The vulnerability of children to HIV/AIDS resulting from political, economic, social, cultural and other factors determines the likelihood of their being left with insufficient support to cope with the impact of HIV/AIDS on their families and communities, exposed to the risk of infection, subjected to inappropriate research, or deprived of access to treatment, care and support if and when HIV infection sets in. Vulnerability to HIV/AIDS is most acute for children living in refugee and internally displaced persons camps, children in detention, children living in institutions, as well as children living in extreme poverty, children living in situations of armed conflict, child soldiers, economically and sexually exploited children, and disabled, migrant, minority, indigenous, and street children. However, all children can be rendered vulnerable by the particular circumstances of their lives. Even in times of severe resource constraints, the Committee wishes to note that the rights of vulnerable members of society must be protected and that many measures can be pursued with minimum resource implications. Reducing vulnerability to HIV/AIDS requires first and foremost that children, their families and communities be empowered to make informed choices about decisions, practices or policies affecting them in relation to HIV/AIDS.

[...]

B. Victims of sexual and economic exploitation

36. Girls and boys who are deprived of the means of survival and development, particularly children orphaned by AIDS, may be subjected to sexual and economic exploitation in a variety of ways, including the exchange of sexual services or hazardous work for money to survive, support their sick or dying parents and younger siblings, or to pay for school fees. Children who

* Source: U.N.Doc. CRC/GC/2003/3.

are infected or directly affected by HIV/AIDS may find themselves at a double disadvantage – experiencing discrimination on the basis of both their social and economic marginalization and their, or their parents', HIV status. Consistent with the right of children under articles 32, 34, 35 and 36 of the Convention, and in order to reduce children's vulnerability to HIV/AIDS, States parties are under obligation to protect children from all forms of economic and sexual exploitation, including ensuring they do not fall prey to prostitution networks, and that they are protected from performing any work likely to be prejudicial to, or to interfere with, their education, health, or physical, mental, spiritual, moral or social development. States parties must take bold action to protect children from sexual and economic exploitation, trafficking and sale and, consistent with the rights under article 39, create opportunities for those who have been subjected to such treatment to benefit from the support and caring services of the State and non-governmental entities engaged in these issues.

C. Victims of violence and abuse

[...]

38. Programmes must be specifically adapted to the environment in which children live, to their ability to recognize and report abuses and to their individual capacity and autonomy. The Committee considers that the relationship between HIV/AIDS and the violence or abuse suffered by children in the context of war and armed conflict requires specific attention. Measures to prevent violence and abuse in these situations are critical, and States parties must ensure the incorporation of HIV/AIDS and child rights issues in addressing and supporting children – girls and boys – who were used by military or other uniformed personnel to provide domestic help or sexual services, or who are internally displaced or living in refugee camps. In keeping with States parties' obligations, including under articles 38 and 39 of the Convention, active information campaigns, combined with the counselling of children and mechanisms for the prevention and early detection of violence and abuse, must be put in place within conflict- and disaster-affected regions, and must form part of national and community responses to HIV/AIDS.

[...]

VI. Recommendations

40. The Committee hereby reaffirms the recommendations, which emerged at the day of general discussion on children living in a world with HIV/AIDS (CRC/C/80), and calls upon States parties:

[...]

(c) To review existing laws or enact new legislation with a view to implementing fully article 2 of the Convention, and in particular to expressly prohibiting discrimination based on real or perceived HIV/AIDS status so as to guarantee equal access for of all children to all relevant services, with particular attention to the child's right to privacy and confidentiality and to other recommendations made by the Committee in the previous paragraphs relevant to legislation;

[...]

(e) To reassess their HIV-related data collection and evaluation to ensure that they adequately cover children as defined under the Convention, are disaggregated by age and gender ideally in five-year age groups, and include, as far as possible, children belonging to vulnerable groups and those in need of special protection;

[...]

CRC General Comment No. 4: Adolescent Health and Development in the Context of the Convention on the Rights of the Child, 2003 [excerpts] *

Adoption: 1 July 2003

[...]

IV. Vulnerability and Risks

[...]

37. Adolescents who are sexually exploited, including in prostitution and pornography, are exposed to significant health risks, including STDs, HIV/AIDS, unwanted pregnancies, unsafe abortions, violence and psychological distress. They have the right to physical and psychological recovery and social reintegration in an environment that fosters health, self respect and dignity (art. 39). It is the obligation of States parties to enact and enforce laws to prohibit all forms of sexual exploitation and related trafficking; to collaborate with other States parties to eliminate intercountry trafficking; and to provide appropriate health and counselling services to adolescents who have been sexually exploited, making sure that they are treated as victims and not as offenders.

38. Additionally, adolescents experiencing poverty, armed conflicts, all forms of injustice, family breakdown, political, social and economic instability and all types of migration may be particularly vulnerable. These situations might seriously hamper their health and development. By investing heavily in preventive policies and measures States parties can drastically reduce levels of vulnerability and risk factors; they will also provide cost-effective ways for society to help adolescents develop harmoniously in a free society.

[...]

* Source: U.N. Doc. CRC/GC/2003/4.

CESCR General Comment No.18: Article 6 (The Right to Work), 2005 [excerpts] *

Adoption: 24 November 2005

I. INTRODUCTION AND BASIC PREMISES

1. The right to work is a fundamental right, recognized in several international legal instruments. The International Covenant on Economic, Social and Cultural Rights (ICESCR), as laid down in article 6, deals more comprehensively than any other instrument with this right. The right to work is essential for realizing other human rights and forms an inseparable and inherent part of human dignity. Every individual has the right to be able to work, allowing him/her to live in dignity. The right to work contributes at the same time to the survival of the individual and to that of his/her family, and insofar as work is freely chosen or accepted, to his/her development and recognition within the community.[1]

2. The ICESCR proclaims the right to work in a general sense in its article 6 and explicitly develops the individual dimension of the right to work through the recognition in article 7 of the right of everyone to the enjoyment of just and favourable conditions of work, in particular the right to safe working conditions. The collective dimension of the right to work is addressed in article 8, which enunciates the right of everyone to form trade unions and join the trade union of his/her choice as well as the right of trade unions to function freely. When drafting article 6 of the Covenant, the Commission on Human Rights affirmed the need to recognize the right to work in a broad sense by laying down specific legal obligations rather than a simple philosophical principle.[2] Article 6 defines the right to work in a general and non-exhaustive manner. In article 6, paragraph 1, States parties recognize "the right to work, which includes the right of everyone to the opportunity to gain his living by work which he freely chooses or accepts, and will take appropriate steps to safeguard this right". In paragraph 2, States parties recognize that "to achieve the full realization of this right" the steps to be taken "shall include technical and vocational guidance and training programmes, policies and techniques to achieve steady economic, social and cultural development and full and productive employment, under conditions safeguarding fundamental political and economic freedoms to the individual".

[...]

4. The right to work, as guaranteed in the ICESCR, affirms the obligation of States parties to assure individuals their right to freely chosen or accepted work, including the right not to be deprived of work unfairly. This definition underlines the fact that respect for the individual and his dignity is expressed through the freedom of the individual regarding the choice to work, while emphasizing the importance of work for personal development as well as for social and economic inclusion. International Labour Organization Convention No.122 concerning Employment Policy (1964) speaks of "full, productive and freely chosen employment", linking the obligation of States parties to create the conditions for full employment with the obligation to ensure the absence of forced labour. Nevertheless, for millions of human beings

* Source: U.N.Doc. E/C.12/GC/18.

[1] See the preamble to ILO Convention No.168, 1988: "... the importance of work and productive employment in any society not only because of the resources which they create for the community, but also because of the income which they bring to workers, the social role which they confer and the feeling of self-esteem which workers derive from them."

[2] Commission on Human Rights, eleventh session, agenda item 31, A/3525 (1957).

throughout the world, full enjoyment of the right to freely chosen or accepted work remains a remote prospect. The Committee recognizes the existence of structural and other obstacles arising from international factors beyond the control of States which hinder the full enjoyment of article 6 in many States parties.

[...]

II. NORMATIVE CONTENT OF THE RIGHT TO WORK

6. The right to work is an individual right that belongs to each person and is at the same time a collective right. It encompasses all forms of work, whether independent work or dependent wage-paid work. The right to work should not be understood as an absolute and unconditional right to obtain employment. Article 6, paragraph 1, contains a definition of the right to work and paragraph 2 cites, by way of illustration and in a non-exhaustive manner, examples of obligations incumbent upon States parties. It includes the right of every human being to decide freely to accept or choose work. This implies not being forced in any way whatsoever to exercise or engage in employment and the right of access to a system of protection guaranteeing each worker access to employment. It also implies the right not to be unfairly deprived of employment.

7. Work as specified in article 6 of the Covenant must be decent work. This is work that respects the fundamental rights of the human person as well as the rights of workers in terms of conditions of work safety and remuneration. It also provides an income allowing workers to support themselves and their families as highlighted in article 7 of the Covenant. These fundamental rights also include respect for the physical and mental integrity of the worker in the exercise of his/her employment.

[...]

Special topics of broad application

Women and the right to work

13. Article 3 of the Covenant prescribes that States parties undertake to "ensure the equal right of men and women to the enjoyment of all economic, social and cultural rights". The Committee underlines the need for a comprehensive system of protection to combat gender discrimination and to ensure equal opportunities and treatment between men and women in relation to their right to work by ensuring equal pay for work of equal value.[3] In particular, pregnancies must not constitute an obstacle to employment and should not constitute justification for loss of employment. Lastly, emphasis should be placed on the link between the fact that women often have less access to education than men and certain traditional cultures which compromise the opportunities for the employment and advancement of women.

Young persons and the right to work

14. Access to a first job constitutes an opportunity for economic self-reliance and in many cases a means to escape poverty. Young persons, particularly young women, generally have great difficulties in finding initial employment. National policies relating to adequate education and vocational training should be adopted and implemented to promote and support access to employment opportunities for young persons, in particular young women.

---

[3] See general comment No.16 (2005) on article 3: the equal right of men and women to the enjoyment of all economic, social and cultural rights, paragraphs 23-25.

Child labour and the right to work

15. The protection of children is covered by article 10 of the Covenant. The Committee recalls its general comment No.14 (2000) and in particular paragraphs 22 and 23 on children's right to health, and emphasizes the need to protect children from all forms of work that are likely to interfere with their development or physical or mental health. The Committee reaffirms the need to protect children from economic exploitation, to enable them to pursue their full development and acquire technical and vocational education as indicated in article 6, paragraph 2. The Committee also recalls its general comment No.13 (1999), in particular the definition of technical and vocational education (paras. 15 and 16) as a component of general education. Several international human rights instruments adopted after the ICESCR, such as the Convention on the Rights of the Child, expressly recognize the need to protect children and young people against any form of economic exploitation or forced labour.[4]

[...]

Migrant workers and the right to work

18. The principle of non-discrimination as set out in article 2.2 of the Covenant and in article 7 of the International Convention on the Protection of the Rights of All Migrant Workers and Members of Their Families should apply in relation to employment opportunities for migrant workers and their families. In this regard the Committee underlines the need for national plans of action to be devised to respect and promote such principles by all appropriate measures, legislative or otherwise.

III. STATES PARTIES' OBLIGATIONS

General legal obligations

19. The principal obligation of States parties is to ensure the progressive realization of the exercise of the right to work. States parties must therefore adopt, as quickly as possible, measures aiming at achieving full employment. While the Covenant provides for progressive realization and acknowledges the constraints due to the limits of available resources, it also imposes on States parties various obligations which are of immediate effect.[5] States parties have immediate obligations in relation to the right to work, such as the obligation to "guarantee" that it will be exercised "without discrimination of any kind" (art. 2, para. 2) and the obligation "to take steps" (art. 2, para. 1) towards the full realization of article 6.[6] Such steps must be deliberate, concrete and targeted towards the full realization of the right to work.

20. The fact that realization of the right to work is progressive and takes place over a period of time should not be interpreted as depriving States parties' obligations of all meaningful content.[7] It means that States parties have a specific and continuing obligation "to move as expeditiously and effectively as possible" towards the full realization of article 6.

21. As with all other rights in the Covenant, retrogressive measures should in principle not be taken in relation to the right to work. If any deliberately retrogressive steps are taken, States

---

[4] See the Convention on the Rights of the Child, 1989, article 32, paragraph 1, reflected in the second preambular paragraph of the Optional Protocol to the Convention on the Rights of the Child on the sale of children, child prostitution and child pornography. See also article 3, paragraph 1, of the Protocol, on forced labour.

[5] See general comment No.3 (1990) on the nature of States parties' obligations, paragraph 1.

[6] Ibid, para. 2.

[7] Ibid, para. 9.

parties have the burden of proving that they have been introduced after consideration of all alternatives and that they are duly justified by reference to the totality of the rights provided for in the Covenant in the context of the full use of the States parties' maximum available resources.[8]

[...]

International obligations

29. In its general comment No.3 (1990) the Committee draws attention to the obligation of all States parties to take steps individually and through international assistance and cooperation, especially economic and technical, towards the full realization of the rights recognized in the Covenant. In the spirit of Article 56 of the Charter of the United Nations and specific provisions of the Covenant (arts. 2.1, 6, 22 and 23), States parties should recognize the essential role of international cooperation and comply with their commitment to take joint and separate action to achieve the full realization of the right to work. States parties should, through international agreements where appropriate, ensure that the right to work as set forth in articles 6, 7 and 8 of the Covenant is given due attention.

30. To comply with their international obligations in relation to article 6, States parties should endeavour to promote the right to work in other countries as well as in bilateral and multilateral negotiations. In negotiations with international financial institutions, States parties should ensure protection of the right to work of their population. States parties that are members of international financial institutions, in particular the International Monetary Fund, the World Bank and regional development banks, should pay greater attention to the protection of the right to work in influencing the lending policies, credit agreements, structural adjustment programmes and international measures of these institutions. The strategies, programmes and policies adopted by States parties under structural adjustment programmes should not interfere with their core obligations in relation to the right to work and impact negatively on the right to work of women, young persons and the disadvantaged and marginalized individuals and groups.

Core obligations

31. In general comment No.3 (1990) the Committee confirms that States parties have a core obligation to ensure the satisfaction of minimum essential levels of each of the rights covered by the Covenant. In the context of article 6, this "core obligation" encompasses the obligation to ensure non-discrimination and equal protection of employment. Discrimination in the field of employment comprises a broad cluster of violations affecting all stages of life, from basic education to retirement, and can have a considerable impact on the work situation of individuals and groups. Accordingly, these core obligations include at least the following requirements:

(a) To ensure the right of access to employment, especially for disadvantaged and marginalized individuals and groups, permitting them to live a life of dignity;

(b) To avoid any measure that results in discrimination and unequal treatment in the private and public sectors of disadvantaged and marginalized individuals and groups or in weakening mechanisms for the protection of such individuals and groups;

(c) To adopt and implement a national employment strategy and plan of action based on and addressing the concerns of all workers on the basis of a participatory and transparent process

---

[8] Ibid, para. 9.

that includes employers' and workers' organizations. Such an employment strategy and plan of action should target disadvantaged and marginalized individuals and groups in particular and include indicators and benchmarks by which progress in relation to the right to work can be measured and periodically reviewed.

[...]

CCPR General Comment No.8: Article 9 (Right to Liberty and Security of Persons), 1982 (See section 7)

CCPR General Comment No.21: Article 10 (Humane Treatment of Persons Deprived of Liberty), 1992 (See section 7)

CCPR General Comment No.23: Article 27 (The Rights of Minorities), 1994 (See section 11)

CERD General Recommendation No.22: Article 5 and Refugees and Displaced Persons, 1996 (See section 12)

CCPR General Comment No.29: Article 4 (States of Emergency), 2001 (See section 6)

2. INTERNATIONAL LABOUR LAW

2.1 International Standards Relating to Migrant Workers

Convention No.97 concerning Migration for Employment (Revised, 1949)*

Adoption: 1 July 1949
Entry into force: 22 January 1952
Parties: 45 (Status as of 1 April 2007)

ALBANIA 2 Mar 2005, ALGERIA 19 Oct 1962 (* Annex II), ARMENIA 27 Jan 2006, BAHAMAS 25 May 1976 (* Annex I-III), BARBADOS 8 May 1967, BELGIUM 27 July 1953 (*Annex III), BELIZE 15 Dec 1983, BOSNIA AND HERZEGOVINA 2 June 1993, BRAZIL 18 June 1965, BURKINA FASO 9 June 1961, CAMEROON 3 Sep 1962(* Annex I-III), CUBA 29 Apr 1952, CYPRUS 23 Sep 1960(* Annex I-III), DOMINICA 28 Feb 1983(* Annex I-III), ECUADOR 5 Apr 1978(* Annex I-III), FRANCE 29 Mar 1954 (*Annex II), GERMANY 22 June 1959, GRENADA 9 July 1979(* Annex I-III), GUATEMALA 13 Feb 1952, GUYANA 8 June 1966(* Annex I-III), ISRAEL 30 Mar 1953, ITALY 22 Oct 1952, JAMAICA 26 Dec 1962(* Annex I-III), KENYA 30 Nov 1965(* Annex I-III), THE FORMER YUGOSLAV REPUBLIC OF MACEDONIA 17 Nov 1991, MADAGASCAR 14 June 2001(* Annex III), MALAWI 22 Mar 1965, MALAYSIA SABAH 3 Mar 1964(* Annex I-III), MAURITIUS 2 Dec 1969(* Annex I-III), REPUBLIC OF MOLDOVA 12 Dec 2005, NETHERLANDS 20 May 1952, NEW ZEALAND 10 Nov 1950 (*Annex I), NIGERIA 17 Oct 1950(* Annex I-III), NORWAY 17 Feb 1955, PORTUGAL 12 Dec 1978, SAINT LUCIA 14 May 1980(* Annex I-III), SERBIA 24 Nov 2000 (*Annex III), SLOVENIA 29 Feb 1992 (*Annex III), SPAIN 21 Mar 1967, TANZANIA ZANZIBAR 22 June 1964(* Annex I-III), TRINIDAD AND TOBAGO 24 May 1963(* Annex I-III), UNITED KINGDOM 22 Jan 1951(* Annex I-III), URUGAY 18 Mar 1954, VENEZUELA (BOLIVARIAN REPUBLIC OF) 9 June 1983, ZAMBIA 2 Dec 1964(* Annex I-III).

The General Conference of the International Labour Organisation,

Having been convened at Geneva by the Governing Body of the International Labour Office, and having met in its Thirty-second Session on 8 June 1949, and

Having decided upon the adoption of certain proposals with regard to the revision of the Migration for Employment Convention, 1939, adopted by the Conference at its Twenty-fifth Session, which is included in the eleventh item on the agenda of the session, and

Considering that these proposals must take the form of an international Convention,

adopts this first day of July of the year one thousand nine hundred and forty-nine the following Convention, which may be cited as the Migration for Employment Convention (Revised), 1949:

---

* Source: International Labour Organization, http://www.ilo.org/ilolex
The ILO shall accept no responsibility for any inaccuracy, errors or omissions or for the consequences arising from the use of the Text.

Article 1

Each Member of the International Labour Organisation for which this Convention is in force undertakes to make available on request to the International Labour Office and to other Members–

(a) information on national policies, laws and regulations relating to emigration and immigration;

(b) information on special provisions concerning migration for employment and the conditions of work and livelihood of migrants for employment;

(c) information concerning general agreements and special arrangements on these questions concluded by the Member.

Article 2

Each Member for which this Convention is in force undertakes to maintain, or satisfy itself that there is maintained, an adequate and free service to assist migrants for employment, and in particular to provide them with accurate information.

Article 3

1. Each Member for which this Convention is in force undertakes that it will, so far as national laws and regulations permit, take all appropriate steps against misleading propaganda relating to emigration and immigration.

2. For this purpose, it will where appropriate act in co-operation with other Members concerned.

Article 4

Measures shall be taken as appropriate by each Member, within its jurisdiction, to facilitate the departure, journey and reception of migrants for employment.

Article 5

Each Member for which this Convention is in force undertakes to maintain, within its jurisdiction, appropriate medical services responsible for–

(a) ascertaining, where necessary, both at the time of departure and on arrival, that migrants for employment and the members of their families authorised to accompany or join them are in reasonable health;

(b) ensuring that migrants for employment and members of their families enjoy adequate medical attention and good hygienic conditions at the time of departure, during the journey and on arrival in the territory of destination.

Article 6

1. Each Member for which this Convention is in force undertakes to apply, without discrimination in respect of nationality, race, religion or sex, to immigrants lawfully within its territory, treatment no less favourable than that which it applies to its own nationals in respect of the following matters:

(a) in so far as such matters are regulated by law or regulations, or are subject to the control of administrative authorities–

(i) remuneration, including family allowances where these form part of remuneration, hours of work, overtime arrangements, holidays with pay, restrictions on home work, minimum age for employment, apprenticeship and training, women's work and the work of young persons;

(ii) membership of trade unions and enjoyment of the benefits of collective bargaining;

(iii) accommodation;

(b) social security (that is to say, legal provision in respect of employment injury, maternity, sickness, invalidity, old age, death, unemployment and family responsibilities, and any other contingency which, according to national laws or regulations, is covered by a social security scheme), subject to the following limitations:

(i) there may be appropriate arrangements for the maintenance of acquired rights and rights in course of acquisition;

(ii) national laws or regulations of immigration countries may prescribe special arrangements concerning benefits or portions of benefits which are payable wholly out of public funds, and concerning allowances paid to persons who do not fulfil the contribution conditions prescribed for the award of a normal pension;

(c) employment taxes, dues or contributions payable in respect of the person employed; and

(d) legal proceedings relating to the matters referred to in this Convention.

2. In the case of a federal State the provisions of this Article shall apply in so far as the matters dealt with are regulated by federal law or regulations or are subject to the control of federal administrative authorities. The extent to which and manner in which these provisions shall be applied in respect of matters regulated by the law or regulations of the constituent States, provinces or cantons, or subject to the control of the administrative authorities thereof, shall be determined by each Member. The Member shall indicate in its annual report upon the application of the Convention the extent to which the matters dealt with in this Article are regulated by federal law or regulations or are subject to the control of federal administrative authorities. In respect of matters which are regulated by the law or regulations of the constituent States, provinces or cantons, or are subject to the control of the administrative authorities thereof, the Member shall take the steps provided for in paragraph 7 (b) of Article 19 of the Constitution of the International Labour Organisation.

Article 7

1. Each Member for which this Convention is in force undertakes that its employment service and other services connected with migration will co-operate in appropriate cases with the corresponding services of other Members.

2. Each Member for which this Convention is in force undertakes to ensure that the services rendered by its public employment service to migrants for employment are rendered free.

Article 8

1. A migrant for employment who has been admitted on a permanent basis and the members of his family who have been authorised to accompany or join him shall not be returned to their territory of origin or the territory from which they emigrated because the migrant is unable to follow his occupation by reason of illness contracted or injury sustained subsequent to entry, unless the person concerned so desires or an international agreement to which the Member is a party so provides.

2. When migrants for employment are admitted on a permanent basis upon arrival in the country of immigration the competent authority of that country may determine that the provisions of paragraph 1 of this Article shall take effect only after a reasonable period which shall in no case exceed five years from the date of admission of such migrants.

Article 9

Each Member for which this Convention is in force undertakes to permit, taking into account the limits allowed by national laws and regulations concerning export and import of currency, the transfer of such part of the earnings and savings of the migrant for employment as the migrant may desire.

Article 10

In cases where the number of migrants going from the territory of one Member to that of another is sufficiently large, the competent authorities of the territories concerned shall, whenever necessary or desirable, enter into agreements for the purpose of regulating matters of common concern arising in connection with the application of the provisions of this Convention.

Article 11

1. For the purpose of this Convention the term migrant for employment means a person who migrates from one country to another with a view to being employed otherwise than on his own account and includes any person regularly admitted as a migrant for employment.

2. This Convention does not apply to–

(a) frontier workers;

(b) short-term entry of members of the liberal professions and artistes; and

(c) seamen.

Article 12

The formal ratifications of this Convention shall be communicated to the Director-General of the International Labour Office for registration.

Article 13

1. This Convention shall be binding only upon those Members of the International Labour Organisation whose ratifications have been registered with the Director-General.

2. It shall come into force twelve months after the date on which the ratifications of two Members have been registered with the Director-General.

3. Thereafter, this Convention shall come into force for any Member twelve months after the date on which its ratification has been registered.

Article 14

1. Each Member ratifying this Convention may, by a declaration appended to its ratification, exclude from its ratification any or all of the Annexes to the Convention.

2. Subject to the terms of any such declaration, the provisions of the Annexes shall have the same effect as the provisions of the Convention.

3. Any Member which makes such a declaration may subsequently by a new declaration notify the Director-General that it accepts any or all of the Annexes mentioned in the declaration; as from the date of the registration of such notification by the Director-General the provisions of such Annexes shall be applicable to the Member in question.

4. While a declaration made under paragraph 1 of this Article remains in force in respect of any Annex, the Member may declare its willingness to accept that Annex as having the force of a Recommendation.

Article 15

1. Declarations communicated to the Director-General of the International Labour Office in accordance with paragraph 2 of Article 35 of the Constitution of the International Labour Organisation shall indicate –

a) the territories in respect of which the Member concerned undertakes that the provisions of the Convention and any or all of the Annexes shall be applied without modification;

b) the territories in respect of which it undertakes that the provisions of the Convention and any or all of the Annexes shall be applied subject to modifications, together with details of the said modifications;

c) the territories in respect of which the Convention and any or all of the Annexes are inapplicable and in such cases the grounds on which they are inapplicable;

d) the territories in respect of which it reserves its decision pending further consideration of the position.

2. The undertakings referred to in subparagraphs (a) and (b) of paragraph 1 of this Article shall be deemed to be an integral part of the ratification and shall have the force of ratification.

3. Any Member may at any time by a subsequent declaration cancel in whole or in part any reservations made in its original declaration in virtue of subparagraph (b), (c) or (d) of paragraph 1 of this Article.

4. Any Member may, at any time at which the Convention is subject to denunciation in accordance with the provisions of Article 17, communicate to the Director-General a declaration modifying in any other respect the terms of any former declaration and stating the present position in respect of such territories as it may specify.

Article 16

1. Declarations communicated to the Director-General of the International Labour Office in accordance with paragraph 4 or 5 of Article 35 of the Constitution of the International Labour Organisation shall indicate whether the provisions of the Convention and any or all of the Annexes will be applied in the territory concerned without modification or subject to modifications; and if the declaration indicates that the provisions of the Convention and any or all of the Annexes will be applied subject to modifications, it shall give details of the said modifications.

2. The Member, Members or international authority concerned may at any time by a subsequent declaration renounce in whole or in part the right to have recourse to any modification indicated in any former declaration.

3. The Member, Members or international authority concerned may, at any time at which this Convention and any or all of the Annexes are subject to denunciation in accordance with the

provisions of Article 17, communicate to the Director-General a declaration modifying in any other respect the terms of any former declaration and stating the present position in respect of the application of the Convention.

Article 17

1. A Member which has ratified this Convention may denounce it after the expiration of ten years from the date on which the Convention first comes into force, by an act communicated to the Director-General of the International Labour Office for registration. Such denunciation shall not take effect until one year after the date on which it is registered.

2. Each Member which has ratified this Convention and which does not, within the year following the expiration of the period of ten years mentioned in the preceding paragraph, exercise the right of denunciation provided for in this Article, will be bound for another period of ten years and, thereafter, may denounce this Convention at the expiration of each period of ten years under the terms provided for in this Article.

3. At any time at which this Convention is subject to denunciation in accordance with the provisions of the preceding paragraphs any Member which does not so denounce it may communicate to the Director-General a declaration denouncing separately any Annex to the Convention which is in force for that Member.

4. The denunciation of this Convention or of any or all of the Annexes shall not affect the rights granted thereunder to a migrant or to the members of his family if he immigrated while the Convention or the relevant Annex was in force in respect of the territory where the question of the continued validity of these rights arises.

Article 18

1. The Director-General of the International Labour Office shall notify all Members of the International Labour Organisation of the registration of all ratifications, declarations and denunciations communicated to him by the Members of the Organisation.

2. When notifying the Members of the Organisation of the registration of the second ratification communicated to him, the Director-General shall draw the attention of the Members of the Organisation to the date upon which the Convention will come into force.

Article 19

The Director-General of the International Labour Office shall communicate to the Secretary-General of the United Nations for registration in accordance with Article 102 of the Charter of the United Nations full particulars of all ratifications, declarations and acts of denunciation registered by him in accordance with the provisions of the preceding articles.

Article 20

At such times as it may consider necessary the Governing Body of the International Labour Office shall present to the General Conference a report on the working of this Convention and shall examine the desirability of placing on the agenda of the Conference the question of its revision in whole or in part.

Article 21

1. Should the Conference adopt a new Convention revising this Convention in whole or in part, then, unless the new Convention otherwise provides:

a) the ratification by a Member of the new revising Convention shall ipso jure involve the immediate denunciation of this Convention, notwithstanding the provisions of Article 17 above, if and when the new revising Convention shall have come into force;

b) as from the date when the new revising Convention comes into force this Convention shall cease to be open to ratification by the Members.

2. This Convention shall in any case remain in force in its actual form and content for those Members which have ratified it but have not ratified the revising Convention.

Article 22

1. The International Labour Conference may, at any session at which the matter is included in its agenda, adopt by a two-thirds majority a revised text of any one or more of the Annexes to this Convention.

2. Each Member for which this Convention is in force shall, within the period of one year, or, in exceptional circumstances, of eighteen months, from the closing of the session of the Conference, submit any such revised text to the authority or authorities within whose competence the matter lies, for the enactment of legislation or other action.

3. Any such revised text shall become effective for each Member for which this Convention is in force on communication by that Member to the Director-General of the International Labour Office of a declaration notifying its acceptance of the revised text.

4. As from the date of the adoption of the revised text of the Annex by the Conference, only the revised text shall be open to acceptance by Members.

Article 23

The English and French versions of the text of this Convention are equally authoritative.

ANNEX I

RECRUITMENT, PLACING AND CONDITIONS OF LABOUR OF MIGRANTS FOR EMPLOYMENT RECRUITED OTHERWISE THAN UNDER GOVERNMENT-SPONSORED ARRANGEMENTS FOR GROUP TRANSFER

Article 1

This Annex applies to migrants for employment who are recruited otherwise than under Government-sponsored arrangements for group transfer.

Article 2

For the purpose of this Annex–

(a) the term recruitment means–

(i) the engagement of a person in one territory on behalf of an employer in another territory, or

(ii) the giving of an undertaking to a person in one territory to provide him with employment in another territory, together with the making of any arrangements in connection with the operations mentioned in (i) and (ii) including the seeking for and selection of emigrants and the preparation for departure of the emigrants;

(b) the term introduction means any operations for ensuring or facilitating the arrival in or admission to a territory of persons who have been recruited within the meaning of paragraph (a) of this Article; and

(c) the term placing means any operations for the purpose of ensuring or facilitating the employment of persons who have been introduced within the meaning of paragraph (b) of this Article.

Article 3

1. Each Member for which this Annex is in force, the laws and regulations of which permit the operations of recruitment, introduction and placing as defined in Article 2, shall regulate such of the said operations as are permitted by its laws and regulations in accordance with the provisions of this Article.

2. Subject to the provisions of the following paragraph, the right to engage in the operations of recruitment, introduction and placing shall be restricted to–

(a) public employment offices or other public bodies of the territory in which the operations take place;

(b) public bodies of a territory other than that in which the operations take place which are authorised to operate in that territory by agreement between the Governments concerned;

(c) any body established in accordance with the terms of an international instrument.

3. In so far as national laws and regulations or a bilateral arrangement permit, the operations of recruitment, introduction and placing may be undertaken by–

(a) the prospective employer or a person in his service acting on his behalf, subject, if necessary in the interest of the migrant, to the approval and supervision of the competent authority;

(b) a private agency, if given prior authorisation so to do by the competent authority of the territory where the said operations are to take place, in such cases and under such conditions as may be prescribed by–

(i) the laws and regulations of that territory, or

(ii) agreement between the competent authority of the territory of emigration or any body established in accordance with the terms of an international instrument and the competent authority of the territory of immigration.

4. The competent authority of the territory where the operations take place shall supervise the activities of bodies and persons to whom authorisations have been issued in pursuance of paragraph 3 (b), other than any body established in accordance with the terms of an international instrument, the position of which shall continue to be governed by the terms of the said instrument or by any agreement made between the body and the competent authority concerned.

5. Nothing in this Article shall be deemed to permit the acceptance of a migrant for employment for admission to the territory of any Member by any person or body other than the competent authority of the territory of immigration.

Article 4

Each Member for which this Annex is in force undertakes to ensure that the services rendered by its public employment service in connection with the recruitment, introduction or placing of migrants for employment are rendered free.

Article 5

1. Each Member for which this Annex is in force which maintains a system of supervision of contracts of employment between an employer, or a person acting on his behalf, and a migrant for employment undertakes to require–

(a) that a copy of the contract of employment shall be delivered to the migrant before departure or, if the Governments concerned so agree, in a reception centre on arrival in the territory of immigration;

(b) that the contract shall contain provisions indicating the conditions of work and particularly the remuneration offered to the migrant;

(c) that the migrant shall receive in writing before departure, by a document which relates either to him individually or to a group of migrants of which he is a member, information concerning the general conditions of life and work applicable to him in the territory of immigration.

2. Where a copy of the contract is to be delivered to the migrant on arrival in the territory of immigration, he shall be informed in writing before departure, by a document which relates either to him individually or to a group of migrants of which he is a member, of the occupational category for which he is engaged and the other conditions of work, in particular the minimum wage which is guaranteed to him.

3. The competent authority shall ensure that the provisions of the preceding paragraphs are enforced and that appropriate penalties are applied in respect of violations thereof.

Article 6

The measures taken under Article 4 of the Convention shall, as appropriate, include–

(a) the simplification of administrative formalities;

(b) the provision of interpretation services;

(c) any necessary assistance during an initial period in the settlement of the migrants and members of their families authorised to accompany or join them; and

(d) the safeguarding of the welfare, during the journey and in particular on board ship, of migrants and members of their families authorised to accompany or join them.

Article 7

1. In cases where the number of migrants for employment going from the territory of one Member to that of another is sufficiently large, the competent authorities of the territories concerned shall, whenever necessary or desirable, enter into agreements for the purpose of regulating matters of common concern arising in connection with the application of the provisions of this Annex.

2. Where the members maintain a system of supervision over contracts of employment, such agreements shall indicate the methods by which the contractual obligations of the employers shall be enforced.

Article 8

Any person who promotes clandestine or illegal immigration shall be subject to appropriate penalties.

ANNEX II

RECRUITMENT, PLACING AND CONDITIONS OF LABOUR OF MIGRANTS FOR EMPLOYMENT RECRUITED UNDER GOVERNMENT-SPONSORED ARRANGEMENTS FOR GROUP TRANSFER

Article 1

This Annex applies to migrants for employment who are recruited under Government-sponsored arrangements for group transfer.

Article 2

For the purpose of this Annex–

(a) the term recruitment means–

(i) the engagement of a person in one territory on behalf of an employer in another territory under a Government-sponsored arrangement for group transfer, or

(ii) the giving of an undertaking to a person in one territory to provide him with employment in another territory under a Government-sponsored arrangement for group transfer,
together with the making of any arrangements in connection with the operations mentioned in (i) and (ii) including the seeking for and selection of emigrants and the preparation for departure of the emigrants;

(b) the term introduction means any operations for ensuring or facilitating the arrival in or admission to a territory of persons who have been recruited under a Government-sponsored arrangement for group transfer within the meaning of subparagraph (a) of this paragraph; and

(c) the term placing means any operations for the purpose of ensuring or facilitating the employment of persons who have been introduced under a Government-sponsored arrangement for group transfer within the meaning of subparagraph (b) of this paragraph.

Article 3

1. Each Member for which this Annex is in force, the laws and regulations of which permit the operations of recruitment, introduction and placing as defined in Article 2, shall regulate such of the said operations as are permitted by its laws and regulations in accordance with the provisions of this Article.

2. Subject to the provisions of the following paragraph, the right to engage in the operations of recruitment, introduction and placing shall be restricted to–

(a) public employment offices or other public bodies of the territory in which the operations take place;

(b) public bodies of a territory other than that in which the operations take place which are authorised to operate in that territory by agreement between the Governments concerned;

(c) any body established in accordance with the terms of an international instrument.

3. In so far as national laws and regulations or a bilateral arrangement permit, and subject, if necessary in the interest of the migrant, to the approval and supervision of the competent authority, the operations of recruitment, introduction and placing may be undertaken by–

(a) the prospective employer or a person in his service acting on his behalf;

(b) private agencies.

4. The right to engage in the operations of recruitment, introduction and placing shall be subject to the prior authorisation of the competent authority of the territory where the said operations are to take place in such cases and under such conditions as may be prescribed by–

(a) the laws and regulations of that territory, or

(b) agreement between the competent authority of the territory of emigration or any body established in accordance with the terms of an international instrument and the competent authority of the territory of immigration.

5. The competent authority of the territory where the operations take place shall, in accordance with any agreements made between the competent authorities concerned, supervise the activities of bodies and persons to whom authorisations have been issued in pursuance of the preceding paragraph, other than any body established in accordance with the terms of an international instrument, the position of which shall continue to be governed by the terms of the said instrument or by any agreement made between the body and the competent authority concerned.

6. Before authorising the introduction of migrants for employment the competent authority of the territory of immigration shall ascertain whether there is not a sufficient number of persons already available capable of doing the work in question.

7. Nothing in this Article shall be deemed to permit the acceptance of a migrant for employment for admission to the territory of any Member by any person or body other than the competent authority of the territory of immigration.

Article 4

1. Each Member for which this Annex is in force undertakes to ensure that the services rendered by its public employment service in connection with the recruitment, introduction or placing of migrants for employment are rendered free.

2. The administrative costs of recruitment, introduction and placing shall not be borne by the migrants.

Article 5

In the case of collective transport of migrants from one country to another necessitating passage in transit through a third country, the competent authority of the territory of transit shall take measures for expediting the passage, to avoid delays and administrative difficulties.

Article 6

1. Each Member for which this Annex is in force which maintains a system of supervision of contracts of employment between an employer, or a person acting on his behalf, and a migrant for employment undertakes to require–

(a) that a copy of the contract of employment shall be delivered to the migrant before departure or, if the Governments concerned so agree, in a reception centre on arrival in the territory of immigration;

(b) that the contract shall contain provisions indicating the conditions of work and particularly the remuneration offered to the migrant;

(c) that the migrant shall receive in writing before departure, by a document which relates either to him individually or to a group of migrants of which he is a member, information concerning the general conditions of life and work applicable to him in the territory of immigration.

2. Where a copy of the contract is to be delivered to the migrant on arrival in the territory of immigration, he shall be informed in writing before departure, by a document which relates either to him individually or to a group of migrants of which he is a member, of the occupational category for which he is engaged and the other conditions of work, in particular the minimum wage which is guaranteed to him.

3. The competent authority shall ensure that the provisions of the preceding paragraphs are enforced and that appropriate penalties are applied in respect of violations thereof.

Article 7

1. The measures taken under Article 4 of this Convention shall, as appropriate, include–

(a) the simplification of administrative formalities;

(b) the provision of interpretation services;

(c) any necessary assistance, during an initial period in the settlement of the migrants and members of their families authorised to accompany or join them;

(d) the safeguarding of the welfare, during the journey and in particular on board ship, of migrants and members of their families authorised to accompany or join them; and

(e) permission for the liquidation and transfer of the property of migrants for employment admitted on a permanent basis.

Article 8

Appropriate measures shall be taken by the competent authority to assist migrants for employment, during an initial period, in regard to matters concerning their conditions of employment; where appropriate, such measures may be taken in co-operation with approved voluntary organisations.

Article 9

If a migrant for employment introduced into the territory of a Member in accordance with the provisions of Article 3 of this Annex fails, for a reason for which he is not responsible, to secure the employment for which he has been recruited or other suitable employment, the cost of his return and that of the members of his family who have been authorised to accompany or join him, including administrative fees, transport and maintenance charges to the final destination, and charges for the transport of household belongings, shall not fall upon the migrant.

Article 10

If the competent authority of the territory of immigration considers that the employment for which a migrant for employment was recruited under Article 3 of this Annex has been found to be unsuitable, it shall take appropriate measures to assist him in finding suitable employment which does not prejudice national workers and shall take such steps as will ensure his maintenance pending placing in such employment, or his return to the area of recruitment if the migrant is willing or agreed to such return at the time of his recruitment, or his resettlement elsewhere.

Article 11

If a migrant for employment who is a refugee or a displaced person and who has entered a territory of immigration in accordance with Article 3 of this Annex becomes redundant in any employment in that territory, the competent authority of that territory shall use its best endeavours to enable him to obtain suitable employment which does not prejudice national workers, and shall take such steps as will ensure his maintenance pending placing in suitable employment or his resettlement elsewhere.

Article 12

1. The competent authorities of the territories concerned shall enter into agreements for the purpose of regulating matters of common concern arising in connection with the application of the provisions of this Annex.

2. Where the Members maintain a system of supervision over contracts of employment, such agreements shall indicate the methods by which the contractual obligations of the employer shall be enforced.

3. Such agreements shall provide, where appropriate, for co-operation between the competent authority of the territory of emigration or a body established in accordance with the terms of an international instrument and the competent authority of the territory of immigration, in respect of the assistance to be given to migrants concerning their conditions of employment in virtue of the provisions of Article 8.

Article 13

Any person who promotes clandestine or illegal immigration shall be subject to appropriate penalties.

ANNEX III

IMPORTATION OF THE PERSONAL EFFECTS, TOOLS AND EQUIPMENT OF MIGRANTS FOR EMPLOYMENT

Article 1

1. Personal effects belonging to recruited migrants for employment and members of their families who have been authorised to accompany or join them shall be exempt from customs duties on arrival in the territory of immigration.

2. Portable hand-tools and portable equipment of the kind normally owned by workers for the carrying out of their particular trades belonging to recruited migrants for employment and members of their families who have been authorised to accompany or join them shall be exempt from customs duties on arrival in the territory of immigration if such tools and equipment can be shown at the time of importation to be in their actual ownership or possession, to have been in their possession and use for an appreciable time, and to be intended to be used by them in the course of their occupation.

Article 2

1. Personal effects belonging to migrants for employment and members of their families who have been authorised to accompany or join them shall be exempt from customs duties on the return of the said persons to their country of origin if such persons have retained the nationality of that country at the time of their return there.

2. Portable hand-tools and portable equipment of the kind normally owned by workers for the carrying out of their particular trades belonging to migrants for employment and members of their families who have been authorised to accompany or join them shall be exempt from customs duties on return of the said persons to their country of origin if such persons have retained the nationality of that country at the time of their return there and if such tools and equipment can be shown at the time of importation to be in their actual ownership or possession, to have been in their possession and use for an appreciable time, and to be intended to be used by them in the course of their occupation.

Recommendation No.86 concerning Migration for Employment (Revised 1949)*

Adoption: 1 July 1949

The General Conference of the International Labour Organisation,

Having been convened at Geneva by the Governing Body of the International Labour Office, and having met its Thirty-second Session on 8 June 1949, and

Having decided upon the adoption of certain proposals with regard to the revision of the Migration for Employment Recommendation, 1939, and the Migration for Employment (Co-operation between States) Recommendation, 1939, adopted by the Conference at its Twenty-fifth Session, which are included in the eleventh item on the agenda of the session, and

Having determined that these proposals shall take the form of a Recommendation,

adopts this first day of July of the year one thousand nine hundred and forty-nine, the following Recommendation, which may be cited as the Migration for Employment Recommendation (Revised), 1949:

The Conference,

Having adopted the Migration for Employment Convention (Revised), 1949, and

Desiring to supplement its provisions by a Recommendation;

Recommends as follows:

I

1.

For the purpose of this Recommendation–

(a) the term migrant for employment means a person who migrates from one country to another with a view to being employed otherwise than on his own account and includes any person regularly admitted as a migrant for employment;

(b) the term recruitment means–

(i) the engagement of a person in one territory on behalf of an employer in another territory, or

(ii) the giving of an undertaking to a person in one territory to provide him with employment in another territory,
together with the making of any arrangements in connection with the operations mentioned in (i) and (ii) including the seeking for and selection of emigrants and the preparation for departure of the emigrants;

(c) the term introduction means any operations for ensuring or facilitating the arrival in or admission to a territory of persons who have been recruited within the meaning of subparagraph (b);

(d) the term placing means any operations for the purpose of ensuring or facilitating the employment of persons who have been introduced within the meaning of subparagraph (c).

* Source: International Labour Organization, http://ilo.org/ilolex/english/
The ILO shall accept no responsibility for any inaccuracy, errors or omissions or for the consequences arising from the use of the Text.

2.

For the purpose of this Recommendation, references to the Government or competent authority of a territory of emigration should be interpreted as referring, in the case of migrants who are refugees or displaced persons, to any body established in accordance with the terms of an international instrument which may be responsible for the protection of refugees and displaced persons who do not benefit from the protection of any Government.

3.

This Recommendation does not apply to–

(a) frontier workers;

(b) short-term entry of members of the liberal professions and artistes; and

(c) seamen.

II

4.

(1) It should be the general policy of Members to develop and utilise all possibilities of employment and for this purpose to facilitate the international distribution of manpower and in particular the movement of manpower from countries which have a surplus of manpower to those countries that have a deficiency.

(2) The measures taken by each Member should have due regard to the manpower situation in the country and the Government should consult the appropriate organisations of employers and workers on all general questions concerning migration for employment.

III

5.

(1) The free service provided in each country to assist migrants and their families and in particular to provide them with accurate information should be conducted–

(a) by public authorities; or

(b) by one or more voluntary organisations not conducted with a view to profit, approved for the purpose by the public authorities, and subject to the supervision of the said authorities; or

(c) partly by the public authorities and partly by one or more voluntary organisations fulfilling the conditions stated in subparagraph (b) of this Paragraph.

(2) The service should advise migrants and their families, in their languages or dialects or at least in a language which they can understand, on matters relating to emigration, immigration, employment and living conditions, including health conditions in the place of destination, return to the country of origin or of emigration, and generally speaking any other question which may be of interest to them in their capacity as migrants.

(3) The service should provide facilities for migrants and their families with regard to the fulfilment of administrative formalities and other steps to be taken in connection with the return of the migrants to the country of origin or of emigration, should the case arise.

(4) With a view to facilitating the adaptation of migrants, preparatory courses should, where necessary, be organised to inform the migrants of the general conditions and the methods of work prevailing in the country of immigration, and to instruct them in the language of that

country. The countries of emigration and immigration should mutually agree to organise such courses.

6.

On request information should be made available by Members to the International Labour Office and to other Members concerning their emigration laws and regulations, including administrative provisions relating to restrictions on emigration and facilities granted to emigrants, and appropriate details concerning the categories of persons wishing to emigrate.

7.

On request information should be made available by Members to the International Labour Office and to other Members concerning their immigration laws and regulations, including administrative provisions, entry permits where needed, number and occupational qualifications of immigrants desired, laws and regulations affecting admission of migrants to employment, and any special facilities granted to migrants and measures to facilitate their adaptation to the economic and social organisation of the country of immigration.

8.

There should, as far as possible, be a reasonable interval between the publication and the coming into force of any measure altering the conditions on which emigration or immigration or the employment of migrants is permitted in order that these conditions may be notified in good time to persons who are preparing to emigrate.

9.

Provision should be made for adequate publicity to be given at appropriate stages to the principal measures referred to in the preceding Paragraph, such publicity to be in the languages most commonly known to the migrants.

10.

Migration should be facilitated by such measures as may be appropriate–

(a) to ensure that migrants for employment are provided in case of necessity with adequate accommodation, food and clothing on arrival in the country of immigration;

(b) to ensure, where necessary, vocational training so as to enable the migrants for employment to acquire the qualifications required in the country of immigration;

(c) to permit, taking into account the limits allowed by national laws and regulations concerning export and import of currency, the transfer of such part of the earnings and savings of migrants for employment as the migrants may desire;

(d) to arrange, in the case of permanent migration, for the transfer, where desired, to the country of immigration, of the capital of migrants for employment, within the limits allowed by national laws and regulations concerning export and import of currency;

(e) to provide access to schools for migrants and members of their families.

11.

Migrants and the members of their families should be assisted in obtaining access to recreation and welfare facilities, and steps should be taken where necessary to ensure that special facilities are made available during the initial period of settlement in the country of immigration.

12.

In the case of migrants under Government-sponsored arrangements for group transfer, medical assistance should be extended to such migrants in the same manner as provided for nationals.

IV

13.

(1) Where necessary in the interest of the migrant, Members should require that any intermediary who undertakes the recruitment, introduction or placing of migrants for employment on behalf of an employer must obtain a written warrant from the employer, or some other document proving that he is acting on the employer's behalf.

(2) This document should be drawn up in, or translated into, the official language of the country of emigration and should set forth all necessary particulars concerning the employer, concerning the nature and scope of the recruitment, introduction or placing which the intermediary is to undertake, and concerning the employment offered, including the remuneration.

14.

(1) The technical selection of migrants for employment should be carried out in such a way as to restrict migration as little as possible while ensuring that the migrants are qualified to perform the required work.

(2) Responsibility for such selection should be entrusted–

(a) to official bodies; or

(b) where appropriate, to private bodies of the territory of immigration duly authorised and, where necessary in the interest of the migrant, supervised by the competent authority of the territory of emigration.

(3) The right to engage in selection should be subject to the prior authorisation of the competent authority of the territory where the said operation takes place, in such cases under such conditions as may be prescribed by the laws and regulations of that territory, or by agreement between the Government of the territory of emigration and the Government of the territory of immigration.

(4) As far as possible, intending migrants for employment should, before their departure from the territory of emigration, be examined for purposes of occupational and medical selection by a representative of the competent authority of the territory of immigration.

(5) If recruitment takes place on a sufficiently large scale there should be arrangements for close liaison and consultation between the competent authorities of the territories of emigration and immigration concerned.

(6) The operations referred to in the preceding subparagraphs of this Paragraph should be carried out as near as possible to the place where the intending migrant is recruited.

15.

(1) Provision should be made by agreement for authorisation to be granted for a migrant for employment introduced on a permanent basis to be accompanied or joined by the members of his family.

(2) The movement of the members of the family of such a migrant authorised to accompany or join him should be specially facilitated by both the country of emigration and the country of immigration.

(3) For the purposes of this Paragraph, the members of the family of a migrant for employment should include his wife and minor children; favourable consideration should be given to requests for the inclusion of other members of the family dependent upon the migrant.

V

16.

(1) Migrants for employment authorised to reside in a territory and the members of their families authorised to accompany or join them should as far as possible be admitted to employment in the same conditions as nationals.

(2) In countries in which the employment of migrants is subject to restrictions, these restrictions should as far as possible–

(a) cease to be applied to migrants who have regularly resided in the country for a period, the length of which should not, as a rule, exceed five years; and

(b) cease to be applied to the wife and children of an age to work who have been authorised to accompany or join the migrant, at the same time as they cease to be applied to the migrant.

17.

In countries where the number of migrants for employment is sufficiently large, the conditions of employment of such workers should be specially supervised, such supervision being undertaken according to circumstances either by a special inspection service or by labour inspectors or other officials specialising in this work.

VI

18.

(1) When a migrant for employment has been regularly admitted to the territory of a Member, the said Member should, as far as possible, refrain from removing such person or the members of his family from its territory on account of his lack of means or the state of the employment market, unless an agreement to this effect has been concluded between the competent authorities of the emigration and immigration territories concerned.

(2) Any such agreement should provide–

(a) that the length of time the said migrant has been in the territory of immigration shall be taken into account and that in principle no migrant shall be removed who has been there for more than five years;

(b) that the migrant must have exhausted his rights to unemployment insurance benefit;

(c) that the migrant must have been given reasonable notice so as to give him time, more particularly to dispose of his property;

(d) that suitable arrangements shall have been made for his transport and that of the members of his family;

(e) that the necessary arrangements shall have been made to ensure that he and the members of his family are treated in a humane manner; and

(f) that the costs of the return of the migrant and the members of his family and of the transport of their household belongings to their final destination shall not fall on him.

19.

Appropriate steps should be taken by the authorities of the territories concerned to consult the employers' and workers' organisations concerning the operations of recruitment, introduction and placing of migrants for employment.

VII

20

When migrants for employment or members of their families who have retained the nationality of their State of origin return there, that country should admit such persons to the benefit of any measures in force for the granting of poor relief and unemployment relief, and for promoting the re-employment of the unemployed, by exempting them from the obligation to comply with any condition as to previous residence or employment in the country or place.

VIII

21

(1) Members should in appropriate cases supplement the Migration for Employment Convention (Revised), 1949, and the preceding Paragraphs of the present Recommendation by bilateral agreements, which should specify the methods of applying the principles set forth in the Convention and in the Recommendation.

(2) In concluding such agreements, Members should take into account the provisions of the Model Agreement annexed to the present Recommendation in framing appropriate clauses for the organisation of migration for employment and the regulation of the conditions of transfer and employment of migrants, including refugees and displaced persons.

ANNEX

Model Agreement on Temporary and Permanent Migration for Employment, including Migration of Refugees and Displaced Persons (Note: The phrases and passages in italics refer primarily to permanent migration; those enclosed within square brackets refer solely to migration of refugees and displaced persons.)

Article 1. Exchange of Information

1. The competent authority of the territory of immigration shall periodically furnish appropriate information to the competent authority of the territory of emigration or in the case of refugees and displaced persons, to any body established in accordance with the terms of an international instrument which may be responsible for the protection of refugees and displaced persons who do not benefit from the protection of any Government concerning:

(a) legislative and administrative provisions relating to entry, employment, residence and settlement of migrants and of their families;

(b) the number, the categories and the occupational qualifications of the migrants desired;

(c) the conditions of life and work for the migrants and, in particular, cost of living and minimum wages according to occupational categories and regions of employment, supplementary allowances, if any, nature of employments available, bonus on engagement, if any, social security systems and medical assistance, provisions concerning transport of migrants and of their tools and belongings, housing conditions and provisions for the supply of food and clothing, measures relating to the transfer of the migrants' savings and other sums due in virtue of this Agreement;

(d) special facilities, if any, for migrants;

(e) facilities for general education and vocational training for migrants;

(f) measures designed to promote rapid adaptation of migrants;

(g) procedure and formalities required for naturalisation.

2. The competent authority of the territory of emigration or in the case of refugees and displaced persons, any body established in accordance with the terms of an international instrument which may be responsible for the protection of refugees and displaced persons who do not benefit from the protection of any Government shall bring this information to the attention of persons or bodies interested.

3. The competent authority of the territory of emigration or in the case of refugees and displaced persons, any body established in accordance with the terms of an international instrument which may be responsible for the protection of refugees and displaced persons who do not benefit from the protection of any Government shall periodically furnish appropriate information to the competent authority of the territory of immigration concerning:

(a) legislative and administrative provisions relating to emigration;

(b) the number and occupational qualifications of intending emigrants, as well as the composition of their families;

(c) the social security system;

(d) special facilities, if any, for migrants;

(e) the environment and living conditions to which migrants are accustomed;

(f) the provisions in force regarding the export of capital.

4. The competent authority of the territory of immigration shall bring this information to the attention of persons or bodies interested.

5. The information mentioned in paragraphs 1 to 4 above shall also be transmitted by the respective parties to the International Labour Office.

Article 2. Action against Misleading Propaganda

1. The parties agree, with regard to their respective territories, to take all practical steps, so far as national laws and regulations permit, against misleading propaganda relating to emigration and immigration.

2. For this purpose the parties will, where appropriate, act in co-operation with the competent authorities of other countries concerned.

Article 3. Administrative Formalities

The parties agree to take measures with a view to accelerating and simplifying the carrying out of administrative formalities relating to departure, travel, entry, residence, and settlement of migrants and as far as possible for the members of their families. Such measures shall include the provision of an interpretation service, where necessary.

Article 4. Validity of Documents

1. The parties shall determine the conditions to be met for purposes of recognition in the territory of immigration of any document issued by the competent authority of the territory of emigration in respect of migrants and members of their families or in the case of refugees and displaced persons, by any body established in accordance with the terms of an international instrument which may be responsible for the protection of refugees and displaced persons who do not benefit from the protection of any Government concerning:

(a) civil status;

(b) legal status;

(c) occupational qualifications;

(d) general education and vocational training; and

(e) participation in social security systems.

2. The parties shall also determine the application of such recognition.

3. In the case of refugees and displaced persons, the competent authority of the territory of immigration shall recognise the validity of any travel document issued in lieu of a national passport by the competent authority of the territory of emigration and, in particular, of travel documents issued in accordance with the terms of an international Agreement (e.g. the travel document established by the Agreement of 15 October 1946, and the Nansen passport).

Article 5. Conditions and Criteria of Migration

1. The parties shall jointly determine:

(a) the requirements for migrants and members of their families, as to age, physical aptitude and health, as well as the occupational qualifications for the various branches of economic activity and for the various occupational categories;

(b) the categories of the members of the migrants' families authorised to accompany or to join them.

2. The parties shall also determine, in accordance with the provisions of Article 28 of this Agreement:

(a) the numbers and occupational categories of migrants to be recruited in the course of a stated period;

(b) the areas of recruitment and the areas of placing and settlement except that in the case of refugees and displaced persons the determination of the areas of recruitment shall be reserved to any body established in accordance with the terms of an international instrument which may be responsible for the protection of refugees and displaced persons who do not benefit from the protection of any Government.

3. In order to recruit migrants required to meet the technical needs of the territory of immigration and who can adapt themselves easily to the conditions in the territory of immigration, the parties shall determine criteria to govern technical selection of the migrants.

4. In drawing up these criteria, the two parties shall take into consideration:

(a) with respect to medical selection:

(i) the nature of the medical examination which migrants shall undergo (general medical examination, X-ray examination, laboratory examination, etc.);

(ii) the drawing up of lists of diseases and physical defects which clearly constitute a disability for employment in certain occupations;

(iii) minimum health provisions prescribed by international health conventions and relating to movement of population from one country to another;

(b) with respect to vocational selection:

(i) qualifications required of migrants with respect to each occupation or groups of occupations;

(ii) enumeration of alternative occupations requiring similar qualifications or capacities on the part of the workers in order to fulfil the needs of specified occupations for which it is difficult to recruit a sufficient number of qualified workers;

(iii) development of psycho-technical testing;

(c) with respect to selection based on the age of migrants, flexibility to be given to the application of age criteria in order to take into consideration on the one hand the requirements of various occupations and, on the other, the varying capacities of different individuals at a given age.

Article 6. Organisation of Recruitment, Introduction and Placing

1. The bodies or persons which engage in the operations of recruitment, introduction and placing of migrants and of members of their families shall be named by the competent authorities of the respective territories or in the case of refugees and displaced persons, by any body established in accordance with the terms of an international instrument which may be responsible for the protection of refugees and displaced persons who do not benefit from the protection of any Government on the one hand and the competent authority of the territory of immigration on the other subject to the approval of both parties.

2. Subject to the provisions of the following paragraphs, the right to engage in the operations of recruitment, introduction and placing shall be restricted to:

(a) public employment offices or other public bodies of the territory in which the operations take place;

(b) public bodies of a territory other than that in which the operations take place which are authorised to operate in that territory by an agreement between the parties;

(c) any body established in accordance with the terms of an international instrument.

3. In addition, in so far as the national laws and regulations of the parties permit and subject to the approval and supervision of the competent authorities of the parties, the operations of recruitment, introduction and placing may be undertaken by:

(a) the prospective employer or a person in his service acting on his behalf; and

(b) private agencies.

4. The administrative costs of recruitment, introduction and placing shall not be borne by the migrants.

Article 7. Selection Testing

1. An intending migrant shall undergo an appropriate examination in the territory of emigration; any such examination should inconvenience him as little as possible.

2. With respect to the organisation of the selection of migrants, the parties shall agree on:

(a) recognition and composition of official agencies or private bodies authorised by the competent authority of the territory of immigration to carry out selection operations in the territory of emigration;

(b) organisation of selection examinations, the centres where they are to be carried out, and allocation of expenses resulting from these examinations;

(c) co-operation of the competent authorities of the two parties and in particular of their employment services in organising selection.

Article 8. Information and Assistance of Migrants

1. The migrant accepted after medical and occupational examination in the assembly or selection centre shall receive, in a language that he understands, all information he may still require as to the nature of the work for which he has been engaged, the region of employment, the undertaking to which he is assigned, travel arrangements and the conditions of life and work including health and related matters in the country and region to which he is going.

2. On arrival in the country of destination, and at a reception centre if such exists, or at the place of residence, migrants and the members of their families shall receive all the documents which they need for their work, their residence and their settlement in the country, as well as information, instruction and advice regarding conditions of life and work, and any other assistance that they may need to adapt themselves to the conditions in the country of immigration.

Article 9. Education and Vocational Training

The parties shall co-ordinate their activities concerning the organisation of educational courses for migrants, which shall include general information on the country of immigration, instruction in the language of that country, and vocational training.

Article 10. Exchange of Trainees

The parties agree to further the exchange of trainees, and to determine in a separate agreement the conditions governing such exchanges.

Article 11. Conditions of Transport

1. During the journey from their place of residence to the assembly or selection centre, as well as during their stay in the said centre, migrants and the members of their families shall receive from the competent authority of the territory of immigration or in the case of refugees and displaced persons, from any body established in accordance with the terms of an international instrument which may be responsible for the protection of refugees and displaced persons who do not benefit from the protection of any Government any assistance which they may require.

2. The competent authorities of the territories of emigration and immigration shall, each within its own jurisdiction, safeguard the health and welfare of, and render assistance to, migrants and the members of their families during the journey from the assembly or selection centre to the place of their employment, as well as during their stay in a reception centre if such exists.

3. Migrants and members of their families shall be transported in a manner appropriate for human beings and in conformity with the laws and regulations in force.

4. The parties shall agree upon the terms and conditions for the application of the provisions of this Article.

Article 12. Travel and Maintenance Expenses

The parties shall agree upon the methods for meeting the cost of travel of the migrants and the members of their families from the place of their residence to the place of their destination, and the cost of their maintenance while travelling, sick or hospitalised, as well as the cost of transport of their personal belongings.

Article 13. Transfer of Funds

1. The competent authority of the territory of emigration shall, as far as possible and in conformity with national laws and regulations concerning the import and export of foreign currency, authorise and provide facilities for migrants and for members of their families to withdraw from their country such sums as they may need for their initial settlement abroad.

2. The competent authority of the territory of immigration shall, as far as possible and in conformity with national laws and regulations concerning the import and export of foreign currency, authorise and provide facilities for the periodical transfer to the territory of emigration of migrants' savings and of any other sums due in virtue of this Agreement.

3. The transfers of funds mentioned in paragraphs 1 and 2 above shall be made at the prevailing official rate of exchange.

4. The parties shall take all measures necessary for the simplification and acceleration of administrative formalities regarding the transfer of funds so that such funds may be available with the least possible delay to those entitled to them.

5. The parties shall determine if and under what conditions a migrant may be required to remit part of his wages for the maintenance of his family remaining in his country or in the territory from which he emigrated.

Article 14. Adaptation and Naturalisation

The competent authority of the territory of immigration shall take measures to facilitate adaptation to national climatic, economic and social conditions and facilitate the procedure of naturalisation of migrants and of members of their families.

Article 15. Supervision of Living and Working Conditions

1. Provision shall be made for the supervision by the competent authority or duly authorised bodies of the territory of immigration of the living and working conditions, including hygienic conditions, to which the migrants are subject.

2. With respect to temporary migrants, the parties shall provide, where appropriate, for authorised representatives of the territory of emigration or in the case of refugees and displaced persons, of any body established in accordance with the terms of an international instrument which may be responsible for the protection of refugees and displaced persons who do not benefit from the protection of any Government to co-operate with the competent authority or duly authorised bodies of the territory of immigration in carrying out this supervision.

3. During a fixed period, the duration of which shall be determined by the parties, migrants shall receive special assistance in regard to matters concerning their conditions of employment.

4. Assistance with respect to the employment and living conditions of the migrants may be given either through the regular labour inspection service of the territory of immigration or through a special service for migrants, in co-operation where appropriate with approved voluntary organisations.

5. Provision shall be made where appropriate for the co-operation of representatives of the territory of emigration or in the case of refugees and displaced persons, of any body established in accordance with the terms of an international instrument which may be responsible for the protection of refugees and displaced persons who do not benefit from the protection of any Government with such services.

Article 16. Settlement of Disputes

1. In case of a dispute between a migrant and his employer, the migrant shall have access to the appropriate courts or shall otherwise obtain redress for his grievances, in accordance with the laws and regulations of the territory of immigration.

2. The authorities shall establish such other machinery as is necessary to settle disputes arising out of the Agreement.

Article 17. Equality of Treatment

1. The competent authority of the territory of immigration shall grant to migrants and to members of their families with respect to employment in which they are eligible to engage treatment no less favourable than that applicable to its won nationals in virtue of legal or administrative provisions or collective labour agreements.

2. Such equality of treatment shall apply, without discrimination in respect of nationality, race, religion or sex, to immigrants lawfully within the territory of immigration in respect of the following matters:

(a) in so far as such matters are regulated by laws or regulations or are subject to the control of administrative authorities,

(i) remuneration, including family allowances where these form part of remuneration, hours of work, weekly rest days, overtime arrangements, holidays with pay and other regulations concerning employment, including limitations on home work, minimum age provisions, women's work, and the work of young persons;

(ii) membership of trade unions and enjoyment of the benefits of collective bargaining;

(iii) admission to schools, to apprenticeship and to courses or schools for vocational or technical training, provided that this does not prejudice nationals of the country of immigration;

(iv) recreation and welfare measures;

(b) employment taxes, dues or contributions payable in respect of the persons employed;

(c) hygiene, safety and medical assistance;

(d) legal proceedings relating to the matters referred to in this Agreement.

Article 18.

Access to Trades and Occupations and the Right to Acquire Property Equality of treatment shall also apply to:

(a) access to trades and occupations to the extent permitted under national laws and regulations;

(b) acquisition, possession and transmission of urban or rural property.

Article 19. Supply of Food

The treatment applied to migrants and the members of their families shall be the same as that applied to national workers in the same occupation as regards the supply of food.

Article 20. Housing Conditions

The competent authority of the territory of immigration shall ensure that migrants and the members of their families have hygienic and suitable housing, in so far as the necessary housing is available.

Article 21. Social Security

1. The two parties shall determine in a separate agreement the methods of applying a system of social security to migrants and their dependants.

2. Such agreement shall provide that the competent authority of the territory of immigration shall take measures to ensure to the migrants and their dependants treatment not less favourable than that afforded by it to its nationals, except where particular residence qualifications apply to nationals.

3. The agreement shall embody appropriate arrangements for the maintenance of migrants' acquired rights and rights in course of acquisition framed with due regard to the principles of the Maintenance of Migrants' Pension Rights Convention, 1935, or of any revision of that Convention.

4. The agreement shall provide that the competent authority of the territory of immigration shall take measures to grant to temporary migrants and their dependants treatment not less favourable than that afforded by it to its nationals, subject in the case of compulsory pension schemes to appropriate arrangements being made for the maintenance of migrants' acquired rights and rights in course of acquisition.

Article 22. Contracts of Employment

1. In countries where a system of model contracts is used, the individual contract of employment for migrants shall be based on a model contract drawn up by the parties for the principal branches of economic activity.

2. The individual contract of employment shall set forth the general conditions of engagement and of employment provided in the relevant model contract and shall be translated into a language which the migrant understands. A copy of the contract shall be delivered to the migrant before departure from the territory of emigration or, if it is agreed between the two parties concerned, in a reception centre on arrival in the territory of immigration. In the latter case before departure the migrant shall be informed in writing by a document which relates either to him individually or to a group of migrants of which he is a member, of the occupational category in which he is to be engaged and the other conditions of work, in particular the minimum wage which is guaranteed to him.

3. The individual contract of employment shall contain necessary information, such as:

(a) the full name of the worker as well as the date and place of birth, his family status, his place of residence and of recruitment;

(b) the nature of the work, and the place where it is to be performed;

(c) the occupational category in which he is placed;

(d) remuneration for ordinary hours of work, overtime, night work and holidays, and the medium for wage payment;

(e) bonuses, indemnities and allowances, if any;

(f) conditions under which and extent to which the employer may be authorised to make any deductions from remuneration;

(g) conditions regarding food if food is to be provided by the employer;

(h) the duration of the contract as well as the conditions of renewal and denunciation of the contract;

(i) the conditions under which entry and residence in the territory of immigration are permitted;

(j) the method of meeting the expenses of the journey of the migrant and the members of his family;

(k) in case of temporary migration, the method of meeting the expenses of return to the home country or the territory of migration, as appropriate;

(l) the grounds on which a contract may be prematurely terminated.

Article 23. Change of Employment

1. If the competent authority of the territory of immigration considers that the employment for which the migrant has been recruited does not correspond to his physical capacity or occupational qualifications, the said authority shall provide facilities for placing the said migrant in an employment corresponding to his capacity or qualifications, and in which he may be employed in accordance with national laws or regulations.

2. During periods of unemployment, if any, the method of maintaining the migrant and the dependent members of his family authorised to accompany or join him shall be determined by arrangements made under a separate agreement.

Article 24. Employment Stability

1. If before the expiration of the period of his contract the migrant for employment becomes redundant in the undertaking or branch of economic activity for which he was engaged, the competent authority of the territory of immigration shall, subject to the provisions of the contract, facilitate the placing of the said migrant in other suitable employment in which he may be employed in accordance with national laws or regulations.

2. If the migrant is not entitled to benefits under an unemployment insurance or assistance scheme, his maintenance, as well as that of dependent members of his family during any period in which he is unemployed shall be determined by a separate agreement in so far as this is not inconsistent with the terms of his contract.

3. The provisions of this Article shall not affect the right of the migrant to benefit from any provisions that may be included in his contract in case it is prematurely terminated by the employer.

Article 25. Provisions Concerning Compulsory Return

1. The competent authority of the territory of immigration undertakes that a migrant and the members of his family who have been authorised to accompany or join him will not be returned to the territory from which he emigrated unless he so desires if, because of illness or injury, he is unable to follow his occupation.

2. The Government of the territory of immigration undertakes not to send refugees and displaced persons or migrants who do not wish to return to their country of origin for political reasons back to their territory of origin as distinct from the territory from which they were recruited, unless they formally express this desire by a request in writing addressed both to

the competent authority of the territory of immigration and the representative of the body set up in accordance with the provisions of an international instrument which may be responsible for the protection of refugees and displaced persons who do not benefit from the protection of any Government.

Article 26. Return Journey

1. The cost of the return journey of a migrant introduced under a plan sponsored by the Government of the territory of immigration, who is obliged to leave his employment for reasons for which he is not responsible, and who cannot, in virtue of national laws and regulations, be placed in an employment for which he is eligible, shall be regulated as follows:

(a) the cost of the return journey of the migrant, and persons dependent upon him, shall in no case fall on the migrant himself;

(b) supplementary bilateral agreements shall specify the method of meeting the cost of this return journey;

(c) in any case, even if no provision to this effect is included in a bilateral agreement, the information given to migrants at the time of their recruitment shall specify what person or agency is responsible for defraying the cost of return in the circumstances mentioned in this Article.

2. In accordance with the methods of co-operation and consultation agreed upon under Article 28 of this Agreement, the two parties shall determine the measures necessary to organise the return home of the said persons and to assure to them in the course of the journey the conditions of health and welfare and the assistance which they enjoyed during the outward journey.

3. The competent authority of the territory of emigration shall exempt from customs duties on their arrival:

(a) personal effects; and

(b) portable hand-tools and portable equipment of the kind normally owned by workers for the carrying out of their particular trades, which have been in possession and use of the said persons for an appreciable time and which are intended to be used by them in the course of their occupation.

Article 27. Double Taxation

The two parties shall determine in a separate agreement the measures to be taken to avoid double taxation on the earnings of a migrant for employment.

Article 28. Methods of Co-operation

1. The two parties shall agree on the methods of consultation and co-operation necessary to carry out the terms of the Agreement.

2. When so requested by the representatives of the two parties the International Labour Office shall be associated with such consultation and co-operation.

Article 29. Final Provisions

1. The parties shall determine the duration of the Agreement as well as the period of notice for termination.

2. The parties shall determine those provisions of this Agreement which shall remain in operation after expiration of this Agreement.

Recommendation No.100 concerning the Protection of Migrant Workers in Underdeveloped Countries and Territories, 1955*

Adoption: 22 June 1955

The General Conference of the International Labour Organisation,

Having been convened at Geneva by the Governing Body of the International Labour Office, and having met in its Thirty-eighth Session on 1 June 1955, and

Having decided upon the adoption of certain proposals concerning the protection of migrant workers in underdeveloped countries and territories, which is the fifth item on the agenda of the session, and

Having determined that these proposals shall take the form of a Recommendation,

adopts this twenty-second day of June of the year one thousand nine hundred and fifty-five, the following Recommendation, which may be cited as the Protection of Migrant Workers (Underdeveloped Countries) Recommendation, 1955:

I. DEFINITIONS AND SCOPE

1.

This Recommendation applies to–

(a) countries and territories in which the evolution from a subsistence form of economy towards more advanced forms of economy, based on wage earning and entailing sporadic and scattered development of industrial and agricultural centres, brings with it appreciable migratory movements of workers and sometimes their families;

(b) countries and territories through which such migratory movements of workers pass on their outward and, where applicable, their return journeys, if existing arrangements in such countries and territories, taken as a whole, afford less protection to the persons concerned during their journeys than is laid down in this Recommendation;

(c) countries and territories of destination of such migratory movements of workers, if existing arrangements in such countries and territories, taken as a whole, afford less protection to the persons concerned during their journeys or employment than is laid down in this Recommendation.

2.

For the purposes of this Recommendation, the term migrant worker means any worker participating in such migratory movements either within the countries and territories described in clause (a) of Paragraph 1 above or from such countries and territories into or through the countries and territories described in clauses (b) and (c) of Paragraph 1 above, whether he has taken up employment, is moving in search of employment or is going to arranged employment, and irrespective of whether he has accepted an offer of employment or entered into a contract. Where applicable, the term migrant worker also means any worker returning temporarily or finally during or at the end of such employment.

* Source: International Labour Organization, http://ilo.org/ilolex/english/.
The ILO shall accept no responsibility for any inaccuracy, errors or omissions or for the consequences arising from the use of the Text.

3.

Nothing in this Recommendation should be construed as giving any person a right to move into or remain in any country or territory except in accordance with the immigration or other laws of that country or territory.

4.

The provisions of this Recommendation are without prejudice to any provision or practice, existing by virtue of law, custom or agreement, which provides for migrant workers conditions more favourable than those provided in this Recommendation.

5.

Any discrimination against migrant workers should be eliminated.

II. PROTECTION OF MIGRANT WORKERS AND THEIR FAMILIES DURING THEIR OUTWARD AND RETURN JOURNEYS AND PRIOR TO THE PERIOD OF THEIR EMPLOYMENT

6.

(1) Arrangements should be made by means of national or local laws or regulations, agreement between governments or any other means, with a view to providing protection for migrant workers and their families during the journey between their point of departure and their place of employment, both in the interests of the migrants themselves and in the interests of the countries or areas whence they come, in which they move about and to which they are making their way.

(2) These arrangements should include–

(a) making available mechanised means of transport, including public passenger transport, for the migrant workers and their families, where that is physically possible; and

(b) providing, at suitable stages along the routes, rest camps where lodging, food, water and essential first aid may be furnished.

7.

All necessary steps should be taken to enable migrant workers to make their journeys in reasonable conditions either–

(a) in the case of recruited or engaged workers, by providing, in the regulations relating to recruitment or to contracts of employment, an obligation on the recruiter, or failing him the employer, to pay the travelling expenses of the workers and, where applicable, of their families;

or

(b) in the case of workers journeying without having entered into a contract or accepted an offer of definite employment, by making provision for reducing travelling expenses to a minimum.

8.

(1) Arrangements should be made for free medical examination of migrant workers on departure for or commencement of employment, and on completion of employment.

(2) Where lack of medical staff in particular regions makes it impossible to submit all migrant workers to this double medical examination, priority should be given to–

(a) migrant workers coming from regions where there are communicable or endemic diseases;

(b) migrant workers who accept or who have been in employment involving special physical risks; and

(c) migrant workers whose journeys are undertaken in accordance with special arrangements for recruitment or engagement.

9.

(1) If the competent authority considers, after consultation with employers' and workers' organisations where both exist, that a period of acclimatisation is necessary in the interest of the health of migrant workers, it should take steps to ensure to them, and particularly to those recruited or bound by a contract, such a period of acclimatisation immediately before commencing their employment.

(2) In making its decision as to the need for a period of acclimatisation the competent authority should take account of the climate, the altitude and the different conditions of life in which the migrant workers may be called upon to work. Where it considers a period of acclimatisation to be necessary it should fix the length thereof according to local circumstances.

(3) During the acclimatisation period, the employer should bear the expense of the adequate maintenance of the migrant worker and of the members of his family authorised to accompany him.

10.

Arrangements should be made to ensure to migrant workers and, where applicable, to their families the right to repatriation, during a period to be determined by the competent authority, after consultation with employers' and workers' organisations where both exist, in the following circumstances:

(a) where the migrant worker has been recruited or has been sent forward to the place of engagement by the recruiter or the employer, his repatriation should be to the place where he was engaged or from which he was sent forward for engagement and at the expense of the recruiter or the employer in all cases where–

(i) the worker becomes incapacitated by sickness or accident during the journey to the place of employment;

(ii) the worker is found on medical examination to be unfit for employment;

(iii) the worker, for a reason for which he is not responsible, is not engaged after having been sent forward for engagement;

(iv) the competent authority finds that the worker has been engaged, or sent forward for engagement, by misrepresentation or mistake; or

(b) where the migrant worker has entered into a contract of employment and has been brought to the place of employment by the employer or by any person acting on behalf of the employer, his repatriation, together with that of the members of his family also so brought, should be to the place where he was engaged or from which he was sent forward for engagement, and at the expense of the employer in all cases where–

(i) the period of service stipulated in the contract has expired;

(ii) the contract is terminated by reason of the inability of the employer to fulfil the contract;

(iii) the contract is terminated by reason of the inability of the migrant worker to fulfil the contract owing to sickness or accident;

(iv) the contract is terminated by agreement between the parties;

(v) the contract is terminated on the application of either of the parties, unless the competent authority otherwise decides.

11.

The competent authority should give sympathetic consideration to the question whether, and if so under what conditions, migrant workers or the members of their families who have not been brought to the place of employment by the employer or by any person acting on behalf of the employer, should have a right to repatriation.

12.

In the event of the death of a migrant worker, the members of his family should have the right, to be exercised within a period to be determined by the competent authority, after consultation with the employers' and workers' organisations where both exist, to be repatriated to the place where the worker was engaged or from which he was sent forward for engagement, at the expense of the recruiter or the employer as the case may be–

(a) where they had been authorised to accompany the worker to the place of employment–

(i) if death has occurred during the journey to the place of employment; or

(ii) if the deceased worker had entered into a contract of employment with the employer; or

(b) in other cases in the circumstances determined by the competent authority under Paragraph 11 above.

13.

(1) Migrant workers should be free to waive the right to repatriation at the expense of the employer, such waiver to be exercised within a period and in a manner to be determined by the competent authority after consultation with employers' and workers' organisations where both exist, and not to become final until the end of such period.

(2) Migrant workers should also be free to postpone the exercise of their rights to repatriation to within a period to be fixed by the competent authority.

14.

Where standard employment contracts, to be entered into between employers and migrant workers, are established by or under the authority of the government or governments concerned, representatives of the employers and workers concerned, including representatives of their respective organisations if such exist, should, whenever practicable, be consulted as to the terms of such contracts.

15.

(1) Arrangements should be made for the proper placing of migrant workers.

(2) These arrangements should include the creation, where appropriate, of a public employment service system which should–

(a) consist of a central office for the country or teritory as a whole and branch offices both in areas from which workers normally migrate and in employment centres, so as to enable information on employment opportunities to be gathered, and to be regularly disseminated in the districts from which labour normally comes to those centres;

(b) establish and maintain arrangements with the employment services in other countries or territories to which workers in a given area usually emigrate, so as to collect information on prevailing employment opportunities there;

(c) establish and maintain, where practicable, vocational guidance facilities and arrangements for ascertaining the general suitability of workers for particular employments; and

(d) seek, where practicable, the advice and co-operation of employers' and workers' organisations in the organisation and operation of the system.

III. MEASURES TO DISCOURAGE MIGRATORY MOVEMENTS WHEN CONSIDERED UNDESIRABLE IN THE INTERESTS OF THE MIGRANT WORKERS AND OF THE COMMUNITIES AND COUNTRIES OF THEIR ORIGIN

16.

The general policy should be to discourage migration of workers when considered undesirable in the interests of the migrant workers and of the communities and countries of their origin by measures designed to improve conditions of life and to raise standards of living in the areas from which the migrations normally start.

17.

The measures to be taken to ensure the application of the policy described in the preceding Paragraph should include–

(a) in emigration areas, the adoption of economic development and vocational training programmes to enable fuller use to be made of available manpower and natural resources, and in particular the adoption of all measures likely to create new jobs and new sources of income for workers who would normally be disposed to emigrate;

(b) in immigration areas, the more rational use of manpower and the increase of productivity through better organisation of work, better training and the development of mechanisation or other measures as local circumstances may require;

(c) the limitation of recruitment in regions where the withdrawal of labour might have untoward effects on the social and economic organisation, and the health, welfare and development of the population concerned.

18.

The governments of the countries and territories of origin and destination of migrant workers should endeavour to bring about a progressive reduction of migratory movements which have not been subject or appeared open to regulation, when such movements are considered undesirable in the interests of the migrant workers and of the communities and countries of their origin. So long as the economic causes of these unregulated migrations persist, the governments concerned should endeavour to exercise appropriate control, to the extent that such action appears practicable and desirable, over voluntary migration as well as organised recruitment. Such reduction and control may be sought by means of arrangements at local or area level and through bilateral agreements.

19.

While unregulated migrations continue the governments concerned should, as far as practicable, strive to secure, for workers who migrate under such conditions, the protection provided for in this Recommendation.

IV. PROTECTION OF MIGRANT WORKERS DURING THE PERIOD OF THEIR EMPLOYMENT

A. General policy

20.

Every effort should be made to assure to migrant workers as favourable working and living conditions as those provided by law or in practice to other workers engaged in the same employment and to apply to them, as to such other workers, the standards of protection set out in the following Paragraphs of this Recommendation.

B. Housing

21.

The arrangements to be made for the housing of migrant workers should include measures to enable such workers to be provided, either at the expense of the employer or by the provision of appropriate financial aid or by other means, with accomodation meeting approved standards and at rents reasonable in relation to the wages earned by the various categories of workers.

22.

The competent authority should be responsible for ensuring the establishment of satisfactory housing conditions for migrant workers. It should define the minimum standards of accomodation and exercise strict control over the enforcement of these standards. It should also define the rights of the worker who may be required to vacate his accommodation on leaving employment and should take all necessary steps to secure the enforcement of these rights.

C. Wages

23.

(1) Arrangements should be made for wage fixing in the case of migrant workers.

(2) Such arrangements should include–

(a) adoption of a scale of minimum wage rates calculated so that its lowest rate, including any allowances, enables a worker starting unskilled work at least to meet his minimum requirements according to the standards accepted in the region and taking into account normal family needs;

(b) the fixing from time to time of minimum wage rates either–

(i) by means of collective agreements freely negotiated between the trade unions which are representative of the workers concerned and the employers or the employers' organisations concerned; or

(ii) where no adequate machinery for fixing minimum wage rates by collective agreements exists, by the competent authority in accordance with the principle stated in clause (a) above.

24.

Where relevant, the competent authority should, when fixing wages, take into consideration the results of any budgetary surveys of household consumption in the region concerned which may be available, it being understood that such surveys should be undertaken with the co-operation of the representative organisations of employers and workers.

25.

Representatives of the employers' and workers' organisations, where they exist and, where they do not, representatives of workers and employers concerned, equal in number and on an equal footing, should collaborate in the operation of statutory machinery for fixing minimum wage rates.

26.

The minimum wage rates in force should be communicated to the employers and workers concerned. Where the rates have been fixed in accordance with subparagraph (2) (b) (ii) of Paragraph 23, they should be binding on the employers and workers concerned so as not to be subject to abatement by them by agreement without the express authorisation of the competent authority.

27.

Employers should be required to keep records of wage payments and deductions in respect of each worker. The amounts of wages and of deductions therefrom should be communicated to the workers concerned.

28.

Deductions from wages should be permitted only under conditions and to the extent prescribed by national laws or regulations or fixed by collective agreement or arbitration award.

29.

Wages should normally be paid in legal tender direct to the individual worker.

30.

Unless there is an established local custom to the contrary, and the competent authority is satisfied, after consulting representatives of the workers or of their representative organisations, that the continuance of this custom is desired by the workers, wages should be paid regularly and at such intervals as will minimise the likelihood of indebtedness among the wage earners.

31.

The substitution of alcohol or any harmful substance for all or any part of wages should be prohibited.

32.

Payment of wages in taverns or stores should be prohibited except in the case of workers employed therein.

33.

Employers should be required to restrict any advances to workers to a small proportion of their monthly remuneration.

34.

Any advance in excess of the amount fixed by the competent authority should not be legally recoverable either by the withholding of amounts of pay due to the worker at a later date or in any other way. No interest should be chargeable on advances.

35.

A worker to whom minimum rates are applicable and who, since they became applicable, has been paid wages at less than these rates, should be entitled to recover, by judicial or other means authorised by law, the amount by which he has been underpaid, subject to such limitation of time as may be determined by law or regulation.

36.

Where food, housing, clothing and other essential supplies and services form part of the remuneration, the competent authority should, with the co-operation of the representative organisations of employers and workers, take all practicable steps to ensure that they are adequate, that their cash value is properly assessed and that the payment in kind does not exceed in value a certain proportion, to be fixed by the competent authority, of the basic cash wage.

D. Admission to skilled jobs without discrimination

37.

The principle of equal opportunity for all sections of the population, including migrant workers, should be accepted.

38.

Subject to the application of national immigration laws, and of special laws concerning the employment of foreigners in the public service, any barriers preventing or restricting, on account of national origin, race, colour, belief, tribal association or trade union affiliation, access of any section of the population, including migrant workers, to particular types of job or employment should be deemed contrary to public policy and the principle of the abolition of any such barriers should be accepted.

39.

Measures should be taken immediately to secure in practice the realisation of the principles set out in Paragraphs 37 and 38 of this Recommendation and to facilitate the performance of an increasing share of skilled work by the least favoured grades of workers.

40.

Such measures should specifically include–

(a) in all countries and territories, provision of equal access for all workers to technical and vocational training facilities and equal possibilities of access for all workers to employment opportunities in new industrial enterprises;

(b) in countries or territories where separate classes distinguished by race or origin have already been permanently formed, the introduction of facilities enabling workers of the least favoured class to be admitted to semi-skilled and skilled jobs;

(c) in countries or territories where separate classes distinguished by race or origin have not been permanently formed, the opening of equal opportunities for all qualified workers to jobs requiring specified skills.

E. Trade union activities

41.

The right of association and freedom for all lawful trade union activities should be granted to migrant workers in the centres where they work and all practicable measures should be taken to assure to trade unions which are representative of the workers concerned the right to conclude collective agreements with employers or employers' organisations.

F. Supply of consumer goods

42.

(1) Steps should be taken to ensure the availability of consumer goods, particularly essential products and foodstuffs, to migrant workers and their families at reasonable prices and in sufficient quantities.

(2) Land for the cultivation of crops should be made available to migrant workers, wherever possible, either by the employer or by the competent authority.

43.

Where the creation of co-operative organisations would be of service, arrangements should be made for their development, including–

(a) the creation, if possible, of stock farms, fish ponds and market gardens on a co-operative basis;

(b) the creation of retail stores run by workers' co-operative;

(c) the granting of assistance by governments by training members of co-operatives, by supervising their administration and by guiding their activities.

44.

(1) Where stores are attached to undertakings, only cash payment should be accepted in them.

(2) If local circumstances do not yet permit the application of the preceding provision, the credit granted to migrant workers should be limited to a proportion of wages, to be fixed by the competent authority, and restricted to a fixed period which should be as short as possible. It should be forbidden to charge interest on credit given or to accept its repayment in work.

(3) There should be no coercion on the migrant workers concerned to make use of such stores.

(4) Where access to other stores is not possible the competent authority should take appropriate measures with the object of ensuring that goods are sold at fair and reasonable prices and that stores operated by the employer are not operated for the purpose of securing a profit but for the benefit of the workers concerned.

G. Social security, industrial safety and hygiene

45.

The steps to be taken for migrant workers should in any case include in the first instance appropriate arrangements, without discrimination on grounds of nationality, race or religion, for workmen's compensation, medical care for workers and their families, industrial hygiene and prevention of accidents and occupational diseases.

46.

These arrangements should include–

(a) medical supervision in accordance with local possibilities by periodical visits in the course of employment, and in case of sickness;

(b) first aid, free medical treatment and hospitalisation facilities in accordance with standards to be prescribed by the competent authority;

(c) a system of workmen's compensation for accidents and for occupational diseases;

(d) suitable assistance measures in case of accident or occupational disease;

(e) measures to secure the health and safety of migrant workers in their places of employment;

(f) measures for reporting accidents and investigating their causes;

(g) an obligation on the employers to bring to the attention of migrant workers by notices, talks or any other means any dangerous or unhealthy features of their work;

(h) special or additional training or instruction to migrant workers on the prevention of accidents and risks to health in places of employment when, on account of lack of familiarity with processes, language difficulties or for other reasons, the training or instruction normally given to other workers employed in the country or territory is unsuitable;

(i) provision for the collaboration of employers and workers in the promotion of safety measures;

(j) special health and social measures for the protection of the migrant worker's wife and children living with him.

47.

Where migrant workers fail to benefit from the same treatment as other workers as regards protection against the risks of invalidity, old age and death, arrangements should be made, to the extent possible and desirable and in collaboration with the workers, for the organisation of friendly societies and works provident funds in order to meet the needs of migrant workers in these cases and as the forerunners of larger schemes on a local, district or territorial basis.

H. Relations of migrant workers with their areas of origin

48.

Arrangements should be made to enable migrant workers to maintain contact with their families and their areas of origin, including–

(a) the granting of such facilities as may be required for the voluntary remittance of funds to the worker's family in his area of origin or elsewhere and for the accumulation, with the assent of the worker, of deferred pay which he should receive at the end of his contract or when he returns to his home or in any other circumstances to be decided in agreement with him;

(b) facilities for the exchange of correspondence between the migrant worker, his family and his area of origin;

(c) facilities for the performance by the migrant worker of those customary obligations to his community of origin which he wishes to observe.

I. Material, intellectual and moral welfare of migrant workers

49.

Arrangements should be made to ensure the material, intellectual and moral welfare of migrant workers, including–

(a) arrangements to encourage voluntary forms of thrift;

(b) arrangements to protect the migrant worker against usury, in particular by action to reduce interest rates on loans, by the control of the operations of money-lenders and by the encouragement of facilities for borrowing money for appropriate purposes through co-operative credit organisations or through institutions under the supervision of the competent authority;

(c) wherever practicable, the maintenance in immigration areas of welfare officers who are familiar with the languages and customs of the migrant workers to facilitate the adaptation of these workers and their families to their new way of living;

(d) measures to ensure educational facilities for migrant workers' children;

(e) facilities to enable migrant workers to satisfy their intellectual and religious aspirations.

V. STABILISATION OF MIGRANT WORKERS

50.

Except where permanent establishment of the migrant workers is clearly against their interest and that of their families or of the economies of the countries or territories concerned, the general policy to be followed should be to seek the stabilisation of the workers and their families in or near the employment centres by all appropriate measures and particularly by those which are set out in Part IV and in Paragraphs 51, 52 and 53 of this Recommendation.

51.

As stated in Paragraph 3, nothing in this Recommendation should be construed as giving any person a right to move into or remain in any country or territory except in accordance with the immigration or other laws of that country or territory. Nevertheless, where such action is not contrary to the policy of the country concerned, the competent authority should consider affording to migrant workers who have been resident for a period of not less than five years in the country to which they have migrated all opportunities of acquiring citizenship of the country of immigration.

52.

(1) Where lasting settlement of migrant workers at or near their place of employment is found to be possible, arrangements should be made to promote their permanent installation.

(2) These arrangements should include–

(a) encouragement of recruitment of migrant workers accompanied by their families;

(b) the granting wherever possible and desirable of facilities to enable the establishment at or near the place of employment of appropriate community organisation;

(c) the provision of housing of an approved standard and at suitable cost to promote the permanent settlement of families;

(d) the allocation, wherever possible and desirable, of sufficient land for the production of foodstuffs;

(e) in the absence of more appropriate facilities and whenever possible and desirable, the creation of villages or settlements of retired migrant workers in places where it is possible for them to contribute to their own subsistence.

VI. APPLICATION OF THE RECOMMENDATION

53.

Provision should be made by the competent authority for the supervision, by the appropriate administrative service or services, and with the co-operation of employers' and workers' organisations where both exist, of the application of the measures for the protection of migrant workers dealt with in this Recommendation.

54.

In particular, in cases where the terms and conditions of employment, the language, customs, or the currency in use in the region of employment are not familiar to migrant workers, the appropriate administrative service or services should ensure the observance of any procedure for entering into employment contracts so as to make certain that each worker understands the terms and conditions of his employment, the provisions of his contract, the details in regard to the rates and payment of wages, and that he has accepted freely and knowingly these terms and conditions.

55.

Each Member of the International Labour Organisation should report to the International Labour Office at appropriate intervals, as requested by the Governing Body, the position of the law and practice in the countries and territories for which the Member is responsible in regard to the matters dealt with in the Recommendation. Such reports should show the extent to which effect has been given, or is proposed to be given, to the provisions of this Recommendation and such modifications of those provisions as it has been found or may be found necessary to make in adopting or applying them.

56.

Each Member of the International Labour Organisation which is responsible for any non-metropolitan territory should take all steps within its competence to secure the effective application in each such territory of the minimum standards set forth in this Recommendation, and in particular should bring the Recommendation before the authority or authorities competent to make effective in each such territory the minimum standards set forth in it.

Convention No.143 concerning Migrations in Abusive Conditions and the Promotion of Equality of Opportunity and Treatment of Migrant Workers, 1975*

Adoption: 24 June 1975
Entry into force: 9 December 1978
Parties: 21 (Status as of 1 April 2007)

ALBANIA 12 Sep 2006, ARMENIA 27 Jan 2006, BENIN 11 June 1980, BOSNIA AND HERZEGOVINA 2 June 1993, BURKINA FASO 9 Dec 1977, CAMEROON 4 July 1978, CYPRUS 28 June 1977, GUINEA 5 June 1978, ITALY 23 June 1981, KENYA 9 Apr 1979, THE FORMER YUGOSLAV REPUBLIC OF MACEDONIA 17 Nov 1991, NORWAY 24 Jan 1979, PHILIPPINES 14 Sep 2006, PORTUGAL 12 Dec 1978, SAN MARINO 23 May 1985, SERBIA 24 Nov 2000, SLOVENIA 29 May 1992, SWEDEN 28 Dec 1982, TOGO 8 Nov 1983, UGANDA 31 Mar 1978, VENEZUELA (BOLIVARIAN REPUBLIC OF) 17 Aug 1983.

The General Conference of the International Labour Organisation,

Having been convened at Geneva by the Governing Body of the International Labour Office, and having met in its Sixtieth Session on 4 June 1975, and

Considering that the Preamble of the Constitution of the International Labour Organisation assigns to it the task of protecting "the interests of workers when employed in countries other than their own", and

Considering that the Declaration of Philadelphia reaffirms, among the principles on which the Organisation is based, that "labour is not a commodity", and that "poverty anywhere constitutes a danger to prosperity everywhere", and recognises the solemn obligation of the ILO to further programmes which will achieve in particular full employment through "the transfer of labour, including for employment...",

Considering the ILO World Employment Programme and the Employment Policy Convention and Recommendation, 1964, and emphasising the need to avoid the excessive and uncontrolled or unassisted increase of migratory movements because of their negative social and human consequences, and

Considering that in order to overcome underdevelopment and structural and chronic unemployment, the governments of many countries increasingly stress the desirability of encouraging the transfer of capital and technology rather than the transfer of workers in accordance with the needs and requests of these countries in the reciprocal interest of the countries of origin and the countries of employment, and

Considering the right of everyone to leave any country, including his own, and to enter his own country, as set forth in the Universal Declaration of Human Rights and the International Covenant on Civil and Political Rights, and

---

* Source: International Labour Organization, http://www.ilo.org/ilolex
The ILO shall accept no responsibility for any inaccuracy, errors or omissions or for the consequences arising from the use of the Text.

Recalling the provisions contained in the Migration for Employment Convention and Recommendation (Revised), 1949, in the Protection of Migrant Workers (Underdeveloped Countries) Recommendation, 1955, in the Employment Policy Convention and Recommendation, 1964, in the Employment Service Convention and Recommendation, 1948, and in the Fee-Charging Employment Agencies Convention (Revised), 1949, which deal with such matters as the regulation of the recruitment, introduction and placing of migrant workers, the provision of accurate information relating to migration, the minimum conditions to be enjoyed by migrants in transit and on arrival, the adoption of an active employment policy and international collaboration in these matters, and

Considering that the migration of workers due to conditions in labour markets should take place under the responsibility of official agencies for employment or in accordance with the relevant bilateral or multilateral agreements, in particular those permitting free circulation of workers, and

Considering that evidence of the existence of illicit and clandestine trafficking in labour calls for further standards specifically aimed at eliminating these abuses, and

Recalling the provisions of the Migration for Employment Convention (Revised), 1949, which require ratifying Members to apply to immigrants lawfully within their territory treatment not less favourable than that which they apply to their nationals in respect of a variety of matters which it enumerates, in so far as these are regulated by laws or regulations or subject to the control of administrative authorities, and

Recalling that the definition of the term "discrimination" in the Discrimination (Employment and Occupation) Convention, 1958, does not mandatorily include distinctions on the basis of nationality, and

Considering that further standards, covering also social security, are desirable in order to promote equality of opportunity and treatment of migrant workers and, with regard to matters regulated by laws or regulations or subject to the control of administrative authorities, ensure treatment at least equal to that of nationals, and

Noting that, for the full success of action regarding the very varied problems of migrant workers, it is essential that there be close co-operation with the United Nations and other specialised agencies, and

Noting that, in the framing of the following standards, account has been taken of the work of the United Nations and of other specialised agencies and that, with a view to avoiding duplication and to ensuring appropriate co-ordination, there will be continuing co-operation in promoting and securing the application of the standards, and

Having decided upon the adoption of certain proposals with regard to migrant workers, which is the fifth item on the agenda of the session, and

Having determined that these proposals shall take the form of an international Convention supplementing the Migration for Employment Convention (Revised), 1949, and the Discrimination (Employment and Occupation) Convention, 1958,

adopts this twenty-fourth day of June of the year one thousand nine hundred and seventy-five the following Convention, which may be cited as the Migrant Workers (Supplementary Provisions) Convention, 1975:

PART I. MIGRATIONS IN ABUSIVE CONDITIONS

Article 1

Each Member for which this Convention is in force undertakes to respect the basic human rights of all migrant workers.

Article 2

1. Each Member for which this Convention is in force shall systematically seek to determine whether there are illegally employed migrant workers on its territory and whether there depart from, pass through or arrive in its territory any movements of migrants for employment in which the migrants are subjected during their journey, on arrival or during their period of residence and employment to conditions contravening relevant international multilateral or bilateral instruments or agreements, or national laws or regulations.

2. The representative organisations of employers and workers shall be fully consulted and enabled to furnish any information in their possession on this subject.

Article 3

Each Member shall adopt all necessary and appropriate measures, both within its jurisdiction and in collaboration with other Members–

(a) to suppress clandestine movements of migrants for employment and illegal employment of migrants, and

(b) against the organisers of illicit or clandestine movements of migrants for employment departing from, passing through or arriving in its territory, and against those who employ workers who have immigrated in illegal conditions,

in order to prevent and to eliminate the abuses referred to in Article 2 of this Convention.

Article 4

In particular, Members shall take such measures as are necessary, at the national and the international level, for systematic contact and exchange of information on the subject with other States, in consultation with representative organisations of employers and workers.

Article 5

One of the purposes of the measures taken under Articles 3 and 4 of this Convention shall be that the authors of manpower trafficking can be prosecuted whatever the country from which they exercise their activities.

Article 6

1. Provision shall be made under national laws or regulations for the effective detection of the illegal employment of migrant workers and for the definition and the application of administrative, civil and penal sanctions, which include imprisonment in their range, in respect of the illegal employment of migrant workers, in respect of the organisation of movements of migrants for employment defined as involving the abuses referred to in Article 2 of this Convention, and in respect of knowing assistance to such movements, whether for profit or otherwise.

2. Where an employer is prosecuted by virtue of the provision made in pursuance of this Article, he shall have the right to furnish proof of his good faith.

Article 7

The representative organisations of employers and workers shall be consulted in regard to the laws and regulations and other measures provided for in this Convention and designed to prevent and eliminate the abuses referred to above, and the possibility of their taking initiatives for this purpose shall be recognised.

Article 8

1. On condition that he has resided legally in the territory for the purpose of employment, the migrant worker shall not be regarded as in an illegal or irregular situation by the mere fact of the loss of his employment, which shall not in itself imply the withdrawal of his authorisation of residence or, as the case may be, work permit.

2. Accordingly, he shall enjoy equality of treatment with nationals in respect in particular of guarantees of security of employment, the provision of alternative employment, relief work and retraining.

Article 9

1. Without prejudice to measures designed to control movements of migrants for employment by ensuring that migrant workers enter national territory and are admitted to employment in conformity with the relevant laws and regulations, the migrant worker shall, in cases in which these laws and regulations have not been respected and in which his position cannot be regularised, enjoy equality of treatment for himself and his family in respect of rights arising out of past employment as regards remuneration, social security and other benefits.

2. In case of dispute about the rights referred to in the preceding paragraph, the worker shall have the possibility of presenting his case to a competent body, either himself or through a representative.

3. In case of expulsion of the worker or his family, the cost shall not be borne by them.

4. Nothing in this Convention shall prevent Members from giving persons who are illegally residing or working within the country the right to stay and to take up legal employment.

PART II. EQUALITY OF OPPORTUNITY AND TREATMENT

Article 10

Each Member for which the Convention is in force undertakes to declare and pursue a national policy designed to promote and to guarantee, by methods appropriate to national conditions and practice, equality of opportunity and treatment in respect of employment and occupation, of social security, of trade union and cultural rights and of individual and collective freedoms for persons who as migrant workers or as members of their families are lawfully within its territory.

Article 11

1. For the purpose of this Part of this Convention, the term migrant worker means a person who migrates or who has migrated from one country to another with a view to being employed otherwise than on his own account and includes any person regularly admitted as a migrant worker.

2. This Part of this Convention does not apply to–

(a) frontier workers;

(b) artistes and members of the liberal professions who have entered the country on a short-term basis;

(c) seamen;

(d) persons coming specifically for purposes of training or education;

(e) employees of organisations or undertakings operating within the territory of a country who have been admitted temporarily to that country at the request of their employer to undertake specific duties or assignments, for a limited and defined period of time, and who are required to leave that country on the completion of their duties or assignments.

Article 12

Each Member shall, by methods appropriate to national conditions and practice–

(a) seek the co-operation of employers' and workers' organisations and other appropriate bodies in promoting the acceptance and observance of the policy provided for in Article 10 of this Convention;

(b) enact such legislation and promote such educational programmes as may be calculated to secure the acceptance and observance of the policy;

(c) take measures, encourage educational programmes and develop other activities aimed at acquainting migrant workers as fully as possible with the policy, with their rights and obligations and with activities designed to give effective assistance to migrant workers in the exercise of their rights and for their protection;

(d) repeal any statutory provisions and modify any administrative instructions or practices which are inconsistent with the policy;

(e) in consultation with representative organisations of employers and workers, formulate and apply a social policy appropriate to national conditions and practice which enables migrant workers and their families to share in advantages enjoyed by its nationals while taking account, without adversely affecting the principle of equality of opportunity and treatment, of such special needs as they may have until they are adapted to the society of the country of employment;

(f) take all steps to assist and encourage the efforts of migrant workers and their families to preserve their national and ethnic identity and their cultural ties with their country of origin, including the possibility for children to be given some knowledge of their mother tongue;

(g) guarantee equality of treatment, with regard to working conditions, for all migrant workers who perform the same activity whatever might be the particular conditions of their employment.

Article 13

1. A Member may take all necessary measures which fall within its competence and collaborate with other Members to facilitate the reunification of the families of all migrant workers legally residing in its territory.

2. The members of the family of the migrant worker to which this Article applies are the spouse and dependent children, father and mother.

Article 14

A Member may–

(a) make the free choice of employment, while assuring migrant workers the right to geographical mobility, subject to the conditions that the migrant worker has resided lawfully in its territory for the purpose of employment for a prescribed period not exceeding two years or, if its laws or regulations provide for contracts for a fixed term of less than two years, that the worker has completed his first work contract;

(b) after appropriate consultation with the representative organisations of employers and workers, make regulations concerning recognition of occupational qualifications acquired outside its territory, including certificates and diplomas;

(c) restrict access to limited categories of employment or functions where this is necessary in the interests of the State.

PART III. FINAL PROVISIONS

Article 15

This Convention does not prevent Members from concluding multilateral or bilateral agreements with a view to resolving problems arising from its application.

Article 16

1. Any Member which ratifies this Convention may, by a declaration appended to its ratification, exclude either Part I or Part II from its acceptance of the Convention.

2. Any Member which has made such a declaration may at any time cancel that declaration by a subsequent declaration.

3. Every Member for which a declaration made under paragraph 1 of this Article is in force shall indicate in its reports upon the application of this Convention the position of its law and practice in regard to the provisions of the Part excluded from its acceptance, the extent to which effect has been given, or is proposed to be given, to the said provision and the reasons for which it has not yet included them in its acceptance of the Convention.

Article 17

The formal ratifications of this Convention shall be communicated to the Director-General of the International Labour Office for registration.

Article 18

1. This Convention shall be binding only upon those Members of the International Labour Organisation whose ratifications have been registered with the Director-General.

2. It shall come into force twelve months after the date on which the ratifications of two Members have been registered with the Director-General.

3. Thereafter, this Convention shall come into force for any Member twelve months after the date on which its ratification has been registered.

Article 19

1. A Member which has ratified this Convention may denounce it after the expiration of ten years from the date on which the Convention first comes into force, by an act communicated to the Director-General of the International Labour Office for registration. Such denunciation shall not take effect until one year after the date on which it is registered.

2. Each Member which has ratified this Convention and which does not, within the year following the expiration of the period of ten years mentioned in the preceding paragraph, exercise the right of denunciation provided for in this Article, will be bound for another period of ten years and, thereafter, may denounce this Convention at the expiration of each period of ten years under the terms provided for in this Article.

Article 20

1. The Director-General of the International Labour Office shall notify all Members of the International Labour Organisation of the registration of all ratifications and denunciations communicated to him by the Members of the Organisation.

2. When notifying the Members of the Organisation of the registration of the second ratification communicated to him, the Director-General shall draw the attention of the Members of the Organisation to the date upon which the Convention will come into force.

Article 21

The Director-General of the International Labour Office shall communicate to the Secretary-General of the United Nations for registration in accordance with Article 102 of the Charter of the United Nations full particulars of all ratifications and acts of denunciation registered by him in accordance with the provisions of the preceding Articles.

Article 22

At such times as it may consider necessary the Governing Body of the International Labour Office shall present to the General Conference a report on the working of this Convention and shall examine the desirability of placing on the agenda of the Conference the question of its revision in whole or in part.

Article 23

1. Should the Conference adopt a new Convention revising this Convention in whole or in part, then, unless the new Convention otherwise provides–

a) the ratification by a Member of the new revising Convention shall ipso jure involve the immediate denunciation of this Convention, notwithstanding the provisions of Article 19 above, if and when the new revising Convention shall have come into force;

b) as from the date when the new revising Convention comes into force this Convention shall cease to be open to ratification by the Members.

2. This Convention shall in any case remain in force in its actual form and content for those Members which have ratified it but have not ratified the revising Convention.

Article 24

The English and French versions of the text of this Convention are equally authoritative.

Recommendation No.151 concerning Migrant Workers, 1975*

Adoption: 24 June 1975

The General Conference of the International Labour Organisation,

Having been convened at Geneva by the Governing Body of the International Labour Office, and having met in its Sixtieth Session on 4 June 1975, and

Considering that the Preamble of the Constitution of the International Labour Organisation assigns to it the task of protecting the interests of workers when employed in countries other than their own, and

Recalling the provisions contained in the Migration for Employment Convention and Recommendation (Revised), 1949, and in the Protection of Migrant Workers (Underdeveloped Countries) Recommendation, 1955, which deal with such matters as the preparation and organisation of migration, social services to be provided to migrant workers and their families, in particular before their departure and during their journey, equality of treatment as regards a variety of matters which they enumerate, and the regulation of the stay and return of migrant workers and their families, and

Having adopted the Migrant Workers (Supplementary Provisions) Convention, 1975, and

Considering that further standards are desirable as regards equality of opportunity and treatment, social policy in regard to migrants and employment and residence, and

Having decided upon the adoption of certain proposals with regard to migrant workers, which is the fifth item on the agenda of the session, and

Having determined that these proposals shall take the form of a Recommendation,

adopts this twenty-fourth day of June of the year one thousand nine hundred and seventy-five, the following Recommendation, which may be cited as the Migrant Workers Recommendation, 1975:

1.

Members should apply the provision of this Recommendation within the framework of a coherent policy on international migration for employment. That policy should be based upon the economic and social needs of both countries of origin and countries of employment; it should take account not only of short-term manpower needs and resources but also of the long-term social and economic consequences of migration for migrants as well as for the communities concerned.

I. Equality of Opportunity and Treatment

2.

Migrant workers and members of their families lawfully within the territory of a Member should enjoy effective equality of opportunity and treatment with nationals of the Member concerned in respect of–

* Source: International Labour Organization, http://ilo.org/ilolex/english/
The ILO shall accept no responsibility for any inaccuracy, errors or omissions or for the consequences arising from the use of the Text.

(a) access to vocational guidance and placement services;

(b) access to vocational training and employment of their own choice on the basis of individual suitability for such training or employment, account being taken of qualifications acquired outside the territory of and in the country of employment;

(c) advancement in accordance with their individual character, experience, ability and diligence;

(d) security of employment, the provision of alternative employment, relief work and retraining;

(e) remuneration for work of equal value;

(f) conditions of work, including hours of work, rest periods, annual holidays with pay, occupational safety and occupational health measures, as well as social security measures and welfare facilities and benefits provided in connection with employment;

(g) membership of trade unions, exercise of trade union rights and eligibility for office in trade unions and in labour-management relations bodies, including bodies representing workers in undertakings;

(h) rights of full membership in any form of co-operative;

(i) conditions of life, including housing and the benefits of social services and educational and health facilities.

3.

Each Member should ensure the application of the principles set forth in Paragraph 2 of this Recommendation in all activities under the control of a public authority and promote its observance in all other activities by methods appropriate to national conditions and practice.

4.

Appropriate measures should be taken, with the collaboration of employers' and workers' organisations and other bodies concerned, with a view to–

(a) fostering public understanding and acceptance of the above-mentioned principles;

(b) examining complaints that these principles are not being observed and securing the correction, by conciliation of other appropriate means, of any practices regarded as in conflict therewith.

5.

Each Member should ensure that national laws and regulations concerning residence in its territory are so applied that the lawful exercise of rights enjoyed in pursuance of these principles cannot be the reason for non-renewal of a residence permit or for expulsion and is not inhibited by the threat of such measures.

6.

A Member may–

(a) make the free choice of employment, while assuring migrant workers the right to geographical mobility, subject to the conditions that the migrant worker has resided lawfully in its territory for the purpose of employment for a prescribed period not exceeding two years or, if its laws or regulations provide for contracts for a fixed term of less than two years, that the worker has completed his first work contract;

(b) after appropriate consultation with the representative organisations of employers and workers, make regulations concerning recognition of occupational qualifications acquired outside its territory, including certificates and diplomas;

(c) restrict access to limited categories of employment or functions where this is necessary in the interests of the State.

7.

(1) In order to enable migrant workers and their families to take full advantage of their rights and opportunities in employment and occupation, such measures as may be necessary should be taken, in consultation with the representative organisations of employers and workers–

(a) to inform them, as far as possible in their mother tongue or, if that is not possible, in a language with which they are familiar, of their rights under national law and practice as regards the matters dealt with in Paragraph 2 of this Recommendation;

(b) to advance their knowledge of the language or languages of the country of employment, as far as possible during paid time;

(c) generally, to promote their adaptation to the society of the country of employment and to assist and encourage the efforts of migrant workers and their families to preserve their national and ethnic identity and their cultural ties with their country of origin, including the possibility for children to be given some knowledge of their mother tongue.

(2) Where agreements concerning the collective recruitment of workers have been concluded between Members, they should jointly take the necessary measures before the migrants' departure from their country of origin to introduce them to the language of the country of employment and also to its economic, social and cultural environment.

8.

(1) Without prejudice to measures designed to ensure that migrant workers and their families enter national territory and are admitted to employment in conformity with the relevant laws and regulations, a decision should be taken as soon as possible in cases in which these laws and regulations have not been respected so that the migrant worker should know whether his position can be regularised or not.

(2) Migrant workers whose position has been regularised should benefit from all rights which, in accordance with Paragraph 2 of this Recommendation, are provided for migrant workers lawfully within the territory of a Member.

(3) Migrant workers whose position has not been or could not be regularised should enjoy equality of treatment for themselves and their families in respect of rights arising out of present and past employment as regards remuneration, social security and other benefits as well as regards trade union membership and exercise of trade union rights.

(4) In case of dispute about the rights referred to in the preceding sub-paragraphs, the worker should have the possibility of presenting his case to a competent body, either himself or through a representative.

(5) In case of expulsion of the worker or his family, the cost should not be borne by them.

II. Social Policy

9.

Each Member should, in consultation with representative organisations of employers and workers, formulate and apply a social policy appropriate to national conditions and practice which enables migrant workers and their families to share in advantages enjoyed by its nationals while taking account, without adversely affecting the principle of equality of opportunity and treatment, of such special needs as they may have until they are adapted to the society of the country of employment.

10.

With a view to making the policy as responsive as possible to the real needs of migrant workers and their families, it should be based, in particular, on an examination not only of conditions in the territory of the Member but also of those in the countries of origin of the migrants.

11.

The policy should take account of the need to spread the social cost of migration as widely and equitably as possible over the entire collectivity of the country of employment, and in particular over those who profit most from the work of migrants.

12.

The policy should be periodically reviewed and evaluated and where necessary revised.

A. Reunification of Families

13.

(1) All possible measures should be taken both by countries of employment and by countries of origin to facilitate the reunification of families of migrant workers as rapidly as possible. These measures should include, as necessary, national laws or regulations and bilateral and multilateral arrangements.

(2) A prerequisite for the reunification of families should be that the worker has, for his family, appropriate accommodation which meets the standards normally applicable to nationals of the country of employment.

14.

Representatives of all concerned, and in particular of employers and workers, should be consulted on the measures to be adopted to facilitate the reunification of families and their co-operation sought in giving effect thereto.

15.

For the purpose of the provisions of this Recommendation relating to the reunification of families, the family of the migrant worker should include the spouse and dependent children, father and mother.

16.

With a view to facilitating the reunification of families as quickly as possible in accordance with Paragraph 13 of this Recommendation, each Member should take full account of the needs of migrant workers and their families in particular in its policy regarding the construction of family housing, assistance in obtaining this housing and the development of appropriate reception services.

17.

Where a migrant worker who has been employed for at least one year in a country of employment cannot be joined by his family in that country, he should be entitled–

(a) to visit the country of residence of his family during the paid annual holiday to which he is entitled under the national law and practice of the country of employment without losing during the absence from that country any acquired rights or rights in course of acquisition and, particularly, without having his employment terminated or his right to residence in the country of employment withdrawn during that period; or

(b) to be visited by his family for a period corresponding at least to the annual holiday with pay to which he is entitled.

18.

Consideration should be given to the possibility of giving the migrant worker financial assistance towards the cost of the travel envisaged in the preceding Paragraph or a reduction in the normal cost of transport, for instance by the arrangement of group travel.

19.

Without prejudice to more favourable provisions which may be applicable to them, persons admitted in pursuance of international arrangements for free movement of labour should have the benefit of the measures provided for in Paragraphs 13 to 18 of this Recommendation.

B. Protection of the Health of Migrant Workers

20.

All appropriate measures should be taken to prevent any special health risks to which migrant workers may be exposed.

21.

(1) Every effort should be made to ensure that migrant workers receive training and instruction in occupational safety and occupational hygiene in connection with their practical training or other work preparation, and, as far as possible, as part thereof.

(2) In addition, a migrant worker should, during paid working hours and immediately after beginning his employment, be provided with sufficient information in his mother tongue or, if that is not possible, in a language with which he is familiar, on the essential elements of laws and regulations and on provisions of collective agreements concerning the protection of workers and the prevention of accidents as well as on safety regulations and procedures particular to the nature of the work.

22.

(1) Employers should take all possible measures so that migrant workers may fully understand instructions, warnings, symbols and other signs relating to safety and health hazards at work.

(2) Where, on account of the migrant workers' lack of familiarity with processes, language difficulties or other reasons, the training or instruction given to other workers is inadequate for them, special measures which ensure their full understanding should be taken.

(3) Members should have laws or regulations applying the principles set out in this Paragraph and provide that where employers or other persons or organisations having responsibility in this regard fail to observe such laws or regulations, administrative, civil and penal sanctions might be imposed.

C. Social Services

23.

In accordance with the provisions of Paragraph 2 of this Recommendation, migrant workers and their families should benefit from the activities of social services and have access thereto under the same conditions as nationals of the country of employment.

24.

In addition, social services should be provided which perform, in particular, the following functions in relation to migrant workers and their families–

(a) giving migrant workers and their families every assistance in adapting to the economic, social and cultural environment of the country of employment;

(b) helping migrant workers and their families to obtain information and advice from appropriate bodies, for instance by providing interpretation and translation services; to comply with administrative and other formalities; and to make full use of services and facilities provided in such fields as education, vocational training and language training, health services and social security, housing, transport and recreation: Provided that migrant workers and their families should as far as possible have the right to communicate with public authorities in the country of employment in their own language or in a language with which they are familiar, particularly in the context of legal assistance and court proceedings;

(c) assisting authorities and bodies with responsibilities relating to the conditions of life and work of migrant workers and their families in identifying their needs and in adapting thereto;

(d) giving the competent authorities information and, as appropriate, advice regarding the formulation, implementation and evaluation of social policy with respect to migrant workers;

(e) providing information for fellow workers and foremen and supervisors about the situation and the problems of migrant workers.

25.

(1) The social services referred to in Paragraph 24 of this Recommendation may be provided, as appropriate to national conditions and practice, by public authorities, by approved non-profit-making organisations or bodies, or by a combination of both. The public authorities should have the over-all responsibility of ensuring that these social services are at the disposal of migrant workers and their families.

(2) Full use should be made of services which are or can be provided by authorities, organisations and bodies serving the nationals of the country of employment, including employers' and workers' organisations.

26.

Each Member should take such measures as may be necessary to ensure that sufficient resources and adequately trained staff are available for the social services referred to in Paragraph 24 of this Recommendation.

27.

Each Member should promote co-operation and co-ordination between different social services on its territory and, as appropriate, between these services and corresponding services in other countries, without, however, this co-operation and co-ordination relieving the States of their responsibilities in this field.

28.

Each Member should organise and encourage the organisation, at the national, regional or local level, or as appropriate in a branch of economic activity employing substantial numbers of migrant workers, of periodic meetings for the exchange of information and experience. Consideration should also be given to the exchange of information and experience with other countries of employment as well as with the countries of origin of migrant workers.

29.

Representatives of all concerned and in particular of employers and workers should be consulted on the organisation of the social services in question and their co-operation sought in achieving the purposes aimed at.

III. Employment and Residence

30.

In pursuance of the provision of Paragraph 18 of the Migration for Employment Recommendation (Revised), 1949, that Members should, as far as possible, refrain from removing from their territory, on account of lack of means or the state of the employment market, a migrant worker regularly admitted thereto, the loss by such migrant worker of his employment should not in itself imply the withdrawal of his authorisation of residence.

31.

A migrant who has lost his employment should be allowed sufficient time to find alternative employment, at least for a period corresponding to that during which he may be entitled to unemployment benefit; the authorisation of residence should be extended accordingly.

32.

(1) A migrant worker who has lodged an appeal against the termination of his employment, under such procedures as may be available, should be allowed sufficient time to obtain a final decision thereon.

(2) If it is established that the termination of employment was not justified, the migrant worker should be entitled, on the same terms as national workers, to reinstatement, to compensation for loss of wages or of other payment which results from unjustified termination, or to access to a new job with a right to indemnification. If he is not reinstated, he should be allowed sufficient time to find alternative employment.

33.

A migrant worker who is the object of an expulsion order should have a right of appeal before an administrative or judicial instance, according to conditions laid down in national laws or regulations. This appeal should stay the execution of the expulsion order, subject to the duly substantiated requirements of national security or public order. The migrant worker should have the same right to legal assistance as national workers and have the possibility of being assisted by an interpreter.

34.

(1) A migrant worker who leaves the country of employment should be entitled, irrespective of the legality of his stay therein–

(a) to any outstanding remuneration for work performed, including severance payments normally due;

(b) to benefits which may be due in respect of any employment injury suffered;

(c) in accordance with national practice–

(i) to compensation in lieu of any holiday entitlement acquired but not used;

(ii) to reimbursement of any social security contributions which have not given and will not give rise to rights under national laws or regulations or international arrangements: Provided that where social security contributions do not permit entitlement to benefits, every effort should be made with a view to the conclusion of bilateral or multilateral agreements to protect the rights of migrants.

(2) Where any claim covered in subparagraph (1) of this Paragraph is in dispute, the worker should be able to have his interests represented before the competent body and enjoy equal treatment with national workers as regards legal assistance.

International Convention on the Protection of the Rights of All Migrant Workers and Members of Their Families, 1990*

Adoption: 18 December 1990
Entry into force: 1 July 2003
Parties: 36 (Status as of 1 April 2007)

ALGERIA 24 Apr 2005 a (*92.1), ARGENTINA 23 Feb 2007, AZERBAIJAN 11 Jan 1999 a, BANGLADESH signed 7 Oct 1998, BELIZE 14 Nov 2001 a, BENIN signed 15 Sep 2005, BOLIVIA 16 Oct 2000 a, BOSNIA AND HERZEGOVINA 13 Dec 1996 a, BURKINA FASO 26 Nov 2003, CAMBODIA signed 27 Sep 2004, CAPE VERDE 16 Sep 1997 a, CHILE 21 Mar 2005 (*22.5, 48.2), COLOMBIA 24 May 1995 a (*15, 46, 47), COMOROS signed 22 Sep 2000, ECUADOR 5 Feb 2002 a, EGYPT 19 Feb 1993 a (*4, 18.6), El SALVADOR 14 Mar 2003 (*32, 46, 47, 48, 61.4, 92.1), GABON 15 Dec 2004, GHANA 7 Sep 2000, GUATEMALA 14 Mar 2003, GUINEA 7 Sep 2000 a, GUINEA-BISSAU signed 12 Sep 2000, GUYANA signed 15 Sep 2005, HONDURAS 9 Aug 2005 a, INDONESIA signed 22 Sep 2004, KYRGYZSTAN 29 Sep 2003 a, LESOTHO 16 Sep 2005, LIBERIA signed 22 Sep 2004, LIBYAN ARAB JAMAHIRIYA 18 June 2004 a, MALI 5 June 2003 a, MEXICO 8 Mar 1999 (*22.4), MONTENEGRO 23 Oct 2006 d, MOROCCO 21 June 1993 (*92.1), NICARAGUA 26 Oct 2005 a (*42.3), PARAGUAY signed 13 Sep 2000, PERU 14 Sep 2005, PHILIPPINES 5 July 1995, REPUBLIC OF SERBIA signed 11 Nov 2004, SAO TOME AND PRINCIPE signed 6 Sep 2000, SENEGAL 9 June 1999 a, SEYCHELLES 15 Dec 1994 a, SIERRA LEONE signed 15 Sep 2000, SRI LANKA 11 Mar 1996 a (*8.2, 29, 49, 54), SYRIAN ARAB REPUBLIC 2 June 2005 a, TAJIKISTAN 8 Jan 2002, TIMOR-LESTE 30 Jan 2004 a, TOGO signed 15 Nov 2001, TURKEY 27 Sep 2004 (*15, 40, 45, 46, 76, 77), UGANDA 14 Nov 1995 a (*18.3d), URUGAY 15 Feb 2001 a.

Preamble

The States Parties to the present Convention,

Taking into account the principles embodied in the basic instruments of the United Nations concerning human rights, in particular the Universal Declaration of Human Rights, the International Covenant on Economic, Social and Cultural Rights, the International Covenant on Civil and Political Rights, the International Convention on the Elimination of All Forms of Racial Discrimination, the Convention on the Elimination of All Forms of Discrimination against Women and the Convention on the Rights of the Child,

Taking into account also the principles and standards set forth in the relevant instruments elaborated within the framework of the International Labour Organisation, especially the Convention concerning Migration for Employment (No.97), the Convention concerning Migrations in Abusive Conditions and the Promotion of Equality of Opportunity and Treatment of Migrant Workers (No.143), the Recommendation concerning Migration for Employment (No.86), the Recommendation concerning Migrant Workers (No.151), the Convention concerning Forced or Compulsory Labour (No.29) and the Convention concerning Abolition of Forced Labour (No.105),

Reaffirming the importance of the principles contained in the Convention against Discrimination in Education of the United Nations Educational, Scientific and Cultural Organization,

* Source: U.N.G.A. Res. 45/158.

Recalling the Convention against Torture and Other Cruel, Inhuman or Degrading Treatment or Punishment, the Declaration of the Fourth United Nations Congress on the Prevention of Crime and the Treatment of Offenders, the Code of Conduct for Law Enforcement Officials, and the Slavery Conventions,

Recalling that one of the objectives of the International Labour Organisation, as stated in its Constitution, is the protection of the interests of workers when employed in countries other than their own, and bearing in mind the expertise and experience of that organization in matters related to migrant workers and members of their families,

Recognizing the importance of the work done in connection with migrant workers and members of their families in various organs of the United Nations, in particular in the Commission on Human Rights and the Commission for Social Development, and in the Food and Agriculture Organization of the United Nations, the United Nations Educational, Scientific and Cultural Organization and the World Health Organization, as well as in other international organizations,

Recognizing also the progress made by certain States on a regional or bilateral basis towards the protection of the rights of migrant workers and members of their families, as well as the importance and usefulness of bilateral and multilateral agreements in this field,

Realizing the importance and extent of the migration phenomenon, which involves millions of people and affects a large number of States in the international community,

Aware of the impact of the flows of migrant workers on States and people concerned, and desiring to establish norms which may contribute to the harmonization of the attitudes of States through the acceptance of basic principles concerning the treatment of migrant workers and members of their families,

Considering the situation of vulnerability in which migrant workers and members of their families frequently find themselves owing, among other things, to their absence from their State of origin and to the difficulties they may encounter arising from their presence in the State of employment,

Convinced that the rights of migrant workers and members of their families have not been sufficiently recognized everywhere and therefore require appropriate international protection,

Taking into account the fact that migration is often the cause of serious problems for the members of the families of migrant workers as well as for the workers themselves, in particular because of the scattering of the family,

Bearing in mind that the human problems involved in migration are even more serious in the case of irregular migration and convinced therefore that appropriate action should be encouraged in order to prevent and eliminate clandestine movements and trafficking in migrant workers, while at the same time assuring the protection of their fundamental human rights,

Considering that workers who are non-documented or in an irregular situation are frequently employed under less favourable conditions of work than other workers and that certain employers find this an inducement to seek such labour in order to reap the benefits of unfair competition,

Considering also that recourse to the employment of migrant workers who are in an irregular situation will be discouraged if the fundamental human rights of all migrant workers are more widely recognized and, moreover, that granting certain additional rights to migrant workers and members of their families in a regular situation will encourage all migrants and employers to respect and comply with the laws and procedures established by the States concerned,

Convinced, therefore, of the need to bring about the international protection of the rights of all migrant workers and members of their families, reaffirming and establishing basic norms in a comprehensive convention which could be applied universally,

Have agreed as follows:

PART I: SCOPE AND DEFINITIONS

Article 1

1. The present Convention is applicable, except as otherwise provided hereafter, to all migrant workers and members of their families without distinction of any kind such as sex, race, colour, language, religion or conviction, political or other opinion, national, ethnic or social origin, nationality, age, economic position, property, marital status, birth or other status.

2. The present Convention shall apply during the entire migration process of migrant workers and members of their families, which comprises preparation for migration, departure, transit and the entire period of stay and remunerated activity in the State of employment as well as return to the State of origin or the State of habitual residence.

Article 2

For the purposes of the present Convention:

1. The term "migrant worker" refers to a person who is to be engaged, is engaged or has been engaged in a remunerated activity in a State of which he or she is not a national.

2. (a) The term "frontier worker" refers to a migrant worker who retains his or her habitual residence in a neighbouring State to which he or she normally returns every day or at least once a week;

(b) The term "seasonal worker" refers to a migrant worker whose work by its character is dependent on seasonal conditions and is performed only during part of the year;

(c) The term "seafarer", which includes a fisherman, refers to a migrant worker employed on board a vessel registered in a State of which he or she is not a national;

(d) The term "worker on an offshore installation" refers to a migrant worker employed on an offshore installation that is under the jurisdiction of a State of which he or she is not a national;

(e) The term "itinerant worker" refers to a migrant worker who, having his or her habitual residence in one State, has to travel to another State or States for short periods, owing to the nature of his or her occupation;

(f) The term "project-tied worker" refers to a migrant worker admitted to a State of employment for a defined period to work solely on a specific project being carried out in that State by his or her employer;

(g) The term "specified-employment worker" refers to a migrant worker:

(i) Who has been sent by his or her employer for a restricted and defined period of time to a State of employment to undertake a specific assignment or duty; or

(ii) Who engages for a restricted and defined period of time in work that requires professional, commercial, technical or other highly specialized skill; or

(iii) Who, upon the request of his or her employer in the State of employment, engages for a restricted and defined period of time in work whose nature is transitory or brief; and who is required to depart from the State of employment either at the expiration of his or her authorized period of stay, or earlier if he or she no longer undertakes that specific assignment or duty or engages in that work;

(h) The term "self-employed worker" refers to a migrant worker who is engaged in a remunerated activity otherwise than under a contract of employment and who earns his or her living through this activity normally working alone or together with members of his or her family, and to any other migrant worker recognized as self-employed by applicable legislation of the State of employment or bilateral or multilateral agreements.

Article 3

The present Convention shall not apply to:

(a) Persons sent or employed by international organizations and agencies or persons sent or employed by a State outside its territory to perform official functions, whose admission and status are regulated by general international law or by specific international agreements or conventions;

(b) Persons sent or employed by a State or on its behalf outside its territory who participate in development programmes and other co-operation programmes, whose admission and status are regulated by agreement with the State of employment and who, in accordance with that agreement, are not considered migrant workers;

(c) Persons taking up residence in a State different from their State of origin as investors;

(d) Refugees and stateless persons, unless such application is provided for in the relevant national legislation of, or international instruments in force for, the State Party concerned;

(e) Students and trainees;

(f) Seafarers and workers on an offshore installation who have not been admitted to take up residence and engage in a remunerated activity in the State of employment.

Article 4

For the purposes of the present Convention the term "members of the family" refers to persons married to migrant workers or having with them a relationship that, according to applicable law, produces effects equivalent to marriage, as well as their dependent children and other dependent persons who are recognized as members of the family by applicable legislation or applicable bilateral or multilateral agreements between the States concerned.

Article 5

For the purposes of the present Convention, migrant workers and members of their families:

(a) Are considered as documented or in a regular situation if they are authorized to enter, to stay and to engage in a remunerated activity in the State of employment pursuant to the law of that State and to international agreements to which that State is a party;

(b) Are considered as non-documented or in an irregular situation if they do not comply with the conditions provided for in subparagraph (a) of the present article.

Article 6

For the purposes of the present Convention:

(a) The term "State of origin" means the State of which the person concerned is a national;

(b) The term "State of employment" means a State where the migrant worker is to be engaged, is engaged or has been engaged in a remunerated activity, as the case may be;

(c) The term "State of transit" means any State through which the person concerned passes on any journey to the State of employment or from the State of employment to the State of origin or the State of habitual residence.

PART II: NON-DISCRIMINATION WITH RESPECT TO RIGHTS

Article 7

States Parties undertake, in accordance with the international instruments concerning human rights, to respect and to ensure to all migrant workers and members of their families within their territory or subject to their jurisdiction the rights provided for in the present Convention without distinction of any kind such as to sex, race, colour, language, religion or conviction, political or other opinion, national, ethnic or social origin, nationality, age, economic position, property, marital status, birth or other status.

PART III: HUMAN RIGHTS OF ALL MIGRANT WORKERS AND MEMBERS OF THEIR FAMILIES

Article 8

1. Migrant workers and members of their families shall be free to leave any State, including their State of origin. This right shall not be subject to any restrictions except those that are provided by law, are necessary to protect national security, public order (ordre public), public health or morals or the rights and freedoms of others and are consistent with the other rights recognized in the present part of the Convention.

2. Migrant workers and members of their families shall have the right at any time to enter and remain in their State of origin.

Article 9

The right to life of migrant workers and members of their families shall be protected by law.

Article 10

No migrant worker or member of his or her family shall be subjected to torture or to cruel, inhuman or degrading treatment or punishment.

Article 11

1. No migrant worker or member of his or her family shall be held in slavery or servitude.

2. No migrant worker or member of his or her family shall be required to perform forced or compulsory labour.

3. Paragraph 2 of the present article shall not be held to preclude, in States where imprisonment with hard labour may be imposed as a punishment for a crime, the performance of hard labour in pursuance of a sentence to such punishment by a competent court.

4. For the purpose of the present article the term “forced or compulsory labour” shall not include:

(a) Any work or service not referred to in paragraph 3 of the present article normally required of a person who is under detention in consequence of a lawful order of a court or of a person during conditional release from such detention;

(b) Any service exacted in cases of emergency or calamity threatening the life or well-being of the community;

(c) Any work or service that forms part of normal civil obligations so far as it is imposed also on citizens of the State concerned.

Article 12

1. Migrant workers and members of their families shall have the right to freedom of thought, conscience and religion. This right shall include freedom to have or to adopt a religion or belief of their choice and freedom either individually or in community with others and in public or private to manifest their religion or belief in worship, observance, practice and teaching.

2. Migrant workers and members of their families shall not be subject to coercion that would impair their freedom to have or to adopt a religion or belief of their choice.

3. Freedom to manifest one’s religion or belief may be subject only to such limitations as are prescribed by law and are necessary to protect public safety, order, health or morals or the fundamental rights and freedoms of others.

4. States Parties to the present Convention undertake to have respect for the liberty of parents, at least one of whom is a migrant worker, and, when applicable, legal guardians to ensure the religious and moral education of their children in conformity with their own convictions.

Article 13

1. Migrant workers and members of their families shall have the right to hold opinions without interference.

2. Migrant workers and members of their families shall have the right to freedom of expression; this right shall include freedom to seek, receive and impart information and ideas of all kinds, regardless of frontiers, either orally, in writing or in print, in the form of art or through any other media of their choice.

3. The exercise of the right provided for in paragraph 2 of the present article carries with it special duties and responsibilities. It may therefore be subject to certain restrictions, but these shall only be such as are provided by law and are necessary:

(a) For respect of the rights or reputation of others;

(b) For the protection of the national security of the States concerned or of public order (ordre public) or of public health or morals;

(c) For the purpose of preventing any propaganda for war;

(d) For the purpose of preventing any advocacy of national, racial or religious hatred that constitutes incitement to discrimination, hostility or violence.

Article 14

No migrant worker or member of his or her family shall be subjected to arbitrary or unlawful interference with his or her privacy, family, home, correspondence or other communications, or to unlawful attacks on his or her honour and reputation. Each migrant worker and member of his or her family shall have the right to the protection of the law against such interference or attacks.

Article 15

No migrant worker or member of his or her family shall be arbitrarily deprived of property, whether owned individually or in association with others. Where, under the legislation in force in the State of employment, the assets of a migrant worker or a member of his or her family are expropriated in whole or in part, the person concerned shall have the right to fair and adequate compensation.

Article 16

1. Migrant workers and members of their families shall have the right to liberty and security of person.

2. Migrant workers and members of their families shall be entitled to effective protection by the State against violence, physical injury, threats and intimidation, whether by public officials or by private individuals, groups or institutions.

3. Any verification by law enforcement officials of the identity of migrant workers or members of their families shall be carried out in accordance with procedure established by law.

4. Migrant workers and members of their families shall not be subjected individually or collectively to arbitrary arrest or detention; they shall not be deprived of their liberty except on such grounds and in accordance with such procedures as are established by law.

5. Migrant workers and members of their families who are arrested shall be informed at the time of arrest as far as possible in a language they understand of the reasons for their arrest and they shall be promptly informed in a language they understand of any charges against them.

6. Migrant workers and members of their families who are arrested or detained on a criminal charge shall be brought promptly before a judge or other officer authorized by law to exercise judicial power and shall be entitled to trial within a reasonable time or to release. It shall not be the general rule that while awaiting trial they shall be detained in custody, but release may be subject to guarantees to appear for trial, at any other stage of the judicial proceedings and, should the occasion arise, for the execution of the judgement.

7. When a migrant worker or a member of his or her family is arrested or committed to prison or custody pending trial or is detained in any other manner:

(a) The consular or diplomatic authorities of his or her State of origin or of a State representing the interests of that State shall, if he or she so requests, be informed without delay of his or her arrest or detention and of the reasons therefor;

(b) The person concerned shall have the right to communicate with the said authorities. Any communication by the person concerned to the said authorities shall be forwarded without delay, and he or she shall also have the right to receive communications sent by the said authorities without delay;

(c) The person concerned shall be informed without delay of this right and of rights deriving from relevant treaties, if any, applicable between the States concerned, to correspond and to meet with representatives of the said authorities and to make arrangements with them for his or her legal representation.

8. Migrant workers and members of their families who are deprived of their liberty by arrest or detention shall be entitled to take proceedings before a court, in order that that court may decide without delay on the lawfulness of their detention and order their release if the detention is not lawful. When they attend such proceedings, they shall have the assistance, if necessary without cost to them, of an interpreter, if they cannot understand or speak the language used.

9. Migrant workers and members of their families who have been victims of unlawful arrest or detention shall have an enforceable right to compensation.

Article 17

1. Migrant workers and members of their families who are deprived of their liberty shall be treated with humanity and with respect for the inherent dignity of the human person and for their cultural identity.

2. Accused migrant workers and members of their families shall, save in exceptional circumstances, be separated from convicted persons and shall be subject to separate treatment appropriate to their status as unconvicted persons. Accused juvenile persons shall be separated from adults and brought as speedily as possible for adjudication.

3. Any migrant worker or member of his or her family who is detained in a State of transit or in a State of employment for violation of provisions relating to migration shall be held, in so far as practicable, separately from convicted persons or persons detained pending trial.

4. During any period of imprisonment in pursuance of a sentence imposed by a court of law, the essential aim of the treatment of a migrant worker or a member of his or her family shall be his or her reformation and social rehabilitation. Juvenile offenders shall be separated from adults and be accorded treatment appropriate to their age and legal status.

5. During detention or imprisonment, migrant workers and members of their families shall enjoy the same rights as nationals to visits by members of their families.

6. Whenever a migrant worker is deprived of his or her liberty, the competent authorities of the State concerned shall pay attention to the problems that may be posed for members of his or her family, in particular for spouses and minor children.

7. Migrant workers and members of their families who are subjected to any form of detention or imprisonment in accordance with the law in force in the State of employment or in the State of transit shall enjoy the same rights as nationals of those States who are in the same situation.

8. If a migrant worker or a member of his or her family is detained for the purpose of verifying any infraction of provisions related to migration, he or she shall not bear any costs arising therefrom.

Article 18

1. Migrant workers and members of their families shall have the right to equality with nationals of the State concerned before the courts and tribunals. In the determination of any criminal charge against them or of their rights and obligations in a suit of law, they shall be entitled to a fair and public hearing by a competent, independent and impartial tribunal established by law.

2. Migrant workers and members of their families who are charged with a criminal offence shall have the right to be presumed innocent until proven guilty according to law.

3. In the determination of any criminal charge against them, migrant workers and members of their families shall be entitled to the following minimum guarantees:

(a) To be informed promptly and in detail in a language they understand of the nature and cause of the charge against them;

(b) To have adequate time and facilities for the preparation of their defence and to communicate with counsel of their own choosing;

(c) To be tried without undue delay;

(d) To be tried in their presence and to defend themselves in person or through legal assistance of their own choosing; to be informed, if they do not have legal assistance, of this right; and to have legal assistance assigned to them, in any case where the interests of justice so require and without payment by them in any such case if they do not have sufficient means to pay;

(e) To examine or have examined the witnesses against them and to obtain the attendance and examination of witnesses on their behalf under the same conditions as witnesses against them;

(f) To have the free assistance of an interpreter if they cannot understand or speak the language used in court;

(g) Not to be compelled to testify against themselves or to confess guilt.

4. In the case of juvenile persons, the procedure shall be such as will take account of their age and the desirability of promoting their rehabilitation.

5. Migrant workers and members of their families convicted of a crime shall have the right to their conviction and sentence being reviewed by a higher tribunal according to law.

6. When a migrant worker or a member of his or her family has, by a final decision, been convicted of a criminal offence and when subsequently his or her conviction has been reversed or he or she has been pardoned on the ground that a new or newly discovered fact shows conclusively that there has been a miscarriage of justice, the person who has suffered punishment as a result of such conviction shall be compensated according to law, unless it is proved that the non-disclosure of the unknown fact in time is wholly or partly attributable to that person.

7. No migrant worker or member of his or her family shall be liable to be tried or punished again for an offence for which he or she has already been finally convicted or acquitted in accordance with the law and penal procedure of the State concerned.

Article 19

1. No migrant worker or member of his or her family shall be held guilty of any criminal offence on account of any act or omission that did not constitute a criminal offence under national or international law at the time when the criminal offence was committed, nor shall a heavier penalty be imposed than the one that was applicable at the time when it was committed. If, subsequent to the commission of the offence, provision is made by law for the imposition of a lighter penalty, he or she shall benefit thereby.

2. Humanitarian considerations related to the status of a migrant worker, in particular with respect to his or her right of residence or work, should be taken into account in imposing a

sentence for a criminal offence committed by a migrant worker or a member of his or her family.

Article 20

1. No migrant worker or member of his or her family shall be imprisoned merely on the ground of failure to fulfil a contractual obligation.

2. No migrant worker or member of his or her family shall be deprived of his or her authorization of residence or work permit or expelled merely on the ground of failure to fulfil an obligation arising out of a work contract unless fulfilment of that obligation constitutes a condition for such authorization or permit.

Article 21

It shall be unlawful for anyone, other than a public official duly authorized by law, to confiscate, destroy or attempt to destroy identity documents, documents authorizing entry to or stay, residence or establishment in the national territory or work permits. No authorized confiscation of such documents shall take place without delivery of a detailed receipt. In no case shall it be permitted to destroy the passport or equivalent document of a migrant worker or a member of his or her family.

Article 22

1. Migrant workers and members of their families shall not be subject to measures of collective expulsion. Each case of expulsion shall be examined and decided individually.

2. Migrant workers and members of their families may be expelled from the territory of a State Party only in pursuance of a decision taken by the competent authority in accordance with law.

3. The decision shall be communicated to them in a language they understand. Upon their request where not otherwise mandatory, the decision shall be communicated to them in writing and, save in exceptional circumstances on account of national security, the reasons for the decision likewise stated. The persons concerned shall be informed of these rights before or at the latest at the time the decision is rendered.

4. Except where a final decision is pronounced by a judicial authority, the person concerned shall have the right to submit the reason he or she should not be expelled and to have his or her case reviewed by the competent authority, unless compelling reasons of national security require otherwise. Pending such review, the person concerned shall have the right to seek a stay of the decision of expulsion.

5. If a decision of expulsion that has already been executed is subsequently annulled, the person concerned shall have the right to seek compensation according to law and the earlier decision shall not be used to prevent him or her from re-entering the State concerned.

6. In case of expulsion, the person concerned shall have a reasonable opportunity before or after departure to settle any claims for wages and other entitlements due to him or her and any pending liabilities.

7. Without prejudice to the execution of a decision of expulsion, a migrant worker or a member of his or her family who is subject to such a decision may seek entry into a State other than his or her State of origin.

8. In case of expulsion of a migrant worker or a member of his or her family the costs of expulsion shall not be borne by him or her. The person concerned may be required to pay his or her own travel costs.

9. Expulsion from the State of employment shall not in itself prejudice any rights of a migrant worker or a member of his or her family acquired in accordance with the law of that State, including the right to receive wages and other entitlements due to him or her.

Article 23

Migrant workers and members of their families shall have the right to have recourse to the protection and assistance of the consular or diplomatic authorities of their State of origin or of a State representing the interests of that State whenever the rights recognized in the present Convention are impaired. In particular, in case of expulsion, the person concerned shall be informed of this right without delay and the authorities of the expelling State shall facilitate the exercise of such right.

Article 24

Every migrant worker and every member of his or her family shall have the right to recognition everywhere as a person before the law.

Article 25

1. Migrant workers shall enjoy treatment not less favourable than that which applies to nationals of the State of employment in respect of remuneration and:

(a) Other conditions of work, that is to say, overtime, hours of work, weekly rest, holidays with pay, safety, health, termination of the employment relationship and any other conditions of work which, according to national law and practice, are covered by these terms;

(b) Other terms of employment, that is to say, minimum age of employment, restriction on home work and any other matters which, according to national law and practice, are considered a term of employment.

2. It shall not be lawful to derogate in private contracts of employment from the principle of equality of treatment referred to in paragraph 1 of the present article.

3. States Parties shall take all appropriate measures to ensure that migrant workers are not deprived of any rights derived from this principle by reason of any irregularity in their stay or employment. In particular, employers shall not be relieved of any legal or contractual obligations, nor shall their obligations be limited in any manner by reason of such irregularity.

Article 26

1. States Parties recognize the right of migrant workers and members of their families:

(a) To take part in meetings and activities of trade unions and of any other associations established in accordance with law, with a view to protecting their economic, social, cultural and other interests, subject only to the rules of the organization concerned;

(b) To join freely any trade union and any such association as aforesaid, subject only to the rules of the organization concerned;

(c) To seek the aid and assistance of any trade union and of any such association as aforesaid.

2. No restrictions may be placed on the exercise of these rights other than those that are prescribed by law and which are necessary in a democratic society in the interests of national security, public order (ordre public) or the protection of the rights and freedoms of others.

Article 27

1. With respect to social security, migrant workers and members of their families shall enjoy in the State of employment the same treatment granted to nationals in so far as they fulfil the requirements provided for by the applicable legislation of that State and the applicable bilateral and multilateral treaties. The competent authorities of the State of origin and the State of employment can at any time establish the necessary arrangements to determine the modalities of application of this norm.

2. Where the applicable legislation does not allow migrant workers and members of their families a benefit, the States concerned shall examine the possibility of reimbursing interested persons the amount of contributions made by them with respect to that benefit on the basis of the treatment granted to nationals who are in similar circumstances.

Article 28

Migrant workers and members of their families shall have the right to receive any medical care that is urgently required for the preservation of their life or the avoidance of irreparable harm to their health on the basis of equality of treatment with nationals of the State concerned. Such emergency medical care shall not be refused them by reason of any irregularity with regard to stay or employment.

Article 29

Each child of a migrant worker shall have the right to a name, to registration of birth and to a nationality.

Article 30

Each child of a migrant worker shall have the basic right of access to education on the basis of equality of treatment with nationals of the State concerned. Access to public pre-school educational institutions or schools shall not be refused or limited by reason of the irregular situation with respect to stay or employment of either parent or by reason of the irregularity of the child's stay in the State of employment.

Article 31

1. States Parties shall ensure respect for the cultural identity of migrant workers and members of their families and shall not prevent them from maintaining their cultural links with their State of origin.

2. States Parties may take appropriate measures to assist and encourage efforts in this respect.

Article 32

Upon the termination of their stay in the State of employment, migrant workers and members of their families shall have the right to transfer their earnings and savings and, in accordance with the applicable legislation of the States concerned, their personal effects and belongings.

Article 33

1. Migrant workers and members of their families shall have the right to be informed by the State of origin, the State of employment or the State of transit as the case may be concerning:

(a) Their rights arising out of the present Convention;

(b) The conditions of their admission, their rights and obligations under the law and practice of the State concerned and such other matters as will enable them to comply with administrative or other formalities in that State.

2. States Parties shall take all measures they deem appropriate to disseminate the said information or to ensure that it is provided by employers, trade unions or other appropriate bodies or institutions. As appropriate, they shall co-operate with other States concerned.

3. Such adequate information shall be provided upon request to migrant workers and members of their families, free of charge, and, as far as possible, in a language they are able to understand.

Article 34

Nothing in the present part of the Convention shall have the effect of relieving migrant workers and the members of their families from either the obligation to comply with the laws and regulations of any State of transit and the State of employment or the obligation to respect the cultural identity of the inhabitants of such States.

Article 35

Nothing in the present part of the Convention shall be interpreted as implying the regularization of the situation of migrant workers or members of their families who are non-documented or in an irregular situation or any right to such regularization of their situation, nor shall it prejudice the measures intended to ensure sound and equitable conditions for international migration as provided in part VI of the present Convention.

PART IV: OTHER RIGHTS OF MIGRANT WORKERS AND MEMBERS OF THEIR FAMILIES WHO ARE DOCUMENTED OR IN A REGULAR SITUATION

Article 36

Migrant workers and members of their families who are documented or in a regular situation in the State of employment shall enjoy the rights set forth in the present part of the Convention in addition to those set forth in part III.

Article 37

Before their departure, or at the latest at the time of their admission to the State of employment, migrant workers and members of their families shall have the right to be fully informed by the State of origin or the State of employment, as appropriate, of all conditions applicable to their admission and particularly those concerning their stay and the remunerated activities in which they may engage as well as of the requirements they must satisfy in the State of employment and the authority to which they must address themselves for any modification of those conditions.

Article 38

1. States of employment shall make every effort to authorize migrant workers and members of their families to be temporarily absent without effect upon their authorization to stay or to work, as the case may be. In doing so, States of employment shall take into account the special needs and obligations of migrant workers and members of their families, in particular in their States of origin.

2. Migrant workers and members of their families shall have the right to be fully informed of the terms on which such temporary absences are authorized.

Article 39

1. Migrant workers and members of their families shall have the right to liberty of movement in the territory of the State of employment and freedom to choose their residence there.

2. The rights mentioned in paragraph 1 of the present article shall not be subject to any restrictions except those that are provided by law, are necessary to protect national security, public order (ordre public), public health or morals, or the rights and freedoms of others and are consistent with the other rights recognized in the present Convention.

Article 40

1. Migrant workers and members of their families shall have the right to form associations and trade unions in the State of employment for the promotion and protection of their economic, social, cultural and other interests.

2. No restrictions may be placed on the exercise of this right other than those that are prescribed by law and are necessary in a democratic society in the interests of national security, public order (ordre public) or the protection of the rights and freedoms of others.

Article 41

1. Migrant workers and members of their families shall have the right to participate in public affairs of their State of origin and to vote and to be elected at elections of that State, in accordance with its legislation.

2. The States concerned shall, as appropriate and in accordance with their legislation, facilitate the exercise of these rights.

Article 42

1. States Parties shall consider the establishment of procedures or institutions through which account may be taken, both in States of origin and in States of employment, of special needs, aspirations and obligations of migrant workers and members of their families and shall envisage, as appropriate, the possibility for migrant workers and members of their families to have their freely chosen representatives in those institutions.

2. States of employment shall facilitate, in accordance with their national legislation, the consultation or participation of migrant workers and members of their families in decisions concerning the life and administration of local communities.

3. Migrant workers may enjoy political rights in the State of employment if that State, in the exercise of its sovereignty, grants them such rights.

Article 43

1. Migrant workers shall enjoy equality of treatment with nationals of the State of employment in relation to:

(a) Access to educational institutions and services subject to the admission requirements and other regulations of the institutions and services concerned;

(b) Access to vocational guidance and placement services;

(c) Access to vocational training and retraining facilities and institutions;

(d) Access to housing, including social housing schemes, and protection against exploitation in respect of rents;

(e) Access to social and health services, provided that the requirements for participation in the respective schemes are met;

(f) Access to co-operatives and self-managed enterprises, which shall not imply a change of their migration status and shall be subject to the rules and regulations of the bodies concerned;

(g) Access to and participation in cultural life.

2. States Parties shall promote conditions to ensure effective equality of treatment to enable migrant workers to enjoy the rights mentioned in paragraph 1 of the present article whenever the terms of their stay, as authorized by the State of employment, meet the appropriate requirements.

3. States of employment shall not prevent an employer of migrant workers from establishing housing or social or cultural facilities for them. Subject to article 70 of the present Convention, a State of employment may make the establishment of such facilities subject to the requirements generally applied in that State concerning their installation.

Article 44

1. States Parties, recognizing that the family is the natural and fundamental group unit of society and is entitled to protection by society and the State, shall take appropriate measures to ensure the protection of the unity of the families of migrant workers.

2. States Parties shall take measures that they deem appropriate and that fall within their competence to facilitate the reunification of migrant workers with their spouses or persons who have with the migrant worker a relationship that, according to applicable law, produces effects equivalent to marriage, as well as with their minor dependent unmarried children.

3. States of employment, on humanitarian grounds, shall favourably consider granting equal treatment, as set forth in paragraph 2 of the present article, to other family members of migrant workers.

Article 45

1. Members of the families of migrant workers shall, in the State of employment, enjoy equality of treatment with nationals of that State in relation to:

(a) Access to educational institutions and services, subject to the admission requirements and other regulations of the institutions and services concerned;

(b) Access to vocational guidance and training institutions and services, provided that requirements for participation are met;

(c) Access to social and health services, provided that requirements for participation in the respective schemes are met;

(d) Access to and participation in cultural life.

2. States of employment shall pursue a policy, where appropriate in collaboration with the States of origin, aimed at facilitating the integration of children of migrant workers in the local school system, particularly in respect of teaching them the local language.

3. States of employment shall endeavour to facilitate for the children of migrant workers the teaching of their mother tongue and culture and, in this regard, States of origin shall collaborate whenever appropriate.

4. States of employment may provide special schemes of education in the mother tongue of children of migrant workers, if necessary in collaboration with the States of origin.

Article 46

Migrant workers and members of their families shall, subject to the applicable legislation of the States concerned, as well as relevant international agreements and the obligations of the States concerned arising out of their participation in customs unions, enjoy exemption from import and export duties and taxes in respect of their personal and household effects as well as the equipment necessary to engage in the remunerated activity for which they were admitted to the State of employment:

(a) Upon departure from the State of origin or State of habitual residence;

(b) Upon initial admission to the State of employment;

(c) Upon final departure from the State of employment;

(d) Upon final return to the State of origin or State of habitual residence.

Article 47

1. Migrant workers shall have the right to transfer their earnings and savings, in particular those funds necessary for the support of their families, from the State of employment to their State of origin or any other State. Such transfers shall be made in conformity with procedures established by applicable legislation of the State concerned and in conformity with applicable international agreements.

2. States concerned shall take appropriate measures to facilitate such transfers.

Article 48

1. Without prejudice to applicable double taxation agreements, migrant workers and members of their families shall, in the matter of earnings in the State of employment:

(a) Not be liable to taxes, duties or charges of any description higher or more onerous than those imposed on nationals in similar circumstances;

(b) Be entitled to deductions or exemptions from taxes of any description and to any tax allowances applicable to nationals in similar circumstances, including tax allowances for dependent members of their families.

2. States Parties shall endeavour to adopt appropriate measures to avoid double taxation of the earnings and savings of migrant workers and members of their families.

Article 49

1. Where separate authorizations to reside and to engage in employment are required by national legislation, the States of employment shall issue to migrant workers authorization of residence for at least the same period of time as their authorization to engage in remunerated activity.

2. Migrant workers who in the State of employment are allowed freely to choose their remunerated activity shall neither be regarded as in an irregular situation nor shall they lose their authorization of residence by the mere fact of the termination of their remunerated activity prior to the expiration of their work permits or similar authorizations.

3. In order to allow migrant workers referred to in paragraph 2 of the present article sufficient time to find alternative remunerated activities, the authorization of residence shall not be withdrawn at least for a period corresponding to that during which they may be entitled to unemployment benefits.

Article 50

1. In the case of death of a migrant worker or dissolution of marriage, the State of employment shall favourably consider granting family members of that migrant worker residing in that State on the basis of family reunion an authorization to stay; the State of employment shall take into account the length of time they have already resided in that State.

2. Members of the family to whom such authorization is not granted shall be allowed before departure a reasonable period of time in order to enable them to settle their affairs in the State of employment.

3. The provisions of paragraphs 1 and 2 of the present article may not be interpreted as adversely affecting any right to stay and work otherwise granted to such family members by the legislation of the State of employment or by bilateral and multilateral treaties applicable to that State.

Article 51

Migrant workers who in the State of employment are not permitted freely to choose their remunerated activity shall neither be regarded as in an irregular situation nor shall they lose their authorization of residence by the mere fact of the termination of their remunerated activity prior to the expiration of their work permit, except where the authorization of residence is expressly dependent upon the specific remunerated activity for which they were admitted. Such migrant workers shall have the right to seek alternative employment, participation in public work schemes and retraining during the remaining period of their authorization to work, subject to such conditions and limitations as are specified in the authorization to work.

Article 52

1. Migrant workers in the State of employment shall have the right freely to choose their remunerated activity, subject to the following restrictions or conditions.

2. For any migrant worker a State of employment may:

(a) Restrict access to limited categories of employment, functions, services or activities where this is necessary in the interests of this State and provided for by national legislation;

(b) Restrict free choice of remunerated activity in accordance with its legislation concerning recognition of occupational qualifications acquired outside its territory. However, States Parties concerned shall endeavour to provide for recognition of such qualifications.

3. For migrant workers whose permission to work is limited in time, a State of employment may also:

(a) Make the right freely to choose their remunerated activities subject to the condition that the migrant worker has resided lawfully in its territory for the purpose of remunerated activity for a period of time prescribed in its national legislation that should not exceed two years;

(b) Limit access by a migrant worker to remunerated activities in pursuance of a policy of granting priority to its nationals or to persons who are assimilated to them for these purposes by virtue of legislation or bilateral or multilateral agreements. Any such limitation shall cease to apply to a migrant worker who has resided lawfully in its territory for the purpose of remunerated activity for a period of time prescribed in its national legislation that should not exceed five years.

4. States of employment shall prescribe the conditions under which a migrant worker who has been admitted to take up employment may be authorized to engage in work on his or her own account. Account shall be taken of the period during which the worker has already been lawfully in the State of employment.

Article 53

1. Members of a migrant worker's family who have themselves an authorization of residence or admission that is without limit of time or is automatically renewable shall be permitted freely to choose their remunerated activity under the same conditions as are applicable to the said migrant worker in accordance with article 52 of the present Convention.

2. With respect to members of a migrant worker's family who are not permitted freely to choose their remunerated activity, States Parties shall consider favourably granting them priority in obtaining permission to engage in a remunerated activity over other workers who seek admission to the State of employment, subject to applicable bilateral and multilateral agreements.

Article 54

1. Without prejudice to the terms of their authorization of residence or their permission to work and the rights provided for in articles 25 and 27 of the present Convention, migrant workers shall enjoy equality of treatment with nationals of the State of employment in respect of:

(a) Protection against dismissal;

(b) Unemployment benefits;

(c) Access to public work schemes intended to combat unemployment;

(d) Access to alternative employment in the event of loss of work or termination of other remunerated activity, subject to article 52 of the present Convention.

2. If a migrant worker claims that the terms of his or her work contract have been violated by his or her employer, he or she shall have the right to address his or her case to the competent authorities of the State of employment, on terms provided for in article 18, paragraph 1, of the present Convention.

Article 55

Migrant workers who have been granted permission to engage in a remunerated activity, subject to the conditions attached to such permission, shall be entitled to equality of treatment with nationals of the State of employment in the exercise of that remunerated activity.

Article 56

1. Migrant workers and members of their families referred to in the present part of the Convention may not be expelled from a State of employment, except for reasons defined in the national legislation of that State, and subject to the safeguards established in part III.

2. Expulsion shall not be resorted to for the purpose of depriving a migrant worker or a member of his or her family of the rights arising out of the authorization of residence and the work permit.

3. In considering whether to expel a migrant worker or a member of his or her family, account should be taken of humanitarian considerations and of the length of time that the person concerned has already resided in the State of employment.

PART V: PROVISIONS APPLICABLE TO PARTICULAR CATEGORIES OF MIGRANT WORKERS AND MEMBERS OF THEIR FAMILIES

Article 57

The particular categories of migrant workers and members of their families specified in the present part of the Convention who are documented or in a regular situation shall enjoy the rights set forth in part III and, except as modified below, the rights set forth in part IV.

Article 58

1. Frontier workers, as defined in article 2, paragraph 2 (a), of the present Convention, shall be entitled to the rights provided for in part IV that can be applied to them by reason of their presence and work in the territory of the State of employment, taking into account that they do not have their habitual residence in that State.

2. States of employment shall consider favourably granting frontier workers the right freely to choose their remunerated activity after a specified period of time. The granting of that right shall not affect their status as frontier workers.

Article 59

1. Seasonal workers, as defined in article 2, paragraph 2 (b), of the present Convention, shall be entitled to the rights provided for in part IV that can be applied to them by reason of their presence and work in the territory of the State of employment and that are compatible with their status in that State as seasonal workers, taking into account the fact that they are present in that State for only part of the year.

2. The State of employment shall, subject to paragraph 1 of the present article, consider granting seasonal workers who have been employed in its territory for a significant period of time the possibility of taking up other remunerated activities and giving them priority over other workers who seek admission to that State, subject to applicable bilateral and multilateral agreements.

Article 60

Itinerant workers, as defined in article 2, paragraph 2 (e), of the present Convention, shall be entitled to the rights provided for in part IV that can be granted to them by reason of their presence and work in the territory of the State of employment and that are compatible with their status as itinerant workers in that State.

Article 61

1. Project-tied workers, as defined in article 2, paragraph 2 (f) of the present Convention, and members of their families shall be entitled to the rights provided for in part IV except the provisions of article 43, paragraphs 1 (b) and (c), article 43, paragraph 1 (d), as it pertains to social housing schemes, article 45, paragraph 1 (b), and articles 52 to 55.

2. If a project-tied worker claims that the terms of his or her work contract have been violated by his or her employer, he or she shall have the right to address his or her case to the competent authorities of the State which has jurisdiction over that employer, on terms provided for in article 18, paragraph 1, of the present Convention.

3. Subject to bilateral or multilateral agreements in force for them, the States Parties concerned shall endeavour to enable project-tied workers to remain adequately protected by the social security systems of their States of origin or habitual residence during their engagement in the project. States Parties concerned shall take appropriate measures with the aim of avoiding any denial of rights or duplication of payments in this respect.

4. Without prejudice to the provisions of article 47 of the present Convention and to relevant bilateral or multilateral agreements, States Parties concerned shall permit payment of the earnings of project-tied workers in their State of origin or habitual residence.

Article 62

1. Specified-employment workers as defined in article 2, paragraph 2 (g), of the present Convention, shall be entitled to the rights provided for in part IV, except the provisions of article 43, paragraphs 1 (b) and (c), article 43, paragraph 1 (d), as it pertains to social housing schemes, article 52, and article 54, paragraph 1 (d).

2. Members of the families of specified-employment workers shall be entitled to the rights relating to family members of migrant workers provided for in part IV of the present Convention, except the provisions of article 53.

Article 63

1. Self-employed workers, as defined in article 2, paragraph 2 (h), of the pre sent Convention, shall be entitled to the rights provided for in part IV with the exception of those rights which are exclusively applicable to workers having a contract of employment.

2. Without prejudice to articles 52 and 79 of the present Convention, the termination of the economic activity of the self-employed workers shall not in itself imply the withdrawal of the authorization for them or for the members of their families to stay or to engage in a remunerated activity in the State of employment except where the authorization of residence is expressly dependent upon the specific remunerated activity for which they were admitted.

PART VI: PROMOTION OF SOUND, EQUITABLE, HUMANE AND LAWFUL CONDITIONS IN CONNECTION WITH INTERNATIONAL MIGRATION OF WORKERS AND MEMBERS OF THEIR FAMILIES

Article 64

1. Without prejudice to article 79 of the present Convention, the States Parties concerned shall as appropriate consult and co-operate with a view to promoting sound, equitable and humane conditions in connection with international migration of workers and members of their families.

2. In this respect, due regard shall be paid not only to labour needs and resources, but also to the social, economic, cultural and other needs of migrant workers and members of their families involved, as well as to the consequences of such migration for the communities concerned.

Article 65

1. States Parties shall maintain appropriate services to deal with questions concerning international migration of workers and members of their families. Their functions shall include, inter alia:

(a) The formulation and implementation of policies regarding such migration;

(b) An exchange of information. consultation and co-operation with the competent authorities of other States Parties involved in such migration;

(c) The provision of appropriate information, particularly to employers, workers and their organizations on policies, laws and regulations relating to migration and employment, on agreements concluded with other States concerning migration and on other relevant matters;

(d) The provision of information and appropriate assistance to migrant workers and members of their families regarding requisite authorizations and formalities and arrangements for departure, travel, arrival, stay, remunerated activities, exit and return, as well as on conditions of work and life in the State of employment and on customs, currency, tax and other relevant laws and regulations.

2. States Parties shall facilitate as appropriate the provision of adequate consular and other services that are necessary to meet the social, cultural and other needs of migrant workers and members of their families.

Article 66

1. Subject to paragraph 2 of the present article, the right to undertake operations with a view to the recruitment of workers for employment in another State shall be restricted to:

(a) Public services or bodies of the State in which such operations take place;

(b) Public services or bodies of the State of employment on the basis of agreement between the States concerned;

(c) A body established by virtue of a bilateral or multilateral agreement.

2. Subject to any authorization, approval and supervision by the public authorities of the States Parties concerned as may be established pursuant to the legislation and practice of those States, agencies, prospective employers or persons acting on their behalf may also be permitted to undertake the said operations.

Article 67

1. States Parties concerned shall co-operate as appropriate in the adoption of measures regarding the orderly return of migrant workers and members of their families to the State of origin when they decide to return or their authorization of residence or employment expires or when they are in the State of employment in an irregular situation.

2. Concerning migrant workers and members of their families in a regular situation, States Parties concerned shall co-operate as appropriate, on terms agreed upon by those States, with a view to promoting adequate economic conditions for their resettlement and to facilitating their durable social and cultural reintegration in the State of origin.

Article 68

1. States Parties, including States of transit, shall collaborate with a view to preventing and eliminating illegal or clandestine movements and employment of migrant workers in an irregular situation. The measures to be taken to this end within the jurisdiction of each State concerned shall include:

(a) Appropriate measures against the dissemination of misleading information relating to emigration and immigration;

(b) Measures to detect and eradicate illegal or clandestine movements of migrant workers and members of their families and to impose effective sanctions on persons, groups or entities which organize, operate or assist in organizing or operating such movements;

(c) Measures to impose effective sanctions on persons, groups or entities which use violence, threats or intimidation against migrant workers or members of their families in an irregular situation.

2. States of employment shall take all adequate and effective measures to eliminate employment in their territory of migrant workers in an irregular situation, including, whenever appropriate, sanctions on employers of such workers. The rights of migrant workers vis-à-vis their employer arising from employment shall not be impaired by these measures.

Article 69

1. States Parties shall, when there are migrant workers and members of their families within their territory in an irregular situation, take appropriate measures to ensure that such a situation does not persist.

2. Whenever States Parties concerned consider the possibility of regularizing the situation of such persons in accordance with applicable national legislation and bilateral or multilateral agreements, appropriate account shall be taken of the circumstances of their entry, the duration of their stay in the States of employment and other relevant considerations, in particular those relating to their family situation.

Article 70

States Parties shall take measures not less favourable than those applied to nationals to ensure that working and living conditions of migrant workers and members of their families in a regular situation are in keeping with the standards of fitness, safety, health and principles of human dignity.

Article 71

1. States Parties shall facilitate, whenever necessary, the repatriation to the State of origin of the bodies of deceased migrant workers or members of their families.

2. As regards compensation matters relating to the death of a migrant worker or a member of his or her family, States Parties shall, as appropriate, provide assistance to the persons concerned with a view to the prompt settlement of such matters. Settlement of these matters shall be carried out on the basis of applicable national law in accordance with the provisions of the present Convention and any relevant bilateral or multilateral agreements.

PART VII: APPLICATION OF THE CONVENTION

Article 72

1. (a) For the purpose of reviewing the application of the present Convention, there shall be established a Committee on the Protection of the Rights of All Migrant Workers and Members of Their Families (hereinafter referred to as "the Committee");

(b) The Committee shall consist, at the time of entry into force of the present Convention, of ten and, after the entry into force of the Convention for the forty-first State Party, of fourteen experts of high moral standing, impartiality and recognized competence in the field covered by the Convention.

2. (a) Members of the Committee shall be elected by secret ballot by the States Parties from a list of persons nominated by the States Parties, due consideration being given to equitable geographical distribution, including both States of origin and States of employment, and to the representation of the principal legal systems. Each State Party may nominate one person from among its own nationals;

(b) Members shall be elected and shall serve in their personal capacity.

3. The initial election shall be held no later than six months after the date of the entry into force of the present Convention and subsequent elections every second year. At least four months before the date of each election, the Secretary-General of the United Nations shall address a letter to all States Parties inviting them to submit their nominations within two months. The Secretary-General shall prepare a list in alphabetical order of all persons thus nominated, indicating the States Parties that have nominated them, and shall submit it to the States Parties not later than one month before the date of the corresponding election, together with the curricula vitae of the persons thus nominated.

4. Elections of members of the Committee shall be held at a meeting of States Parties convened by the Secretary-General at United Nations Headquarters. At that meeting, for which two thirds of the States Parties shall constitute a quorum, the persons elected to the Committee shall be those nominees who obtain the largest number of votes and an absolute majority of the votes of the States Parties present and voting.

5. (a) The members of the Committee shall serve for a term of four years. However, the terms of five of the members elected in the first election shall expire at the end of two years; immediately after the first election, the names of these five members shall be chosen by lot by the Chairman of the meeting of States Parties;

(b) The election of the four additional members of the Committee shall be held in accordance with the provisions of paragraphs 2, 3 and 4 of the present article, following the entry into force of the Convention for the forty-first State Party. The term of two of the additional members elected on this occasion shall expire at the end of two years; the names of these members shall be chosen by lot by the Chairman of the meeting of States Parties;

(c) The members of the Committee shall be eligible for re-election if renominated.

6. If a member of the Committee dies or resigns or declares that for any other cause he or she can no longer perform the duties of the Committee, the State Party that nominated the expert shall appoint another expert from among its own nationals for the remaining part of the term. The new appointment is subject to the approval of the Committee.

7. The Secretary-General of the United Nations shall provide the necessary staff and facilities for the effective performance of the functions of the Committee.

8. The members of the Committee shall receive emoluments from United Nations resources on such terms and conditions as the General Assembly may decide.

9. The members of the Committee shall be entitled to the facilities, privileges and immunities of experts on mission for the United Nations as laid down in the relevant sections of the Convention on the Privileges and Immunities of the United Nations.

Article 73

1. States Parties undertake to submit to the Secretary-General of the United Nations for consideration by the Committee a report on the legislative, judicial, administrative and other measures they have taken to give effect to the provisions of the present Convention:

(a) Within one year after the entry into force of the Convention for the State Party concerned;

(b) Thereafter every five years and whenever the Committee so requests.

2. Reports prepared under the present article shall also indicate factors and difficulties, if any, affecting the implementation of the Convention and shall include information on the characteristics of migration flows in which the State Party concerned is involved.

3. The Committee shall decide any further guidelines applicable to the content of the reports.

4. States Parties shall make their reports widely available to the public in their own countries.

Article 74

1. The Committee shall examine the reports submitted by each State Party and shall transmit such comments as it may consider appropriate to the State Party concerned. This State Party may submit to the Committee observations on any comment made by the Committee in accordance with the present article. The Committee may request supplementary information from States Parties when considering these reports.

2. The Secretary-General of the United Nations shall, in due time before the opening of each regular session of the Committee, transmit to the Director-General of the International Labour Office copies of the reports submitted by States Parties concerned and information relevant to the consideration of these reports, in order to enable the Office to assist the Committee with the expertise the Office may provide regarding those matters dealt with by the present Convention that fall within the sphere of competence of the International Labour Organisation. The Committee shall consider in its deliberations such comments and materials as the Office may provide.

3. The Secretary-General of the United Nations may also, after consultation with the Committee, transmit to other specialized agencies as well as to intergovernmental organizations, copies of such parts of these reports as may fall within their competence.

4. The Committee may invite the specialized agencies and organs of the United Nations, as well as intergovernmental organizations and other concerned bodies to submit, for consideration by the Committee, written information on such matters dealt with in the present Convention as fall within the scope of their activities.

5. The International Labour Office shall be invited by the Committee to appoint representatives to participate, in a consultative capacity, in the meetings of the Committee.

6. The Committee may invite representatives of other specialized agencies and organs of the United Nations, as well as of intergovernmental organizations, to be present and to be heard in its meetings whenever matters falling within their field of competence are considered.

7. The Committee shall present an annual report to the General Assembly of the United Nations on the implementation of the present Convention, containing its own considerations and recommendations, based, in particular, on the examination of the reports and any observations presented by States Parties.

8. The Secretary-General of the United Nations shall transmit the annual reports of the Committee to the States Parties to the present Convention, the Economic and Social Council, the Commission on Human Rights of the United Nations, the Director-General of the International Labour Office and other relevant organizations.

Article 75

1. The Committee shall adopt its own rules of procedure.

2. The Committee shall elect its officers for a term of two years.

3. The Committee shall normally meet annually.

4. The meetings of the Committee shall normally be held at United Nations Headquarters.

Article 76

1. A State Party to the present Convention may at any time declare under this article that it recognizes the competence of the Committee to receive and consider communications to the effect that a State Party claims that another State Party is not fulfilling its obligations under the present Convention. Communications under this article may be received and considered only if submitted by a State Party that has made a declaration recognizing in regard to itself the competence of the Committee. No communication shall be received by the Committee if it concerns a State Party which has not made such a declaration. Communications received under this article shall be dealt with in accordance with the following procedure:

(a) If a State Party to the present Convention considers that another State Party is not fulfilling its obligations under the present Convention, it may, by written communication, bring the matter to the attention of that State Party. The State Party may also inform the Committee of the matter. Within three months after the receipt of the communication the receiving State shall afford the State that sent the communication an explanation, or any other statement in writing clarifying the matter which should include, to the extent possible and pertinent, reference to domestic procedures and remedies taken, pending or available in the matter;

(b) If the matter is not adjusted to the satisfaction of both States Parties concerned within six months after the receipt by the receiving State of the initial communication, either State shall have the right to refer the matter to the Committee, by notice given to the Committee and to the other State;

(c) The Committee shall deal with a matter referred to it only after it has ascertained that all available domestic remedies have been invoked and exhausted in the matter, in conformity with the generally recognized principles of international law. This shall not be the rule where, in the view of the Committee, the application of the remedies is unreasonably prolonged;

(d) Subject to the provisions of subparagraph (c) of the present paragraph, the Committee shall make available its good offices to the States Parties concerned with a view to a friendly solution of the matter on the basis of the respect for the obligations set forth in the present Convention;

(e) The Committee shall hold closed meetings when examining communications under the present article;

(f) In any matter referred to it in accordance with subparagraph (b) of the present paragraph, the Committee may call upon the States Parties concerned, referred to in subparagraph (b), to supply any relevant information;

(g) The States Parties concerned, referred to in subparagraph (b) of the present paragraph, shall have the right to be represented when the matter is being considered by the Committee and to make submissions orally and/or in writing;

(h) The Committee shall, within twelve months after the date of receipt of notice under subparagraph (b) of the present paragraph, submit a report, as follows:

(i) If a solution within the terms of subparagraph (d) of the present paragraph is reached, the Committee shall confine its report to a brief statement of the facts and of the solution reached;

(ii) If a solution within the terms of subparagraph (d) is not reached, the Committee shall, in its report, set forth the relevant facts concerning the issue between the States Parties concerned. The written submissions and record of the oral submissions made by the States Parties concerned shall be attached to the report. The Committee may also communicate only to the States Parties concerned any views that it may consider relevant to the issue between them. In every matter, the report shall be communicated to the States Parties concerned.

2. The provisions of the present article shall come into force when ten States Parties to the present Convention have made a declaration under paragraph 1 of the present article. Such declarations shall be deposited by the States Parties with the Secretary-General of the United Nations, who shall transmit copies thereof to the other States Parties. A declaration may be withdrawn at any time by notification to the Secretary-General. Such a withdrawal shall not prejudice the consideration of any matter that is the subject of a communication already transmitted under the present article; no further communication by any State Party shall be received under the present article after the notification of withdrawal of the declaration has been received by the Secretary-General, unless the State Party concerned has made a new declaration.

Article 77

1. A State Party to the present Convention may at any time declare under the present article that it recognizes the competence of the Committee to receive and consider communications from or on behalf of individuals subject to its jurisdiction who claim that their individual rights as established by the present Convention have been violated by that State Party. No communication shall be received by the Committee if it concerns a State Party that has not made such a declaration.

2. The Committee shall consider inadmissible any communication under the present article which is anonymous or which it considers to be an abuse of the right of submission of such communications or to be incompatible with the provisions of the present Convention.

3. The Committee shall not consider any communication from an individual under the present article unless it has ascertained that:

(a) The same matter has not been, and is not being, examined under another procedure of international investigation or settlement;

(b) The individual has exhausted all available domestic remedies; this shall not be the rule where, in the view of the Committee, the application of the remedies is unreasonably prolonged or is unlikely to bring effective relief to that individual.

4. Subject to the provisions of paragraph 2 of the present article, the Committee shall bring any communications submitted to it under this article to the attention of the State Party to the present Convention that has made a declaration under paragraph 1 and is alleged to be violating any provisions of the Convention. Within six months, the receiving State shall submit to the Committee written explanations or statements clarifying the matter and the remedy, if any, that may have been taken by that State.

5. The Committee shall consider communications received under the present article in the light of all information made available to it by or on behalf of the individual and by the State Party concerned.

6. The Committee shall hold closed meetings when examining communications under the present article.

7. The Committee shall forward its views to the State Party concerned and to the individual.

8. The provisions of the present article shall come into force when ten States Parties to the present Convention have made declarations under paragraph 1 of the present article. Such declarations shall be deposited by the States Parties with the Secretary-General of the United Nations, who shall transmit copies thereof to the other States Parties. A declaration may be withdrawn at any time by notification to the Secretary-General. Such a withdrawal shall not prejudice the consideration of any matter that is the subject of a communication already transmitted under the present article; no further communication by or on behalf of an individual shall be received under the present article after the notification of withdrawal of the declaration has been received by the Secretary-General, unless the State Party has made a new declaration.

Article 78

The provisions of article 76 of the present Convention shall be applied without prejudice to any procedures for settling disputes or complaints in the field covered by the present Convention laid down in the constituent instruments of, or in conventions adopted by, the United Nations and the specialized agencies and shall not prevent the States Parties from having recourse to any procedures for settling a dispute in accordance with international agreements in force between them.

PART VIII: GENERAL PROVISIONS

Article 79

Nothing in the present Convention shall affect the right of each State Party to establish the criteria governing admission of migrant workers and members of their families. Concerning other matters related to their legal situation and treatment as migrant workers and members of their families, States Parties shall be subject to the limitations set forth in the present Convention.

Article 80

Nothing in the present Convention shall be interpreted as impairing the provisions of the Charter of the United Nations and of the constitutions of the specialized agencies which define the respective responsibilities of the various organs of the United Nations and of the specialized agencies in regard to the matters dealt with in the present Convention.

Article 81

1. Nothing in the present Convention shall affect more favourable rights or freedoms granted to migrant workers and members of their families by virtue of:

(a) The law or practice of a State Party; or

(b) Any bilateral or multilateral treaty in force for the State Party concerned.

2. Nothing in the present Convention may be interpreted as implying for any State, group or person any right to engage in any activity or perform any act that would impair any of the rights and freedoms as set forth in the present Convention.

Article 82

The rights of migrant workers and members of their families provided for in the present Convention may not be renounced. It shall not be permissible to exert any form of pressure upon migrant workers and members of their families with a view to their relinquishing or foregoing any of the said rights. It shall not be possible to derogate by contract from rights recognized in the present Convention. States Parties shall take appropriate measures to ensure that these principles are respected.

Article 83

Each State Party to the present Convention undertakes:

(a) To ensure that any person whose rights or freedoms as herein recognized are violated shall have an effective remedy, notwithstanding that the violation has been committed by persons acting in an official capacity;

(b) To ensure that any persons seeking such a remedy shall have his or her claim reviewed and decided by competent judicial, administrative or legislative authorities, or by any other competent authority provided for by the legal system of the State, and to develop the possibilities of judicial remedy;

(c) To ensure that the competent authorities shall enforce such remedies when granted.

Article 84

Each State Party undertakes to adopt the legislative and other measures that are necessary to implement the provisions of the present Convention.

PART IX: FINAL PROVISIONS

Article 85

The Secretary-General of the United Nations is designated as the depositary of the present Convention.

Article 86

1. The present Convention shall be open for signature by all States. It is subject to ratification.

2. The present Convention shall be open to accession by any State.

3. Instruments of ratification or accession shall be deposited with the Secretary-General of the United Nations.

Article 87

1. The present Convention shall enter into force on the first day of the month following a period of three months after the date of the deposit of the twentieth instrument of ratification or accession.

2. For each State ratifying or acceding to the present Convention after its entry into force, the Convention shall enter into force on the first day of the month following a period of three months after the date of the deposit of its own instrument of ratification or accession.

Article 88

A State ratifying or acceding to the present Convention may not exclude the application of any Part of it, or, without prejudice to article 3, exclude any particular category of migrant workers from its application.

Article 89

1. Any State Party may denounce the present Convention, not earlier than five years after the Convention has entered into force for the State concerned, by means of a notification in writing addressed to the Secretary-General of the United Nations.

2. Such denunciation shall become effective on the first day of the month following the expiration of a period of twelve months after the date of the receipt of the notification by the Secretary-General of the United Nations.

3. Such a denunciation shall not have the effect of releasing the State Party from its obligations under the present Convention in regard to any act or omission which occurs prior to the date at which the denunciation becomes effective, nor shall denunciation prejudice in any way the continued consideration of any matter which is already under consideration by the Committee prior to the date at which the denunciation becomes effective.

4. Following the date at which the denunciation of a State Party becomes effective, the Committee shall not commence consideration of any new matter regarding that State.

Article 90

1. After five years from the entry into force of the Convention a request for the revision of the Convention may be made at any time by any State Party by means of a notification in writing addressed to the Secretary-General of the United Nations. The Secretary-General

shall thereupon communicate any proposed amendments to the States Parties with a request that they notify him whether they favour a conference of States Parties for the purpose of considering and voting upon the proposals. In the event that within four months from the date of such communication at least one third of the States Parties favours such a conference, the Secretary-General shall convene the conference under the auspices of the United Nations. Any amendment adopted by a majority of the States Parties present and voting shall be submitted to the General Assembly for approval.

2. Amendments shall come into force when they have been approved by the General Assembly of the United Nations and accepted by a two-thirds majority of the States Parties in accordance with their respective constitutional processes.

3. When amendments come into force, they shall be binding on those States Parties that have accepted them, other States Parties still being bound by the provisions of the present Convention and any earlier amendment that they have accepted.

Article 91

1. The Secretary-General of the United Nations shall receive and circulate to all States the text of reservations made by States at the time of signature, ratification or accession.

2. A reservation incompatible with the object and purpose of the present Convention shall not be permitted.

3. Reservations may be withdrawn at any time by notification to this effect addressed to the Secretary-General of the United Nations, who shall then inform all States thereof. Such notification shall take effect on the date on which it is received.

Article 92

1. Any dispute between two or more States Parties concerning the interpretation or application of the present Convention that is not settled by negotiation shall, at the request of one of them, be submitted to arbitration. If within six months from the date of the request for arbitration the Parties are unable to agree on the organization of the arbitration, any one of those Parties may refer the dispute to the International Court of Justice by request in conformity with the Statute of the Court.

2. Each State Party may at the time of signature or ratification of the present Convention or accession thereto declare that it does not consider itself bound by paragraph 1 of the present article. The other States Parties shall not be bound by that paragraph with respect to any State Party that has made such a declaration.

3. Any State Party that has made a declaration in accordance with paragraph 2 of the present article may at any time withdraw that declaration by notification to the Secretary-General of the United Nations.

Article 93

1. The present Convention, of which the Arabic, Chinese, English, French, Russian and Spanish texts are equally authentic, shall be deposited with the Secretary-General of the United Nations.

2. The Secretary-General of the United Nations shall transmit certified copies of the present Convention to all States.

In witness whereof the undersigned plenipotentiaries, being duly authorized thereto by their respective Governments, have signed the present Convention.

ILO Declaration on Fundamental Principles and Rights at Work, 1998*

Adoption: June 1998

Whereas the ILO was founded in the conviction that social justice is essential to universal and lasting peace;

Whereas economic growth is essential but not sufficient to ensure equity, social progress and the eradication of poverty, confirming the need for the ILO to promote strong social policies, justice and democratic institutions;

Whereas the ILO should, now more than ever, draw upon all its standard-setting, technical cooperation and research resources in all its areas of competence, in particular employment, vocational training and working conditions, to ensure that, in the context of a global strategy for economic and social development, economic and social policies are mutually reinforcing components in order to create broad-based sustainable development;

Whereas the ILO should give special attention to the problems of persons with special social needs, particularly the unemployed and migrant workers, and mobilize and encourage international, regional and national efforts aimed at resolving their problems, and promote effective policies aimed at job creation;

Whereas, in seeking to maintain the link between social progress and economic growth, the guarantee of fundamental principles and rights at work is of particular significance in that it enables the persons concerned, to claim freely and on the basis of equality of opportunity, their fair share of the wealth which they have helped to generate, and to achieve fully their human potential;

Whereas the ILO is the constitutionally mandated international organization and the competent body to set and deal with international labour standards, and enjoys universal support and acknowledgement in promoting Fundamental Rights at Work as the expression of its constitutional principles;

Whereas it is urgent, in a situation of growing economic interdependence, to reaffirm the immutable nature of the fundamental principles and rights embodied in the Constitution of the Organization and to promote their universal application;

The International Labour Conference

1. Recalls:

(a) that in freely joining the ILO, all Members have endorsed the principles and rights set out in its Constitution and in the Declaration of Philadelphia, and have undertaken to work towards attaining the overall objectives of the Organization to the best of their resources and fully in line with their specific circumstances;

(b) that these principles and rights have been expressed and developed in the form of specific rights and obligations in Conventions recognized as fundamental both inside and outside the Organization.

---

* Source: Source: International Labour Organization, http://ilo.org/ilolex/english/
The ILO shall accept no responsibility for any inaccuracy, errors or omissions or for the consequences arising from the use of the Text.

2. Declares that all Members, even if they have not ratified the Conventions in question, have an obligation arising from the very fact of membership in the Organization to respect, to promote and to realize, in good faith and in accordance with the Constitution, the principles concerning the fundamental rights which are the subject of those Conventions, namely:

(a) freedom of association and the effective recognition of the right to collective bargaining;

(b) the elimination of all forms of forced or compulsory labour;

(c) the effective abolition of child labour; and

(d) the elimination of discrimination in respect of employment and occupation.

3. Recognizes the obligation on the Organization to assist its Members, in response to their established and expressed needs, in order to attain these objectives by making full use of its constitutional, operational and budgetary resources, including, by the mobilization of external resources and support, as well as by encouraging other international organizations with which the ILO has established relations, pursuant to article 12 of its Constitution, to support these efforts:

(a) by offering technical cooperation and advisory services to promote the ratification and implementation of the fundamental Conventions;

(b) by assisting those Members not yet in a position to ratify some or all of these Conventions in their efforts to respect, to promote and to realize the principles concerning fundamental rights which are the subject of these Conventions; and

(c) by helping the Members in their efforts to create a climate for economic and social development.

4. Decides that, to give full effect to this Declaration, a promotional follow-up, which is meaningful and effective, shall be implemented in accordance with the measures specified in the annex hereto, which shall be considered as an integral part of this Declaration.

5. Stresses that labour standards should not be used for protectionist trade purposes, and that nothing in this Declaration and its follow-up shall be invoked or otherwise used for such purposes; in addition, the comparative advantage of any country should in no way be called into question by this Declaration and its follow-up.

Report of the Special Rapporteur on Human Rights of Migrant Workers, 2002
(See section 6)

2.2 International Standards Relating to Seafarers

Convention No.109 concerning Wages, Hours of Work on Board Ship and Manning (Revised, 1958)*

Adoption: 14 May 1958
Entry into force: Not yet in force
Parties: 11 (Status as of 1 April 2007)

BOSNIA AND HERZEGOVINA 2 June 1993, BRAZIL 30 Nov 1966 (* Part II), CROATIA 8 Oct 1991, FRANCE 8 June 1967 (denounced on 27 Apr 2004), GUATEMALA 2 Aug 1961, IRAQ 23 Sep 1986, ITALY 23 June 1981, LEBANON 6 Dec 1993, THE FORMER YUGOSLAV REPUBLIC OF MACEDONIA 17 Nov 1991, MEXICO 11 Sep 1961, NORWAY 30 Aug 1966 (denounced on 22 Oct 2003), PORTUGAL 9 Jan 1981, SERBIA 24 Nov 2000, SLOVENIA 29 May 1992 (denounced on 21 July 2004), SPAIN 14 July 1971 (denounced on 7 Jan 2004).

The General Conference of the International Labour Organisation,

Having been convened at Geneva by the Governing Body of the International Labour Office, and having met in its Forty-first Session on 29 April 1958, and

Having decided upon the adoption of certain proposals with regard to the general revision of the Wages, Hours of Work and Manning (Sea) Convention (Revised), 1949, which is the second item on the agenda of the session, and

Considering that these proposals must take the form of an international Convention,

adopts this fourteenth day of May of the year one thousand nine hundred and fifty-eight the following Convention, which may be cited as the Wages, Hours of Work and Manning (Sea) Convention (Revised), 1958:

PART I. GENERAL PROVISIONS

Article 1

Nothing in this Convention shall be deemed to prejudice any provision concerning wages, hours of work on board ship, or manning, by law, award, custom or agreement between shipowners and seafarers, which ensures the seafarers conditions more favourable than those provided for by this Convention.

Article 2

1. This Convention applies to every vessel, whether publicly or privately owned, which is–

(a) mechanically propelled;

(b) registered in a territory for which the Convention is in force;

* Source: International Labour Organization, http://ilo.org/ilolex/english/
The ILO shall accept no responsibility for any inaccuracy, errors or omissions or for the consequences arising from the use of the Text.

(c) engaged in the transport of cargo or passengers for the purpose of trade; and

(d) engaged in a voyage by sea.

2. This Convention does not apply to–

(a) vessels of less than 500 gross register tons;

(b) wooden vessels of primitive build such as dhows and junks;

(c) vessels engaged in fishing or in operations directly connected therewith;

(d) estuarial craft.

Article 3

This Convention applies to every person who is engaged in any capacity on board a vessel except–

(a) a master;

(b) a pilot not a member of the crew;

(c) a doctor;

(d) nursing staff engaged exclusively on nursing duties and hospital staff;

(e) a chaplain;

(f) persons engaged exclusively on educational duties;

(g) a musician;

(h) persons whose duties are connected solely with the cargo on board;

(i) persons working exclusively on their own account or remunerated exclusively by a share of profits or earnings;

(j) persons not remunerated for their services or remunerated only by a nominal salary or wage;

(k) persons, excluding those in the service of a wireless telegraphy company, who are employed on board by an employer other than the shipowner;

(l) travelling dockers (longshoremen) not members of the crew;

(m) persons employed in whale-catching, floating factory or transport vessels or otherwise for the purpose of whaling or similar operations under conditions regulated by legislation or by the provisions of a special collective whaling or similar agreement determining hours of work and other conditions of service concluded by an organisation of seafarers;

(n) persons who are not members of the crew (whether working on or off articles) but are employed while the vessel is in port on repairing, cleaning, loading or unloading the vessel or similar work or on port relief, maintenance, watch or caretaking duties.

Article 4

In this Convention–

(a) the term officer means a person other than a master who is described in the ship's articles as an officer or who is serving in a capacity which by law, collective agreement or custom is recognised as that of an officer;

(b) the term rating means a member of the crew other than a master or officer and includes a certificated seaman;

(c) the term able seaman means any person who by national laws or regulations, or in the absence of such laws or regulations by collective agreement, is deemed to be competent to perform any duty which may be required of a rating serving in the deck department other than the duties of a leading or specialist rating;

(d) the term basic pay or wages means the remuneration of an officer or rating in cash exclusive of the cost of food, overtime, premiums or any other allowances either in cash or in kind.

Article 5

1. Each Member ratifying this Convention may, by a declaration appended to its ratification, exclude from its ratification Part II of the Convention.

2. Subject to the terms of any such declaration, the provisions of Part II of the Convention shall have the same effect as the other provisions of the Convention.

3. Any Member which makes such a declaration shall also supply information showing the basic pay or wages for a calendar month of service of an able seaman employed in a vessel to which the Convention applies.

4. Any Member which makes such a declaration may subsequently, by a new declaration, notify the Director-General that it accepts Part II; as from the date of the registration of such notification by the Director-General the provisions of Part II shall be applicable to the Member in question.

5. While a declaration made under paragraph 1 of this Article remains in force in respect of Part II, the Member may declare its willingness to accept Part II as having the force of a Recommendation.

PART II. WAGES

Article 6

1. The basic pay or wages for a calendar month of service of an able seaman employed in a vessel to which this Convention applies shall not be less than sixteen pounds in currency of the United Kingdom of Great Britain and Northern Ireland or sixty-four dollars in currency of the United States of America or the equivalent thereof in other currency.

2. In respect of any change in the par value of the pound or the dollar notified to the International Monetary Fund since 29 June 1946, or in the event of any further such change being notified subsequent to the adoption of this Convention–

(a) the minimum basic wage prescribed in paragraph 1 of this Article in terms of the currency in respect of which such notification has been made shall be adjusted so as to maintain equivalence with the other currency;

(b) the adjustment shall be notified by the Director-General of the International Labour Office to the Members of the International Labour Organisation; and

(c) the minimum basic wage so adjusted shall be binding upon Members which have ratified the Convention in the same manner as the wage prescribed in paragraph 1 of this Article, and shall take effect for each such Member not later than the beginning of the second calendar month following that in which the Director-General communicates the change to Members.

Article 7

1. In the case of ships in which are employed such groups of ratings as necessitate the employment of larger groups of ratings than would otherwise be employed the minimum basic pay or wages of an able seaman shall be an amount fixed as the adjusted equivalent of the minimum basic pay or wages stipulated in the preceding Article.

2. The adjusted equivalent shall be fixed in accordance with the principle of equal pay for equal work and due allowance shall be made for–

(a) the extra number of ratings of such groups who are employed; and

(b) any increase or decrease in cost to the shipowner consequent on the employment of such groups of ratings.

3. The adjusted equivalent shall be determined by collective agreement between the organisations of shipowners and seafarers concerned or, failing such agreement and subject to both countries concerned having ratified the Convention, by the competent authority of the territory of the group of seafarers concerned.

Article 8

If meals are not provided free of charge, the minimum basic pay or wages shall be increased by an amount to be determined by collective agreement between the organisations of shipowners and seafarers concerned or, failing such agreement, by the competent authority.

Article 9

1. The rate to be used for determining the equivalent in other currency of the minimum basic pay or wages prescribed in Article 6 shall be the ratio between the par value of that currency and the par value of the pound of the United Kingdom of Great Britain and Northern Ireland or of the dollar of the United States of America.

2. In the case of the currency of a Member of the International Labour Organisation which is a Member of the International Monetary Fund, the par value shall be that currently in effect under the Articles of Agreement of the International Monetary Fund.

3. In the case of the currency of a Member of the International Labour Organisation which is not a Member of the International Monetary Fund, the par value shall be the official rate of exchange, in terms of gold or of the dollar of the United States of America of the weight and fineness in effect on 1 July 1944, currently in effect for payments and transfers for current international transactions.

4. In the case of any currency which cannot be dealt with under the provisions of either of the two preceding paragraphs–

(a) the rate to be adopted for the purpose of this Article shall be determined by the Member of the International Labour Organisation concerned;

(b) the Member concerned shall notify its decision to the Director-General of the International Labour Office, who shall forthwith inform the other Members which have ratified this Convention;

(c) within a period of six months from the date on which the information is communicated by the Director-General, any other Member which has ratified the Convention may inform the Director-General of the International Labour Office that it objects to the decision, and the Director-General shall thereupon inform the Member concerned and the other Members which have ratified the Convention and shall report the matter to the Committee provided for in Article 22;

(d) the foregoing provisions shall apply in the event of any change in the decision of the Member concerned.

5. A change in basic pay or wages as a result of a change in the rate for determining the equivalent in other currency shall take effect not later than the beginning of the second calendar month following that in which the change in the relative par values of the currencies concerned becomes effective.

Article 10

Each Member shall take the necessary measures–

(a) to ensure, by way of a system of supervision and sanctions, that remuneration is paid at not less than the rate required by this Convention; and

(b) to ensure that any person who has been paid at a rate less than that required by this Convention is enabled to recover, by an inexpensive and expeditious judicial or other procedure, the amount by which he has been underpaid.

PART III. HOURS OF WORK ON BOARD SHIP

Article 11

This Part of this Convention does not apply to–

(a) a chief officer or chief engineer;

(b) a purser;

(c) any other officer in charge of a department who does not keep watch;

(d) a person employed in the clerical or catering department of a vessel who is–

(i) serving in a superior grade as defined by a collective agreement between the organisations of shipowners and seafarers concerned; or

(ii) working chiefly on his own account; or

(iii) remunerated solely on a commission basis or chiefly by a share of profits or earnings.

Article 12

In this Part of this Convention–

(a) the term near trade ship means a vessel exclusively engaged in voyages upon which it does not proceed farther from the country from which it trades than the near-by ports of neighbouring countries within geographical limits which–

(i) are clearly specified by national laws, regulations or by collective agreement between organisations of shipowners and seafarers;

(ii) are uniform in respect of the application of all the provisions of this Part of the Convention;

(iii) have been notified by the Member when registering its ratification by a declaration annexed thereto; and

(iv) have been fixed after consultation with the other Members concerned;

(b) the term distant trade ship means a vessel other than a near trade ship;

(c) the term passenger ship means a vessel licensed to carry more than twelve passengers;

(d) the term hours of work means time during which a person is required by the orders of a superior to do work on account of the vessel or the owner.

Article 13

1. This Article applies to officers and ratings employed in the deck, engine-room and radio departments of near trade ships.

2. The normal hours of work of an officer or rating shall not exceed–

(a) when the vessel is at sea, twenty-four hours in any period of two consecutive days;

(b) when the vessel is in port–

(i) on the weekly day of rest, such time not exceeding two hours as is necessary for ordinary routine and sanitary duties;

(ii) on other days, eight hours except where a collective agreement provides for less on any day;

(c) one hundred and twelve hours in a period of two consecutive weeks.

3. Time worked in excess of the limits prescribed in subparagraphs (a) and (b) of paragraph 2 shall be regarded as overtime for which the officer or rating concerned shall be entitled to compensation in accordance with the provisions of Article 18 of this Convention.

4. When the total number of hours worked in a period of two consecutive weeks, excluding hours regarded as overtime, exceeds one hundred and twelve, the officer or rating concerned shall be compensated by time off in port or otherwise as may be determined by collective agreement between the organisations of shipowners and seafarers concerned.

5. National laws or regulations or collective agreements shall determine when a ship is to be regarded as being at sea and when it is to be regarded as being in port for the purposes of this Article.

Article 14

1. This Article applies to officers and ratings employed in the deck, engine room and radio departments of distant trade ships.

2. When the vessel is at sea and on days of sailing and arrival, the normal hours of work of an officer or rating shall not exceed eight hours in any one day.

3. When the vessel is in port, the normal hours of work of an officer or rating shall not exceed–

(a) on the weekly day of rest, such time not exceeding two hours as is necessary for ordinary routine and sanitary duties;

(b) on other days, eight hours except where a collective agreement provides for less on any day.

4. Time worked in excess of the daily limits prescribed in the preceding paragraphs shall be regarded as overtime for which the officer or rating shall be entitled to compensation in accordance with the provisions of Article 18 of this Convention.

5. When the total number of hours worked in a period of one week, excluding hours regarded as overtime, exceeds forty-eight, the officer or rating shall be compensated by time off in port or otherwise as may be determined by collective agreement between the organisations of shipowners and seafarers concerned.

6. National laws or regulations or collective agreements shall determine when a ship is to be regarded as being at sea and when it is to be regarded as being in port for the purposes of this Article.

Article 15

1. This Article applies to persons employed in the catering department of a vessel.

2. In the case of a passenger ship, normal hours of work shall not exceed–

(a) when the vessel is at sea and on days of sailing and arrival, ten hours in any consecutive period of fourteen hours;

(b) when the vessel is in port–

(i) when passengers are on board, ten hours in any period of fourteen hours;

(ii) in other cases–

on the day preceding the weekly day of rest, five hours;

on the weekly day of rest, five hours for persons engaged in messing duties and such time not exceeding two hours as is necessary for ordinary routine and sanitary duties in the case of other persons;

on any other day, eight hours.

3. In the case of a vessel not a passenger ship, normal hours of work shall not exceed–

(a) when the vessel is at sea and on days of sailing and arrival, nine hours in any period of thirteen hours;

(b) when the vessel is in port–

on the weekly day of rest, five hours;

on the day preceding the weekly day of rest, six hours;

on any other days, eight hours in any period of twelve hours.

4. When the total number of hours worked in a period of two consecutive weeks exceeds one hundred and twelve the person concerned shall be compensated by time off in port or otherwise as may be determined by collective agreement between the organisations of shipowners and seafarers concerned.

5. National laws or regulations or collective agreements between the organisations of shipowners and seafarers concerned may make special arrangements for the regulation of the hours of work of night watchmen.

Article 16

1. This Article applies to officers and ratings employed in near and distant trade ships.

2. Time off in port should be the subject of negotiations between the organisations of shipowners and seafarers concerned on the basis that officers and ratings should receive the maximum time off in port that is practicable and that such time off should not count as leave.

Article 17

1. The competent authority may exempt from the application of this Part of this Convention officers not already excluded therefrom by virtue of Article 11, subject to the following conditions:

(a) the officers must be entitled in virtue of a collective agreement to conditions of employment which the competent authority certifies constitute full compensation for the non-application of this Part of the Convention;

(b) the collective agreement must have been originally concluded before 30 June 1946 and the agreement or a renewal thereof must be still in force.

2. A Member having recourse to the provisions of paragraph 1 shall supply to the Director-General of the International Labour Office full particulars of any such collective agreement and the Director-General shall lay a summary of the information received by him before the Committee referred to in Article 22.

3. The said Committee shall consider whether the collective agreements reported to it provide for conditions of employment which constitute full compensation for the non-application of this Part of this Convention. Each Member ratifying the Convention undertakes to give consideration to any observations or suggestions made by the Committee concerning such agreements and further undertakes to bring any such observations or suggestions to the notice of the organisations of shipowners and officers who are parties to such agreements.

Article 18

1. The rate or rates of compensation for overtime shall be prescribed by national laws or regulations or be fixed by collective agreement, but in no case shall the hourly rate of payment for overtime be less than one-and-a-quarter times the basic pay or wages per hour.

2. Collective agreements may provide for compensation by equivalent time off duty and off the vessel in lieu of cash payment or for any other method of compensation.

Article 19

1. The consistent working of overtime shall be avoided whenever possible.

2. Time spent in the following work shall not be included in normal hours of work or be regarded as overtime for the purpose of this Part of this Convention:

(a) work that the master deems to be necessary and urgent for the safety of the vessel, cargo or persons on board;

(b) work required by the master for the purpose of giving assistance to other vessels or persons in distress;

(c) musters, fire, lifeboat and similar drills of the kind prescribed by the International Convention for the Safety of Life at Sea for the time being in force;

(d) extra work for the purposes of customs or quarantine or other health formalities;

(e) normal and necessary work by officers for the determination of the position of the ship and for making meteorological observations;

(f) extra time required for the normal relieving of watches.

3. Nothing in this Convention shall be deemed to impair the right and duty of the master of a vessel to require, or the duty of an officer or rating to perform, any work deemed by the master to be necessary for the safe and efficient operation of the vessel.

Article 20

1. No person under the age of sixteen years shall work at night.

2. For the purpose of this Article, night means a period of at least nine consecutive hours between times before and after midnight to be prescribed by national laws or regulations or collective agreements.

PART IV. MANNING

Article 21

1. Every vessel to which this Convention applies shall be sufficiently and efficiently manned for the purposes of–

(a) ensuring the safety of life at sea;

(b) giving effect to the provisions of Part III of this Convention; and

(c) preventing excessive strain upon the crew and avoiding or minimising as far as practicable the working of overtime.

2. Each Member undertakes to maintain, or to satisfy itself that there is maintained, efficient machinery for the investigation and settlement of any complaint or dispute concerning the manning of a vessel.

3. Representatives of the organisations of shipowners and seafarers shall participate, with or without other persons or authorities, in the operation of such machinery.

PART V. APPLICATION OF THE CONVENTION

Article 22

1. Effect may be given to this Convention by (a) laws or regulations; (b) collective agreements between shipowners and seafarers (except as regards paragraph 2 of Article 21); or (c) a combination of laws or regulations and collective agreements between shipowners and seafarers. Except as may be otherwise provided herein, the provisions of this Convention shall be made applicable to every vessel registered in the territory of the ratifying Member and to every person engaged on any such vessel.

2. Where effect has been given to any provision of this Convention by a collective agreement in pursuance of paragraph 1 of this Article, then notwithstanding anything contained in Article 10 of this Convention the Member shall not be required to take any measures in pursuance of Article 10 of this Convention in respect of the provisions of the Convention to which effect has been so given by collective agreement.

3. Each Member ratifying this Convention shall supply to the Director-General of the International Labour Office information on the measures by which the Convention is applied, including particulars of any collective agreements in force which give effect to any of its provisions.

4. Each Member ratifying this Convention undertakes to take part, by means of a tripartite delegation, in any Committee representative of governments and shipowners' and seafarers' organisations, and including, in an advisory capacity, representatives of the Joint Maritime Commission of the International Labour Office, which may be set up for the purpose of examining the measures taken to give effect to the Convention.

5. The Director-General shall lay before the said Committee a summary of the information received by him under paragraph 3 above.

6. The Committee shall consider whether the collective agreements reported to it give full effect to the provisions of the Convention. Each Member ratifying the Convention undertakes to give consideration to any observations or suggestions concerning the application of the Convention made by the Committee, and further undertakes to bring to the notice of the organisations of shipowners and of seafarers who are parties to any of the collective agreements mentioned in paragraph 1 any observations or suggestions of the aforesaid Committee concerning the degree to which such agreements give effect to the provisions of the Convention.

Article 23

1. Each Member which ratifies this Convention shall be responsible for the application of its provisions to vessels registered in its territory and shall, except where effect is given to the Convention by collective agreements, maintain in force laws or regulations which–

(a) determine the respective responsibilities of the shipowner and the master for ensuring compliance therewith;

(b) prescribe adequate penalties for any violation thereof;

(c) provide for adequate public supervision of compliance with Part IV of the Convention;

(d) require the keeping of the records of hours worked necessary for the purposes of Part III of the Convention and of the compensation granted in respect of overtime and of excess hours of work;

(e) ensure to seafarers the same remedies for recovering payments due to them in respect of compensation for overtime and for excess hours of work as they have for recovering other arrears of pay.

2. The organisations of shipowners and seafarers concerned shall, so far as is reasonable and practicable, be consulted in the framing of all laws or regulations for giving effect to the provisions of this Convention.

Article 24

For the purpose of giving mutual assistance in the enforcement of this Convention, every Member which ratifies the Convention undertakes to require the competent authority in every port in its territory to inform the consular or other appropriate authority of any other such Member of any case in which it comes to the notice of such authority that the requirements of the Convention are not being complied with in a vessel registered in the territory of that other Member.

PART VI. FINAL PROVISIONS

Article 25

1. This Convention revises the Wages, Hours of Work and Manning (Sea) Conventions, 1946 and 1949.

2. For the purpose of Article 28 of the Hours of Work and Manning (Sea) Convention, 1936, this Convention shall also be regarded as a Convention revising that Convention.

Article 26

The formal ratifications of this Convention shall be communicated to the Director-General of the International Labour Office for registration.

Article 27

1. This Convention shall be binding only upon those Members of the International Labour Organisation whose ratifications have been registered with the Director-General.

2. It shall first come into force six months after the date at which the following conditions have been fulfilled:

(a) the ratifications of nine of the following Members have been registered: Argentina, Australia, Belgium, Brazil, Canada, Chile, China, Denmark, Finland, France, Federal Republic of Germany, Greece, India, Ireland, Italy, Japan, Netherlands, Norway, Poland, Portugal, Spain, Sweden, Turkey, Union of Soviet Socialist Republics, United Kingdom of Great Britain and Northern Ireland, United States of America, Yugoslavia;

(b) at least five of the Members whose ratifications have been registered have at the date of registration each not less than 1 million gross register tons of shipping;

(c) the aggregate tonnage of shipping possessed at the time of registration by the Members whose ratifications have been registered is not less than 15 million gross register tons.

3. The provisions of the preceding paragraph are included for the purpose of facilitating and encouraging early ratification of the Convention by member States.

4. After the Convention has first come into force, it shall come into force for any Member six months after the date on which its ratification has been registered.

Article 28

1. A Member which has ratified this Convention may denounce it after the expiration of ten years from the date on which the Convention first comes into force, by an act communicated to the Director-General of the International Labour Office for registration. Such denunciation shall not take effect until one year after the date on which it is registered.

2. Each Member which has ratified this Convention and which does not, within the year following the expiration of the period of five years mentioned in the preceding paragraph, exercise the right of denunciation provided for in this Article will be bound for another period of five years and, thereafter, may denounce this Convention at the expiration of each period of ten years under the terms provided for in this Article.

Article 29

1. The Director-General of the International Labour Office shall notify all the Members of the International Labour Organisation of the registration of all ratifications, declarations and denunciations communicated to him by the Members of the Organisation.

2. When notifying the Members of the Organisation of the registration of the last of the ratifications required to bring the Convention into force, the Director-General shall draw the attention of the Members of the Organisation to the date upon which the Convention will come into force.

Article 30

The Director-General of the International Labour Office shall communicate to the Secretary-General of the United Nations for registration in accordance with Article 102 of the Charter of the United Nations full particulars of all ratifications, declarations and acts of denunciation registered by him in accordance with the provisions of the preceding Articles.

Article 31

At such times as it may consider necessary the Governing Body of the International Labour Office shall present to the General Conference a report on the working of this Convention and shall examine the desirability of placing on the agenda of the Conference the question of its revision in whole or in part.

Article 32

1. Should the Conference adopt a new Convention revising this Convention in whole or in part, then, unless the new Convention otherwise provides:

a) the ratification by a Member of the new revising Convention shall ipso jure involve the immediate denunciation of this Convention, notwithstanding the provisions of Article 28 above, if and when the new revising Convention shall have come into force;

b) as from the date when the new revising Convention comes into force, this Convention shall cease to be open to ratification by the Members.

2. This Convention shall in any case remain in force in its actual form and content for those Members which have ratified it but have not ratified the revising Convention.

Article 33

The English and French versions of the text of this Convention are equally authoritative.

Convention No.166 concerning the Repatriation of Seafarers (Revised, 1987)*

Adoption: 9 October 1987
Entry into force: 3 July 1991
Parties: 13 (Status as of 1 April 2007)

AUSTRALIA 29 Aug 1995, BRAZIL 4 Mar 1997, BULGARIA 30 July 2003, EGYPT 28 May 2004, FRANCE 27 Apr 2004, GERMANY 14 Nov 2006, GUYANA 10 June 1996, HUNGARY 14 Mar 1989, LUXEMBOURG 15 Feb 1991, MEXICO 5 Oct 1990, ROMANIA 11 Oct 2000, SPAIN 3 July 1990, TURKEY 17 Mar 2005.

The General Conference of the International Labour Organisation,

Having been convened in Geneva by the Governing Body of the International Labour Office and having met at its Seventy-fourth Session on 24 September 1987, and

Noting that since the adoption of the Repatriation of Seamen Convention, 1926, and of the Repatriation (Ship Masters and Apprentices) Recommendation, 1926, developments in the shipping industry have made it necessary to revise the Convention to incorporate appropriate elements of the Recommendation, and

Noting further that considerable progress has been made through national legislation and practice in providing for the repatriation of seafarers in various matters not covered by the Repatriation of Seamen Convention, 1926, and

Considering that further action by means of a new international instrument as regards certain additional aspects of the repatriation of seafarers would accordingly be desirable taking into account the widespread growth in employment of non-national seafarers in the shipping industry, and

Having decided upon the adoption of certain proposals with regard to the Revision of the Repatriation of Seamen Convention, 1926 (No.23), and of the Repatriation (Ship Masters and Apprentices) Recommendation, 1926 (No.27), which is the fifth item on the agenda of the session, and

Having determined that these proposals shall take the form of an international Convention,

adopts this ninth day of October of the year one thousand nine hundred and eighty-seven the following Convention which may be cited as the Repatriation of Seafarers Convention (Revised), 1987.

PART I. SCOPE AND DEFINITIONS

Article 1

1. This Convention applies to every seagoing ship whether publicly or privately owned which is registered in the territory of any Member for which the Convention is in force and which

---

* Source: International Labour Organization, http://www.ilo.org/ilolex
The ILO shall accept no responsibility for any inaccuracy, errors or omissions or for the consequences arising from the use of the Text.

is ordinarily engaged in commercial maritime navigation and to the owners and seafarers of such ships.

2. To the extent it deems practicable, after consultation with the representative organisations of fishing vessel owners and fishermen, the competent authority shall apply the provisions of this Convention to commercial maritime fishing.

3. In the event of doubt as to whether or not any ships are to be regarded as engaged in commercial maritime navigation or commercial maritime fishing for the purpose of this Convention, the question shall be determined by the competent authority after consultation with the organisations of shipowners, seafarers and fishermen concerned.

4. For the purpose of this Convention the term seafarer means any person who is employed in any capacity on board a seagoing ship to which this Convention applies.

PART II. ENTITLEMENTS

Article 2

1. A seafarer shall be entitled to repatriation in the following circumstances:

(a) if an engagement for a specific period or for a specific voyage expires abroad;

(b) upon the expiry of the period of notice given in accordance with the provisions of the articles of agreement or the seafarer's contract of employment;

(c) in the event of illness or injury or other medical condition which requires his or her repatriation when found medically fit to travel;

(d) in the event of shipwreck;

(e) in the event of the shipowner not being able to continue to fulfil his or her legal or contractual obligations as an employer of the seafarer by reason of bankruptcy, sale of ship, change of ship's registration or any other similar reason;

(f) in the event of a ship being bound for a war zone, as defined by national laws or regulations or collective agreements, to which the seafarer does not consent to go;

(g) in the event of termination or interruption of employment in accordance with an industrial award or collective agreement, or termination of employment for any other similar reason.

2. National laws or regulations or collective agreements shall prescribe the maximum duration of service periods on board following which a seafarer is entitled to repatriation; such periods shall be less than 12 months. In determining the maximum periods, account shall be taken of factors affecting the seafarers' working environment. Each Member shall seek, wherever possible, to reduce these periods in the light of technological changes and developments and may be guided by any recommendations made on the matter by the Joint Maritime Commission.

PART III. DESTINATION

Article 3

1. Each Member for which this Convention is in force shall prescribe by national laws or regulations the destinations to which seafarers may be repatriated.

2. The destinations so prescribed shall include the place at which the seafarer agreed to enter into the engagement, the place stipulated by collective agreement, the seafarer's country of

residence or such other place as may be mutually agreed at the time of engagement. The seafarer shall have the right to choose from among the prescribed destinations the place to which he or she is to be repatriated.

PART IV. ARRANGEMENTS FOR REPATRIATION

Article 4

1. It shall be the responsibility of the shipowner to arrange for repatriation by appropriate and expeditious means. The normal mode of transport shall be by air.

2. The cost of repatriation shall be borne by the shipowner.

3. Where repatriation has taken place as a result of a seafarer being found, in accordance with national laws or regulations or collective agreements, to be in serious default of his or her employment obligations, nothing in this Convention shall prejudice the right of recovery from the seafarer of repatriation costs or part thereof in accordance with national laws or regulations or collective agreements.

4. The cost to be borne by the shipowner shall include:

(a) passage to the destination selected for repatriation in accordance with Article 3 above;

(b) accommodation and food from the moment the seafarer leaves the ship until he or she reaches the repatriation destination;

(c) pay and allowances from the moment he or she leaves the ship until he or she reaches the repatriation destination, if provided for by national laws or regulations or collective agreements;

(d) transportation of 30 kg of the seafarer's personal luggage to the repatriation destination;

(e) medical treatment when necessary until the seafarer is medically fit to travel to the repatriation destination.

5. The shipowner shall not require the seafarer to make an advance payment towards the cost of repatriation at the beginning of his or her employment, nor shall the shipowner recover the cost of repatriation from the seafarer's wages or other entitlements except as provided for in paragraph 3 above.

6. National laws or regulations shall not prejudice any right of the shipowner to recover the cost of repatriation of seafarers not employed by the shipowner from their employer.

Article 5

If a shipowner fails to make arrangements for or to meet the cost of repatriation of a seafarer who is entitled to be repatriated-

(a) the competent authority of the Member in whose territory the ship is registered shall arrange for and meet the cost of the repatriation of the seafarer concerned; if it fails to do so, the State from which the seafarer is to be repatriated or the State of which he or she is a national may arrange for his or her repatriation and recover the cost from the Member in whose territory the ship is registered;

(b) costs incurred in repatriating the seafarer shall be recoverable from the shipowner by the Member in whose territory the ship is registered;

(c) the expenses of repatriation shall in no case be a charge upon the seafarer, except as provided for in paragraph 3 of Article 4 above.

PART V. OTHER ARRANGEMENTS

Article 6

Seafarers who are to be repatriated shall be able to obtain their passport and other identity documents for the purpose of repatriation.

Article 7

Time spent awaiting repatriation and repatriation travel time shall not be deducted from paid leave accrued to the seafarer.

Article 8

A seafarer shall be deemed to have been duly repatriated when he or she is landed at a destination prescribed pursuant to Article 3 above, or when the seafarer does not claim his or her entitlement to repatriation within a reasonable period of time to be defined by national laws or regulations or collective agreements.

Article 9

The provisions of this Convention in so far as they are not otherwise made effective by means of collective agreements or in such other manner as may be appropriate under national conditions shall be given effect by national laws or regulations.

Article 10

Each Member shall facilitate the repatriation of seafarers serving on ships which call at its ports or pass through its territorial or internal waters, as well as their replacement on board.

Article 11

The competent authority of each Member shall ensure by means of adequate supervision that the owners of ships registered in its territory comply with the provisions of the Convention, and shall provide relevant information to the International Labour Office.

Article 12

The text of this Convention shall be available in an appropriate language to the crew members of every ship which is registered in the territory of any Member for which it is in force.

PART VI. FINAL PROVISIONS

Article 13

This Convention revises the Repatriation of Seamen Convention, 1926.

Article 14

The formal ratifications of this Convention shall be communicated to the Director-General of the International Labour Office for registration.

Article 15

1. This Convention shall be binding only upon those Members of the International Labour Organisation whose ratifications have been registered with the Director-General of the International Labour Office.

2. It shall come into force twelve months after the date on which the ratifications of two Members have been registered with the Director-General of the International Labour Office.

3. Thereafter, this Convention shall come into force for any Member twelve months after the date on which its ratification has been registered.

Article 16

1. A Member which has ratified this Convention may denounce it after the expiration of ten years from the date on which the Convention first comes into force, by an act communicated to the Director-General of the International Labour Office for registration. Such denunciation shall not take effect until one year after the date on which it is registered.

2. Each Member which has ratified this Convention and which does not, within the year following the expiration of the period of ten years mentioned in the preceding paragraph, exercise the right of denunciation provided for in this Article, will be bound for another period of ten years and, thereafter, may denounce this Convention at the expiration of each period of ten years under the terms provided for in this Article.

Article 17

1. The Director-General of the International Labour Office shall notify all Members of the International Labour Organisation of the registration of all ratifications and denunciations communicated to him by the Members of the Organisation.

2. When notifying the Members of the Organisation of the registration of the second ratification communicated to him, the Director-General of the International Labour Office shall draw the attention of the Members of the Organisation to the date upon which the Convention will come into force.

Article 18

The Director-General of the International Labour Office shall communicate to the Secretary-General of the United Nations for registration in accordance with Article 102 of the Charter of the United Nations full particulars of all ratifications and acts of denunciation registered by him in accordance with the provisions of the preceding Articles.

Article 19

At such times as it may consider necessary, the Governing Body of the International Labour Office shall present to the General Conference a report on the working of this Convention and shall examine the desirability of placing on the agenda of the Conference the question of its revision in whole or in part.

Article 20

1. Should the Conference adopt a new Convention revising this Convention in whole or in part, then, unless the new Convention otherwise provides-

(a) the ratification by a Member of the new revising Convention shall ipso jure involve the immediate denunciation of this Convention, notwithstanding the provisions of Article 16 above, if and when the new revising Convention shall have come into force;

(b) as from the date when the new revising Convention comes into force this Convention shall cease to be open to ratification by the Members.

2. This Convention shall in any case remain in force in its actual form and content for those Members which have ratified it but have not ratified the revising Convention.

Article 21

The English and French versions of the text of this Convention are equally authoritative.

Recommendation No.174 concerning the Repatriation of Seafarers, 1987*

Adoption: 9 October 1987

The General Conference of the International Labour Organisation,

Having been convened in Geneva by the Governing Body of the International Labour Office and having met at its Seventy-fourth Session on 24 September 1987, and

Having decided upon the adoption of certain proposals with regard to the revision of the Repatriation of Seamen Convention, 1926 (No.23), and of the Repatriation (Ship Masters and Apprentices) Recommendation, 1926 (No.27), which is the fifth item on the agenda of the session, and

Having determined that these proposals shall take the form of an international Recommendation supplementing the Repatriation of Seafarers Convention (Revised), 1987,

adopts this ninth day of October of the year one thousand nine hundred eighty-seven, the following Recommendation which may be cited as the Repatriation of Seafarers Recommendation, 1987:

Whenever a seafarer is entitled to be repatriated pursuant to the provisions of the Repatriation of Seafarers Convention (Revised), 1987, but both the shipowner and the Member in whose territory the ship is registered fail to meet their obligations under the Convention to arrange for and meet the cost of repatriation, the State from which the seafarer is to be repatriated or the State of which he or she is a national should arrange for his or her repatriation, and recover the cost from the Member in whose territory the ship is registered in accordance with Article 5 (a) of the Convention.

* Source: International Labour Organization, http://ilo.org/ilolex/english/
The ILO shall accept no responsibility for any inaccuracy, errors or omissions or for the consequences arising from the use of the Text.

Convention No.185 revising the Seafarers' Identity Documents Convention (Revised), 2003 [excerpts]*

Adoption: 19 June 2003
Entry into force: 9 February 2005
Parties: 10 (Status as of 1 April 2007)

AZERBAIJAN 17 July 2006, BAHAMAS 14 Dec 2006, FRANCE 27 Apr 2004, HUNGARY 30 Mar 2005, JORDAN 9 Aug 2004, LITHUANIA 14 Aug 2006 (*provisional application), NIGERIA 19 Aug 2004, PAKISTAN 21 Dec 2006, REPUBLIC OF MOLDOVA 28 Aug 2006, VANUATU 28 July 2006.

The General Conference of the International Labour Organization,

Having been convened at Geneva by the Governing Body of the International Labour Office, and having met in its Ninety-first Session on 3 June 2003, and Mindful of the continuing threat to the security of passengers and crews and the safety of ships, to the national interest of States and to individuals, and

Mindful also of the core mandate of the Organization, which is to promote decent conditions of work, and

Considering that, given the global nature of the shipping industry, seafarers need special protection, and

Recognizing the principles embodied in the Seafarers' Identity Documents Convention, 1958, concerning the facilitation of entry by seafarers into the territory of Members, for the purposes of shore leave, transit, transfer or repatriation, and

Noting the Convention on the Facilitation of International Maritime Traffic, 1965, as amended, of the International Maritime Organization, in particular, Standards 3.44 and 3.45, and

Noting further that United Nations General Assembly Resolution A/RES/57/219 (Protection of human rights and fundamental freedoms while countering terrorism) affirms that States must ensure that any measure taken to combat terrorism complies with their obligations under international law, in particular international human rights, refugee and humanitarian law, and

Being aware that seafarers work and live on ships involved in international trade and that access to shore facilities and shore leave are vital elements of seafarers' general well-being and, therefore, to the achievement of safer shipping and cleaner oceans, and

Being aware also that the ability to go ashore is essential for joining a ship and leaving after the agreed period of service, and

Noting the amendments to the International Convention for the Safety of Life at Sea, 1974, as amended, concerning special measures to enhance maritime safety and security, that were adopted by the International Maritime Organization Diplomatic Conference on 12 December 2002, and

---

* Source: International Labour Organization, http://www.ilo.org/ilolex
The ILO shall accept no responsibility for any inaccuracy, errors or omissions or for the consequences arising from the use of the Text.

Having decided upon the adoption of certain proposals with regard to the improved security of seafarers' identification, which is the seventh item on the agenda of the session, and

Having decided that these proposals shall take the form of an international Convention revising the Seafarers' Identity Documents Convention, 1958,

adopts this nineteenth day of June of the year two thousand and three, the following Convention, which may be cited as the Seafarers' Identity Documents Convention (Revised), 2003.

Article 1

Scope

1. For the purposes of this Convention, the term seafarer means any person who is employed or is engaged or works in any capacity on board a vessel, other than a ship of war, ordinarily engaged in maritime navigation.

2. In the event of any doubt whether any categories of persons are to be regarded as seafarers for the purpose of this Convention, the question shall be determined in accordance with the provisions of this Convention by the competent authority of the State of nationality or permanent residence of such persons after consulting with the shipowners' and seafarers' organizations concerned.

3. After consulting the representative organizations of fishing-vessel owners and persons working on board fishing vessels, the competent authority may apply the provisions of this Convention to commercial maritime fishing.

Article 2

Issuance of seafarers' identity documents

1. Each Member for which this Convention is in force shall issue to each of its nationals who is a seafarer and makes an application to that effect a seafarers' identity document conforming to the provisions of Article 3 of this Convention.

2. Unless otherwise provided for in this Convention, the issuance of seafarers' identity documents may be subject to the same conditions as those prescribed by national laws and regulations for the issuance of travel documents.

3. Each Member may also issue seafarers' identity documents referred to in paragraph 1 to seafarers who have been granted the status of permanent resident in its territory. Permanent residents shall in all cases travel in conformity with the provisions of Article 6, paragraph 7.

4. Each Member shall ensure that seafarers' identity documents are issued without undue delay.

5. Seafarers shall have the right to an administrative appeal in the case of a rejection of their application.

6. This Convention shall be without prejudice to the obligations of each Member under international arrangements relating to refugees and stateless persons.

Article 3

Content and form

1. The seafarers' identity document covered by this Convention shall conform - in its content - to the model set out in Annex I[1] hereto. The form of the document and the materials used in it shall be consistent with the general specifications set out in the model, which shall be based on the criteria set out below. Provided that any amendment is consistent with the following paragraphs, Annex I may, where necessary, be amended in accordance with Article 8 below, in particular to take account of technological developments. The decision to adopt the amendment shall specify when the amendment will enter into effect, taking account of the need to give Members sufficient time to make any necessary revisions of their national seafarers' identity documents and procedures.

2. The seafarers' identity document shall be designed in a simple manner, be made of durable material, with special regard to conditions at sea and be machine-readable. The materials used shall:

(a) prevent tampering with the document or falsification, as far as possible, and enable easy detection of alterations; and

(b) be generally accessible to governments at the lowest cost consistent with reliably achieving the purpose set out in (a) above.

3. Members shall take into account any available guidelines developed by the International Labour Organization on standards of the technology to be used which will facilitate the use of a common international standard.

4. The seafarers' identity document shall be no larger than a normal passport.

5. The seafarers' identity document shall contain the name of the issuing authority, indications enabling rapid contact with that authority, the date and place of issue of the document, and the following statements:

(a) this document is a seafarers' identity document for the purpose of the Seafarers' Identity Documents Convention (Revised), 2003, of the International Labour Organization; and

(b) this document is a stand-alone document and not a passport.

6. The maximum validity of a seafarers' identity document shall be determined in accordance with the laws and regulations of the issuing State and shall in no case exceed ten years, subject to renewal after the first five years.

7. Particulars about the holder included in the seafarer's identity document shall be restricted to the following:

(a) full name (first and last names where applicable);

(b) sex;

(c) date and place of birth;

(d) nationality;

(e) any special physical characteristics that may assist identification;

(f) digital or original photograph; and

(g) signature.

[1] Annexes are not reproduced here.

8. Notwithstanding paragraph 7 above, a template or other representation of a biometric of the holder which meets the specification provided for in Annex I shall also be required for inclusion in the seafarers' identity document, provided that the following preconditions are satisfied:

(a) the biometric can be captured without any invasion of privacy of the persons concerned, discomfort to them, risk to their health or offence against their dignity;

(b) the biometric shall itself be visible on the document and it shall not be possible to reconstitute it from the template or other representation;

(c) the equipment needed for the provision and verification of the biometric is user-friendly and is generally accessible to governments at low cost;

(d) the equipment for the verification of the biometric can be conveniently and reliably operated in ports and in other places, including on board ship, where verification of identity is normally carried out by the competent authorities; and

(e) the system in which the biometric is to be used (including the equipment, technologies and procedures for use) provides results that are uniform and reliable for the authentication of identity.

9. All data concerning the seafarer that are recorded on the document shall be visible. Seafarers shall have convenient access to machines enabling them to inspect any data concerning them that is not eye-readable. Such access shall be provided by or on behalf of the issuing authority.

10. The content and form of the seafarers' identity document shall take into account the relevant international standards cited in Annex I.

Article 4

National electronic database

1. Each Member shall ensure that a record of each seafarers' identity document issued, suspended or withdrawn by it is stored in an electronic database. The necessary measures shall be taken to secure the database from interference or unauthorized access.

2. The information contained in the record shall be restricted to details which are essential for the purposes of verifying a seafarers' identity document or the status of a seafarer and which are consistent with the seafarer's right to privacy and which meet all applicable data protection requirements. The details are set out in Annex II hereto, which may be amended in the manner provided for in Article 8 below, taking account of the need to give Members sufficient time to make any necessary revisions of their national database systems.

3. Each Member shall put in place procedures which will enable any seafarer to whom it has issued a seafarers' identity document to examine and check the validity of all the data held or stored in the electronic database which relate to that individual and to provide for correction if necessary, at no cost to the seafarer concerned.

4. Each Member shall designate a permanent focal point for responding to inquiries, from the immigration or other competent authorities of all Members of the Organization, concerning the authenticity and validity of the seafarers' identity document issued by its authority. Details of the permanent focal point shall be communicated to the International Labour Office, and the Office shall maintain a list which shall be communicated to all Members of the Organization.

5. The details referred to in paragraph 2 above shall at all times be immediately accessible to the immigration or other competent authorities in member States of the Organization, either electronically or through the focal point referred to in paragraph 4 above.

6. For the purposes of this Convention, appropriate restrictions shall be established to ensure that no data - in particular, photographs - are exchanged, unless a mechanism is in place to ensure that applicable data protection and privacy standards are adhered to.

7. Members shall ensure that the personal data on the electronic database shall not be used for any purpose other than verification of the seafarers' identity document.

Article 5

Quality control and evaluations

1. Minimum requirements concerning processes and procedures for the issue of seafarers' identity documents, including quality-control procedures, are set out in Annex III to this Convention. These minimum requirements establish mandatory results that must be achieved by each Member in the administration of its system for issuance of seafarers' identity documents.

2. Processes and procedures shall be in place to ensure the necessary security for:

(a) the production and delivery of blank seafarers' identity documents;

(b) the custody, handling and accountability for blank and completed seafarers' identity documents;

(c) the processing of applications, the completion of the blank seafarers' identity documents into personalized seafarers' identity documents by the authority and unit responsible for issuing them and the delivery of the seafarers' identity documents;

(d) the operation and maintenance of the database; and

(e) the quality control of procedures and periodic evaluations.

3. Subject to paragraph 2 above, Annex III may be amended in the manner provided for in Article 8, taking account of the need to give Members sufficient time to make any necessary revisions to their processes and procedures.

4. Each Member shall carry out an independent evaluation of the administration of its system for issuing seafarers' identity documents, including quality-control procedures, at least every five years. Reports on such evaluations, subject to the removal of any confidential material, shall be provided to the Director-General of the International Labour Office with a copy to the representative organizations of shipowners and seafarers in the Member concerned. This reporting requirement shall be without prejudice to the obligations of Members under article 22 of the Constitution of the International Labour Organisation.

5. The International Labour Office shall make these evaluation reports available to Members. Any disclosure, other than those authorized by this Convention, shall require the consent of the reporting Member.

6. The Governing Body of the International Labour Office, acting on the basis of all relevant information in accordance with arrangements made by it, shall approve a list of Members which fully meet the minimum requirements referred to in paragraph 1 above.

7. The list must be available to Members of the Organization at all times and be updated as appropriate information is received. In particular, Members shall be promptly notified where

the inclusion of any Member on the list is contested on solid grounds in the framework of the procedures referred to in paragraph 8.

8. In accordance with procedures established by the Governing Body, provision shall be made for Members which have been or may be excluded from the list, as well as interested governments of ratifying Members and representative shipowners' and seafarers' organizations, to make their views known to the Governing Body, in accordance with the arrangements referred to above and to have any disagreements fairly and impartially settled in a timely manner.

9. The recognition of seafarers' identity documents issued by a Member is subject to its compliance with the minimum requirements referred to in paragraph 1 above.

Article 6

Facilitation of shore leave and transit and transfer of seafarers

1. Any seafarer who holds a valid seafarers' identity document issued in accordance with the provisions of this Convention by a Member for which the Convention is in force shall be recognized as a seafarer within the meaning of the Convention unless clear grounds exist for doubting the authenticity of the seafarers' identity document.

2. The verification and any related inquiries and formalities needed to ensure that the seafarer for whom entry is requested pursuant to paragraphs 3 to 6 or 7 to 9 below is the holder of a seafarers' identity document issued in accordance with the requirements of this Convention shall be at no cost to the seafarers or shipowners.

Shore leave

3. Verification and any related inquiries and formalities referred to in paragraph 2 above shall be carried out in the shortest possible time provided that reasonable advance notice of the holder's arrival was received by the competent authorities. The notice of the holder's arrival shall include the details specified in section 1 of Annex II.

4. Each Member for which this Convention is in force shall, in the shortest possible time, and unless clear grounds exist for doubting the authenticity of the seafarers' identity document, permit the entry into its territory of a seafarer holding a valid seafarer's identity document, when entry is requested for temporary shore leave while the ship is in port.

5. Such entry shall be allowed provided that the formalities on arrival of the ship have been fulfilled and the competent authorities have no reason to refuse permission to come ashore on grounds of public health, public safety, public order or national security.

6. For the purpose of shore leave seafarers shall not be required to hold a visa. Any Member which is not in a position to fully implement this requirement shall ensure that its laws and regulations or practice provide arrangements that are substantially equivalent.

Transit and transfer

7. Each Member for which this Convention is in force shall, in the shortest possible time, also permit the entry into its territory of seafarers holding a valid seafarers' identity document supplemented by a passport, when entry is requested for the purpose of:

(a) joining their ship or transferring to another ship;

(b) passing in transit to join their ship in another country or for repatriation; or any other purpose approved by the authorities of the Member concerned.

8. Such entry shall be allowed unless clear grounds exist for doubting the authenticity of the seafarers' identity document, provided that the competent authorities have no reason to refuse entry on grounds of public health, public safety, public order or national security.

9. Any Member may, before permitting entry into its territory for one of the purposes specified in paragraph 7 above, require satisfactory evidence, including documentary evidence of a seafarer's intention and ability to carry out that intention. The Member may also limit the seafarer's stay to a period considered reasonable for the purpose in question.

Article 7

Continuous possession and withdrawal

1. The seafarers' identity document shall remain in the seafarer's possession at all times, except when it is held for safekeeping by the master of the ship concerned, with the seafarer's written consent.

2. The seafarers' identity document shall be promptly withdrawn by the issuing State if it is ascertained that the seafarer no longer meets the conditions for its issue under this Convention. Procedures for suspending or withdrawing seafarers' identity documents shall be drawn up in consultation with the representative shipowners' and seafarers' organizations and shall include procedures for administrative appeal.

Article 8

Amendment of the Annexes

1. Subject to the relevant provisions of this Convention, amendments to the Annexes may be made by the International Labour Conference, acting on the advice of a duly constituted tripartite maritime body of the International Labour Organization. The decision shall require a majority of two-thirds of the votes cast by the delegates present at the Conference, including at least half the Members that have ratified this Convention.

2. Any Member that has ratified this Convention may give written notice to the Director-General within six months of the date of the adoption of such an amendment that it shall not enter into force for that Member, or shall only enter into force at a later date upon subsequent written notification.

Article 9

Transitional provision

Any Member which is a party to the Seafarers' Identity Documents Convention, 1958, and which is taking measures, in accordance with article 19 of the Constitution of the International Labour Organisation, with a view to ratification of this Convention may notify the Director-General of its intention to apply the present Convention provisionally. A seafarers' identity document issued by such a Member shall be treated for the purposes of this Convention as a seafarers' identity document issued under it provided that the requirements of Articles 2 to 5 of this Convention are fulfilled and that the Member concerned accepts seafarers' identity documents issued under this Convention.

Final provisions

Article 10

This Convention revises the Seafarers' Identity Documents Convention, 1958.

Article 11

The formal ratifications of this Convention shall be communicated to the Director-General of the International Labour Office for registration.

Article 12

1. This Convention shall be binding only upon those Members of the International Labour Organization whose ratifications have been registered with the Director-General.

2. It shall come into force six months after the date on which the ratifications of two Members have been registered with the Director-General.

3. Thereafter, this Convention shall come into force for any Member six months after the date on which its ratification has been registered.

Article 13

1. A Member which has ratified this Convention may denounce it after the expiration of ten years from the date on which the Convention first comes into force, by an act communicated to the Director-General for registration. Such denunciation shall take effect twelve months after the date on which it is registered.

2. Each Member which has ratified this Convention and which does not, within the year following the expiration of the period of ten years mentioned in the preceding paragraph, exercise the right of denunciation provided for in this Article, shall be bound for another period of ten years and, thereafter, may denounce this Convention at the expiration of each period of ten years under the terms provided for in this Article.

Article 14

1. The Director-General shall notify all Members of the registration of all ratifications, declarations and acts of denunciation communicated by the Members.

2. When notifying the Members of the registration of the second ratification of this Convention, the Director-General shall draw the attention of the Members to the date upon which the Convention shall come into force.

3. The Director-General shall notify all Members of the registration of any amendments made to the Annexes in accordance with Article 8, as well as of notifications relating thereto.

Article 15

The Director-General of the International Labour Office shall communicate to the Secretary-General of the United Nations, for registration in accordance with article 102 of the Charter of the United Nations, full particulars of all ratifications, declarations and acts of denunciation registered by the Director-General in accordance with the provisions of the preceding Articles.

Article 16

At such times as it may consider necessary, the Governing Body of the International Labour Office shall present to the General Conference a report on the working of this Convention and shall examine the desirability of placing on the agenda of the Conference the question of its revision in whole or in part, taking account also of the provisions of Article 8.

Article 17

1. Should the Conference adopt a new Convention revising this Convention in whole or in part, then, unless the new Convention otherwise provides:

(a) the ratification by a Member of the new revising Convention shall ipso jure involve the immediate denunciation of this Convention, notwithstanding the provisions of Article 13, if and when the new revising Convention shall have come into force;

(b) as from the date when the new revising Convention comes into force, this Convention shall cease to be open to ratification by the Members.

2. This Convention shall in any case remain in force in its actual form and content for those Members which have ratified it but have not ratified the revising Convention.

Article 18

The English and French versions of the text of this Convention are equally authoritative.

[…]

Maritime Labour Convention, 2006 [excerpts]*

Adoption: 7 Feb 2006
Entry into force: Not yet in force
Parties: 1 (Status as of 1 April 2007)

LIBERIA 7 June 2006.

The General Conference of the International Labour Organization,

Having been convened at Geneva by the Governing Body of the International Labour Office, and having met in its Ninety-fourth Session on 7 February 2006, and

Desiring to create a single, coherent instrument embodying as far as possible all up-to-date standards of existing international maritime labour Conventions and Recommendations, as well as the fundamental principles to be found in other international labour Conventions, in particular:

[...]

Mindful of the core mandate of the Organization, which is to promote decent conditions of work, and

Recalling the ILO Declaration on Fundamental Principles and Rights at Work, 1998, and

Mindful also that seafarers are covered by the provisions of other ILO instruments and have other rights which are established as fundamental rights and freedoms applicable to all persons, and

Considering that, given the global nature of the shipping industry, seafarers need special protection, and

Mindful also of the international standards on ship safety, human security and quality ship management in the International Convention for the Safety of Life at Sea, 1974, as amended, the Convention on the International Regulations for Preventing Collisions at Sea, 1972, as amended, and the seafarer training and competency requirements in the International Convention on Standards of Training, Certification and Watchkeeping for Seafarers, 1978, as amended, and

Recalling that the United Nations Convention on the Law of the Sea, 1982, sets out a general legal framework within which all activities in the oceans and seas must be carried out and is of strategic importance as the basis for national, regional and global action and cooperation in the marine sector, and that its integrity needs to be maintained, and

Recalling that Article 94 of the United Nations Convention on the Law of the Sea, 1982, establishes the duties and obligations of a flag State with regard to, inter alia, labour conditions, crewing and social matters on ships that fly its flag, and

Recalling paragraph 8 of article 19 of the Constitution of the International Labour Organisation which provides that in no case shall the adoption of any Convention or Recommendation by the Conference or the ratification of any Convention by any Member be deemed to affect any

* Source: International Labour Organization, http://www.ilo.org/ilolex
The ILO shall accept no responsibility for any inaccuracy, errors or omissions or for the consequences arising from the use of the Text.

law, award, custom or agreement which ensures more favourable conditions to the workers concerned than those provided for in the Convention or Recommendation, and

Determined that this new instrument should be designed to secure the widest possible acceptability among governments, shipowners and seafarers committed to the principles of decent work, that it should be readily updateable and that it should lend itself to effective implementation and enforcement, and

Having decided upon the adoption of certain proposals for the realization of such an instrument, which is the only item on the agenda of the session, and

Having determined that these proposals shall take the form of an international Convention;

adopts this twenty-third day of February of the year two thousand and six the following Convention, which may be cited as the Maritime Labour Convention, 2006.

General Obligations

Article I

1. Each Member which ratifies this Convention undertakes to give complete effect to its provisions in the manner set out in Article VI in order to secure the right of all seafarers to decent employment.

2. Members shall cooperate with each other for the purpose of ensuring the effective implementation and enforcement of this Convention.

Definitions and Scope of Application

Article II

1. For the purpose of this Convention and unless provided otherwise in particular provisions, the term:

(a) competent authority means the minister, government department or other authority having power to issue and enforce regulations, orders or other instructions having the force of law in respect of the subject matter of the provision concerned;

(b) declaration of maritime labour compliance means the declaration referred to in Regulation 5.1.3;

(c) gross tonnage means the gross tonnage calculated in accordance with the tonnage measurement regulations contained in Annex I to the International Convention on Tonnage Measurement of Ships, 1969, or any successor Convention; for ships covered by the tonnage measurement interim scheme adopted by the International Maritime Organization, the gross tonnage is that which is included in the REMARKS column of the International Tonnage Certificate (1969);

(d) maritime labour certificate means the certificate referred to in Regulation 5.1.3;

(e) requirements of this Convention refers to the requirements in these Articles and in the Regulations and Part A of the Code[1] of this Convention;

(f) seafarer means any person who is employed or engaged or works in any capacity on board a ship to which this Convention applies;

[1] Not reproduced.

(g) seafarers' employment agreement includes both a contract of employment and articles of agreement;

(h) seafarer recruitment and placement service means any person, company, institution, agency or other organization, in the public or the private sector, which is engaged in recruiting seafarers on behalf of shipowners or placing seafarers with shipowners;

(i) ship means a ship other than one which navigates exclusively in inland waters or waters within, or closely adjacent to, sheltered waters or areas where port regulations apply;

(j) shipowner means the owner of the ship or another organization or person, such as the manager, agent or bareboat charterer, who has assumed the responsibility for the operation of the ship from the owner and who, on assuming such responsibility, has agreed to take over the duties and responsibilities imposed on shipowners in accordance with this Convention, regardless of whether any other organization or persons fulfil certain of the duties or responsibiities on behalf of the shipowner.

2. Except as expressly provided otherwise, this Convention applies to all seafarers.

3. In the event of doubt as to whether any categories of persons are to be regarded as seafarers for the purpose of this Convention, the question shall be determined by the competent authority in each Member after consultation with the shipowners' and seafarers' organizations concerned with this question.

4. Except as expressly provided otherwise, this Convention applies to all ships, whether publicly or privately owned, ordinarily engaged in commercial activities, other than ships engaged in fishing or in similar pursuits and ships of traditional build such as dhows and junks. This Convention does not apply to warships or naval auxiliaries.

5. In the event of doubt as to whether this Convention applies to a ship or particular category of ships, the question shall be determined by the competent authority in each Member after consultation with the shipowners' and seafarers' organizations concerned.

6. Where the competent authority determines that it would not be reasonable or practicable at the present time to apply certain details of the Code referred to in Article VI, paragraph 1, to a ship or particular categories of ships flying the flag of the Member, the relevant provisions of the Code shall not apply to the extent that the subject matter is dealt with differently by national laws or regulations or collective bargaining agreements or other measures. Such a determination may only be made in consultation with the shipowners' and seafarers' organizations concerned and may only be made with respect to ships of less than 200 gross tonnage not engaged in international voyages.

7. Any determinations made by a Member under paragraph 3 or 5 or 6 of this Article shall be communicated to the Director-General of the International Labour Office, who shall notify the Members of the Organization.

8. Unless expressly provided otherwise, a reference to this Convention constitutes at the same time a reference to the Regulations and the Code.

Fundamental Rights and Principles

Article III

Each Member shall satisfy itself that the provisions of its law and regulations respect, in the context of this Convention, the fundamental rights to:

(a) freedom of association and the effective recognition of the right to collective bargaining;

(b) the elimination of all forms of forced or compulsory labour;

(c) the effective abolition of child labour; and

(d) the elimination of discrimination in respect of employment and occupation.

Seafarers' Employment and Social Rights

Article IV

1. Every seafarer has the right to a safe and secure workplace that complies with safety standards.

2. Every seafarer has a right to fair terms of employment.

3. Every seafarer has a right to decent working and living conditions on board ship.

4. Every seafarer has a right to health protection, medical care, welfare measures and other forms of social protection.

5. Each Member shall ensure, within the limits of its jurisdiction, that the seafarers' employment and social rights set out in the preceding paragraphs of this Article are fully implemented in accordance with the requirements of this Convention. Unless specified otherwise in the Convention, such implementation may be achieved through national laws or regulations, through applicable collective bargaining agreements or through other measures or in practice.

Implementation and Enforcement Responsibilities

Article V

1. Each Member shall implement and enforce laws or regulations or other measures that it has adopted to fulfil its commitments under this Convention with respect to ships and seafarers under its jurisdiction.

2. Each Member shall effectively exercise its jurisdiction and control over ships that fly its flag by establishing a system for ensuring compliance with the requirements of this Convention, including regular inspections, reporting, monitoring and legal proceedings under the applicable laws.

3. Each Member shall ensure that ships that fly its flag carry a maritime labour certificate and a declaration of maritime labour compliance as required by this Convention.

4. A ship to which this Convention applies may, in accordance with international law, be inspected by a Member other than the flag State, when the ship is in one of its ports, to determine whether the ship is in compliance with the requirements of this Convention.

5. Each Member shall effectively exercise its jurisdiction and control over seafarer recruitment and placement services, if these are established in its territory.

6. Each Member shall prohibit violations of the requirements of this Convention and shall, in accordance with international law, establish sanctions or require the adoption of corrective measures under its laws which are adequate to discourage such violations.

7. Each Member shall implement its responsibilities under this Convention in such a way as to ensure that the ships that fly the flag of any State that has not ratified this Convention do not receive more favourable treatment than the ships that fly the flag of any State that has ratified it.

Regulations and Parts A and B of the Code

Article VI

1. The Regulations and the provisions of Part A of the Code are mandatory. The provisions of Part B of the Code are not mandatory.

2. Each Member undertakes to respect the rights and principles set out in the Regulations and to implement each Regulation in the manner set out in the corresponding provisions of Part A of the Code. In addition, the Member shall give due consideration to implementing its responsibilities in the manner provided for in Part B of the Code.

3. A Member which is not in a position to implement the rights and principles in the manner set out in Part A of the Code may, unless expressly provided otherwise in this Convention, implement Part A through provisions in its laws and regulations or other measures which are substantially equivalent to the provisions of Part A.

4. For the sole purpose of paragraph 3 of this Article, any law, regulation, collective agreement or other implementing measure shall be considered to be substantially equivalent, in the context of this Convention, if the Member satisfies itself that:

(a) it is conducive to the full achievement of the general object and purpose of the provision or provisions of Part A of the Code concerned; and

(b) it gives effect to the provision or provisions of Part A of the Code concerned.

Consultation with Shipowners' and Seafarers' Organizations

Article VII

Any derogation, exemption or other flexible application of this Convention for which the Convention requires consultation with shipowners' and seafarers' organizations may, in cases where representative organizations of shipowners or of seafarers do not exist within a Member, only be decided by that Member through consultation with the Committee referred to in Article XIII.

Entry into Force

Article VIII

1. The formal ratifications of this Convention shall be communicated to the Director-General of the International Labour Office for registration.

2. This Convention shall be binding only upon those Members of the International Labour Organization whose ratifications have been registered by the Director-General.

3. This Convention shall come into force 12 months after the date on which there have been registered ratifications by at least 30 Members with a total share in the world gross tonnage of ships of 33 per cent.

4. Thereafter, this Convention shall come into force for any Member 12 months after the date on which its ratification has been registered.

Denunciation

Article IX

1. A Member which has ratified this Convention may denounce it after the expiration of ten years from the date on which the Convention first comes into force, by an act communicated

to the Director-General of the International Labour Office for registration. Such denunciation shall not take effect until one year after the date on which it is registered.

2. Each Member which does not, within the year following the expiration of the period of ten years mentioned in paragraph 1 of this Article, exercise the right of denunciation provided for in this Article, shall be bound for another period of ten years and, thereafter, may denounce this Convention at the expiration of each new period of ten years under the terms provided for in this Article.

Effect of Entry into Force

Article X

This Convention revises the following Conventions:

[...]

Depositary Functions

Article XI

1. The Director-General of the International Labour Office shall notify all Members of the International Labour Organization of the registration of all ratifications, acceptances and denunciations under this Convention.

2. When the conditions provided for in paragraph 3 of Article VIII have been fulfilled, the Director-General shall draw the attention of the Members of the Organization to the date upon which the Convention will come into force.

Article XII

The Director-General of the International Labour Office shall communicate to the Secretary-General of the United Nations for registration in accordance with Article 102 of the Charter of the United Nations full particulars of all ratifications, acceptances and denunciations registered under this Convention.

Special Tripartite Committee

Article XIII

1. The Governing Body of the International Labour Office shall keep the working of this Convention under continuous review through a committee established by it with special competence in the area of maritime labour standards.

2. For matters dealt with in accordance with this Convention, the Committee shall consist of two representatives nominated by the Government of each Member which has ratified this Convention, and the representatives of Shipowners and Seafarers appointed by the Governing Body after consultation with the Joint Maritime Commission.

3. The Government representatives of Members which have not yet ratified this Convention may participate in the Committee but shall have no right to vote on any matter dealt with in accordance with this Convention. The Governing Body may invite other organizations or entities to be represented on the Committee by observers.

4. The votes of each Shipowner and Seafarer representative in the Committee shall be weighted so as to ensure that the Shipowners' group and the Seafarers' group each have half the voting power of the total number of governments which are represented at the meeting concerned and entitled to vote.

Amendment of this Convention

Article XIV

1. Amendments to any of the provisions of this Convention may be adopted by the General Conference of the International Labour Organization in the framework of article 19 of the Constitution of the International Labour Organisation and the rules and procedures of the Organization for the adoption of Conventions. Amendments to the Code may also be adopted following the procedures in Article XV.

2. In the case of Members whose ratifications of this Convention were registered before the adoption of the amendment, the text of the amendment shall be communicated to them for ratification.

3. In the case of other Members of the Organization, the text of the Convention as amended shall be communicated to them for ratification in accordance with article 19 of the Constitution.

4. An amendment shall be deemed to have been accepted on the date when there have been registered ratifications, of the amendment or of the Convention as amended, as the case may be, by at least 30 Members with a total share in the world gross tonnage of ships of at least 33 per cent.

5. An amendment adopted in the framework of article 19 of the Constitution shall be binding only upon those Members of the Organization whose ratifications have been registered by the Director-General of the International Labour Office.

6. For any Member referred to in paragraph 2 of this Article, an amendment shall come into force 12 months after the date of acceptance referred to in paragraph 4 of this Article or 12 months after the date on which its ratification of the amendment has been registered, whichever date is later.

7. Subject to paragraph 9 of this Article, for Members referred to in paragraph 3 of this Article, the Convention as amended shall come into force 12 months after the date of acceptance referred to in paragraph 4 of this Article or 12 months after the date on which their ratifications of the Convention have been registered, whichever date is later.

8. For those Members whose ratification of this Convention was registered before the adoption of an amendment but which have not ratified the amendment, this Convention shall remain in force without the amendment concerned.

9. Any Member whose ratification of this Convention is registered after the adoption of the amendment but before the date referred to in paragraph 4 of this Article may, in a declaration accompanying the instrument of ratification, specify that its ratification relates to the Convention without the amendment concerned. In the case of a ratification with such a declaration, the Convention shall come into force for the Member concerned 12 months after the date on which the ratification was registered. Where an instrument of ratification is not accompanied by such a declaration, or where the ratification is registered on or after the date referred to in paragraph 4, the Convention shall come into force for the Member concerned 12 months after the date on which the ratification was registered and, upon its entry into force in accordance with paragraph 7 of this Article, the amendment shall be binding on the Member concerned unless the amendment provides otherwise.

Amendments to the Code

Article XV

1. The Code may be amended either by the procedure set out in Article XIV or, unless expressly provided otherwise, in accordance with the procedure set out in the present Article.

[…]

2.3 International Labour Standards Relating to Forced Labour and Slavery

Convention No.29 concerning Forced or Compulsory Labour, 1930*

Adoption: 28 June 1930
Entry into force: 1 May 1932
Parties: 171 (Status as of 1 April 2007)

ALBANIA 25 May 1957, ALGERIA 19 Oct 1962, ANGOLA 4 June 1976, ANTIGUA AND BARBUDA 2 Feb 1983, ARGENTINA 14 Mar 1950, ARMENIA 17 Dec 2004, AUSTRALIA 2 Jan 1932, AUSTRIA 7 June 1960, AZERBAIJAN 19 May 1992, BAHAMAS 25 May 1976, BAHRAIN 11 June 1981, BANGLADESH 22 June 1972, BARBADOS 8 May 1967, BELARUS 21 Aug 1956, BELGIUM 20 Jan 1944, BELIZE 15 Dec 1983, BENIN 12 Dec 1960, BOLIVIA 31 May 2005, BOSNIA AND HERZEGOVINA 2 June 1993, BOTSWANA 5 June 1997, BRAZIL 24 May 1957, BULGARIA 22 Sep 1932, BURKINA FASO 21 Nov 1960, BURUNDI 11 Mar 1963, CAMBODIA 24 Feb 1969, CAMEROON 7 June 1960, CAPE VERDE 3 Apr 1979, CENTRAL AFRICAN REPUBLIC 27 Oct 1960, CHAD A10 Nov 1960, CHILE 31 May 1933, COLOMBIA 4 Mar 1969, COMOROS 23 Oct 1978, CONGO 10 Nov 1960, DEMOCRATIC REPUBLIC OF CONGO 20 Sep 1960, COSTA RICA 2 June 1960, COTE D'IVOIRE 21 Nov 1960, CROATIA 8 Oct 1991, CUBA 20 July 1953, CYPRUS 23 Sep 1960, CZECH REPUBLIC 1 Jan 1993, DENMARK 11 Feb 1932, DJIBOUTI 3 Aug 1978, DOMINICA 28 Feb 1983, DOMINICAN REPUBLIC 5 Dec 1956, ECUADOR 6 July 1954, EGYPT 29 Nov 1955, EL SALVADOR 15 June 1995, EQUATORIAL GUINEA 13 Aug 2001, ERITREA 22 Feb 2000, ESTONIA 7 Feb 1996, ETHIOPIA 2 Sep 2003, FIJI 19 Apr 1974, FINLAND 13 Jan 1936, FRANCE 24 June 1937, GABON 14 Oct 1960, GAMBIA 4 Sep 2000, GEORGIA 22 June 1997, GERMANY 13 June 1956, GHANA 20 May 1957, GREECE 13 June 1952, GRENADA 9 July 1979, GUATEMALA 13 June 1989, GUINEA-BISSAU 21 Feb 1977, GUINEA 21 Jan 1959, GUYANA 8 June 1966, HAITI 4 Mar 1958, HONDURAS 21 Feb 1957, HUNGARY 8 June 1956, ICELAND 17 Feb 1958, INDIA 30 Nov 1954, INDONESIA 12 June 1950, IRAN (THE ISLAMIC REPUBLIC OF) 10 June 1957, IRAQ 27 Nov 1962, IRELAND 2 Mar 1931, ISRAEL 7 June 1955, ITALY 18 June 1934, JAMAICA 26 Dec 1962, JAPAN 21 Nov 1932, JORDAN 6 June 1966, KAZAKHSTAN 18 May 2001, KENYA 13 Jan 1964, KIRIBATI 3 Feb 2000, KUWAIT 23 Sep 1968, KYRGYZSTAN 31 Mar 1992, LAO PEOPLE'S DEMOCRATIC REPUBLIC 23 Jan 1964, LATVIA 2 June 2006, LEBANON 1 June 1977, LESOTHO 31 Oct 1966, LIBERIA 1 May 1931, LIBYAN ARAB JAMAHIRIYA 13 June 1961, LITHUANIA 26 Sep 1994, LUXEMBOURG 24 July 1964, THE FORMER YUGOSLAV REPUBLIC OF MACEDONIA 17 Nov 1991, MADAGASCAR 1 Nov 1960, MALAWI 19 Nov 1999, MALAYSIA 11 Nov 1957, MALI 22 Sep 1960, MALTA 4 Jan 1965, MAURITANIA 20 June 1961, MAURITIUS 2 Dec 1969, MEXICO 12 May 1934, REPUBLIC OF MOLDOVA 23 Mar 2000, MONGOLIA 15 Mar 2005, MOROCCO 20 May 1957, MOZAMBIQUE 16 June 2003, MYANMAR 4 Mar 1955, NAMIBIA 15 Nov 2000, NEPAL 3 Jan 2002, NETHERLANDS 31 Mar 1933, NEW ZEALAND 29 Mar 1938, NICARAGUA 12 Apr 1934, NIGER 27 Feb 1961, NIGERIA 17 Oct 1960, NORWAY 1 July 1932, OMAN 30 Oct 1998, PAKISTAN 23 Dec 1957, PANAMA 16 May 1966, PAPUA NEW

* Source: International Labour Organization, http://www.ilo.org/ilolex
The ILO shall accept no responsibility for any inaccuracy, errors or omissions or for the consequences arising from the use of the Text.

GUINEA 1 May 1976, PARAGUAY 28 Aug 1967, PERU 1 Feb 1960, PHILIPPINES 15 July 2005, POLAND 30 July 1958, PORTUGAL 26 June 1956, QATAR 12 Mar 1998, REPUBLIC OF SERBIA 24 Nov 2000, ROMANIA 28 May 1957, RUSSIAN FEDERATION 23 June 1956, RWANDA 23 May 2001, SAINT KITTS AND NEVIS 12 Oct 2000, SAINT LUCIA 14 May 1980, SAINT VINCENT AND THE GRENADINES 21 Oct 1998, SAN MARINO 1 Feb 1995, SAO TOME AND PRINCIPE 4 May 2005, SAUDI ARABIA 15 June 1978, SENEGAL 4 Nov 1960, SEYCHELLES 6 Feb 1978, SIERRA LEONE 13 June 1961, SINGAPORE 25 Oct 1965, SLOVAKIA 1 Jan 1993, SLOVENIA 29 May 1992, SOLOMON ISLANDS 6 Aug 1985, SOMALIA 18 Nov 1960, SOUTH AFRICA 5 Mar 1997, SPAIN 29 Aug 1932, SRI LANKA 5 Apr 1950, SUDAN 18 June 1957, SURINAME 15 June 1976, SWAZILAND 26 Apr 1978, SWEDEN 22 Dec 1931, SWITZERLAND 23 May 1940, SYRIAN ARAB REPUBLIC 26 July 1960, TAJIKISTAN 26 Nov 1993, TANZANIA (UNITED REPUBLIC OF) 30 Jan 1962, THAILAND 26 Feb 1969, TOGO 7 June 1960, TRINIDAD AND TOBAGO 24 May 1963, TUNISIA 17 Dec 1962, TURKEY 30 Oct 1998, TURKMENISTAN 15 May 1997, UGANDA 4 June 1963, UKRAINE 10 Aug 1956, UNITED ARAB EMIRATES 27 May 1982, UNITED KINGDOM 3 June 1931, URUGUAY 6 Sep 1995, UZBEKISTAN 13 July 1992, VANUATU 28 Aug 2006, VENEZUELA (BOLIVARIAN REPUBLIC OF) 20 Nov 1944, VIET NAM 5 Mar 2007, YEMEN 14 Apr 1969, ZAMBIA 2 Dec 1964, ZIMBABWE 27 Aug 1998.

The General Conference of the International Labour Organisation,

Having been convened at Geneva by the Governing Body of the International Labour Office, and having met in its Fourteenth Session on 10 June 1930, and

Having decided upon the adoption of certain proposals with regard to forced or compulsory labour, which is included in the first item on the agenda of the Session, and

Having determined that these proposals shall take the form of an international Convention,

adopts this twenty-eighth day of June of the year one thousand nine hundred and thirty the following Convention, which may be cited as the Forced Labour Convention, 1930, for ratification by the Members of the International Labour Organisation in accordance with the provisions of the Constitution of the International Labour Organisation:

Article 1

1. Each Member of the International Labour Organisation which ratifies this Convention undertakes to suppress the use of forced or compulsory labour in all its forms within the shortest possible period.

2. With a view to this complete suppression, recourse to forced or compulsory labour may be had, during the transitional period, for public purposes only and as an exceptional measure, subject to the conditions and guarantees hereinafter provided.

3. At the expiration of a period of five years after the coming into force of this Convention, and when the Governing Body of the International Labour Office prepares the report provided for in Article 31 below, the said Governing Body shall consider the possibility of the suppression of forced or compulsory labour in all its forms without a further transitional period and the desirability of placing this question on the agenda of the Conference.

Article 2

1. For the purposes of this Convention the term forced or compulsory labour shall mean all work or service which is exacted from any person under the menace of any penalty and for which the said person has not offered himself voluntarily.

2. Nevertheless, for the purposes of this Convention, the term forced or compulsory labour shall not include–

(a) any work or service exacted in virtue of compulsory military service laws for work of a purely military character;

(b) any work or service which forms part of the normal civic obligations of the citizens of a fully self-governing country;

(c) any work or service exacted from any person as a consequence of a conviction in a court of law, provided that the said work or service is carried out under the supervision and control of a public authority and that the said person is not hired to or placed at the disposal of private individuals, companies or associations;

(d) any work or service exacted in cases of emergency, that is to say, in the event of war or of a calamity or threatened calamity, such as fire, flood, famine, earthquake, violent epidemic or epizootic diseases, invasion by animal, insect or vegetable pests, and in general any circumstance that would endanger the existence or the well-being of the whole or part of the population;

(e) minor communal services of a kind which, being performed by the members of the community in the direct interest of the said community, can therefore be considered as normal civic obligations incumbent upon the members of the community, provided that the members of the community or their direct representatives shall have the right to be consulted in regard to the need for such services.

Article 3

For the purposes of this Convention the term competent authority shall mean either an authority of the metropolitan country or the highest central authority in the territory concerned.

Article 4

1. The competent authority shall not impose or permit the imposition of forced or compulsory labour for the benefit of private individuals, companies or associations.

2. Where such forced or compulsory labour for the benefit of private individuals, companies or associations exists at the date on which a Member's ratification of this Convention is registered by the Director-General of the International Labour Office, the Member shall completely suppress such forced or compulsory labour from the date on which this Convention comes into force for that Member.

Article 5

1. No concession granted to private individuals, companies or associations shall involve any form of forced or compulsory labour for the production or the collection of products which such private individuals, companies or associations utilise or in which they trade.

2. Where concessions exist containing provisions involving such forced or compulsory labour, such provisions shall be rescinded as soon as possible, in order to comply with Article 1 of this Convention.

Article 6

Officials of the administration, even when they have the duty of encouraging the populations under their charge to engage in some form of labour, shall not put constraint upon the said populations or upon any individual members thereof to work for private individuals, companies or associations.

Article 7

1. Chiefs who do not exercise administrative functions shall not have recourse to forced or compulsory labour.

2. Chiefs who exercise administrative functions may, with the express permission of the competent authority, have recourse to forced or compulsory labour, subject to the provisions of Article 10 of this Convention.

3. Chiefs who are duly recognised and who do not receive adequate remuneration in other forms may have the enjoyment of personal services, subject to due regulation and provided that all necessary measures are taken to prevent abuses.

Article 8

1. The responsibility for every decision to have recourse to forced or compulsory labour shall rest with the highest civil authority in the territory concerned.

2. Nevertheless, that authority may delegate powers to the highest local authorities to exact forced or compulsory labour which does not involve the removal of the workers from their place of habitual residence. That authority may also delegate, for such periods and subject to such conditions as may be laid down in the regulations provided for in Article 23 of this Convention, powers to the highest local authorities to exact forced or compulsory labour which involves the removal of the workers from their place of habitual residence for the purpose of facilitating the movement of officials of the administration, when on duty, and for the transport of Government stores.

Article 9

Except as otherwise provided for in Article 10 of this Convention, any authority competent to exact forced or compulsory labour shall, before deciding to have recourse to such labour, satisfy itself–

(a) that the work to be done or the service to be rendered is of important direct interest for the community called upon to do work or render the service;

(b) that the work or service is of present or imminent necessity;

(c) that it has been impossible to obtain voluntary labour for carrying out the work or rendering the service by the offer of rates of wages and conditions of labour not less favourable than those prevailing in the area concerned for similar work or service; and

(d) that the work or service will not lay too heavy a burden upon the present population, having regard to the labour available and its capacity to undertake the work.

Article 10

1. Forced or compulsory labour exacted as a tax and forced or compulsory labour to which recourse is had for the execution of public works by chiefs who exercise administrative functions shall be progressively abolished.

2. Meanwhile, where forced or compulsory labour is exacted as a tax, and where recourse is had to forced or compulsory labour for the execution of public works by chiefs who exercise administrative functions, the authority concerned shall first satisfy itself–

(a) that the work to be done or the service to be rendered is of important direct interest for the community called upon to do the work or render the service;

(b) that the work or the service is of present or imminent necessity;

(c) that the work or service will not lay too heavy a burden upon the present population, having regard to the labour available and its capacity to undertake the work;

(d) that the work or service will not entail the removal of the workers from their place of habitual residence;

(e) that the execution of the work or the rendering of the service will be directed in accordance with the exigencies of religion, social life and agriculture.

Article 11

1. Only adult able-bodied males who are of an apparent age of not less than 18 and not more than 45 years may be called upon for forced or compulsory labour. Except in respect of the kinds of labour provided for in Article 10 of this Convention, the following limitations and conditions shall apply:

(a) whenever possible prior determination by a medical officer appointed by the administration that the persons concerned are not suffering from any infectious or contagious disease and that they are physically fit for the work required and for the conditions under which it is to be carried out;

(b) exemption of school teachers and pupils and officials of the administration in general;

(c) the maintenance in each community of the number of adult able-bodied men indispensable for family and social life;

(d) respect for conjugal and family ties.

2. For the purposes of subparagraph (c) of the preceding paragraph, the regulations provided for in Article 23 of this Convention shall fix the proportion of the resident adult able-bodied males who may be taken at any one time for forced or compulsory labour, provided always that this proportion shall in no case exceed 25 per cent. In fixing this proportion the competent authority shall take account of the density of the population, of its social and physical development, of the seasons, and of the work which must be done by the persons concerned on their own behalf in their locality, and, generally, shall have regard to the economic and social necessities of the normal life of the community concerned.

Article 12

1. The maximum period for which any person may be taken for forced or compulsory labour of all kinds in any one period of twelve months shall not exceed sixty days, including the time spent in going to and from the place of work.

2. Every person from whom forced or compulsory labour is exacted shall be furnished with a certificate indicating the periods of such labour which he has completed.

Article 13

1. The normal working hours of any person from whom forced or compulsory labour is exacted shall be the same as those prevailing in the case of voluntary labour, and the hours worked in excess of the normal working hours shall be remunerated at the rates prevailing in the case of overtime for voluntary labour.

2. A weekly day of rest shall be granted to all persons from whom forced or compulsory labour of any kind is exacted and this day shall coincide as far as possible with the day fixed by tradition or custom in the territories or regions concerned.

Article 14

1. With the exception of the forced or compulsory labour provided for in Article 10 of this Convention, forced or compulsory labour of all kinds shall be remunerated in cash at rates not less than those prevailing for similar kinds of work either in the district in which the labour is employed or in the district from which the labour is recruited, whichever may be the higher.

2. In the case of labour to which recourse is had by chiefs in the exercise of their administrative functions, payment of wages in accordance with the provisions of the preceding paragraph shall be introduced as soon as possible.

3. The wages shall be paid to each worker individually and not to his tribal chief or to any other authority.

4. For the purpose of payment of wages the days spent in travelling to and from the place of work shall be counted as working days.

5. Nothing in this Article shall prevent ordinary rations being given as a part of wages, such rations to be at least equivalent in value to the money payment they are taken to represent, but deductions from wages shall not be made either for the payment of taxes or for special food, clothing or accommodation supplied to a worker for the purpose of maintaining him in a fit condition to carry on his work under the special conditions of any employment, or for the supply of tools.

Article 15

1. Any laws or regulations relating to workmen's compensation for accidents or sickness arising out of the employment of the worker and any laws or regulations providing compensation for the dependants of deceased or incapacitated workers which are or shall be in force in the territory concerned shall be equally applicable to persons from whom forced or compulsory labour is exacted and to voluntary workers.

2. In any case it shall be an obligation on any authority employing any worker on forced or compulsory labour to ensure the subsistence of any such worker who, by accident or sickness arising out of his employment, is rendered wholly or partially incapable of providing for himself, and to take measures to ensure the maintenance of any persons actually dependent upon such a worker in the event of his incapacity or decease arising out of his employment.

Article 16

1. Except in cases of special necessity, persons from whom forced or compulsory labour is exacted shall not be transferred to districts where the food and climate differ so considerably from those to which they have been accustomed as to endanger their health.

2. In no case shall the transfer of such workers be permitted unless all measures relating to hygiene and accommodation which are necessary to adapt such workers to the conditions and to safeguard their health can be strictly applied.

3. When such transfer cannot be avoided, measures of gradual habituation to the new conditions of diet and of climate shall be adopted on competent medical advice.

4. In cases where such workers are required to perform regular work to which they are not accustomed, measures shall be taken to ensure their habituation to it, especially as regards progressive training, the hours of work and the provision of rest intervals, and any increase or amelioration of diet which may be necessary.

Article 17

Before permitting recourse to forced or compulsory labour for works of construction or maintenance which entail the workers remaining at the workplaces for considerable periods, the competent authority shall satisfy itself–

(1) that all necessary measures are taken to safeguard the health of the workers and to guarantee the necessary medical care, and, in particular, (a) that the workers are medically examined before commencing the work and at fixed intervals during the period of service, (b) that there is an adequate medical staff, provided with the dispensaries, infirmaries, hospitals and equipment necessary to meet all requirements, and (c) that the sanitary conditions of the workplaces, the supply of drinking water, food, fuel, and cooking utensils, and, where necessary, of housing and clothing, are satisfactory;

(2) that definite arrangements are made to ensure the subsistence of the families of the workers, in particular by facilitating the remittance, by a safe method, of part of the wages to the family, at the request or with the consent of the workers;

(3) that the journeys of the workers to and from the workplaces are made at the expense and under the responsibility of the administration, which shall facilitate such journeys by making the fullest use of all available means of transport;

(4) that, in case of illness or accident causing incapacity to work of a certain duration, the worker is repatriated at the expense of the administration;

(5) that any worker who may wish to remain as a voluntary worker at the end of his period of forced or compulsory labour is permitted to do so without, for a period of two years, losing his right to repatriation free of expense to himself.

Article 18

1. Forced or compulsory labour for the transport of persons or goods, such as the labour of porters or boatmen, shall be abolished within the shortest possible period. Meanwhile the competent authority shall promulgate regulations determining, inter alia, (a) that such labour shall only be employed for the purpose of facilitating the movement of officials of the administration, when on duty, or for the transport of Government stores, or, in cases of very urgent necessity, the transport of persons other than officials, (b) that the workers so employed shall be medically certified to be physically fit, where medical examination is possible, and that where such medical examination is not practicable the person employing such workers shall be held responsible for ensuring that they are physically fit and not suffering from any infectious or contagious disease, (c) the maximum load which these workers may carry, (d) the maximum distance from their homes to which they may be taken, (e) the maximum number of days per month or other period for which they may be taken, including the days spent in returning to their homes, and (f) the persons entitled to demand this form of forced or compulsory labour and the extent to which they are entitled to demand it.

2. In fixing the maxima referred to under (c), (d) and (e) in the foregoing paragraph, the competent authority shall have regard to all relevant factors, including the physical development of the

population from which the workers are recruited, the nature of the country through which they must travel and the climatic conditions.

3. The competent authority shall further provide that the normal daily journey of such workers shall not exceed a distance corresponding to an average working day of eight hours, it being understood that account shall be taken not only of the weight to be carried and the distance to be covered, but also of the nature of the road, the season and all other relevant factors, and that, where hours of journey in excess of the normal daily journey are exacted, they shall be remunerated at rates higher than the normal rates.

Article 19

1. The competent authority shall only authorise recourse to compulsory cultivation as a method of precaution against famine or a deficiency of food supplies and always under the condition that the food or produce shall remain the property of the individuals or the community producing it.

2. Nothing in this Article shall be construed as abrogating the obligation on members of a community, where production is organised on a communal basis by virtue of law or custom and where the produce or any profit accruing from the sale thereof remain the property of the community, to perform the work demanded by the community by virtue of law or custom.

Article 20

Collective punishment laws under which a community may be punished for crimes committed by any of its members shall not contain provisions for forced or compulsory labour by the community as one of the methods of punishment.

Article 21

Forced or compulsory labour shall not be used for work underground in mines.

Article 22

The annual reports that Members which ratify this Convention agree to make to the International Labour Office, pursuant to the provisions of Article 22 of the Constitution of the International Labour Organisation, on the measures they have taken to give effect to the provisions of this Convention, shall contain as full information as possible, in respect of each territory concerned, regarding the extent to which recourse has been had to forced or compulsory labour in that territory, the purposes for which it has been employed, the sickness and death rates, hours of work, methods of payment of wages and rates of wages, and any other relevant information.

Article 23

1. To give effect to the provisions of this Convention the competent authority shall issue complete and precise regulations governing the use of forced or compulsory labour.

2. These regulations shall contain, inter alia, rules permitting any person from whom forced or compulsory labour is exacted to forward all complaints relative to the conditions of labour to the authorities and ensuring that such complaints will be examined and taken into consideration.

Article 24

Adequate measures shall in all cases be taken to ensure that the regulations governing the employment of forced or compulsory labour are strictly applied, either by extending the duties of any existing labour inspectorate which has been established for the inspection of voluntary labour to cover the inspection of forced or compulsory labour or in some other appropriate manner. Measures shall also be taken to ensure that the regulations are brought to the knowledge of persons from whom such labour is exacted.

Article 25

The illegal exaction of forced or compulsory labour shall be punishable as a penal offence, and it shall be an obligation on any Member ratifying this Convention to ensure that the penalties imposed by law are really adequate and are strictly enforced.

Article 26

1. Each Member of the International Labour Organisation which ratifies this Convention undertakes to apply it to the territories placed under its sovereignty, jurisdiction, protection, suzerainty, tutelage or authority, so far as it has the right to accept obligations affecting matters of internal jurisdiction; provided that, if such Member may desire to take advantage of the provisions of article 35 of the Constitution of the International Labour Organisation, it shall append to its ratification a declaration stating–

(1) the territories to which it intends to apply the provisions of this Convention without modification;

(2) the territories to which it intends to apply the provisions of this Convention with modifications, together with details of the said modifications;

(3) the territories in respect of which it reserves its decision.

2. The aforesaid declaration shall be deemed to be an integral part of the ratification and shall have the force of ratification. It shall be open to any Member, by a subsequent declaration, to cancel in whole or in part the reservations made, in pursuance of the provisions of subparagraphs (2) and (3) of this Article, in the original declaration.

Article 27

The formal ratifications of this Convention under the conditions set forth in the Constitution of the International Labour Organisation shall be communicated to the Director-General of the International Labour Office for registration.

Article 28

1. This Convention shall be binding only upon those Members whose ratifications have been registered with the International Labour Office.

2. It shall come into force twelve months after the date on which the ratifications of two Members of the International Labour Organisation have been registered with the Director-General.

3. Thereafter, this Convention shall come into force for any Member twelve months after the date on which the ratification has been registered.

Article 29

As soon as the ratifications of two Members of the International Labour Organisation have been registered with the International Labour Office, the Director-General of the International Labour Office shall so notify all the Members of the International Labour Organisation. He shall likewise notify them of the registration of ratifications which may be communicated subsequently by other Members of the Organisation.

Article 30

1. A Member which has ratified this Convention may denounce it after the expiration of ten years from the date on which the Convention first comes into force, by an act communicated to the Director-General of the International Labour Office for registration. Such denunciation shall not take effect until one year after the date on which it is registered with the International Labour Office.

2. Each Member which has ratified this Convention and which does not, within the year following the expiration of the period of ten years mentioned in the preceding paragraph, exercise the right of denunciation provided for in this Article, will be bound for another period of five years and, thereafter, may denounce this Convention at the expiration of each period of five years under the terms provided for in this Article.

Article 31

At such times as it may consider necessary the Governing Body of the International Labour Office shall present to the General Conference a report on the working of this Convention and shall examine the desirability of placing on the agenda of the Conference the question of its revision in whole or in part.

Article 32

1. Should the Conference adopt a new Convention revising this Convention in whole or in part, the ratification by a Member of the new revising Convention shall ipso jure involve denunciation of this Convention without any requirement of delay, notwithstanding the provisions of Article 30 above, if and when the new revising Convention shall have come into force.

2. As from the date of the coming into force of the new revising Convention, the present Convention shall cease to be open to ratification by the Members.

3. Nevertheless, this Convention shall remain in force in its actual form and content for those Members which have ratified it but have not ratified the revising convention.

Article 33

The French and English texts of this Convention shall both be authentic.

Recommendation No. 35 concerning Indirect Compulsion to Labour, 1930*

Adoption: 28 June 1930

This Recommendation is related to a fundamental Convention and is considered up to date.

The General Conference of the International Labour Organisation,

Having been convened at Geneva by the Governing Body of the International Labour Office, and having met in its Fourteenth Session on 10 June 1930, and

Having decided upon the adoption of certain proposals with regard to indirect compulsion to labour, which is included in the first item on the agenda of the Session, and

Having determined that these proposals should take the form of a Recommendation,

adopts this twenty-eighth day of June of the year one thousand nine hundred thirty, the following Recommendation, which may be cited as the Forced Labour (Indirect Compulsion) Recommendation, 1930, to be submitted to the Members of the International Labour Organisation for consideration with a view to effect being given to it by national legislation or otherwise, in accordance with the provisions of the Constitution of the International Labour Organisation:

Having adopted a Convention concerning forced or compulsory labour, and

Desiring to supplement this Convention by a statement of the principles which appear best fitted to guide the policy of the Members in endeavouring to avoid any indirect compulsion to labour which would lay too heavy a burden upon the populations of territories to which the Convention may apply,

The Conference recommends that each Member should take the following principles into consideration:

I

The amount of labour available, the capacities for labour of the population, and the evil effects which too sudden changes in the habits of life and labour may have on the social conditions of the population, are factors which should be taken into consideration in deciding questions connected with the economic development of territories in a primitive stage of development, and, in particular, when deciding upon:

(a) increases in the number and extent of industrial, mining and agricultural undertakings in such territories;

(b) the non-indigenous settlement, if any, which is to be permitted;

(c) the granting of forest or other concessions, with or without the character of monopolies.

---

* Source: International Labour Organization, http://www.ilo.org/ilolex
The ILO shall accept no responsibility for any inaccuracy, errors or omissions or for the consequences arising from the use of the Text.

II

The desirability of avoiding indirect means of artificially increasing the economic pressure upon populations to seek wage-earning employment, and particularly such means as:

(a) imposing such taxation upon populations as would have the effect of compelling them to seek wage-earning employment with private undertakings;

(b) imposing such restrictions on the possession, occupation, or use of land as would have the effect of rendering difficult the gaining of a living by independent cultivation;

(c) extending abusively the generally accepted meaning of vagrancy;

(d) adopting such pass laws as would have the effect of placing workers in the service of others in a position of advantage as compared with that of other workers.

III

The desirability of avoiding any restrictions on the voluntary flow of labour from one form of employment to another or from one district to another which might have the indirect effect of compelling workers to take employment in particular industries or districts, except where such restrictions are considered necessary in the interest of the population or of the workers concerned.

Convention No.105 concerning the Abolition of Forced Labour, 1957*

Adoption: 25 June 1957
Entry into force: 17 January 1959
Parties: 165 (Status as of 1 April 2007)

AFGHANISTAN 16 May 1963, ALBANIA 27 Feb 1997, ALGERIA 12 June 1969, ANGOLA 4 June 1976, ANTIGUA AND BARBUDA 2 Feb 1983, ARGENTINA 18 Jan 1960, ARMENIA 17 Dec 2004, AUSTRALIA 7 June 1960, AUSTRIA 5 Mar 1958, AZRBAIJAN 9 Aug 2000, BAHAMAS 25 May 1976, BAHRAIN 14 July 1998, BANGLADESH 22 June 1972, BARBADOS 8 May 1967, BELARUS 25 Sep 1995, BELGIUM 23 Jan 1961, BELIZE 15 Dec 1983, BENIN 22 May 1961, BOLIVIA 11 June 1990, BOSNIA AND HERZEGOVINA 15 Nov 2000, BOTSWANA 5 June 1997, BRAZIL 18 June 1965, BULGARIA 23 Mar 1999, BURKINA FASO 25 Aug 1997, BURUNDI 11 Mar 1963, CAMBODIA 23 Aug 1999, CAMEROON 3 Sep 1962, CANADA 14 July 1959, CAPE VERDE 3 Apr 1979, CENTRAL AFRICAN REPUBLIC 9 June 1964, CHAD 8 June 1961, CHILE 1 Feb 1999, COLOMBIA 7 June 1963, COMOROS 23 Oct 1978, CONGO 26 Nov 1999, DEMOCRATIC REPUBLIC OF CONGO 20 June 2001, COSTA RICA 4 May 1959, COTE D'IVOIRE 5 May 1961, CROATIA 5 Mar 1997, CUBA 2 June 1958, CYPRUS 23 Sep 1960, CZECH REPUBLIC 6 Aug 1996, DENMARK 17 Jan 1958, DJIBOUTI 3 Aug 1978, DOMINICA 28 Feb 1983, DOMINICAN REPUBLIC 23 June 1958, ECUADOR 5 Feb 1962, EGYPT 23 Oct 1958, EL SALVADOR 18 Nov 1958, EQUATORIAL GUINEA 13 Aug 2001, ERITREA 22 Feb 2000, ESTONIA 7 Feb 1996, ETHIOPIA 24 Mar 1999, FIJI 19 Apr 1974, FINLAND 27 May 1960, FRANCE 18 Dec 1969, GABON 29 May 1961, GAMBIA 4 Sep 2000, GEORGIA 23 Sep 1996, GERMANY 22 June 1959, GHANA 15 Dec 1958, GREECE 30 Mar 1962, GRENADA 9 July 1979, GUATEMALA 9 Dec 1959, GUINEA-BISSAU 21 Feb 1977, GUINEA 11 July 1961, GUYANA 8 June 1966, HAITI 4 Mar 1958, HONDURAS 4 Aug 1958, HUNGARY 4 Jan 1994, ICELAND 29 Nov 1960, INDIA 18 May 2000, INDONESIA 7 June 1999, IRAN (ISLAMIC REPUBLIC OF) 13 Apr 1959, IRAQ 15 June 1959, IRELAND 11 June 1958, ISRAEL 10 Apr 1958, ITALY 15 Mar 1968, JAMAICA 26 Dec 1962, JORDAN 31 Mar 1958, KAZAKHSTAN 18 May 2001, KENYA 13 Jan 1964, KIRIBATI 3 Feb 2000, KUWAIT 21 Sep 1961, KYRGYZSTAN 18 Feb 1999, LATVIA 27 Jan 1992, LEBANON 1 June 1977, LESOTHO 14 June 2001, LIBERIA 25 May 1962, LIBYAN ARAB JAMAHIRIYA 13 June 1961, LITHUANIA 26 Sep 1994, LUXEMBOURG 24 July 1964, THE FORMER YUGOSLAV REPUBLIC OF MACEDONIA 15 July 2003, MALAWI 19 Nov 1999, MALAYSIA 13 Oct 1958 (denounced on 10 Jan 1990), MALI 28 May 1962, MALTA 4 Jan 1965, MAURITANIA 3 Apr 1997, MAURITIUS 2 Dec 1969, MEXICO 1 June 1959, REPUBLIC OF MOLDOVA 10 Mar 1993, MONGOLIA 15 Mar 2005, MOROCCO 1 Dec 1966, MOZAMBIQUE 6 June 1977, NAMIBIA 15 Nov 2000, NETHERLANDS 18 Feb 1959, NEW ZEALAND 14 June 1968, NICARAGUA 31 Oct 1967, NIGER 23 Mar 1962, NIGERIA 17 Oct 1960, NORWAY 14 Apr 1958, OMAN 21 July 2005, PAKISTAN 15 Feb 1960, PANAMA 16 May 1966, PAPUA NEW GUINEA 1 May 1976, PARAGUAY 16 May 1968, PERU 6 Dec 1960, PHILIPPINES 17 Nov 1960, POLAND 30 July 1958, PORTUGAL 23 Nov 1959, QATAR 2 Feb 2007, REPUBLIC OF SERBIA 10 July 2003, ROMANIA 3 Aug 1998, RUSSIAN FEDERATION 2 July 1998, RWANDA 18 Sep 1962, SAINT KITTS AND NEVIS 12 Oct 2000, SAINT LUCIA 14 May 1980, SAINT VINCENT AND THE GRENADINES 21 Oct 1998, SAN MARINO 1 Feb

* Source: International Labour Organization, http://www.ilo.org/ilolex
The ILO shall accept no responsibility for any inaccuracy, errors or omissions or for the consequences arising from the use of the Text.

1995, SAO TOME AND PRINCIPE 4 May 2005, SAUDI ARABIA 15 June 1978, SENEGAL 28 July 1961, SEYCHELLES 6 Feb 1978, SIERRA LEONE 13 June 1961, SINGAPORE 25 Oct 1965 (denounced on 19 Apr 1979), SLOVAKIA 29 Sep 1997, SLOVENIA 24 June 1997, SOMALIA 8 Dec 1961, SOUTH AFRICA 5 Mar 1997, SPAIN 6 Nov 1967, SRI LANKA 7 Jan 2003, SUDAN 22 Oct 1970, SURINAME 15 June 1976, SWAZILAND 28 Feb 1979, SWEDEN 2 June 1958, SWITZERLAND 18 July 1958, SYRIAN ARAB REPUBLIC 23 Oct 1958, TAJIKISTAN 23 Sep 1999, TANZANIA (UNITED REPUBLIC OF) 30 Jan 1962, THAILAND 2 Dec 1969, TOGO 10 July 1999, TRINIDAD AND TOBAGO 24 May 1963, TUNISIA 12 Jan 1959, TURKEY 29 May 1961, TURKMENISTAN 15 May 1997, UGANDA 4 June 1963, UKRAINE 14 Dec 2000, UNITED ARAB EMIRATES 24 Feb 1997, UNITED KINGDOM 30 Dec 1957, UNITED STATES 25 Sep 1991, URUGAY 22 Nov 1968, UZBEKISTAN 15 Dec 1997, VANUATU 28 Aug 2006, VENEZUELA (BOLIVARIAN REPUBLIC OF) 16 Nov 1964, YEMEN 14 Apr 1969, ZAMBIA 22 Feb 1965, ZIMBABWE 27 Aug 1998.

The General Conference of the International Labour Organisation,

Having been convened at Geneva by the Governing Body of the International Labour Office, and having met in its Fortieth Session on 5 June 1957, and

Having considered the question of forced labour, which is the fourth item on the agenda of the session, and

Having noted the provisions of the Forced Labour Convention, 1930, and

Having noted that the Slavery Convention, 1926, provides that all necessary measures shall be taken to prevent compulsory or forced labour from developing into conditions analogous to slavery and that the Supplementary Convention on the Abolition of Slavery, the Slave Trade and Institutions and Practices Similar to Slavery, 1956, provides for the complete abolition of debt bondage and serfdom, and

Having noted that the Protection of Wages Convention, 1949, provides that wages shall be paid regularly and prohibits methods of payment which deprive the worker of a genuine possibility of terminating his employment, and

Having decided upon the adoption of further proposals with regard to the abolition of certain forms of forced or compulsory labour constituting a violation of the rights of man referred to in the Charter of the United Nations and enunciated by the Universal Declaration of Human Rights, and

Having determined that these proposals shall take the form of an international Convention,

adopts this twenty-fifth day of June of the year one thousand nine hundred and fifty-seven the following Convention, which may be cited as the Abolition of Forced Labour Convention, 1957:

Article 1

Each Member of the International Labour Organisation which ratifies this Convention undertakes to suppress and not to make use of any form of forced or compulsory labour–

(a) as a means of political coercion or education or as a punishment for holding or expressing political views or views ideologically opposed to the established political, social or economic system;

(b) as a method of mobilising and using labour for purposes of economic development;

(c) as a means of labour discipline;

(d) as a punishment for having participated in strikes;

(e) as a means of racial, social, national or religious discrimination.

Article 2

Each Member of the International Labour Organisation which ratifies this Convention undertakes to take effective measures to secure the immediate and complete abolition of forced or compulsory labour as specified in Article 1 of this Convention.

Article 3

The formal ratifications of this Convention shall be communicated to the Director-General of the International Labour Office for registration.

Article 4

1. This Convention shall be binding only upon those Members of the International Labour Organisation whose ratifications have been registered with the Director-General.

2. It shall come into force twelve months after the date on which the ratifications of two Members have been registered with the Director-General.

3. Thereafter, this Convention shall come into force for any Member twelve months after the date on which its ratification has been registered.

Article 5

1. A Member which has ratified this Convention may denounce it after the expiration of ten years from the date on which the Convention first comes into force, by an act communicated to the Director-General of the International Labour Office for registration. Such denunciation shall not take effect until one year after the date on which it is registered.

2. Each Member which has ratified this Convention and which does not, within the year following the expiration of the period of ten years mentioned in the preceding paragraph, exercise the right of denunciation provided for in this Article, will be bound for another period of ten years and, thereafter, may denounce this Convention at the expiration of each period of ten years under the terms provided for in this Article.

Article 6

1. The Director-General of the International Labour Office shall notify all Members of the International Labour Organisation of the registration of all ratifications and denunciations communicated to him by the Members of the Organisation.

2. When notifying the Members of the Organisation of the registration of the second ratification communicated to him, the Director-General shall draw the attention of the Members of the Organisation to the date upon which the Convention will come into force.

Article 7

The Director-General of the International Labour Office shall communicate to the Secretary-General of the United Nations for registration in accordance with Article 102 of the Charter of the United Nations full particulars of all ratifications and acts of denunciation registered by him in accordance with the provisions of the preceding Articles.

Article 8

At such times as it may consider necessary the Governing Body of the International Labour Office shall present to the General Conference a report on the working of this Convention and shall examine the desirability of placing on the agenda of the Conference the question of its revision in whole or in part.

Article 9

1. Should the Conference adopt a new Convention revising this Convention in whole or in part, then, unless the new Convention otherwise provides:

a) the ratification by a Member of the new revising Convention shall ipso jure involve the immediate denunciation of this Convention, notwithstanding the provisions of Article 5 above, if and when the new revising Convention shall have come into force;

b) as from the date when the new revising Convention comes into force this Convention shall cease to be open to ratification by the Members.

2. This Convention shall in any case remain in force in its actual form and content for those Members which have ratified it but have not ratified the revising Convention.

Article 10

The English and French versions of the text of this Convention are equally authoritative.

Convention No. 138 concerning Minimum Age for Admission to Employment, 1973*

Adoption: 26 June 1973
Entry into force: 19 June 1976
Parties: 148 (Status as of 1 April 2007)

ALBANIA 16 Feb 1998, ALGERIA 30 Apr 1984, ANGOLA 13 June 2001, ANTIGUA AND BARBUDA 17 Mar 1983, ARGENTINA 11 Nov 1996, ARMENIA 27 Jan 2006, AUSTRIA 18 Sep 2000, AZERBAIJAN 19 May 1992, BAHAMAS 31 Oct 2001, BARBADOS 4 Jan 2000, BELARUS 3 May 1979, BELGIUM 19 Apr 1988, BELIZE 6 Mar 2000, BENIN 11 June 2001, BOLIVIA 11 June 1997, BOSNIA AND HERZEGOVINA 2 June 1993, BOTSWANA 5 June 1997, BRAZIL 28 June 2001, BULGARIA 23 Apr 1980, BURKINA FASO 11 Feb 1999, BURUNDI 19 July 2000, CAMBODIA 23 Aug 1999, CAMEROON 13 Aug 2001, CENTRAL AFRICAN REPUBLIC 28 June 2000, CHAD 21 Mar 2005, CHILE 1 Feb 1999, CHINA 28 Apr 1999, COLOMBIA 2 Feb 2001, COMOROS 17 Mar 2004, CONGO 26 Nov 1999, DEMOCRATIC REPUBLIC OF CONGO 20 June 2001, COSTA RICA 11 June 1976, COTE D'IVOIRE 7 Feb 2003, CROATIA 8 Oct 1991, CUBA 7 Mar 1975, CYPRUS 2 Oct 1997, DENMARK 13 Nov 1997, DJIBOUTI 14 June 2005, DOMINICA 27 Sep 1983, DOMINICAN REPUBLIC 15 June 1999, ECUADOR 19 Sep 2000, EGYPT 9 June 1999, EL SALVADOR 23 Jan 1996, EQUATORIAL GUINEA 12 June 1985, ERITREA 22 Feb 2000, ETHIOPIA 27 May 1999, FIJI 3 Jan 2003, FINLAND 13 Jan 1976, FRANCE 13 July 1990, GAMBIA 4 Sep 2000, GEORGIA 23 Sep 1996, GERMANY 8 Apr 1976, GREECE 14 Mar 1986, GRENADA 14 May 2003, GUATEMALA 27 Apr 1990, GUINEA 6 June 2003, GUYANA 15 Apr 1998, HONDURAS 9 June 1980, HUNGARY 28 May 1998, ICELAND 6 Dec 1999, INDONESIA 7 June 1999, IRAQ 13 Feb 1985, IRELAND 22 June 1978, ISRAEL 21 June 1979, ITALY 28 July 1981, JAMAICA 13 Oct 2003, JAPAN 5 June 2000, JORDAN 23 Mar 1998, KAZAKHSTAN 18 May 2001, KENYA 9 Apr 1979, REPUBLIC OF KOREA 28 Jan 1999, KUWAIT 15 Nov 1999, KYRGYZSTAN 31 Mar 1992, LAO PEOPLE'S DEMOCRATIC REPUBLIC 13 June 2005, LATVIA 2 June 2006, LEBANON 10 June 2003, LESOTHO 14 June 2001, LIBYAN ARAB JAMAHIRIYA 19 June 1975, LITHUANIA 22 June 1998, LUXEMBOURHG 24 Mar 1977, THE FORMER YUGOSLAV REPUBLIC OF MACEDONIA 17 Nov 1991, MADAGASCAR 31 May 2000, MALAWI 19 Nov 1999, MALAYSIA 9 Sep 1997, MALI 11 Mar 2002, MALTA 9 June 1988, MAURITANIA 3 Dec 2001, MAURITIUS 30 July 1990, MONGOLIA 16 Dec 2002, MOROCCO 6 Jan 2000, MOZAMBIQUE 16 June 2003, NAMIBIA 15 Nov 2000, NEPAL 30 May 1997, NETHERLANDS 14 Sep 1976, NICARAGUA 2 Nov 1981, NIGER 4 Dec 1978, NIGERIA 2 Oct 2002, NORWAY 8 July 1980, OMAN 21 July 2005, PAKISTAN 6 July 2006, PANAMA 31 Oct 2000, PAPUA NEW GUINEA 2 June 2000, PARAGUAY 3 Mar 2004, PERU 13 Nov 2002, PHILIPPINES 4 June 1998, POLAND 22 Mar 1978, PORTUGAL 20 May 1998, QATAR 3 Jan 2006, REPUBLIC OF MOLDOVA 21 Sep 1999, ROMANIA 19 Nov 1975, RUSSIAN FEDERATION 3 May 1979, RWANDA 15 Apr 1981, SAINT KITTS AND NEVIS 3 June 2005, SAINT VINCENT AND THE GRENADINES 25 July 2006, SAN MARINO 1 Feb 1995, SAO TOME AND PRINCIPE 4 May 2005, SENEGAL 15 Dec 1999, REPUBLIC OF SERBIA 24 Nov 2000, SEYCHELLES 7 Mar 2000, SINGAPORE 7 Nov 2005, SLOVAKIA 29 Sep 1997, SLOVENIA 29 May 1992, SOUTH AFRICA 30 Mar 2000,

* Source: International Labour Organization, http://www.ilo.org/ilolex
The ILO shall accept no responsibility for any inaccuracy, errors or omissions or for the consequences arising from the use of the Text.

SPAIN 16 May 1977, SRI LANKA 11 Feb 2000, SUDAN 7 Mar 2002, SWAZILAND 23 Oct 2002, SWEDEN 23 Apr 1990, SWITZERLAND 17 Aug 1999, SYRIAN ARAB REPUBLIC 18 Sep 2001, TAJIKISTAN 26 Nov 1993, TANZANIA (UNITED REPUBLIC OF) 16 Dec 1998, THAILAND 11 May 2004, TOGO 16 Mar 1984, TRINIDAD AND TOBAGO 3 Sep 2004, TUNISIA 19 Oct 1995, TURKEY 30 Oct 1998, UGANDA 25 Mar 2003, UKRAINE 3 May 1979, UNITED ARAB EMIRATES 2 Oct 1998, UNITED KINGDOM 7 June 2000, URUGAY 2 June 1977, VENEZUELA (BOLIVARIAN REPUBLIC OF) 15 July 1987, VIETNAM 24 June 2003, YEMEN 15 June 2000, ZAMBIA 9 Feb 1976, ZIMBABWE 6 June 2000.

The General Conference of the International Labour Organization,

Having been convened at Geneva by the Governing Body of the International Labour Office, and having met in its Fifty-eighth Session on 6 June 1973, and

Having decided upon the adoption of certain proposals with regard to minimum age for admission to employment, which is the fourth item on the agenda of the session, and

Noting the terms of the Minimum Age (Industry) Convention, 1919, the Minimum Age (Sea) Convention, 1920, the Minimum Age (Agriculture) Convention, 1921, the Minimum Age (Trimmers and Stokers) Convention, 1921, the Minimum Age (Non-Industrial Employment) Convention, 1932, the Minimum Age (Sea) Convention (Revised), 1936, the Minimum Age (Industry) Convention (Revised), 1937, the Minimum Age (Non-Industrial Employment) Convention (Revised), 1937, the Minimum Age (Fishermen) Convention, 1959, and the Minimum Age (Underground Work) Convention, 1965, and

Considering that the time has come to establish a general instrument on the subject, which would gradually replace the existing ones applicable to limited economic sectors, with a view to achieving the total abolition of child labour, and

Having determined that these proposals shall take the form of an international Convention,

adopts this twenty-sixth day of June of the year one thousand nine hundred and seventy-three the following Convention, which may be cited as the Minimum Age Convention, 1973:

Article 1

Each Member for which this Convention is in force undertakes to pursue a national policy designed to ensure the effective abolition of child labour and to raise progressively the minimum age for admission to employment or work to a level consistent with the fullest physical and mental development of young persons.

Article 2

1. Each Member which ratifies this Convention shall specify, in a declaration appended to its ratification, a minimum age for admission to employment or work within its territory and on means of transport registered in its territory; subject to Articles 4 to 8 of this Convention, no one under that age shall be admitted to employment or work in any occupation.

2. Each Member which has ratified this Convention may subsequently notify the Director-General of the International Labour Office, by further declarations, that it specifies a minimum age higher than that previously specified.

3. The minimum age specified in pursuance of paragraph 1 of this Article shall not be less than the age of completion of compulsory schooling and, in any case, shall not be less than 15 years.

4. Notwithstanding the provisions of paragraph 3 of this Article, a Member whose economy and educational facilities are insufficiently developed may, after consultation with the organizations of employers and workers concerned, where such exist, initially specify a minimum age of 14 years.

5. Each Member which has specified a minimum age of 14 years in pursuance of the provisions of the preceding paragraph shall include in its reports on the application of this Convention submitted under article 22 of the Constitution of the International Labour Organization a statement–

(a) that its reason for doing so subsists; or

(b) that it renounces its right to avail itself of the provisions in question as from a stated date.

Article 3

1. The minimum age for admission to any type of employment or work which by its nature or the circumstances in which it is carried out is likely to jeopardise the health, safety or morals of young persons shall not be less than 18 years.

2. The types of employment or work to which paragraph 1 of this Article applies shall be determined by national laws or regulations or by the competent authority, after consultation with the organizations of employers and workers concerned, where such exist.

3. Notwithstanding the provisions of paragraph 1 of this Article, national laws or regulations or the competent authority may, after consultation with the organizations of employers and workers concerned, where such exist, authorize employment or work as from the age of 16 years on condition that the health, safety and morals of the young persons concerned are fully protected and that the young persons have received adequate specific instruction or vocational training in the relevant branch of activity.

Article 4

1. In so far as necessary, the competent authority, after consultation with the organizations of employers and workers concerned, where such exist, may exclude from the application of this Convention limited categories of employment or work in respect of which special and substantial problems of application arise.

2. Each Member which ratifies this Convention shall list in its first report on the application of the Convention submitted under article 22 of the Constitution of the International Labour Organization any categories which may have been excluded in pursuance of paragraph 1 of this Article, giving the reasons for such exclusion, and shall state in subsequent reports the position of its law and practice in respect of the categories excluded and the extent to which effect has been given or is proposed to be given to the Convention in respect of such categories.

3. Employment or work covered by Article 3 of this Convention shall not be excluded from the application of the Convention in pursuance of this Article.

Article 5

1. A Member whose economy and administrative facilities are insufficiently developed may, after consultation with the organizations of employers and workers concerned, where such exist, initially limit the scope of application of this Convention.

2. Each Member which avails itself of the provisions of paragraph 1 of this Article shall specify, in a declaration appended to its ratification, the branches of economic activity or types of undertakings to which it will apply the provisions of the Convention.

3. The provisions of the Convention shall be applicable as a minimum to the following: mining and quarrying; manufacturing; construction; electricity, gas and water; sanitary services; transport, storage and communication; and plantations and other agricultural undertakings mainly producing for commercial purposes, but excluding family and small-scale holdings producing for local consumption and not regularly employing hired workers.

4. Any Member which has limited the scope of application of this Convention in pursuance of this Article–

(a) shall indicate in its reports under Article 22 of the Constitution of the International Labour Organization the general position as regards the employment or work of young persons and children in the branches of activity which are excluded from the scope of application of this Convention and any progress which may have been made towards wider application of the provisions of the Convention;

(b) may at any time formally extend the scope of application by a declaration addressed to the Director-General of the International Labour Office.

Article 6

This Convention does not apply to work done by children and young persons in schools for general, vocational or technical education or in other training institutions, or to work done by persons at least 14 years of age in undertakings, where such work is carried out in accordance with conditions prescribed by the competent authority, after consultation with the organizations of employers and workers concerned, where such exist, and is an integral part of–

(a) a course of education or training for which a school or training institution is primarily responsible;

(b) a programme of training mainly or entirely in an undertaking, which programme has been approved by the competent authority; or

(c) a programme of guidance or orientation designed to facilitate the choice of an occupation or of a line of training.

Article 7

1. National laws or regulations may permit the employment or work of persons 13 to 15 years of age on light work which is–

(a) not likely to be harmful to their health or development; and

(b) not such as to prejudice their attendance at school, their participation in vocational orientation or training programmes approved by the competent authority or their capacity to benefit from the instruction received.

2. National laws or regulations may also permit the employment or work of persons who are at least 15 years of age but have not yet completed their compulsory schooling on work which meets the requirements set forth in sub-paragraphs (a) and (b) of paragraph 1 of this Article.

3. The competent authority shall determine the activities in which employment or work may be permitted under paragraphs 1 and 2 of this Article and shall prescribe the number of hours during which and the conditions in which such employment or work may be undertaken.

4. Notwithstanding the provisions of paragraphs 1 and 2 of this Article, a Member which has availed itself of the provisions of paragraph 4 of Article 2 may, for as long as it continues to do so, substitute the ages 12 and 14 for the ages 13 and 15 in paragraph 1 and the age 14 for the age 15 in paragraph 2 of this Article.

Article 8

1. After consultation with the organizations of employers and workers concerned, where such exist, the competent authority may, by permits granted in individual cases, allow exceptions to the prohibition of employment or work provided for in Article 2 of this Convention, for such purposes as participation in artistic performances.

2. Permits so granted shall limit the number of hours during which and prescribe the conditions in which employment or work is allowed.

Article 9

1. All necessary measures, including the provision of appropriate penalties, shall be taken by the competent authority to ensure the effective enforcement of the provisions of this Convention.

2. National laws or regulations or the competent authority shall define the persons responsible for compliance with the provisions giving effect to the Convention.

3. National laws or regulations or the competent authority shall prescribe the registers or other documents which shall be kept and made available by the employer; such registers or documents shall contain the names and ages or dates of birth, duly certified wherever possible, of persons whom he employs or who work for him and who are less than 18 years of age.

Article 10

1. This Convention revises, on the terms set forth in this Article, the Minimum Age (Industry) Convention, 1919, the Minimum Age (Sea) Convention, 1920, the Minimum Age (Agriculture) Convention, 1921, the Minimum Age (Trimmers and Stokers) Convention, 1921, the Minimum Age (Non-Industrial Employment) Convention, 1932, the Minimum Age (Sea) Convention (Revised), 1936, the Minimum Age (Industry) Convention (Revised), 1937, the Minimum Age (Non-Industrial Employment) Convention (Revised), 1937, the Minimum Age (Fishermen) Convention, 1959, and the Minimum Age (Underground Work) Convention, 1965.

2. The coming into force of this Convention shall not close the Minimum Age (Sea) Convention (Revised), 1936, the Minimum Age (Industry) Convention (Revised), 1937, the Minimum Age (Non-Industrial Employment) Convention (Revised), 1937, the Minimum Age (Fishermen) Convention, 1959, or the Minimum Age (Underground Work) Convention, 1965, to further ratification.

3. The Minimum Age (Industry) Convention, 1919, the Minimum Age (Sea) Convention, 1920, the Minimum Age (Agriculture) Convention, 1921, and the Minimum Age (Trimmers and Stokers) Convention, 1921, shall be closed to further ratification when all the parties thereto have consented to such closing by ratification of this Convention or by a declaration communicated to the Director-General of the International Labour Office.

4. When the obligations of this Convention are accepted–

(a) by a Member which is a party to the Minimum Age (Industry) Convention (Revised), 1937, and a minimum age of not less than 15 years is specified in pursuance of Article 2 of this Convention, this shall ipso jure involve the immediate denunciation of that Convention,

(b) in respect of non-industrial employment as defined in the Minimum Age (Non-Industrial Employment) Convention, 1932, by a Member which is a party to that Convention, this shall ipso jure involve the immediate denunciation of that Convention,

(c) in respect of non-industrial employment as defined in the Minimum Age (Non-Industrial Employment) Convention (Revised), 1937, by a Member which is a party to that Convention, and a minimum age of not less than 15 years is specified in pursuance of Article 2 of this Convention, this shall ipso jure involve the immediate denunciation of that Convention,

(d) in respect of maritime employment, by a Member which is a party to the Minimum Age (Sea) Convention (Revised), 1936, and a minimum age of not less than 15 years is specified in pursuance of Article 2 of this Convention or the Member specifies that Article 3 of this Convention applies to maritime employment, this shall ipso jure involve the immediate denunciation of that Convention,

(e) in respect of employment in maritime fishing, by a Member which is a party to the Minimum Age (Fishermen) Convention, 1959, and a minimum age of not less than 15 years is specified in pursuance of Article 2 of this Convention or the Member specifies that Article 3 of this Convention applies to employment in maritime fishing, this shall ipso jure involve the immediate denunciation of that Convention,

(f) by a Member which is a party to the Minimum Age (Underground Work) Convention, 1965, and a minimum age of not less than the age specified in pursuance of that Convention is specified in pursuance of Article 2 of this Convention or the Member specifies that such an age applies to employment underground in mines in virtue of Article 3 of this Convention, this shall ipso jure involve the immediate denunciation of that Convention, if and when this Convention shall have come into force.

5. Acceptance of the obligations of this Convention–

(a) shall involve the denunciation of the Minimum Age (Industry) Convention, 1919, in accordance with Article 12 thereof,

(b) in respect of agriculture shall involve the denunciation of the Minimum Age (Agriculture) Convention, 1921, in accordance with Article 9 thereof,

(c) in respect of maritime employment shall involve the denunciation of the Minimum Age (Sea) Convention, 1920, in accordance with Article 10 thereof, and of the Minimum Age (Trimmers and Stokers) Convention, 1921, in accordance with Article 12 thereof, if and when this Convention shall have come into force.

Article 11

The formal ratifications of this Convention shall be communicated to the Director-General of the International Labour Office for registration.

Article 12

1. This Convention shall be binding only upon those Members of the International Labour Organization whose ratifications have been registered with the Director-General.

2. It shall come into force twelve months after the date on which the ratifications of two Members have been registered with the Director-General.

3. Thereafter, this Convention shall come into force for any Member twelve months after the date on which its ratifications have been registered.

Article 13

1. A Member which has ratified this Convention may denounce it after the expiration of ten years from the date on which the Convention first comes into force, by an act communicated to the Director-General of the International Labour Office for registration. Such denunciation shall not take effect until one year after the date on which it is registered.

2. Each Member which has ratified this Convention and which does not, within the year following the expiration of the period of ten years mentioned in the preceding paragraph, exercise the right of denunciation provided for in this Article, will be bound for another period of ten years and, thereafter, may denounce this Convention at the expiration of each period of ten years under the terms provided for in this Article.

Article 14

1. The Director-General of the International Labour Office shall notify all Members of the International Labour Organization of the registration of all ratifications and denunciations communicated to him by the Members of the Organization.

2. When notifying the Members of the Organization of the registration of the second ratification communicated to him, the Director-General shall draw the attention of the Members of the Organization to the date upon which the Convention will come into force.

Article 15

The Director-General of the International Labour Office shall communicate to the Secretary-General of the United Nations for registration in accordance with Article 102 of the Charter of the United Nations full particulars of all ratifications and acts of denunciation registered by him in accordance with the provisions of the preceding Articles.

Article 16

At such times as it may consider necessary the Governing Body of the International Labour Office shall present to the General Conference a report on the working of this Convention and shall examine the desirability of placing on the agenda of the Conference the question of its revision in whole or in part.

Article 17

1. Should the Conference adopt a new Convention revising this Convention in whole or in part, then, unless the new Convention otherwise provides:

a) the ratification by a Member of the new revising Convention shall ipso jure involve the immediate denunciation of this Convention, notwithstanding the provisions of Article 13 above, if and when the new revising Convention shall have come into force;

b) as from the date when the new revising Convention comes into force this Convention shall cease to be open to ratification by the Members.

2. This Convention shall in any case remain in force in its actual form and content for those Members which have ratified it but have not ratified the revising Convention.

Article 18

The English and French versions of the text of this Convention are equally authoritative.

Convention No.182 concerning the Prohibition and Immediate Action for the Elimination of the Worst Forms of Child Labour, 1999*

Adoption: 17 June 1999
Entry into force: 19 November 2000
Parties: 163 (Status as of 1 April 2007)

ALBANIA 2 Aug 2001, ALGERIA 9 Feb 2001, ANGOLA 13 June 2001, ANTIGUA AND BARBUDA 16 Sep 2002, ARGENTINA 5 Feb 2001, ARMENIA 2 Jan 2006, AUSTRIA 4 Dec 2001, AUSTRALIA 19 Dec 2006, AZERBAIJAN 30 Mar 2004, BAHAMAS 14 June 2001, BAHRAIN 23 Mar 2001, BANGLADESH 12 Mar 2001, BARBADOS 23 Oct 2000, BELARUS 31 Oct 2000, BELGIUM 8 May 2002, BELIZE 6 Mar 2000, BENIN 6 Nov 2001, BOLIVIA 6 June 2003, BOSNIA AND HERZEGOVINA 5 Oct 2001, BOTSWANA 3 Jan 2000, BRAZIL 2 Feb 2000, BULGARIA 28 July 2000, BURKINA FASO 25 July 2001, BURUNDI 11 June 2002, CAMBODIA 14 Mar 2006, CAMEROON 5 June 2002, CANADA 6 June 2000, CAPE VERDE 23 Oct 2001, CENTRAL AFRICAN REPUBLIC 28 June 2000, CHAD 6 Nov 2000, CHILE 17 July 2000, CHINA 8 Aug 2002, COLOMBIA 28 Jan 2005, COMOROS 17 Mar 2004, CONGO 23 Aug 2002, DEMOCRATIC REPUBLIC OF CONGO 20 June 2001, COSTA RICA 10 Sep 2001, COTE D'IVOIRE 7 Feb 2003, CROATIA 17 July 2001, CYPRUS 27 Nov 2000, CZECH REPUBLIC 19 June 2001, DENMARK 14 Aug 2000, DJIBOUTI 28 Feb 2005, DOMINICA 4 Jan 2001, DOMINICAN REPUBLIC 15 Nov 2000, ECUADOR 19 Sep 2000, EGYPT 6 May 2002, EL SALVADOR 12 Oct 2000, EQUATORIAL GUINEA 13 Aug 2001, ESTONIA 24 Sep 2001, ETHIOPIA 2 Sep 2003, FIJI 17 Apr 2002, FINLAND 17 Jan 2000, FRANCE 11 Sep 2001, GABON 28 Mar 2001, GAMBIA 3 July 2001, GEORGIA 24 July 2002, GERMANY 18 Apr 2002, GHANA 13 June 2000, GREECE 6 Nov 2001, GRENADA 14 May 2003, GUATEMALA 11 Oct 2001, GUINEA 6 June 2003, GUYANA 15 Jan 2001, HONDURAS 25 Oct 2001, HUNGARY 20 Apr 2000, ICELAND 29 May 2000, INDONESIA 28 Mar 2000, IRAN (THE ISLAMIC REPUBLIC OF) 8 May 2002, IRAQ 9 July 2001, IRELAND 20 Dec 1999, ISRAEL 15 Mar 2005, ITALY 7 June 2000, JAMAICA 13 Oct 2003, JAPAN 18 June 2001, JORDAN 20 Apr 2000, KAZAKHSTAN 26 Feb 2003, KENYA 7 May 2001, REPUBLIC OF KOREA 29 Mar 2001, KUWAIT 15 Aug 2000, KYRGYZSTAN 11 May 2004, LAO PEOPLE'S DEMOCRATIC REPUBLIC 13 June 2005, LATVIA 2 June 2006, LEBANON 11 Sep 2001, LESOTHO 14 June 2001, LIBERIA 2 June 2003, LIBYAN ARAB JAMAHIRIYA 4 Oct 2000, LITHUANIA 29 Sep 2003, LUXEMBOURG 21 Mar 2001, THE FORMER YUGOSLAV REPUBLIC OF MACEDONIA 30 May 2002, MADAGASCAR 4 Oct 2001, MALAWI 19 Nov 1999, MALAYSIA 10 Nov 2000, MALI 14 July 2000, MALTA 15 June 2001, MAURITANIA 3 Dec 2001, MAURITIUS 8 June 2000, MEXICO 30 June 2000, REPUBLIC OF MOLDOVA 14 June 2002, MONGOLIA 26 Feb 2001, MOROCCO 26 Jan 2001, MOZAMBIQUE 16 June 2003, NAMIBIA 15 Nov 2000, NEPAL 3 Jan 2002, NETHERLANDS 14 Feb 2002, NEW ZEALAND 14 June 2001, NICARAGUA 6 Nov 2000, NIGER 23 Oct 2000, NIGERIA 2 Oct 2002, NORWAY 21 Dec 2000, OMAN 11 June 2001, PAKISTAN 11 Oct 2001, PANAMA 31 Oct 2000, PAPUA NEW GUINEA 2 June 2000, PARAGUAY 7 Mar 2001, PERU 10 Jan 2002, PHILIPPINES 28 Nov 2000, POLAND 9 Aug 2002, PORTUGAL 15 June 2000, QATAR 30 May 2000, ROMANIA 13 Dec 2000, RUSSIAN FEDERATION 25 Mar 2003, RWANDA 23 May 2000, SAINT KITTS AND NEVIS 12 Oct 2000, SAINT LUCIA 6 Dec 2000, SAINT VINCENT AND THE GRENADINES 4 Dec 2001,

* Source: International Labour Organization, http://www.ilo.org/ilolex
The ILO shall accept no responsibility for any inaccuracy, errors or omissions or for the consequences arising from the use of the Text.

SAN MARINO 15 Mar 2000, SAO TOME AND PRINCIPE 4 May 2005, SAUDI ARABIA 8 Oct 2001, SENEGAL 1 June 2000, REPUBLIC OF SERBIA 10 July 2003, SEYCHELLES 28 Sep 1999, SINGAPORE 14 June 2001, SLOVAKIA 10 Dec 1999, SLOVENIA 8 May 2001, SOUTH AFRICA 7 June 2000, SPAIN 2 Apr 2001, SRI LANKA 1 Mar 2001, SUDAN 7 Mar 2003, SURINAME 12 Apr 2006, SWAZILAND 23 Oct 2002, SWEDEN 13 June 2001, SWITZERLAND 28 June 2000, SYRIAN ARAB REPUBLIC 22 May 2003, TAJIKISTAN 8 June 2005, TANZANIA (UNITED REPUBLIC OF) 12 Sep 2001, THAILAND 16 Feb 2001, TOGO 19 Sep 2000, TRINIDAD AND TOBAGO 23 Apr 2003, TUNISIA 28 Feb 2000, TURKEY 2 Aug 2001, UGANDA 21 June 2001, UKRAINE 14 Dec 2000, UNITED ARAB EMIRATES 28 June 2001, UNITED KINGDOM 22 Mar 2000, UNITED STATES 2 Dec 1999, URUGAY 3 Aug 2001, VANUATU 28 Aug 2006, VENEZUELA (BOLIVARIAN REPUBLIC OF) 26 Oct 2005, VIETNAM 19 Dec 2000, YEMEN 15 June 2000, ZAMBIA 10 Dec 2001, ZIMBABWE 11 Dec 2000.

The General Conference of the International Labour Organization,

Having been convened at Geneva by the Governing Body of the International Labour Office, and having met in its 87th Session on 1 June 1999, and

Considering the need to adopt new instruments for the prohibition and elimination of the worst forms of child labour, as the main priority for national and international action, including international cooperation and assistance, to complement the Convention and the Recommendation concerning Minimum Age for Admission to Employment, 1973, which remain fundamental instruments on child labour, and

Considering that the effective elimination of the worst forms of child labour requires immediate and comprehensive action, taking into account the importance of free basic education and the need to remove the children concerned from all such work and to provide for their rehabilitation and social integration while addressing the needs of their families, and

Recalling the resolution concerning the elimination of child labour adopted by the International Labour Conference at its 83rd Session in 1996, and

Recognizing that child labour is to a great extent caused by poverty and that the long-term solution lies in sustained economic growth leading to social progress, in particular poverty alleviation and universal education, and

Recalling the Convention on the Rights of the Child adopted by the United Nations General Assembly on 20 November 1989, and

Recalling the ILO Declaration on Fundamental Principles and Rights at Work and its Follow-up, adopted by the International Labour Conference at its 86th Session in 1998, and

Recalling that some of the worst forms of child labour are covered by other international instruments, in particular the Forced Labour Convention, 1930, and the United Nations Supplementary Convention on the Abolition of Slavery, the Slave Trade, and Institutions and Practices Similar to Slavery, 1956, and

Having decided upon the adoption of certain proposals with regard to child labour, which is the fourth item on the agenda of the session, and

Having determined that these proposals shall take the form of an international Convention;

adopts this seventeenth day of June of the year one thousand nine hundred and ninety-nine the following Convention, which may be cited as the Worst Forms of Child Labour Convention, 1999.

Article 1

Each Member which ratifies this Convention shall take immediate and effective measures to secure the prohibition and elimination of the worst forms of child labour as a matter of urgency.

Article 2

For the purposes of this Convention, the term *child* shall apply to all persons under the age of 18.

Article 3

For the purposes of this Convention, the term *the worst forms of child labour* comprises:

(a) all forms of slavery or practices similar to slavery, such as the sale and trafficking of children, debt bondage and serfdom and forced or compulsory labour, including forced or compulsory recruitment of children for use in armed conflict;

(b) the use, procuring or offering of a child for prostitution, for the production of pornography or for pornographic performances;

(c) the use, procuring or offering of a child for illicit activities, in particular for the production and trafficking of drugs as defined in the relevant international treaties;

(d) work which, by its nature or the circumstances in which it is carried out, is likely to harm the health, safety or morals of children.

Article 4

1. The types of work referred to under Article 3(d) shall be determined by national laws or regulations or by the competent authority, after consultation with the organizations of employers and workers concerned, taking into consideration relevant international standards, in particular Paragraphs 3 and 4 of the Worst Forms of Child Labour Recommendation, 1999.

2. The competent authority, after consultation with the organizations of employers and workers concerned, shall identify where the types of work so determined exist.

3. The list of the types of work determined under paragraph 1 of this Article shall be periodically examined and revised as necessary, in consultation with the organizations of employers and workers concerned.

Article 5

Each Member shall, after consultation with employers' and workers' organizations, establish or designate appropriate mechanisms to monitor the implementation of the provisions giving effect to this Convention.

Article 6

1. Each Member shall design and implement programmes of action to eliminate as a priority the worst forms of child labour.

2. Such programmes of action shall be designed and implemented in consultation with relevant government institutions and employers' and workers' organizations, taking into consideration the views of other concerned groups as appropriate.

Article 7

1. Each Member shall take all necessary measures to ensure the effective implementation and enforcement of the provisions giving effect to this Convention including the provision and application of penal sanctions or, as appropriate, other sanctions.

2. Each Member shall, taking into account the importance of education in eliminating child labour, take effective and time-bound measures to:

(a) prevent the engagement of children in the worst forms of child labour;

(b) provide the necessary and appropriate direct assistance for the removal of children from the worst forms of child labour and for their rehabilitation and social integration;

(c) ensure access to free basic education, and, wherever possible and appropriate, vocational training, for all children removed from the worst forms of child labour;

(d) identify and reach out to children at special risk; and

(e) take account of the special situation of girls.

3. Each Member shall designate the competent authority responsible for the implementation of the provisions giving effect to this Convention.

Article 8

Members shall take appropriate steps to assist one another in giving effect to the provisions of this Convention through enhanced international cooperation and/or assistance including support for social and economic development, poverty eradication programmes and universal education.

Article 9

The formal ratifications of this Convention shall be communicated to the Director-General of the International Labour Office for registration.

Article 10

1. This Convention shall be binding only upon those Members of the International Labour Organization whose ratifications have been registered with the Director-General of the International Labour Office.

2. It shall come into force 12 months after the date on which the ratifications of two Members have been registered with the Director-General.

3. Thereafter, this Convention shall come into force for any Member 12 months after the date on which its ratification has been registered.

Article 11

1. A Member which has ratified this Convention may denounce it after the expiration of ten years from the date on which the Convention first comes into force, by an act communicated to the Director-General of the International Labour Office for registration. Such denunciation shall not take effect until one year after the date on which it is registered.

2. Each Member which has ratified this Convention and which does not, within the year following the expiration of the period of ten years mentioned in the preceding paragraph, exercise the right of denunciation provided for in this Article, will be bound for another period of ten years and, thereafter, may denounce this Convention at the expiration of each period of ten years under the terms provided for in this Article.

Article 12

1. The Director-General of the International Labour Office shall notify all Members of the International Labour Organization of the registration of all ratifications and acts of denunciation communicated by the Members of the Organization.

2. When notifying the Members of the Organization of the registration of the second ratification, the Director-General shall draw the attention of the Members of the Organization to the date upon which the Convention shall come into force.

Article 13

The Director-General of the International Labour Office shall communicate to the Secretary-General of the United Nations, for registration in accordance with article 102 of the Charter of the United Nations, full particulars of all ratifications and acts of denunciation registered by the Director-General in accordance with the provisions of the preceding Articles.

Article 14

At such times as it may consider necessary, the Governing Body of the International Labour Office shall present to the General Conference a report on the working of this Convention and shall examine the desirability of placing on the agenda of the Conference the question of its revision in whole or in part.

Article 15

1. Should the Conference adopt a new Convention revising this Convention in whole or in part, then, unless the new Convention otherwise provides –

(a) the ratification by a Member of the new revising Convention shall ipso jure involve the immediate denunciation of this Convention, notwithstanding the provisions of Article 11 above, if and when the new revising Convention shall have come into force;

(b) as from the date when the new revising Convention comes into force, this Convention shall cease to be open to ratification by the Members.

2. This Convention shall in any case remain in force in its actual form and content for those Members which have ratified it but have not ratified the revising Convention.

Article 16

The English and French versions of the text of this Convention are equally authoritative.

Recommendation No.190 concerning the Prohibition and Immediate Action for the Elimination of the Worst Forms of Child Labour, 1999*

Adoption: 17 June 1999

The General Conference of the International Labour Organization,

Having been convened at Geneva by the Governing Body of the International Labour Office, and having met in its Eighty-seventh Session on 1 June 1999, and

Having adopted the Worst Forms of Child Labour Convention, 1999, and

Having decided upon the adoption of certain proposals with regard to child labour, which is the fourth item on the agenda of the session, and

Having determined that these proposals shall take the form of a Recommendation supplementing the Worst Forms of Child Labour Convention, 1999;

adopts this seventeenth day of June of the year one thousand nine hundred and ninety-nine the following Recommendation, which may be cited as the Worst Forms of Child Labour Recommendation, 1999.

1. The provisions of this Recommendation supplement those of the Worst Forms of Child Labour Convention, 1999 (hereafter referred to as "the Convention"), and should be applied in conjunction with them.

I. Programmes of action

2. The programmes of action referred to in Article 6 of the Convention should be designed and implemented as a matter of urgency, in consultation with relevant government institutions and employers' and workers' organizations, taking into consideration the views of the children directly affected by the worst forms of child labour, their families and, as appropriate, other concerned groups committed to the aims of the Convention and this Recommendation. Such programmes should aim at, inter alia:

(a) identifying and denouncing the worst forms of child labour;

(b) preventing the engagement of children in or removing them from the worst forms of child labour, protecting them from reprisals and providing for their rehabilitation and social integration through measures which address their educational, physical and psychological needs;

(c) giving special attention to:

(i) younger children;

(ii) the girl child;

(iii) the problem of hidden work situations, in which girls are at special risk;

(iv) other groups of children with special vulnerabilities or needs;

(d) identifying, reaching out to and working with communities where children are at special risk;

---

* Source: International Labour Organization, http://www.ilo.org/ilolex

The ILO shall accept no responsibility for any inaccuracy, errors or omissions or for the consequences arising from the use of the Text.

(e) informing, sensitizing and mobilizing public opinion and concerned groups, including children and their families.

II. Hazardous work

3. In determining the types of work referred to under Article 3(d) of the Convention, and in identifying where they exist, consideration should be given, inter alia, to:

(a) work which exposes children to physical, psychological or sexual abuse;

(b) work underground, under water, at dangerous heights or in confined spaces;

(c) work with dangerous machinery, equipment and tools, or which involves the manual handling or transport of heavy loads;

(d) work in an unhealthy environment which may, for example, expose children to hazardous substances, agents or processes, or to temperatures, noise levels, or vibrations damaging to their health;

(e) work under particularly difficult conditions such as work for long hours or during the night or work where the child is unreasonably confined to the premises of the employer.

4. For the types of work referred to under Article 3(d) of the Convention and Paragraph 3 above, national laws or regulations or the competent authority could, after consultation with the workers' and employers' organizations concerned, authorize employment or work as from the age of 16 on condition that the health, safety and morals of the children concerned are fully protected, and that the children have received adequate specific instruction or vocational training in the relevant branch of activity.

III. Implementation

5. (1) Detailed information and statistical data on the nature and extent of child labour should be compiled and kept up to date to serve as a basis for determining priorities for national action for the abolition of child labour, in particular for the prohibition and elimination of its worst forms as a matter of urgency.

(2) As far as possible, such information and statistical data should include data disaggregated by sex, age group, occupation, branch of economic activity, status in employment, school attendance and geographical location. The importance of an effective system of birth registration, including the issuing of birth certificates, should be taken into account.

(3) Relevant data concerning violations of national provisions for the prohibition and elimination of the worst forms of child labour should be compiled and kept up to date.

6. The compilation and processing of the information and data referred to in Paragraph 5 above should be carried out with due regard for the right to privacy.

7. The information compiled under Paragraph 5 above should be communicated to the International Labour Office on a regular basis.

8. Members should establish or designate appropriate national mechanisms to monitor the implementation of national provisions for the prohibition and elimination of the worst forms of child labour, after consultation with employers' and workers' organizations.

9. Members should ensure that the competent authorities which have responsibilities for implementing national provisions for the prohibition and elimination of the worst forms of child labour cooperate with each other and coordinate their activities.

10. National laws or regulations or the competent authority should determine the persons to be held responsible in the event of non-compliance with national provisions for the prohibition and elimination of the worst forms of child labour.

11. Members should, in so far as it is compatible with national law, cooperate with international efforts aimed at the prohibition and elimination of the worst forms of child labour as a matter of urgency by:

(a) gathering and exchanging information concerning criminal offences, including those involving international networks;

(b) detecting and prosecuting those involved in the sale and trafficking of children, or in the use, procuring or offering of children for illicit activities, for prostitution, for the production of pornography or for pornographic performances;

(c) registering perpetrators of such offences.

12. Members should provide that the following worst forms of child labour are criminal offences:

(a) all forms of slavery or practices similar to slavery, such as the sale and trafficking of children, debt bondage and serfdom and forced or compulsory labour, including forced or compulsory recruitment of children for use in armed conflict;

(b) the use, procuring or offering of a child for prostitution, for the production of pornography or for pornographic performances; and

(c) the use, procuring or offering of a child for illicit activities, in particular for the production and trafficking of drugs as defined in the relevant international treaties, or for activities which involve the unlawful carrying or use of firearms or other weapons.

13. Members should ensure that penalties including, where appropriate, criminal penalties are applied for violations of the national provisions for the prohibition and elimination of any type of work referred to in Article 3(d) of the Convention.

14. Members should also provide as a matter of urgency for other criminal, civil or administrative remedies, where appropriate, to ensure the effective enforcement of national provisions for the prohibition and elimination of the worst forms of child labour, such as special supervision of enterprises which have used the worst forms of child labour, and, in cases of persistent violation, consideration of temporary or permanent revoking of permits to operate.

15. Other measures aimed at the prohibition and elimination of the worst forms of child labour might include the following:

(a) informing, sensitizing and mobilizing the general public, including national and local political leaders, parliamentarians and the judiciary;

(b) involving and training employers' and workers' organizations and civic organizations;

(c) providing appropriate training for the government officials concerned, especially inspectors and law enforcement officials, and for other relevant professionals;

(d) providing for the prosecution in their own country of the Member's nationals who commit offences under its national provisions for the prohibition and immediate elimination of the worst forms of child labour even when these offences are committed in another country;

(e) simplifying legal and administrative procedures and ensuring that they are appropriate and prompt;

(f) encouraging the development of policies by undertakings to promote the aims of the Convention;

(g) monitoring and giving publicity to best practices on the elimination of child labour;

(h) giving publicity to legal or other provisions on child labour in the different languages or dialects;

(i) establishing special complaints procedures and making provisions to protect from discrimination and reprisals those who legitimately expose violations of the provisions of the Convention, as well as establishing helplines or points of contact and ombudspersons;

(j) adopting appropriate measures to improve the educational infrastructure and the training of teachers to meet the needs of boys and girls;

(k) as far as possible, taking into account in national programmes of action:

(i) the need for job creation and vocational training for the parents and adults in the families of children working in the conditions covered by the Convention; and

(ii) the need for sensitizing parents to the problem of children working in such conditions.

16. Enhanced international cooperation and/or assistance among Members for the prohibition and effective elimination of the worst forms of child labour should complement national efforts and may, as appropriate, be developed and implemented in consultation with employers' and workers' organizations. Such international cooperation and/or assistance should include:

(a) mobilizing resources for national or international programmes;

(b) mutual legal assistance;

(c) technical assistance including the exchange of information;

(d) support for social and economic development, poverty eradication programmes and universal education.

2.4 International Labour Standards on Equality of Opportunity and Treatment

Convention No. 87 concerning Freedom of Association and Protection of the Right to Organise, 1948*

Adopion: 9 July 1948
Entry into force: 4 July 1950
Parties: 147 (Status as of 1 April 2007)

ALBANIA 3 June 1957, ALGERIA 19 Oct 1962, ANGOLA 13 June 2001, ANTIGUA AND BARBUDA 2 Feb 1983, ARGENTINA 18 Jan 1960, ARMENIA 2 Jan 2006, AUSTRALIA 28 Feb 1973, AUSTRIA 18 Oct 1950, AZERBAIJAN 19 May 1992, BAHAMAS 14 June 2001, BANGLADESH 22 June 1972, BARBADOS 8 May 1967, BELARUS 6 Nov 1956, BELGIUM 23 Oct 1951, BELIZE 15 Dec 1983, BENIN 12 Dec 1960, BOLIVIA 4 Jan 1965, BOSNIA AND HERZEGOVINA 2 June 1993, BOTSWANA 22 Dec 1997, BULGARIA 8 June 1959, BURKINA FASO 21 Nov 1960, BURUNDI 25 June 1993, CAMBODIA 23 Aug 1999, CAMEROON 7 June 1960, CANADA 23 Mar 1972, CAPE VERDE 1 Feb 1999, CENTRAL AFRICAN REPUBLIC 27 Oct 1960, CHAD 10 Nov 1960, CHILE 1 Feb 1999, COLOMBIA 16 Nov 1976, COMOROS 23 Oct 1978, CONGO 10 Nov 1960, DEMOCRATIC REPUBLIC OF CONGO 20 June 2001, COSTA RICA 2 June 1960, COTE D'IVOIRE 21 Nov 1960, CROATIA 8 Oct 1991, CUBA 25 June 1952, CYPRUS 24 May 1966, CZECH REPUBLIC 1 Jan 1993, DENMARK 13 June 1951, DJIBOUTI 3 Aug 1978, DOMINICA 28 Feb 1983, DOMINICAN REPUBLIC 5 Dec 1956, ECUADOR 29 May 1967, EGYPT 6 Nov 1957, EL SALVADOR 6 Sep 2006, EQUATORIAL GUINEA 13 Aug 2001, ERITREA 22 Feb 2000, ESTONIA 22 Mar 1994, ETHIOPIA 4 June 1963, FIJI 17 Apr 2002, FINLAND 20 Jan 1950, FRANCE 28 June 1951, GABON 14 Oct 1960, GAMBIA 4 Sep 2000, GEORGIA 3 Aug 1999, GERMANY 20 Mar 1957, GHANA 2 June 1965, GREECE 30 Mar 1962, GRENADA 25 Oct 1994, GUATEMALA 13 Feb 1952, GUINEA 21 Jan 1959, GUYANA 25 Sep 1967, HAITI 5 June 1979, HONDURAS 27 June 1956, HUNGARY 6 June 1957, ICELAND 19 Aug 1950, INDONESIA 9 June 1998, IRELAND 4 June 1955, ISRAEL 28 Jan 1957, ITALY 13 May 1958, JAMAICA 26 Dec 1962, JAPAN 14 June 1965, KAZAKHSTAN 13 Dec 2000, KIRIBATI 3 Feb 2000, KUWAIT 21 Sep 1961, KYRGYZSTAN 31 Mar 1992, LATVIA 27 Jan 1992, LESOTHO 31 Oct 1966, LIBERIA 25 May 1962, LIBYAN ARAB JAMAHIRIYA 4 Oct 2000, LITHUANIA 26 Sep 1994, LUXEMBOURG 3 Mar 1958, THE FORMER YUGOSLAV REPUBLIC OF MACEDONIA 17 Nov 1991, MADAGASCAR 1 Nov 1960, MALAWI 19 Nov 1999, MALI 22 Sep 1960, MALTA 4 Jan 1965, MAURITANIA 20 June 1961, MAURITIUS 1 Apr 2005, MEXICO 1 Apr 1950, REPUBLIC OF MOLDOVA 12 Aug 1996, MONGOLIA 3 June 1969, MOZAMBIQUE 23 Dec 1996, MYANMAR 4 Mar 1955, NAMIBIA 3 Jan 1995, NETHERLANDS 7 Mar 1950, NICARAGUA 31 Oct 1967, NIGER 27 Feb 1961, NIGERIA 17 Oct 1960, NORWAY 4 July 1949, PAKISTAN 14 Feb 1951, PANAMA 3 June 1958, PAPUA NEW GUINEA 2 June 2000, PARAGUAY 28 June 1962, PERU 2 Mar 1960, PHILIPPINES 29 Dec 1953, POLAND 25 Feb 1957, PORTUGAL 14 Oct 1977, ROMANIA 28 May 1957, RUSSIAN FEDERATION 10 Aug 1956, RWANDA 8 Nov 1988, SAINT KITTS AND NEVIS 25 Aug 2000, SAINT LUCIA 14 May 1980, SAINT VINCENT AND THE GRENADINES 9 Nov 2001, SAN MARINO 19 Dec 1986, SAO TOME AND

* Source: International Labour Organization, http://www.ilo.org/ilolex.
The ILO shall accept no responsibility for any inaccuracy, errors or omissions or for the consequences arising from the use of the Text.

PRINCIPE 17 June 1992, SENEGAL 4 Nov 1960, SERBIA 24 Nov 2000, SEYCHELLES 6 Feb 1978, SIERRA LEONE 15 June 1961, SLOVAKIA 1 Jan 1993, SLOVENIA 29 May 1992, SOUTH AFRICA 19 Feb 1996, SPAIN 20 Apr 1977, SRI LANKA 15 Sep 1995, SURINAME 15 June 1976, SWAZILAND 26 Apr 1978, SWEDEN 25 Nov 1949, SWITZERLAND 25 Mar 1975, SYRIAN ARAB REPUBLIC 26 July 1960, TAJIKISTAN 26 Nov 1993, TANZANIA (UNITED REPUBLIC OF) 18 Apr 2000, TOGO 7 June 1960, TRINIDAD AND TOBAGO 24 May 1963, TUNISIA 18 June 1957, TURKEY 12 July 1993, TURKMENISTAN 15 May 1997, UGANDA 2 June 2005, UKRAINE 14 Sep 1956, UNITED KINGDOM 27 June 1949, URUGAY 18 Mar 1954, VANUATU 28 Aug 2006, VENEZUELA (BOLIVARIAN REPUBLIC OF) 20 Sep 1982, YEMEN 29 July 1976, ZAMBIA 2 Sep 1996, ZIMBABWE 9 Apr 2003.

The General Conference of the International Labour Organisation,

Having been convened at San Francisco by the Governing Body of the International Labour Office, and having met in its Thirty-first Session on 17 June 1948;

Having decided to adopt, in the form of a Convention, certain proposals concerning freedom of association and protection of the right to organise, which is the seventh item on the agenda of the session;

Considering that the Preamble to the Constitution of the International Labour Organisation declares "recognition of the principle of freedom of association" to be a means of improving conditions of labour and of establishing peace;

Considering that the Declaration of Philadelphia reaffirms that "freedom of expression and of association are essential to sustained progress";

Considering that the International Labour Conference, at its Thirtieth Session, unanimously adopted the principles which should form the basis for international regulation;

Considering that the General Assembly of the United Nations, at its Second Session, endorsed these principles and requested the International Labour Organisation to continue every effort in order that it may be possible to adopt one or several international Conventions;

adopts this ninth day of July of the year one thousand nine hundred and forty-eight the following Convention, which may be cited as the Freedom of Association and Protection of the Right to Organise Convention, 1948:

PART I. FREEDOM OF ASSOCIATION

Article 1

Each Member of the International Labour Organisation for which this Convention is in force undertakes to give effect to the following provisions.

Article 2

Workers and employers, without distinction whatsoever, shall have the right to establish and, subject only to the rules of the organisation concerned, to join organisations of their own choosing without previous authorisation.

Article 3

1. Workers' and employers' organisations shall have the right to draw up their constitutions and rules, to elect their representatives in full freedom, to organise their administration and activities and to formulate their programmes.

2. The public authorities shall refrain from any interference which would restrict this right or impede the lawful exercise thereof.

Article 4

Workers' and employers' organisations shall not be liable to be dissolved or suspended by administrative authority.

Article 5

Workers' and employers' organisations shall have the right to establish and join federations and confederations and any such organisation, federation or confederation shall have the right to affiliate with international organisations of workers and employers.

Article 6

The provisions of Articles 2, 3 and 4 hereof apply to federations and confederations of workers' and employers' organisations.

Article 7

The acquisition of legal personality by workers' and employers' organisations, federations and confederations shall not be made subject to conditions of such a character as to restrict the application of the provisions of Articles 2, 3 and 4 hereof.

Article 8

1. In exercising the rights provided for in this Convention workers and employers and their respective organisations, like other persons or organised collectivities, shall respect the law of the land.

2. The law of the land shall not be such as to impair, nor shall it be so applied as to impair, the guarantees provided for in this Convention.

Article 9

1. The extent to which the guarantees provided for in this Convention shall apply to the armed forces and the police shall be determined by national laws or regulations.

2. In accordance with the principle set forth in paragraph 8 of Article 19 of the Constitution of the International Labour Organisation the ratification of this Convention by any Member shall not be deemed to affect any existing law, award, custom or agreement in virtue of which members of the armed forces or the police enjoy any right guaranteed by this Convention.

Article 10

In this Convention the term organisation means any organisation of workers or of employers for furthering and defending the interests of workers or of employers.

PART II. PROTECTION OF THE RIGHT TO ORGANISE

Article 11

Each Member of the International Labour Organisation for which this Convention is in force undertakes to take all necessary and appropriate measures to ensure that workers and employers may exercise freely the right to organise.

PART III. MISCELLANEOUS PROVISIONS

Article 12

1.In respect of the territories referred to in Article 35 of the Constitution of the International Labour Organisation as amended by the Constitution of the International Labour Organisation Instrument of Amendment 1946, other than the territories referred to in paragraphs 4 and 5 of the said article as so amended, each Member of the Organisation which ratifies this Convention shall communicate to the Director-General of the International Labour Office with or as soon as possible after its ratification a declaration stating:

a) the territories in respect of which it undertakes that the provisions of the Convention shall be applied without modification;

b) the territories in respect of which it undertakes that the provisions of the Convention shall be applied subject to modifications, together with details of the said modifications;

c) the territories in respect of which the Convention is inapplicable and in such cases the grounds on which it is inapplicable;

d) the territories in respect of which it reserves its decision.

2. The undertakings referred to in subparagraphs (a) and (b) of paragraph 1 of this Article shall be deemed to be an integral part of the ratification and shall have the force of ratification.

3. Any Member may at any time by a subsequent declaration cancel in whole or in part any reservations made in its original declaration in virtue of subparagraphs (b), (c) or (d) of paragraph 1 of this Article.

4. Any Member may, at any time at which the Convention is subject to denunciation in accordance with the provisions of Article 16, communicate to the Director-General a declaration modifying in any other respect the terms of any former declaration and stating the present position in respect of such territories as it may specify.

Article 13

1. Where the subject-matter of this Convention is within the self-governing powers of any non-metropolitan territory, the Member responsible for the international relations of that territory may, in agreement with the government of the territory, communicate to the Director-General of the International Labour Office a declaration accepting on behalf of the territory the obligations of this Convention.

2. A declaration accepting the obligations of this Convention may be communicated to the Director-General of the International Labour Office:

a) by two or more Members of the Organisation in respect of any territory which is under their joint authority; or

b) by any international authority responsible for the administration of any territory, in virtue of the Charter of the United Nations or otherwise, in respect of any such territory.

3. Declarations communicated to the Director-General of the International Labour Office in accordance with the preceding paragraphs of this Article shall indicate whether the provisions of the Convention will be applied in the territory concerned without modification or subject to modifications; when the declaration indicates that the provisions of the Convention will be applied subject to modifications it shall give details of the said modifications.

4. The Member, Members or international authority concerned may at any time by a subsequent declaration renounce in whole or in part the right to have recourse to any modification indicated in any former declaration.

5. The Member, Members or international authority concerned may, at any time at which this Convention is subject to denunciation in accordance with the provisions of Article 16, communicate to the Director-General a declaration modifying in any other respect the terms of any former declaration and stating the present position in respect of the application of the Convention.

PART IV. FINAL PROVISIONS

Article 14

The formal ratifications of this Convention shall be communicated to the Director-General of the International Labour Office for registration.

Article 15

1. This Convention shall be binding only upon those Members of the International Labour Organisation whose ratifications have been registered with the Director-General.

2. It shall come into force twelve months after the date on which the ratifications of two Members have been registered with the Director-General.

3. Thereafter, this Convention shall come into force for any Member twelve months after the date on which its ratifications has been registered.

Article 16

1. A Member which has ratified this Convention may denounce it after the expiration of ten years from the date on which the Convention first comes into force, by an act communicated to the Director-General of the International Labour Office for registration. Such denunciation shall not take effect until one year after the date on which it is registered.

2. Each Member which has ratified this Convention and which does not, within the year following the expiration of the period of ten years mentioned in the preceding paragraph, exercise the right of denunciation provided for in this Article, will be bound for another period of ten years and, thereafter, may denounce this Convention at the expiration of each period of ten years under the terms provided for in this Article.

Article 17

1. The Director-General of the International Labour Office shall notify all Members of the International Labour Organisation of the registration of all ratifications, declarations and denunciations communicated to him by the Members of the Organisation.

2. When notifying the Members of the Organisation of the registration of the second ratification communicated to him, the Director-General shall draw the attention of the Members of the Organisation to the date upon which the Convention will come into force.

Article 18

The Director-General of the International Labour Office shall communicate to the Secretary-General of the United Nations for registration in accordance with Article 102 of the Charter of the United Nations full particulars of all ratifications, declarations and acts of denunciation registered by him in accordance with the provisions of the preceding articles.

Article 19

At such times as it may consider necessary the Governing Body of the International Labour Office shall present to the General Conference a report on the working of this Convention and shall examine the desirability of placing on the agenda of the Conference the question of its revision in whole or in part.

Article 20

1. Should the Conference adopt a new Convention revising this Convention in whole or in part, then, unless the new Convention otherwise provides:

a) the ratification by a Member of the new revising Convention shall ipso jure involve the immediate denunciation of this Convention, notwithstanding the provisions of Article 16 above, if and when the new revising Convention shall have come into force;

b) as from the date when the new revising Convention comes into force this Convention shall cease to be open to ratification by the Members.

2. This Convention shall in any case remain in force in its actual form and content for those Members which have ratified it but have not ratified the revising Convention.

Article 21

The English and French versions of the text of this Convention are equally authoritative.

Convention No.100 concerning Equal Remuneration for Men and Women Workers for Work of Equal Value, 1951*

Adoption: 29 June 1951
Entry into force: 23 May 1953
Parties: 163 (status as of 1 April 2007)

ALBANIA 3 Jun 1957, ALGERIA 10 Oct 1962, ANGOLA 4 Jun 1976, ANTIGUA AND BARBUDA 2 May 2003, ARGENTINA 24 Sep 1956, ARMENIA 29 Jul 1994, AUSTRALIA 10 Dec 1974, AUSTRIA 29 Oct 1953, AZERBAIJAN 19 May 1992, BAHAMAS 14 Jun 1002, BANGLADESH 28 Jan 1998, BARBADOS 19 Sep 1974, BELARUS 21 Aug 1956, BELGIUM 23 May 1953, BELIZE 22 Jun 1999, BENIN 16 May 1968, BOLIVIA 15 Nov 1973, BOSNIA AND HERZEGOVINA 2 Jun 1993, BOTSWANA 5 Jun 1997, BRAZIL 25 Apr 1957, BULGARIA 7 Nov 1955, BURKINA FASO 30 Jun 1969, BURINDI 25 Jun 1969, CAMBODIA 23 Aug 1993, CAMEROON 25 May 1970, CANADA 16 Nov 1972, CAPE VERDE 16 Oct 1979, CENTRAL AFRICAN REPUBLIC 9 Jun 1964, CHAD 29 Mar 19656, CHILE 20 Sep 1971, CHINA 2 Nov 1990, COLOMBIA 7 Jun 1963, COMOROS 23 Oct 1978, CONGO 26 Nov 1999, DEMOCRATIC REPUBLIC OF THE CONGO 16 Jun 1969, COSTA RICA 2 Jun 1960, CÔTE D'IVOIRE 5 May 1961, CROATIA 8 Oct 1991, CUBA 13 Jan 1954, CYPRUS 19 Nov 1987, CZECH REPUBLIC 1 Jan 1993, DENMARK 22 Jun 1960, DJIBOUTI 3 Aug 1978, DOMINCA 28 Feb 1983, DEOMINICAN REPUBLIC 22 Sep 1953, ECUADOR 11 Mar 1957, EGYPT 26 Jul 1960, EL SALVADOR 12 Oct 2000, EQUATORIAL GUINEA 12 Jun 1985, ERITREA 22 Feb 2000, ESTONIA 10 May 1996, ETHIOPIA 24 Mar 1999, FIJI 17 Apr 2002, FINLAND 14 Jan 1963, FRANCE 10 Apr 1953, GABON 13 Jun 1961, GAMBIA 4 Sep 2000, GEORGIA 22 Jun 1993, GERMANY 8 Jun 1956, GHANA 14 Mar 1968, GREECE Jun 6 1975, GRENADA 25 Oct 1994, GUATEMALA 2 Aug 1961, GUINEA-BISSAU 21 Feb 1977, GUINEA 11 Aug 1967, GUYUNA 13 Jun 1975, HAITI Mar 1958, HONDURAS 9 Aug 1956, HUNGARY 8 Jun 1956, ICELAND 17 Feb 1958, INDIA 25 Sep 1958, INDONESIA 11 Aug 1958, THE ISLAMIC REPUBLIC OF IRAN 10 Jun 1972, IRAQ 28 Aug 1963, IRELAND 18 Dec 1974, ISRAEL 9 Jun 1965, ITALY 8 Jun 1956, JAMAICA 14 Jan 1975, JAPAN 24 Aug 1967, JORDAN 22 Sep 1966, KAZAKHSTAN 18 May 2001, KENYA 7 May 2001, REPUBLIC KOREA 8 Dec 1997, KYRGYZSTAN 31 Mar 1992, LATVIA 27 Jan 1992, LEBANON 1 Jun 1977, LESOTHO 27 Jan 1998, LIBYAN ARAB JAMAHIRIYA 10 Jun 1962, LITHUANIA 26 Sep 1994, LUXEMBOURG 23 Aug 1967, THE FORMER REPUBLIC OF MACEDONIA 17 Nov 1991, MADAGASCAR 10 Aug 1962, MALAWI 22 Mar 1965, MALAYSIA 9 Aug 1997, MALI 12 Jul 1968, MALTA 9 Jun 1988, MAURITANIA 3 Dec 2001, MAURITIUS 18 Dec 2002, MEXICO 23 Aug 1952, REPUBLIC OF MOLDOVA 23 Mar 2000, MONGOLIA 3 Jun 1969, MOROCCO 11 May 1979, MOZAMBIQUE 6 Jun 1977, NEPAL 10 Jun 1976, NETHERLANDS 16 Jun 1971, NEW ZELAND 3 Jun 1983, NICARAGUA 31 Oct 1967, NIGER 9 Aug 1866, NIGERIA 8 May 1974, NORWAY 24 Sep 1959, PAKISTAN 11 Oct 2001, PANAMA 3 Jun 1958, PAPUA NEW GUINEA 2 Jun 2000, PARAGUAY 24 Jun 1964, PERU 1 Feb 1960, PHILIPPINES 29 Dec 1953, POLAND 25 Oct 1954, PORTUGAL 20 Feb 1967, ROMANIA 28 May 1957, RUSSIAN FEDERATION 30 Apr 1956, RWANDA 2 Dec 1980, SAINT KITTS AND NEVIS 25 Oct 2000, SAINT LUCIA 18 Aug 1983, SAINT VINCENT AND THE GRENADINES 4 Dec 2001, SAN MARINO 23 May 1985, SAO TOME AND PRINCIPE 1 Jun 1982, SAUDI

* Source: International Labour Organization, http://www.ilo.org/ilolex.
The ILO shall accept no responsibility for any inaccuracy, errors or omissions or for the consequences arising from the use of the Text.

ARABIA 15 Jun 1978, SENEGAL 22 Oct 1962, SERBIA 24 Nov 2000, SEYCHELLES 23 Nov 1999, SIERRA LEONE 15 Nov 1968, SINGAPORE 30 May 2002, SLOVAKIA 1 Jan 1993, SLOVENIA 29 May 1992, SOUTH AFRICA 30 Mar 2000, SPAIN 6 Nov 1967, SRI LANKA 1 Apr 1993, SUDAN 22 Oct 1970, SWAZILAND 5 Jun 1981, SWEDEN 20 Jun 1962, SWITZERLAND 25 Oct 1972, SYRIAN ARAB REPUBLIC 7 Jun 1957, TAJIKISTAN 26 Nov 1993, TANZANIA (UNITED REPUBLC OF) 26 Feb 2002, THAILAND 8 Feb 1992, TOGO 8 Nov 1983, TRINIDAD AND TOBAGO 29 May 1997, TUNISIA 11 Oct 1968, TURKEY 19 Jul 1967, TURKMENISTAN 15 May 1997, UGANDA 2 Jun 2005, UKRAINE 10 Aug 1956, UNITED ARAB EMIRATES 24 Feb 1997, UNITED KINGDOM 15 Jun 1971, URUGUAY 16 Nov 1989, UZBEKISTAN 13 Jul 1992, VANUATU 28 July 2006, VENEZUELA (BOLIVARIAN REPUBLIC OF) 10 Aug 1982, VIET NAM 7 Oct 1997, YEMEN 29 Jul 1976, ZAMBIA 20 Jun 1972, ZIMBABWE 14 Dec.

The General Conference of the International Labour Organisation,

Having been convened at Geneva by the Governing Body of the International Labour Office, and having met in its Thirty-fourth Session on 6 June 1951, and

Having decided upon the adoption of certain proposals with regard to the principle of equal remuneration for men and women workers for work of equal value, which is the seventh item on the agenda of the session, and

Having determined that these proposals shall take the form of an international Convention,

adopts this twenty-ninth day of June of the year one thousand nine hundred and fifty-one the following Convention, which may be cited as the Equal Remuneration Convention, 1951:

Article 1

For the purpose of this Convention–

(a) the term remuneration includes the ordinary, basic or minimum wage or salary and any additional emoluments whatsoever payable directly or indirectly, whether in cash or in kind, by the employer to the worker and arising out of the worker's employment;

(b) the term equal remuneration for men and women workers for work of equal value refers to rates of remuneration established without discrimination based on sex.

Article 2

1. Each Member shall, by means appropriate to the methods in operation for determining rates of remuneration, promote and, in so far as is consistent with such methods, ensure the application to all workers of the principle of equal remuneration for men and women workers for work of equal value.

2. This principle may be applied by means of–

(a) national laws or regulations;

(b) legally established or recognised machinery for wage determination;

(c) collective agreements between employers and workers; or

(d) a combination of these various means.

Article 3

1. Where such action will assist in giving effect to the provisions of this Convention measures shall be taken to promote objective appraisal of jobs on the basis of the work to be performed.

2. The methods to be followed in this appraisal may be decided upon by the authorities responsible for the determination of rates of remuneration, or, where such rates are determined by collective agreements, by the partíes thereto.

3. Differential rates between workers which correspond, without regard to sex, to differences, as determined by such objective appraisal, in the work to be performed shall not be considered as being contrary to the principle of equal remuneration for men and women workers for work of equal value.

Article 4

Each Member shall co-operate as appropriate with the employers' and workers' organisations concerned for the purpose of giving effect to the provisions of this Convention.

Article 5

The formal ratifications of this Convention shall be communicated to the Director-General of the International Labour Office for registration.

Article 6

1. This Convention shall be binding only upon those Members of the International Labour Organisation whose ratifications have been registered with the Director-General.

2. It shall come into force twelve months after the date on which the ratifications of two Members have been registered with the Director-General.

3. Thereafter, this Convention shall come into force for any Member twelve months after the date on which its ratification has been registered.

Article 7

1. Declarations communicated to the Director-General of the International Labour Office in accordance with paragraph 2 of Article 35 of the Constitution of the International Labour Organisation shall indicate –

a) the territories in respect of which the Member concerned undertakes that the provisions of the Convention shall be applied without modification;

b) the territories in respect of which it undertakes that the provisions of the Convention shall be applied subject to modifications, together with details of the said modifications;

c) the territories in respect of which the Convention is inapplicable and in such cases the grounds on which it is inapplicable;

d) the territories in respect of which it reserves its decision pending further consideration of the position.

2. The undertakings referred to in subparagraphs (a) and (b) of paragraph 1 of this Article shall be deemed to be an integral part of the ratification and shall have the force of ratification.

3. Any Member may at any time by a subsequent declaration cancel in whole or in part any reservation made in its original declaration in virtue of subparagraph (b), (c) or (d) of paragraph 1 of this Article.

4. Any Member may, at any time at which the Convention is subject to denunciation in accordance with the provisions of Article 9, communicate to the Director-General a declaration modifying in any other respect the terms of any former declaration and stating the present position in respect of such territories as it may specify.

Article 8

1. Declarations communicated to the Director-General of the International Labour Office in accordance with paragraph 4 or 5 of Article 35 of the Constitution of the International Labour Organisation shall indicate whether the provisions of the Convention will be applied in the territory concerned without modification or subject to modifications; when the declaration indicates that the provisions of the Convention will be applied subject to modifications, it shall give details of the said modifications.

2. The Member, Members or international authority concerned may at any time by a subsequent declaration renounce in whole or in part the right to have recourse to any modification indicated in any former declaration.

3. The Member, Members or international authority concerned may, at any time at which this Convention is subject to denunciation in accordance with the provisions of Article 9, communicate to the Director-General a declaration modifying in any other respect the terms of any former declaration and stating the present position in respect of the application of the Convention.

Article 9

1. A Member which has ratified this Convention may denounce it after the expiration of ten years from the date on which the Convention first comes into force, by an act communicated to the Director-General of the International Labour Office for registration. Such denunciation shall not take effect until one year after the date on which it is registered.

2. Each Member which has ratified this Convention and which does not, within the year following the expiration of the period of ten years mentioned in the preceding paragraph, exercise the right of denunciation provided for in this Article, will be bound for another period of ten years and, thereafter, may denounce this Convention at the expiration of each period of ten years under the terms provided for in this Article.

Article 10

1. The Director-General of the International Labour Office shall notify all Members of the International Labour Organisation of the registration of all ratifications, declarations and denunciations communicated to him by the Members of the Organisation.

2. When notifying the Members of the Organisation of the registration of the second ratification communicated to him, the Director-General shall draw the attention of the Members of the Organisation to the date upon which the Convention will come into force.

Article 11

The Director-General of the International Labour Office shall communicate to the Secretary-General of the United Nations for registration in accordance with Article 102 of the Charter of the United Nations full particulars of all ratifications, declarations and acts of denunciation registered by him in accordance with the provisions of the preceding articles.

Article 12

At such times as may consider necessary the Governing Body of the International Labour Office shall present to the General Conference a report on the working of this Convention and shall examine the desirability of placing on the agenda of the Conference the question of its revision in whole or in part.

Article 13

1. Should the Conference adopt a new Convention revising this Convention in whole or in part, then, unless the new Convention otherwise provides–

a) the ratification by a Member of the new revising Convention shall ipso jure involve the immediate denunciation of this Convention, notwithstanding the provisions of Article 9 above, if and when the new revising Convention shall have come into force;

b) as from the date when the new revising Convention comes into force this Convention shall cease to be open to ratification by the Members.

2. This Convention shall in any case remain in force in its actual form and content for those Members which have ratified it but have not ratified the revising Convention.

Article 14

The English and French versions of the text of this Convention are equally authoritative.

Recommendation No. 90 concerning Equal Remuneration for Men and Women Workers for Work of Equal Value, 1951*

Date of adoption: 29 June 1951

The General Conference of the International Labour Organisation,

Having been convened at Geneva by the Governing Body of the International Labour Office, and having met in its Thirty-fourth Session on 6 June 1951, and

Having decided upon the adoption of certain proposals with regard to the principle of equal remuneration for men and women workers for work of equal value, which is the seventh item on the agenda of the session, and

Having determined that these proposals shall take the form of a Recommendation, supplementing the Equal Remuneration Convention, 1951,

adopts this twenty-ninth day of June of the year one thousand nine hundred and fifty-one, the following Recommendation, which may be cited as the Equal Remuneration Recommendation, 1951:

Whereas the Equal Remuneration Convention, 1951, lays down certain general principles concerning equal remuneration for men and women workers for work of equal value;

Whereas the Convention provides that the application of the principle of equal remuneration for men and women workers for work of equal value shall be promoted or ensured by means appropriate to the methods in operation for determining rates of remuneration in the countries concerned;

Whereas it is desirable to indicate certain procedures for the progressive application of the principles laid down in the Convention;

Whereas it is at the same time desirable that all Members should, in applying these principles, have regard to methods of application which have been found satisfactory in certain countries;

The Conference recommends that each Member should, subject to the provisions of Article 2 of the Convention, apply the following provisions and report to the International Labour Office as requested by the Governing Body concerning the measures taken to give effect thereto:

1. Appropriate action should be taken, after consultation with the workers' organisations concerned or, where such organisations do not exist, with the workers concerned–

(a) to ensure the application of the principle of equal remuneration for men and women workers for work of equal value to all employees of central Government departments or agencies; and

(b) to encourage the application of the principle to employees of State, provincial or local Government departments or agencies, where these have jurisdiction over rates of remuneration.

2. Appropriate action should be taken, after consultation with the employers' and workers' organisations concerned, to ensure, as rapidly as practicable, the application of the principle

* Source: International Labour Organization, http://www.ilo.org/ilolex
The ILO shall accept no responsibility for any inaccuracy, errors or omissions or for the consequences arising from the use of the Text.

of equal remuneration for men and women workers for work of equal value in all occupations, other than those mentioned in Paragraph 1, in which rates of remuneration are subject to statutory regulation or public control, particularly as regards–

(a) the establishment of minimum or other wage rates in industries and services where such rates are determined under public authority;

(b) industries and undertakings operated under public ownership or control; and

(c) where appropriate, work executed under the terms of public contracts.

3. (1) Where appropriate in the light of the methods in operation for the determination of rates of remuneration, provision should be made by legal enactment for the general application of the principle of equal remuneration for men and women workers for work of equal value.

(2) The competent public authority should take all necessary and appropriate measures to ensure that employers and workers are fully informed as to such legal requirements and, where appropriate, advised on their application.

4. When, after consultation with the organisations of workers and employers concerned, where such exist, it is not deemed feasible to implement immediately the principle of equal remuneration for men and women workers for work of equal value, in respect of employment covered by Paragraph 1, 2 or 3, appropriate provision should be made or caused to be made, as soon as possible, for its progressive application, by such measures as–

(a) decreasing the differentials between rates of remuneration for men and rates of remuneration for women for work of equal value;

(b) where a system of increments is in force, providing equal increments for men and women workers performing work of equal value.

5. Where appropriate for the purpose of facilitating the determination of rates or remuneration in accordance with the principle of equal remuneration for men and women workers for work of equal value, each Member should, in agreement with the employers' and workers' organisations concerned, establish or encourage the establishment of methods for objective appraisal of the work to be performed, whether by job analysis or by other procedures, with a view to providing a classification of jobs without regard to sex; such methods should be applied in accordance with the provisions of Article 2 of the Convention.

6. In order to facilitate the application of the principle of equal remuneration for men and women workers for work of equal value, appropriate action should be taken, where necessary, to raise the productive efficiency of women workers by such measures as–

(a) ensuring that workers of both sexes have equal or equivalent facilities for vocational guidance or employment counselling, for vocational training and for placement;

(b) taking appropriate measures to encourage women to use facilities for vocational guidance or employment counselling, for vocational training and for placement;

(c) providing welfare and social services which meet the needs of women workers, particularly those with family responsibilities, and financing such services from general public funds or from social security or industrial welfare funds financed by payments made in respect of workers without regard to sex; and

(d) promoting equality of men and women workers as regards access to occupations and posts without prejudice to the provisions of international regulations and of national laws and regulations concerning the protection of the health and welfare of women.

7. Every effort should be made to promote public understanding of the grounds on which it is considered that the principle of equal remuneration for men and women workers for work of equal value should be implemented.

8. Such investigations as may be desirable to promote the application of the principle should be undertaken.

Convention No. 111 concerning Discrimination in Respect of Employment and Occupation, 1958*

Adoption: 25 June 1958
Entry into force: 15 June 1960
Parties: 165 (Status as of 1 April 2007)

AFGHANISTAN 1 Oct 1969, ALBANIA 27 Feb 1997, ALGERIA 12 June 1969, ANGOLA 4 June 1976, ANTIGUA AND BARBUDA 2 Feb 1983, ARGENTINA 18 June 1968, ARMENIA 29 July 1994, AUSTRALIA 15 June 1973, AUSTRIA 10 Jan 1973, AZERBAIJAN 19 May 1992, BAHAMAS 14 June 2001, BAHRAIN 26 Sep 2000, BANGLADESH 22 June 1972, BARBADOS 14 Oct 1974, BELARUS 4 Aug 1961, BELGIUM 22 Mar 1977, BELIZE 22 June 1999, BENIN 22 May 1961, BOLIVIA 31 Jan 1977, BOSNIA AND HERZEGOVINA 2 June 1993, BOTSWANA 5 June 1997, BRAZIL 26 Nov 1965, BULGARIA 22 July 1960, BURKINA FASO 16 Apr 1962, BURUNDI 25 June 1993, CAMBODIA 23 Aug 1999, CAMEROON 13 May 1988, CANADA 26 Nov 1964, CAPE VERDE 3 Apr 1979, CENTRAL AFRICAN REPUBLIC 9 June 1964, CHAD 29 Mar 1966, CHILE 20 Sep 1971, CHINA 12 Jan 2006, COLOMBIA 4 Mar 1969, COMOROS 17 Mar 2004, CONGO 26 Nov 1999, DEMOCRATIC REPUBLIC OF CONGO 20 June 2001, COSTA RICA 1 Mar 1962, COTE D'IVOIRE 5 May 1961, CROATIA 8 Oct 1991, CUBA 26 Aug 1965, CYPRUS 2 Feb 1968, CZECH REPUBLIC 1 Jan 1993, DENMARK 22 June 1960, DJIBOUTI 28 Feb 2005, DOMINICA 28 Feb 1983, DOMINICAN REPUBLIC 13 July 1964, ECUADOR 10 July 1962, EGYPT 10 May 1960, EL SALVADOR 15 June 1995, EQUATORIAL GUINEA 13 Aug 2001, ERITREA 22 Feb 2000, ESTONIA 17 Aug 2005, ETHIOPIA 11 Nov 1966, FIJI 17 Apr 2002, FINLAND 23 Apr 1970, FRANCE 28 May 1981, GABON 29 May 1961, GAMBIA 4 Sep 2000, GEORGIA 22 June 1993, GERMANY 15 June 1961, GHANA 4 Apr 1961, GREECE 7 May 1984, GRENADA 14 May 2003, GUATEMALA 11 Oct 1960, GUINEA-BISSAU 21 Feb 1977, GUINEA 1 Sep 1960, GUYANA 13 June 1975, HAITI 9 Nov 1976, HONDURAS 20 June 1960, HUNGARY 20 June 1961, ICELAND 29 July 1963, INDIA 3 June 1960, INDONESIA 7 June 1999, IRAN (THE ISLAMIC REPUBLIC OF) 30 June 1964, IRAQ 15 June 1959, IRELAND 22 Apr 1999, ISRAEL 12 Jan 1959, ITALY 12 Aug 1963, JAMAICA 10 Jan 1975, JORDAN 4 July 1963, KAZAKHSTAN 6 Dec 1999, KENYA 7 May 2001, REPUBLIC OF KOREA 4 Dec 1998, KUWAIT 1 Dec 1966, KYRGYZSTAN 31 Mar 1992, LATVIA 27 Jan 1992, LEBANON 1 June 1977, LESOTHO 27 Jan 1998, LIBERIA 22 July 1959, LIBYAN ARAB JAMAHIRIYA 13 June 1961, LITHUANIA 26 Sep 1994, LUXEMBOURG 21 Mar 2001, THE FORMER YUGOSLAV REPUBLIC OF MACEDONIA 17 Nov 1991, MADAGASCAR 11 Aug 1961, MALAWI 22 Mar 1965, MALI 2 Mar 1964, MALTA 1 July 1968, MAURITANIA 8 Nov 1963, MAURITIUS 18 Dec 2002, MEXICO 11 Sep 1961, REPUBLIC OF MOLDOVA 12 Aug 1996, MONGOLIA 3 June 1969, MOROCCO 27 Mar 1963, MOZAMBIQUE 6 June 1977, NAMIBIA 13 Nov 2001, NEPAL 19 Sep 1974, NETHERLANDS 15 Mar 1973, NEW ZEALAND 3 June 1983, NICARAGUA 31 Oct 1967, NIGER 23 Mar 1962, NIGERIA 2 Oct 2002, NORWAY 24 Sep 1959, PAKISTAN 24 Jan 1961, PANAMA 16 May 1966, PAPUA NEW GUINEA 2 June 2000, PARAGUAY 10 July 1967, PERU 10 Aug 1970, PHILIPPINES 17 Nov 1960, POLAND 30 May 1961, PORTUGAL 19 Nov 1959, QATAR 18 Aug 1976, ROMANIA 6 June 1973, RUSSIAN FEDERATION 4 May 1961, RWANDA 2 Feb 1981, SAINT KITTS AND NEVIS 25 Aug 2000, SAINT LUCIA 18

* Source: International Labour Organization, http://www.ilo.org/ilolex.
The ILO shall accept no responsibility for any inaccuracy, errors or omissions or for the consequences arising from the use of the Text.

Aug 1983, SAINT VINCENT AND THE GRENADINES 9 Nov 2001, SAN MARINO 19 Dec 1986, SAO TOME AND PRINCIPE 1 June 1982, SAUDI ARABIA 15 June 1978, SENEGAL 13 Nov 1967, REPUBLIC OF SERBIA 24 Nov 2000, SEYCHELLES 23 Nov 1999, SIERRA LEONE 14 Oct 1966, SLOVAKIA 1 Jan 1993, SLOVENIA 29 May 1992, SOMALIA 8 Dec 1961, SOUTH AFRICA 5 Mar 1997, SPAIN 6 Nov 1967, SRI LANKA 27 Nov 1998, SUDAN 22 Oct 1970, SWAZILAND 5 June 1981, SWEDEN 20 June 1962, SWITZERLAND 13 July 1961, SYRIAN ARAB REPUBLIC 10 May 1960, TAJIKISTAN 26 Nov 1993, TANZANIA (UNITED REPUBLIC OF) 26 Feb 2002, TOGO 8 Nov 1983, TRINIDAD AND TOBAGO 26 Nov 1970, TUNISIA 14 Sep 1959, TURKEY 19 July 1967, TURKMENISTAN 15 May 1997, UGANDA 2 June 2005, UKRAINE 4 Aug 1961, UNITED ARAB EMIRATES 28 June 2001, UNITED KINGDOM 8 June 1999, URUGAY 16 Nov 1989, UZBEKISTAN 13 July 1992, VANUATU 28 July 2006, VENEZUELA (BOLIVARIAN REPUBLIC OF) 3 June 1971, VIETNAM 7 Oct 1997, YEMEN 22 Aug 1969, ZAMBIA 23 Oct 1979, ZIMBABWE 23 June 1999.

The General Conference of the International Labour Organization,

Having been convened at Geneva by the Governing Body of the International Labour Office, and having met in its Forty-second Session on 4 June 1958, and

Having decided upon the adoption of certain proposals with regard to discrimination in the field of employment and occupation, which is the fourth item on the agenda of the session, and

Having determined that these proposals shall take the form of an international Convention, and

Considering that the Declaration of Philadelphia affirms that all human beings, irrespective of race, creed or sex, have the right to pursue both their material well-being and their spiritual development in conditions of freedom and dignity, of economic security and equal opportunity, and

Considering further that discrimination constitutes a violation of rights enunciated by the Universal Declaration of Human Rights,

Adopts this twenty-fifth day of June of the year one thousand nine hundred and fifty-eight the following Convention, which may be cited as the Discrimination (Employment and Occupation) Convention, 1958:

Article 1

1. For the purpose of this Convention the term discrimination includes–

(a) any distinction, exclusion or preference made on the basis of race, colour, sex, religion, political opinion, national extraction or social origin, which has the effect of nullifying or impairing equality of opportunity or treatment in employment or occupation;

(b) such other distinction, exclusion or preference which has the effect of nullifying or impairing equality of opportunity or treatment in employment or occupation as may be determined by the Member concerned after consultation with representative employers' and workers' organizations, where such exist, and with other appropriate bodies.

2. Any distinction, exclusion or preference in respect of a particular job based on the inherent requirements thereof shall not be deemed to be discrimination.

3. For the purpose of this Convention the terms employment and occupation include access to vocational training, access to employment and to particular occupations, and terms and conditions of employment.

Article 2

Each Member for which this Convention is in force undertakes to declare and pursue a national policy designed to promote, by methods appropriate to national conditions and practice, equality of opportunity and treatment in respect of employment and occupation, with a view to eliminating any discrimination in respect thereof.

Article 3

Each Member for which this Convention is in force undertakes, by methods appropriate to national conditions and practice–

(a) to seek the co-operation of employers' and workers' organizations and other appropriate bodies in promoting the acceptance and observance of this policy;

(b) to enact such legislation and to promote such educational programmes as may be calculated to secure the acceptance and observance of the policy;

(c) to repeal any statutory provisions and modify any administrative instructions or practices which are inconsistent with the policy;

(d) to pursue the policy in respect of employment under the direct control of a national authority;

(e) to ensure observance of the policy in the activities of vocational guidance, vocational training and placement services under the direction of a national authority;

(f) to indicate in its annual reports on the application of the Convention the action taken in pursuance of the policy and the results secured by such action.

Article 4

Any measures affecting an individual who is justifiably suspected of, or engaged in, activities prejudicial to the security of the State shall not be deemed to be discrimination, provided that the individual concerned shall have the right to appeal to a competent body established in accordance with national practice.

Article 5

1. Special measures of protection or assistance provided for in other Conventions or Recommendations adopted by the International Labour Conference shall not be deemed to be discrimination.

2. Any Member may, after consultation with representative employers' and workers' organizations, where such exist, determine that other special measures designed to meet the particular requirements of persons who, for reasons such as sex, age, disablement, family responsibilities or social or cultural status, are generally recognized to require special protection or assistance, shall not be deemed to be discrimination.

Article 6

Each Member which ratifies this Convention undertakes to apply it to non-metropolitan territories in accordance with the provisions of the Constitution of the International Labour Organization.

Article 7

The formal ratifications of this Convention shall be communicated to the Director-General of the International Labour Office for registration.

Article 8

1. This Convention shall be binding only upon those Members of the International Labour Organization whose ratifications have been registered with the Director-General.

2. It shall come into force twelve months after the date on which the ratifications of two Members have been registered with the Director-General.

3. Thereafter, this Convention shall come into force for any Member twelve months after the date on which its ratification has been registered.

Article 9

1. A Member which has ratified this Convention may denounce it after the expiration of ten years from the date on which the Convention first comes into force, by an act communicated to the Director-General of the International Labour Office for registration. Such denunciation shall not take effect until one year after the date on which it is registered.

2. Each Member which has ratified this Convention and which does not, within the year following the expiration of the period of ten years mentioned in the preceding paragraph, exercise the right of denunciation provided for in this Article, will be bound for another period of ten years and, thereafter, may denounce this Convention at the expiration of each period of ten years under the terms provided for in this Article.

Article 10

1. The Director-General of the International Labour Office shall notify all Members of the International Labour Organization of the registration of all ratifications and denunciations communicated to him by the Members of the Organization.

2. When notifying the Members of the Organization of the registration of the second ratification communicated to him, the Director-General shall draw the attention of the Members of the Organization to the date upon which the Convention will come into force.

Article 11

The Director-General of the International Labour Office shall communicate to the Secretary-General of the United Nations for registration in accordance with Article 102 of the Charter of the United Nations full particulars of all ratifications and acts of denunciation registered by him in accordance with the provisions of the preceding Articles.

Article 12

At such times as it may consider necessary the Governing Body of the International Labour Office shall present to the General Conference a report on the working of this Convention and shall examine the desirability of placing on the agenda of the Conference the question of its revision in whole or in part.

Article 13

1. Should the Conference adopt a new Convention revising this Convention in whole or in part, then, unless the new Convention otherwise provides:

a) the ratification by a Member of the new revising Convention shall ipso jure involve the immediate denunciation of this Convention, notwithstanding the provisions of Article 9 above, if and when the new revising Convention shall have come into force;

b) as from the date when the new revising Convention comes into force, this Convention shall cease to be open to ratification by the Members.

2. This Convention shall in any case remain in force in its actual form and content for those Members which have ratified it but have not ratified the revising Convention.

Article 14

The English and French versions of the text of this Convention are equally authoritative.

Recommendation No. 111 concerning Discrimination in Respect of Employment and Occupation, 1958*

Adoption: 25 June 1958

The General Conference of the International Labour Organisation,

Having been convened at Geneva by the Governing Body of the International Labour Office, and having met in its Forty-second Session on 4 June 1958, and

Having decided upon the adoption of certain proposals with regard to discrimination in the field of employment and occupation, which is the fourth item on the agenda of the session, and

Having determined that these proposals shall take the form of a Recommendation supplementing the Discrimination (Employment and Occupation) Convention, 1958,

Adopts this twenty-fifth day of June of the year one thousand nine hundred and fifty-eight, the following Recommendation, which may be cited as the Discrimination (Employment and Occupation) Recommendation, 1958:

The Conference recommends that each Member should apply the following provisions:

I. Definitions

1.

(1) For the purpose of this Recommendation the term discrimination includes–

(a) any distinction, exclusion or preference made on the basis of race, colour, sex, religion, political opinion, national extraction or social origin, which has the effect of nullifying or impairing equality of opportunity or treatment in employment or occupation;

(b) such other distinction, exclusion or preference which has the effect of nullifying or impairing equality of opportunity or treatment in employment or occupation as may be determined by the Member concerned after consultation with representative employers' and workers' organizations, where such exist, and with other appropriate bodies.

(2) Any distinction, exclusion or preference in respect of a particular job based on the inherent requirements thereof is not deemed to be discrimination. (3) For the purpose of this Recommendation the terms employment and occupation include access to vocational training, access to employment and to particular occupations, and terms and conditions of employment.

II. Formulation and Application of Policy

2.

Each Member should formulate a national policy for the prevention of discrimination in employment and occupation. This policy should be applied by means of legislative measures, collective agreements between representative employers' and workers' organizations or in any other manner consistent with national conditions and practice, and should have regard to the following principles:

* Source: International Labour Organization, http://www.ilo.org/ilolex/
The ILO shall accept no responsibility for any inaccuracy, errors or omissions or for the consequences arising from the use of the Text.

(a) the promotion of equality of opportunity and treatment in employment and occupation is a matter of public concern;

(b) all persons should, without discrimination, enjoy equality of opportunity and treatment in respect of–

(i) access to vocational guidance and placement services;

(ii) access to training and employment of their own choice on the basis of individual suitability for such training or employment;

(iii) advancement in accordance with their individual character, experience, ability and diligence;

(iv) security of tenure of employment;

(v) remuneration for work of equal value;

(vi) conditions of work including hours of work, rest periods, annual holidays with pay, occupational safety and occupational health measures, as well as social security measures and welfare facilities and benefits provided in connection with employment;

(c) government agencies should apply non-discriminatory employment policies in all their activities;

(d) employers should not practise or countenance discrimination in engaging or training any person for employment, in advancing or retaining such person in employment, or in fixing terms and conditions of employment; nor should any person or organization obstruct or interfere, either directly or indirectly, with employers in pursuing this principle;

(e) in collective negotiations and industrial relations the parties should respect the principle of equality of opportunity and treatment in employment and occupation, and should ensure that collective agreements contain no provisions of a discriminatory character in respect of access to, training for, advancement in or retention of employment or in respect of the terms and conditions of employment;

(f) employers' and workers' organizations should not practise or countenance discrimination in respect of admission, retention of membership or participation in their affairs.

3.

Each Member should–

(a) ensure application of the principles of non-discrimination–

(i) in respect of employment under the direct control of a national authority;

(ii) in the activities of vocational guidance, vocational training and placement services under the direction of a national authority;

(b) promote their observance, where practicable and necessary, in respect of other employment and other vocational guidance, vocational training and placement services by such methods as–

(i) encouraging state, provincial or local government departments or agencies and industries and undertakings operated under public ownership or control to ensure the application of the principles;

(ii) making eligibility for contracts involving the expenditure of public funds dependent on observance of the principles;

(iii) making eligibility for grants to training establishments and for a licence to operate a private employment agency or a private vocational guidance office dependent on observance of the principles.

4.

Appropriate agencies, to be assisted where practicable by advisory committees composed of representatives of employers' and workers' organizations, where such exist, and of other interested bodies, should be established for the purpose of promoting application of the policy in all fields of public and private employment, and in particular–

(a) to take all practicable measures to foster public understanding and acceptance of the principles of non-discrimination;

(b) to receive, examine and investigate complaints that the policy is not being observed and, if necessary by conciliation, to secure the correction of any practices regarded as in conflict with the policy; and

(c) to consider further any complaints which cannot be effectively settled by conciliation and to render opinions or issue decisions concerning the manner in which discriminatory practices revealed should be corrected.

5.

Each Member should repeal any statutory provisions and modify any administrative instructions or practices which are inconsistent with the policy.

6.

Application of the policy should not adversely affect special measures designed to meet the particular requirements of persons who, for reasons such as sex, age, disablement, family responsibilities or social or cultural status are generally recognized to require special protection or assistance.

7.

Any measures affecting an individual who is justifiably suspected of, or engaged in, activities prejudicial to the security of the State should not be deemed to be discrimination, provided that the individual concerned has the right to appeal to a competent body established in accordance with national practice.

8.

With respect to immigrant workers of foreign nationality and the members of their families, regard should be had to the provisions of the Migration for Employment Convention (Revised), 1949, relating to equality of treatment and the provisions of the Migration for Employment Recommendation (Revised), 1949, relating to the lifting of restrictions on access to employment.

9.

There should be continuing co-operation between the competent authorities, representatives of employers and workers and appropriate bodies to consider what further positive measures may be necessary in the light of national conditions to put the principles of non-discrimination into effect.

III. Co-ordination of Measures for the Prevention of Discrimination in All Fields

10.

The authorities responsible for action against discrimination in employment and occupation should co-operate closely and continuously with the authorities responsible for action against discrimination in other fields in order that measures taken in all fields may be co-ordinated.

Convention No.122 concerning Employment Policy, 1964*

Adoption: 9 July 1964
Entry into force: 15 July 1966
Parties: 96 (Status as of 1 April 2007)

ALGERIA 12 June 1969, ANTIGUA AND BARBUDA 16 Sep 2002, ARMENIA 29 July 1994, AUSTRALIA 12 Nov 1969, AUSTRIA 27 July 1972, AZERBAIJAN 19 May 1992, BARBADOS 15 Mar 1976, BELARUS 26 Feb 1968, BELGIUM 8 July 1969, BOLIVIA 31 Jan 1977, BOSNIA AND HERZEGOVINA 2 June 1993, BRAZIL 24 Mar 1969, CAMBODIA 28 Sep 1971, CAMEROON 25 May 1970, CANADA 16 Sep 1966, CENTRAL AFRICAN REPUBLIC 5 June 2006, CHILE 24 Oct 1968, CHINA 17 Dec 1997, COMOROS 23 Oct 1978, COSTA RICA 27 Jan 1966, CROATIA 8 Oct 1991, CUBA 5 Feb 1971, CYPRUS 28 July 1966, CZECH REPUBLIC 1 Jan 1993, DENMARK 17 June 1970, DJIBOUTI 3 Aug 1978, DOMINICAN REPUBLIC 29 Mar 2001, ECUADOR 13 Nov 1972, EL SALVADOR 15 June 1995, ESTONIA 12 Mar 2003, FINLAND 23 Sep 1968, FRANCE 5 Aug 1971, GEORGIA 22 June 1993, GERMANY 17 June 1971, GREECE 7 May 1984, GUATEMALA 14 Sep 1988, GUINEA 12 Dec 1966, HONDURAS 9 Sep 1980, HUNGARY 18 June 1969, ICELAND 22 June 1990, INDIA 17 Nov 1998, IRAN (THE ISLAMIC REPUBLIC OF) 10 June 1972, IRAQ 2 Mar 1970, IRELAND 20 June 1967, ISRAEL 26 Jan 1970, ITALY 5 May 1971, JAMAICA 10 Jan 1975, JAPAN 10 June 1986, JORDAN 10 Mar 1966, KAZAKHSTAN 6 Dec 1999, REPUBLIC OF KOREA 9 Dec 1992, KYRGYZSTAN 31 Mar 1992, LATVIA 27 jan 1992, LEBANON 1 June 1977, LIBYAN ARAB JAMAHIRIYA 27 May 1971, LITHUANIA 3 Mar 2004, THE FORMER YUGOSLAV REPUBLIC OF MACEDONIA 17 Nov 1991, MADAGASCAR 21 Nov 1966, MAURITANIA 30 July 1971, REPUBLIC OF MOLDOVA 12 Aug 1996, MONGOLIA 24 Nov 1976, MOROCCO 11 May 1979, MOZAMBIQUE 23 Dec 1996, NETHERLANDS 9 Jan 1967, NEW ZEALAND 15 July 1965, NICARAGUA 1 Oct 1981, NORWAY 6 June 1966, PANAMA 19 June 1970, PAPUA NEW GUINEA 1 May 1976, PARAGUAY 20 Feb 1969, PERU 27 July 1967, PHILIPPINES 13 Jan 1976, POLAND 24 Nov 1966, PORTUGAL 9 Jan 1981, REPUBLIC OF SERBIA 24 Nov 2000, ROMANIA 6 June 1973, RUSSIAN FEDERATION 22 Sep 1967, SENEGAL 25 Apr 1966, SLOVAKIA 1 Jan 1993, SLOVENIA 29 May 1992, SPAIN 28 Dec 1970, SUDAN 22 Oct 1970, SURINAME 15 June 1976, SWEDEN 11 June 1965, TAJIKISTAN 26 Nov 1993, THAILAND 26 Feb 1969, TUNISIA 17 Feb 1966, TURKEY 13 Dec 1977, UGANDA 23 June 1967, UKRAINE 19 June 1968, UNITED KINGDOM 27 June 1966, URUGUAY 2 June 1977, UZBEKISTAN 13 July 1992, VENEZUELA (BOLIVARIAN REPUBLIC OF) 10 Aug 1982, YEMEN 30 Jan 1989, ZAMBIA 23 Oct 1979.

The General Conference of the International Labour Organisation,

Having been convened at Geneva by the Governing Body of the International Labour Office, and having met in its Forty-eighth Session on 17 June 1964, and

Considering that the Declaration of Philadelphia recognises the solemn obligation of the International Labour Organisation to further among the nations of the world programmes which will achieve full employment and the raising of standards of living, and that the Preamble

---

* Source: International Labour Organization, http://www.ilo.org/ilolex
The ILO shall accept no responsibility for any inaccuracy, errors or omissions or for the consequences arising from the use of the Text.

to the Constitution of the International Labour Organisation provides for the prevention of unemployment and the provision of an adequate living wage, and

Considering further that under the terms of the Declaration of Philadelphia it is the responsibility of the International Labour Organisation to examine and consider the bearing of economic and financial policies upon employment policy in the light of the fundamental objective that "all human beings, irrespective of race, creed or sex, have the right to pursue both their material well-being and their spiritual development in conditions of freedom and dignity, of economic security and equal opportunity", and

Considering that the Universal Declaration of Human Rights provides that "everyone has the right to work, to free choice of employment, to just and favourable conditions of work and to protection against unemployment", and

Noting the terms of existing international labour Conventions and Recommendations of direct relevance to employment policy, and in particular of the Employment Service Convention and Recommendation, 1948, the Vocational Guidance Recommendation, 1949, the Vocational Training Recommendation, 1962, and the Discrimination (Employment and Occupation) Convention and Recommendation, 1958, and

Considering that these instruments should be placed in the wider framework of an international programme for economic expansion on the basis of full, productive and freely chosen employment, and

Having decided upon the adoption of certain proposals with regard to employment policy, which are included in the eighth item on the agenda of the session, and

Having determined that these proposals shall take the form of an international Convention,

adopts this ninth day of July of the year one thousand nine hundred and sixty-four the following Convention, which may be cited as the Employment Policy Convention, 1964:

Article 1

1. With a view to stimulating economic growth and development, raising levels of living, meeting manpower requirements and overcoming unemployment and underemployment, each Member shall declare and pursue, as a major goal, an active policy designed to promote full, productive and freely chosen employment.

2. The said policy shall aim at ensuring that–

(a) there is work for all who are available for and seeking work;

(b) such work is as productive as possible;

(c) there is freedom of choice of employment and the fullest possible opportunity for each worker to qualify for, and to use his skills and endowments in, a job for which he is well suited, irrespective of race, colour, sex, religion, political opinion, national extraction or social origin.

3. The said policy shall take due account of the stage and level of economic development and the mutual relationships between employment objectives and other economic and social objectives, and shall be pursued by methods that are appropriate to national conditions and practices.

Article 2

Each Member shall, by such methods and to such extent as may be appropriate under national conditions–

(a) decide on and keep under review, within the framework of a co-ordinated economic and social policy, the measures to be adopted for attaining the objectives specified in Article 1;

(b) take such steps as may be needed, including when appropriate the establishment of programmes, for the application of these measures.

Article 3

In the application of this Convention, representatives of the persons affected by the measures to be taken, and in particular representatives of employers and workers, shall be consulted concerning employment policies, with a view to taking fully into account their experience and views and securing their full co-operation in formulating and enlisting support for such policies.

Article 4

The formal ratifications of this Convention shall be communicated to the Director-General of the International Labour Office for registration.

Article 5

1. This Convention shall be binding only upon those Members of the International Labour Organisation whose ratifications have been registered with the Director-General.

2. It shall come into force twelve months after the date on which the ratifications of two Members have been registered with the Director-General.

3. Thereafter, this Convention shall come into force for any Member twelve months after the date on which its ratification has been registered.

Article 6

1. A Member which has ratified this Convention may denounce it after the expiration of ten years from the date on which the Convention first comes into force, by an act communicated to the Director-General of the International Labour Office for registration. Such denunciation shall not take effect until one year after the date on which it is registered.

2. Each Member which has ratified this Convention and which does not, within the year following the expiration of the period of ten years mentioned in the preceding paragraph, exercise the right of denunciation provided for in this Article, will be bound for another period of ten years and, thereafter, may denounce this Convention at the expiration of each period of ten years under the terms provided for in this Article.

Article 7

1. The Director-General of the International Labour Office shall notify all Members of the International Labour Organisation of the registration of all ratifications and denunciations communicated to him by the Members of the Organisation.

2. When notifying the Members of the Organisation of the registration of the second ratification communicated to him, the Director-General shall draw the attention of the Members of the Organisation to the date upon which the Convention will come into force.

Article 8

The Director-General of the International Labour Office shall communicate to the Secretary-General of the United Nations for registration in accordance with Article 102 of the Charter of the United Nations full particulars of all ratifications and acts of denunciation registered by him in accordance with the provisions of the preceding Articles.

Article 9

At such times as it may consider necessary the Governing Body of the International Labour Office shall present to the General Conference a report on the working of this Convention and shall examine the desirability of placing on the agenda of the Conference the question of its revision in whole or in part.

Article 10

1. Should the Conference adopt a new Convention revising this Convention in whole or in part, then, unless the new Convention otherwise provides–

a) the ratification by a Member of the new revising Convention shall ipso jure involve the immediate denunciation of this Convention, notwithstanding the provisions of Article 6 above, if and when the new revising Convention shall have come into force;

b) as from the date when the new revising Convention comes into force this Convention shall cease to be open to ratification by the Members.

2. This Convention shall in any case remain in force in its actual form and content for those Members which have ratified it but have not ratified the revising Convention.

Article 11

The English and French versions of the text of this Convention are equally authoritative.

Convention No. 156 concerning Equal Opportunities and Equal Treatment for Men and Women Workers: Workers with Family Responsibilities, 1981*

Adoption: 23 June 1981
Entry into force: 11 August 1983
Parties: 37 (Status as of 1 April 2007)

ARGENTINA 17 Mar 1988, AUSTRALIA 30 Mar 1990, BELIZE 22 June 1999, BOLIVIA 1 Sep 1998, BOSNIA AND HERZEGOVINA 2 June 1993, BULGARIA 3 Apr 2006, CHILE 10 Oct 1994, CROATIA 8 Oct 1991, EL SALVADOR 12 Oct 2000, ETHIOPIA 28 Jan 1991, FINLAND 9 Feb 1983, FRANCE 16 Mar 1989, GREECE 10 June 1988, GUATEMALA 6 Jan 1994, GUINEA 16 Oct 1995, ICELAND 22 June 2000, JAPAN 9 June 1995, REPUBLIC OF KOREA 29 Mar 2001, LITHUANIA 6 May 2004, THE FORMER YUGOSLAV REPUBLIC OF MACEDONIA 17 Nov 1991, MAURITIUS 5 Apr 2004, NETHERLANDS 24 Mar 1988, NIGER 5 June 1985, NORWAY 22 June 1982, PERU 16 June 1986, PORTUGAL 2 May 1985, REPUBLIC OF SERBIA 24 Nov 2000, RUSSIAN FEDERATION 13 Feb 1998, SAN MARINO 19 Apr 1988, SLOVAKIA 14 June 2002, SLOVENIA 29 May 1992, SPAIN 11 Sep 1985, SWEDEN 11 Aug 1982, UKRAINE 11 Apr 2000, URUGAY 16 Nov 1989, VENEZUELA (BOLIVARIAN REPUBLIC OF) 27 Nov 1984, YEMEN 13 Mar 1989.

The General Conference of the International Labour Organisation,

Having been convened at Geneva by the Governing Body of the International Labour Office and having met in its Sixty-seventh Session on 3 June 1981, and

Noting the Declaration of Philadelphia concerning the Aims and Purposes of the International Labour Organisation which recognises that "all human beings, irrespective of race, creed or sex, have the right to pursue their material well-being and their spiritual development in conditions of freedom and dignity, of economic security and equal opportunity", and

Noting the terms of the Declaration on Equality of Opportunity and Treatment for Women Workers and of the resolution concerning a plan of action with a view to promoting equality of opportunity and treatment for women workers, adopted by the International Labour Conference in 1975, and

Noting the provisions of international labour Conventions and Recommendations aimed at ensuring equality of opportunity and treatment for men and women workers, namely the Equal Remuneration Convention and Recommendation, 1951, the Discrimination (Employment and Occupation) Convention and Recommendation, 1958, and Part VIII of the Human Resources Development Recommendation, 1975, and

Recalling that the Discrimination (Employment and Occupation) Convention, 1958, does not expressly cover distinctions made on the basis of family responsibilities, and considering that supplementary standards are necessary in this respect, and

Noting the terms of the Employment (Women with Family Responsibilities) Recommendation, 1965, and considering the changes which have taken place since its adoption, and

* Source: International Labour Organization, http://www.ilo.org/ilolex/.
The ILO shall accept no responsibility for any inaccuracy, errors or omissions or for the consequences arising from the use of the Text.

Noting that instruments on equality of opportunity and treatment for men and women have also been adopted by the United Nations and other specialised agencies, and recalling, in particular, the fourteenth paragraph of the Preamble of the United Nations Convention on the Elimination of All Forms of Discrimination against Women, 1979, to the effect that States Parties are " aware that a change in the traditional role of men as well as the role of women in society and in the family is needed to achieve full equality between men and women", and

Recognising that the problems of workers with family responsibilities are aspects of wider issues regarding the family and society which should be taken into account in national policies, and

Recognising the need to create effective equality of opportunity and treatment as between men and women workers with family responsibilities and between such workers and other workers, and

Considering that many of the problems facing all workers are aggravated in the case of workers with family responsibilities and recognising the need to improve the conditions of the latter both by measures responding to their special needs and by measures designed to improve the conditions of workers in general, and

Having decided upon the adoption of certain proposals with regard to equal opportunities and equal treatment for men and women workers: workers with family responsibilities, which is the fifth item on the agenda of the session, and

Having determined that these proposals shall take the form of an international Convention,

adopts this twenty-third day of June of the year one thousand nine hundred and eighty-one the following Convention, which may be cited as the Workers with Family Responsibilities Convention, 1981:

Article 1

1. This Convention applies to men and women workers with responsibilities in relation to their dependent children, where such responsibilities restrict their possibilities of preparing for, entering, participating in or advancing in economic activity.

2. The provisions of this Convention shall also be applied to men and women workers with responsibilities in relation to other members of their immediate family who clearly need their care or support, where such responsibilities restrict their possibilities of preparing for, entering, participating in or advancing in economic activity.

3. For the purposes of this Convention, the terms dependent child and other member of the immediate family who clearly needs care or support mean persons defined as such in each country by one of the means referred to in Article 9 of this Convention.

4. The workers covered by virtue of paragraphs 1 and 2 of this Article are hereinafter referred to as workers with family responsibilities.

Article 2

This Convention applies to all branches of economic activity and all categories of workers.

Article 3

1. With a view to creating effective equality of opportunity and treatment for men and women workers, each Member shall make it an aim of national policy to enable persons with family

responsibilities who are engaged or wish to engage in employment to exercise their right to do so without being subject to discrimination and, to the extent possible, without conflict between their employment and family responsibilities.

2. For the purposes of paragraph 1 of this Article, the term discrimination means discrimination in employment and occupation as defined by Articles 1 and 5 of the Discrimination (Employment and Occupation) Convention, 1958.

Article 4

With a view to creating effective equality of opportunity and treatment for men and women workers, all measures compatible with national conditions and possibilities shall be taken–

(a) to enable workers with family responsibilities to exercise their right to free choice of employment; and

(b) to take account of their needs in terms and conditions of employment and in social security.

Article 5

All measures compatible with national conditions and possibilities shall further be taken–

(a) to take account of the needs of workers with family responsibilities in community planning; and

(b) to develop or promote community services, public or private, such as child-care and family services and facilities.

Article 6

The competent authorities and bodies in each country shall take appropriate measures to promote information and education which engender broader public understanding of the principle of equality of opportunity and treatment for men and women workers and of the problems of workers with family responsibilities, as well as a climate of opinion conducive to overcoming these problems.

Article 7

All measures compatible with national conditions and possibilities, including measures in the field of vocational guidance and training, shall be taken to enable workers with family responsibilities to become and remain integrated in the labour force, as well as to re-enter the labour force after an absence due to those responsibilities.

Article 8

Family responsibilities shall not, as such, constitute a valid reason for termination of employment.

Article 9

The provisions of this Convention may be applied by laws or regulations, collective agreements, works rules, arbitration awards, court decisions or a combination of these methods, or in any other manner consistent with national practice which may be appropriate, account being taken of national conditions.

Article 10

1. The provisions of this Convention may be applied by stages if necessary, account being taken of national conditions: Provided that such measures of implementation as are taken shall apply in any case to all the workers covered by Article 1, paragraph 1.

2. Each Member which ratifies this Convention shall indicate in the first report on the application of the Convention submitted under Article 22 of the Constitution of the International Labour Organisation in what respect, if any, it intends to make use of the faculty given by paragraph 1 of this Article, and shall state in subsequent reports the extent to which effect has been given or is proposed to be given to the Convention in that respect.

Article 11

Employers' and workers' organisations shall have the right to participate, in a manner appropriate to national conditions and practice, in devising and applying measures designed to give effect to the provisions of this Convention.

Article 12

The formal ratifications of this Convention shall be communicated to the Director-General of the International Labour Office for registration.

Article 13

1. This Convention shall be binding only upon those Members of the International Labour Organisation whose ratifications have been registered with the Director-General.

2. It shall come into force twelve months after the date on which the ratifications of two Members have been registered with the Director-General.

3. Thereafter, this Convention shall come into force for any Member twelve months after the date on which its ratification has been registered.

Article 14

1. A Member which has ratified this Convention may denounce it after the expiration of ten years from the date on which the Convention first comes into force, by an act communicated to the Director-General of the International Labour Office for registration. Such denunciation shall not take effect until one year after the date on which it is registered.

2. Each Member which has ratified this Convention and which does not, within the year following the expiration of the period of ten years mentioned in the preceding paragraph, exercise the right of denunciation provided for in this Article, will be bound for another period of ten years and, thereafter, may denounce this Convention at the expiration of each period of ten years under the terms provided for in this Article.

Article 15

1. The Director-General of the International Labour Office shall notify all Members of the International Labour Organisation of the registration of all ratifications and denunciations communicated to him by the Members of the Organisation.

2. When notifying the Members of the Organisation of the registration of the second ratification communicated to him, the Director-General shall draw the attention of the Members of the Organisation to the date upon which the Convention will come into force.

Article 16

The Director-General of the International Labour Office shall communicate to the Secretary-General of the United Nations for registration in accordance with Article 102 of the Charter of the United Nations full particulars of all ratifications and acts of denunciation registered by him in accordance with the provisions of the preceding Articles.

Article 17

At such times as it may consider necessary the Governing Body of the International Labour Office shall present to the General Conference a report on the working of this Convention and shall examine the desirability of placing on the agenda of the Conference the question of its revision in whole or in part.

Article 18

1. Should the Conference adopt a new Convention revising this Convention in whole or in part, then, unless the new Convention otherwise provides:

a) the ratification by a Member of the new revising Convention shall ipso jure involve the immediate denunciation of this Convention, notwithstanding the provisions of Article 14 above, if and when the new revising Convention shall have come into force;

b) as from the date when the new revising Convention comes into force this Convention shall cease to be open to ratification by the Members.

2. This Convention shall in any case remain in force in its actual form and content for those Members which have ratified it but have not ratified the revising Convention.

Article 19

The English and French versions of the text of this Convention are equally authoritative.

Recommendation No. 165 concerning Equal Opportunities and Equal Treatment for Men and Women Workers: Workers with Family Responsibilities, 1981*

Adoption: 23 June 1981

The General Conference of the International Labour Organisation,

Having been convened at Geneva by the Governing Body of the International Labour Office and having met in its Sixty-seventh Session on 3 June 1981, and

Noting the Declaration of Philadelphia concerning the Aims and Purposes of the International Labour Organisation which recognises that all human beings, irrespective of race, creed or sex, have the right to pursue their material well-being and their spiritual development in conditions of freedom and dignity, of economic security and equal opportunity, and

Noting the terms of the Declaration on Equality of Opportunity and Treatment for Women Workers and of the resolution concerning a plan of action with a view to promoting equality of opportunity and treatment for women workers, adopted by the International Labour Conference in 1975, and

Noting the provisions of international labour Conventions and Recommendations aimed at ensuring equality of opportunity and treatment for men and women workers, namely the Equal Remuneration Convention and Recommendation, 1951, the Discrimination (Employment and Occupation) Convention and Recommendation, 1958, and Part VIII of the Human Resources Development Recommendation, 1975, and

Recalling that the Discrimination (Employment and Occupation) Convention, 1958, does not expressly cover distinctions made on the basis of family responsibilities, and considering that supplementary standards are necessary in this respect, and

Noting the terms of the Employment (Women with Family Responsibilities) Recommendation, 1965, and considering the changes which have taken place since its adoption, and

Noting that instruments on equality of opportunity and treatment for men and women have also been adopted by the United Nations and other specialised agencies, and recalling, in particular, the fourteenth paragraph of the Preamble of the United Nations Convention on the Elimination of All Forms of Discrimination against Women, 1979, to the effect that States Parties are aware that a change in the traditional role of men as well as the role of women in society and in the family is needed to achieve full equality between men and women, and

Recognising that the problems of workers with family responsibilities are aspects of wider issues regarding the family and society which should be taken into account in national policies, and

Recognising the need to create effective equality of opportunity and treatment as between men and women workers with family responsibilities and between such workers and other workers, and

Considering that many of the problems facing all workers are aggravated in the case of workers with family responsibilities and recognising the need to improve the conditions of the

* Source: International Labour Organization, http://www.ilo.org/ilolex/
The ILO shall accept no responsibility for any inaccuracy, errors or omissions or for the consequences arising from the use of the Text.

latter both by measures responding to their special needs and by measures designed to improve the conditions of workers in general, and

Having decided upon the adoption of certain proposals with regard to equal opportunities and equal treatment for men and women workers: workers with family responsibilities, which is the fifth item on the agenda of the session, and

Having determined that these proposals shall take the form of a Recommendation,

adopts this twenty-third day of June of the year one thousand nine hundred and eighty-one, the following Recommendation, which may be cited as the Workers with Family Responsibilities Recommendation, 1981:

I. Definition, Scope and Means of Implementation

1. (1) This Recommendation applies to men and women workers with responsibilities in relation to their dependent children, where such responsibilities restrict their possibilities of preparing for, entering, participating in or advancing in economic activity.

(2) The provision of this Recommendation should also be applied to men and women workers with responsibilities in relation to other members of their immediate family who need their care or support, where such responsibilities restrict their possibilities of preparing for, entering, participating or advancing in economic activity.

(3) For the purposes of this Recommendation, the terms dependent child and other member of the immediate family who needs care or support mean persons defined as such in each country by one of the means referred to in Paragraph 3 of this Recommendation.

(4) The workers covered by virtue of subparagraphs (1) and (2) of this Paragraph are hereinafter referred to as workers with family responsibilities.

2. This Recommendation applies to all branches of economic activity and all categories of workers.

3. The provisions of this Recommendation may be applied by laws or regulations, collective agreements, works rules, arbitration awards, court decisions or a combination of these methods, or in any other manner consistent with national practice which may be appropriate, account being taken of national conditions.

4. The provisions of this Recommendation may be applied by stages if necessary, account being taken of national conditions: Provided that such measures of implementation as are taken should apply in any case to all the workers covered by Paragraph 1, subgaragraph (1).

5. Employers' and workers' organisations should have the right to participate, in a manner appropriate to national conditions and practice, in devising and applying measures designed to give effect to the provisions of this Recommendation.

II. National Policy

6. With a view to creating effective equality of opportunity and treatment for men and women workers, each Member should make it an aim of national policy to enable persons with family responsibilities who are engaged or wish to engage in employment to exercise their right to do so without being subject to discrimination and, to the extent possible, without conflict between their employment and family responsibilities.

7. Within the framework of a national policy to promote equality of opportunity and treatment for men and women workers, measures should be adopted and applied with a view to

preventing direct or indirect discrimination on the basis of marital status or family responsibilities.

8. (1) For the purposes of Paragraphs 6 and 7 above, the term discrimination means discrimination in employment and occupation as defined by Articles 1 and 5 of the Discrimination (Employment and Occupation) Convention, 1958.

(2) During a transitional period special measures aimed at achieving effective equality between men and women workers should not be regarded as discriminatory.

9. With a view to creating effective equality of opportunity and treatment for men and women workers, all measures compatible with national conditions and possibilities should be taken–

(a) to enable workers with family responsibilities to exercise their right to vocational training and to free choice of employment;

(b) to take account of their needs in terms and conditions of employment and in social security; and

(c) to develop or promote child-care, family and other community services, public or private, responding to their needs.

10. The competent authorities and bodies in each country should take appropriate measures to promote information and education which engender broader public understanding of the principle of equality of opportunity and treatment for men and women workers and of the problems of workers with family responsibilities, as well as a climate of opinion conducive to overcoming these problems.

11. The competent authorities and bodies in each country should take appropriate measures–

(a) to undertake or promote such research as may be necessary into the various aspects of the employment of workers with family responsibilities with a view to providing objective information on which sound policies and measures may be based; and

(b) to promote such education as will encourage the sharing of family responsibilities between men and women and enable workers with family responsibilities better to meet their employment and family responsibilities.

III. Training and Employment

12. All measures compatible with national conditions and possibilities should be taken to enable workers with family responsibilities to become and remain integrated in the labour force, as well as to re-enter the labour force after an absence due to those responsibilities.

13. In accordance with national policy and practice, vocational training facilities and, where possible, paid educational leave arrangements to use such facilities should be made available to workers with family responsibilities.

14. Such services as may be necessary to enable workers with family responsibilities to enter or re-enter employment should be available, within the framework of existing services for all workers or, in default thereof, along lines appropriate to national conditions; they should include, free of charge to the workers, vocational guidance, counselling, information and placement services which are staffed by suitably trained personnel and are able to respond adequately to the special needs of workers with family responsibilities.

15. Workers with family responsibilities should enjoy equality of opportunity and treatment with other workers in relation to preparation for employment, access to employment, advancement within employment and employment security.

16. Marital status, family situation or family responsibilities should not, as such, constitute valid reasons for refusal or termination of employment.

IV. Terms and Conditions of Employment

17. All measures compatible with national conditions and possibilities and with the legitimate interests of other workers should be taken to ensure that terms and conditions of employment are such as to enable workers with family responsibilities to reconcile their employment and family responsibilities.

18. Particular attention should be given to general measures for improving working conditions and the quality of working life, including measures aiming at–

(a) the progressive reduction of daily hours of work and the reduction of overtime, and

(b) more flexible arrangements as regards working schedules, rest periods and holidays, account being taken of the stage of development and the particular needs of the country and of different sectors of activity.

19. Whenever practicable and appropriate, the special needs of workers, including those arising from family responsibilities, should be taken into account in shift-work arrangements and assignments to night work.

20. Family responsibilities and considerations such as the place of employment of the spouse and the possibilities of educating children should be taken into account when transferring workers from one locality to another.

21. (1) With a view to protecting part-time workers, temporary workers and homeworkers, many of whom have family responsibilities, the terms and conditions on which these types of employment are performed should be adequately regulated and supervised.

(2) The terms and conditions of employment, including social security coverage, of part-time workers and temporary workers should be, to the extent possible, equivalent to those of full-time and permanent workers respectively; in appropriate cases, their entitlement may be calculated on a pro rata basis. (3) Part-time workers should be given the option to obtain or return to full-time employment when a vacancy exists and when the circumstances which determined assignment to part-time employment no longer exist.

22. (1) Either parent should have the possibility, within a period immediately following maternity leave, of obtaining leave of absence (parental leave), without relinquishing employment and with rights resulting from employment being safeguarded.

(2) The length of the period following maternity leave and the duration and conditions of the leave of absence referred to in subparagraph (1) of this Paragraph should be determined in each country by one of the means referred to in Paragraph 3 of this Recommendation.

(3) The leave of absence referred to in subparagraph (1) of this Paragraph may be introduced gradually.

23. (1) It should be possible for a worker, man or woman, with family responsibilities in relation to a dependent child to obtain leave of absence in the case of its illness.

(2) It should be possible for a worker with family responsibilities to obtain leave of absence in the case of the illness of another member of the worker's immediate family who needs that worker's care or support.

(3) The duration and conditions of the leave of absence referred to in subparagraphs (1) and (2) of this Paragraph should be determined in each country by one of the means referred to in Paragraph 3 of this Recommendation.

V. Child-care and Family Services and Facilities

24. With a view to determining the scope and character of the child-care and family services and facilities needed to assist workers with family responsibilities to meet their employment and family responsibilities, the competent authorities should, in co-operation with the public and private organisations concerned, in particular employers' and workers' organisations, and within the scope of their resources for collecting information, take such measures as may be necessary and appropriate–

(a) to collect and publish adequate statistics on the number of workers with family responsibilities engaged in or seeking employment and on the number and age of their children and of other dependants requiring care; and

(b) to ascertain, through systematic surveys conducted more particularly in local communities, the needs and preferences for child-care and family services and facilities.

25. The competent authorities should, in co-operation with the public and private organisations concerned, take appropriate steps to ensure that child-care and family services and facilities meet the needs and preferences so revealed; to this end they should, taking account of national and local circumstances and possibilities, in particular–

(a) encourage and facilitate the establishment, particularly in local communities, of plans for the systematic development of child-care and family services and facilities, and

(b) themselves organise or encourage and facilitate the provision of adequate and appropriate child-care and family services and facilities, free of charge or at a reasonable charge in accordance with the workers' ability to pay, developed along flexible lines and meeting the needs of children of different ages, of other dependants requiring care and of workers with family responsibilities.

26. (1) Child-care and family services and facilities of all types should comply with standards laid down and supervised by the competent authorities.

(2) Such standards should prescribe in particular the equipment and hygienic and technical requirements of the services and facilities provided and the number and qualifications of the staff.

(3) The competent authorities should provide or help to ensure the provision of adequate training at various levels for the personnel needed to staff child-care and family services and facilities.

VI. Social Security

27. Social security benefits, tax relief, or other appropriate measures consistent with national policy should, when necessary, be available to workers with family responsibilities.

28. During the leave of absence referred to in Paragraphs 22 and 23, the workers concerned may, in conformity with national conditions and practice, and by one of the means referred to in Paragraph 3 of this Recommendation, be protected by social security.

29. A worker should not be excluded from social security coverage by reference to the occupational activity of his or her spouse and entitlement to benefits arising from that activity.

30. (1) The family responsibilities of a worker should be an element to be taken into account in determining whether employment offered is suitable in the sense that refusal of the offer may lead to loss or suspension of unemployment benefit.

(2) In particular, where the employment offered involves moving to another locality, the considerations to be taken into account should include the place of employment of the spouse and the possibilities of educating children.

31. In applying Paragraphs 27 to 30 of this Recommendation, a Member whose economy is insufficiently developed may take account of the national resources and social security arrangements available.

VII. Help in Exercise of Family Responsibilities

32. The competent authorities and bodies in each country should promote such public and private action as is possible to lighten the burden deriving from the family responsibilities of workers.

33. All measures compatible with national conditions and possibilities should be taken to develop home-help and home-care services which are adequately regulated and supervised and which can provide workers with family responsibilities, as necessary, with qualified assistance at a reasonable charge in accordance with their ability to pay.

34. Since many measures designed to improve the conditions of workers in general can have a favourable impact on those of workers with family responsibilities, the competent authorities and bodies in each country should promote such public and private action as is possible to make the provision of services in the community, such as public transport, supply of water and energy in or near workers' housing and housing with labour-saving layout, responsive to the needs of workers.

VIII. Effect on Existing Recommendations

35. This Recommendation supersedes the Employment (Women with Family Responsibilities) Recommendation, 1965.

Recommendation No. 166 concerning Termination of Employment at the Initiative of the Employer, 1982*

Adoption: 22 June 1982

The General Conference of the International Labour Organisation,

Having been convened at Geneva by the Governing Body of the International Labour Office, and having met in its Sixty-eighth Session on 2 June 1982, and

Having decided upon the adoption of certain proposals with regard to termination of employment at the initiative of the employer, which is the fifth item on the agenda of the session, and

Having determined that these proposals shall take the form of a Recommendation supplementing the Termination of Employment Convention, 1982;

adopts this twenty-second day of June of the year one thousand nine hundred and eighty-two, the following Recommendation, which may be cited as the Termination of Employment Recommendation, 1982:

I. METHODS OF IMPLEMENTATION, SCOPE AND DEFINITIONS

1.

The provisions of this Recommendation may be applied by national laws or regulations, collective agreements, works rules, arbitration awards or court decisions or in such other manner consistent with national practice as may be appropriate under national conditions.

2.

(1) This Recommendation applies to all branches of economic activity and to all employed persons.

(2) A Member may exclude the following categories of employed persons from all or some of the provisions of this Recommendation:

(a) workers engaged under a contract of employment for a specified period of time or a specified task;

(b) workers serving a period of probation or a qualifying period of employment, determined in advance and of reasonable duration;

(c) workers engaged on a casual basis for a short period.

(3) In so far as necessary, measures may be taken by the competent authority or through the appropriate machinery in a country, after consultation with the organisations of employers and workers concerned, where such exist, to exclude from the application of this Recommendation or certain provisions thereof categories of employed persons whose terms and conditions of employment are governed by special arrangements, which as a whole provide protection that is at least equivalent to the protection afforded under the Recommendation.

(4) In so far as necessary, measures may be taken by the competent authority or through the appropriate machinery in a country, after consultation with the organisations of employers and

* Source: International Labour Organization, http://ilo.org/ilolex/english/
The ILO shall accept no responsibility for any inaccuracy, errors or omissions or for the consequences arising from the use of the Text.

workers concerned, where such exist, to exclude from the application of this Recommendation or certain provisions thereof other limited categories of employed persons in respect of which special problems of a substantial nature arise in the light of the particular conditions of employment of the workers concerned or the size or nature of the undertaking that employs them.

3.

(1) Adequate safeguards should be provided against recourse to contracts of employment for a specified period of time the aim of which is to avoid the protection resulting from the Termination of Employment Convention, 1982, and this Recommendation.

(2) To this end, for example, provision may be made for one or more of the following:

(a) limiting recourse to contracts for a specified period of time to cases in which, owing either to the nature of the work to be effected or to the circumstances under which it is to be effected or to the interests of the worker, the employment relationship cannot be of indeterminate duration;

(b) deeming contracts for a specified period of time, other than in the cases referred to in clause (a) of this subparagraph, to be contracts of employment of indeterminate duration;

(c) deeming contracts for a specified period of time, when renewed on one or more occasions, other than in the cases mentioned in clause (a) of this subparagraph, to be contracts of employment of indeterminate duration.

4.

For the purpose of this Recommendation the terms termination and termination of employment mean termination of employment at the initiative of the employer.

II. STANDARDS OF GENERAL APPLICATION

Justification for Termination

5.

In addition to the grounds referred to in Article 5 of the Termination of Employment Convention, 1982, the following should not constitute valid reasons for termination:

(a) age, subject to national law and practice regarding retirement;

(b) absence from work due to compulsory military service or other civic obligations, in accordance with national law and practice.

6.

(1) Temporary absence from work because of illness or injury should not constitute a valid reason for termination.

(2) The definition of what constitutes temporary absence from work, the extent to which medical certification should be required and possible limitations to the application of subparagraph (1) of this Paragraph should be determined in accordance with the methods of implementation referred to in Paragraph 1 of this Recommendation.

Procedure Prior to or at the Time of Termination

7.

The employment of a worker should not be terminated for misconduct of a kind that under national law or practice would justify termination only if repeated on one or more occasions, unless the employer has given the worker appropriate written warning.

8.

The employment of a worker should not be terminated for unsatisfactory performance, unless the employer has given the worker appropriate instructions and written warning and the worker continues to perform his duties unsatisfactorily after a reasonable period of time for improvement has elapsed.

9.

A worker should be entitled to be assisted by another person when defending himself, in accordance with Article 7 of the Termination of Employment Convention, 1982, against allegations regarding his conduct or performance liable to result in the termination of his employment; this right may be specified by the methods of implementation referred to in Paragraph 1 of this Recommendation.

10.

The employer should be deemed to have waived his right to terminate the employment of a worker for misconduct if he has failed to do so within a reasonable period of time after he has knowledge of the misconduct.

11.

The employer may consult workers' representatives before a final decision is taken on individual cases of termination of employment.

12.

The employer should notify a worker in writing of a decision to terminate his employment.

13.

(1) A worker who has been notified of termination of employment or whose employment has been terminated should be entitled to receive, on request, a written statement from his employer of the reason or reasons for the termination.

(2) Subparagraph (1) of this Paragraph need not be applied in the case of collective termination for the reasons referred to in Articles 13 and 14 of the Termination of Employment Convention, 1982, if the procedure provided for therein is followed.

Procedure of Appeal against Termination

14.

Provision may be made for recourse to a procedure of conciliation before or during appeal proceedings against termination of employment.

15.

Efforts should be made by public authorities, workers' representatives and organisations of workers to ensure that workers are fully informed of the possibilities of appeal at their disposal.

Time Off from Work during the Period of Notice

16.

During the period of notice referred to in Article 11 of the Termination of Employment Convention, 1982, the worker should, for the purpose of seeking other employment, be entitled to a reasonable amount of time off without loss of pay, taken at times that are convenient to both parties.

Certificate of Employment

17.

A worker whose employment has been terminated should be entitled to receive, on request, a certificate from the employer specifying only the dates of his engagement and termination of his employment and the type or types of work on which he was employed; nevertheless, and at the request of the worker, an evaluation of his conduct and performance may be given in this certificate or in a separate certificate.

Severance Allowance and Other Income Protection

18.

(1) A worker whose employment has been terminated should be entitled, in accordance with national law and practice, to-

(a) a severance allowance or other separation benefits, the amount of which should be based, inter alia, on length of service and the level of wages, and paid directly by the employer or by a fund constituted by employers' contributions; or

(b) benefits from unemployment insurance or assistance or other forms of social security, such as old-age or invalidity benefits, under the normal conditions to which such benefits are subject; or

(c) a combination of such allowance and benefits.

(2) A worker who does not fulfil the qualifying conditions for unemployment insurance or assistance under a scheme of general scope need not be paid any allowance or benefit referred to in subparagraph (1) (a) of this Paragraph solely because he is not receiving an unemployment benefit under subparagraph (1) (b).

(3) Provision may be made by the methods of implementation referred to in Paragraph 1 of this Recommendation for loss of entitlement to the allowance or benefits referred to in subparagraph (1) (a) of this Paragraph in the event of termination for serious misconduct.

III. SUPPLEMENTARY PROVISIONS CONCERNING TERMINATIONS OF EMPLOYMENT FOR ECONOMIC, TECHNOLOGICAL, STRUCTURAL OR SIMILAR REASONS

19.

(1) All parties concerned should seek to avert or minimise as far as possible termination of employment for reasons of an economic, technological, structural or similar nature, without prejudice to the efficient operation of the undertaking, establishment or service, and to mitigate the adverse effects of any termination of employment for these reasons on the worker or workers concerned.

(2) Where appropriate, the competent authority should assist the parties in seeking solutions to the problems raised by the terminations contemplated.

Consultations on Major Changes in the Undertaking

20.

(1) When the employer contemplates the introduction of major changes in production, programme, organisation, structure or technology that are likely to entail terminations, the employer should consult the workers' representatives concerned as early as possible on, inter alia, the introduction of such changes, the effects they are likely to have and the measures for averting or mitigating the adverse effects of such changes.

(2) To enable the workers' representatives concerned to participate effectively in the consultations referred to in subparagraph (1) of this Paragraph, the employer should supply them in good time with all relevant information on the major changes contemplated and the effects they are likely to have.

(3) For the purposes of this Paragraph the term the workers' representatives concerned means the workers' representatives recognised as such by national law or practice, in conformity with the Workers' Representatives Convention, 1971.

Measures to Avert or Minimise Termination

21.

The measures which should be considered with a view to averting or minimising terminations of employment for reasons of an economic, technological, structural or similar nature might include, inter alia, restriction of hiring, spreading the workforce reduction over a certain period of time to permit natural reduction of the workforce, internal transfers, training and retraining, voluntary early retirement with appropriate income protection, restriction of overtime and reduction of normal hours of work.

22.

Where it is considered that a temporary reduction of normal hours of work would be likely to avert or minimise terminations of employment due to temporary economic difficulties, consideration should be given to partial compensation for loss of wages for the normal hours not worked, financed by methods appropriate under national law and practice.

Criteria for Selection for Termination

23.

(1) The selection by the employer of workers whose employment is to be terminated for reasons of an economic, technological, structural or similar nature should be made according to criteria,

established wherever possible in advance, which give due weight both to the interests of the undertaking, establishment or service and to the interests of the workers.

(2) These criteria, their order of priority and their relative weight, should be determined by the methods of implementation referred to in Paragraph 1 of this Recommendation.

Priority of Rehiring

24.

(1) Workers whose employment has been terminated for reasons of an economic, technological, structural or similar nature, should be given a certain priority of rehiring if the employer again hires workers with comparable qualifications, subject to their having, within a given period from the time of their leaving, expressed a desire to be rehired.

(2) Such priority of rehiring may be limited to a specified period of time.

(3) The criteria for the priority of rehiring, the question of retention of rights-particularly seniority rights-in the event of rehiring, as well as the terms governing the wages of rehired workers, should be determined according to the methods of implementation referred to in Paragraph 1 of this Recommendation.

Mitigating the Effects of Termination

25.

(1) In the event of termination of employment for reasons of an economic, technological, structural or similar nature, the placement of the workers affected in suitable alternative employment as soon as possible, with training or retraining where appropriate, should be promoted by measures suitable to national circumstances, to be taken by the competent authority, where possible with the collaboration of the employer and the workers' representatives concerned.

(2) Where possible, the employer should assist the workers affected in the search for suitable alternative employment, for example through direct contacts with other employers.

(3) In assisting the workers affected in obtaining suitable alternative employment or training or retraining, regard may be had to the Human Resources Development Convention and Recommendation, 1975.

26.

(1) With a view to mitigating the adverse effects of termination of employment for reasons of an economic, technological, structural or similar nature, consideration should be given to providing income protection during any course of training or retraining and partial or total reimbursement of expenses connected with training or retraining and with finding and taking up employment which requires a change of residence.

(2) The competent authority should consider providing financial resources to support in full or in part the measures referred to in subparagraph (1) of this Paragraph, in accordance with national law and practice.

IV. EFFECT ON EARLIER RECOMMENDATION

27.

This Recommendation and the Termination of Employment Convention, 1982, supersede the Termination of Employment Recommendation, 1963.

Recommendation No. 169 concerning Employment Policy, 1984 (Supplementary Provisions)*

Adoption: 26 June 1984

The General Conference of the International Labour Organisation,

Having been convened at Geneva by the Governing Body of the International Labour Office, and having met in its Seventieth Session on 6 June 1984, and

Noting the existing international standards contained in the Employment Policy Convention and Recommendation, 1964, as well as in other international labour instruments relating to certain categories of workers, in particular the Workers with Family Responsibilities Convention and Recommendation, 1981, the Older Workers Recommendation, 1980, the Migration for Employment Convention and Recommendation (Revised), 1949, the Migrant Workers (Supplementary Provisions) Convention, 1975, and the Migrant Workers Recommendation, 1975,

Recalling the responsibility of the International Labour Organisation, resulting from the Declaration of Philadelphia, to examine and consider the bearing of economic and financial policies upon employment policy in the light of the fundamental objective that all human beings, irrespective of race, creed or sex, have the right to pursue both their material well-being and their spiritual development in conditions of freedom and dignity, of economic security and equal opportunity,

Recalling that the International Covenant on Economic, Social and Cultural Rights, adopted by the United Nations General Assembly in 1966, provides for the recognition of inter alia the right to work, which includes the right of everyone to the opportunity to gain his living by work which he freely chooses or accepts, and for the taking of appropriate steps to achieve progressively the full realisation of, and to safeguard, this right,

Recalling also the provisions of the Convention on the Elimination of All Forms of Discrimination against Women, adopted by the United Nations General Assembly in 1979,

Recognising, in the light of increasing interdependence within the world economy and of low economic growth rates in recent years, the need to coordinate economic, monetary and social policies at the national and international levels, to strive for the reduction of disparities between developed and developing countries and for the establishment of the new international economic order, in order to make the fullest possible use of resources for development and for the creation of employment opportunities, and thus to combat unemployment and underemployment,

Noting the deterioration of employment opportunities in most industrialised and developing countries and expressing the conviction that poverty, unemployment and inequality of opportunity are unacceptable in terms of humanity and social justice, can provoke social tension and thus create conditions which can endanger peace and prejudice the exercise of the right to work, which includes free choice of employment, just and favourable conditions of work and protection against unemployment,

---

* Source: International Labour Organization, http://ilo.org/ilolex/english/
The ILO shall accept no responsibility for any inaccuracy, errors or omissions or for the consequences arising from the use of the Text.

Considering that the Employment Policy Convention and Recommendation, 1964, should be placed in the wider framework of the Declaration of Principles and Programme of Action adopted in 1976 by the Tripartite World Conference on Employment, Income Distribution and Social Progress and the International Division of Labour, and of the resolution concerning follow-up to the World Employment Conference adopted by the International Labour Conference in 1979,

Having decided upon the adoption of certain proposals with regard to employment policy which is the fourth item on the agenda of the session, and

Having determined that these proposals shall take the form of a Recommendation supplementing the Employment Policy Convention and Recommendation, 1964:

adopts this twenty-sixth day of June of the year one thousand nine hundred and eighty-four, the following Recommendation, which may be cited as the Employment Policy (Supplementary Provisions) Recommendation, 1984.

I. General Principles of Employment Policy

1.

The promotion of full, productive and freely chosen employment provided for in the Employment Policy Convention and Recommendation, 1964, should be regarded as the means of achieving in practice the realisation of the right to work.

2.

Full recognition by Members of the right to work should be linked with the implementation of economic and social policies, the purpose of which is the promotion of full, productive and freely chosen employment.

3.

The promotion of full, productive and freely chosen employment should be the priority in, and an integral part of, economic and social policies of Members and, where appropriate, their plans for the satisfaction of the basic needs of the population.

4.

Members should give special attention to the most efficient means of increasing employment and production and draw up policies and, if appropriate, programmes designed to facilitate the increased production and fair distribution of essential goods and services and the fair distribution of income throughout the country, with a view to satisfying the basic needs of the population in accordance with the Declaration of Principles and Programme of Action of the World Employment Conference.

5.

In accordance with national practice, the policies, plans and programmes referred to in Paragraphs 3 and 4 of this Recommendation should be drawn up and implemented in consultation and co-operation with the organisations of employers and workers and other organisations representative of the persons concerned, particularly those in the rural sector covered by the Rural Workers' Organisations Convention and Recommendation, 1975.

6.

Economic and financial policies, at both the national and international levels, should reflect the priority to be attached to the goals referred to in Paragraphs 3 and 4 of this Recommendation.

7.

The policies, plans and programmes referred to in Paragraphs 3 and 4 of this Recommendation should aim at eliminating any discrimination and ensuring for all workers equal opportunity and treatment in respect of access to employment, conditions of employment, wages and income, vocational guidance and training and career development.

8.

Members should take measures to combat effectively illegal employment, that is employment which does not comply with the requirements of national laws, regulations and practice.

9.

Members should take measures to enable the progressive transfer of workers from the informal sector, where it exists, to the formal sector to take place.

10.

Members should adopt policies and take measures which, while taking account of national law and practice, should-

(a) facilitate adjustment to structural change at the global, sectoral and enterprise levels and the re-employment of workers who have lost their jobs as a result of structural and technological changes; and

(b) safeguard the employment or facilitate the re-employment of workers affected in the case of sale, transfer, closure or relocation of a company, establishment or equipment.

11.

In accordance with national law and practice, the methods of giving effect to employment policies might include negotiating collective agreements on questions having a bearing on employment such as-

(a) the promotion and safeguarding of employment;

(b) the economic and social consequences of restructuring and rationalisation of branches of economic activity and undertakings;

(c) the reorganisation and reduction of working time;

(d) the protection of particular groups; and

(e) information on economic, financial and employment issues.

12.

Members should, after consultation with the organisations of employers and workers, take effective measures to encourage multinational enterprises to undertake and promote in particular the employment policies set forth in the Tripartite Declaration of Principles concerning Multinational Enterprises and Social Policy, 1977, and to ensure that negative effects of the investments of multinational enterprises on employment are avoided and that positive effects are encouraged.

13.

In view of increasing interdependence within the world economy, Members should, in addition to the measures taken at the national level, strengthen international co-operation in order to ensure the success of the fight against unemployment.

II. Population Policy

14.

(1) While ensuring that sufficient employment opportunities exist, development and employment policies might, where appropriate and in accordance with national law and practice, include population policies and programmes designed to ensure promotion of family welfare and family planning through programmes of information and voluntary education on population issues.

(2) Members, particularly developing countries, in collaboration with both national and international non-governmental organisations might-

(a) pay particular attention in their population policies and programmes to educating actual and potential parents on the benefits of family planning;

(b) in rural areas, increase the number of health facilities and community centres offering family planning services and the number of trained personnel to provide these services; and

(c) in urban areas, pay particular attention to the urgent need to develop appropriate infrastructures and improve living conditions, especially in slum areas.

III. Employment of Youth and Disadvantaged Groups and Persons

15.

In the context of an overall employment policy, Members should adopt measures to respond to the needs of all categories of persons frequently having difficulties in finding lasting employment, such as certain women, certain young workers, disabled persons, older workers, the long-term unemployed and migrant workers lawfully within their territory. These measures should be consistent with the provisions of international labour Conventions and Recommendations relating to the employment of these groups and with the conditions of employment established under national law and practice.

16.

While taking account of national conditions and in accordance with national law and practice, the measures referred to in Paragraph 15 of this Recommendation might include, inter alia-

(a) general education accessible to all and vocational guidance and training programmes to assist these persons to find work and to improve their employment opportunities and their income;

(b) the creation of a training system linked with both the educational system and the world of work;

(c) counselling and employment services to assist individuals to enter the labour market and to help them to find employment which corresponds to their skills and aptitudes;

(d) programmes which create gainful employment in specific regions, areas or sectors;

(e) programmes of adjustment to structural change;

(f) measures of continuing training and retraining;

(g) measures of vocational rehabilitation;

(h) assistance for voluntary mobility; and

(i) programmes for the promotion of self-employment and workers' co-operatives.

17.

(1) Other special measures should be taken for young people. In particular-

(a) public and private institutions and undertakings should be encouraged to engage and to train young people by means appropriate to national conditions and practice;

(b) although priority should be given to integrating young persons into regular employment, special programmes might be set up with a view to employing young people on a voluntary basis for the execution of community projects, in particular local projects having a social character, bearing in mind the provisions of the Special Youth Schemes Recommendation, 1970;

(c) special programmes should be set up in which training and work alternate so as to assist young people in finding their first job;

(d) training opportunities should be adapted to technical and economic development and the quality of training should be improved;

(e) measures should be taken to ease the transition from school to work and to promote opportunities for employment on completion of training;

(f) research on employment prospects should be promoted as a basis for a rational vocational training policy; and

(g) the safety and health of young workers should be protected.

(2) The measures referred to in subparagraph (1) of this Paragraph should be carefully monitored to ensure that they result in beneficial effects on young people's employment.

(3) These measures should be consistent with the provisions of international labour Conventions and Recommendations relating to the employment of young persons and with the conditions of employment established under national law and practice.

18.

Incentives appropriate to national conditions and practice might be provided in order to facilitate the implementation of the measures referred to in Paragraphs 15 to 17 of this Recommendation.

19.

In accordance with national law and practice, full and timely consultations should be held on the formulation, application and monitoring of the measures and programmes referred to in Paragraphs 15 to 18 of this Recommendation between the competent authorities and the organisations of employers and workers and other organisations concerned.

IV. Technology Policies

20.

One of the major elements of national development policy should be to facilitate the development of technology as a means of increasing productive potential and achieving the major development objectives of creation of employment opportunities and the satisfaction of basic needs. Technology policies should, taking into account the stage of economic development, contribute to the improvement of working conditions and reduction of working time, and include measures to prevent loss of jobs.

21.

Members should-

(a) encourage research on the selection, adoption and development of new technologies and on their effects on the volume and structure of employment, conditions of employment, training, job content and skill requirements; and

(b) encourage research on the technologies most appropriate to the specific conditions of countries, by ensuring the involvement of independent research institutes.

22.

Members should endeavour to ensure by appropriate measures-

(a) that the education and training systems, including schemes for retraining, offer workers sufficient opportunities for adjusting to altered employment requirements resulting from technological change;

(b) that particular attention is given to the best possible use of existing and future skills; and

(c) that negative effects of technological changes on employment, working and living conditions and on occupational safety and health are eliminated to the extent possible, in particular through the incorporation of ergonomic, safety and health considerations at the design stage of new technologies.

23.

Members should, through all methods suited to national conditions and practice, promote the use of appropriate new technologies and assure or improve liaison and consultation between the different units and organisations concerned with these questions and the representative organisations of employers and workers.

24.

The organisations of employers and workers concerned and undertakings should be encouraged to assist in the dissemination of general information on technological choices, in the promotion of technological linkages between large-scale and small-scale undertakings and in the setting up of relevant training programmes.

25.

In accordance with national practice, Members should encourage employers' and workers' organisations to enter into collective agreements at national, sectoral or undertaking levels on the social consequences of the introduction of new technologies.

26.

Members should, as far as possible and in accordance with national law and practice, encourage undertakings, when introducing into their operations technological changes which are liable to have major effects upon workers in the undertaking-

(a) to associate workers and/or their representatives in the planning, introduction and use of new technologies, that is to inform them of the opportunities offered by and the effects of such new technologies and to consult them in advance with a view to arriving at agreements;

(b) to promote a better organisation of working time and a better distribution of employment;

(c) to prevent and mitigate to the greatest extent practicable any adverse effects of the technological changes on workers; and

(d) to promote investments in technology that would encourage, directly or indirectly, the creation of employment and contribute to a progressive increase in production and the satisfaction of the basic needs of the population.

V. Informal Sector

27.

(1) National employment policy should recognise the importance as a provider of jobs of the informal sector, that is economic activities which are carried on outside the institutionalised economic structures.

(2) Employment promotion programmes should be elaborated and implemented to encourage family work and independent work in individual workshops, both in urban and rural areas.

28.

Members should take measures to promote complementary relationships between the formal and informal sectors and to provide greater access of undertakings in the informal sector to resources, product markets, credit, infrastructure, training facilities, technical expertise and improved technologies.

29.

(1) While taking measures to increase employment opportunities and improve conditions of work in the informal sector, Members should seek to facilitate its progressive integration into the national economy.

(2) Members should take into account that integration of the informal sector into the formal sector may reduce its ability to absorb labour and generate income. Nevertheless, they should seek progressively to extend measures of regulation to the informal sector.

VI. Small Undertakings

30.

National employment policy should take account of the importance of small undertakings as providers of jobs, and recognise the contribution of local employment creation initiatives to the fight against unemployment and to economic growth. These undertakings, which can take diverse forms, such as small traditional undertakings, co-operatives and associations, offer employment opportunities, especially for workers who have particular difficulties.

31.

After consultation and in co-operation with employers' and workers' organisations, Members should take the necessary measures to promote complementary relationships between the undertakings referred to in Paragraph 30 of this Recommendation and other undertakings, to improve working conditions in these undertakings, and to improve their access to product markets, credit, technical expertise and advanced technology.

VII. Regional Development Policies

32.

In accordance with national law and practice, Members should recognise the importance of balanced regional development as a means of mitigating the social and employment problems created by the unequal distribution of natural resources and the inadequate mobility of the means of production, and of correcting the uneven spread of growth and employment between regions and areas within a country.

33.

Measures should be taken, after consultation and in co-operation with the representatives of the populations concerned and in particular with the organisations of employers and workers, with a view to promoting employment in underdeveloped or backward areas, declining industrial and agricultural areas, frontier zones and, in general, parts of the country which have not benefited satisfactorily from national development.

34.

Taking account of national conditions and of each Member's plans and programmes, the measures referred to in Paragraph 33 of this Recommendation might include, inter alia-

(a) creating and developing growth poles and growth centres with good prospects for generating employment;

(b) developing and intensifying regional potential taking into account the human and natural resources of each region and the need for coherent and balanced regional development;

(c) expanding the number and size of medium-sized and small towns in order to counterbalance the growth of large cities;

(d) improving the availability and distribution of and access to essential services required for meeting basic needs;

(e) encouraging the voluntary mobility of workers within each region and between different regions of the country by appropriate social welfare measures, while making an effort to promote satisfactory living and working conditions in their areas of origin;

(f) investing in improvements to the regional infrastructures, services and administrative structures, including the allocation of the necessary staff and the provision of training and retraining opportunities; and

(g) promoting the participation of the community in the definition and implementation of regional development measures.

VIII. Public Investment and Special Public Works Programmes

35.

Members might implement economically and socially viable public investment and special public works programmes, particularly with a view to creating and maintaining employment and raising incomes, reducing poverty and better meeting basic needs in areas of widespread unemployment and underemployment. Such programmes should, where possible and appropriate-

(a) pay special attention to the creation of employment opportunities for disadvantaged groups;

(b) include rural and urban infrastructure projects as well as the construction of facilities for basic-needs satisfaction in rural, urban and suburban areas, and increased productive investments in sectors such as energy and telecommunications;

(c) contribute to raising the standard of social services in fields such as education and health;

(d) be designed and implemented within the framework of development plans where they exist and in consultation with the organisations of employers and workers concerned;

(e) identify the persons whom the programmes are to benefit, determine the available manpower and define the criteria for project selection;

(f) ensure that workers are recruited on a voluntary basis;

(g) ensure that manpower is not diverted from other productive activities;

(h) provide conditions of employment consistent with national law and practice, and in particular with legal provisions governing access to employment, hours of work, remuneration, holidays with pay, occupational safety and health and compensation for employment injuries; and

(i) facilitate the vocational training of workers engaged in such programmes as well as the retraining of those who, because of structural changes in production and employment, have to change their jobs.

IX. International Economic Co-Operation and Employment

36.

Members should promote the expansion of international trade in order to help one another to attain employment growth. To this end, they should co-operate in international bodies which are engaged in facilitating sustainable and mutually beneficial increases in international trade, technical assistance and investment.

37.

Bearing in mind their responsibilities in relation to other competent international bodies Members should, with a view to ensuring the effectiveness of employment policies, adopt the following objectives:

(a) to promote the growth of production and world trade in conditions of economic stability and growing employment, within the context of international co-operation for development and on the basis of equality of rights and mutual advantage;

(b) to recognise that the interdependence between States, resulting from the increasing integration of the world economy, should help to create a climate in which States can, wherever appropriate, define joint policies designed to promote a fair distribution of the social costs and benefits of structural adjustment as well as a fairer international distribution of income and wealth, in such a way as to enable developing countries to absorb the increase in their labour force, and the developed countries to raise their levels of employment and reduce the adjustment cost for the workers concerned;

(c) to co-ordinate national policies concerning trade and structural change and adjustment so as to make possible a greater participation of developing countries in world industrial production within an open and fair world trading system, to stabilise commodity prices at remunerative levels which are acceptable to both producers and consumers, and to encourage investment in the production and processing of commodities in developing countries;

(d) to encourage the peaceful resolution of disputes among nations and negotiated arms reduction agreements which will achieve security for all nations, as well as the progressive transfer of expenditure on armaments and the reconversion of the armaments industry to the production of essential goods and services, especially those which satisfy the basic needs of the population and the needs of developing countries;

(e) to seek agreement on concerted action at the international level with a view to improving the international economic system, especially in the financial sphere, so as to promote employment in developed as well as developing countries;

(f) to increase mutual economic and technical co-operation, especially between countries at different levels of economic development and with different social and economic systems, through exchange of experience and the development of complementary capacities, particularly in the fields of employment and human resources and the choice, development and transfer of technology in accordance with mutually accepted law and practice concerning private property rights;

(g) to create conditions for sustained, non-inflationary growth of the world economy, and for the establishment of an improved international monetary system which would lead to the establishment of the new international economic order; and

(h) to ensure greater stability in exchange rates, a reduction of the debt burden of developing countries, the provision of long-term, low-cost financial assistance to developing countries and the adoption of adjustment policies which promote employment and the satisfaction of basic needs.

38.

Members should-

(a) promote the transfer of technologies with a view to enabling developing countries to adopt, on fair and reasonable commercial terms, those which are most appropriate for the promotion of employment and the satisfaction of basic needs; and

(b) take appropriate measures for the creation and maintenance of employment and for the provision of training and retraining opportunities. Such measures might include the establishment of national, regional or international readjustment funds for the purpose of assisting in the positive adjustment of industries and workers affected by changes in the world economy.

X. International Migration and Employment

39.

Members, taking account of international labour Conventions and Recommendations on migrant workers, should, where international migration takes place, adopt policies designed-

(a) to create more employment opportunities and better conditions of work in countries of emigration so as to reduce the need to migrate to find employment; and

(b) to ensure that international migration takes place under conditions designed to promote full, productive and freely chosen employment.

40.

Members which habitually or repeatedly admit significant numbers of foreign workers with a view to employment should, when such workers come from developing countries, endeavour to co-operate more fully in the development of such countries, by appropriate intensified capital movements, the expansion of trade, the transfer of technical knowledge and assistance in the vocational training of local workers, in order to establish an effective alternative to migration for employment and to assist the countries in question in improving their economic and employment situation.

41.

Members which habitually or repeatedly experience significant outflows of their nationals for the purpose of employment abroad should, provided that such measures are not inconsistent with the right of everyone to leave any country including his own, take measures by means of legislation, agreements with employers' and workers' organisations, or in any other manner consistent with national conditions and practice, to prevent malpractices at the stage of recruitment or departure liable to result in illegal entry to, or stay or employment in, another country.

42.

Developing emigration countries, in order to facilitate the voluntary return of their nationals who possess scarce skills, should-

(a) provide the necessary incentives; and

(b) enlist the co-operation of the countries employing their nationals as well as of the International Labour Office and other international or regional bodies concerned with the matter.

43.

Members, both countries of employment and countries of origin, should take appropriate measures to-

(a) prevent abuse in the recruitment of labour for work abroad;

(b) prevent the exploitation of migrant workers; and

(c) ensure the full exercise of the rights to freedom of association and to organise and bargain collectively.

44.

Members, both countries of employment and countries of origin, should, when it is necessary, taking fully into account existing international labour Conventions and Recommendations on migrant workers, conclude bilateral and multilateral agreements covering issues such as right of entry and stay, the protection of rights resulting from employment, the promotion of education and training opportunities for migrant workers, social security, and assistance to workers and members of their families wishing to return to their country of origin.

2.5 International Standards Relating to Social Security

Convention No. 102 concerning Minimum Standards of Social Security, 1952* [excerpts]

Adoption: 28 June 1952
Entry into force: 27 April 1955
Parties: 42 (Status as of 1 April 2007)

ALBANIA 18 Jan 2006 (II-VI, VIII-X), AUSTRIA 4 Nov 1969 (II, IV, V, VII, VIII), BARBADOS 11 July 1972 (III, V, VI, IX, X), BELGIUM 26 Nov 1959 (II-V, VII-X), BOLIVIA 31 Jan 1977 (II, III, V-X), BOSNIA AND HERZEGOVINA 2 June 1993 (II-VI, VIII, X), DEMOCRATIC REPUBLIC OF CONGO 3 Apr 1987 (V, VII, IX, X), COSTA RICA 16 Mar 1972 (II, V-X), CROATIA 8 Oct 1991 (II-VI, VII, X), CYPRUS 3 Sep 1991 (III, IV, V, VI, IX, X), CZECH REPUBLIC 1 Jan 1993 (II, III, V, VII-X), DENMARK 15 Aug 1955 (II, IV-VI, IX), ECUADOR 25 Oct 1974 (III, V, VI, IX, X), FRANCE 14 June 1974 (II, IV-X), GERMANY 21 Feb 1958 (II-X), GREECE 16 June 1955 (II-Vi, VIII-X), ICELAND 20 Feb 1961 (V, VII, IX), IRELAND 17 June 1968 (III, IV, X), ISRAEL 16 Dec 1955 (V, VI, X), ITALY 8 June 1956 (V, VII, VIII), JAPAN 2 Feb 1976 (III-VI), LIBYAN ARAB JAMAHIRIYA 16 June 1975 (II-X), LUXEMBOURG 31 Aug 1964 (II-X), THE FORMER YOUGOSLAV REPUBLIC OF MACEDONIA 17 Nov 1991 (II-VI, VII, X), MAURITANIA 15 July 1968 (V-VIII, IX, X), MEXICO 12 Oct 1961 (II, III, V, VI, VIII-X), NETHERLANDS 11 Oct 1962 (II, IV, V, VII-X), NIGER 9 Aug 1966 (V-VIII), NORWAY 30 Sep 1954 (II-VII), PERU 23 Aug 1961 (II, III, V, VII, IX), POLAND 3 Dec 2003 (II, V, VII, VIII, IX), PORTUGAL 17 Mar 1994 (II-X), REPUBLIC OF SERBIA 24 Nov 2000 (II-VI, VIII, X), SENEGAL 22 Oct 1962 (VI-VIII), SLOVAKIA 1 Jan 1993 (II, III, V, VII-X), SLOVENIA 29 May 1992 (II-VI, VIII, X), SPAIN 29 June 1988 (II-IV, VI), SWEDEN 12 Aug 1953 (II-IV, VI-VIII), SWITZERLAND 18 Oct 1977 (V-VII, IX, X), TURKEY 29 Jan 1975 (II, III, V, VI, VIII-X), UNITED KINGDOM 27 Apr 1954 (II-V, VII, X), BOLIVARIAN REPUBLIC OF VENEZUELA 5 Nov 1982 (II, III, V, VI, VIII, X).**

The General Conference of the International Labour Organisation,

Having been convened at Geneva by the Governing Body of the International Labour Office, and having met in its Thirty-fifth Session on 4 June 1952, and

Having decided upon the adoption of certain proposals with regard to minimum standards of social security, which are included in the fifth item on the agenda of the session, and

Having determined that these proposals shall take the form of an international Convention,

adopts this twenty-eighth day of June of the year one thousand nine hundred and fifty-two the following Convention, which may be cited as the Social Security (Minimum Standards) Convention, 1952:

[...]

---

* Source: International Labour Organization, http://www.ilo.org/ilolex
The ILO shall accept no responsibility for any inaccuracy, errors or omissions or for the consequences arising from the use of the Text.

** The ratification information provided in brackets refers to relevant parts of the Convention by which the State Parties declared to be bound (obligatory declaration).

PART II. MEDICAL CARE

Article 7

Each Member for which this Part of this Convention is in force shall secure to the persons protected the provision of benefit in respect of a condition requiring medical care of a preventive or curative nature in accordance with the following Articles of this Part.

Article 8

The contingencies covered shall include any morbid condition, whatever its cause, and pregnancy and confinement and their consequences.

Article 9

The persons protected shall comprise–

(a) prescribed classes of employees, constituting not less than 50 per cent. of all employees, and also their wives and children; or

(b) prescribed classes of economically active population, constituting not less than 20 per cent. of all residents, and also their wives and children; or

(c) prescribed classes of residents, constituting not less than 50 per cent. of all residents; or

(d) where a declaration made in virtue of Article 3 is in force, prescribed classes of employees constituting not less than 50 per cent. of all employees in industrial workplaces employing 20 persons or more, and also their wives and children.

Article 10

1. The benefit shall include at least–

(a) in case of a morbid condition–

(i) general practitioner care, including domiciliary visiting;

(ii) specialist care at hospitals for in-patients and out-patients, and such specialist care as may be available outside hospitals;

(iii) the essential pharmaceutical supplies as prescribed by medical or other qualified practitioners; and

(iv) hospitalisation where necessary; and

(b) in case of pregnancy and confinement and their consequences–

(i) pre-natal, confinement and post-natal care either by medical practitioners or by qualified midwives; and

(ii) hospitalisation where necessary.

2. The beneficiary or his breadwinner may be required to share in the cost of the medical care the beneficiary receives in respect of a morbid condition; the rules concerning such cost-sharing shall be so designed as to avoid hardship.

3. The benefit provided in accordance with this Article shall be afforded with a view to maintaining, restoring or improving the health of the person protected and his ability to work and to attend to his personal needs.

4. The institutions or Government departments administering the benefit shall, by such means as may be deemed appropriate, encourage the persons protected to avail themselves of the general health services placed at their disposal by the public authorities or by other bodies recognised by the public authorities.

Article 11

The benefit specified in Article 10 shall, in a contingency covered, be secured at least to a person protected who has completed, or whose breadwinner has completed, such qualifying period as may be considered necessary to preclude abuse.

Article 12

1. The benefit specified in Article 10 shall be granted throughout the contingency covered, except that, in case of a morbid condition, its duration may be limited to 26 weeks in each case, but benefit shall not be suspended while a sickness benefit continues to be paid, and provision shall be made to enable the limit to be extended for prescribed diseases recognised as entailing prolonged care.

2. Where a declaration made in virtue of Article 3 is in force, the duration of the benefit may be limited to 13 weeks in each case.

PART III. SICKNESS BENEFIT

Article 13

Each Member for which this Part of this Convention is in force shall secure to the persons protected the provision of sickness benefit in accordance with the following Articles of this Part.

Article 14

The contingency covered shall include incapacity for work resulting from a morbid condition and involving suspension of earnings, as defined by national laws or regulations.

Article 15

The persons protected shall comprise–

(a) prescribed classes of employees, constituting not less than 50 per cent. of all employees; or

(b) prescribed classes of the economically active population, constituting not less than 20 per cent. of all residents; or

(c) all residents whose means during the contingency do not exceed limits prescribed in such a manner as to comply with the requirements of Article 67; or

(d) where a declaration made in virtue of Article 3 is in force, prescribed classes of employees, constituting not less than 50 per cent. of all employees in industrial workplaces employing 20 persons or more.

Article 16

1. Where classes of employees or classes of the economically active population are protected, the benefit shall be a periodical payment calculated in such a manner as to comply either with the requirements of Article 65 or with the requirements of Article 66.

2. Where all residents whose means during the contingency do not exceed prescribed limits are protected, the benefit shall be a periodical payment calculated in such a manner as to comply with the requirements of Article 67.

Article 17

The benefit specified in Article 16 shall, in a contingency covered, be secured at least to a person protected who has completed such qualifying period as may be considered necessary to preclude abuse.

Article 18

1. The benefit specified in Article 16 shall be granted throughout the contingency, except that the benefit may be limited to 26 weeks in each case of sickness, in which event it need not be paid for the first three days of suspension of earnings.

2. Where a declaration made in virtue of Article 3 is in force, the duration of the benefit may be limited–

(a) to such period that the total number of days for which the sickness benefit is granted in any year is not less than ten times the average number of persons protected in that year; or

(b) to 13 weeks in each case of sickness, in which event it need not be paid for the first three days of suspension of earnings.

PART IV. UNEMPLOYMENT BENEFIT

Article 19

Each Member for which this Part of this Convention is in force shall secure to the persons protected the provision of unemployment benefit in accordance with the following Articles of this Part.

Article 20

The contingency covered shall include suspension of earnings, as defined by national laws or regulations, due to inability to obtain suitable employment in the case of a person protected who is capable of, and available for, work.

Article 21

The persons protected shall comprise–

(a) prescribed classes of employees, constituting not less than 50 per cent. of all employees; or

(b) all residents whose means during the contingency do not exceed limits prescribed in such a manner as to comply with the requirements of Article 67; or

(c) where a declaration made in virtue of Article 3 is in force, prescribed classes of employees, constituting not less than 50 per cent. of all employees in industrial workplaces employing 20 persons or more.

Article 22

1. Where classes of employees are protected, the benefit shall be a periodical payment calculated in such manner as to comply either with the requirements of Article 65 or with the requirements of Article 66.

2. Where all residents whose means during the contingency do not exceed prescribed limits are protected, the benefit shall be a periodical payment calculated in such a manner as to comply with the requirements of Article 67.

Article 23

The benefit specified in Article 22 shall, in a contingency covered, be secured at least to a person protected who has completed such qualifying period as may be considered necessary to preclude abuse.

Article 24

1. The benefit specified in Article 22 shall be granted throughout the contingency, except that its duration may be limited–

(a) where classes of employees are protected, to 13 weeks within a period of 12 months, or

(b) where all residents whose means during the contingency do not exceed prescribed limits are protected, to 26 weeks within a period of 12 months.

2. Where national laws or regulations provide that the duration of the benefit shall vary with the length of the contribution period and/or the benefit previously received within a prescribed period, the provisions of subparagraph (a) of paragraph 1 shall be deemed to be fulfilled if the average duration of benefit is at least 13 weeks within a period of 12 months.

3. The benefit need not be paid for a waiting period of the first seven days in each case of suspension of earnings, counting days of unemployment before and after temporary employment lasting not more than a prescribed period as part of the same case of suspension of earnings.

4. In the case of seasonal workers the duration of the benefit and the waiting period may be adapted to their conditions of employment.

PART V. OLD-AGE BENEFIT

Article 25

Each Member for which this Part of this Convention is in force shall secure to the persons protected the provision of old-age benefit in accordance with the following Articles of this Part.

Article 26

1. The contingency covered shall be survival beyond a prescribed age.

2. The prescribed age shall be not more than 65 years or such higher age as may be fixed by the competent authority with due regard to the working ability of elderly persons in the country concerned.

3. National laws or regulations may provide that the benefit of a person otherwise entitled to it may be suspended if such person is engaged in any prescribed gainful activity or that the benefit, if contributory, may be reduced where the earnings of the beneficiary exceed a prescribed

amount and, if non-contributory, may be reduced where the earnings of the beneficiary or his other means or the two taken together exceed a prescribed amount.

Article 27

The persons protected shall comprise–

(a) prescribed classes of employees, constituting not less than 50 per cent. of all employees; or

(b) prescribed classes of the economically active population, constituting not less than 20 per cent. of all residents; or

(c) all residents whose means during the contingency do not exceed limits prescribed in such a manner as to comply with the requirements of Article 67; or

(d) where a declaration made in virtue of Article 3 is in force, prescribed classes of employees, constituting not less than 50 per cent. of all employees in industrial workplaces employing 20 persons or more.

Article 28

The benefit shall be a periodical payment calculated as follows:

(a) where classes of employees or classes of the economically active population are protected, in such a manner as to comply either with the requirements of Article 65 or with the requirements of Article 66;

(b) where all residents whose means during the contingency do not exceed prescribed limits are protected, in such a manner as to comply with the requirements of Article 67.

Article 29

1. The benefit specified in Article 28 shall, in a contingency covered, be secured at least–

(a) to a person protected who has completed, prior to the contingency, in accordance with prescribed rules, a qualifying period which may be 30 years of contribution or employment, or 20 years of residence; or

(b) where, in principle, all economically active persons are protected, to a person protected who has completed a prescribed qualifying period of contribution and in respect of whom, while he was of working age, the prescribed yearly average number of contributions has been paid.

2. Where the benefit referred to in paragraph 1 is conditional upon a minimum period of contribution or employment, a reduced benefit shall be secured at least–

(a) to a person protected who has completed, prior to the contingency, in accordance with prescribed rules, a qualifying period of 15 years of contribution or employment; or

(b) where, in principle, all economically active persons are protected, to a person protected who has completed a prescribed qualifying period of contribution and in respect of whom, while he was of working age, half the yearly average number of contributions prescribed in accordance with subparagraph (b) of paragraph 1 of this Article has been paid.

3. The requirements of paragraph 1 of this Article shall be deemed to be satisfied where a benefit calculated in conformity with the requirements of Part XI but at a percentage of ten

points lower than shown in the Schedule appended to that Part for the standard beneficiary concerned is secured at least to a person protected who has completed, in accordance with prescribed rules, ten years of contribution or employment, or five years of residence.

4. A proportional reduction of the percentage indicated in the Schedule appended to Part XI may be effected where the qualifying period for the benefit corresponding to the reduced percentage exceeds ten years of contribution or employment but is less than 30 years of contribution or employment; if such qualifying period exceeds 15 years, a reduced benefit shall be payable in conformity with paragraph 2 of this Article.

5. Where the benefit referred to in paragraphs 1, 3 or 4 of this Article is conditional upon a minimum period of contribution or employment, a reduced benefit shall be payable under prescribed conditions to a person protected who, by reason only of his advanced age when the provisions concerned in the application of this Part come into force, has not satisfied the conditions prescribed in accordance with paragraph 2 of this Article, unless a benefit in conformity with the provisions of paragraphs 1, 3 or 4 of this Article is secured to such person at an age higher than the normal age.

Article 30

The benefits specified in Articles 28 and 29 shall be granted throughout the contingency.

PART VI. EMPLOYMENT INJURY BENEFIT

Article 31

Each Member for which this Part of this Convention is in force shall secure to the persons protected the provision of employment injury benefit in accordance with the following Articles of this Part.

Article 32

The contingencies covered shall include the following where due to accident or a prescribed disease resulting from employment:

(a) a morbid condition;

(b) incapacity for work resulting from such a condition and involving suspension of earnings, as defined by national laws or regulations;

(c) total loss of earning capacity or partial loss thereof in excess of a prescribed degree, likely to be permanent, or corresponding loss of faculty; and

(d) the loss of support suffered by the widow or child as the result of the death of the breadwinner; in the case of a widow, the right to benefit may be made conditional on her being presumed, in accordance with national laws or regulations, to be incapable of self-support.

Article 33

The persons protected shall comprise–

(a) prescribed classes of employees, constituting not less than 50 per cent. of all employees, and, for benefit in respect of death of the breadwinner, also their wives and children; or

(b) where a declaration made in virtue of Article 3 is in force, prescribed classes of employees, constituting not less than 50 per cent. of all employees in industrial workplaces employing 20 persons or more, and, for benefit in respect of death of the breadwinner, also their wives and children.

Article 34

1. In respect of a morbid condition, the benefit shall be medical care as specified in paragraphs 2 and 3 of this Article.

2. The medical care shall comprise–

(a) general practitioner and specialist in-patient care and out-patient care, including domiciliary visiting;

(b) dental care;

(c) nursing care at home or in hospital or other medical institutions;

(d) maintenance in hospitals, convalescent homes, sanatoria or other medical institutions;

(e) dental, pharmaceutical and other medical or surgical supplies, including prosthetic appliances, kept in repair, and eyeglasses; and

(f) the care furnished by members of such other professions as may at any time be legally recognised as allied to the medical profession, under the supervision of a medical or dental practitioner.

3. Where a declaration made in virtue of Article 3 is in force, the medical care shall include at least–

(a) general practitioner care, including domiciliary visiting;

(b) specialist care at hospitals for in-patients and out-patients, and such specialist care as may be available outside hospitals;

(c) the essential pharmaceutical supplies as prescribed by a medical or other qualified practitioner; and

(d) hospitalisation where necessary.

4. The medical care provided in accordance with the preceding paragraphs shall be afforded with a view to maintaining, restoring or improving the health of the person protected and his ability to work and to attend to his personal needs.

Article 35

1. The institutions or Government departments administering the medical care shall co-operate, wherever appropriate, with the general vocational rehabilitation services, with a view to the re-establishment of handicapped persons in suitable work.

2. National laws or regulations may authorise such institutions or departments to ensure provision for the vocational rehabilitation of handicapped persons.

Article 36

1. In respect of incapacity for work, total loss of earning capacity likely to be permanent or corresponding loss of faculty, or the death of the breadwinner, the benefit shall be a periodical payment calculated in such a manner as to comply either with the requirements of Article 65 or with the requirements of Article 66.

2. In case of partial loss of earning capacity likely to be permanent, or corresponding loss of faculty, the benefit, where payable, shall be a periodical payment representing a suitable proportion of that specified for total loss of earning capacity or corresponding loss of faculty.

3. The periodical payment may be commuted for a lump sum–

(a) where the degree of incapacity is slight; or

(b) where the competent authority is satisfied that the lump sum will be properly utilised.

Article 37

The benefit specified in Articles 34 and 36 shall, in a contingency covered, be secured at least to a person protected who was employed in the territory of the Member at the time of the accident if the injury is due to accident or at the time of contracting the disease if the injury is due to a disease and, for periodical payments in respect of death of the breadwinner, to the widow and children of such person.

Article 38

The benefit specified in Articles 34 and 36 shall be granted throughout the contingency, except that, in respect of incapacity for work, the benefit need not be paid for the first three days in each case of suspension of earnings.

PART VII. FAMILY BENEFIT

Article 39

Each Member for which this Part of this Convention is in force shall secure to the persons protected the provision of family benefit in accordance with the following Articles of this Part.

Article 40

The contingency covered shall be responsibility for the maintenance of children as prescribed.

Article 41

The persons protected shall comprise–

(a) prescribed classes of employees, constituting not less than 50 per cent. of all employees; or

(b) prescribed classes of the economically active population, constituting not less than 20 per cent. of all residents; or

(c) all residents whose means during the contingency do not exceed prescribed limits; or

(d) where a declaration made in virtue of Article 3 is in force, prescribed classes of employees, constituting not less than 50 per cent. of all employees in industrial workplaces employing 20 persons or more.

Article 42

The benefit shall be–

(a) a periodical payment granted to any person protected having completed the prescribed qualifying period; or

(b) the provision to or in respect of children, of food, clothing, housing, holidays or domestic help; or

(c) a combination of (a) and (b).

Article 43

The benefit specified in Article 42 shall be secured at least to a person protected who, within a prescribed period, has completed a qualifying period which may be three months of contribution or employment, or one year of residence, as may be prescribed.

Article 44

The total value of the benefits granted in accordance with Article 42 to the persons protected shall be such as to represent–

(a) 3 per cent. of the wage of an ordinary adult male labourer, as determined in accordance with the rules laid down in Article 66, multiplied by the total number of children of persons protected; or

(b) 1.5 per cent. of the said wage, multiplied by the total number of children of all residents.

Article 45

Where the benefit consists of a periodical payment, it shall be granted throughout the contingency.

PART VIII. MATERNITY BENEFIT

Article 46

Each Member for which this Part of this Convention is in force shall secure to the persons protected the provision of maternity benefit in accordance with the following Articles of this Part.

Article 47

The contingencies covered shall include pregnancy and confinement and their consequences, and suspension of earnings, as defined by national laws or regulations, resulting therefrom.

Article 48

The persons protected shall comprise–

(a) all women in prescribed classes of employees, which classes constitute not less than 50 per cent. of all employees and, for maternity medical benefit, also the wives of men in these classes; or

(b) all women in prescribed classes of the economically active population, which classes constitute not less than 20 per cent. of all residents, and, for maternity medical benefit, also the wives of men in these classes; or

(c) where a declaration made in virtue of Article 3 is in force, all women in prescribed classes of employees, which classes constitute not less than 50 per cent. of all employees in industrial workplaces employing 20 persons or more, and, for maternity medical benefit, also the wives of men in these classes.

Article 49

1. In respect of pregnancy and confinement and their consequences, the maternity medical benefit shall be medical care as specified in paragraphs 2 and 3 of this Article.

2. The medical care shall include at least–

(a) pre-natal, confinement and post-natal care either by medical practitioners or by qualified midwives; and

(b) hospitalisation where necessary.

3. The medical care specified in paragraph 2 of this Article shall be afforded with a view to maintaining, restoring or improving the health of the woman protected and her ability to work and to attend to her personal needs.

4. The institutions or Government departments administering the maternity medical benefit shall, by such means as may be deemed appropriate, encourage the women protected to avail themselves of the general health services placed at their disposal by the public authorities or by other bodies recognised by the public authorities.

Article 50

In respect of suspension of earnings resulting from pregnancy and from confinement and their consequences, the benefit shall be a periodical payment calculated in such a manner as to comply either with the requirements of Article 65 or with the requirements of Article 66. The amount of the periodical payment may vary in the course of the contingency, subject to the average rate thereof complying with these requirements.

Article 51

The benefit specified in Articles 49 and 50 shall, in a contingency covered, be secured at least to a woman in the classes protected who has completed such qualifying period as may be considered necessary to preclude abuse, and the benefit specified in Article 49 shall also be secured to the wife of a man in the classes protected where the latter has completed such qualifying period.

Article 52

The benefit specified in Articles 49 and 50 shall be granted throughout the contingency, except that the periodical payment may be limited to 12 weeks, unless a longer period of abstention from work is required or authorised by national laws or regulations, in which event it may not be limited to a period less than such longer period.

PART IX. INVALIDITY BENEFIT

Article 53

Each Member for which this Part of this Convention is in force shall secure to the persons protected the provision of invalidity benefit in accordance with the following Articles of this Part.

Article 54

The contingency covered shall include inability to engage in any gainful activity, to an extent prescribed, which inability is likely to be permanent or persists after the exhaustion of sickness benefit.

Article 55

The persons protected shall comprise–

(a) prescribed classes of employees, constituting not less than 50 per cent. of all employees; or

(b) prescribed classes of the economically active population, constituting not less than 20 per cent. of all residents; or

(c) all residents whose means during the contingency do not exceed limits prescribed in such a manner as to comply with the requirements of Article 67; or

(d) where a declaration made in virtue of Article 3 is in force, prescribed classes of employees, constituting not less than 50 per cent. of all employees in industrial workplaces employing 20 persons or more.

Article 56

The benefit shall be a periodical payment calculated as follows:

(a) where classes of employees or classes of the economically active population are protected, in such a manner as to comply either with the requirements of Article 65 or with the requirements of Article 66;

(b) where all residents whose means during the contingency do not exceed prescribed limits are protected, in such a manner as to comply with the requirements of Article 67.

Article 57

1. The benefit specified in Article 56 shall, in a contingency covered, be secured at least–

(a) to a person protected who has completed, prior to the contingency, in accordance with prescribed rules, a qualifying period which may be 15 years of contribution or employment, or 10 years of residence; or

(b) where, in principle, all economically active persons are protected, to a person protected who has completed a qualifying period of three years of contribution and in respect of whom, while he was of working age, the prescribed yearly average number of contributions has been paid.

2. Where the benefit referred to in paragraph 1 is conditional upon a minimum period of contribution or employment, a reduced benefit shall be secured at least–

(a) to a person protected who has completed, prior to the contingency, in accordance with prescribed rules, a qualifying period of five years of contribution or employment; or

(b) where, in principle, all economically active persons are protected, to a person protected who has completed a qualifying period of three years of contribution and in respect of whom, while he was of working age, half the yearly average number of contributions prescribed in accordance with subparagraph (b) of paragraph 1 of this Article has been paid.

3. The requirements of paragraph 1 of this Article shall be deemed to be satisfied where a benefit calculated in conformity with the requirements of Part XI but at a percentage of ten points lower than shown in the Schedule appended to that Part for the standard beneficiary concerned is secured at least to a person protected who has completed, in accordance with prescribed rules, five years of contribution, employment or residence.

4. A proportional reduction of the percentage indicated in the Schedule appended to Part XI may be effected where the qualifying period for the pension corresponding to the reduced percentage exceeds five years of contribution or employment but is less than 15 years of contribution or employment; a reduced pension shall be payable in conformity with paragraph 2 of this Article.

Article 58

The benefit specified in Articles 56 and 57 shall be granted throughout the contingency or until an old-age benefit becomes payable.

PART X. SURVIVORS' BENEFIT

Article 59

Each Member for which this Part of this Convention is in force shall secure to the persons protected the provision of survivors' benefit in accordance with the following Articles of this Part.

Article 60

1. The contingency covered shall include the loss of support suffered by the widow or child as the result of the death of the breadwinner; in the case of a widow, the right to benefit may be made conditional on her being presumed, in accordance with national laws or regulations, to be incapable of self-support.

2. National laws or regulations may provide that the benefit of a person otherwise entitled to it may be suspended if such person is engaged in any prescribed gainful activity or that the benefit, if contributory, may be reduced where the earnings of the beneficiary exceed a prescribed amount, and, if non-contributory, may be reduced where the earnings of the beneficiary or his other means or the two taken together exceed a prescribed amount.

Article 61

The persons protected shall comprise–

(a) the wives and the children of breadwinners in prescribed classes of employees, which classes constitute not less than 50 per cent. of all employees; or

(b) the wives and the children of breadwinners in prescribed classes of the economically active population, which classes constitute not less than 20 per cent. of all residents; or

(c) all resident widows and resident children who have lost their breadwinner and whose means during the contingency do not exceed limits prescribed in such a manner as to comply with the requirements of Article 67; or

(d) where a declaration made in virtue of Article 3 is in force, the wives and the children of breadwinners in prescribed classes of employees, which classes constitute not less than 50 per cent. of all employees in industrial workplaces employing 20 persons or more.

Article 62

The benefit shall be a periodical payment calculated as follows:

(a) where classes of employees or classes of the economically active population are protected, in such a manner as to comply either with the requirements of Article 65 or with the requirements of Article 66;

(b) where all residents whose means during the contingency do not exceed prescribed limits are protected, in such a manner as to comply with the requirements of Article 67.

Article 63

1. The benefit specified in Article 62 shall, in a contingency covered, be secured at least–

(a) to a person protected whose breadwinner has completed, in accordance with prescribed rules, a qualifying period which may be 15 years of contribution or employment, or 10 years of residence; or

(b) where, in principle, the wives and children of all economically active persons are protected, to a person protected whose breadwinner has completed a qualifying period of three years of contribution and in respect of whose breadwinner, while he was of working age, the prescribed yearly average number of contributions has been paid.

2. Where the benefit referred to in paragraph 1 is conditional upon a minimum period of contribution or employment, a reduced benefit shall be secured at least–

(a) to a person protected whose breadwinner has completed, in accordance with prescribed rules, a qualifying period of five years of contribution or employment; or

(b) where, in principle, the wives and children of all economically active persons are protected, to a person protected whose breadwinner has completed a qualifying period of three years of contribution and in respect of whose breadwinner, while he was of working age, half the yearly average number of contributions prescribed in accordance with subparagraph (b) of paragraph 1 of this Article has been paid.

3. The requirements of paragraph 1 of this Article shall be deemed to be satisfied where a benefit calculated in conformity with the requirements of Part XI but a percentage of ten points lower than shown in the Schedule appended to that Part for the standard beneficiary concerned is secured at least to a person protected whose breadwinner has completed, in accordance with prescribed rules, five years of contribution, employment or residence.

4. A proportional reduction of the percentage indicated in the Schedule appended to Part XI may be effected where the qualifying period for the benefit corresponding to the reduced percentage exceeds five years of contribution or employment but is less than 15 years of contribution or employment; a reduced benefit shall be payable in conformity with paragraph 2 of this Article.

5. In order that a childless widow presumed to be incapable of self-support may be entitled to a survivor's benefit, a minimum duration of the marriage may be required.

Article 64

The benefit specified in Articles 62 and 63 shall be granted throughout the contingency.

[…]

PART XII. EQUALITY OF TREATMENT OF NON-NATIONAL RESIDENTS

Article 68

1. Non-national residents shall have the same rights as national residents: Provided that special rules concerning non-nationals and nationals born outside the territory of the Member may be prescribed in respect of benefits or portions of benefits which are payable wholly or mainly out of public funds and in respect of transitional schemes.

2. Under contributory social security schemes which protect employees, the persons protected who are nationals of another Member which has accepted the obligations of the relevant Part of the Convention shall have, under that Part, the same rights as nationals of the Member concerned: Provided that the application of this paragraph may be made subject to the existence of a bilateral or multilateral agreement providing for reciprocity.

[...]

Convention No. 117 concerning Basic Aims and Standards of Social Policy, 1962*

Adoption: 22 June 1962
Entry into force: 23 April 1964
Parties: 32 (Status as of 1 April 2007)

BAHAMAS 25 May 1976, BOLIVIA 31 Jan 1977, BRAZIL 24 Mar 1969, CENTRAL AFRICAN REPUBLIC 9 June 1964, DEMOCRATIC REPUBLIC OF CONGO 5 Sep 1967, COSTA RICA 27 Jan 1966, ECUADOR 3 Oct 1969, GEORGIA 21 Oct 1997, GHANA 18 June 1964, GUATEMALA 13 June 1989, GUINEA 12 Dec 1966, ISRAEL 15 Jan 1964, ITALY 27 Dec 1966, JAMAICA 4 Jan 1966, JORDAN 7 Mar 1963, KUWAIT 23 Apr 1963, MADAGASCAR 1 June 1964, MALTA 9 June 1988, REPUBLIC OF MOLDOVA 12 Aug 1966, NICARAGUA 1 Oct 1981, NIGER 23 Nov 1964, PANAMA 4 June 1971, PARAGUAY 20 Feb 1969, PORTUGAL 9 Jan 1981, ROMANIA 6 June 1973, SENEGAL 13 Nov 1967, SPAIN 8 May 1973, SUDAN 22 Oct 1970, SYRIAN ARAB REPUBLIC 11 Dec 1964, TUNISIA 14 Apr 1970, VENEZUELA (BOLIVARIAN REPUBLIC OF) 6 Sep 1983, ZAMBIA 2 Dec 1964.

The General Conference of the International Labour Organisation,

Having been convened at Geneva by the Governing Body of the International Labour Office, and having met in its Forty-sixth Session on 6 June 1962, and

Having decided upon the adoption of certain proposals concerning the revision of the Social Policy (Non-Metropolitan Territories) Convention, 1947, which is the tenth item on the agenda of the Session, primarily with a view to making its continued application and ratification possible for independent States, and

Considering that these proposals must take the form of an international Convention, and

Considering that economic development must serve as a basis for social progress, and

Considering that every effort should be made, on an international, regional or national basis, to secure financial and technical assistance safeguarding the interests of the population, and Considering that, in appropriate cases, international, regional or national action should be taken with a view to establishing conditions of trade which would encourage production at a high level of efficiency and make possible the maintenance of a reasonable standard of living, and

Considering that all possible steps should be taken by appropriate international, regional and national measures to promote improvement in such fields as public health, housing, nutrition, education, the welfare of children, the status of women, conditions of employment, the remuneration of wage earners and independent producers, the protection of migrant workers, social security, standards of public services and general production, and

Considering that all possible steps should be taken effectively to interest and associate the population in the framing and execution of measures of social progress,

---

* Source: International Labour Organization, http://www.ilo.org/ilolex
The ILO shall accept no responsibility for any inaccuracy, errors or omissions or for the consequences arising from the use of the Text.

adopts this twenty-second day of June of the year one thousand nine hundred and sixty-two the following Convention, which may be cited as the Social Policy (Basic Aims and Standards) Convention, 1962:

PART I. GENERAL PRINCIPLES

Article 1

1. All policies shall be primarily directed to the well-being and development of the population and to the promotion of its desire for social progress.

2. All policies of more general application shall be formulated with due regard to their effect upon the well-being of the population.

PART II. IMPROVEMENT OF STANDARDS OF LIVING

Article 2

The improvement of standards of living shall be regarded as the principal objective in the planning of economic development.

Article 3

1. All practicable measures shall be taken in the planning of economic development to harmonise such development with the healthy evolution of the communities concerned.

2. In particular, efforts shall be made to avoid the disruption of family life and of traditional social units, especially by–

(a) close study of the causes and effect of migratory movements and appropriate action where necessary;

(b) the promotion of town and village planning in areas where economic needs result in the concentration of population;

(c) the prevention and elimination of congestion in urban areas;

(d) the improvement of living conditions in rural areas and the establishment of suitable industries in rural areas where adequate manpower is available.

Article 4

The measures to be considered by the competent authorities for the promotion of productive capacity and the improvement of standards of living of agricultural producers shall include–

(a) the elimination to the fullest practicable extent of the causes of chronic indebtedness;

(b) the control of the alienation of agricultural land to non-agriculturalists so as to ensure that such alienation takes place only when it is in the best interests of the country;

(c) the control, by the enforcement of adequate laws or regulations, of the ownership and use of land resources to ensure that they are used, with due regard to customary rights, in the best interests of the inhabitants of the country;

(d) the supervision of tenancy arrangements and of working conditions with a view to securing for tenants and labourers the highest practicable standards of living and an equitable share in any advantages which may result from improvements in productivity or in price levels;

(e) the reduction of production and distribution costs by all practicable means and in particular by forming, encouraging and assisting producers' and consumers co-operatives.

Article 5

1. Measures shall be taken to secure for independent producers and wage earners conditions which will give them scope to improve living standards by their own efforts and will ensure the maintenance of minimum standards of living as ascertained by means of official inquiries into living conditions, conducted after consultation with the representative organisations of employers and workers.

2. In ascertaining the minimum standards of living, account shall be taken of such essential family needs of the workers as food and its nutritive value, housing, clothing, medical care and education.

PART III. PROVISIONS CONCERNING MIGRANT WORKERS

Article 6

Where the circumstances under which workers are employed involve their living away from their homes, the terms and conditions of their employment shall take account of their normal family needs.

Article 7

Where the labour resources of one area are used on a temporary basis for the benefit of another area, measures shall be taken to encourage the transfer of part of the workers' wages and savings from the area of labour utilisation to the area of labour supply.

Article 8

1. Where the labour resources of a country are used in an area under a different administration, the competent authorities of the countries concerned shall, whenever necessary or desirable, enter into agreements for the purpose of regulating matters of common concern arising in connection with the application of the provisions of this Convention.

2. Such agreements shall provide that the worker shall enjoy protection and advantages not less than those enjoyed by workers resident in the area of labour utilisation.

3. Such agreements shall provide for facilities for enabling the worker to transfer part of his wages and savings to his home.

Article 9

Where workers and their families move from low-cost to higher-cost areas, account shall be taken of the increased cost of living resulting from the change.

PART IV. REMUNERATION OF WORKERS AND RELATED QUESTIONS

Article 10

1. The fixing of minimum wages by collective agreements freely negotiated between trade unions which are representative of the workers concerned and employers or employers' organisations shall be encouraged.

2. Where no adequate arrangements exist for the fixing of minimum wages by collective agreement, the necessary arrangements shall be made whereby minimum rates of wages can be fixed in consultation with representatives of the employers and workers, including representatives of their respective organisations, where such exist.

3. The necessary measures shall be taken to ensure that the employers and workers concerned are informed of the minimum wage rates in force and that wages are not paid at less than these rates in cases where they are applicable.

4. A worker to whom minimum rates are applicable and who, since they became applicable, has been paid wages at less than these rates shall be entitled to recover, by judicial or other means authorised by law, the amount by which he has been underpaid, subject to such limitation of time as may be determined by law or regulation.

Article 11

1. The necessary measures shall be taken to ensure the proper payment of all wages earned and employers shall be required to keep registers of wage payments, to issue to workers statements of wage payments and to take other appropriate steps to facilitate the necessary supervision.

2. Wages shall normally be paid in legal tender only.

3. Wages shall normally be paid direct to the individual worker.

4. The substitution of alcohol or other spirituous beverages for all or any part of wages for services performed by the worker shall be prohibited.

5. Payment of wages shall not be made in taverns or stores, except in the case of workers employed therein.

6. Unless there is an established local custom to the contrary, and the competent authority is satisfied that the continuance of this custom is desired by the workers, wages shall be paid regularly at such intervals as will lessen the likelihood of indebtedness among the wage earners.

7. Where food, housing, clothing and other essential supplies and services form part of remuneration, all practicable steps shall be taken by the competent authority to ensure that they are adequate and their cash value properly assessed.

8. All practicable measures shall be taken–

(a) to inform the workers of their wage rights;

(b) to prevent any unauthorised deductions from wages; and

(c) to restrict the amounts deductible from wages in respect of supplies and services forming part of remuneration to the proper cash value thereof.

Article 12

1. The maximum amounts and manner of repayment of advances on wages shall be regulated by the competent authority.

2. The competent authority shall limit the amount of advances which may be made to a worker in consideration of his taking up employment; the amount of advances permitted shall be clearly explained to the worker.

3. Any advance in excess of the amount laid down by the competent authority shall be legally irrecoverable and may not be recovered by the withholding of amounts of pay due to the worker at a later date.

Article 13

1. Voluntary forms of thrift shall be encouraged among wage earners and independent producers.

2. All practicable measures shall be taken for the protection of wage earners and independent producers against usury, in particular by action aiming at the reduction of rates of interest on loans, by the control of the operations of money lenders, and by the encouragement of facilities for borrowing money for appropriate purposes through co-operative credit organisations or through institutions which are under the control of the competent authority.

PART V. NON-DISCRIMINATION ON GROUNDS OF RACE, COLOUR, SEX, BELIEF, TRIBAL ASSOCIATION OR TRADE UNION AFFILIATION

Article 14

1. It shall be an aim of policy to abolish all discrimination among workers on grounds of race, colour, sex, belief, tribal association or trade union affiliation in respect of–

(a) labour legislation and agreements which shall afford equitable economic treatment to all those lawfully resident or working in the country;

(b) admission to public or private employment;

(c) conditions of engagement and promotion;

(d) opportunities for vocational training;

(e) conditions of work;

(f) health, safety and welfare measures;

(g) discipline;

(h) participation in the negotiation of collective agreements;

(i) wage rates, which shall be fixed according to the principle of equal pay for work of equal value in the same operation and undertaking.

2. All practicable measures shall be taken to lessen, by raising the rates applicable to the lower-paid workers, any existing differences in wage rates due to discrimination by reason of race, colour, sex, belief, tribal association or trade union affiliation.

3. Workers from one country engaged for employment in another country may be granted in addition to their wages benefits in cash or in kind to meet any reasonable personal or family expenses resulting from employment away from their homes.

4. The foregoing provisions of this Article shall be without prejudice to such measures as the competent authority may think it necessary or desirable to take for the safeguarding of motherhood and for ensuring the health, safety and welfare of women workers.

PART VI. EDUCATION AND TRAINING

Article 15

1. Adequate provision shall be made to the maximum extent possible under local conditions, for the progressive development of broad systems of education, vocational training and apprenticeship, with a view to the effective preparation of children and young persons of both sexes for a useful occupation.

2. National laws or regulations shall prescribe the school-leaving age and the minimum age for and conditions of employment.

3. In order that the child population may be able to profit by existing facilities for education and in order that the extension of such facilities may not be hindered by a demand for child labour, the employment of persons below the school-leaving age during the hours when the schools are in session shall be prohibited in areas where educational facilities are provided on a scale adequate for the majority of the children of school age.

Article 16

1. In order to secure high productivity through the development of skilled labour, training in new techniques of production shall be provided in suitable cases.

2. Such training shall be organised by or under the supervision of the competent authorities, in consultation with the employers' and workers' organisations of the country from which the trainees come and of the country of training.

PART VII. FINAL PROVISIONS

Article 17

The formal ratifications of this Convention shall be communicated to the Director-General of the International Labour Office for registration.

Article 18

1. This Convention shall be binding only upon those Members of the International Labour Organisation whose ratification have been registered with the Director-General.

2. It shall come into force twelve months after the date on which the ratifications of two Members have been registered with the Director-General.

3. Thereafter, this Convention shall come into force for any Member twelve months after the date on which its ratification has been registered.

Article 19

The coming into force of this Convention shall not involve the ipso jure denunciation of the Social Policy (Non-Metropolitan Territories) Convention, 1947, by any Member for which that Convention continues to remain in force, nor shall it close that Convention to further ratification.

Article 20

1. A Member which has ratified this Convention may denounce it after the expiration of ten years from the date on which the Convention first comes into force, by an act communicated

to the Director-General of the International Labour Office for registration. Such denunciation shall not take effect until one year after the date on which it is registered.

2. Each Member which has ratified this Convention and which does not, within the year following the expiration of the period of ten years mentioned in the preceding paragraph, exercise the right of denunciation provided for in this Article, will be bound for another period of ten years and, thereafter, may denounce this Convention at the expiration of each period of ten years under the terms provided for in this Article.

Article 12

1. The Director-General of the International Labour Office shall notify all Members of the International Labour Organisation of the registration of all ratifications and denunciations communicated to him by the Members of the Organisation.

2. When notifying the Members of the Organisation of the registration of the second ratification communicated to him, the Director-General shall draw the attention of the Members of the Organisation to the date upon which the Convention will come into force.

Article 22

The Director-General of the International Labour Office shall communicate to the Secretary-General of the United Nations for registration in accordance with Article 102 of the Charter of the United Nations full particulars of all ratifications and acts of denunciation registered by him in accordance with the provisions of the preceding Articles.

Article 23

At such times as it may consider necessary the Governing Body of the International Labour Office shall present to the General Conference a report on the working of this Convention and shall consider the desirability of placing on the agenda of the Conference the question of its revision in whole or in part.

Article 24

1. Should the Conference adopt a new Convention revising this Convention in whole or in part, then, unless the new Convention otherwise provides–

a) the ratification by a Member of the new revising Convention shall ipso jure involve the immediate denunciation of this Convention, notwithstanding the provisions of Article 20 above, if and when the new revising Convention shall have come into force;

b) as from the date when the new revising Convention comes into force this Convention shall cease to be open to ratification by the Members.

2. This Convention shall in any case remain in force in its actual form and content for those Members which have ratified it but have not ratified the revising Convention.

Article 25

The English and French versions of the text of this Convention are equally authoritative.

Convention No. 118 concerning Equality of Treatment of Nationals and Non-Nationals in Social Security, 1962*

Adoption: 28 June 1962
Entry into force: 25 April 1964
Parties: 38 (Status as of 1 April 2007)

BANGLADESH 22 June 1972 (*2.1 c, g), BARBADOS 14 Oct 1974 (*2.1 b, c, e-g), BOLIVIA 31 Jan 1977 (*2.1 a-c, i), BRAZIL 24 Mar 1969 (*2.1 a-g), CAPE VERDE 8 July 1987 (*2.1 a-g, i), CENTRAL AFRICAN REPUBLIC 8 Oct 1964(*2.1 c, e, g, i), DEMOCRATIC REPUBLIC OF CONGO 1 Nov 1967 (*2.1 d, e, g), DENMARK 17 June 1969 (*2.1 a, b, g, h), ECUADOR 9 Mar 1970 (*2.1 a-d, f, g), EGYPT 12 Jan 1993 (*2.1 a-h), FINLAND 15 Aug 1969 (*2.1 a, b, g), FRANCE 13 May 1974 (*2.1 a-d, f, g, i), GERMANY 19 Mar 1971 (*2.1 a-c, g, h), GUATEMALA 4 Nov 1963 (*2.1 c), GUINEA 11 Aug 1967 (*2.1 a-c, e-g, i), INDIA 19 Aug 1964 (*2.1 a-c), IRAQ 28 Apr 1978 (*2.1 a-g), IRELAND 26 Nov 1964 (*2.1 a, b, g,h, i), ISRAEL 9 June 1965 (*2.1 c, e-g, i), ITALY 5 May 1967(*2.1 a-i), JORDAN 7 Mar 1963 (*2.1 c, d, f, g), KENYA 9 Feb 1971 (*2.1 d-f), LIBYAN ARAB JAMAHIRIYA 19 June 1975 (*2.1 a-i), MADAGASCAR 22 June 1964 (*2.1 b-d, g), MAURITANIA 15 July 1968 (*2.1 d-g, i), MEXICO 6 Jan 1978 (*2.1 a-g), NETHERLANDS 3 July 1964 (*2.1 a-i, denounced 20 Dec 2004), NORWAY 28 Aug 1963 (*2.1 f, i), PAKISTAN 27 Mar 1969 (*2.1 c-g), PHILIPPINES 26 Apr 1994 (*2.1 a-g), RWANDA 21 Sep 1989 (*2.1 d-g), SURINAME 15 June 1976 (*2.1 g), SWEDEN 25 Apr 1963 (*2.1 a-c, g, h), SYRIAN ARAB REPUBLIC 18 Nov 1963 (*2.1 d-g), TUNISIA 20 Sep 1965 (*2.1 a-g, i), TURKEY 25 June 1974 (*2.1 a-g), URUGUAY 22 Feb 1983 (*2.1 a-c, g-i), VENEZUELA (BOLIVARIAN REPUBLIC OF) 5 Nov 1982 (*2.1 a-g).

The General Conference of the International Labour Organisation,

Having been convened at Geneva by the Governing Body of the International Labour Office, and having met in its Forty-sixth Session on 6 June 1962, and

Having decided upon the adoption of certain proposals with regard to equality of treatment of nationals and non-nationals in social security, which is the fifth item on the agenda of the session, and

Having determined that these proposals shall take the form of an international Convention,

adopts this twenty-eighth day of June of the year one thousand nine hundred and sixty-two the following Convention, which may be cited as the Equality of Treatment (Social Security) Convention, 1962:

Article 1

In this Convention–

(a) the term legislation includes any social security rules as well as laws and regulations;

(b) the term benefits refers to all benefits, grants and pensions, including any supplements or increments;

* Source: International Labour Organization, http://www.ilo.org/ilolex
The ILO shall accept no responsibility for any inaccuracy, errors or omissions or for the consequences arising from the use of the Text.

(c) the term benefits granted under transitional schemes means either benefits granted to persons who have exceeded a prescribed age at the date when the legislation applicable came into force, or benefits granted as a transitional measure in consideration of events occurring or periods completed outside the present boundaries of the territory of a Member;

(d) the term death grant means any lump sum payable in the event of death;

(e) the term residence means ordinary residence;

(f) the term prescribed means determined by or in virtue of national legislation as defined in subparagraph (a) above;

(g) the term refugee has the meaning assigned to it in Article 1 of the Convention relating to the Status of Refugees of 28 July 1951;

(h) the term stateless person has the meaning assigned to it in Article 1 of the Convention relating to the Status of Stateless Persons of 28 September 1954.

Article 2

1. Each Member may accept the obligations of this Convention in respect of any one or more of the following branches of social security for which it has in effective operation legislation covering its own nationals within its own territory:

(a) medical care;

(b) sickness benefit;

(c) maternity benefit;

(d) invalidity benefit;

(e) old-age benefit;

(f) survivors' benefit;

(g) employment injury benefit;

(h) unemployment benefit; and

(i) family benefit.

2. Each Member for which this Convention is in force shall comply with its provisions in respect of the branch or branches of social security for which it has accepted the obligations of the Convention.

3. Each Member shall specify in its ratification in respect of which branch or branches of social security it accepts the obligations of this Convention.

4. Each Member which has ratified this Convention may subsequently notify the Director-General of the International Labour Office that it accepts the obligations of the Convention in respect of one or more branches of social security not already specified in its ratification.

5. The undertakings referred to in paragraph 4 of this Article shall be deemed to be an integral part of the ratification and to have the force of ratification as from the date of notification.

6. For the purpose of the application of this Convention, each Member accepting the obligations thereof in respect of any branch of social security which has legislation providing for benefits of the type indicated in clause (a) or (b) below shall communicate to the Director-General of the International Labour Office a statement indicating the benefits provided for by its legislation which it considers to be–

(a) benefits other than those the grant of which depends either on direct financial participation by the persons protected or their employer, or on a qualifying period of occupational activity; or

(b) benefits granted under transitional schemes.

7. The communication referred to in paragraph 6 of this Article shall be made at the time of ratification or at the time of notification in accordance with paragraph 4 of this Article; as regards any legislation adopted subsequently, the communication shall be made within three months of the date of the adoption of such legislation.

Article 3

1. Each Member for which this Convention is in force shall grant within its territory to the nationals of any other Member for which the Convention is in force equality of treatment under its legislation with its own nationals, both as regards coverage and as regards the right to benefits, in respect of every branch of social security for which it has accepted the obligations of the Convention.

2. In the case of survivors' benefits, such equality of treatment shall also be granted to the survivors of the nationals of a Member for which the Convention is in force, irrespective of the nationality of such survivors.

3. Nothing in the preceding paragraphs of this Article shall require a Member to apply the provisions of these paragraphs, in respect of the benefits of a specified branch of social security, to the nationals of another Member which has legislation relating to that branch but does not grant equality of treatment in respect thereof to the nationals of the first Member.

Article 4

1. Equality of treatment as regards the grant of benefits shall be accorded without any condition of residence: Provided that equality of treatment in respect of the benefits of a specified branch of social security may be made conditional on residence in the case of nationals of any Member the legislation of which makes the grant of benefits under that branch conditional on residence on its territory.

2. Notwithstanding the provisions of paragraph 1 of this Article, the grant of the benefits referred to in paragraph 6 (a) of Article 2–other than medical care, sickness benefit, employment injury benefit and family benefit–may be made subject to the condition that the beneficiary has resided on the territory of the Member in virtue of the legislation of which the benefit is due, or, in the case of a survivor, that the deceased had resided there, for a period which shall not exceed–

(a) six months immediately preceding the filing of claim, for grant of maternity benefit and unemployment benefit;

(b) five consecutive years immediately preceding the filing of claim, for grant of invalidity benefit, or immediately preceding death, for grant of survivors' benefit;

(c) ten years after the age of 18, which may include five consecutive years immediately preceding the filing of claim, for grant of old-age benefit.

3. Special provisions may be prescribed in respect of benefits granted under transitional schemes.

4. The measures necessary to prevent the cumulation of benefits shall be determined, as necessary, by special arrangements between the Members concerned.

Article 5

1. In addition to the provisions of Article 4, each Member which has accepted the obligations of this Convention in respect of the branch or branches of social security concerned shall guarantee both to its own nationals and to the nationals of any other Member which has accepted the obligations of the Convention in respect of the branch or branches in question, when they are resident abroad, provision of invalidity benefits, old-age benefits, survivors' benefits and death grants, and employment injury pensions, subject to measures for this purpose being taken, where necessary, in accordance with Article 8.

2. In case of residence abroad, the provision of invalidity, old-age and survivors' benefits of the type referred to in paragraph 6 (a) of Article 2 may be made subject to the participation of the Members concerned in schemes for the maintenance of rights as provided for in Article 7.

3. The provisions of this Article do not apply to benefits granted under transitional schemes.

Article 6

In addition to the provisions of Article 4, each Member which has accepted the obligations of this Convention in respect of family benefit shall guarantee the grant of family allowances both to its own nationals and to the nationals of any other Member which has accepted the obligations of this Convention for that branch, in respect of children who reside on the territory of any such Member, under conditions and within limits to be agreed upon by the Members concerned.

Article 7

1. Members for which this Convention is in force shall, upon terms being agreed between the Members concerned in accordance with Article 8, endeavour to participate in schemes for the maintenance of the acquired rights and rights in course of acquisition under their legislation of the nationals of Members for which the Convention is in force, for all branches of social security in respect of which the Members concerned have accepted the obligations of the Convention.

2. Such schemes shall provide, in particular, for the totalisation of periods of insurance, employment or residence and of assimilated periods for the purpose of the acquisition, maintenance or recovery of rights and for the calculation of benefits.

3. The cost of invalidity, old-age and survivors' benefits as so determined shall either be shared among the Members concerned, or be borne by the Member on whose territory the beneficiaries reside, as may be agreed upon by the Members concerned.

Article 8

The Members for which this Convention is in force may give effect to their obligations under the provisions of Articles 5 and 7 by ratification of the Maintenance of Migrants' Pension Rights Convention, 1935, by the application of the provisions of that Convention as between particular Members by mutual agreement, or by any multilateral or bilateral agreement giving effect to these obligations.

Article 9

The provisions of this Convention may be derogated from by agreements between Members which do not affect the rights and duties of other Members and which make provision for the maintenance of rights in course of acquisition and of acquired rights under conditions at least as favourable on the whole as those provided for in this Convention.

Article 10

1. The provisions of this Convention apply to refugees and stateless persons without any condition of reciprocity.

2. This Convention does not apply to special schemes for civil servants, special schemes for war victims, or public assistance.

3. This Convention does not require any Member to apply the provisions thereof to persons who, in accordance with the provisions of international instruments, are exempted from its national social security legislation.

Article 11

The Members for which this Convention is in force shall afford each other administrative assistance free of charge with a view to facilitating the application of the Convention and the execution of their respective social security legislation.

Article 12

1. This Convention does not apply to benefits payable prior to the coming into force of the Convention for the Member concerned in respect of the branch of social security under which the benefit is payable.

2. The extent to which the Convention applies to benefits attributable to contingencies occurring before its coming into force for the Member concerned in respect of the branch of social security under which the benefit is payable thereafter shall be determined by multilateral or bilateral agreement or in default thereof by the legislation of the Member concerned.

Article 13

This Convention shall not be regarded as revising any existing Convention.

Article 14

The formal ratifications of this Convention shall be communicated to the Director-General of the International Labour Office for registration.

Article 15

1. This Convention shall be binding only upon those Members of the International Labour Organisation whose ratifications have been registered with the Director-General.

2. It shall come into force twelve months after the date on which the ratifications of two Members have been registered with the Director-General.

3. Thereafter, this Convention shall come into force for any Member twelve months after the date on which its ratification has been registered.

Article 16

1. A Member which has ratified this Convention may denounce it after the expiration of ten years from the date on which the Convention first comes into force, by an act communicated to the Director-General of the International Labour Office for registration. Such denunciation shall not take effect until one year after the date on which it is registered.

2. Each Member which has ratified this Convention and which does not, within the year following the expiration of the period of ten years mentioned in the preceding paragraph,

exercise the right of denunciation provided for in this Article, will be bound for another period of ten years and, thereafter, may denounce this Convention at the expiration of each period of ten years under the terms provided for in this Article.

Article 17

1. The Director-General of the International Labour Office shall notify all Members of the International Labour Organisation of the registration of all ratifications and denunciations communicated to him by the Members of the Organisation.

2. When notifying the Members of the Organisation of the registration of the second ratification communicated to him, the Director-General shall draw the attention of the Members of the Organisation to the date upon which the Convention will come into force.

Article 18

The Director-General of the International Labour Office shall communicate to the Secretary-General of the United Nations for registration in accordance with Article 102 of the Charter of the United Nations full particulars of all ratifications and acts of denunciation registered by him in accordance with the provisions of the preceding Articles.

Article 19

At such times as it may consider necessary the Governing Body of the International Labour Office shall present to the General Conference a report on the working of this Convention and shall examine the desirability of placing on the agenda of the Conference the question of its revision in whole or in part.

Article 20

1. Should the Conference adopt a new Convention revising this Convention in whole or in part, then, unless the new Convention otherwise provides:

a) the ratification by a Member of the new revising Convention shall ipso jure involve the immediate denunciation of this Convention, notwithstanding the provisions of Article 16 above, if and when the new revising Convention shall have come into force;

b) as from the date when the new revising Convention comes into force this Convention shall cease to be open to ratification by the Members.

2. This Convention shall in any case remain in force in its actual form and content for those Members which have ratified it but have not ratified the revising Convention.

Article 21

The English and French versions of the text of this Convention are equally authoritative.

Convention No. 157 concerning the Establishment of an International System for the Maintenance of Rights in Social Security, 1982*

Adoption: 21 June 1982
Entry into force: 11 September 1986
Parties: 3 (Status as of 1 April 2007)

PHILIPPINES 26 Apr 1994, SPAIN 11 Sep 1985, SWEDEN 18 Apr 1984.

The General Conference of the International Labour Organisation,

Having been convened at Geneva by the Governing Body of the International Labour Office, and having met in its Sixty-eighth Session on 2 June 1982, and

Recalling the principles established by the Equality of Treatment (Social Security) Convention, 1962, which relate not only to equality of treatment but also to the maintenance of acquired rights and of rights in course of acquisition, and

Considering it necessary to provide for the application of the principles of the maintenance of rights in course of acquisition and of acquired rights in respect of all the branches of social security covered by the Social Security (Minimum Standards) Convention, 1952, and

Having decided upon the adoption of certain proposals with regard to maintenance of migrant workers' rights in social security (revision of Convention No.48), which is the fourth item on the agenda of the session, and

Having determined that these proposals shall take the form of an international Convention;

adopts this twenty-first day of June of the year one thousand nine hundred and eighty-two the following Convention, which may be cited as the Maintenance of Social Security Rights Convention, 1982:

PART I. GENERAL PROVISIONS

Article 1

In this Convention-

(a) the term Member means any Member of the International Labour Organisation that is bound by the Convention;

(b) the term legislation includes any social security rules as well as laws and regulations;

(c) the term competent Member means the Member under whose legislation the person concerned can claim benefit;

(d) the term institution means the body or authority directly responsible for applying all or part of the legislation of a Member;

(e) the term refugee has the meaning assigned to it in Article 1 of the Convention relating to the Status of Refugees of 28 July 1951 and in paragraph 2 of Article 1 of the Protocol relating to the Status of Refugees of 31 January 1967;

---

* Source: International Labour Organization, http://www.ilo.org/ilolex
The ILO shall accept no responsibility for any inaccuracy, errors or omissions or for the consequences arising from the use of the Text.

(f) the term stateless person has the meaning assigned to it in Article 1 of the Convention relating to the Status of Stateless Persons of 28 September 1954;

(g) the term members of the family means persons defined or recognised as such or as members of the household by the legislation under which benefits are awarded or provided, as appropriate, or persons determined by mutual agreement between the Members concerned; where persons are defined or recognised as members of the family or as members of the household under the relevant legislation only on the condition that they are living with the person concerned, this condition shall be deemed to be satisfied in respect of persons who obtain their main support from the person concerned;

(h) the term survivors means persons defined or recognised as such by the legislation under which benefits are awarded; where persons are defined or recognised as survivors under the relevant legislation only on the condition that they were living with the deceased, this condition shall be deemed to be satisfied in respect of persons who obtained their main support from the deceased;

(i) the term residence means ordinary residence;

(j) the term temporary residence means a temporary stay;

(k) the term periods of insurance means periods of contribution, employment, occupational activity or residence which are defined or recognised as periods of insurance by the legislation under which they were completed, and such other periods as are regarded by that legislation as equivalent to periods of insurance;

(l) the terms periods of employment and periods of occupational activity mean periods defined or recognised as such by the legislation under which they were completed and such other periods as are regarded by that legislation as equivalent to periods of employment or periods of occupational activity respectively;

(m) the term periods of residence means periods of residence defined or recognised as such by the legislation under which they were completed;

(n) the term non-contributory applies to benefits the award of which does not depend on direct financial participation by the persons protected or by their employer, or on a qualifying period of occupational activity, and to any scheme which exclusively awards such benefits;

(o) the term benefits awarded under transitional arrangements covers benefits awarded to persons who are over a given age on the date of entry into force of the legislation applicable, as well as benefits awarded, as a transitional measure, in consideration of events that have occurred or periods that have been completed outside the current frontiers of the territory of a Member.

Article 2

1. Subject to the provisions of paragraph 1 and of paragraph 3, subparagraph (a), of Article 4, this Convention applies to those of the following branches of social security for which a Member has legislation in force:

(a) medical care;

(b) sickness benefit;

(c) maternity benefit;

(d) invalidity benefit;

(e) old-age benefit;

(f) survivors' benefit;

(g) employment injury benefit, namely benefit in respect of occupational injuries and diseases;

(h) unemployment benefit; and

(i) family benefit.

2. This Convention applies to rehabilitation benefits provided by legislation concerning any of the branches of social security referred to in paragraph 1 of this Article.

3. This Convention applies to all general and special social security schemes, both contributory and non-contributory, as well as to schemes consisting of obligations imposed on employers by legislation in respect of any branch of social security referred to in paragraph 1 of this Article.

4. This Convention does not apply to special schemes for civil servants, to special schemes for war victims or to social or medical assistance schemes.

Article 3

1. Subject to the provisions of paragraph 1 and paragraph 3, subparagraph (b), of Article 4 and of paragraph 1 of Article 9, this Convention applies to persons who are or have been subject to the legislation of one or more Members, as well as to the members of their families and to their survivors, in all cases in which the international system for the maintenance of rights established by this Convention requires that account be taken of the legislation of a Member other than the Member in whose territory the persons concerned are resident or temporarily resident.

2. This Convention does not require any Member to apply its provisions to persons who, by virtue of international instruments, are exempted from the application of the legislation of that Member.

Article 4

1. Members may give effect to their obligations under the terms of Parts II to VI of this Convention by bilateral or multilateral instruments giving effect to these obligations, under conditions to be determined by mutual agreement between the Members concerned.

2. Notwithstanding the provisions of paragraph 1 of this Article, the provisions of paragraph 4 of Article 7, of paragraphs 2 and 3 of Article 8, of paragraphs 1 and 4 of Article 9, of Article 11, of Article 12, of Article 14 and of paragraph 3 of Article 18 of this Convention shall be immediately applied by each Member as from the coming into force of this Convention for that Member.

3. The instruments referred to in paragraph 1 of this Article shall specify in particular-

(a) the branches of social security to which they apply, having regard to the requirement of reciprocity referred to in Articles 6 and 10 of this Convention; these branches shall, where the Members concerned have legislation covering them, comprise at least invalidity benefits, old-age benefits, survivors' benefits and pensions in respect of employment injuries, including death grants, as well as, subject to the provisions of paragraph 1 of Article 10 of this Convention, medical care, sickness benefits, maternity benefits and benefits in respect of employment injuries, other than pensions and death grants;

(b) the categories of persons to which they are applicable; these categories shall comprise at least employees (including, as appropriate, frontier workers and seasonal workers), as well as the members of their families and their survivors, who are nationals of one of the Members concerned or who are refugees or stateless persons resident in the territory of one of these Members;

(c) the arrangements for the reimbursement of the benefits provided and other costs borne by the institution of one Member on behalf of the institution of another Member unless it has been agreed that there shall be no reimbursement;

(d) the rules to avoid undue plurality of contributions or other liabilities or of benefits.

PART II. APPLICABLE LEGISLATION

Article 5

1. The legislation applicable in respect of the persons covered by this Convention shall be determined by mutual agreement between the Members concerned, with a view to avoiding conflicts of laws and the undesirable consequences that might ensue for those concerned either through lack of protection, or as a result of undue plurality of contributions or other liabilities or of benefits, in accordance with the following rules:

(a) employees who are normally employed in the territory of a Member shall be subject to the legislation of that Member, even if they are resident in the territory of another Member or if the undertaking which employs them has its registered office, or their employer has his place of residence, in the territory of another Member;

(b) self-employed persons who normally engage in their occupation in the territory of a Member shall be subject to the legislation of that Member, even if they are resident in the territory of another Member;

(c) employees and self-employed persons sailing on board a ship flying the flag of a Member shall be subject to the legislation of that Member even if they are resident in the territory of another Member or if the undertaking which employs them has its registered office, or their employer has his place of residence, in the territory of another Member;

(d) persons who are not part of the economically active population shall be subject to the legislation of the Member in whose territory they are resident, in so far as they are not protected in virtue of subparagraphs (a) to (c) of this paragraph.

2. Notwithstanding the provisions of subparagraphs (a) to (c) of paragraph 1 of this Article, Members concerned may agree that certain categories of persons, in particular self-employed persons, shall be subject to the legislation of the Member in whose territory they are resident.

3. Members concerned may determine by mutual agreement other exceptions to the rules set forth in paragraph 1 of this Article, in the interest of the persons concerned.

PART III. MAINTENANCE OF RIGHTS IN COURSE OF ACQUISITION

Article 6

Subject to the provisions of paragraph 3, subparagraph (a), of Article 4 of this Convention, each Member shall endeavour to participate with every other Member concerned in schemes for the maintenance of rights in course of acquisition, as regards each branch of social security referred to in paragraph 1 of Article 2 of this Convention and for which every one of these Members has legislation in force, for the benefit of persons who have been subject successively or alternately to the legislation of the said Members.

Article 7

1. The schemes for the maintenance of rights in course of acquisition referred to in Article 6 of this Convention shall provide for the adding together, to the extent necessary, of periods of insurance, employment, occupational activity or residence, as the case may be, completed under the legislation of the Members concerned for the purposes of:

(a) participation in voluntary insurance or optional continued insurance, where appropriate;

(b) acquisition, maintenance or recovery of rights and, as the case may be, calculation of benefits.

2. Periods completed concurrently under the legislation of two or more Members shall be reckoned only once.

3. The Members concerned shall, where necessary, determine by mutual agreement special arrangements for adding together periods which are different in nature and periods qualifying for right to benefits under special schemes.

4. Where a person has completed periods under the legislation of three or more Members which are parties to different bilateral or multilateral instruments, each Member which is concurrently bound by two or more of the instruments in question shall add these periods together, to the extent necessary, in accordance with the provisions of these instruments, for the purposes of acquisition, maintenance or recovery of rights to benefit.

Article 8

1. The schemes for the maintenance of rights in course of acquisition referred to in Article 6 of this Convention shall determine the formula of awarding:

(a) invalidity, old-age and survivors' benefits, and

(b) pensions, in respect of occupational diseases,

as well as the apportionment, where appropriate, of the costs involved.

2. In the case referred to in paragraph 4 of Article 7 of this Convention, each Member which is concurrently bound by two or more of the instruments in question shall apply the provisions of these instruments for the purpose of calculating benefits to which there is a right under its legislation, taking into account the periods added together in accordance with the legislation of the Members concerned.

3. Where in application of the provisions of paragraph 2 of this Article a Member would have to award benefits of the same nature to the same person in pursuance of two or more bilateral or multilateral instruments, that Member shall be required to award only the benefit most favourable to the person concerned as determined on the initial award of these benefits.

4. Notwithstanding the provisions of paragraph 2 of this Article the Members concerned may, where necessary, agree on supplementary provisions for the calculation of the benefits specified in that paragraph.

PART IV. MAINTENANCE OF ACQUIRED RIGHTS AND PROVISION OF BENEFITS ABROAD

Article 9

1. Each Member shall guarantee the provision of invalidity, old-age and survivors' cash benefits, pensions in respect of employment injuries and death grants, to which a right is acquired under its legislation, to beneficiaries who are nationals of a Member or refugees or stateless persons,

irrespective of their place of residence, subject to measures for this purpose to be taken, where necessary, by agreement between the Members or with the states concerned.

2. Notwithstanding the provisions of paragraph 1 of this Article, the Members concerned which participate in the schemes for the maintenance of rights in course of acquisition referred to in Article 6 of this Convention may agree to guarantee the provision of the benefits referred to in the said paragraph to beneficiaries resident in the territory of a Member other than the competent Member, within the framework of the bilateral or multilateral agreements referred to in paragraph 1 of Article 4 of this Convention.

3. In addition, notwithstanding the provisions of paragraph 1 of this Article, in the case of non-contributory benefits, the Members concerned shall determine by mutual agreement the conditions under which the provision of these benefits shall be guaranteed to beneficiaries resident in the territory of a Member other than the competent member.

4. The provisions of paragraphs 1, 2 and 3 of this Article need not be applied to:

(a) special non-contributory benefits awarded as a form of assistance or in cases of need;

(b) benefits awarded under transitional schemes.

Article 10

1. Members concerned shall endeavour to participate in schemes for the maintenance of rights acquired under their legislation, taking into account the provisions of Part III of this Convention, as regards each of the following branches of social security for which each of these Members has legislation in force: medical care, sickness benefit, maternity benefit and benefit in respect of employment injuries, other than pensions and death grants. These schemes shall guarantee such benefits to persons resident or temporarily resident in the territory of one of these Members other than the competent Member, under conditions and within limits to be determined by mutual agreement between the Members concerned.

2. When not assured by existing legislation, the reciprocity required by paragraph 1 of this Article may be assured by measures taken by a Member to guarantee benefits corresponding to the benefits provided under the legislation of another Member, subject to the agreement of that Member.

3. Members concerned shall endeavour to participate in schemes for the maintenance of rights acquired under their legislation, taking into account the provisions of Part III of this Convention, as regards each of the following branches of social security for which each of these Members has legislation in force: unemployment benefit, family benefit and, notwithstanding the provisions of paragraph 1 of Article 9 of this Convention and paragraph 1 of this Article, rehabilitation benefit. These schemes shall guarantee such benefits to persons resident in the territory of one of these Members other than the competent Member, under conditions and within limits to be determined by mutual agreement between the Members concerned.

Article 11

The rules for the adjustment of benefits provided for under the legislation of a Member shall be applicable to the benefits payable under that legislation by virtue of the provisions of this Convention.

PART V. ADMINISTRATIVE ASSISTANCE AND ASSISTANCE TO PERSONS COVERED BY THIS CONVENTION

Article 12

1. The authorities and institutions of Members shall afford one another assistance with a view to facilitating the application of this Convention and of their respective legislation.

2. In principle, the administrative assistance given by these authorities and institutions to one another shall be free of charge. Members may agree to reimburse certain expenses.

3. The authorities, institutions and jurisdictions of one Member may not reject claims or other documents submitted to them by reason of the fact that they are written in an official language of another Member.

Article 13

1. Where a claimant is resident in the territory of a Member other than the competent Member, he may present his claim validly to the institution of his place of residence, which shall forward it to the institution or institutions referred to in the claim.

2. Any claim, declaration or appeal that should have been submitted, under the legislation of a Member, within a specified time to an authority, institution or jurisdiction of that Member, shall be admissible if it is submitted within that time-limit to an authority, institution or jurisdiction of another Member in the territory of which the claimant is resident. In such event, the authority, institution or jurisdiction receiving the claim, declaration or appeal shall forward it without delay to the competent authority, institution or jurisdiction of the first Member. The date on which any claim, declaration or appeal was submitted to an authority, institution or jurisdiction of the second Member shall be deemed to be the date of its submission to the authority, institution or jurisdiction competent to deal with it.

3. Benefits to be provided by a Member to a beneficiary resident or temporarily resident in the territory of another Member may be provided either directly by the institution liable for the payment, or through the intermediary of an institution designated by the latter Member, at the place where the beneficiary is resident or temporarily resident, subject to the agreement of the Members concerned.

Article 14

Each Member shall promote the development of social services to assist persons covered by this Convention, particularly migrant workers, in their dealings with the authorities, institutions and jurisdictions, particularly with respect to the award and receipt of benefits to which they are entitled and the exercise of their right of appeal, as well as in order to promote their personal and family welfare.

PART VI. MISCELLANEOUS PROVISIONS

Article 15

Except for invalidity, old-age and survivors' benefits and benefits in respect of occupational disease, the costs of which are apportioned among two or more Members, this Convention shall not confer or maintain a right to several benefits of the same nature based on the same period of compulsory insurance, employment, occupational activity or residence.

Article 16

1. The benefits provided and other costs borne by an institution of a Member on behalf of an institution of another Member shall be reimbursed in accordance with the modalities

determined by mutual agreement among these Members, unless they have agreed that there shall be no reimbursement.

2. Transfers of sums resulting from the application of this Convention shall be effected, if need be, in accordance with the agreements in force between the Members concerned at the date of transfer. In the absence of such agreements, the necessary arrangements shall be agreed between them.

Article 17

1. Members may derogate from the provisions of this Convention by special arrangements within the framework of the bilateral or multilateral instruments concluded amongst two or more of them, on condition that they do not affect the rights and obligations of other Members and settle the maintenance of rights on terms which, in the aggregate, are at least as favourable as those of this Convention.

2. A Member shall be deemed to satisfy the provisions of paragraph 1 of Article 9 and of Article 11 of this Convention:

(a) if it guarantees at the date of its ratification the provision of the relevant benefits in a substantial amount prescribed under its legislation, to all beneficiaries regardless of their nationality and irrespective of their place of residence; and

(b) if it gives effect to the provisions of paragraph 1 of Article 9 and of Article 11 of this Convention within the framework of the bilateral or multilateral instruments referred to in paragraph 1 of Article 4 of this Convention.

3. Each Member which has taken advantage of the provisions of paragraph 2 of this Article shall indicate in its reports on the application of this Convention submitted under article 22 of the Constitution of the International Labour Organisation:

(a) that its reasons for doing so subsist; or

(b) that it renounces its right to avail itself of the provisions of the above-mentioned paragraph of this Article as from a stated date.

PART VII. TRANSITIONAL AND FINAL PROVISIONS

Article 18

1. This Convention does not confer any right to benefit in respect of a period prior to its coming into force for the Members concerned.

2. For the application of the provisions of this Convention, all periods of insurance, employment, occupational activity or residence completed under the legislation of a Member before the date on which a scheme for the maintenance of rights in course of acquisition referred to in Article 6 of this Convention enters into force for the Member concerned shall be taken into account for the purpose of determining whether rights arise under that scheme as from the date of its entry into force, subject to specific provisions to be agreed upon, if necessary, between the Members concerned.

3. Any benefit referred to in paragraph 1 of Article 9 of this Convention, which has not been awarded or which has been suspended on account of the residence of the claimant in the territory of a State other than the competent Member, shall be awarded or resumed, at the request of the person concerned, as from the date on which this Convention enters into force for the latter Member or from the date of its entry into force for the Member of which he is a national, whichever is the later, unless the person concerned has previously obtained a

lumpsum settlement in place of this benefit. The provisions of the legislation of the competent Member concerning the extinction of rights shall not be invoked against the person concerned if he submits his request within two years following this date or the date of the coming into effect of the measures provided for in paragraph 1 of Article 9, as the case may be.

4. Members concerned shall determine by mutual agreement the extent to which a scheme for the maintenance of rights in course of acquisition referred to in Article 6 of this Convention applies to a contingency arising before the entry into force of the scheme for these Members.

Article 19

1. The denunciation of this Convention by a Member shall not affect the Member's obligations with respect to contingencies arising before the date on which denunciation has taken effect.

2. Rights in course of acquisition which are maintained by virtue of this Convention shall not lapse by reason of its denunciation by a Member; their further maintenance during the period subsequent to the date on which this Convention ceased to be in force shall be determined by the bilateral or multilateral social security instruments concluded by the Member, or, in the absence of such instruments, by the legislation of the said Member.

Article 20

1. This Convention, revises, on the terms set forth in the following paragraphs of this Article, the Maintenance of Migrants' Pension Rights Convention, 1935.

2. The coming into force of this Convention for any Member bound by the obligations of the Maintenance of Migrants' Pension Rights Convention, 1935, shall not, ipso jure, involve the immediate denunciation of that Convention.

3. The Maintenance of Migrants' Pension Rights Convention, 1935, shall cease to have effect in the relations between any Members parties thereto as and when a scheme for the maintenance of rights in course of acquisition in pursuance of Article 6 of this Convention has become applicable in these relations.

Article 21

The formal ratifications of this Convention shall be communicated to the Director-General of the International Labour Office for registration.

Article 22

1. This Convention shall be binding only upon those Members of the International Labour Organisation whose ratifications have been registered with the Director-General.

2. It shall come into force twelve months after the date on which the ratifications of two Members have been registered with the Director-General.

3. Thereafter, this Convention shall come into force for any Member twelve months after the date on which its ratification has been registered.

Article 23

1. A Member which has ratified this Convention may denounce it after the expiration of ten years from the date on which the Convention first comes into force, by an act communicated to the Director-General of the International Labour Office for registration. Such denunciation shall not take effect until one year after the date on which it is registered.

2. Each Member which has ratified this Convention and which does not, within the year following the expiration of the period of ten years mentioned in the preceding paragraph, exercise the right of denunciation provided for in this Article, will be bound for another period of ten years and, thereafter, may denounce this Convention at the expiration of each period of ten years under the terms provided for in this Article.

Article 24

1. The Director-General of the International Labour Office shall notify all Members of the International Labour Organisation of the registration of all ratifications and denunciations communicated to him by the Members of the Organisation.

2. When notifying the Members of the Organisation of the registration of the second ratification communicated to him, the Director-General shall draw the attention of the Members of the Organisation to the date upon which the Convention will come into force.

Article 25

The Director-General of the International Labour Office shall communicate to the Secretary-General of the United Nations for registration in accordance with article 102 of the Charter of the United Nations full particulars of all ratifications and acts of denunciation registered by him in accordance with the provisions of the preceding Articles.

Article 26

At such times as it may consider necessary the Governing Body of the International Labour Office shall present to the General Conference a report on the working of this Convention and shall examine the desirability of placing on the agenda of the Conference the question of its revision in whole or in part.

Article 27

1. Should the Conference adopt a new Convention revising this Convention in whole or in part, then, unless the new Convention otherwise provides-

(a) the ratification by a Member of the new revising Convention shall ipso jure involve the immediate denunciation of this Convention, notwithstanding the provisions of Article 23 above, if and when the new revising Convention shall have come into force;

(b) as from the date when the new revising Convention comes into force this Convention shall cease to be open to ratification by the Members.

2. This Convention shall in any case remain in force in its actual form and content for those Members which have ratified it but have not ratified the revising Convention.

Article 28

The English and French versions of the text of this Convention are equally authoritative.

2.6 International Labour Standards Relating to Indigenous Peoples

Convention No. 169 concerning Indigenous and Tribal Peoples in Independent Countries, 1989*

Adoption: 27 June 1989
Entry into force: 5 September 1991
Parties: 18 (Status as of 1 April 2007)

ARGENTINA 3 July 2000, BOLIVIA 11 Dec 1991, BRAZIL 25 July 2002, COLOMBIA 7 Aug 1991, COSTA RICA 2 Apr 1993, DENMARK 22 Feb 1996, DOMINICA 25 June 2002, ECUADOR 15 May 1998, FIJI 3 Mar 1998, GUATEMALA 5 June 1996, HONDURAS 28 Mar 1995, MEXICO 5 Sep 1990, NETHERLANDS 2 Feb 1998, NORWAY 19 June 1990, PARAGUAY 10 Aug 1993, PERU 2 Feb 1994, SPAIN 15 Feb 2007, VENEZUELA (BOLIVARIAN REPUBLIC OF) 22 May 2002.

The General Conference of the International Labour Organisation,

Having been convened at Geneva by the Governing Body of the International Labour Office, and having met in its 76th Session on 7 June 1989, and

Noting the international standards contained in the Indigenous and Tribal Populations Convention and Recommendation, 1957, and

Recalling the terms of the Universal Declaration of Human Rights, the International Covenant on Economic, Social and Cultural Rights, the International Covenant on Civil and Political Rights, and the many international instruments on the prevention of discrimination, and

Considering that the developments which have taken place in international law since 1957, as well as developments in the situation of indigenous and tribal peoples in all regions of the world, have made it appropriate to adopt new international standards on the subject with a view to removing the assimilationist orientation of the earlier standards, and

Recognising the aspirations of these peoples to exercise control over their own institutions, ways of life and economic development and to maintain and develop their identities, languages and religions, within the framework of the States in which they live, and

Noting that in many parts of the world these peoples are unable to enjoy their fundamental human rights to the same degree as the rest of the population of the States within which they live, and that their laws, values, customs and perspectives have often been eroded, and

Calling attention to the distinctive contributions of indigenous and tribal peoples to the cultural diversity and social and ecological harmony of humankind and to international co-operation and understanding, and

Noting that the following provisions have been framed with the co-operation of the United Nations, the Food and Agriculture Organisation of the United Nations, the United Nations Educational, Scientific and Cultural Organisation and the World Health Organisation, as well as of the Inter-American Indian Institute, at appropriate levels and in their respective fields,

* Source: International Labour Organization, http://www.ilo.org/ilolex
The ILO shall accept no responsibility for any inaccuracy, errors or omissions or for the consequences arising from the use of the Text.

and that it is proposed to continue this co-operation in promoting and securing the application of these provisions, and

Having decided upon the adoption of certain proposals with regard to the partial revision of the Indigenous and Tribal Populations Convention, 1957 (No.107), which is the fourth item on the agenda of the session, and

Having determined that these proposals shall take the form of an international Convention revising the Indigenous and Tribal Populations Convention, 1957;

adopts this twenty-seventh day of June of the year one thousand nine hundred and eighty-nine the following Convention, which may be cited as the Indigenous and Tribal Peoples Convention, 1989;

Part I. General policy

Article 1

1. This Convention applies to:

(a) tribal peoples in independent countries whose social, cultural and economic conditions distinguish them from other sections of the national community, and whose status is regulated wholly or partially by their own customs or traditions or by special laws or regulations;

(b) peoples in independent countries who are regarded as indigenous on account of their descent from the populations which inhabited the country, or a geographical region to which the country belongs, at the time of conquest or colonisation or the establishment of present state boundaries and who, irrespective of their legal status, retain some or all of their own social, economic, cultural and political institutions.

2. Self-identification as indigenous or tribal shall be regarded as a fundamental criterion for determining the groups to which the provisions of this Convention apply.

3. The use of the term peoples in this Convention shall not be construed as having any implications as regards the rights which may attach to the term under international law.

Article 2

1. Governments shall have the responsibility for developing, with the participation of the peoples concerned, co-ordinated and systematic action to protect the rights of these peoples and to guarantee respect for their integrity.

2. Such action shall include measures for:

(a) ensuring that members of these peoples benefit on an equal footing from the rights and opportunities which national laws and regulations grant to other members of the population;

(b) promoting the full realisation of the social, economic and cultural rights of these peoples with respect for their social and cultural identity, their customs and traditions and their institutions;

(c) assisting the members of the peoples concerned to eliminate socio-economic gaps that may exist between indigenous and other members of the national community, in a manner compatible with their aspirations and ways of life.

Article 3

1. Indigenous and tribal peoples shall enjoy the full measure of human rights and fundamental freedoms without hindrance or discrimination. The provisions of the Convention shall be applied without discrimination to male and female members of these peoples.

2. No form of force or coercion shall be used in violation of the human rights and fundamental freedoms of the peoples concerned, including the rights contained in this Convention.

Article 4

1. Special measures shall be adopted as appropriate for safeguarding the persons, institutions, property, labour, cultures and environment of the peoples concerned.

2. Such special measures shall not be contrary to the freely-expressed wishes of the peoples concerned.

3. Enjoyment of the general rights of citizenship, without discrimination, shall not be prejudiced in any way by such special measures.

Article 5

In applying the provisions of this Convention:

(a) the social, cultural, religious and spiritual values and practices of these peoples shall be recognised and protected, and due account shall be taken of the nature of the problems which face them both as groups and as individuals;

(b) the integrity of the values, practices and institutions of these peoples shall be respected;

(c) policies aimed at mitigating the difficulties experienced by these peoples in facing new conditions of life and work shall be adopted, with the participation and co-operation of the peoples affected.

Article 6

1. In applying the provisions of this Convention, governments shall:

(a) consult the peoples concerned, through appropriate procedures and in particular through their representative institutions, whenever consideration is being given to legislative or administrative measures which may affect them directly;

(b) establish means by which these peoples can freely participate, to at least the same extent as other sectors of the population, at all levels of decision-making in elective institutions and administrative and other bodies responsible for policies and programmes which concern them;

(c) establish means for the full development of these peoples' own institutions and initiatives, and in appropriate cases provide the resources necessary for this purpose.

2. The consultations carried out in application of this Convention shall be undertaken, in good faith and in a form appropriate to the circumstances, with the objective of achieving agreement or consent to the proposed measures.

Article 7

1. The peoples concerned shall have the right to decide their own priorities for the process of development as it affects their lives, beliefs, institutions and spiritual well-being and the lands they occupy or otherwise use, and to exercise control, to the extent possible, over

their own economic, social and cultural development. In addition, they shall participate in the formulation, implementation and evaluation of plans and programmes for national and regional development which may affect them directly.

2. The improvement of the conditions of life and work and levels of health and education of the peoples concerned, with their participation and co-operation, shall be a matter of priority in plans for the overall economic development of areas they inhabit. Special projects for development of the areas in question shall also be so designed as to promote such improvement.

3. Governments shall ensure that, whenever appropriate, studies are carried out, in co-operation with the peoples concerned, to assess the social, spiritual, cultural and environmental impact on them of planned development activities. The results of these studies shall be considered as fundamental criteria for the implementation of these activities.

4. Governments shall take measures, in co-operation with the peoples concerned, to protect and preserve the environment of the territories they inhabit.

Article 8

1. In applying national laws and regulations to the peoples concerned, due regard shall be had to their customs or customary laws.

2. These peoples shall have the right to retain their own customs and institutions, where these are not incompatible with fundamental rights defined by the national legal system and with internationally recognised human rights. Procedures shall be established, whenever necessary, to resolve conflicts which may arise in the application of this principle.

3. The application of paragraphs 1 and 2 of this Article shall not prevent members of these peoples from exercising the rights granted to all citizens and from assuming the corresponding duties.

Article 9

1. To the extent compatible with the national legal system and internationally recognised human rights, the methods customarily practised by the peoples concerned for dealing with offences committed by their members shall be respected.

2. The customs of these peoples in regard to penal matters shall be taken into consideration by the authorities and courts dealing with such cases.

Article 10

1. In imposing penalties laid down by general law on members of these peoples account shall be taken of their economic, social and cultural characteristics.

2. Preference shall be given to methods of punishment other than confinement in prison.

Article 11

The exaction from members of the peoples concerned of compulsory personal services in any form, whether paid or unpaid, shall be prohibited and punishable by law, except in cases prescribed by law for all citizens.

Article 12

The peoples concerned shall be safeguarded against the abuse of their rights and shall be able to take legal proceedings, either individually or through their representative bodies, for the effective protection of these rights. Measures shall be taken to ensure that members of these peoples can understand and be understood in legal proceedings, where necessary through the provision of interpretation or by other effective means.

PART II. LAND

Article 13

1. In applying the provisions of this Part of the Convention governments shall respect the special importance for the cultures and spiritual values of the peoples concerned of their relationship with the lands or territories, or both as applicable, which they occupy or otherwise use, and in particular the collective aspects of this relationship.

2. The use of the term lands in Articles 15 and 16 shall include the concept of territories, which covers the total environment of the areas which the peoples concerned occupy or otherwise use.

Article 14

1. The rights of ownership and possession of the peoples concerned over the lands which they traditionally occupy shall be recognised. In addition, measures shall be taken in appropriate cases to safeguard the right of the peoples concerned to use lands not exclusively occupied by them, but to which they have traditionally had access for their subsistence and traditional activities. Particular attention shall be paid to the situation of nomadic peoples and shifting cultivators in this respect.

2. Governments shall take steps as necessary to identify the lands which the peoples concerned traditionally occupy, and to guarantee effective protection of their rights of ownership and possession.

3. Adequate procedures shall be established within the national legal system to resolve land claims by the peoples concerned.

Article 15

1. The rights of the peoples concerned to the natural resources pertaining to their lands shall be specially safeguarded. These rights include the right of these peoples to participate in the use, management and conservation of these resources.

2. In cases in which the State retains the ownership of mineral or sub-surface resources or rights to other resources pertaining to lands, governments shall establish or maintain procedures through which they shall consult these peoples, with a view to ascertaining whether and to what degree their interests would be prejudiced, before undertaking or permitting any programmes for the exploration or exploitation of such resources pertaining to their lands. The peoples concerned shall wherever possible participate in the benefits of such activities, and shall receive fair compensation for any damages which they may sustain as a result of such activities.

Article 16

1. Subject to the following paragraphs of this Article, the peoples concerned shall not be removed from the lands which they occupy.

2. Where the relocation of these peoples is considered necessary as an exceptional measure, such relocation shall take place only with their free and informed consent. Where their consent

cannot be obtained, such relocation shall take place only following appropriate procedures established by national laws and regulations, including public inquiries where appropriate, which provide the opportunity for effective representation of the peoples concerned.

3. Whenever possible, these peoples shall have the right to return to their traditional lands, as soon as the grounds for relocation cease to exist.

4. When such return is not possible, as determined by agreement or, in the absence of such agreement, through appropriate procedures, these peoples shall be provided in all possible cases with lands of quality and legal status at least equal to that of the lands previously occupied by them, suitable to provide for their present needs and future development. Where the peoples concerned express a preference for compensation in money or in kind, they shall be so compensated under appropriate guarantees.

5. Persons thus relocated shall be fully compensated for any resulting loss or injury.

Article 17

1. Procedures established by the peoples concerned for the transmission of land rights among members of these peoples shall be respected.

2. The peoples concerned shall be consulted whenever consideration is being given to their capacity to alienate their lands or otherwise transmit their rights outside their own community.

3. Persons not belonging to these peoples shall be prevented from taking advantage of their customs or of lack of understanding of the laws on the part of their members to secure the ownership, possession or use of land belonging to them.

Article 18

Adequate penalties shall be established by law for unauthorised intrusion upon, or use of, the lands of the peoples concerned, and governments shall take measures to prevent such offences.

Article 19

National agrarian programmes shall secure to the peoples concerned treatment equivalent to that accorded to other sectors of the population with regard to:

(a) the provision of more land for these peoples when they have not the area necessary for providing the essentials of a normal existence, or for any possible increase in their numbers;

(b) the provision of the means required to promote the development of the lands which these peoples already possess.

PART III. RECRUITMENT AND CONDITIONS OF EMPLOYMENT

Article 20

1. Governments shall, within the framework of national laws and regulations, and in co-operation with the peoples concerned, adopt special measures to ensure the effective protection with regard to recruitment and conditions of employment of workers belonging to these peoples, to the extent that they are not effectively protected by laws applicable to workers in general.

2. Governments shall do everything possible to prevent any discrimination between workers belonging to the peoples concerned and other workers, in particular as regards:

(a) admission to employment, including skilled employment, as well as measures for promotion and advancement;

(b) equal remuneration for work of equal value;

(c) medical and social assistance, occupational safety and health, all social security benefits and any other occupationally related benefits, and housing;

(d) the right of association and freedom for all lawful trade union activities, and the right to conclude collective agreements with employers or employers' organisations.

3. The measures taken shall include measures to ensure:

(a) that workers belonging to the peoples concerned, including seasonal, casual and migrant workers in agricultural and other employment, as well as those employed by labour contractors, enjoy the protection afforded by national law and practice to other such workers in the same sectors, and that they are fully informed of their rights under labour legislation and of the means of redress available to them;

(b) that workers belonging to these peoples are not subjected to working conditions hazardous to their health, in particular through exposure to pesticides or other toxic substances;

(c) that workers belonging to these peoples are not subjected to coercive recruitment systems, including bonded labour and other forms of debt servitude;

(d) that workers belonging to these peoples enjoy equal opportunities and equal treatment in employment for men and women, and protection from sexual harassment.

4. Particular attention shall be paid to the establishment of adequate labour inspection services in areas where workers belonging to the peoples concerned undertake wage employment, in order to ensure compliance with the provisions of this Part of this Convention.

PART IV. VOCATIONAL TRAINING, HANDICRAFTS AND RURAL INDUSTRIES

Article 21

Members of the peoples concerned shall enjoy opportunities at least equal to those of other citizens in respect of vocational training measures.

Article 22

1. Measures shall be taken to promote the voluntary participation of members of the peoples concerned in vocational training programmes of general application.

2. Whenever existing programmes of vocational training of general application do not meet the special needs of the peoples concerned, governments shall, with the participation of these peoples, ensure the provision of special training programmes and facilities.

3. Any special training programmes shall be based on the economic environment, social and cultural conditions and practical needs of the peoples concerned. Any studies made in this connection shall be carried out in co-operation with these peoples, who shall be consulted on the organisation and operation of such programmes. Where feasible, these peoples shall progressively assume responsibility for the organisation and operation of such special training programmes, if they so decide.

Article 23

1. Handicrafts, rural and community-based industries, and subsistence economy and traditional activities of the peoples concerned, such as hunting, fishing, trapping and gathering, shall be

recognised as important factors in the maintenance of their cultures and in their economic self-reliance and development. Governments shall, with the participation of these people and whenever appropriate, ensure that these activities are strengthened and promoted.

2. Upon the request of the peoples concerned, appropriate technical and financial assistance shall be provided wherever possible, taking into account the traditional technologies and cultural characteristics of these peoples, as well as the importance of sustainable and equitable development.

PART V. SOCIAL SECURITY AND HEALTH

Article 24

Social security schemes shall be extended progressively to cover the peoples concerned, and applied without discrimination against them.

Article 25

1. Governments shall ensure that adequate health services are made available to the peoples concerned, or shall provide them with resources to allow them to design and deliver such services under their own responsibility and control, so that they may enjoy the highest attainable standard of physical and mental health.

2. Health services shall, to the extent possible, be community-based. These services shall be planned and administered in co-operation with the peoples concerned and take into account their economic, geographic, social and cultural conditions as well as their traditional preventive care, healing practices and medicines.

3. The health care system shall give preference to the training and employment of local community health workers, and focus on primary health care while maintaining strong links with other levels of health care services.

4. The provision of such health services shall be co-ordinated with other social, economic and cultural measures in the country.

PART VI. EDUCATION AND MEANS OF COMMUNICATION

Article 26

Measures shall be taken to ensure that members of the peoples concerned have the opportunity to acquire education at all levels on at least an equal footing with the rest of the national community.

Article 27

1. Education programmes and services for the peoples concerned shall be developed and implemented in co-operation with them to address their special needs, and shall incorporate their histories, their knowledge and technologies, their value systems and their further social, economic and cultural aspirations.

2. The competent authority shall ensure the training of members of these peoples and their involvement in the formulation and implementation of education programmes, with a view to the progressive transfer of responsibility for the conduct of these programmes to these peoples as appropriate.

3. In addition, governments shall recognise the right of these peoples to establish their own educational institutions and facilities, provided that such institutions meet minimum standards established by the competent authority in consultation with these peoples. Appropriate resources shall be provided for this purpose.

Article 28

1. Children belonging to the peoples concerned shall, wherever practicable, be taught to read and write in their own indigenous language or in the language most commonly used by the group to which they belong. When this is not practicable, the competent authorities shall undertake consultations with these peoples with a view to the adoption of measures to achieve this objective.

2. Adequate measures shall be taken to ensure that these peoples have the opportunity to attain fluency in the national language or in one of the official languages of the country.

3. Measures shall be taken to preserve and promote the development and practice of the indigenous languages of the peoples concerned.

Article 29

The imparting of general knowledge and skills that will help children belonging to the peoples concerned to participate fully and on an equal footing in their own community and in the national community shall be an aim of education for these peoples.

Article 30

1. Governments shall adopt measures appropriate to the traditions and cultures of the peoples concerned, to make known to them their rights and duties, especially in regard to labour, economic opportunities, education and health matters, social welfare and their rights deriving from this Convention.

2. If necessary, this shall be done by means of written translations and through the use of mass communications in the languages of these peoples.

Article 31

Educational measures shall be taken among all sections of the national community, and particularly among those that are in most direct contact with the peoples concerned, with the object of eliminating prejudices that they may harbour in respect of these peoples. To this end, efforts shall be made to ensure that history textbooks and other educational materials provide a fair, accurate and informative portrayal of the societies and cultures of these peoples.

PART VII. CONTACTS AND CO-OPERATION ACROSS BORDERS

Article 32

Governments shall take appropriate measures, including by means of international agreements, to facilitate contacts and co-operation between indigenous and tribal peoples across borders, including activities in the economic, social, cultural, spiritual and environmental fields.

PART VIII. ADMINISTRATION

Article 33

1. The governmental authority responsible for the matters covered in this Convention shall ensure that agencies or other appropriate mechanisms exist to administer the programmes affecting the peoples concerned, and shall ensure that they have the means necessary for the proper fulfilment of the functions assigned to them.

2. These programmes shall include:

(a) the planning, co-ordination, execution and evaluation, in co-operation with the peoples concerned, of the measures provided for in this Convention;

(b) the proposing of legislative and other measures to the competent authorities and supervision of the application of the measures taken, in co-operation with the peoples concerned.

PART IX. GENERAL PROVISIONS

Article 34

The nature and scope of the measures to be taken to give effect to this Convention shall be determined in a flexible manner, having regard to the conditions characteristic of each country.

Article 35

The application of the provisions of this Convention shall not adversely affect rights and benefits of the peoples concerned pursuant to other Conventions and Recommendations, international instruments, treaties, or national laws, awards, custom or agreements.

PART X. FINAL PROVISIONS

Article 36

This Convention revises the Indigenous and Tribal Populations Convention, 1957.

Article 37

The formal ratifications of this Convention shall be communicated to the Director-General of the International Labour Office for registration.

Article 38

1. This Convention shall be binding only upon those Members of the International Labour Organisation whose ratifications have been registered with the Director-General.

2. It shall come into force twelve months after the date on which the ratifications of two Members have been registered with the Director-General.

3. Thereafter, this Convention shall come into force for any Member twelve months after the date on which its ratification has been registered.

Article 39

1. A Member which has ratified this Convention may denounce it after the expiration of ten years from the date on which the Convention first comes into force, by an act communicated to the Director-General of the International Labour Office for registration. Such denunciation shall not take effect until one year after the date on which it is registered.

2. Each Member which has ratified this Convention and which does not, within the year following the expiration of the period of ten years mentioned in the preceding paragraph, exercise the right of denunciation provided for in this Article, will be bound for another period of ten years and, thereafter, may denounce this Convention at the expiration of each period of ten years under the terms provided for in this Article.

Article 40

1. The Director-General of the International Labour Office shall notify all Members of the International Labour Organisation of the registration of all ratifications and denunciations communicated to him by the Members of the Organisation.

2. When notifying the Members of the Organisation of the registration of the second ratification communicated to him, the Director-General shall draw the attention of the Members of the Organisation to the date upon which the Convention will come into force.

Article 41

The Director-General of the International Labour Office shall communicate to the Secretary-General of the United Nations for registration in accordance with Article 102 of the Charter of the United Nations full particulars of all ratifications and acts of denunciation registered by him in accordance with the provisions of the preceding Articles.

Article 42

At such times as it may consider necessary the Governing Body of the International Labour Office shall present to the General Conference a report on the working of this Convention and shall examine the desirability of placing on the agenda of the Conference the question of its revision in whole or in part.

Article 43

1. Should the Conference adopt a new Convention revising this Convention in whole or in part, then, unless the new Convention otherwise provides-

(a) the ratification by a Member of the new revising Convention shall ipso jure involve the immediate denunciation of this Convention, notwithstanding the provisions of Article 39 above, if and when the new revising Convention shall have come into force;

(b) as from the date when the new revising Convention comes into force this Convention shall cease to be open to ratification by the Members.

2. This Convention shall in any case remain in force in its actual form and content for those Members which have ratified it but have not ratified the revising Convention.

Article 44

The English and French versions of the text of this Convention are equally authoritative.

3. NATIONALITY AND STATELESSNESS

Convention on Certain Questions relating to the Conflict of Nationality Laws, 1930*

Date of adoption: 12 April 1930
Entry into force: 1 July 1937
Parties: 21 (Status as of 1 April 2007)**

AUSTRALIA 10 Nov 1937, BELGIUM 4 Apr 1939 (*16), BRAZIL 19 Sep 1931 (*5, 6, 7, 16, 17), CANADA 6 Apr 1934 (*denunciation 15 May 1996), CHINA 14 Feb 1935 (*4), CYPRUS 27 Mar 1970 d, FIJI 12 Jun 1971 d, INDIA 7 Oct 1935, KIRABATI 29 Nov 1983 d, LESOTHO 4 Nov 1974 (*6), LIBERIA 16 Sep 2005 a, MALTA 16 Aug 1966 (*6, 16), MAURITIUS 18 Jul 1969 d (*6), MONACO 27 Apr 1931, NETHERLANDS 2 Apr 1937 (*8, 9, 10), NORWAY 16 Mar 1931, PAKISTAN 29 Jul 1953, POLAND 15 Jun 1934, SWAZILAND 18 Sep 1970, SWEDEN 6 Jul 1933 (*11), THE UNITED KINGDOM OF GREAT BRITAIN AND NORTHERN IRELAND 6 Apr 1934, ZIMBABWE 1 Dec 1998 d.

The President of the German Reich; the Federal President of the Austrian Republic; His Majesty the King of the Belgians; His Majesty the King of Great Britain, Ireland and the British Dominions beyond the Seas, Emperor of India; the President of the Republic of Chile; the President of the National Government of the Republic of China; the President of the Republic of Colombia; the President of the Republic of Cuba; His Majesty the King of Denmark and Iceland; the President of the Polish Republic, for the Free City of Danzig; His Majesty the King of Egypt; His Majesty the King of Spain; the Government of the Estonian Republic; the President of the French Republic; the President of the Hellenic Republic; His Serene Highness the Regent of the Kingdom of Hungary; His Majesty the King of Denmark and Iceland, for Iceland; His Majesty the King of Italy; His Majesty the Emperor of Japan; the President of the Latvian Republic; Her Royal Highness the Grand-Duchess of Luxemburg; the President of the United States of Mexico; Her Majesty the Queen of the Netherlands; the President of the Republic of Peru; the President of the Polish Republic; the President of the Portuguese Republic; the President of the Republic of Salvador; His Majesty the King of Sweden; the Swiss Federal Council; the President of the Czechoslovak Republic; the President of the Republic of Uruguay; His Majesty the King of Yugoslavia,

CONSIDERING that it is of importance to settle by international agreement questions relating to the conflict of nationality laws;

BEING CONVINCED that it is in the general interest of the international community to secure that all its members should recognise that every person should have a nationality and should have one nationality only;

RECOGNISING accordingly that the ideal towards which the efforts of humanity should be directed in this domain is the abolition of all cases both of statelessness and of double nationality;

BEING OF OPINION that, under the economic and social conditions which at present exist in the various countries, it is not possible to reach immediately a uniform solution of all the abovementioned problems;

* Source: League of Nations, 179 L.N.T.S. 89.

** The list does not include States which have signed but not ratified the Convention.

BEING DESIROUS, nevertheless, as a first step toward this great achievement, of settling in a first attempt at progressive codification, those questions relating to the conflict of nationality laws on which it is possible at the present time to reach international agreement,

HAVE DECIDED to conclude a Convention and have for this purpose appointed as their Plenipotentiaries:

[Names of plenipotentiaries not reproduced here.]

WHO, having deposited their full powers found in good and due form,

HAVE AGREED AS FOLLOWS:

CHAPTER I. GENERAL PRINCIPLES

Article 1

It is for each State to determine under its own law who are its nationals. This law shall be recognised by other States in so far as it is consistent with international conventions, international custom, and the principles of law generally recognised with regard to nationality.

Article 2

Any question as to whether a person possesses the nationality of a particular State shall be determined in accordance with the law of that State.

Article 3

Subject to the provisions of the present Convention, a person having two or more nationalities may be regarded as its national by each of the States whose nationality he possesses.

Article 4

A State may not afford diplomatic protection to one of its nationals against a State whose nationality such person also possesses.

Article 5

Within a third State, a person having more than one nationality shall be treated as if he had only one. Without prejudice to the application of its law in matters of personal status and of any conventions in force, a third State shall, of the nationalities which any such person possesses, recognise exclusively in its territory either the nationality of the country in which he is habitually and principally resident, or the nationality of the country with which in the circumstances he appears to be in fact most closely connected.

Article 6

Without prejudice to the liberty of a State to accord wider rights to renounce its nationality, a person possessing two nationalities acquired without any voluntary act on his part may renounce one of them with the authorisation of the State whose nationality he desires to surrender.

This authorisation may not be refused in the case of a person who has his habitual and principal residence abroad, if the conditions laid down in the law of the State whose nationality he desires to surrender are satisfied.

CHAPTER II. EXPATRIATION PERMITS

Article 7

In so far as the law of a State provides for the issue of an expatriation permit, such a permit shall not entail the loss of the nationality of the State which issues it, unless the person to whom it is issued possesses another nationality or unless and until he acquires another nationality.

An expatriation permit shall lapse if the holder does not acquire a new nationality within the period fixed by the State which has issued the permit. This provision shall not apply in the case of an individual who, at the time when he receives the expatriation permit, already possesses a nationality other than that of the State by which the permit is issued to him.

The State whose nationality is acquired by a person to whom an expatriation permit has been issued, shall notify such acquisition to the State which has issued the permit.

CHAPTER III. NATIONALITY OF MARRIED WOMEN

Article 8

If the national law of the wife causes her to lose her nationality on marriage with a foreigner, this consequence shall be conditional on her acquiring the nationality of the husband.

Article 9

If the national law of the wife causes her to lose her nationality upon a change in the nationality of her husband occurring during marriage, this consequence shall be conditional on her acquiring her husband's new nationality.

Article 10

Naturalisation of the husband during marriage shall not involve a change in the nationality of the wife except with her consent.

Article 11

The wife who, under the law of her country, lost her nationality on marriage shall not recover it after the dissolution of the marriage except on her own application and in accordance with the law of that country. If she does recover it, she shall lose the nationality which she acquired by reason of the marriage.

CHAPTER IV. NATIONALITY OF CHILDREN

Article 12

Rules of law which confer nationality by reason of birth on the territory of a State shall not apply automatically to children born to persons enjoying diplomatic immunities in the country where the birth occurs.

The law of each State shall permit children of consuls de carrière, or of officials of foreign States charged with official missions by their Governments, to become divested, by repudiation or otherwise, of the nationality of the State in which they were born, in any case in which on birth they acquired dual nationality, provided that they retain the nationality of their parents.

Article 13

Naturalisation of the parents shall confer on such of their children as, according to its law, are minors the nationality of the State by which the naturalisation is granted. In such case the law of that State may specify the conditions governing the acquisition of its nationality by the minor children as a result of the naturalisation of the parents. In cases where minor children do not acquire the nationality of their parents as the result of the naturalisation of the latter, they shall retain their existing nationality.

Article 14

A child whose parents are both unknown shall have the nationality of the country of birth. If the child's parentage is established, its nationality shall be determined by the rules applicable in cases where the parentage is known.

A foundling is, until the contrary is proved, presumed to have been born on the territory of the State in which it was found.

Article 15

Where the nationality of a State is not acquired automatically by reason of birth on its territory, a child born on the territory of that State of parents having no nationality, or of unknown nationality, may obtain the nationality of the said State. The law of that State shall determine the conditions governing the acquisition of its nationality in such cases.

Article 16

If the law of the State, whose nationality an illegitimate child possesses, recognises that such nationality may be lost as a consequence of a change in the civil status of the child (legitimation, recognition), such loss shall be conditional on the acquisition by the child of the nationality of another State under the law of such State relating to the effect upon nationality of changes in civil status.

CHAPTER V. ADOPTION

Article 17

If the law of a State recognises that its nationality may be lost as the result of adoption, this loss shall be conditional upon the acquisition by the person adopted of the nationality of the person by whom he is adopted, under the law of the State of which the latter is a national relating to the effect of adoption upon nationality.

CHAPTER VI. GENERAL AND FINAL PROVISIONS

Article 18

The High Contracting Parties agree to apply the principles and rules contained in the preceding Articles in their relations with each other, as from the date of the entry into force of the present Convention.

The inclusion of the abovementioned principles and rules in the Convention shall in no way be deemed to prejudice the question whether they do or do not already form part of international law.

It is understood that, in so far as any point is not covered by any of the provisions of the preceding Articles, the existing principles and rules of international law shall remain in force.

Article 19

Nothing in the present Convention shall affect the provisions of any treaty, convention or agreement in force between any of the High Contracting Parties relating to nationality or matters connected therewith.

Article 20

Any High Contracting Party may, when signing or ratifying the present Convention or acceding thereto, append an express reservation excluding any one or more of the provisions of Articles 1 to 17 and 21.

The provisions thus excluded cannot be applied against the Contracting Party who has made the reservation nor relied on by that Party against any other Contracting Party.

Article 21

If there should arise between the High Contracting Parties a dispute of any kind relating to the interpretation or application of the present Convention and if such dispute cannot be satisfactorily settled by diplomacy, it shall be settled in accordance with any applicable agreements in force between the parties providing for the settlement of international disputes.

In case there is no such agreement in force between the parties, the dispute shall be referred to arbitration or judicial settlement, in accordance with the constitutional procedure of each of the parties to the dispute. In the absence of agreement on the choice of another tribunal, the dispute shall be referred to the Permanent Court of International Justice, if all the parties to the dispute are parties to the Protocol of 16 December 1920 relating to the Statute of that Court, and if any of the parties to the dispute is not a party to the Protocol of 16 December 1920, the dispute shall be referred to an arbitral tribunal constituted in accordance with the Hague Convention of 18 October 1907 for the Pacific Settlement of International Conflicts.

Article 22

The present Convention shall remain open until 31 December 1930 for signature on behalf of any Member of the League of Nations or of any non-Member State invited to the First Codification Conference or to which the Council of the League of Nations has communicated a copy of the Convention for this purpose.

Article 23

The present Convention is subject to ratification. Ratifications shall be deposited with the Secretariat of the League of Nations.

The Secretary-General shall give notice of the deposit of each ratification to the Members of the League of Nations and to the non-Member States mentioned in Article 22, indicating the date of its deposit.

Article 24

As from 1 January 1931, any Member of the League of Nations and any non-Member State mentioned in Article 22 on whose behalf the Convention has not been signed before that date, may accede thereto.

Accession shall be effected by an instrument deposited with the Secretariat of the League of Nations. The Secretary-General of the League of Nations shall give notice of each accession to the Members of the League of Nations and to the non-Member States mentioned in Article 22, indicating the date of the deposit of the instrument.

Article 25

A procès-verbal shall be drawn up by the Secretary-General of the League of Nations as soon as ratifications or accessions on behalf of ten Members of the League of Nations or non-Member States have been deposited.

A certified copy of this procès-verbal shall be sent by the Secretary-General of the League of Nations to each Member of the League of Nations and to each non-Member State mentioned in Article 22.

Article 26

The present Convention shall enter into force on the 90th day after the date of the procès-verbal mentioned in Article 25 as regards all Members of the League of Nations or non-Member States on whose behalf ratifications or accessions have been deposited on the date of the procès-verbal.

As regards any Member of the League or non-Member State on whose behalf a ratification or accession is subsequently deposited, the Convention shall enter into force on the 90th day after the date of the deposit of a ratification or accession on its behalf.

Article 27

As from 1 January 1936, any Member of the League of Nations or any non-Member State in regard to which the present Convention is then in force, may address to the Secretary-General of the League of Nations a request for the revision of any or all of the provisions of this Convention. If such a request, after being communicated to the other Members of the League and non-Member States in regard to which the Convention is then in force, is supported within one year by at least nine of them, the Council of the League of Nations shall decide, after consultation with the Members of the League of Nations and the non-Member States mentioned in Article 22, whether a conference should be specially convoked for that purpose or whether such revision should be considered at the next conference for the codification of international law.

The High Contracting Parties agree that, if the present Convention is revised, the revised Convention may provide that upon its entry into force some or all of the provisions of the present Convention shall be abrogated in respect of all of the Parties to the present Convention.

Article 28

The present Convention may be denounced.

Denunciation shall be effected by a notification in writing addressed to the Secretary-General of the League of Nations, who shall inform all Members of the League of Nations and the non-Member States mentioned in Article 22.

Each denunciation shall take effect one year after the receipt by the Secretary-General of the notification but only as regards the Member of the League or non-Member State on whose behalf it has been notified.

Article 29

1. Any High Contracting Party may, at the time of signature, ratification or accession, declare that, in accepting the present Convention, he does not assume any obligations in respect of all or any of his colonies, protectorates, overseas territories or territories under suzerainty or mandate, or in respect of certain parts of the population of the said territories; and the present Convention shall not apply to any territories or to the parts of their population named in such declaration.

2. Any High Contracting Party may give notice to the Secretary-General of the League of Nations at any time subsequently that he desires that the Convention shall apply to all or any of his territories or to the parts of their population which have been made the subject of a declaration under the preceding paragraph, and the Convention shall apply to all the territories or the parts of their population named in such notice six months after its receipt by the Secretary-General of the League of Nations.

3. Any High Contracting Party may, at any time, declare that he desires that the present Convention shall cease to apply to all or any of his colonies, protectorates, overseas territories or territories under suzerainty or mandate, or in respect of certain parts of the population of the said territories, and the Convention shall cease to apply to the territories or to the parts of their population named in such declaration one year after its receipt by the Secretary-General of the League of Nations.

4. Any High Contracting Party may make the reservations provided for in Article 20 in respect of all or any of his colonies, protectorates, overseas territories or territories under suzerainty or mandate, or in respect of certain parts of the population of these territories, at the time of signature, ratification or accession to the Convention or at the time of making a notification under the second paragraph of this Article.

5. The Secretary-General of the League of Nations shall communicate to all the Members of the League of Nations and the non-Member States mentioned in Article 22 all declarations and notices received in virtue of this Article.

Article 30

The present Convention shall be registered by the Secretary-General of the League of Nations as soon as it has entered into force.

Article 31

The French and English texts of the present Convention shall both be authoritative.

IN FAITH WHEREOF the Plenipotentiaries have signed the present Convention.

DONE at The Hague on the twelfth day of April, one thousand nine hundred and thirty, in a single copy, which shall be deposited in the archives of the Secretariat of the League of Nations and of which certified true copies shall be transmitted by the Secretary-General to all the Members of the League of Nations and all the non-Member States invited to the First Conference for the Codification of International Law.

Protocol Relating to a Certain Case of Statelessness, 1930*

Adoption: 12 April 1930
Entry into Force: 1 July 1937
Parties: 24 (Status as of 1 April 2007) **

AUSTRALIA 8 July 1935, BRAZIL 19 Sep 1931 a, BURMA (no date given), CHILE 20 Mar 1935, CHINA 14 Feb 1935, CYPRUS 3 Apr 1978 d, EL SALVADOR 14 Oct 1935 a, FIJI 12 Jun 1972 d, INDIA 28 Sep 1932, JAMAICA 12 Jun 1968 a, KIRIBATI 29 Nov 1983 d, LESOTHO 4 Nov 1974 d, MALAWI 11 Jul 1967 a, MALTA 16 Aug 1966 d, MAURITIUS 18 Jul 1969 d, NETHERLANDS 2 Apr 1937, NIGER 18 Jul 1968 a, PAKISTAN 29 Jul 1953 d, POLAND 15 Jun 1934, SERBIA (REPUBLIC OF) 12 Mar 2001 d, SOUTH AFRICA 9 Apr 1936, THE FORMER YUGOSLAV REPUBLIC OF MACEDONIA 18 Jan 1994 d, UNITED KINGDOM OF GREAT BRITAIN AND NORTHERN IRELAND 14 Jan 1932, ZIMBABWE 1 Dec 1998 d.

The undersigned Plenipotentiaries, on behalf of their respective Governments,

With a view to preventing statelessness arising in certain circumstances,

Have agreed as follows:

Article 1

In a State whose nationality is not conferred by the mere fact of birth in its territory, a person born in its territory of a mother possessing the nationality of that State and of a father without nationality or of unknown nationality shall have the nationality of the said State.

Article 2

The High Contracting Parties agree to apply the principles and rules contained in the preceding article in their relation with each other, as from the date of the entry into force of the present Protocol.

The inclusion of the above-mentioned principles and rules in the said article shall in no way be deemed to prejudice the question whether they do or do not already form part of international law.

It is understood that, in so far as any point is not covered by any of the provisions of the preceding article, the existing principles and rules of international law shall remain in force.

Article 3

Nothing in the present Protocol shall affect the provisions of any treaty, convention or agreement in force between any of the High Contracting Parties relating to nationality or matters connected therewith.

Article 4

Any High Contracting Party may, when signing or ratifying the present Protocol or acceding

* Source: League of Nations, 179 L.T.N.S. 115.

** The list does not include States which have signed but not ratified the Convention.

thereto, append an express reservation excluding any one or more of the provisions of Articles 1 and 5.

The provisions thus excluded cannot be applied against the High Contracting Party who has made the reservation nor relied on by that Party against any other High Contracting Party.

Article 5

If there should arise between the High Contracting Parties a dispute of any kind relating to the interpretation or application of the present Protocol and if such dispute cannot be satisfactorily settled by diplomacy, it shall be settled in accordance with any applicable agreements in force between the Parties providing for the settlement of international disputes.

In case there is no such agreement in force between the Parties, the dispute shall be referred to arbitration or judicial settlement, in accordance with the constitutional procedure of each of the Parties to the dispute. In the absence of agreement on the choice of another tribunal, the dispute shall be referred to the Permanent Court of International Justice, if any the Parties to the dispute are Parties to the Protocol[1] of the 16th December, 1920, relating to the Statute of that Court, and if any of the Parties to the dispute is not a Party to the Protocol of the 16th December, 1920, the dispute shall be referred to an arbitral tribunal constituted in accordance with the Hague Convention[2] of the 18th October, 1907, for the Pacific Settlement of International Conflicts.

Article 6

The present Protocol shall remain open until the 31st December, 1930, for signature on behalf of any Member of the League of Nations or of any non-Member State invited to the First Codification Conference or to which the Council of the League of Nations has communicated a copy of the Protocol for this purpose.

Article 7

The present Protocol is subject to ratification. Ratifications shall be deposited with the Secretariat of the League of Nations.

The Secretary-General shall give notice of the deposit of each ratification to the Members of the League of Nations and to the non-Member States mentioned in Article 6, indicating the date of its deposit.

Article 8

As from January 1st, 1931, any Member of the League of Nations and any non-Member State mentioned in Article 6 on whose behalf the Protocol has not been signed before that date, may accede thereto.

---

[1] Vol. VI, page 379; Vol. XI, page 405; Vol. XV, page 305; Vol.XXIV, page 153; Vol XXVII, page 417; Vol. XXXIX, page 165 ; Vol. XLV, page 96, Vol. L, page 159 ; Vol LIV, page 387 ; Vol. LXIX, page 70 ; Vol. LXXII, page 452 ; Vol. LXXVIII, page 435 ; Vol. LXXXVIIII, page 272 ; Vol. XCII, page 362 ; Vol. XCVI, page 180 ; Vol. C, page 153 ; Vol. CIV, page 492 ; Vol. CVII, page 461 ; Vol. CXI, page 402 ; Vol. CXVII, page 46 ; Vol. CXXVI, page 430 ; Vol. CXXX, page 440 ; Vol. CXXXXIV, page 392, Vol. CXLVII, page 318 ; Vol. CLII, page 282 ; Vol CLVI, page 1976 ; Vol. CLX, page 325 ; Vol. CLXIV, page 352 ; Vol. CLXVIII, page 228 ; Vol. CLXXII, page 388 ; and Vol. CLXXVII, page 382, of this Series.

[2] *British and Foreign State Papers*, Vol. 100, page 298.

Accession shall be effected by an instrument deposited with the Secretariat of the League of Nations. The Secretary-General of the League of Nations shall give notice of each accession to the Members of the League of Nations and to the non-Member States mentioned in Article 6, indicating the date of the deposit of the instrument.

Article 9

A procès-verbal shall be drawn up by the Secretary-General of the League of Nations as soon as ratifications or accessions on behalf of ten Members of the League of Nations or non-Member States have been deposited.

A certified copy of this procès-verbal shall be sent by the Secretary-General to each Member of the League of Nations and to each non-Member State mentioned in Article 6.

Article 10

The present Protocol shall enter into force on the 90th day after the date of the procès-verbal mentioned in Article 9 as regards all Members of the League of Nations or non-Member States on whose behalf ratifications or accessions have been deposited on the date of the procès-verbal.

As regards any Member of the League or non-Member State on whose behalf a ratification or accession is subsequently deposited, the Protocol shall enter into force on the 90th day after the date of the deposit of a ratification or accession on its behalf.

Article 11

As from January 1st, 1936, any Member of the League of Nations or any non-Member State in regard to which the present Protocol is then in force, may address to the Secretary-General of the League of Nations a request for the revision of any or all of the provisions of this Protocol. If such a request, after being communicated to the other Members of the League and non-Member States in regard to which the Protocol is then in force, is supported within one year by at least nine of them, the Council and the non-Member States mentioned, in Article 6, whether a conference should be specially convoked for that purpose or whether such revision should be considered at the next conference for the codification of international law.

The High Contracting Parties agree that, if the present Protocol is revised, the new Agreement may provide that upon its entry into force some or all of the provisions of the present Protocol shall be abrogated in respect of all of the Parties to the present Protocol.

Article 12

The present Protocol may be denounced.

Denunciation shall be effected by a notification in writing addressed to the Secretary-General of the League of Nations, who shall inform all Members of the League of Nations and non-Member States mentioned in Article 6.

Each denunciation shall take effect one year after the receipt by the Secretary-General of the notification but only as regards the Member of the League or non-Member State on whose behalf it has been notified.

Article 13

1. Any High Contracting Party may, at the time of signature, ratification or accession, declare that, in accepting the present Protocol, he does not assume any obligations in respect of all or any of his colonies, protectorates, overseas territories under suzerainty or mandate, or in respect of certain parts of the population of the said territories; and the present Protocol shall not apply to any territories or to the parts of their population named in such declaration.

2. Any High Contracting Party may give notice to the Secretary-General of the League of Nations at any time subsequently that he desires that the Protocol shall apply to all or any of his territories or to the parts of their population which have been made the subject of a declaration under the preceding paragraph, and the Protocol shall apply to all the territories or the parts of their population named in such notice six months after its receipt by the Secretary-General of the League of Nations.

3. Any High Contracting Party may, at any time, declare that he desires that the present Protocol shall cease to apply to all or any of his colonies, protectorates, overseas territories or territories under suzerainty or mandate, or in respect of certain parts of the population of the said territories, and the Protocol shall cease to apply to the territories or to the parts of their population named in such declaration one year after its receipt by the Secretary-General of the League of Nations.

4. Any High Contracting Party may make the reservations provided for in Article 4 in respect of all or any of his colonies, protectorates, overseas territories or territories under suzerainty or mandate, or in respect of certain parts of the population of these territories, at the time of signature, ratification or accession to the Protocol or at the time of making a notification under the second paragraph of this article.

5. The Secretary-General of the League of Nations shall communicate to all the Members of the League of Nations and the non-Member States mentioned in Article 6 all declarations and notices received in virtue of this article.

Article 14

The present Protocol shall be registered by the Secretary-General of the League of Nations as soon as it has entered into force.

Article 15

The French and English texts of the present Protocol shall be both authoritative.

IN FAITH WHEREOF the Plenipotentiaries have signed the present Protocol.

DONE at The Hague on the twelfth day of April, one thousand nine hundred and thirty, in a single copy, which shall be deposited in the archives of the Secretariat of the League of Nations and of which certified true copies shall be transmitted by the Secretary-General to all the Members of the League of Nations and all the non-Member States invited to the First Conference for the Codification of International Law.

[Signatures not reproduced here.]

Protocol relating to Military Obligations in Certain Cases of Double Nationality, 1930*

Adoption: 12 April 1930
Entry into force: 25 May 1937
Parties: 26 (Status as of 1 April 2007) **

AUSTRIA 28 Jul 1958, AUSTRALIA 8 Jul 1935, BELGIUM 4 Apr 1939, BRAZIL 19 Sep 1931 a, COLOMBIA 24 Feb 1937, CUBA 22 Oct 1936 (*2), CYPRUS 27 Mar 1970 d, EL SALVADOR 14 Oct 1935, FIJI 12 Jun 1972 d, INDIA 28 Sep 1932 (*territorial), KIRIBATI 29 Nov 1983 d, LESOTHO 4 Nov 1983 d, LIBERIA 16 Sep 2005 a, MALAWI 13 Oct 1966 a, MALTA 16 Aug 1966 d, MAURITANIA 2 Mar 1966, MAURITIUS 18 Jul 1969 d, NETHERLANDS 2 Apr 1937, NIGER 25 Jul 1966 a, NIGERIA 17 Mar 1967 a, SOUTH AFRICA 9 Oct 1935 (*2), SWAZILAND 18 Sep 1970 a, SWEDEN 6 Jul 1933, UNITED KINGDOM OF GREAT BRITAIN AND NORTHERN IRELAND 14 Jan 1932, UNITED STATES OF AMERICA 3 Aug 1932, ZIMBABWE 1 Dec 1998 d.

THE UNDERSIGNED PLENIPOTENTIARIES, on behalf of their respective Governments,

With a view to determining in certain cases the position as regards their military obligations of persons possessing two or more nationalities,

HAVE AGREED as follows:

Article 1

A person possessing two or more nationalities who habitually resides in one of the countries whose nationality he possesses, and who is in fact most closely connected with that country, shall be exempt from all military obligations in the other country or countries.

This exemption may involve the loss of the nationality of the other country or countries.

Article 2

Without prejudice to the provisions of Article 1 of the present Protocol, if a person possesses the nationality of two or more States and, under the law of any one of such States, has the right, on attaining his majority, to renounce or decline the nationality of that State, he shall be exempt from military service in such State during his minority.

Article 3

A person who has lost the nationality of a State under the law of that State and has acquired another nationality, shall be exempt from military obligations in the State of which he has lost the nationality.

Article 4

The High Contracting Parties agree to apply the principles and rules contained in the preceding Articles in their relations with each other, as from the date of the entry into force of the present Protocol.

* Source: League of Nations, 178 L.N.T.S. 227.

** The list does not include States which have signed but not ratified the Convention.

The inclusion of the above mentioned principles and rules in the said Articles shall in no way be deemed to prejudice the question whether they do or do not already form part of international law.

It is understood that, in so far as any point is not covered by any of the provisions of the preceding Articles, the existing principles and rules of international law shall remain in force.

Article 5

Nothing in the present Protocol shall affect the provisions of any treaty, convention or agreement in force between any of the High Contracting Parties relating to nationality or matters connected therewith.

Article 6

Any High Contracting Party may, when signing or ratifying the present Protocol or acceding thereto, append an express reservation excluding any one or more of the provisions of Articles 1 to 3 and 7.

The provisions thus excluded cannot be applied against the High Contracting Party who has made the reservation nor relied on by that Party against any other High Contracting Party.

Article 7

If there should arise between the High Contracting Parties a dispute of any kind relating to the interpretation or application of the present Protocol and if such dispute cannot be satisfactorily settled by diplomacy, it shall be settled in accordance with any applicable agreements in force between the Parties providing for the settlement of international disputes.

In case there is no such agreement in force between the Parties, the dispute shall be referred to arbitration or judicial settlement, in accordance with the constitutional procedure of each of the Parties to the dispute. In the absence of agreement on the choice of another tribunal, the dispute shall be referred to the Permanent Court of International Justice, if all the Parties to the dispute are Parties to the Protocol of 16 December 1920, relating to the Statute of that Court, and if any of the Parties to the dispute is not a Party to the Protocol of 16 December 1920, the dispute shall be referred to an arbitral tribunal constituted in accordance with the Hague Convention of 18 October 1907, for the Pacific Settlement of International Conflicts.

Article 8

The present Protocol shall remain open until 31 December 1930 for signature on behalf of any Member of the League of Nations or of any non-Member State invited to the First Codification Conference or to which the Council of the League of Nations has communicated a copy of the Protocol for this purpose.

Article 9

The present Protocol is subject to ratification. Ratifications shall be deposited with the Secretariat of the League of Nations.

The Secretary-General shall give notice of the deposit of each ratification to the Members of the League of Nations and to the non-Member States mentioned in Article 8, indicating the date of its deposit.

Article 10

As from 1 January 1931, any Member of the League of Nations and any non-Member State mentioned in Article 8 on whose behalf the Protocol has not been signed before that date may accede thereto.

Accession shall be effected by an instrument deposited with the Secretariat of the League of Nations. The Secretary-General of the League of Nations shall give notice of each accession to the Members of the League of Nations and to the non-Member States mentioned in Article 8, indicating the date of the deposit of the instrument.

Article 11

A procès-verbal shall be drawn up by the Secretary-General of the League of Nations as soon as ratifications or accessions on behalf of ten Members of the League of Nations or non-Member States have been deposited.

A certified copy of this procès-verbal shall be sent by the Secretary-General to each Member of the League of Nations and to each non-Member State mentioned in Article 8.

Article 12

The present Protocol shall enter into force on the 90th day after the date of the procès-verbal mentioned in Article 11 as regards all Members of the League of Nations or non-Member States on whose behalf ratifications or accessions have been deposited on the date of the procès-verbal.

As regards any Member of the League or non-Member State on whose behalf a ratification or accession is subsequently deposited, the Protocol shall enter into force on the 90th day after the date of the deposit of a ratification or accession on its behalf.

Article 13

As from 1 January 1936, any Member of the League of Nations or any non-Member State in regard to which the present Protocol is then in force, may address to the Secretary-General of the League of Nations a request for the revision of any or all of the provisions of this Protocol. If such a request, after being communicated to the other Members of the League and non-Member States in regard to which the Protocol is then in force, is supported within one year by at least nine of them, the Council of the League of Nations shall decide, after consultation with the Members of the League of Nations and the non-Member States mentioned in Article 8, whether a conference should be specially convoked for that purpose or whether such revision should be considered at the next conference for the codification of international law.

The High Contracting Parties agree that, if the present Protocol is revised, the new Agreement may provide that upon its entry into force some or all of the provisions of the present Protocol shall be abrogated in respect of all of the Parties to the present Protocol.

Article 14

The present Protocol may be denounced.

Denunciation shall be effected by a notification in writing addressed to the Secretary-General of the League of Nations, who shall inform all Members of the League of Nations and the non-Member States mentioned in Article 8.

Each denunciation shall take effect one year after the receipt by the Secretary-General of the notification but only as regards the Member of the League or non-Member State on whose behalf it has been notified.

Article 15

1. Any High Contracting Party may, at the time of signature, ratification or accession, declare that, in accepting the present Protocol, he does not assume any obligations in respect of all or any of his colonies, protectorates, overseas territories or territories under suzerainty or mandate, or in respect of certain parts of the population of the said territories; and the present Protocol shall not apply to any territories or to the parts of their population named in such declaration.

2. Any High Contracting Party may give notice to the Secretary-General of the League of Nations at any time subsequently that he desires that the Protocol shall apply to all or any of his territories or to the parts of their population which have been made the subject of a declaration under the preceding paragraph, and the Protocol shall apply to all the territories or the parts of their population named in such notice six months after its receipt by the Secretary-General of the League of Nations.

3. Any High Contracting Party may, at any time, declare that he desires that the present Protocol shall cease to apply to all or any of his colonies, protectorates, overseas territories or territories under suzerainty or mandate, or in respect of certain parts of the population of the said territories, and the Protocol shall cease to apply to the territories or to the parts of their population named in such declaration one year after its receipt by the Secretary-General of the League of Nations.

4. Any High Contracting Party may make the reservations provided for in Article 6 in respect of all or any of his colonies, protectorates, overseas territories or territories under suzerainty or mandate, or in respect of certain parts of the population of these territories, at the time of signature, ratification or accession to the Protocol or at the time of making a notification under the second paragraph of this Article.

5. The Secretary-General of the League of Nations shall communicate to all the Members of the League of Nations and the non-Member States mentioned in Article 8 all declarations and notices received in virtue of this Article.

Article 16

The present Protocol shall be registered by the Secretary-General of the League of Nations as soon as it has entered into force.

Article 17

The French and English texts of the present Protocol shall both be authoritative.
IN FAITH WHEREOF the Plenipotentiaries have signed the present Protocol.

DONE at The Hague on the twelfth day of April, one thousand nine hundred and thirty, in a single copy, which shall be deposited in the archives of the Secretariat of the League of Nations and of which certified true copies shall be transmitted by the Secretary-General to all the Members of the League of Nations and all the non-Member States invited to the First Conference for the Codification of International Law.

[Signatures not reproduced here.]

Convention relating to the Status of Stateless Persons, 1954*

Adoption: 28 September 1954
Entry into force: 6 June 1960
Parties: 62 (Status as of 1 April 2007)

ALBANIA 23 Jun 2003 a, ALGERIA 15 Jul 1964 a, ANTIGUA AND BARBUDA 25 Oct 1988 d (*general), ARGENTINA 1 Jun 1972 a (*general), ARMENIA 18 May 1994 a, AUSTRALIA 13 Dec 1973 a, AZERBAIJAN 16 Aug 1996 a, BARBADOS 6 Mar 1972 d (*general), BELGIUM 27 May 1960, BELIZE 14 Sep 2006 a, BOLIVIA 6 Oct 1983 a, BOSNIA AND HERZEGOVINA 1 Sep 1993 d, BOTSWANA 25 Feb 1969 d (*7, 12, 31), BRAZIL 13 Aug 1996, CHAD 12 Aug 1999 a, COLOMBIA signed 30 Dec 1954, COSTA RICA 2 Nov 1977, CROATIA 12 Oct 1992 d, CZECH REPUBLIC 19 Jul 2004 a (*23, 24, 27, 28), DENMARK 17 Jan 1956 (*24, 31), ECUADOR 2 Oct 1970, EL SALVADOR signed 28 Sep 1954 (*general), FIJI 12 Jun 1972 d (*8, 9, 25, general), FINLAND 10 Oct 1968 a (*7, 8, 24, 25, 28, general), FRANCE 8 Mar 1960 (*10), GERMANY 26 Oct 1976 (*23, 27), GREECE 4 Nov 1975 a, GUATEMALA 28 Nov 2000 (*general), GUINEA 21 Mar 1962 a, HOLY SEE signed 28 Sep 1954 (*general), HONDURAS signed 28 Sep 1954, HUNGARY 21 Nov 2001 a (*23, 24, 28), IRELAND 17 Dec 1962 a (*29, 31), ISRAEL 23 Dec 1958, ITALY 3 Dec 1962 (*17, 18), KIRIBATI 29 Nov 1983 d (*8, 9, 24, 25), LATVIA 5 Nov 1999 a (*24, 27), LESOTHO 4 Nov 1974 d (*8, 9, 25, 31), LIBERIA 11 Sep 1964 a, LIBYAN ARAB JAMAHIRIYA 16 May 1989 a, LIECHTENSTEIN signed 28 Nov 1954, LITHUANIA 7 Feb 2000 a, LUXEMBOURG 27 Jun 1960, MADAGASCAR 20 Feb 1962 a, MEXICO 7 Jun 2000 a (*17, 31, 32), MONTENEGRO 23 Oct 2006 d, NETHERLANDS 12 Apr 1962 (*8, 26), NORWAY 19 Nov 1956, PHILIPPINES signed 22 Jun 1955 (*17, 31), REPUBLIC OF KOREA 22 Aug 1962 a, ROMANIA 27 Jan 2006 a (*23, 27, 31), RWANDA 4 Oct 2006 a, SAINT VINCENT AND THE GRENADINES 27 Apr 1999 d (*23-25, 31), SENEGAL 21 Sep 2005 a, SERBIA (REPUBLIC OF) 12 Mar 2001 d, SLOVAKIA 3 Apr 2000 a (*27), SLOVENIA 6 Jul 1992 d, SPAIN 12 May 1997 a (*29), SWAZILAND 16 Nov 1999 a, SWEDEN 2 Apr 1965 (*8, 12, 24, 25), SWITZERLAND 3 Jul 1972, THE FORMER YUGOSLAV REPUBLIC OF MACEDONIA 18 Jan 1994 d, TRINIDAD AND TOBAGO 11 Apr 1966 d, TUNISIA 29 Jul 1969 a, UGANDA 15 Apr 1965 a, UNITED KINGDOM OF GREAT BRITAIN AND NORTHERN IRELAND 16 Apr 1959 (*24, 25, 36, 38, territorial), URUGUAY 2 Apr 2004 a, ZAMBIA 1 Nov 1974 d (*22, 26, 28, 31), ZIMBABWE 1 Dec 1998 d.

Preamble

The High Contracting Parties,

Considering that the Charter of the United Nations and the Universal Declaration of Human Rights approved on 10 December 1948 by the General Assembly of the United Nations have affirmed the principle that human beings shall enjoy fundamental rights and freedoms without discrimination,

Considering that the United Nations has, on various occasions, manifested its profound concern for stateless persons and endeavoured to assure stateless persons the widest possible exercise of these fundamental rights and freedoms,

---

* Source: 360 U.N.T.S. 130.

Considering that only those stateless persons who are also refugees are covered by the Convention relating to the Status of Refugees of 28 July 1951, and that there are many stateless persons who are not covered by that Convention,

Considering that it is desirable to regulate and improve the status of stateless persons by an international agreement,

Have agreed as follows:

CHAPTER I

GENERAL PROVISIONS

Article 1. - Definition of the term "stateless person"

1. For the purpose of this Convention, the term "stateless person" means a person who is not considered as a national by any State under the operation of its law.

2. This Convention shall not apply:

(i) To persons who are at present receiving from organs or agencies of the United Nations other than the United Nations High Commissioner for Refugees protection or assistance so long as they are receiving such protection or assistance;

(ii) To persons who are recognized by the competent authorities of the country in which they have taken residence as having the rights and obligations which are attached to the possession of the nationality of that country;

(iii) To persons with respect to whom there are serious reasons for considering that:

(a) They have committed a crime against peace, a war crime, or a crime against humanity, as defined in the international instruments drawn up to make provisions in respect of such crimes;

(b) They have committed a serious non-political crime outside the country of their residence prior to their admission to that country;

(c) They have been guilty of acts contrary to the purposes and principles of the United Nations.

Article 2. - General obligations

Every stateless person has duties to the country in which he finds himself, which require in particular that he conform to its laws and regulations as well as to measures taken for the maintenance of public order.

Article 3. - Non-discrimination

The Contracting States shall apply the provisions of this Convention to stateless persons without discrimination as to race, religion or country of origin.

Article 4. - Religion

The Contracting States shall accord to stateless persons within their territories treatment at least as favourable as that accorded to their nationals with respect to freedom to practise their religion and freedom as regards the religious education of their children.

Article 5. - Rights granted apart from this Convention

Nothing in this Convention shall be deemed to impair any rights and benefits granted by a Contracting State to stateless persons apart from this Convention.

Article 6. - The term "in the same circumstances"

For the purpose of this Convention, the term "in the same circumstances" implies that any requirements (including requirements as to length and conditions of sojourn or residence) which the particular individual would have to fulfil for the enjoyment of the right in question, if he were not a stateless person, must be fulfilled by him, with the exception of requirements which by their nature a stateless person is incapable of fulfilling.

Article 7. - Exemption from reciprocity

1. Except where this Convention contains more favourable provisions, a Contracting State shall accord to stateless persons the same treatment as is accorded to aliens generally.

2. After a period of three years' residence, all stateless persons shall enjoy exemption from legislative reciprocity in the territory of the Contracting States.

3. Each Contracting State shall continue to accord to stateless persons the rights and benefits to which they were already entitled, in the absence of reciprocity, at the date of entry into force of this Convention for that State.

4. The Contracting States shall consider favourably the possibility of according to stateless persons, in the absence of reciprocity, rights and benefits beyond those to which they are entitled according to paragraphs 2 and 3, and to extending exemption from reciprocity to stateless persons who do not fulfil the conditions provided for in paragraphs 2 and 3.

5. The provisions of paragraphs 2 and 3 apply both to the rights and benefits referred to in articles 13, 18, 19, 21 and 22 of this Convention and to rights and benefits for which this Convention does not provide.

Article 8. - Exemption from exceptional measures

With regard to exceptional measures which may be taken against the person, property or interests of nationals or former nationals of a foreign State, the Contracting States shall not apply such measures to a stateless person solely on account of his having previously possessed the nationality of the foreign State in question. Contracting States which, under their legislation, are prevented from applying the general principle expressed in this article shall, in appropriate cases, grant exemptions in favour of such stateless persons.

Article 9. - Provisional measures

Nothing in this Convention shall prevent a Contracting State, in time of war or other grave and exceptional circumstances, from taking provisionally measures which it considers to be essential to the national security in the case of a particular person, pending a determination by the Contracting State that that person is in fact a stateless person and that the continuance of such measures is necessary in his case in the interests of national security.

Article 10. - Continuity of residence

1. Where a stateless person has been forcibly displaced during the Second World War and removed to the territory of a Contracting State, and is resident there, the period of such enforced sojourn shall be considered to have been lawful residence within that territory.

2. Where a stateless person has been forcibly displaced during the Second World War from the territory of a Contracting State and has, prior to the date of entry into force of this Convention, returned there for the purpose of taking up residence, the period of residence before and after such enforced displacement shall be regarded as one uninterrupted period for any purposes for which uninterrupted residence is required.

Article 11. - Stateless seamen

In the case of stateless persons regularly serving as crew members on board a ship flying the flag of a Contracting State, that State shall give sympathetic consideration to their establishment on its territory and the issue of travel documents to them or their temporary admission to its territory particularly with a view to facilitating their establishment in another country.

CHAPTER II

JURIDICAL STATUS

Article 12. - Personal status

1. The personal status of a stateless person shall be governed by the law of the country of his domicile or, if he has no domicile, by the law of the country of his residence.

2. Rights previously acquired by a stateless person and dependent on personal status, more particularly rights attaching to marriage, shall be respected by a Contracting State, subject to compliance, if this be necessary, with the formalities required by the law of that State, provided that the right in question is one which would have been recognized by the law of that State had he not become stateless.

Article 13. - Movable and immovable property

The Contracting States shall accord to a stateless person treatment as favourable as possible and, in any event, not less favourable than that accorded to aliens generally in the same circumstances, as regards the acquisition of movable and immovable property and other rights pertaining thereto, and to leases and other contracts relating to movable and immovable property.

Article 14. - Artistic rights and industrial property

In respect of the protection of industrial property, such as inventions, designs or models, trade marks, trade names, and of rights in literary, artistic and scientific works, a stateless person shall be accorded in the country in which he has his habitual residence the same protection as is accorded to nationals of that country. In the territory of any other Contracting State, he shall be accorded the same protection as is accorded in that territory to nationals of the country in which he has his habitual residence.

Article 15. - Right of association

As regards non-political and non-profit-making associations and trade unions the Contracting States shall accord to stateless persons lawfully staying in their territory treatment as favourable as possible, and in any event, not less favourable than that accorded to aliens generally in the same circumstances.

Article 16. - Access to courts

1. A stateless person shall have free access to the courts of law on the territory of all Contracting States.

2. A stateless person shall enjoy in the Contracting State in which he has his habitual residence the same treatment as a national in matters pertaining to access to the courts, including legal assistance and exemption from cautio judicatum solvi.

3. A stateless person shall be accorded in the matters referred to in paragraph 2 in countries other than that in which he has his habitual residence the treatment granted to a national of the country of his habitual residence.

CHAPTER III

GAINFUL EMPLOYMENT

Article 17. - Wage-earning employment

1. The Contracting States shall accord to stateless persons lawfully staying in their territory treatment as favourable as possible and, in any event, not less favourable that that accorded to aliens generally in the same circumstances, as regards the right to engage in wage-earning employment.

2. The Contracting States shall give sympathetic consideration to assimilating the rights of all stateless persons with regard to wage-earning employment to those of nationals, and in particular of those stateless persons who have entered their territory pursuant to programmes of labour recruitment or under immigration schemes.

Article 18. - Self-employment

The Contracting States shall accord to a stateless person lawfully in their territory treatment as favourable as possible and, in any event, not less favourable than that accorded to aliens generally in the same circumstances, as regards the right to engage on his own account in agriculture, industry, handicrafts and commerce and to establish commercial and industrial companies.

Article 19. - Liberal professions

Each Contracting State shall accord to stateless persons lawfully staying in their territory who hold diplomas recognized by the competent authorities of that State, and who are desirous of practising a liberal profession, treatment as favourable as possible and, in any event, not less favourable than that accorded to aliens generally in the same circumstances.

CHAPTER IV

WELFARE

Article 20. - Rationing

Where a rationing system exists, which applies to the population at large and regulates the general distribution of products in short supply, stateless persons shall be accorded the same treatment as nationals.

Article 21. - Housing

As regards housing, the Contracting States, in so far as the matter is regulated by laws or regulations or is subject to the control of public authorities, shall accord to stateless persons lawfully staying in their territory treatment as favourable as possible and, in any event, not less favourable than that accorded to aliens generally in the same circumstances.

Article 22. - Public education

1. The Contracting States shall accord to stateless persons the same treatment as is accorded to nationals with respect to elementary education.

2. The Contracting States shall accord to stateless persons treatment as favourable as possible and, in any event, not less favourable than that accorded to aliens generally in the same circumstances, with respect to education other than elementary education and, in particular, as regards access to studies, the recognition of foreign school certificates, diplomas and degrees, the remission of fees and charges and the award of scholarships.

Article 23. - Public relief

The Contracting States shall accord to stateless persons lawfully staying in their territory the same treatment with respect to public relief and assistance as is accorded to their nationals.

Article 24. - Labour legislation and social security

1. The Contracting States shall accord to stateless persons lawfully staying in their territory the same treatment as is accorded to nationals in respect of the following matters:

(a) In so far as such matters are governed by laws or regulations or are subject to the control of administrative authorities; remuneration, including family allowances where these form part of remuneration, hours of work, overtime arrangements, holidays with pay, restrictions on home work, minimum age of employment, apprenticeship and training, women's work and the work of young persons, and the enjoyment of the benefits of collective bargaining;

(b) Social security (legal provisions in respect of employment injury, occupational diseases, maternity, sickness, disability, old age, death, unemployment, family responsibilities and any other contingency which, according to national laws or regulations, is covered by a social security scheme), subject to the following limitations:

(i) There may be appropriate arrangements for the maintenance of acquired rights and rights in course of acquisition;

(ii) National laws or regulations of the country of residence may prescribe special arrangements concerning benefits or portions of benefits which are payable wholly out of public funds, and concerning allowances paid to persons who do not fulfil the contribution conditions prescribed for the award of a normal pension.

2. The right to compensation for the death of a stateless person resulting from employment injury or from occupational disease shall not be affected by the fact that the residence of the beneficiary is outside the territory of the Contracting State.

3. The Contracting States shall extend to stateless persons the benefits of agreements concluded between them, or which may be concluded between them in the future, concerning the maintenance of acquired rights and rights in the process of acquisition in regard to social security, subject only to the conditions which apply to nationals of the States signatory to the agreements in question.

4. The Contracting States will give sympathetic consideration to extending to stateless persons so far as possible the benefits of similar agreements which may at any time be in force between such Contracting States and non-contracting States.

CHAPTER V

ADMINISTRATIVE MEASURES

Article 25. - Administrative assistance

1. When the exercise of a right by a stateless person would normally require the assistance of authorities of a foreign country to whom he cannot have recourse, the Contracting State in whose territory he is residing shall arrange that such assistance be afforded to him by their own authorities.

2. The authority or authorities mentioned in paragraph 1 shall deliver or cause to be delivered under their supervision to stateless persons such documents or certifications as would normally be delivered to aliens by or through their national authorities.

3. Documents or certifications so delivered shall stand in the stead of the official instruments delivered to aliens by or through their national authorities and shall be given credence in the absence of proof to the contrary.

4. Subject to such exceptional treatment as may be granted to indigent persons, fees may be charged for the services mentioned herein, but such fees shall be moderate and commensurate with those charged to nationals for similar services.

5. The provisions of this article shall be without prejudice to articles 27 and 28.

Article 26. - Freedom of movement

Each Contracting State shall accord to stateless persons lawfully in its territory the right to choose their place of residence and to move freely within its territory, subject to any regulations applicable to aliens generally in the same circumstances.

Article 27. - Identity papers

The Contracting States shall issue identity papers to any stateless person in their territory who does not possess a valid travel document.

Article 28. - Travel documents

The Contracting States shall issue to stateless persons lawfully staying in their territory travel documents for the purpose of travel outside their territory, unless compelling reasons of national security or public order otherwise require, and the provisions of the schedule to this Convention shall apply with respect to such documents. The Contracting States may issue such a travel document to any other stateless person in their territory; they shall in particular give sympathetic consideration to the issue of such a travel document to stateless persons in their territory who are unable to obtain a travel document from the country of their lawful residence.

Article 29. - Fiscal charges

1. The Contracting States shall not impose upon stateless persons duties, charges or taxes, of any description whatsoever, other or higher than those which are or may be levied on their nationals in similar situations.

2. Nothing in the above paragraph shall prevent the application to stateless persons of the laws and regulations concerning charges in respect of the issue to aliens of administrative documents including identity papers.

Article 30. - Transfer of assets

1. A Contracting State shall, in conformity with its laws and regulations, permit stateless persons to transfer assets which they have brought into its territory, to another country where they have been admitted for the purposes of resettlement.

2. A Contracting State shall give sympathetic consideration to the application of stateless persons for permission to transfer assets wherever they may be and which are necessary for their resettlement in another country to which they have been admitted.

Article 31. - Expulsion

1. The Contracting States shall not expel a stateless person lawfully in their territory save on grounds of national security or public order.

2. The expulsion of such a stateless person shall be only in pursuance of a decision reached in accordance with due process of law. Except where compelling reasons of national security otherwise require, the stateless person shall be allowed to submit evidence to clear himself, and to appeal to and be represented for the purpose before competent authority or a person or persons specially designated by the competent authority.

3. The Contracting States shall allow such a stateless person a reasonable period within which to seek legal admission into another country. The Contracting States reserve the right to apply during that period such internal measures as they may deem necessary.

Article 32. - Naturalization

The Contracting States shall as far as possible facilitate the assimilation and naturalization of stateless persons. They shall in particular make every effort to expedite naturalization proceedings and to reduce as far as possible the charges and costs of such proceedings.

CHAPTER VI

FINAL CLAUSES

Article 33. - Information on national legislation

The Contracting States shall communicate to the Secretary-General of the United Nations the laws and regulations which they may adopt to ensure the application of this Convention.

Article 34. - Settlement of disputes

Any dispute between Parties to this Convention relating to its interpretation or application, which cannot be settled by other means, shall be referred to the International Court of Justice at the request of any one of the parties to the dispute.

Article 35. - Signature, ratification and accession

1. This Convention shall be open for signature at the Headquarters of the United Nations until 31 December 1955.

2. It shall be open for signature on behalf of:

(a) Any State Member of the United Nations;

(b) Any other State invited to attend the United Nations Conference on the Status of Stateless Persons; and

(c) Any State to which an invitation to sign or to accede may be addressed by the General Assembly of the United Nations.

3. It shall be ratified and the instruments of ratification shall be deposited with the Secretary-General of the United Nations.

4. It shall be open for accession by the States referred to in paragraph 2 of this article. Accession shall be effected by the deposit of an instrument of accession with the Secretary-General of the United Nations.

Article 36. - Territorial application clause

1. Any State may, at the time of signature, ratification or accession, declare that this Convention shall extend to all or any of the territories for the international relations of which it is responsible. Such a declaration shall take effect when the Convention enters into force for the State concerned.

2. At any time thereafter any such extension shall be made by notification addressed to the Secretary-General of the United Nations and shall take effect as from the ninetieth day after the day of receipt by the Secretary-General of the United Nations of this notification, or as from the date of entry into force of the Convention for the State concerned, whichever is the later.

3. With respect to those territories to which this Convention is not extended at the time of signature, ratification or accession, each State concerned shall consider the possibility of taking the necessary steps in order to extend the application of this Convention to such territories, subject, where necessary for constitutional reasons, to the consent of the Governments of such territories.

Article 37. - Federal clause

In the case of a Federal or non-unitary State, the following provisions shall apply

(a) With respect to those articles of this Convention that come within the legislative jurisdiction of the federal legislative authority, the obligations of the Federal Government shall to this extent be the same as those of Parties which are not Federal States;

(b) With respect to those articles of this Convention that come within the legislative jurisdiction of constituent States, provinces or cantons which are not, under the constitutional system of the Federation, bound to take legislative action, the Federal Government shall bring such articles with a favourable recommendation to the notice of the appropriate authorities of States, provinces or cantons at the earliest possible moment;

(c) A Federal State Party to this Convention shall, at the request of any other Contracting State transmitted through the Secretary-General of the United Nations, supply a statement of the law and practice of the Federation and its constituent units in regard to any particular provision of the Convention showing the extent to which effect has been given to that provision by legislative or other action.

Article 38. - Reservations

1. At the time of signature, ratification or accession, any State may make reservations to articles of the Convention other than to articles 1, 3, 4, 16 (1) and 33 to 42 inclusive.

2. Any State making a reservation in accordance with paragraph 1 of this article may at any time withdraw the reservation by a communication to that effect addressed to the Secretary-General of the United Nations.

Article 39. - Entry into force

1. This Convention shall come into force on the ninetieth day following the day of deposit of the sixth instrument of ratification or accession.

2. For each State ratifying or acceding to the Convention after the deposit of the sixth instrument of ratification or accession, the Convention shall enter into force on the ninetieth day following the date of deposit by such State of its instrument of ratification or accession.

Article 40. - Denunciation

1. Any Contracting State may denounce this Convention at any time by a notification addressed to the Secretary-General of the United Nations.

2. Such denunciation shall take effect for the Contracting State concerned one year from the date upon which it is received by the Secretary-General of the United Nations.

3. Any State which has made a declaration or notification under article 36 may, at any time thereafter, by a notification to the Secretary-General of the United Nations, declare that the Convention shall cease to extend to such territory one year after the date of receipt of the notification by the Secretary-General.

Article 41. - Revision

1. Any Contracting State may request revision of this Convention at any time by a notification addressed to the Secretary-General of the United Nations.

2. The General Assembly of the United Nations shall recommend the steps, if any, to be taken in respect of such request.

Article 42. - Notifications by the Secretary-General of the United Nations

The Secretary-General of the United Nations shall inform all Members of the United Nations and non-member States referred to in article 35:

(a) Of signatures, ratifications and accessions in accordance with article 35;

(b) Of declarations and notifications in accordance with article 36;

(c) Of reservations and withdrawals in accordance with article 38;

(d) Of the date on which this Convention will come into force in accordance with article 39;

(e) Of denunciations and notifications in accordance with article 40;

(f) Of request for revision in accordance with article 41.

In faith whereof the undersigned, duly authorized, have signed this Convention on behalf of their respective Governments.

Done at New York, this twenty-eighth day of September, one thousand nine hundred and fifty-four, in a single copy, of which the English, French and Spanish texts are equally authentic and which shall remain deposited in the archives of the United Nations, and certified true copies of which shall be delivered to all Members of the United Nations and to the non-member States referred to in article 35.

Convention on the Nationality of Married Women, 1957*

Adoption: 29 January 1957
Entry into force: 11 August 1958
Parties: 74 (Status as of 1 April 2007)

ALBANIA 27 Jul 1960 a, ANTIGUA AND BARBUDA 25 Oct 1988 d, ARGENTINA 10 Oct 1963 a (*7, 10), ARMENIA 18 May 1994 a, AUSTRALIA 14 Mar 1961 a (*territorial), AUSTRIA 19 Jan 1968 a, AZERBAIJAN 16 Aug 1996 a, BAHAMAS 10 Jun 1976 d, BARBADOS 26 Oct 1979 a, BELARUS 23 Dec 1958, BELGIUM signed 15 May 1972, BOSNIA AND HERZEGOVINA 1 Sep 1993 d, BRAZIL 4 Dec 1968 (*10), BULGARIA 22 Jun 1960, CAMBODIA signed 11 Nov 2001, CANADA 21 Oct 1959, CHILE signed 18 Mar 1957 (*10), CHINA 22 Sep 1958, COLOMBIA signed 20 Feb 1957, CÔTE D'IVOIRE 2 Nov 1999 a, CROATIA 12 Oct 1992 d, CUBA 5 Dec 1957, CYPRUS 26 Apr 1971 d, CZECH REPUBLIC 22 Feb 1993 d, DENMARK 22 Jun 1959, DOMINICAN REPUBLIC 10 Oct 1957, ECUADOR 29 Mar 1960, FIJI 12 Jun 1972 d, FINLAND 15 May 1968 a, GERMANY 7 Feb 1974 a, GHANA 15 Aug 1966 a, GUATEMALA 13 Jul 1960 (*10), GUINEA signed 19 Mar 1975, HUNGARY 3 Dec 1959, ICELAND 18 Oct 1977 a, INDIA signed 15 May 1957 (*10), IRELAND 25 Nov 1957, ISRAEL 7 Jun 1957, JAMAICA 30 Jul 1964 d, JORDAN 1 Jul 1992 a, KAZAKHSTAN 28 Mar 2000 a, KYRGYZSTAN 10 Feb 1997 a, LATVIA 14 Apr 1992 a, LESOTHO 4 Nov 1974 d, LIBERIA 16 Sep 2005 a, LIBYAN ARAB JAMAHIRIYA 16 May 1989 a, LUXEMBOURG 22 Jul 1977, MADAGASCAR signed 12 Sep 2002, MALAWI 8 Sep 1966 a, MALAYSIA 24 Feb 1959 a, MALI 2 Feb 1973 a, MALTA 7 Jun 1967 d, MAURITIUS 18 Jul 1969 d, MEXICO 4 Apr 1979 a, MONTENEGRO 23 Oct 2006 d, NETHERLANDS 8 Aug 1966 a (*territorial), NEW ZEALAND 17 Dec 1958 (*territorial), NICARAGUA 9 Jan 1986 a, NORWAY 20 May 1958, PAKISTAN signed 10 Apr 1958, POLAND 3 Jul 1959 a, PORTUGAL signed 21 Feb 1957, ROMANIA 2 Dec 1960 a, RUSSIAN FEDERATION 17 Sep 1958, RWANDA 26 Sep 2003 a, SAINT LUCIA 14 Oct 1991 d, SAINT VINCENT AND THE GRENADINES 27 Apr 1999 d, REPUBLIC OF SERBIA 12 Mar 2001 d, SIERRA LEONE 13 Mar 1962 d, SINGAPORE 18 Mar 1966 d, SINGAPORE 18 Mar 1966 d, SLOVAKIA 28 May 1993 d, SLOVENIA 6 Jul 1992 d, SOUTH AFRICA 17 Dec 2002, SRI LANKA 30 May 1958 a, SWAZILAND 18 Sep 1970 a, SWEDEN 13 May 1958, THE FORMER YUGOSLAV REPUBLIC OF MACEDONIA 20 Apr 1994 d, TRINIDAD AND TOBAGO 11 Apr 1966 d, TUNISIA 24 Jan 1968 a (*10), UGANDA 15 Apr 1965 a, UKRAINE 3 Dec 1958, UNITED KINGDOM OF GREAT BRITAIN AND NORTHERN IRELAND 28 Aug 1957 (*territorial), UNITED REPUBLIC OF TANZANIA 28 Nov 1962 a, URUGUAY signed 20 Feb 1957, VENEZUELA (BOLIVARIAN REPUBLIC OF) 31 May 1983 a, ZAMBIA 22 Jan 1975 d, ZIMBABWE 1 Dec 1998 d.

The Contracting States,

Recognizing that, conflicts in law in practice with reference to nationality arise as a result of provisions concerning the loss or acquisition of nationality by women as a result of marriage, of its dissolution or of the change of nationality by the husband during marriage,

Recognizing that, in article 15 of the Universal Declaration of Human Rights, the General Assembly of the United Nations has proclaimed that "everyone has the right to a nationality" and that "no one shall be arbitrarily deprived of his nationality nor denied the right to change his nationality",

* Source: U.N.G.A. Res. 1040 (XI), 309 U.N.T.S. 65.

Desiring to co-operate with the United Nations in promoting universal respect for, and observance of, human rights and fundamental freedoms for all without distinction as to sex,
Hereby agree as hereinafter provided:

Article 1

Each Contracting State agrees that neither the celebration nor the dissolution of a marriage between one of its nationals and an alien, nor the change of nationality by the husband during marriage, shall automatically affect the nationality of the wife.

Article 2

Each Contracting State agrees that neither the voluntary acquisition of the nationality of another State nor the renunciation of its nationality by one of its nationals shall prevent the retention of its nationality by the wife of such national.

Article 3

1. Each Contracting State agrees that the alien wife of one of its nationals may, at her request, acquire the nationality of her husband through specially privileged naturalization procedures; the grant of such nationality may be subject to such limitations as may be imposed in the interests of national security or public policy.

2. Each Contracting State agrees that the present Convention shall not be construed as affecting any legislation or judicial practice by which the alien wife of one of its nationals may, at her request, acquire her husband's nationality as a matter of right.

Article 4

1. The present Convention shall be open for signature and ratification on behalf of any State Member of the United Nations and also on behalf of any other State which is or hereafter becomes a member of any specialized agency of the United Nations, or which is or hereafter becomes a Party to the Statute of the International Court of Justice, or any other State to which an invitation has been addressed by the General Assembly of the United Nations.

2. The present Convention shall be ratified and the instruments of ratification shall be deposited with the Secretary-General of the United Nations

Article 5

1. The present Convention shall be open for accession to all States referred to in paragraph I of article 4.

2. Accession shall be effected by the deposit of an instrument of accession with the Secretary-General of the United Nations.

Article 6

1. The present Convention shall come into force on the ninetieth day following the date of deposit of the sixth instrument of ratification or accession.

2. For each State ratifying or acceding to the Convention after the deposit of the sixth instrument of ratification or accession, the Convention shall enter into force on the ninetieth day after deposit by such State of its instrument of ratification or accession.

Article 7

1. The present Convention shall apply to all non-self-governing, trust, colonial and other non-metropolitan territories for the international relations of which any Contracting State is responsible; the Contracting State concerned shall, subject to the provisions of paragraph 2 of the present article, at the time of signature, ratification or accession declare the non-metropolitan territory or territories to which the Convention shall apply ipso facto as a result of such signature, ratification or accession.

2. In any case in which, for the purpose of nationality, a non-metropolitan territory is not treated as one with the metropolitan territory, or in any case in which the previous consent of a non-metropolitan territory is required by the constitutional laws or practices of the Contracting State or of the non-metropolitan territory for the application of the Convention to that territory, that Contracting State shall endeavour to secure the needed consent of the non-metropolitan territory within the period of twelve months from the date of signature of the Convention by that Contracting State, and when such consent has been obtained the Contracting State shall notify the Secretary-General of the United Nations. The present Convention shall apply to the territory or territories named in such notification from the date of its receipt by the Secretary-General.

3. After the expiry of the twelve-month period mentioned in paragraph 2 of the present article, the Contracting States concerned shall inform the Secretary-General of the results of the consultations with those non-metropolitan territories for whose international relations they are responsible and whose consent to the application of the present Convention may have been withheld.

Article 8

1. At the time of signature, ratification or accession, any State may make reservations to any article of the present Convention other than articles 1 and 2.

2. If any State makes a reservation in accordance with paragraph 1 of the present article, the Convention, with the exception of those provisions to which the reservation relates, shall have effect as between the reserving State and the other Parties. The Secretary-General of the United Nations shall communicate the text of the reservation to all States which are or may become Parties to the Convention. Any State Party to the Convention or which thereafter becomes a Party may notify the Secretary-General that it does not agree to consider itself bound by the Convention with respect to the State making the reservation. This notification must be made, in the case of a State already a Party, within ninety days from the date of the communication by the Secretary-General; and, in the case of a State subsequently becoming a Party, within ninety days from the date when the instrument of ratification or accession is deposited. In the event that such a notification is made, the Convention shall not be deemed to be in effect as between the State making the notification and the State making the reservation.

3. Any State making a reservation in accordance with paragraph 1 of the present article may at any time withdraw the reservation, in whole or in part, after it has been accepted, by a notification to this effect addressed to the Secretary-General of the United Nations. Such notification shall take effect on the date on which it is received.

Article 9

1. Any Contracting State may denounce the present Convention by written notification to the Secretary-General of the United Nations. Denunciation shall take effect one year after the date of receipt of the notification by the Secretary-General.

2. The present Convention shall cease to be in force as from the date when the denunciation which reduces the number of Parties to less than six becomes effective.

Article 10

Any dispute which may arise between any two or more Contracting States concerning the interpretation or application of the present Convention which is not settled by negotiation, shall, at the request of any one of the parties to the dispute, be referred to the International Court of Justice for decision, unless the parties agree to another mode of settlement.

Article 11

The Secretary-General of the United Nations shall notify all States Members of the United Nations and the non-member States contemplated in paragraph 1 of article 4 of the present Convention of the following:

(a) Signatures and instruments of ratification received in accordance with article 4;

(b) Instruments of accession received in accordance with article 5;

(c) The date upon which the present Convention enters into force in accordance with article 6;

(d) Communications and notifications received in accordance with article 8;

(e) Notifications of denunciation received in accordance with paragraph 1 of article 9;

(f) Abrogation in accordance with paragraph 2 of article 9.

Article 12

1. The present Convention, of which the Chinese, English, French, Russian and Spanish texts shall be equally authentic, shall be deposited in the archives of the United Nations.

2. The Secretary-General of the United Nations shall transmit a certified copy of the Convention to all States Members of the United Nations and to the non-member States contemplated in paragraph 1 of article 4.

Convention on the Reduction of Statelessness, 1961*

Adoption: 30 August 1961
Entry into force: 13 December 1975
Parties: 33 (Status as of 1 April 2007)

ALBANIA 9 Jul 2003 a, ARMENIA 18 May 1994 a, AUSTRALIA 13 Dec 1973 a, AUSTRIA 22 Sep 1972 a (*8.3a), AZERBAIJAN 16 Aug 1996 a, BOLIVIA 6 Oct 1983 a, BOSNIA AND HERZEGOVINA 13 Dec 1996 a, CANADA 17 Jul 1978 a, CHAD 12 Aug 1999 a, COSTA RICA 2 Nov 1977 a, CZECH REPUBLIC 19 Dec 2001 a, DENMARK 11 Jul 1977 a, DOMINICAN REPUBLIC signed 5 Dec 1961, FRANCE signed 31 May 1962 (*8.3, 11, 14), GERMANY 31 Aug 1977 a, GUATEMALA 19 Jul 2001 a, IRELAND 18 Jan 1973 a (*8.3), ISRAEL signed 30 Aug 1961, KIRIBATI 29 Nov 1983 d, LATVIA 14 Apr 1992 a, LESOTHO 24 Sep 2004 a, LIBERIA 22 Sep 2004 a, LIBYAN ARAB JAMAHIRIYA 16 May 1989 a, NETHERLANDS 13 May 1985, NEW ZEALAND 20 Sep 2006 a, NIGER 17 Jun 1985 a (*11, 14, 15), NORWAY 11 Aug 1971 a, ROMANIA 27 Jan 2006 a, RWANDA 4 Oct 2006 a, SENEGAL 21 Sep 2005 a, SLOVAKIA 3 Apr 2000 a, SWAZILAND 16 Nov 1999 a, SWEDEN 19 Feb 1969 a, TUNISIA 12 May 2000 a (*8.3, 11, 14), UNITED KINGDOM OF GREAT BRITAIN AND NORTHERN IRELAND 29 Mar 1966 (*8.3), URUGUAY 21 Sep 2001 a.

The Contracting States,

Acting in pursuance of resolution 896 (IX), adopted by the General Assembly of the United Nations on 4 December 1954,

Considering it desirable to reduce statelessness by international agreement,

Have agreed as follows:

Article 1

1. A Contracting State shall grant its nationality to a person born in its territory who would otherwise be stateless. Such nationality shall be granted:

(a) At birth, by operation of law, or

(b) Upon an application being lodged with the appropriate authority, by or on behalf of the person concerned, in the manner prescribed by the national law. Subject to the provisions of paragraph 2 of this article, no such application may be rejected.

A Contracting State which provides for the grant of its nationality in accordance with subparagraph (b) of this paragraph may also provide for the grant of its nationality by operation of law at such age and subject to such conditions as may be prescribed by the national law.

2. A Contracting State may make the grant of its nationality in accordance with subparagraph (b) of paragraph 1 of this article subject to one or more of the following conditions:

(a) That the application is lodged during a period, fixed by the Contracting State, beginning not later than at the age of eighteen years and ending not earlier than at the age of twenty-one years, so, however, that the person concerned shall be allowed at least one year during which he may himself make the application without having to obtain legal authorization to do so;

* Source: 989 U.N.T.S. 175.

(b) That the person concerned has habitually resided in the territory of the Contracting State for such period as may be fixed by that State, not exceeding five years immediately preceding the lodging of the application nor ten years in all;

(c) That the person concerned has neither been convicted of an offence against national security nor has been sentenced to imprisonment for a term of five years or more on a criminal charge;

(d) That the person concerned has always been stateless.

3. Notwithstanding the provisions of paragraphs 1 (b) and 2 of this article, a child born in wedlock in the territory of a Contracting State, whose mother has the nationality of that State, shall acquire at birth that nationality if it otherwise would be stateless.

4. A Contracting State shall grant its nationality to a person who would otherwise be stateless and who is unable to acquire the nationality of the Contracting State in whose territory he was born because he has passed the age for lodging his application or has not fulfilled the required residence conditions, if the nationality of one of his parents at the time of the person's birth was that of the Contracting State first above-mentioned. If his parents did not possess the same nationality at the time of his birth, the question whether the nationality of the person concerned should follow that of the father or that of the mother shall be determined by the national law of such Contracting State. If application for such nationality is required, the application shall be made to the appropriate authority by or on behalf of the applicant in the manner prescribed by the national law. Subject to the provisions of paragraph 5 of this article, such application shall not be refused.

5. The Contracting State may make the grant of its nationality in accordance with the provisions of paragraph 4 of this article subject to one or more of the following conditions:

(a) That the application is lodged before the applicant reaches an age, being not less than twenty-three years, fixed by the Contracting State;

(b) That the person concerned has habitually resided in the territory of the Contracting State for such period immediately preceding the lodging of the application, not exceeding three years, as may be fixed by that State;

(c) That the person concerned has always been stateless.

Article 2

A foundling found in the territory of a Contracting State shall, in the absence of proof to the contrary, be considered to have been born within that territory of parents possessing the nationality of that State.

Article 3

For the purpose of determining the obligations of Contracting States under this Convention, birth on a ship or in an aircraft shall be deemed to have taken place in the territory of the State whose flag the ship flies or in the territory of the State in which the aircraft is registered, as the case may be.

Article 4

1. A Contracting State shall grant its nationality to a person, not born in the territory of a Contracting State, who would otherwise be stateless, if the nationality of one of his parents at the time of the person's birth was that of that State. If his parents did not possess the same

nationality at the time of his birth, the question whether the nationality of the person concerned should follow that of the father or that of the mother shall be determined by the national law of such Contracting State. Nationality granted in accordance with the provisions of this paragraph shall be granted:

(a) At birth, by operation of law, or

(b) Upon an application being lodged with the appropriate authority, by or on behalf of the person concerned, in the manner prescribed by the national law. Subject to the provisions of paragraph 2 of this article, no such application may be rejected.

2. A Contracting State may make the grant of its nationality in accordance with the provisions of paragraph 1 of this article subject to one or more of the following conditions:

(a) That the application is lodged before the applicant reaches an age, being not less than twenty-three years, fixed by the Contracting State;

(b) That the person concerned has habitually resided in the territory of the Contracting State for such period immediately preceding the lodging of the application, not exceeding three years, as may be fixed by that State;

(c) That the person concerned has not been convicted of an offence against national security;

(d) That the person concerned has always been stateless.

Article 5

1. If the law of a Contracting State entails loss of nationality as a consequence of any change in the personal status of a person such as marriage, termination of marriage, legitimation, recognition or adoption, such loss shall be conditional upon possession or acquisition of another nationality.

2. If, under the law of a Contracting State, a child born out of wedlock loses the nationality of that State in consequence of a recognition of affiliation, he shall be given an opportunity to recover that nationality by written application to the appropriate authority, and the conditions governing such application shall not be more rigorous than those laid down in paragraph 2 of article 1 of this Convention.

Article 6

If the law of a Contracting State provides for loss of its nationality by a person's spouse or children as a consequence of that person losing or being deprived of that nationality, such loss shall be conditional upon their possession or acquisition of another nationality.

Article 7

1. (a) If the law of a Contracting State entails loss or renunciation of nationality, such renunciation shall not result in loss of nationality unless the person concerned possesses or acquires another nationality;

(b) The provisions of subparagraph (a) of this paragraph shall not apply where their application would be inconsistent with the principles stated in articles 13 and 14 of the Universal Declaration of Human Rights approved on 10 December 1948 by the General Assembly of the United Nations.

2. A national of a Contracting State who seeks naturalization in a foreign country shall not lose his nationality unless he acquires or has been accorded assurance of acquiring the nationality of that foreign country.

3. Subject to the provisions of paragraphs 4 and 5 of this article, a national of a Contracting State shall not lose his nationality, so as to become stateless, on the ground of departure, residence abroad, failure to register or on any similar ground.

4. A naturalized person may lose his nationality on account of residence abroad for a period, not less than seven consecutive years, specified by the law of the Contracting State concerned if he fails to declare to the appropriate authority his intention to retain his nationality.

5. In the case of a national of a Contracting State, born outside its territory, the law of that State may make the retention of its nationality after the expiry of one year from his attaining his majority conditional upon residence at that time in the territory of the State or registration with the appropriate authority.

6. Except in the circumstances mentioned in this article, a person shall not lose the nationality of a Contracting State, if such loss would render him stateless, notwithstanding that such loss is not expressly prohibited by any other provision of this Convention.

Article 8

1. A Contracting State shall not deprive a person of his nationality if such deprivation would render him stateless.

2. Notwithstanding the provisions of paragraph 1 of this article, a person may be deprived of the nationality of a Contracting State:

(a) In the circumstances in which, under paragraphs 4 and 5 of article 7, it is permissible that a person should lose his nationality;

(b) Where the nationality has been obtained by misrepresentation or fraud.

3. Notwithstanding the provisions of paragraph 1 of this article, a Contracting State may retain the right to deprive a person of his nationality, if at the time of signature, ratification or accession it specifies its retention of such right on one or more of the following grounds, being grounds existing in its national law at that time:

(a) That, inconsistently with his duty of loyalty to the Contracting State, the person:

(i) Has, in disregard of an express prohibition by the Contracting State rendered or continued to render services to, or received or continued to receive emoluments from, another State, or

(ii) Has conducted himself in a manner seriously prejudicial to the vital interests of the State;

(b) That the person has taken an oath, or made a formal declaration, of allegiance to another State, or given definite evidence of his determination to repudiate his allegiance to the Contracting State.

4. A Contracting State shall not exercise a power of deprivation permitted by paragraphs 2 or 3 of this article except in accordance with law, which shall provide for the person concerned the right to a fair hearing by a court or other independent body.

Article 9

A Contracting State may not deprive any person or group of persons of their nationality on racial, ethnic, religious or political grounds.

Article 10

1. Every treaty between Contracting States providing for the transfer of territory shall include provisions designed to secure that no person shall become stateless as a result of the transfer. A

Contracting State shall use its best endeavours to secure that any such treaty made by it with a State which is not a Party to this Convention includes such provisions.

2. In the absence of such provisions a Contracting State to which territory is transferred or which otherwise acquires territory shall confer its nationality on such persons as would otherwise become stateless as a result of the transfer or acquisition.

Article 11

The Contracting States shall promote the establishment within the framework of the United Nations, as soon as may be after the deposit of the sixth instrument of ratification or accession, of a body to which a person claiming the benefit of this Convention may apply for the examination of his claim and for assistance in presenting it to the appropriate authority.

Article 12

1. In relation to a Contracting State which does not, in accordance with the provisions of paragraph 1 of article 1 or of article 4 of this Convention, grant its nationality at birth by operation of law, the provisions of paragraph 1 of article 1 or of article 4, as the case may be, shall apply to persons born before as well as to persons born after the entry into force of this Convention.

2. The provisions of paragraph 4 of article 1 of this Convention shall apply to persons born before as well as to persons born after its entry into force.

3. The provisions of article 2 of this Convention shall apply only to foundlings found in the territory of a Contracting State after the entry into force of the Convention for that State.

Article 13

This Convention shall not be construed as affecting any provisions more conducive to the reduction of statelessness which may be contained in the law of any Contracting State now or hereafter in force, or may be contained in any other convention, treaty or agreement now or hereafter in force between two or more Contracting States.

Article 14

Any dispute between Contracting States concerning the interpretation or application of this Convention which cannot be settled by other means shall be submitted to the International Court of Justice at the request of any one of the parties to the dispute.

Article 15

1. This Convention shall apply to all non-self-governing, trust, colonial and other non-metropolitan territories for the international relations of which any Contracting State is responsible; the Contracting State concerned shall, subject to the provisions of paragraph 2 of this article, at the time of signature, ratification or accession, declare the non-metropolitan territory or territories to which the Convention shall apply ipso facto as a result of such signature, ratification or accession.

2. In any case in which, for the purpose of nationality, a non-metropolitan territory is not treated as one with the metropolitan territory, or in any case in which the previous consent of a non-metropolitan territory is required by the constitutional laws or practices of the Contracting State or of the non-metropolitan territory for the application of the Convention to that territory,

that Contracting State shall endeavour to secure the needed consent of the non-metropolitan territory within the period of twelve months from the date of signature of the Convention by that Contracting State, and when such consent has been obtained the Contracting State shall notify the Secretary-General of the United Nations. This Convention shall apply to the territory or territories named in such notification from the date of its receipt by the Secretary-General.

3. After the expiry of the twelve-month period mentioned in paragraph 2 of this article, the Contracting States concerned shall inform the Secretary-General of the results of the consultations with those non-metropolitan territories for whose international relations they are responsible and whose consent to the application of this Convention may have been withheld.

Article 16

1. This Convention shall be open for signature at the Headquarters of the United Nations from 30 August 1961 to 31 May 1962.

2. This Convention shall be open for signature on behalf of:

(a) Any State Member of the United Nations;

(b) Any other State invited to attend the United Nations Conference on the Elimination or Reduction of Future Statelessness;

(c) Any State to which an invitation to sign or to accede may be addressed by the General Assembly of the United Nations.

3. This Convention shall be ratified and the instruments of ratification shall be deposited with the Secretary-General of the United Nations.

4. This Convention shall be open for accession by the States referred to in paragraph 2 of this article. Accession shall be effected by the deposit of an instrument of accession with the Secretary-General of the United Nations.

Article 17

1. At the time of signature, ratification or accession any State may make a reservation in respect of articles 11, 14 or 15.

2. No other reservations to this Convention shall be admissible.

Article 18

1. This Convention shall enter into force two years after the date of the deposit of the sixth instrument of ratification or accession.

2. For each State ratifying or acceding to this Convention after the deposit of the sixth instrument of ratification or accession, it shall enter into force on the ninetieth day after the deposit by such State of its instrument of ratification or accession or on the date on which this Convention enters into force in accordance with the provisions of paragraph 1 of this article, whichever is the later.

Article 19

1. Any Contracting State may denounce this Convention at any time by a written notification addressed to the Secretary-General of the United Nations. Such denunciation shall take effect for the Contracting State concerned one year after the date of its receipt by the Secretary-General.

2. In cases where, in accordance with the provisions of article 15, this Convention has become applicable to a non-metropolitan territory of a Contracting State, that State may at any time thereafter, with the consent of the territory concerned, give notice to the Secretary-General of the United Nations denouncing this Convention separately in respect to that territory. The denunciation shall take effect one year after the date of the receipt of such notice by the Secretary-General, who shall notify all other Contracting States of such notice and the date of receipt thereof.

Article 20

1. The Secretary-General of the United Nations shall notify all Members of the United Nations and the non-member States referred to in article 16 of the following particulars:

(a) Signatures, ratifications and accessions under article 16;

(b) Reservations under article 17;

(c) The date upon which this Convention enters into force in pursuance of article 18;

(d) Denunciations under article 19.

2. The Secretary-General of the United Nations shall, after the deposit of the sixth instrument of ratification or accession at the latest, bring to the attention of the General Assembly the question of the establishment, in accordance with article 11, of such a body as therein mentioned.

Article 21

This Convention shall be registered by the Secretary-General of the United Nations on the date of its entry into force.

In witness whereof the undersigned Plenipotentiaries have signed this Convention.

Done at New York, this thirtieth day of August, one thousand nine hundred and sixty-one, in a single copy, of which the Chinese, English, French, Russian and Spanish texts are equally authentic and which shall be deposited in the archives of the United Nations, and certified copies of which shall be delivered by the Secretary-General of the United Nations to all members of the United Nations and to the non-member States referred to in article 16 of this Convention.

4. TRAFFICKING AND SMUGGLING

4.1 Slavery

Slavery Convention, signed at Geneva on 25 September 1926 and amended by the 1953 Protocol*

Adoption: 7 December 1953
Entry into force: 7 July 1955
Parties: 96 (Status as of 1 April 2007)

AFGHANISTAN signed 16 Aug 1954, ALBANIA 2 Jul 1957 a, ALGERIA 20 Nov 1963 a, AUSTRALIA signed 9 Dec 1953, AUSTRIA signed 16 Jul 1954, AZERBAIJAN signed 16 Aug 1996, BAHAMAS signed 10 Jun 1976, BAHRAIN 27 Mar 1990 a, BANGLADESH signed 7 Jan 1985, BARBADOS signed 22 Jul 1976, BELARUS 13 Sep 1956 a, BELGIUM signed 13 Dec 1962, BOLIVIA signed 6 Oct 1983, BOSNIA AND HERZEGOVINA 1 Sep 1993 d, BRAZIL 6 Jan 1966 a, CAMEROON signed 27 Jun 1984, CANADA signed 17 Dec 1953, CHILE signed 20 Jun 1995, CROATIA 12 Oct 1992 d, CUBA signed 28 Jun 1954, CYPRUS 21 Apr 1986 d, DENMARK signed 3 Mar 1954, DOMINICA signed 17 Aug 1994, ECUADOR signed 17 Aug 1955, EGYPT signed 29 Sep 1954, ETHIOPIA 21 Jan 1969, FIJI signed 12 Jun 1972, FINLAND signed 19 Mar 1954, FRANCE signed 14 Feb 1963, GERMANY signed 29 May 1973, GREECE signed 12 Dec 1955, GUATEMALA signed 11 Nov 1983, GUINEA signed 12 Jul 1963, HUNGARY signed 26 Feb 1958, INDIA signed 12 Mar 1954, IRAQ signed 23 May 1955, IRELAND signed 31 Aug 1961, ISRAEL signed 12 Sep 1955, ITALY signed 4 Feb 1954, JAMAICA 30 Jul 1964 d, JORDAN 5 May 1959 a, KUWAIT 28 May 1963 a, KYRGYZSTAN 5 Sep 1997 a, LESOTHO 4 Nov 1974 d, LIBERIA signed 7 Dec 1953, LIBYAN ARAB JAMAHIRIYA 14 Feb 1957 a, MADAGASCAR 12 Feb 1964 a, MALAWI 2 Aug 1965 a, MALI signed 2 Feb 1973, MALTA 3 Jan 1966 d, MAURITANIA signed 6 Jun 1986, MAURITIUS 18 Jul 1969 d, MEXICO signed 3 Feb 1954, MONACO signed 12 Nov 1954, MONGOLIA 20 Dec 1968 a, MOROCCO signed 11 May 1959, MYANMAR signed 29 Apr 1957, NEPAL 7 Jan 1963 a, NETHERLANDS signed 7 Jul 1955, NEW ZEALAND signed 16 Dec 1953, NICARAGUA signed 14 Jan 1986, NIGER signed 7 Dec 1964, NIGERIA 26 Jun 1961 d, NORWAY signed 11 Apr 1957, PAKISTAN 30 Sep 1955 a, PAPUA NEW GUINEA 27 Jan 1982 a, PHILIPPINES 12 Jul 1955 a, ROMANIA signed 13 Nov 1957, RUSSIAN FEDERATION 8 Aug 1956 a, SAINT LUCIA signed 14 Feb 1990, SAINT VINCENT AND THE GRENADINES 9 Nov 1981, SAUDI ARABIA 5 Jul 1973 a, SIERRA LEONE 13 Mar 1962 d, SOLOMON ISLANDS signed 3 Sep 1981, SOUTH AFRICA signed 29 Dec 1953, SPAIN signed 10 Nov 1976, SRI LANKA 21 Mar 1958 a, SUDAN 9 Sep 1957 d, SWEDEN signed 17 Aug 1954, SWITZERLAND signed 7 Dec 1953, SYRIAN ARAB REPUBLIC signed 4 Aug 1954, TRINIDAD AND TOBAGO 11 Apr 1966 d, TUNISIA 15 Jul 1966 a, TURKEY signed 14 Jan 1955, TURMENISTAN signed 1 May 1997, UGANDA 12 Aug 1964 a, UKRAINE 27 Jan 1959 a, UNITED KINGDOM OF GREAT BRITAIN AND NORTHERN IRELAND signed 7 Dec 1953, UNITED REPUBLIC OF TANZANIA 28 Nov 1962 a, UNITED STATES OF AMERICA signed 7 Mar 1956, URUGUAY 7 Jun 2001 a, VIET NAM 14 Aug 1956 a, YEMEN 9 Feb 1987 a, YUGOSLAVIA 12 Mar 2001 d, ZAMBIA 26 Mar 1973 d.

* Source: 212 U.N.T.S. 17.

Article I

For the purpose of the present Convention, the following definitions are agreed upon:

(1) Slavery is the status or condition of a person over whom any or all of the powers attaching to the right of ownership are exercised.

(2) The slave trade includes all acts involved in the capture, acquisition or disposal of a person with intent to reduce him to slavery; all acts involved in the acquisition of a slave with a view to selling or exchanging him; all acts of disposal by sale or exchange of a slave acquired with a view to being sold or exchanged, and, in general, every act of trade or transport in slaves.

Article 2

The High Contracting Parties undertake, each in respect of the territories placed under its sovereignty, jurisdiction, protection, suzerainty or tutelage, so far as they have not already taken the necessary steps:

(a) To prevent and suppress the slave trade;

(b) To bring about, progressively and as soon as possible, the complete abolition of slavery in all its forms.

Article 3

The High Contracting Parties undertake to adopt all appropriate measures with a view to preventing and suppressing the embarkation, disembarkation and transport of slaves in their territorial waters and upon all vessels flying their respective flags.

The High Contracting Parties undertake to negotiate as soon as possible a general Convention with regard to the slave trade which will give them rights and impose upon them duties of the same nature as those provided for in the Convention of June 17th, 1925, relative to the International Trade in Arms (Articles 12, 20, 21, 22, 23, 24 and paragraphs 3, 4 and 5 of Section II of Annex II), with the necessary adaptations, it being understood that this general Convention will not place the ships (even of small tonnage) of any High Contracting Parties in a position different from that of the other High Contracting Parties.

It is also understood that, before or after the coming into force of this general Convention, the High Contracting Parties are entirely free to conclude between themselves, without, however, derogating from the principles laid down in the preceding paragraph, such special agreements as, by reason of their peculiar situation, might appear to be suitable in order to bring about as soon as possible the complete disappearance of the slave trade.

Article 4

The High Contracting Parties shall give to one another every assistance with the object of securing the abolition of slavery and the slave trade.

Article 5

The High Contracting Parties recognise that recourse to compulsory or forced labour may have grave consequences and undertake, each in respect of the territories placed under its sovereignty, jurisdiction, protection, suzerainty or tutelage, to take all necessary measures to prevent compulsory or forced labour from developing into conditions analogous to slavery.

It is agreed that:

(1) Subject to the transitional provisions laid down in paragraph (2) below, compulsory or forced labour may only be exacted for public purposes.

(2) In territories in which compulsory or forced labour for other than public purposes still survives, the High Contracting Parties shall endeavour progressively and as soon as possible to put an end to the practice. So long as such forced or compulsory labour exists, this labour shall invariably be of an exceptional character, shall always receive adequate remuneration, and shall not involve the removal of the labourers from their usual place of residence.

(3) In all cases, the responsibility for any recourse to compulsory or forced labour shall rest with the competent central authorities of the territory concerned.

Article 6

Those of the High Contracting Parties whose laws do not at present make adquate provision for the punishment of infractions of laws and regulations enacted with a view to giving effect to the purposes of the present Convention undertake to adopt the necessary measures in order that severe penalties may be imposed in respect of such infractions.

Article 7

The High Contracting Parties undertake to communicate to each other and to the Secretary-General of the United Nations any laws and regulations which they may enact with a view to the application of the provisions of the present Convention.

Article 8

The High Contracting Parties agree that disputes arising between them relating to the interpretation or application of this Convention shall, if they cannot be settled by direct negotiation, be referred for decision to the International Court of Justice. In case either or both of the States Parties to such a dispute should not be Parties to the Statute of the International Court of Justice, the dispute shall be referred, at the choice of the Parties and in accordance with the constitutional procedure of each State, either to the International Court of Justice or to a court of arbitration constituted in accordance with the Convention of October 18th, 1907, for the Pacific Settlement of International Disputes, or to some other court of arbitration

Article 9

At the time of signature or of ratification or of accession, any High Contracting Party may declare that its acceptance of the present Convention does not bind some or all of the territories placed under its sovereignty, jurisdiction, protection, suzerainty or tutelage in respect of all or any provisions of the Convention; it may subsequently accede separately on behalf of any one of them or in respect of any provision to which any one of them is not a Party.

Article 10

In the event of a High Contracting Party wishing to denounce the present Convention, the denunciation shall be notified in writing to the Secretary-General of the United Nations, who will at once communicate a certified true copy of the notification to all the other High Contracting Parties, informing them of the date on which it was received.

The denunciation shall only have effect in regard to the notifying State, and one year after the notification has reached the Secretary-General of the United Nations.

Denunciation may also be made separately in respect of any territory placed under its sovereignty, jurisdiction, protection, suzerainty or tutelage.

Article 11

The present Convention, which will bear this day's date and of which the French and English texts are both authentic, will remain open for signature by the States Members of the League of Nations until April 1st, 1927.

The present Convention shall be open to accession by all States, including States which are not Members of the United Nations, to which the Secretary-General of the United Nations shall have communicated a certified copy of the Convention.

Accession shall be effected by the deposit of a formal instrument with the Secretary-General of the United Nations, who shall give notice thereof to all States Parties to the Convention and to all other States contemplated in the present article, informing them of the date on which each such instrument of accession was received in deposit.

Article 12

The present Convention will be ratified and the instruments of ratification shall be deposited in the office of the Secretary-General of the United Nations. The Secretary-General will inform all the High Contracting Parties of such deposit.

The Convention will come into operation for each State on the date of the deposit of its ratification or of its accession.

Supplementary Convention on the Abolition of Slavery, the Slave Trade, and Institutions and Practices Similar to Slavery, 1956*

Adoption: 7 September 1956
Entry into force: 30 April 1957
Parties: 121 (Status as of 1 April 2007)

AFGHANISTAN 16 Nov 1966 a, ALBANIA 6 Nov 1958 a, ALGERIA 31 Oct 1963 a, ANTIGUA AND BARBUDA 25 Oct 1988 d, ARGENTINA 13 Aug 1964 a, AUSTRALIA 6 Jan 1958, AUSTRIA 7 Oct 1963 a, AZERBAIJAN 16 Aug 1996 a, BAHAMAS 10 Jun 1976 d, BAHRAIN 27 Mar 1990 a, BANGLADESH 5 Feb 1985 a, BARBADOS 9 Aug 1972 d, BELARUS 5 Jun 1957, BELGIUM 13 Dec 1962, BOLIVIA 6 Oct 1983 a, BOSNIA AND HERZEGOVINA 1 Sep 1993 d, BRAZIL 6 Jan 1966 a, BULGARIA 21 Aug 1958, CAMBODIA 12 Jun 1957 a, CAMEROON 27 Jun 1984 a, CANADA 10 Jan 1963, CENTRAL AFRICAN REPUBLIC 30 Dec 1970 a, CHILE 20 Jun 1995 a, CONGO 25 Aug 1977 a, CÔTE D'IVOIRE 10 Dec 1970 a, CROATIA 12 Oct 1992 d, CUBA 21 Aug 1963, CYPRUS 11 May 1962 d, CZECH REPUBLIC 22 Feb 1993 d, DEMOCRATIC REPUBLIC OF CONGO 28 Feb 1975 a, DENMARK 24 Apr 1958, DJIBOUTI 21 Mar 1979 a, DOMINICA 17 Aug 1994 d, DOMINICAN REPUBLIC 31 Oct 1962 a, ECUADOR 29 Mar 1960 a, EGYPT 17 Apr 1958 a, EL SALVADOR signed 7 Sep 1956, ETHIOPIA 21 Jan 1969 a, FIJI 12 Jun 1972 d, FINLAND 1 Apr 1959 a, FRANCE 26 May 1964, GERMANY 14 Jan 1959, GHANA 3 May 1963 a, GREECE 13 Dec 1972, GUATEMALA 11 Nov 1983, GUINEA 14 Mar 1977 a, HAITI 12 Feb 1958, HUNGARY 26 Feb 1958, ICELAND 17 Nov 1965 a, INDIA 23 Jun 1960, IRAN (ISLAMIC REPUBLIC OF) 30 Dec 1959 a, IRAQ 30 Sep 1963, IRELAND 18 Sep 1961 a, ISRAEL 23 Oct 1957, ITALY 12 Feb 1958, JAMAICA 30 Jul 1964 d, JORDAN 27 Sep 1957 a, KUWAIT 18 Jan 1963 a, KYRGYZSTAN 5 Sep 1997 a, LAO PEOPLE'S DEMOCRATIC REPUBLIC 9 Sep 1957 a, LATVIA 14 Apr 1992 a, LESOTHO 4 Nov 1974 d, LIBERIA signed 7 Sep 1956, LIBYAN ARAB JAMAHIRIYA 16 May 1989 a, LUXEMBOURG 1 May 1967, MADAGASCAR 29 Feb 1972 a, MALAWI 2 Aug 1965 a, MALAYSIA 18 Nov 1957 a, MALI 2 Feb 1973 a, MALTA 3 Jan 1966 d, MAURITANIA 6 Jun 1986 a, MAURITIUS 18 Jul 1969 d, MEXICO 30 Jun 1959, MONGOLIA 20 Dec 1968 a, MONTENEGRO 23 Oct 2006 d, MOROCCO 11 May 1959 a, NEPAL 7 Jan 1963 a, NETHERLANDS 3 Dec 1957, NEW ZEALAND 26 Apr 1962 a, NICARAGUA 14 Jan 1986 a, NIGER 22 Jul 1963 a, NIGERIA 26 Jun 1961 d, NORWAY 3 May 1960, PAKISTAN 20 Mar 1958, PERU signed 7 Sep 1956, PHILIPPINES 17 Nov 1964 a, POLAND 10 Jan 1963, PORTUGAL 10 Aug 1959, ROMANIA 13 Nov 1957, RUSSIAN FEDERATION 12 Apr 1957, RWANDA 4 Oct 2006 a, SAINT LUCIA 14 Feb 1990 d, SAINT VINCENT AND THE GRENADINES 9 Nov 1981 a, SAN MARINO 29 Aug 1967, SAUDI ARABIA 5 Jul 1973 a, SENEGAL 19 Jul 1979 a, SEYCHELLES 5 May 1992 a, SIERRA LEONE 13 Mar 1962 d, SINGAPORE 28 Mar 1972 d, SLOVAKIA 28 May 1993 d, SLOVENIA 6 Jul 1992 s, SOLOMON ISLANDS 3 Sep 1981 d, SPAIN 21 Nov 1967 a, SRI LANKA 21 Mar 1958, SUDAN 9 Sep 1957, SURINAME 12 Oct 1979 d, SWEDEN 28 Oct 1979 d, SWITZERLAND 28 Jul 1964 a, SYRIAN ARAB REPUBLIC 17 Apr 1958 a, THE FORMER YUGOSLAV REPUBLIC 18 Jan 1994 d, TOGO 8 Jul 1980 a, TRINIDAD AND TOBAGO 11 Apr 1966 d, TUNISIA 15 Jul 1966 a, TURKEY 17 Jul 1964, TURKMENISTAN 1 May 1997 a, UGANDA 12 Aug 1964 a, UKRAINE 3 Dec 1958, UNITED KINGDOM OF GREAT BRITAIN AND NORTHERN IRELAND 30 Apr 1957, UNITED REPUBLIC OF TANZANIA 28 Nov 1962 a, UNITED STATES OF AMERICA 6 Dec 1967 a, URUGUAY 7 Jun 2001 a, YUGOSLAVIA 12 Mar 2001 d, ZAMBIA 26 Mar 1973 d, ZIMBABWE 1 Dec 1998 d.

* Source: 226 U.N.T.S. 3.

The States Parties to the present Convention,

Considering that freedom is the birthright of every human being,

Mindful that the peoples of the United Nations reaffirmed in the Charter their faith in the dignity and worth of the human person,

Considering that the Universal Declaration of Human Rights, proclaimed by the General Assembly of the United Nations as a common standard of achievement for all peoples and all nations, states that no one shall be held in slavery or servitude and that slavery and the slave trade shall be prohibited in all their forms,

Recognizing that, since the conclusion of the Slavery Convention signed at Geneva on 25 September 1926, which was designed to secure the abolition of slavery and of the slave trade, further progress has been made towards this end,

Having regard to the Forced Labour Convention of 1930 and to subsequent action by the International Labour Organisation in regard to forced or compulsory labour,

Being aware, however, that slavery, the slave trade and institutions and practices similar to slavery have not yet been eliminated in all parts of the world,

Having decided, therefore, that the Convention of 1926, which remains operative, should now be augmented by the conclusion of a supplementary convention designed to intensify national as well as international efforts towards the abolition of slavery, the slave trade and institutions and practices similar to slavery,

Have agreed as follows:

SECTION I.

INSTITUTIONS AND PRACTICES SIMILAR TO SLAVERY

Article 1

Each of the States Parties to this Convention shall take all practicable and necessary legislative and other measures to bring about progressively and as soon as possible the complete abolition or abandonment of the following institutions and practices, where they still exist and whether or not they are covered by the definition of slavery contained in article 1 of the Slavery Convention signed at Geneva on 25 September 1926:

(a) Debt bondage, that is to say, the status or condition arising from a pledge by a debtor of his personal services or of those of a person under his control as security for a debt, if the value of those services as reasonably assessed is not applied towards the liquidation of the debt or the length and nature of those services are not respectively limited and defined;

(b) Serfdom, that is to say, the condition or status of a tenant who is by law, custom or agreement bound to live and labour on land belonging to another person and to render some determinate service to such other person, whether for reward or not, and is not free to change his status;

(c) Any institution or practice whereby:

(i) A woman, without the right to refuse, is promised or given in marriage on payment of a consideration in money or in kind to her parents, guardian, family or any other person or group; or

(ii) The husband of a woman, his family, or his clan, has the right to transfer her to another person for value received or otherwise; or

(iii) A woman on the death of her husband is liable to be inherited by another person;

(d) Any institution or practice whereby a child or young person under the age of 18 years, is delivered by either or both of his natural parents or by his guardian to another person, whether for reward or not, with a view to the exploitation of the child or young person or of his labour.

Article 2

With a view to bringing to an end the institutions and practices mentioned in article 1 (c) of this Convention, the States Parties undertake to prescribe, where appropriate, suitable minimum ages of marriage, to encourage the use of facilities whereby the consent of both parties to a marriage may be freely expressed in the presence of a competent civil or religious authority, and to encourage the registration of marriages.

SECTION II.

THE SLAVE TRADE

Article 3

1. The act of conveying or attempting to convey slaves from one country to another by whatever means of transport, or of being accessory thereto, shall be a criminal offence under the laws of the States Parties to this Convention and persons convicted thereof shall be liable to very severe penalties.

2. (a) The States Parties shall take all effective measures to prevent ships and aircraft authorized to fly their flags from conveying slaves and to punish persons guilty of such acts or of using national flags for that purpose.

(b) The States Parties shall take all effective measures to ensure that their ports, airfields and coasts are not used for the conveyance of slaves.

3. The States Parties to this Convention shall exchange information in order to ensure the practical co-ordination of the measures taken by them in combating the slave trade and shall inform each other of every case of the slave trade, and of every attempt to commit this criminal offence, which comes to their notice.

Article 4

Any slave who takes refuge on board any vessel of a State Party to this Convention shall ipso facto be free.

SECTION III.

SLAVERY AND INSTITUTIONS AND PRACTICES SIMILAR TO SLAVERY

Article 5

In a country where the abolition or abandonment of slavery, or of the institutions or practices mentioned in article 1 of this Convention, is not yet complete, the act of mutilating, branding or otherwise marking a slave or a person of servile status in order to indicate his status, or as a punishment, or for any other reason, or of being accessory thereto, shall be a criminal offence under the laws of the States Parties to this Convention and persons convicted thereof shall be liable to punishment.

Article 6

1. The act of enslaving another person or of inducing another person to give himself or a person dependent upon him into slavery, or of attempting these acts, or being accessory thereto, or being a party to a conspiracy to accomplish any such acts, shall be a criminal offence under the laws of the States Parties to this Convention and persons convicted thereof shall be liable to punishment.

2. Subject to the provisions of the introductory paragraph of article 1 of this Convention, the provisions of paragraph 1 of the present article shall also apply to the act of inducing another person to place himself or a person dependent upon him into the servile status resulting from any of the institutions or practices mentioned in article 1, to any attempt to perform such acts, to being accessory thereto, and to being a party to a conspiracy to accomplish any such acts.

SECTION IV.

DEFINITIONS

Article 7

For the purposes of the present Convention:

(a) "Slavery" means, as defined in the Slavery Convention of 1926, the status or condition of a person over whom any or all of the powers attaching to the right of ownership are exercised, and "slave" means a person in such condition or status;

(b) "A person of servile status" means a person in the condition or status resulting from any of the institutions or practices mentioned in article 1 of this Convention;

(c) "Slave trade" means and includes all acts involved in the capture, acquisition or disposal of a person with intent to reduce him to slavery; all acts involved in the acquisition of a slave with a view to selling or exchanging him; all acts of disposal by sale or exchange of a person acquired with a view to being sold or exchanged; and, in general, every act of trade or transport in slaves by whatever means of conveyance.

SECTION V.

CO-OPERATION BETWEEN STATES PARTIES AND COMMUNICATION OF INFORMATION

Article 8

1. The States Parties to this Convention undertake to co-operate with each other and with the United Nations to give effect to the foregoing provisions.

2. The Parties undertake to communicate to the Secretary-General of the United Nations copies of any laws, regulations and administrative measures enacted or put into effect to implement the provisions of this Convention.

3. The Secretary-General shall communicate the information received under paragraph 2 of this article to the other Parties and to the Economic and Social Council as part of the documentation for any discussion which the Council might undertake with a view to making

further recommendations for the abolition of slavery, the slave trade or the institutions and practices which are the subject of this Convention.

SECTION VI.

FINAL CLAUSES

Article 9

No reservations may be made to this Convention.

Article 10

Any dispute between States Parties to this Convention relating to its interpretation or application, which is not settled by negotiation, shall be referred to the International Court of Justice at the request of any one of the parties to the dispute, unless the parties concerned agree on another mode of settlement.

Article 11

1. This Convention shall be open until I July 1957 for signature by any State Member of the United Nations or of a specialized agency. It shall be subject to ratification by the signatory States, and the instruments of ratification shall be deposited with the Secretary-General of the United Nations, who shall inform each signatory and acceding State.

2. After 1 July 1957 this Convention shall be open for accession by any State Member of the United Nations or of a specialized agency, or by any other State to which an invitation to accede has been addressed by the General Assembly of the United Nations. Accession shall be effected by the deposit of a formal instrument with the Secretary-General of the United Nations, who shall inform each signatory and acceding State.

Article 12

1. This Convention shall apply to all non-self-governing trust, colonial and other non-metropolitan territories for the international relations of which any State Party is responsible; the Party concerned shall, subject to the provisions of paragraph 2 of this article, at the time of signature, ratification or accession declare the non-metropolitan territory or territories to which the Convention shall apply ipso facto as a result of such signature, ratification or accession.

2. In any case in which the previous consent of a non-metropolitan territory is required by the constitutional laws or practices of the Party or of the non-metropolitan territory, the Party concerned shall endeavour to secure the needed consent of the non-metropolitan territory within the period of twelve months from the date of signature of the Convention by the metropolitan State, and when such consent has been obtained the Party shall notify the Secretary-General. This Convention shall apply to the territory or territories named in such notification from the date of its receipt by the Secretary-General.

3. After the expiry of the twelve-month period mentioned in the preceding paragraph, the States Parties concerned shall inform the Secretary-General of the results of the consultations with those non-metropolitan territories for whose international relations they are responsible and whose consent to the application of this Convention may have been withheld.

Article 13

1. This Convention shall enter into force on the date on which two States have become Parties thereto.

2. It shall thereafter enter into force with respect to each State and territory on the date of deposit of the instrument of ratification or accession of that State or notification of application to that territory.

Article 14

1. The application of this Convention shall be divided into successive periods of three years, of which the first shall begin on the date of entry into force of the Convention in accordance with paragraph 1 of article 13.

2. Any State Party may denounce this Convention by a notice addressed by that State to the Secretary-General not less than six months before the expiration of the current three-year period. The Secretary-General shall notify all other Parties of each such notice and the date of the receipt thereof.

3. Denunciations shall take effect at the expiration of the current three-year period. The Secretary- General shall notify other Parties of each such notice and the date of the receipt thereof.

4. In cases where, in accordance with the provisions of article 12, this Convention has become applicable to a non-metropolitan territory of a Party, that Party may at any time thereafter, with the consent of the territory concerned, give notice to the Secretary-General of the United Nations denouncing this Convention separately in respect of that territory. The denunciation shall take effect one year after the date of the receipt of such notice by the Secretary-General, who shall notify all other Parties of such notice and the date of the receipt thereof.

Article 15

This Convention, of which the Chinese, English, French, Russian and Spanish texts are equally authentic, shall be deposited in the archives of the United Nations Secretariat. The Secretary-General shall prepare a certified copy thereof for communication to States Parties to this Convention, as well as to all other States Members of the United Nations and of the specialized agencies.

IN WITNESS WHEREOF the undersigned, being duly authorized thereto by their respective Governments, have signed this Convention on the date appearing opposite their respective signatures.

DONE at the European Office of the United Nations at Geneva, this seventh day of September one thousand nine hundred and fifty-six.

Convention No.29 concerning Forced or Compulsory Labour, 1930 (See section 2.3)

Recommendation No.35 concerning Indirect Compulsion to Labour, 1930 (See section 2.3)

Convention No.105 concerning the Abolition of Forced Labour, 1957 (See section 2.3)

Convention No.138 concerning Minimum Age for Admission to Employment, 1973 (See section 2.3)

Convention No.182 concerning the Prohibition and Immediate Action for the Elimination of the Worst Forms of Child Labour, 1999 (See section 2.3)

Recommendation No.190 concerning Worst Forms of Child Labour, 1999 (See section 2.3)

4.2 Trafficking

Convention for the Suppression of the Traffic in Persons and of the Exploitation of the Prostitution of Others, 1949*

Adoption: 2 December 1949**
Entry into force: 25 July 1951
Parties: 80 (Status as of 1 April 2007)

AFGHANISTAN 21 May 1985 a (*22), ALBANIA 6 Nov 1958 a (*22), ALGERIA 31 Oct 1963 a (*22), ARGENTINA 15 Nov 1957 a, AZERBAIJAN 16 Aug 1996 a, BANGLADESH 11 Jan 1985 a, BELARUS 24 Aug 1956 a, BELGIUM 22 Jun 1965 a, BENIN signed 25 Sep 2003, BOLIVIA 6 Oct 1983 a, BOSNIA AND HERZEGOVINA 1 Sep 1993 d, BRAZIL 12 Sep 1958, BULGARIA 18 Jan 1955 a, BURKINA FASO 27 Aug 1962 a, CAMBODIA signed 27 Sep 2004, CAMEROON 19 Feb 1982 a, CENTRAL AFRICAN REPUBLIC 29 Sep 1981 a, CONGO 25 Aug 1977 a, COTE D'IVOIRE 2 Nov 1999 a, CROATIA 12 Oct 1992 d, CUBA 4 Sep 1952 a, CYPRUS 5 Oct 1983 a, CZECH REPUBLIC 30 Dec 1993 d, DENMARK signed 12 Feb 1951, DJIBOUTI 21 Mar 1979 a, ECUADOR 3 Apr 1979, EGYPT 12 Jun 1959 a, ETHIOPIA 10 Sep 1981 a (*22), FINLAND 8 Jun 1972 (*9), FRANCE 19 Nov 1960 a (*territorial), GHANA signed 24 Sep 2003, HAITI 26 Aug 1953 a, HONDURAS 15 Jun 1993, HUNGARY 29 Sep 1955 a, INDIA 9 Jan 1953, INDONESIA signed 25 Sep 2003, IRAN (ISLAMIC REPUBLIC OF) signed 16 Jul 1953, Iraq 22 Sep 1955 a, ISRAEL 28 Dec 1950 a, ITALY 18 Jan 1980 a, JAPAN 1 May 1958 a, JORDAN 13 Apr 1976 a, KAZAKHSTAN 24 Jan 2006, KUWAIT 20 Nov 1968 a, KYRGYZSTAN 5 Sep 1997 a, LAO PEOPLE'S DEMOCRATIC REPUBLIC 14 Apr 1978 a (*22), LATVIA 14 Apr 1992 a, LIBERIA signed 21 Mar 1950, LIBYAN ARAB JAMAHIRIYA 3 Dec 1956 a, LUXEMBOURG 5 Oct 1983, MADAGASCAR signed 1 Oct 2001, MALAWI 13 Oct 1965 a (*22), MALI 23 Dec 1964 a, MAURITANIA 6 Jun 1986 a, MAURITIUS signed 24 Sep 2003, MEXICO 21 Feb 1956 a, MICRONESIA (FEDERATED STATES OF) signed 23 Sep 2003, MONTENEGRO 23 Oct 2006 d, MOROCCO 17 Aug 1973 a, MYANMAR signed 14 Mar 1956, NIGER 10 Jun 1977 a, NIGERIA signed 25 Sep 2003, NORWAY 23 Jan 1952 a, PAKISTAN 11 Jul 1952, PHILIPPINES 19 Sep 1952, POLAND 2 Jun 1952 a, PORTUGAL 30 Sep 1992 a, REPUBLIC OF KOREA 13 Feb 1962 a, ROMANIA 15 Feb 1955 a, RUSSIAN FEDERATION 11 Aug 1954 a, RWANDA 26 Sep 2003 a, SENEGAL 19 Jul 1979 a, SEYCHELLES 5 May 1992 a, SIERRA LEONE 26 Sep 2003, SINGAPORE 26 Oct 1966 a, SLOVAKIA 28 May 1993 d, SOUTH AFRICA 10 Oct 1951, SPAIN 18 Jun 1962 a, SRI LANKA 15 Apr 1958 a, SYRIAN ARAB REPUBLIC 12 Jun 1959◊ a, TAJIKISTAN 19 Oct 2001 a, THE FORMER YUGOSLAV REPUBLIC OF MACEDONIA 18 Jan 1994 d, TOGO 14 Mar 1990 a, UZBEKISTAN 27 Feb 2004 a, UKRAINE 15 Nov 1954 a, VENEZUELA 18 Dec 1968 a, YEMEN 6 Apr 1989 a, ZIMBABWE 15 Nov 1995.

Whereas prostitution and the accompanying evil of the traffic in persons for the purpose of prostitution are incompatible with the dignity and worth of the human person and endanger the welfare of the individual, the family and the community, Whereas, with respect to the suppression of the traffic in women and children, the following international instruments are in force:

* Source: U.N.G.A. Res. 317 (IV).

** The Convention was opened for signature on 21 March 1950.

(1) International Agreement of 18 May 1904 for the Suppression of the White Slave Traffic, as amended by the Protocol approved by the General Assembly of the United Nations on 3 December 1948,

(2) International Convention of 4 May 1910 for the Suppression of the White Slave Traffic, as amended by the above-mentioned Protocol,

(3) International Convention of 30 September 1921 for the Suppression of the Traffic in Women and Children, as amended by the Protocol approved by the General Assembly of the United Nations on 20 October 1947,

(4) International Convention of 11 October 1933 for the Suppression of the Traffic in Women of Full Age, as amended by the aforesaid Protocol,

Whereas the League of Nations in 1937 prepared a draft Convention extending the scope of the above-mentioned instruments, and

Whereas developments since 1937 make feasible the conclusion of a convention consolidating the above-mentioned instruments and embodying the substance of the 1937 draft Convention as well as desirable alterations therein:

Now therefore
The Contracting parties
Hereby agree as hereinafter provided:

Article 1

The Parties to the present Convention agree to punish any person who, to gratify the passions of another:

(1) Procures, entices or leads away, for purposes of prostitution, another person, even with the consent of that person;

(2) Exploits the prostitution of another person, even with the consent of that person.

Article 2

The Parties to the present Convention further agree to punish any person who:

(1) Keeps or manages, or knowingly finances or takes part in the financing of a brothel;

(2) Knowingly lets or rents a building or other place or any part thereof for the purpose of the prostitution of others.

Article 3

To the extent permitted by domestic law, attempts to commit any of the offences referred to in articles 1 and 2, and acts preparatory to the commission thereof, shall also be punished.

Article 4

To the extent permitted by domestic law, intentional participation in the acts referred to in articles 1 and 2 above shall also be punishable.

To the extent permitted by domestic law, acts of participation shall be treated as separate offences whenever this is necessary to prevent impunity.

Article 5

In cases where injured persons are entitled under domestic law to be parties to proceedings in respect of any of the offences referred to in the present Convention, aliens shall be so entitled upon the same terms as nationals.

Article 6

Each Party to the present Convention agrees to take all the necessary measures to repeal or abolish any existing law, regulation or administrative provision by virtue of which persons who engage in or are suspected of engaging in prostitution are subject either to special registration or to the possession of a special document or to any exceptional requirements for supervision or notification.

Article 7

Previous convictions pronounced in foreign States for offences referred to in the present Convention shall, to the extent permitted by domestic law, be taken into account for the purposes of:

(1) Establishing recidivism;

(2) Disqualifying the offender from the exercise of civil rights.

Article 8

The offences referred to in articles 1 and 2 of the present Convention shall be regarded as extraditable offences in any extradition treaty which has been or may hereafter be concluded between any of the Parties to this Convention.

The Parties to the present Convention which do not make extradition conditional on the existence of a treaty shall henceforward recognize the offences referred to in articles 1 and 2 of the present Convention as cases for extradition between themselves.

Extradition shall be granted in accordance with the law of the State to which the request is made.

Article 9

In States where the extradition of nationals is not permitted by law, nationals who have returned to their own State after the commission abroad of any of the offences referred to in articles 1 and 2 of the present Convention shall be prosecuted in and punished by the courts of their own State.

This provision shall not apply if, in a similar case between the Parties to the present Convention, the extradition of an alien cannot be granted.

Article 10

The provisions of article 9 shall not apply when the person charged with the offence has been tried in a foreign State and, if convicted, has served his sentence or had it remitted or reduced in conformity with the laws of that foreign State.

Article 11

Nothing in the present Convention shall be interpreted as determining the attitude of a Party towards the general question of the limits of criminal jurisdiction under international law.

Article 12

The present Convention does not affect the principle that the offences to which it refers shall in each State be defined, prosecuted and punished in conformity with its domestic law.

Article 13

The Parties to the present Convention shall be bound to execute letters of request relating to offences referred to in the Convention in accordance with their domestic law and practice.

The transmission of letters of request shall be effected:

(1) By direct communication between the judicial authorities; or

(2) By direct communication between the Ministers of Justice of the two States, or by direct communication from another competent authority of the State making the request to the Minister of Justice of the State to which the request is made; or

(3) Through the diplomatic or consular representative of the State making the request in the State to which the request is made; this representative shall send the letters of request direct to the competent judicial authority or to the authority indicated by the Government of the State to which the request is made, and shall receive direct from such authority the papers constituting the execution of the letters of request.

In cases 1 and 3 a copy of the letters of request shall always be sent to the superior authority of the State to which application is made.

Unless otherwise agreed, the letters of request shall be drawn up in the language of the authority making the request, provided always that the State to which the request is made may require a translation in its own language, certified correct by the authority making the request.

Each Party to the present Convention shall notify to each of the other Parties to the Convention the method or methods of transmission mentioned above which it will recognize for the letters of request of the latter State.

Until such notification is made by a State, its existing procedure in regard to letters of request shall remain in force.

Execution of letters of request shall not give rise to a claim for reimbursement of charges or expenses of any nature whatever other than expenses of experts.

Nothing in the present article shall be construed as an undertaking on the part of the Parties to the present Convention to adopt in criminal matters any form or methods of proof contrary to their own domestic laws.

Article 14

Each Party to the present Convention shall establish or maintain a service charged with the co-ordination and centralization of the results of the investigation of offences referred to in the present Convention.

Such services should compile all information calculated to facilitate the prevention and punishment of the offences referred to in the present Convention and should be in close contact with the corresponding services in other States.

Article 15

To the extent permitted by domestic law and to the extent to which the authorities responsible for the services referred to in article 14 may judge desirable, they shall furnish to the authorities responsible for the corresponding services in other States the following information:

(1) Particulars of any offence referred to in the present Convention or any attempt to commit such offence;

(2) Particulars of any search for any prosecution, arrest, conviction, refusal of admission or expulsion of persons guilty of any of the offences referred to in the present Convention, the movements of such persons and any other useful information with regard to them.

The information so furnished shall include descriptions of the offenders, their fingerprints, photographs, methods of operation, police records and records of conviction.

Article 16

The Parties to the present Convention agree to take or to encourage, through their public and private educational, health, social, economic and other related services, measures for the prevention of prostitution and for the rehabilitation and social adjustment of the victims of prostitution and of the offences referred to in the present Convention.

Article 17

The Parties to the present Convention undertake, in connection with immigration and emigration, to adopt or maintain such measures as are required, in terms of their obligations under the present Convention, to check the traffic in persons of either sex for the purpose of prostitution.

In particular they undertake:

(1) To make such regulations as are necessary for the protection of immigrants or emigrants, and in particular, women and children, both at the place of arrival and departure and while en route;

(2) To arrange for appropriate publicity warning the public of the dangers of the aforesaid traffic;

(3) To take appropriate measures to ensure supervision of railway stations, airports, seaports and en route, and of other public places, in order to prevent international traffic in persons for the purpose of prostitution;

(4) To take appropriate measures in order that the appropriate authorities be informed of the arrival of persons who appear, prima facie, to be the principals and accomplices in or victims of such traffic.

Article 18

The Parties to the present Convention undertake, in accordance with the conditions laid down by domestic law, to have declarations taken from aliens who are prostitutes, in order to establish their identity and civil status and to discover who has caused them to leave their State. The information obtained shall be communicated to the authorities of the State of origin of the said persons with a view to their eventual repatriation.

Article 19

The Parties to the present Convention undertake, in accordance with the conditions laid down by domestic law and without prejudice to prosecution or other action for violations thereunder and so far as possible:

(1) Pending the completion of arrangements for the repatriation of destitute victims of international traffic in persons for the purpose of prostitution, to make suitable provisions for their temporary care and maintenance;

(2) To repatriate persons referred to in article 18 who desire to be repatriated or who may be claimed by persons exercising authority over them or whose expulsion is ordered in conformity with the law. Repatriation shall take place only after agreement is reached with the State of destination as to identity and nationality as well as to the place and date of arrival at frontiers. Each Party to the present Convention shall facilitate the passage of such persons through its territory.

Where the persons referred to in the preceding paragraph cannot themselves repay the cost of repatriation and have neither spouse, relatives nor guardian to pay for them, the cost of repatriation as far as the nearest frontier or port of embarkation or airport in the direction of the State of origin shall be borne by the State where they are in residence, and the cost of the remainder of the journey shall be borne by the State of origin.

Article 20

The Parties to the present Convention shall, if they have not already done so, take the necessary measures for the supervision of employment agencies in order to prevent persons seeking employment, in particular women and children, from being exposed to the danger of prostitution.

Article 21

The Parties to the present Convention shall communicate to the Secretary-General of the United Nations such laws and regulations as have already been promulgated in their States, and thereafter annually such laws and regulations as may be promulgated, relating to the subjects of the present Convention, as well as all measures taken by them concerning the application of the Convention. The information received shall be published periodically by the Secretary-General and sent to all Members of the United Nations and to non-member States to which the present Convention is officially communicated in accordance with article 23.

Article 22

If any dispute shall arise between the Parties to the present Convention relating to its interpretation or application and if such dispute cannot be settled by other means, the dispute shall, at the request of any one of the Parties to the dispute, be referred to the International Court of Justice.

Article 23

The present Convention shall be open for signature on behalf of any Member of the United Nations and also on behalf of any other State to which an invitation has been addressed by the Economic and Social Council.

The present Convention shall be ratified and the instruments of ratification shall be deposited with the Secretary-General of the United Nations.

The States mentioned in the first paragraph which have not signed the Convention may accede to it.

Accession shall be effected by deposit of an instrument of accession with the Secretary-General of the United Nations.

For the purposes of the present Convention the word "State" shall include all the colonies and Trust Territories of a State signatory or acceding to the Convention and all territories for which such State is internationally responsible.

Article 24

The present Convention shall come into force on the ninetieth day following the date of deposit of the second instrument of ratification or accession.

For each State ratifying or acceding to the Convention after the deposit of the second instrument of ratification or accession, the Convention shall enter into force ninety days after the deposit by such State of its instrument of ratification or accession.

Article 25

After the expiration of five years from the entry into force of the present Convention, any Party to the Convention may denounce it by a written notification addressed to the Secretary-General of the United Nations.

Such denunciation shall take effect for the Party making it one year from the date upon which it is received by the Secretary-General of the United Nations.

Article 26

The Secretary-General of the United Nations shall inform all Members of the United Nations and non-member States referred to in article 23:

(a) Of signatures, ratifications and accessions received in accordance with article 23;

(b) Of the date on which the present Convention will come into force in accordance with article 24;

(c) Of denunciations received in accordance with article 25.

Article 27

Each Party to the present Convention undertakes to adopt, in accordance with its Constitution, the legislative or other measures necessary to ensure the application of the Convention.

Article 28

The provisions of the present Convention shall supersede in the relations between the Parties thereto the provisions of the international instruments referred to in subparagraphs 1, 2, 3 and 4 of the second paragraph of the Preamble, each of which shall be deemed to be terminated when all the Parties thereto shall have become Parties to the present Convention.

FINAL PROTOCOL

Nothing in the present Convention shall be deemed to prejudice any legislation which ensures, for the enforcement of the provisions for securing the suppression of the traffic in persons and of the exploitation of others for purposes of prostitution, stricter conditions than those provided by the present Convention.

The provisions of articles 23 to 26 inclusive of the Convention shall apply to the present Protocol.

Declaration of Basic Principles of Justice for Victims of Crime and Abuse of Power, 1985*

Adoption: 29 November 1985

A. Victims of crime

1. "Victims" means persons who, individually or collectively, have suffered harm, including physical or mental injury, emotional suffering, economic loss or substantial impairment of their fundamental rights, through acts or omissions that are in violation of criminal laws operative within Member States, including those laws proscribing criminal abuse of power.

2. A person may be considered a victim, under this Declaration, regardless of whether the perpetrator is identified, apprehended, prosecuted or convicted and regardless of the familial relationship between the perpetrator and the victim. The term "victim" also includes, where appropriate, the immediate family or dependants of the direct victim and persons who have suffered harm in intervening to assist victims in distress or to prevent victimization.

3. The provisions contained herein shall be applicable to all, without distinction of any kind, such as race, colour, sex, age, language, religion, nationality, political or other opinion, cultural beliefs or practices, property, birth or family status, ethnic or social origin, and disability.

Access to justice and fair treatment

4. Victims should be treated with compassion and respect for their dignity. They are entitled to access to the mechanisms of justice and to prompt redress, as provided for by national legislation, for the harm that they have suffered.

5. Judicial and administrative mechanisms should be established and strengthened where necessary to enable victims to obtain redress through formal or informal procedures that are expeditious, fair, inexpensive and accessible. Victims should be informed of their rights in seeking redress through such mechanisms.

6. The responsiveness of judicial and administrative processes to the needs of victims should be facilitated by:

(a) Informing victims of their role and the scope, timing and progress of the proceedings and of the disposition of their cases, especially where serious crimes are involved and where they have requested such information;

(b) Allowing the views and concerns of victims to be presented and considered at appropriate stages of the proceedings where their personal interests are affected, without prejudice to the accused and consistent with the relevant national criminal justice system;

(c) Providing proper assistance to victims throughout the legal process;

(d) Taking measures to minimize inconvenience to victims, protect their privacy, when necessary, and ensure their safety, as well as that of their families and witnesses on their behalf, from intimidation and retaliation;

(e) Avoiding unnecessary delay in the disposition of cases and the execution of orders or decrees granting awards to victims.

* Source: U.N.G.A. Res. 40/34.

7. Informal mechanisms for the resolution of disputes, including mediation, arbitration and customary justice or indigenous practices, should be utilized where appropriate to facilitate conciliation and redress for victims.

Restitution

8. Offenders or third parties responsible for their behaviour should, where appropriate, make fair restitution to victims, their families or dependants. Such restitution should include the return of property or payment for the harm or loss suffered, reimbursement of expenses incurred as a result of the victimization, the provision of services and the restoration of rights.

9. Governments should review their practices, regulations and laws to consider restitution as an available sentencing option in criminal cases, in addition to other criminal sanctions.

10. In cases of substantial harm to the environment, restitution, if ordered, should include, as far as possible, restoration of the environment, reconstruction of the infrastructure, replacement of community facilities and reimbursement of the expenses of relocation, whenever such harm results in the dislocation of a community.

11. Where public officials or other agents acting in an official or quasi-official capacity have violated national criminal laws, the victims should receive restitution from the State whose officials or agents were responsible for the harm inflicted. In cases where the Government under whose authority the victimizing act or omission occurred is no longer in existence, the State or Government successor in title should provide restitution to the victims.

Compensation

12. When compensation is not fully available from the offender or other sources, States should endeavour to provide financial compensation to:

(a) Victims who have sustained significant bodily injury or impairment of physical or mental health as a result of serious crimes;

(b) The family, in particular dependants of persons who have died or become physically or mentally incapacitated as a result of such victimization.

13. The establishment, strengthening and expansion of national funds for compensation to victims should be encouraged. Where appropriate, other funds may also be established for this purpose, including in those cases where the State of which the victim is a national is not in a position to compensate the victim for the harm.

Assistance

14. Victims should receive the necessary material, medical, psychological and social assistance through governmental, voluntary, community-based and indigenous means.

15. Victims should be informed of the availability of health and social services and other relevant assistance and be readily afforded access to them.

16. Police, justice, health, social service and other personnel concerned should receive training to sensitize them to the needs of victims, and guidelines to ensure proper and prompt aid.

17. In providing services and assistance to victims, attention should be given to those who have special needs because of the nature of the harm inflicted or because of factors such as those mentioned in paragraph 3 above.

B. Victims of abuse of power

18. "Victims" means persons who, individually or collectively, have suffered harm, including physical or mental injury, emotional suffering, economic loss or substantial impairment of their fundamental rights, through acts or omissions that do not yet constitute violations of national criminal laws but of internationally recognized norms relating to human rights.

19. States should consider incorporating into the national law norms proscribing abuses of power and providing remedies to victims of such abuses. In particular, such remedies should include restitution and/or compensation, and necessary material, medical, psychological and social assistance and support.

20. States should consider negotiating multilateral international treaties relating to victims, as defined in paragraph 18.

21. States should periodically review existing legislation and practices to ensure their responsiveness to changing circumstances, should enact and enforce, if necessary, legislation proscribing acts that constitute serious abuses of political or economic power, as well as promoting policies and mechanisms for the prevention of such acts, and should develop and make readily available appropriate rights and remedies for victims of such acts.

United Nations Convention Against Transnational Organized Crime, 2000*

Adoption: 15 November 2000
Entry into force: 29 September 2003
Parties: 132 (Status as of 1 April 2007)

AFGHANISTAN 24 Sep 2003, ALBANIA 21 Aug 2002, ALGERIA 7 Oct 2002 (*35.2), ANDORRA signed 11 Nov 2001, ANGOLA signed 13 Dec 2000, ANTIGUA AND BARBUDA 24 July 2002, ARGENTINA 19 Nov 2002, ARMENIA 1 July 2003, AUSTRALIA 27 May 2004, AUSTRIA 23 Sep 2004, AZERBAIJAN 30 Oct 2003 (*35.2), BAHAMAS signed 9 Apr 2001, BAHRAIN 7 June 2004 a (*35.2), BARBADOS signed 26 Sep 2001, BELARUS 25 June 2003 (*10), BELGIUM 11 Aug 2004 (territorial), BELIZE 26 Sep 2003 a (*35.2), BENIN 30 Aug 2004, BOLIVIA 10 Oct 2005, BOSNIA AND HERZEGOVINA 24 Apr 2002, BOTSWANA 29 Aug 2002, BRAZIL 29 Jan 2004, BULGARIA 5 Dec 2001, BURKINA FASO 15 May 2002, BURUNDI signed 14 Dec 2000, CAMBODIA 12 Dec 2005, CAMEROON 6 Feb 2006, CANADA 13 May 2002, CAPE VERDE 15 July 2004, CENTRAL AFRICAN REPUBLIC 14 Sep 2004 a, CHILE 29 Nov 2004, CHINA 23 Sep 2003 (* 35.2, territorial), COLOMBIA 4 Aug 2004 (*35.2), COMOROS 25 Sep 2003 a, CONGO signed 14 Dec 2000, COOK ISLANDS 4 Mar 2004 a, COSTA RICA 24 July 2003, COTE D'IVOIRE signed 15 Dec 2000, CROATIA 24 Jan 2003, CUBA 9 Feb 2007, CYPRUS 22 Apr 2003, CZECH REPUBLIC signed 12 Dec 2000, DEMOCRATIC REPUBLIC OF THE CONGO 28 Oct 2005 a, DENMARK 30 Sep 2003 (territorial), DJIBOUTI 20 Apr 2005 a, DOMINICAN REPUBLIC 26 Oct 2006, ECUADOR 17 Sep 2002 (*10, 35.2), EGYPT 5 Mar 2004 (*35.2), EL SALVADOR 18 Mar 2004 (*35.2), EQUATORIAL GUINEA 7 Feb 2003, ESTONIA 10 Feb 2003, ETHIOPIA signed 14 Dec 2000, EUROPEAN COMMUNITY 21 May 2004 AA (*35.2, territorial), FINLAND 10 Feb 2004, FRANCE 29 Oct 2002, GABON 15 Dec 2004 a, GAMBIA 5 May 2003, GEORGIA 5 Sep 2006, GERMANY 14 June 2006, GREECE signed 13 Dec 2000, GRENADA 21 May 2004 a, GUATEMALA 25 Sep 2003, GUINEA 9 Nov 2004 a, GUINEA-BISSAU signed 14 Dec 2000, GUAYANA 14 Sep 2004 a, HAITI signed 13 Dec 2000, HONDURAS 2 Dec 2003, HUNGARY 22 Dec 2006, ICELAND signed 13 Dec 2000, INDIA signed 12 Dec 2002, INDONESIA signed 12 Dec 2000, IRAN (ISLAMIC REPUBLIC OF) signed 12 Dec 2000, IRELAND signed 13 Dec 2000, ISRAEL 27 Dec 2006, ITALY 2 Aug 2006, JAMAICA 29 Sep 2003, JAPAN signed 12 Dec 2000, JORDAN signed 26 Nov 2002 (*35.2), KAZAKHSTAN signed 13 Dec 2000, KENYA 16 June 2004 a, KIRIBATI 15 Sep 2005 a, KUWAIT 12 May 2006, KYRGYZSTAN 2 Oct 2003, LAO'S PEOPLE'S DEMOCRATIC REPUBLIC 26 Sep 2003 a (*35.2), LATVIA 7 Dec 2001, LEBANON 5 Oct 2005, LESOTHO 24 Sep 2003, LIBERIA 22 Sep 2004 a, LIBYAN ARAB JAMAHIRIYA 18 June 2004, LIECHTENSTEIN signed 12 Dec 2000, LITHUANIA 9 May 2002 (* 35.2, LUXEMBOURG signed 13 Dec 2000, MADAGASCAR 15 Sep 2005, MALAWI 17 Mar 2005, MALAYSIA 24 Sep 2004 (*35.2), MALI 12 Apr 2002, MALTA 24 Sep 2003, MAURITANIA 22 July 2005 a, MAURITIUS 21 Apr 2003, MEXICO 4 Mar 2003, MICRONESIA (FEDERAL STATES OF) 24 May 2004 a (*35.2), MONACO 5 June 2001, MONTENEGRO 23 Oct 2006 d, MOROCCO 19 Sep 2002, MOZAMBIQUE 20 Sep 2006, MYANMAR 30 Mar 2004 a (*16, 35.2), NAMIBIA 16 Aug 2002, NAURU signed 12 Nov 2001, NEPAL signed 12 Dec 2002, NETHERLANDS 26 May 2004 (territorial), NEW ZEALAND 19 July 2002 (territorial), NICARAGUA 9 Sep 2002, NIGER 30 Sep 2004, NIGERIA 28 June 2001, NORWAY 23 Sep

* Source: U.N.G.A. Res. 55/25.

2003, OMAN 13 May 2005 a, PAKISTAN signed 14 Dec 2000, PANAMA 18 Aug 2004 (*16, 18), PARAGUAY 22 Sep 2004, PERU 23 Jan 2002, PHILIPPINES 28 May 2002, POLAND 12 Nov 2001, PORTUGAL 10 May 2004, REPUBLIC OF KOREA signed 13 Dec 2000, REPUBLIC OF MOLDOVA 16 Sep 2005, REPUBLIC OF SERBIA 6 Sep 2001, ROMANIA 4 Dec 2002, RUSSIAN FEDERATION 26 May 2004, RWANDA 26 Sep 2003, SAINT KITTS & NEVIS 21 May 2004, SAINT LUCIA signed 26 Sep 2001, SAINT VINCENT AND THE GRENADINES signed 24 July 2002, SAN MARINO signed 14 Dec 2000, SAO TOME AND PRINCIPE 12 Apr 2006 a, SAUDI ARABIA 18 Jan 2005 (*35.2), SENEGAL 27 Oct 2003, SEYCHELLES 22 Apr 2003, SIERRA LEONE signed 27 Nov 2001, SINGAPORE signed 13 Dec 2000, SLOVAKIA 3 Dec 2003, SLOVENIA 21 May 2004, SOUTH AFRICA 20 Feb 2004 (*35.2), SPAIN 1 Mar 2002, SRI LANKA 22 Sep 2006, SUDAN 10 Dec 2004, SWAZILAND signed 14 Dec 2000, SWEDEN 30 Apr 2004, SWITZERLAND 27 Oct 2006, SYRIAN ARAB REPUBLIC signed 13 Dec 2000, TAJIKISTAN 8 July 2002, THAILAND 13 Dec 2000, THE FORMER YUGOSLAV REPUBLIC OF MACEDONIA 12 Jan 2005 (*35.2), TOGO 2 July 2004, TRINIDAD AND TOBAGO signed 26 Sep 2001, TUNISIA 19 June 2003 (*35.2), TURKEY 25 Mar 2003, TURKMENISTAN 28 Mar 2005 a, UGANDA 9 Mar 2005, UKRAINE 21 May 2004 (*2.b), 13.2), UNITED ARAB EMIRATES signed 9 Dec 2002, UNITED KINGDOM OF GREAT BRITAIN AND NORTHERN IRELAND 9 Feb 2006, UNITED REPUBLIC OF TANZANIA 24 May 2006, UNITED STATES OF AMERICA 3 Nov 2005, URUGAY 4 Mar 2005, UZBEKISTAN 9 Dec 2003 (*35.2), VANUATU 4 Jan 2006 a, VENEZUELA (BOLIVARIAN REPUBLIC OF) A13 May 2002 (*35.2), VIETNAM signed 13 Dec 2000, YEMEN signed 15 Dec 2000, ZAMBIA 24 Apr 2005 a, ZIMBABWE signed 12 Dec 2000.

Article 1
Statement of purpose

The purpose of this Convention is to promote cooperation to prevent and combat transnational organized crime more effectively.

Article 2
Use of terms

For the purposes of this Convention:

a) "Organized criminal group" shall mean a structured group of three or more persons, existing for a period of time and acting in concert with the aim of committing one or more serious crimes or offences established in accordance with this Convention, in order to obtain, directly or indirectly, a financial or other material benefit;

b) "Serious crime" shall mean conduct constituting an offence punishable by a maximum deprivation of liberty of at least four years or a more serious penalty;

c) "Structured group" shall mean a group that is not randomly formed for the immediate commission of an offence and that does not need to have formally defined roles for its members, continuity of its membership or a developed structure;

d) "Property" shall mean assets of every kind, whether corporeal or incorporeal, movable or immovable, tangible or intangible, and legal documents or instruments evidencing title to, or interest in, such assets;

e) "Proceeds of crime" shall mean any property derived from or obtained, directly or indirectly, through the commission of an offence;

f) "Freezing" or "seizure" shall mean temporarily prohibiting the transfer, conversion, disposition or movement of property or temporarily assuming custody or control of property on the basis of an order issued by a court or other competent authority;

g) "Confiscation", which includes forfeiture where applicable, shall mean the permanent deprivation of property by order of a court or other competent authority;

h) "Predicate offence" shall mean any offence as a result of which proceeds have been generated that may become the subject of an offence as defined in article 6 of this Convention;

i) "Controlled delivery" shall mean the technique of allowing illicit or suspect consignments to pass out of, through or into the territory of one or more States, with the knowledge and under the supervision of their competent authorities, with a view to the investigation of an offence and the identification of persons involved in the commission of the offence;

j) "Regional economic integration organization" shall mean an organization constituted by sovereign States of a given region, to which its member States have transferred competence in respect of matters governed by this Convention and which has been duly authorized, in accordance with its internal procedures, to sign, ratify, accept, approve or accede to it; references to "States Parties" under this Convention shall apply to such organizations within the limits of their competence.

Article 3
Scope of application

1. This Convention shall apply, except as otherwise stated herein, to the prevention, investigation and prosecution of:

a) The offences established in accordance with articles 5, 6, 8 and 23 of this Convention; and

b) Serious crime as defined in article 2 of this Convention;

c) Where the offence is transnational in nature and involves an organized criminal group.

2. For the purpose of paragraph 1 of this article, an offence is transnational in nature if:

a. It is committed in more than one State;

b. It is committed in one State but a substantial part of its preparation, planning, direction or control takes place in another State;

c. It is committed in one State but involves an organized criminal group that engages in criminal activities in more than one State; or

d. It is committed in one State but has substantial effects in another State.

Article 4
Protection of sovereignty

1. States Parties shall carry out their obligations under this Convention in a manner consistent with the principles of sovereign equality and territorial integrity of States and that of non-intervention in the domestic affairs of other States.

2. Nothing in this Convention entitles a State Party to undertake in the territory of another State the exercise of jurisdiction and performance of functions that are reserved exclusively for the authorities of that other State by its domestic law.

Article 5
Criminalization of participation in an organized criminal group

1. Each State Party shall adopt such legislative and other measures as may be necessary to establish as criminal offences, when committed intentionally:

(a) Either or both of the following as criminal offences distinct from those involving the attempt or completion of the criminal activity:

(i) Agreeing with one or more other persons to commit a serious crime for a purpose relating directly or indirectly to the obtaining of a financial or other material benefit and, where required by domestic law, involving an act undertaken by one of the participants in furtherance of the agreement or involving an organized criminal group;

(ii) Conduct by a person who, with knowledge of either the aim and general criminal activity of an organized criminal group or its intention to commit the crimes in question, takes an active part in:

a. Criminal activities of the organized criminal group;

b. Other activities of the organized criminal group in the knowledge that his or her participation will contribute to the achievement of the above-described criminal aim;

(b) Organizing, directing, aiding, abetting, facilitating or counselling the commission of serious crime involving an organized criminal group.

2. The knowledge, intent, aim, purpose or agreement referred to in paragraph 1 of this article may be inferred from objective factual circumstances.

3. States Parties whose domestic law requires involvement of an organized criminal group for purposes of the offences established in accordance with paragraph 1 (a) (i) of this article shall ensure that their domestic law covers all serious crimes involving organized criminal groups. Such States Parties, as well as States Parties whose domestic law requires an act in furtherance of the agreement for purposes of the offences established in accordance with paragraph 1 (a) (i) of this article, shall so inform the Secretary-General of the United Nations at the time of their signature or of deposit of their instrument of ratification, acceptance or approval of or accession to this Convention.

Article 6
Criminalization of the laundering of proceeds of crime

1. Each State Party shall adopt, in accordance with fundamental principles of its domestic law, such legislative and other measures as may be necessary to establish as criminal offences, when committed intentionally:

(a) (i) The conversion or transfer of property, knowing that such property is the proceeds of crime, for the purpose of concealing or disguising the illicit origin of the property or of helping any person who is involved in the commission of the predicate offence to evade the legal consequences of his or her action;

(ii) The concealment or disguise of the true nature, source, location, disposition, movement or ownership of or rights with respect to property, knowing that such property is the proceeds of crime;

(b) Subject to the basic concepts of its legal system:

(i) The acquisition, possession or use of property, knowing, at the time of receipt, that such property is the proceeds of crime;

(ii) Participation in, association with or conspiracy to commit, attempts to commit and aiding, abetting, facilitating and counselling the commission of any of the offences established in accordance with this article.

2. For purposes of implementing or applying paragraph 1 of this article:

(a) Each State Party shall seek to apply paragraph 1 of this article to the widest range of predicate offences;

(b) Each State Party shall include as predicate offences all serious crime as defined in article 2 of this Convention and the offences established in accordance with articles 5, 8 and 23 of this Convention. In the case of States Parties whose legislation sets out a list of specific predicate offences, they shall, at a minimum, include in such list a comprehensive range of offences associated with organized criminal groups;

(c) For the purposes of subparagraph (b), predicate offences shall include offences committed both within and outside the jurisdiction of the State Party in question. However, offences committed outside the jurisdiction of a State Party shall constitute predicate offences only when the relevant conduct is a criminal offence under the domestic law of the State where it is committed and would be a criminal offence under the domestic law of the State Party implementing or applying this article had it been committed there;

(d) Each State Party shall furnish copies of its laws that give effect to this article and of any subsequent changes to such laws or a description thereof to the Secretary-General of the United Nations;

(e) If required by fundamental principles of the domestic law of a State Party, it may be provided that the offences set forth in paragraph 1 of this article do not apply to the persons who committed the predicate offence;

(f) Knowledge, intent or purpose required as an element of an offence set forth in paragraph 1 of this article may be inferred from objective factual circumstances.

Article 7
Measures to combat money-laundering

1. Each State Party:

(a) Shall institute a comprehensive domestic regulatory and supervisory regime for banks and non-bank financial institutions and, where appropriate, other bodies particularly susceptible to money-laundering, within its competence, in order to deter and detect all forms of money-laundering, which regime shall emphasize requirements for customer identification, record-keeping and the reporting of suspicious transactions;

(b) Shall, without prejudice to articles 18 and 27 of this Convention, ensure that administrative, regulatory, law enforcement and other authorities dedicated to combating money-laundering (including, where appropriate under domestic law, judicial authorities) have the ability to cooperate and exchange information at the national and international levels within the conditions prescribed by its domestic law and, to that end, shall consider the establishment of a financial intelligence unit to serve as a national centre for the collection, analysis and dissemination of information regarding potential money-laundering.

2. States Parties shall consider implementing feasible measures to detect and monitor the movement of cash and appropriate negotiable instruments across their borders, subject to

safeguards to ensure proper use of information and without impeding in any way the movement of legitimate capital. Such measures may include a requirement that individuals and businesses report the cross-border transfer of substantial quantities of cash and appropriate negotiable instruments.

3. In establishing a domestic regulatory and supervisory regime under the terms of this article, and without prejudice to any other article of this Convention, States Parties are called upon to use as a guideline the relevant initiatives of regional, interregional and multilateral organizations against money-laundering.

4. States Parties shall endeavour to develop and promote global, regional, sub regional and bilateral cooperation among judicial, law enforcement and financial regulatory authorities in order to combat money-laundering.

Article 8
Criminalization of corruption

1. Each State Party shall adopt such legislative and other measures as may be necessary to establish as criminal offences, when committed intentionally:

(a) The promise, offering or giving to a public official, directly or indirectly, of an undue advantage, for the official himself or herself or another person or entity, in order that the official act or refrain from acting in the exercise of his or her official duties;

(b) The solicitation or acceptance by a public official, directly or indirectly, of an undue advantage, for the official himself or herself or another person or entity, in order that the official act or refrain from acting in the exercise of his or her official duties.

2. Each State Party shall consider adopting such legislative and other measures as may be necessary to establish as criminal offences conduct referred to in paragraph 1 of this article involving a foreign public official or international civil servant. Likewise, each State Party shall consider establishing as criminal offences other forms of corruption.

3. Each State Party shall also adopt such measures as may be necessary to establish as a criminal offence participation as an accomplice in an offence established in accordance with this article.

4. For the purposes of paragraph 1 of this article and article 9 of this Convention, "public official" shall mean a public official or a person who provides a public service as defined in the domestic law and as applied in the criminal law of the State Party in which the person in question performs that function.

Article 9
Measures against corruption

1. In addition to the measures set forth in article 8 of this Convention, each State Party shall, to the extent appropriate and consistent with its legal system, adopt legislative, administrative or other effective measures to promote integrity and to prevent, detect and punish the corruption of public officials.

2. Each State Party shall take measures to ensure effective action by its authorities in the prevention, detection and punishment of the corruption of public officials, including providing such authorities with adequate independence to deter the exertion of inappropriate influence on their actions.

Article 10
Liability of legal persons

1. Each State Party shall adopt such measures as may be necessary, consistent with its legal principles, to establish the liability of legal persons for participation in serious crimes involving an organized criminal group and for the offences established in accordance with articles 5, 6, 8 and 23 of this Convention.

2. Subject to the legal principles of the State Party, the liability of legal persons may be criminal, civil or administrative.

3. Such liability shall be without prejudice to the criminal liability of the natural persons who have committed the offences.

4. Each State Party shall, in particular, ensure that legal persons held liable in accordance with this article are subject to effective, proportionate and dissuasive criminal or non-criminal sanctions, including monetary sanctions.

Article 11
Prosecution, adjudication and sanctions

1. Each State Party shall make the commission of an offence established in accordance with articles 5, 6, 8 and 23 of this Convention liable to sanctions that take into account the gravity of that offence.

2. Each State Party shall endeavour to ensure that any discretionary legal powers under its domestic law relating to the prosecution of persons for offences covered by this Convention are exercised to maximize the effectiveness of law enforcement measures in respect of those offences and with due regard to the need to deter the commission of such offences.

3. In the case of offences established in accordance with articles 5, 6, 8 and 23 of this Convention, each State Party shall take appropriate measures, in accordance with its domestic law and with due regard to the rights of the defence, to seek to ensure that conditions imposed in connection with decisions on release pending trial or appeal take into consideration the need to ensure the presence of the defendant at subsequent criminal proceedings.

4. Each State Party shall ensure that its courts or other competent authorities bear in mind the grave nature of the offences covered by this Convention when considering the eventuality of early release or parole of persons convicted of such offences.

5. Each State Party shall, where appropriate, establish under its domestic law a long statute of limitations period in which to commence proceedings for any offence covered by this Convention and a longer period where the alleged offender has evaded the administration of justice.

6. Nothing contained in this Convention shall affect the principle that the description of the offences established in accordance with this Convention and of the applicable legal defences or other legal principles controlling the lawfulness of conduct is reserved to the domestic law of a State Party and that such offences shall be prosecuted and punished in accordance with that law.

Article 12
Confiscation and seizure

1. States Parties shall adopt, to the greatest extent possible within their domestic legal systems, such measures as may be necessary to enable confiscation of:

(a) Proceeds of crime derived from offences covered by this Convention or property the value of which corresponds to that of such proceeds;

(b) Property, equipment or other instrumentalities used in or destined for use in offences covered by this Convention.

2. States Parties shall adopt such measures as may be necessary to enable the identification, tracing, freezing or seizure of any item referred to in paragraph 1 of this article for the purpose of eventual confiscation.

3. If proceeds of crime have been transformed or converted, in part or in full, into other property, such property shall be liable to the measures referred to in this article instead of the proceeds.

4. If proceeds of crime have been intermingled with property acquired from legitimate sources, such property shall, without prejudice to any powers relating to freezing or seizure, be liable to confiscation up to the assessed value of the intermingled proceeds.

5. Income or other benefits derived from proceeds of crime, from property into which proceeds of crime have been transformed or converted or from property with which proceeds of crime have been intermingled shall also be liable to the measures referred to in this article, in the same manner and to the same extent as proceeds of crime.

6. For the purposes of this article and article 13 of this Convention, each State Party shall empower its courts or other competent authorities to order that bank, financial or commercial records be made available or be seized. States Parties shall not decline to act under the provisions of this paragraph on the ground of bank secrecy.

7. States Parties may consider the possibility of requiring that an offender demonstrate the lawful origin of alleged proceeds of crime or other property liable to confiscation, to the extent that such a requirement is consistent with the principles of their domestic law and with the nature of the judicial and other proceedings.

8. The provisions of this article shall not be construed to prejudice the rights of bona fide third parties.

9. Nothing contained in this article shall affect the principle that the measures to which it refers shall be defined and implemented in accordance with and subject to the provisions of the domestic law of a State Party.

Article 13
International cooperation for purposes of confiscation

1. A State Party that has received a request from another State Party having jurisdiction over an offence covered by this Convention for confiscation of proceeds of crime, property, equipment or other instrumentalities referred to in article 12, paragraph 1, of this Convention situated in its territory shall, to the greatest extent possible within its domestic legal system:

(a) Submit the request to its competent authorities for the purpose of obtaining an order of confiscation and, if such an order is granted, give effect to it; or

(b) Submit to its competent authorities, with a view to giving effect to it to the extent requested, an order of confiscation issued by a court in the territory of the requesting State Party in accordance with article 12, paragraph 1, of this Convention insofar as it relates to proceeds of crime, property, equipment or other instrumentalities referred to in article 12, paragraph 1, situated in the territory of the requested State Party.

2. Following a request made by another State Party having jurisdiction over an offence covered by this Convention, the requested State Party shall take measures to identify, trace and freeze

or seize proceeds of crime, property, equipment or other instrumentalities referred to in article 12, paragraph 1, of this Convention for the purpose of eventual confiscation to be ordered either by the requesting State Party or, pursuant to a request under paragraph 1 of this article, by the requested State Party.

3. The provisions of article 18 of this Convention are applicable, mutatis mutandis, to this article. In addition to the information specified in article 18, paragraph 15, requests made pursuant to this article shall contain:

(a) In the case of a request pertaining to paragraph 1 (a) of this article, a description of the property to be confiscated and a statement of the facts relied upon by the requesting State Party sufficient to enable the requested State Party to seek the order under its domestic law;

(b) In the case of a request pertaining to paragraph 1 (b) of this article, a legally admissible copy of an order of confiscation upon which the request is based issued by the requesting State Party, a statement of the facts and information as to the extent to which execution of the order is requested;

(c) In the case of a request pertaining to paragraph 2 of this article, a statement of the facts relied upon by the requesting State Party and a description of the actions requested.

4. The decisions or actions provided for in paragraphs 1 and 2 of this article shall be taken by the requested State Party in accordance with and subject to the provisions of its domestic law and its procedural rules or any bilateral or multilateral treaty, agreement or arrangement to which it may be bound in relation to the requesting State Party.

5. Each State Party shall furnish copies of its laws and regulations that give effect to this article and of any subsequent changes to such laws and regulations or a description thereof to the Secretary-General of the United Nations.

6. If a State Party elects to make the taking of the measures referred to in paragraphs 1 and 2 of this article conditional on the existence of a relevant treaty, that State Party shall consider this Convention the necessary and sufficient treaty basis.

7. Cooperation under this article may be refused by a State Party if the offence to which the request relates is not an offence covered by this Convention.

8. The provisions of this article shall not be construed to prejudice the rights of bona fide third parties.

9. States Parties shall consider concluding bilateral or multilateral treaties, agreements or arrangements to enhance the effectiveness of international cooperation undertaken pursuant to this article.

Article 14
Disposal of confiscated proceeds of crime or property

1. Proceeds of crime or property confiscated by a State Party pursuant to articles 12 or 13, paragraph 1, of this Convention shall be disposed of by that State Party in accordance with its domestic law and administrative procedures.

2. When acting on the request made by another State Party in accordance with article 13 of this Convention, States Parties shall, to the extent permitted by domestic law and if so requested, give priority consideration to returning the confiscated proceeds of crime or property to the requesting State Party so that it can give compensation to the victims of the crime or return such proceeds of crime or property to their legitimate owners.

3. When acting on the request made by another State Party in accordance with articles 12 and 13 of this Convention, a State Party may give special consideration to concluding agreements or arrangements on:

(a) Contributing the value of such proceeds of crime or property or funds derived from the sale of such proceeds of crime or property or a part thereof to the account designated in accordance with article 30, paragraph 2 (c), of this Convention and to intergovernmental bodies specializing in the fight against organized crime;

(b) Sharing with other States Parties, on a regular or case-by-case basis, such proceeds of crime or property, or funds derived from the sale of such proceeds of crime or property, in accordance with its domestic law or administrative procedures.

Article 15
Jurisdiction

1. Each State Party shall adopt such measures as may be necessary to establish its jurisdiction over the offences established in accordance with articles 5, 6, 8 and 23 of this Convention when:

(a) The offence is committed in the territory of that State Party; or

(b) The offence is committed on board a vessel that is flying the flag of that State Party or an aircraft that is registered under the laws of that State Party at the time that the offence is committed.

2. Subject to article 4 of this Convention, a State Party may also establish its jurisdiction over any such offence when:

(a) The offence is committed against a national of that State Party;

(b) The offence is committed by a national of that State Party or a stateless person who has his or her habitual residence in its territory; or

(c) The offence is:

(i) One of those established in accordance with article 5, paragraph 1, of this Convention and is committed outside its territory with a view to the commission of a serious crime within its territory;

(ii) One of those established in accordance with article 6, paragraph 1 (b) (ii), of this Convention and is committed outside its territory with a view to the commission of an offence established in accordance with article 6, paragraph 1 (a) (i) or (ii) or (b) (i), of this Convention within its territory.

3. For the purposes of article 16, paragraph 10, of this Convention, each State Party shall adopt such measures as may be necessary to establish its jurisdiction over the offences covered by this Convention when the alleged offender is present in its territory and it does not extradite such person solely on the ground that he or she is one of its nationals.

4. Each State Party may also adopt such measures as may be necessary to establish its jurisdiction over the offences covered by this Convention when the alleged offender is present in its territory and it does not extradite him or her.

5. If a State Party exercising its jurisdiction under paragraph 1 or 2 of this article has been notified, or has otherwise learned, that one or more other States Parties are conducting an investigation, prosecution or judicial proceeding in respect of the same conduct, the competent authorities of those States Parties shall, as appropriate, consult one another with a view to coordinating their actions.

6. Without prejudice to norms of general international law, this Convention does not exclude the exercise of any criminal jurisdiction established by a State Party in accordance with its domestic law.

Article 16
Extradition

1. This article shall apply to the offences covered by this Convention or in cases where an offence referred to in article 3, paragraph 1 (a) or (b), involves an organized criminal group and the person who is the subject of the request for extradition is located in the territory of the requested State Party, provided that the offence for which extradition is sought is punishable under the domestic law of both the requesting State Party and the requested State Party.

2. If the request for extradition includes several separate serious crimes, some of which are not covered by this article, the requested State Party may apply this article also in respect of the latter offences.

3. Each of the offences to which this article applies shall be deemed to be included as an extraditable offence in any extradition treaty existing between States Parties. States Parties undertake to include such offences as extraditable offences in every extradition treaty to be concluded between them.

4. If a State Party that makes extradition conditional on the existence of a treaty receives a request for extradition from another State Party with which it has no extradition treaty, it may consider this Convention the legal basis for extradition in respect of any offence to which this article applies.

5. States Parties that make extradition conditional on the existence of a treaty shall:

(a) At the time of deposit of their instrument of ratification, acceptance, approval of or accession to this Convention, inform the Secretary-General of the United Nations whether they will take this Convention as the legal basis for cooperation on extradition with other States Parties to this Convention; and

(b) If they do not take this Convention as the legal basis for cooperation on extradition, seek, where appropriate, to conclude treaties on extradition with other States Parties to this Convention in order to implement this article.

6. States Parties that do not make extradition conditional on the existence of a treaty shall recognize offences to which this article applies as extraditable offences between themselves.

7. Extradition shall be subject to the conditions provided for by the domestic law of the requested State Party or by applicable extradition treaties, including, inter alia, conditions in relation to the minimum penalty requirement for extradition and the grounds upon which the requested State Party may refuse extradition.

8. States Parties shall, subject to their domestic law, endeavour to expedite extradition procedures and to simplify evidentiary requirements relating thereto in respect of any offence to which this article applies.

9. Subject to the provisions of its domestic law and its extradition treaties, the requested State Party may, upon being satisfied that the circumstances so warrant and are urgent and at the request of the requesting State Party, take a person whose extradition is sought and who is present in its territory into custody or take other appropriate measures to ensure his or her presence at extradition proceedings.

10. A State Party in whose territory an alleged offender is found, if it does not extradite such person in respect of an offence to which this article applies solely on the ground that he or she

is one of its nationals, shall, at the request of the State Party seeking extradition, be obliged to submit the case without undue delay to its competent authorities for the purpose of prosecution. Those authorities shall take their decision and conduct their proceedings in the same manner as in the case of any other offence of a grave nature under the domestic law of that State Party. The States Parties concerned shall cooperate with each other, in particular on procedural and evidentiary aspects, to ensure the efficiency of such prosecution.

11. Whenever a State Party is permitted under its domestic law to extradite or otherwise surrender one of its nationals only upon the condition that the person will be returned to that State Party to serve the sentence imposed as a result of the trial or proceedings for which the extradition or surrender of the person was sought and that State Party and the State Party seeking the extradition of the person agree with this option and other terms that they may deem appropriate, such conditional extradition or surrender shall be sufficient to discharge the obligation set forth in paragraph 10 of this article.

12. If extradition, sought for purposes of enforcing a sentence, is refused because the person sought is a national of the requested State Party, the requested Party shall, if its domestic law so permits and in conformity with the requirements of such law, upon application of the requesting Party, consider the enforcement of the sentence that has been imposed under the domestic law of the requesting Party or the remainder thereof.

13. Any person regarding whom proceedings are being carried out in connection with any of the offences to which this article applies shall be guaranteed fair treatment at all stages of the proceedings, including enjoyment of all the rights and guarantees provided by the domestic law of the State Party in the territory of which that person is present.

14. Nothing in this Convention shall be interpreted as imposing an obligation to extradite if the requested State Party has substantial grounds for believing that the request has been made for the purpose of prosecuting or punishing a person on account of that person's sex, race, religion, nationality, ethnic origin or political opinions or that compliance with the request would cause prejudice to that person's position for any one of these reasons.

15. States Parties may not refuse a request for extradition on the sole ground that the offence is also considered to involve fiscal matters.

16. Before refusing extradition, the requested State Party shall, where appropriate, consult with the requesting State Party to provide it with ample opportunity to present its opinions and to provide information relevant to its allegation.

17. States Parties shall seek to conclude bilateral and multilateral agreements or arrangements to carry out or to enhance the effectiveness of extradition.

Article 17
Transfer of sentenced persons

States Parties may consider entering into bilateral or multilateral agreements or arrangements on the transfer to their territory of persons sentenced to imprisonment or other forms of deprivation of liberty for offences covered by this Convention, in order that they may complete their sentences there.

Article 18
Mutual legal assistance

1. States Parties shall afford one another the widest measure of mutual legal assistance in investigations, prosecutions and judicial proceedings in relation to the offences covered by this Convention as provided for in article 3 and shall reciprocally extend to one another similar

assistance where the requesting State Party has reasonable grounds to suspect that the offence referred to in article 3, paragraph 1 (a) or (b), is transnational in nature, including that victims, witnesses, proceeds, instrumentalities or evidence of such offences are located in the requested State Party and that the offence involves an organized criminal group.

2. Mutual legal assistance shall be afforded to the fullest extent possible under relevant laws, treaties, agreements and arrangements of the requested State Party with respect to investigations, prosecutions and judicial proceedings in relation to the offences for which a legal person may be held liable in accordance with article 10 of this Convention in the requesting State Party.

3. Mutual legal assistance to be afforded in accordance with this article may be requested for any of the following purposes:

(a) Taking evidence or statements from persons;

(b) Effecting service of judicial documents;

(c) Executing searches and seizures, and freezing;

(d) Examining objects and sites;

(e) Providing information, evidentiary items and expert evaluations;

(f) Providing originals or certified copies of relevant documents and records, including government, bank, financial, corporate or business records;

(g) Identifying or tracing proceeds of crime, property, instrumentalities or other things for evidentiary purposes;

(h) Facilitating the voluntary appearance of persons in the requesting State Party;

(i) Any other type of assistance that is not contrary to the domestic law of the requested State Party.

4. Without prejudice to domestic law, the competent authorities of a State Party may, without prior request, transmit information relating to criminal matters to a competent authority in another State Party where they believe that such information could assist the authority in undertaking or successfully concluding inquiries and criminal proceedings or could result in a request formulated by the latter State Party pursuant to this Convention.

5. The transmission of information pursuant to paragraph 4 of this article shall be without prejudice to inquiries and criminal proceedings in the State of the competent authorities providing the information. The competent authorities receiving the information shall comply with a request that said information remain confidential, even temporarily, or with restrictions on its use. However, this shall not prevent the receiving State Party from disclosing in its proceedings information that is exculpatory to an accused person. In such a case, the receiving State Party shall notify the transmitting State Party prior to the disclosure and, if so requested, consult with the transmitting State Party. If, in an exceptional case, advance notice is not possible, the receiving State Party shall inform the transmitting State Party of the disclosure without delay.

6. The provisions of this article shall not affect the obligations under any other treaty, bilateral or multilateral, that governs or will govern, in whole or in part, mutual legal assistance.

7. Paragraphs 9 to 29 of this article shall apply to requests made pursuant to this article if the States Parties in question are not bound by a treaty of mutual legal assistance. If those States Parties are bound by such a treaty, the corresponding provisions of that treaty shall apply unless the States Parties agree to apply paragraphs 9 to 29 of this article in lieu thereof. States Parties are strongly encouraged to apply these paragraphs if they facilitate cooperation.

8. States Parties shall not decline to render mutual legal assistance pursuant to this article on the ground of bank secrecy.

9. States Parties may decline to render mutual legal assistance pursuant to this article on the ground of absence of dual criminality. However, the requested State Party may, when it deems appropriate, provide assistance, to the extent it decides at its discretion, irrespective of whether the conduct would constitute an offence under the domestic law of the requested State Party.

10. A person who is being detained or is serving a sentence in the territory of one State Party whose presence in another State Party is requested for purposes of identification, testimony or otherwise providing assistance in obtaining evidence for investigations, prosecutions or judicial proceedings in relation to offences covered by this Convention may be transferred if the following conditions are met:

(a) The person freely gives his or her informed consent;

(b) The competent authorities of both States Parties agree, subject to such conditions as those States Parties may deem appropriate.

11. For the purposes of paragraph 10 of this article:

(a) The State Party to which the person is transferred shall have the authority and obligation to keep the person transferred in custody, unless otherwise requested or authorized by the State Party from which the person was transferred;

(b) The State Party to which the person is transferred shall without delay implement its obligation to return the person to the custody of the State Party from which the person was transferred as agreed beforehand, or as otherwise agreed, by the competent authorities of both States Parties;

(c) The State Party to which the person is transferred shall not require the State Party from which the person was transferred to initiate extradition proceedings for the return of the person;

(d) The person transferred shall receive credit for service of the sentence being served in the State from which he or she was transferred for time spent in the custody of the State Party to which he or she was transferred.

12. Unless the State Party from which a person is to be transferred in accordance with paragraphs 10 and 11 of this article so agrees, that person, whatever his or her nationality, shall not be prosecuted, detained, punished or subjected to any other restriction of his or her personal liberty in the territory of the State to which that person is transferred in respect of acts, omissions or convictions prior to his or her departure from the territory of the State from which he or she was transferred.

13. Each State Party shall designate a central authority that shall have the responsibility and power to receive requests for mutual legal assistance and either to execute them or to transmit them to the competent authorities for execution. Where a State Party has a special region or territory with a separate system of mutual legal assistance, it may designate a distinct central authority that shall have the same function for that region or territory. Central authorities shall ensure the speedy and proper execution or transmission of the requests received. Where the central authority transmits the request to a competent authority for execution, it shall encourage the speedy and proper execution of the request by the competent authority. The Secretary-General of the United Nations shall be notified of the central authority designated for this purpose at the time each State Party deposits its instrument of ratification, acceptance or approval of or accession to this Convention. Requests for mutual legal assistance and any communication related thereto shall be transmitted to the central authorities designated by the States Parties. This requirement shall be without prejudice to the right of a State Party to

require that such requests and communications be addressed to it through diplomatic channels and, in urgent circumstances, where the States Parties agree, through the International Criminal Police Organization, if possible.

14. Requests shall be made in writing or, where possible, by any means capable of producing a written record, in a language acceptable to the requested State Party, under conditions allowing that State Party to establish authenticity. The Secretary-General of the United Nations shall be notified of the language or languages acceptable to each State Party at the time it deposits its instrument of ratification, acceptance or approval of or accession to this Convention. In urgent circumstances and where agreed by the States Parties, requests may be made orally, but shall be confirmed in writing forthwith.

15. A request for mutual legal assistance shall contain:

(a) The identity of the authority making the request;

(b) The subject matter and nature of the investigation, prosecution or judicial proceeding to which the request relates and the name and functions of the authority conducting the investigation, prosecution or judicial proceeding;

(c) A summary of the relevant facts, except in relation to requests for the purpose of service of judicial documents;

(d) A description of the assistance sought and details of any particular procedure that the requesting State Party wishes to be followed;

(e) Where possible, the identity, location and nationality of any person concerned; and

(f) The purpose for which the evidence, information or action is sought.

16. The requested State Party may request additional information when it appears necessary for the execution of the request in accordance with its domestic law or when it can facilitate such execution.

17. A request shall be executed in accordance with the domestic law of the requested State Party and, to the extent not contrary to the domestic law of the requested State Party and where possible, in accordance with the procedures specified in the request.

18. Wherever possible and consistent with fundamental principles of domestic law, when an individual is in the territory of a State Party and has to be heard as a witness or expert by the judicial authorities of another State Party, the first State Party may, at the request of the other, permit the hearing to take place by video conference if it is not possible or desirable for the individual in question to appear in person in the territory of the requesting State Party. States Parties may agree that the hearing shall be conducted by a judicial authority of the requesting State Party and attended by a judicial authority of the requested State Party.

19. The requesting State Party shall not transmit or use information or evidence furnished by the requested State Party for investigations, prosecutions or judicial proceedings other than those stated in the request without the prior consent of the requested State Party. Nothing in this paragraph shall prevent the requesting State Party from disclosing in its proceedings information or evidence that is exculpatory to an accused person. In the latter case, the requesting State Party shall notify the requested State Party prior to the disclosure and, if so requested, consult with the requested State Party. If, in an exceptional case, advance notice is not possible, the requesting State Party shall inform the requested State Party of the disclosure without delay.

20. The requesting State Party may require that the requested State Party keep confidential the fact and substance of the request, except to the extent necessary to execute the request. If the

requested State Party cannot comply with the requirement of confidentiality, it shall promptly inform the requesting State Party.

21. Mutual legal assistance may be refused:

(a) If the request is not made in conformity with the provisions of this article;

(b) If the requested State Party considers that execution of the request is likely to prejudice its sovereignty, security, ordre public or other essential interests;

(c) If the authorities of the requested State Party would be prohibited by its domestic law from carrying out the action requested with regard to any similar offence, had it been subject to investigation, prosecution or judicial proceedings under their own jurisdiction;

(d) If it would be contrary to the legal system of the requested State Party relating to mutual legal assistance for the request to be granted.

22. States Parties may not refuse a request for mutual legal assistance on the sole ground that the offence is also considered to involve fiscal matters.

23. Reasons shall be given for any refusal of mutual legal assistance.

24. The requested State Party shall execute the request for mutual legal assistance as soon as possible and shall take as full account as possible of any deadlines suggested by the requesting State Party and for which reasons are given, preferably in the request. The requested State Party shall respond to reasonable requests by the requesting State Party on progress of its handling of the request. The requesting State Party shall promptly inform the requested State Party when the assistance sought is no longer required.

25. Mutual legal assistance may be postponed by the requested State Party on the ground that it interferes with an ongoing investigation, prosecution or judicial proceeding.

26. Before refusing a request pursuant to paragraph 21 of this article or postponing its execution pursuant to paragraph 25 of this article, the requested State Party shall consult with the requesting State Party to consider whether assistance may be granted subject to such terms and conditions as it deems necessary. If the requesting State Party accepts assistance subject to those conditions, it shall comply with the conditions.

27. Without prejudice to the application of paragraph 12 of this article, a witness, expert or other person who, at the request of the requesting State Party, consents to give evidence in a proceeding or to assist in an investigation, prosecution or judicial proceeding in the territory of the requesting State Party shall not be prosecuted, detained, punished or subjected to any other restriction of his or her personal liberty in that territory in respect of acts, omissions or convictions prior to his or her departure from the territory of the requested State Party. Such safe conduct shall cease when the witness, expert or other person having had, for a period of fifteen consecutive days or for any period agreed upon by the States Parties from the date on which he or she has been officially informed that his or her presence is no longer required by the judicial authorities, an opportunity of leaving, has nevertheless remained voluntarily in the territory of the requesting State Party or, having left it, has returned of his or her own free will.

28. The ordinary costs of executing a request shall be borne by the requested State Party, unless otherwise agreed by the States Parties concerned. If expenses of a substantial or extraordinary nature are or will be required to fulfil the request, the States Parties shall consult to determine the terms and conditions under which the request will be executed, as well as the manner in which the costs shall be borne.

29. The requested State Party:

(a) Shall provide to the requesting State Party copies of government records, documents or information in its possession that under its domestic law are available to the general public;

(b) May, at its discretion, provide to the requesting State Party in whole, in part or subject to such conditions as it deems appropriate, copies of any government records, documents or information in its possession that under its domestic law are not available to the general public.

30. States Parties shall consider, as may be necessary, the possibility of concluding bilateral or multilateral agreements or arrangements that would serve the purposes of, give practical effect to or enhance the provisions of this article.

Article 19
Joint investigations

States Parties shall consider concluding bilateral or multilateral agreements or arrangements whereby, in relation to matters that are the subject of investigations, prosecutions or judicial proceedings in one or more States, the competent authorities concerned may establish joint investigative bodies. In the absence of such agreements or arrangements, joint investigations may be undertaken by agreement on a case-by-case basis. The States Parties involved shall ensure that the sovereignty of the State Party in whose territory such investigation is to take place is fully respected.

Article 20
Special investigative techniques

1. If permitted by the basic principles of its domestic legal system, each State Party shall, within its possibilities and under the conditions prescribed by its domestic law, take the necessary measures to allow for the appropriate use of controlled delivery and, where it deems appropriate, for the use of other special investigative techniques, such as electronic or other forms of surveillance and undercover operations, by its competent authorities in its territory for the purpose of effectively combating organized crime.

2. For the purpose of investigating the offences covered by this Convention, States Parties are encouraged to conclude, when necessary, appropriate bilateral or multilateral agreements or arrangements for using such special investigative techniques in the context of cooperation at the international level. Such agreements or arrangements shall be concluded and implemented in full compliance with the principle of sovereign equality of States and shall be carried out strictly in accordance with the terms of those agreements or arrangements.

3. In the absence of an agreement or arrangement as set forth in paragraph 2 of this article, decisions to use such special investigative techniques at the international level shall be made on a case-by-case basis and may, when necessary, take into consideration financial arrangements and understandings with respect to the exercise of jurisdiction by the States Parties concerned.

4. Decisions to use controlled delivery at the international level may, with the consent of the States Parties concerned, include methods such as intercepting and allowing the goods to continue intact or be removed or replaced in whole or in part.

Article 21
Transfer of criminal proceedings

States Parties shall consider the possibility of transferring to one another proceedings for the prosecution of an offence covered by this Convention in cases where such transfer is considered to be in the interests of the proper administration of justice, in particular in cases where several jurisdictions are involved, with a view to concentrating the prosecution.

Article 22
Establishment of criminal record

Each State Party may adopt such legislative or other measures as may be necessary to take into consideration, under such terms as and for the purpose that it deems appropriate, any previous conviction in another State of an alleged offender for the purpose of using such information in criminal proceedings relating to an offence covered by this Convention.

Article 23
Criminalization of obstruction of justice

Each State Party shall adopt such legislative and other measures as may be necessary to establish as criminal offences, when committed intentionally:

(a) The use of physical force, threats or intimidation or the promise, offering or giving of an undue advantage to induce false testimony or to interfere in the giving of testimony or the production of evidence in a proceeding in relation to the commission of offences covered by this Convention;

(b) The use of physical force, threats or intimidation to interfere with the exercise of official duties by a justice or law enforcement official in relation to the commission of offences covered by this Convention. Nothing in this subparagraph shall prejudice the right of States Parties to have legislation that protects other categories of public officials.

Article 24
Protection of witnesses

1. Each State Party shall take appropriate measures within its means to provide effective protection from potential retaliation or intimidation for witnesses in criminal proceedings who give testimony concerning offences covered by this Convention and, as appropriate, for their relatives and other persons close to them.

2. The measures envisaged in paragraph 1 of this article may include, inter alia, without prejudice to the rights of the defendant, including the right to due process:

(a) Establishing procedures for the physical protection of such persons, such as, to the extent necessary and feasible, relocating them and permitting, where appropriate, non-disclosure or limitations on the disclosure of information concerning the identity and whereabouts of such persons;

(b) Providing evidentiary rules to permit witness testimony to be given in a manner that ensures the safety of the witness, such as permitting testimony to be given through the use of communications technology such as video links or other adequate means.

3. States Parties shall consider entering into agreements or arrangements with other States for the relocation of persons referred to in paragraph 1 of this article.

4. The provisions of this article shall also apply to victims insofar as they are witnesses.

Article 25
Assistance to and protection of victims

1. Each State Party shall take appropriate measures within its means to provide assistance and protection to victims of offences covered by this Convention, in particular in cases of threat of retaliation or intimidation.

2. Each State Party shall establish appropriate procedures to provide access to compensation and restitution for victims of offences covered by this Convention.

3. Each State Party shall, subject to its domestic law, enable views and concerns of victims to be presented and considered at appropriate stages of criminal proceedings against offenders in a manner not prejudicial to the rights of the defence.

Article 26
Measures to enhance cooperation with law enforcement authorities

1. Each State Party shall take appropriate measures to encourage persons who participate or who have participated in organized criminal groups:

(a) To supply information useful to competent authorities for investigative and evidentiary purposes on such matters as:

(i) The identity, nature, composition, structure, location or activities of organized criminal groups;

(ii) Links, including international links, with other organized criminal groups;

(iii) Offences that organized criminal groups have committed or may commit;

(b) To provide factual, concrete help to competent authorities that may contribute to depriving organized criminal groups of their resources or of the proceeds of crime.

2. Each State Party shall consider providing for the possibility, in appropriate cases, of mitigating punishment of an accused person who provides substantial cooperation in the investigation or prosecution of an offence covered by this Convention.

3. Each State Party shall consider providing for the possibility, in accordance with fundamental principles of its domestic law, of granting immunity from prosecution to a person who provides substantial cooperation in the investigation or prosecution of an offence covered by this Convention.

4. Protection of such persons shall be as provided for in article 24 of this Convention.

5. Where a person referred to in paragraph 1 of this article located in one State Party can provide substantial cooperation to the competent authorities of another State Party, the States Parties concerned may consider entering into agreements or arrangements, in accordance with their domestic law, concerning the potential provision by the other State Party of the treatment set forth in paragraphs 2 and 3 of this article.

Article 27
Law enforcement cooperation

1. States Parties shall cooperate closely with one another, consistent with their respective domestic legal and administrative systems, to enhance the effectiveness of law enforcement action to combat the offences covered by this Convention. Each State Party shall, in particular, adopt effective measures:

(a) To enhance and, where necessary, to establish channels of communication between their competent authorities, agencies and services in order to facilitate the secure and rapid exchange of information concerning all aspects of the offences covered by this Convention, including, if the States Parties concerned deem it appropriate, links with other criminal activities;

(b) To cooperate with other States Parties in conducting inquiries with respect to offences covered by this Convention concerning:

(i) The identity, whereabouts and activities of persons suspected of involvement in such offences or the location of other persons concerned;

(ii) The movement of proceeds of crime or property derived from the commission of such offences;

(iii) The movement of property, equipment or other instrumentalities used or intended for use in the commission of such offences;

(c) To provide, when appropriate, necessary items or quantities of substances for analytical or investigative purposes;

(d) To facilitate effective coordination between their competent authorities, agencies and services and to promote the exchange of personnel and other experts, including, subject to bilateral agreements or arrangements between the States Parties concerned, the posting of liaison officers;

(e) To exchange information with other States Parties on specific means and methods used by organized criminal groups, including, where applicable, routes and conveyances and the use of false identities, altered or false documents or other means of concealing their activities;

(f) To exchange information and coordinate administrative and other measures taken as appropriate for the purpose of early identification of the offences covered by this Convention.

2. With a view to giving effect to this Convention, States Parties shall consider entering into bilateral or multilateral agreements or arrangements on direct cooperation between their law enforcement agencies and, where such agreements or arrangements already exist, amending them. In the absence of such agreements or arrangements between the States Parties concerned, the Parties may consider this Convention as the basis for mutual law enforcement cooperation in respect of the offences covered by this Convention. Whenever appropriate, States Parties shall make full use of agreements or arrangements, including international or regional organizations, to enhance the cooperation between their law enforcement agencies.

3. States Parties shall endeavour to cooperate within their means to respond to transnational organized crime committed through the use of modern technology.

Article 28
Collection, exchange and analysis of information on the nature of organized crime

1. Each State Party shall consider analyzing, in consultation with the scientific and academic communities, trends in organized crime in its territory, the circumstances in which organized crime operates, as well as the professional groups and technologies involved.

2. States Parties shall consider developing and sharing analytical expertise concerning organized criminal activities with each other and through international and regional organizations. For that purpose, common definitions, standards and methodologies should be developed and applied as appropriate.

3. Each State Party shall consider monitoring its policies and actual measures to combat organized crime and making assessments of their effectiveness and efficiency.

Article 29
Training and technical assistance

1. Each State Party shall, to the extent necessary, initiate, develop or improve specific training programmes for its law enforcement personnel, including prosecutors, investigating magistrates and customs personnel, and other personnel charged with the prevention, detection and control of the offences covered by this Convention. Such programmes may include secondments and exchanges of staff. Such programmes shall deal, in particular and to the extent permitted by domestic law, with the following:

(a) Methods used in the prevention, detection and control of the offences covered by this Convention;

(b) Routes and techniques used by persons suspected of involvement in offences covered by this Convention, including in transit States, and appropriate countermeasures;

(c) Monitoring of the movement of contraband;

(d) Detection and monitoring of the movements of proceeds of crime, property, equipment or other instrumentalities and methods used for the transfer, concealment or disguise of such proceeds, property, equipment or other instrumentalities, as well as methods used in combating money-laundering and other financial crimes;

(e) Collection of evidence;

(f) Control techniques in free trade zones and free ports;

(g) Modern law enforcement equipment and techniques, including electronic surveillance, controlled deliveries and undercover operations;

(h) Methods used in combating transnational organized crime committed through the use of computers, telecommunications networks or other forms of modern technology; and

(i) Methods used in the protection of victims and witnesses.

2. States Parties shall assist one another in planning and implementing research and training programmes designed to share expertise in the areas referred to in paragraph 1 of this article and to that end shall also, when appropriate, use regional and international conferences and seminars to promote cooperation and to stimulate discussion on problems of mutual concern, including the special problems and needs of transit States.

3. States Parties shall promote training and technical assistance that will facilitate extradition and mutual legal assistance. Such training and technical assistance may include language training, secondments and exchanges between personnel in central authorities or agencies with relevant responsibilities.

4. In the case of existing bilateral and multilateral agreements or arrangements, States Parties shall strengthen, to the extent necessary, efforts to maximize operational and training activities within international and regional organizations and within other relevant bilateral and multilateral agreements or arrangements.

Article 30
Other measures: implementation of the Convention through economic development and technical assistance

1. States Parties shall take measures conducive to the optimal implementation of this Convention to the extent possible, through international cooperation, taking into account the negative effects of organized crime on society in general, in particular on sustainable development.

2. States Parties shall make concrete efforts to the extent possible and in coordination with each other, as well as with international and regional organizations:

(a) To enhance their cooperation at various levels with developing countries, with a view to strengthening the capacity of the latter to prevent and combat transnational organized crime;

(b) To enhance financial and material assistance to support the efforts of developing countries to fight transnational organized crime effectively and to help them implement this Convention successfully;

(c) To provide technical assistance to developing countries and countries with economies in transition to assist them in meeting their needs for the implementation of this Convention. To that end, States Parties shall endeavour to make adequate and regular voluntary contributions to an account specifically designated for that purpose in a United Nations funding mechanism. States Parties may also give special consideration, in accordance with their domestic law and the provisions of this Convention, to contributing to the aforementioned account a percentage of the money or of the corresponding value of proceeds of crime or property confiscated in accordance with the provisions of this Convention;

(d) To encourage and persuade other States and financial institutions as appropriate to join them in efforts in accordance with this article, in particular by providing more training programmes and modern equipment to developing countries in order to assist them in achieving the objectives of this Convention.

3. To the extent possible, these measures shall be without prejudice to existing foreign assistance commitments or to other financial cooperation arrangements at the bilateral, regional or international level.

4. States Parties may conclude bilateral or multilateral agreements or arrangements on material and logistical assistance, taking into consideration the financial arrangements necessary for the means of international cooperation provided for by this Convention to be effective and for the prevention, detection and control of transnational organized crime.

Article 31
Prevention

1. States Parties shall endeavour to develop and evaluate national projects and to establish and promote best practices and policies aimed at the prevention of transnational organized crime.

2. States Parties shall endeavour, in accordance with fundamental principles of their domestic law, to reduce existing or future opportunities for organized criminal groups to participate in lawful markets with proceeds of crime, through appropriate legislative, administrative or other measures. These measures should focus on:

(a) The strengthening of cooperation between law enforcement agencies or prosecutors and relevant private entities, including industry;

(b) The promotion of the development of standards and procedures designed to safeguard the integrity of public and relevant private entities, as well as codes of conduct for relevant professions, in particular lawyers, notaries public, tax consultants and accountants;

(c) The prevention of the misuse by organized criminal groups of tender procedures conducted by public authorities and of subsidies and licences granted by public authorities for commercial activity;

(d) The prevention of the misuse of legal persons by organized criminal groups; such measures could include:

(i) The establishment of public records on legal and natural persons involved in the establishment, management and funding of legal persons;

(ii) The introduction of the possibility of disqualifying by court order or any appropriate means for a reasonable period of time persons convicted of offences covered by this Convention from acting as directors of legal persons incorporated within their jurisdiction;

(iii) The establishment of national records of persons disqualified from acting as directors of legal persons; and

(iv) The exchange of information contained in the records referred to in subparagraphs (d) (i) and (iii) of this paragraph with the competent authorities of other States Parties.

3. States Parties shall endeavour to promote the reintegration into society of persons convicted of offences covered by this Convention.

4. States Parties shall endeavour to evaluate periodically existing relevant legal instruments and administrative practices with a view to detecting their vulnerability to misuse by organized criminal groups.

5. States Parties shall endeavour to promote public awareness regarding the existence, causes and gravity of and the threat posed by transnational organized crime. Information may be disseminated where appropriate through the mass media and shall include measures to promote public participation in preventing and combating such crime.

6. Each State Party shall inform the Secretary-General of the United Nations of the name and address of the authority or authorities that can assist other States Parties in developing measures to prevent transnational organized crime.

7. States Parties shall, as appropriate, collaborate with each other and relevant international and regional organizations in promoting and developing the measures referred to in this article. This includes participation in international projects aimed at the prevention of transnational organized crime, for example by alleviating the circumstances that render socially marginalized groups vulnerable to the action of transnational organized crime.

Article 32
Conference of the Parties to the Convention

1. A Conference of the Parties to the Convention is hereby established to improve the capacity of States Parties to combat transnational organized crime and to promote and review the implementation of this Convention.

2. The Secretary-General of the United Nations shall convene the Conference of the Parties not later than one year following the entry into force of this Convention. The Conference of the Parties shall adopt rules of procedure and rules governing the activities set forth in paragraphs 3 and 4 of this article (including rules concerning payment of expenses incurred in carrying out those activities).

3. The Conference of the Parties shall agree upon mechanisms for achieving the objectives mentioned in paragraph 1 of this article, including:

(a) Facilitating activities by States Parties under articles 29, 30 and 31 of this Convention, including by encouraging the mobilization of voluntary contributions;

(b) Facilitating the exchange of information among States Parties on patterns and trends in transnational organized crime and on successful practices for combating it;

(c) Cooperating with relevant international and regional organizations and non-governmental organizations;

(d) Reviewing periodically the implementation of this Convention;

(e) Making recommendations to improve this Convention and its implementation.

4. For the purpose of paragraphs 3 (d) and (e) of this article, the Conference of the Parties shall acquire the necessary knowledge of the measures taken by States Parties in implementing this Convention and the difficulties encountered by them in doing so through information provided by them and through such supplemental review mechanisms as may be established by the Conference of the Parties.

5. Each State Party shall provide the Conference of the Parties with information on its programmes, plans and practices, as well as legislative and administrative measures to implement this Convention, as required by the Conference of the Parties.

Article 33
Secretariat

1. The Secretary-General of the United Nations shall provide the necessary secretariat services to the Conference of the Parties to the Convention.

2. The secretariat shall:

(a) Assist the Conference of the Parties in carrying out the activities set forth in article 32 of this Convention and make arrangements and provide the necessary services for the sessions of the Conference of the Parties;

(b) Upon request, assist States Parties in providing information to the Conference of the Parties as envisaged in article 32, paragraph 5, of this Convention; and

(c) Ensure the necessary coordination with the secretariats of relevant international and regional organizations.

Article 34
Implementation of the Convention

1. Each State Party shall take the necessary measures, including legislative and administrative measures, in accordance with fundamental principles of its domestic law, to ensure the implementation of its obligations under this Convention.

2. The offences established in accordance with articles 5, 6, 8 and 23 of this Convention shall be established in the domestic law of each State Party independently of the transnational nature or the involvement of an organized criminal group as described in article 3, paragraph 1, of this Convention, except to the extent that article 5 of this Convention would require the involvement of an organized criminal group.

3. Each State Party may adopt more strict or severe measures than those provided for by this Convention for preventing and combating transnational organized crime.

Article 35
Settlement of disputes

1. States Parties shall endeavour to settle disputes concerning the interpretation or application of this Convention through negotiation.

2. Any dispute between two or more States Parties concerning the interpretation or application of this Convention that cannot be settled through negotiation within a reasonable time shall, at the request of one of those States Parties, be submitted to arbitration. If, six months after the date of the request for arbitration, those States Parties are unable to agree on the organization of the arbitration, any one of those States Parties may refer the dispute to the International Court of Justice by request in accordance with the Statute of the Court.

3. Each State Party may, at the time of signature, ratification, acceptance or approval of or accession to this Convention, declare that it does not consider itself bound by paragraph 2 of this article. The other States Parties shall not be bound by paragraph 2 of this article with respect to any State Party that has made such a reservation.

4. Any State Party that has made a reservation in accordance with paragraph 3 of this article may at any time withdraw that reservation by notification to the Secretary-General of the United Nations.

Article 36
Signature, ratification, acceptance, approval and accession

1. This Convention shall be open to all States for signature from 12 to 15 December 2000 in Palermo, Italy, and thereafter at United Nations Headquarters in New York until 12 December 2002.

2. This Convention shall also be open for signature by regional economic integration organizations provided that at least one member State of such organization has signed this Convention in accordance with paragraph 1 of this article.

3. This Convention is subject to ratification, acceptance or approval. Instruments of ratification, acceptance or approval shall be deposited with the Secretary-General of the United Nations. A regional economic integration organization may deposit its instrument of ratification, acceptance or approval if at least one of its member States has done likewise. In that instrument of ratification, acceptance or approval, such organization shall declare the extent of its competence with respect to the matters governed by this Convention. Such organization shall also inform the depositary of any relevant modification in the extent of its competence.

4. This Convention is open for accession by any State or any regional economic integration organization of which at least one member State is a Party to this Convention. Instruments of accession shall be deposited with the Secretary-General of the United Nations. At the time of its accession, a regional economic integration organization shall declare the extent of its competence with respect to matters governed by this Convention. Such organization shall also inform the depositary of any relevant modification in the extent of its competence.

Article 37
Relation with protocols

1. This Convention may be supplemented by one or more protocols.

2. In order to become a Party to a protocol, a State or a regional economic integration organization must also be a Party to this Convention.

3. A State Party to this Convention is not bound by a protocol unless it becomes a Party to the protocol in accordance with the provisions thereof.

4. Any protocol to this Convention shall be interpreted together with this Convention, taking into account the purpose of that protocol.

Article 38
Entry into force

1. This Convention shall enter into force on the ninetieth day after the date of deposit of the fortieth instrument of ratification, acceptance, approval or accession. For the purpose of this paragraph, any instrument deposited by a regional economic integration organization shall not be counted as additional to those deposited by member States of such organization.

2. For each State or regional economic integration organization ratifying, accepting, approving or acceding to this Convention after the deposit of the fortieth instrument of such action, this Convention shall enter into force on the thirtieth day after the date of deposit by such State or organization of the relevant instrument.

Article 39
Amendment

1. After the expiry of five years from the entry into force of this Convention, a State Party may propose an amendment and file it with the Secretary-General of the United Nations, who shall thereupon communicate the proposed amendment to the States Parties and to the Conference of the Parties to the Convention for the purpose of considering and deciding on the proposal. The Conference of the Parties shall make every effort to achieve consensus on each amendment. If all efforts at consensus have been exhausted and no agreement has been reached, the amendment shall, as a last resort, require for its adoption a two-thirds majority vote of the States Parties present and voting at the meeting of the Conference of the Parties.

2. Regional economic integration organizations, in matters within their competence, shall exercise their right to vote under this article with a number of votes equal to the number of their member States that are Parties to this Convention. Such organizations shall not exercise their right to vote if their member States exercise theirs and vice versa.

3. An amendment adopted in accordance with paragraph 1 of this article is subject to ratification, acceptance or approval by States Parties.

4. An amendment adopted in accordance with paragraph 1 of this article shall enter into force in respect of a State Party ninety days after the date of the deposit with the Secretary-General of the United Nations of an instrument of ratification, acceptance or approval of such amendment.

5. When an amendment enters into force, it shall be binding on those States Parties which have expressed their consent to be bound by it. Other States Parties shall still be bound by the provisions of this Convention and any earlier amendments that they have ratified, accepted or approved.

Article 40
Denunciation

1. A State Party may denounce this Convention by written notification to the Secretary-General of the United Nations. Such denunciation shall become effective one year after the date of receipt of the notification by the Secretary-General.

2. A regional economic integration organization shall cease to be a Party to this Convention when all of its member States have denounced it.

3. Denunciation of this Convention in accordance with paragraph 1 of this article shall entail the denunciation of any protocols thereto.

Article 41
Depositary and languages

1. The Secretary-General of the United Nations is designated depositary of this Convention.

2. The original of this Convention, of which the Arabic, Chinese, English, French, Russian and Spanish texts are equally authentic, shall be deposited with the Secretary-General of the United Nations.

IN WITNESS WHEREOF, the undersigned plenipotentiaries, being duly authorized thereto by their respective Governments, have signed this Convention.

Protocol to Prevent, Suppress and Punish Trafficking in Persons Especially Women and Children, supplementing the United Nations Convention against Transnational Organized Crime, 2000*

Adoption: 15 November 2000
Entry into force: 25 December 2003
Parties: 111 (Status as of 1 April 2007)

ALBANIA 21 Aug 2002, ALGERIA 9 Mar 2004 (*15.2), ARGENTINA 19 Nov 2002, ARMENIA 1 July 2003, AUSTRALIA 14 Sep 2005 (*territorial), AUSTRIA 15 Sep 2005, AZERBAIJAN 30 Oct (*15.2, territorial) 2003, BAHRAIN 7 June 2004 (*15.2) a, BELARUS 25 June 2003, BELGIUM 11 Aug 2004(*territorial), BELIZE 26 Sep 2003 a, BENIN 30 Aug 2004, BOLIVIA 18 May 2006, BOSNIA AND HERZEGOVINA 24 Apr 2002, BOTSWANA 29 Aug 2002, BRAZIL 29 Jan 2004, BULGARIA 5 Dec 2001, BURKINA FASO 15 May 2002, BURUNDI signed 14 Dec 2000, CAMBODIA signed 11 Nov 2001, CAMEROON 6 Feb 2006, CANADA 13 May 2002, CAPE VERDE 15 July 2004, CENTRAL AFRICAN REPUBLIC 6 Oct 2006 a, CHILE 29 Nov 2004, COLOMBIA 4 Aug 2004 (*15.2), CONGO signed 14 Dec 2000, COSTA RICA 9 Sep 2003, CROATIA 24 Jan 2003, CYPRUS 6 Aug 2003, CZECH REPUBLIC signed 10 Dec 2002, DEMOCCRATIC REPUBLIC OF CONGO 28 Oct 2005a, DENMARK 30 Sep 2003 (*territorial), DJIBOUTI 20 Apr 2005a, DOMINICAN REPUBLIC signed 15 Dec 2000, ECUADOR 17 Sep 2002 (*15.2), EGYPT 5 Mar 2004, EL SALVADOR 18 Mar 2004 (*15.2), EQUATORIAL GUINEA 7 Feb 2003, ESTONIA 12 May 2004, EUROPEAN COMMUNITY 6 Sep 2006 AA, FINLAND 7 Sep 2006 a, FRANCE 29 Oct 2002, GAMBIA 5 May 2003, GEORGIA 5 Sep 2006, GERMANY 14 June 2006, GREECE signed 13 Dec 2000, GRENADA 21 May 2004a, GUATEMALA 1 Apr 2004a, GUINEA 9 Nov 2004a, GUINEA-BISSAU signed 14 Dec 2000, GUYANA 14 Sep 2004a, HAITI signed 13 Dec 2000, HUNGARY 22 Dec 2006, ICELAND signed 13 Dec 2000, INDIA signed 12 Dec 2002, INDONESIA signed 12 Dec 2000, IRELAND signed 13 Dec 2000, ISRAEL signed 14 Nov 2001, ITALY 2 Aug 2006, JAMAICA 29 Sep 2003, JAPAN signed 9 Dec 2002, KENYA 5 Jan 2005a, KIRIBATI 15 Sep 2005a, KUWAIT 12 May 2006a, KYRGYZSTAN 2 Oct 2003, LAO PEOPLE'S DEMOCRATIC REPUBLIC 26 Sep 2003a (*15.2), LATVIA 25 May 2004, LEBANON 5 Oct 2005, LESOTHO 24 Sep 2003, LIBERIA 22 Sep 2004a, LIBYIAN ARAB JAMAHIRIYA 24 Sep 2004, LICHTENSTEIN signed 14 Mar 2001, LITHUANIA 23 June 2003 (*15.2), LUXEMBOURG signed 13 Dec 2000, MADAGASCAR 15 Sep 2005, MALAWI 17 Mar 2005a (*16.4, 15.2), MALI 12 Apr 2002, MALTA 24 Sep 2003, MAURITANIA 22 July 2005a, MAURITIUS 24 Sep 2003a, MEXICO 4 May 2003, MONACO 5 June 2001, MONTENEGRO 23 Oct 2006 d, MOZAMBIQUE 20 Sep 2006, MYANMAR 30 Mar 2004 a (*15.2, 20), NAMIBIA 16 Aug 2002, NAURU signed 12 Nov 2001, NETHERLANDS 27 July 2005 a (*territorial), NEW ZEALAND 19 July 2002 (*territorial), NICARAGUA 12 Oct 2004a, NIGERIA 28 June 2001, NIGER 30 Sep 2004, NORWAY 23 Sep 2003, OMAN 13 May 2005a, PANAMA 18 Aug 2004, PARAGUAY 22 Sep 2004, PERU 23 Jan 2002, PHILIPPINES 28 May 2002, POLAND 26 Sep 2003, PORTUGAL 10 May 2004, REPUBLIC OF KOREA signed 13 Dec 2000, REPUBLIC OF MOLDOVA 16 Sep 2005, REPUBLIC OF SERBIA 6 Sep 2001, ROMANIA 4 Dec 2002, RUSSIAN FEDERATION 26 May 2004, RWANDA 26 Sep 2003, SAINT KITTS AND NEVIS 21 May 2004a, SAINT VINCENT AND THE GRENADINES signed 20 Nov 2002, SAN MARINO 14 Dec 2000, SAO TOME AND PRINCIPE 23 Aug 2006 a, SAUDI ARABIA 10 Dec 2002 (*3a),

* Source: U.N.G.A. Res. 55/25.

15.2, 6.3d), 7.1), SENEGAL 27 Oct 2003, SEYCHELLES 22 June 2004, SIERRA LEONE signed 27 Nov 2001, SLOVAKIA 21 Sep 2004, SLOVENIA 21 May 2004, SOUTH AFRICA 20 Feb 2004 (*15.2), SPAIN 1 Mar 2002, SRI LANKA signed 13 Dec 2000, SWAZILAND signed 8 Jan 2001, SWEDEN 1 July 2004, SWITZERLAND 27 Oct 2006, SYRIAN ARAB REPUBLIC signed 13 Dec 2000, TAJIKISTAN 8 July 2002a, THAILAND signed 18 Dec 2001, THE FORMER YOUGOSLAV REPUBLIC OF MACEDONIA 12 Jan 2005, TOGO signed 12 Dec 2000, TRINIDAD AND TOBAGO signed 26 Sep 2001, TUNISIA 14 July 2003 (*15.2), TURKEY 25 Mar 2003, TURKMENISTAN 28 Mar 2005a, UGANDA signed 12 Dec 2000, UKRAINE 21 May 2004, UNITED KINGDOM OF GREAT BRITAIN AND NOTHERN IRELAND 9 Feb 2006, UNITED REPUBLIC OF TANZANIA 24 May 2006, UNITED STATES OF AMERICA 3 Nov 2005, URUGUAY 4 Mar 2005, UZBEKISTAN signed 28 June 2001, VENEZUELA 13 May 2002, ZAMBIA 24 Apr 2005a.

Preamble

The States Parties to this Protocol,

Declaring that effective action to prevent and combat trafficking in persons, especially women and children, requires a comprehensive international approach in the countries of origin, transit and destination that includes measures to prevent such trafficking, to punish the traffickers and to protect the victims of such trafficking, including by protecting their internationally recognized human rights,

Taking into account the fact that, despite the existence of a variety of international instruments containing rules and practical measures to combat the exploitation of persons, especially women and children, there is no universal instrument that addresses all aspects of trafficking in persons,

Concerned that, in the absence of such an instrument, persons who are vulnerable to trafficking will not be sufficiently protected,

Recalling General Assembly resolution 53/111 of 9 December 1998, in which the Assembly decided to establish an open-ended intergovernmental ad hoc committee for the purpose of elaborating a comprehensive international convention against transnational organized crime and of discussing the elaboration of, inter alia, an international instrument addressing trafficking in women and children,

Convinced that supplementing the United Nations Convention against Transnational Organized Crime with an international instrument for the prevention, suppression and punishment of trafficking in persons, especially women and children, will be useful in preventing and combating that crime,

Have agreed as follows:

I. GENERAL PROVISIONS

Article 1

Relation with the United Nations Convention against Transnational Organized Crime

1. This Protocol supplements the United Nations Convention against Transnational Organized Crime. It shall be interpreted together with the Convention.

2. The provisions of the Convention shall apply, mutatis mutandis, to this Protocol unless otherwise provided herein.

3. The offences established in accordance with article 5 of this Protocol shall be regarded as offences established in accordance with the Convention.

Article 2

Statement of purpose

The purposes of this Protocol are:

(a) To prevent and combat trafficking in persons, paying particular attention to women and children;

(b) To protect and assist the victims of such trafficking, with full respect for their human rights; and

(c) To promote cooperation among States Parties in order to meet those objectives.

Article 3

Use of terms

For the purposes of this Protocol:

(a) "Trafficking in persons" shall mean the recruitment, transportation, transfer, harbouring or receipt of persons, by means of the threat or use of force or other forms of coercion, of abduction, of fraud, of deception, of the abuse of power or of a position of vulnerability or of the giving or receiving of payments or benefits to achieve the consent of a person having control over another person, for the purpose of exploitation. Exploitation shall include, at a minimum, the exploitation of the prostitution of others or other forms of sexual exploitation, forced labour or services, slavery or practices similar to slavery, servitude or the removal of organs;

(b) The consent of a victim of trafficking in persons to the intended exploitation set forth in subparagraph (a) of this article shall be irrelevant where any of the means set forth in subparagraph (a) have been used;

(c) The recruitment, transportation, transfer, harbouring or receipt of a child for the purpose of exploitation shall be considered "trafficking in persons" even if this does not involve any of the means set forth in subparagraph (a) of this article;

(d) "Child" shall mean any person under eighteen years of age.

Article 4

Scope of application

This Protocol shall apply, except as otherwise stated herein, to the prevention, investigation and prosecution of the offences established in accordance with article 5 of this Protocol, where those offences are transnational in nature and involve an organized criminal group, as well as to the protection of victims of such offences.

Article 5

Criminalization

1. Each State Party shall adopt such legislative and other measures as may be necessary to establish as criminal offences the conduct set forth in article 3 of this Protocol, when committed intentionally.

2. Each State Party shall also adopt such legislative and other measures as may be necessary to establish as criminal offences:

(a) Subject to the basic concepts of its legal system, attempting to commit an offence established in accordance with paragraph 1 of this article;

(b) Participating as an accomplice in an offence established in accordance with paragraph 1 of this article; and

(c) Organizing or directing other persons to commit an offence established in accordance with paragraph 1 of this article.

II. PROTECTION OF VICTIMS OF TRAFFICKING IN PERSONS

Article 6

Assistance to and protection of victims of trafficking in persons

1. In appropriate cases and to the extent possible under its domestic law, each State Party shall protect the privacy and identity of victims of trafficking in persons, including, inter alia, by making legal proceedings relating to such trafficking confidential.

2. Each State Party shall ensure that its domestic legal or administrative system contains measures that provide to victims of trafficking in persons, in appropriate cases:

(a) Information on relevant court and administrative proceedings;

(b) Assistance to enable their views and concerns to be presented and considered at appropriate stages of criminal proceedings against offenders, in a manner not prejudicial to the rights of the defence.

3. Each State Party shall consider implementing measures to provide for the physical, psychological and social recovery of victims of trafficking in persons, including, in appropriate cases, in cooperation with non-governmental organizations, other relevant organizations and other elements of civil society, and, in particular, the provision of:

(a) Appropriate housing;

(b) Counselling and information, in particular as regards their legal rights, in a language that the victims of trafficking in persons can understand;

(c) Medical, psychological and material assistance; and

(d) Employment, educational and training opportunities.

4. Each State Party shall take into account, in applying the provisions of this article, the age, gender and special needs of victims of trafficking in persons, in particular the special needs of children, including appropriate housing, education and care.

5. Each State Party shall endeavour to provide for the physical safety of victims of trafficking in persons while they are within its territory.

6. Each State Party shall ensure that its domestic legal system contains measures that offer victims of trafficking in persons the possibility of obtaining compensation for damage suffered.

Article 7

Status of victims of trafficking in persons in receiving States

1. In addition to taking measures pursuant to article 6 of this Protocol, each State Party shall consider adopting legislative or other appropriate measures that permit victims of trafficking in persons to remain in its territory, temporarily or permanently, in appropriate cases.

2. In implementing the provision contained in paragraph 1 of this article, each State Party shall give appropriate consideration to humanitarian and compassionate factors.

Article 8

Repatriation of victims of trafficking in persons

1. The State Party of which a victim of trafficking in persons is a national or in which the person had the right of permanent residence at the time of entry into the territory of the receiving State Party shall facilitate and accept, with due regard for the safety of that person, the return of that person without undue or unreasonable delay.

2. When a State Party returns a victim of trafficking in persons to a State Party of which that person is a national or in which he or she had, at the time of entry into the territory of the receiving State Party, the right of permanent residence, such return shall be with due regard for the safety of that person and for the status of any legal proceedings related to the fact that the person is a victim of trafficking and shall preferably be voluntary.

3. At the request of a receiving State Party, a requested State Party shall, without undue or unreasonable delay, verify whether a person who is a victim of trafficking in persons is its national or had the right of permanent residence in its territory at the time of entry into the territory of the receiving State Party.

4. In order to facilitate the return of a victim of trafficking in persons who is without proper documentation, the State Party of which that person is a national or in which he or she had the right of permanent residence at the time of entry into the territory of the receiving State Party shall agree to issue, at the request of the receiving State Party, such travel documents or other authorization as may be necessary to enable the person to travel to and re-enter its territory.

5. This article shall be without prejudice to any right afforded to victims of trafficking in persons by any domestic law of the receiving State Party.

6. This article shall be without prejudice to any applicable bilateral or multilateral agreement or arrangement that governs, in whole or in part, the return of victims of trafficking in persons.

III. PREVENTION, COOPERATION AND OTHER MEASURES

Article 9

Prevention of trafficking in persons

1. States Parties shall establish comprehensive policies, programmes and other measures:

(a) To prevent and combat trafficking in persons; and

(b) To protect victims of trafficking in persons, especially women and children, from revictimization.

2. States Parties shall endeavour to undertake measures such as research, information and mass media campaigns and social and economic initiatives to prevent and combat trafficking in persons.

3. Policies, programmes and other measures established in accordance with this article shall, as appropriate, include cooperation with non-governmental organizations, other relevant organizations and other elements of civil society.

4. States Parties shall take or strengthen measures, including through bilateral or multilateral cooperation, to alleviate the factors that make persons, especially women and children, vulnerable to trafficking, such as poverty, underdevelopment and lack of equal opportunity.

5. States Parties shall adopt or strengthen legislative or other measures, such as educational, social or cultural measures, including through bilateral and multilateral cooperation, to discourage the demand that fosters all forms of exploitation of persons, especially women and children, that leads to trafficking.

Article 10

Information exchange and training

1. Law enforcement, immigration or other relevant authorities of States Parties shall, as appropriate, cooperate with one another by exchanging information, in accordance with their domestic law, to enable them to determine:

(a) Whether individuals crossing or attempting to cross an international border with travel documents belonging to other persons or without travel documents are perpetrators or victims of trafficking in persons;

(b) The types of travel document that individuals have used or attempted to use to cross an international border for the purpose of trafficking in persons; and

(c) The means and methods used by organized criminal groups for the purpose of trafficking in persons, including the recruitment and transportation of victims, routes and links between and among individuals and groups engaged in such rafficking, and possible measures for detecting them.

2. States Parties shall provide or strengthen training for law enforcement, immigration and other relevant officials in the prevention of trafficking in persons. The training should focus on methods used in preventing such trafficking, prosecuting the traffickers and protecting the rights of the victims, including protecting the victims from the traffickers. The training should also take into account the need to consider human rights and child- and gender-sensitive issues and it should encourage cooperation with non-governmental organizations, other relevant organizations and other elements of civil society.

3. A State Party that receives information shall comply with any request by the State Party that transmitted the information that places restrictions on its use.

Article 11

Border measures

1. Without prejudice to international commitments in relation to the free movement of people, States Parties shall strengthen, to the extent possible, such border controls as may be necessary to prevent and detect trafficking in persons.

2. Each State Party shall adopt legislative or other appropriate measures to prevent, to the extent possible, means of transport operated by commercial carriers from being used in the commission of offences established in accordance with article 5 of this Protocol.

3. Where appropriate, and without prejudice to applicable international conventions, such measures shall include establishing the obligation of commercial carriers, including any

transportation company or the owner or operator of any means of transport, to ascertain that all passengers are in possession of the travel documents required for entry into the receiving State.

4. Each State Party shall take the necessary measures, in accordance with its domestic law, to provide for sanctions in cases of violation of the obligation set forth in paragraph 3 of this article.

5. Each State Party shall consider taking measures that permit, in accordance with its domestic law, the denial of entry or revocation of visas of persons implicated in the commission of offences established in accordance with this Protocol.

6. Without prejudice to article 27 of the Convention, States Parties shall consider strengthening cooperation among border control agencies by, inter alia, establishing and maintaining direct channels of communication.

Article 12

Security and control of documents

Each State Party shall take such measures as may be necessary, within available means:

(a) To ensure that travel or identity documents issued by it are of such quality that they cannot easily be misused and cannot readily be falsified or unlawfully altered, replicated or issued; and

(b) To ensure the integrity and security of travel or identity documents issued by or on behalf of the State Party and to prevent their unlawful creation, issuance and use.

Article 13

Legitimacy and validity of documents

At the request of another State Party, a State Party shall, in accordance with its domestic law, verify within a reasonable time the legitimacy and validity of travel or identity documents issued or purported to have been issued in its name and suspected of being used for trafficking in persons.

IV. FINAL PROVISIONS

Article 14

Saving clause

1. Nothing in this Protocol shall affect the rights, obligations and responsibilities of States and individuals under international law, including international humanitarian law and international human rights law and, in particular, where applicable, the 1951 Convention and the 1967 Protocol relating to the Status of Refugees and the principle of non-refoulement as contained therein.

2. The measures set forth in this Protocol shall be interpreted and applied in a way that is not discriminatory to persons on the ground that they are victims of trafficking in persons. The interpretation and application of those measures shall be consistent with internationally recognized principles of non-discrimination.

Article 15

Settlement of disputes

1. States Parties shall endeavour to settle disputes concerning the interpretation or application of this Protocol through negotiation.

2. Any dispute between two or more States Parties concerning the interpretation or application of this Protocol that cannot be settled through negotiation within a reasonable time shall, at the request of one of those States Parties, be submitted to arbitration. If, six months after the date of the request for arbitration, those States Parties are unable to agree on the organization of the arbitration, any one of those States Parties may refer the dispute to the International Court of Justice by request in accordance with the Statute of the Court.

3. Each State Party may, at the time of signature, ratification, acceptance or approval of or accession to this Protocol, declare that it does not consider itself bound by paragraph 2 of this article. The other States Parties shall not be bound by paragraph 2 of this article with respect to any State Party that has made such a reservation.

4. Any State Party that has made a reservation in accordance with paragraph 3 of this article may at any time withdraw that reservation by notification to the Secretary-General of the United Nations.

Article 16

Signature, ratification, acceptance, approval and accession

1. This Protocol shall be open to all States for signature from 12 to 15 December 2000 in Palermo, Italy, and thereafter at United Nations Headquarters in New York until 12 December 2002.

2. This Protocol shall also be open for signature by regional economic integration organizations provided that at least one member State of such organization has signed this Protocol in accordance with paragraph 1 of this article.

3. This Protocol is subject to ratification, acceptance or approval. Instruments of ratification, acceptance or approval shall be deposited with the Secretary-General of the United Nations. A regional economic integration organization may deposit its instrument of ratification, acceptance or approval if at least one of its member States has done likewise. In that instrument of ratification, acceptance or approval, such organization shall declare the extent of its competence with respect to the matters governed by this Protocol. Such organization shall also inform the depositary of any relevant modification in the extent of its competence.

4. This Protocol is open for accession by any State or any regional economic integration organization of which at least one member State is a Party to this Protocol. Instruments of accession shall be deposited with the Secretary-General of the United Nations. At the time of its accession, a regional economic integration organization shall declare the extent of its competence with respect to matters governed by this Protocol. Such organization shall also inform the depositary of any relevant modification in the extent of its competence.

Article 17

Entry into force

1. This Protocol shall enter into force on the ninetieth day after the date of deposit of the fortieth instrument of ratification, acceptance, approval or accession, except that it shall not enter into force before the entry into force of the Convention. For the purpose of this paragraph, any

instrument deposited by a regional economic integration organization shall not be counted as additional to those deposited by member States of such organization.

2. For each State or regional economic integration organization ratifying, accepting, approving or acceding to this Protocol after the deposit of the fortieth instrument of such action, this Protocol shall enter into force on the thirtieth day after the date of deposit by such State or organization of the relevant instrument or on the date this Protocol enters into force pursuant to paragraph 1 of this article, whichever is the later.

Article 18

Amendment

1. After the expiry of five years from the entry into force of this Protocol, a State Party to the Protocol may propose an amendment and file it with the Secretary-General of the United Nations, who shall thereupon communicate the proposed amendment to the States Parties and to the Conference of the Parties to the Convention for the purpose of considering and deciding on the proposal. The States Parties to this Protocol meeting at the Conference of the Parties shall make every effort to achieve consensus on each amendment. If all efforts at consensus have been exhausted and no agreement has been reached, the amendment shall, as a last resort, require for its adoption a two-thirds majority vote of the States Parties to this Protocol present and voting at the meeting of the Conference of the Parties.

2. Regional economic integration organizations, in matters within their competence, shall exercise their right to vote under this article with a number of votes equal to the number of their member States that are Parties to this Protocol. Such organizations shall not exercise their right to vote if their member States exercise theirs and vice versa.

3. An amendment adopted in accordance with paragraph 1 of this article is subject to ratification, acceptance or approval by States Parties.

4. An amendment adopted in accordance with paragraph 1 of this article shall enter into force in respect of a State Party ninety days after the date of the deposit with the Secretary-General of the United Nations of an instrument of ratification, acceptance or approval of such amendment.

5. When an amendment enters into force, it shall be binding on those States Parties which have expressed their consent to be bound by it. Other States Parties shall still be bound by the provisions of this Protocol and any earlier amendments that they have ratified, accepted or approved.

Article 19

Denunciation

1. A State Party may denounce this Protocol by written notification to the Secretary-General of the United Nations. Such denunciation shall become effective one year after the date of receipt of the notification by the Secretary-General.

2. A regional economic integration organization shall cease to be a Party to this Protocol when all of its member States have denounced it.

Article 20

Depositary and languages

1. The Secretary-General of the United Nations is designated depositary of this Protocol.

2. The original of this Protocol, of which the Arabic, Chinese, English, French, Russian and Spanish texts are equally authentic, shall be deposited with the Secretary-General of the United Nations.

In witness whereof, the undersigned plenipotentiaries, being duly authorized thereto by their respective Governments, have signed this Protocol.

Optional Protocol to the Convention on the Rights of the Child on the Sale of Children, Child Prostitution and Child Pornography, 2000*

Adoption: 25 May 2000
Entry into force: 18 January 2002
Parties: 118 (Status as of 1 April 2007)

AFGHANISTAN 19 Sep 2002 a, ALGERIA 27 Dec 2006 a, ANDORRA 30 Apr 2001, ANGOLA 24 Mar 2005 a, ANTIGUA AND BARBUDA 30 Apr 2002, ARGENTINA 25 Sep 2003 (*3), ARMENIA 30 Jun 2005, AUSTRALIA 8 Jan 2007, AUSTRIA 6 May 2004, AZERBAIJAN 3 Jul 2002, BAHRAIN 21 Sep 2004 a, BANGLADESH 6 Sep 2000, BELARUS 23 Jan 2002 a, BELGIUM 17 Mar 2006, BELIZE 1 Dec 2003, BENIN 31 Jan 2005, BHUTAN signed 15 Sep 2005, BOLIVIA 3 Jun 2003, BOSNIA AND HERZEGOVINA 4 Sep 2002, BOTSWANA 24 Sep 2003 a, BRAZIL 27 Jan 2004, BRUNEI DARUSSALAM 21 Nov 2006 a, BULGARIA 12 Feb 2002, BURKINA FASO 31 Mar 2006, CAMBODIA 30 May 2002, CAMEROON signed 5 Oct 2001, CANADA 14 Sep 2005, CAPE VERDE 10 May 2002 a, CHAD 28 Aug 2002, CHILE 6 Feb 2003, CHINA 3 Dec 2002, COLOMBIA 11 Nov 2003 (*7), COMOROS 23 Feb 2007 a, COSTA RICA 9 Apr 2002, CROATIA 13 May 2002, CUBA 25 Sep 2001, CYPRUS 6 Apr 2006, CZECH REPUBLIC signed 26 Jan 2005, DEMOCRATIC REPUBLIC OF THE CONGO 11 Nov 2001 a, DENMARK 24 Jul 2003 (*2), DOMINICA 20 Sep 2002 a, DOMINICAN REPUBLIC 6 Dec 2006 a, ECUADOR 30 Jan 2004, EGYPT 12 Jul 2002 a, EL SALVADOR 17 May 2004, EQUATORIAL GUINEA 7 Feb 2003 a, ERITREA 16 Feb 2005 a, ESTONIA 3 Aug 2004, FIJI signed 16 Sep 2005, FINLAND signed 7 Sep 2000, FRANCE 5 Feb 2003, GABON signed 8 Sep 2000, GAMBIA signed 21 Dec 2000, GEORGIA 28 Jun 2005 a, GERMANY signed 6 Sep 2000, GHANA signed 24 Sep 2003, GREECE signed 7 Sep 2000, GUATEMALA 9 May 2002, GUINEA-BISSAU signed 8 Sep 2000, HAITI signed 15 Aug 2002, HOLY SEE 24 Oct 2001, HONDURAS 8 May 2002 a, HUNGARY signed 11 May 2002, ICELAND 9 Jul 2001, INDIA 16 Aug 2005, INDONESIA signed 24 Sep 2001, IRELAND signed 7 Sep 2000, ISRAEL signed 14 Nov 2001, ITALY 9 May 2002, JAMAICA signed 8 Sep 2000, JAPAN 24 Jam 2005, JORDAN 4 Dec 2006, KAZAKHSTAN 24 Aug 2001, KENYA signed 8 Sep 2000, KUWAIT 26 Aug 2004 a (*3.5), KYRGYZSTAN 12 Feb 2003 a, LAO PEOPLE'S DEMOCRATIC REPUBLIC 20 Sep 2006 a, LATVIA 22 Feb 2006, LEBANON 8 Nov 2004, LESOTHO 24 Sep 2003, LIBERIA signed 22 Sep 2004, LIBYAN ARAB JAMAHIRIYA 18 Jun 2004 a, LIECHTENSTEIN signed 8 Sep 2000, LITHUANIA 5 Aug 2004 a, LUXEMBOURG signed 8 Sep 2000, MADAGASCAR 22 Sep 2004, MALAWI signed 7 Sep 2000, MALDIVES 10 May 2002, MALI 16 May 2002 a, MALTA signed 7 Sep 2000, MAURITIUS signed 11 Nov 2001, MEXICO 15 Mar 2002, MICRONESIA (FEDERATED STATES OF) signed 8 May 2002, MONACO signed 26 Jun 2000, MONGOLIA 27 Jun 2003, MONTENEGRO 23 Oct 2006 a, MOROCCO 2 Oct 2001, MOZAMBIQUE 6 Mar 2003 a, NAMIBIA 16 Apr 2002, NAURU signed 8 Sep 2000, NEPAL 20 Jan 2006, NETHERLANDS 23 Aug 2005, NEW ZEALAND 7 Sep 2000, NICARAGUA 2 Dec 2004 a, NIGER 26 Oct 2004, NIGERIA signed 8 Sep 2000, NORWAY 2 Oct 2001, OMAN 17 Sep 2004 a, PAKISTAN signed 26 Sep 2001, PANAMA 9 Feb 2001, PARAGUAY 18 Aug 2003, PERU 8 May 2002, PHILIPPINES 28 May 2002, POLAND 4 Feb 2005, PORTUGAL 16 May 2003, QATAR 14 Dec 2001 a (*general), REPUBLIC OF KOREA 24 Sep 2004 (*3.1a), REPUBLIC OF MOLDOVA signed 8 Feb 2002, REPUBLIC OF SERBIA 10 Oct 2002, ROMANIA 18 Oct 2001, RWANDA 14 Mar 2002 a, SAINT VINCENT AND THE GRENADINES 15 Sep 2005 a, SAN MARINO signed 5 Jun 2000,

* Source: U.N.G.A. Res. 54/263.

SENEGAL 5 Nov 2003, SEYCHELLES signed 23 Jan 2001, SIERRA LEONE 17 Sep 2001, SLOVAKIA 25 Jun 2004, SLOVENIA 23 Sep 2004, SOUTH AFRICA 30 Jun 2003 a, SPAIN 18 Dec 2001, SRI LANKA 22 Sep 2006, SUDAN 2 Nov 2004 a, SURINAME signed 10 May 2002, SWEDEN 19 Jan 2007 (*2), SWITZERLAND 19 Sep 2006, SYRIAN ARAB REPUBLIC 15 May 2003 a (*3.1a, 3.5), TAJIKISTAN 5 Aug 2002 a, THAILAND 11 Jan 2006 a, THE FORMER YUGOSLAV REPUBLIC OF MACEDONIA 17 Oct 2003, TOGO 2 Jul 2004, TUNISIA 13 Sep 2002, TURKEY 19 Aug 2002, TURKMENISTAN 28 Mar 2005 a, UGANDA 30 Nov 2001 a, UKRAINE 3 Jul 2003, UNITED KINGDOM OF GREAT BRITAIN AND NORTHERN IRELAND signed 7 Sep 2000, UNITED REPUBLIC OF TANZANIA 24 Apr 2003 a, UNITED STATES OF AMERICA 23 Dec 2002 (*2, 3, general), URUGUAY 3 Jul 2003, VANUATU signed 16 Sep 2005, VENEZUELA (BOLIVERIAN REPUBLIC OF) 8 May 2002, VIET NAM 20 Dec 2001 (*5), YEMEN 15 Dec 2004 a.

The States Parties to the present Protocol,

Considering that, in order further to achieve the purposes of the Convention on the Rights of the Child and the implementation of its provisions, especially articles 1, 11, 21, 32, 33, 34, 35 and 36, it would be appropriate to extend the measures that States Parties should undertake in order to guarantee the protection of the child from the sale of children, child prostitution and child pornography,

Considering also that the Convention on the Rights of the Child recognizes the right of the child to be protected from economic exploitation and from performing any work that is likely to be hazardous or to interfere with the child's education, or to be harmful to the child's health or physical, mental, spiritual, moral or social development,

Gravely concerned at the significant and increasing international traffic in children for the purpose of the sale of children, child prostitution and child pornography,

Deeply concerned at the widespread and continuing practice of sex tourism, to which children are especially vulnerable, as it directly promotes the sale of children, child prostitution and child pornography,

Recognizing that a number of particularly vulnerable groups, including girl children, are at greater risk of sexual exploitation and that girl children are disproportionately represented among the sexually exploited,

Concerned about the growing availability of child pornography on the Internet and other evolving technologies, and recalling the International Conference on Combating Child Pornography on the Internet, held in Vienna in 1999, in particular its conclusion calling for the worldwide criminalization of the production, distribution, exportation, transmission, importation, intentional possession and advertising of child pornography, and stressing the importance of closer cooperation and partnership between Governments and the Internet industry,

Believing that the elimination of the sale of children, child prostitution and child pornography will be facilitated by adopting a holistic approach, addressing the contributing factors, including underdevelopment, poverty, economic disparities, inequitable socio-economic structure, dysfunctioning families, lack of education, urban-rural migration, gender discrimination, irresponsible adult sexual behaviour, harmful traditional practices, armed conflicts and trafficking in children,

Believing also that efforts to raise public awareness are needed to reduce consumer demand for the sale of children, child prostitution and child pornography, and believing further in the importance of strengthening global partnership among all actors and of improving law enforcement at the national level,

Noting the provisions of international legal instruments relevant to the protection of children, including the Hague Convention on Protection of Children and Cooperation in Respect of Intercountry Adoption, the Hague Convention on the Civil Aspects of International Child Abduction, the Hague Convention on Jurisdiction, Applicable Law, Recognition, Enforcement and Cooperation in Respect of Parental Responsibility and Measures for the Protection of Children, and International Labour Organization Convention No.182 on the Prohibition and Immediate Action for the Elimination of the Worst Forms of Child Labour,

Encouraged by the overwhelming support for the Convention on the Rights of the Child, demonstrating the widespread commitment that exists for the promotion and protection of the rights of the child,

Recognizing the importance of the implementation of the provisions of the Programme of Action for the Prevention of the Sale of Children, Child Prostitution and Child Pornography and the Declaration and Agenda for Action adopted at the World Congress against Commercial Sexual Exploitation of Children, held in Stockholm from 27 to 31 August 1996, and the other relevant decisions and recommendations of pertinent international bodies,

Taking due account of the importance of the traditions and cultural values of each people for the protection and harmonious development of the child,

Have agreed as follows:

Article 1

States Parties shall prohibit the sale of children, child prostitution and child pornography as provided for by the present Protocol.

Article 2

For the purposes of the present Protocol:

(a) Sale of children means any act or transaction whereby a child is transferred by any person or group of persons to another for remuneration or any other consideration;

(b) Child prostitution means the use of a child in sexual activities for remuneration or any other form of consideration;

(c) Child pornography means any representation, by whatever means, of a child engaged in real or simulated explicit sexual activities or any representation of the sexual parts of a child for primarily sexual purposes.

Article 3

1. Each State Party shall ensure that, as a minimum, the following acts and activities are fully covered under its criminal or penal law, whether such offences are committed domestically or transnationally or on an individual or organized basis:

(a) In the context of sale of children as defined in article 2:

(i) Offering, delivering or accepting, by whatever means, a child for the purpose of:

a. Sexual exploitation of the child;

b. Transfer of organs of the child for profit;

c. Engagement of the child in forced labour;

(ii) Improperly inducing consent, as an intermediary, for the adoption of a child in violation of applicable international legal instruments on adoption;

(b) Offering, obtaining, procuring or providing a child for child prostitution, as defined in article 2;

(c) Producing, distributing, disseminating, importing, exporting, offering, selling or possessing for the above purposes child pornography as defined in article 2.

2. Subject to the provisions of the national law of a State Party, the same shall apply to an attempt to commit any of the said acts and to complicity or participation in any of the said acts.

3. Each State Party shall make such offences punishable by appropriate penalties that take into account their grave nature.

4. Subject to the provisions of its national law, each State Party shall take measures, where appropriate, to establish the liability of legal persons for offences established in paragraph 1 of the present article. Subject to the legal principles of the State Party, such liability of legal persons may be criminal, civil or administrative.

5. States Parties shall take all appropriate legal and administrative measures to ensure that all persons involved in the adoption of a child act in conformity with applicable international legal instruments.

Article 4

1. Each State Party shall take such measures as may be necessary to establish its jurisdiction over the offences referred to in article 3, paragraph 1, when the offences are commited in its territory or on board a ship or aircraft registered in that State.

2. Each State Party may take such measures as may be necessary to establish its jurisdiction over the offences referred to in article 3, paragraph 1, in the following cases:

(a) When the alleged offender is a national of that State or a person who has his habitual residence in its territory;

(b) When the victim is a national of that State.

3. Each State Party shall also take such measures as may be necessary to establish its jurisdiction over the aforementioned offences when the alleged offender is present in its territory and it does not extradite him or her to another State Party on the ground that the offence has been committed by one of its nationals.

4. The present Protocol does not exclude any criminal jurisdiction exercised in accordance with internal law.

Article 5

1. The offences referred to in article 3, paragraph 1, shall be deemed to be included as extraditable offences in any extradition treaty existing between States Parties and shall be included as extraditable offences in every extradition treaty subsequently concluded between them, in accordance with the conditions set forth in such treaties.

2. If a State Party that makes extradition conditional on the existence of a treaty receives a request for extradition from another State Party with which it has no extradition treaty, it may consider the present Protocol to be a legal basis for extradition in respect of such offences. Extradition shall be subject to the conditions provided by the law of the requested State.

3. States Parties that do not make extradition conditional on the existence of a treaty shall recognize such offences as extraditable offences between themselves subject to the conditions provided by the law of the requested State.

4. Such offences shall be treated, for the purpose of extradition between States Parties, as if they had been committed not only in the place in which they occurred but also in the territories of the States required to establish their jurisdiction in accordance with article 4.

5. If an extradition request is made with respect to an offence described in article 3, paragraph 1, and the requested State Party does not or will not extradite on the basis of the nationality of the offender, that State shall take suitable measures to submit the case to its competent authorities for the purpose of prosecution.

Article 6

1. States Parties shall afford one another the greatest measure of assistance in connection with investigations or criminal or extradition proceedings brought in respect of the offences set forth in article 3, paragraph 1, including assistance in obtaining evidence at their disposal necessary for the proceedings.

2. States Parties shall carry out their obligations under paragraph 1 of the present article in conformity with any treaties or other arrangements on mutual legal assistance that may exist between them. In the absence of such treaties or arrangements, States Parties shall afford one another assistance in accordance with their domestic law.

Article 7

States Parties shall, subject to the provisions of their national law:

(a) Take measures to provide for the seizure and confiscation, as appropriate, of:

(i) Goods, such as materials, assets and other instrumentalities used to commit or facilitate offences under the present protocol;

(ii) Proceeds derived from such offences;

(b) Execute requests from another State Party for seizure or confiscation of goods or proceeds referred to in subparagraph (a);

(c) Take measures aimed at closing, on a temporary or definitive basis, premises used to commit such offences.

Article 8

1. States Parties shall adopt appropriate measures to protect the rights and interests of child victims of the practices prohibited under the present Protocol at all stages of the criminal justice process, in particular by:

(a) Recognizing the vulnerability of child victims and adapting procedures to recognize their special needs, including their special needs as witnesses;

(b) Informing child victims of their rights, their role and the scope, timing and progress of the proceedings and of the disposition of their cases;

(c) Allowing the views, needs and concerns of child victims to be presented and considered in proceedings where their personal interests are affected, in a manner consistent with the procedural rules of national law;

(d) Providing appropriate support services to child victims throughout the legal process;

(e) Protecting, as appropriate, the privacy and identity of child victims and taking measures in accordance with national law to avoid the inappropriate dissemination of information that could lead to the identification of child victims;

(f) Providing, in appropriate cases, for the safety of child victims, as well as that of their families and witnesses on their behalf, from intimidation and retaliation;

(g) Avoiding unnecessary delay in the disposition of cases and the execution of orders or decrees granting compensation to child victims.

2. States Parties shall ensure that uncertainty as to the actual age of the victim shall not prevent the initiation of criminal investigations, including investigations aimed at establishing the age of the victim.

3. States Parties shall ensure that, in the treatment by the criminal justice system of children who are victims of the offences described in the present Protocol, the best interest of the child shall be a primary consideration.

4. States Parties shall take measures to ensure appropriate training, in particular legal and psychological training, for the persons who work with victims of the offences prohibited under the present Protocol.

5. States Parties shall, in appropriate cases, adopt measures in order to protect the safety and integrity of those persons and/or organizations involved in the prevention and/or protection and rehabilitation of victims of such offences.

6. Nothing in the present article shall be construed to be prejudicial to or inconsistent with the rights of the accused to a fair and impartial trial.

Article 9

1. States Parties shall adopt or strengthen, implement and disseminate laws, administrative measures, social policies and programmes to prevent the offences referred to in the present Protocol. Particular attention shall be given to protect children who are especially vulnerable to such practices.

2. States Parties shall promote awareness in the public at large, including children, through information by all appropriate means, education and training, about the preventive measures and harmful effects of the offences referred to in the present Protocol. In fulfilling their obligations under this article, States Parties shall encourage the participation of the community and, in particular, children and child victims, in such information and education and training programmes, including at the international level.

3. States Parties shall take all feasible measures with the aim of ensuring all appropriate assistance to victims of such offences, including their full social reintegration and their full physical and psychological recovery.

4. States Parties shall ensure that all child victims of the offences described in the present Protocol have access to adequate procedures to seek, without discrimination, compensation for damages from those legally responsible.

5. States Parties shall take appropriate measures aimed at effectively prohibiting the production and dissemination of material advertising the offences described in the present Protocol.

Article 10

1. States Parties shall take all necessary steps to strengthen international cooperation by multilateral, regional and bilateral arrangements for the prevention, detection, investigation,

prosecution and punishment of those responsible for acts involving the sale of children, child prostitution, child pornography and child sex tourism. States Parties shall also promote international cooperation and coordination between their authorities, national and international non-governmental organizations and international organizations.

2. States Parties shall promote international cooperation to assist child victims in their physical and psychological recovery, social reintegration and repatriation.

3. States Parties shall promote the strengthening of international cooperation in order to address the root causes, such as poverty and underdevelopment, contributing to the vulnerability of children to the sale of children, child prostitution, child pornography and child sex tourism.

4. States Parties in a position to do so shall provide financial, technical or other assistance through existing multilateral, regional, bilateral or other programmes.

Article 11

Nothing in the present Protocol shall affect any provisions that are more conducive to the realization of the rights of the child and that may be contained in:

(a) The law of a State Party;

(b) International law in force for that State.

Article 12

1. Each State Party shall, within two years following the entry into force of the present Protocol for that State Party, submit a report to the Committee on the Rights of the Child providing comprehensive information on the measures it has taken to implement the provisions of the Protocol.

2. Following the submission of the comprehensive report, each State Party shall include in the reports they submit to the Committee on the Rights of the Child, in accordance with article 44 of the Convention, any further information with respect to the implementation of the present Protocol. Other States Parties to the Protocol shall submit a report every five years.

3. The Committee on the Rights of the Child may request from States Parties further information relevant to the implementation of the present Protocol.

Article 13

1. The present Protocol is open for signature by any State that is a party to the Convention or has signed it.

2. The present Protocol is subject to ratification and is open to accession by any State that is a party to the Convention or has signed it. Instruments of ratification or accession shall be deposited with the Secretary- General of the United Nations.

Article 14

1. The present Protocol shall enter into force three months after the deposit of the tenth instrument of ratification or accession.

2. For each State ratifying the present Protocol or acceding to it after its entry into force, the Protocol shall enter into force one month after the date of the deposit of its own instrument of ratification or accession.

Article 15

1. Any State Party may denounce the present Protocol at any time by written notification to the Secretary- General of the United Nations, who shall thereafter inform the other States Parties to the Convention and all States that have signed the Convention. The denunciation shall take effect one year after the date of receipt of the notification by the Secretary-General.

2. Such a denunciation shall not have the effect of releasing the State Party from its obligations under the present Protocol in regard to any offence that occurs prior to the date on which the denunciation becomes effective. Nor shall such a denunciation prejudice in any way the continued consideration of any matter that is already under consideration by the Committee on the Rights of the Child prior to the date on which the denunciation becomes effective.

Article 16

1. Any State Party may propose an amendment and file it with the Secretary-General of the United Nations. The Secretary-General shall thereupon communicate the proposed amendment to States Parties with a request that they indicate whether they favour a conference of States Parties for the purpose of considering and voting upon the proposals. In the event that, within four months from the date of such communication, at least one third of the States Parties favour such a conference, the Secretary-General shall convene the conference under the auspices of the United Nations. Any amendment adopted by a majority of States Parties present and voting at the conference shall be submitted to the General Assembly of the United Nations for approval.

2. An amendment adopted in accordance with paragraph 1 of the present article shall enter into force when it has been approved by the General Assembly and accepted by a two-thirds majority of States Parties.

3. When an amendment enters into force, it shall be binding on those States Parties that have accepted it, other States Parties still being bound by the provisions of the present Protocol and any earlier amendments they have accepted.

Article 17

1. The present Protocol, of which the Arabic, Chinese, English, French, Russian and Spanish texts are equally authentic, shall be deposited in the archives of the United Nations.

2. The Secretary-General of the United Nations shall transmit certified copies of the present Protocol to all States Parties to the Convention and all States that have signed the Convention.

IMO Interim Measures for Combating Unsafe Practices Associated with the Trafficking or Transport of Migrants by Sea, 2001*

Adoption: 12 June 2001

1. Pending entry into force of a Convention against transnational organized crime including trafficking in migrants this circular provides interim, non-binding measures for the prevention and suppression of unsafe practices associated with the trafficking or transport of migrants by sea.

Definitions

2. For purposes of this circular:

2.1 "Ship" means every description of water craft, including non-displacement craft and seaplanes, used or capable of being used as a means of transportation on water, except a warship, naval auxiliary, or other ship owned or operated by a Government and used, for the time being, only on government non-commercial service;

2.2 "Organization" means the International Maritime Organization; and

2.3 "unsafe practices" means any practice which involves operating a ship that is:
.1 obviously in conditions which violate fundamental principles of safety at sea, in particular those of the SOLAS Convention; or
.2 not properly manned, equipped or licensed for carrying passengers on international voyages, and thereby constitute a serious danger for the lives or the health of the persons on board, including the conditions for embarkation and disembarkation.

Purpose

3. The purpose of this circular is to promote awareness and co-operation among Contracting Governments of the Organization so that they may address more effectively unsafe practices associated with the trafficking or transport of migrants by sea which have an international dimension.

Recommended actions by States

Compliance with international obligations

4. Experience has shown that migrants often are transported on ships that are not properly manned, equipped or licensed for carrying passengers on international voyages. States should take steps relating to maritime safety, in accordance with domestic and international law, to eliminate these unsafe practices associated with the trafficking or transport of migrants by sea, including:

* Source: International Maritime Organization, Doc. No.MSC/Circ.896/Rev.1; for more information, see: www.imo.org.

1 ensuring compliance with the International Convention for the Safety of Life at Sea, 1974, as amended (SOLAS)[1];

.2 collecting and disseminating information on ships believed to be engaged in unsafe practices associated with trafficking or transporting migrants;

.3 taking appropriate action against masters, officers and crew members engaged in such unsafe practices; and

.4 preventing any such ship:

.1 from again engaging in unsafe practices; and

.2 if in port, from sailing.

5. Measures taken, adopted or implemented pursuant to this circular to combat unsafe practices associated with the trafficking or transport of migrants by sea should be in conformity with the international law of the sea and all generally accepted relevant international instruments, such as the United Nations 1951 Convention and the 1967 Protocol Relating to the Status of Refugees.

6. States should take, adopt or implement such measures in conformity with international law with due regard to:

.1 the authority of the flag State to exercise jurisdiction and control in administrative, technical and social matters involving the ship; and

.2 the rights and obligations of the coastal State.

7. If any measures are taken against any ship suspected of unsafe practices associated with trafficking or transport of migrants by sea, the State concerned should take into account the need not to endanger the safety of human life at sea and the security of the ship and the cargo, or to prejudice the commercial and/or legal interests of the flag State or any other interested State.

Co-operation

8. States should co-operate to the fullest extent possible to prevent and suppress unsafe practices associated with the trafficking or transport of migrants by sea, in conformity with the international law of the sea and all generally accepted relevant international instruments. It is consistent with international law for a flag State to authorize a vessel flying its flag to be boarded and inspected by a warship of another State, as described in paragraphs 12 and 20 below.

9. States should consider entering into bilateral or regional agreements to facilitate co-operation in applying appropriate, efficient and effective measures to prevent and suppress unsafe practices associated with the trafficking or transport of migrants by sea.

---

[1] It is recalled that:
– regulation 1 of chapter I of SOLAS Convention provides that SOLAS applies to ships engaged on international voyages;
– regulation 2 of the same chapter defines as:
international voyage, a voyage from a country to which the present Convention applies to a port outside such country, or conversely.
passenger ship, a ship which carries more than twelve passengers.
cargo ship, any ship which is not a passenger ship.
The trafficking of migrants will normally constitute an international voyage. When this practice occurs on board cargo ships, multiple infringements of the SOLAS Convention are therefore committed.

10. States should also encourage the conclusion of operational arrangements in relation to specific cases.

Measures and Procedures

11. A State, which has reasonable grounds to suspect that a ship which:

.1 is flying its flag or claiming its registry, or

.2 is without nationality, or

.3 though flying a foreign flag or refusing to show its flag is, in reality, of the same nationality as the State concerned,

is engaged in unsafe practices associated with the trafficking or transport of migrants by sea, may request the assistance of other States in suppressing its use for that purpose. The States so requested should render such assistance as is reasonable under these circumstances.

12. A State which has reasonable grounds to suspect that a ship exercising freedom of navigation in accordance with international law and flying the flag or displaying marks of registry of another State is engaged in unsafe practices associated with the trafficking or transport of migrants by sea may so notify the flag State, request confirmation of registry and, if confirmed[2], request authorization from the flag State to take appropriate measures in regard to that ship. The flag State may authorize the requesting State to, inter alia:

.1 board the ship;

.2 inspect and carry out a safety examination of the ship, and

.3 if evidence is found that the ship is engaged in unsafe practices, take appropriate action with respect to the ship, persons and cargo on board, as authorized by the flag State.

A State which has taken any action in accordance with this paragraph should promptly inform the flag State concerned of the results of that action.

13. A flag State may, consistent with paragraph 8, subject its authorization to conditions to be mutually agreed between it and the requesting State, including conditions relating to responsibility and to the extent of effective measures to be taken including the use of force. A State shall take no additional actions without the express authorization of the flag State, except those necessary to relieve imminent danger or those that follow from relevant bilateral or multilateral agreements.

14. A State should respond expeditiously to a request from another State to determine whether a ship that is claiming its registry or flying its flag is entitled to do so, and to a request for authorization made pursuant to paragraph 12.

15. When a ship is found engaged in unsafe practices associated with the trafficking or transport of migrants by sea, States should:

.1 immediately report the findings of the safety examinations conducted pursuant to paragraph 12 to the administration of the State whose flag the ship is entitled to fly or in which it is registered; and

.2 immediately consult on the further actions to be taken after giving or receiving reports on the ship involved.

[2] If registry is refuted, the situation is that described in paragraph 11.2 above.

16. When there are reasonable grounds to suspect that a ship is engaged in unsafe practices associated with trafficking or transport of migrants by sea and it is concluded in accordance with the international law of the sea that the ship is without nationality, or has been assimilated to a ship without nationality, States should conduct a safety examination of the ship, as necessary. If the results of the safety examination indicate that the ship is engaged in unsafe practices, States should take appropriate measures in accordance with relevant domestic and international law.

17. When evidence exists that a ship is engaged in unsafe practices associated with the trafficking or transport of migrants by sea, States, in taking action pursuant to paragraphs 12 or 16, should:

.1 ensure the safety and the humanitarian handling of the persons on board and that any actions taken with regard to the ship are environmentally sound; and

.2 take appropriate action in accordance with relevant domestic and international law. 18 States should take required steps, in accordance with international law including SOLAS regulation I/19(c), to ensure that a ship involved in unsafe practices associated with the trafficking or transport of migrants by sea does not sail until it can proceed to sea without endangering the ship or persons on board, and to report promptly to the State whose flag the ship is entitled to fly, or in which it is registered, all incidents concerning such unsafe practices which come to their attention.

19. Contracting Governments to SOLAS 1974, as amended, should ensure that, when a request is received to transfer a ship to their flag or registry, the requirements listed in regulation I/14(g)(ii) are met, and appropriate inspections and surveys are conducted to ensure the ship will be used for the service specified in the certificates issued in accordance with chapter I of the 1974 SOLAS Convention.

20. Any action taken at sea pursuant to this circular shall be carried out only by warships or military aircraft, or other ships or aircraft clearly marked and identifiable as being on government service and authorized to that effect.

21. Each State should designate an authority or, where necessary, authorities to receive reports of unsafe practices, and to respond to requests for assistance, confirmation of registry or right to fly its flag and authorization to take appropriate measures.

22. Notwithstanding paragraph 20, ships providing assistance to persons in distress at sea, as required by the international law of the sea including SOLAS regulation V/10, and ships providing assistance in accordance with this circular, should not be considered as engaging in unsafe practices associated with the trafficking or transport of migrants by sea.

Reports

23. To prevent and suppress unsafe practices associated with trafficking or transport of migrants by sea, reports on incidents and the measures taken should be provided to the Organization by States concerned as soon as possible. This information will be used for the purpose of updating or revising this circular, as necessary.

24. Use of the report form given in the Appendix is recommended for conveying information for the purposes mentioned in paragraphs 12, 15 and 22.

[Appendix not included in the present excerpt]

Recommended Principles and Guidelines on Human Rights and Human Trafficking, 2002*[1]

Adoption: 20 May 2002

The primacy of human rights

1. The human rights of trafficked persons shall be at the centre of all efforts to prevent and combat trafficking and to protect, assist and provide redress to victims.

2. States have a responsibility under international law to act with due diligence to prevent trafficking, to investigate and prosecute traffickers and to assist and protect trafficked persons.

3. Anti-trafficking measures shall not adversely affect the human rights and dignity of persons, in particular the rights of those who have been trafficked, and of migrants, internally displaced persons, refugees and asylum-seekers.

Preventing trafficking

4. Strategies aimed at preventing trafficking shall address demand as a root cause of trafficking.

5. States and intergovernmental organizations shall ensure that their interventions address the factors that increase vulnerability to trafficking, including inequality, poverty and all forms of discrimination.

6. States shall exercise due diligence in identifying and eradicating public-sector involvement or complicity in trafficking. All public officials suspected of being implicated in trafficking shall be investigated, tried and, if convicted, appropriately punished.

Protection and assistance

7. Trafficked persons shall not be detained, charged or prosecuted for the illegality of their entry into or residence in countries of transit and destination, or for their involvement in unlawful activities to the extent that such involvement is a direct consequence of their situation as trafficked persons.

8. States shall ensure that trafficked persons are protected from further exploitation and harm and have access to adequate physical and psychological care. Such protection and care shall not be made conditional upon the capacity or willingness of the trafficked person to cooperate in legal proceedings.

* Source: United Nations Doc. No.E/2002/68/Add.1.

[1] The term "trafficking", as used in the present Principles and Guidelines, refers to the recruitment, transportation, transfer, harbouring or receipt of persons, by means of the threat or use of force or other forms of coercion, of abduction, of fraud, of deception, of the abuse of power or of a position of vulnerability or of the giving or receiving of payments or benefits to achieve the consent of a person having control over another person, for the purpose of exploitation. Exploitation shall include, at a minimum, the exploitation of the prostitution of others or other forms of sexual exploitation, forced labour or services, slavery or practices similar to slavery, servitude or the removal of organs. Source: Protocol to Prevent, Suppress and Punish Trafficking in Persons, Especially Women and Children, supplementing the United Nations Convention against Transnational Organized Crime (article 3 (a)).

9. Legal and other assistance shall be provided to trafficked persons for the duration of any criminal, civil or other actions against suspected traffickers. States shall provide protection and temporary residence permits to victims and witnesses during legal proceedings.

10. Children who are victims of trafficking shall be identified as such. Their best interests shall be considered paramount at all times. Child victims of trafficking shall be provided with appropriate assistance and protection. Full account shall be taken of their special vulnerabilities, rights and needs.

11. Safe (and, to the extent possible, voluntary) return shall be guaranteed to trafficked persons by both the receiving State and the State of origin. Trafficked persons shall be offered legal alternatives to repatriation in cases where it is reasonable to conclude that such repatriation would pose a serious risk to their safety and/or to the safety of their families.

Criminalization, punishment and redress

12. States shall adopt appropriate legislative and other measures necessary to establish, as criminal offences, trafficking, its component acts[2] and related conduct.[3]

13. States shall effectively investigate, prosecute and adjudicate trafficking, including its component acts and related conduct, whether committed by governmental or by non-State actors.

14. States shall ensure that trafficking, its component acts and related offences constitute extraditable offences under national law and extradition treaties. States shall cooperate to ensure that the appropriate extradition procedures are followed in accordance with international law.

15. Effective and proportionate sanctions shall be applied to individuals and legal persons found guilty of trafficking or of its component or related offences.

16. States shall, in appropriate cases, freeze and confiscate the assets of individuals and legal persons involved in trafficking. To the extent possible, confiscated assets shall be used to support and compensate victims of trafficking.

17. States shall ensure that trafficked persons are given access to effective and appropriate legal remedies.

RECOMMENDED GUIDELINES ON HUMAN RIGHTS AND HUMAN TRAFFICKING

Guideline 1: Promotion and protection of human rights

Violations of human rights are both a cause and a consequence of trafficking in persons. Accordingly, it is essential to place the protection of all human rights at the centre of any

[2] For the purposes of the present Principles and Guidelines, the "component acts" and component offences" of trafficking are understood to include the recruitment, transportation, ransfer, harbouring or receipt of persons over eighteen years of age by means of threat, force, oercion or deception for the purpose of exploitation. The recruitment, transportation, transfer, arbouring or receipt of a person under eighteen years of age constitute component acts and omponent offences of trafficking in children. Source: Protocol to Prevent, Suppress and Punish rafficking in Persons, Especially Women and Children, supplementing the United Nations Convention against Transnational Organized Crime, articles 3 (a) and 3 (c).

[3] For the purposes of the present Principles and Guidelines, conduct and offences "related to" trafficking are understood to include: exploitation of the prostitution of others or other forms of sexual exploitation, forced labour or services, slavery or practices similar to slavery and ervitude. Source: Protocol to Prevent, Suppress and Punish Trafficking in Persons, Especially women and Children, supplementing the United Nations Convention against Transnational rganized Crime, article 3 (a).

measures taken to prevent and end trafficking. Anti-trafficking measures should not adversely affect the human rights and dignity of persons and, in particular, the rights of those who have been trafficked, migrants, internally displaced persons, refugees and asylum-seekers.

States and, where applicable, intergovernmental and non-governmental organizations, should consider:

1. Taking steps to ensure that measures adopted for the purpose of preventing and combating trafficking in persons do not have an adverse impact on the rights and dignity of persons, including those who have been trafficked.

2. Consulting with judicial and legislative bodies, national human rights institutions and relevant sectors of civil society in the development, adoption, implementation and review of anti-trafficking legislation, policies and programmes.

3. Developing national plans of action to end trafficking. This process should be used to build links and partnerships between governmental institutions involved in combating trafficking and/or assisting trafficked persons and relevant sectors of civil society.

4. Taking particular care to ensure that the issue of gender-based discrimination is addressed systematically when anti-trafficking measures are proposed with a view to ensuring that such measures are not applied in a discriminatory manner.

5. Protecting the right of all persons to freedom of movement and ensuring that anti-trafficking measures do not infringe upon this right.

6. Ensuring that anti-trafficking laws, policies, programmes and interventions do not affect the right of all persons, including trafficked persons, to seek and enjoy asylum from persecution in accordance with international refugee law, in particular through the effective application of the principle of non-refoulement.

7. Establishing mechanisms to monitor the human rights impact of anti-trafficking laws, policies, programmes and interventions. Consideration should be given to assigning this role to independent national human rights institutions where such bodies exist. Non-governmental organizations working with trafficked persons should be encouraged to participate in monitoring and evaluating the human rights impact of anti-trafficking measures.

8. Presenting detailed information concerning the measures that they have taken to prevent and combat trafficking in their periodic reports to the United Nations human rights treaty-monitoring bodies.[4]

9. Ensuring that bilateral, regional and international cooperation agreements and other laws and policies concerning trafficking in persons do not affect the rights, obligations or responsibilities of States under international law, including human rights law, humanitarian law and refugee law.

10. Offering technical and financial assistance to States and relevant sectors of civil society for the purpose of developing and implementing human rights-based anti-trafficking strategies.

---

[4] The human rights treaty-monitoring bodies include the Human Rights Committee; the Committee on Economic, Social and Cultural Rights; the Committee on the Elimination of Discrimination against Women; the Committee on the Elimination of Racial Discrimination; the Committee against Torture; and the Committee on the Rights of the Child.

Guideline 2: Identification of trafficked persons and traffickers

Trafficking means much more than the organized movement of persons for profit. The critical additional factor that distinguishes trafficking from migrant smuggling is the presence of force, coercion and/or deception throughout or at some stage in the process — such deception, force or coercion being used for the purpose of exploitation. While the additional elements that distinguish trafficking from migrant smuggling may sometimes be obvious, in many cases they are difficult to prove without active investigation. A failure to identify a trafficked person correctly is likely to result in a further denial of that person's rights. States are therefore under an obligation to ensure that such identification can and does take place.

States are also obliged to exercise due diligence in identifying traffickers,[5] including those who are involved in controlling and exploiting trafficked persons.

States and, where applicable, intergovernmental and non-governmental organizations, should consider:

1. Developing guidelines and procedures for relevant State authorities and officials such as police, border guards, immigration officials and others involved in the detection, detention, reception and processing of irregular migrants, to permit the rapid and accurate identification of trafficked persons.

2. Providing appropriate training to relevant State authorities and officials in the identification of trafficked persons and correct application of the guidelines and procedures referred to above.

3. Ensuring cooperation between relevant authorities, officials and non-governmental organizations to facilitate the identification and provision of assistance to trafficked persons. The organization and implementation of such cooperation should be formalized in order to maximize its effectiveness.

4. Identifying appropriate points of intervention to ensure that migrants and potential migrants are warned about possible dangers and consequences of trafficking and receive information that enables them to seek assistance if required.

5. Ensuring that trafficked persons are not prosecuted for violations of immigration laws or for the activities they are involved in as a direct consequence of their situation as trafficked persons.

6. Ensuring that trafficked persons are not, in any circumstances, held in immigration detention or other forms of custody.

7. Ensuring that procedures and processes are in place for receipt and consideration of asylum claims from both trafficked persons and smuggled asylum seekers and that the principle of non-refoulement is respected and upheld at all times.

Guideline 3: Research, analysis, evaluation and dissemination

Effective and realistic anti-trafficking strategies must be based on accurate and current information, experience and analysis. It is essential that all parties involved in developing and implementing these strategies have and maintain a clear understanding of the issues.

---

[5] The term "traffickers", where it appears in the present Principles and Guidelines, is used to refer to: recruiters; transporters; those who exercise control over trafficked persons; those who transfer and/or maintain trafficked persons in exploitative situations; those involved in related crimes; and those who profit either directly or indirectly from trafficking, its component acts and related offences.

The media has an important role to play in increasing public understanding of the trafficking phenomenon by providing accurate information in accordance with professional ethical standards.
States and, where appropriate, intergovernmental and non-governmental organizations, should consider:

1. Adopting and consistently using the internationally agreed definition of trafficking contained in the Palermo Protocol.[6]

2. Standardizing the collection of statistical information on trafficking and related movements (such as migrant smuggling) that may include a trafficking element.

3. Ensuring that data concerning individuals who are trafficked is disaggregated on the basis of age, gender, ethnicity and other relevant characteristics.

4. Undertaking, supporting and bringing together research into trafficking. Such research should be firmly grounded in ethical principles, including an understanding of the need not to re-traumatize trafficked persons. Research methodologies and interpretative techniques should be of the highest quality.

5. Monitoring and evaluating the relationship between the intention of anti-trafficking laws, policies and interventions, and their real impact. In particular, ensuring that distinctions are made between measures which actually reduce trafficking and measures which may have the effect of transferring the problem from one place or group to another.

6. Recognizing the important contribution that survivors of trafficking can, on a strictly voluntary basis, make to developing and implementing anti-trafficking interventions and evaluating their impact.

7. Recognizing the central role that non-governmental organizations can play in improving the law enforcement response to trafficking by providing relevant authorities with information on trafficking incidents and patterns taking into account the need to preserve the privacy of trafficked persons.

Guideline 4: Ensuring an adequate legal framework

The lack of specific and/or adequate legislation on trafficking at the national level has been identified as one of the major obstacles in the fight against trafficking. There is an urgent need to harmonize legal definitions, procedures and cooperation at the national and regional levels in accordance with international standards. The development of an appropriate legal framework that is consistent with relevant international instruments and standards will also play an important role in the prevention of trafficking and related exploitation.

---

[6] The Protocol to Prevent, Suppress and Punish Trafficking in Persons, Especially Women and Children (Palermo Protocol), supplementing the United Nations Convention against Transnational Organized Crime, defines trafficking in persons as: "...the recruitment, transportation, transfer, harbouring or receipt of persons, by means of the threat or use of force or other forms of coercion, of abduction, of fraud, of deception, of the abuse of power or of a position of vulnerability or of the giving or receiving of payments or benefits to achieve the consent of a person having control over another person for the purpose of exploitation. Exploitation shall include, at a minimum, the exploitation of the prostitution of others or other forms of sexual exploitation, forced labour or services, slavery or practices similar to slavery, servitude or the removal of organs (article 3 (a)). The Protocol further states that the recruitment, transportation, transfer, harbouring or receipt of a child for the purpose of exploitation shall be considered "trafficking in persons" even if this does not involve any of the means set forth above (article 3 (c)).

States should consider:

1. Amending or adopting national legislation in accordance with international standards so that the crime of trafficking is precisely defined in national law and detailed guidance is provided as to its various punishable elements. All practices covered by the definition of trafficking such as debt bondage, forced labour and enforced prostitution should also be criminalized.

2. Enacting legislation to provide for the administrative, civil and, where appropriate, criminal liability of legal persons for trafficking offences in addition to the liability of natural persons. Reviewing current laws, administrative controls and conditions relating to the licensing and operation of businesses that may serve as cover for trafficking such as marriage bureaux, employment agencies, travel agencies, hotels and escort services.

3. Making legislative provision for effective and proportional criminal penalties (including custodial penalties giving rise to extradition in the case of individuals). Where appropriate, legislation should provide for additional penalties to be applied to persons found guilty of trafficking in aggravating circumstances, including offences involving trafficking in children or offences committed or involving complicity by State officials.

4. Making legislative provision for confiscation of the instruments and proceeds of trafficking and related offences. Where possible, the legislation should specify that the confiscated proceeds of trafficking will be used for the benefit of victims of trafficking. Consideration should be given to the establishment of a compensation fund for victims of trafficking and the use of confiscated assets to finance such a fund.

5. Ensuring that legislation prevents trafficked persons from being prosecuted, detained or punished for the illegality of their entry or residence or for the activities they are involved in as a direct consequence of their situation as trafficked persons.

6. Ensuring that the protection of trafficked persons is built into anti-trafficking legislation, including protection from summary deportation or return where there are reasonable grounds to conclude that such deportation or return would represent a significant security risk to the trafficked person and/or her/his family.

7. Providing legislative protection for trafficked persons who voluntarily agree to cooperate with law enforcement authorities, including protection of their right to remain lawfully within the country of destination for the duration of any legal proceedings.

8. Making effective provision for trafficked persons to be given legal information and assistance in a language they understand as well as appropriate social support sufficient to meet their immediate needs. States should ensure that entitlement to such information, assistance and immediate support is not discretionary but is available as a right for all persons who have been identified as trafficked.

9. Ensuring that the right of trafficking victims to pursue civil claims against alleged traffickers is enshrined in law.

10. Guaranteeing that protections for witnesses are provided for in law.

11. Making legislative provision for the punishment of public sector involvement or complicity in trafficking and related exploitation.

Guideline 5: Ensuring an adequate law enforcement response

Although there is evidence to suggest that trafficking in persons is increasing in all regions of the world, few traffickers have been apprehended. More effective law enforcement will create a disincentive for traffickers and will therefore have a direct impact upon demand.

An adequate law enforcement response to trafficking is dependent on the cooperation of trafficked persons and other witnesses. In many cases, individuals are reluctant or unable to report traffickers or to serve as witnesses because they lack confidence in the police and the judicial system and/or because of the absence of any effective protection mechanisms. These problems are compounded when law enforcement officials are involved or complicit in trafficking. Strong measures need to be taken to ensure that such involvement is investigated, prosecuted and punished. Law enforcement officials must also be sensitized to the paramount requirement of ensuring the safety of trafficked persons. This responsibility lies with the investigator and cannot be abrogated.

States and, where applicable, intergovernmental and non-governmental organizations should consider:

1. Sensitizing law enforcement authorities and officials to their primary responsibility to ensure the safety and immediate well-being of trafficked persons.

2. Ensuring that law enforcement personnel are provided with adequate training in the investigation and prosecution of cases of trafficking. This training should be sensitive to the needs of trafficked persons, particularly those of women and children, and should acknowledge the practical value of providing incentives for trafficked persons and others to come forward to report traffickers. The involvement of relevant non-governmental organizations in such training should be considered as a means of increasing its relevance and effectiveness.

3. Providing law enforcement authorities with adequate investigative powers and techniques to enable effective investigation and prosecution of suspected traffickers. States should encourage and support the development of proactive investigatory procedures that avoid over-reliance on victim testimony.

4. Establishing specialist anti-trafficking units (comprising both women and men) in order to promote competence and professionalism.

5. Guaranteeing that traffickers are and will remain the focus of anti-trafficking strategies and that law enforcement efforts do not place trafficked persons at risk of being punished for offences committed as a consequence of their situation.

6. Implementing measures to ensure that "rescue" operations do not further harm the rights and dignity of trafficked persons. Such operations should only take place once appropriate and adequate procedures for responding to the needs of trafficked persons released in this way have been put in place.

7. Sensitizing police, prosecutors, border, immigration and judicial authorities, and social and public health workers to the problem of trafficking and ensuring the provision of specialized training in identifying trafficking cases, combating trafficking and protecting the rights of victims.

8. Making appropriate efforts to protect individual trafficked persons during the investigation and trial process and any subsequent period when the safety of the trafficked person so requires. Appropriate protection programmes may include some or all of the following elements: identification of a safe place in the country of destination; access to independent legal counsel; protection of identity during legal proceedings; identification of options for continued stay, resettlement or repatriation.

9. Encouraging law enforcement authorities to work in partnership with non-governmental agencies in order to ensure that trafficked persons receive necessary support and assistance.

Guideline 6: Protection and support for trafficked persons

The trafficking cycle cannot be broken without attention to the rights and needs of those who have been trafficked. Appropriate protection and support should be extended to all trafficked persons without discrimination.

States and, where applicable, intergovernmental and non-governmental organizations, should consider:

1. Ensuring, in cooperation with non-governmental organizations, that safe and adequate shelter that meets the needs of trafficked persons is made available. The provision of such shelter should not be made contingent on the willingness of the victims to give evidence in criminal proceedings. Trafficked persons should not be held in immigration detention centres, other detention facilities or vagrant houses.

2. Ensuring, in partnership with non-governmental organizations, that trafficked persons are given access to primary health care and counselling. Trafficked persons should not be required to accept any such support and assistance and they should not be subject to mandatory testing for diseases, including HIV/AIDS.

3. Ensuring that trafficked persons are informed of their right of access to diplomatic and consular representatives from their State of nationality. Staff working in embassies and consulates should be provided with appropriate training in responding to requests for information and assistance from trafficked persons. These provisions would not apply to trafficked asylum-seekers.

4. Ensuring that legal proceedings in which trafficked persons are involved are not prejudicial to their rights, dignity or physical or psychological well-being.

5. Providing trafficked persons with legal and other assistance in relation to any criminal, civil or other actions against traffickers/exploiters. Victims should be provided with information in a language that they understand.

6. Ensuring that trafficked persons are effectively protected from harm, threats or intimidation by traffickers and associated persons. To this end, there should be no public disclosure of the identity of trafficking victims and their privacy should be respected and protected to the extent possible, while taking into account the right of any accused person to a fair trial. Trafficked persons should be given full warning, in advance, of the difficulties inherent in protecting identities and should not be given false or unrealistic expectations regarding the capacities of law enforcement agencies in this regard.

7. Ensuring the safe and, where possible, voluntary return of trafficked persons and exploring the option of residency in the country of destination or third-country resettlement in specific circumstances (e.g. to prevent reprisals or in cases where re-trafficking is considered likely).

8. In partnership with non-governmental organizations, ensuring that trafficked persons who do return to their country of origin are provided with the assistance and support necessary to ensure their well-being, facilitate their social integration and prevent re-trafficking. Measures should be taken to ensure the provision of appropriate physical and psychological health care, housing and educational and employment services for returned trafficking victims.

Guideline 7: Preventing trafficking

Strategies aimed at preventing trafficking should take into account demand as a root cause. States and intergovernmental organizations should also take into account the factors that increase vulnerability to trafficking, including inequality, poverty and all forms of discrimination and prejudice. Effective prevention strategies should be based on existing experience and accurate information.

States, in partnership with intergovernmental and non-governmental organizations and where appropriate, using development cooperation policies and programmes, should consider:

1. Analysing the factors that generate demand for exploitative commercial sexual services and exploitative labour and taking strong legislative, policy and other measures to address these issues.

2. Developing programmes that offer livelihood options, including basic education, skills training and literacy, especially for women and other traditionally disadvantaged groups.

3. Improving children's access to educational opportunities and increasing the level of school attendance, in particular by girl children.

4. Ensuring that potential migrants, especially women, are properly informed about the risks of migration (e.g. exploitation, debt bondage and health and security issues, including exposure to HIV/AIDS) as well as avenues available for legal, non-exploitative migration.

5. Developing information campaigns for the general public aimed at promoting awareness of the dangers associated with trafficking. Such campaigns should be informed by an understanding of the complexities surrounding trafficking and of the reasons why individuals may make potentially dangerous migration decisions.

6. Reviewing and modifying policies that may compel people to resort to irregular and vulnerable labour migration. This process should include examining the effect on women of repressive and/or discriminatory nationality, property, immigration, emigration and migrant labour laws.

7. Examining ways of increasing opportunities for legal, gainful and non-exploitative labour migration. The promotion of labour migration by the State should be dependent on the existence of regulatory and supervisory mechanisms to protect the rights of migrant workers.

8. Strengthening the capacity of law enforcement agencies to arrest and prosecute those involved in trafficking as a preventive measure. This includes ensuring that law enforcement agencies comply with their legal obligations.

9. Adopting measures to reduce vulnerability by ensuring that appropriate legal documentation for birth, citizenship and marriage is provided and made available to all persons.

Guideline 8: Special measures for the protection and support of child victims of trafficking

The particular physical, psychological and psychosocial harm suffered by trafficked children and their increased vulnerability to exploitation require that they be dealt with separately from adult trafficked persons in terms of laws, policies, programmes and interventions. The best interests of the child must be a primary consideration in all actions concerning trafficked children, whether undertaken by public or private social welfare institutions, courts of law, administrative authorities or legislative bodies. Child victims of trafficking should be provided with appropriate assistance and protection and full account should be taken of their special rights and needs.

States and, where applicable, intergovernmental and non-governmental organizations, should consider, in addition to the measures outlined under Guideline 6:

1. Ensuring that definitions of trafficking in children in both law and policy reflect their need for special safeguards and care, including appropriate legal protection. In particular, and in accordance with the Palermo Protocol, evidence of deception, force, coercion, etc. should not form part of the definition of trafficking where the person involved is a child.

2. Ensuring that procedures are in place for the rapid identification of child victims of trafficking.

3. Ensuring that children who are victims of trafficking are not subjected to criminal procedures or sanctions for offences related to their situation as trafficked persons.

4. In cases where children are not accompanied by relatives or guardians, taking steps to identify and locate family members. Following a risk assessment and consultation with the child, measures should be taken to facilitate the reunion of trafficked children with their families where this is deemed to be in their best interest.

5. In situations where the safe return of the child to his or her family is not possible, or where such return would not be in the child's best interests, establishing adequate care arrangements that respect the rights and dignity of the trafficked child.

6. In both the situations referred to in the two paragraphs above, ensuring that a child who is capable of forming his or her own views enjoys the right to express those views freely in all matters affecting him or her, in particular concerning decisions about his or her possible return to the family, the views of the child being given due weight in accordance with his or her age and maturity.

7. Adopting specialized policies and programmes to protect and support children who have been victims of trafficking. Children should be provided with appropriate physical, psychosocial, legal, educational, housing and health-care assistance.

8. Adopting measures necessary to protect the rights and interests of trafficked children at all stages of criminal proceedings against alleged offenders and during procedures for obtaining compensation.

9. Protecting, as appropriate, the privacy and identity of child victims and taking measures to avoid the dissemination of information that could lead to their identification.

10. Taking measures to ensure adequate and appropriate training, in particular legal and psychological training, for persons working with child victims of trafficking.

Guideline 9: Access to remedies

Trafficked persons, as victims of human rights violations, have an international legal right to adequate and appropriate remedies. This right is often not effectively available to trafficked persons as they frequently lack information on the possibilities and processes for obtaining remedies, including compensation, for trafficking and related exploitation. In order to overcome this problem, legal and other material assistance should be provided to trafficked persons to enable them to realize their right to adequate and appropriate remedies.

States and, where applicable, intergovernmental and non-governmental organizations, should consider:

1. Ensuring that victims of trafficking have an enforceable right to fair and adequate remedies, including the means for as full a rehabilitation as possible. These remedies may be criminal, civil or administrative in nature.

2. Providing information as well as legal and other assistance to enable trafficked persons to access remedies. The procedures for obtaining remedies should be clearly explained in a language that the trafficked person understands.

3. Making arrangements to enable trafficked persons to remain safely in the country in which the remedy is being sought for the duration of any criminal, civil or administrative proceedings.

Guideline 10: Obligations of peacekeepers, civilian police and humanitarian and diplomatic personnel

The direct or indirect involvement of peacekeeping, peace-building, civilian policing, humanitarian and diplomatic personnel in trafficking raises special concerns. States, intergovernmental and non-governmental organizations are responsible for the actions of those working under their authority and are therefore under an obligation to take effective measures to prevent their nationals and employees from engaging in trafficking and related exploitation. They are also required to investigate thoroughly all allegations of trafficking and related exploitation and to provide for and apply appropriate sanctions to personnel found to have been involved in trafficking.

States and, where appropriate, intergovernmental and non-governmental organizations, should consider:

1. Ensuring that pre- and post-deployment training programmes for all peacekeeping, peace-building, civilian policing, humanitarian and diplomatic staff adequately address the issue of trafficking and clearly set out the expected standard of behaviour. This training should be developed within a human rights framework and delivered by appropriately experienced trainers.

2. Ensuring that recruitment, placement and transfer procedures (including those of private contractors and sub-contractors) are rigorous and transparent.

3. Ensuring that staff employed in the context of peacekeeping, peace-building, civilian policing, humanitarian and diplomatic missions do not engage in trafficking and related exploitation or use the services of persons in relation to which there are reasonable grounds to suspect they may have been trafficked. This obligation also covers complicity in trafficking through corruption or affiliation with any person or group of persons who could reasonably be suspected of engaging in trafficking and related exploitation.

4. Developing and adopting specific regulations and codes of conduct setting out expected standards of behaviour and the consequences of failure to adhere to these standards.

5. Requiring all personnel employed in the context of peacekeeping, peace-building, civilian policing, humanitarian and diplomatic missions to report on any instances of trafficking and related exploitation that come to their attention.

6. Establishing mechanisms for the systematic investigation of all allegations of trafficking and related exploitation involving personnel employed in the context of peacekeeping, peace-building, civilian policing, humanitarian and diplomatic missions.

7. Consistently applying appropriate criminal, civil and administrative sanctions to personnel shown to have engaged in or been complicit in trafficking and related exploitation. Intergovernmental and non-governmental organizations should, in appropriate cases, apply disciplinary sanctions to staff members found to be involved in trafficking and related exploitation in addition to and independently of any criminal or other sanctions decided on by the State concerned. Privileges and immunities attached to the status of an employee should not be invoked in order to shield that person from sanctions for serious crimes such as trafficking and related offences.

Guideline 11: Cooperation and coordination between States and regions

Trafficking is a regional and global phenomenon that cannot always be dealt with effectively at the national level: a strengthened national response can often result in the operations of traffickers moving elsewhere. International, multilateral and bilateral cooperation can play an important role in combating trafficking activities. Such cooperation is particularly critical between countries involved in different stages of the trafficking cycle.

States and, where applicable, intergovernmental and non-governmental organizations, should consider:

1. Adopting bilateral agreements aimed at preventing trafficking, protecting the rights and dignity of trafficked persons and promoting their welfare.

2. Offering, either on a bilateral basis or through multilateral organizations, technical and financial assistance to States and relevant sectors of civil society for the purpose of promoting the development and implementation of human rights-based anti-trafficking strategies.

3. Elaborating regional and subregional treaties on trafficking, using the Palermo Protocol and relevant international human rights standards as a baseline and framework.

4. Adopting labour migration agreements, which may include provision for minimum work standards, model contracts, modes of repatriation, etc., in accordance with existing international standards. States are encouraged effectively to enforce all such agreements in order to help eliminate trafficking and related exploitation.

5. Developing cooperation arrangements to facilitate the rapid identification of trafficked persons including the sharing and exchange of information in relation to their nationality and right of residence.

6. Establishing mechanisms to facilitate the exchange of information concerning traffickers and their methods of operation.

7. Developing procedures and protocols for the conduct of proactive joint investigations by law enforcement authorities of different concerned States. In recognition of the value of direct contacts, provision should be made for direct transmission of requests for assistance between locally competent authorities in order to ensure that such requests are rapidly dealt with and to foster the development of cooperative relations at the working level.

8. Ensuring judicial cooperation between States in investigations and judicial processes relating to trafficking and related offences, in particular through common prosecution methodologies and joint investigations. This cooperation should include assistance in: identifying and interviewing witnesses with due regard for their safety; identifying, obtaining and preserving evidence; producing and serving the legal documents necessary to secure evidence and witnesses; and the enforcement of judgements.

9. Ensuring that requests for extradition for offences related to trafficking are dealt with by the authorities of the requested State without undue delay.

10. Establishing cooperative mechanisms for the confiscation of the proceeds of trafficking. This cooperation should include the provision of assistance in identifying, tracing, freezing and confiscating assets connected to trafficking and related exploitation.

11. Exchanging information and experience relating to the implementation of assistance, return and integration programmes with a view to maximizing impact and effectiveness.

12. Encouraging and facilitating cooperation between non-governmental organizations and other civil society organizations in countries of origin, transit and destination. This is particularly important to ensure support and assistance to trafficked persons who are repatriated.

UNHCR Guidelines on International Protection: The Application of Article 1 A(2) of the 1951 Convention and/or 1967 Protocol relating to the Status of Refugees to victims of trafficking and persons at risk of being trafficked, 2006 [excerpts]*

Adoption: 7 April 2006

[...]

I. INTRODUCTION

[...]

5. UNHCR's involvement with the issue of trafficking is essentially twofold. Firstly, the Office has a responsibility to ensure that refugees, asylum-seekers, internally displaced persons (IDPs), stateless persons and other persons of concern do not fall victim to trafficking. Secondly, the Office has a responsibility to ensure that individuals who have been trafficked and who fear being subjected to persecution upon a return to their country of origin, or individuals who fear being trafficked, whose claim to international protection falls within the refugee definition contained in the 1951 Convention and/or its 1967 Protocol relating to the Status of Refugees (hereinafter "the 1951 Convention") are recognized as refugees and afforded the corresponding international protection.

6. Not all victims or potential victims of trafficking fall within the scope of the refugee definition. To be recognized as a refugee, all elements of the refugee definition have to be satisfied. These Guidelines are intended to provide guidance on the application of Article 1A(2) of the 1951 Convention to victims or potential victims of trafficking. They also cover issues concerning victims of trafficking arising in the context of the 1954 Convention Relating to the Status of Stateless Persons and the 1961 Convention on the Reduction of Statelessness. The protection of victims or potential victims of trafficking as set out in these Guidelines is additional to and distinct from the protection contemplated by Part II of the Trafficking Protocol.

II. SUBSTANTIVE ANALYSIS

a) Definitional issues

[...]

12. Some victims or potential victims of trafficking may fall within the definition of a refugee contained in Article 1A(2) of the 1951 Convention and may therefore be entitled to international refugee protection. Such a possibility is not least implicit in the saving clause contained in Article 14 of the Trafficking Protocol, which states:

"1. Nothing in this Protocol shall affect the rights, obligations and responsibilities of States and individuals under international law, including international humanitarian law and international human rights law and, in particular, where applicable, the 1951 Convention and the 1967 Protocol relating to the Status of Refugees and the principle of non-refoulement as contained therein.

2. The measures set forth in this Protocol shall be interpreted and applied in a way that is not discriminatory to persons on the ground that they are victims of trafficking in persons.

* Source: HCR/GIP/06/07; for more information, see: www.unhcr.org.

The interpretation and application of those measures shall be consistent with internationally recognized principles of non-discrimination."

13. A claim for international protection presented by a victim or potential victim of trafficking can arise in a number of distinct sets of circumstances. The victim may have been trafficked abroad, may have escaped her or his traffickers and may seek the protection of the State where she or he now is. The victim may have been trafficked within national territory, may have escaped from her or his traffickers and have fled abroad in search of international protection. The individual concerned may not have been trafficked but may fear becoming a victim of trafficking and may have fled abroad in search of international protection. In all these instances, the individual concerned must be found to have a "well-founded fear of persecution" linked to one or more of the Convention grounds in order to be recognized as a refugee.

b) Well-founded fear of persecution

14. What amounts to a well-founded fear of persecution will depend on the particular circumstances of each individual case. Persecution can be considered to involve serious human rights violations, including a threat to life or freedom, as well as other kinds of serious harm or intolerable predicament, as assessed in the light of the opinions, feelings and psychological make-up of the asylum applicant.

15. In this regard, the evolution of international law in criminalizing trafficking can help decision-makers determine the persecutory nature of the various acts associated with trafficking. Asylum claims lodged by victims of trafficking or potential victims of trafficking should thus be examined in detail to establish whether the harm feared as a result of the trafficking experience, or as a result of its anticipation, amounts to persecution in the individual case. Inherent in the trafficking experience are such forms of severe exploitation as abduction, incarceration, rape, sexual enslavement, enforced prostitution, forced labour, removal of organs, physical beatings, starvation, the deprivation of medical treatment. Such acts constitute serious violations of human rights which will generally amount to persecution.

[...]

c) Women and children victims of trafficking

19. The forcible or deceptive recruitment of women and children for the purposes of forced prostitution or sexual exploitation is a form of gender-related violence, which may constitute persecution. Trafficked women and children can be particularly susceptible to serious reprisals by traffickers after their escape and/or upon return, as well as to a real possibility of being re-trafficked or of being subjected to severe family or community ostracism and/or severe discrimination.

[...]

d) Agents of persecution

21. There is scope within the refugee definition to recognize both State and non-State agents of persecution. While persecution is often perpetrated by the authorities of a country, it can also be perpetrated by individuals if the persecutory acts are "knowingly tolerated by the authorities or if the authorities refuse, or prove unable to offer effective protection". In most situations involving victims or potential victims of trafficking, the persecutory acts emanate from individuals, that is, traffickers or criminal enterprises or, in some situations, family or community members. Under these circumstances, it is also necessary to examine whether the authorities of the country of origin are able and willing to protect the victim or potential victim upon return.

[...]

24. There may also be situations where trafficking activities are de facto tolerated or condoned by the authorities or even actively facilitated by corrupt State officials. In these circumstances, the agent of persecution may well be the State itself, which becomes responsible, whether directly or as a result of inaction, for a failure to protect those within its jurisdiction. Whether this is so will depend on the role played by the officials concerned and on whether they are acting in their personal capacity outside the framework of governmental authority or on the basis of the position of authority they occupy within governmental structures supporting or condoning trafficking. In the latter case, the persecutory acts may be deemed to emanate from the State itself.

e) Place of persecution

25. In order to come within the scope of Article 1A(2) of the 1951 Convention, the applicant must be outside her or his country of origin and, owing to a well-founded fear of persecution, be unable or unwilling to avail her- or himself of the protection of that country. The requirement of being outside one's country does not, however, mean that the individual must have left on account of a well-founded fear of persecution. Where this fear arises after she or he has left the country of origin, she or he would be a refugee sur place, providing the other elements in the refugee definition were fulfilled. Thus, while victims of trafficking may not have left their country owing to a well-founded fear of persecution, such a fear may arise after leaving their country of origin. In such cases, it is on this basis that the claim to refugee status should be assessed.

[...]

f) The causal link ("for reasons of")

29. To qualify for refugee status, an individual's well-founded fear of persecution must be related to one or more of the Convention grounds, that is, it must be "for reasons of" race, religion, nationality, membership of a particular social group or political opinion. It is sufficient that the Convention ground be a relevant factor contributing to the persecution; it is not necessary that it be the sole, or even dominant, cause. In many jurisdictions, the causal link ("for reasons of") must be explicitly established, while in other States, causation is not treated as a separate question for analysis but is subsumed within the holistic analysis of the refugee definition. In relation to asylum claims involving trafficking, the difficult issue for a decision-maker is likely to be linking the well-founded fear of persecution to a Convention ground. Where the persecutor attributes or imputes a Convention ground to the applicant, this is sufficient to satisfy the causal link.

30. In cases where there is a risk of being persecuted at the hands of a non-State actor for reasons related to one of the Convention grounds, the causal link is established, whether or not the absence of State protection is Convention-related. Alternatively, where a risk of persecution at the hands of a non-State actor is unrelated to a Convention ground, but the inability or unwillingness of the State to offer protection is for reasons of a Convention ground, the causal link is also established.

31. Trafficking in persons is a commercial enterprise, the prime motivation of which is likely to be profit rather than persecution on a Convention ground. In other words, victims are likely to be targeted above all because of their perceived or potential commercial value to the traffickers. This overriding economic motive does not, however, exclude the possibility of Convention-related grounds in the targeting and selection of victims of trafficking. Scenarios in which trafficking can flourish frequently coincide with situations where potential victims may be vulnerable to trafficking precisely as a result of characteristics contained in the 1951 Convention refugee definition. For instance, States where there has been significant social

upheaval and/or economic transition or which have been involved in armed conflict resulting in a breakdown in law and order are prone to increased poverty, deprivation and dislocation of the civilian population. Opportunities arise for organized crime to exploit the inability, or lack of will, of law enforcement agencies to maintain law and order, in particular the failure to ensure adequate security for specific or vulnerable groups.

32. Members of a certain race or ethnic group in a given country may be especially vulnerable to trafficking and/or less effectively protected by the authorities of the country of origin. Victims may be targeted on the basis of their ethnicity, nationality, religious or political views in a context where individuals with specific profiles are already more vulnerable to exploitation and abuse of varying forms. Individuals may also be targeted by reason of their belonging to a particular social group. As an example, among children or women generally in a particular society some subsets of children or women may be especially vulnerable to being trafficked and may constitute a social group within the terms of the refugee definition. Thus, even if an individual is not trafficked solely and exclusively for a Convention reason, one or more of these Convention grounds may have been relevant for the trafficker's selection of the particular victim.

f) Convention grounds

33. The causal link may be established to any one single Convention ground or to a combination of these grounds. Although a successful claim to refugee status only needs to establish a causal link to one ground, a full analysis of trafficking cases may frequently reveal a number of interlinked, cumulative grounds.

[...]

III. STATELESSNESS AND TRAFFICKING

41. The 1954 Convention relating to the Status of Stateless Persons and the 1961 Convention on the Reduction of Statelessness establish a legal framework setting out the rights of stateless persons, the obligations of States Parties to avoid actions that would result in statelessness and the steps to be taken to remedy situations of statelessness. The 1954 Convention applies to anyone who is "not considered as a national by any State under the operation of its law", that is, it applies for the benefit of those who are denied citizenship under the laws of any State. The 1961 Convention generally requires States to avoid actions that would result in statelessness and explicitly forbids the deprivation of nationality if this would result in statelessness. This constitutes a prohibition on actions that would cause statelessness, as well as an obligation to avoid situations where statelessness may arise by default or neglect. The only exception to this prohibition is when the nationality was acquired fraudulently.

42. When seeking to assess and address the situation of someone who has been trafficked, it is important to recognize potential implications as regards statelessness. The mere fact of being a victim of trafficking will not per se render someone stateless. Victims of trafficking continue to possess the citizenship they had when they fell under the control of their traffickers. If, however, these traffickers have confiscated their identity documents, as commonly happens as a way of establishing and exerting control over their victims, they may be unable to prove citizenship. This lack of documentation and temporary inability to establish identity is not necessarily unique to victims of trafficking. It should be, and in many cases is, easily overcome with the assistance of the authorities of the State of origin.

[...]

IV. PROCEDURAL ISSUES

45. Given the broad range of situations in which trafficking cases come to light and victims of trafficking can be identified, it is important that mechanisms be put in place at the national level to provide for the physical, psychological and social recovery of victims of trafficking. This includes the provision of housing, legal counselling and information, medical, psychological and material assistance, as well as employment, educational and training opportunities in a manner which takes into account the age, gender and special needs of victims of trafficking. It is also necessary to ensure that victims of trafficking have access to fair and efficient asylum procedures as appropriate and to proper legal counselling, if they are to be able to lodge an asylum claim effectively. In view of the complexities of asylum claims presented by victims or potential victims of trafficking, such claims normally require an examination on their merits in regular procedures.

[…]

4.3 Smuggling

Protocol against the Smuggling of Migrants by Land, Sea and Air, supplementing the United Nations Convention against Transnational Organized Crime, 2000*

Adoption: 15 November 2000
Entry into force: 28 January 2004
Parties: 105 (Status as of 1 April 2007)

ALBANIA 21 Aug 2002, ALGERIA 09 Mar 2004 (*20.2), ARGENTINA 19 Nov 2002, ARMENIA 01 July 2003, AUSTRALIA 27 May 2004, AZERBAIJAN 30 Oct 2003 (*20.2), BAHRAIN 7 Jun 2004 a (*20.2), BELARUS 25 Jun 2003, BELGIUM 11 Aug 2004, BELIZE 14 Sep 2006 a, BENIN 30 Aug 2004, BOSNIA AND HERZEGOVINA 24 Apr 2002, BOTSWANA 29 Aug 2002, BRAZIL 29 Jan 2004, BULGARIA 5 Dec 2001, BURKINA FASO 15 May 2002, BURUNDI 14 Dec 2000, CAMBODIA 12 Dec 2005, CAMEROON 06 Feb 2006, CANADA 13 May 2002, CAPE VERDE 15 Jul 2004, CENTRAL AFRICAN REPUBLIC 06 Oct 2006 a, CHILE 29 Nov 2004, COSTA RICA 07 Aug 2003, CROATIA 24 Jan 2003, CYPRUS 06 Aug 2003, DEMOCRATIC REPUBLIC OF THE CONGO 28 Oct 2005 a, DENMARK 8 Dec 2006, DJIBOUTI 20 Apr 2005 a, ECUADOR 17 Sep 2002 (*20.2), EGYPT 1 Mar 2005 a, EL SALVADOR 18 Mar 2004 (*20.2, 9.2, 18), ESTONIA 12 May 2002, EUROPEAN COMMUNITY 06 Sep 2006 AA, FINLAND 07 Sep 2006 A, FRANCE 29 Oct 2002, GAMBIA 14 05 May 2003, GEORGIA 13 05 Sep 2006, GERMANY 14 Jun 2006, GRENADA 21 May 2004 a, GUATEMALA 01 Apr 2004 a, GUINEA 08 Jun 2005 a, HUNGARY 22 Dec 2006, ITALY 02 Aug 2006, JAMAICA 29 Sep 2003, KENYA 5 Jan 2005 a, KIRIBATI 15 Sep 2005 a, KUWAIT 12 May 2006 a, KYRGYZSTAN 02 Oct 2003, LAO'S PEOPLE'S DEMOCRATIC REPUBLIC 26 Sep 2003 a (*20.2), LATVIA 23 Apr 2003, LEBANON 05 Oct 2005, LESOTHO 24 Sep 2004, LIBERIA 22 Sep 2004 a, LIBYAN ARAB JAMAHIRIYA 24 Sep 2004, LIECHTENSTEIN 14 Mar 2001, LITHUANIA 12 May 2003 (*20.2), MADAGASCAR 15 Sep 2005, MALAWI 17 Mar 2005 a, MALI 12 Apr 2002, MALTA 24 Sep 2003, MAURITANIA 22 July 2005 a, MAURITIUS 24 Sep 2003 a, MEXICO 04 Mar 2003, MONACO 5 Jun 2001, MONTENEGRO 23 Oct 2006 d, MOZAMBIQUE 20 Sep 2006, MYANMAR 30 Mar 2004 a (*20.2), NAMIBIA 16 Aug 2002, NETHERLANDS 27 July 2005 A, NEW ZEALAND 19 July 2002, NICARAGUA 15 Feb 2006 a, NIGERIA 27 Sep 2001, NORWAY 23 Sep 2003, OMAN 13 May 2005 a, PANAMA 18 Aug 2004, PERU 23 Jan 2002, PHILIPPINES 28 May 2002, POLAND 26 Sep 2003, PORTUGAL 10 May 2004, REPUBLIC OF MOLDOVA 16 Sep 2005, ROMANIA 04 Dec 2002, RUSSIAN FEDERATION 26 May 2004, RWANDA 04 Oct 2006, SAINT KITTS AND NEVIS 21 May 2004 a, SAO TOME AND PRINCIPE 12 Apr 2006 a, SAUDI ARABIA 10 Dec 2002 (*20.2), SENEGAL 27 Oct 2003, SERBIA 6 Sep 2001, SEYCHELLES 22 Jun 2004, SLOVAKIA 21 Sep 2004, SLOVENIA 21 May 2004, SOUTH AFRICA 20 Feb 2004 (*20.2), SPAIN 01 Mar 2002, SWEDEN 06 Sep 2006, SWITZERLAND 27 Oct 2006, TAJIKISTAN 08 July 2002 a, THAILAND 18 Dec 2001, THE FORMER YUGOSLAV REPUBLIC OF MACEDONIA 12 Jan 2005, TRINIDAD AND TOBAGO 26 Sep 2001, TUNISIA 14 July 2003 (*20.2), TURKEY 25 Mar 2003, TURKMENISTAN 28 Mar 2005 a, UKRAINE 21 May 2004, UNITED KINGDOM OF GREAT BRITAIN AND NORTHERN IRELAND 09 Feb 2006, UNITED REPUBLIC OF TANZANIA 24 May 2006, UNITED STATES OF AMERICA 03

* Source: U.N.G.A. Res. 55/25.

Nov 2005 (*6, 20.2), URUGUAY 4 Mar 2005, VENEZUELA 19 Apr 2005 (*20.2), ZAMBIA 24 Apr 2005 a.

Preamble

The States Parties to this Protocol,

Declaring that effective action to prevent and combat the smuggling of migrants by land, sea and air requires a comprehensive international approach, including cooperation, the exchange of information and other appropriate measures, including socio-economic measures, at the national, regional and international levels,

Recalling General Assembly resolution 54/212 of 22 December 1999, in which the Assembly urged Member States and the United Nations system to strengthen international cooperation in the area of international migration and development in order to address the root causes of migration, especially those related to poverty, and to maximize the benefits of international migration to those concerned, and encouraged, where relevant, interregional, regional and subregional mechanisms to continue to address the question of migration and development,

Convinced of the need to provide migrants with humane treatment and full protection of their rights,

Taking into account the fact that, despite work undertaken in other international forums, there is no universal instrument that addresses all aspects of smuggling of migrants and other related issues,

Concerned at the significant increase in the activities of organized criminal groups in smuggling of migrants and other related criminal activities set forth in this Protocol, which bring great harm to the States concerned,

Also concerned that the smuggling of migrants can endanger the lives or security of the migrants involved,

Recalling General Assembly resolution 53/111 of 9 December 1998, in which the Assembly decided to establish an open-ended intergovernmental ad hoc committee for the purpose of elaborating a comprehensive international convention against transnational organized crime and of discussing the elaboration of, inter alia, an international instrument addressing illegal trafficking in and transporting of migrants, including by sea,

Convinced that supplementing the United Nations Convention against Transnational Organized Crime with an international instrument against the smuggling of migrants by land, sea and air will be useful in preventing and combating that crime,

Have agreed as follows:

I. GENERAL PROVISIONS

Article 1

Relation with the United Nations Convention against Transnational Organized Crime

1. This Protocol supplements the United Nations Convention against Transnational Organized Crime. It shall be interpreted together with the Convention.

2. The provisions of the Convention shall apply, mutatis mutandis, to this Protocol unless otherwise provided herein.

3. The offences established in accordance with article 6 of this Protocol shall be regarded as offences established in accordance with the Convention.

Article 2

Statement of purpose

The purpose of this Protocol is to prevent and combat the smuggling of migrants, as well as to promote cooperation among States Parties to that end, while protecting the rights of smuggled migrants.

Article 3

Use of terms

For the purposes of this Protocol:

(a) "Smuggling of migrants" shall mean the procurement, in order to obtain, directly or indirectly, a financial or other material benefit, of the illegal entry of a person into a State Party of which the person is not a national or a permanent resident;

(b) "Illegal entry" shall mean crossing borders without complying with the necessary requirements for legal entry into the receiving State;

(c) "Fraudulent travel or identity document" shall mean any travel or identity document:

(i) That has been falsely made or altered in some material way by anyone other than a person or agency lawfully authorized to make or issue the travel or identity document on behalf of a State; or

(ii) That has been improperly issued or obtained through misrepresentation, corruption or duress or in any other unlawful manner; or

(iii) That is being used by a person other than the rightful holder;

(d) "Vessel" shall mean any type of water craft, including non-displacement craft and seaplanes, used or capable of being used as a means of transportation on water, except a warship, naval auxiliary or other vessel owned or operated by a Government and used, for the time being, only on government non-commercial service.

Article 4

Scope of application

This Protocol shall apply, except as otherwise stated herein, to the prevention, investigation and prosecution of the offences established in accordance with article 6 of this Protocol, where the offences are transnational in nature and involve an organized criminal group, as well as to the protection of the rights of persons who have been the object of such offences.

Article 5

Criminal liability of migrants

Migrants shall not become liable to criminal prosecution under this Protocol for the fact of having been the object of conduct set forth in article 6 of this Protocol.

Article 6

Criminalization

1. Each State Party shall adopt such legislative and other measures as may be necessary to establish as criminal offences, when committed intentionally and in order to obtain, directly or indirectly, a financial or other material benefit:

(a) The smuggling of migrants;

(b) When committed for the purpose of enabling the smuggling of migrants:

(i) Producing a fraudulent travel or identity document;

(ii) Procuring, providing or possessing such a document;

(c) Enabling a person who is not a national or a permanent resident to remain in the State concerned without complying with the necessary requirements for legally remaining in the State by the means mentioned in subparagraph (b) of this paragraph or any other illegal means.

2. Each State Party shall also adopt such legislative and other measures as may be necessary to establish as criminal offences:

(a) Subject to the basic concepts of its legal system, attempting to commit an offence established in accordance with paragraph 1 of this article;

(b) Participating as an accomplice in an offence established in accordance with paragraph 1 (a), (b) (i) or (c) of this article and, subject to the basic concepts of its legal system, participating as an accomplice in an offence established in accordance with paragraph 1 (b) (ii) of this article;

(c) Organizing or directing other persons to commit an offence established in accordance with paragraph 1 of this article.

3. Each State Party shall adopt such legislative and other measures as may be necessary to establish as aggravating circumstances to the offences established in accordance with paragraph 1 (a), (b) (i) and (c) of this article and, subject to the basic concepts of its legal system, to the offences established in accordance with paragraph 2 (b) and (c) of this article, circumstances:

(a) That endanger, or are likely to endanger, the lives or safety of the migrants concerned; or

(b) That entail inhuman or degrading treatment, including for exploitation, of such migrants.

4. Nothing in this Protocol shall prevent a State Party from taking measures against a person whose conduct constitutes an offence under its domestic law.

II. SMUGGLING OF MIGRANTS BY SEA

Article 7

Cooperation

States Parties shall cooperate to the fullest extent possible to prevent and suppress the smuggling of migrants by sea, in accordance with the international law of the sea.

Article 8

Measures against the smuggling of migrants by sea

1. A State Party that has reasonable grounds to suspect that a vessel that is flying its flag or claiming its registry, that is without nationality or that, though flying a foreign flag or refusing to show a flag, is in reality of the nationality of the State Party concerned is engaged in the smuggling of migrants by sea may request the assistance of other States Parties in suppressing the use of the vessel for that purpose. The States Parties so requested shall render such assistance to the extent possible within their means.

2. A State Party that has reasonable grounds to suspect that a vessel exercising freedom of navigation in accordance with international law and flying the flag or displaying the marks of

registry of another State Party is engaged in the smuggling of migrants by sea may so notify the flag State, request confirmation of registry and, if confirmed, request authorization from the flag State to take appropriate measures with regard to that vessel. The flag State may authorize the requesting State, inter alia:

(a) To board the vessel;

(b) To search the vessel; and

(c) If evidence is found that the vessel is engaged in the smuggling of migrants by sea, to take appropriate measures with respect to the vessel and persons and cargo on board, as authorized by the flag State.

3. A State Party that has taken any measure in accordance with paragraph 2 of this article shall promptly inform the flag State concerned of the results of that measure.

4. A State Party shall respond expeditiously to a request from another State Party to determine whether a vessel that is claiming its registry or flying its flag is entitled to do so and to a request for authorization made in accordance with paragraph 2 of this article.

5. A flag State may, consistent with article 7 of this Protocol, subject its authorization to conditions to be agreed by it and the requesting State, including conditions relating to responsibility and the extent of effective measures to be taken. A State Party shall take no additional measures without the express authorization of the flag State, except those necessary to relieve imminent danger to the lives of persons or those which derive from relevant bilateral or multilateral agreements.

6. Each State Party shall designate an authority or, where necessary, authorities to receive and respond to requests for assistance, for confirmation of registry or of the right of a vessel to fly its flag and for authorization to take appropriate measures. Such designation shall be notified through the Secretary-General to all other States Parties within one month of the designation.

7. A State Party that has reasonable grounds to suspect that a vessel is engaged in the smuggling of migrants by sea and is without nationality or may be assimilated to a vessel without nationality may board and search the vessel. If evidence confirming the suspicion is found, that State Party shall take appropriate measures in accordance with relevant domestic and international law.

Article 9

Safeguard clauses

1. Where a State Party takes measures against a vessel in accordance with article 8 of this Protocol, it shall:

(a) Ensure the safety and humane treatment of the persons on board;

(b) Take due account of the need not to endanger the security of the vessel or its cargo;

(c) Take due account of the need not to prejudice the commercial or legal interests of the flag State or any other interested State;

(d) Ensure, within available means, that any measure taken with regard to the vessel is environmentally sound.

2. Where the grounds for measures taken pursuant to article 8 of this Protocol prove to be unfounded, the vessel shall be compensated for any loss or damage that may have been sustained, provided that the vessel has not committed any act justifying the measures taken.

3. Any measure taken, adopted or implemented in accordance with this chapter shall take due account of the need not to interfere with or to affect:

(a) The rights and obligations and the exercise of jurisdiction of coastal States in accordance with the international law of the sea; or

(b) The authority of the flag State to exercise jurisdiction and control in administrative, technical and social matters involving the vessel.

4. Any measure taken at sea pursuant to this chapter shall be carried out only by warships or military aircraft, or by other ships or aircraft clearly marked and identifiable as being on government service and authorized to that effect.

III. PREVENTION, COOPERATION AND OTHER MEASURES

Article 10

Information

1. Without prejudice to articles 27 and 28 of the Convention, States Parties, in particular those with common borders or located on routes along which migrants are smuggled, shall, for the purpose of achieving the objectives of this Protocol, exchange among themselves, consistent with their respective domestic legal and administrative systems, relevant information on matters such as:

(a) Embarkation and destination points, as well as routes, carriers and means of transportation, known to be or suspected of being used by an organized criminal group engaged in conduct set forth in article 6 of this Protocol;

(b) The identity and methods of organizations or organized criminal groups known to be or suspected of being engaged in conduct set forth in article 6 of this Protocol;

(c) The authenticity and proper form of travel documents issued by a State Party and the theft or related misuse of blank travel or identity documents;

(d) Means and methods of concealment and transportation of persons, the unlawful alteration, reproduction or acquisition or other misuse of travel or identity documents used in conduct set forth in article 6 of this Protocol and ways of detecting them;

(e) Legislative experiences and practices and measures to prevent and combat the conduct set forth in article 6 of this Protocol; and

(f) Scientific and technological information useful to law enforcement, so as to enhance each other's ability to prevent, detect and investigate the conduct set forth in article 6 of this Protocol and to prosecute those involved.

2. A State Party that receives information shall comply with any request by the State Party that transmitted the information that places restrictions on its use.

Article 11

Border measures

1. Without prejudice to international commitments in relation to the free movement of people, States Parties shall strengthen, to the extent possible, such border controls as may be necessary to prevent and detect the smuggling of migrants.

2. Each State Party shall adopt legislative or other appropriate measures to prevent, to the extent possible, means of transport operated by commercial carriers from being used in the

commission of the offence established in accordance with article 6, paragraph 1 (a), of this Protocol.

3. Where appropriate, and without prejudice to applicable international conventions, such measures shall include establishing the obligation of commercial carriers, including any transportation company or the owner or operator of any means of transport, to ascertain that all passengers are in possession of the travel documents required for entry into the receiving State.

4. Each State Party shall take the necessary measures, in accordance with its domestic law, to provide for sanctions in cases of violation of the obligation set forth in paragraph 3 of this article.

5. Each State Party shall consider taking measures that permit, in accordance with its domestic law, the denial of entry or revocation of visas of persons implicated in the commission of offences established in accordance with this Protocol.

6. Without prejudice to article 27 of the Convention, States Parties shall consider strengthening cooperation among border control agencies by, inter alia, establishing and maintaining direct channels of communication.

Article 12

Security and control of documents

Each State Party shall take such measures as may be necessary, within available means:

(a) To ensure that travel or identity documents issued by it are of such quality that they cannot easily be misused and cannot readily be falsified or unlawfully altered, replicated or issued; and

(b) To ensure the integrity and security of travel or identity documents issued by or on behalf of the State Party and to prevent their unlawful creation, issuance and use.

Article 13

Legitimacy and validity of documents

At the request of another State Party, a State Party shall, in accordance with its domestic law, verify within a reasonable time the legitimacy and validity of travel or identity documents issued or purported to have been issued in its name and suspected of being used for purposes of conduct set forth in article 6 of this Protocol.

Article 14

Training and technical cooperation

1. States Parties shall provide or strengthen specialized training for immigration and other relevant officials in preventing the conduct set forth in article 6 of this Protocol and in the humane treatment of migrants who have been the object of such conduct, while respecting their rights as set forth in this Protocol.

2. States Parties shall cooperate with each other and with competent international organizations, non-governmental organizations, other relevant organizations and other elements of civil society as appropriate to ensure that there is adequate personnel training in their territories to prevent, combat and eradicate the conduct set forth in article 6 of this Protocol and to protect the rights of migrants who have been the object of such conduct. Such training shall include:

(a) Improving the security and quality of travel documents;

(b) Recognizing and detecting fraudulent travel or identity documents;

(c) Gathering criminal intelligence, relating in particular to the identification of organized criminal groups known to be or suspected of being engaged in conduct set forth in article 6 of this Protocol, the methods used to transport smuggled migrants, the misuse of travel or identity documents for purposes of conduct set forth in article 6 and the means of concealment used in the smuggling of migrants;

(d) Improving procedures for detecting smuggled persons at conventional and non-conventional points of entry and exit; and

(e) The humane treatment of migrants and the protection of their rights as set forth in this Protocol.

3. States Parties with relevant expertise shall consider providing technical assistance to States that are frequently countries of origin or transit for persons who have been the object of conduct set forth in article 6 of this Protocol. States Parties shall make every effort to provide the necessary resources, such as vehicles, computer systems and document readers, to combat the conduct set forth in article 6.

Article 15

Other prevention measures

1. Each State Party shall take measures to ensure that it provides or strengthens information programmes to increase public awareness of the fact that the conduct set forth in article 6 of this Protocol is a criminal activity frequently perpetrated by organized criminal groups for profit and that it poses serious risks to the migrants concerned.

2. In accordance with article 31 of the Convention, States Parties shall cooperate in the field of public information for the purpose of preventing potential migrants from falling victim to organized criminal groups.

3. Each State Party shall promote or strengthen, as appropriate, development programmes and cooperation at the national, regional and international levels, taking into account the socio-economic realities of migration and paying special attention to economically and socially depressed areas, in order to combat the root socio-economic causes of the smuggling of migrants, such as poverty and underdevelopment.

Article 16

Protection and assistance measures

1. In implementing this Protocol, each State Party shall take, consistent with its obligations under international law, all appropriate measures, including legislation if necessary, to preserve and protect the rights of persons who have been the object of conduct set forth in article 6 of this Protocol as accorded under applicable international law, in particular the right to life and the right not to be subjected to torture or other cruel, inhuman or degrading treatment or punishment.

2. Each State Party shall take appropriate measures to afford migrants appropriate protection against violence that may be inflicted upon them, whether by individuals or groups, by reason of being the object of conduct set forth in article 6 of this Protocol.

3. Each State Party shall afford appropriate assistance to migrants whose lives or safety are endangered by reason of being the object of conduct set forth in article 6 of this Protocol.

4. In applying the provisions of this article, States Parties shall take into account the special needs of women and children.

5. In the case of the detention of a person who has been the object of conduct set forth in article 6 of this Protocol, each State Party shall comply with its obligations under the Vienna Convention on Consular Relations, where applicable, including that of informing the person concerned without delay about the provisions concerning notification to and communication with consular officers.

Article 17

Agreements and arrangements

States Parties shall consider the conclusion of bilateral or regional agreements or operational arrangements or understandings aimed at:

(a) Establishing the most appropriate and effective measures to prevent and combat the conduct set forth in article 6 of this Protocol; or

(b) Enhancing the provisions of this Protocol among themselves.

Article 18

Return of smuggled migrants

1. Each State Party agrees to facilitate and accept, without undue or unreasonable delay, the return of a person who has been the object of conduct set forth in article 6 of this Protocol and who is its national or who has the right of permanent residence in its territory at the time of return.

2. Each State Party shall consider the possibility of facilitating and accepting the return of a person who has been the object of conduct set forth in article 6 of this Protocol and who had the right of permanent residence in its territory at the time of entry into the receiving State in accordance with its domestic law.

3. At the request of the receiving State Party, a requested State Party shall, without undue or unreasonable delay, verify whether a person who has been the object of conduct set forth in article 6 of this Protocol is its national or has the right of permanent residence in its territory.

4. In order to facilitate the return of a person who has been the object of conduct set forth in article 6 of this Protocol and is without proper documentation, the State Party of which that person is a national or in which he or she has the right of permanent residence shall agree to issue, at the request of the receiving State Party, such travel documents or other authorization as may be necessary to enable the person to travel to and re-enter its territory.

5. Each State Party involved with the return of a person who has been the object of conduct set forth in article 6 of this Protocol shall take all appropriate measures to carry out the return in an orderly manner and with due regard for the safety and dignity of the person.

6. States Parties may cooperate with relevant international organizations in the implementation of this article.

7. This article shall be without prejudice to any right afforded to persons who have been the object of conduct set forth in article 6 of this Protocol by any domestic law of the receiving State Party.

8. This article shall not affect the obligations entered into under any other applicable treaty, bilateral or multilateral, or any other applicable operational agreement or arrangement that

governs, in whole or in part, the return of persons who have been the object of conduct set forth in article 6 of this Protocol.

IV. FINAL PROVISIONS

Article 19

Saving clause

1. Nothing in this Protocol shall affect the other rights, obligations and responsibilities of States and individuals under international law, including international humanitarian law and international human rights law and, in particular, where applicable, the 1951 Convention and the 1967 Protocol relating to the Status of Refugees and the principle of non-refoulement as contained therein.

2. The measures set forth in this Protocol shall be interpreted and applied in a way that is not discriminatory to persons on the ground that they are the object of conduct set forth in article 6 of this Protocol. The interpretation and application of those measures shall be consistent with internationally recognized principles of non-discrimination.

Article 20

Settlement of disputes

1. States Parties shall endeavour to settle disputes concerning the interpretation or application of this Protocol through negotiation.

2. Any dispute between two or more States Parties concerning the interpretation or application of this Protocol that cannot be settled through negotiation within a reasonable time shall, at the request of one of those States Parties, be submitted to arbitration. If, six months after the date of the request for arbitration, those States Parties are unable to agree on the organization of the arbitration, any one of those States Parties may refer the dispute to the International Court of Justice by request in accordance with the Statute of the Court.

3. Each State Party may, at the time of signature, ratification, acceptance or approval of or accession to this Protocol, declare that it does not consider itself bound by paragraph 2 of this article. The other States Parties shall not be bound by paragraph 2 of this article with respect to any State Party that has made such a reservation.

4. Any State Party that has made a reservation in accordance with paragraph 3 of this article may at any time withdraw that reservation by notification to the Secretary-General of the United Nations.

Article 21

Signature, ratification, acceptance, approval and accession

1. This Protocol shall be open to all States for signature from 12 to 15 December 2000 in Palermo, Italy, and thereafter at United Nations Headquarters in New York until 12 December 2002.

2. This Protocol shall also be open for signature by regional economic integration organizations provided that at least one member State of such organization has signed this Protocol in accordance with paragraph 1 of this article.

3. This Protocol is subject to ratification, acceptance or approval. Instruments of ratification, acceptance or approval shall be deposited with the Secretary-General of the United Nations. A regional economic integration organization may deposit its instrument of ratification,

acceptance or approval if at least one of its member States has done likewise. In that instrument of ratification, acceptance or approval, such organization shall declare the extent of its competence with respect to the matters governed by this Protocol. Such organization shall also inform the depositary of any relevant modification in the extent of its competence.

4. This Protocol is open for accession by any State or any regional economic integration organization of which at least one member State is a Party to this Protocol. Instruments of accession shall be deposited with the Secretary-General of the United Nations. At the time of its accession, a regional economic integration organization shall declare the extent of its competence with respect to matters governed by this Protocol. Such organization shall also inform the depositary of any relevant modification in the extent of its competence.

Article 22

Entry into force

1. This Protocol shall enter into force on the ninetieth day after the date of deposit of the fortieth instrument of ratification, acceptance, approval or accession, except that it shall not enter into force before the entry into force of the Convention. For the purpose of this paragraph, any instrument deposited by a regional economic integration organization shall not be counted as additional to those deposited by member States of such organization.

2. For each State or regional economic integration organization ratifying, accepting, approving or acceding to this Protocol after the deposit of the fortieth instrument of such action, this Protocol shall enter into force on the thirtieth day after the date of deposit by such State or organization of the relevant instrument or on the date this Protocol enters into force pursuant to paragraph 1 of this article, whichever is the later.

Article 23

Amendment

1. After the expiry of five years from the entry into force of this Protocol, a State Party to the Protocol may propose an amendment and file it with the Secretary-General of the United Nations, who shall thereupon communicate the proposed amendment to the States Parties and to the Conference of the Parties to the Convention for the purpose of considering and deciding on the proposal. The States Parties to this Protocol meeting at the Conference of the Parties shall make every effort to achieve consensus on each amendment. If all efforts at consensus have been exhausted and no agreement has been reached, the amendment shall, as a last resort, require for its adoption a two-thirds majority vote of the States Parties to this Protocol present and voting at the meeting of the Conference of the Parties.

2. Regional economic integration organizations, in matters within their competence, shall exercise their right to vote under this article with a number of votes equal to the number of their member States that are Parties to this Protocol. Such organizations shall not exercise their right to vote if their member States exercise theirs and vice versa.

3. An amendment adopted in accordance with paragraph 1 of this article is subject to ratification, acceptance or approval by States Parties.

4. An amendment adopted in accordance with paragraph 1 of this article shall enter into force in respect of a State Party ninety days after the date of the deposit with the Secretary-General of the United Nations of an instrument of ratification, acceptance or approval of such amendment.

5. When an amendment enters into force, it shall be binding on those States Parties which have expressed their consent to be bound by it. Other States Parties shall still be bound by the provisions of this Protocol and any earlier amendments that they have ratified, accepted or approved.

Article 24

Denunciation

1. A State Party may denounce this Protocol by written notification to the Secretary-General of the United Nations. Such denunciation shall become effective one year after the date of receipt of the notification by the Secretary-General.

2. A regional economic integration organization shall cease to be a Party to this Protocol when all of its member States have denounced it.

Article 25

Depositary and languages

1. The Secretary-General of the United Nations is designated depositary of this Protocol.

2. The original of this Protocol, of which the Arabic, Chinese, English, French, Russian and Spanish texts are equally authentic, shall be deposited with the Secretary-General of the United Nations.

In witness whereof, the undersigned plenipotentiaries, being duly authorized thereto by their respective Governments, have signed this Protocol.

5. INTERNATIONAL MARITIME LAW

Convention on Facilitation of International Maritime Traffic, 1965 [excerpts]*

Adoption: 9 April 1965
Entry into force: 5 March 1967
Parties: 107 (Status as of 31 December 2005)

ALBANIA 19 Dec 2005 a, ALGERIA 28 Nov 1983, ARGENTINA 29 Jan 1980, AUSTRALIA 28 Apr 1986 a, AUSTRIA 20 June 1975 a, BAHAMAS 22 July 1976 a, BANGLADESH 21 Sep 2000 a, BARBADOS 30 Sep 1982 a, BELGIUM 4 Jan 1967, BENIN 2 Mar 1992 a, BRAZIL 22 Aug 1977, BULGARIA 22 Apr 1999 a, BURUNDI 29 Sep 1998 a, CAMEROON 10 Apr 1997 a, CANADA 18 July 1967, CAPE VERDE 28 Apr 1977 a, CHILE 14 Feb 1975 a, CHINA 16 Jan 1995 a, COLOMBIA 3 June 1991 a, CONGO 7 Aug 2002 a, COTE D'IVOIRE 16 Feb 1967, CROATIA 8 Oct 1991 a, CUBA 27 Nov 1984 a, CYPRUS 9 Mar 2004 a, CZECH REPUBLIC 1 Jan 1993 a, DEMOCRATIC PEOPLE'S REPUBLIC OF KOREA 24 Apr 1992 a, DENMARK 9 Jan 1968, DOMINICA 31 Aug 2001 a, DOMINICAN REPUBLIC 11 July 1966, ECUADOR 17 May 1988, EGYPT 19 Feb 1987, ESTONIA 22 Mar 2002 a, FIJI 29 Nov 1972 a, FINLAND 20 Mar 1967, FRANCE 29 Nov 1967, GABON 12 Apr 2005 a, GAMBIA 1 Nov 1991 a, GEORGIA 25 Aug 1995 a, GERMANY 26 July 1967, GHANA 5 Nov 1965, GREECE 8 June 1972, GUINEA 19 Jan 1981 a, GUYANA 10 Dec 1997 a, HUNGARY 15 Dec 1976, ICELAND 24 Jan 1967 a, INDIA 25 May 1976 a, INDONESIA 4 Nov 2002 a, IRAN (ISLAMIC REPUBLIC OF) 27 Mar 1995 a, IRAQ 15 Nov 1976 a, IRELAND 18 June 1971, ISRAEL 13 Oct 1967, ITALY 25 Sep 1972, JAPAN 2 Sep 2005, JORDAN 27 Mar 1997 a, LATVIA 20 Jan 1998 a, LEBANON 17 July 2001, LIBERIA 14 Fev 1978 a, LIBYAN ARAB JAMAHIRIYA 28 Apr 2005 a, LITHUANIA 25 Jan 2000 a, LUXEMBOURG 14 Feb 1991 a, MADAGASCAR 8 July 1970, MALI 12 Oct 2004 a, MALTA 24 Sep 2002 a, MARSHALL ISLANDS 29 Nov 1994 a, MAURITIUS 18 June 1990 a, MEXICO 31 May 1983 a, MONACO 9 Apr 1965 a, NETHERLANDS 21 Sep 1967, NEW ZEALAND 27 July 1973 a, NIGERIA 24 Jan 1967 a, NORWAY 8 Sep 1966, PERU 16 July 1982 a, POLAND 25 July 1969, PORTUGAL 6 Aug 1990 a, REPUBLIC OF KOREA 6 Mar 2001, REPUBLIC OF SERBIA 27 Apr 1992, ROMANIA 25 Apr 2001 a, RUSSIAN FEDERATION 25 Oct 1966, SAINT KITTS AND NEVIS 7 Oct 2004 a, SAINT LUCIA 20 May 2004 a, SAMOA 18 May 2004 a, SENEGAL 17 Oct 1980, SEYCHELLES 13 Dec 1989 a, SINGAPORE 3 Apr 1967 a, SLOVAKIA 1 Jan 1993, SLOVENIA 25 June 1991, SPAIN 24 Aug 1973, SRI LANKA 6 Mar 1998 a, SURINAME 25 Nov 1975, SWEDEN 28 July 1967, SWITZERLAND 23 Apr 1968, SYRIAN ARAB REPUBLIC 6 Feb 1975 a, THAILAND 28 Nov 1991 a, TONGA 18 Sep 2003 a, TRINIDAD AND TOBAGO 16 Mar 1967, TUNISIA 27 Jan 1969 a, UKRAINE 25 Oct 1993, UNITED KINGDOM 24 Feb 1966, UNITED STATES 17 Mar 1967, URUGUAY 2 Dec 1992 a, VANUATU 13 Jan 1989 a, VENEZUELA 10 May 2002 a, YEMEN 6 Mar 1979 a, ZAMBIA 14 Dec 1965 a.

THE CONTRACTING GOVERNMENTS:

DESIRING to facilitate maritime traffic by simplifying and reducing to a minimum the formalities, documentary requirements and procedures on the arrival, stay and departure of ships engaged in international voyages;

---

* Source:http://www.admiraltylawguide.com/conven/facilitation1965.html, for more information see: www.imo.org.

HAVE AGREED as follows:

Article I

The Contracting Governments undertake to adopt, in accordance with the provisions of the present Convention and its Annex, all appropriate measures to facilitate and expedite international maritime traffic and to prevent unnecessary delays to ships and to persons and property on board.

[...]

ANNEX

[...]

SECTION 2 – ARRIVAL, STAY AND DEPARTURE OF THE SHIP

[...]

B. Contents and purpose of documents

[...]

2.7 Standard. The Passenger List shall be the basic document providing public authorities with information relating to passengers on the arrival and departure of a ship.

2.7.1 Recommended Practice. Public authorities should not require Passenger Lists on short sea routes or combined ship/railway services between neighbouring countries.

2.7.2 Recommended Practice. Public authorities should not require Embarkation or Disembarkation Cards in addition to Passenger Lists in respect of passengers whose names appear on those Lists. However, where public authorities have special problems constituting a grave danger to public health a person on an international voyage may on arrival be required to give a destination address in writing.

2.7.3 Recommended Practice. In the Passenger List public authorities should not require more than the following information:

– Name and nationality of the ship

– Family name

– Given names

– Nationality

– Date of birth

– Place of birth

– Port embarkation

– Port of disembarkation

– Port and date of arrival of the ship.

2.7.4 Recommended Practice. A list compiled by shipping companies for their own use should be accepted in place of the Passenger List, provided it contains at least the information required in accordance with Recommended Practice 2.7.3 and is dated and signed in accordance with Standard 2.7.5.

2.7.5 Standard. Public authorities shall accept a Passenger List dated and signed by the master, the ship's agent or some other person duly authorized by the master.

2.7.6 Standard. Public authorities should ensure that shipowners notify them on arrival of the presence of any stowaway discovered on board.

2.8 Standard. Public authorities shall not require on arrival or departure of the ship any written declaration in respect of mail other than that prescribed in the Universal Postal Convention.

2.9 Standard. The Maritime Declaration of Health shall be the basic document providing information required by Port Health authorities relating to the state of health on board a ship during the voyage and on arrival at a port.

[...]

H. Special measures of facilitation for ships calling at ports in order to put ashore sick or injured crew members, passengers or other persons for emergency medical treatment

2.17 Standard. Public authorities shall seek the co-operation of shipowners to ensure that, when ships intend to call at ports for the sole purpose of putting ashore sick or injured crew members, passengers or other persons for emergency medical treatment, the master shall give the public authorities as much notice as possible of that intention, with the fullest possible details of the sickness or injury and of the identity and status of the persons.

2.18 Standard. Public authorities shall by radio whenever possible, but in any case by the fastest channels available, inform the master, before the arrival of the ship, of the documentation and the procedures necessary to put the sick or injured persons ashore expeditiously and to clear the ship without delay.

2.19 Standard. With regard to ships calling at ports for this purpose and intending to leave again immediately, public authorities shall give priority in berthing if the state of the sick person or the sea conditions do not allow a safe disembarkation in the roads or harbour approaches.

2.20 Standard. With regard to ships calling at ports for this purpose and intending to leave again immediately, public authorities shall not normally require the documents mentioned in Standard 2.1 with the exception of the Maritime Declaration of Health and, if it is indispensable, the General Declaration.

2.21 Standard. Where public authorities require the General Declaration, this document shall not contain more information than that mentioned in Recommended Practice 2.2.2 and, wherever possible, shall contain less.

2.22 Standard. Where the public authorities apply control measures related to the arrival of a ship prior to sick or injured persons being put ashore, emergency medical treatment and measures for the protection of public health shall take precedence over these control measures.

2.23 Standard. Where guarantees or undertakings are required in respect of costs of treatment or eventual removal or repatriation of the persons concerned, emergency medical treatment shall not be withheld or delayed while these guarantees or undertakings are being obtained.

2.24 Standard. Emergency medical treatment and measures for the protection of public health shall take precedence over any control measures which public authorities may apply to sick or injured persons being put ashore.

SECTION 3 – ARRIVAL AND DEPARTURE OF PERSONS

This section contains the provisions concerning the formalities required by public authorities from crew and passengers on the arrival or departure of a ship.

A. Arrival and departure requirements and procedures

3.1 Standard. A valid passport shall be the basic document providing public authorities with information relating to the individual passenger on arrival or departure of a ship.

3.1.1 Recommended Practice. Contracting Governments should as far as possible agree, by bilateral or multilateral agreements, to accept official documents of identity in lieu of passports.

3.2 Recommended Practice. Public authorities should make arrangements whereby passports, or official documents of identity accepted in their place, from ship's passengers need be inspected by the immigration authorities only once at the time of arrival and once at the time of departure. In addition these passports or official documents of identity may be required to be produced for the purpose of verification or identification in connexion with customs and other formalities on arrival and departure.

3.3 Recommended Practice. After individual presentation of passports or official documents of identity accepted in their place, public authorities should hand back such documents immediately after examination rather than withholding them for the purpose of obtaining additional control, unless there is some obstacle to the admission of a passenger to the territory.

3.4 Recommended Practice. Public authorities should not require from embarking or disembarking passengers, or from shipowners on their behalf, any information in writing supplementary to or repeating that already presented in their passports or official documents of identity, other than as necessary to complete any documents provided for in this Annex.

[...]

D. Special measures of facilitation for passengers in transit

3.17.1 Standard. A passenger in transit who remains on board the ship on which he arrived and departs with it shall not normally be subjected to routine control by public authorities.

3.17.2 Recommended Practice. A passenger in transit should be allowed to retain his passport or other identity document.

3.17.3 Recommended Practice. A passenger in transit should not be required to complete a Disembarkation/Embarkation Card.

3.17.4 Recommended Practice. A passenger in transit who is continuing his journey from the same port in the same ship should normally be granted temporary permission to go ashore during the ship's stay in port if he so wishes.

3.17.5 Recommended Practice. A passenger in transit who is continuing his journey from the same port in the same ship should not be required to have a visa, except in special circumstances determined by the public authorities concerned.

3.17.6 Recommended Practice. A passenger in transit who is continuing his journey from the same port in the same ship should not normally be required to give a written Customs Declaration.

3.17.7 Recommended Practice. A passenger in transit who leaves the ship at one port and embarks in the same ship at a different port in the same country should enjoy the same facilities as a passenger who arrives and departs in the same ship at the same port.

[...]

International Convention for the Safety of Life at Sea, 1974, as amended [excerpts]*

Adoption: 1 November 1974
Entry into force: 25 May 1980
Parties: 156 (Status as of 31 December 2005)

ALBANIA 7 June 2004 a, ALGERIA 3 Nov 1983 a, ANGOLA 3 Oct 1991 a, ANTIGUA AND BARBUDA 9 Feb 1987 a, ARGENTINA 5 Dec 1979, AUSTRALIA 27 May 1983 a, AUSTRIA 27 May 1988 a, AZERBAIJAN 1 July 1997 a, BAHAMAS 16 Feb 1979 a, BAHRAIN 21 Oct 1985 a, BANGLADESH 6 Nov 1981 a, BARBADOS 1 Sep 1982 a, BELARUS 7 Jan 1994 a, BELGIUM 24 Sep 1979, BELIZE 2 Apr 1991 a, BENIN 1 Nov 1985 a, BOLIVIA 4 June 1999 a, BRAZIL 22 May 1980 a, BRUNEI DARUSSALAM 23 Oct 1986 a, BULGARIA 2 Nov 1983 a, CAMBODIA 28 Nov 1994 a, CAMEROON 14 May 1984 a, CANADA 8 May 1978 a, CAPE VERDE 28 Apr 1977 a, CHILE 28 Mar 1980, CHINA 7 Jan 1980 (*territorial), COLOMBIA 31 Oct 1980 a, COMOROS 22 Nov 2000 a, CONGO 10 Sep 1985, COOK ISLANDS 30 June 2003 a, COTE D'IVOIRE 5 Oct 1987 a, CROATIA 8 Oct 1991, CUBA 19 June 1992 a, CYPRUS 11 Oct 1985 a, CZECH REPUBLIC 1 Jan 1993, DOMINICA 21 June 2000 a, DEMOCRATIC PEOPLE'S REPUBLIC OF KOREA 1 May 1985 a, DEMOCRATIC REPUBLIC OF CONGO 17 Dec 2004 a, DENMARK 8 Mar 1978, DJIBOUTI 1 Mar 1984 a, DOMINICAN REPUBLIC 10 Apr 1980 a, ECUADOR 28 May 1982 a, EGYTPT 4 Sep 1981, EQUATORIAL GUINEA 24 Apr 1996 a, ERITREA 22 Apr 1996 a, ESTONIA 16 Dec 1991 a, ETHIOPIA 18 July 1985 a, FIJI 4 Mar 1983 a, FINLAND 21 Nov 1980 a, FRANCE 25 May 1977, GABON 21 Jan 1982 a, GAMBIA 1 Nov 1991 a, GEORGIA 19 Apr 1994 a, GERMANY 26 Mar 1979, GHANA 19 May 1983, GREECE 12 May 1980, GRENADA 28 June 2004 a, GUATEMALA 20 Oct 1982 a, GUINEA 19 Jan 1981 a, GUYANA 10 Dec 1997 a, HAITI 6 Apr 1989 a, HONDURAS 24 Sep 1985 a, HUNGARY 9 Jan 1980, ICELAND 6 July 1983, INDIA 16 June 1976 a, INDONESIA 17 Feb 1981, IRAN (ISLAMIC REPUBLIC OF) 17 Oct 1994, IRAQ 14 Dec 1990 a, IRELAND 29 Nov 1983, ISRAEL 15 May 1979, ITALY 11 June 1980 a, JAMAICA 14 Oct 1983 a, JAPAN 15 May 1980 a, JORDAN 7 Aug 1985 a, KAZAKHSTAN 7 Mar 1994 a, KENYA 21 July 1999 a, KUWAIT 29 June 1979 a, LATVIA 20 May 1992 a, LEBANON 29 Nov 1983 a, LIBERIA 14 Nov 1977, LIBYAN ARAB JAMAHIRIYA 2 July 1981 a, LITHUANIA 4 Dec 1991 a, LUXEMBOURG 14 Feb 1991 a, MADAGASCAR 7 Mar 1996 a, MALAWI 9 Mar 1993 a, MALAYSIA 19 Oct 1983 a, MALDIVES 14 Jan 1981 a, MALTA 8 Aug 1986 a, MARSHALL ISLANDS 26 Apr 1988 a, MAURITANIA 24 Nov 1997 a, MAURITIUS 1 Feb 1988 a, MEXICO 28 Mar 1977, MOLDOVA 11 Oct 2005 a, MONACO 1 Nov 1974, MONGOLIA 26 June 2002 a, MOROCCO 28 June 1990 a, MOZAMBIQUE 23 Dec 1996 a, MYANMAR 11 Nov 1987 a, NAMIBIA 27 Nov 2000 a, NETHERLANDS 10 July 1978 a (* territorial), NEW ZEALAND 23 Feb 1990 a (*territorial), NICARAGUA 17 Dec 2004 a, NIGERIA 7 May 1981 a, NORWAY 15 Feb 1977, OMAN 25 Apr 1985 a, PAKISTAN 10 Apr 1985 a, PANAMA 9 Mar 1978 a, PAPUA NEW GUINEA 12 Nov 1980 a, PARAGUAY 15 June 2004 a, PERU 4 Dec 1979 a, PHILIPPINES 15 Dec 1981 a, POLAND 15 Mar 1984, PORTUGAL 7 Nov 1983, QUATAR 22 Dec 1980 a, REPUBLIC OF KOREA 31 Dec 1980 a, ROMANIA 24 May 1979 a, RUSSIAN FEDERATION 9 Jan 1980, SAINT KITTS AND NEVIS 11 June 2004 a, SAINT LUCIA 20 May 2004 a, SAINT VINCENT AND THE GRENADINES 28 Oct 1983 a, SAMOA 14 Mar 1997 a, SAO TOME AND PRINCIPE

* Source: http://www.austlii.edu.au/au/other/dfat/treaties/1983/22.html
Amendments by IMO Res. MSC.153 (78), adopted on 20 May 2004 (see: MSC 78/26/Add.1). The amendments entered into force on 1 July 2006. For more information, see: www.imo.org.

29 Oct 1998 a, SAUDI ARABIA 24 Apr 1985 a, SENEGAL 16 Jan 1997 a, REPUBLIC OF SERBIA 27 Apr 1992 a, SEYCHELLES 10 May 1998 a, SIERRA LEONE 13 Aug 1993 a, SINGAPORE 16 Mar 1981 a, SLOVAKIA 1 Jan 1993 a, SLOVENIA 25 June 1991 a, SOLOMON ISLANDS 30 June 2004 a, SOUTH AFRICA 23 May 1980 a, SPAIN 5 Sep 1978, SRI LANKA 30 Aug 1983 a, SUDAN 15 May 1990 a, SURINAME 4 Nov 1988 a, SWEDEN 7 July 1978, SWITZERLAND 1 Oct 1981, SYRIAN ARAB REPUBLIC 20 July 2001 a, THAILAND 18 Dec 1984 a, TOGO 19 July 1989 a, TONGA 12 Apr 1977 a, TRINIDAD AND TOBAGO 15 Feb 1979 a, TUNISIA 6 Aug 1980 a, TURKEY 31 July 1980 a, TUVALU 22 Aug 1985 a, UKRAINE 1 Nov 1974, UNITED ARAB EMIRATES 15 Dec 1983 a, UNITED KINGDOM 7 Oct 1977 (*territorial), UNITED REPUBLIC OF TANZANIA 28 Mar 2001 a, UNITED STATES 7 Sep 1978, URUGUAY 30 Apr 1979 a, VANUATU 28 July 1982 a, VENEZUELA 29 Mar 1983 a, VIETNAM 18 Dec 1990 a, YEMEN 6 Mar 1979 a.

[...]

Article IV

Cases of *force majeure*

[...]

b) Persons who are on board a ship by reason of *force majeure* or in consequence of the obligation laid upon the master to carry shipwrecked or other persons shall not be taken into account for the purpose of ascertaining the application to a ship of any provisions of the present Convention.

Article V

Carriage of persons in emergencies

(a) For the purpose of evacuating persons in order to avoid a threat to the security of their lives a Contracting Government may permit the carriage of a larger number of persons in its ships than is otherwise permissible under the present Convention.

(b) Such permission shall not deprive other Contracting Governments of any right of control under the present Convention over such ships which come within their ports.

(c) Notice of any such permission, together with a statement of the circumstances, shall be sent to the Secretary-General of the Organization by the Contracting Government granting such permission.

[...]

ANNEX

[...]

CHAPTER V

SAFETY OF NAVIGATION

[...]

Regulation 2

Definitions

For the purpose of this chapter:

[...]

5. *Search and rescue service.* The performance of distress monitoring, communication, co-ordination and search and rescue functions, including provisions of medical advice, initial medical assistance, or medical evacuation, through the use of public and private resources including co-operating aircraft, ships, vessels and other craft and installations.

[...]

Regulation 7

Search and rescue services

1. Each Contracting Government undertakes to ensure that necessary arrangements are made for distress communication and co-ordination in their area of responsibility and for the rescue of persons in distress at sea around its coasts. These arrangements shall include the establishment, operation and maintenance of such search and rescue facilities as are deemed practicable and necessary, having regard to the density of the seagoing traffic and the navigational dangers, and shall, so far as possible, provide adequate means of locating and rescuing such persons.[1]

[...]

Regulation 33

Distress situations - obligations and procedures

1. The master of a ship at sea, which is in a position to be able to provide assistance, on receiving information from any source that persons are in distress at sea, is bound to proceed with all speed to the assistance, if possible informing them or the search and rescue service that the ship is doing so. If the ship receiving the distress alert is unable or, in the special circumstances of the case, considers it unreasonable or unnecessary to proceed to their assistance, the master must enter in the log-book the reason for failing to proceed to the assistance of the persons in distress, taking into account the recommendation of the Organization to inform the appropriate search and rescue service accordingly. This obligation to provide assistance applies regardless of the nationality or status of such persons or the circumstances in which they are found.

1-1. Contracting Governments shall co-ordinate and co-operate to ensure that masters of ships providing assistance by embarking persons in distress at sea are released from their obligations with minimum further deviation from the ships' intended voyage, provided that releasing the master of the ship from the obligations under the current regulation does not further endanger the safety of life at sea. The Contracting Government responsible for the search and rescue region in which such assistance is rendered shall exercise primary responsibility for ensuring such co-ordination and co-operation occurs, so that survivors assisted are disembarked from the assisting ship and delivered to a place of safety, taking into account the particular circumstances of the case and guidelines developed by the Organization. In these cases the relevant Contracting Governments shall arrange for such disembarkation to be effected as soon as reasonably practicable.

2. The master of a ship in distress or the search and rescue service concerned, after consultation, so far as may be possible, with the masters of ships which answer the distress alert, has the

[1] Refer to the International Convention on Maritime Search and Rescue (SAR), 1979, and to the following resolutions adopted by the Organization: Homing capability of search and rescue (SAR) aircraft (resolution A.225 (VII)), Use of radar transponders for search and rescue purposes (resolution A.530 (13)), Search and rescue homing capability (resolution A.616 (15)) and International Aeronautical and Maritime Search and Rescue (IAMSAR) Manual (resolution A.894 (21)).

right to requisition such one or more of those ships as the master of the ship in distress or the search and rescue service considers best able to render assistance, and it shall be the duty of the master or masters of the ship or ships requisitioned to comply with the requisition by continuing to proceed with all speed to the assistance of persons in distress.

3. Masters of ships shall be released from the obligation imposed by paragraph 1 on learning that their ships have not been requisitioned and that one or more other ships have been requisitioned and are complying with the requisition. This decision shall, if possible, be communicated to the other requisitioned ships and to the search and rescue service.

4. The master of a ship shall be released from the obligation imposed by paragraph 1 and, if his ship has been requisitioned, from the obligation imposed by paragraph 2 on being informed by the persons in distress or by the search and rescue service or by the master of another ship which has reached such persons that assistance is no longer necessary.

5. The provisions of this Regulation do not prejudice the Convention for the Unification of Certain Rules of Law relating to Assistance and Salvage at Sea, signed at Brussels on 23 September 1910, particularly the obligation to render assistance imposed by Article 11 of that Convention.[2]

6. Masters of ships who have embarked persons in distress at sea shall treat them with humanity, within the capabilities and limitations of the ship.

[...]

Regulation 34 -1

Master's discretion

The owner, charterer, the company operating the ship as defined in regulation IX71, or any other person shall not prevent or restrict the master of the ship from taking or executing any decision which, in the master's professional judgement, is necessary for safety of life at sea and protection of the marine environment.

[...]

[2] International Convention on Salvage, 1989, done at London on 28 April 1989, entered into force on 14 July 1996.

International Convention on Maritime Search and Rescue, 1979, as amended [excerpts]*

Adoption: 27 April 1979
Entry into force: 22 June 1985
Parties: 88 (Status as of 31 December 2005)

ALBANIA 19 June 2003 a, ALGERIA 5 Jan 1983 a, ANGOLA 4 Oct 2001 a, ARGENTINA 18 May 1981 a, AUSTRALIA 7 Nov 1983 a, BARBADOS 25 July 1983 a, BELGIUM 28 Feb 1985 a, BRAZIL 22 Sep 1982, BULGARIA 8 July 1999 a, CAMEROON 9 Jan 1987 a, CANADA 18 June 1982 a, CAPE VERDE 4 July 2003 a, CHILE 7 Oct 1981, CHINA 24 June 1985 (* territorial), COLOMBIA 10 July 2001 a, CONGO 7 Aug 2002 a, COTE D'IVOIRE 5 Oct 1987 a, CROATIA 12 Jan 1998 a, CUBA 16 July 1998 a, CYPRUS 29 July 1994 a, DENMARK 21 June 1984, DOMINICA 31 Aug 2001 a, ECUADOR 17 May 1988 a, ESTONIA 30 Apr 2001 a, FINLAND 6 Nov 1986 a, FRANCE 9 Apr 1980, GAMBIA 1 Nov 1991 a, GEORGIA 25 Aug 1995 a, GERMANY 21 Jan 1982, GREECE 4 Sep 1989 a, HUNGARY 27 Jan 2000 a, ICELAND 21 Mar 1995 a, INDIA 17 Apr 2001 a, IRAN (ISLAMIC REPUBLIC OF) 26 Sep 1995 a, IRELAND 1 Nov 1993 a, ITALY 2 June 1989 a, JAMAICA 10 June 1988 a, JAPAN 10 June 1985 a, KENYA 15 Ded 1992 a, LATVIA 30 Nov 1998 a, LIBYAN ARAB JAMAHIRIYA 28 Arp 2005 a, LITHUANIA 23 Jan 2001 a, LUXEMBOURG 14 Feb 1991 a, MALTA 24 Sep 2002 a, MAURITIUS 4 May 1999 a, MEXICO 26 Mar 1986 a, MONACO 19 Nov 1991 a, MOROCCO 10 May 1999 a, MOZAMBIQUE 23 Dec 1996 a, NAMIBIA 12 Mar 2004 a, NETHERLANDS 8 July 1982, NEW ZEALAND 26 Apr 1985 a (*territorial), NIGERIA 24 May 2002 a, NORWAY 9 Dec 1981, OMAN 17 May 1993 a, PAKISTAN 11 Nov 1985 a, PAPUA NEW GUINEA 3 Aug 1992 a, PERU 4 July 1988 a, POLAND 26 Feb 1988, PORTUGAL 30 Oct 1985 a, REPUBLIC OF KOREA 4 Sep 1995 a, ROMANIA 19 Mar 1999 a, RUSSIAN FEDERATION 25 Mar 1988, SAINT KITTS AND NEVIS 7 Oct 2004 a, SAINT LUCIA 20 May 2004 a, SAMOA 18 May 2004 a, SENEGAL 24 Mar 1994 a, REPUBLIC OF SERBIA 20 Jan 1997 a, SINGAPORE 20 Jan 1997 a, SLOVENIA 31 May 2001 a, SOUTH AFRICA 25 Aug 1987 a, SPAIN 11 Feb 1993 a, SWEDEN 27 Sep 1982 a, SYRIAN ARAB REPUBLIC 18 June 2003 a, TONGA 18 Sept 2003 a, TRINIDAD AND TOBAGO 4 May 1989 a, TUNISIA 31 July 1998 a, TURKEY 21 Nov 1985, UKRAINE 5 Mar 1993 a, UNITED ARAB EMIRATES 4 Oct 1993 a, UNITED KINGDOM 22 May 1980 (*territorial), UNITED STATES 12 Aug 1980, URUGUAY 15 Dec 1987 a, VANUATU 14 Sep 1992 a, VENEZUELA 8 July 1986 a.

[...]

ANNEX

[...]

CHAPTER 2

ORGANIZATION

2.1 Arrangements for provision and co-ordination of search and rescue services

* Source: http://www.admiraltylawguide.com/conven/searchrescue1979.html
Amendments by IMO Res. 155 (78), adopted on 20 May 2004 (see: MSC 78/26 Add.1). The amendments entered into force on 1 July 2006. For more information, see: www.imo.org.

2.1.1 Parties shall ensure that necessary arrangements are made for the provision of adequate search and rescue services for persons in distress at sea round their coasts. The notion of a person in distress at sea also includes persons in need of assistance who have found refuge on a coast in a remote location within an ocean area inaccessible to any rescue facility other than as provided for in the annex.

[…]

2.1.7 The delimitation of search and rescue regions is not related to and shall not prejudice the delimitation of any boundary between States.

[…]

2.1.10 Parties shall ensure that assistance be provided to any person in distress at sea. They shall do so regardless of the nationality or status of such a person or the circumstances in which that person is found.

[…]

CHAPTER 3

CO-OPERATION

3.1 Co-operation between States

3.1.1 Parties shall co-ordinate their search and rescue organizations and should, whenever necessary, co-ordinate search and rescue operations with those of neighbouring States.

3.1.2 Unless otherwise agreed between the States concerned, a Party should authorize, subject to applicable national laws, rules and regulations, immediate entry into or over its territorial sea or territory of rescue units of other Parties solely for the purpose of searching for the position of maritime casualties and rescuing the survivors of such casualties. In such cases, search and rescue operations shall, as far as practicable, be co-ordinated by the appropriate rescue co-ordination centre of the Party which has authorized entry, or such other authority as has been designated by that Party.

[…]

3.1.9 Parties shall co-ordinate and co-operate to ensure that masters of ships providing assistance by embarking persons in distress at sea are released from their obligations with minimum further deviation from the ships′ intended voyage, provided that releasing the master of the ship from these obligations does not further endanger the safety of life at sea. The Party responsible for the search and rescue region in which such assistance is rendered shall exercise primary responsibility for ensuring such co-ordination and co-operation occurs, so that survivors assisted are disembarked from the assisting ship and delivered to a place of safety, taking into account the particular circumstances of the case and guidelines developed by the Organization. In these cases, the relevant Parties shall arrange for such disembarkation to be effected as soon as reasonably practicable.

United Nations Convention on the Law of the Sea, 1982 [excerpts]*

Adoption: 10 December 1982
Entry into Force: 16 November 1994
Parties: 153 (Status as of 1 April 2007)

ALBANIA 25 Jun 2003 a, ALGERIA 11 Jun 1996 (*3, 287, general), ANGOLA 5 Dec 1990 (*general), ANTIGUA AND BARBUDA 2 Feb 1989, ARGENTINA 1 Dec 1995 (*general, territorial), ARMENIA 9 Dec 2002 a, AUSTRALIA 5 Oct 1994 (*287, 298), AUSTRIA 14 Jul 1995 (*287, general), BAHAMAS 29 Jul 1983, BAHRAIN 30 Mar 1985, BANGLADESH 27 Jul 2001 (*general), BARBADOS 12 Oct 1993, BELARUS 30 Aug 2006 (*287, 292, general), BELGIUM 13 Nov 1998 (*general), BELIZE 13 Aug 1983, BENIN 16 Oct 1997, BOLIVIA 38 Apr 1995 (*general), BOSNIA AND HERZEGOVINA 12 Jan 1994 s, BOTSWANA 2 May 1990, BRAZIL 22 Dec 1988 (*general), BRUNEI AND DARUSSALAM 5 Nov 1996, BULGARIA 15 May 1996, BURKINA FASO 25 Jan 2005, CAMEROON 19 Nov 1985, CANADA 7 Nov 2003 (*general), CAPE VERDE 10 Aug 1987 (*general), CHILE 25 Aug 1997 (*general), CHINA 7 Jun 1996 (*territorial, general), COMOROS 21 Jun 1994, COOK ISLANDS 15 Feb 1995, COSTA RICA 21 Sep 1992 (*general), COTE D'IVOIRE 26 Mar 1984, CROATIA 5 Apr 1995 s (*general), CUBA 15 Aug 1984 (*general), CYPRUS 12 Dec 1988, CZECH REPUBLIC 21 Jun 1996, DEMOCRATIC REPUBLIC OF THE CONGO 17 Feb 1989, DEMOCRATIC PEOPLE'S REPUBLIC OF KOREA signed 10 Dec 1982, DENMARK 16 Nov 2004 (*general), DJIBOUTI 8 Oct 19991, DOMINICA 24 Oct 1991, DOMINICAN REPUBLIC signed 10 Dec 1982, EGYPT 26 Aug 1983 (*general), EQUATORIAL GUINEA 21 Jul 1997 (*general), ESTONIA 26 Aug 2005 a (*general), EUROPEAN COMMUNITY 1 Apr 1998 (*general), FIJI 10 Dec 1982, FINLAND 21 Jun 1996 (*general), FRANCE 11 Apr 1996 (*general), GABON 11 Mar 1998, GAMBIA 11 May 1984, GEORGIA 22 May 1984, GERMANY 14 Oct 1994 a (*general), GHANA 7 Jun 1983, GREECE 21 Jul 1995 (*general), GRENADA 25 Apr 1991, GUATEMALA 11 Feb 1997 (*territorial, general), GUINEA 6 Sep 1985 (*general), GUINEA-BISSAU 25 Aug 1986 (*general), GUYANA 16 Nov 1993, HAITI 31 Jul 1996, HONDURAS 5 Oct 1993 (*general), HUNGARY 5 Feb 2002 (*general), ICELAND 21 Jun 1985 (*general), INDIA 29 Jun 1995 (*general), INDONESIA 3 Feb 1986, IRAN (ISLAMIC REPUBLIC OF) (*general, territorial), IRAQ 30 Jul 1985 (*general), IRELAND 21 Jun 1996 (*general), ITALY 13 Jan 1995 (*general), JAMAICA 21 Mar 1983, JAPAN 20 Jun 1996, JORDAN 27 Nov 1995 a, KENYA 2 Mar 1989, KIRIBATI 24 Feb 2003 a (*general), KUWAIT 2 May 1986 (*general), LAO PEOPLE'S DEMOCRATIC REPUBLIC 5 Jun 1998, LATVIA 23 Dec 2004 a (*general), LEBANON 5 Jan 1995, LESOTHO signed 10 Dec 1982, LIBERIA signed 10 Dec 1982, LIBYAN ARAB JAMAHIRIYA signed 3 Dec 1984, LIECHTENSTEIN signed 30 Nov 1984, LITHUANIA 12 Nov 2003 a (*general), LUXEMBOURG 5 Oct 2000 (*general), MADAGASCAR 22 Aug 2001, MALAWI signed 7 Dec 1984, MALAYSIA 14 Oct 1996 (*general), MALDIVES 7 Sep 2000, MALI 16 Jul 1985, MALTA 20 May 1993 (*general), MARSHALL ISLANDS 9 Aug 1991 a, MAURITANIA 17 Jul 1996, MAURITIUS 4 Nov 1994, MEXICO 18 Mar 1983 (*general), MICRONESIA (FEDERATED STATES OF) 29 Apr 1991 a, MOLDOVA 6 Feb 2007 a, MONACO 20 Mar 1996, MONGOLIA 13 Aug 1996, MONTENEGRO 23 Oct 2006 d, MOROCCO signed 10 Dec 1982, MOZAMBIQUE 13 Mar 1997, MYANMAR 21 May 1996, NAMIBIA 18 Apr 1983, NAURU 23 Jan 1996, NEPAL 2 Nov 1998, NETHERLANDS 28 Jun 1996 (*general), NEW ZEALAND 19 Jul 1996, NICARAGUA 3 May 2000 (*general), NIGER signed 10 Dec 1982, NIGERIA 14 Aug 1986, NIUE 11 Oct 2006, NORWAY 24 Jun 1996 (*general), OMAN

* Source: 1833 U.N.T.S. 3.

17 Aug 1989 (*general, territorial), PAKISTAN 26 Feb 1997 (*general, territorial), PALAU 30 Sep 1996 a (*general), PANAMA 1 Jul 1996 (*general), PAPUA NEW GUINEA 14 Jan 1997, PARAGUAY 26 Sep 1986, PHILIPPINES 8 May 1984 (*general), POLAND 13 Nov 1998, PORTUGAL 3 Nov 1997 (*general), QATAR 9 Dec 2002, REPUBLIC OF KOREA 29 Jan 1996 (*general), ROMANIA 17 Dec 1996 (*general), RUSSIAN FEDERATION 12 Mar 1997 (*general), RWANDA signed 10 Dec 1982, SAINT KITTS AND NEVIS 7 Jan 1993, SAINT LUCIA 27 Mar 1985, SAINT VINCENT AND THE GRENADINES 1 Oct 1993, SAMOA 14 Aug 1995, SAO TOME AND PRINCIPE 3 Nov 1987 (*general), SAUDI ARABIA 24 Apr 1996 (*general), SENEGAL 25 Oct 1984, SERBIA 12 Mar 2001 s (*general), SEYCHELLES 16 Sep 1991, SIERRA LEONE 12 Dec 1994, SINGAPORE 17 Nov 1994, SLOVAKIA 8 May 1996, SLOVENIA 16 Jun 1995 s (*general), SOLOMON ISLANDS 23 Jun 1997, SOMALIA 24 Jul 1989, SOUTH AFRICA 23 Dec 1997 (*general), SPAIN 15 Jan 1997 (*general), SRI LANKA 19 Jul 1994, SUDAN 23 Jan 1985 (*general), SURINAME 9 Jul 1998, SWAZILAND signed 18 Jan 1984, SWEDEN 25 Jun 1996 (*general), SWITZERLAND signed 17 Oct 1984, THAILAND signed 10 Dec 1982, THE FORMER YUGOSLAV REPUBLIC OF MACEDONIA 19 Aug 1994 s, TOGO 16 Apr 1985, TONGA 2 Aug 1995 s, TRINIDAD AND TOBAGO 25 Apr 1986, TUNISIA 24 Apr 1985 (*general), TUVALU 9 Dec 2002, UGANDA 9 Nov 1990, UKRAINE 26 Jul 1999 (*general), UNITED ARAB EMIRATES signed 10 Dec 1982, UNITED KINGDOM OF GREAT BRITAIN AND NORTHERN IRELAND 25 Jul 1997 a (*general, territorial), UNITED REPUBLIC OF TANZANIA 30 Sep 1985 (*general), URUGUAY 10 Dec 1992 (*general), VANUATU 10 Aug 1999, VIET NAM 25 Jul 1994 (*general), YEMEN 21 Jul 1987 (*general), ZAMBIA 7 Mar 1983, ZIMBABWE 24 Feb 1983.

[…]

PART II

TERRITORIAL SEA AND CONTIGUOUS ZONE

[…]

SECTION 3. INNOCENT PASSAGE IN THE TERRITORIAL SEA

SUBSECTION A. RULES APPLICABLE TO ALL SHIPS

Article 17

Right of innocent passage

Subject to this Convention, ships of all States, whether coastal or land-locked, enjoy the right of innocent passage through the territorial sea.

Article 18

Meaning of passage

1. Passage means navigation through the territorial sea for the purpose of:

(a) traversing that sea without entering internal waters or calling at a roadstead or port facility outside internal waters; or

(b) proceeding to or from internal waters or a call at such roadstead or port facility.

2. Passage shall be continuous and expeditious. However, passage includes stopping and anchoring, but only in so far as the same are incidental to ordinary navigation or are rendered

necessary by force majeure or distress or for the purpose of rendering assistance to persons, ships or aircraft in danger or distress.

Article 19

Meaning of innocent passage

1. Passage is innocent so long as it is not prejudicial to the peace, good order or security of the coastal State. Such passage shall take place in conformity with this Convention and with other rules of international law.

2. Passage of a foreign ship shall be considered to be prejudicial to the peace, good order or security of the coastal State if in the territorial sea it engages in any of the following activities:

[...]

(g) the loading or unloading of any commodity, currency or person contrary to the customs, fiscal, immigration or sanitary laws and regulations of the coastal State;

[...]

Article 21

Laws and regulations of the coastal State relating to innocent passage

1. The coastal State may adopt laws and regulations, in conformity with the provisions of this Convention and other rules of international law, relating to innocent passage through the territorial sea, in respect of all or any of the following:

[...]

(h) the prevention of infringement of the customs, fiscal, immigration or sanitary laws and regulations of the coastal State.

[...]

SECTION 4. CONTIGUOUS ZONE

Article 33

Contiguous zone

1. In a zone contiguous to its territorial sea, described as the contiguous zone, the coastal State may exercise the control necessary to:

(a) prevent infringement of its customs, fiscal, immigration or sanitary laws and regulations within its territory or territorial sea;

(b) punish infringement of the above laws and regulations committed within its territory or territorial sea.

2. The contiguous zone may not extend beyond 24 nautical miles from the baselines from which the breadth of the territorial sea is measured.

PART III

STRAITS USED FOR INTERNATIONAL NAVIGATION

[...]

SECTION 2. TRANSIT PASSAGE

[...]

Article 42

Laws and regulations of States bordering straits relating to transit passage

1. Subject to the provisions of this section, States bordering straits may adopt laws and regulations relating to transit passage through straits, in respect of all or any of the following:

[...]

(d) the loading or unloading of any commodity, currency or person in contravention of the customs, fiscal, immigration or sanitary laws and regulations of States bordering straits.

[...]

PART V

EXCLUSIVE ECONOMIC ZONE

[...]

Article 60

Artificial islands, installations and structures in the exclusive economic zone

1. In the exclusive economic zone, the coastal State shall have the exclusive right to construct and to authorize and regulate the construction, operation and use of:

(a) artificial islands;

(b) installations and structures for the purposes provided for in article 56 and other economic purposes;

(c) installations and structures which may interfere with the exercise of the rights of the coastal State in the zone.

2. The coastal State shall have exclusive jurisdiction over such artificial islands, installations and structures, including jurisdiction with regard to customs, fiscal, health, safety and immigration laws and regulations.

[...]

Guidelines on the Allocation of Responsibilities to Seek the Successful Resolution of Stowaways Cases, 1997 [excerpts] *

Adoption: 27 November 1997

[...]

ANNEX

1 Masters, shipowners[1], port authorities, national administrations, and other bodies including security operators all have a responsibility to cooperate to prevent illegal access to a vessel while it is in port. However, no matter how effective routine port and ship security is, there will still be occasions when stowaways gain access to vessels, either secreted in the cargo or by surreptitious boarding.

2 For the purposes of the Guidelines a stowaway is defined as a person who is secreted on a ship, or in cargo which is subsequently loaded on the ship, without the consent of the shipowner or the master or any other responsible person, and who is detected on board after the ship has departed from a port and reported as a stowaway by the master to the appropriate authorities.

3 The resolution of stowaway cases is difficult because of different national legislation in each of the potentially several countries involved: the country of embarkation, the country of disembarkation, the flag State of the vessel, the country of apparent, claimed or actual nationality/citizenship of the stowaway, and countries of transit during repatriation.

4 There are, however, some basic principles which can be applied generally. These are as follows:

.1 A recognition that stowaways arriving at or entering a country without the required documents are, in general, illegal entrants. Decisions on dealing with such situations are the prerogative of the countries where such arrival or entry occurs.

.2 Stowaway asylum-seekers should be treated in compliance with international protection principles as set out in international instruments[2] and relevant national legislation.

.3 The shipowner and his representative on the spot, the master, as well as port authorities and national administrations, should cooperate as far as possible in dealing with stowaway cases.

.4 Shipowners and their representatives on the spot, masters, port authorities and national administrations should have security arrangements in place which, as far as practicable, will prevent intending stowaways from getting aboard a ship or, if this fails, will detect them before a ship arrives at port. Where national legislation permits, national authorities should consider prosecution of stowaways for trespassing upon or damaging the property of the shipping company, or the cargo.

.5 All Parties should be aware that an adequate search may minimize the risk of having to deal with a stowaway case and may also save the life of a stowaway who may, for example, be hiding in a place which is subsequently sealed and/or chemically treated.

* Source: www.marisec.org, IMO Resolution A.871(20). For more information, see: www.imo.org.

[1] Including any persons or party acting on behalf of the owner of the vessel.

[2] Reference is made to the provisions of the United Nations Convention relating to the Status of Refugees of 28 July 1951 and of the United Nations Protocol relating to the Status of Refugees of 31 January 1967.

.6 Countries should admit returned stowaways with full nationality/citizenship status of that country or a right of residence.

.7 The country of the original port of embarkation of a stowaway should normally accept the return of such a stowaway for examination pending final case disposition.

.8 Every effort should be made to avoid situations where a stowaway has to be detained on board a ship indefinitely. In this regard countries should co-operate with the shipowner in arranging the return of a stowaway to an appropriate country.

.9 Stowaway incidents should be dealt with humanely by all parties involved. Due consideration must always be given to the operational safety of the ship and to the well-being of the stowaway.

5 As a first step in addressing the issue, a framework of the various responsibilities, rights and liabilities of the parties involved needs to be identified and agreed. The following allocation of responsibility is suggested:

.1 The master

.1.1 to make every effort to determine immediately the port of embarkation of the stowaway;

.1.2 to make every effort to establish the identity, including the nationality/citizenship of the stowaway;

.1.3 to prepare a statement containing all information relevant to the stowaway, in accordance with information specified in the standard document annexed to these Guidelines, for presentation to the appropriate authorities;

.1.4 to notify the existence of a stowaway and any relevant details to his shipowner and appropriate authorities at the port of embarkation, the next port of call and the flag State;

.1.5 not to depart from his planned voyage to seek the disembarkation of a stowaway to any country unless repatriation has been arranged with sufficient documentation and permission given for disembarkation, or unless there are extenuating security or compassionate reasons;

.1.6 to ensure that the stowaway is presented to the appropriate authorities at the next port of call in accordance with their requirements;

.1.7 to take appropriate measures to ensure the security, general health, welfare and safety of the stowaway until disembarkation;

.2 The shipowner or operator

.2.1 to ensure that the existence of, and any relevant information on, the stowaway has been notified to the appropriate authorities at the port of embarkation, the next port of call and the flag State;

.2.2 to comply with any removal directions made by the competent national authorities at the port of disembarkation;

.3 Country of first scheduled port of call after discovery of the stowaway (port of disembarkation)

.3.1 to accept the stowaway for examination in accordance with the national laws of that country and, where the competent national authority considers that it would facilitate matters, to allow the shipowner and his named representative and the competent or appointed P&I Club correspondent to have access to the stowaway;

.3.2 to consider allowing disembarkation and provide, as necessary and in accordance with national law, secure accommodation which may be at the expense of the shipowner or agents, where:

.3.2.1 a case under.3.1 is unresolved at the time of sailing, or

.3.2.2 national authorities are satisfied that arrangements have been made and will be effected for the early return or repatriation of the stowaway by other means (which may be at the expense of the shipowner or agents), or

.3.2.3 a stowaway's presence on board would endanger the safe operation of the vessel;

.3.3 to assist, as necessary, in the identification of the stowaway and the establishment of his or her nationality/citizenship;

.3.4 to assist, as necessary, in establishing the validity and authenticity of a stowaway's documents;

.3.5 to give directions for the removal of the stowaway to the port of embarkation, country of nationality/citizenship or to some other country to which lawful directions may be made, in co-operation with the shipowner and his nominated representative;

.3.6 in co-operation with the shipowner and his and his nominated representatives to discuss repatriation or removal arrangements or directions with the master/shipowner or their appointed representatives, keeping them informed, as far as practicable, of the level of detention costs, while keeping these to a minimum;

.3.7 to consider mitigation of charges that might otherwise be applicable when shipowners have cooperated with the control authorities to the satisfaction of those authorities in measures designed to prevent the transportation of stowaways;

.3.8 to issue, if necessary, in the event that the stowaway has no identification and/or travel documents, a document attesting to the circumstances of embarkation and arrival to enable the return of the stowaway either to his country of origin, to the country of the port of embarkation, or to any other country to which lawful directions can be made, by any means of transport;

.3.9 to band over the document to the transport operator effecting the removal of the stowaway;

.3.10 to take proper account of the interests of, and implications for, the shipowner or agent when directing detention and setting removal directions, so far as is consistent with the maintenance of control, their duties or obligations to the stowaway under the law, and the cost to public funds.

.4 The country of the original port of embarkation of the stowaway (i.e. the country where the stowaway first boarded the ship)

.4.1 to accept any returned stowaway having nationality/citizenship or right of residence;

.4.2 to accept, in normal circumstances, a stowaway back for examination where the port of embarkation is identified to the satisfaction of the authorities of the receiving country;

.4.3 to apprehend and detain the stowaway, where permitted by national legislation, if the stowaway is discovered before sailing either on the vessel or in cargo due to be loaded; to refer the intended stowaway to local authorities for prosecution, and/or, where applicable, to the immigration authorities for examination and possible removal: no charge to be imposed on the shipowner in respect of detention or removal costs, and no penalty to be imposed;

.4.4 to apprehend and detain the stowaway, where permitted by national legislation, if the stowaway is discovered while the vessel is still in the territorial waters of the country of the port of his embarkation, or in another port in the same country (not having called at a port in another country in the meantime) no charge to be imposed on the shipowner in respect of detention or removal costs, and no penalty to be imposed.

.5 The apparent or claimed country of nationality/citizenship of the stowaway

.5.1 to make every effort to assist in determining the identity and nationality/citizenship of the stowaway and to document the stowaway, accordingly once satisfied that he or she holds the nationality/citizenship claimed;

.5.2 to accept the stowaway where nationality/citizenship is established.

.6 The flag State of the vessel

.6.1 to be willing, if practicable, to assist the master/shipowner or the appropriate authority at the port of disembarkation in identifying the stowaway and determining his or her nationality/citizenship;

.6.2 to be prepared to make representations to the relevant authority to assist in the removal of the stowaway from the vessel at the first available opportunity;

.6.3 to be prepared to assist the master/shipowner or the authority at the port of disembarkation in making arrangements for the removal or repatriation of the stowaway.

.7 Any countries of transit during repatriation

to allow, subject to normal visa requirements, the transit through their ports and airports of stowaways travelling under the removal instructions or directions of the country of the port of disembarkation.

[...]

Interim Measures for Combating Unsafe Practices Associated with the Trafficking or Transport of Migrants by Sea, 1998 (Revised, 2001)*

Adoption: 11 December 1998

1. The Maritime Safety Committee, at its sixty-ninth session (11 to 20 May 1998), being concerned about the unsafe practices associated with the trafficking or transport of migrants by sea and recalling resolution A. 867 (20) on Combating unsafe practices associated with the trafficking or transport of migrants by sea, in particular operative paragraph 6 thereof, established a correspondence group to prepare Interim Measures for combating unsafe practices associated with the trafficking or transport of migrants by sea, which were eventually considered and approved by the Committee, at its seventieth session (7 to 11 December 1998) and disseminated by means of MSC/Circ.896.

2. To prevent and suppress unsafe practices associated with the trafficking or transport of migrants by sea, the Committee invited Member Governments to promptly convey to the Organization reports on relevant incidents and the measures taken, to enable the updating or revising of that circular, as necessary.

3. The Committee, at its seventy-third session (27 November to 6 December 2000), established a biannual reporting procedure; instructed the Secretariat to issue biannual reports (MSC.3/Circ. series); and urged Governments and international organizations to promptly communicate all unsafe practices associated with the trafficking or transport of migrants by sea.

4. The Committee, at its seventy-fourth session (30 May to 8 June 2001), in the light of reports recorded and proposals made by Governments, approved amendments to the annex to MSC/Circ.896, the revised text of which is given at annex.

5. The use of the report format given in the Appendix to the annex is recommended for conveying information for the purposes mentioned in paragraphs 12, 15 and 22 of the Interim Measures.

6. Member Governments are invited to bring this circular and annex to the attention of all parties concerned.

7. The circular will be further revised in the light of the consideration of incident reports received by IMO and further submission by Member Governments, following the adoption, in December 2000, of the Convention against transnational organized crime, developed by the United Nations Commission on Crime Prevention and Criminal Justice together with the Protocol against smuggling of migrants by land, sea and air.

***

ANNEX

INTERIM MEASURES FOR COMBATING UNSAFE PRACTICES ASSOCIATED WITH THE TRAFFICKING OR TRANSPORT OF MIGRANTS BY SEA

1. Pending entry into force of a Convention against transnational organized crime including trafficking in migrants this circular provides interim, non-binding measures for the prevention and suppression of unsafe practices associated with the trafficking or transport of migrants by sea.

* Source: IMO Doc. MSC/Circ.896/Rev.1, dated 12 June 2001; for more information, see: www.imo.org.

Definitions

2. For purposes of this circular:

2.1. "Ship" means every description of water craft, including non-displacement craft and seaplanes, used or capable of being used as a means of transportation on water, except a warship, naval auxiliary, or other ship owned or operated by a Government and used, for the time being, only on government non-commercial service;

2.2. "Organization" means the International Maritime Organization; and

2.3. "unsafe practices" means any practice which involves operating a ship that is:

.1. obviously in conditions which violate fundamental principles of safety at sea, in particular those of the SOLAS Convention; or

.2. not properly manned, equipped or licensed for carrying passengers on international voyages, and thereby constitute a serious danger for the lives or the health of the persons on board, including the conditions for embarkation and disembarkation.

Purpose

3. The purpose of this circular is to promote awareness and co-operation among Contracting Governments of the Organization so that they may address more effectively unsafe practices associated with the trafficking or transport of migrants by sea which have an international dimension.

Recommended actions by States

Compliance with international obligations.

4. Experience has shown that migrants often are transported on ships that are not properly manned, equipped or licensed for carrying passengers on international voyages. States should take steps relating to maritime safety, in accordance with domestic and international law, to eliminate these unsafe practices associated with the trafficking or transport of migrants by sea, including:

.1. ensuring compliance with the International Convention for the Safety of Life at Sea, 1974, as amended (SOLAS)[1];

.2. collecting and disseminating information on ships believed to be engaged in unsafe practices associated with trafficking or transporting migrants;

.3. taking appropriate action against masters, officers and crew members engaged in such unsafe practices; and

---

[1] It is recalled that:
– regulation 1 of chapter I of SOLAS Convention provides that SOLAS applies to ships engaged on international voyages;
– regulation 2 of the same chapter defines as:
international voyage, a voyage from a country to which the present Convention applies to a port outside such country, or conversely.
passenger ship, a ship which carries more than twelve passengers.
cargo ship, any ship which is not a passenger ship.

The trafficking of migrants will normally constitute an international voyage. When this practice occurs on board cargo ships, multiple infringements of the SOLAS Convention are therefore committed.

.4. preventing any such ship:

.1. from again engaging in unsafe practices; and

.2. if in port, from sailing.

5. Measures taken, adopted or implemented pursuant to this circular to combat unsafe practices associated with the trafficking or transport of migrants by sea should be in conformity with the international law of the sea and all generally accepted relevant international instruments, such as the United Nations 1951 Convention and the 1967 Protocol Relating to the Status of Refugees.

6. States should take, adopt or implement such measures in conformity with international law with due regard to:

.1. the authority of the flag State to exercise jurisdiction and control in administrative, technical and social matters involving the ship; and

.2. the rights and obligations of the coastal State.

7. If any measures are taken against any ship suspected of unsafe practices associated with trafficking or transport of migrants by sea, the State concerned should take into account the need not to endanger the safety of human life at sea and the security of the ship and the cargo, or to prejudice the commercial and/or legal interests of the flag State or any other interested State.

Co-operation.

8. States should co-operate to the fullest extent possible to prevent and suppress unsafe practices associated with the trafficking or transport of migrants by sea, in conformity with the international law of the sea and all generally accepted relevant international instruments. It is consistent with international law for a flag State to authorize a vessel flying its flag to be boarded and inspected by a warship of another State, as described in paragraphs 12 and 20 below.

9. States should consider entering into bilateral or regional agreements to facilitate co-operation in applying appropriate, efficient and effective measures to prevent and suppress unsafe practices associated with the trafficking or transport of migrants by sea.

10. States should also encourage the conclusion of operational arrangements in relation to specific cases.

Measures and Procedures.

11. A State, which has reasonable grounds to suspect that a ship which:

.1. is flying its flag or claiming its registry, or

.2. is without nationality, or

.3. though flying a foreign flag or refusing to show its flag is, in reality, of the same nationality as the State concerned, is engaged in unsafe practices associated with the trafficking or transport of migrants by sea, may request the assistance of other States in suppressing its use for that purpose. The States so requested should render such assistance as is reasonable under these circumstances.

12. A State which has reasonable grounds to suspect that a ship exercising freedom of navigation in accordance with international law and flying the flag or displaying marks of

registry of another State is engaged in unsafe practices associated with the trafficking or transport of migrants by sea may so notify the flag State, request confirmation of registry and, if confirmed[2], request authorization from the flag State to take appropriate measures in regard to that ship. The flag State may authorize the requesting State to, inter alia:

.1. board the ship;

.2. inspect and carry out a safety examination of the ship, and

.3. if evidence is found that the ship is engaged in unsafe practices, take appropriate action with respect to the ship, persons and cargo on board, as authorized by the flag State.

A State which has taken any action in accordance with this paragraph should promptly inform the flag State concerned of the results of that action.

13. A flag State may, consistent with paragraph 8, subject its authorization to conditions to be mutually agreed between it and the requesting State, including conditions relating to responsibility and to the extent of effective measures to be taken including the use of force. A State shall take no additional actions without the express authorization of the flag State, except those necessary to relieve imminent danger or those that follow from relevant bilateral or multilateral agreements.

14. A State should respond expeditiously to a request from another State to determine whether a ship that is claiming its registry or flying its flag is entitled to do so, and to a request for authorization made pursuant to paragraph 12.

15. When a ship is found engaged in unsafe practices associated with the trafficking or transport of migrants by sea, States should:

.1. immediately report the findings of the safety examinations conducted pursuant to paragraph 12 to the administration of the State whose flag the ship is entitled to fly or in which it is registered; and

.2. immediately consult on the further actions to be taken after giving or receiving reports on the ship involved.

16. When there are reasonable grounds to suspect that a ship is engaged in unsafe practices associated with trafficking or transport of migrants by sea and it is concluded in accordance with the international law of the sea that the ship is without nationality, or has been assimilated to a ship without nationality, States should conduct a safety examination of the ship, as necessary. If the results of the safety examination indicate that the ship is engaged in unsafe practices, States should take appropriate measures in accordance with relevant domestic and international law.

17. When evidence exists that a ship is engaged in unsafe practices associated with the trafficking or transport of migrants by sea, States, in taking action pursuant to paragraphs 12 or 16, should:

.1 ensure the safety and the humanitarian handling of the persons on board and that any actions taken with regard to the ship are environmentally sound; and

.2 take appropriate action in accordance with relevant domestic and international law.

18. States should take required steps, in accordance with international law including SOLAS regulation I/19(c), to ensure that a ship involved in unsafe practices associated with the

[2] If registry is refuted, the situation is that described in paragraph 11.2 above.

trafficking or transport of migrants by sea does not sail until it can proceed to sea without endangering the ship or persons on board, and to report promptly to the State whose flag the ship is entitled to fly, or in which it is registered, all incidents concerning such unsafe practices which come to their attention.

19. Contracting Governments to SOLAS 1974, as amended, should ensure that, when a request is received to transfer a ship to their flag or registry, the requirements listed in regulation I/14(g)(ii) are met, and appropriate inspections and surveys are conducted to ensure the ship will be used for the service specified in the certificates issued in accordance with chapter I of the 1974 SOLAS Convention.

20. Any action taken at sea pursuant to this circular shall be carried out only by warships or military aircraft, or other ships or aircraft clearly marked and identifiable as being on government service and authorized to that effect.

21. Each State should designate an authority or, where necessary, authorities to receive reports of unsafe practices, and to respond to requests for assistance, confirmation of registry or right to fly its flag and authorization to take appropriate measures.

22. Notwithstanding paragraph 20, ships providing assistance to persons in distress at sea, as required by the international law of the sea including SOLAS regulation V/10, and ships providing assistance in accordance with this circular, should not be considered as engaging in unsafe practices associated with the trafficking or transport of migrants by sea.

Reports

23. To prevent and suppress unsafe practices associated with trafficking or transport of migrants by sea, reports on incidents and the measures taken should be provided to the Organization by States concerned as soon as possible. This information will be used for the purpose of updating or revising this circular, as necessary.

24. Use of the report form given in the Appendix is recommended for conveying information for the purposes mentioned in paragraphs 12, 15 and 22.

Guidelines on the Treatment of Persons Rescued at Sea, 2004*

Adoption: 20 May 2004

The Maritime Safety Committee,

Recalling Article 28(b) of the Convention on the International Maritime Organization concerning the functions of the Committee,

Noting resolution A.920(22) entitled "Review of safety measures and procedures for the treatment of persons rescued at sea",

Recalling also the provisions of the International Convention for the Safety of Life at Sea (SOLAS), 1974, as amended relating to the obligation of:

- shipmasters to proceed with all speed to the assistance of persons in distress at sea; and

- Governments to ensure arrangements for coast watching and for the rescue of persons in distress at sea round their coasts,

Recalling further the provisions of the International Convention on Maritime Search and Rescue (SAR), 1979, as amended relating to the provision of assistance to any person in distress at sea regardless of the nationality or status of such person or the circumstances in which that person is found,

Noting also article 98 of the United Nations Convention on the Law of the Sea, 1982, regarding the duty to render assistance,

Noting further the initiative taken by the Secretary-General to involve competent United Nations specialized agencies and programmes in the consideration of the issues addressed in this resolution, for the purpose of agreeing on a common approach which will resolve them in an efficient and consistent manner,

Realizing the need for clarification of existing procedures to guarantee that persons rescued at sea will be provided a place of safety regardless of their nationality, status or the circumstances in which they are found,

Having adopted, as its [seventy-eighth session], by resolution MSC.153(78) amendments to the SOLAS Convention, proposed and circulated in accordance with article VIII(b)(i) thereof, and by resolution MSC.155(78) amendments to the SAR Convention proposed and circulated in accordance with article III(2)(a) thereof,

Realizing further that the intent of the new paragraph 1-1 of SOLAS regulation V/33, as adopted by resolution MSC.153(78) and paragraph 3.1.9 of the Annex to the SAR Convention as adopted by resolution MSC.155(78), is to ensure that in every case a place of safety is provided within a reasonable time. It is further intended that the responsibility to provide a place of safety, or to ensure that a place of safety is provided, falls on the Contracting Government/Party responsible for the SAR region in which the survivors were recovered,

1. ADOPTS Guidelines on the treatment of persons rescued at sea the text of which is set out in the Annex to the present resolution;

2. INVITES Governments, rescue co-ordination centres and masters to establish procedures consistent with the annexed Guidelines as soon as possible;

* Source: IMO Doc. MSC 78/26/Add.2, Annex 34; for more information, see: www.imo.org.

3. INVITES Governments to bring the annexed Guidelines to the attention of authorities concerned and to ship owners, operators and masters;

4. REQUESTS the Secretary-General to take appropriate action in further pursuing his inter-agency initiative, informing the Maritime Safety Committee of developments, in particular with respect to procedures to assist in the provision of places of safety for persons in distress at sea, for action as the Committee may deem appropriate;

5. DECIDES to keep this resolution under review.

ANNEX

GUIDELINES ON THE TREATMENT OF PERSONS RESCUED AT SEA

1 PURPOSE

1.1 The purpose of these Guidelines are to provide guidance to Governments[1] and to shipmasters with regard to humanitarian obligations and obligations under the relevant international law relating to treatment of persons rescued at sea.

1.2 The obligation of the master to render assistance should complement the corresponding obligation of IMO Member Governments to co-ordinate and co-operate in relieving the master of the responsibility to provide follow up care of survivors and to deliver the persons retrieved at sea to a place of safety. These Guidelines are intended to help Governments and masters better understand their obligations under international law and provide helpful guidance with regard to carrying out these obligations.

2 BACKGROUND

IMO Assembly resolution A.920(22)

2.1 The IMO Assembly, at its twenty-second session, adopted resolution A.920(22) on the review of safety measures and procedures for the treatment of persons rescued at sea. That resolution requested various IMO bodies to review selected IMO Conventions to identify any gaps, inconsistencies, ambiguities, vagueness or other inadequacies associated with the treatment of persons rescued at sea. The objectives were to help ensure that:

.1 survivors of distress incidents are provided assistance regardless of nationality or status or the circumstances in which they are found;

.2 ships, which have retrieved persons in distress at sea, are able to deliver the survivors to a place of safety; and

.3 survivors, regardless of nationality or status, including undocumented migrants, asylum seekers and refugees, and stowaways, are treated, while on board, in the manner prescribed in the relevant IMO instruments and in accordance with relevant international agreements and long-standing humanitarian maritime traditions.

2.2 Pursuant to resolution A.920(22), the Secretary-General brought the issue of persons rescued at sea to the attention of a number of competent United Nations specialized agencies and programmes highlighting the need for a co-ordinated approach among United Nations

[1] Where the term Government is used in these Guidelines, it should be read to mean Contracting Government to the International Convention for the Safety of Life at Sea (SOLAS), 1974, as amended, or Party to the International Convention on Maritime Search and Rescue, 1979, as amended, respectively.

agencies, and soliciting the input of relevant agencies within the scope of their respective mandates. Such an inter-agency effort focusing on State responsibilities for non-rescue issues, such as immigration and asylum that are beyond the competence of IMO, is an essential complement to IMO efforts.

SOLAS and SAR Convention amendments

2.3 At its seventy-eighth session, the Maritime Safety Committee (MSC) adopted pertinent amendments to chapter V of the International Convention for the Safety of Life at Sea (SOLAS) and to chapters 2, 3 and 4 of the Annex to the International Convention on Maritime Search and Rescue Convention (SAR Convention). These amendments are expected to enter into force on 1 July 2006. At the same session the MSC adopted the current guidelines; these amendments provide for the development of such guidelines. The purpose of these amendments and the current guidelines is to help ensure that persons in distress are assisted, while minimizing the inconvenience to assisting ships and ensuring the continued integrity of SAR services.

2.4 Specifically, paragraph 1-1 of SOLAS regulation V/33 and paragraph 3.1.9 of the Annex to the SAR Convention, as amended, impose upon Governments an obligation to co-ordinate and co-operate to ensure that masters of ships providing assistance by embarking persons in distress at sea are released from their obligations with minimum further deviation from the ship's intended voyage.

2.5 As realized by the MSC in adopting the amendments, the intent of new paragraph 1-1 of SOLAS regulation V/33 and paragraph 3.1.9 of the Annex to the International Convention on Maritime Search and Rescue, 1979, as amended, is to ensure that in every case a place of safety is provided within a reasonable time. The responsibility to provide a place of safety, or to ensure that a place of safety is provided, falls on the Government responsible for the SAR region in which the survivors were recovered.

2.6 Each case, however, can involve different circumstances. These amendments give the responsible Government the flexibility to address each situation on a case-by-case basis, while assuring that the masters of ships providing assistance are relieved of their responsibility within a reasonable time and with as little impact on the ship as possible.

2.7 Some comments on relevant international law are set out at the appendix.

3 PRIORITIES

3.1 When ships assist persons in distress at sea, co-ordination will be needed among all concerned to ensure that all of the following priorities are met in a manner that takes due account of border control, sovereignty and security concerns consistent with international law:

Lifesaving

All persons in distress at sea should be assisted without delay. Preservation of the integrity and effectiveness of SAR services Prompt assistance provided by ships at sea is an essential element of global SAR services; therefore it must remain a top priority for shipmasters, shipping companies and flag States.

Relieving masters of obligations after assisting persons

Flag and coastal States should have effective arrangements in place for timely assistance to shipmasters in relieving them of persons recovered by ships at sea.

4 INTERNATIONAL AERONAUTICAL AND MARITIME SEARCH AND RESCUE MANUAL

4.1 The three-volume *International Aeronautical and Maritime Search and Rescue Manual* (IAMSAR Manual) has been developed and is maintained to assist Governments in meeting their SAR needs, and the obligations they have accepted under the SOLAS Convention, the SAR Convention and the Convention on International Civil Aviation. Governments are encouraged to develop and improve their SAR services, co operate with neighbouring States and to consider SAR services to be part of a global system.

4.2 Each volume of the IAMSAR Manual is written with specific SAR system duties in mind and can be used as a stand-alone document, or, in conjunction with the other guidance documents, as a means to attain a full view of the SAR system.

4.3 Volume I – *Organization and Management* discusses the global SAR system concept, establishment of national and regional SAR systems and co-operation with neighbouring States to provide effective and economical SAR services.

4.4 Volume II – *Mission Co-ordination* assists personnel who plan and co-ordinate SAR operations and exercises.

4.5 Volume III – *Mobile Facilities* – is intended to be carried aboard ships, aircraft and rescue units to help with performance of search, rescue or on-scene co-ordinator functions and with aspects of SAR that pertain to their own emergencies.

5 SHIPMASTERS

General guidance

5.1 SAR services throughout the world depend on ships at sea to assist persons in distress. It is impossible to arrange SAR services that depend totally upon dedicated shore-based rescue units to provide timely assistance to all persons in distress at sea. Shipmasters have certain duties that must be carried out in order to provide for safety of life at sea, preserve the integrity of global SAR services of which they are part, and to comply with humanitarian and legal obligations. In this regard, shipmasters should:

.1 understand and heed obligations under international law to assist persons in distress at sea (such assistance should always be carried out without regard to the nationality or status of the persons in distress, or to the circumstances in which they are found);

.2 do everything possible, within the capabilities and limitations of the ship, to treat the survivors humanely and to meet their immediate needs;

.3 carry out SAR duties in accordance with the provisions of Volume III of the IAMSAR Manual;

.4 in a case where the RCC responsible for the area where the survivors are recovered cannot be contacted, attempt to contact another RCC, or if that is impractical, any other Government authority that may be able to assist, while recognizing that responsibility still rests with the RCC of the area in which the survivors are recovered;

.5 keep the RCC informed about conditions, assistance needed, and actions taken or planned for the survivors (see paragraph 6.10 regarding other information the RCC may wish to obtain);

.6 seek to ensure that survivors are not disembarked to a place where their safety would be further jeopardized; and

.7 comply with any relevant requirements of the Government responsible for the SAR region where the survivors were recovered, or of another responding coastal State, and seek additional guidance from those authorities where difficulties arise in complying with such requirements.

5.2 In order to more effectively contribute to safety of life at sea, ships are urged to participate in ship reporting systems established for the purpose of facilitating SAR operations.

6 GOVERNMENTS AND RESCUE CO-ORDINATION CENTRES

Responsibilities and preparedness

6.1 Governments should ensure that their respective rescue co-ordination centres (RCCs) and other national authorities concerned have sufficient guidance and authority to fulfil their duties consistent with their treaty obligations and the current guidelines contained in this resolution.

6.2 Governments should ensure that their RCCs and rescue units are operating in accordance with the standards and procedures in the IAMSAR Manual and that all ships operating under their flag have on board Volume III of the IAMSAR Manual.

6.3 A ship should not be subject to undue delay, financial burden or other related difficulties after assisting persons at sea; therefore coastal States should relieve the ship as soon as practicable.

6.4 Normally, any SAR co-ordination that takes place between an assisting ship and any coastal State(s) should be handled via the responsible RCC. States may delegate to their respective RCCs the authority to handle such co-ordination on a 24-hour basis, or may task other national authorities to promptly assist the RCC with these duties. RCCs should be prepared to act quickly on their own, or have processes in place, as necessary, to involve other authorities, so that timely decisions can be reached with regard to handling survivors.

6.5 Each RCC should have effective plans of operation and arrangements (interagency or international plans and agreements if appropriate) in place for responding to all types of SAR situations. Such plans and arrangements should cover incidents that occur within its associated SAR region, and should also cover incidents outside its own SAR region if necessary until the RCC responsible for the region in which assistance is being rendered (see paragraph 6.7) or another RCC better situated to handle the case accept responsibility. These plans and arrangements should cover how the RCC could co-ordinate:

.1 a recovery operation;

.2 disembarkation of survivors from a ship;

.3 delivery of survivors to a place of safety; and

.4 its efforts with other entities (such as customs and immigration authorities, or the ship owner or flag State), should non-SAR issues arise while survivors are still aboard the assisting ship with regard to nationalities, status or circumstances of the survivors; and quickly address initial border control or immigration issues to minimize delays that might negatively impact the assisting ship, including temporary provisions for hosting survivors while such issues are being resolved.

6.6 Plans of operation, liaison activities and communications arrangements should provide for proper co-ordination in advance of and during a rescue operation with shipping companies and with national or international authorities that may need to be involved in response or disembarkation efforts.

6.7 When appropriate, the first RCC contacted should immediately begin efforts to transfer the case to the RCC responsible for the region in which the assistance is being rendered. When the RCC responsible for the SAR region in which assistance is needed is informed about the situation, that RCC should immediately accept responsibility for co-ordinating the rescue efforts, since related responsibilities, including arrangements for a place of safety for survivors, fall primarily on the Government responsible for that region. The first RCC, however, is responsible for co-ordinating the case until the responsible RCC or other competent authority assumes responsibility.

6.8 Governments and the responsible RCC should make every effort to minimize the time survivors remain aboard the assisting ship.

6.9 Responsible State authorities should make every effort to expedite arrangements to disembark survivors from the ship; however, the master should understand that in some cases necessary co-ordination may result in unavoidable delays.

6.10 The RCC should seek to obtain the following information from the master of the assisting ship:

.1 information about the survivors, including name, age, gender, apparent health and medical condition and any special medical needs;

.2 the master's judgment about the continuing safety of the assisting ship;

.3 actions completed or intended to be taken by the master;

.4 assisting ship's current endurance with the additional persons on board;

.5 assisting ship's next intended port of call;

.6 the master's preferred arrangements for disembarking the survivors;

.7 any help that the assisting ship may need during or after the recovery operation; and

.8 any special factors (e.g., prevailing weather, time sensitive cargo).

6.11 Potential health and safety concerns aboard a ship that has recovered persons in distress include insufficient lifesaving equipment, water, provisions, medical care, and accommodations for the number of persons on board, and the safety of the crew and passengers if persons on board might become aggressive or violent. In some cases it may be advisable for the RCC to arrange for SAR or other personnel to visit the assisting ship to better assess the situation onboard, to help meet needs on board, or to facilitate safe and secure disembarkation of the survivors.

Place of safety

6.12 A place of safety (as referred to in the Annex to the 1979 SAR Convention, paragraph 1.3.2) is a location where rescue operations are considered to terminate. It is also a place where the survivors' safety of life is no longer threatened and where their basic human needs (such as food, shelter and medical needs) can be met. Further, it is a place from which transportation arrangements can be made for the survivors' next or final destination.

6.13 An assisting ship should not be considered a place of safety based solely on the fact that the survivors are no longer in immediate danger once aboard the ship. An assisting ship may not have appropriate facilities and equipment to sustain additional persons on board without endangering its own safety or to properly care for the survivors. Even if the ship is capable of safely accommodating the survivors and may serve as a temporary place of safety, it should be relieved of this responsibility as soon as alternative arrangements can be made.

6.14 A place of safety may be on land, or it may be aboard a rescue unit or other suitable vessel or facility at sea that can serve as a place of safety until the survivors are disembarked to their next destination.

6.15 The Conventions, as amended, indicate that delivery to a place of safety should take into account the particular circumstances of the case. These circumstances may include factors such as the situation on board the assisting ship, on scene conditions, medical needs, and availability of transportation or other rescue units. Each case is unique, and selection of a place of safety may need to account for a variety of important factors.

6.16 Governments should co-operate with each other with regard to providing suitable places of safety for survivors after considering relevant factors and risks.

6.17 The need to avoid disembarkation in territories where the lives and freedoms of those alleging a well-founded fear of persecution would be threatened is a consideration in the case of asylum-seekers and refugees recovered at sea.

6.18 Often the assisting ship or another ship may be able to transport the survivors to a place of safety. However, if performing this function would be a hardship for the ship, RCCs should attempt to arrange use of other reasonable alternatives for this purpose.

Non-SAR considerations

6.19 If survivor status or other non-SAR matters need to be resolved, the appropriate authorities can often handle these matters once the survivors have been delivered to a place of safety. Until then, RCCs are responsible for co-operation with any national or international authorities or others involved in the situation. Examples of non-SAR considerations that may require attention include oil spills, onscene investigations, salvage, survivors who are migrants or asylum seekers, needs of survivors once they have been delivered to a place of safety, or security or law enforcement concerns. National authorities other than the RCC typically have primary responsibility for such efforts.

6.20 Any operations and procedures such as screening and status assessment of rescued persons that go beyond rendering assistance to persons in distress should not be allowed to hinder the provision of such assistance or unduly delay disembarkation of survivors from the assisting ship(s).

6.21 Although issues other than rescue relating to asylum seekers, refugees and migratory status are beyond the remit of IMO, and beyond the scope of the SOLAS and SAR Conventions, Governments should be aware of assistance that international organizations or authorities of other countries might be able to provide in such cases, be able to contact them rapidly, and provide any instructions that their RCCs may need in this regard, including how to alert and involve appropriate national authorities. States should ensure that their response mechanisms are sufficiently broad to account for the full range of State responsibilities.

6.22 Authorities responsible for such matters may request that RCCs obtain from the assisting ship certain information about a ship or other vessel in distress, or certain information about the persons assisted. Relevant national authorities should also be made aware of what they need to do to co-operate with the RCC (especially with regard to contacting ships), and to respond as a matter of urgency to situations involving assisted persons aboard ships.

APPENDIX

SOME COMMENTS ON RELEVANT INTERNATIONAL LAW

1 A shipmaster's obligation to render assistance at sea is a longstanding maritime tradition. It is an obligation that is recognized by international law. Article 98 of the United Nations Convention on the Law of the Sea, 1982 (UNCLOS) codifies this obligation in that every "State shall require the master of a ship flying its flag, in so far as he can do so without serious danger to the ship, the crew, or the passengers... to render assistance to any person found at sea in danger of being lost …". in addition to imposing an obligation on States to "promote the establishment, operation and maintenance of an adequate and effective search and rescue service regarding safety on and over the sea …".

2 The SAR Convention defines rescue as "an operation to retrieve persons in distress, provide for their initial medical or other needs, and deliver them to a place of safety." SAR services are defined as "the performance of distress monitoring, communication, co-ordination and search and rescue functions, including provision of medical advice, initial medical assistance, or medical evacuation, through the use of public and private resources including co-operating aircraft, vessels and other craft and installations." SAR services include making arrangements for disembarkation of survivors from assisting ships. The SAR Convention establishes the principle that States delegate to their rescue co-ordination centres (RCCs) the responsibility and authority to be the main point of contact for ships, rescue units, other RCCs, and other authorities for co-ordination of SAR operations. The SAR Convention also discusses, with regard to obligations of States, the need for making arrangements for SAR services, establishment of RCCs, international co-operation, RCC operating procedures, and use of ship reporting systems for SAR.

3 The SAR Convention does not define "place of safety". However, it would be inconsistent with the intent of the SAR Convention to define a place of safety solely by reference to geographical location. For example, a place of safety may not necessarily be on land. Rather, a place of safety should be determined by reference to its characteristics and by what it can provide for the survivors. It is a location where the rescue operation is considered to terminate. It is also a place where the survivors' safety of life is no longer threatened and where their basic human needs (such as food, shelter and medical needs) can be met. Further, it is a place from which transportation arrangements can be made for the survivors' next or final destination.

4 The SOLAS Convention regulation V/33.1 provides that the "master of a ship at sea which is in a position to be able to provide assistance, on receiving information from any source that persons are in distress at sea, is bound to proceed with all speed to their assistance, if possible informing them or the search and rescue service that the ship is doing so." Comparable obligations are contained in other international instruments. Nothing in these guidelines is intended in any way to affect those obligations. Compliance with this obligation is essential in order to preserve the integrity of search and rescue services. The SOLAS Convention, Article IV (cases of force majeure) protects the shipmaster insofar as the existence of persons on board the ship by reason of force majeure or due to the obligation for the master to carry shipwrecked or other persons, will not be a basis for determining application of the Convention's provisions to the ship. The SOLAS Convention also addresses in chapter V, regulation 7, the responsibility of Governments to arrange rescue services.

5 As a general principle of international law, a State's sovereignty allows that State to control its borders, to exclude aliens from its territory and to prescribe laws governing the entry of aliens into its territory. A State's sovereignty extends beyond its land territory and internal waters to the territorial sea, subject to the provisions of UNCLOS and other rules of

international law. Further, as provided in Article 21 of UNCLOS, a coastal State may adopt laws and regulations relating to innocent passage in the territorial sea to prevent, among other things, the infringement of that coastal State's immigration laws.

6 Pursuant to Article 18 of UNCLOS, a ship exercising innocent passage may stop or anchor in the coastal State's territorial sea "only in so far as the same are incidental to ordinary navigation or are rendered by force majeure or distress or for the purpose of rendering assistance to persons, ships or aircraft in danger or distress." UNCLOS does not specifically address the question of whether there exists a right to enter a port in cases of distress, although under customary international law, there may be a universal, albeit not absolute, right for a ship in distress to enter a port or harbour when there exists a clear threat to safety of persons aboard the ship. Such threats often worsen with time and immediate port entry is needed to ensure the safety of the vessel and those onboard. Nevertheless, the right of the ship in distress to enter a port involves a balancing of the nature and immediacy of the threat to the ship's safety against the risks to the port that such entry may pose. Thus, a coastal State might refuse access to its ports where the ship poses a serious and unacceptable safety, environmental, health or security threat to that coastal State after the safety of persons onboard is assured.

7 The Refugee Convention's prohibition of expulsion or return "refoulement" contained in Article 33.1 prohibits Contracting States from expelling or returning a refugee to the frontiers of territories where his or her life or freedom would be threatened on account of the person's race, religion, nationality, membership of a particular social group or political opinion. Other relevant international law also contains prohibition on return to a place where there are substantial grounds for believing that the person would be in danger of being subjected to torture.

8 Other relevant provisions, not all of which are under the competence of IMO, inter alia, include the following:

International Convention on Maritime Search and Rescue, 1979, as amended, in entirety

International Convention for the Safety of Life at Sea, 1974, as amended, chapter V, regulation 33

Convention on Facilitation of International Maritime Traffic, 1965, in particular Section 6.C, Standards 6.8-6.10

International Convention on Salvage, 1983, Article 11

United Nations Convention on the Law of the Sea, 1982, Article 98

Resolution A.773(18) on Enhancement of safety of life at sea by the prevention and suppression of unsafe practices associated with alien smuggling by ships

Resolution A.871(20) on Guidelines on the allocation of responsibilities to seek the successful resolution of stowaway cases

Resolution A.867(20) on Combating unsafe practices associated with the trafficking or transport of migrants by sea

IMO Global SAR Plan – SAR.8/Circ.1 and addenda addresses (the Admiralty List of Radio Signals, Volume 5, is a practical alternative)

United Nations Convention relating to the Status of Refugees, 1951 and its 1967 Protocol UN Convention against Transnational Organized Crime, 2000 and its Protocols, Protocol against the smuggling of migrants by land, sea and air; and Protocol to Prevent, Suppress and Punish Trafficking in Persons, Especially Women and Children.

MSC/Circ.896/Rev.1 on Interim measures for combating unsafe practices associated with the trafficking or transport of immigrants by sea

IMO Interim Measures for Combating Unsafe Practices Associated with the Trafficking or Transport of Migrants by Sea, 2001 (See section 4.2)

Convention for the Suppression of Unlawful Acts against the Safety of Maritime Navigation, 1988 (See section 6)

6. STATE SECURITY

Convention on International Civil Aviation, 1944 [excerpts]*

Adoption: 7 December 1944
Entry into force: 4 April 1947
Parties: 190 (Status as of 1 April 2007)

AFGHANISTAN 28 Mar 1991 a, ALGERIA 7 May 1963 a, ANDORRA 26 Jan 2001, ANGOLA 11 Mar 1977 a, ANTIGUA AND BARBUDA 10 Nov 1981 a, ARGENTINA 4 Jun 1946 a, ARMENIA 18 Jun 1946 a, AUSTRALIA 1 Mar 1947, AUSTRIA 27 Aug 1948, AZERBAIJAN 9 Oct 1992 a, BAHAMAS 27 May 1975 a, BAHRAIN 20 Aug 1971 a, BANGLADESH 22 Dec 1972 a, BARBADOS 21 Mar 1967 a, BELARUS 4 Jun 1993 a, BELGIUM 5 May 1947, BELIZE 7 Dec 1990 a, BENIN 29 May 1961 a, BHUTAN 17 May 1989 a BOLIVIA 4 Apr 1947, BOSNIA AND HERZEGOVINA 13 Jan 1993 a, BOTSWANA 28 Dec 1978 a, BRAZIL 8 Jul 1946, BRUNEI DARUSSALAM 4 Dec 1984 a, BULGARIA 8 Jun 1967 a, BURKINA FASO 21 Mar 1962 a, BURUNDI 19 Jan 1968 a, CAMBODIA 16 Jan 1956 a, CAMEROON 15 Jan 1960 a, CANADA 13 Feb 1946, CAPE VERDE 19 Aug 1976 a, CENTRAL AFRICAN REPUBLIC 28 Jun 1961 a, CHAD 3 Jul 1962 a, CHILE 11 Mar 1947, CHINA 20 Feb 1946, COLOMBIA 31 Oct 1947, COMOROS 15 Jan 1985 a, CONGO 26 Apr 1962 a, COOK ISLANDS 20 Aug 1986 a, COSTA RICA 1 May 1958, CÔTE D'IVOIRE 31 Oct 1960 a, CROATIA 9 Apr 1992 a, CUBA 11 May 1949, CYPRUS 17 Jan 1961 a, CZECH REPUBLIC 4 Mar 1993 a, DEMOCRATIC PEOPLE'S REPUBLIC OF KOREA 16 Aug 1977 a, DEMOCRATIC REPUBLIC OF THE CONGO 27 Jul 1961 a, DENMARK 28 Feb 1947, DJIBOUTI 30 Jun 1978 a, DOMINICAN REPUBLIC 25 Jan 1946, ECUADOR 20 Aug 1954, EGYPT 13 Mar 1947, EL SALVADOR 11 Jun 1947, EQUATORIAL GUINEA 22 Feb 1972 a, ERITREA 17 Sep 1993 a, ESTONIA 24 Jan 1992 a, ETHIOPIA 1 Mar 1947, FIJI 5 Mar 1973 a, FINLAND 30 Mar 1949 a, FRANCE 25 Mar 1947, GABON 18 Jan 1962 a, GAMBIA 13 May 1977 a, GEORGIA 21 Jan 1994 a, GERMANY 9 May 1956 a, GHANA 9 May 1957 a, GREECE 13 Mar 1947, GRENADA 31 Aug 1981 a, GUATEMALA 28 Apr 1947, GUINEA 27 Mar 1959 a, GUINEA-BISSAU 15 Dec 1977 a, GUYUNA 3 Feb 1967 a, HAITI 25 Mar 1948, HONDURAS 7 May 1953, HUNGARY 30 Sep 1969 a, ICELAND 21 Mar 1947, INDIA 1 Mar 1947, INDONESIA 27 Apr 1950 a, IRAN (ISLAMIC REPUBLIC OF) 19 Apr 1950, IRAQ 2 Jun 1947, IRELAND 31 Oct 1946, ISRAEL 24 May 1949 a, ITALY 31 Oct 1947 a, JAMAICA 26 Mar 1963 a, JAPAN 8 Sep 1953 a, JORDAN 18 Mar 1947 a, KAZAKHSTAN 21 Aug 1992 a, KENYA 1 May 1964 a, KIRIBATI 14 Apr 1981 a, KUWAIT 18 May 1960 a, KYRGYZSTAN 25 Feb 1993 a, LAO PEOPLE'S DEMOCRATIC REPUBLIC 13 Jun 1955 a, LATVIA 13 Jul 1992 a, LEBANON 19 Sep 1949, LESOTHO 19 May 1975 a, LIBERIA 11 Feb 1947, LIBYAN ARAB JAMAHIRIYA 29 Jan 1953 a, LITHUANIA 8 Jan 1992 a, LUXEMBOURG 28 Apr 1948 a, MALAWI 11 Sep 1964 a, MALAYSIA 12 Mar 1974 a, MALI 8 Nov 1960 a, MALTA 5 Jan 1965 a, MARSHALL ISLANDS 18 Mar 1988 a, MAURITANIA 12 Jan 1962 a, MAURITIUS 30 Jan 1970 a, MEXICO 25 Jun 1946, MICRONESIA (FEDERATED STATES OF) 27 Sep 1988 a, MONACO 4 Jan 1980 a, MONGOLIA 7 Sep 1989 a, MONTENEGRO 12 Feb 2007 a, MOROCCO 13 Nov 1956 a, MOZAMBIQUE 5 Jan 1977 a, MYANMAR 8 Jul 1948 a, NAMIBIA 30 Apr 1991 a, NAURU 25 Aug 1975 a, NEPAL 29 Jun 1960 a, NETHERLANDS 26 Mar 1947, NEW ZEALAND 7 Mar 1947, NICARAGUA 28 Dec 1945, NIGER 29 May 1961 a, NORWAY 5 May 1947, OMAN 24 Jan 1973 a, PAKISTAN 6 Nov 1947 a, PALAU 4 Oct 1995 a, PANAMA 18 Jan 1960 a (*2), PAPUA NEW GUINEA 15 Dec

* Source: 15 U.N.T.S. 295.

1975 a, PARAGUAY 21 Jan 1946, PERU 8 Apr 1946, PHILIPPINES 1 Mar 1947, POLAND 6 Apr 1945, PORTUGAL 27 Feb 1947, QATAR 5 Sep 1971 a, REPUBLIC OF KOREA 11 Nov 1952 a, REPUBLIC OF MOLDOVA 1 Jun 1992 a, ROMANIA 30 Apr 1965 a, RUSSIAN FEDERATION 15 Oct 1970 a, RWANDA 3 Feb 1964 a, SAINT KITTS AND NEVIS 21 May 2002 a, SAINT LUCIA 20 Nov 1979 a, SAINT VINCENT AND THE GRENADINES 15 Nov 1983 a, SAMOA 21 Nov 1996 a, SAN MARINO 13 May 1988 a, SAO TOME AND PRINCIPE 28 Feb 1877 a, SAUDI ARABIA 19 Feb 1962 a, SENEGAL 11 Nov 1960 a, SERBIA (REPUBLIC OF) 14 Dec 2000, SEYCHELLES 25 Apr 1977 a, SIERRA LEONE 22 Nov 1961 a, SINGAPORE 20 May 1966, SLOVAKIA 15 Mar 1993 a, SLOVENIA 13 May 1992 a, SOLOMON ISLANDS 11 Apr 1985 a, SOMALIA 2 Mar 1964 a, SOUTH AFRICA 1 Mar 1947, SPAIN 5 Mar 1947, SRI LANKA 1 Jun 1948 a, SUDAN 29 Jun 1956 a, SURINAME 5 Mar 1976 a, SWAZILAND 14 Feb 1973 a, SWEDEN 7 Nov 1946, SWITZERLAND 6 Feb 1947 (*territorial), SYRIAN ARAB REPUBLIC 21 Dec 1949, TAJIKISTAN 3 Sep 1993 a, THAILAND 4 Apr 1947, THE FORMER YUGOSLAV REPUBLIC OF MACEDONIA 10 Dec 1992 a, TIMOR-LESTE 4 Aug 2005 a, TOGO 18 May 1965 a, TONGA 2 Nov 1984 a, TRINIDAD AND TOBAGO 14 Mar 1963 a, TUNISIA 18 Nov 1957 a, TURKEY 20 Dec 1945, TURKMENISTAN 15 Mar 1993 a, UGANDA 10 Apr 1967 a, UKRAINE 10 Aug 1992 a, UNITED ARAB EMIRATES 25 Apr 1972 a, UNITED KINGDOM 1 Mar 1947, UNITED REPUBLIC OF TANZANIA 23 Apr 1962 a, UNITED STATES OF AMERICA 9 Aug 1946, URUGUAY 14 Jan 1954, UZBEKISTAN 13 Oct 1992 a, VANUATU 17 Aug 1983 a, VENEZUELA 1 Apr 1947 a, VIET NAM 13 Mar 1980 a, YEMEN 17 Apr 1964 a, ZAMBIA 30 Oct 1964 a, ZIMBABWE 11 Feb 1981 a.

[...]

PART I

AIR NAVIGATION

CHAPTER I

GENERAL PRINCIPLES AND APPLICATION OF THE CONVENTION

Article 1

Sovereignty

The contracting States recognize that every State has complete and exclusive sovereignty over the airspace above its territory.

[...]

CHAPTER II

FLIGHT OVER TERRITORY OF CONTRACTING STATES

[...]

Article 7

Cabotage

Each contracting State shall have the right to refuse permission to the aircraft of other contracting States to take on in its territory passengers, mail and cargo carried for remuneration or hire and destined for another point within its territory. Each contracting State undertakes not to enter into any arrangements which specifically grant any such privilege on an exclusive basis to any other State or an airline of any other State, and not to obtain any such exclusive privilege from any other State.

[...]

Article 13

Entry and clearance regulations

The laws and regulations of a contracting State as to the admission to or departure from its territory of passengers, crew or cargo of aircraft, such as regulations relating to entry, clearance, immigration, passports, customs, and quarantine shall be complied with by or on behalf of such passengers, crew or cargo upon entrance into or departure from, or while within the territory of that State.

Article 14

Prevention of spread of disease

Each contracting State agrees to take effective measures to prevent the spread by means of air navigation of cholera, typhus (epidemic), smallpox, yellow fever, plague, and such other communicable diseases as the contracting States shall from time to time decide to designate, and to that end contracting States will keep in close consultation with the agencies concerned with international regulations relating to sanitary measures applicable to aircraft. Such consultation shall be without prejudice to the application of any existing international convention on this subject to which the contracting States may be parties.

[...]

Article 16

Search of Aircraft

The appropriate authorities of each of the contracting States shall have the right, without unreasonable delay, to search aircraft of the other contracting States on landing or departure, and to inspect the certificates and other documents prescribed by this Convention.

[...]

CHAPTER IV

MEASURES TO FACILITATE AIR NAVIGATION

Article 22

Facilitation of formalities

Each contracting State agrees to adopt all practicable measures, through the issuance of special regulations or otherwise, to facilitate and expedite navigation by aircraft between the territories of contracting States, and to prevent unnecessary delays to aircraft, crews, passengers and cargo, especially in the administration of the laws relating to immigration, quarantine, customs and clearance.

Article 23

Customs and immigration procedures

Each contracting State undertakes, so far as it may find practicable, to establish customs and immigration procedures affecting international air navigation in accordance with the practices which may be established or recommended from time to time, pursuant to this Convention. Nothing in this Convention shall be construed as preventing the establishment of customs-free airports.

[...]

CHAPTER V

CONDITIONS TO BE FULFILLED WITH RESPECT TO AIRCRAFT

Article 29

Documents carried in aircraft

Every aircraft of a contracting State, engaged in international navigation, shall carry the following documents in conformity with the conditions prescribed in this Convention:

[...]

(f) If it carries passengers, a list of their names and places of embarkation and destination;

[...]

Convention on Offences and Certain Other Acts Committed on Board Aircraft, 1963 [excerpts]*

Adoption: 14 September 1963
Entry into force: 4 December 1969
Parties: 182 (Status as of 1 April 2007)

AFGHANISTAN 15 April 1977, ALBANIA 1 Dec 1997, ALGERIA 12 Oct 1995 (*24.1), ANDORRA 17 May 2006, ANGOLA 24 Feb 1998, ANTINGUA AND BARBUDA 19 Jul 1985, ARGENTINA 23 Jul 1971, ARMENIA 23 Jan 2003, AUSTRALIA 22 Jun 1970, AUSTRIA 7 Feb 1974, AZERBAIJAN 5 Feb 2004 (*24.1), BAHAMAS 12 Jun 1975, BAHRAIN 9 Feb 1984 (*24.1), BANGLADESH 25 Jul 1978, BARBADOS 25 Jun 1969, BELARUS 3 Feb 1988 (*24.1, general), BELGIUM 20 Dec 1968, BELIZE 19 May, BENIN 30 Mar 2004, BHUTAN 25 Jan 1989, BOLIVIA 5 Jul 1979, BOSNIA AND HERZEGOVINA 7 Mar 1995, BOTSWANA 26 Jan 1979, BRAZIL 28 Feb 1969, BRUNEI DARUSSALAM 23 May 1986, BULGARIA 28 Sep 1989 (*general), BURKINA FASO 14 Sep 1963, BURUNDI 14 Jul 1971, CAMBODIA 22 Oct 1996, CAMEROON 24 Mar 1988, CANADA 4 Nov 1964, CAPE VERDE 4 Oct 1989, CENTRAL AFRICAN REPUBLIC 11 Jun 1991, CHAD 30 Jun 1970, CHILE 24 Jan 1974, CHINA 14 Nov 1978 (*24.1), COLOMBIA 6 Jul 1973, COMOROS 21 Aug 1991, CONGO 13 Nov 1978, COOK ISLANDS 12 Apr 2005, COSTA RICA 24 Oct 1972, CÖTE D'IVOIRE 3 Jun 1970, CROATIA 5 Oct 1993, CUBA 12 Feb 2001 (*24.1), CYPRUS 31 May 1972, CZECH REPUBLIC 25 Mar 1993, DEMOCRATIC PEOPLE'S REPUBLIC OF KOREA 9 May 1983 (*24.1), DEMOCRATIC REPUBLIC OF THE CONGO 20 Jul 1977, DENMARK 17 Jan 1967, DJIBOUTI 10 Jun 1992, DOMINICAN REPUBLIC 3 Dec 1970, ECUADOR 8 Jul 1969, EGYPT 12 Feb 1975 (*24.1), EL SALVADOR 13 Feb 1980, EQUATORIAL GUINEA 27 Feb 1991, ESTONIA 31 Dec 1993, ETHIOPIA 27 Mar 1979 (*24.1), FIJI 31 Jan 1972, FINLAND 24 Oct 1969, FRANCE 11 Jul 1969, GABON 14 Jan 1970, GAMBIA 4 Jan 1979, GEORGIA 16 Jun 1994, GERMANY 16 Dec 1969, GHANA 2 Jan 1974, GREECE 31 May 1971, GRENADA 28 Aug 1978, GUATEMALA 17 Nov 1970 (*24.1), GUINEA 20 Dec 1972, HAITI 26 Apr 1984, HOLY SEE signed 14 Sep 1963, HONDURAS 8 Apr 1987 (*24.1), HUNGARY 3 Dec 1970, ICELAND 16 Mar 1970, INDIA 22 Jul 1975 (*24.1), INDONESIA 7 Sep 1976 (*24.1), IRAN (ISLAMIC REPUBLIC OF) 28 Jun 1976, IRAQ 15 May 1974, IRELAND 14 Nov 1975, ISRAEL 19 Sep 1969, ITALY 18 Oct 1968, JAMAICA 16 Sep 1983, JAPAN 26 May 1970, JORDAN 3 May 1973, KAZAKHSTAN 18 May 1995, KENYA 22 Jun 1970, KUWAIT 27 Nov 1979, KYRGYZSTAN 28 Feb 2000, LAO PEOPLE'S DEMOCRATIC REPUBLIC 21 Jan 1973, LATVIA 10 Jun 1997, LEBANON 11 Jun 1974, LESOTHO 28 Apr 1972, LIBERIA 10 Mar 2003, LIBYAN ARAB JAMAHIRIYA 21 Jun 1972, LIECHENSTEIN 26 Feb 2001, LITHUANIA 21 Nov 1996, LUXEMBOURG 21 Sep 1972, MADAGASCAR 2 Dec 1969, MALAWI 28 Dec 1972 (*24.1), MALAYSIA 5 Mar 1985, MALDIVES 28 Sep 1987, MALI 31 May 1971, MALTA 28 Jun 1991, MARSHALL ISLANDS 15 May 1989, MAURITANIA 30 Jun 1977, MAURITIUS 5 Apr 1983, MEXICO 18 Mar 1969, MONACO 2 Jun 1983, MONGOLIA 24 Jul 1990, MOROCCO 21 Oct 1975, MOZAMBIQUE 6 Jan 2003 (*24.1), MYANMAR 23 May 1996, NAMIBIA 19 Dec 2005, NAURU 17 May 1984, NEPAL 15 Jan 1979, NETHERLANDS 9 Jun 1967 (*territorial), NEW ZEALAND 12 Feb 1974, NICARAGUA 24 Aug 1973, NIGER 27 Jun 1969, NORWAY 17 Jan 1967, OMAN 9 Feb 1977 (*24.1), PAKISTAN 11 Sep 1973, PALAU 12 Oct 1995, PANAMA 16 Nov 1970, PAPUA NEW GUINEA 15 Dec 1975 (*24.1), PARAGUAY 9 Aug 1971, PERU 12 May 1978 (*24.1), PHILIPPINES 26 Nov 1965, POLAND 19 Mar 1971, PORTUGAL 25 Nov 1964,

* Source: 704 U.N.T.S 219.

QATAR 6 Aug 1981, REPUBLIC OF KOREA 19 Feb 1971, REPUBLIC OF MOLDOVA 20 Jun 1997, ROMANIA 15 1974 (*24.1), RUSSIAN FEDERATION 3 Feb 1988 (*24.1, general), RWANDA 17 May 1971, SAINT LUCIA 31 Oct 1983, SAINT VINCENT AND THE GRENADINES 18 Nov 1991, SAMOA 9 Jul 1998, SAO TOME AND PRINCIPE 4 May 2006, SAUDI ARABIA 21 Nov 1969, SENEGAL 9 Mar 1972, SERBIA (REPUBLIC OF) 6 Sep 2001, SEYCHELLES 4 Jan 1979, SIERRA LEONE 9 Nov 1970, SINGAPORE 1 Mar 1971, SLOVAKIA 20 Mar 1995, SLOVENIA 18 Dec 1992, SOLOMON ISLANDS 23 Mar 1982, SOUTH AFRICA 26 May 1972 (*24.1), SPAIN 1 Oct 1969, SRI LANKA 30 May 1978, SUDAN 25 May 2000, SURINAME 10 Sep 1979, SWAZILAND 15 Nov 1999, SWEDEN 17 Jan 1967, SWITZERLAND 21 Dec 1970, SYRIAN ARAB REPUBLIC 31 Jul 1980 (*24.1), TAJIKISTAN 20 Mar 1996, THAILAND 6 Mar 1972, THE FORMER REPUBLIC OF MACEDONIA 30 Aug 1994, TOGO 26 Jul 1971, TONGA 13 Feb 2002, TRINIDAD AND TOBAGO 9 Feb 1972, TUNISIA 25 Feb 1975 (*24.1), TURKEY 17 Dec 1975, TURKMENISTAN 30 Jun 1999, UGANDA 25 Jun 1982, UKRAINE 29 Feb 1988 (*24.1), UNITED ARAB EMIRATES 16 Apr 1981, UNITED KINGDOM OF GREAT BRITAIN AND NORTHERN IRELAND 29 Nov 1968, UNITED REPUBLIC OF TANZANIA 12 Aug 1983, UNITED STATES OF AMERICA 5 Sep 1969, URUGUAY 26 Jan 1977, UZBEKISTAN 31 Jul 1995, VANUATU 31 Jan 1989, VENEZUELA 4 Feb 1983 (*24.1), VIET NAM 10 Oct 1979 (*24.1), YEMEN 26 Sep 1971, ZAMBIA 14 Sep 1971, ZIMBABWE 8 Mar 1989.

[...]

Article 4

A Contracting State which is not the State of registration may not interfere with an aircraft in flight in order to exercise its criminal jurisdiction over an offence committed on board except in the following cases:

a) the offence has effect on the territory of such State;

b) the offence has been committed by or against a national or permanent resident of such State;

c) the offence is against the security of such State;

d) the offence consists of a breach of any rules or regulations relating to the flight or manoeuvre of aircraft in force in such State;

e) the exercise of jurisdiction is necessary to ensure the observance of any obligation of such State under a multilateral international agreement.

[...]

Article 9

1. The aircraft commander may deliver to the competent authorities of any Contracting State in the territory of which the aircraft lands any person who he has reasonable grounds to believe has committed on board the aircraft an act which, in his opinion, is a serious offence according to the penal law of the State of registration of the aircraft.

[...]

Article 11

1. When a person on board has unlawfully committed by force or threat thereof an act of interference, seizure, or other wrongful exercise of control of an aircraft in flight or when such

an act is about to be committed, Contracting States shall take all appropriate measures to restore control of the aircraft to its lawful commander or to preserve his control of the aircraft.

[...]

Article 13

1. Any Contracting State shall take delivery of any person whom the aircraft commander delivers pursuant to Article 9, paragraph 1.

2. Upon being satisfied that the circumstances so warrant, any Contracting State shall take custody or other measures to ensure the presence of any person suspected of an act contemplated in Article 11, paragraph 1 and of any person of whom it has taken delivery. The custody and other measures shall be as provided in the law of that State but may only be continued for such time as is reasonably necessary to enable any criminal or extradition proceedings to be instituted.

3. Any person in custody pursuant to the previous paragraph shall be assisted in communicating immediately with the nearest appropriate representative of the State of which he is a national.

4. Any Contracting State, to which a person is delivered pursuant to Article 9, paragraph 1, or in whose territory an aircraft lands following the commission of an act contemplated in Article 11, paragraph 1, shall immediately make a preliminary enquiry into the facts.

5. When a State, pursuant to this Article, has taken a person into custody, it shall immediately notify the State of registration of the aircraft and the State of nationality of the detained person and, if it considers it advisable, any other interested State of the fact that such person is in custody and of the circumstance which warrant his detention. The State which makes the preliminary enquiry contemplated in paragraph 4 of this Article shall promptly report its findings to the said States and shall indicate whether it intends to exercise jurisdiction.

Article 14

1. When any person has been disembarked in accordance with Article 8, paragraph 1, or delivered in accordance with Article 9, paragraph 1, or has disembarked after committing an act contemplated in Article 11, paragraph 1, and when such person cannot or does not desire to continue his journey and the State of landing refuses to admit him, that State may, if the person in question is not a national or permanent resident of that State, return him to the territory of the State of which he is a national or permanent resident or to the territory of the State in which he began his journey by air.

2. Neither disembarkation, nor delivery, nor the taking of custody or other measures contemplated in Article 13, paragraph 2, nor return of the person concerned, shall be considered as admission to the territory of the Contracting State concerned for the purpose of its law relating to entry or admission of persons and nothing in this Convention shall affect the law of a Contracting State relating to the expulsion of persons from its territory.

Article 15

1. Without prejudice to Article 14, any person who has been disembarked in accordance with Article 8, paragraph 1, or delivered in accordance with Article 9, paragraph 1, or has disembarked after committing an act contemplated in Article 11, paragraph 1, and who desires to continue his journey shall be at liberty as soon as practicable by the law of the State of landing for the purpose of extradition or criminal proceedings.

2. Without prejudice to its law as to entry and admission to, and extradition and expulsion from its territory, a Contracting State in whose territory a person has been disembarked in accordance with Article 8, paragraph 1, or delivered in accordance with Article 9, paragraph 1 or has disembarked and is suspected of having committed an act contemplated in Article 11, paragraph 1, shall accord to such person treatment which is no less favourable for his protection and security than that accorded to nationals of such Contracting State in like circumstances.

[...]

Convention for the Suppression of Unlawful Seizure of Aircraft, 1970 [excerpts]*

Adoption: 16 December 1970
Entry into force: 14 October 1971
Parties: 182 (Status as of 1 April 2007)

AFGHANISTAN 29 Aug 1979, ALBANIA 21 Oct 1997, ALGERIA 6 Oct 1995 (*12.1, 14.1, 24.1), ANDORRA 23 Sep 2004 (*no airport), ANGOLA 12 Mar 1998, ANTIGUA AND BARBUDA 22 Jul 1985, ARGENTINA 11 Sep 1972 (*general), ARMENIA 10 Sep 2002, AUSTRALIA 9 Sep 1972, AUSTRIA 11 Feb 1974, AZERBAIJAN 3 Mar 2000, BAHAMAS 13 Aug 1976, BAHRAIN 3 Feb 1984 (*12.1), BANGLADESH 28 Jun, BARBADOS 2 Apr 1973, BELARUS 30 Dec 1971 (*12.1), BELGIUM 24 Aug 1973, BELIZE 10 Jun 1998, BENIN 13 Mar 1972, BHUTAN 28 Dec 1988, BOLIVIA 18 Jul 1979, BOSNIA AND HERZEGOVINA 15 Aug 1994, BOTSWANA 28 Dec 1978, BRAZIL 14 Jan 1972 (*12.1), BRUNEI DARRUSSALAM 6 Apr 1986, BULGARIA 19 May 1971 (*12.1), BURKINA FASO 19 Oct 1987, BURUNDI signed 17 Feb 1971, CAMBODIA 8 Nov 1996, CAMEROON 4 Apr 1988, CANADA 20 Jun 1972, CAPE VERDE 20 Oct 1977, CENTRAL AFRICAN REPUBLIC 1 Jul 1991, CHAD 12 Jul 1972, CHILE 2 Feb 1972, CHINA 10 Sep 1980 (*12.1), COLOMBIA 3 Jul 1973, COMOROS 1 Aug 1991, CONGO 24 Nov 1989, COOK ISLANDS 14 Apr 2005, COSTA RICA 9 Jul 1971, CÖTE D'IVOIRE 9 Jan 1973, CROATIA 8 Jun 1993, CUBA 27 Nov 2001 (*12.1), CYPRUS 5 Jul 1972, CZECH REPBULIC 14 Nov 1994, DEMOCRATIC PEOPLE'S REPUBLIC OF KOREA 28 Apr 1983, DEMOCRATIC REPUBLIC OF THE CONGO 6 Jul 1977, DENMARK 17 Oct 1972, DJIBOUTI 24 Nov 1992, DOMINICA 26 Jul 2005, DOMINICAN REPUBLIC 22 Jun 1978, ECUADOR 14 Jun 1971, EGYPT 28 Feb 1975 (*12.1), EL SALVADOR 16 Jan 1973, EQUATORIAL GUINEA 2 Jan 1991, ESTONIA 22 Dec 1993, ETHIOPIA 26 Mar 1970, FIJI 27 Jul 1972, FINLAND 15 Dec 1971, FRANCE 18 Sep 1972, GABON 14 Jul 1971, GAMBIA 28 Nov 1978, GEORGIA 20 Apr 1994, GERMANY 11 Oct 1974, GHANA 12 Dec 1973, GREECE 20 Sep 1973, GRENADA 10 Aug 1978, GUATEMALA 16 May 1979 (*12.1), GUINEA 2 May 1984, GUINEA-BISSAU 20 Aug 1976, GUYANA 21 Dec 1972, HAITI 9 May 1984, HONDURAS 13 Apr 1987, HUNGARY 13 Aug 1971, ICELAND 29 Jun 1973, INDIA 12 Nov 1982 (*12.1), INDONESIA 27 Aug 1976 (*12.1), IRAN (ISLAMIC REPUBLIC OF) 25 Jan 1972, IRAQ 3 Dec 1971, IRELAND 24 Nov 1975, ISRAEL 16 Aug 1971, ITALY 19 Feb 1974, JAMAICA 15 Sep 1983, JAPAN 19 Apr 1971, JORDAN 18 Nov 1971, KAZAKHSTAN 4 Apr 1995, KENYA 11 Jan 1977, KUWAIT 25 May 1979, KYRGYZSTAN 25 Fen 2000, LAO PEOPLE'S DEMOCRATIC REPUBLIC 6 Apr 1989, LATVIA 23 Oct 1998, LEBANON 10 Aug 1973, LESOTHO 27 Jul 1978, LIBERIA 1 Feb 1982, LIBYAN ARAB JAMAHIRIYA 4 Oct 1978, LIECHTENSTEIN 23 Feb 2001, LITHUANIA 4 Dec 1996, LUXEMBOURG 22 Nov 1978, MADAGASCAR 18 Nov 1986, MALAWI 21 Dec 1972 (*12.1), MALAYSIA 4 May 1985, MALDIVES 1 Sep 1987, MALI 29 Sep 1971, MALTA 14 Jun 1991, MARSHALL ISLANDS 31 May 1989, MAURITANIA 1 Nov 1978, MAURITIUS 25 Apr 1983, MEXICO 19 Jul 1972, MONACO 3 Jun 1983, MONGOLIA 8 Oct 1971, MOROCCO 24 Oct 1975, MOZAMBIQUE 16 Jan 2003 (*12.1), MYANMAR 22 May 1996, NAMIBIA 4 Nov 2005, NAURU 17 May 1984, NEPAL 11 Jan 1979, NETHERLANDS 27 Aug 1973 (*general), NEW ZEALAND 12 Feb 1974, NICARAGUA 6 Nov 1973, NIGER 15 Oct 1971, NIGERIA 3 Jul 1973, NORWAY 23 Aug 1971, OMAN 2 Feb 1977 (*12.1), PAKISTAN 28 Nov 1973, PALAU 3 Aug 1995, PANAMA 10 Mar 1972, PAPUA NEW GUINEA 15 Dec 1975 (*12.1),

* Source: 860 U.N.T.S. 105.

PARAGUAY 4 Feb 1972, PERU 28 Apr 1978 (*12.1), PHILLIPINES 26 Mar 1973, POLAND 21 Mar 1972, PORTUGAL 27 Nov 1972, QATAR 26 Aug 1981 (*12.1), REPUBLIC OF KOREA 18 Jan 1973, REPUBLIC OF MOLDOVA 21 May 1997, ROMANIA 10 Jul 1972 (*12.1), RUSSIAN FEDERATION 24 Sep 1971 (*12.1), RWANDA 3 Nov 1987, SAINT LUCIA 8 Nov 1983, SAINT VINCENT AND THE GRENADINES 29 Nov 1991, SAMOA 9 Jul 1998, SAO TOME AND PRINCIPE 8 May 2006, SAUDI ARABIA 14 Jun 1974 (*12.1), SENEGAL 3 Feb 1978, SERBIA (REPUBLIC OF) 23 Jul 2001, SEYCHELLES 29 Dec 1978, SIERRA LEONE 13 Nov 1974, SINGAPORE 12 Apr 1978, SLOVAKIA 13 Dec 1995, SLOVENIA 27 May 1992, SOUTH AFRICA 30 May 1972 (*12.1), SPAIN 20 Oct 1972, SRI LANKA 30 May 1978, SUDAN 18 Jan 1979, SURINAME 27 Oct 1978, SWAZILAND 27 Dec 1999, SWEDEN 7 Jul 1971, SWITZERLAND 14 Sep 1971, SYRIAN ARAB REPUBLIC 10 Jul 1980 (*12.1), TAJIKISTAN 29 Feb 1996, THAILAND 16 May 1978, THE FORMER REPUBLIC OF MACEDONIA 7 Jan 1998, TOGO 9 Feb 1979, TONGA 21 Feb 1977, TRINIDAD AND TOBAGO 21 Jan 1972, TUNISIA 16 Nov 1981 (*12.1), TURKEY 17 Apr 1973, TURKMENISTAN 25 May 1999, UGANDA 27 Mar 1972, UKRAINE 21 Feb 1972 (*12.1), UNITED ARAB EMIRATES 10 Apr 1981, UNITED KINGDOM OF GREAT BRITAIN AND NORTHERN IRELAND 22 Dec 1971, UNITED REPUBLIC OF TANZANIA 9 Aug 1983, UNITED STATES OF AMERICA 14 Sep 1971, URUGUAY 12 Jan 1977, UZBEKISTAN 7 Feb 1994, VANUATU 22 Feb 1989, VENEZUELA 7 Jul 1983, VIET NAM 17 Sep 1979 (*12.1), YEMEN 29 Sep 1986, ZAMBIA 3 Mar 1987, ZIMBABWE 6 Feb 1989.

[...]

Article 4

1. Each Contracting State shall take such measures as may be necessary to establish its jurisdiction over the offence and any other act of violence against passengers or crew committed by the alleged offender in connection with the offence, in the following cases:

a) when the offence is committed on board an aircraft registered in that State;

b) when the aircraft on board which the offence is committed lands in its territory with the alleged offender still on board;

c) when the offence is committed on board an aircraft lease without crew to a lessee who has his principal place of business or, if the lessee has no such place of business, his permanent residence, in that State.

[...]

Article 6

1. Upon being satisfied that the circumstances so warrant, any Contracting State in the territory of which the offender or the alleged offender is present, shall take him into custody or take other measures to ensure his presence. The custody and other measures shall be as provided in the law of that State but may only be continued for such time as is necessary to enable any criminal or extradition proceedings to be instituted.

2. Such State shall immediately make a preliminary enquiry into the facts.

3. Any person in custody pursuant to paragraph 1 of this article shall be assisted in communicating immediately with the nearest appropriate representative of the State of which he is a national.

4. When a State, pursuant to this article, has taken a person into custody, it shall immediately notify the State of registration of the aircraft, the State mentioned in article 4, paragraph 1 c), the State of nationality of the detained person and, if it considers it advisable any other interested States of the fact that such person is in custody and of the circumstances which warrant his detention. The State which makes the preliminary enquiry contemplated in paragraph 2 of this Article shall promptly report its findings to the said States and shall indicate whether it intends to exercise jurisdiction.

Article 7

The Contracting State in the territory of which the alleged offender is found shall, if it does not extradite him, be obliged, wihtout exception whatsoever and whether or not the offence was committed in its territory, to submit the case to its competent authorities for the purpose of prosecution. Those authorities shall take their decision in the same manner as in the case of any ordinary offence of a serious nature under the law of that State.

Article 8

1. The offence shall be deemed to be included as an extraditable offence in any extradition treaty existing between Contracting States. Contracting States undertake to include the offence as an extraditable offence in every extradition treaty to be concluded between them.

[...]

Convention for the Suppression of Unlawful Acts against the Safety of Civil Aviation, 1971 [excerpts]*

Adoption: 23 September 1971
Entry into force: 26 January 1973
Parties: 185 (Status as of 1 April 2007)

AFGHANISTAN 26 Sep 1984, ALBANIA 21 Oct 1997, ALGERIA 9 Oct 1995 (*12.1, 14.1, 24.1), ANDORRA 22 May 2006 (*no airport), ANGOLA 12 Mar 1998, ANTIGUA AND BARBUDA 22 Jul 1985, ARGENTINA 26 Nov 1973, ARMENIA 10 Sep 2002, AUSTRALIA 12 Jul 1973, AUSTRIA 11 Feb 1974, AZERBAIJAN 15 Mar 2000, BAHAMAS 27 Dec 1984, BAHRAIN 20 Feb 1984 (*14.1), BANGLADESH 28 Jun 1978, BARBADOS 6 Aug 1976, BELARUS 31 Jan 1973 (*14.1), BELGIUM 12 Aug 1976, BELIZE 10 Jun 1998, BELIZE 19 Apr 2004, BHUTAN 28 Dec 1988, BOLIVIA 18 Jul 1979, BOSNIA AND HERZEGOVINA 15 Aug 1994, BOTSWANA 28 Dec 1989, BRAZIL 24 Jul 1972 (*14.1), BRUNEI DARUSSALAM 16 Apr 1986, BULGARIA 28 Mar 1973, BURKINA FASO 19 Oct 1987, BURUNDI 11 Feb 1999, CAMBODIA 11 Jul 1973, CANADA 19 Jun 1972, CAPE VERDE 20 Oct 1977, CENTRAL AFRICAN REPUBLIC 1 Jul 1991, CHAD 12 Jul 1972, CHILE 28 Feb 1974, CHINA 10 Sep 1980 (*14.1), COLOMBIA 4 Dec 1974, COMOROS 1 Aug 1991, CONGO 19 Mar 1987, COOK ISLANDS 14 Apr 2005, COSTA RICA 21 Sep 1973, CÖTE D'IVOIRE 9 Jan 1973, CROATIA 8 Jun 1993, CUBA 31 Oct 2001 (*14.1), CYPRUS 27 Jul 1973, CZECH REPUBLIC 14 Nov 1994, DEMOCRATIC PEOPLE'S REPUBLIC OF KOREA 13 Aug 1980, DEMOCRATIC REPUBLIC OF THE CONGO 6 Jul 1977, DENMARK 17 Jan 1973, DJIBOUTI 24 Nov 1992, DOMINICA 26 Jul 2005, DOMINICAN REPUBLIC 28 Nov 1973, ECUADOR 12 Jan 1977, EGYPT 20 May 1975 (*14.1), EL SALVADOR 25 Sep 1979, EQUATORIAL GUINEA 2 Jan 1991, ESTONIA 22 Dec 1993, ETHIOPIA 26 Mar 1979 (*14.1), FIJI 5 Mar 1973, FINLAND 13 Jul 1973, FRANCE 30 Jun 1976 (*14.1), GABON 29 Jun 1976, GAMBIA 28 Nov 1978, GEORGIA 20 Apr 1994, GERMANY 3 Feb 1978, GHANA 12 Dec 1973, GREECE 15 Jan 1974, GRENADA 10 Aug 1978, GUATEMALA 19 Oct 1978 (*14.1), GUINEA 2 May 1984, GUINEA-BISSAU 20 Aug 1976, GUYANA 21 Dec 1972, HAITI 9 May 1984, HONDURAS 13 Apr 1987, HUNGARY 27 Dec 1972, ICELAND 29 Jun 1973, INDIA 12 Nov 1982, INDONESIA 27 Aug 1976 (*14.1), IRAN (ISLAMIC REPUBLIC OF) 10 Jul 1973, IRAQ 10 Sep 1974, IRELAND 12 Oct 1976, ISRAEL 30 Jun 1972, ITALY 12 Feb 1974, JAMAICA 15 Sep 1983, JAPAN 12 Jun 1974, JORDAN 13 Feb 1973, KAZAKHSTAN 4 Apr 1995, KENYA 11 Jan 1977, KUWAIT 23 Nov 1979, KYRGYZSTAN 25 Feb 2000, LAO PEOPLE'S DEMOCRATIC REPUBLIC 6 Apr 1989, LATVIA 13 Apr 1997, LEBANON 23 Dec 1977, LESOTHO 27 Jul 1978, LIBERIA 1 Feb 1982, LIBYAN ARAB JAMAHIRIYAH 19 Feb 1974, LIECHTENSTEIN 23 Feb 2001, LITHUANIA 4 Dec 1996, LUXEMBOURG 18 May 1982, MADAGASCAR 18 Nov 1986, MALAWI 21 Dec 1972 (*14.1), MALAYSIA 4 May 1985, MALDIVES 1 Sep 1987, MALI 24 Aug 1972, MALTA 14 Jun 1991, MARSHALL ISLANDS 31 May 1989, MAURITANIA 1 Nov 1978, MAURITIUS 25 Apr 1983, MEXICO 12 Sep 1974, MICRONESIA (FEDERATED STATES OF) 19 Mar 2003, MONACO 3 Jun 1983, MONGOLIA 14 Sep 1972 (*14.1), MOROCCO 24 Oct 1975, MOZAMBIQUE 16 Jan 2003 (*14.1), MYANMAR 22 May 1996, NAMIBIA 4 Nov 2005, NAURU 17 May 1984, NEPAL 11 Jan 1979, NETHERLANDS 27 Aug 1973 (*territorial), NEW ZEALAND 12 Feb 1974, NICARAGUA 6 Nov 1973, NIGER 1 Sep 1972, NIGERIA 3 Jul 1973, NORWAY 1 Aug 1973, OMAN 2 Feb 1977 (*14.1), PAKISTAN 24 Jan

* Source: 974 UNTS 178.

1974, PALAU 3 Aug 1995, PANAMA 24 Apr 1972, PAPUA NEW GUINEA 15 Dec 1975 (*14.1), PARAGUAY 5 Mar 1974, PERU 28 Apr 1978 (*14.1), PHILIPPINES 26 Mar 1973, POLAND 28 Jan 1975, PORTUGAL 15 Jan 1973, QATAR 26 Aug 1981 (*14.1), REPUBLIC OF KOREA 2 Aug 1973, REPUBLIC OF MOLDOVA 21 May 1997, ROMANIA 15 Aug 1975 (*14.1), RUSSIAN FEDERATION 19 Feb 1973, RWANDA 3 Nov 1987 SAINT LUCIA 8 Nov 1983, SAINT VINCENT AND THE GRENADINES 29 Nov 1991, SAMOA 9 Jul 1998, SAO TOME AND PRINCIPE 8 May 2006, SAUDI ARABIA 14 Jun 1974 (*14.1), SENEGAL 3 Feb 1978, SERBIA (REPUBLIC OF), SEYCHELLES 29 Dec 1978, SIERRA LEONE 20 Sep 1979, SINGAPORE 12 Apr 1978, SLOVAKIA 6 Mar 1995, SLOVENIA 27 May 1992, SOLOMON ISLANDS 13 Apr 1982, SOUTH AFRICA 30 May 1972 (*14.1), SPAIN 30 Oct 1972, SRI LANKA 30 May 1978, SUDAN 18 Jan 1979, SURINAME 27 Oct 1978, SWAZILAND 27 Dec 1999, SWEDEN 10 Jul 1973, SWITZERLAND 17 Jan 1978, SYRIAN ARAB REPUBLIC 10 Jul 1980 (*14.1), TAJIKISTAN 29 Feb 1996, THAILAND 16 May 1978, THE FORMER YUGOSLAV REPUBLIC OF MACEDONIA 4 Jan 1995, TOGO 9 Fen 1979, TONGA 21 Feb 1977, TRINIDAD AND TOBAGO 9 Feb 1972, TUNISIA 16 Nov 1981 (*14.1), TURKEY 23 Dec 1975, TURKMENISTAN 25 May 1999, UGANDA 19 Jul 1982, UKRAINE 26 Jan 1973 (*14.1), UNITED ARAB EMIRATES 10 Apr 1981, UNITED KINGDOM OF GREAT BRITAIN AND NORTHERN IRELAND 25 Oct 1973, UNITED REPUBLIC OF TANZANIA 9 Aug 1983, UNITED STATES OF AMERICA 1 Nov 1972, URUGUAY 12 Jan 1977, UZBEKISTAN 7 Feb 1994, VANUATU 6 Nov 1989, VENEZUELA 21 Nov 1983 (*4, 7, 8), VIET NAM 17 Sep 1979, YEMEN 29 Sep 1986, ZAMBIA 3 Mar 1987, ZIMBABWE 6 Feb 1989.

[...]

Article 5

1. Each Contracting State shall take such measures as may be necessary to establish its jurisdiction over the offences in the following cases:

a) when the offence is committed in the territory of that State;

b) when the offence is committed against or on board an aircraft registered in that State;

c) when the aircraft on board which the offence is committed lands in its territory with the alleged offender still on board;

d) when the offence is committed against or on board an aircraft leased without crew to a lessee who has his principal place of business or, if the lessee has no such place of business, his permanent residence, in that State.

2. Each Contracting State shall likewise take such measures as may be necessary to establish its jurisdiction over the offences mentioned in Article 1, paragraph 1 a), b) and c), and in Article 1, paragraph 2, in so far as that paragraph relates to those offences, in the case where the alleged offender is present in its territory and it does not extradite him pursuant to Article 8 to any of the States mentioned in paragraph 1 of this Article.

[...]

Article 6

1. Upon being satisfied that the circumstances so warrant, any Contracting State in the territory of which the offender or the alleged offender is present, shall take him into custody or take

other measures to ensure his presence. The custody and other measures shall be as provided in the law of that State but may only be continued for such time as is necessary to enable any criminal or extradition proceedings to be instituted.

2. Such State shall immediately make a preliminary enquiry into the facts.

3. Any person in custody pursuant to paragraph 1 of this Article shall be assisted in communicating immediately with the nearest appropriate representative of the State of which he is a national.

4. When a State, pursuant to this Article, has taken a person into custody, it shall immediately notigy the States mentioned in Article 5, paragraph 1, the State of nationality of the detained person and, if it considers it advisable, any other interested State of the fact that such person is in custody and of the circumstances which warrant his detention. The State which makes the preliminrary enquiry contemplated in paragraph 2 of this Article shall promptly report its findings to the said States and shal indicate whether it intends to exercise jurisdiction.

Article 7

The Contracting State in the territory of which the alleged offender is found shall, if it does not extradite him, be obliged, without exception whatsoever and whether or not the offence was committed in its territory, to submit the case to its competent authorities for the purpose of prosecution. Those authorities shall take their decision in the same manner as in the case of any ordinary offence of a serious nature under the law of that State.

Article 8

1. The offences shall be deemed to be included as extraditable offences in any extradition treaty existing between Contracting States. Contracting States undertake to include the offences as extraditable offences in every etradition treaty to be concluded between them.

[…]

Protocol on the Suppression of Unlawful Acts of Violence at Airports Serving International Civil Aviation, supplementary to the Convention for the Suppression of Unlawful Acts against the Safety of Civil Aviation, 1988 [excerpt]*

Adoption: 24 February 1988
Entry into force: 6 August 1989
Parties: 161 (Status as of 1 April 2007)

ALBANIA 29 Apr 2002, ALGERIA 6 Oct 1995, ANDORRA 22 May 2006, ARGENTINA 24 Feb 1988, AUSTRALIA 23 Oct 1990, AUSTRIA 4 Jul 1989, AZERBAIJAN 23 Mar 2000, BAHRAIN 12 Feb 1996, BANGLADESH 27 Jun 2005, BARBADOS 12 Sep 2002, BELARUS 24 Feb 1988, BELGIUM 15 Mar 1989, BELIZE 10 Jun 1998, BENIN 19 Apr 2004, BHUTAN 26 Aug 2005, BOLIVIA 1 Feb 2002, BOSNIA AND HERZEGOVINA 15 Aug 1994, BOTSWANA 30 Oct 2000, Brazil 24 Feb 1988, BRUNEI DARUSSALAM 20 Dec 2000, BULGARIA 26 Mar 1991, BURKINA FASO 8 Dec 1998, CAMBODIA 8 Nov 1996, CAMEROON 13 Mar 2003, CANADA 2 Aug 1993, CAPE VERDE 12 Sep 2002, CENTRAL AFRICAN REPUBLIC 1 Jul 1991, CHILE 15 Aug 1989, CHINA 5 Mar 1999 (*14.1, general), COLOMBIA 14 Jan 2004, CONGO signed 13 Apr 1989, COOK ISLANDS 14 Apr 2005, COSTA RICA 22 Apr 2003, CÔTE D'IVOIRE signed 21 Mar 1988, CROATIA 8 Jun 1993, CUBA 31 Oct 2001, CYPRUS 23 Apr 2002, CZECH REPUBLIC 25 Mar 1993, DEMOCRATIC PEOPLE'S REPUBLIC OF KOREA 19 Jul 1995, DEMOCRATIC REPUBLIC OF THE CONGO signed 24 Feb 1988, DENMARK 23 Nov 1989, DJIBOUTI 11 Jun 2004, DOMINICA 26 Jul 2005, ECUADOR 4 Mar 2004, EGYPT 25 Jul 2000, EL SALVADOR 8 Apr 1998, EQUATORIAL GUINEA 14 Jan 2004, ESTONIA 22 Dec 1993, ETHIOPIA 15 Dec 1999, FIJI 21 Sep 1992, FINLAND 3 Apr 1998, FRANCE 6 Sep 1989 (*14.1), GABON 13 Aug 2003, GAMBIA 16 Jun 2000, GEORGIA 15 Feb 1999, GERMANY 25 Apr 1994, GHANA 15 Jul 1997, GREECE 25 Apr 1991, GRENADA 15 Jan 2002, GUATEMALA 11 Oct 1994, GUINEA 1 Oct 1998, GUYANA 19 Jun 2002, HONDURAS 20 Jan 2004, HUNGARY 7 Sep 1988, ICELAND 9 May 1990, INDIA 22 Mar 1995, INDONESIA signed 24 Feb 1988, IRAN (ISLAMIC REPUBLIC OF) 14 Feb 2002, IRAQ 31 Jan 1990, IRELAND 26 Jul 1991, ISRAEL 2 Apr 1993, ITALY 13 Mar 1990, JAMAICA 18 Aug 2005, JAPAN 24 Apr 1998, JORDAN 18 Sep 1992, KAZAKHSTAN 18 May 1995, KENYA 5 Oct 1995, KUWAIT 8 Mar 1989, KYRGYZSTAN 28 Feb 2000, LAO PEOPLE'S DEMOCRATIC REPUBLIC 7 Oct 2002, LATVIA 13 Apr 1997, LEBANON 27 May 1996, LIBERIA 10 Mar 2003, LIBYAN ARAB JAMAHIRIYA 26 Jul 1996, LIECHTENSTEIN 26 Feb 2001, LITHUANIA 4 Dec 1996, LUXEMBOURG 14 Nov 2003, MADAGASCAR 30 Mar 1998, MALAWI signed 24 Feb 1988, MALAYSIA 8 Oct 2006, MALDIVES 22 Mar 1999, Mali 31 Oct 1990, MALTA 14 Jun 1991, MARSHALL ISLANDS 30 May 1989, MAURITANIA 8 Jul 2003, MAURITIUS 17 Aug 1989, MEXICO 11 Oct 1990, MICRONESIA (FEDERATED STATES OF) 19 Mar 2003, MONACO 22 Dec 1993, MONGOLIA 22 Sep 1999, MOROCCO 15 Feb 2002, MOZAMBIQUE 16 Jan 2003, MYANMAR 22 May 1996, NAMIBIA 4 Nov 2005, NAURU 19 Aug 2005, NETHERLANDS 11 Jul 1995 (*2, 3), NEW ZEALAND 2 Aug 1999, NICARAGUA 25 Apr 2002, NIGER signed 24 Feb 1988, NIGERIA 25 Mar 2003, NORWAY 29 May 1990, OMAN 27 Nov 1992, PAKISTAN 26 Sep 2000, PALAU 12 Oct 1995, PANAMA 10 Apr 1996, PAPUA NEW GUINEA 11 Jul 2002, PARAGUAY 23 Jul 2002, PERU 7 Jun 1989, PHILIPPINES 17 Dec 2003, POLAND 12 Aug 2004, PORTUGAL 18 Dec 2001, QATAR 17

* Source: 974 U.N.T.S. 177.

Jun 2003, REPUBLIC OF KOREA 27 Jun 1990, REPUBLIC OF MOLDOVA 20 Jun 1997, ROMANIA 3 Sep 1998, RUSSIAN FEDERATION 31 Mar 1989, RWANDA 16 May 2002, SAINT LUCIA 11 Jun 1990, SAINT VINCENT AND THE GRENADINES 29 Nov 1991, SAMOA 9 Jul 1998, SAO TOME AND PRINCIPE 8 May 2006, SAUDI ARABIA 21 Feb 1989, SENEGAL 24 Mar 2003, SERBIA (REPUBLIC OF) 6 Sep 2001, SEYCHELLES 21 May 2004, SINGAPORE 22 Nov 1996, SLOVAKIA 20 Mar 1995, SLOVENIA 27 May 1992, SOUTH AFRICA 21 Sep 1998, SPAIN 8 May 1991, SRI LANKA 11 Feb 1997, SUDAN 15 May 2000, SURINAME 27 Mar 2003, SWEDEN 26 Jul 1990, SWITZERLAND 9 Oct 1990, SYRIAN ARAB REPUBLIC 18 Jul 2002, TAJIKISTAN 29 Feb 1996, THAILAND 14 May 1996, THE FORMER YUGOSLAV REPUBLIC OF MACEDONIA 4 Jan 1995, TOGO 9 Feb 1990, TONGA 10 Dec 2002, TRINIDAD AND TOBAGO 3 Apr 2001, TUNISIA 7 Jun 1994, TURKEY 7 Jul 1989, TURKMENISTAN 25 May 1999, UGANDA 17 Mar 1994, UKRAINE 3 Jan 1990, UNITED ARAB EMIRATES 9 Mar 1989, UNITED KINGDOM OF GREAT BRITAIN AND NORTHERN IRELAND 15 Nov 1990, UNITED REPUBLIC OF TANZANIA 9 Mar 2004, UNITED STATES OF AMERICA 19 Oct 1994, URUGUAY 3 Dec 1998, UZBEKISTAN 7 Feb 1994, VANUATU 9 Nov 2005, VENEZUELA signed 24 Feb 1988, VIET NAM 25 Aug 1999, YEMEN 4 Feb 2007.

[...]

Article IIII

In Article 5 of the Convention, the following shall be added as paragraph 2 *bis*:

"2 *bis*. Each Contracting State shall likewise take such measures as may be necessary to establish its jurisdiction over the offences mentioned in Article 1, paragraph 1 *bis*, and in Article 1, paragraph 2, in so far as that paragraph relates to those offences, in the case where the alleged offender is present in its territory and it does not extradite him pursuant to Article 8 to the State mentioned in paragraph 1(a) of this Article."

[...]

Convention for the Suppression of Unlawful Acts against the Safety of Maritime Navigation, 1988 [excerpts]*

Adoption: 10 March 1988
Entry into force: 1 March 1992
Parties: 142 (Status as of 1 January 2007)

AFGHANISTAN 23 Sep 2003 a, ALBANIA 19 Jul 2002 a, ALGERIA 11 Feb 1998 a (*16.1), ARGENTINA 17 Aug 1993 (*16.2), ARMENIA 8 Jun 2005 a (*16.1), AUSTRALIA 19 Feb 1993, AUSTRIA 28 Dec 1989, AZERBAIJAN 26 Jan 2004 (*16.1), BAHAMAS 25 Oct 2005, BAHRAIN 21 Oct 2005 a, BANGLADESH 9 Jun 2005 a, BARBADOS 6 May 1994 a, BELARUS 4 Dec 2002 a, BELGIUM 11 Apr 2005 a, BOLIVIA 13 Feb 2002 a, BOSNIA & HERZEGOVINA 28 Jul 2003 a, BOTSWANA 14 Sep 200 a, BRAZIL 25 Oct 2005 (*6.2, 8, 16.1), BRUNEI DARUSSALAM 4 Dec 2003, BULGARIA 8 Jul 1999, BURKINA FASO 15 Jan 2004 a, CANADA 18 Jun 1993, CAPE VERDE 3 Jan 2003 a, CHILE 22 Apr 1994 (*4), CHINA 20 Aug 1991 (*16.1), COSTA RICA 25 Mar 2003, CROATIA 18 Aug 2005 a, CUBA 20 Nov 2001 a (*16.1, 16.2), CYPRUS 2 Feb 2000 a, CZECH REPUBLIC 10 Dec 2004 a, DENMARK 25 Aug 1995 (*general), DJIBOUTI 9 Jun 2004, DOMINICA 31 Aug 2001 a, ECUADOR 10 Mar 2003 a, EGYPT 8 Jan 1993 (*16, 6.2, 3.2), EL SALVADOR 7 Dec 2000 a, EQUATORIAL GUINEA 15 Jan 2004 a, ESTONIA 15 Feb 2002 a, FINLAND 12 Nov 1998, FRANCE 2 Dec 1991 (*3.2, 16.1), GAMBIA 1 Nov 1991 a, GERMANY 6 Nov 1990 a (*16), GHANA 1 Nov 2002 a, GREECE 11 Jun 1993, GRENADA 9 Jan 2002 a, GUINEA 1 Feb 2005 a, GUYANA 2 Jan 2003 a, HONDURAS 17 May 2005 a, HUNGARY 9 Nov 1989, ICELAND 28 May 2002 a, INDIA 15 Oct 1999 a (*16), IRELAND 10 Sept 2004 a, ITALY 26 Jan 1990, JAMAICA 17 Aug 2005 a, JAPAN 24 Apr 1998 a, JORDAN 2 Jul 2004 a, KAZAKHSTAN 24 Nov 2003 a, KENYA 21 Jan 2002 a, KIRIBATI 17 Nov 2005 a, KUWAIT 30 Jun 2003 a, LATVIA 4 Dec 2002 a, LEBANON 16 Dec 1994 a, LIBERIA 5 Oct 1995, LIBYAN ARAB JAMAHIRIYAH 8 Aug 2002 a, LIECHTENSTEIN 8 Nov 2002 a, LITHUANIA 30 Jan 2003 a, MADAGASCAR 15 Sep 2006 a, MALI 29 Apr 2002 a, MALTA 20 Nov 2001 a, MARSHALL ISLANDS 29 Nov 1994 a, MAURITIUS 3 Aug 2004 a, MEXICO 13 May 1994 a (*11), MICRONESIA 16 Feb 2003 a, MOLDOVA 11 Oct 2005 a (*8.1, 6.2, 16), MONACO 8 Jan 2002, MOZAMBIQUE 8 Jan 2003 a (16), MYANMAR 19 Sep 2003 a (*16.1), NAMIBIA 10 Jul 2004 a, NAURU 11 Aug 2005 a, NETHERLANDS 5 Mar 1992, NEW ZEALAND 10 Jun 1999, NIGERIA 24 Feb 2004 a, NORWAY 18 Apr 1991 a, OMAN 24 Sep 1990 a, PAKISTAN 20 Sep 2000 a, PALAU 4 Dec 2001 a, PANAMA 3 Jul 2002 a, PARAGUAY 12 Nov 2004 a, PERU 19 Jul 2001 a, PHILIPPINES 6 Jan 2004, POLAND 25 Jun 1991, PORTUGAL 5 Jan 1996 a (*8.3), QATAR 18 Sep 2003 a (*16(a)), REPUBLIC OF KOREA 14 May 2003 a, ROMANIA 2 Jun 1993 a, RUSSIAN FEDERATION 4 May 2001 (*8.1), SAINT KITTS AND NEVIS 17 Jan 2002 a, SAINT LUCIA 20 May 2004 a, ST. VINCENT AND THE GRENADINES 9 Oct 2001 a, SAMOA 18 May 2004 a, SAO TOME & SENEGAL 9 Aug 2004 a, SERBIA 10 May 2004 a, SEYCHELLES 24 Jan 1989, SINGAPORE 3 Feb 2004 a, SLOVAKIA 8 Dec 2000 a, SLOVENIA 18 Jul 2003 a, SOUTH AFRICA 8 July 2005 a, SPAIN 7 Jul 1989, SRI LANKA 4 Sep 2000 a, SUDAN 22 May 2000 a, SWAZI LAND 17 Apr 2003 a, SWEDEN 13 Sep 1990, SWITZERLAND 12 Mar 1993, SYRIAN ARAB REPUBLIC 24 Mar 2003 a, TAJIKISTAN 12 Aug 2005 a, TOGO 10 Mar 2003 a, TRINIDAD AND TOBAGO 24 Jul 1989 a, TUNISIA 6 Mar 1998 a (*16.1), TURKEY 6 Mar 1998 (*16), TURKMENISTAN 8 Jun 1999 a, TUVALU 2 Dec 2005 a, UGANDA 11 Nov 2003 a, UKRAINE 21 Apr 1994, UNITED ARAB EMIRATES 15 Sep 2005 a (*16.1),

* Source: 1589 U.N.T.S. 474.

UNITED KINGDOM 3 May 1991, UNITED REPUBLIC OF TANZANIA 11 May 2005 a, UNITED STATES 6 Dec 1994, URUGUAY 10 Aug 2001 a, VANUATU 18 Feb 1999 a, VIET NAM 12 Jul 2000 a, YEMEN 30 Jun 2000 a.

[…]

Article 3

1. Any person commits an offence if that person unlawfully and intentionally:

a) seizes or exercises control over a ship by force or threat thereof or any other form of intimidation; or

b) performs an act of violence against a person on board a ship if that act is likely to endanger the safe navigation of that ship; or

c) destroys a ship or causes damage to a ship or to its cargo which is likely to endanger the safe navigation of that ship; or

d) places or causes to be placed on a ship, by any means whatsoever, a device or substance which is likely to destroy that ship, or cause damage to that ship or its cargo which endangers or is likely to endanger the safe navigation of that ship; or

e) destroys or seriously damages maritime navigational facilities or seriously interferes with their operation, if any such act is likely to endanger the safe navigation of a ship; or

f) communicates information which he knows to be false, thereby endangering the safe navigation of a ship; or

g) injures or kills any person, in connection with the commission or the attempted commission of any of the offences set forth in subparagraphs (a) to (f).

[…]

Article 6

1. Each State Party shall take such measures as may be necessary to establish its jurisdiction over the offences set forth in article 3 when the offence is committed:

a) against or on board a ship flying the flag of the State at the time the offence is committed; or

b) in the territory of that State, including its territorial sea; or

c) by a national of that State.

2. A State Party may also establish its jurisdiction over any such offence when:

a) it is committed by a stateless person whose habitual residence is in that State; or

b) during its commission a national of that State is seized, threatened, injured or killed; or

c) it is committed in an attempt to compel that State to do or abstain from doing any act.

[…]

Article 7

1. Upon being satisfied that the circumstances so warrant, any State Party in the territory of which the offender or the alleged offender is present shall, in accordance with its law, take

him into custody or take other measures to ensure his presence for such time as is necessary to enable any criminal or extradition proceedings to be instituted.

2. Such State shall immediately make a preliminary inquiry into the facts, in accordance with its own legislation.

3. Any person regarding whom the measures referred to in paragraph 1 are being taken shall be entitled to:

a) communicate without delay with the nearest appropriate representative of the State of which he is a national or which is otherwise entitled to establish such communication or, if he is a stateless person, the State in the territory of which he has his habitual residence;

b) be visited by a representative of that State.

4. The rights referred to in paragraph 3 shall be exercised in conformity with the laws and regulations of the State in the territory of which the offender or the alleged offender is present, subject to the proviso that the said laws and regulations must enable full effect to be given to the purposes for which the rights accorded under paragraph 3 are intended.

5. When a State Party, pursuant to this article, has taken a person into custody, it shall immediately notify the States which have established jurisdiction in accordance with article 6, paragraph 1 and, if it considers it advisable, any other interested States, of the fact that such person is in custody and of the circumstances which warrant his detention. The State which makes the preliminary inquiry contemplated in paragraph 2 of this article shall promptly report its findings to the said States and shall indicate whether it intends to exercise jurisdiction.

[...]

Article 11

1. The offences set forth in article 3 shall be deemed to be included as extraditable offences in any extradition treaty existing between any of the States Parties. States Parties undertake to include such offences as extraditable offences in every extradition treaty to be concluded between them.

[...]

Declaration on Measures to Eliminate International Terrorism, 1994 [excerpts]*

Adoption: 9 December 1994

[…]

I

[…]

2. Acts, methods and practices of terrorism constitute a grave violation of the purposes and principles of the United Nations, which may pose a threat to international peace and security, jeopardize friendly relations among States, hinder international cooperation and aim at the destruction of human rights, fundamental freedoms and the democratic bases of society;

[…]

4. States, guided by the purposes and principles of the Charter of the United Nations and other relevant rules of international law, must refrain from organizing, instigating, assisting or participating in terrorist acts in territories of other States, or from acquiescing in or encouraging activities within their territories directed towards the commission of such acts;

5. States must also fulfil their obligations under the Charter of the United Nations and other provisions of international law with respect to combating international terrorism and are urged to take effective and resolute measures in accordance with the relevant provisions of international law and international standards of human rights for the speedy and final elimination of international terrorism, in particular:

[…]

(b) To ensure the apprehension and prosecution or extradition of perpetrators of terrorist acts, in accordance with the relevant provisions of their national law;

[…]

(f) To take appropriate measures, before granting asylum, for the purpose of ensuring that the asylum seeker has not engaged in terrorist activities and, after granting asylum, for the purpose of ensuring that the refugee status is not used in a manner contrary to the provisions set out in subparagraph (a) above;

[…]

* Source: U.N.G.A. Res. 49/60.

Declaration to Supplement the 1994 Declaration on Measures to Eliminate International Terrorism, 1996*

Adoption: 17 December 1996

The General Assembly,

Guided by the purposes and principles of the Charter of the United Nations,

Recalling the Declaration on Measures to Eliminate International Terrorism adopted by the General Assembly by its resolution 49/60 of 9 December 1994,

Recalling also the Declaration on the Occasion of the Fiftieth Anniversary of the United Nations,

Deeply disturbed by the worldwide persistence of acts of international terrorism in all its forms and manifestations, including those in which States are directly or indirectly involved, which endanger or take innocent lives, have a deleterious effect on international relations and may jeopardize the security of States,

Underlining the importance of States developing extradition agreements or arrangements as necessary in order to ensure that those responsible for terrorist acts are brought to justice,

Noting that the Convention relating to the Status of Refugees, done at Geneva on 28 July 1951, does not provide a basis for the protection of perpetrators of terrorist acts, noting also in this context articles 1, 2, 32 and 33 of the Convention, and emphasizing in this regard the need for States parties to ensure the proper application of the Convention,

Stressing the importance of full compliance by States with their obligations under the provisions of the 1951 Convention and the 1967 Protocol relating to the Status of Refugees, including the principle of non-refoulement of refugees to places where their life or freedom would be threatened on account of their race, religion, nationality, membership in a particular social group or political opinion, and affirming that the present Declaration does not affect the protection afforded under the terms of the Convention and Protocol and other provisions of international law,

Recalling article 4 of the Declaration on Territorial Asylum adopted by the General Assembly by its resolution 2312 (XXII) of 14 December 1967,

Stressing the need further to strengthen international cooperation between States in order to prevent, combat and eliminate terrorism in all its forms and manifestations,

Solemnly declares the following:

1. The States Members of the United Nations solemnly reaffirm their unequivocal condemnation of all acts, methods and practices of terrorism as criminal and unjustifiable, wherever and by whomsoever committed, including those which jeopardize friendly relations among States and peoples and threaten the territorial integrity and security of States;

2. The States Members of the United Nations reaffirm that acts, methods and practices of terrorism are contrary to the purposes and principles of the United Nations; they declare that knowingly financing, planning and inciting terrorist acts are also contrary to the purposes and principles of the United Nations;

* Source: U.N.G.A. Res. 51/210, Annex.

3. The States Members of the United Nations reaffirm that States should take appropriate measures in conformity with the relevant provisions of national and international law, including international standards of human rights, before granting refugee status, for the purpose of ensuring that the asylum-seeker has not participated in terrorist acts, considering in this regard relevant information as to whether the asylum-seeker is subject to investigation for or is charged with or has been convicted of offences connected with terrorism and, after granting refugee status, for the purpose of ensuring that that status is not used for the purpose of preparing or organizing terrorist acts intended to be committed against other States or their citizens;

4. The States Members of the United Nations emphasize that asylum- seekers who are awaiting the processing of their asylum applications may not thereby avoid prosecution for terrorist acts;

5. The States Members of the United Nations reaffirm the importance of ensuring effective cooperation between Member States so that those who have participated in terrorist acts, including their financing, planning or incitement, are brought to justice; they stress their commitment, in conformity with the relevant provisions of international law, including international standards of human rights, to work together to prevent, combat and eliminate terrorism and to take all appropriate steps under their domestic laws either to extradite terrorists or to submit the cases to their competent authorities for the purpose of prosecution;

6. In this context, and while recognizing the sovereign rights of States in extradition matters, States are encouraged, when concluding or applying extradition agreements, not to regard as political offences excluded from the scope of those agreements offences connected with terrorism which endanger or represent a physical threat to the safety and security of persons, whatever the motives which may be invoked to justify them;

7. States are also encouraged, even in the absence of a treaty, to consider facilitating the extradition of persons suspected of having committed terrorist acts, insofar as their national laws permit;

8. The States Members of the United Nations emphasize the importance of taking steps to share expertise and information about terrorists, their movements, their support and their weapons and to share information regarding the investigation and prosecution of terrorist acts.

International Convention for the Suppression of Terrorist Bombings, 1997 [excerpts]*

Adoption: 15 December 1997
Entry into force: 23 May 2001
Parties: 149 (Status as of 1 April 2007)

AFGHANISTAN 24 Sep 2003 a, ALBANIA 22 Jan 2002 a, ALGERIA 8 Nov 2001 (*20.1), ANDORRA 23 Sep 2004 a, ARGENTINA 25 Sep 2003, ARMENIA 16 Mar 2004 a, AUSTRALIA 9 Aug 2002 a, AUSTRIA 6 Sep 2000, AZERBAIJAN 2 Apr 2001 a, BAHRAIN 21 Sep 2004 a (*20.1), BANGLADESH 20 May 2005 a, BARBADOS 18 Sep 2002 a, BELARUS 1 Oct 2001, BELGIUM 20 May 2005 (*11), BELIZE 14 Nov 2001 a, BENIN 31 Jul 2003 a, BOLIVIA 22 Jan 2002 a, BOSNIA AND HERZEGOVINA 11 Aug 2003 a, BOTSWANA 8 Sep 2000 a, BRAZIL 23 Aug 2002 (*20.1), BRUNEI DARUSSALAM 14 Mar 2002 a, BULGARIA 12 Feb 2002 a, BURKINA FASO 1 Oct 2003 a, BURUNDI signed 4 Mar 1998, CAMBODIA 31 July 2006 a, CAMEROON 21 Mar 2005 a, CANADA 3 Apr 2002 (*2.3c), CAPE VERDE 10 May 2002 a, CHILE 10 Nov 2001 a, CHINA 13 Nov 2001 a, COLOMBIA 14 Sep 2004 a (*6.3, 20.1), COMOROS 25 Sep 2003, COSTA RICA 20 Sep 2001, CÔTE D'IVOIRE 13 Mar 2002, CROATIA 2 Jun 2005 a, CUBA 15 Nov 2001 a (*19.2, 20.1, general), CYPRUS 24 Jan 2001, CZECH REPUBLIC 6 Sep 2000, DENMARK 31 Aug 2001, DJIBOUTI 1 Jun 2004 a, DOMINICA 24 Sep 2004 a, EGYPT 9 Aug 2005 (*6.5, 19.2), EL SALVADOR 15 May 2003 a (*20.1), ESTONIA 10 Apr 2002, ETHIOPIA 16 Apr 2003 a (*20.1), FINLAND 28 May 2002 a, FRANCE 19 Aug 1999, GABON 10 Mar 2005 a, GEORGIA 18 Feb 2004 a, GERMANY 23 Apr 2003 (*1.4), GHANA 6 Sep 2002 a, GREECE 27 May 2003, GRENADA 13 Dec 2001 a, GUATEMALA 12 Feb 2002 a, GUINEA 7 Sep 2000 a, HONDURAS 25 Mar 2003 a, HUNGARY 13 Nov 2001, ICELAND 15 Apr 2002, INDIA 22 Sep 1999 (*20.1), INDONESIA 29 Jun 2006 a (*6, 20.1), IRELAND 30 Jun 2005, ISRAEL 10 Feb 2003 (*1.4, 19, 20.1), ITALY 16 Apr 2003, JAMAICA 9 Aug 2005 a, JAPAN 16 Nov 2001 a, KAZAKHSTAN 6 Nov 2002 a, KENYA 16 Nov 2001 a, KIRABATI 15 Sep 2005 a, KUWAIT 19 Apr 2004 a (*20.1), KYRGYZSTAN 1 May 2001 a, LAO PEOPLE'S DEMOCRATIC REPUBLIC 22 Aug 2002 a (*20.1), LATVIA 25 Nov 2002 a, LESOTHO 12 Nov 2001 a, LIBERIA 5 Mar 2003 a, LIBYAN ARAB JAMAHIRIYA 22 Sep 2000 a, LIECHTENSTEIN 26 Nov 2002 a, LITHUANIA 17 Mar 2004, LUXEMBOURG 6 Feb 2004, MADAGASCAR 24 Sep 2003, MALAWI 11 Aug 2003 a, MALAYSIA 24 Sep 2003 a (*1.4, 8.1, 20.1), MALDIVES 7 Sep 2000 a, MALI 28 Mar 2002 a, MALTA 11 Nov 2001 a, MARSHALL ISLANDS 27 Jan 2003 a, MAURITANIA 30 Apr 2003 a, MAURITIUS 24 Jan 2003 a, MEXICO 20 Jan 2003 a, MICRONESIA (FEDERATED STATES OF) 23 Sep 2002 a, MONACO 6 Sep 2001, MONGOLIA 7 Sep 2000 a, MONTENEGRO 23 Oct 2006 d, MOZAMBIQUE 14 Jan 2003 a (*20.1), MYANMAR 12 Nov 2001 a (20.1), NAURU 2 Aug 2005 a, NEPAL signed 24 Sep 1999, NETHERLANDS 7 Sep 2002 a (*8.1), NEW ZEALAND 4 Nov 2002 a, NICARAGUA 17 Jan 2003 a, NIGER 26 Oct 2004 a, NORWAY 20 Sep 1999, PAKISTAN 13 Aug 2002 a (*general), PALAU 14 Nov 2001 a, PANAMA 5 Mar 1999, PAPUA NEW GUINEA 30 Sep 2003 a, PARAGUAY 22 Sep 2004 a, PERU 10 Nov 2001 a, PHILIPPINES 7 Jan 2004, PORTUGAL 10 Nov 2001 (*8.2, general), REPUBLIC OF KOREA 17 Feb 2004, REPUBLIC OF MOLDOVA 10 Oct 2002 a (*12, 20.1), ROMANIA 29 Jul 2004, RUSSIAN FEDERATION 8 May 2001 (*12), RWANDA 13 May 2002 a, SAINT KITTS AND NEVIS 16 Nov 2001 a, SAINT VINCENT AND THE GRENADINES 15 Sep 2005 a, SAN MARINO 12 Mar 2002 a, SAO TOME AND PRINCIPE 12 Apr 2006,

* Source: U.N.G.A. Res. 52/164.

SENEGAL 27 Oct 2003 a, SERBIA 31 Jul 2003, SEYCHELLES 22 Aug 2003 a, SIERRA LEONE 26 Sep 2003 a, SLOVAKIA 8 Dec 2000, SLOVENIA 25 Sep 2003, SOUTH AFRICA 1 May 2003, SPAIN 30 Apr 1999 (*6.2, 23), SRI LANKA 23 Mar 1999, SUDAN 8 Sep 2000 (*19.2, 20.1), SWAZILAND 4 Apr 2003 a, SWEDEN 6 Sep 2001, SWITZERLAND 23 Sep 2003 a, TAJIKISTAN 29 Jul 2002 a, THE FORMER REPUBLIC OF MACEDONIA 30 Aug 2004, TOGO 10 Mar 2003, TONGA 9 Dec 2002 a, TRINIDAD AND TOBAGO 2 Apr 2001 a, TUNISIA 22 Apr 2005 a (*20.1), TURKEY 30 May 2002 (*9, 12, 19, 20.1), TURKMENISTAN 25 Jun 1999, UGANDA 5 Nov 2003, UKRAINE 26 Mar 2002 a (*19.2), UNITED ARAB EMIRATES 23 Sep 2005 a (*6.2, 20.1), UNITED KINGDOM OF GREAT BRITAIN AND NORTHERN IRELAND 7 Mar 2001, UNITED REPUBLIC OF TANZANIA 22 Jan 2003 a, UNITED STATES OF AMERICA 26 Jun 2002 (*1.4, 19, 20.1), URUGUAY 10 Nov 2001, UZBEKISTAN 30 Nov 1998, VENEZUELA (BOLIVARIAN REPUBLIC OF) 23 Sep 2003 (*20.1), YEMEN 23 Apr 2001 a.

[…]

Article 2

1. Any person commits an offence within the meaning of this Convention if that person unlawfully and intentionally delivers, places, discharges or detonates an explosive or other lethal device in, into or against a place of public use, a State or government facility, a public transportation system or an infrastructure facility:

a) With the intent to cause death or serious bodily injury; or

b) With the intent to cause extensive destruction of such a place, facility or system, where such destruction results in or is likely to result in major economic loss.

[…]

Article 6

1. Each State Party shall take such measures as may be necessary to establish its jurisdiction over the offences set forth in article 2 when:

a) The offence is committed in the territory of that State; or

b) The offence is committed on board a vessel flying the flag of that State or an aircraft which is registered under the laws of that State at the time the offence is committed; or

c) The offence is committed by a national of that State.

2. A State Party may also establish its jurisdiction over any such offence when:

a) The offence is committed against a national of that State; or

b) The offence is committed against a State or government facility of that State abroad, including an embassy or other diplomatic or consular premises of that State; or

c) The offence is committed by a stateless person who has his or her habitual residence in the territory of that State; or

d) The offence is committed in an attempt to compel that State to do or abstain from doing any act; or

e) The offence is committed on board an aircraft which is operated by the Government of that State.

[...]

Article 7

[...]

3. Any person regarding whom the measures referred to in paragraph 2 of the present article are being taken shall be entitled to:

a) Communicate without delay with the nearest appropriate representative of the State of which that person is a national or which is otherwise entitled to protect that person's rights or, if that person is a stateless person, the State in the territory of which that person habitually resides;

b) Be visited by a representative of that State;

c) Be informed of that person's rights under subparagraphs (a) and (b).

4. The rights referred to in paragraph 3 of the present article shall be exercised in conformity with the laws and regulations of the State in the territory of which the offender or alleged offender is present, subject to the provision that the said laws and regulations must enable full effect to be given to the purposes for which the rights accorded under paragraph 3 are intended.

[...]

Article 9

1. The offences set forth in article 2 shall be deemed to be included as extraditable offences in any extradition treaty existing between any of the States Parties before the entry into force of this Convention. States Parties undertake to include such offences as extraditable offences in every extradition treaty to be subsequently concluded between them.

[...]

Article 12

Nothing in this Convention shall be interpreted as imposing an obligation to extradite or to afford mutual legal assistance, if the requested State Party has substantial grounds for believing that the request for extradition for offences set forth in article 2 or for mutual legal assistance with respect to such offences has been made for the purpose of prosecuting or punishing a person on account of that person's race, religion, nationality, ethnic origin or political opinion or that compliance with the request would cause prejudice to that person's position for any of these reasons.

[...]

Article 14

Any person who is taken into custody or regarding whom any other measures are taken or proceedings are carried out pursuant to this Convention shall be guaranteed fair treatment, including enjoyment of all rights and guarantees in conformity with the law of the State in the territory of which that person is present and applicable provisions of international law, including international law of human rights.

International Convention for the Suppression of the Financing of Terrorism, 1999 [excerpts]*

Adoption: 9 December 1999
Entry into force: 10 April 2002
Parties: 156 (Status as of 1 April 2007)

AFGHANISTAN 24 Sep 2003 a, ALBANIA 10 Apr 2002, ALGERIA 8 Nov 2001(*24.1), ANDORRA signed 11 Nov 2001, ANTIGUA AND BARBUDA 11 Mar 2002 a, ARGENTINA 22 Aug 2005 (*24.1), ARMENIA 16 Mar 2004, AUSTRALIA 26 Sep 2002, AUSTRIA 15 Apr 2002, AZERBAIJAN 26 Oct 2001, BAHAMAS 1 Nov 2005 (*2.2), BAHRAIN 21 Sep 2004 (*2.1, 24.1), BANGLADESH 26 Aug 2005 a (*24.1, general), BARBADOS 18 Sep 2002, BELARUS 6 Oct 2004, BELGIUM 17 May 2004 (*2, 14), BELIZE 1 Dec 2003, BENIN 30 Aug 2004, BHUTAN 22 Mar 2004, BOLIVIA 7 Jan 2002, BOSNIA AND HERZEGOVINA 10 Jun 2003, BOTSWANA 8 Sep 2000, BRAZIL 16 Sep 2005 (*2, 24.1), BRUNEI DARUSSALAM 4 Dec 2002 a, BULGARIA 15 Apr 2002, BURKINA FASO 1 Oct 2003 a, BURUNDI signed 13 Nov 2001, CAMEROON 6 Feb 2006 a, CANADA 19 Feb 2002, CAPE VERDE 10 May 2002, CENTRAL AFRICAN REPUBLIC signed 19 Dec 2001, CHILE 10 Nov 2001, CHINA 19 Apr 2006 (*2, 24.1), COLOMBIA 14 Sep 2004 (*7, 24.1), COMOROS 25 Sep 2003, CONGO signed 14 Nov 2001, COOK ISLANDS 4 Mar 2004 (*2), COSTA RICA 24 Jan 2003, CÔTE D'IVOIRE 13 Mar 2002 a, CROATIA 1 Dec 2003 (*2), CUBA 15 Nov 2001 (*24.1), CYPRUS 30 Nov 2001, CZECH REPUBLIC 27 Dec 2005, DEMOCRATIC PEOPLE'S REPUBLIC OF KOREA signed 12 Nov 2001 (*2.1, 14, 24.1), DEMOCRATIC REPUBLIC OF THE CONGO 28 Oct 2005, DENMARK 27 Aug 2002, DJIBOUTI 13 Mar 2006, DOMINICA 24 Sep 2004 a, DOMINICAN REPUBLIC signed 15 Nov 2001, ECUADOR 9 Dec 2003, EGYPT 1 Mar 2005 (*2.2a, 24.1), EL SALVADOR 15 May 2003 a (*2.2a, 24.1), EQUATORIAL GUINEA 7 Feb 2003 a, ESTONIA 22 May 2002, FINLAND 28 Jun 2002 a, FRANCE 7 Jan 2002 (*2.2a), GABON 10 Mar 2005, GEORGIA 27 Sep 2002 (*2.2), GERMANY 17 Jun 2004, GHANA 6 Sep 2002, GREECE 16 Apr 2004, GRENADA 13 Dec 2001 a, GUATEMALA 12 Feb 2002 (*2.2a), GUINEA 14 Jul 2003, GUINEA-BISSAU signed 14 Nov 2001, HONDRUAS 25 Mar 2003, HUNGARY 14 Oct 2002, ICELAND 15 Apr 2002, INDIA 22 Apr 2003, INDONESIA 29 Jun 2006 (*2.2a, 24.1), IRELAND 30 Jun 2005, ISRAEL 10 Feb 2003 (*2.2a, 21, 24.1), ITALY 27 Mar 2003, JAMAICA 16 Sep 2005, JAPAN 11 Jun 2002 a, JORDAN 28 Aug 2003 (*2, general), KAZAKHSTAN 24 Feb 2003 a, KENYA 27 Jun 2003, KIRIBATI 15 Sep 2005 a, KYRGYZSTAN 2 Oct 2003 a, LATVIA 14 Nov 2002 (*2.2), LESOTHO 12 Nov 2001, LIBERIA 5 Mar 2003 a, LIBYAN ARAB JAMAHIRIYA 9 Jul 2002, LIECHTENSTEIN 9 Jul 2003, LITHUANIA 20 Feb 2003 a (*2, 24.1), LUXEMBOURG 5 Nov 2003 (*2.2), MADAGASCAR 24 Sep 2003, MALAWI 11 Aug 2003 a, MALDIVES 20 Apr 2004 a, MALI 28 Mar 2002, MALTA 11 Nov 2001, MARSHALL ISLANDS 27 Jan 2003 a, MAURITANIA 30 Apr 2003 a, MAURITIUS 14 Dec 2004 (*2.2, 24.1), MEXICO 20 Jan 2003, MICRONESIA (FEDERATED STATES OF) 23 Sep 2002, MONACO 10 Nov 2001, MONGOLIA 25 Feb 2004, MONTENEGRO 23 Oct 2006 d, MOROCCO 19 Sep 2002, MOZAMBIQUE 14 Jan 2003 (*24.1, general), MYANMAR 16 Aug 2006 (*24.1), NAMIBIA signed 10 Nov 2001, NAURU 24 May 2005, NETHERLANDS 7 Feb 2002 a (*10.1), NEW ZEALAND 4 Nov 2002 (*2.2a), NICARAGUA 14 Nov 2002 (*2.2a), NIGER 30 Sep 2004 a, NIGERIA 16 Jun 2003, NORWAY 15 Jul 2002, PALAU 14 Nov 2001 a, PANAMA 3 Jul 2002, PAPUA NEW GUINEA 30 Sep 2003 a, PARAGUAY 30 Nov 2004, PERU 10 Nov 2001, PHILIPPINES 7 Jan 2004 (*2.2a), POLAND 26 Sep 2003, PORTUGAL 18 Oct 2002, REPUBLIC OF KOREA 17 Feb

* Source: U.N.G.A. Res. 54/109.

2004, REPUBLIC OF MOLDOVA 10 Oct 2002 (*2.2a, 24.1), ROMANIA 9 Jan 2003 (*2.2a), RUSSIAN FEDERATION 27 Nov 2002 (*15), RWANDA 13 May 2002, SAINT KITTS AND NEVIS 16 Nov 2001, SAINT VINCENT AND THE GRENADINES 28 Mar 2002 (*2.2a, 24.1), SAMOA 27 Sep 2002, SAN MARINO 12 Mar 2002, SAO TOME AND PRINCIPE 12 Apr 2006 a, SAUDI ARABIA signed 29 Nov 2001, SENEGAL 24 Sep 2004 a, SERBIA 10 Oct 2002, SEYCHELLES 30 Mar 2004, SIERRA LEONE 26 Sep 2003, SINGAPORE 30 Dec 2002 (*2.2a, 21, 24.1), SLOVAKIA 13 Sep 2002, SLOVENIA 23 Sep 2004, SOMALIA signed 19 Dec 2001, SOUTH AFRICA 1 May 2003, SPAIN 9 Apr 2002, SRI LANKA 8 Sep 2000, SUDAN 5 May 2003, SWAZILAND 4 Apr 2003 a, SWEDEN 6 Jun 2002, SWITZERLAND 23 Sep 2003, SYRIAN ARAB REPUBLIC 24 Apr 2005 a (*2, 24.1), TAJIKISTAN 16 Jul 2004, THAILAND 29 Sep 2004 (*2.2a, 24.1), THE FORMER YUGOSLAV REPUBLIC OF MACEDONIA 30 Aug 2004 (*2), TOGO 10 Mar 2003, TONGA 9 Dec 2002 a, TUNISIA 10 Jun 2003 (*24.1), TURKEY 28 Jun 2002 (*2, 21, 24.1), TURMENISTAN 7 Jan 2005 a, UGANDA 5 Nov 2003, UKRAINE 6 Dec 2002, UNITED ARAB EMIRATES 23 Sep 2005 a (*24.1), UNITED KINGDOM OF GREAT BRITAIN AND NORTHERN IRELAND, UNITED REPUBLIC OF TANZANIA 22 Jan 2003 a, UNITED STATES OF AMERICA 26 Jun 2002 (*2, 24.1, general), URUGUAY 8 Jan 2004, UZBEKISTAN 9 Jul 2001, VANUATU 31 Oct 2005 a, VENEZUELA (BOLIVERIAN REPUBLIC OF) 23 Sep 2003 (*2.2a, 24.1), VIET NAM 25.

[...]

Article 2

1. Any person commits an offence within the meaning of this Convention if that person by any means, directly or indirectly, unlawfully and wilfully, provides or collects funds with the intention that they should be used or in the knowledge that they are to be used, in full or in part, in order to carry out:

(a) An act which constitutes an offence within the scope of and as defined in one of the treaties listed in the annex; or

(b) Any other act intended to cause death or serious bodily injury to a civilian, or to any other person not taking an active part in the hostilities in a situation of armed conflict, when the purpose of such act, by its nature or context, is to intimidate a population, or to compel a government or an international organization to do or to abstain from doing any act.

[...]

Article 7

1. Each State Party shall take such measures as may be necessary to establish its jurisdiction over the offences set forth in article 2 when: (a) The offence is committed in the territory of that State;

(b) The offence is committed on board a vessel flying the flag of that State or an aircraft registered under the laws of that State at the time the offence is committed;

(c) The offence is committed by a national of that State.

2. A State Party may also establish its jurisdiction over any such offence when:

(a) The offence was directed towards or resulted in the carrying out of an offence referred to in article 2, paragraph 1, subparagraph (a) or (b), in the territory of or against a national of that State;

(b) The offence was directed towards or resulted in the carrying out of an offence referred to in article 2, paragraph 1, subparagraph (a) or (b), against a State or government facility of that State abroad, including diplomatic or consular premises of that State;

(c) The offence was directed towards or resulted in an offence referred to in article 2, paragraph 1, subparagraph (a) or (b), committed in an attempt to compel that State to do or abstain from doing any act;

(d) The offence is committed by a stateless person who has his or her habitual residence in the territory of that State;

(e) The offence is committed on board an aircraft which is operated by the Government of that State.

[...]

Article 9

1. Upon receiving information that a person who has committed or who is alleged to have committed an offence set forth in article 2 may be present in its territory, the State Party concerned shall take such measures as may be necessary under its domestic law to investigate the facts contained in the information.

2. Upon being satisfied that the circumstances so warrant, the State Party in whose territory the offender or alleged offender is present shall take the appropriate measures under its domestic law so as to ensure that person's presence for the purpose of prosecution or extradition.

3. Any person regarding whom the measures referred to in paragraph 2 are being taken shall be entitled to:

(a) Communicate without delay with the nearest appropriate representative of the State of which that person is a national or which is otherwise entitled to protect that person's rights or, if that person is a stateless person, the State in the territory of which that person habitually resides;

(b) Be visited by a representative of that State;

(c) Be informed of that person's rights under subparagraphs (a) and (b).

4. The rights referred to in paragraph 3 shall be exercised in conformity with the laws and regulations of the State in the territory of which the offender or alleged offender is present, subject to the provision that the said laws and regulations must enable full effect to be given to the purposes for which the rights accorded under paragraph 3 are intended.

5. The provisions of paragraphs 3 and 4 shall be without prejudice to the right of any State Party having a claim to jurisdiction in accordance with article 7, paragraph 1, subparagraph (b), or paragraph 2, subparagraph (b), to invite the International Committee of the Red Cross to communicate with and visit the alleged offender.

6. When a State Party, pursuant to the present article, has taken a person into custody, it shall immediately notify, directly or through the Secretary-General of the United Nations, the States Parties which have established jurisdiction in accordance with article 7, paragraph 1 or 2, and, if it considers it advisable, any other interested States Parties, of the fact that such person is in custody and of the circumstances which warrant that person's detention. The State which makes the investigation contemplated in paragraph 1 shall promptly inform the said States Parties of its findings and shall indicate whether it intends to exercise jurisdiction.

[...]

Article 11

1. The offences set forth in article 2 shall be deemed to be included as extraditable offences in any extradition treaty existing between any of the States Parties before the entry into force of this Convention. States Parties undertake to include such offences as extraditable offences in every extradition treaty to be subsequently concluded between them.

[…]

Article 17

Any person who is taken into custody or regarding whom any other measures are taken or proceedings are carried out pursuant to this Convention shall be guaranteed fair treatment, including enjoyment of all rights and guarantees in conformity with the law of the State in the territory of which that person is present and applicable provisions of international law, including international human rights law.

[…]

Security Council Resolution 1373, 2001 [excerpts]*

Adoption: 28 September 2001

The Security Council

[...]

3. Calls upon States to:

[...]

(d) Become parties as soon as possible to the relevant international conventions and protocols relating to terrorism, including the International Convention for the Suppression of the Financing of Terrorism of 9 December 1999;

(e) Increase cooperation and fully implement the relevant international conventions and protocols relating to terrorism and Security Council resolutions 1269 (1999) and 1368 (2001);

(f) Take appropriate measures in conformity with the relevant provisions of national and international law, including international standards of human rights, before granting refugee status, for the purpose of ensuring that the asylum-seeker has not planned, facilitated or participated in the commission of terrorist acts;

(g) Ensure, in conformity with international law, that refugee status is not abused by the perpetrators, organizers or facilitators of terrorist acts, and that claims of political motivation are not recognized as grounds for refusing requests for the extradition of alleged terrorists;

[...]

* Source: Resolution 1373 (2001), adopted by the Security Council at its 4385th meeting [S/RES/1373(2001)].

CCPR General Comment No.29: Article 4 (States of Emergency), 2001*

Adoption: 24 July 2001

1. Article 4 of the Covenant is of paramount importance for the system of protection for human rights under the Covenant. On the one hand, it allows for a State party unilaterally to derogate temporarily from a part of its obligations under the Covenant. On the other hand, article 4 subjects both this very measure of derogation, as well as its material consequences, to a specific regime of safeguards. The restoration of a state of normalcy where full respect for the Covenant can again be secured must be the predominant objective of a State party derogating from the Covenant. In this general comment, replacing its General Comment No 5, adopted at the thirteenth session (1981), the Committee seeks to assist States parties to meet the requirements of article 4.

2. Measures derogating from the provisions of the Covenant must be of an exceptional and temporary nature. Before a State moves to invoke article 4, two fundamental conditions must be met: the situation must amount to a public emergency which threatens the life of the nation, and the State party must have officially proclaimed a state of emergency. The latter requirement is essential for the maintenance of the principles of legality and rule of law at times when they are most needed. When proclaiming a state of emergency with consequences that could entail derogation from any provision of the Covenant, States must act within their constitutional and other provisions of law that govern such proclamation and the exercise of emergency powers; it is the task of the Committee to monitor the laws in question with respect to whether they enable and secure compliance with article 4. In order that the Committee can perform its task, States parties to the Covenant should include in their reports submitted under article 40 sufficient and precise information about their law and practice in the field of emergency powers.

3. Not every disturbance or catastrophe qualifies as a public emergency which threatens the life of the nation, as required by article 4, paragraph 1. During armed conflict, whether international or non-international, rules of international humanitarian law become applicable and help, in addition to the provisions in article 4 and article 5, paragraph 1, of the Covenant, to prevent the abuse of a State's emergency powers. The Covenant requires that even during an armed conflict measures derogating from the Covenant are allowed only if and to the extent that the situation constitutes a threat to the life of the nation. If States parties consider invoking article 4 in other situations than an armed conflict, they should carefully consider the justification and why such a measure is necessary and legitimate in the circumstances. On a number of occasions the Committee has expressed its concern over States parties that appear to have derogated from rights protected by the Covenant, or whose domestic law appears to allow such derogation in situations not covered by article 4.[1]

4. A fundamental requirement for any measures derogating from the Covenant, as set forth in article 4, paragraph 1, is that such measures are limited to the extent strictly required by the

* Source: U.N. Doc. No.CCPR/C/21/Rev.1/Add.11.

[1] See the following comments/concluding observations: United Republic of Tanzania (1992), CCPR/C/79/Add.12, para. 7; Dominican Republic (1993), CCPR/C/79/Add.18, para. 4; United Kingdom of Great Britain and Northern Ireland (1995), CCPR/C/79/Add.55, para. 23; Peru (1996), CCPR/C/79/Add.67, para. 11; Bolivia (1997), CCPR/C/79/Add.74, para. 14; Colombia (1997), CCPR/C/79/Add.76, para. 25; Lebanon (1997), CCPR/C/79/Add.78, para. 10; Uruguay (1998), CCPR/C/79/Add.90, para. 8; Israel (1998), CCPR/C/79/Add.93, para. 11.

exigencies of the situation. This requirement relates to the duration, geographical coverage and material scope of the state of emergency and any measures of derogation resorted to because of the emergency. Derogation from some Covenant obligations in emergency situations is clearly distinct from restrictions or limitations allowed even in normal times under several provisions of the Covenant.[2] Nevertheless, the obligation to limit any derogations to those strictly required by the exigencies of the situation reflects the principle of proportionality which is common to derogation and limitation powers. Moreover, the mere fact that a permissible derogation from a specific provision may, of itself, be justified by the exigencies of the situation does not obviate the requirement that specific measures taken pursuant to the derogation must also be shown to be required by the exigencies of the situation. In practice, this will ensure that no provision of the Covenant, however validly derogated from will be entirely inapplicable to the behaviour of a State party. When considering States parties' reports the Committee has expressed its concern over insufficient attention being paid to the principle of proportionality.[3]

5. The issues of when rights can be derogated from, and to what extent, cannot be separated from the provision in article 4, paragraph 1, of the Covenant according to which any measures derogating from a State party's obligations under the Covenant must be limited "to the extent strictly required by the exigencies of the situation". This condition requires that States parties provide careful justification not only for their decision to proclaim a state of emergency but also for any specific measures based on such a proclamation. If States purport to invoke the right to derogate from the Covenant during, for instance, a natural catastrophe, a mass demonstration including instances of violence, or a major industrial accident, they must be able to justify not only that such a situation constitutes a threat to the life of the nation, but also that all their measures derogating from the Covenant are strictly required by the exigencies of the situation. In the opinion of the Committee, the possibility of restricting certain Covenant rights under the terms of, for instance, freedom of movement (article 12) or freedom of assembly (article 21) is generally sufficient during such situations and no derogation from the provisions in question would be justified by the exigencies of the situation.

6. The fact that some of the provisions of the Covenant have been listed in article 4 (paragraph 2), as not being subject to derogation does not mean that other articles in the Covenant may be subjected to derogations at will, even where a threat to the life of the nation exists. The legal obligation to narrow down all derogations to those strictly required by the exigencies of the situation establishes both for States parties and for the Committee a duty to conduct a careful analysis under each article of the Covenant based on an objective assessment of the actual situation.

7. Article 4, paragraph 2, of the Covenant explicitly prescribes that no derogation from the following articles may be made: article 6 (right to life), article 7 (prohibition of torture or cruel, inhuman or degrading punishment, or of medical or scientific experimentation without consent), article 8, paragraphs 1 and 2 (prohibition of slavery, slave-trade and servitude), article 11 (prohibition of imprisonment because of inability to fulfil a contractual obligation), article 15 (the principle of legality in the field of criminal law, i.e. the requirement of both criminal liability and punishment being limited to clear and precise provisions in the law that was in place and applicable at the time the act or omission took place, except in cases where a later law imposes a lighter penalty), article 16 (the recognition of everyone as a person before the law), and article 18 (freedom of thought, conscience and religion). The rights enshrined in these provisions are non-derogable by the very fact that they are listed in article 4, paragraph

[2] See, for instance, articles 12 and 19 of the Covenant.

[3] See, for example, concluding observations on Israel (1998), CCPR/C/79/Add.93, para. 11.

2. The same applies, in relation to States that are parties to the Second Optional Protocol to the Covenant, aiming at the abolition of the death penalty, as prescribed in article 6 of that Protocol. Conceptually, the qualification of a Covenant provision as a non-derogable one does not mean that no limitations or restrictions would ever be justified. The reference in article 4, paragraph 2, to article 18, a provision that includes a specific clause on restrictions in its paragraph 3, demonstrates that the permissibility of restrictions is independent of the issue of derogability. Even in times of most serious public emergencies, States that interfere with the freedom to manifest one's religion or belief must justify their actions by referring to the requirements specified in article 18, paragraph 3. On several occasions the Committee has expressed its concern about rights that are non-derogable according to article 4, paragraph 2, being either derogated from or under a risk of derogation owing to inadequacies in the legal regime of the State party.[4]

8. According to article 4, paragraph 1, one of the conditions for the justifiability of any derogation from the Covenant is that the measures taken do not involve discrimination solely on the ground of race, colour, sex, language, religion or social origin. Even though article 26 or the other Covenant provisions related to non-discrimination (articles 2, 3, 14, paragraph 1, 23, paragraph 4, 24, paragraph 1, and 25) have not been listed among the non-derogable provisions in article 4, paragraph 2, there are elements or dimensions of the right to non-discrimination that cannot be derogated from in any circumstances. In particular, this provision of article 4, paragraph 1, must be complied with if any distinctions between persons are made when resorting to measures that derogate from the Covenant.

9. Furthermore, article 4, paragraph 1, requires that no measure derogating from the provisions of the Covenant may be inconsistent with the State party's other obligations under international law, particularly the rules of international humanitarian law. Article 4 of the Covenant cannot be read as justification for derogation from the Covenant if such derogation would entail a breach of the State's other international obligations, whether based on treaty or general international law. This is reflected also in article 5, paragraph 2, of the Covenant according to which there shall be no restriction upon or derogation from any fundamental rights recognized in other instruments on the pretext that the Covenant does not recognize such rights or that it recognizes them to a lesser extent.

10. Although it is not the function of the Human Rights Committee to review the conduct of a State party under other treaties, in exercising its functions under the Covenant the Committee has the competence to take a State party's other international obligations into account when it considers whether the Covenant allows the State party to derogate from specific provisions of the Covenant. Therefore, when invoking article 4, paragraph 1, or when reporting under article 40 on the legal framework related to emergencies, States parties should present information on their other international obligations relevant for the protection of the rights in question, in particular those obligations that are applicable in times of emergency.[5] In this respect, States

---

[4] See the following comments/concluding observations: Dominican Republic (1993), CCPR/C/79/Add.18, para. 4; Jordan (1994) CCPR/C/79/Add.35, para. 6; Nepal (1994) CCPR/C/79/Add.42, para. 9; Russian Federation (1995), CCPR/C/79/Add.54, para. 27; Zambia (1996), CCPR/C/79/Add.62, para. 11; Gabon (1996), CCPR/C/79/Add.71, para. 10; Colombia (1997) CCPR/C/79/Add.76, para. 25; Israel (1998), CCPR/C/79/Add.93, para. 11; Iraq (1997), CCPR/C/79/Add.84, para. 9; Uruguay (1998) CCPR/C/79/Add.90, para. 8; Armenia (1998), CCPR/C/79/Add.100, para. 7; Mongolia (2000), CCPR/C/79/Add.120, para. 14; Kyrgyzstan (2000), CCPR/CO/69/KGZ, para. 12.

[5] Reference is made to the Convention on the Rights of the Child which has been ratified by almost all States parties to the Covenant and does not include a derogation clause. As article 38 of the Convention clearly indicates, the Convention is applicable in emergency situations.

parties should duly take into account the developments within international law as to human rights standards applicable in emergency situations.[6]

11. The enumeration of non-derogable provisions in article 4 is related to, but not identical with, the question whether certain human rights obligations bear the nature of peremptory norms of international law. The proclamation of certain provisions of the Covenant as being of a non derogable nature, in article 4, paragraph 2, is to be seen partly as recognition of the peremptory nature of some fundamental rights ensured in treaty form in the Covenant (e.g., articles 6 and 7). However, it is apparent that some other provisions of the Covenant were included in the list of non-derogable provisions because it can never become necessary to derogate from these rights during a state of emergency (e.g., articles 11 and 18). Furthermore, the category of peremptory norms extends beyond the list of non-derogable provisions as given in article 4, paragraph 2. States parties may in no circumstances invoke article 4 of the Covenant as justification for acting in violation of humanitarian law or peremptory norms of international law, for instance by taking hostages, by imposing collective punishments, through arbitrary deprivations of liberty or by deviating from fundamental principles of fair trial, including the presumption of innocence.

12. In assessing the scope of legitimate derogation from the Covenant, one criterion can be found in the definition of certain human rights violations as crimes against humanity. If action conducted under the authority of a State constitutes a basis for individual criminal responsibility for a crime against humanity by the persons involved in that action, article 4 of the Covenant cannot be used as justification that a state of emergency exempted the State in question from its responsibility in relation to the same conduct. Therefore, the recent codification of crimes against humanity, for jurisdictional purposes, in the Rome Statute of the International Criminal Court is of relevance in the interpretation of article 4 of the Covenant.[7]

13. In those provisions of the Covenant that are not listed in article 4, paragraph 2, there are elements that in the Committee's opinion cannot be made subject to lawful derogation under article 4. Some illustrative examples are presented below.

---

[6] Reference is made to reports of the Secretary General to the Commission on Human Rights submitted pursuant to Commission resolutions 1998/29, 1996/65 and 2000/69 on minimum humanitarian standards (later: fundamental standards of humanity), E/CN.4/1999/92, E/CN.4/2000/94 and E/CN.4/2001/91, and to earlier efforts to identify fundamental rights applicable in all circumstances, for instance the Paris Minimum Standards of Human Rights Norms in a State of Emergency (International Law Association, 1984), the Siracusa Principles on the Limitation and Derogation Provisions in the International Covenant on Civil and Political Rights, the final report of Mr. Leandro Despouy, Special Rapporteur of the Sub-Commission, on human rights and states of emergency (E/CN.4/Sub.2/1997/19 and Add.1), the Guiding Principles on Internal Displacement (E/CN.4/1998/53/Add.2), the Turku (Åbo) Declaration of Minimum Humanitarian Standards (1990), (E/CN.4/1995/116). As a field of ongoing further work reference is made to the decision of the 26th International Conference of the Red Cross and Red Crescent (1995) to assign the International Committee of the Red Cross the task of preparing a report on the customary rules of international humanitarian law applicable in international and non-international armed conflicts.

[7] See articles 6 (genocide) and 7 (crimes against humanity) of the Statute which by 1 July 2001 had been ratified by 35 States. While many of the specific forms of conduct listed in article 7 of the Statute are directly linked to violations against those human rights that are listed as non derogable provisions in article 4, paragraph 2, of the Covenant, the category of crimes against humanity as defined in that provision covers also violations of some provisions of the Covenant that have not been mentioned in the said provision of the Covenant. For example, certain grave violations of article 27 may at the same time constitute genocide under article 6 of the Rome Statute, and article 7, in turn, covers practices that are related to, besides articles 6, 7 and 8 of the Covenant, also articles 9, 12, 26 and 27.

(a) All persons deprived of their liberty shall be treated with humanity and with respect for the inherent dignity of the human person. Although this right, prescribed in article 10 of the Covenant, is not separately mentioned in the list of non-derogable rights in article 4, paragraph 2, the Committee believes that here the Covenant expresses a norm of general international law not subject to derogation. This is supported by the reference to the inherent dignity of the human person in the preamble to the Covenant and by the close connection between articles 7 and 10.

(b) The prohibitions against taking of hostages, abductions or unacknowledged detention are not subject to derogation. The absolute nature of these prohibitions, even in times of emergency, is justified by their status as norms of general international law.

(c) The Committee is of the opinion that the international protection of the rights of persons belonging to minorities includes elements that must be respected in all circumstances. This is reflected in the prohibition against genocide in international law, in the inclusion of a non-discrimination clause in article 4 itself (paragraph 1), as well as in the non-derogable nature of article 18.

(d) As confirmed by the Rome Statute of the International Criminal Court, deportation or forcible transfer of population without grounds permitted under international law, in the form of forced displacement by expulsion or other coercive means from the area in which the persons concerned are lawfully present, constitutes a crime against humanity.[8] The legitimate right to derogate from article 12 of the Covenant during a state of emergency can never be accepted as justifying such measures.

(e) No declaration of a state of emergency made pursuant to article 4, paragraph 1, may be invoked as justification for a State party to engage itself, contrary to article 20, in propaganda for war, or in advocacy of national, racial or religious hatred that would constitute incitement to discrimination, hostility or violence.

14. Article 2, paragraph 3, of the Covenant requires a State party to the Covenant to provide remedies for any violation of the provisions of the Covenant. This clause is not mentioned in the list of non-derogable provisions in article 4, paragraph 2, but it constitutes a treaty obligation inherent in the Covenant as a whole. Even if a State party, during a state of emergency, and to the extent that such measures are strictly required by the exigencies of the situation, may introduce adjustments to the practical functioning of its procedures governing judicial or other remedies, the State party must comply with the fundamental obligation, under article 2, paragraph 3, of the Covenant to provide a remedy that is effective.

15. It is inherent in the protection of rights explicitly recognized as non-derogable in article 4, paragraph 2, that they must be secured by procedural guarantees, including, often, judicial guarantees. The provisions of the Covenant relating to procedural safeguards may never be made subject to measures that would circumvent the protection of non-derogable rights. Article 4 may not be resorted to in a way that would result in derogation from non-derogable rights. Thus, for example, as article 6 of the Covenant is non-derogable in its entirety, any trial leading to the imposition of the death penalty during a state of emergency must conform to the provisions of the Covenant, including all the requirements of articles 14 and 15.

16. Safeguards related to derogation, as embodied in article 4 of the Covenant, are based on the principles of legality and the rule of law inherent in the Covenant as a whole. As certain elements of the right to a fair trial are explicitly guaranteed under international humanitarian

[8] See article 7 (1) (d) and 7 (2) (d) of the Rome Statute.

law during armed conflict, the Committee finds no justification for derogation from these guarantees during other emergency situations. The Committee is of the opinion that the principles of legality and the rule of law require that fundamental requirements of fair trial must be respected during a state of emergency. Only a court of law may try and convict a person for a criminal offence. The presumption of innocence must be respected. In order to protect non-derogable rights, the right to take proceedings before a court to enable the court to decide without delay on the lawfulness of detention, must not be diminished by a State party's decision to derogate from the Covenant.[9]

17. In paragraph 3 of article 4, States parties, when they resort to their power of derogation under article 4, commit themselves to a regime of international notification. A State party availing itself of the right of derogation must immediately inform the other States parties, through the United Nations Secretary General, of the provisions it has derogated from and of the reasons for such measures. Such notification is essential not only for the discharge of the Committee's functions, in particular in assessing whether the measures taken by the State party were strictly required by the exigencies of the situation, but also to permit other States parties to monitor compliance with the provisions of the Covenant. In view of the summary character of many of the notifications received in the past, the Committee emphasizes that the notification by States parties should include full information about the measures taken and a clear explanation of the reasons for them, with full documentation attached regarding their law. Additional notifications are required if the State party subsequently takes further measures under article 4, for instance by extending the duration of a state of emergency. The requirement of immediate notification applies equally in relation to the termination of derogation. These obligations have not always been respected: States parties have failed to notify other States parties, through the Secretary-General, of a proclamation of a state of emergency and of the resulting measures of derogation from one or more provisions of the Covenant, and States parties have sometimes neglected to submit a notification of territorial or other changes in the exercise of their emergency powers.[10] 'Sometimes, the existence of a state of emergency and the question of whether a State party has derogated from provisions of the Covenant have come to the attention of the Committee only incidentally, in the course of the consideration of a State party's report. The Committee emphasizes the obligation of immediate international notification whenever a State party takes measures derogating from its obligations under the Covenant. The duty of the Committee to monitor the law and practice of a State party for compliance with article 4 does not depend on whether that State party has submitted a notification.

---

[9] See the Committee's concluding observations on Israel (1998) (CCPR/C/79/Add.93), para. 21: "… The Committee considers the present application of administrative detention to be incompatible with articles 7 and 16 of the Covenant, neither of which allows for derogation in times of public emergency …. The Committee stresses, however, that a State party may not depart from the requirement of effective judicial review of detention." See also the recommendation by the Committee to the Sub-Commission on Prevention of Discrimination and Protection of Minorities concerning a draft third optional protocol to the Covenant: "The Committee is satisfied that States parties generally understand that the right to habeas corpus and amparo should not be limited in situations of emergency. Furthermore, the Committee is of the view that the remedies provided in article 9, paragraphs 3 and 4, read in conjunction with article 2 are inherent to the Covenant as a whole." Official Records of the General Assembly, Forty-ninth session, Supplement No.40 (A/49/40), vol. I, annex XI, para. 2.

[10] See comments/concluding observations on Peru (1992) CCPR/C/79/Add.8, para. 10; Ireland (1993) CCPR/C/79/Add.21, para. 11; Egypt (1993), CCPR/C/79/Add.23, para. 7; Cameroon (1994) CCPR/C/79/Add.33, para. 7; Russian Federation (1995), CCPR/C/79/Add.54, para. 27; Zambia (1996), CCPR/C/79/Add.62, para. 11; Lebanon (1997), CCPR/C/79/Add.78, para. 10; India (1997), CCPR/C/79/Add.81, para. 19; Mexico (1999), CCPR/C/79/Add.109, para. 12.

Report of the Working Group on Arbitrary Detention, 2004 (See section 7)

7. DETAINEES

Standard Minimum Rules for the Treatment of Prisoners, 1955*

Adoption: 30 August 1955

PRELIMINARY OBSERVATIONS

1. The following rules are not intended to describe in detail a model system of penal institutions. They seek only, on the basis of the general consensus of contemporary thought and the essential elements of the most adequate systems of today, to set out what is generally accepted as being good principle and practice in the treatment of prisoners and the management of institutions.

2. In view of the great variety of legal, social, economic and geographical conditions of the world, it is evident that not all of the rules are capable of application in all places and at all times. They should, however, serve to stimulate a constant endeavour to overcome practical difficulties in the way of their application, in the knowledge that they represent, as a whole, the minimum conditions which are accepted as suitable by the United Nations.

3. On the other hand, the rules cover a field in which thought is constantly developing. They are not intended to preclude experiment and practices, provided these are in harmony with the principles and seek to further the purposes which derive from the text of the rules as a whole. It will always be justifiable for the central prison administration to authorize departures from the rules in this spirit.

4. (1) Part I of the rules covers the general management of institutions, and is applicable to all categories of prisoners, criminal or civil, untried or convicted, including prisoners subject to "security measures" or corrective measures ordered by the judge.

(2) Part II contains rules applicable only to the special categories dealt with in each section. Nevertheless, the rules under section A, applicable to prisoners under sentence, shall be equally applicable to categories of prisoners dealt with in sections B, C and D, provided they do not conflict with the rules governing those categories and are for their benefit.

5. (1) The rules do not seek to regulate the management of institutions set aside for young persons such as Borstal institutions or correctional schools, but in general part I would be equally applicable in such institutions.

(2) The category of young prisoners should include at least all young persons who come within the jurisdiction of juvenile courts. As a rule, such young persons should not be sentenced to imprisonment.

PART I

RULES OF GENERAL APPLICATION

Basic principle

6. (1) The following rules shall be applied impartially. There shall be no discrimination on grounds of race, colour, sex, language, religion, political or other opinion, national or social origin, property, birth or other status.

---

* Source: U.N. Doc. A/CONF/611, Annex I; approved and amended by the Economic and Social Council by its resolutions 663 C (XXIV) of 31 July 1957 and 2076 (LXII) of 13 May 1977.

(2) On the other hand, it is necessary to respect the religious beliefs and moral precepts of the group to which a prisoner belongs.

Register

7. (1) In every place where persons are imprisoned there shall be kept a bound registration book with numbered pages in which shall be entered in respect of each prisoner received:

(a) Information concerning his identity;

(b) The reasons for his commitment and the authority therefor;

(c) The day and hour of his admission and release.

(2) No person shall be received in an institution without a valid commitment order of which the details shall have been previously entered in the register.

Separation of categories

8. The different categories of prisoners shall be kept in separate institutions or parts of institutions taking account of their sex, age, criminal record, the legal reason for their detention and the necessities of their treatment. Thus,

(a) Men and women shall so far as possible be detained in separate institutions; in an institution which receives both men and women the whole of the premises allocated to women shall be entirely separate;

(b) Untried prisoners shall be kept separate from convicted prisoners;

(c) Persons imprisoned for debt and other civil prisoners shall be kept separate from persons imprisoned by reason of a criminal offence;

(d) Young prisoners shall be kept separate from adults.

Accommodation

9. (1) Where sleeping accommodation is in individual cells or rooms, each prisoner shall occupy by night a cell or room by himself. If for special reasons, such as temporary overcrowding, it becomes necessary for the central prison administration to make an exception to this rule, it is not desirable to have two prisoners in a cell or room.

(2) Where dormitories are used, they shall be occupied by prisoners carefully selected as being suitable to associate with one another in those conditions. There shall be regular supervision by night, in keeping with the nature of the institution.

10. All accommodation provided for the use of prisoners and in particular all sleeping accommodation shall meet all requirements of health, due regard being paid to climatic conditions and particularly to cubic content of air, minimum floor space, lighting, heating and ventilation.

11. In all places where prisoners are required to live or work,

(a) The windows shall be large enough to enable the prisoners to read or work by natural light, and shall be so constructed that they can allow the entrance of fresh air whether or not there is artificial ventilation;

(b) Artificial light shall be provided sufficient for the prisoners to read or work without injury to eyesight.

12. The sanitary installations shall be adequate to enable every prisoner to comply with the needs of nature when necessary and in a clean and decent manner.

13. Adequate bathing and shower installations shall be provided so that every prisoner may be enabled and required to have a bath or shower, at a temperature suitable to the climate, as frequently as necessary for general hygiene according to season and geographical region, but at least once a week in a temperate climate.

14. All parts of an institution regularly used by prisoners shall be properly maintained and kept scrupulously clean at all times.

Personal hygiene

15. Prisoners shall be required to keep their persons clean, and to this end they shall be provided with water and with such toilet articles as are necessary for health and cleanliness.

16. In order that prisoners may maintain a good appearance compatible with their self-respect, facilities shall be provided for the proper care of the hair and beard, and men shall be enabled to shave regularly.

Clothing and bedding

17. (1) Every prisoner who is not allowed to wear his own clothing shall be provided with an outfit of clothing suitable for the climate and adequate to keep him in good health. Such clothing shall in No.manner be degrading or humiliating.

(2) All clothing shall be clean and kept in proper condition. Underclothing shall be changed and washed as often as necessary for the maintenance of hygiene.

(3) In exceptional circumstances, whenever a prisoner is removed outside the institution for an authorized purpose, he shall be allowed to wear his own clothing or other inconspicuous clothing.

18. If prisoners are allowed to wear their own clothing, arrangements shall be made on their admission to the institution to ensure that it shall be clean and fit for use.

19. Every prisoner shall, in accordance with local or national standards, be provided with a separate bed, and with separate and sufficient bedding which shall be clean when issued, kept in good order and changed often enough to ensure its cleanliness.

Food

20. (1) Every prisoner shall be provided by the administration at the usual hours with food of nutritional value adequate for health and strength, of wholesome quality and well prepared and served.

(2) Drinking water shall be available to every prisoner whenever he needs it.

Exercise and sport

21. (1) Every prisoner who is not employed in outdoor work shall have at least one hour of suitable exercise in the open air daily if the weather permits.

(2) Young prisoners, and others of suitable age and physique, shall receive physical and recreational training during the period of exercise. To this end space, installations and equipment should be provided.

Medical services

22. (1) At every institution there shall be available the services of at least one qualified medical officer who should have some knowledge of psychiatry. The medical services should be organized in close relationship to the general health administration of the community or nation. They shall include a psychiatric service for the diagnosis and, in proper cases, the treatment of states of mental abnormality.

(2) Sick prisoners who require specialist treatment shall be transferred to specialized institutions or to civil hospitals. Where hospital facilities are provided in an institution, their equipment, furnishings and pharmaceutical supplies shall be proper for the medical care and treatment of sick prisoners, and there shall be a staff of suitable trained officers.

(3) The services of a qualified dental officer shall be available to every prisoner.

23. (1) In women's institutions there shall be special accommodation for all necessary pre-natal and post-natal care and treatment. Arrangements shall be made wherever practicable for children to be born in a hospital outside the institution. If a child is born in prison, this fact shall not be mentioned in the birth certificate.

(2) Where nursing infants are allowed to remain in the institution with their mothers, provision shall be made for a nursery staffed by qualified persons, where the infants shall be placed when they are not in the care of their mothers.

24. The medical officer shall see and examine every prisoner as soon as possible after his admission and thereafter as necessary, with a view particularly to the discovery of physical or mental illness and the taking of all necessary measures; the segregation of prisoners suspected of infectious or contagious conditions; the noting of physical or mental defects which might hamper rehabilitation, and the determination of the physical capacity of every prisoner for work.

25. (1) The medical officer shall have the care of the physical and mental health of the prisoners and should daily see all sick prisoners, all who complain of illness, and any prisoner to whom his attention is specially directed.

(2) The medical officer shall report to the director whenever he considers that a prisoner's physical or mental health has been or will be injuriously affected by continued imprisonment or by any condition of imprisonment.

26. (1) The medical officer shall regularly inspect and advise the director upon:

(a) The quantity, quality, preparation and service of food;

(b) The hygiene and cleanliness of the institution and the prisoners;

(c) The sanitation, heating, lighting and ventilation of the institution;

(d) The suitability and cleanliness of the prisoners' clothing and bedding;

(e) The observance of the rules concerning physical education and sports, in cases where there is no technical personnel in charge of these activities.

(2) The director shall take into consideration the reports and advice that the medical officer submits according to rules 25 (2) and 26 and, in case he concurs with the recommendations made, shall takeimmediate steps to give effect to those recommendations; if they are not within his competence or if he does not concur with them, he shall immediately submit his own report and the advice of the medical officer to higher authority.

Discipline and punishment

27. Discipline and order shall be maintained with firmness, but with no more restriction than is necessary for safe custody and well-ordered community life.

28. (1) No prisoner shall be employed, in the service of the institution, in any disciplinary capacity.

(2) This rule shall not, however, impede the proper functioning of systems based on self-government, under which specified social, educational or sports activities or responsibilities are entrusted, under supervision, to prisoners who are formed into groups for the purposes of treatment.

29. The following shall always be determined by the law or by the regulation of the competent administrative authority:

(a) Conduct constituting a disciplinary offence;

(b) The types and duration of punishment which may be inflicted;

(c) The authority competent to impose such punishment.

30. (1) No prisoner shall be punished except in accordance with the terms of such law or regulation, and never twice for the same offence.

(2) No prisoner shall be punished unless he has been informed of the offence alleged against him and given a proper opportunity of presenting his defence. The competent authority shall conduct a thorough examination of the case.

(3) Where necessary and practicable the prisoner shall be allowed to make his defence through an interpreter.

31. Corporal punishment, punishment by placing in a dark cell, and all cruel, inhuman or degrading punishments shall be completely prohibited as punishments for disciplinary offences.

32. (1) Punishment by close confinement or reduction of diet shall never be inflicted unless the medical officer has examined the prisoner and certified in writing that he is fit to sustain it.

(2) The same shall apply to any other punishment that may be prejudicial to the physical or mental health of a prisoner. In no case may such punishment be contrary to or depart from the principle stated in rule 31.

(3) The medical officer shall visit daily prisoners undergoing such punishments and shall advise the director if he considers the termination or alteration of the punishment necessary on grounds of physical or mental health.

Instruments of restraint

33. Instruments of restraint, such as handcuffs, chains, irons and strait-jackets, shall never be applied as a punishment. Furthermore, chains or irons shall not be used as restraints. Other instruments of restraint shall not be used except in the following circumstances:

(a) As a precaution against escape during a transfer, provided that they shall be removed when the prisoner appears before a judicial or administrative authority;

(b) On medical grounds by direction of the medical officer;

(c) By order of the director, if other methods of control fail, in order to prevent a prisoner from injuring himself or others or from damaging property; in such instances the director shall at once consult the medical officer and report to the higher administrative authority.

34. The patterns and manner of use of instruments of restraint shall be decided by the central prison administration. Such instruments must not be applied for any longer time than is strictly necessary.

Information to and complaints by prisoners

35. (1) Every prisoner on admission shall be provided with written information about the regulations governing the treatment of prisoners of his category, the disciplinary requirements of the institution, the authorized methods of seeking information and making complaints, and all such other matters as are necessary to enable him to understand both his rights and his obligations and to adapt himself to the life of the institution.

(2) If a prisoner is illiterate, the aforesaid information shall be conveyed to him orally.

36. (1) Every prisoner shall have the opportunity each week day of making requests or complaints to the director of the institution or the officer authorized to represent him.

(2) It shall be possible to make requests or complaints to the inspector of prisons during his inspection. The prisoner shall have the opportunity to talk to the inspector or to any other inspecting officer without the director or other members of the staff being present.

(3) Every prisoner shall be allowed to make a request or complaint, without censorship as to substance but in proper form, to the central prison administration, the judicial authority or other proper authorities through approved channels.

(4) Unless it is evidently frivolous or groundless, every request or complaint shall be promptly dealt with and replied to without undue delay.

Contact with the outside world

37. Prisoners shall be allowed under necessary supervision to communicate with their family and reputable friends at regular intervals, both by correspondence and by receiving visits.

38. (1) Prisoners who are foreign nationals shall be allowed reasonable facilities to communicate with the diplomatic and consular representatives of the State to which they belong.

(2) Prisoners who are nationals of States without diplomatic or consular representation in the country and refugees or stateless persons shall be allowed similar facilities to communicate with the diplomatic representative of the State which takes charge of their interests or any national or international authority whose task it is to protect such persons.

39. Prisoners shall be kept informed regularly of the more important items of news by the reading of newspapers, periodicals or special institutional publications, by hearing wireless transmissions, by lectures or by any similar means as authorized or controlled by the administration.

Books

40. Every institution shall have a library for the use of all categories of prisoners, adequately stocked with both recreational and instructional books, and prisoners shall be encouraged to make full use of it.

Religion

41. (1) If the institution contains a sufficient number of prisoners of the same religion, a qualified representative of that religion shall be appointed or approved. If the number of prisoners justifies it and conditions permit, the arrangement should be on a full-time basis.

(2) A qualified representative appointed or approved under paragraph (1) shall be allowed to hold regular services and to pay pastoral visits in private to prisoners of his religion at proper times.

(3) Access to a qualified representative of any religion shall not be refused to any prisoner. On the other hand, if any prisoner should object to a visit of any religious representative, his attitude shall be fully respected.

42. So far as practicable, every prisoner shall be allowed to satisfy the needs of his religious life by attending the services provided in the institution and having in his possession the books of religious observance and instruction of his denomination.

Retention of prisoners' property

43. (1) All money, valuables, clothing and other effects belonging to a prisoner which under the regulations of the institution he is not allowed to retain shall on his admission to the institution be placed in safe custody. An inventory thereof shall be signed by the prisoner. Steps shall be taken to keep them in good condition.

(2) On the release of the prisoner all such articles and money shall be returned to him except in so far as he has been authorized to spend money or send any such property out of the institution, or it has been found necessary on hygienic grounds to destroy any article of clothing. The prisoner shall sign a receipt for the articles and money returned to him.

(3) Any money or effects received for a prisoner from outside shall be treated in the same way.

(4) If a prisoner brings in any drugs or medicine, the medical officer shall decide what use shall be made of them.

Notification of death, illness, transfer, etc.

44. (1) Upon the death or serious illness of, or serious injury to a prisoner, or his removal to an institution for the treatment of mental affections, the director shall at once inform the spouse, if the prisoner is married, or the nearest relative and shall in any event inform any other person previously designated by the prisoner.

(2) A prisoner shall be informed at once of the death or serious illness of any near relative. In case of the critical illness of a near relative, the prisoner should be authorized, whenever circumstances allow, to go to his bedside either under escort or alone.

(3) Every prisoner shall have the right to inform at once his family of his imprisonment or his transfer to another institution.

Removal of prisoners

45. (1) When the prisoners are being removed to or from an institution, they shall be exposed to public view as little as possible, and proper safeguards shall be adopted to protect them from insult, curiosity and publicity in any form.

(2) The transport of prisoners in conveyances with inadequate ventilation or light, or in any way which would subject them to unnecessary physical hardship, shall be prohibited.

(3) The transport of prisoners shall be carried out at the expense of the administration and equal conditions shall obtain for all of them.

Institutional personnel

46. (1) The prison administration shall provide for the careful selection of every grade of the personnel, since it is on their integrity, humanity, professional capacity and personal suitability for the work that the proper administration of the institutions depends.

(2) The prison administration shall constantly seek to awaken and maintain in the minds both of the personnel and of the public the conviction that this work is a social service of great importance, and to this end all appropriate means of informing the public should be used.

(3) To secure the foregoing ends, personnel shall be appointed on a full-time basis as professional prison officers and have civil service status with security of tenure subject only to good conduct, efficiency and physical fitness. Salaries shall be adequate to attract and retain suitable men and women; employment benefits and conditions of service shall be favourable in view of the exacting nature of the work.

47. (1) The personnel shall possess an adequate standard of education and intelligence.

(2) Before entering on duty, the personnel shall be given a course of training in their general and specific duties and be required to pass theoretical and practical tests.

(3) After entering on duty and during their career, the personnel shall maintain and improve their knowledge and professional capacity by attending courses of in-service training to be organized at suitable intervals.

48. All members of the personnel shall at all times so conduct themselves and perform their duties as to influence the prisoners for good by their example and to command their respect.

49. (1) So far as possible, the personnel shall include a sufficient number of specialists such as psychiatrists, psychologists, social workers, teachers and trade instructors.

(2) The services of social workers, teachers and trade instructors shall be secured on a permanent basis, without thereby excluding part-time or voluntary workers.

50. (1) The director of an institution should be adequately qualified for his task by character, administrative ability, suitable training and experience.

(2) He shall devote his entire time to his official duties and shall not be appointed on a part-time basis.

(3) He shall reside on the premises of the institution or in its immediate vicinity.

(4) When two or more institutions are under the authority of one director, he shall visit each of them at frequent intervals. A responsible resident official shall be in charge of each of these institutions.

51. (1) The director, his deputy, and the majority of the other personnel of the institution shall be able to speak the language of the greatest number of prisoners, or a language understood by the greatest number of them.

(2) Whenever necessary, the services of an interpreter shall be used.

52. (1) In institutions which are large enough to require the services of one or more full-time medical officers, at least one of them shall reside on the premises of the institution or in its immediate vicinity.

(2) In other institutions the medical officer shall visit daily and shall reside near enough to be able to attend without delay in cases of urgency.

53. (1) In an institution for both men and women, the part of the institution set aside for women shall be under the authority of a responsible woman officer who shall have the custody of the keys of all that part of the institution.

(2) No male member of the staff shall enter the part of the institution set aside for women unless accompanied by a woman officer.

(3) Women prisoners shall be attended and supervised only by women officers. This does not, however, preclude male members of the staff, particularly doctors and teachers, from carrying out their professional duties in institutions or parts of institutions set aside for women.

54. (1) Officers of the institutions shall not, in their relations with the prisoners, use force except in self-defence or in cases of attempted escape, or active or passive physical resistance to an order based on law or regulations. Officers who have recourse to force must use no more than is strictly necessary and must report the incident immediately to the director of the institution.

(2) Prison officers shall be given special physical training to enable them to restrain aggressive prisoners.

(3) Except in special circumstances, staff performing duties which bring them into direct contact with prisoners should not be armed. Furthermore, staff should in no circumstances be provided with arms unless they have been trained in their use.

Inspection

55. There shall be a regular inspection of penal institutions and services by qualified and experienced inspectors appointed by a competent authority. Their task shall be in particular to ensure that these institutions are administered in accordance with existing laws and regulations and with a view to bringing about the objectives of penal and correctional services.

PART II

RULES APPLICABLE TO SPECIAL CATEGORIES

A. Prisoners under sentence

Guiding principles

56. The guiding principles hereafter are intended to show the spirit in which penal institutions should be administered and the purposes at which they should aim, in accordance with the declaration made under Preliminary Observation 1 of the present text.

57. Imprisonment and other measures which result in cutting off an offender from the outside world are afflictive by the very fact of taking from the person the right of self-determination by depriving him of his liberty. Therefore the prison system shall not, except as incidental to justifiable segregation or the maintenance of discipline, aggravate the suffering inherent in such a situation.

58. The purpose and justification of a sentence of imprisonment or a similar measure deprivative of liberty is ultimately to protect society against crime. This end can only be achieved if the period of imprisonment is used to ensure, so far as possible, that upon his return to society the offender is not only willing but able to lead a law-abiding and self-supporting life.

59. To this end, the institution should utilize all the remedial, educational, moral, spiritual and other forces and forms of assistance which are appropriate and available, and should seek to apply them according to the individual treatment needs of the prisoners.

60. (1) The regime of the institution should seek to minimize any differences between prison life and life at liberty which tend to lessen the responsibility of the prisoners or the respect due to their dignity as human beings.

(2) Before the completion of the sentence, it is desirable that the necessary steps be taken to ensure for the prisoner a gradual return to life in society. This aim may be achieved, depending on the case, by a pre-release regime organized in the same institution or in another appropriate institution, or by release on trial under some kind of supervision which must not be entrusted to the police but should be combined with effective social aid.

61. The treatment of prisoners should emphasize not their exclusion from the community, but their continuing part in it. Community agencies should, therefore, be enlisted wherever possible to assist the staff of the institution in the task of social rehabilitation of the prisoners. There should be in connection with every institution social workers charged with the duty of maintaining and improving all desirable relations of a prisoner with his family and with valuable social agencies. Steps should be taken to safeguard, to the maximum extent compatible with the law and the sentence, the rights relating to civil interests, social security rights and other social benefits of prisoners.

62. The medical services of the institution shall seek to detect and shall treat any physical or mental illnesses or defects which may hamper a prisoner's rehabilitation. All necessary medical, surgical and psychiatric services shall be provided to that end.

63. (1) The fulfilment of these principles requires individualization of treatment and for this purpose a flexible system of classifying prisoners in groups; it is therefore desirable that such groups should be distributed in separate institutions suitable for the treatment of each group.

(2) These institutions need not provide the same degree of security for every group. It is desirable to provide varying degrees of security according to the needs of different groups. Open institutions, by the very fact that they provide no physical security against escape but rely on the self-discipline of the inmates, provide the conditions most favourable to rehabilitation for carefully selected prisoners.

(3) It is desirable that the number of prisoners in closed institutions should not be so large that the individualization of treatment is hindered. In some countries it is considered that the population of such institutions should not exceed five hundred. In open institutions the population should be as small as possible.

(4) On the other hand, it is undesirable to maintain prisons which are so small that proper facilities cannot be provided.

64. The duty of society does not end with a prisoner's release. There should, therefore, be governmental or private agencies capable of lending the released prisoner efficient after-care directed towards the lessening of prejudice against him and towards his social rehabilitation.

Treatment

65. The treatment of persons sentenced to imprisonment or a similar measure shall have as its purpose, so far as the length of the sentence permits, to establish in them the will to lead law-abiding and self-supporting lives after their release and to fit them to do so. The treatment shall be such as will encourage their self-respect and develop their sense of responsibility.

66. (1) To these ends, all appropriate means shall be used, including religious care in the countries where this is possible, education, vocational guidance and training, social casework, employment counselling, physical development and strengthening of moral character, in accordance with the individual needs of each prisoner, taking account of his social and criminal

history, his physical and mental capacities and aptitudes, his personal temperament, the length of his sentence and his prospects after release.

(2) For every prisoner with a sentence of suitable length, the director shall receive, as soon as possible after his admission, full reports on all the matters referred to in the foregoing paragraph. Such reports shall always include a report by a medical officer, wherever possible qualified in psychiatry, on the physical and mental condition of the prisoner.

(3) The reports and other relevant documents shall be placed in an individual file. This file shall be kept up to date and classified in such a way that it can be consulted by the responsible personnel whenever the need arises.

Classification and individualization

67. The purposes of classification shall be:

(a) To separate from others those prisoners who, by reason of their criminal records or bad characters, are likely to exercise a bad influence;

(b) To divide the prisoners into classes in order to facilitate their treatment with a view to their social rehabilitation.

68. So far as possible separate institutions or separate sections of an institution shall be used for the treatment of the different classes of prisoners.

69. As soon as possible after admission and after a study of the personality of each prisoner with a sentence of suitable length, a programme of treatment shall be prepared for him in the light of the knowledge obtained about his individual needs, his capacities and dispositions.

Privileges

70. Systems of privileges appropriate for the different classes of prisoners and the different methods of treatment shall be established at every institution, in order to encourage good conduct, develop a sense of responsibility and secure the interest and co-operation of the prisoners in their treatment.

Work

71. (1) Prison labour must not be of an afflictive nature.

(2) All prisoners under sentence shall be required to work, subject to their physical and mental fitness as determined by the medical officer.

(3) Sufficient work of a useful nature shall be provided to keep prisoners actively employed for a normal working day.

(4) So far as possible the work provided shall be such as will maintain or increase the prisoners, ability to earn an honest living after release.

(5) Vocational training in useful trades shall be provided for prisoners able to profit thereby and especially for young prisoners.

(6) Within the limits compatible with proper vocational selection and with the requirements of institutional administration and discipline, the prisoners shall be able to choose the type of work they wish to perform.

72. (1) The organization and methods of work in the institutions shall resemble as closely as possible those of similar work outside institutions, so as to prepare prisoners for the conditions of normal occupational life.

(2) The interests of the prisoners and of their vocational training, however, must not be subordinated to the purpose of making a financial profit from an industry in the institution.

73. (1) Preferably institutional industries and farms should be operated directly by the administration and not by private contractors.

(2) Where prisoners are employed in work not controlled by the administration, they shall always be under the supervision of the institution's personnel. Unless the work is for other departments of the government the full normal wages for such work shall be paid to the administration by the persons to whom the labour is supplied, account being taken of the output of the prisoners.

74. (1) The precautions laid down to protect the safety and health of free workmen shall be equally observed in institutions.

(2) Provision shall be made to indemnify prisoners against industrial injury, including occupational disease, on terms not less favourable than those extended by law to free workmen.

75. (1) The maximum daily and weekly working hours of the prisoners shall be fixed by law or by administrative regulation, taking into account local rules or custom in regard to the employment of free workmen.

(2) The hours so fixed shall leave one rest day a week and sufficient time for education and other activities required as part of the treatment and rehabilitation of the prisoners.

76. (1) There shall be a system of equitable remuneration of the work of prisoners.

(2) Under the system prisoners shall be allowed to spend at least a part of their earnings on approved articles for their own use and to send a part of their earnings to their family.

(3) The system should also provide that a part of the earnings should be set aside by the administration so as to constitute a savings fund to be handed over to the prisoner on his release.

Education and recreation

77. (1) Provision shall be made for the further education of all prisoners capable of profiting thereby, including religious instruction in the countries where this is possible. The education of illiterates and young prisoners shall be compulsory and special attention shall be paid to it by the administration.

(2) So far as practicable, the education of prisoners shall be integrated with the educational system of the country so that after their release they may continue their education without difficulty. 78. Recreational and cultural activities shall be provided in all institutions for the benefit of the mental and physical health of prisoners.

Social relations and after-care

79. Special attention shall be paid to the maintenance and improvement of such relations between a prisoner and his family as are desirable in the best interests of both.

80. From the beginning of a prisoner's sentence consideration shall be given to his future after release and he shall be encouraged and assisted to maintain or establish such relations with

persons or agencies outside the institution as may promote the best interests of his family and his own social rehabilitation.

81. (1) Services and agencies, governmental or otherwise, which assist released prisoners to reestablish themselves in society shall ensure, so far as is possible and necessary, that released prisoners be provided with appropriate documents and identification papers, have suitable homes and work to go to, are suitably and adequately clothed having regard to the climate and season, and have sufficient means to reach their destination and maintain themselves in the period immediately following their release.

(2) The approved representatives of such agencies shall have all necessary access to the institution and to prisoners and shall be taken into consultation as to the future of a prisoner from the beginning of his sentence.

(3) It is desirable that the activities of such agencies shall be centralized or co-ordinated as far as possible in order to secure the best use of their efforts.

B. Insane and mentally abnormal prisoners

82. (1) Persons who are found to be insane shall not be detained in prisons and arrangements shall be made to remove them to mental institutions as soon as possible.

(2) Prisoners who suffer from other mental diseases or abnormalities shall be observed and treated in specialized institutions under medical management.

(3) During their stay in a prison, such prisoners shall be placed under the special supervision of a medical officer.

(4) The medical or psychiatric service of the penal institutions shall provide for the psychiatric treatment of all other prisoners who are in need of such treatment.

83. It is desirable that steps should be taken, by arrangement with the appropriate agencies, to ensure if necessary the continuation of psychiatric treatment after release and the provision of socialpsychiatric after-care.

C. Prisoners under arrest or awaiting trial

84. (1) Persons arrested or imprisoned by reason of a criminal charge against them, who are detained either in police custody or in prison custody (jail) but have not yet been tried and sentenced, will be referred to as "untried prisoners" hereinafter in these rules.

(2) Unconvicted prisoners are presumed to be innocent and shall be treated as such.

(3) Without prejudice to legal rules for the protection of individual liberty or prescribing the procedure to be observed in respect of untried prisoners, these prisoners shall benefit by a special regime which is described in the following rules in its essential requirements only.

85. (1) Untried prisoners shall be kept separate from convicted prisoners.

(2) Young untried prisoners shall be kept separate from adults and shall in principle be detained in separate institutions.

86. Untried prisoners shall sleep singly in separate rooms, with the reservation of different local custom in respect of the climate.

87. Within the limits compatible with the good order of the institution, untried prisoners may, if they so desire, have their food procured at their own expense from the outside, either through the administration or through their family or friends. Otherwise, the administration shall provide their food.

88. (1) An untried prisoner shall be allowed to wear his own clothing if it is clean and suitable.

(2) If he wears prison dress, it shall be different from that supplied to convicted prisoners.

89. An untried prisoner shall always be offered opportunity to work, but shall not be required to work. If he chooses to work, he shall be paid for it.

90. An untried prisoner shall be allowed to procure at his own expense or at the expense of a third party such books, newspapers, writing materials and other means of occupation as are compatible with the interests of the administration of justice and the security and good order of the institution. 91. An untried prisoner shall be allowed to be visited and treated by his own doctor or dentist if there is reasonable ground for his application and he is able to pay any expenses incurred.

92. An untried prisoner shall be allowed to inform immediately his family of his detention and shall be given all reasonable facilities for communicating with his family and friends, and for receiving visits from them, subject only to restrictions and supervision as are necessary in the interests of the administration of justice and of the security and good order of the institution.

93. For the purposes of his defence, an untried prisoner shall be allowed to apply for free legal aid where such aid is available, and to receive visits from his legal adviser with a view to his defence and to prepare and hand to him confidential instructions. For these purposes, he shall if he so desires be supplied with writing material. Interviews between the prisoner and his legal adviser may be within sight but not within the hearing of a police or institution official.

D. Civil prisoners

94. In countries where the law permits imprisonment for debt, or by order of a court under any other non-criminal process, persons so imprisoned shall not be subjected to any greater restriction or severity than is necessary to ensure safe custody and good order. Their treatment shall be not less favourable than that of untried prisoners, with the reservation, however, that they may possibly be required to work.

E. Persons arrested or detained without charge

95. Without prejudice to the provisions of article 9 of the International Covenant on Civil and Political Rights, persons arrested or imprisoned without charge shall be accorded the same protection as that accorded under part I and part II, section C. Relevant provisions of part II, section A, shall likewise be applicable where their application may be conducive to the benefit of this special group of persons in custody, provided that no measures shall be taken implying that re-education or rehabilitation is in any way appropriate to persons not convicted of any criminal offence.

Code of Conduct for Law Enforcement Officials, 1979 [excerpts]*

Adoption: 17 December 1979

[…]

Article 2

In the performance of their duty, law enforcement officials shall respect and protect human dignity and maintain and uphold the human rights of all persons.

[…]

Article 5

No law enforcement official may inflict, instigate or tolerate any act of torture or other cruel, inhuman or degrading treatment or punishment, nor may any law enforcement official invoke superior orders or exceptional circumstances such as a state of war or a threat of war, a threat to national security, internal political instability or any other public emergency as a justification of torture or other cruel, inhuman or degrading treatment or punishment.

Article 6

Law enforcement officials shall ensure the full protection of the health of persons in their custody and, in particular, shall take immediate action to secure medical attention whenever required.

[…]

* Source: U.N.G.A. Res. 34/169.

CCPR General Comment No.8: Article 9 (Right to Liberty and Security of Persons), 1982*

Adoption: 30 June 1982

1. Article 9 which deals with the right to liberty and security of persons has often been somewhat narrowly understood in reports by States parties, and they have therefore given incomplete information. The Committee points out that paragraph 1 is applicable to all deprivations of liberty, whether in criminal cases or in other cases such as, for example, mental illness, vagrancy, drug addiction, educational purposes, immigration control, etc. It is true that some of the provisions of article 9 (part of paragraph 2 and the whole of paragraph 3) are only applicable to persons against whom criminal charges are brought. But the rest, and in particular the important guarantee laid down in paragraph 4, i.e. the right to control by a court of the legality of the detention, applies to all persons deprived of their liberty by arrest or detention. Furthermore, States parties have in accordance with article 2 (3) also to ensure that an effective remedy is provided in other cases in which an individual claims to be deprived of his liberty in violation of the Covenant.

2. Paragraph 3 of article 9 requires that in criminal cases any person arrested or detained has to be brought "promptly" before a judge or other officer authorized by law to exercise judicial power. More precise time limits are fixed by law in most States parties and, in the view of the Committee, delays must not exceed a few days. Many States have given insufficient information about the actual practices in this respect.

3. Another matter is the total length of detention pending trial. In certain categories of criminal cases in some countries this matter has caused some concern within the Committee, and members have questioned whether their practices have been in conformity with the entitlement "to trial within a reasonable time or to release" under paragraph 3. Pre trial detention should be an exception and as short as possible. The Committee would welcome information concerning mechanisms existing and measures taken with a view to reducing the duration of such detention.

4. Also if so called preventive detention is used, for reasons of public security, it must be controlled by these same provisions, i.e. it must not be arbitrary, and must be based on grounds and procedures established by law (para. 1), information of the reasons must be given (para. 2) and court control of the detention must be available (para. 4) as well as compensation in the case of a breach (para. 5). And if, in addition, criminal charges are brought in such cases, the full protection of article 9 (2) and (3), as well as article 14, must also be granted.

* Source: U.N.Doc. HRI/GEN/1/Rev.7 p. 130.

Principles of Medical Ethics relevant to the Role of Health Personnel, particularly Physicians, in the Protection of Prisoners and Detainees against Torture and Other Cruel, Inhuman or Degrading Treatment or Punishment, 1982*

Adoption: 18 December 1982

Principle 1

Health personnel, particularly physicians, charged with the medical care of prisoners and detainees have a duty to provide them with protection of their physical and mental health and treatment of disease of the same quality and standard as is afforded to those who are not imprisoned or detained.

Principle 2

It is a gross contravention of medical ethics, as well as an offence under applicable international instruments, for health personnel, particularly physicians, to engage, actively or passively, in acts which constitute participation in, complicity in, incitement to or attempts to commit torture or other cruel, inhuman or degrading treatment or punishment.[1]

Principle 3

It is a contravention of medical ethics for health personnel, particularly physicians, to be involved in any professional relationship with prisoners or detainees the purpose of which is not solely to evaluate, protect or improve their physical and mental health.

Principle 4

It is a contravention of medical ethics for health personnel, particularly physicians:

(a) To apply their knowledge and skills in order to assist in the interrogation of prisoners and detainees in a manner that may adversely affect the physical or mental health or condition of such prisoners or detainees and which is not in accordance with the relevant international instruments;[2]

(b) To certify, or to participate in the certification of, the fitness of prisoners or detainees for any form of treatment or punishment that may adversely affect their physical or mental health and which is not in accordance with the relevant international instruments, or to participate in any way in the infliction of any such treatment or punishment which is not in accordance with the relevant international instruments.

* Source: U.N.G.A. Res. 37/194.

[1] See the Declaration on the Protection of All Persons from Being Subjected to Torture and Other Cruel. Inhuman or Degrading Treatment or Punishment (resolution 3452 (XXX), annex).

[2] Particularly the Universal Declaration of Human Rights (resolution 217 A (III)), the International Covenants on Human Rights (resolution 2200 A (XXI). annex), the Declaration on the Protection of All Persons from Being Subjected to Torture and Other Cruel, Inhuman or Degrading Treatment or Punishment (resolution 3452 (XXX), annex) and the Standard Minimum Rules for the Treatment of Prisoners (First United Nations Congress on the Prevention of Crime and the Treatment of Offenders: report by the Secretariat (United Nations publication, Sales No.E.1956.IV.4, annex I.A)).

Principle 5

It is a contravention of medical ethics for health personnel, particularly physicians, to participate in any procedure for restraining a prisoner or detainee unless such a procedure is determined in accordance with purely medical criteria as being necessary for the protection of the physical or mental health or the safety of the prisoner or detainee himself, of his fellow prisoners or detainees, or of his guardians, and presents no hazard to his physical or mental health.

Principle 6

There may be no derogation from the foregoing principles on any ground whatsoever, including public emergency.

Body of Principles for the Protection of All Persons under Any Form of Detention or Imprisonment, 1988*

Adoption: 9 December 1988

The General Assembly,

Recalling its resolutions 35/177 of 15 December 1980, in which it referred the task of elaborating the draft Body of Principles for the Protection of All Persons under Any Form of Detention or Imprisonment[1] *to the Sixth Committee and decided to establish an open-ended working group for that purpose,*

Taking note of the report of the Working Group on the Draft Body of Principles for the Protection of All Persons under Any Form of Detention or Imprisonment, which met during the forty-third session of the General Assembly and completed the elaboration of the draft Body of Principles,

Considering that the Working Group decided to submit the text of the draft Body of Principles to the Sixth Committee for its consideration and adoption,[2]

Convinced that the adoption of the draft Body of Principles would make an important contribution to the protection of human rights,

Considering the need to ensure the wide dissemination of the text of the Body of Principles,

1. Approves the Body of Principles for the Protection of All Persons under Any Form of Detention or Imprisonment, the text of which is annexed to the present resolution;

2. Expresses its appreciation to the Working Group on the Draft Body of Principles for the Protection of All Persons under Any Form of Detention or Imprisonment for its important contribution to the elaboration of the Body of Principles;

3. Requests the Secretary-General to inform States Members of the United Nations or members of specialized agencies of the adoption of the Body of Principles;

4. Urges that every effort be made so that the Body of Principles becomes generally known and respected.

76th plenary meeting
9 December 1988

ANNEX

Scope of the Body of Principles

These principles apply for the protection of all persons under any form of detention or imprisonment.

---

* Source: U.N.G.A. Res. 43/173.

1 A/C.6/43/L.9

2 *Ibid.*, para 4.

Use of Terms

For the purposes of the Body of Principles:

(a) "Arrest" means the act of apprehending a person for the alleged commission of an offence or by the action of an authority;

(b) "Detained person" means any person deprived of personal liberty except as a result of conviction for an offence;

(c) "Imprisoned person" means any person deprived of personal liberty as a result of conviction for an offence;

(d) "Detention" means the condition of detained persons as defined above;

(e) "Imprisonment" means the condition of imprisoned persons as defined above;

(f) The words "a judicial or other authority" means a judicial or other authority under the law whose status and tenure should afford the strongest possible guarantees of competence, impartiality and independence.

Principle 1

All persons under any form of detention or imprisonment shall be treated in a humane manner and with respect for the inherent dignity of the human person.

Principle 2

Arrest, detention or imprisonment shall only be carried out strictly in accordance with the provisions of the law and by competent officials or persons authorized for that purpose.

Principle 3

There shall be no restriction upon or derogation from any of the human rights of persons under any form of detention or imprisonment recognized or existing in any State pursuant to law, conventions, regulations or custom on the pretext that this Body of Principles does not recognize such rights or that it recognizes them to a lesser extent.

Principle 4

Any form of detention or imprisonment and all measures affecting the human rights of a person under any form of detention or imprisonment shall be ordered by, or be subject to the effective control of, a judicial or other authority.

Principle 5

1. These principles shall be applied to all persons within the territory of any given State, without distinction of any kind, such as race, colour, sex, language, religion or religious belief, political or other opinion, national, ethnic or social origin, property, birth or other status.

2. Measures applied under the law and designed solely to protect the rights and special status of women, especially pregnant women and nursing mothers, children and juveniles, aged, sick or handicapped persons shall not be deemed to be discriminatory. The need for, and the application of, such measures shall always be subject to review by a judicial or other authority.

Principle 6

No person under any form of detention or imprisonment shall be subjected to torture or to cruel, inhuman or degrading treatment or punishment.[3] No circumstance whatever may be invoked as a justification for torture or other cruel, inhuman or degrading treatment or punishment.

Principlc 7

1. States should prohibit by law any act contrary to the rights and duties contained in these principles, make any such act subject to appropriate sanctions and conduct impartial investigations upon complaints.

2. Officials who have reason to believe that a violation of this Body of Principles has occurred or is about to occur shall report the matter to their superior authorities and, where necessary, to other appropriate authorities or organs vested with reviewing or remedial powers.

3. Any other person who has ground to believe that a violation of this Body of Principles has occurred or is about to occur shall have the right to report the matter to the superiors of the officials involved as well as to other appropriate authorities or organs vested with reviewing or remedial powers.

Principle 8

Persons in detention shall be subject to treatment appropriate to their unconvicted status. Accordingly, they shall, whenever possible, be kept separate from imprisoned persons.

Principle 9

The authorities which arrest a person, keep him under detention or investigate the case shall exercise only the powers granted to them under the law and the exercise of these powers shall be subject to recourse to a judicial or other authority.

Principle 10

Anyone who is arrested shall be informed at the time of his arrest of the reason for his arrest and shall be promptly informed of any charges against him.

Principle 11

1. A person shall not be kept in detention without being given an effective opportunity to be heard promptly by a judicial or other authority. A detained person shall have the right to defend himself or to be assisted by counsel as prescribed by law.

2. A detained person and his counsel, if any, shall receive prompt and full communication of any order of detention, together with the reasons therefor.

3. A judicial or other authority shall be empowered to review as appropriate the continuance of detention.

---

[3] The term "cruel, inhuman or degrading treatment or punishment" should be interpreted so as to extend the widest possible protection against abuses, whether physical or mental, including the holding of a detained or imprisoned person in conditions which deprive him, temporarily or permanently, of the use of any of his natural senses, such as sight or hearing, or of his awareness of place and the passing of time.

Principle 12

1. There shall be duly recorded:

(a) The reasons for the arrest;

(b) The time of the arrest and the taking of the arrested person to a place of custody as well as that of his first appearance before a judicial or other authority;

(c) The identity of the law enforcement officials concerned;

(d) Precise information concerning the place of custody.

2. Such records shall be communicated to the detained person, or his counsel, if any, in the form prescribed by law.

Principle 13

Any person shall, at the moment of arrest and at the commencement of detention or imprisonment, or promptly thereafter, be provided by the authority responsible for his arrest, detention or imprisonment, respectively with information on and an explanation of his rights and how to avail himself of such rights.

Principle 14

A person who does not adequately understand or speak the language used by the authorities responsible for his arrest, detention or imprisonment is entitled to receive promptly in a language which he understands the information referred to in principle 10, principle 11, paragraph 2, principle 12, paragraph 1, and principle 13 and to have the assistance, free of charge, if necessary, of an interpreter in connection with legal proceedings subsequent to his arrest.

Principle 15

Notwithstanding the exceptions contained in principle 16, paragraph 4, and principle 18, paragraph 3, communication of the detained or imprisoned person with the outside world, and in particular his family or counsel, shall not be denied for more than a matter of days.

Principle 16

1. Promptly after arrest and after each transfer from one place of detention or imprisonment to another, a detained or imprisoned person shall be entitled to notify or to require the competent authority to notify members of his family or other appropriate persons of his choice of his arrest, detention or imprisonment or of the transfer and of the place where he is kept in custody.

2. If a detained or imprisoned person is a foreigner, he shall also be promptly informed of his right to communicate by appropriate means with a consular post or the diplomatic mission of the State of which he is a national or which is otherwise entitled to receive such communication in accordance with international law or with the representative of the competent international organization, if he is a refugee or is otherwise under the protection of an intergovernmental organization.

3. If a detained or imprisoned person is a juvenile or is incapable of understanding his entitlement, the competent authority shall on its own initiative undertake the notification referred to in the present principle. Special attention shall be given to notifying parents or guardians.

4. Any notification referred to in the present principle shall be made or permitted to be made without delay. The competent authority may however delay a notification for a reasonable period where exceptional needs of the investigation so require.

Principle 17

1. A detained person shall be entitled to have the assistance of a legal counsel. He shall be informed of his right by the competent authority promptly after arrest and shall be provided with reasonable facilities for exercising it.

2. If a detained person does not have a legal counsel of his own choice, he shall be entitled to have a legal counsel assigned to him by a judicial or other authority in all cases where the interests of justice so require and without payment by him if he does not have sufficient means to pay.

Principle 18

1. A detained or imprisoned person shall be entitled to communicate and consult with his legal counsel.

2. A detained or imprisoned person shall be allowed adequate time and facilities for consultation with his legal counsel.

3. The right of a detained or imprisoned person to be visited by and to consult and communicate, without delay or censorship and in full confidentiality, with his legal counsel may not be suspended or restricted save in exceptional circumstances, to be specified by law or lawful regulations, when it is considered indispensable by a judicial or other authority in order to maintain security and good order.

4. Interviews between a detained or imprisoned person and his legal counsel may be within sight, but not within the hearing, of a law enforcement official.

5. Communications between a detained or imprisoned person and his legal counsel mentioned in the present principle shall be inadmissible as evidence against the detained or imprisoned person unless they are connected with a continuing or contemplated crime.

Principle 19

A detained or imprisoned person shall have the right to be visited by and to correspond with, in particular, members of his family and shall be given adequate opportunity to communicate with the outside world, subject to reasonable conditions and restrictions as specified by law or lawful regulations.

Principle 20

If a detained or imprisoned person so requests, he shall if possible be kept in a place of detention or imprisonment reasonably near his usual place of residence.

Principle 21

1. It shall be prohibited to take undue advantage of the situation of a detained or imprisoned person for the purpose of compelling him to confess, to incriminate himself otherwise or to testify against any other person.

2. No detained person while being interrogated shall be subject to violence, threats or methods of interrogation which impair his capacity of decision or his judgement.

Principle 22

No detained or imprisoned person shall, even with his consent, be subjected to any medical or scientific experimentation which may be detrimental to his health.

Principle 23

1. The duration of any interrogation of a detained or imprisoned person and of the intervals between interrogations as well as the identity of the officials who conducted the interrogations and other persons present shall be recorded and certified in such form as may be prescribed by law.

2. A detained or imprisoned person, or his counsel when provided by law, shall have access to the information described in paragraph 1 of the present principle.

Principle 24

A proper medical examination shall be offered to a detained or imprisoned person as promptly as possible after his admission to the place of detention or imprisonment, and thereafter medical care and treatment shall be provided whenever necessary. This care and treatment shall be provided free of charge.

Principle 25

A detained or imprisoned person or his counsel shall, subject only to reasonable conditions to ensure security and good order in the place of detention or imprisonment, have the right to request or petition a judicial or other authority for a second medical examination or opinion.

Principle 26

The fact that a detained or imprisoned person underwent a medical examination, the name of the physician and the results of such an examination shall be duly recorded. Access to such records shall be ensured. Modalities therefore shall be in accordance with relevant rules of domestic law.

Principle 27

Non-compliance with these principles in obtaining evidence shall be taken into account in determining the admissibility of such evidence against a detained or imprisoned person.

Principle 28

A detained or imprisoned person shall have the right to obtain within the limits of available resources, if from public sources, reasonable quantities of educational, cultural and informational material, subject to reasonable conditions to ensure security and good order in the place of detention or imprisonment.

Principle 29

1. In order to supervise the strict observance of relevant laws and regulations, places of detention shall be visited regularly by qualified and experienced persons appointed by, and responsible to, a competent authority distinct from the authority directly in charge of the administration of the place of detention or imprisonment.

2. A detained or imprisoned person shall have the right to communicate freely and in full confidentiality with the persons who visit the places of detention or imprisonment in accordance with paragraph 1 of the present principle, subject to reasonable conditions to ensure security and good order in such places.

Principle 30

1. The types of conduct of the detained or imprisoned person that constitute disciplinary offences during detention or imprisonment, the description and duration of disciplinary punishment that may be inflicted and the authorities competent to impose such punishment shall be specified by law or lawful regulations and duly published.

2. A detained or imprisoned person shall have the right to be heard before disciplinary action is taken. He shall have the right to bring such action to higher authorities for review.

Principle 31

The appropriate authorities shall endeavour to ensure, according to domestic law, assistance when needed to dependent and, in particular, minor members of the families of detained or imprisoned persons and shall devote a particular measure of care to the appropriate custody of children left with out supervision.

Principle 32

1. A detained person or his counsel shall be entitled at any time to take proceedings according to domestic law before a judicial or other authority to challenge the lawfulness of his detention in order to obtain his release without delay, if it is unlawful.

2. The proceedings referred to in paragraph 1 of the present principle shall be simple and expeditious and at no cost for detained persons without adequate means. The detaining authority shall produce without unreasonable delay the detained person before the reviewing authority.

Principle 33

1. A detained or imprisoned person or his counsel shall have the right to make a request or complaint regarding his treatment, in particular in case of torture or other cruel, inhuman or degrading treatment, to the authorities responsible for the administration of the place of detention and to higher authorities and, when necessary, to appropriate authorities vested with reviewing or remedial powers.

2. In those cases where neither the detained or imprisoned person nor his counsel has the possibility to exercise his rights under paragraph 1 of the present principle, a member of the family of the detained or imprisoned person or any other person who has knowledge of the case may exercise such rights.

3. Confidentiality concerning the request or complaint shall be maintained if so requested by the complainant.

4. Every request or complaint shall be promptly dealt with and replied to without undue delay. If the request or complaint is rejected or, in case of inordinate delay, the complainant shall be entitled to bring it before a judicial or other authority. Neither the detained or imprisoned person nor any complainant under paragraph 1 of the present principle shall suffer prejudice for making a request or complaint.

Principle 34

Whenever the death or disappearance of a detained or imprisoned person occurs during his detention or imprisonment, an inquiry into the cause of death or disappearance shall be held by a judicial or other authority, either on its own motion or at the instance of a member of the family of such a person or any person who has knowledge of the case. When circumstances so warrant, such an inquiry shall be held on the same procedural basis whenever the death or disappearance occurs shortly after the termination of the detention or imprisonment. The findings of such inquiry or a report thereon shall be made available upon request, unless doing so would jeopardize an ongoing criminal investigation.

Principle 35

1. Damage incurred because of acts or omissions by a public official contrary to the rights contained in these principles shall be compensated according to the applicable rules or liability provided by domestic law.

2. Information required to be recorded under these principles shall be available in accordance with procedures provided by domestic law for use in claiming compensation under the present principle.

Principle 36

1. A detained person suspected of or charged with a criminal offence shall be presumed innocent and shall be treated as such until proved guilty according to law in a public trial at which he has had all the guarantees necessary for his defence.

2. The arrest or detention of such a person pending investigation and trial shall be carried out only for the purposes of the administration of justice on grounds and under conditions and procedures specified by law. The imposition of restrictions upon such a person which are not strictly required for the purpose of the detention or to prevent hindrance to the process of investigation or the administration of justice, or for the maintenance of security and good order in the place of detention shall be forbidden.

Principle 37

A person detained on a criminal charge shall be brought before a judicial or other authority provided by law promptly after his arrest. Such authority shall decide without delay upon the lawfulness and necessity of detention. No person may be kept under detention pending investigation or trial except upon the written order of such an authority. A detained person shall, when brought before such an authority, have the right to make a statement on the treatment received by him while in custody.

Principle 38

A person detained on a criminal charge shall be entitled to trial within a reasonable time or to release pending trial.

Principle 39

Except in special cases provided for by law, a person detained on a criminal charge shall be entitled, unless a judicial or other authority decides otherwise in the interest of the administration of justice, to release pending trial subject to the conditions that may be imposed in accordance with the law. Such authority shall keep the necessity of detention under review.

General clause

Nothing in this Body of Principles shall be construed as restricting or derogating from any right defined in the International Covenant on Civil and Political Rights.

Basic Principles on the Role of Lawyers, 1990 [excerpts]*

Adoption: 7 September 1990

[...]

Access to lawyers and legal services

1. All persons are entitled to call upon the assistance of a lawyer of their choice to protect and establish their rights and to defend them in all stages of criminal proceedings.

2. Governments shall ensure that efficient procedures and responsive mechanisms for effective and equal access to lawyers are provided for all persons within their territory and subject to their jurisdiction, without distinction of any kind, such as discrimination based on race, colour, ethnic origin, sex, language, religion, political or other opinion, national or social origin, property, birth, economic or other status.

3. Governments shall ensure the provision of sufficient funding and other resources for legal services to the poor and, as necessary, to other disadvantaged persons. Professional associations of lawyers shall cooperate in the organization and provision of services, facilities and other resources.

4. Governments and professional associations of lawyers shall promote programmes to inform the public about their rights and duties under the law and the important role of lawyers in protecting their fundamental freedoms. Special attention should be given to assisting the poor and other disadvantaged persons so as to enable them to assert their rights and where necessary call upon the assistance of lawyers.

Special safeguards in criminal justice matters

5. Governments shall ensure that all persons are immediately informed by the competent authority of their right to be assisted by a lawyer of their own choice upon arrest or detention or when charged with a criminal offence.

6. Any such persons who do not have a lawyer shall, in all cases in which the interests of justice so require, be entitled to have a lawyer of experience and competence commensurate with the nature of the offence assigned to them in order to provide effective legal assistance, without payment by them if they lack sufficient means to pay for such services.

7. Governments shall further ensure that all persons arrested or detained, with or without criminal charge, shall have prompt access to a lawyer, and in any case not later than forty-eight hours from the time of arrest or detention.

8. All arrested, detained or imprisoned persons shall be provided with adequate opportunities, time and facilities to be visited by and to communicate and consult with a lawyer, without delay, interception or censorship and in full confidentiality. Such consultations may be within sight, but not within the hearing, of law enforcement officials.

[...]

* Source: U.N. Doc. A/CONF.144/28/Rev.1.

Basic Principles for the Treatment of Prisoners, 1990*

Adoption: 14 December 1990

1. All prisoners shall be treated with the respect due to their inherent dignity and value as human beings.

2. There shall be no discrimination on the grounds of race, colour, sex, language, religion, political or other opinion, national or social origin, property, birth or other status.

3. It is, however, desirable to respect the religious beliefs and cultural precepts of the group to which prisoners belong, whenever local conditions so require.

4. The responsibility of prisons for the custody of prisoners and for the protection of society against crime shall be discharged in keeping with a State's other social objectives and its fundamental responsibilities for promoting the well-being and development of all members of society.

5. Except for those limitations that are demonstrably necessitated by the fact of incarceration, all prisoners shall retain the human rights and fundamental freedoms set out in the Universal Declaration of Human Rights, and, where the State concerned is a party, the International Covenant on Economic, Social and Cultural Rights, and the International Covenant on Civil and Political Rights and the Optional Protocol thereto, as well as such other rights as are set out in other United Nations covenants.

6. All prisoners shall have the right to take part in cultural activities and education aimed at the full development of the human personality.

7. Efforts addressed to the abolition of solitary confinement as a punishment, or to the restriction of its use, should be undertaken and encouraged.

8. Conditions shall be created enabling prisoners to undertake meaningful remunerated employment which will facilitate their reintegration into the country's labour market and permit them to contribute to their own financial support and to that of their families.

9. Prisoners shall have access to the health services available in the country without discrimination on the grounds of their legal situation.

10. With the participation and help of the community and social institutions, and with due regard to the interests of victims, favourable conditions shall be created for the reintegration of the ex-prisoner into society under the best possible conditions.

11. The above Principles shall be applied impartially.

* Source: U.N.G.A. Res. 45/111.

United Nations Rules for the Protection of Juveniles Deprived of their Liberty, 1990*

Adoption: 14 December 1990

I. FUNDAMENTAL PERSPECTIVES

1. The juvenile justice system should uphold the rights and safety and promote the physical and mental well-being of juveniles. Imprisonment should be used as a last resort.

2. Juveniles should only be deprived of their liberty in accordance with the principles and procedures set forth in these Rules and in the United Nations Standard Minimum Rules for the Administration of Juvenile Justice (The Beijing Rules). Deprivation of the liberty of a juvenile should be a disposition of last resort and for the minimum necessary period and should be limited to exceptional cases. The length of the sanction should be determined by the judicial authority, without precluding the possibility of his or her early release.

3. The Rules are intended to establish minimum standards accepted by the United Nations for the protection of juveniles deprived of their liberty in all forms, consistent with human rights and fundamental freedoms, and with a view to counteracting the detrimental effects of all types of detention and to fostering integration in society.

4. The Rules should be applied impartially, without discrimination of any kind as to race, colour, sex, age, language, religion, nationality, political or other opinion, cultural beliefs or practices, property, birth or family status, ethnic or social origin, and disability. The religious and cultural beliefs, practices and moral concepts of the juvenile should be respected.

5. The Rules are designed to serve as convenient standards of reference and to provide encouragement and guidance to professionals involved in the management of the juvenile justice system.

6. The Rules should be made readily available to juvenile justice personnel in their national languages.

Juveniles who are not fluent in the language spoken by the personnel of the detention facility should have the right to the services of an interpreter free of charge whenever necessary, in particular during medical examinations and disciplinary proceedings.

7. Where appropriate, States should incorporate the Rules into their legislation or amend it accordingly and provide effective remedies for their breach, including compensation when injuries are inflicted on juveniles. States should also monitor the application of the Rules.

8. The competent authorities should constantly seek to increase the awareness of the public that the care of detained juveniles and preparation for their return to society is a social service of great importance, and to this end active steps should be taken to foster open contacts between the juveniles and the local community.

9. Nothing in the Rules should be interpreted as precluding the application of the relevant United Nations and human rights instruments and standards, recognized by the international community, that are more conducive to ensuring the rights, care and protection of juveniles, children and all young persons.

* Source: U.N.G.A. Res. 45/113.

10. In the event that the practical application of particular Rules contained in sections II to V, inclusive, presents any conflict with the Rules contained in the present section, compliance with the latter shall be regarded as the predominant requirement.

II. SCOPE AND APPLICATION OF THE RULES

11. For the purposes of the Rules, the following definitions should apply:

(a) A juvenile is every person under the age of 18. The age limit below which it should not be permitted to deprive a child of his or her liberty should be determined by law;

(b) The deprivation of liberty means any form of detention or imprisonment or the placement of a person in a public or private custodial setting, from which this person is not permitted to leave at will, by order of any judicial, administrative or other public authority.

12. The deprivation of liberty should be effected in conditions and circumstances which ensure respect for the human rights of juveniles. Juveniles detained in facilities should be guaranteed the benefit of meaningful activities and programmes which would serve to promote and sustain their health and selfrespect, to foster their sense of responsibility and encourage those attitudes and skills that will assist them in developing their potential as members of society.

13. Juveniles deprived of their liberty shall not for any reason related to their status be denied the civil, economic, political, social or cultural rights to which they are entitled under national or international law, and which are compatible with the deprivation of liberty.

14. The protection of the individual rights of juveniles with special regard to the legality of the execution of the detention measures shall be ensured by the competent authority, while the objectives of social integration should be secured by regular inspections and other means of control carried out, according to international standards, national laws and regulations, by a duly constituted body authorized to visit the juveniles and not belonging to the detention facility.

15. The Rules apply to all types and forms of detention facilities in which juveniles are deprived of their liberty. Sections I, II, IV and V of the Rules apply to all detention facilities and institutional settings in which juveniles are detained, and section III applies specifically to juveniles under arrest or awaiting trial.

16. The Rules shall be implemented in the context of the economic, social and cultural conditions prevailing in each Member State.

III. JUVENILES UNDER ARREST OR AWAITING TRIAL

17. Juveniles who are detained under arrest or awaiting trial ("untried") are presumed innocent and shall be treated as such. Detention before trial shall be avoided to the extent possible and limited to exceptional circumstances. Therefore, all efforts shall be made to apply alternative measures. When preventive detention is nevertheless used, juvenile courts and investigative bodies shall give the highest priority to the most expeditious processing of such cases to ensure the shortest possible duration of detention. Untried detainees should be separated from convicted juveniles.

18. The conditions under which an untried juvenile is detained should be consistent with the rules set out below, with additional specific provisions as are necessary and appropriate, given the requirements of the presumption of innocence, the duration of the detention and the legal status and circumstances of the juvenile. These provisions would include, but not necessarily be restricted to, the following:

(a) Juveniles should have the right of legal counsel and be enabled to apply for free legal aid, where such aid is available, and to communicate regularly with their legal advisers. Privacy and confidentiality shall be ensured for such communications;

(b) Juveniles should be provided, where possible, with opportunities to pursue work, with remuneration, and continue education or training, but should not be required to do so. Work, education or training should not cause the continuation of the detention;

(c) Juveniles should receive and retain materials for their leisure and recreation as are compatible with the interests of the administration of justice.

IV. THE MANAGEMENT OF JUVENILE FACILITIES

A. Records

19. All reports, including legal records, medical records and records of disciplinary proceedings, and all other documents relating to the form, content and details of treatment, should be placed in a confidential individual file, which should be kept up to date, accessible only to authorized persons and classified in such a way as to be easily understood. Where possible, every juvenile should have the right to contest any fact or opinion contained in his or her file so as to permit rectification of inaccurate, unfounded or unfair statements. In order to exercise this right, there should be procedures that allow an appropriate third party to have access to and to consult the file on request. Upon release, the records of juveniles shall be sealed, and, at an appropriate time, expunged.

20. No juvenile should be received in any detention facility without a valid commitment order of a judicial, administrative or other public authority. The details of this order should be immediately entered in the register. No juvenile should be detained in any facility where there is no such register.

B. Admission, registration, movement and transfer

21. In every place where juveniles are detained, a complete and secure record of the following information should be kept concerning each juvenile received:

(a) Information on the identity of the juvenile;

(b) The fact of and reasons for commitment and the authority therefor;

(c) The day and hour of admission, transfer and release;

(d) Details of the notifications to parents and guardians on every admission, transfer or release of the juvenile in their care at the time of commitment;

(e) Details of known physical and mental health problems, including drug and alcohol abuse.

22. The information on admission, place, transfer and release should be provided without delay to the parents and guardians or closest relative of the juvenile concerned.

23. As soon as possible after reception, full reports and relevant information on the personal situation and circumstances of each juvenile should be drawn up and submitted to the administration.

24. On admission, all juveniles shall be given a copy of the rules governing the detention facility and a written description of their rights and obligations in a language they can understand, together with the address of the authorities competent to receive complaints, as well as the address of public or private agencies and organizations which provide legal assistance. For

those juveniles who are illiterate or who cannot understand the language in the written form, the information should be conveyed in a manner enabling full comprehension.

25. All juveniles should be helped to understand the regulations governing the internal organization of the facility, the goals and methodology of the care provided, the disciplinary requirements and procedures, other authorized methods of seeking information and of making complaints and all such other matters as are necessary to enable them to understand fully their rights and obligations during detention.

26. The transport of juveniles should be carried out at the expense of the administration in conveyances with adequate ventilation and light, in conditions that should in no way subject them to hardship or indignity. Juveniles should not be transferred from one facility to another arbitrarily.

C. Classification and placement

27. As soon as possible after the moment of admission, each juvenile should be interviewed, and a psychological and social report identifying any factors relevant to the specific type and level of care and programme required by the juvenile should be prepared. This report, together with the report prepared by a medical officer who has examined the juvenile upon admission, should be forwarded to the director for purposes of determining the most appropriate placement for the juvenile within the facility and the specific type and level of care and programme required and to be pursued. When special rehabilitative treatment is required, and the length of stay in the facility permits, trained personnel of the facility should prepare a written, individualized treatment plan specifying treatment objectives and time-frame and the means, stages and delays with which the objectives should be approached.

28. The detention of juveniles should only take place under conditions that take full account of their particular needs, status and special requirements according to their age, personality, sex and type of offence, as well as mental and physical health, and which ensure their protection from harmful influences and risk situations. The principal criterion for the separation of different categories of juveniles deprived of their liberty should be the provision of the type of care best suited to the particular needs of the individuals concerned and the protection of their physical, mental and moral integrity and well-being.

29. In all detention facilities juveniles should be separated from adults, unless they are members of the same family. Under controlled conditions, juveniles may be brought together with carefully selected adults as part of a special programme that has been shown to be beneficial for the juveniles concerned.

30. Open detention facilities for juveniles should be established. Open detention facilities are those with no or minimal security measures. The population in such detention facilities should be as small as possible. The number of juveniles detained in closed facilities should be small enough to enable individualized treatment. Detention facilities for juveniles should be decentralized and of such size as to facilitate access and contact between the juveniles and their families. Small-scale detention facilities should be established and integrated into the social, economic and cultural environment of the community.

D. Physical environment and accommodation

31. Juveniles deprived of their liberty have the right to facilities and services that meet all the requirements of health and human dignity.

32. The design of detention facilities for juveniles and the physical environment should be in keeping with the rehabilitative aim of residential treatment, with due regard to the need of the

juvenile for privacy, sensory stimuli, opportunities for association with peers and participation in sports, physical exercise and leisure-time activities. The design and structure of juvenile detention facilities should be such as to minimize the risk of fire and to ensure safe evacuation from the premises. There should be an effective alarm system in case of fire, as well as formal and drilled procedures to ensure the safety of the juveniles. Detention facilities should not be located in areas where there are known health or other hazards or risks.

33. Sleeping accommodation should normally consist of small group dormitories or individual bedrooms, while bearing in mind local standards. During sleeping hours there should be regular, unobtrusive supervision of all sleeping areas, including individual rooms and group dormitories, in order to ensure the protection of each juvenile. Every juvenile should, in accordance with local or national standards, be provided with separate and sufficient bedding, which should be clean when issued, kept in good order and changed often enough to ensure cleanliness.

34. Sanitary installations should be so located and of a sufficient standard to enable every juvenile to comply, as required, with their physical needs in privacy and in a clean and decent manner.

35. The possession of personal effects is a basic element of the right to privacy and essential to the psychological well-being of the juvenile. The right of every juvenile to possess personal effects and to have adequate storage facilities for them should be fully recognized and respected. Personal effects that the juvenile does not choose to retain or that are confiscated should be placed in safe custody. An inventory thereof should be signed by the juvenile. Steps should be taken to keep them in good condition. All such articles and money should be returned to the juvenile on release, except in so far as he or she has been authorized to spend money or send such property out of the facility. If a juvenile receives or is found in possession of any medicine, the medical officer should decide what use should be made of it.

36. To the extent possible juveniles should have the right to use their own clothing. Detention facilities should ensure that each juvenile has personal clothing suitable for the climate and adequate to ensure good health, and which should in no manner be degrading or humiliating. Juveniles removed from or leaving a facility for any purpose should be allowed to wear their own clothing.

37. Every detention facility shall ensure that every juvenile receives food that is suitably prepared and presented at normal meal times and of a quality and quantity to satisfy the standards of dietetics, hygiene and health and, as far as possible, religious and cultural requirements. Clean drinking water should be available to every juvenile at any time.

E. Education, vocational training and work

38. Every juvenile of compulsory school age has the right to education suited to his or her needs and abilities and designed to prepare him or her for return to society. Such education should be provided outside the detention facility in community schools wherever possible and, in any case, by qualified teachers through programmes integrated with the education system of the country so that, after release, juveniles may continue their education without difficulty. Special attention should be given by the administration of the detention facilities to the education of juveniles of foreign origin or with particular cultural or ethnic needs. Juveniles who are illiterate or have cognitive or learning difficulties should have the right to special education.

39. Juveniles above compulsory school age who wish to continue their education should be permitted and encouraged to do so, and every effort should be made to provide them with access to appropriate educational programmes.

40. Diplomas or educational certificates awarded to juveniles while in detention should not indicate in any way that the juvenile has been institutionalized.

41. Every detention facility should provide access to a library that is adequately stocked with both instructional and recreational books and periodicals suitable for the juveniles, who should be encouraged and enabled to make full use of it.

42. Every juvenile should have the right to receive vocational training in occupations likely to prepare him or her for future employment.

43. With due regard to proper vocational selection and to the requirements of institutional administration, juveniles should be able to choose the type of work they wish to perform.

44. All protective national and international standards applicable to child labour and young workers should apply to juveniles deprived of their liberty.

45. Wherever possible, juveniles should be provided with the opportunity to perform remunerated labour, if possible within the local community, as a complement to the vocational training provided in order to enhance the possibility of finding suitable employment when they return to their communities.

The type of work should be such as to provide appropriate training that will be of benefit to the juveniles following release. The organization and methods of work offered in detention facilities should resemble as closely as possible those of similar work in the community, so as to prepare juveniles for the conditions of normal occupational life.

46. Every juvenile who performs work should have the right to an equitable remuneration. The interests of the juveniles and of their vocational training should not be subordinated to the purpose of making a profit for the detention facility or a third party. Part of the earnings of a juvenile should normally be set aside to constitute a savings fund to be handed over to the juvenile on release. The juvenile should have the right to use the remainder of those earnings to purchase articles for his or her own use or to indemnify the victim injured by his or her offence or to send it to his or her family or other persons outside the detention facility.

F. Recreation

47. Every juvenile should have the right to a suitable amount of time for daily free exercise, in the open air whenever weather permits, during which time appropriate recreational and physical training should normally be provided. Adequate space, installations and equipment should be provided for these activities. Every juvenile should have additional time for daily leisure activities, part of which should be devoted, if the juvenile so wishes, to arts and crafts skill development. The detention facility should ensure that each juvenile is physically able to participate in the available programmes of physical education. Remedial physical education and therapy should be offered, under medical supervision, to juveniles needing it.

G. Religion

48. Every juvenile should be allowed to satisfy the needs of his or her religious and spiritual life, in particular by attending the services or meetings provided in the detention facility or by conducting his or her own services and having possession of the necessary books or items of religious observance and instruction of his or her denomination. If a detention facility contains a sufficient number of juveniles of a given religion, one or more qualified representatives of that religion should be appointed or approved and allowed to hold regular services and to pay pastoral visits in private to juveniles at their request.

Every juvenile should have the right to receive visits from a qualified representative of any religion of his or her choice, as well as the right not to participate in religious services and freely to decline religious education, counselling or indoctrination.

H. Medical care

49. Every juvenile shall receive adequate medical care, both preventive and remedial, including dental, ophthalmological and mental health care, as well as pharmaceutical products and special diets as medically indicated. All such medical care should, where possible, be provided to detained juveniles through the appropriate health facilities and services of the community in which the detention facility is located, in order to prevent stigmatization of the juvenile and promote self-respect and integration into the community.

50. Every juvenile has a right to be examined by a physician immediately upon admission to a detention facility, for the purpose of recording any evidence of prior ill-treatment and identifying any physical or mental condition requiring medical attention.

51. The medical services provided to juveniles should seek to detect and should treat any physical or mental illness, substance abuse or other condition that may hinder the integration of the juvenile into society. Every detention facility for juveniles should have immediate access to adequate medical facilities and equipment appropriate to the number and requirements of its residents and staff trained in preventive health care and the handling of medical emergencies. Every juvenile who is ill, who complains of illness or who demonstrates symptoms of physical or mental difficulties, should be examined promptly by a medical officer.

52. Any medical officer who has reason to believe that the physical or mental health of a juvenile has been or will be injuriously affected by continued detention, a hunger strike or any condition of detention should report this fact immediately to the director of the detention facility in question and to the independent authority responsible for safeguarding the well-being of the juvenile.

53. A juvenile who is suffering from mental illness should be treated in a specialized institution under independent medical management. Steps should be taken, by arrangement with appropriate agencies, to ensure any necessary continuation of mental health care after release.

54. Juvenile detention facilities should adopt specialized drug abuse prevention and rehabilitation programmes administered by qualified personnel. These programmes should be adapted to the age, sex and other requirements of the juveniles concerned, and detoxification facilities and services staffed by trained personnel should be available to drug- or alcohol-dependent juveniles.

55. Medicines should be administered only for necessary treatment on medical grounds and, when possible, after having obtained the informed consent of the juvenile concerned. In particular, they must not be administered with a view to eliciting information or a confession, as a punishment or as a means of restraint. Juveniles shall never be testees in the experimental use of drugs and treatment.

The administration of any drug should always be authorized and carried out by qualified medical personnel.

I. Notification of illness, injury and death

56. The family or guardian of a juvenile and any other person designated by the juvenile have the right to be informed of the state of health of the juvenile on request and in the event of any

important changes in the health of the juvenile. The director of the detention facility should notify immediately the family or guardian of the juvenile concerned, or other designated person, in case of death, illness requiring transfer of the juvenile to an outside medical facility, or a condition requiring clinical care within the detention facility for more than 48 hours. Notification should also be given to the consular authorities of the State of which a foreign juvenile is a citizen.

57. Upon the death of a juvenile during the period of deprivation of liberty, the nearest relative should have the right to inspect the death certificate, see the body and determine the method of disposal of the body. Upon the death of a juvenile in detention, there should be an independent inquiry into the causes of death, the report of which should be made accessible to the nearest relative. This inquiry should also be made when the death of a juvenile occurs within six months from the date of his or her release from the detention facility and there is reason to believe that the death is related to the period of detention.

58. A juvenile should be informed at the earliest possible time of the death, serious illness or injury of any immediate family member and should be provided with the opportunity to attend the funeral of the deceased or go to the bedside of a critically ill relative.

J. Contacts with the wider community

59. Every means should be provided to ensure that juveniles have adequate communication with the outside world, which is an integral part of the right to fair and humane treatment and is essential to the preparation of juveniles for their return to society. Juveniles should be allowed to communicate with their families, friends and other persons or representatives of reputable outside organizations, to leave detention facilities for a visit to their home and family and to receive special permission to leave the detention facility for educational, vocational or other important reasons. Should the juvenile be serving a sentence, the time spent outside a detention facility should be counted as part of the period of sentence.

60. Every juvenile should have the right to receive regular and frequent visits, in principle once a week and not less than once a month, in circumstances that respect the need of the juvenile for privacy, contact and unrestricted communication with the family and the defence counsel.

61. Every juvenile should have the right to communicate in writing or by telephone at least twice a week with the person of his or her choice, unless legally restricted, and should be assisted as necessary in order effectively to enjoy this right. Every juvenile should have the right to receive correspondence.

62. Juveniles should have the opportunity to keep themselves informed regularly of the news by reading newspapers, periodicals and other publications, through access to radio and television programmes and motion pictures, and through the visits of the representatives of any lawful club or organization in which the juvenile is interested.

K. Limitations of physical restraint and the use of force

63. Recourse to instruments of restraint and to force for any purpose should be prohibited, except as set forth in rule 64 below.

64. Instruments of restraint and force can only be used in exceptional cases, where all other control methods have been exhausted and failed, and only as explicitly authorized and specified by law and regulation. They should not cause humiliation or degradation, and should be used restrictively and only for the shortest possible period of time. By order of the director of the administration, such instruments might be resorted to in order to prevent the juvenile from

inflicting self-injury, injuries to others or serious destruction of property. In such instances, the director should at once consult medical and other relevant personnel and report to the higher administrative authority.

65. The carrying and use of weapons by personnel should be prohibited in any facility where juveniles are detained.

L. Disciplinary procedures

66. Any disciplinary measures and procedures should maintain the interest of safety and an ordered community life and should be consistent with the upholding of the inherent dignity of the juvenile and the fundamental objective of institutional care, namely, instilling a sense of justice, self-respect and respect for the basic rights of every person.

67. All disciplinary measures constituting cruel, inhuman or degrading treatment shall be strictly prohibited, including corporal punishment, placement in a dark cell, closed or solitary confinement or any other punishment that may compromise the physical or mental health of the juvenile concerned.

The reduction of diet and the restriction or denial of contact with family members should be prohibited for any purpose. Labour should always be viewed as an educational tool and a means of promoting the self-respect of the juvenile in preparing him or her for return to the community and should not be imposed as a disciplinary sanction. No juvenile should be sanctioned more than once for the same disciplinary infraction. Collective sanctions should be prohibited.

68. Legislation or regulations adopted by the competent administrative authority should establish norms concerning the following, taking full account of the fundamental characteristics, needs and rights of juveniles:

(a) Conduct constituting a disciplinary offence;

(b) Type and duration of disciplinary sanctions that may be inflicted;

(c) The authority competent to impose such sanctions;

(d) The authority competent to consider appeals.

69. A report of misconduct should be presented promptly to the competent authority, which should decide on it without undue delay. The competent authority should conduct a thorough examination of the case.

70. No juvenile should be disciplinarily sanctioned except in strict accordance with the terms of the law and regulations in force. No juvenile should be sanctioned unless he or she has been informed of the alleged infraction in a manner appropriate to the full understanding of the juvenile, and given a proper opportunity of presenting his or her defence, including the right of appeal to a competent impartial authority. Complete records should be kept of all disciplinary proceedings.

71. No juveniles should be responsible for disciplinary functions except in the supervision of specified social, educational or sports activities or in self-government programmes.

M. Inspection and complaints

72. Qualified inspectors or an equivalent duly constituted authority not belonging to the administration of the facility should be empowered to conduct inspections on a regular basis and to undertake unannounced inspections on their own initiative, and should enjoy full guarantees

of independence in the exercise of this function. Inspectors should have unrestricted access to all persons employed by or working in any facility where juveniles are or may be deprived of their liberty, to all juveniles and to all records of such facilities.

73. Qualified medical officers attached to the inspecting authority or the public health service should participate in the inspections, evaluating compliance with the rules concerning the physical environment, hygiene, accommodation, food, exercise and medical services, as well as any other aspect or conditions of institutional life that affect the physical and mental health of juveniles. Every juvenile should have the right to talk in confidence to any inspecting officer.

74. After completing the inspection, the inspector should be required to submit a report on the findings. The report should include an evaluation of the compliance of the detention facilities with the present rules and relevant provisions of national law, and recommendations regarding any steps considered necessary to ensure compliance with them. Any facts discovered by an inspector that appear to indicate that a violation of legal provisions concerning the rights of juveniles or the operation of a juvenile detention facility has occurred should be communicated to the competent authorities for investigation and prosecution.

75. Every juvenile should have the opportunity of making requests or complaints to the director of the detention facility and to his or her authorized representative.

76. Every juvenile should have the right to make a request or complaint, without censorship as to substance, to the central administration, the judicial authority or other proper authorities through approved channels, and to be informed of the response without delay.

77. Efforts should be made to establish an independent office (ombudsman) to receive and investigate complaints made by juveniles deprived of their liberty and to assist in the achievement of equitable settlements.

78. Every juvenile should have the right to request assistance from family members, legal counsellors, humanitarian groups or others where possible, in order to make a complaint. Illiterate juveniles should be provided with assistance should they need to use the services of public or private agencies and organizations which provide legal counsel or which are competent to receive complaints.

N. Return to the community

79. All juveniles should benefit from arrangements designed to assist them in returning to society, family life, education or employment after release. Procedures, including early release, and special courses should be devised to this end.

80. Competent authorities should provide or ensure services to assist juveniles in re-establishing themselves in society and to lessen prejudice against such juveniles. These services should ensure, to the extent possible, that the juvenile is provided with suitable residence, employment, clothing, and sufficient means to maintain himself or herself upon release in order to facilitate successful reintegration. The representatives of agencies providing such services should be consulted and should have access to juveniles while detained, with a view to assisting them in their return to the community.

V. PERSONNEL

81. Personnel should be qualified and include a sufficient number of specialists such as educators, vocational instructors, counsellors, social workers, psychiatrists and psychologists. These and other specialist staff should normally be employed on a permanent basis. This should not preclude part-time or volunteer workers when the level of support and training they

can provide is appropriate and beneficial. Detention facilities should make use of all remedial, educational, moral, spiritual, and other resources and forms of assistance that are appropriate and available in the community, according to the individual needs and problems of detained juveniles.

82. The administration should provide for the careful selection and recruitment of every grade and type of personnel, since the proper management of detention facilities depends on their integrity, humanity, ability and professional capacity to deal with juveniles, as well as personal suitability for the work.

83. To secure the foregoing ends, personnel should be appointed as professional officers with adequate remuneration to attract and retain suitable women and men. The personnel of juvenile detention facilities should be continually encouraged to fulfil their duties and obligations in a humane, committed, professional, fair and efficient manner, to conduct themselves at all times in such a way as to deserve and gain the respect of the juveniles, and to provide juveniles with a positive role model and perspective.

84. The administration should introduce forms of organization and management that facilitate communications between different categories of staff in each detention facility so as to enhance cooperation between the various services engaged in the care of juveniles, as well as between staff and the administration, with a view to ensuring that staff directly in contact with juveniles are able to function in conditions favourable to the efficient fulfilment of their duties.

85. The personnel should receive such training as will enable them to carry out their responsibilities effectively, in particular training in child psychology, child welfare and international standards and norms of human rights and the rights of the child, including the present Rules. The personnel should maintain and improve their knowledge and professional capacity by attending courses of in-service training, to be organized at suitable intervals throughout their career.

86. The director of a facility should be adequately qualified for his or her task, with administrative ability and suitable training and experience, and should carry out his or her duties on a full-time basis.

87. In the performance of their duties, personnel of detention facilities should respect and protect the human dignity and fundamental human rights of all juveniles, in particular, as follows:

(a) No member of the detention facility or institutional personnel may inflict, instigate or tolerate any act of torture or any form of harsh, cruel, inhuman or degrading treatment, punishment, correction or discipline under any pretext or circumstance whatsoever;

(b) All personnel should rigorously oppose and combat any act of corruption, reporting it without delay to the competent authorities;

(c) All personnel should respect the present Rules. Personnel who have reason to believe that a serious violation of the present Rules has occurred or is about to occur should report the matter to their superior authorities or organs vested with reviewing or remedial power;

(d) All personnel should ensure the full protection of the physical and mental health of juveniles, including protection from physical, sexual and emotional abuse and exploitation, and should take immediate action to secure medical attention whenever required;

(e) All personnel should respect the right of the juvenile to privacy, and, in particular, should safeguard all confidential matters concerning juveniles or their families learned as a result of their professional capacity;

(f) All personnel should seek to minimize any differences between life inside and outside the detention facility which tend to lessen due respect for the dignity of juveniles as human beings.

CCPR General Comment No. 21: Article 10 (Humane Treatment of Persons Deprived of Liberty), 1992 (Replaces General Comment No.9)*

Adoption: 10 April 1992

1. This general comment replaces general comment 9 (the sixteenth session, 1982) reflecting and further developing it.

2. Article 10, paragraph 1, of the International Covenant on Civil and Political Rights applies to any one deprived of liberty under the laws and authority of the State who is held in prisons, hospitals - particularly psychiatric hospitals - detention camps or correctional institutions or elsewhere. States parties should ensure that the principle stipulated therein is observed in all institutions and establishments within their jurisdiction where persons are being held.

3. Article 10, paragraph 1, imposes on States parties a positive obligation towards persons who are particularly vulnerable because of their status as persons deprived of liberty, and complements for them the ban on torture or other cruel, inhuman or degrading treatment or punishment contained in article 7 of the Covenant. Thus, not only may persons deprived of their liberty not be subjected to treatment that is contrary to article 7, including medical or scientific experimentation, but neither may they be subjected to any hardship or constraint other than that resulting from the deprivation of liberty; respect for the dignity of such persons must be guaranteed under the same conditions as for that of free persons. Persons deprived of their liberty enjoy all the rights set forth in the Covenant, subject to the restrictions that are unavoidable in a closed environment.

4. Treating all persons deprived of their liberty with humanity and with respect for their dignity is a fundamental and universally applicable rule. Consequently, the application of this rule, as a minimum, cannot be dependent on the material resources available in the State party. This rule must be applied without distinction of any kind, such as race, colour, sex, language, religion, political or other opinion, national or social origin, property, birth or other status.

5. States parties are invited to indicate in their reports to what extent they are applying the relevant United Nations standards applicable to the treatment of prisoners: the Standard Minimum Rules for the Treatment of Prisoners (1957), the Body of Principles for the Protection of All Persons under Any Form of Detention or Imprisonment (1988), the Code of Conduct for Law Enforcement Officials (1978) and the Principles of Medical Ethics relevant to the Role of Health Personnel, particularly Physicians, in the Protection of Prisoners and Detainees against Torture and Other Cruel, Inhuman or Degrading Treatment or Punishment (1982).

6. The Committee recalls that reports should provide detailed information on national legislative and administrative provisions that have a bearing on the right provided for in article 10, paragraph 1. The Committee also considers that it is necessary for reports to specify what concrete measures have been taken by the competent authorities to monitor the effective application of the rules regarding the treatment of persons deprived of their liberty. States parties should include in their reports information concerning the system for supervising penitentiary establishments, the specific measures to prevent torture and cruel, inhuman or degrading treatment, and how impartial supervision is ensured.

7. Furthermore, the Committee recalls that reports should indicate whether the various applicable provisions form an integral part of the instruction and training of the personnel who have authority over persons deprived of their liberty and whether they are strictly adhered to by

* Source: U.N. Doc. HRI\GEN\1\Rev.1 at 33.

such personnel in the discharge of their duties. It would also be appropriate to specify whether arrested or detained persons have access to such information and have effective legal means enabling them to ensure that those rules are respected, to complain if the rules are ignored and to obtain adequate compensation in the event of a violation.

8. The Committee recalls that the principle set forth in article 10, paragraph 1, constitutes the basis for the more specific obligations of States parties in respect of criminal justice, which are set forth in article 10, paragraphs 2 and 3.

9. Article 10, paragraph 2 (a), provides for the segregation, save in exceptional circumstances, of accused persons from convicted ones. Such segregation is required in order to emphasize their status as unconvicted persons who at the same time enjoy the right to be presumed innocent as stated in article 14, paragraph 2. The reports of States parties should indicate how the separation of accused persons from convicted persons is effected and explain how the treatment of accused persons differs from that of convicted persons.

10. As to article 10, paragraph 3, which concerns convicted persons, the Committee wishes to have detailed information on the operation of the penitentiary system of the State party. No penitentiary system should be only retributory; it should essentially seek the reformation and social rehabilitation of the prisoner. States parties are invited to specify whether they have a system to provide assistance after release and to give information as to its success.

11. In a number of cases, the information furnished by the State party contains no specific reference either to legislative or administrative provisions or to practical measures to ensure the re-education of convicted persons. The Committee requests specific information concerning the measures taken to provide teaching, education and re-education, vocational guidance and training and also concerning work programmes for prisoners inside the penitentiary establishment as well as outside.

12. In order to determine whether the principle set forth in article 10, paragraph 3, is being fully respected, the Committee also requests information on the specific measures applied during detention, e.g., how convicted persons are dealt with individually and how they are categorized, the disciplinary system, solitary confinement and high-security detention and the conditions under which contacts are ensured with the outside world (family, lawyer, social and medical services, non-governmental organizations).

13. Moreover, the Committee notes that in the reports of some States parties no information has been provided concerning the treatment accorded to accused juvenile persons and juvenile offenders. Article 10, paragraph 2 (b), provides that accused juvenile persons shall be separated from adults. The information given in reports shows that some States parties are not paying the necessary attention to the fact that this is a mandatory provision of the Covenant. The text also provides that cases involving juveniles must be considered as speedily as possible. Reports should specify the measures taken by States parties to give effect to that provision. Lastly, under article 10, paragraph 3, juvenile offenders shall be segregated from adults and be accorded treatment appropriate to their age and legal status in so far as conditions of detention are concerned, such as shorter working hours and contact with relatives, with the aim of furthering their reformation and rehabilitation. Article 10 does not indicate any limits of juvenile age. While this is to be determined by each State party in the light of relevant social, cultural and other conditions, the Committee is of the opinion that article 6, paragraph 5, suggests that all persons under the age of 18 should be treated as juveniles, at least in matters relating to criminal justice. States should give relevant information about the age groups of persons treated as juveniles. In that regard, States parties are invited to indicate whether they are applying the United Nations Standard Minimum Rules for the Administration of Juvenile Justice, known as the Beijing Rules (1987).

Guidelines for Action on Children in the Criminal Justice System, 1997 [excerpts]*

Adoption: 21 July 1997

[...]

II. Plans for the Implementation of the Convention on the Rights of the Child, the pursuit of its goals and the use and application of international standards and norms in juvenile justice

[...]

17. Appropriate action should be ensured to alleviate the problem of children in need of special protection measures, such as children working or living on the streets or children permanently deprived of a family environment, children with disabilities, children of minorities, immigrants and indigenous peoples and other vulnerable groups of children.

[...]

III. Plans concerned with child victims and witnesses

43. In accordance with the Declaration of Basic Principles of Justice for Victims of Crime and Abuse of Power, States should undertake to ensure that child victims and witnesses are provided with appropriate access to justice and fair treatment, restitution, compensation and social assistance. If applicable, measures should be taken to prevent the settling of penal matters through compensation outside the justice system, when doing so is not in the best interests of the child.

44. Police, lawyers, the judiciary and other court personnel should receive training in dealing with cases where children are victims. States should consider establishing, if they have not yet done so, specialized offices and units to deal with cases involving offences against children. States should establish, as appropriate, a code of practice for proper management of cases involving child victims.

45. Child victims should be treated with compassion and respect for their dignity. They are entitled to access to the mechanisms of justice and to prompt redress, as provided for by national legislation, for the harm they have suffered.

46. Child victims should have access to assistance that meets their needs, such as advocacy, protection, economic assistance, counselling, health and social services, social reintegration and physical and psychological recovery services. Special assistance should be given to those children who are disabled or ill. Emphasis should be placed upon family- and communitybased rehabilitation rather than institutionalization.

47. Judicial and administrative mechanisms should be established and strengthened where necessary to enable child victims to obtain redress through formal or informal procedures

* Recommended by Economic and Social Council Resolution 1997/30.
In resolution 1997/30, paragraph 1, the Economic and Social Council welcomed the Guidelines for Action on Children in the Criminal Justice System annexed to the resolution and invited all parties concerned to make use of the Guidelines in the implementation of the Convention on the Rights of the Child with regard to juvenile justice.

that are prompt, fair and accessible. Child victims and/or their legal representatives should be informed accordingly.

48. Access should be allowed to fair and adequate compensation for all child victims of violations of human rights, specifically torture and other cruel, inhuman or degrading treatment or punishment, including rape and sexual abuse, unlawful or arbitrary deprivation of liberty, unjustifiable detention and miscarriage of justice. Necessary legal representation to bring an action within an appropriate court or tribunal, as well as interpretation into the native language of the child, if necessary, should be available.

49. Child witnesses need assistance in the judicial and administrative processes. States should review, evaluate and improve, as necessary, the situation for children as witnesses of crime in their evidential and procedural law to ensure that the rights of children are fully protected. In accordance with the different law traditions, practices and legal framework, direct contact should be avoided between the child victim and the offender during the process of investigation and prosecution as well as during trial hearings as much as possible. The identification of the child victim in the media should be prohibited, where necessary to protect the privacy of the child. Where prohibition is contrary to the fundamental legal principles of Member States, such identification should be discouraged.

50. States should consider, if necessary, amendments of their penal procedural codes to allow for, inter alia, videotaping of the child's testimony and presentation of the videotaped testimony in court as an official piece of evidence. In particular, police, prosecutors, judges and magistrates should apply more child-friendly practices, for example, in police operations and interviews of child witnesses.

51. The responsiveness of judicial and administrative processes to the needs of child victims and witnesses should be facilitated by:

(a) Informing child victims of their role and the scope, timing and progress of the proceedings and of the disposition of their cases, especially where serious crimes are involved;

(b) Encouraging the development of child witness preparation schemes to familiarize children with the criminal justice process prior to giving evidence. Appropriate assistance should be provided to child victims and witnesses throughout the legal process;

(c) Allowing the views and concerns of child victims to be presented and considered at appropriate stages of the proceedings where their personal interests are affected, without prejudice to the accused and in accordance with the relevant national criminal justice system;

(d) Taking measures to minimize delays in the criminal justice process, protecting the privacy of child victims and witnesses and, when necessary, ensuring their safety from intimidation and retaliation.

52. Children displaced illegally or wrongfully retained across borders are as a general principle to be returned to the country of origin. Due attention should be paid to their safety, and they should be treated humanely and receive necessary assistance, pending their return. They should be returned promptly to ensure compliance with the Convention on the Rights of the Child. Where the Hague Convention on the Civil Aspects of International Child Abduction of 1980 or the Hague Convention on the Protection of Children and Cooperation in respect of Inter-Country Adoption of 1993, approved by the Hague Conference on Private International Law, the Convention on Jurisdiction, Applicable Law, Recognition, Enforcement and Cooperation in Respect of Parental Responsibility and Measures for the Protection of the Child are applicable, the provisions of these conventions with regard to the return of the child should be promptly applied. Upon the return of the child, the country of origin should treat the child with respect,

in accordance with international principles of human rights, and offer adequate family-based rehabilitation measures.

53. The United Nations Crime Prevention and Criminal Justice Programme, including the institutes comprising the Programme network, the Office of the United Nations High Commissioner for Human Rights/Centre for Human Rights, the United Nations Children's Fund, the United Nations Development Programme, the Committee on the Rights of the Child, the United Nations Educational, Scientific and Cultural Organization, the World Bank and interested non-governmental organizations should assist Member States, at their request, within the overall appropriations of the United Nations budgets or from extrabudgetary resources, in developing multidisciplinary training, education and information activities for law enforcement and other criminal justice personnel, including police officers, prosecutors, judges and magistrates.

Report of the Working Group on Arbitrary Detention, 1998 [excerpts]*

Adoption: 18 December 1998

[...]

II. SITUATION REGARDING IMMIGRANTS AND ASYLUM SEEKERS

62. In its resolution 1997/50, the Commission on Human Rights requested the Working Group to devote all necessary attention to reports concerning the situation of immigrants and asylum seekers who are allegedly being held in prolonged administrative custody without the possibility of administrative or judicial remedy, and to include observations on this question in its report.

63. Taking into account the preliminary observations submitted to the Commission regarding the definition of the mandate, the applicable international and regional standards and the places of deprivation of liberty concerned (see E/CN.4/1998/44, paras. 2842), as well as the experience gained from the first two field missions conducted in this area in SeptemberOctober 1998 (see E/CN.4/1999/62/Add.3 and 4), the Working Group has set the following guidelines for the accomplishment of its mission.

A. Scope

64. It follows from the abovecited resolution that the Working Group's mandate relates essentially to situations in which aliens, asylum seekers or immigrants, are deprived of liberty for the time necessary to consider their applications for admission into the territory concerned and, in the event of refusal, for the period preceding their expulsion as appropriate.

65. The Working Group, following the terminology used by the Commission, describes this form of deprivation of liberty as "custody" ("rétention") (see E/CN.4/1998/44, para. 38).

66. Measures assimilated with such custody are house arrest under the conditions set forth in deliberation 01 of the Working Group (see the Group's report for 1993, E/CN.4/1993/24, para. 20) and confinement on board a ship, aircraft, road vehicle or train. However, resolution 1997/50 does not cover the situation of aliens deprived of their liberty in connection with extradition proceedings or following prosecution or a criminal conviction, except in those cases where the offence under domestic law is related to illegal entry into the territory.

67. The Working Group also considers that its specific mandate does not include determining the lawfulness and conformity with international standards of procedures for granting asylum or conferring refugee status, or for permitting temporary residence where immigrants are concerned, unless they have a direct bearing on the juridical aspects of the custody and its possible arbitrary character.

68. The places of deprivation of liberty concerned may be places of custody situated in border areas, police premises, premises under the authority of a prison administration, ad hoc centres, so called "international" or "transit" areas (ports or international airports), gathering centres or certain hospital premises (see E/CN.4/1998/44, paras. 2841).

* Source: U.N.Doc. E/CN.4/1999/63.

B. Criteria for determining whether or not the custody is arbitrary

69. In order to determine the arbitrary character or otherwise of the custody, the Working Group considers whether or not the alien is able to enjoy all or some of the following guarantees:

Guarantee 1: To be informed, at least orally, when held for questioning at the border, or in the territory concerned if he has entered illegally, in a language which he understands, of the nature of and grounds for the measure refusing admission at the border, or permission for temporary residence in the territory, that is being contemplated with respect to him.

Guarantee 2: Decision involving administrative custody taken by a duly authorized official with a sufficient level of responsibility in accordance with the criteria laid down by law and subject to guarantees 3 and 4.

Guarantee 3: Determination of the lawfulness of the administrative custody pursuant to legislation providing to this end for:

(a) The person concerned to be brought automatically and promptly before a judge or a body affording equivalent guarantees of competence, independence and impartiality;

(b) Alternatively, the possibility of appealing to a judge or to such a body.

Guarantee 4: To be entitled to have the decision reviewed by a higher court or an equivalent competent, independent and impartial body.

Guarantee 5: Written and reasoned notification of the measure of custody in a language understood by the applicant.

Guarantee 6: Possibility of communicating by an effective medium such as the telephone, fax or electronic mail, from the place of custody, in particular with a lawyer, a consular representative and relatives.

Guarantee 7: To be assisted by counsel of his own choosing (or, alternatively, by officially appointed counsel) both through visits in the place of custody and at any hearing.

Guarantee 8: Custody effected in public premises intended for this purpose; otherwise, the individual in custody shall be separated from persons imprisoned under criminal law.

Guarantee 9: Keeping up to date a register of persons entering and leaving custody, and specifying the reasons for the measure.

Guarantee 10: Not to be held in custody for an excessive or unlimited period, with a maximum period being set, as appropriate, by the regulations.

Guarantee 11: To be informed of the guarantees provided for in the disciplinary rules, if any.

Guarantee 12: Existence of a procedure for holding a person incommunicado and the nature of such a procedure, where applicable.

Guarantee 13: Possibility for the alien to benefit from alternatives to administrative custody.

Guarantee 14: Possibility for the Office of the United Nations High Commissioner for Refugees, the International Committee of the Red Cross and specialized nongovernmental organizations to have access to places of custody.

70. Where the absence of such guarantees or their violation, circumvention or nonimplementation constitutes a matter of a high degree of gravity, the Working Group may conclude that the custody is arbitrary.

[...]

UNHCR Revised Guidelines on Applicable Criteria and Standards Relating to the Detention of Asylum Seekers, 1999*[1]

Adoption: 1 February 1999

Introduction

1. The detention of asylum-seekers is, in the view of UNHCR inherently undesirable. This is even more so in the case of vulnerable groups such as single women, children, unaccompanied minors and those with special medical or psychological needs. Freedom from arbitrary detention is a fundamental human right and the use of detention is, in many instances, contrary to the norms and principles of international law.

2. Of key significance to the issue of detention is Article 31 of the 1951 Convention[2]. Article 31 exempts refugees coming directly from a country of persecution from being punished on account of their illegal entry or presence, provided they present themselves without delay to the authorities and show good cause for their illegal entry or presence. The Article also provides that Contracting States shall not apply to the movements of such refugees restrictions other than those which are necessary, and that any restrictions shall only be applied until such time as their status is regularised, or they obtain admission into another country.

3. Consistent with this Article, detention should only be resorted to in cases of necessity. The detention of asylum-seekers who come "directly" in an irregular manner should, therefore, not be automatic, or unduly prolonged. This provision applies not only to recognised refugees but also to asylum-seekers pending determination of their status, as recognition of refugee status does not make an individual a refugee but declares him to be one. Conclusion No.44(XXXVII) of the Executive Committee on the Detention of Refugees and Asylum-Seekers examines more concretely what is meant by the term "necessary". This Conclusion also provides guidelines to States on the use of detention and recommendations as to certain procedural guarantees to which detainees should be entitled.

4. The expression "coming directly" in Article 31(1), covers the situation of a person who enters the country in which asylum is sought directly from the country of origin, or from another country where his protection, safety and security could not be assured. It is understood that this term also covers a person who transits an intermediate country for a short period of time without having applied for, or received, asylum there. No strict time limit can be applied to the concept "coming directly" and each case must be judged on its merits. Similarly, given the special situation of asylum-seekers, in particular the effects of trauma, language problems, lack of information, previous experiences which often result in a suspicion of those in authority, feelings of insecurity, and the fact that these and other circumstances may vary enormously from one asylum seeker to another, there is no time limit which can be mechanically applied or associated with the expression "without delay". The expression "good cause", requires a consideration of the circumstances under which the asylum-seeker fled. The term "asylum-seeker" in these guidelines applies to those whose claims are being considered under an admissibility or pre-screening procedure as well as those who are being considered under

* Source: http://www.unhcr.org.

[1] These Guidelines address exclusively the detention of asylum seekers. The detention of refugees is generally covered by national law and subject to the principles, norms and standards contained in the 1951 Convention, and the applicable human rights instruments.

[2] The Geneva Convention of 28 July 1951 Relating to the Status of Refugees.

refugee status determination procedures. It also includes those exercising their right to seek judicial and/or administrative review of their asylum request.

5. Asylum-seekers are entitled to benefit from the protection afforded by various International and Regional Human Rights instruments which set out the basic standards and norms of treatment. Whereas each State has a right to control those entering into their territory, these rights must be exercised in accordance with a prescribed law which is accessible and formulated with sufficient precision for the regulation of individual conduct. For detention of asylum-seekers to be lawful and not arbitrary, it must comply not only with the applicable national law, but with Article 31 of the Convention and international law. It must be exercised in a non-discriminatory manner and must be subject to judicial or administrative review to ensure that it continues to be necessary in the circumstances, with the possibility of release where no grounds for its continuation exist.[3]

6. Although these guidelines deal specifically with the detention of asylum-seekers the issue of the detention of stateless persons needs to be highlighted.[4] While the majority of stateless persons are not asylum-seekers, a paragraph on the detention of stateless persons is included in these guidelines in recognition of UNHCR's formal responsibilities for this group and also because the basic standards and norms of treatment contained in international human rights instruments applicable to detainees generally should be applied to both asylum-seekers and stateless persons. The inability of stateless persons who have left their countries of habitual residence to return to them, has been a reason for unduly prolonged or arbitrary detention of these persons in third countries. Similarly, individuals whom the State of nationality refuses to accept back on the basis that nationality was withdrawn or lost while they were out of the country, or who are not acknowledged as nationals without proof of nationality, which in the circumstances is difficult to acquire, have also been held in prolonged or indefinite detention only because the question of where to send them remains unresolved.

Guideline 1: Scope of the Guidelines

These guidelines apply to all asylum-seekers who are being considered for, or who are in, detention or detention-like situations. For the purpose of these guidelines, UNHCR considers detention as: confinement within a narrowly bounded or restricted location, including prisons, closed camps, detention facilities or airport transit zones, where freedom of movement is substantially curtailed, and where the only opportunity to leave this limited area is to leave the territory. There is a qualitative difference between detention and other restrictions on freedom of movement.

Persons who are subject to limitations on domicile and residency are not generally considered to be in detention.

When considering whether an asylum-seeker is in detention, the cumulative impact of the restrictions as well as the degree and intensity of each of them should also be assessed.

Guideline 2: General Principle

As a general principle asylum-seekers should not be detained.

[3] Views of the Human Rights Committee on Communication No.560/1993, 59th Session, CCPR/C/D/560/1993.

[4] UNHCR has been requested to provide technical and advisory services to states on nationality legislation or practice resulting in statelessness. EXCOM Conclusion No.78(XLVI) (1995), General Assembly Resolution 50/152, 1996. See also Guidelines: Field Office Activities Concerning Statelessness (IOM/66/98-FOM70/98).

According to Article 14 of the Universal Declaration of Human Rights, the right to seek and enjoy asylum is recognised as a basic human right. In exercising this right asylum-seekers are often forced to arrive at, or enter, a territory illegally. However the position of asylum-seekers differs fundamentally from that of ordinary immigrants in that they may not be in a position to comply with the legal formalities for entry. This element, as well as the fact that asylum-seekers have often had traumatic experiences, should be taken into account in determining any restrictions on freedom of movement based on illegal entry or presence.

Guideline 3: Exceptional Grounds for Detention

Detention of asylum-seekers may exceptionally be resorted to for the reasons set out below as long as this is clearly prescribed by a national law which is in conformity with general norms and principles of international human rights law. These are contained in the main human rights instruments.[5]

There should be a presumption against detention. Where there are monitoring mechanisms which can be employed as viable alternatives to detention, (such as reporting obligations or guarantor requirements [see Guideline 4]), these should be applied first unless there is evidence to suggest that such an alternative will not be effective in the individual case. Detention should therefore only take place after a full consideration of all possible alternatives, or when monitoring mechanisms have been demonstrated not to have achieved the lawful and legitimate purpose.

In assessing whether detention of asylum-seekers is necessary, account should be taken of whether it is reasonable to do so and whether it is proportional to the objectives to be achieved. If judged necessary it should only be imposed in a non discriminatory manner for a minimal period.[6]

The permissible exceptions to the general rule that detention should normally be avoided must be prescribed by law. In conformity with EXCOM Conclusion No.44 (XXXVII) the detention of asylum-seekers may only be resorted to, if necessary:

(i) to verify identity.

This relates to those cases where identity may be undetermined or in dispute.

(ii) to determine the elements on which the claim for refugee status or asylum is based.

This statement means that the asylum-seeker may be detained exclusively for the purposes of a preliminary interview to identify the basis of the asylum claim.[7] This would involve obtaining essential facts from the asylum-seeker as to why asylum is being sought and would not extend to a determination of the merits or otherwise of the claim. This exception to the general principle cannot be used to justify detention for the entire status determination procedure, or for an unlimited period of time.

(iii) in cases where asylum-seekers have destroyed their travel and /or identity documents or have used fraudulent documents in order to mislead the authorities of the State, in which they intend to claim asylum.

---

[5] Article 9(1) International Covenant on Civil and Political Rights (ICCPR); Article 37(b) UN Convention on the Rights of the Child (CRC); Article 5(1) European Convention for the Protection of Human Rights and Fundamental Freedoms (ECHR); Article 7(2) American Convention on Human Rights 1969 (American Convention); Article 5 African Charter on Human and People's Rights (African Charter).

[6] Article 9(1), Article 12 ICCPR ; Article 37(b) CRC ; Article 5(1)(f) ECHR ; Article 7(3) American Convention ; Article 6 African Charter ; EXCOM Conclusion No.44(XXXVII).

[7] EXCOM Conclusion No.44 (XXXVII).

What must be established is the absence of good faith on the part of the applicant to comply with the verification of identity process. As regards asylum-seekers using fraudulent documents or travelling with no documents at all, detention is only permissible when there is an intention to mislead, or a refusal to co-operate with the authorities. Asylum-seekers who arrive without documentation because they are unable to obtain any in their country of origin should not be detained solely for that reason.

(iv) to protect national security and public order.

This relates to cases where there is evidence to show that the asylum-seeker has criminal antecedents and/or affiliations which are likely to pose a risk to public order or national security should he/she be allowed entry.

Detention of asylum-seekers which is applied for purposes other than those listed above, for example, as part of a policy to deter future asylum-seekers, or to dissuade those who have commenced their claims from pursuing them, is contrary to the norms of refugee law. It should not be used as a punitive or disciplinary measure for illegal entry or presence in the country. Detention should also be avoided for failure to comply with the administrative requirements or other institutional restrictions related residency at reception centres, or refugee camps. Escape from detention should not lead to the automatic discontinuation of the asylum procedure, or to return to the country of origin, having regard to the principle of non- refoulement.[8]

Guideline 4: Alternatives to Detention

Alternatives to the detention of an asylum-seeker until status is determined should be considered. The choice of an alternative would be influenced by an individual assessment of the personal circumstances of the asylum-seeker concerned and prevailing local conditions.

Alternatives to detention which may be considered are as follows:

(i) Monitoring Requirements.

Reporting Requirements: Whether an asylum-seeker stays out of detention may be conditional on compliance with periodic reporting requirements during the status determination procedures. Release could be on the asylum-seeker's own recognisance, and/or that of a family member, NGO or community group who would be expected to ensure the asylum-seeker reports to the authorities periodically, complies with status determination procedures, and appears at hearings and official appointments.

Residency Requirements: Asylum-seekers would not be detained on condition they reside at a specific address or within a particular administrative region until their status has been determined. Asylum-seekers would have to obtain prior approval to change their address or move out of the administrative region. However this would not be unreasonably withheld where the main purpose of the relocation was to facilitate family reunification or closeness to relatives.[9]

(ii) Provision of a Guarantor/ Surety. Asylum seekers would be required to provide a guarantor who would be responsible for ensuring their attendance at official appointments and hearings, failure of which a penalty most likely the forfeiture of a sum of money, levied against the guarantor.

(iii) Release on Bail. This alternative allows for asylum-seekers already in detention to apply for release on bail, subject to the provision of recognisance and surety. For this to be genuinely

[8] Sub Committee of the Whole of International Protection Note EC/SCP/44 Paragraph 51(c).

[9] Art 16, Art 12 UDHR.

available to asylum-seekers they must be informed of its availability and the amount set must not be so high as to be prohibitive.

(iv) Open Centres. Asylum-seekers may be released on condition that they reside at specific collective accommodation centres where they would be allowed permission to leave and return during stipulated times.

These alternatives are not exhaustive. They identify options which provide State authorities with a degree of control over the whereabouts of asylum-seekers while allowing asylum-seekers basic freedom of movement.

Guideline 5: Procedural Safeguards[10]

If detained, asylum-seekers should be entitled to the following minimum procedural guarantees:

(i) to receive prompt and full communication of any order of detention, together with the reasons for the order, and their rights in connection with the order, in a language and in terms which they understand;

(ii) to be informed of the right to legal counsel. Where possible, they should receive free legal assistance;

(iii) to have the decision subjected to an automatic review before a judicial or administrative body independent of the detaining authorities. This should be followed by regular periodic reviews of the necessity for the continuation of detention, which the asylum-seeker or his representative would have the right to attend;

(iv) either personally or through a representative, to challenge the necessity of the deprivation of liberty at the review hearing, and to rebut any findings made. Such a right should extend to all aspects of the case and not simply the executive discretion to detain;

(v) to contact and be contacted by the local UNHCR Office, available national refugee bodies or other agencies and an advocate. The right to communicate with these representatives in private, and the means to make such contact should be made available.

Detention should not constitute an obstacle to an asylum-seekers' possibilities to pursue their asylum application.

Guideline 6: Detention of Persons under the Age of 18 years[11]

In accordance with the general principle stated at Guideline 2 and the UNHCR Guidelines on Refugee Children, minors who are asylum-seekers should not be detained.

In this respect particular reference is made to the Convention on the Rights of the Child in particular:

• Article 2 which requires that States take all measures appropriate to ensure that children are protected from all forms of discrimination or punishment on the basis of the status, activities, expressed opinions, or beliefs of the child's parents, legal guardians or family members;

[10] Article 9(2) and (4) ICCPR; Article 37(d) CRC; Article 5(2) and (4) ECHR; Article 7(1) African Charter; Article 7(4) and (5) American Convention; EXCOM Conclusion No.44 (XXXVII); UN Body of Principles for the Protection of All Persons under any Form of Detention or Imprisonment; 1988 UN Standard Minimum Rules for the Treatment of Prisoners 1955.

[11] See also UN Rules for the Protection of Juveniles Deprived of their Liberty 1990.

• Article 3 which provides that in any action taken by States Parties concerning children, the best interests of the child shall be a primary consideration;

• Article 9 which grants children the right not to be separated from their parents against their will;

• Article 22 which requires that States Parties take appropriate measures to ensure that minors who are seeking refugee status or who are recognised refugees, whether accompanied or not, receive appropriate protection and assistance;

• Article 37 by which States Parties are required to ensure that the detention of minors be used only as a measure of last resort and for the shortest appropriate period of time.

Unaccompanied minors should not, as a general rule, be detained. Where possible they should be released into the care of family members who already have residency within the asylum country. Where this is not possible, alternative care arrangements should be made by the competent child care authorities for unaccompanied minors to receive adequate accommodation and appropriate supervision. Residential homes or foster care placements may provide the necessary facilities to ensure their proper development, (both physical and mental), is catered for while longer term solutions are being considered.

All appropriate alternatives to detention should be considered in the case of children accompanying their parents. Children and their primary caregivers should not be detained unless this is the only means of maintaining family unity.

If none of the alternatives can be applied and States do detain children, this should, in accordance with Article 37 of the Convention on the Rights of the Child, be as a measure of last resort, and for the shortest period of time.

If children who are asylum-seekers are detained at airports, immigration-holding centres or prisons, they must not be held under prison- like conditions. All efforts must be made to have them released from detention and placed in other accommodation. If this proves impossible, special arrangements must be made for living quarters which are suitable for children and their families.

During detention, children have a right to education which should optimally take place outside the detention premises in order to facilitate the continuation of their education upon release. Provision should be made for their recreation and play which is essential to a child's mental development and will alleviate stress and trauma.

Children who are detained, benefit from the same minimum procedural guarantees (listed at Guideline 5) as adults. A legal guardian or adviser should be appointed for unaccompanied minors.[12]

Guideline 7: Detention of Vulnerable Persons

Given the very negative effects of detention on the psychological well being of those detained, active consideration of possible alternatives should precede any order to detain asylum-seekers falling within the following vulnerable categories:[13]

---

12 An adult who is familiar with the child's language and culture may also alleviate the stress and trauma of being alone in unfamiliar surroundings.

13 Although it must be recognised that most individuals will be able to articulate their claims, this may not be the case in those who are victims of trauma. Care must be taken when dealing with these individuals as their particular problems may not be apparent, and it will require care and skill to assess the situation of a person with mental disability or a disoriented older refugee who is alone.

Unaccompanied elderly persons.

Torture or trauma victims.

Persons with a mental or physical disability.

In the event that individuals falling within these categories are detained, it is advisable that this should only be on the certification of a qualified medical practitioner that detention will not adversely affect their health and well being. In addition there must be regular follow up and support by a relevant skilled professional. They must also have access to services, hospitalisation, medication counselling etc. should it become necessary.

Guideline 8: Detention of Women

Women asylum-seekers and adolescent girls, especially those who arrive unaccompanied, are particularly at risk when compelled to remain in detention centres. As a general rule the detention of pregnant women in their final months and nursing mothers, both of whom may have special needs, should be avoided.

Where women asylum-seekers are detained they should be accommodated separately from male asylum-seekers, unless these are close family relatives. In order to respect cultural values and improve the physical protection of women in detention centres, the use of female staff is recommended.

Women asylum-seekers should be granted access to legal and other services without discrimination as to their gender,[14] and specific services in response to their special needs.[15] In particular they should have access to gynaecological and obstetrical services.

Guideline 9: Detention of Stateless Persons

Everyone has the right to a nationality and the right not to be arbitrarily deprived of their nationality.[16]

Stateless persons, those who are not considered to be nationals by any State under the operation of its law, are entitled to benefit from the same standards of treatment as those in detention generally.[17] Being stateless and therefore not having a country to which automatic claim might be made for the issue of a travel document should not lead to indefinite detention. Statelessness cannot be a bar to release. The detaining authorities should make every effort to resolve such cases in a timely manner, including through practical steps to identify and confirm the individual's nationality status in order to determine which State they may be returned to, or through negotiations with the country of habitual residence to arrange for their re-admission.

In the event of serious difficulties in this regard, UNHCR's technical and advisory service pursuant to its mandated responsibilities for stateless persons may, as appropriate, be sought.

---

[14] See UNHCR Guidelines on The Protection of Refugee Women.

[15] Women particularly those who have travelled alone may have been exposed to violence and exploitation prior to and during their flight and will require counselling.

[16] Art 15 UDHR. See EXCOM No.78(XLVI).

[17] Article 10(1) ICCPR; 1988 UN Body of Principles for the Protection of All Persons under any Form of Detention or Imprisonment; UN Standard Minimum Rules for the Treatment of Prisoners 1955; 1990 UN Rules for the Protection of Juveniles Deprived of their Liberty.

Guideline 10: Conditions of Detention[18]

Conditions of detention for asylum-seekers should be humane with respect shown for the inherent dignity of the person. They should be prescribed by law.

Reference is made to the applicable norms and principles of international law and standards on the treatment of such persons. Of particular relevance are the 1988 UN Body of Principles for the Protection of all Persons under any form of Detention or Imprisonment, 1955 UN Standard Minimum Rules for the Treatment of Prisoners, and the 1990 UN Rules for the Protection of Juveniles Deprived of their Liberty.

The following points in particular should be emphasised:

(i) the initial screening of all asylum seekers at the outset of detention to identify trauma or torture victims, for treatment in accordance with Guideline 7.

(ii) the segregation within facilities of men and women; children from adults(unless these are relatives);

(iii) the use of separate detention facilities to accommodate asylum-seekers. The use of prisons should be avoided. If separate detention facilities are not used, asylum-seekers should be accommodated separately from convicted criminals or prisoners on remand. There should be no co-mingling of the two groups;

(iv) the opportunity to make regular contact and receive visits from friends, relatives, religious, social and legal counsel. Facilities should be made available to enable such visits. Where possible such visits should take place in private unless there are compelling reasons to warrant the contrary;

(v) the opportunity to receive appropriate medical treatment, and psychological counselling where appropriate;

(vi) the opportunity to conduct some form of physical exercise through daily indoor and outdoor recreational activities;

(vii) the opportunity to continue further education or vocational training;

(viii) the opportunity to exercise their religion and to receive a diet in keeping with their religion;

(ix) the opportunity to have access to basic necessities i.e. beds, shower facilities, basic toiletries etc.;

(x) access to a complaints mechanism, (grievance procedures) where complaints may be submitted either directly or confidentially to the detaining authority. Procedures for lodging complaints, including time limits and appeal procedures, should be displayed and made available to detainees in different languages.

Conclusion

The increasing use of detention as a restriction on the freedom of movement of asylum seekers on the grounds of their illegal entry is a matter of major concern to UNHCR, NGOs, other

[18] Article 10(1) ICCPR; 1988 UN Body of Principles for the Protection of All Persons under any Form of Detention or Imprisonment; 1955 UN Standard Minimum Rules for the Treatment of Prisoners; 1990 UN Rules for the Protection of Juveniles Deprived of their Liberty.

agencies as well as Governments. The issue is not a straight-forward one and these guidelines have addressed the legal standards and norms applicable to the use of detention. Detention as a mechanism which seeks to address the particular concerns of States related to illegal entry requires the exercise of great caution in its use to ensure that it does not serve to undermine the fundamental principles upon which the regime of international protection is based.

Report of the Working Group on Arbitrary Detention, 1999 [excerpts]*

Adoption: 28 December 1999

[...]

ANNEX II

Deliberation No. 5

Situation regarding immigrants and asylum-seekers

By resolution 1997/50, the Working Group was requested by the Commission to devote all necessary attention to reports concerning the situation of immigrants and asylum-seekers who are allegedly being held in prolonged administrative custody without the possibility of administrative or judicial remedy.

In the light of the experience gained from its missions carried out in this framework, the Working Group took the initiative to develop criteria for determining whether or not the deprivation of liberty of asylum seekers and immigrants may be arbitrary.

After consultation, in particular with the Office of the United Nations High Commissioner for Refugees, the Working Group, in order to determine whether the above situations of administrative detentions were of an arbitrary nature, adopted the following deliberation:

Deliberation No. 5

For the purposes of the Body of Principles for the Protection of All Persons under Any Form of Detention or Imprisonment:

The term "a judicial or other authority" means a judicial or other authority which is duly empowered by law and has a status and length of mandate affording sufficient guarantees of competence, impartiality and independence.

House arrest under the conditions set forth in deliberation No.1 of the Working Group (E/CN.4/1993/24, para. 20) and confinement on board a ship, aircraft, road vehicle or train are assimilated with custody of immigrants and asylum-seekers.

The places of deprivation of liberty concerned by the present principles may be places of custody situated in border areas, on police premises, premises under the authority of a prison administration, ad hoc centres (centres de rétention), so called international or transit zones in ports or international airports, gathering centres or certain hospital premises (see E/CN.4/1998/44, paras. 28-41).

In order to determine the arbitrary character of the custody, the Working Group considers whether or not the alien is enabled to enjoy all or some of the following guarantees:

I. Guarantees concerning persons held in custody

<u>Principle 1:</u> Any asylum-seeker or immigrant, when held for questioning at the border, or inside national territory in the case of illegal entry, must be informed at least orally, and in a language which he or she understands, of the nature of and grounds for the decision refusing entry at the border, or permission for temporary residence in the territory, that is being contemplated with respect to the person concerned.

* Source: U.N.Doc. E/CN.4/2000/4.

Principle 2: Any asylum-seeker or immigrant must have the possibility, while in custody, of communicating with the outside world, including by telephone, fax or electronic mail, and of contacting a lawyer, a consular representative and relatives.

Principle 3: Any asylum-seeker or immigrant placed in custody must be brought promptly before a judicial or other authority.

Principle 4: Any asylum-seeker or immigrant, when placed in custody, must enter his or her signature in a register which is numbered and bound, or affords equivalent guarantees, indicating the person's identity, the grounds for the custody and the competent authority which decided on the measure, as well as the time and date of admission into and release from custody.

Principle 5: Any asylum-seeker or immigrant, upon admission to a centre for custody, must be informed of the internal regulations and, where appropriate, of the applicable disciplinary rules and any possibility of his or her being held incommunicado, as well as of the guarantees accompanying such a measure.

II. Guarantees concerning detention

Principle 6: The decision must be taken by a duly empowered authority with a sufficient level of responsibility and must be founded on criteria of legality established by the law.

Principle 7: A maximum period should be set by law and the custody may in no case be unlimited or of excessive length.

Principle 8: Notification of the custodial measure must be given in writing, in a language understood by the asylum-seeker or immigrant, stating the grounds for the measure; it shall set out the conditions under which the asylum-seeker or immigrant must be able to apply for a remedy to a judicial authority, which shall decide promptly on the lawfulness of the measure and, where appropriate, order the release of the person concerned.

Principle 9: Custody must be effected in a public establishment specifically intended for this purpose; when, for practical reasons, this is not the case, the asylum-seeker or immigrant must be placed in premises separate from those for persons imprisoned under criminal law.

Principle 10: The Office of the United Nations High Commissioner for Refugees (UNHCR), the International Committee of the Red Cross (ICRC) and, where appropriate, duly authorized non-governmental organizations must be allowed access to the places of custody.

Report of the Special Rapporteur on Human Rights of Migrant Workers, 2003 [excerpts]*

Adoption: 30 December 2002

[...]

II. THE HUMAN RIGHTS OF MIGRANTS DEPRIVED OF THEIR LIBERTY

12. On 1 August 2002, the Special Rapporteur sent a request for information on the issue of migrants deprived of their liberty through a questionnaire which was distributed to all permanent missions in Geneva, NGOs, United Nations special procedures mandate holders, OHCHR field presences, United Nations and other agencies and programmes, and international experts in this field.

13. The questionnaire comprised 23 questions, grouped under three main areas: legislative framework; safeguards for the protection of migrants in detention;[1] and conditions of detention. The Special Rapporteur would like to thank all Governments, organizations, experts and individuals who provided written responses to the questionnaire.[2]

14. In the following paragraphs, fundamental international human rights obligations are reviewed in the context of national legislation and practices, with a view to identifying the most frequent violations and abuses suffered by migrants. The analysis is based on the information provided through answers to the questionnaire and on practices personally observed by the Special Rapporteur.

A. Deprivation of liberty in the context of migration management

15. Deprivation of liberty of migrants must comply not only with national law, but also with international legislation.[3] It is a fundamental principle of international law that no one

* Source: U.N. Doc. E/CN.4/2003/85.

[1] For the purposes of this report, the term "detention" is used to indicate both administrative deprivation of liberty, or remand custody, and incarceration or imprisonment resulting from criminal charges or sentencing. The Special Rapporteur considers detention as confinement within a narrowly bounded or restricted location which the detainee cannot leave. Other restrictive measures such as limitations on residency do not fall within the scope of the present study.

[2] The following Governments responded to the questionnaire: Argentina, Azerbaijan, Belarus, Bulgaria, Canada, Costa Rica, Croatia, Cyprus, Czech Republic, El Salvador, Finland, Germany, Greece, Honduras, Italy, Jordan, Lebanon, Mexico, Nicaragua, Norway, Poland, Qatar, Slovenia, Russian Federation, Spain, Togo and Uruguay. Information provided by NGOs supplemented or complemented that provided by Governments. No information was received on the situation, legislation and practices of a considerable number of countries.

[3] See Views of the Human Rights Committee, A. v. Australia, communication No.560/1993 (CCPR/C/D/560/1993). The deliberation of the Working Group on Arbitrary Detention on the "Situation regarding immigrants and asylum-seekers" (E/CN.4/2000/4, annex II, Deliberation No.5) and the UNHCR Revised Guidelines on Applicable Criteria and Standards Relating to the Detention of Asylum-Seekers set the conditions under which detention of migrants can be carried out. Other international forums, such as the World Conference against Racism, Racial Discrimination, Xenophobia and Related Intolerance held in South Africa in 2001, have highlighted that detention of migrants shall respect international human rights standards (see Durban Programme of Action (A/CONF.189/12, chap. I), paragraph 36). Guarantees against arbitrary detention are also enshrined in regional human rights instruments; in particular, see article 7 of the American Convention on Human Rights, article 5 of the European Convention for the Protection of Human Rights and Fundamental Freedoms and article 6 of the African Charter on Human and Peoples' Rights.

should be subjected to arbitrary detention. International human rights norms, principles and standards define the content of that principle. Such norms, principles and standards apply to all individuals, including migrants and asylum-seekers, and to both criminal and administrative proceedings.

16. The Special Rapporteur observed that irregular migrants are particularly vulnerable to deprivation of liberty both in the context of criminal and administrative proceedings and that, especially in case of administrative detention, the above-mentioned rights and guarantees are often not respected in practice.

17. Migrants are detained in connection with criminal offences like any other citizens of a State. The Special Rapporteur, however, is concerned by the fact that under the legislation of a considerable number of countries violations of the immigration law constitute a criminal offence. Undocumented and irregular migrants therefore become particularly vulnerable to criminal detention, which is punitive in nature, for such infractions as irregularly crossing the State border, using false documents, leaving their residence without authorization, irregular stay, overstaying their or breaching conditions of stay. The Special Rapporteur notes with concern that criminalization of irregular migration is increasingly being used by Governments to discourage it.

18. The Special Rapporteur also received worrying reports that there have been cases of evidence of criminal offences, such as theft or robbery, being planted by immigration officials on irregular migrants. Such incidents are often inspired by racist attitudes and beliefs. The Special Rapporteur further observed that the tendency to arbitrary resort to criminal proceedings for administrative infractions is more frequent where corruption of immigration officials is widespread.

19. Migrants are also liable to administrative detention in connection with violations of immigration laws and regulations, including staying after the permit has expired, non-possession of identification documents, using somebody else's travel documents, not leaving the country after the prescribed period of time has expired, etc. The objective of administrative detention is to guarantee that another measure, such as deportation or expulsion, can be implemented. Under the legislation of some countries, administrative detention is also admitted on grounds of public security and public order, among others. Unless otherwise specified, this analysis focuses on the administrative detention of migrants.

Procedural guarantees in the context of administrative detention of migrants

20. According to the information provided to the Special Rapporteur, under the legislation of many countries, those detained under judicial proceedings enjoy far more guarantees than those held in administrative detention. In some countries migrants who are the subject of judicial proceedings have the right to free legal counsel and interpretation, while the costs of these services (or of one of them) must be borne by the alien in administrative proceedings. The right to judicial or administrative review of the lawfulness of detention, as well as the right to appeal against the detention/deportation decision/order or to apply for bail or other non-custodial measures, are not always guaranteed in cases of administrative detention.

21. The Special Rapporteur was informed that grounds for detention of migrants vary greatly from country to country and within the same country according to the infraction or offence of which migrants are suspected. In several countries the legislative criteria for administrative detention allow for a high degree of discretion in ordering it: foreign nationals can be detained when immigration officers have "reasonable" grounds to believe that the person is inadmissible, is a danger to the public, that the individual is unlikely to appear for an examination or a hearing,

or where the officer is not satisfied about identity of the person. This often leads to situation in which migrants themselves have to prove to the satisfaction of officials circumstances relating to their documentation, entry, or migratory status in order to avoid deprivation of liberty.

22. The high degree of discretion and the broad power to detain accorded to immigration and other law enforcement officials can give rise to abuses and to human rights violations. The failure to provide legal criteria can result in de facto discriminatory patterns of arrest and deportation of irregular migrants. The Special Rapporteur was informed that at times migration authorities stop migrants at the border and take them arbitrarily to the police station where they are asked for money or sexual favours in exchange for their release. Cases of prolonged detention because of refusal to pay were reported. Information received by the Special Rapporteur shows patterns of discrimination whereby migrants belonging to certain ethnic groups or of a specific nationality are more likely to be intercepted and detained than others. Furthermore, the Special Rapporteur personally observed that migration and other police authorities with vast power to detain are often not adequately trained. In some instances migrants have been requested to produce documents other than or in addition to those prescribed by law.

23. Article 9 of the Universal Declaration of Human Rights establishes that "no one shall be subjected to arbitrary arrest or detention". This universally recognized principle is also enshrined in article 9 of the International Covenant on Civil and Political Rights (ICCPR), which also sets that "anyone who is deprived of his liberty by arrest or detention shall be entitled to take proceedings before a court, in order that the court may decide without delay on the lawfulness of his detention and order his release if the detention is not lawful". In its General Comment No.8, the Human Rights Committee states that these provisions are applicable to all deprivations of liberty by arrest or detention, including in cases of immigration control. The Body of Principles for the Protection of All Persons under Any Form of Detention or Imprisonment (General Assembly 43/173 of 9 December 1988) reiterates that any form of detention or imprisonment shall be ordered by, or be subject to the effective control of a judicial or other authority. In addition, a person shall not be kept in detention without being given an effective opportunity to be heard promptly by a judicial or other authority and a detained person shall be entitled at any time to take proceedings before a judicial or other authority to challenge the lawfulness of his/her detention.

24. However, according to the information provided to the Special Rapporteur, national laws often do not provide for judicial review of administrative detention of migrants. In some countries, judicial review of administrative detention is automatic within a prescribed period of time, in other instances it is initiated only upon request of the migrant. Sometimes only an administrative review of the decision to detain is possible. Even when the law guarantees the right to judicial review, other circumstances may undermine it. When the migrant must take the initiative for such review, lack of awareness of the right to appeal and lack of access to free legal counsel can prevent the migrant from exercising his/her right in practice. It was reported that even when the law requires that detained migrants be brought before an administrative or other court, this is often not done within the prescribed time limit.

25. In the context of anti-terrorism measures adopted after 11 September 2001, the legislation of some countries allows for long periods of detention of non-nationals, without basic guarantees.[4] Information was received according to which migrants, including asylum-

[4] See E/CN.4/2003/85/Add.1, communications sent by the Special Rapporteur on the human rights of migrants and the Special Rapporteur on the independence of judges and lawyer to the Governments of the United Kingdom of Great Britain and Northern Ireland and of the United States.

seekers, are sometimes detained at airport transit zones,[5] under no clear authority, either with the knowledge of government officials at the airport or simply on the instructions of airline companies,[6] before being returned to their countries.[7] The difficulty or impossibility of reaching any outside assistance impedes the exercise of the right of the persons concerned to challenge the lawfulness of the detention and deportation decision and to apply for asylum, even in the presence of legitimate claims.

26. The 1963 Vienna Convention on Consular Relations (art. 36) provides that, if so requested, the competent authorities of the receiving State shall, without delay, inform the consular post of the sending State that its national has been deprived of his/her liberty. Any communication to the consular post by the person detained shall be forwarded by the competent authorities without delay.

27. It was reported that consular posts are not always informed in a timely manner of detentions, often because detainees are not aware of this right. In many instances, consulates are informed only when migrants are taken to prison after several days of detention in police stations. The Special Rapporteur visited some facilities where the absence of public telephones and the fact that the migrants had to pay for calls discouraged or prevented contacts with consular representatives.

28. According to the Body of Principles, persons under any form of detention or imprisonment shall be informed at the time of arrest of the reason for the arrest, as well as of their rights and how to avail themselves of those rights in a language they understand. Also, detained persons should have the assistance, free of charge, of an interpreter in connection with legal proceedings subsequent to arrest. Further, a detained person is entitled to have the assistance of a legal counsel, to be informed of that right and to be provided with facilities for exercising it. Detained persons also should have the right to be visited by and correspond with members of their families.

29. In practice detainees are often not informed of their right to appeal and of the status of their situation. Often they are unaware of the grounds for their detention and of its duration. It was reported that in some cases it is difficult for migrants under administrative detention to have access to their files and often migrants are only informed at a very late stage of the date of hearings. All these circumstances, coupled at times with the absence of legal assistance, seriously curtail migrants' right to defence.

30. Under the legislation of a number of countries no free legal services are available for administrative proceedings. Furthermore, often migrants are not informed, in a language they understand, of their rights to instruct and retain counsel. The Special Rapporteur received information that some migrant holding facilities do not allow visits from or confidential conversations with lawyers. Incidents in which detainees have been denied access to lawyers have also been reported to the Special Rapporteur, as well as cases of lawyers who had difficulty in locating their clients after a transfer.

31. During her visits and through answers to the questionnaire the Special Rapporteur was informed that migrants who do not speak the language of the country where they are detained have no access to translation services. Pertinent information on rights and procedures is sometimes only provided in the national language, and sometimes a few other languages.

[5] See ibid., communications sent to the Governments of Japan, South Africa and Spain.

[6] Reportedly, in some countries fines are imposed on companies that allow into the country people not in possession of valid papers.

[7] E/CN.4/2003/85/Add.1, letter dated 25 September sent by the Special Rapporteur to the Government of South Africa.

Detainees with some knowledge of the local language are sometimes requested to act as interpreters for others or translation is provided by telephone. According to the information received, in many instances interpretation is available only during judicial or administrative proceedings.

32. As for visits of families and friends, time and conditions vary from facility to facility and from country to country. The Special Rapporteur received information about migrants in administrative detention who were allowed to meet with their relatives and friends only for a very short period, separated by glass and in the presence of immigration or other officials. Incidents in which families were not informed of the whereabouts of the detainees were reported to the Special Rapporteur.

33. When administrative custody centres are not monitored and inspected by external mechanisms, and in particular when migrants are held in facilities that are not easily accessible, abuse and violence are more frequent. In the absence of a lawyer and interpreters, migrants often feel intimidated and obliged to sign papers without understanding their content. Incidents were reported in which migrants waived their right to appeal against a deportation decision without understanding that they were doing so.

34. Often a lack of resources represents an obstacle to respecting procedural safeguards. Resources might in fact not be available to allow countries of destination to provide free legal counsel and interpretation services to all migrants. Equally, countries of origin might not have consular representation owing to financial constraints. The Special Rapporteur believes that efforts should be made to find imaginative and cost-effective solutions to guarantee migrants' rights. These could include using the voluntary services of NGOs, individuals, universities, or other national, regional and international organizations; the creation of toll-free services run by volunteers to provide information and assistance to migrants; the conclusion of bilateral and multilateral agreements between countries to provide assistance to migrants in distress; and greater use of non-custodial measures.

Length of administrative detention

35. Administrative deprivation of liberty should last only for the time necessary for the deportation/expulsion to become effective. Deprivation of liberty should never be indefinite. The Human Rights Committee found that "detention should not continue beyond the period for which the State can provide appropriate justification. For example, the fact of illegal entry may indicate a need for investigation and there may be other factors particular to the individual, such as the likelihood of absconding and lack of cooperation, which may justify detention for a period. Without such factors detention may be considered arbitrary, even if entry was illegal". [8] The Working Group on Arbitrary Detention[9] further states that a maximum period should be set by law and the custody may in no case be unlimited or of excessive length.

36. Only in some countries' legislation is a specific time limit set beyond which deprivation of liberty should cease when deportation is not possible for reasons not imputable to the migrant, and even where time limits are prescribed by law, they are often disregarded.

37. According to the information received or personally witnessed by the Special Rapporteur, migrants often remain in administrative detention for long periods of time. The deportation procedure can in fact be very lengthy: consulates have to process travel documents, travel arrangements made, asylum claims and appeals against deportation reviewed.[10] The procedure

[8] CCPR/C/D/560/1993, op.cit., para. 9.4.

[9] E/CN.4/2000/4, op.cit., supra at note 3.

[10] See E/CN.4/2003/85/Add.1, communication sent on 7 November 2002 by the Special Rapporteur to the Government of Australia.

can be particularly time consuming in circumstances such as the absence of diplomatic representation of the country of citizenship of the alien; the lack of means of the country of destination to finance the deportation; the refusal of the State of origin or the receiving country to accept the migrant. The case of stateless detainees, i.e. those who crossed the border irregularly and whose Governments refuse to recognize them, is another circumstance that may lead to indefinite detention. At times migrants remain in detention because, owing to the situation in their countries of origin, they cannot be deported.[11] The Special Rapporteur is particularly concerned that recently enacted anti-terrorism legislation, allowing for the detention of migrants on the basis of vague, unspecified allegations of threats to national security, can lead to indefinite detention when migrants cannot be immediately deported because that would imply a threat to their security and human rights.[12]

38. According to the information received by the Special Rapporteur, only the legislation of a limited number of countries provides for an automatic review of detention at set intervals to determine whether it should continue.[13] In the majority of cases the review is not undertaken automatically, but mechanisms exist that allow the migrant to request it. However, access to such mechanisms can be seriously undermined by the lack of procedural safeguards.

Application of non-custodial measures

39. The Working Group on Arbitrary Detention recommended that "alternative and non custodial measures, such as reporting requirements, should always be considered before resorting to detention".[14] Similarly, in its resolution 2000/21, the Sub-Commission on the Promotion and Protection of Human Rights encouraged "States to adopt alternatives to detention such as those enumerated in the Guidelines on the Applicable Criteria and Standards relating to the Detention of Asylum Seekers" (para. 6). The legislation of several countries provides for alternatives to administrative detention, such as release on bail, release on parole, home detention, semi-liberty, payment of a certain sum as guarantee, police supervision, ban on leaving the country, obligation to reside at a given address with periodic reporting to the authorities, withdrawal of passport.

40. Reportedly, there is an element of discretion in many countries as to when such measures can be granted, as often the law itself does not prescribe them in the presence of specific criteria. Often, in the absence of statistics it is not possible to assess how often alternative measures are granted. However, it was reported that even when the laws provides expressly for non-custodial measures, they are hardly accessible. Bail, when granted, is usually set at a sum not affordable by migrants. The request for sureties is a further obstacle given the absence of relatives or friends who can stand surety for migrants. Similarly, home detention or social work is hard to obtain due to the fact that migrants often do not have stable work and lodgings.

Detention of victims of trafficking and smuggling

41. Victims of trafficking and smuggling commit infractions or offences, such as irregular entry, use of false documents and other violations of immigration laws and regulations, which

[11] See ibid., letter dated 4 September 2002 sent by the Special Rapporteur, together with the Special Rapporteur on torture to the Government of Greece.
[12] See also the report of the Special Rapporteur on torture to the General Assembly (A/57/173).
[13] Among the factors considered in undertaking such reviews are the reasons for detention, elements to determine the length of time that detention is likely to continue, unexplained delays or lack of diligence on the part of the authority in charge or by the person concerned, the existence of alternatives to detention.
[14] E/CN.4/1999/63/Add.3.

make them liable to detention.[15] The law of some countries punishes as criminal offences or administrative infractions irregular entry, entry without valid documents or engaging in prostitution, including forced prostitution. Victims of trafficking are thus often detained and deported without regard for their victimization and without consideration for the risks they may be exposed to if returned to their country of origin.

42. The victims' needs for specific medical, psychological or legal assistance are often not taken into account.[16] The Special Rapporteur received information and testimonies of women and children who had been held in slavery-like conditions and who had suffered physical and sexual abuse and who were arrested and detained as irregular migrants after managing to escape from their exploiters, suffering further traumas. Furthermore, the Special Rapporteur received information according to which, for fear of being deported or criminalized, often victims of trafficking do not denounce their traffickers and do not seek protection from local authorities against their abusers.

Detention of women, children and other vulnerable groups

43. The Special Rapporteur observed that very often national legislation does not contain special provision regarding administrative detention of vulnerable groups, such as children, pregnant women, the elderly and the physically and mentally ill. Administrative detention should never be punitive in nature and special arrangements should be sought to protect vulnerable groups. In these cases the harm inflicted seems to the Special Rapporteur to be wholly disproportionate to the policy aim of immigration control.

44. Undocumented migrants often do not denounce violations and abuses for fear of being detained and deported. In the experience of the Special Rapporteur, this is particularly the case for migrants working in the informal and private sectors, such as women domestic workers, who are particularly vulnerable to exploitation and abuse.

45. Article 37 of the Convention on the Rights of the Child requires States parties to ensure that minors are detained as a measure of last resort and for the shortest possible period of time. In accordance with article 3 of the Convention, the best interests of the child shall be the primary consideration in any action taken by States parties.

46. The detention of migrant children for administrative infractions is forbidden under the legislation of some countries, which provides for unaccompanied irregular migrant children to be entrusted to foster families or institutions for minors. However, in other countries, immigration laws and regulations are silent with respect to the detention of minors, including unaccompanied children. In these cases decisions are taken on individual cases, often with

---

[15] See provision against criminalization in the Protocol to Prevent, Suppress and Punish Trafficking in Persons, Especially Women and Children, and the Protocol against the Smuggling of Migrants by Land, Sea and Air, Supplementing the United Nations Convention against Transnational Organized Crime.

[16] The legislation of some countries provides for some forms of assistance and protection of victims of trafficking. In the Netherlands, victims of trafficking are temporarily regularized and given protection and support so that they may decide to cooperate with law enforcement authorities. In Belgium the Act on Human Trafficking provides that victims of trafficking should be granted residence permits and social assistance if they agree to testify against the perpetrators. In the United States, the Act on the Protection of Victims of Trafficking provides that victims of trafficking should not be detained unless individual circumstances or the law require otherwise. In any case, if in detention, they should be placed in facilities appropriate to their victim's status. In January 2002, the "T" visa programme for victims of trafficking was created. It is a procedure for attaining permanent residency status for certain trafficking victims who cooperate with law enforcement agencies to prosecute those responsible for their enslavement. After three years under this status they may apply for permanent residency status.

reference to other national provisions and regional and international obligations. Even when administrative detention of migrant children is prohibited, other legislative provisions of the same country may allow for minors to be detained for criminal offences where breaches of immigration law are considered as such.

47. According to the Special Rapporteur's information and personal observations, minors, including unaccompanied children, are at times detained for long or undetermined periods and deported under no clear authority and on discretional grounds, with no possibility of challenging the legality of the measure before a court or other competent, independent and impartial authority. The legislation or regulations of several countries provide for "family detention", whereby children under a certain age are detained with their parents, either in special facilities or in separate rooms within centres for migrants or penitentiaries. However, accompanied and unaccompanied children are often detained in punitive and inadequate conditions, deprived of the care, protection and rights to which they are entitled under the Convention on the Rights of the Child and other international human rights norms, including the right to education, physical and mental health, privacy, information, and rest and leisure, among others. During her visits the Special Rapporteur personally met women with newborn babies who did not even have blankets to protect them from the cold.

48. When the age of migrants is disputed, they are often reportedly treated like adults until credible documentary or medical evidence is produced which demonstrates that they are minors. Cases of migrant child victims of trafficking or smuggling who were detained and subsequently deported without consideration for their status as victims were brought to the attention of the Special Rapporteur, who also personally interviewed some of them.

49. The Special Rapporteur notices with concern that while the legislation of the majority of countries provides that minors subjected to criminal proceedings should be detained only as a measure of last resort and protected by a set of judicial safeguards and guarantees to ensure that the children's rights are protected, at the same time it allows for administrative detention of foreign children without any such guarantees.

50. Often elderly people, persons with disabilities, pregnant women and ill people, including the mentally ill, are detained without any particular regard for their conditions and specific needs. It was reported that detention has a heavy impact on pregnant women and their children, as well as the elderly, disabled and mentally ill. Pregnant women, for example, need to have access to proper nutrition for the well-being of the baby and to medical and support service that are not available in detention facilities.

51. Furthermore, detention produces anxiety, depression and isolation, especially in women. Detained migrants have often suffered previous traumas and the absence of psychological support, coupled with the conditions of detention, the lack of safeguards and uncertainty about the future, can have serious consequences for their mental and physical health. Several instances of migrants committing or attempting to commit suicide in detention were reported to the Special Rapporteur. It was also reported that migrants who attempt suicide are not always provided with the necessary medical and psychological assistance. It has been reported that migrants who had attempted suicide were moved to special rooms where they remained isolated and under constant surveillance, instead of being provided with necessary care and support.

B. Conditions of detention

52. Detention facilities for migrants vary from country to country and according to the type of regime to which migrants are subjected.

53. Migrants sentenced to imprisonment for immigration offences are detained with common criminals and subjected to the same punitive regime; they are not always separated from the rest of the prison population and have difficulties in understanding and communicating. The fact that their families are often far away and are difficult to keep in touch with further increases their sense of isolation. There are often no arrangements to provide culturally appropriate foods and to allow them to practise their faiths. Racist attacks against migrants detained with common prisoners were also reported. Prison personnel in most of the cases do not receive specific training on how to deal with foreign detainees.

54. Administrative detention should never be of a punitive nature. Furthermore, as enshrined in article 10 of ICCPR, all persons deprived of their liberty shall be treated with humanity and with respect for the inherent dignity of the human person. This implies not only the right not to be subjected to torture or to cruel, inhuman or degrading treatment or punishment,[17] but also that migrants deprived of their liberty should be subjected to conditions of detention that take into account their status and needs. In this respect, the Special Rapporteur would like to refer to General Comment No.15 of the Human Rights Committee, which states: "if lawfully deprived of their liberty, [aliens] shall be treated with humanity and with respect for the inherent dignity of their person". Article 37 of the Convention on the Rights of the Child also establishes that every child deprived of liberty shall be treated with humanity and respect for the inherent dignity of the human person, and in a manner which takes into account the needs of persons of his or her age. In particular, every child deprived of liberty shall be separated from adults unless it is considered in the child's best interest not to do so and shall have the right to maintain contact with his or her family through correspondence and visits, save in exceptional circumstances.

55. The Body of Principles for the Protection of All Persons under Any Form of Detention or Imprisonment, the Standard Minimum Rules for the Treatment of Prisoners, the United Nations Rules for the Protection of Juveniles Deprived of their Liberty and the UNHCR Revised Guidelines on Applicable Criteria and Standards Relating to the Detention of Asylum Seekers also provide an extensive list of guarantees for the protection of the human dignity of persons, including migrants, deprived of their liberty. Despite their non-binding nature, they reflect internationally recognized principles.

56. According to the information received by the Special Rapporteur, conditions of administrative detention are well below international standards.[18] In many instances migrants under administrative detention are detained in common prisons, either because no other specific facility exists, or because those that exist are full. The Special Rapporteur received reports according to which migrants awaiting deportation were kept in penitentiaries with common criminals and subjected to the same regime, with severe restrictions on their freedom of movement, rights to communicate with families and receive visits, and limited access to outdoor recreational activities. Reports of migrants held in solitary confinement and heavily shackled and tightly handcuffed during visits or court appearances were brought to the attention of the Special Rapporteur.

57. In some countries special facilities for administrative detention of migrants have been built. Elsewhere, places such as schools, warehouses, airport terminals, sports stadiums and

[17] The freedom from torture or cruel, inhuman or degrading treatment or punishment is an underogable right guaranteed by both customary and conventional law. See, in particular, article 5 of the Universal Declaration of Human Rights, article 7 of the International Covenant on Civil and Political Rights and the Convention against Torture and Other Cruel, Inhuman or Degrading Treatment or Punishment.

[18] See E/CN.4/2003/Add.1, letter sent on 4 September 2002 by the Special Rapporteur on the human rights of migrants to the Government of Spain.

similar facilities have been converted into centres for the administrative custody of migrants. Both types of facility are usually thought of as being for the short term, however, it often happens that migrants remain detained in these centres for months, and in some cases years. In most cases there is no provision for either education for children or for adequate recreational activities. Facilities converted into detention centres often lack basic infrastructures, such as ventilation systems, outdoor spaces, or rooms allowing for private conversations with lawyers or family members.

58. Special centres for the detention of migrants are often overcrowded,[19] leading to a serious deterioration in living conditions, including lack of bedding, poor hygienic conditions, inadequate access to medical treatment and other services, the impossibility of separating men from women and adults from minors and of keeping families together, and lack of privacy. For security reasons, freedom of movement is limited within the facility and migrants remain locked up for most of the day.

59. The Special Rapporteur observed during her visits that many of the facilities where migrants are held do not have public telephones. Sometimes detention facilities are not regularly cleaned and basic products for personal use, such as soap, are not available and have to be provided by families and friends or by NGOs and humanitarian organizations. The Special Rapporteur personally interviewed detained women who were obliged to cook for male detainees and to sell food in order to be able to purchase basic items for personal use.

60. A very few centres provide a medical check-up upon arrival. The Special Rapporteur met with migrants who had open wounds, some of them suffered during their apprehension or resulting from excessive use of force by immigration officials, and migrants with serious skin diseases, other illnesses and psychological traumas who had no access to medical care.

61. Some of the recently built facilities for migrants provide for a general doctor to visit detainees every day. In many instances, however, only urgent medical care is provided. Also, it was reported that in some countries all medical expenses apart from general check-ups or emergency interventions must be borne by the detainees. Often, no translation or interpretation services are available, making it difficult for migrants to request medical attention and to understand medical prescriptions and diagnoses. Other inmates are sometimes used as interpreters. This practice is a source of concern as it breaches confidentiality, and when consent is sought and obtained, there are questions as to whether that consent is sufficiently informed. Furthermore, in these circumstances a detainee may be prevented from disclosing vital information about trauma suffered. Access to medical assistance is curtailed when migrants are detained in police stations and holding facilities that are not easily accessible. The Special Rapporteur received information about incidents of denial of medical care to migrants in administrative custody.

62. Mechanisms of external oversight of migrant holding facilities are not always in place. Some countries allow regular visits by external actors, such as the Red Cross, representatives of human rights institutions, NGOs, humanitarian organizations, the Office of the United Nations High Commissioner for Refugees (UNHCR), the International Organization for Migration (IOM), or regional mechanisms such as the European Committee for the Prevention of Torture. However, the Special Rapporteur received information according to which representatives of NGOs were denied access to detained migrants. In some countries inspections are only carried out by representatives of hierarchically superior bodies of the ministry or department to which

[19] See ibid., letter dated 11 November 2002, sent by the Special Rapporteur on the human rights of migrants together with the Special Rapporteur on torture to the Government of Thailand.

the police or the immigration service running the centre belongs. This raises concerns as to the objectiveness and impartiality of the supervision.

63. The regulations of some migrants holding facilities provide for internal complaint or grievance mechanisms. It was reported that internal complaint mechanisms are not always easily accessible, due to linguistic barriers, and scarcely used due to the fear of being labelled troublemakers or of retaliation, given the lack of confidentiality of such procedures. Reportedly, often the internal complaint procedure is not transparent and answers are not provided in a timely manner. The decision of internal review mechanism is usually final and such mechanisms frequently allow only for internal disciplinary measures, while a separate procedure must be initiated to start criminal proceedings. As repeatedly stated, such procedures are very difficult to access, especially if there are no external mechanisms of oversight and support that can provide assistance.

64. Holding centres for migrants under administrative detention are often run by immigration or other police. Immigration authorities in some countries have the power to detain migrants in police stations while their identity or migratory status is verified. In some countries migrant holding centres are staffed with or run by private personnel who often do not receive adequate training and are not prepared to discharge their functions in a way that is respectful of the human rights of migrants. Incidents of abuse and discrimination, and even of ill-treatment and torture of migrants in detention facilities at the hands of prison guards, police and immigration officers and private staff were brought to the attention of the Special Rapporteur.[20]

[...]

[20] See E/CN.4/2003/85/Add.1, communication sent by the Special Rapporteur, together with the Special Rapporteur on torture, to the Government of Japan.

Report of the Working Group on Arbitrary Detention, 2004 [excerpts]*

Adoption: 1 December 2004

[...]

III. DEVELOPMENTS CONCERNING DEPRIVATION OF LIBERTY AS A MEASURE IN COUNTERING TERRORISM

59. On 21 April 2004, the Commission on Human Rights adopted resolution 2004/87 entitled "Protection of human rights and fundamental freedoms while countering terrorism", in which it requested "all relevant special procedures and mechanisms of the Commission, as well as the United Nations human rights treaty bodies, to consider, within their mandates, the protection of human rights and fundamental freedoms in the context of measures to combat terrorism and to coordinate their efforts where appropriate in order to promote a consistent approach on this subject".

60. The Working Group recalls that, in implementing Commission resolution 2003/68 concerning the same matter, it dedicated a substantial part of its 2004 annual report to the Commission to the question of the misuse of detention in the context of the fight against terrorism. Taking note of resolution 2004/87, the Working Group informs the Commission that, during the period covered by the present report, it was seized by individual communications and issued opinions in six cases concerning 18 persons in five countries. The Working Group considered that detention was arbitrary in five cases concerning 12 persons, the other persons having been released at the time of adoption of the Working Group's opinion.

61. The Working Group expresses its concern about the frequent use of various forms of administrative detention, entailing restrictions on fundamental rights. It notes a further expansion of States' recourse to emergency legislation diluting the right of habeas corpus or amparo and limiting the fundamental rights of persons detained in the context of the fight against terrorism. In this respect, several States enacted new anti-terror or internal security legislation, or toughened existing ones, allowing persons to be detained for an unlimited time or for very long periods, without charges being raised, without the detainees being brought before a judge, and without a remedy to challenge the legality of the detention. This kind of administrative detention, which often is also secret, aims at circumventing the legal time limits governing police custody and pre-trial detention and at depriving the persons concerned of the judicial guarantees recognized to all persons suspected or accused of having committed an offence.

62. In other countries, legislation newly enacted contains definitions of terrorism that are so wide or vague as to result in a substantial risk that they may be used to suppress legitimate political opposition and other forms of dissent. The risks of abuse posed by such vague definitions of terrorism are compounded where the offence is punishable with the death penalty or life imprisonment.

63. The Working Group is also aware of several instances in which Governments, purportedly in order to more effectively combat terrorism, made use of existing legislation allowing deprivation of liberty in ways that raise serious concerns of arbitrariness. The Working Group received numerous reports according to which detention on charges of terrorism, with the ensuing limitations on the right of habeas corpus, is used to detain political opponents, religious dissenters, and other persons exercising their freedoms of opinion, expression, conscience and

* Source: U.N. Doc. E/CN.4/2005/6.

religion. According to information received, anti-terror legislation, entailing longer terms of pre-trial detention and facilitated recourse by the prosecution to anonymous witnesses, is used to prosecute and try indigenous leaders in cases concerning conflicts with the Government over land use. In another country, persons suspected of involvement in terrorist activities are reportedly secretly detained by the security forces as "material witnesses" to a crime in order to circumvent the requirement of showing a reasonable suspicion for arrest and detention of a crime suspect. Allegations were also received that administrative detention is being used in certain cases to obtain information from witnesses in pending cases or from persons who may be charged at a later stage.

64. Finally, the Working Group recalls several decisions by courts of appeal in actions challenging detention ordered under provisions of anti-terror legislation. The Working Group welcomes several of these decisions. The supreme court of one State found that the remedy of habeas corpus had extraterritorial effect, whether for citizens or not.[1] In another encouraging development in the same State, a court ruled that it is for the judiciary and not for the executive power to establish whether the Third Geneva Convention applies to persons deprived of their liberty during the hostilities. The same court stated that the exclusion of the defendant from certain hearings and from access to evidence used against him was unlawful.[2] The appeals court of a second State quashed a judgement convicting a defendant on terrorism charges on the grounds that the trial court had not taken into sufficient account that the Government had denied the accused access to evidence potentially in his favour on grounds of national security.[3] The constitutional court of a third State held that, contrary to the claims of its Government, an anti-terror law widening the definition of punishable conduct and introducing the death sentence could not be applied retroactively.[4] The Working Group is, however, deeply concerned about other decisions. In this respect, it notes the decision of a court of appeal, which not only upheld the use of secret evidence to justify the indefinite detention without charges of foreign nationals, but also stated that evidence extracted under torture of a third party in another country can be adduced and relied upon in the proceedings concerning confirmation of this form of detention.[5]

65. The Working Group has also been informed that new immigration laws jeopardizing the rights of immigrants to be free from arbitrary detention, to claim asylum, to receive a full and fair deportation hearing, and to be protected from deportation to countries where they are at risk of torture, were enacted in several countries. The Working Group is gravely concerned by this trend towards administrative detention of aliens, which is gaining strength amidst general agreement, and regrets the abusive tendency to equate terrorism and aliens, including refugees and asylum-seekers, aimed at exploiting the fears created by the terrorist threat.

[...]

[1] Supreme Court of the United States of America, Rasul & Others v. Bush, decision of 28 June 2004.

[2] United States District Court for the District of Columbia, Hamdan v. Rumsfeld, decision of 8 November 2004.

[3] Germany, Bundesgerichtshof decision of 4 March 2004 in the case of Mounir El Motassadeq.

[4] Indonesia, Constitutional Court decision of 24 July 2004 on the constitutionality of Law No.16/2003.

[5] United Kingdom, Court of Appeal, A. and others v. Secretary of State for the Home Department, decision of 11 August 2004.

Principles on the Effective Investigation and Documentation of Torture and Other Cruel, Inhuman or Degrading Treatment or Punishment, 2000 (See section 1.2)

8. DIPLOMATIC AND CONSULAR RELATIONS

Vienna Convention on Diplomatic Relations, 1961 [excerpts]*

Adoption: 18 April 1961
Entry into force: 24 April 1964
Parties: 185 (Status as of 1 April 2007)

AFGHANISTAN 6 Oct 1965 a, ALBANIA 8 Feb 1988, ALGERIA 14 Apr 1964 a, ANDORRA 3 Jul 1996 a, ANGOLA 9 Aug 1990 a, ARGENTINA 10 Oct 1963, ARMENIA 23 Jun 1993 a, AUSTRALIA 26 Jan 1968, AUSTRIA 28 Apr 1966, AZERBAIJAN 13 Aug 1992 a, BAHAMAS 17 Mar 1977 d, BAHRAIN 2 Nov 1971 a, BANGLADESH 13 Jan 1978 d, BARBADOS 6 May 1968 d, BELARUS 14 May 1964, BELGIUM 2 May 1968, BELIZE 30 Nov 2000 a, BENIN 27 Mar 1967 a, BHUTAN 7 Dec 1972 a, BOLIVIA 28 Dec 1977 a, BOSNIA AND HERZEGOVINA 1 Sep 1993 d, BOTSWANA 11 Apr 1969 a, BRAZIL 25 Mar 1965, BULGARIA 17 Jan 1968, BURKINA FASO 4 May 1987 a, BURUNDI 1 May 1968 a, CAMBODIA 31 Aug 1965 a, CAMEROON 4 Mar 1977 a, CANADA 26 May 1966, CAPE VERDE 30 Jul 1979 a, CENTRAL AFRICAN REPUBLIC 19 Mar 1973, CHAD 3 Nov 1977 a, CHILE 9 Jan 1968, CHINA 25 Nov 1975 a, COLOMBIA 5 Apr 1973, COMOROS 27 Sep 2004 a, CONGO 11 Mar 1963 a, COSTA RICA 9 Nov 1964, CÔTE D'IVOIRE 1 Oct 1962 a, CROATIA 12 Oct 1992 d, CUBA 26 Sep 1963, CYPRUS 10 Sep 1968 a, CZECH REPUBLIC 22 Feb 1993 d, DEMOCRATIC PEOPLE'S REPUBLIC OF KOREA 29 Oct 1980 a, DEMOCRATIC REPUBLIC OF THE CONGO 19 Jul 1965, DENMARK 2 Oct 1968, DJIBOUTI 2 Nov 1978 a, DOMINICA 24 Nov 1987 d, DOMINICAN REPUBLIC 14 Jan 1964, ECUADOR 21 Sep 1964, EGYPT 9 Jun 1964 a, EL SALVADOR 9 Dec 1965 a, EQUATORIAL GUINEA 30 Aug 1976 a, ERITREA 14 Jan 1997 a, ESTONIA 21 Oct 1991 a, ETHIOPIA 22 Mar 1979 a, FIJI 21 Jun 1971 d, FINLAND 9 Dec 1969, FRANCE 31 Dec 1970, GABON 2 Apr 1964 a, GEORGIA 12 Jul 1993 a, GERMANY 11 Nov 1964, GHANA 28 Jun 1962, GREECE 16 Jul 1970, GRENADA 2 Sep 1992 a, GUATEMALA 1 Oct 1963, GUINEA 10 Jan 1968 a, GUINEA-BISSAU 11 Aug 1993 a, GUYUNA 28 Dec 1972 a, HAITI 2 Feb 1978 a, HOLY SEE 17 Apr 1964, HONDURAS 13 Feb 1968 a, HUNGARY 24 Sep 1965, ICELAND 18 May 1971 a, INDIA 15 Oct 1965 a, INDONESIA 4 Jun 1982 a, IRAN (ISLAMIC REPUBLIC OF) 3 Feb 1965, IRAQ 15 Oct 1963, IRELAND 10 May 1967, ISRAEL 11 Aug 1970, ITALY 25 Jun 1969, JAMAICA 5 Jun 1963 a, JAPAN 8 Jun 1964, JORDAN 29 Jul 1971 a, KAZAKHSTAN 5 Jan 1994 a, KENYA 1 Jul 1965 a, KIRIBATI 2 Apr 1982 d, KUWAIT 23 Jul 1969 a, KYRGYZSTAN 7 Oct 1994 a, LAO PEOPLE'S DEMOCRATIC REPUBLIC 3 Dec 1962 a, LATVIA 13 Feb 1992 a, LEBANON 16 Mar 1971, LESOTHO 26 Nov 1969 a, LIBERIA 15 May 1962, LIBYAN ARAB JAMAHIRIYAH 7 Jun 1977 a, LIECHTENSTEIN 8 May 1964, LITHUANIA 15 Jan 1992 a, LUXEMBOURG 17 Aug 1966, MADAGASCAR 31 Jul 1963 a, MALAWI 19 May 1965 a, MALAYSIA 9 Nov 1965 a, MALI 28 Mar 1968 a, MALTA 7 Mar 1967 d, MARSHALL ISLANDS 9 Aug 1991 a, MAURITANIA 16 Jul 1962 a, MAURITIUS 18 Jul 1969 d, MEXICO 16 Jun 1965, MICRONESIA (FEDERATED STATES OF) 29 Apr 1991 a, MONACO 4 Oct 2005 a, MONGOLIA 5 Jan 1967 a, MONTENEGRO 23 Oct 2006 d, MOZAMBIQUE 18 Nov 1981 a, MYANMAR 7 Mar 1980 a, NAMIBIA 14 Sep 1992 a, NAURU 5 May 1978 d, NEPAL 28 Sep 1965 a, NETHERLANDS 7 Sep 1984 a, NEW ZEALAND 23 Sep 1970, NICARAGUA 31 Oct 1975 a, NIGER 5 Dec 1962 a, NIGERIA 19 Jun 1967, NORWAY 24 Oct 1967, OMAN 31 May 1974 a, PAKISTAN 29 Mar 1962, PANAMA 4 Dec 1963, PAPUA NEW GUINEA 4 Dec 1975 d, PARAGUAY 23 Dec 1969 a, PERU 18 Dec 1968 a, PHILIPPINES 15 Nov

* Source: 500 U.N.T.S. 96.

1965, POLAND 19 Apr 1965, PORTUGAL 11 Sep 1968 a, QATAR 6 Jun 1986 a, REPUBLIC OF KOREA 28 Dec 1970, REPUBLIC OF MOLDOVA 26 Jan 1993 a, ROMANIA 15 Nov 1968, RUSSIAN FEDERATION 25 Mar 1964, RWANDA 15 Apr 1964 a, SAINT LUCIA 27 Aug 1986 d, SAINT VINCENT AND THE GRENADINES 27 Apr 1999 d, SAMOA 26 Oct 1987 a, SAN MARINO 8 Sep 1965, SAO TOME AND PRINCIPE 3 May 1983 a, SAUDI ARABIA 10 Feb 1981 a, SENEGAL 12 Oct 1972, SERBIA (REPUBLIC OF) 12 Mar 2001 d, SEYCHELLES 29 May 1979, SIERRA LEONE 13 Aug 1962 a, SINGAPORE 1 Apr 2005 a, SLOVAKIA 28 May 1993 d, SLOVENIA 6 Jul 1992 d, SOMALIA 29 Mar 1968 a, SOUTH AFRICA 21 Aug 1989, SPAIN 21 Nov 1967 a, SRI LANKA 2 Jun 1978, SUDAN 13 Apr 1981 a, SURINAME 28 Oct 1992 a, SWAZILAND 25 Apr 1969 a, SWEDEN 21 Mar 1967, SWITZERLAND 30 Oct 1963, SYRIAN ARAB REPUBLIC 4 Aug 1978 a, TAJIKISTAN 6 May 1996 a, THAILAND 23 Jan 1985, THE FORMER REPUBLIC OF MACEDONIA 18 Aug 1993 d, TIMOR-LESTE 30 Jan 2004 a, TOGO 27 Nov 1970 a, TONGA 31 Jan 1973 d, TRINIDAD AND TOBAGO 19 Oct 1965 a, TUNISIA 24 Jan 1968 a, TURKEY 6 Mar 1985 a, TURKMENISTAN 25 Sep 1996 a, TUVALU 15 Sep 1982 d, UGANDA 15 Apr 1965 a, UKRAINE 12 Jun 1964, UNITED ARAB EMIRATES 24 Feb 1977 a, UNITED KINGDOM OF GREAT BRITAIN AND NORTHERN IRELAND 1 Sep 1964, UNITED REPUBLIC OF TANZANIA 5 Nov 1962, UNITED STATES OF AMERICA 13 Nov 1972, URUGUAY 10 Mar 1970, UZBEKISTAN 2 Mar 1992 a, VENEZUELA (BOLIVERIAN REPUBLIC OF) 16 Mar 1965.

[...]

Article 3

1. The functions of a diplomatic mission consist inter alia in:

(a) representing the sending State in the receiving State;

(b) protecting in the receiving State the interests of the sending State and of its nationals, within the limits permitted by international law;

(c) negotiating with the Government of the receiving State;

(d) ascertaining by all lawful means conditions and developments in the receiving State, and reporting thereon to the Government of the sending State;

(e) promoting friendly relations between the sending State and the receiving State, and developing their economic, cultural and scientific relations.

2. Nothing in the present Convention shall be construed as preventing the performance of consular functions by a diplomatic mission.

[...]

Article 45

If diplomatic relations are broken off between two States, or if a mission is permanently or temporarily recalled:

(a) the receiving State must, even in case of armed conflict, respect and protect the premises of the mission, together with its property and archives;

(b) the sending State may entrust the custody of the premises of the mission, together with its property and archives, to a third State acceptable to the receiving State;

(c) the sending State may entrust the protection of its interests and those of its nationals to a third State acceptable to the receiving State.

Article 46

A sending State may with the prior consent of a receiving State, and at the request of a third State not represented in the receiving State, undertake the temporary protection of the interests of the third State and of its nationals.

[...]

Vienna Convention on Consular Relations, 1963 [excerpts]*

Adoption: 24 April 1963
Entry into force: 19 March 1967
Parties: 171 (Status as of 1 April 2007)

ALBANIA 4 Oct 1991 a, ALGERIA 14 Apr 1964 a, ANDORRA 3 Jul 1996 a, ANGOLA 21 Nov 1990 a, ANTIGUA AND BARBUDA 25 Oct 1988 d (*44.3), ARGENTINA 7 Mar 1967, ARMENIA 23 Jun 1993 a, AUSTRALIA 12 Feb 1973, AUSTRIA 12 Jun 1969, AZERBAIJAN 13 Aug 1992 a, BAHAMAS 17 Mar 1977 d, BAHRAIN 17 Sep 1992 a, BANGLADESH 13 Jan 1978 d, BARBADOS 11 May 1992 a, BELARUS 21 Mar 1989 a, BELGIUM 9 Sep 1970, BELIZE 30 Nov 2000 a (*44.3), BENIN 27 Apr 1979, BHUTAN 28 Jul 1981 a, BOLIVIA 22 Sep 1970, BOSNIA AND HERZEGOVINA 1 Sep 1993 d, BRAZIL 11 May 1967, BULGARIA 11 Jul 1989 a (*31.2), BURKINA FASO 11 Aug 1964 a, CAMBODIA 10 Mar 2006 a, CAMEROON 22 May 1967, CANADA 18 Jul 1974 a, CAPE VERDE 30 Jul 1979 a, CENTRAL AFRICAN REPUBLIC signed 24 Apr 1963, CHILE 9 Jan 1968, CHINA 2 Jul 1979 a, COLOMBIA 6 Sep 1972, CONGO signed 24 Apr 1963, COSTA RICA 29 Dec 1966, CÖTE D'IVOIRE signed 24 Apr 1963, CROATIA 12 Oct 1992 d, CUBA 15 Oct 1965 (*74, 76), CYPRUS 14 Apr 1976 a, CZECH REPUBLIC 22 Feb 1993 d, DEMOCRATIC PEOPLE'S REPUBLIC OF KOREA 8 Aug 1984 a, DEMOCRATIC REPUBLIC OF THE CONGO 15 Jul 1976, DENMARK 15 Nov 1972 (*5, 22, 68), DJIBOUTI 2 Nov 1978 a, DOMINICA 24 Nov 1987 d, DOMINICAN REPUBLIC 4 Mar 1964, ECUADOR 11 Mar 1965, EGYPT 21 Jun 1965 a (*46, 49, 62, 65), EL SALVADOR 19 Jan 1973 a, EQUATORIAL GUINEA 30 Aug 1976 a, ERITREA 14 Jan 1997 a, ESTONIA 21 Oct 1991 a, FIJI 28 Apr 1972 a (*44.3), FINLAND 2 Jul 1980 (*22, 35, 49, 58), FRANCE 31 Dec 1970, GABON 23 Feb 1965, GEORGIA 12 Jul 1993 a, GERMANY 7 Sep 1971 (*general), GHANA 4 Oct 1963, GREECE 14 Oct 1975 a, GRENADA 2 Sep 1992 a, GUATEMALA 9 Feb 1973 a, GUINEA 30 Jun 1988 a, GUYUNA 13 Sep 1973 a, HAITI 2 Feb 1978 a, HOLY SEE 8 Oct 1970, HONDURAS 13 Feb 1968 a, HUNGARY 19 Jun 1987 a, ICELAND 1 Jun 1978 a (*22), INDIA 28 Nov 1977 a, INDONESIA 4 Jun 1982 a, IRAN (ISLAMIC REPUBLIC OF) 5 Jun 1975, IRAQ 14 Jan 1970 a, IRELAND 10 May 1967, ISRAEL signed 25 Feb 1964, ITALY 25 Jun 1969 (*36), JAMAICA 9 Feb 1976 a, JAPAN 3 Oct 1983 a, JORDAN 7 Mar 1973 a, KAZAKHSTAN 5 Jan 1994 a, KENYA 1 Jul 1965 a, KIRIBATI 2 Apr 1982 d, KUWAIT 31 Jul 1975, KYRGYZSTAN 7 Oct 1994 a, LAO PEOPLE'S DEMOCRATIC REPUBLIC 9 Aug 1973 a, LATVIA 13 Feb 1992 a, LEBANON 20 Mar 1975, LESOTHO 26 Jul 1972 a (*44.3), LIBERIA 28 Aug 1984, LIBYAN ARAB JAMAHIRIYAH 4 Sep 1998 a, LIECHTENSTEIN 18 May 1966, LITHUANIA 15 Jan 1992 a, LUXEMBOURG 8 Mar 1972, MADAGASCAR 17 Feb 1967 a, MALAWI 29 Apr 1980 a, MALAYSIA 1 Oct 1991 a, MALDIVES 21 Jan 1991 a, MALI 28 Mar 1968 a, MALTA 10 Dec 1997 a (*5, 44.3), MARSHALL ISLANDS 9 Aug 1991 a, MAURITANIA 21 Jul 2000 a, MAURITIUS 13 May 1970 a, MEXICO 16 Jan 1965 (*31), MICRONESIA (FEDERATED STATES OF) 29 Apr 1991 a, MONACO 4 Oct 2005 a, MONGOLIA 14 Mar 1989 a, MONTENEGRO 23 Oct 2006 d, MOROCCO 23 Feb 1977 a (*62, 65), MOZAMBIQUE 18 Apr 1983 a (*74, 76), MYANMAR 2 Jan 1997 a (*35, 58, 62), NAMIBIA 14 Sep 1992 a, NEPAL 28 Sep 1965 a, NETHERLANDS 17 Dec 1985 a (*general), NEW ZEALAND 10 Sep 1974 a, NICARAGUA 31 Oct 1975 a, NIGER 26 Apr 1966, NIGERIA 22 Jan 1968 a, NORWAY 13 Feb 1980 (*22), OMAN 31 May 1974 a, PAKISTAN 14 Apr 1969 a, PANAMA 28 Aug 1967, PAPUA NEW GUINEA 4 Dec 1975 d, PARAGUAY 23 Dec 1969 a, PERU 17 Feb 1978, PHILIPPINES 15 Nov 1965, POLAND

* Source: 596 U.N.T.S. 261.

13 Oct 1981, PORTUGAL 13 Sep 1972 a, QATAR 4 Nov 1998 a (*35, 36, 49), REPUBLIC OF KOREA 7 Mar 1977 a, REPUBLIC OF MOLDOVA 26 Jan 1993 a, ROMANIA 24 Feb 1972 a (*74, 76), RUSSIAN FEDERATION 15 Mar 1989 a, RWANDA 31 May 1974 a, SAINT LUCIA 27 Aug 1986 d, SAINT VINCENT AND THE GRENADINES 27 Apr 1999 d, SAMOA 26 Oct 1987 a, SAO TOME AND PRINCIPE 3 May 1983 a, SAUDI ARABIA 29 Jun 1988 a (*35, general), SENEGAL 29 Apr 1966 a, SERBIA 12 Mar 2001 d, SEYCHELLES 29 May 1979 a, SINGAPORE 1 Apr 2005 a, SLOVAKIA 28 May 1993 d, SLOVENIA 6 Jul 1992 d, SOMALIA 29 Mar 1968 a, SOUTH AFRICA 21 Aug 1989 a, SPAIN 3 Feb 1970 a, SRI LANKA 4 May 2006 a, SUDAN 23 Mar 1995 a, SURINAME 11 Sep 1980 a, SWEDEN 19 Mar 1974 (*22, 35, 58), SWITZERLAND 3 May 1965, SYRIAN ARAB REPUBLIC 13 Oct 1978 a (*49), TAJIKISTAN 6 May 1996 a, THAILAND 15 Apr 1999 a (*41), THE FORMER YUGOSLAV REPUBLIC OF MACEDONIA 18 Aug 1993 d, TIMOR-LESTE 30 Jan 2004 a, TOGO 26 Sep 1983 a, TONGA 7 Jan 1972 a, TRINIDAD AND TOBAGO 19 Oct 1965 a, TUNISIA 8 Jul 1964 a, TURKEY 19 Feb 1976 a, TURKMENISTAN 25 Sep 1996 a, TUVALU 15 Sep 1982 d, UKRAINE 27 Apr 1989 a, UNITED ARAB EMIRATES 24 Feb 1977 a, UNITED KINGDOM OF GREAT BRITAIN AND NORTHERN IRELAND 9 May 1972 (*44.3), UNITED REPUBLIC OF TANZANIA 18 Apr 1977 a, UNITED STATES OF AMERICA 24 Nov 1969, URUGUAY 10 Mar 1970, UZBEKISTAN 2 Mar 1992 a, VANUATU 18 Aug 1987 a, VENEZUELA (BOLIVARIAN REPUBLIC OF) 27 Oct 1965, VIET NAM 8 Sep 1992 a (*general), YEMEN 10 1986 a (*35, 46, 49, general), ZIMABAWE 13 May 1991 a.

[...]

CHAPTER I

CONSULAR RELATIONS IN GENERAL

SECTION I

ESTABLISHMENT AND CONDUCT OF CONSULAR RELATIONS

[...]

Article 5

Consular Functions

Consular functions consist in:

(a) protecting in the receiving State the interests of the sending State and of its nationals, both individuals and bodies corporate, within the limits permitted by international law;

(b) furthering the development of commercial, economic, cultural and scientific relations between the sending State and the receiving State and otherwise promoting friendly relations between them in accordance with the provisions of the present Convention;

(c) ascertaining by all lawful means conditions and developments in the commercial, economic, cultural and scientific life of the receiving State, reporting thereon to the Government of the sending State and giving information to persons interested;

(d) issuing passports and travel documents to nationals of the sending State, and visas or appropriate documents to persons wishing to travel to the sending State;

(e) helping and assisting nationals, both individuals and bodies corporate, of the sending State;

(f) acting as notary and civil registrar and in capacities of a similar kind, and performing certain functions of an administrative nature, provided that there is nothing contrary thereto in the laws and regulations of the receiving State;

(g) safeguarding the interests of nationals, both individuals and bodies corporate, of the sending State in cases of succession mortis causa in the territory of the receiving State, in accordance with the laws and regulations of the receiving State;

(h) safeguarding, within the limits imposed by the laws and regulations of the receiving State, the interests of minors and other persons lacking full capacity who are nationals of the sending State, particularly where any guardianship or trusteeship is required with respect to such persons;

(i) subject to the practices and procedures obtaining in the receiving State, representing or arranging appropriate representation for nationals of the sending State before the tribunals and other authorities of the receiving State, for the purpose of obtaining, in accordance with the laws and regulations of the receiving State, provisional measures for the preservation of the rights and interests of these nationals, where, because of absence or any other reason, such nationals are unable at the proper time to assume the defence of their rights and interests;

(j) transmitting judicial and extrajudicial documents or executing letters rogatory or commissions to take evidence for the courts of the sending State in accordance with international agreements in force or, in the absence of such international agreements, in any other manner compatible with the laws and regulations of the receiving State;

(k) exercising rights of supervision and inspection provided for in the laws and regulations of the sending State in respect of vessels having the nationality of the sending State, and of aircraft registered in that State, and in respect of their crews;

(l) extending assistance to vessels and aircraft mentioned in sub-paragraph (k) of this Article and to their crews, taking statements regarding the voyage of a vessel, examining and stamping the ship's papers, and, without prejudice to the powers of the authorities of the receiving State, conducting investigations into any incidents which occurred during the voyage, and settling disputes of any kind between the master, the officers and the seamen in so far as this may be authorized by the laws and regulations of the sending State;

(m) performing any other functions entrusted to a consular post by the sending State which are not prohibited by the laws and regulations of the receiving State or to which no objection is taken by the receiving State or which are referred to in the international agreements in force between the sending State and the receiving State.

[…]

CHAPTER II

FACILITIES, PRIVILEGES AND IMMUNITIES RELATING TO CONSULAR POSTS, CAREER CONSULAR OFFICERS AND OTHER MEMBERS OF A CONSULAR POST

SECTION I

FACILITIES, PRIVILEGES AND IMMUNITIES RELATING TO A CONSULAR POST

[...]

Article 36

Communication and Contact with Nationals of the Sending State

1. With a view to facilitating the exercise of consular functions relating to nationals of the sending State:

(a) consular officers shall be free to communicate with nationals of the sending State and to have access to them. Nationals of the sending State shall have the same freedom with respect to communication with and access to consular officers of the sending State;

(b) if he so requests, the competent authorities of the receiving State shall, without delay, inform the consular post of the sending State if, within its consular district, a national of that State is arrested or committed to prison or to custody pending trial or is detained in any other manner. Any communication addressed to the consular post by the person arrested, in prison, custody or detention shall also be forwarded by the said authorities without delay. The said authorities shall inform the person concerned without delay of his rights under this sub-paragraph;

(c) consular officers shall have the right to visit a national of the sending State who is in prison, custody or detention, to converse and correspond with him and to arrange for his legal representation. They shall also have the right to visit any national of the sending State who is in prison, custody or detention in their district in pursuance of a judgment. Nevertheless, consular officers shall refrain from taking action on behalf of a national who is in prison, custody or detention if he expressly opposes such action.

2. The rights referred to in paragraph 1 of this Article shall be exercised in conformity with the laws and regulations of the receiving State, subject to the proviso, however, that the said laws and regulations must enable full effect to be given to the purposes for which the rights accorded under this Article are intended.

Article 37

Information in Cases of Deaths, Guardianship or Trusteeship, Wrecks and Air Accidents

If the relevant information is available to the competent authorities of the receiving State, such authorities shall have the duty:

(a) in the case of the death of a national of the sending State, to inform without delay the consular post in whose district the death occurred;

(b) to inform the competent consular post without delay of any case where the appointment of a guardian or trustee appears to be in the interests of a minor or other person lacking full capacity who is a national of the sending State. The giving of this information shall, however, be without prejudice to the operation of the laws and regulations of the receiving State concerning such appointments;

(c) if a vessel, having the nationality of the sending State, is wrecked or runs aground in the territorial sea or internal waters of the receiving State, or if an aircraft registered in the sending State suffers an accident on the territory of the receiving State, to inform without delay the consular post nearest to the scene of the occurrence.

Article 38

Communication with the Authorities of the Receiving State

In the exercise of their functions, consular officers may address:

(a) the competent local authorities of their consular district;

(b) the competent central authorities of the receiving State if and to the extent that this is allowed by the laws, regulations and usages of the receiving State or by the relevant international agreements.

[...]

9. INTERNATIONAL TRADE LAW

General Agreement on Trade in Services, 1994 [excerpts][*] (GATS)[**]

Adoption: 15 April 1994

[...]

Part I

SCOPE AND DEFINITION

Article I

Scope and Definition

1. This Agreement applies to measures by Members affecting trade in services.

2. For the purposes of this Agreement, trade in services is defined as the supply of a service:

(a) from the territory of one Member into the territory of any other Member;

(b) in the territory of one Member to the service consumer of any other Member;

(c) by a service supplier of one Member, through commercial presence in the territory of any other Member;

(d) by a service supplier of one Member, through presence of natural persons of a Member in the territory of any other Member.

3. For the purposes of this Agreement:

(a) "measures by Members" means measures taken by:

(i) central, regional or local governments and authorities; and

---

* Source: www.wto.org.

** GATS provides for the liberalisation of trade in services, including trade-related temporary movements of persons (also referred to as Mode 4). Concerning the free movement of service providers, GATS Mode 4 offers a multilateral framework for negotiations, with a set of principles (covering domestic regulations, transparency requirements and other issues) designed to facilitate the removal of trade barriers. However, GATS does not create universal criteria for admission of defined categories of service providers and their access to labour markets. Indeed, it does not provide for a definition of service providers nor does it prescribe the range, depth or sectoral coverage of country commitments. Inclusion of individual sectors within GATS schedules is at the discretion of the Member States, which must define the commitment they are prepared to make on market access and national treatment on a sector-by-sector basis. States can also make 'horizontal commitments' i.e., cross-sectoral commitments given by Member State for market access (e.g. categories of stay of natural persons; durations of stay for natural persons; and conditions of entry). GATS does not require its members to offer market access or conditions that are more liberal than those present in national policy settings. Departures from market access and national treatment are not prohibited per se under the GATS, but must be identified in schedules as limitations. Therefore, each party defines in its commitments the category of service providers to whom it is providing freer access. It is noteworthy, however, that to date, countries do not generally grant access to service providers pursant to GATS Mode 4 beyond that which they already permit under their existing immigration policies. (S. Nonnenmacher, IOM)

(ii) non-governmental bodies in the exercise of powers delegated by central, regional or local governments or authorities;

In fulfilling its obligations and commitments under the Agreement, each Member shall take such reasonable measures as may be available to it to ensure their observance by regional and local governments and authorities and non-governmental bodies within its territory;

(b) "services" includes any service in any sector except services supplied in the exercise of governmental authority;

(c) "a service supplied in the exercise of governmental authority" means any service which is supplied neither on a commercial basis, nor in competition with one or more service suppliers.

[...]

Part III

SPECIFIC COMMITMENTS

Article XVI

Market Access

1. With respect to market access through the modes of supply identified in Article I, each Member shall accord services and service suppliers of any other Member treatment no less favourable than that provided for under the terms, limitations and conditions agreed and specified in its Schedule.[1]

2. In sectors where market-access commitments are undertaken, the measures which a Member shall not maintain or adopt either on the basis of a regional subdivision or on the basis of its entire territory, unless otherwise specified in its Schedule, are defined as:

(a) limitations on the number of service suppliers whether in the form of numerical quotas, monopolies, exclusive service suppliers or the requirements of an economic needs test;

(b) limitations on the total value of service transactions or assets in the form of numerical quotas or the requirement of an economic needs test;

(c) limitations on the total number of service operations or on the total quantity of service output expressed in terms of designated numerical units in the form of quotas or the requirement of an economic needs test; [2]

(d) limitations on the total number of natural persons that may be employed in a particular service sector or that a service supplier may employ and who are necessary for, and directly related to, the supply of a specific service in the form of numerical quotas or the requirement of an economic needs test;

[1] If a Member undertakes a market-access commitment in relation to the supply of a service through the mode of supply referred to in subparagraph 2(a) of Article I and if the cross-border movement of capital is an essential part of the service itself, that Member is thereby committed to allow such movement of capital. If a Member undertakes a market-access commitment in relation to the supply of a service through the mode of supply referred to in subparagraph 2(c) of Article I, it is thereby committed to allow related transfers of capital into its territory.

[2] Subparagraph 2(c) does not cover measures of a Member which limit inputs for the supply of services.

(e) measures which restrict or require specific types of legal entity or joint venture through which a service supplier may supply a service; and

(f) limitations on the participation of foreign capital in terms of maximum percentage limit on foreign shareholding or the total value of individual or aggregate foreign investment.

Article XVII

National Treatment

1. In the sectors inscribed in its Schedule, and subject to any conditions and qualifications set out therein, each Member shall accord to services and service suppliers of any other Member, in respect of all measures affecting the supply of services, treatment no less favourable than that it accords to its own like services and service suppliers.[3]

2. A Member may meet the requirement of paragraph 1 by according to services and service suppliers of any other Member, either formally identical treatment or formally different treatment to that it accords to its own like services and service suppliers.

3. Formally identical or formally different treatment shall be considered to be less favourable if it modifies the conditions of competition in favour of services or service suppliers of the Member compared to like services or service suppliers of any other Member.

Article XVIII

Additional Commitments

Members may negotiate commitments with respect to measures affecting trade in services not subject to scheduling under Articles XVI or XVII, including those regarding qualifications, standards or licensing matters. Such commitments shall be inscribed in a Member's Schedule.

[...]

Part VI

FINAL PROVISIONS

[...]

Article XXVIII

Definitions

For the purpose of this Agreement:

[...]

(k) "natural person of another Member" means a natural person who resides in the territory of that other Member or any other Member, and who under the law of that other Member:

(i) is a national of that other Member; or

(ii) has the right of permanent residence in that other Member, in the case of a Member which:

---

[3] Specific commitments assumed under this Article shall not be construed to require any Member to compensate for any inherent competitive disadvantages which result from the foreign character of the relevant services or service suppliers.

1. does not have nationals; or

2. accords substantially the same treatment to its permanent residents as it does to its nationals in respect of measures affecting trade in services, as notified in its acceptance of or accession to the WTO Agreement, provided that no Member is obligated to accord to such permanent residents treatment more favourable than would be accorded by that other Member to such permanent residents. Such notification shall include the assurance to assume, with respect to those permanent residents, in accordance with its laws and regulations, the same responsibilities that other Member bears with respect to its nationals;

[...]

Annexes

The Annexes to this Agreement are an integral part of this Agreement.

[...]

ANNEX ON MOVEMENT OF NATURAL PERSONS SUPPLYING SERVICES UNDER THE AGREEMENT

1. This Annex applies to measures affecting natural persons who are service suppliers of a Member, and natural persons of a Member who are employed by a service supplier of a Member, in respect of the supply of a service.

2. The Agreement shall not apply to measures affecting natural persons seeking access to the employment market of a Member, nor shall it apply to measures regarding citizenship, residence or employment on a permanent basis.

3. In accordance with Parts III and IV of the Agreement, Members may negotiate specific commitments applying to the movement of all categories of natural persons supplying services under the Agreement. Natural persons covered by a specific commitment shall be allowed to supply the service in accordance with the terms of that commitment.

4. The Agreement shall not prevent a Member from applying measures to regulate the entry of natural persons into, or their temporary stay in, its territory, including those measures necessary to protect the integrity of, and to ensure the orderly movement of natural persons across, its borders, provided that such measures are not applied in such a manner as to nullify or impair the benefits accruing to any Member under the terms of a specific commitment.[4]

[...]

[4] The sole fact of requiring a visa for natural persons of certain Members and not for those of others shall not be regarded as nullifying or impairing benefits under a specific commitment.

10. MIGRATION AND DEVELOPMENT

Programme of Action of the International Conference on Population and Development, Cairo, 5–13 September 1994 [excerpts]*

Adoption: 13 September 1994

[...]

Chapter X

INTERNATIONAL MIGRATION

A. International migration and development

Basis for action

10.1. International economic, political and cultural interrelations play an important role in the flow of people between countries, whether they are developing, developed or with economies in transition. In its diverse types, international migration is linked to such interrelations and both affects and is affected by the development process. International economic imbalances, poverty and environmental degradation, combined with the absence of peace and security, human rights violations and the varying degrees of development of judicial and democratic institutions are all factors affecting international migration. Although most international migration flows occur between neighbouring countries, interregional migration, particularly that directed to developed countries, has been growing. It is estimated that the number of international migrants in the world, including refugees, is in excess of 125 million, about half of them in the developing countries. In recent years, the main receiving countries in the developed world registered a net migration intake of approximately 1.4 million persons annually, about two thirds of whom originated in developing countries. Orderly international migration can have positive impacts on both the communities of origin and the communities of destination, providing the former with remittances and the latter with needed human resources. International migration also has the potential of facilitating the transfer of skills and contributing to cultural enrichment. However, international migration entails the loss of human resources for many countries of origin and may give rise to political, economic or social tensions in countries of destination. To be effective, international migration policies need to take into account the economic constraints of the receiving country, the impact of migration on the host society and its effects on countries of origin. The long-term manageability of international migration hinges on making the option to remain in one's country a viable one for all people. Sustainable economic growth with equity and development strategies consistent with this aim are a necessary means to that end. In addition, more effective use can be made of the potential contribution that expatriate nationals can make to the economic development of their countries of origin.

Objectives

10.2. The objectives are:

(a) To address the root causes of migration, especially those related to poverty;

(b) To encourage more cooperation and dialogue between countries of origin and countries of destination in order to maximize the benefits of migration to those concerned and increase the

* Source: http://www.un.org/popin/icpd2.htm; U.N.Doc. A/CONF.171/13.

likelihood that migration has positive consequences for the development of both sending and receiving countries;

(c) To facilitate the reintegration process of returning migrants.

Actions

10.3. Governments of countries of origin and of countries of destination should seek to make the option of remaining in one's country viable for all people. To that end, efforts to achieve sustainable economic and social development, ensuring a better economic balance between developed and developing countries and countries with economies in transition, should be strengthened. It is also necessary to increase efforts to defuse international and internal conflicts before they escalate; to ensure that the rights of persons belonging to ethnic, religious or linguistic minorities, and indigenous people are respected; and to respect the rule of law, promote good governance, strengthen democracy and promote human rights. Furthermore, greater support should be provided for the attainment of national and household food security, for education, nutrition, health and population-related programmes and to ensure effective environmental protection. Such efforts may require national and international financial assistance, reassessment of commercial and tariff relations, increased access to world markets and stepped-up efforts on the part of developing countries and countries with economies in transition to create a domestic framework for sustainable economic growth with an emphasis on job creation. The economic situation in those countries is likely to improve only gradually and, therefore, migration flows from those countries are likely to decline only in the long term; in the interim, the acute problems currently observed will cause migration flows to continue for the short-to-medium term, and Governments are accordingly urged to adopt transparent international migration policies and programmes to manage those flows.

10.4. Governments of countries of origin wishing to foster the inflow of remittances and their productive use for development should adopt sound exchange rate, monetary and economic policies, facilitate the provision of banking facilities that enable the safe and timely transfer of migrants' funds, and promote the conditions necessary to increase domestic savings and channel them into productive investment.

10.5. Governments of countries of destination are invited to consider the use of certain forms of temporary migration, such as short-term and project-related migration, as a means of improving the skills of nationals of countries of origin, especially developing countries and countries with economies in transition. To that end, they should consider, as appropriate, entering into bilateral or multilateral agreements. Appropriate steps should be taken to safeguard the wages and working conditions of both migrant and native workers in the affected sectors. Governments of countries of origin are urged to facilitate the return of migrants and their reintegration into their home communities, and to devise ways of using their skills. Governments of countries of origin should consider collaborating with countries of destination and engaging the support of appropriate international organizations in promoting the return on a voluntary basis of qualified migrants who can play a crucial role in the transfer of knowledge, skills and technology. Countries of destination are encouraged to facilitate return migration by adopting flexible policies, such as the transferability of pensions and other work benefits.

10.6. Governments of countries affected by international migration are invited to cooperate, with a view to integrating the issue into their political and economic agendas and engaging in technical cooperation to aid developing countries and countries with economies in transition in addressing the impact of international migration. Governments are urged to exchange information regarding their international migration policies and the regulations governing the admission and stay of migrants in their territories. States that have not already done so are invited to consider ratifying the International Convention on the Protection of the Rights of All Migrant Workers and Members of Their Families.

10.7. Governments are encouraged to consider requests for migration from countries whose existence, according to available scientific evidence, is imminently threatened by global warming and climate change.

10.8. In cooperation with international and non-governmental organizations and research institutions, Governments should support the gathering of data on flows and stocks of international migrants and on factors causing migration, as well as the monitoring of international migration. The identification of strategies to ensure that migration contributes to development and international relations should also be supported. The role of international organizations with mandates in the area of migration should be strengthened so that they can deliver adequate technical support to developing countries, advise in the management of international migration flows and promote intergovernmental cooperation through, inter alia, bilateral and multilateral negotiations, as appropriate.

[…]

Resolution of the Commission on Population and Development No.2006/2 on International Migration and Development, 2006*

Adoption: 10 May 2006

The Commission on Population and Development,

Recalling the Programme of Action of the International Conference on Population and Development adopted at Cairo,[1] *in particular chapter X on international migration, and the key actions for the further implementation of the Programme of Action,*[2] *in particular section II.C on international migration,*

Recognizing that the implementation of the Programme of Action of the International Conference on Population and Development and the key actions for its further implementation is integrally linked to global efforts to eradicate poverty and achieve sustainable development and that the achievement of the goals of the Programme of Action is consistent with and makes an essential contribution to the achievement of the internationally agreed development goals, including the Millennium Development Goals,

Recalling the relevant provisions on international migration contained, inter alia, in the Copenhagen Declaration on Social Development,[3] *the Programme of Action of the World Summit for Social Development,*[4] *the Beijing Declaration and Platform for Action*[5] *and their periodic reviews, and the Durban Declaration and Programme of Action adopted by the World Conference against Racism, Racial Discrimination, Xenophobia and Related Intolerance on 8 September 2001,*[6]

Recalling also the 2005 World Summit Outcome of 16 September 2005,[7]

Recalling further General Assembly resolution 57/270 B of 23 June 2003 on the integrated and coordinated implementation of and follow-up to the outcomes of the major United Nations conferences and summits in the economic and social fields,

Recalling all General Assembly resolutions relevant to international migration and development,

Recalling also General Assembly resolutions 58/208 of 23 December 2003, 59/241 of 22 December 2004 and 60/227 of 23 December 2005, which are relevant to the setting up and organizing of the High-level Dialogue on International Migration and Development which will be held during the sixty-first session of the Assembly and which will discuss the overall

* Source: U.N.Doc. E/2006/25, E/CN.9/2006/9; in Report of the Commission on Population and Development on the thirty-ninth session (14 April 2005 and 3-7 April and 10 May 2006), Economic and Social Council, Official Records, 2006 Supplement No. 5.

1 See Report of the International Conference on Population and Development, Cairo, 5-13 September 1994 (United Nations publication, Sales No. E.95.XIII.18).

2 See General Assembly resolution S-21/2 of 2 July 1999, annex, and Official Records of the General Assembly, Twenty-first Special Session, Supplement No. 3 (A/S-21/5/Rev.1) and A/S-21/PV.9.

3 Report of the World Summit for Social Development, Copenhagen, 6-12 March 1995 (United Nations publication, Sales No. E.96.IV.8), chap. I, resolution 1, annex I.

4 Ibid., annex II.

5 Report of the Fourth World Conference on Women, Beijing, 4-15 September 1995 (United Nations publication, Sales No. E.96.IV.13), chap. I, resolution 1, annexes I and II.

6 See A/CONF.189/12 and Corr.1, chap. I.

7 See General Assembly resolution 60/1.

theme of the multidimensional aspects of international migration and development in order to identify appropriate ways and means to maximize the development benefits and minimize the negative impacts,

Reaffirming the resolve expressed by the Heads of State and Government[8] *to take measures to ensure respect for and protection of the human rights of migrants, migrant workers and members of their families,*

Recalling the Universal Declaration of Human Rights,[9] *the International Convention on the Elimination of All Forms of Racial Discrimination,*[10] *the Convention on the Elimination of All Forms of Discrimination against Women*[11] *and the Convention on the Rights of the Child,*[12]

Recalling also the International Convention on the Protection of the Rights of All Migrant Workers and Members of Their Families,[13] *which entered into force in July 2003,*

Recalling further the United Nations Convention against Transnational Organized Crime and the supplementing protocols thereto, namely, the Protocol to Prevent, Suppress and Punish Trafficking in Persons, Especially Women and Children, and the Protocol against the Smuggling of Migrants by Land, Sea and Air,[14]

Acknowledging the important nexus between international migration and development and the need to deal with the challenges and opportunities that migration presents to countries of origin, transit and destination and recognizing that migration brings benefits as well as challenges to the global community,

Bearing in mind that policies and initiatives on the issue of migration, including those that refer to the orderly management of migration, should promote holistic approaches that take into account the causes and consequences of the phenomenon, as well as the full respect of the human rights and fundamental freedoms of migrants,

Recognizing that remittance flows constitute one of the important aspects of international migration,

Noting that the proportion of women and girls among international migrants amounted to nearly 50 per cent in 2005 and deeply concerned about the risks that women and girls, including women migrant workers, are exposed to in the context of migration, such as gender-based discrimination, multiple aggravated forms of discrimination, violence, including sexual violence, migrant smuggling, trafficking in persons, commercial sexual exploitation and economic exploitation, sexual abuse and other forms of abuse,

Recognizing that the increasing feminization of international migration requires greater gender sensitivity in all policies and efforts related to the subject of international migration,

Recognizing also the impact of migration on the effectiveness of public services, and the need to address, as appropriate, the shortages of workers, including health and education workers, giving appropriate attention to enhancing the capacity of developing countries in this regard,

---

[8] See the United Nations Millennium Declaration, as contained in General Assembly resolution 55/2 of 8 September 2000, and the 2005 World Summit Outcome.

[9] General Assembly resolution 217 A (III).

[10] General Assembly resolution 2106 A (XX), annex.

[11] General Assembly resolution 34/180, annex.

[12] United Nations, Treaty Series, vol. 1577, No. 27531.

[13] General Assembly resolution 45/158, annex.

[14] General Assembly resolution 55/25, annexes I to III.

Noting the efforts of Member States, relevant United Nations bodies, organizations, funds and programmes, and international and intergovernmental organizations, including the International Organization for Migration, in respect of convening events at the national, regional and international levels with a view to advancing the dialogue on the issue of international migration and development,

Taking note of the reports of the Secretary-General on world population monitoring[15] *and on the monitoring of population programmes,*[16] *both focusing on international migration and development, and taking note also of the report of the Secretary-General on the flow of financial resources for assisting in the implementation of the Programme of Action of the International Conference on Population and Development,*[17]

Taking note also of the report of the Global Commission on International Migration entitled "Migration in an interconnected world: new directions for action",[18] *including its contribution to the debate on international migration and development, and taking note further of the report as an input for consideration at the High-level Dialogue,*

1. *Reaffirms* the Programme of Action of the International Conference on Population and Development[1] and the key actions for its further implementation;[2]

2. *Acknowledges* the important contribution made by migrants and migration to development in countries of origin and destination;

3. *Recognizes* the need for Member States to consider the multidimensional aspects of international migration and development in order to identify appropriate ways and means of maximizing the development benefits and minimizing the negative impacts;

4. *Requests* States to effectively promote and protect the human rights and fundamental freedoms of all migrants regardless of their immigration status, especially those of women and children, in conformity with the Universal Declaration of Human Rights[9] and the international instruments to which they are party;

5. *Reaffirms* the responsibility of Governments to safeguard and protect the rights of migrants against illegal or violent acts, in particular acts of racial discrimination and crimes perpetrated with racist or xenophobic motivation by individuals or groups, and urges them to reinforce measures in this regard;

6. *Recognizes* that trafficking in persons and smuggling of migrants continue to pose a serious challenge to humanity and require a concerted international response, and to that end urges all States to devise, enforce and strengthen effective measures to prevent, combat and eliminate all forms of trafficking in persons, to counter the demand for trafficked victims and to protect the victims, in particular women and children subjected to forced labour, or sexual or commercial exploitation, violence or sexual abuse;

7. *Requests* all Member States, in accordance with their relevant international obligations and commitments, to promote cooperation at all levels in addressing the challenge of undocumented or irregular migration so as to foster a secure, regular and orderly process of migration;

---

[15] E/CN.9/2006/3.
[16] E/CN.9/2006/4.
[17] E/CN.9/2006/5.
[18] Geneva, Global Commission on International Migration, October 2005.

8. *Calls upon* States that have not yet done so to enact domestic legislation and to take further effective measures to combat and prosecute international trafficking in persons and smuggling of migrants;

9. *Reaffirms* the right of Governments to enforce their migration laws, consistent with their international obligations;

10. *Invites* Governments, with the assistance of the international community, where appropriate, to seek to make the option of remaining in one's own country viable for all people, in particular through efforts to achieve sustainable development, leading to a better economic balance between developed and developing countries;

11. *Calls upon* States to facilitate family reunification in an expeditious and effective manner, with due regard for applicable laws, as such reunification has a positive effect on the integration of migrants;

12. *Recognizes* the importance of public awareness of opportunities, limitations and rights in the event of migration;

13. *Urges* Member States and relevant international organizations to incorporate a gender perspective in all policies and programmes on international migration in order to, inter alia, reinforce the positive contributions that migrant women can make to the economic, social and human development of their countries of origin and their host countries as well as to strengthen protection of women migrants from all forms of violence, discrimination, trafficking, exploitation and abuse, by promoting their rights and welfare, while recognizing in this regard the importance of joint and collaborative approaches and strategies at the bilateral, regional, interregional and international levels;

14. *Reiterates* the need to consider how the migration of highly skilled persons and those with advanced education impacts the development efforts of developing countries;

15. *Acknowledges* the need to analyse the impact of certain forms of temporary migration and return migration;

16. *Reaffirms* that there is a need to address and to promote conditions for cheaper, faster and safer transfers of remittances in both source and recipient countries and, as appropriate, to encourage opportunities for development-oriented investment in recipient countries by beneficiaries that are willing and able to undertake such action;

17. *Invites* the countries of origin and destination, in accordance with domestic legislation, to undertake appropriate measures to facilitate the contribution of migrants and migrant communities to the development of their countries of origin;

18. *Recalls* the commitments contained in the 2001 Declaration of Commitment on HIV/AIDS[19] to develop and begin to implement national, regional and international strategies that would facilitate access to HIV/AIDS prevention programmes for migrants and mobile workers, including the provision of information on health and social services;[20]

19. *Invites* Governments to set up or, where they already exist and where necessary, to strengthen relevant institutions and mechanisms for, inter alia, data collection, analysis, the subsequent elaboration of policies, programmes and projects, and their monitoring and evaluation, including by improving skills and increasing resources, with a view to their providing timely,

---

[19] General Assembly resolution S-26/2, annex.

[20] Ibid., para. 50.

reliable and disaggregated information, including, inter alia, sex- and age-specific information, on international migration flows in countries of origin, transit and destination and their effects on development, and in this regard invites the international community to provide financial and technical assistance to developing countries;

20. *Invites* relevant international organizations and multilateral institutions to enhance their cooperation on methodologies for the collection and processing of statistical data on international migration and the situation of migrants;

21. *Encourages* efforts by Member States and the international community to promote a balanced and comprehensive approach to international migration and development, particularly by building partnerships and ensuring coordinated action to develop capacities, including for the management of migration;

22. *Invites* Governments, where appropriate, to consider the linkages between international migration and development in policy formulation by, inter alia, promoting, through a comprehensive approach at the national level, collaboration and coordination among the governmental authorities in charge of international migration, and those focusing on development or development cooperation, and other relevant policy areas;

23. *Recognizes* the need to take concrete actions to strengthen bilateral, regional and international cooperation and dialogue in the area of international migration and development and, where appropriate, to develop and implement national policies and cooperative strategies to ensure that migration contributes to the development of both countries of origin and countries of destination;

24. *Urges* the relevant United Nations bodies, organizations, funds and programmes, and other relevant intergovernmental organizations working on international migration, including the International Organization for Migration, to enhance within their respective mandates the coordination of their activities, and to strengthen cooperation and collaboration;

25. Requests the Secretary-General to continue his substantive work on international migration and development and, in collaboration with other relevant international organizations, funds and programmes, to continue assessing the progress made in achieving the goals and objectives on international migration and development set out in the outcomes of major United Nations conferences and summits;

26. Looks forward to the High-level Dialogue on International Migration and Development to be held during the sixty-first session of the General Assembly;

27. Recommends in this regard that the Economic and Social Council transmit the report of the Commission on its thirty-ninth session to the High-level Dialogue.

Summary of the High-level Dialogue on International Migration and Development, New York, 14–15 September 2006 [excerpts]*

Note by the President of the General Assembly

[...]

II. Key issues

6. The High-level Dialogue on International Migration and Development demonstrated the strong commitment of Member States, United Nations entities, observers, non-governmental organizations, civil society and the private sector to examining the relationship and synergies between international migration and development. There was general consensus that the High-level Dialogue presented a unique opportunity to identify ways and means to maximize the developmental benefits of international migration and to reduce its negative impacts.

7. Participants stressed the global character of international migration. They affirmed that international migration was a growing phenomenon, both in scope and in complexity, affecting virtually all countries in the world. They agreed that international migration could be a positive force for development in both countries of origin and countries of destination, provided that it was supported by the right set of policies.

8. Participants noted that international migrants contributed to development in both developing and developed countries. In some countries, migrants were essential in meeting labour shortages. A number of participants also underscored the social and cultural contributions of migrants. Some countries reported on their long experience in receiving and integrating international migrants. Other countries had only recently become migrant receiving countries. Many participants mentioned how their countries had benefited from the emigration of their citizens and from the financial and other contributions that migrant communities had made to the development of their countries. The role of migrant entrepreneurs in reinvigorating urban areas was mentioned.

9. Participants felt that it was essential to address the root causes of international migration to ensure that people migrated out of choice rather than necessity. They observed that people often had to migrate because of poverty, conflict, human rights violations, poor governance or lack of employment. There was widespread support for incorporating international migration issues in national development plans, including poverty reduction strategies. Participants noted that international migration could contribute to the achievement of the internationally agreed development goals, including the Millennium Development Goals, but cautioned against viewing international migration by itself as a long-term development strategy. The need to generate jobs with decent working conditions and to ensure that sustainable livelihoods were possible in all countries was emphasized.

10. Participants recognized that international migration, development and human rights were intrinsically interconnected. Respect for the fundamental rights and freedoms of all migrants was considered essential for reaping the full benefits of international migration. Many noted that some vulnerable groups, such as migrant women and children, needed special protection. Governments were called upon to ratify and implement the core human rights conventions and other relevant international instruments, including the International Convention on the Protection of the Rights of All Migrant Workers and Members of Their Families. Participants

* Source: U.N. Doc. A/61/515, dated 13 October 2006.

underlined the need for concerted efforts on the part of Governments to combat xenophobia, discrimination, racism and the social exclusion of migrant populations.

11. Participants emphasized that the social consequences of international migration deserved urgent attention. The integration of international migrants in receiving countries required mutual adaptation and acceptance by both the host society and the migrants themselves. It was important to combat all types of intolerance. Information campaigns about the positive contribution of international migrants to the host society and about the rights and responsibilities of international migrants were deemed useful.

12. Participants acknowledged that remittances were the most tangible benefit of international migration for countries of origin. They noted that the volume of remittances had increased markedly in recent years. While remittances benefited millions of families of migrants, participants believed that their development potential could be enhanced by appropriate measures. These encompassed increasing competition among money-transfer companies and banks to reduce transfer fees, improving the access to banking services, including credit, of migrants and their families and expanding financial literacy in countries of origin. There was consensus that remittances were private flows and should not be considered a substitute for official development assistance, direct foreign investment or debt relief. Some participants warned about the potentially negative consequences of remittances, including the culture of dependency that they might foster at both the household and national levels.

13. Participants agreed that migrant communities had significant potential to contribute to the development of their countries of origin. A number of countries had taken measures to strengthen ties with their nationals abroad and to encourage highly skilled workers in the direction of return and circular migration. Several participants noted that, through co-development projects, migrant entrepreneurs had been agents of development in their countries of origin. The role of international migrants in transferring know-how, skills, technology, expertise and new ways of thinking to their countries of origin was also underscored.

14. Participants also focused on ways of minimizing the negative consequences of highly skilled emigration from developing countries. The outflow of highly skilled workers from the health and education sectors was of particular concern, since it compromised the delivery of services in countries of origin. Participants urged the implementation of measures to retain highly skilled workers by, among other things, ensuring equitable pay and decent working conditions. The promotion of return, even on a temporary basis, of skilled workers to their countries of origin was also recommended. Some participants noted that their countries had adopted or were about to adopt codes of conduct barring the active recruitment of health workers from developing countries affected by labour shortages in the health and education sectors. A number of participants suggested that cooperative arrangements could be made to train skilled workers in developing countries and others argued for different mechanisms for compensation.

15. Participants remarked that labour migration was crucial for the world economy. In some countries, the labour market was highly dependent on foreign workers. In others, temporary labour migration allowed for the filling of specific labour needs. Participants noted that the relatively high participation of women in labour migration had prompted some countries to re-examine their labour migration regulations and procedures to ensure that they were gender sensitive and that they offered adequate protection for female migrants.

16. Participants noted that about half of all international migrants were female. Women, like men, migrated in order to improve their livelihoods. For many women migration was a means of empowerment. The entrepreneurial potential of female migrants deserved support, and the contribution of migrant women to development in both countries of origin

and those of destination had to be recognized. However, migration also entailed risks that were often more serious for women than for men, especially when women were relegated to undesirable low-paying jobs. It was important, therefore, to adopt policies that addressed the particular circumstances and experiences of female migrants and reduced their vulnerability to exploitation and abuse. Women and girls who were victims of trafficking were entitled to special protection.

17. Participants expressed concern about the increase in irregular migration and the exploitation and abuse of migrants in an irregular situation. There was general consensus that trafficking in persons and the smuggling of migrants, especially women and children, should be combated with urgency at the national, bilateral, regional and global levels. Some participants noted that restrictive migration policies contributed to an increase in irregular migration and argued for an increase in legal avenues for migration and for the regularization of migrants in an irregular situation. Participants suggested that information campaigns highlighting the dangers involved in migrating without authorization could help in reducing irregular flows. Although effective border control was considered necessary by many participants, there was recognition that security and control measures alone would not eliminate irregular migration. Hence, there was a call for migration policies that could produce a better balance between unmet labour demand and the inflows of workers from abroad. Participants also underscored that measures to control irregular migration should not prevent persons fleeing persecution and other vulnerable populations from seeking international protection.

18. Most participants considered that national strategies to address the impact of international migration on development should be complemented by strengthened bilateral, regional and multilateral cooperation. They considered that such cooperation was needed to promote legal, safe and orderly migration, reduce irregular migration and improve the chances of reaping the full benefits of international migration. The proliferation of regional consultative processes was seen by participants as proof that cooperation was particularly effective at the regional level. Many participants provided examples of regional mechanisms that, through improved dialogue and better mutual understanding, had led to practical measures to address migration issues.

19. Participants also recognized the usefulness of bilateral agreements and cited examples of those addressing labour migration, the portability of pensions, the readmission of nationals or the fight against trafficking in persons and the smuggling of migrants. Many participants considered that regional and bilateral initiatives had to be complemented by initiatives at the global level, noting that the United Nations was a natural venue for such initiatives. Participants also mentioned the work of the Global Commission on International Migration, whose report provided useful guidance, the International Agenda for Migration Management, produced by the Berne Initiative, and the annual dialogue on migration policy sponsored by IOM.

[...]

General Assembly Resolution No. 61/208 on International Migration and Development, 2006 [excerpts]*

Adoption: 20 December 2006

The General Assembly,

[...]

1. *Takes note* of the report of the Secretary-General; [1]

2. *Welcomes* the convening of the High-level Dialogue on International Migration and Development in New York on 14 and 15 September 2006, and the high level and broad participation that provided an opportunity to discuss the multidimensional aspects of international migration and development;

3. *Takes note* of the summary of the High-level Dialogue by the President of the General Assembly; [2]

4. *Welcomes* the heightened awareness achieved by the High-level Dialogue on the issue, and decides to consider, at its sixty-third session, possible options for appropriate follow-up to the High-level Dialogue;

5. *Also welcomes* the ongoing efforts of Governments in the area of regional and interregional cooperation and regional consultative processes, where they exist, on migration and encourages consideration of development dimensions in such processes, towards facilitating the dialogue and the exchange of information and experiences, fostering coordination at the regional and national levels, building common understanding, promoting cooperation, contributing to capacity-building and strengthening partnerships among countries of origin, transit and destination;

6. *Takes note with interest* of the establishment of the Global Migration Group; [3]

7. *Calls upon* all relevant bodies, agencies, funds and programmes of the United Nations system and other relevant intergovernmental, regional and subregional organizations, within their respective mandates, to continue to address the issue of international migration and development, with a view to integrating migration issues, including a gender perspective and cultural diversity, in a more coherent way within the broader context of the implementation of internationally agreed development goals, including the Millennium Development Goals and respect for human rights;

[...]

10. Decides to include in the provisional agenda of its sixty-third session the sub-item entitled “International migration and development”.

* Source: U.N.G.A. Res. A/RES/61/208.

1 See resolutions 55/2 and 60/1.

2 A/60/871.

3 A/61/515.

11. MINORITIES

Declaration on the Rights of Persons Belonging to National or Ethnic, Religious and Linguistic Minorities, 1992*

Adoption: 18 December 1992

The General Assembly,

Reaffirming that one of the basic aims of the United Nations, as proclaimed in the Charter, is to promote and encourage respect for human rights and for fundamental freedoms for all, without distinction as to race, sex, language or religion,

Reaffirming faith in fundamental human rights, in the dignity and worth of the human person, in the equal rights of men and women and of nations large and small,

Desiring to promote the realization of the principles contained in the Charter, the Universal Declaration of Human Rights, the Convention on the Prevention and Punishment of the Crime of Genocide, the International Convention on the Elimination of All Forms of Racial Discrimination, the International Covenant on Civil and Political Rights, the International Covenant on Economic, Social and Cultural Rights, the Declaration on the Elimination of All Forms of Intolerance and of Discrimination Based on Religion or Belief, and the Convention on the Rights of the Child, as well as other relevant international instruments that have been adopted at the universal or regional level and those concluded between individual States Members of the United Nations,

Inspired by the provisions of article 27 of the International Covenant on Civil and Political Rights concerning the rights of persons belonging to ethnic, religious and linguistic minorities,

Considering that the promotion and protection of the rights of persons belonging to national or ethnic, religious and linguistic minorities contribute to the political and social stability of States in which they live,

Emphasizing that the constant promotion and realization of the rights of persons belonging to national or ethnic, religious and linguistic minorities, as an integral part of the development of society as a whole and within a democratic framework based on the rule of law, would contribute to the strengthening of friendship and cooperation among peoples and States,

Considering that the United Nations has an important role to play regarding the protection of minorities,

Bearing in mind the work done so far within the United Nations system, in particular by the Commission on Human Rights, the Subcommission on Prevention of Discrimination and Protection of Minorities and the bodies established pursuant to the International Covenants on Human Rights and other relevant international human rights instruments in promoting and protecting the rights of persons belonging to national or ethnic, religious and linguistic minorities,

Taking into account the important work which is done by intergovernmental and non-governmental organizations in protecting minorities and in promoting and protecting the rights of persons belonging to national or ethnic, religious and linguistic minorities,

* Source: U.N.G.A. 47/135.

Recognizing the need to ensure even more effective implementation of international human rights instruments with regard to the rights of persons belonging to national or ethnic, religious and linguistic minorities,

Proclaims this Declaration on the Rights of Persons Belonging to National or Ethnic, Religious and Linguistic Minorities:

Article 1

1. States shall protect the existence and the national or ethnic, cultural, religious and linguistic identity of minorities within their respective territories and shall encourage conditions for the promotion of that identity.

2. States shall adopt appropriate legislative and other measures to achieve those ends.

Article 2

1. Persons belonging to national or ethnic, religious and linguistic minorities (hereinafter referred to as persons belonging to minorities) have the right to enjoy their own culture, to profess and practise their own religion, and to use their own language, in private and in public, freely and without interference or any form of discrimination.

2. Persons belonging to minorities have the right to participate effectively in cultural, religious, social, economic and public life.

3. Persons belonging to minorities have the right to participate effectively in decisions on the national and, where appropriate, regional level concerning the minority to which they belong or the regions in which they live, in a manner not incompatible with national legislation.

4. Persons belonging to minorities have the right to establish and maintain their own associations.

5. Persons belonging to minorities have the right to establish and maintain, without any discrimination, free and peaceful contacts with other members of their group and with persons belonging to other minorities, as well as contacts across frontiers with citizens of other States to whom they are related by national or ethnic, religious or linguistic ties.

Article 3

1. Persons belonging to minorities may exercise their rights, including those set forth in the present Declaration, individually as well as in community with other members of their group, without any discrimination.

2. No disadvantage shall result for any person belonging to a minority as the consequence of the exercise or non-exercise of the rights set forth in the present Declaration.

Article 4

1. States shall take measures where required to ensure that persons belonging to minorities may exercise fully and effectively all their human rights and fundamental freedoms without any discrimination and in full equality before the law.

2. States shall take measures to create favourable conditions to enable persons belonging to minorities to express their characteristics and to develop their culture, language, religion, traditions and customs, except where specific practices are in violation of national law and contrary to international standards.

3. States should take appropriate measures so that, wherever possible, persons belonging to minorities may have adequate opportunities to learn their mother tongue or to have instruction in their mother tongue.

4. States should, where appropriate, take measures in the field of education, in order to encourage knowledge of the history, traditions, language and culture of the minorities existing within their territory. Persons belonging to minorities should have adequate opportunities to gain knowledge of the society as a whole.

5. States should consider appropriate measures so that persons belonging to minorities may participate fully in the economic progress and development in their country.

Article 5

1. National policies and programmes shall be planned and implemented with due regard for the legitimate interests of persons belonging to minorities.

2. Programmes of cooperation and assistance among States should be planned and implemented with due regard for the legitimate interests of persons belonging to minorities.

Article 6

States should cooperate on questions relating to persons belonging to minorities, inter alia, exchanging information and experiences, in order to promote mutual understanding and confidence.

Article 7

States should cooperate in order to promote respect for the rights set forth in the present Declaration.

Article 8

1. Nothing in the present Declaration shall prevent the fulfilment of international obligations of States in relation to persons belonging to minorities. In particular, States shall fulfil in good faith the obligations and commitments they have assumed under international treaties and agreements to which they are parties.

2. The exercise of the rights set forth in the present Declaration shall not prejudice the enjoyment by all persons of universally recognized human rights and fundamental freedoms.

3. Measures taken by States to ensure the effective enjoyment of the rights set forth in the present Declaration shall not prima facie be considered contrary to the principle of equality contained in the Universal Declaration of Human Rights.

4. Nothing in the present Declaration may be construed as permitting any activity contrary to the purposes and principles of the United Nations, including sovereign equality, territorial integrity and political independence of States.

Article 9

The specialized agencies and other organizations of the United Nations system shall contribute to the full realization of the rights and principles set forth in the present Declaration, within their respective fields of competence.

CCPR General Comment No.23: Article 27 (The Rights of Minorities), 1994 [excerpts]*

Adoption: 8 April 1994

[...]

4. The Covenant also distinguishes the rights protected under article 27 from the guarantees under articles 2.1 and 26. The entitlement, under article 2.1, to enjoy the rights under the Covenant without discrimination applies to all individuals within the territory or under the jurisdiction of the State whether or not those persons belong to a minority. In addition, there is a distinct right provided under article 26 for equality before the law, equal protection of the law, and non-discrimination in respect of rights granted and obligations imposed by the States. It governs the exercise of all rights, whether protected under the Covenant or not, which the State party confers by law on individuals within its territory or under its jurisdiction, irrespective of whether they belong to the minorities specified in article 27 or not.[1] Some States parties who claim that they do not discriminate on grounds of ethnicity, language or religion, wrongly contend, on that basis alone, that they have no minorities.

5.1. The terms used in article 27 indicate that the persons designed to be protected are those who belong to a group and who share in common a culture, a religion and/or a language. Those terms also indicate that the individuals designed to be protected need not be citizens of the State party. In this regard, the obligations deriving from article 2.1 are also relevant, since a State party is required under that article to ensure that the rights protected under the Covenant are available to all individuals within its territory and subject to its jurisdiction, except rights which are expressly made to apply to citizens, for example, political rights under article 25. A State party may not, therefore, restrict the rights under article 27 to its citizens alone.

5.2. Article 27 confers rights on persons belonging to minorities which "exist" in a State party. Given the nature and scope of the rights envisaged under that article, it is not relevant to determine the degree of permanence that the term "exist" connotes. Those rights simply are that individuals belonging to those minorities should not be denied the right, in community with members of their group, to enjoy their own culture, to practise their religion and speak their language. Just as they need not be nationals or citizens, they need not be permanent residents. Thus, migrant workers or even visitors in a State party constituting such minorities are entitled not to be denied the exercise of those rights. As any other individual in the territory of the State party, they would, also for this purpose, have the general rights, for example, to freedom of association, of assembly, and of expression. The existence of an ethnic, religious or linguistic minority in a given State party does not depend upon a decision by that State party but requires to be established by objective criteria.

[...]

* Source: U.N.Doc. CCPR/C/21/Rev.1/Add.5.

[1] See ibid. [Official Records of the General Assembly], Forty-second Session, Supplement No.40 (A/42/40), annex VIII, sect. D, Communication No.182/1984 (F.H. Zwaan-de Vries v. the Netherlands), views adopted on 9 April 1987; ibid., sect. C, Communication No.180/1984 (L.G. Danning v. the Netherlands), views adopted on 9 April 1987.

Universal Declaration on Cultural Diversity, 2001*

Adoption: 2 November 2001

The General Conference,

Committed to the full implementation of the human rights and fundamental freedoms proclaimed in the Universal Declaration of Human Rights and other universally recognized legal instruments, such as the two International Covenants of 1966 relating respectively to civil and political rights and to economic, social and cultural rights,

Recalling that the Preamble to the Constitution of UNESCO affirms "that the wide diffusion of culture, and the education of humanity for justice and liberty and peace are indispensable to the dignity of man and constitute a sacred duty which all the nations must fulfil in a spirit of mutual assistance and concern",

Further recalling Article 1 of the Constitution, which assigns to UNESCO among other purposes that of recommending "such international agreements as may be necessary to promote the free flow of ideas by word and image",

Referring to the provisions relating to cultural diversity and the exercise of cultural rights in the international instruments enacted by UNESCO,[1]

Reaffirming that culture should be regarded as the set of distinctive spiritual, material, intellectual and emotional features of society or a social group, and that it encompasses, in addition to art and literature, lifestyles, ways of living together, value systems, traditions and beliefs,[2]

Noting that culture is at the heart of contemporary debates about identity, social cohesion, and the development of a knowledge-based economy,

Affirming that respect for the diversity of cultures, tolerance, dialogue and cooperation, in a climate of mutual trust and understanding are among the best guarantees of international peace and security,

Aspiring to greater solidarity on the basis of recognition of cultural diversity, of awareness of the unity of humankind, and of the development of intercultural exchanges,

Considering that the process of globalization, facilitated by the rapid development of new information and communication technologies, though representing a challenge for cultural diversity, creates the conditions for renewed dialogue among cultures and civilizations,

---

* Source: http://unesdoc.unesco.org/images/0012/001271/127160m.pdf

[1] Among which, in particular, the Florence Agreement of 1950 and its Nairobi Protocol of 1976, the Universal Copyright Convention of 1952, the Declaration of Principles on International Cultural Co-operation of 1966, the Convention on the Means of Prohibiting and Preventing the Illicit Import, Export and Transfer of Ownership of Cultural Property (1970), the Convention for the Protection of World Cultural and Natural Heritage of 1972, the UNESCO Declaration on Race and Racial Prejudice of 1978, the Recommendation concerning the Status of the Artist of 1980, and the Recommendation on Safeguarding Traditional and Popular Culture of 1989.

[2] This definition is in line with the conclusions of the World Conference on Cultural Policies (MONDIACULT, Mexico City, 1982), of the World Commission on Culture and Development (Our Creative Diversity, 1995), and of the Intergovernmental Conference on Cultural Policies for Development (Stockholm, 1998).

Aware of the specific mandate which has been entrusted to UNESCO, within the United Nations system, to ensure the preservation and promotion of the fruitful diversity of cultures,

Proclaims the following principles and adopts the present Declaration:

IDENTITY, DIVERSITY AND PLURALISM

Article 1 - Cultural diversity: the common heritage of humanity

Culture takes diverse forms across time and space. This diversity is embodied in the uniqueness and plurality of the identities of the groups and societies making up humankind. As a source of exchange, innovation and creativity, cultural diversity is as necessary for humankind as biodiversity is for nature. In this sense, it is the common heritage of humanity and should be recognized and affirmed for the benefit of present and future generations.

Article 2 - From cultural diversity to cultural pluralism

In our increasingly diverse societies, it is essential to ensure harmonious interaction among people and groups with plural, varied and dynamic cultural identities as well as their willingness to live together. Policies for the inclusion and participation of all citizens are guarantees of social cohesion, the vitality of civil society and peace. Thus defined, cultural pluralism gives policy expression to the reality of cultural diversity. Indissociable from a democratic framework, cultural pluralism is conducive to cultural exchange and to the flourishing of creative capacities that sustain public life.

Article 3 - Cultural diversity as a factor in development

Cultural diversity widens the range of options open to everyone; it is one of the roots of development, understood not simply in terms of economic growth, but also as a means to achieve a more satisfactory intellectual, emotional, moral and spiritual existence.

CULTURAL DIVERSITY AND HUMAN RIGHTS

Article 4 - Human rights as guarantees of cultural diversity

The defence of cultural diversity is an ethical imperative, inseparable from respect for human dignity. It implies a commitment to human rights and fundamental freedoms, in particular the rights of persons belonging to minorities and those of indigenous peoples. No one may invoke cultural diversity to infringe upon human rights guaranteed by international law, nor to limit their scope.

Article 5 - Cultural rights as an enabling environment for cultural diversity

Cultural rights are an integral part of human rights, which are universal, indivisible and interdependent. The flourishing of creative diversity requires the full implementation of cultural rights as defined in Article 27 of the Universal Declaration of Human Rights and in Articles 13 and 15 of the International Covenant on Economic, Social and cultural Rights. All persons should therefore be able to express themselves and to create and disseminate their work in the language of their choice, and particularly in their mother tongue; all persons should be entitled to quality education and training that fully respect their cultural identity; and all persons have the right to participate in the cultural life of their choice and conduct their own cultural practices, subject to respect for human rights and fundamental freedoms.

Article 6 - Towards access for all to cultural diversity

While ensuring the free flow of ideas by word and image, care should be exercised so that all cultures can express themselves and make themselves known. Freedom of expression, media pluralism, multilingualism, equal access to art and to scientific and technological knowledge, including in digital form, and the possibility for all cultures to have access to the means of expression and dissemination are the guarantees of cultural diversity.

CULTURAL DIVERSITY AND CREATIVITY

Article 7 - Cultural heritage as the wellspring of creativity

Creation draws on the roots of cultural tradition, but flourishes in contact with other cultures. For this reason, heritage in all its forms must be preserved, enhanced and handed on to future generations as a record of human experience and aspirations, so as to foster creativity in all its diversity and to inspire genuine dialogue among cultures.

Article 8 - Cultural goods and services: commodities of a unique kind

In the face of present-day economic and technological change, opening up vast prospects for creation and innovation, particular attention must be paid to the diversity of the supply of creative work, to due recognition of the rights of authors and artists and to the specificity of cultural goods and services which, as vectors of identity, values and meaning, must not be treated as mere commodities or consumer goods.

Article 9 - Cultural policies as catalysts of creativity

While ensuring the free circulation of ideas and works, cultural policies must create conditions conducive to the production and dissemination of diversified cultural goods and services through cultural industries that have the means to assert themselves at the local and global level. It is for each State, with due regard to its international obligations, to define its cultural policy and to implement it through the means it considers fit, whether by operational support or appropriate regulations.

CULTURAL DIVERSITY AND INTERNATIONAL SOLIDARITY

Article 10 - Strengthening capacities for creation and dissemination worldwide

In the face of current imbalances in flows and exchanges of cultural goods and services at the global level, it is necessary to reinforce international cooperation and solidarity aimed at enabling all countries, especially developing countries and countries in transition, to establish cultural industries that are viable and competitive at national and international level.

Article 11 - Building partnerships between the public sector, the private sector and civil society

Market forces alone cannot guarantee the preservation and promotion of cultural diversity, which is the key to sustainable human development. From this perspective, the pre-eminence of public policy, in partnership with the private sector and civil society, must be reaffirmed.

Article 12 - The role of UNESCO

UNESCO, by virtue of its mandate and functions, has the responsibility to:

(a) Promote the incorporation of the principles set out in the present Declaration into the development strategies drawn up within the various intergovernmental bodies;

(b) Serve as a reference point and a forum where States, international governmental and non-governmental organizations, civil society and the private sector may join together in elaborating concepts, objectives and policies in favour of cultural diversity;

(c) Pursue its activities in standard-setting, awareness-raising and capacity-building in the areas related to the present Declaration within its fields of competence;

(d) Facilitate the implementation of the Action Plan, the main lines of which are appended to the present Declaration.

12. REFUGEE LAW

Convention relating to the Status of Refugees, 1951*

Adoption: 28 July 1951
Entry into force: 22 April 1954
Parties: 144 (Status as of 1 April 2007)

AFGHANISTAN 30 Aug 2005 a, ALBANIA 18 Aug 1992 a, ALGERIA 21 Feb 1963 d, ANGOLA 23 Jun 1981 a (*7, 8, 9, 13, 15, 17, 18, 24, 27), ANTIGUA AND BARBUDA 7 Sep 1995 a, ARGENTINA 15 Nov 1961 a, ARMENIA 6 Jul 1993 a, AUSTRALIA 22 Jan 1954 a, AUSTRIA 1 Nov 1954 (*17, 21), AZERBAIJAN 12 Feb 1993 a, BAHAMAS 15 Sep 1993 a (*general), BELARUS 23 Aug 2001 a, BELGIUM 22 Jul 1953 (*15, general), BELIZE 27 Jun 1990 a, BENIN 4 Apr 1962 d, BOLIVIA 9 Feb 1982 a, BONSIA AND HERZEGOVINA 1 Sep 1993 a, BOTSWANA 6 Jan 1969 a (*7, 12.1, 17, 26, 31, 32, 34), BRAZIL 16 Nov 1960, BULGARIA 12 May 1993 a, BURKINA FASO 18 Jun 1980 a, BURUNDI 19 Jul 1963 a, CAMBODIA 15 Oct 1992 a, CAMEROON 23 Oct 1961 d, CANADA 4 Jun 1969 a (*23, 24), CENTRAL AFRICAN REPUBLIC 4 Sep 1962 d, CHAD 19 Aug 1981 a, CHILE 28 Jan 1972 a (*17, 34), CHINA 24 Sep 1982 (*14, 16), COLOMBIA 10 Oct 1961, CONGO 15 Oct 1962 d, COSTA RICA 28 Mar 1978 a, COTE D'IVOIRE 8 Dec 1961 d, CROATIA 12 Oct 1992 d, CYPRUS 16 May 1963 d, CZECH REPUBLIC 11 May 1993 d, DEMOCRATIC REPUBLIC OF THE CONGO 19 Jul 1965 a, DENMARK 4 Dec 1952 (*17), DJIBOUTI 9 Aug 1977 d, DOMINICA 17 Feb 1994 a, DOMINICAN REPUBLIC 4 Jan 1978 a, ECUADOR 17 Aug 1955 a (*1, 15), EGYPT 22 May 1981 a (*12, 20, 22, 23, 24), EL SALVADOR 28 Apr 1983 a, EQUATORIAL GUINEA 7 Feb 1986 a, ESTONIA 10 Apr 1997 a (*23, 24 25, 28), ETHIOPIA 10 Nov 1969 a (*8, 9, 17, 22), FIJI 12 Jun 1972 d (*8, 9, 25), FINLAND 10 Oct 1968 a (*7, 8, 12, 24, 25, 28, general), FRANCE 23 Jun 1954 (*17, 29), GABON 27 Apr 1964 a, GAMBIA 7 Sep 1966 d, GEORGIA 9 Aug 1999 a (*territorial), GERMANY 1 Dec 1953, GHANA 18 Mar 1963 a, GREECE 5 Apr 1960 (*26), GUATEMALA 22 Sep 1983 a (*general), GUINEA 28 Dec 1965 d, GUINEA-BISSAU 11 Feb 1976 a, HAITI 25 Sep 1984 a, HOLY SEE 15 Mar 1956 (*general), HONDURAS 23 Mar 1992 a (*7, 17, 24, 26, 31, 34), HUNGARY 14 Mar 1989 a, ICELAND 30 Nov 1955 a, IRAN (ISLAMIC REPUBLIC OF) 28 Jul 1976 a (*17, 23, 24, 26, general), IRELAND 29 Nov 1956 a (*17, 25, 29, 32), ISRAEL 1 Oct 1954 (*8, 12, 28, 30), ITALY 15 Nov 1954, JAMAICA 30 Jul 1964 d (*8, 9, 17, 24, 25), JAPAN 3 Oct 1981 a, KAZAKHSTAN 15 Jan 1999 a, KENYA 16 May 1966 a, KYRGYZSTAN 8 Oct 1996 a, LATVIA 31 Jul 1997 a (*8, 17, 24, 26, 34, general), LESOTHO 14 May 1981 a, LIBERIA 15 Oct 1964 a, LIECHTENSTEIN 8 Mar 1957 (*17, 24), LITHUANIA 28 Apr 1997 a, LUXEMBOURG 23 Jul 1963 (*general), MADAGASCAR 18 Dec 1967 a (*7, 8, 9, 17), MALAWI 10 Dec 1987 a (*7, 13, 15, 17, 19, 22, 24, 26, 34), MALI 2 Feb 1973 d, MALTA 17 Jun 1971 a (*7, 8, 9, 11, 14, 17, 18, 23, 27, 28, 31, 32, 34), MAURITANIA 5 May 1987 a, MEXICO 7 Jun 2000 a (*17, 26, 31-33, general), MONACO 18 May 1954 a (*7, 15, 22-24), MONTENEGRO 10 Oct 2006 d, MOROCCO 7 Nov 1956 d, MOZAMBIQUE 16 Dec 1983 a (*13, 15, 17, 19, 26, 34), NAMIBIA 17 Feb 1995 a (*26), NETHERLANDS 3 May 1956 (*26, 40, general), NEW ZEALAND 30 Jun 1960 a (*24), NICARAGUA 28 Mar 1980 a, NIGER 25 Aug 1961 d, NIGERIA 23 Oct 1967 a, NORWAY 23 Mar 1953 (*17), PANAMA 2 Aug 1978 a, PAPUA NEW GUINEA 17 Jul 1986 a (*17, 21, 22, 26, 31, 32, 34), PARAGUAY 1 Apr 1970 a, PERU 21 Dec 1964 a, PHILIPPINES 22 Jul 1981 a, POLAND 27 Sep 1991 a, PORTUGAL

* Source: 189 U.N.T.S 150.

22 Dec 1960 a (*Brazilian nationals), REPUBLIC OF KOREA 3 Dec 1992 a (*7), REPUBLIC OF MOLDOVA 31 Jan 2002 a, ROMANIA 7 Aug 1991 a, RUSSIAN FEDERATION 2 Feb 1993 a, RWANDA 3 Jan 1980 a (*26), SAINT KITTS AND NEVIS 1 Feb 2002 a, SAINT VINCENT AND THE GRENADINES 3 Nov 1993 a, SAMOA 21 Sep 1988 a, SAO TOME AND PRINCIPE 1 Feb 1978 a, SENEGAL 2 May 1963 d, SEYCHELLES 23 Apr 1980 a, SIERRA LEONE 22 May 1981 a (*17, 29), SLOVAKIA 4 Feb 1993 d, SLOVENIA 6 Jul 1992 d, SOLOMON ISLANDS 28 Feb 1995 a, SOMALIA 10 Oct 1978 a (*general), SOUTH AFRICA 12 Jan 1996 a, SPAIN 14 Aug 1978 a (*8, 12, 26, general), SUDAN 22 Feb 1974 a (*26), SURINAME 29 Nov 1978 d, SWAZILAND 14 Feb 2000 a, SWEDEN 26 Oct 1954 (*12, 17, 24, 25, general), SWITZERLAND 21 Jan 1955, TAJIKISTAN 7 Dec 1993 a, THE FORMER YUGOSLAV REPUBLIC OF MACEDONIA 18 Jan 1994 d, TIMOR LESTE 7 May 2003 a, TOGO 27 Feb 1962 d, TRINIDAD AND TOBAGO 10 Nov 2000 a, TUNISIA 24 Oct 1957 d, TURKEY 30 Mar 1962 (*1, general), TURKMENISTAN 2 Mar 1998 a, TUVALU 7 Mar 1986 d, UGANDA 27 Sep 1976 a (*7, 8, 9, 13, 15-17, 25, 32), UNITED KINGDOM OF GREAT BRITAIN AND NORTHERN IRELAND 11 Mar 1954 (*8, 9, 17, 24, 25), UNITED REPUBLIC OF TANZANIA 12 May 1964 a, URUGUAY 22 Sep 1970 a, YEMEN 18 Jan 1980 a, YUGOSLAVIA 12 Mar 2001 d, ZAMBIA 24 Sep 1969 d (*17, 22, 26, 28), ZIMBABWE 25 Aug 1981 a (*17, 22-24, 26, territorial).

Preamble

The High Contracting Parties,

Considering that the Charter of the United Nations and the Universal Declaration of Human Rights approved on 10 December 1948 by the General Assembly have affirmed the principle that human beings shall enjoy fundamental rights and freedoms without discrimination,

Considering that the United Nations has, on various occasions, manifested its profound concern for refugees and endeavoured to assure refugees the widest possible exercise of these fundamental rights and freedoms,

Considering that it is desirable to revise and consolidate previous international agreements relating to the status of refugees and to extend the scope of and the protection accorded by such instruments by means of a new agreement,

Considering that the grant of asylum may place unduly heavy burdens on certain countries, and that a satisfactory solution of a problem of which the United Nations has recognized the international scope and nature cannot therefore be achieved without international co-operation,

Expressing the wish that all States, recognizing the social and humanitarian nature of the problem of refugees, will do everything within their power to prevent this problem from becoming a cause of tension between States,

Noting that the United Nations High Commissioner for Refugees is charged with the task of supervising international conventions providing for the protection of refugees, and recognizing that the effective co-ordination of measures taken to deal with this problem will depend upon the co-operation of States with the High Commissioner,

Have agreed as follows:

CHAPTER I

GENERAL PROVISIONS

Article 1. - Definition of the term "refugee"

A. For the purposes of the present Convention, the term "refugee" shall apply to any person who:

(1) Has been considered a refugee under the Arrangements of 12 May 1926 and 30 June 1928 or under the Conventions of 28 October 1933 and 10 February 1938, the Protocol of 14 September 1939 or the Constitution of the International Refugee Organization;

Decisions of non-eligibility taken by the International Refugee Organization during the period of its activities shall not prevent the status of refugee being accorded to persons who fulfil the conditions of paragraph 2 of this section;

(2) As a result of events occurring before 1 January 1951 and owing to well-founded fear of being persecuted for reasons of race, religion, nationality, membership of a particular social group or political opinion, is outside the country of his nationality and is unable or, owing to such fear, is unwilling to avail himself of the protection of that country; or who, not having a nationality and being outside the country of his former habitual residence as a result of such events, is unable or, owing to such fear, is unwilling to return to it.

In the case of a person who has more than one nationality, the term "the country of his nationality" shall mean each of the countries of which he is a national, and a person shall not be deemed to be lacking the protection of the country of his nationality if, without any valid reason based on well-founded fear, he has not availed himself of the protection of one of the countries of which he is a national.

B. (1) For the purposes of this Convention, the words "events occurring before 1 January 1951" in article 1, section A, shall be understood to mean either (a) "events occurring in Europe before 1 January 1951"; or (b) "events occurring in Europe or elsewhere before 1 January 1951"; and each Contracting State shall make a declaration at the time of signature, ratification or accession, specifying which of these meanings it applies for the purpose of its obligations under this Convention.

(2) Any Contracting State which has adopted alternative (a) may at any time extend its obligations by adopting alternative (b) by means of a notification addressed to the Secretary-General of the United Nations.

C. This Convention shall cease to apply to any person falling under the terms of section A if:

(1) He has voluntarily re-availed himself of the protection of the country of his nationality; or

(2) Having lost his nationality, he has voluntarily reacquired it; or

(3) He has acquired a new nationality, and enjoys the protection of the country of his new nationality; or

(4) He has voluntarily re-established himself in the country which he left or outside which he remained owing to fear of persecution; or

(5) He can no longer, because the circumstances in connection with which he has been recognized as a refugee have ceased to exist, continue to refuse to avail himself of the protection of the country of his nationality;

Provided that this paragraph shall not apply to a refugee falling under section A (1) of this article who is able to invoke compelling reasons arising out of previous persecution for refusing to avail himself of the protection of the country of nationality;

(6) Being a person who has no nationality he is, because the circumstances in connection with which he has been recognized as a refugee have ceased to exist, able to return to the country of his former habitual residence;

Provided that this paragraph shall not apply to a refugee falling under section A (1) of this article who is able to invoke compelling reasons arising out of previous persecution for refusing to return to the country of his former habitual residence.

D. This Convention shall not apply to persons who are at present receiving from organs or agencies of the United Nations other than the United Nations High Commissioner for Refugees protection or assistance.

When such protection or assistance has ceased for any reason, without the position of such persons being definitively settled in accordance with the relevant resolutions adopted by the General Assembly of the United Nations, these persons shall ipso facto be entitled to the benefits of this Convention.

E. This Convention shall not apply to a person who is recognized by the competent authorities of the country in which he has taken residence as having the rights and obligations which are attached to the possession of the nationality of that country.

F. The provisions of this Convention shall not apply to any person with respect to whom there are serious reasons for considering that:

(a) He has committed a crime against peace, a war crime, or a crime against humanity, as defined in the international instruments drawn up to make provision in respect of such crimes;

(b) He has committed a serious non-political crime outside the country of refuge prior to his admission to that country as a refugee;

(c) He has been guilty of acts contrary to the purposes and principles of the United Nations.

Article 2. - General obligations

Every refugee has duties to the country in which he finds himself, which require in particular that he conform to its laws and regulations as well as to measures taken for the maintenance of public order.

Article 3. - Non-discrimination

The Contracting States shall apply the provisions of this Convention to refugees without discrimination as to race, religion or country of origin.

Article 4. - Religion

The Contracting States shall accord to refugees within their territories treatment at least as favourable as that accorded to their nationals with respect to freedom to practise their religion and freedom as regards the religious education of their children.

Article 5. - Rights granted apart from this Convention

Nothing in this Convention shall be deemed to impair any rights and benefits granted by a Contracting State to refugees apart from this Convention.

Article 6. - The term "in the same circumstances"

For the purposes of this Convention, the term "in the same circumstances" implies that any requirements (including requirements as to length and conditions of sojourn or residence) which the particular individual would have to fulfil for the enjoyment of the right in question, if he were not a refugee, must be fulfilled by him, with the exception of requirements which by their nature a refugee is incapable of fulfilling.

Article 7. - Exemption from reciprocity

1. Except where this Convention contains more favourable provisions, a Contracting State shall accord to refugees the same treatment as is accorded to aliens generally.

2. After a period of three years' residence, all refugees shall enjoy exemption from legislative reciprocity in the territory of the Contracting States.

3. Each Contracting State shall continue to accord to refugees the rights and benefits to which they were already entitled, in the absence of reciprocity, at the date of entry into force of this Convention for that State.

4. The Contracting States shall consider favourably the possibility of according to refugees, in the absence of reciprocity, rights and benefits beyond those to which they are entitled according to paragraphs 2 and 3, and to extending exemption from reciprocity to refugees who do not fulfil the conditions provided for in paragraphs 2 and 3.

5. The provisions of paragraphs 2 and 3 apply both to the rights and benefits referred to in articles 13, 18, 19, 21 and 22 of this Convention and to rights and benefits for which this Convention does not provide.

Article 8. - Exemption from exceptional measures

With regard to exceptional measures which may be taken against the person, property or interests of nationals of a foreign State, the Contracting States shall not apply such measures to a refugee who is formally a national of the said State solely on account of such nationality. Contracting States which, under their legislation, are prevented from applying the general principle expressed in this article, shall, in appropriate cases, grant exemptions in favour of such refugees.

Article 9. - Provisional measures

Nothing in this Convention shall prevent a Contracting State, in time of war or other grave and exceptional circumstances, from taking provisionally measures which it considers to be essential to the national security in the case of a particular person, pending a determination by the Contracting State that that person is in fact a refugee and that the continuance of such measures is necessary in his case in the interests of national security.

Article 10. - Continuity of residence

1. Where a refugee has been forcibly displaced during the Second World War and removed to the territory of a Contracting State, and is resident there, the period of such enforced sojourn shall be considered to have been lawful residence within that territory.

2. Where a refugee has been forcibly displaced during the Second World War from the territory of a Contracting State and has, prior to the date of entry into force of this Convention, returned there for the purpose of taking up residence, the period of residence before and after such enforced displacement shall be regarded as one uninterrupted period for any purposes for which uninterrupted residence is required.

Article 11. - Refugee seamen

In the case of refugees regularly serving as crew members on board a ship flying the flag of a Contracting State, that State shall give sympathetic consideration to their establishment on its territory and the issue of travel documents to them or their temporary admission to its territory particularly with a view to facilitating their establishment in another country.

CHAPTER II

JURIDICAL STATUS

Article 12. - Personal status

1. The personal status of a refugee shall be governed by the law of the country of his domicile or, if he has no domicile, by the law of the country of his residence.

2. Rights previously acquired by a refugee and dependent on personal status, more particularly rights attaching to marriage, shall be respected by a Contracting State, subject to compliance, if this be necessary, with the formalities required by the law of that State, provided that the right in question is one which would have been recognized by the law of that State had he not become a refugee.

Article 13. - Movable and immovable property

The Contracting States shall accord to a refugee treatment as favourable as possible and, in any event, not less favourable than that accorded to aliens generally in the same circumstances, as regards the acquisition of movable and immovable property and other rights pertaining thereto, and to leases and other contracts relating to movable and immovable property.

Article 14. - Artistic rights and industrial property

In respect of the protection of industrial property, such as inventions, designs or models, trade marks, trade names, and of rights in literary, artistic and scientific works, a refugee shall be accorded in the country in which he has his habitual residence the same protection as is accorded to nationals of that country. In the territory of any other Contracting States, he shall be accorded the same protection as is accorded in that territory to nationals of the country in which he has his habitual residence.

Article 15. - Right of association

As regards non-political and non-profit-making associations and trade unions the Contracting States shall accord to refugees lawfully staying in their territory the most favourable treatment accorded to nationals of a foreign country, in the same circumstances.

Article 16. - Access to courts

1. A refugee shall have free access to the courts of law on the territory of all Contracting States.

2. A refugee shall enjoy in the Contracting State in which he has his habitual residence the same treatment as a national in matters pertaining to access to the courts, including legal assistance and exemption from cautio judicatum solvi.

3. A refugee shall be accorded in the matters referred to in paragraph 2 in countries other than that in which he has his habitual residence the treatment granted to a national of the country of his habitual residence.

CHAPTER III

GAINFUL EMPLOYMENT

Article 17. - Wage-earning employment

1. The Contracting States shall accord to refugees lawfully staying in their territory the most favourable treatment accorded to nationals of a foreign country in the same circumstances, as regards the right to engage in wage-earning employment.

2. In any case, restrictive measures imposed on aliens or the employment of aliens for the protection of the national labour market shall not be applied to a refugee who was already exempt from them at the date of entry into force of this Convention for the Contracting State concerned, or who fulfils one of the following conditions:

(a) He has completed three years' residence in the country;

(b) He has a spouse possessing the nationality of the country of residence. A refugee may not invoke the benefit of this provision if he has abandoned his spouse;

(c) He has one or more children possessing the nationality of the country of residence.

3. The Contracting States shall give sympathetic consideration to assimilating the rights of all refugees with regard to wage-earning employment to those of nationals, and in particular of those refugees who have entered their territory pursuant to programmes of labour recruitment or under immigration schemes.

Article 18. - Self-employment

The Contracting States shall accord to a refugee lawfully in their territory treatment as favourable as possible and, in any event, not less favourable than that accorded to aliens generally in the same circumstances, as regards the right to engage on his own account in agriculture, industry, handicrafts and commerce and to establish commercial and industrial companies.

Article 19. - Liberal professions

1. Each Contracting State shall accord to refugees lawfully staying in their territory who hold diplomas recognized by the competent authorities of that State, and who are desirous of practising a liberal profession, treatment as favourable as possible and, in any event, not less favourable than that accorded to aliens generally in the same circumstances.

2. The Contracting States shall use their best endeavours consistently with their laws and constitutions to secure the settlement of such refugees in the territories, other than the metropolitan territory, for whose international relations they are responsible.

CHAPTER IV

WELFARE

Article 20. - Rationing

Where a rationing system exists, which applies to the population at large and regulates the general distribution of products in short supply, refugees shall be accorded the same treatment as nationals.

Article 21. - Housing

As regards housing, the Contracting States, in so far as the matter is regulated by laws or regulations or is subject to the control of public authorities, shall accord to refugees lawfully staying in their territory treatment as favourable as possible and, in any event, not less favourable than that accorded to aliens generally in the same circumstances.

Article 22. - Public education

1. The Contracting States shall accord to refugees the same treatment as is accorded to nationals with respect to elementary education.

2. The Contracting States shall accord to refugees treatment as favourable as possible, and, in any event, not less favourable than that accorded to aliens generally in the same circumstances, with respect to education other than elementary education and, in particular, as regards access to studies, the recognition of foreign school certificates, diplomas and degrees, the remission of fees and charges and the award of scholarships.

Article 23. - Public relief

The Contracting States shall accord to refugees lawfully staying in their territory the same treatment with respect to public relief and assistance as is accorded to their nationals.

Article 24. - Labour legislation and social security

1. The Contracting States shall accord to refugees lawfully staying in their territory the same treatment as is accorded to nationals in respect of the following matters;

(a) In so far as such matters are governed by laws or regulations or are subject to the control of administrative authorities: remuneration, including family allowances where these form part of remuneration, hours of work, overtime arrangements, holidays with pay, restrictions on home work, minimum age of employment, apprenticeship and training, women's work and the work of young persons, and the enjoyment of the benefits of collective bargaining;

(b) Social security (legal provisions in respect of employment injury, occupational diseases, maternity, sickness, disability, old age, death, unemployment, family responsibilities and any other contingency which, according to national laws or regulations, is covered by a social security scheme), subject to the following limitations:

(i) There may be appropriate arrangements for the maintenance of acquired rights and rights in course of acquisition;

(ii) National laws or regulations of the country of residence may prescribe special arrangements concerning benefits or portions of benefits which are payable wholly out of public funds, and concerning allowances paid to persons who do not fulfil the contribution conditions prescribed for the award of a normal pension.

2. The right to compensation for the death of a refugee resulting from employment injury or from occupational disease shall not be affected by the fact that the residence of the beneficiary is outside the territory of the Contracting State.

3. The Contracting States shall extend to refugees the benefits of agreements concluded between them, or which may be concluded between them in the future, concerning the maintenance of acquired rights and rights in the process of acquisition in regard to social security, subject only to the conditions which apply to nationals of the States signatory to the agreements in question.

4. The Contracting States will give sympathetic consideration to extending to refugees so far as possible the benefits of similar agreements which may at any time be in force between such Contracting States and non-contracting States.

CHAPTER V

ADMINISTRATIVE MEASURES

Article 25. - Administrative assistance

1. When the exercise of a right by a refugee would normally require the assistance of authorities of a foreign country to whom he cannot have recourse, the Contracting States in whose territory he is residing shall arrange that such assistance be afforded to him by their own authorities or by an international authority.

2. The authority or authorities mentioned in paragraph 1 shall deliver or cause to be delivered under their supervision to refugees such documents or certifications as would normally be delivered to aliens by or through their national authorities.

3. Documents or certifications so delivered shall stand in the stead of the official instruments delivered to aliens by or through their national authorities, and shall be given credence in the absence of proof to the contrary.

4. Subject to such exceptional treatment as may be granted to indigent persons, fees may be charged for the services mentioned herein, but such fees shall be moderate and commensurate with those charged to nationals for similar services.

5. The provisions of this article shall be without prejudice to articles 27 and 28.

Article 26. - Freedom of movement

Each Contracting State shall accord to refugees lawfully in its territory the right to choose their place of residence and to move freely within its territory subject to any regulations applicable to aliens generally in the same circumstances.

Article 27. - Identity papers

The Contracting States shall issue identity papers to any refugee in their territory who does not possess a valid travel document.

Article 28. - Travel documents

1. The Contracting States shall issue to refugees lawfully staying in their territory travel documents for the purpose of travel outside their territory, unless compelling reasons of national security or public order otherwise require, and the provisions of the Schedule to this Convention shall apply with respect to such documents. The Contracting States may issue such a travel document to any other refugee in their territory; they shall in particular give sympathetic consideration to the issue of such a travel document to refugees in their territory who are unable to obtain a travel document from the country of their lawful residence.

2. Travel documents issued to refugees under previous international agreements by Parties thereto shall be recognized and treated by the Contracting States in the same way as if they had been issued pursuant to this article.

Article 29. - Fiscal charges

1. The Contracting States shall not impose upon refugees duties, charges or taxes, of any description whatsoever, other or higher than those which are or may be levied on their nationals in similar situations.

2. Nothing in the above paragraph shall prevent the application to refugees of the laws and regulations concerning charges in respect of the issue to aliens of administrative documents including identity papers.

Article 30. - Transfer of assets

1. A Contracting State shall, in conformity with its laws and regulations, permit refugees to transfer assets which they have brought into its territory, to another country where they have been admitted for the purposes of resettlement.

2. A Contracting State shall give sympathetic consideration to the application of refugees for permission to transfer assets wherever they may be and which are necessary for their resettlement in another country to which they have been admitted.

Article 31. - Refugees unlawfully in the country of refuge

1. The Contracting States shall not impose penalties, on account of their illegal entry or presence, on refugees who, coming directly from a territory where their life or freedom was threatened in the sense of article 1, enter or are present in their territory without authorization, provided they present themselves without delay to the authorities and show good cause for their illegal entry or presence.

2. The Contracting States shall not apply to the movements of such refugees restrictions other than those which are necessary and such restrictions shall only be applied until their status in the country is regularized or they obtain admission into another country. The Contracting States shall allow such refugees a reasonable period and all the necessary facilities to obtain admission into another country.

Article 32. - Expulsion

1. The Contracting States shall not expel a refugee lawfully in their territory save on grounds of national security or public order.

2. The expulsion of such a refugee shall be only in pursuance of a decision reached in accordance with due process of law. Except where compelling reasons of national security otherwise require, the refugee shall be allowed to submit evidence to clear himself, and to appeal to and be represented for the purpose before competent authority or a person or persons specially designated by the competent authority.

3. The Contracting States shall allow such a refugee a reasonable period within which to seek legal admission into another country. The Contracting States reserve the right to apply during that period such internal measures as they may deem necessary.

Article 33. - Prohibition of expulsion or return ("refoulement")

1. No Contracting State shall expel or return (" refouler ") a refugee in any manner whatsoever to the frontiers of territories where his life or freedom would be threatened on account of his race, religion, nationality, membership of a particular social group or political opinion.

2. The benefit of the present provision may not, however, be claimed by a refugee whom there are reasonable grounds for regarding as a danger to the security of the country in which he is,

or who, having been convicted by a final judgement of a particularly serious crime, constitutes a danger to the community of that country.

Article 34. - Naturalization

The Contracting States shall as far as possible facilitate the assimilation and naturalization of refugees. They shall in particular make every effort to expedite naturalization proceedings and to reduce as far as possible the charges and costs of such proceedings.

CHAPTER VI

EXECUTORY AND TRANSITORY PROVISIONS

Article 35. - Co-operation of the national authorities with the United Nations

1. The Contracting States undertake to co-operate with the Office of the United Nations High Commissioner for Refugees, or any other agency of the United Nations which may succeed it, in the exercise of its functions, and shall in particular facilitate its duty of supervising the application of the provisions of this Convention.

2. In order to enable the Office of the High Commissioner or any other agency of the United Nations which may succeed it, to make reports to the competent organs of the United Nations, the Contracting States undertake to provide them in the appropriate form with information and statistical data requested concerning:

(a) The condition of refugees,

(b) The implementation of this Convention, and

(c) Laws, regulations and decrees which are, or may hereafter be, in force relating to refugees.

Article 36. - Information on national legislation

The Contracting States shall communicate to the Secretary-General of the United Nations the laws and regulations which they may adopt to ensure the application of this Convention.

Article 37. - Relation to previous conventions

Without prejudice to article 28, paragraph 2, of this Convention, this Convention replaces, as between Parties to it, the Arrangements of 5 July 1922, 31 May 1924, 12 May 1926, 30 June 1928 and 30 July 1935, the Conventions of 28 October 1933 and 10 February 1938, the Protocol of 14 September 1939 and the Agreement of 15 October 1946.

CHAPTER VII

FINAL CLAUSES

Article 38. - Settlement of disputes

Any dispute between Parties to this Convention relating to its interpretation or application, which cannot be settled by other means, shall be referred to the International Court of Justice at the request of any one of the parties to the dispute.

Article 39. - Signature, ratification and accession

1. This Convention shall be opened for signature at Geneva on 28 July 1951 and shall thereafter be deposited with the Secretary-General of the United Nations. It shall be open for signature at the European Office of the United Nations from 28 July to 31 August 1951 and shall be re-opened for signature at the Headquarters of the United Nations from 17 September 1951 to 31 December 1952.

2. This Convention shall be open for signature on behalf of all States Members of the United Nations, and also on behalf of any other State invited to attend the Conference of Plenipotentiaries on the Status of Refugees and Stateless Persons or to which an invitation to sign will have been addressed by the General Assembly. It shall be ratified and the instruments of ratification shall be deposited with the Secretary-General of the United Nations.

3. This Convention shall be open from 28 July 1951 for accession by the States referred to in paragraph 2 of this article. Accession shall be effected by the deposit of an instrument of accession with the Secretary-General of the United Nations.

Article 40. - Territorial application clause

1. Any State may, at the time of signature, ratification or accession, declare that this Convention shall extend to all or any of the territories for the international relations of which it is responsible. Such a declaration shall take effect when the Convention enters into force for the State concerned.

2. At any time thereafter any such extension shall be made by notification addressed to the Secretary-General of the United Nations and shall take effect as from the ninetieth day after the day of receipt by the Secretary-General of the United Nations of this notification, or as from the date of entry into force of the Convention for the State concerned, whichever is the later.

3. With respect to those territories to which this Convention is not extended at the time of signature, ratification or accession, each State concerned shall consider the possibility of taking the necessary steps in order to extend the application of this Convention to such territories, subject, where necessary for constitutional reasons, to the consent of the Governments of such territories.

Article 41. - Federal clause

In the case of a Federal or non-unitary State, the following provisions shall apply:

(a) With respect to those articles of this Convention that come within the legislative jurisdiction of the federal legislative authority, the obligations of the Federal Government shall to this extent be the same as those of parties which are not Federal States;

(b) With respect to those articles of this Convention that come within the legislative jurisdiction of constituent States, provinces or cantons which are not, under the constitutional system of the Federation, bound to take legislative action, the Federal Government shall bring such articles with a favourable recommendation to the notice of the appropriate authorities of States, provinces or cantons at the earliest possible moment;

(c) A Federal State Party to this Convention shall, at the request of any other Contracting State transmitted through the Secretary-General of the United Nations, supply a statement of the law and practice of the Federation and its constituent units in regard to any particular provision of the Convention showing the extent to which effect has been given to that provision by legislative or other action.

Article 42. - Reservations

1. At the time of signature, ratification or accession, any State may make reservations to articles of the Convention other than to articles 1, 3, 4, 16 (1), 33, 36-46 inclusive.

2. Any State making a reservation in accordance with paragraph 1 of this article may at any time withdraw the reservation by a communication to that effect addressed to the Secretary-General of the United Nations.

Article 43. - Entry into force

1. This Convention shall come into force on the ninetieth day following the day of deposit of the sixth instrument of ratification or accession.

2. For each State ratifying or acceding to the Convention after the deposit of the sixth instrument of ratification or accession, the Convention shall enter into force on the ninetieth day following the date of deposit by such State of its instrument of ratification or accession.

Article 44. - Denunciation

1. Any Contracting State may denounce this Convention at any time by a notification addressed to the Secretary-General of the United Nations.

2. Such denunciation shall take effect for the Contracting State concerned one year from the date upon which it is received by the Secretary-General of the United Nations.

3. Any State which has made a declaration or notification under article 40 may, at any time thereafter, by a notification to the Secretary-General of the United Nations, declare that the Convention shall cease to extend to such territory one year after the date of receipt of the notification by the Secretary-General.

Article 45. - Revision

1. Any Contracting State may request revision of this Convention at any time by a notification addressed to the Secretary-General of the United Nations.

2. The General Assembly of the United Nations shall recommend the steps, if any, to be taken in respect of such request.

Article 46. - Notifications by the Secretary-General of the United Nations

The Secretary-General of the United Nations shall inform all Members of the United Nations and non-member States referred to in article 39:

(a) Of declarations and notifications in accordance with section B of article 1;

(b) Of signatures, ratifications and accessions in accordance with article 39;

(c) Of declarations and notifications in accordance with article 40;

(d) Of reservations and withdrawals in accordance with article 42;

(e) Of the date on which this Convention will come into force in accordance with article 43;

(f) Of denunciations and notifications in accordance with article 44;

(g) Of requests for revision in accordance with article 45.

In faith whereof the undersigned, duly authorized, have signed this Convention on behalf of their respective Governments.

Done at Geneva, this twenty-eighth day of July, one thousand nine hundred and fifty-one, in a single copy, of which the English and French texts are equally authentic and which shall remain deposited in the archives of the United Nations, and certified true copies of which shall be delivered to all Members of the United Nations and to the non-member States referred to in article 39.

Agreement relating to Refugee Seamen, 1957*

Adoption: 23 November 1957
Entry into force: 27 December 1961
Parties: 21 (Status as of 1 April 2007)

AUSTRALIA 18 Apr 1973, BELGIUM 16 May 1959, BOSNIA AND HERZEGOVINA 23 Aug 1993, CANADA 30 May 1969, DENMARK 2 Sep 1959, FIJI 20 Mar 1972 (termination 20 Mar 1973), FRANCE 20 Jun 1958, GERMANY 28 Sep 1961, IRELAND 21 Apr 1964, ITALY 31 Oct 1966, MAURITIUS 24 Aug 1970, MONACO 11 Apr 1960, MOROCCO 20 May 1959, NETHERLANDS 27 Aug 1959, NEW ZEALAND 21 Oct 1974, NORWAY 28 May 1959, PORTUGAL 3 Mar 1965, SLOVENIA 14 Jun 1993, SWITZERLAND 12 Dec 1962, UNITED KINGDOM OF GREAT BRITAIN AND NORTHERN IRELAND, YUGOSLAVIA 4 Dec 1963.

PREAMBLE

The Governments of the Kingdom of Belgium, the Kingdom of Denmark, the French Republic, the Federal Republic of Germany, the United Kingdom of Great Britain and Northern Ireland, the Kingdom of the Netherlands, the Kingdom of Norway and the Kingdom of Sweden,

BEING Governments of States Parties to the Convention of the 28th of July 1951 relating to the Status of Refugees,

DESIROUS of making further progress towards a solution of the problem of refugee seamen in the spirit of Article 11 and of maintaining co-operation with the United Nations High Commissioner for Refugees in the fulfillment of his functions, especially having regard to Article 35 of the above-mentioned Convention,

HAVE AGREED as follows:

CHAPTER I

Article 1

For the purpose of this Agreement:

(a) the term "Convention" shall apply to the Convention relating to the Status of Refugees of 28 July 1951;

(b) the term "refugee seaman" shall apply to any person who, being a refugee according to the definition in Article 1 of the Convention and the declaration or notification made by the Contracting State concerned in accordance with Section B of that Article, is serving as a seafarer in any capacity on a mercantile ship, or habitually earns his living as a seafarer on such a ship.

CHAPTER II

Article 2

A refugee seaman who is not lawfully staying in the territory of any State and who is not entitled to admission for the purpose of so staying to the territory of any State, other than a State where he has well-founded fear of being persecuted for reasons of race, religion,

* Source: 506 U.N.T.S. 125.

nationality, membership of a particular social group or political opinion, shall become entitled to be regarded, for the purpose of Article 28 of the Convention, as lawfully staying in the territory:

(a) of the Contracting Party under whose flag he, while a refugee, has served as a seafarer for a total of 600 days within the three years preceding the application of this Agreement to his case on ships calling at least twice a year at ports in that territory, provided that for the purposes of this paragraph no account shall be taken of any service performed while or before he had a residence established in the territory of another State;

or, if there is no such Contracting Party,

(b) of the Contracting Party where he, while a refugee, has had his last lawful residence in the three years preceding the application of this Agreement to his case, provided that he has not, in the meantime, had a residence established in the territory of another State.

Article 3

A refugee seaman who on the date when this Agreement enters into force:

(i) is not lawfully staying in the territory of any State and is not entitled to admission for the purpose of so staying to the territory of any State, other than a State where he has well-founded fear of being persecuted for reasons of race, religion, nationality, membership of a particular social group or political opinion, and

(ii) is not in accordance with Article 2 of this Agreement regarded as lawfully staying in the territory of a Contracting Party

shall become entitled to be regarded, for the purpose of Article 28 of the Convention, as lawfully staying in the territory:

(a) of the Contracting Party which after 31 December 1945 and before the entry into force of this Agreement last issued to, or extended or renewed for him, while a refugee, a travel document valid for return to that territory whether or not that document is still in force;

or, if there is no such Contracting Party,

(b) of the Contracting Party where he, while a refugee, after 31 December 1945 and before the entry into force of this Agreement was last lawfully staying;

or, if there is no such Contracting Party,

(c) of the Contracting Party under whose flag he, while a refugee, after 31 December 1945 and before the entry into force of this Agreement last has served as a seafarer for a total of 600 days within any period of three years on ships calling at least twice a year at ports in that territory.

Article 4

Unless otherwise decided by the Contracting Party concerned, a refugee seaman will cease to be regarded as lawfully staying in the territory of a Contracting Party when he, after the date upon which he, in accordance with Article 2 or 3 of this Agreement, last became entitled to be so regarded:

(a) has established his residence in the territory of another State, or

(b) within any period of six years following that date, has been serving a total of 1350 days on ships flying the flag of one other State, or

(c) within any period of three years following that date, neither has served at least a total of 30 days as a seafarer on ships flying the flag of that Contracting Party and calling at least twice a year at ports in its territory nor has stayed for at least a total of 10 days in the territory of that Party.

Article 5

For the purpose of improving the position of the greatest possible number of refugee seamen, a Contracting Party shall give sympathetic consideration to extending the benefits of this Agreement to refugee seamen who, according to its provisions, do not qualify for those benefits.

CHAPTER III

Article 6

A Contracting Party shall grant to a refugee seaman in possession of a travel document issued by another Contracting Party and valid for return to the territory of that Contracting Party the same treatment as regards admission to its territory in pursuance of a previous arrangement to serve on a ship, or for shore-leave, as is granted to seafarers who are nationals of the last mentioned Party, or at least treatment not less favourable than is granted to alien seafarers generally.

Article 7

A Contracting Party shall give sympathetic consideration to a request for temporary admission to its territory by a refugee seaman who holds a travel document valid for return to the territory of another Contracting Party with a view to facilitating his establishment in another State or for other good reasons.

Article 8

A Contracting Party shall endeavour to ensure that any refugee seaman who serves under its flag and cannot obtain a valid travel document is provided with identity papers.

Article 9

No refugee seaman shall be forced, as far as it is in the power of the Contracting Parties, to stay on board a ship if his physical or mental health would thereby be seriously endangered.

Article 10

No refugee seaman shall be forced, as far as it is in the power of the Contracting Parties, to stay on board a ship which is bound for a port, or is due to sail through waters, where he has well-founded fear of persecution for reasons of race, religion, nationality, membership of a particular social group or political opinion.

Article 11

The Contracting Party in the territory of which a refugee seaman is lawfully staying or, in accordance with this Agreement, is for the purpose of Article 28 of the Convention regarded as lawfully staying, shall admit him to its territory if so requested by the Contracting Party in whose territory that seaman finds himself.

Article 12

Nothing in this Agreement shall be deemed to impair any rights or benefits granted by a Contracting Party to refugee seamen apart from this Agreement.

Article 13

(1) A Contracting Party may, for compelling reasons of national security or public order, consider itself released from the obligations incumbent on it under this Agreement with regard to a refugee seaman. The refugee seaman in question shall be allowed such period as may be reasonable in the circumstances to submit to the competent authority evidence to clear himself, except where there are reasonable grounds for regarding the refugee seaman in question as a danger to the security of the country where he is.

(2) A decision made in accordance with paragraph 1 of this Article does not, however, release the Contracting Party in question from its obligations under Article 11 of this Agreement with respect to a refugee seaman to whom it has issued a travel document, unless the request for admission to its territory is presented to that Party by another Contracting Party more than 120 days after the expiration of that travel document.

CHAPTER IV

Article 14

Any dispute between the Contracting Parties relating to the interpretation or application of this Agreement, which cannot be settled by other means, shall be referred to the International Court of Justice at the request of any one of the parties to the dispute.

Article 15

This Agreement shall be subject to ratification. Instruments of ratification shall be deposited with the Government of the Kingdom of the Netherlands.

Article 16

This Agreement shall come into force on the 90th day following the day of deposit of the eighth instrument of ratification.

Article 17

(1) Any Government which undertakes obligations with respect to refugee seamen under Article 28 of the Convention or obligations corresponding thereto may accede to this Agreement.

(2) Instruments of accession shall be deposited with the Government of the Kingdom of the Netherlands.

(3) This Agreement shall come into force with respect to each acceding Government on the 90th day following the day upon which its instrument of accession was deposited, but not before the date of entry into force as defined in Article 16.

Article 18

(1) Any Government may, at the time of ratification or accession or at any time thereafter, declare that this Agreement shall extend to any territory or territories for the international relations of which it is responsible, provided that it has undertaken in relation thereto such obligations as are mentioned in paragraph (1) of Article 17.

(2) Such extension shall be made by a notification addressed to the Government of the Kingdom of the Netherlands.

(3) The extension shall take effect on the 90th day following the day upon which the notification was received by the Government of the Kingdom of the Netherlands, but not before the date of entry into force as defined in Article 16.

Article 19

(1) A Contracting Party may denounce this Agreement at any time by a notification addressed to the Government of the Kingdom of the Netherlands.

(2) The denunciation shall take effect one year from the date upon which the notification was received by the Government of the Kingdom of the Netherlands, provided that where the Agreement has been denounced by a Contracting Party, any other Contracting Party after consulting the remaining Parties, may denounce the Agreement with effect from the same date, so however, that not less than six months notice is given.

Article 20

(1) A Contracting Party which has made a notification under Article 18 may, at any time thereafter, by a notification addressed to the Government of the Kingdom of the Netherlands, declare that the Agreement shall cease to apply to the territory or territories specified in the notification.

(2) The Agreement shall cease to apply to the territory concerned one year from the date upon which the notification was received by the Government of the Kingdom of the Netherlands.

Article 21

The Government of the Kingdom of the Netherlands shall inform the Governments mentioned in the Preamble and all acceding Governments of deposits and notifications made in accordance with Articles 15, 17, 18, 19 and 20.

IN WITNESS WHEREOF, the undersigned, duly authorized to that effect, have signed this Agreement.

DONE at The Hague, this twenty-third day of November 1957, in the English and French languages, both texts being equally authoritative, in a single copy which shall remain deposited in the archives of the Government of the Kingdom of the Netherlands, which shall transmit certified true copies thereof to the Governments mentioned in the Preamble and all acceding Governments.

[Signatures not reproduced here.]

Protocol relating to the Status of Refugees, 1967*

Adoption: 31 January 1967
Entry into force: 4 October 1967
Parties: 144 (Status as of 1 April 2007)

AFGHANISTAN 30 Aug 2005 a, ALBANIA 18 Aug 1992 a, ALGERIA 8 Nov 1967 a, ANGOLA 23 Jun 1981 a (*4), ANTIGUA AND BARBUDA 7 Sep 1995 a, ARGENTINA 6 Dec 1967 a, ARMENIA 6 Jul 1993 a, AUSTRALIA 13 Dec 1973 a, AUSTRIA 5 Sep 1973 a, AZERBAIJAN 12 Feb 1993 a, BAHAMAS 15 Sep 1993 a, BELARUS 23 Aug 2001 a, BELGIUM 8 Apr 1969 a, BELIZE 27 Jun 1990 a, BENIN 6 Jul 1970 a, BOLIVIA 9 Feb 1982 a, BONSIA AND HERZEGOVINA 1 Sep 1993 d, BOTSWANA 6 Jan 1969 a (*4), BRAZIL 7 Apr 1972 a, BULGARIA 12 May 1993 a, BURKINA FASO 18 Jun 1980 a, BURUNDI 15 Mar 1971 a (*22, 17, 26, general), CAMBODIA 15 Oct 1992 a, CAMEROON Sep 1967 a, CANDA 4 Jun 1969 a, CAPE VERDE 9 Jul 1987 a (*general), CENTRAL AFRICAN REPUBLIC 30 Aug 1967 a, CHAD 19 Aug 1981 a, CHILE 27 Apr 1972 a, CHINA 24 Sep 1982 a (*4), COLOMBIA 4 Mar 1980 a, CONGO 10 Jul 1970 a (*4), COSTA RICA 28 Mar 1978 a, CÔTE D'IVOIRE 16 Feb 1970 a, CROATIA 12 Oct 1992 d, CYPRUS 9 Jul 1968 a, CZECH REPUBLIC 11 May 1993 d, DEMOCRATIC REPUBLIC OF THE CONGO 13 Jan 1975 a, DENMARK 29 Jan 1968 a, DJIBOUTI 9 Aug 1977 d, DOMINICA 17 Feb 1994 a, DOMINICAN REPUBLIC 4 Jan 1978 a, ECUADOR 6 Mar 1969 a, EGYPT 22 May 1981 a, EL SALVADOR 28 Apr 1083 a (*4), EQUATORIAL GUINEA 7 Feb 1986 a, ESTONIA 10 Apr 1997 a, ETHIOPIA 10 Nov 1969 a, FIJI 12 Jun 1972 d, FINLAND 10 Oct 1968 a, FRANCE 3 Feb 1971 a, GABON 28 Aug 1973 a, GAMBIA 29 Sep 1967 a, GEORGIA 9 Aug 1999 a, GERMANY 5 Nov 1969 a, GHANA 30 Oct 1968 a (*4), GREECE 7 Aug 1968 a, GUATEMALA 22 Sep 1983 a, GUINEA 16 May 1968 a, GUINEA-BISSAU 11 Feb 1976 a, HAITI 25 Sep 1984 a, HOLY SEE 8 Jun 1967 a, HONDURAS 23 Mar 1992 a (*1.1), HUNGARY 14 Mar 1989 a, ICELAND 26 Apr 1968 a, IRAN (ISLAMIC REPUBLIC OF) 28 Jul 1976 a, IRELAND 6 Nov 1968 a, ISRAEL 14 Jun 1968 a (*7.2), ITALY 26 Jan 1972 a, JAMAICA 30 Oct 1980 a (*4), JAPAN 1 Jan 1982 a, KAZAKHSTAN 15 Jan 1999 a, KENYA 13 Nov 1981 a, KYRGYZSTAN 8 Oct 1996 a, LATVIA 31 Jul 1997 a (*41), LESOTHO 14 May 1981 a, LIBERIA 27 Feb 1980 a, LIECHTENSTEIN 20 May 1968 a, LITHUANIA 28 Apr 1997 a, LUXEMBOURG 22 Apr 1971 a, MALAWI 10 Dec 1987 a (*4), MALI 2 Feb 1973 a, MALTA 15 Sep 1971 a (*general), MAURITANIA 5 May 1987 a, MEXICO 7 Jun 2000, MONTENEGRO 10 Oct 2006 d, MOROCCO 20 Apr 1971 a, MOZAMBIQUE 1 May 1989 a, NAMIBIA 17 Feb 1995 a, NETHERLANDS 29 Nov 1968 a (*general), NEW ZEALAND 6 Aug 1973 a, NICARAGUA 28 Mar 1980 a, NIGER 2 Feb 1970 a, NIGERIA 2 May 1968 a, NORWAY 28 Nov 1967 a, PANAMA 2 Aug 1978 a, PAPUA NEW GUINEA 17 Jul 1986 a, PARAGUAY 1 Apr 1970 a, PERU 15 Sep 1983 a (*1, 2), PHILIPPINES 22 Jul 1981 a, POLAND 27 Sep 1991 a, PORTUGAL 13 Jul 1976 a (*general), REPUBLIC Of KOREA 3 Dec 1992 a (*7), REPUBLIC OF MOLDOVA 31 Jan 2002 a, ROMANIA 7 Aug 1991 a, RUSSIAN FEDERATION 2 Feb 1993 a, RWANDA 3 Jan 1980 a (*4), SAINT VINCENT AND THE GRENADINES 3 Nov 2003 a (*4), SAMOA 29 Nov 1994 a, SAO TOME AND PRINCIPE 1 Feb 1978 a, SENEGAL 3 Oct 1967 a, SERBIA (REPUBLIC OF) 12 Mar 2001 d, SEYCHELLES 23 Apr 1980 a, SIERRA LEONE 22 May 1981 a, SLOVAKIA 4 Feb 1993 d, SLOVENIA 6 Jul 1992 d, SOLOMON ISLANDS 12 Apr 1995 a, SOMALIA 10 Oct 1978 a, SOUTH AFRICA 12 Jan 1996 a, SPAIN 14 Aug 1978 a, SUDAN 23 May 1974 a, SURINAME 29 Nov 1978 d, SWAZILAND 28 Jan 1969 a (*22, 34), SWEDEN 4 Oct 1967 a,

* Source: 606 U.N.T.S. 267.

SWITZERLAND 20 May 1968 a,, TAJIKISTAN 7 Dec 1993 a, THE FORMER YUGOSLAV REPUBLIC OF MACEDONIA 18 Jan 1994 d, TIMOR-LESTE 7 May 2003 a (*general), TOGO 1 Dec 1969 a, TRINIDAD AND TOBAGO 10 Nov 2000 a, TUNISIA 16 Oct 1968 a, TURKEY 31 Jul 1968 a (*general), TURKMENISTAN 2 Mar 1998 a, TUVALU 7 Mar 1986 d, UGANDA 27 Sep 1976 a, UKRAINE 4 Apr 2002 a, UNITED KINGDOM OF GREAT BRITAIN AND NORTHERN IRELAND 4 Sep 1968 a (*general), UNITED REPUBLIC OF TANZANIA 4 Sep 1968 a (*4), UNITED STATES Of AMERICA 1 Nov 1968 a (*general), URUGUAY 22 Sep 1970 a, VENEZUELA (BOLIVERIAN REPUBLIC OF) 19 Sep 1986 a (*4, general), YEMEN 18 Jan 1980 a, ZAMBIA 24 Sep 1969 a, ZIMBABWE 25 Aug 1981 a.

The States Parties to the present Protocol,

Considering that the Convention relating to the Status of Refugees done at Geneva on 28 July 1951 (hereinafter referred to as the Convention) covers only those persons who have become refugees as a result of events occurring before I January 1951,

Considering that new refugee situations have arisen since the Convention was adopted and that the refugees concerned may therefore not fall within the scope of the Convention,

Considering that it is desirable that equal status should be enjoyed by all refugees covered by the definition in the Convention irrespective of the dateline I January 1951,

Have agreed as follows:

Article 1. General provision

1. The States Parties to the present Protocol undertake to apply articles 2 to 34 inclusive of the Convention to refugees as hereinafter defined.

2. For the purpose of the present Protocol, the term “refugee” shall, except as regards the application of paragraph 3 of this article, mean any person within the definition of article I of the Convention as if the words “As a result of events occurring before 1 January 1951 and...” and the words “...as a result of such events”, in article 1 A (2) were omitted.

3. The present Protocol shall be applied by the States Parties hereto without any geographic limitation, save that existing declarations made by States already Parties to the Convention in accordance with article I B (I) (a) of the Convention, shall, unless extended under article I B (2) thereof, apply also under the present Protocol.

Article 2. Co-operation of the national authorities with the United Nations

1. The States Parties to the present Protocol undertake to co-operate with the Office of the United Nations High Commissioner for Refugees, or any other agency of the United Nations which may succeed it, in the exercise of its functions, and shall in particular facilitate its duty of supervising the application of the provisions of the present Protocol.

2. In order to enable the Office of the High Commissioner or any other agency of the United Nations which may succeed it, to make reports to the competent organs of the United Nations, the States Parties to the present Protocol undertake to provide them with the information and statistical data requested, in the appropriate form, concerning:

(a) The condition of refugees;

(b) The implementation of the present Protocol;

(c) Laws, regulations and decrees which are, or may hereafter be, in force relating to refugees.

Article 3. Information on national legislation

The States Parties to the present Protocol shall communicate to the Secretary-General of the United Nations the laws and regulations which they may adopt to ensure the application of the present Protocol.

Article 4. Settlement of disputes

Any dispute between States Parties to the present Protocol which relates to its interpretation or application and which cannot be settled by other means shall be referred to the International Court of Justice at the request of any one of the parties to the dispute.

Article 5. Accession

The present Protocol shall be open for accession on behalf of all States Parties to the Convention and of any other State Member of the United Nations or member of any of the specialized agencies or to which an invitation to accede may have been addressed by the General Assembly of the United Nations. Accession shall be effected by the deposit of an instrument of accession with the Secretary-General of the United Nations.

Article 6. Federal clause

In the case of a Federal or non-unitary State, the following provisions shall apply:

(a) With respect to those articles of the Convention to be applied in accordance with article I, paragraph 1, of the present Protocol that come within the legislative jurisdiction of the federal legislative authority, the obligations of the Federal Government shall to this extent be the same as those of States Parties which are not Federal States;

(b) With respect to those articles of the Convention to be applied in accordance with article I, paragraph 1, of the present Protocol that come within the legislative jurisdiction of constituent States, provinces or cantons which are not, under the constitutional system of the Federation, bound to take legislative action, the Federal Government shall bring such articles with a favourable recommendation to the notice of the appropriate authorities of States, provinces or cantons at the earliest possible moment;

(c) A Federal State Party to the present Protocol shall, at the request of any other State Party hereto transmitted through the Secretary-General of the United Nations, supply a statement of the law and practice of the Federation and its constituent units in regard to any particular provision of the Convention to be applied in accordance with article I, paragraph 1, of the present Protocol, showing the extent to which effect has been given to that provision by legislative or other action.

Article 7. Reservations and declarations

1. At the time of accession, any State may make reservations in respect of article IV of the present Protocol and in respect of the application in accordance with article I of the present Protocol of any provisions of the Convention other than those contained in articles 1, 3, 4, 16(1) and 33 thereof, provided that in the case of a State Party to the Convention reservations made under this article shall not extend to refugees in respect of whom the Convention applies.

2. Reservations made by States Parties to the Convention in accordance with article 42 thereof shall, unless withdrawn, be applicable in relation to their obligations under the present Protocol.

3. Any State making a reservation in accordance with paragraph I of this article may at any time withdraw such reservation by a communication to that effect addressed to the Secretary-General of the United Nations.

4. Declarations made under article 40, paragraphs I and 2, of the Convention by a State Party thereto which accedes to the present Protocol shall be deemed to apply in respect of the present Protocol, unless upon accession a notification to the contrary is addressed by the State Party concerned to the Secretary-General of the United Nations. The provisions of article 40, paragraphs 2 and 3, and of article 44, paragraph 3, of the Convention shall be deemed to apply mutatis mutandis to the present Protocol.

Article 8. Entry into Protocol

1. The present Protocol shall come into force on the day of deposit of the sixth instrument of accession.

2. For each State acceding to the Protocol after the deposit of the sixth instrument of accession, the Protocol shall come into force on the date of deposit by such State of its instrument of accession.

Article 9. Denunciation

1. Any State Party hereto may denounce this Protocol at any time by a notification addressed to the Secretary-General of the United Nations.

2. Such denunciation shall take effect for the State Party concerned one year from the date on which it is received by the Secretary-General of the United Nations.

Article 10. Notifications by the Secretary-General of the United Nations

The Secretary-General of the United Nations shall inform the States referred to in article V above of the date of entry into force, accessions, reservations and withdrawals of reservations to and denunciations of the present Protocol, and of declarations and notifications relating hereto.

Article 11. Deposit in the archives of the Secretariat of the United Nations

A copy of the present Protocol, of which the Chinese, English, French, Russian and Spanish texts are equally authentic, signed by the President of the General Assembly and by the Secretary-General of the United Nations, shall be deposited in the archives of the Secretariat of the United Nations. The Secretary-General will transmit certified copies thereof to all States Members of the United Nations and to the other States referred to in article 5 above.

Declaration on Territorial Asylum, 1967*

Adoption: 14 December 1967

The General Assembly,

Recalling its resolutions 1839 (XVII) of 19 December 1962, 2100 (XX) of 20 December 1965 and 2203 (XXI) of 16 December 1966 concerning a declaration on the right of asylum,

Considering the work of codification to be undertaken by the International Law Commission in accordance with General Assembly resolution 1400 (XIV) of 21 November 1959,

Adopts the following Declaration:

DECLARATION ON TERRITORIAL ASYLUM

The General Assembly,

Noting that the purposes proclaimed in the Charter of the United Nations are to maintain international peace and security, to develop friendly relations among all nations and to achieve international co-operation in solving international problems of an economic, social, cultural or humanitarian character and in promoting and encouraging respect for human rights and for fundamental freedoms for all without distinction as to race, sex, language or religion,

Mindful of the Universal Declaration of Human Rights, which declares in article 14 that:

"1. Everyone has the right to seek and to enjoy in other countries asylum from persecution.

"2. This right may not be invoked in the case of prosecutions genuinely arising from non-political crimes or from acts contrary to the purposes and principles of the United Nations,",

Recalling also article 13, paragraph 2, of the Universal Declaration of Human Rights, which states:

"Everyone has the right to leave any country, including his own, and to return to his country",

Recognizing that the grant of asylum by a State to persons entitled to invoke article 14 of the Universal Declaration of Human Rights is a peaceful and humanitarian act and that, as such, it cannot be regarded as unfriendly by any other State,

Recommends that, without prejudice to existing instruments dealing with asylum and the status of refugees and stateless persons, States should base themselves in their practices relating to territorial asylum on the following principles:

Article 1

1. Asylum granted by a State, in the exercise of its sovereignty, to persons entitled to invoke article 14 of the Universal Declaration of Human Rights, including persons struggling against colonialism, shall be respected by all other States.

2. The right to seek and to enjoy asylum may not be invoked by any person with respect to whom there are serious reasons for considering that he has committed a crime against peace, a

* Source: U.N.G.A. res. 2312 (XXII).

war crime or a crime against humanity, as defined in the international instruments drawn up to make provision in respect of such crimes.

3. It shall rest with the State granting asylum to evaluate the grounds for the grant of asylum.

Article 2

1. The situation of persons referred to in article 1, paragraph 1, is, without prejudice to the sovereignty of States and the purposes and principles of the United Nations, of concern to the international community.

2. Where a State finds difficulty in granting or continuing to grant asylum, States individually or jointly or through the United Nations shall consider, in a spirit of international solidarity, appropriate measures to lighten the burden on that State.

Article 3

1. No person referred to in article 1, paragraph 1, shall be subjected to measures such as rejection at the frontier or, if he has already entered the territory in which he seeks asylum, expulsion or compulsory return to any State where he may be subjected to persecution.

2. Exception may be made to the foregoing principle only for overriding reasons of national security or in order to safeguard the population, as in the case of a mass influx of persons.

3. Should a State decide in any case that exception to the principle stated in paragraph I of this article would be justified, it shall consider the possibility of granting to the persons concerned, under such conditions as it may deem appropriate, an opportunity, whether by way of provisional asylum or otherwise, of going to another State.

Article 4

States granting asylum shall not permit persons who have received asylum to engage in activities contrary to the purposes and principles of the United Nations.

Protocol relating to Refugee Seamen, 1973*

Adopted: 12 June 1973
Entry into force: 30 March 1975
Parties: 16 (Status as of 1 April 2007)

AUSTRALIA 10 Dec 1973, BELGIUM 22 Mar 1977, BOSNIA AND HERZEGOVINA 1 Oct 1993, CANADA 9 Jan 1975, DENMARK 24 Jan 1974, FRANCE 16 Jul 1975, GERMANY 13 Aug 1975, ITALY 23 Feb 1981, MOROCCO 18 Sep 1974, NETHERLANDS 9 Oct 1973, NORWAY 12 Feb 1974, SLOVENIA 14 Jun 1993, SWEDEN 25 Sep 1973, SWITZERLAND 30 Dec 1974, UNITED KINGDOM OF GREAT BRITAIN AND NORTHERN IRELAND 12 Nov 1974, YUGOSLAVIA 23 Sep 1976.

THE CONTRACTING PARTIES TO THE PRESENT PROTOCOL,

CONSIDERING that the application of the Agreement relating to Refugee Seamen done at The Hague on 23 November 1957 (hereinafter referred to as the Agreement) is closely connected with the application of the Convention relating to the Status of Refugees done at Geneva on 28 July 1951 (hereinafter referred to as the Convention), which applies only to those persons who have become refugees as a result of events occurring before 1 January 1951,

CONSIDERING that new refugee situations have arisen since the Convention was adopted and that it is desirable that equal status should be enjoyed by all refugees covered by the definition of the Convention irrespective of the dateline of 1 January 1951, and that to this end a Protocol relating to the Status of Refugees was opened for accession at New York on 31 January 1967,

DESIRING to establish a similar regime with regard to refugee seamen,

HAVE AGREED as follows:

Article I

(1) The Contracting Parties to the present Protocol undertake to apply Articles 2 and 4 to 13 inclusive of the Agreement to refugee seamen as hereinafter defined.

(2) For the purpose of the present Protocol, the term "refugee seaman" shall apply to any person who, being a refugee according to the definition in paragraph 2 of Article I of the Protocol relating to the Status of Refugees of 31 January 1967, is serving as a seafarer in any capacity on a mercantile ship, or habitually earns his living as a seafarer on such a ship.

(3) The present Protocol shall be applied without any geographic limitation, save that existing declarations made by the States already Parties to the Convention in accordance with Article 1B(1)(a) of the Convention, shall, unless extended under Article 1B(2) thereof, apply also under the present Protocol.

Article II

Any dispute between the Contracting Parties to the present Protocol relating to the interpretation or application of any of its provisions which cannot be settled by other means shall be referred to the International Court of Justice at the request of any one of the Parties to the dispute.

* Source: 965 U.N.T.S. 445.

Article III

(1) The present Protocol shall be open for acceptance or approval on behalf of all the Governments which have signed the Agreement or have acceded thereto and of any other Government which undertakes obligations with respect to refugee seamen under Article 28 of the Convention or obligations corresponding thereto.

(2) Instruments of acceptance or approval shall be deposited with the Government of the Kingdom of the Netherlands.

Article IV

(1) The present Protocol shall come into force on the 90th day following the date of deposit of the eighth instrument of acceptance or approval.

(2) For each Government accepting or approving the present Protocol after the deposit of the eighth instrument of acceptance or approval, the present Protocol shall come into force on the date of deposit by such Government of its instrument of acceptance or approval.

Article V

(1) Any Government may, at the time of the deposit of its instrument of acceptance or approval, or at any time thereafter, declare that the present Protocol shall extend to any territory or territories for the international relations of which it is responsible, provided that it has undertaken in relation thereto such obligations as are mentioned in paragraph 1 of Article III.

(2) Such extension shall be made by notification addressed to the Government of the Kingdom of the Netherlands.

(3) The extension shall take effect on the 90th day following the date upon which the notification was received by the Government of the Kingdom of the Netherlands, but not before the date of the entry into force of the present Protocol for the notifying Government as specified in Article IV.

Article VI

(1) A Contracting Party may denounce the present Protocol at any time by a notification addressed to the Government of the Kingdom of the Netherlands.

(2) The denunciation shall take effect one year from the date upon which the notification was received by the Government of the Kingdom of the Netherlands. Where the present Protocol has been denounced by a Contracting Party, any other Contracting Party after consulting the remaining Parties, may denounce the Protocol with effect from the same date, provided not less than six months' notice is given.

Article VII

(1) A Contracting Party which has made a notification under Article V may at any time thereafter declare by a notification addressed to the Government of the Kingdom of the Netherlands that the present Protocol shall cease to apply to any territory or territories specified in the notification.

(2) The present Protocol shall cease to apply to any territory or territories concerned one year from the date upon which the notification was received by the Government of the Kingdom of the Netherlands.

Article VIII

The Government of the Kingdom of the Netherlands shall inform all the Governments which have signed the Agreement or have acceded thereto and all other Governments which have accepted or approved the present Protocol of any deposits and notifications made in accordance with Articles III, V, VI and VII.

Article IX

A copy of the present Protocol, of which the English and French texts are equally authentic, signed by the Minister for Foreign Affairs of the Kingdom of the Netherlands, shall be deposited in the archives of the Government of the Kingdom of the Netherlands, which shall transmit certified true copies thereof to the Governments referred to in Article VIII.

IN ACCORDANCE WITH Article IX of the Protocol, I have appended my signature this twelfth day of June one thousand nine hundred and seventy-three.

[Signed:]

M. VAN DER STOEL

Minister for Foreign Affairs of the Kingdom of the Netherlands

CERD General Recommendation No.22: Article 5 and Refugees and Displaced Persons, 1996*

Adoption: 24 August 1996

The Committee on the Elimination of Racial Discrimination,

Conscious of the fact that foreign military, non-military and/or ethnic conflicts have resulted in massive flows of refugees and the displacement of persons on the basis of ethnic criteria in many parts of the world,

Considering that the Universal Declaration of Human Rights and the Convention on the Elimination of All Forms of Racial Discrimination proclaim that all human beings are born free and equal in dignity and rights and that everyone is entitled to all the rights and freedoms set out therein, without distinction of any kind, in particular as to race, colour, descent or national or ethnic origin,

Recalling the 1951 Convention and the 1967 Protocol relating to the status of refugees as the main source of the international system for the protection of refugees in general,

1. Draws the attention of States parties to article 5 of the International Convention on the Elimination of All Forms of Racial Discrimination as well as Committee's General Recommendation XX (48) on article 5, and reiterates that the Convention obliges States parties to prohibit and eliminate racial discrimination in the enjoyment of civil, political, economic, social and cultural rights and freedoms;

2. Emphasizes in this respect that:

(a) All such refugees and displaced persons have the right freely to return to their homes of origin under conditions of safety;

(b) States parties are obliged to ensure that the return of such refugees and displaced persons is voluntary and to observe the principle of non-refoulement and non-expulsion of refugees;

(c) All such refugees and displaced persons have, after their return to their homes of origin, the right to have restored to them property of which they were deprived in the course of the conflict and to be compensated appropriately for any such property that cannot be restored to them. Any commitments or statements relating to such property made under duress are null and void;

(d) All such refugees and displaced persons have, after their return to their homes of origin, the right to participate fully and equally in public affairs at all levels and to have equal access to public services and to receive rehabilitation assistance.

* Source: U.N.Doc. A/51/18, Annex VIII.

UNHCR Guidelines on Policies and Procedures in Dealing with Unaccompanied Children Seeking Asylum, 1997 [excerpts]*

Adoption: 1 February 1997

Executive Summary

General principles

The basic guiding principle in any child care and protection action is the principle of the "best interests of the child".

Effective protection and assistance should be delivered to unaccompanied children in a systematic, comprehensive and integrated manner.

Definition

An unaccompanied child is a person who is under the age of eighteen, unless, under the law applicable to the child, majority is, attained earlier and who is "separated from both parents and is not being cared for by an adult who by law or custom has responsibility to do so.

Access to the territory

Because of their vulnerability, unaccompanied children seeking asylum should not be refused access to the territory.

Identification and initial action

Authorities at ports of entry should take necessary measures to ensure that unaccompanied children seeking admission to the territory are identified as such promptly and on a priority basis.

Unaccompanied children should be registered through interviews. Effective documentation of the child will help to ensure that subsequent actions are in the 'best interests' of the child.

A guardian or adviser should be appointed as soon as the unaccompanied child is identified. The guardian or adviser should have the necessary expertise in the field of childcaring, so as to ensure that the interests of the child are safeguarded and that his/her needs are appropriately met.

Initial interviews of unaccompanied children to collect biodata and social history information should be done immediately after arrival and in an age-appropriate manner.

It is desirable that all interviews with unaccompanied children be carried out by professionally qualified and persons, specially trained in refugee and children's issues. Insofar as possible, interpreters should also be specially trained persons.

In all cases, the views and wishes of the child should be elicited, and considered.

Access to asylum procedures

Children should always have access to asylum procedures, regardless of their age.

* Source: www.unhcr.org.

Interim care and protection of children seeking asylum

Children seeking asylum, particularly if they are unaccompanied, are entitled to special care and protection.

Children seeking asylum should not be kept in detention. This is particularly important in the case of unaccompanied children.

Refugee status determination

Considering their vulnerability and special needs, it is essential that children's refugee status applications be given priority and that every effort be made to reach a decision promptly and fairly.

Not being legally independent, an asylum-seeking child should be represented by an adult who is familiar with the child's background and who would protect his/her interests.

Interviews should be conducted by specially qualified and trained officials.

Appeals should be processed as expeditiously as possible.

In the examination of the factual elements of the claim of an unaccompanied child, particular regard should be given to circumstances such as the child's stage of development, his/her possibly limited knowledge of conditions in the country of origin, and their significance to the legal concept of refugee status, as well as his/her special vulnerability.

Identification of durable solutions

If the child is granted asylum or permitted to stay on grounds, possible durable solutions are either local integration or resettlement in a third country, normally on the grounds of family reunification.

If the child is found not to qualify for asylum, either as a refugee or on humanitarian grounds, an assessment of the solution that is in the best interests of the child should follow as soon as practicable after the negative result of his/her application is confirmed.

The identification of the most appropriate solution requires that all the various aspects of the case be duly considered and weighed. One way in which this objective may be ensured is by the establishment of multidisciplinary Panels in charge of considering on a case-by-case basis which solution is in the best interests of the child, and making appropriate recommendations.

Implementation of durable solution

In recognition of the particular vulnerability of unaccompanied children, every effort should be made to ensure that decisions relating to them are taken and implemented without any undue delays.

As soon as the child has been recognized refugee status or permitted to stay on humanitarian grounds, long-term placement in a community should be arranged.

Should repatriation be considered as the most appropriate durable solution, the return will not be carried out unless, prior to the return, a suitable care-giver such as a parent, other relative, other adult care-taker, a government agency, a child-care agency in the country of origin has agreed, and is able to take responsibility for the child and provide him/her with appropriate protection and care.

Special efforts must be made to ensure the provision of appropriate counselling for a child who is to be returned.

The possibility of using the expertise of international agencies could be explored, notably for initiating contacts and establishing an assistance programme for the family.

Cooperation and coordination

The process above will involve information-sharing and networking between agencies and individuals. The close cooperation of a variety of government bodies, specialized agencies and individuals in delivering an effective continuum or care is crucial.

[…]

UNHCR Revised Guidelines on Applicable Criteria and Standards Relating to the Detention of Asylum Seekers, 1999 (See section 7)

UNHCR Guidelines on International Protection: The Application of Article 1 A(2) of the 1951 Convention and/or 1967 Protocol relating to the Status of Refugees to victims of trafficking and persons at risk of being trafficked, 2006 (See section 4.2)

13. INTERNALLY DISPLACED PERSONS

Guiding Principles on Internal Displacement, 1998*

Adoption: 11 February 1998

INTRODUCTION: SCOPE AND PURPOSE

1. These Guiding Principles address the specific needs of internally displaced persons worldwide. They identify rights and guarantees relevant to the protection of persons from forced displacement and to their protection and assistance during displacement as well as during return or resettlement and reintegration.

2. For the purposes of these Principles, internally displaced persons are persons or groups of persons who have been forced or obliged to flee or to leave their homes or places of habitual residence, in particular as a result of or in order to avoid the effects of armed conflict, situations of generalized violence, violations of human rights or natural or human-made disasters, and who have not crossed an internationally recognized State border.

3. These Principles reflect and are consistent with international human rights law and international humanitarian law. They provide guidance to:

(a) The Representative of the Secretary-General on internally displaced persons in carrying out his mandate;

(b) States when faced with the phenomenon of internal displacement;

(c) All other authorities, groups and persons in their relations with internally displaced persons; and

(d) Intergovernmental and non-governmental organizations when addressing internal displacement.

4. These Guiding Principles should be disseminated and applied as widely as possible.

SECTION I - GENERAL PRINCIPLES

Principle 1

1. Internally displaced persons shall enjoy, in full equality, the same rights and freedoms under international and domestic law as do other persons in their country. They shall not be discriminated against in the enjoyment of any rights and freedoms on the ground that they are internally displaced.

2. These Principles are without prejudice to individual criminal responsibility under international law, in particular relating to genocide, crimes against humanity and war crimes.

Principle 2

1. These Principles shall be observed by all authorities, groups and persons irrespective of their legal status and applied without any adverse distinction. The observance of these Principles shall not affect the legal status of any authorities, groups or persons involved.

* Source: U.N. doc. E/CN.4/1998/53/Add.2.

2. These Principles shall not be interpreted as restricting, modifying or impairing the provisions of any international human rights or international humanitarian law instrument or rights granted to persons under domestic law. In particular, these Principles are without prejudice to the right to seek and enjoy asylum in other countries.

Principle 3

1. National authorities have the primary duty and responsibility to provide protection and humanitarian assistance to internally displaced persons within their jurisdiction.

2. Internally displaced persons have the right to request and to receive protection and humanitarian assistance from these authorities. They shall not be persecuted or punished for making such a request.

Principle 4

1. These Principles shall be applied without discrimination of any kind, such as race, colour, sex, language, religion or belief, political or other opinion, national, ethnic or social origin, legal or social status, age, disability, property, birth, or on any other similar criteria.

2. Certain internally displaced persons, such as children, especially unaccompanied minors, expectant mothers, mothers with young children, female heads of household, persons with disabilities and elderly persons, shall be entitled to protection and assistance required by their condition and to treatment which takes into account their special needs.

SECTION II - PRINCIPLES RELATING TO PROTECTION FROM DISPLACEMENT

Principle 5

All authorities and international actors shall respect and ensure respect for their obligations under international law, including human rights and humanitarian law, in all circumstances, so as to prevent and avoid conditions that might lead to displacement of persons.

Principle 6

1. Every human being shall have the right to be protected against being arbitrarily displaced from his or her home or place of habitual residence.

2. The prohibition of arbitrary displacement includes displacement:

(a) When it is based on policies of apartheid, "ethnic cleansing" or similar practices aimed at/or resulting in altering the ethnic, religious or racial composition of the affected population;

(b) In situations of armed conflict, unless the security of the civilians involved or imperative military reasons so demand;

(c) In cases of large-scale development projects, which are not justified by compelling and overriding public interests;

(d) In cases of disasters, unless the safety and health of those affected requires their evacuation; and

(e) When it is used as a collective punishment.

3. Displacement shall last no longer than required by the circumstances.

Principle 7

1. Prior to any decision requiring the displacement of persons, the authorities concerned shall ensure that all feasible alternatives are explored in order to avoid displacement altogether. Where no alternatives exist, all measures shall be taken to minimize displacement and its adverse effects.

2. The authorities undertaking such displacement shall ensure, to the greatest practicable extent, that proper accommodation is provided to the displaced persons, that such displacements are effected in satisfactory conditions of safety, nutrition, health and hygiene, and that members of the same family are not separated.

3. If displacement occurs in situations other than during the emergency stages of armed conflicts and disasters, the following guarantees shall be complied with:

(a) A specific decision shall be taken by a State authority empowered by law to order such measures;

(b) Adequate measures shall be taken to guarantee to those to be displaced full information on the reasons and procedures for their displacement and, where applicable, on compensation and relocation;

(c) The free and informed consent of those to be displaced shall be sought;

(d) The authorities concerned shall endeavour to involve those affected, particularly women, in the planning and management of their relocation;

(e) Law enforcement measures, where required, shall be carried out by competent legal authorities; and

(f) The right to an effective remedy, including the review of such decisions by appropriate judicial authorities, shall be respected.

Principle 8

Displacement shall not be carried out in a manner that violates the rights to life, dignity, liberty and security of those affected.

Principle 9

States are under a particular obligation to protect against the displacement of indigenous peoples, minorities, peasants, pastoralists and other groups with a special dependency on and attachment to their lands.

SECTION III - PRINCIPLES RELATING TO PROTECTION DURING DISPLACEMENT

Principle 10

1. Every human being has the inherent right to life which shall be protected by law. No one shall be arbitrarily deprived of his or her life. Internally displaced persons shall be protected in particular against:

(a) Genocide;

(b) Murder;

(c) Summary or arbitrary executions; and

(d) Enforced disappearances, including abduction or unacknowledged detention, threatening or resulting in death.

Threats and incitement to commit any of the foregoing acts shall be prohibited.

2. Attacks or other acts of violence against internally displaced persons who do not or no longer participate in hostilities are prohibited in all circumstances. Internally displaced persons shall be protected, in particular, against:

(a) Direct or indiscriminate attacks or other acts of violence, including the creation of areas wherein attacks on civilians are permitted;

(b) Starvation as a method of combat;

(c) Their use to shield military objectives from attack or to shield, favour or impede military operations;

(d) Attacks against their camps or settlements; and

(e) The use of anti-personnel landmines.

Principle 11

1. Every human being has the right to dignity and physical, mental and moral integrity.

2. Internally displaced persons, whether or not their liberty has been restricted, shall be protected in particular against:

(a) Rape, mutilation, torture, cruel, inhuman or degrading treatment or punishment, and other outrages upon personal dignity, such as acts of gender-specific violence, forced prostitution and any form of indecent assault;

(b) Slavery or any contemporary form of slavery, such as sale into marriage, sexual exploitation, or forced labour of children; and

(c) Acts of violence intended to spread terror among internally displaced persons.

Threats and incitement to commit any of the foregoing acts shall be prohibited.

Principle 12

1. Every human being has the right to liberty and security of person. No one shall be subjected to arbitrary arrest or detention.

2. To give effect to this right for internally displaced persons, they shall not be interned in or confined to a camp. If in exceptional circumstances such internment or confinement is absolutely necessary, it shall not last longer than required by the circumstances.

3. Internally displaced persons shall be protected from discriminatory arrest and detention as a result of their displacement.

4. In no case shall internally displaced persons be taken hostage.

Principle 13

1. In no circumstances shall displaced children be recruited nor be required or permitted to take part in hostilities.

2. Internally displaced persons shall be protected against discriminatory practices of recruitment into any armed forces or groups as a result of their displacement. In particular any

cruel, inhuman or degrading practices that compel compliance or punish non-compliance with recruitment are prohibited in all circumstances.

Principle 14

1. Every internally displaced person has the right to liberty of movement and freedom to choose his or her residence.

2. In particular, internally displaced persons have the right to move freely in and out of camps or other settlements.

Principle 15

Internally displaced persons have:

(a) The right to seek safety in another part of the country;

(b) The right to leave their country;

(c) The right to seek asylum in another country; and

(d) The right to be protected against forcible return to or resettlement in any place where their life, safety, liberty and/or health would be at risk.

Principle 16

1. All internally displaced persons have the right to know the fate and whereabouts of missing relatives.

2. The authorities concerned shall endeavour to establish the fate and whereabouts of internally displaced persons reported missing, and cooperate with relevant international organizations engaged in this task. They shall inform the next of kin on the progress of the investigation and notify them of any result.

3. The authorities concerned shall endeavour to collect and identify the mortal remains of those deceased, prevent their despoliation or mutilation, and facilitate the return of those remains to the next of kin or dispose of them respectfully.

4. Grave sites of internally displaced persons should be protected and respected in all circumstances. Internally displaced persons should have the right of access to the grave sites of their deceased relatives.

Principle 17

1. Every human being has the right to respect of his or her family life.

2. To give effect to this right for internally displaced persons, family members who wish to remain together shall be allowed to do so.

3. Families which are separated by displacement should be reunited as quickly as possible. All appropriate steps shall be taken to expedite the reunion of such families, particularly when children are involved. The responsible authorities shall facilitate inquiries made by family members and encourage and cooperate with the work of humanitarian organizations engaged in the task of family reunification.

4. Members of internally displaced families whose personal liberty has been restricted by internment or confinement in camps shall have the right to remain together.

Principle 18

1. All internally displaced persons have the right to an adequate standard of living.

2. At the minimum, regardless of the circumstances, and without discrimination, competent authorities shall provide internally displaced persons with and ensure safe access to:

(a) Essential food and potable water;

(b) Basic shelter and housing;

(c) Appropriate clothing; and

(d) Essential medical services and sanitation.

3. Special efforts should be made to ensure the full participation of women in the planning and distribution of these basic supplies.

Principle 19

1. All wounded and sick internally displaced persons as well as those with disabilities shall receive to the fullest extent practicable and with the least possible delay, the medical care and attention they require, without distinction on any grounds other than medical ones. When necessary, internally displaced persons shall have access to psychological and social services.

2. Special attention should be paid to the health needs of women, including access to female health care providers and services, such as reproductive health care, as well as appropriate counselling for victims of sexual and other abuses.

3. Special attention should also be given to the prevention of contagious and infectious diseases, including AIDS, among internally displaced persons.

Principle 20

1. Every human being has the right to recognition everywhere as a person before the law.

2. To give effect to this right for internally displaced persons, the authorities concerned shall issue to them all documents necessary for the enjoyment and exercise of their legal rights, such as passports, personal identification documents, birth certificates and marriage certificates. In particular, the authorities shall facilitate the issuance of new documents or the replacement of documents lost in the course of displacement, without imposing unreasonable conditions, such as requiring the return to one's area of habitual residence in order to obtain these or other required documents.

3. Women and men shall have equal rights to obtain such necessary documents and shall have the right to have such documentation issued in their own names.

Principle 21

1. No one shall be arbitrarily deprived of property and possessions.

2. The property and possessions of internally displaced persons shall in all circumstances be protected, in particular, against the following acts:

(a) Pillage;

(b) Direct or indiscriminate attacks or other acts of violence;

(c) Being used to shield military operations or objectives;

(d) Being made the object of reprisal; and

(e) Being destroyed or appropriated as a form of collective punishment.

3. Property and possessions left behind by internally displaced persons should be protected against destruction and arbitrary and illegal appropriation, occupation or use.

Principle 22

1. Internally displaced persons, whether or not they are living in camps, shall not be discriminated against as a result of their displacement in the enjoyment of the following rights:

(a) The rights to freedom of thought, conscience, religion or belief, opinion and expression;

(b) The right to seek freely opportunities for employment and to participate in economic activities;

(c) The right to associate freely and participate equally in community affairs;

(d) The right to vote and to participate in governmental and public affairs, including the right to have access to the means necessary to exercise this right; and

(e) The right to communicate in a language they understand.

Principle 23

1. Every human being has the right to education.

2. To give effect to this right for internally displaced persons, the authorities concerned shall ensure that such persons, in particular displaced children, receive education which shall be free and compulsory at the primary level. Education should respect their cultural identity, language and religion.

3. Special efforts should be made to ensure the full and equal participation of women and girls in educational programmes.

4. Education and training facilities shall be made available to internally displaced persons, in particular adolescents and women, whether or not living in camps, as soon as conditions permit.

SECTION IV - PRINCIPLES RELATING TO HUMANITARIAN ASSISTANCE

Principle 24

1. All humanitarian assistance shall be carried out in accordance with the principles of humanity and impartiality and without discrimination.

2. Humanitarian assistance to internally displaced persons shall not be diverted, in particular for political or military reasons.

Principle 25

1. The primary duty and responsibility for providing humanitarian assistance to internally displaced persons lies with national authorities.

2. International humanitarian organizations and other appropriate actors have the right to offer their services in support of the internally displaced. Such an offer shall not be regarded as an unfriendly act or an interference in a State's internal affairs and shall be considered in good faith. Consent thereto shall not be arbitrarily withheld, particularly when authorities concerned are unable or unwilling to provide the required humanitarian assistance.

3. All authorities concerned shall grant and facilitate the free passage of humanitarian assistance and grant persons engaged in the provision of such assistance rapid and unimpeded access to the internally displaced.

Principle 26

Persons engaged in humanitarian assistance, their transport and supplies shall be respected and protected. They shall not be the object of attack or other acts of violence.

Principle 27

1. International humanitarian organizations and other appropriate actors when providing assistance should give due regard to the protection needs and human rights of internally displaced persons and take appropriate measures in this regard. In so doing, these organizations and actors should respect relevant international standards and codes of conduct.

2. The preceding paragraph is without prejudice to the protection responsibilities of international organizations mandated for this purpose, whose services may be offered or requested by States.

SECTION V - PRINCIPLES RELATING TO RETURN, RESETTLEMENT AND REINTEGRATION

Principle 28

1. Competent authorities have the primary duty and responsibility to establish conditions, as well as provide the means, which allow internally displaced persons to return voluntarily, in safety and with dignity, to their homes or places of habitual residence, or to resettle voluntarily in another part of the country. Such authorities shall endeavour to facilitate the reintegration of returned or resettled internally displaced persons.

2. Special efforts should be made to ensure the full participation of internally displaced persons in the planning and management of their return or resettlement and reintegration.

Principle 29

1. Internally displaced persons who have returned to their homes or places of habitual residence or who have resettled in another part of the country shall not be discriminated against as a result of their having been displaced. They shall have the right to participate fully and equally in public affairs at all levels and have equal access to public services.

2. Competent authorities have the duty and responsibility to assist returned and/or resettled internally displaced persons to recover, to the extent possible, their property and possessions which they left behind or were dispossessed of upon their displacement. When recovery of such property and possessions is not possible, competent authorities shall provide or assist these persons in obtaining appropriate compensation or another form of just reparation.

Principle 30

All authorities concerned shall grant and facilitate for international humanitarian organizations and other appropriate actors, in the exercise of their respective mandates, rapid and unimpeded access to internally displaced persons to assist in their return or resettlement and reintegration.

General Assembly Resolution No.56/164 on the Protection of and Assistance to Internally Displaced Persons, 2002*

Adoption: 19 December 2001

The General Assembly,

Deeply disturbed by the alarmingly high numbers of internally displaced persons throughout the world who receive inadequate protection and assistance, and conscious of the serious problem that this is creating for the international community,

Conscious of the human rights and the humanitarian dimensions of the problem of internally displaced persons and the responsibilities that this poses for States and the international community to explore methods and means better to address the protection and assistance needs of those persons,

Noting the growing awareness of the international community of the issue of internally displaced persons worldwide and the urgency of addressing the root causes of their displacement and finding durable solutions, including voluntary return in safety and with dignity or local integration,

Emphasizing that national authorities have the primary responsibility to provide protection and assistance to internally displaced persons within their jurisdiction as well as to address the root causes for the displacement problem in cooperation with the international community,

Recalling the relevant norms of international human rights law, international humanitarian law and analogous refugee law, and recognizing that the protection of internally displaced persons has been strengthened by identifying, reaffirming and consolidating specific standards for their protection, in particular through the Guiding Principles on Internal Displacement,[1]

Taking note of Commission on Human Rights resolution 2001/54 of 24 April 2001,[2] *and recalling the Vienna Declaration and Programme of Action adopted by the World Conference on Human Rights on 25 June 1993,*[3] *regarding the need to develop global strategies to address the problem of internal displacement,*

Deploring practices of forced displacement and their negative consequences for the enjoyment of fundamental human rights by large groups of populations,

Noting with appreciation the work of the Representative of the Secretary-General on internally displaced persons in developing a normative framework, in particular a compilation and analysis of legal norms and the development of guiding principles, analysing institutional arrangements, undertaking dialogue with Governments and issuing a series of reports on particular country situations together with proposals for remedial measures,

Welcoming the cooperation established between the Representative of the Secretary-General and the United Nations and other international and regional organizations, in particular the participation of the Representative of the Secretary-General in the meetings of the Inter-Agency Standing Committee and its subsidiary bodies, and encouraging further strengthening of this

---

* Source: U.N.G.A. Res. A/RES/56/164.

[1] E/CN.4/1998/53/Add.2, annex.

[2] See Official Records of the Economic and Social Council, 2001, Supplement No.3 (E/2001/23), chap. II, sect. A.

[3] A/CONF.157/24 (Part I), chap. III.

collaboration in order to promote better protection, assistance and development strategies for internally displaced persons,

Recognizing the central role of the Emergency Relief Coordinator for the interagency coordination of protection of and assistance to internally displaced persons, and in this regard welcoming the establishment of the Senior Inter-Agency Network on Internal Displacement and the decision to set up within the Office for the Coordination of Humanitarian Affairs of the Secretariat a unit for coordinating activities regarding internally displaced persons in order to promote better protection, assistance and development strategies for internally displaced persons, as well as to enhance further accountability by the United Nations system,

Acknowledging with appreciation the independent coordination within, as well as the independent work of, the International Red Cross and Red Crescent Movement and other humanitarian agencies in protecting and assisting internally displaced persons in cooperation with relevant international bodies,

Recalling its resolution 54/167 of 17 December 1999,

1. *Welcomes* the report of the Representative of the Secretary-General on internally displaced persons;[4]

2. *Commends* the Representative of the Secretary-General for the activities undertaken so far, for the catalytic role that he continues to play in raising the level of consciousness about the plight of internally displaced persons and for his efforts to promote a comprehensive strategy that focuses on prevention as well as better protection, assistance and development for internally displaced persons;

3. *Expresses its appreciation* to those Governments and intergovernmental and non-governmental organizations that have provided protection and assistance to internally displaced persons and have supported the work of the Representative of the Secretary-General;

4. *Encourages* the Representative of the Secretary-General, through continuous dialogue with Governments and all intergovernmental and non- governmental organizations concerned, to continue his analysis of the causes of internal displacement, the needs and rights of those displaced, measures of prevention and ways to strengthen protection, assistance and solutions for internally displaced persons, taking into account specific situations, and to include information thereon in his reports to the Commission on Human Rights and the General Assembly;

5. *Welcomes* the specific attention paid by the Representative of the Secretary-General to the special protection, assistance and development needs of internally displaced women, children and other groups with specific needs and his commitment to pay more systematic and in-depth attention to their needs;

6. *Also welcomes* the fact that the Representative of the Secretary-General has made use of the Guiding Principles on Internal Displacement1 in his dialogue with Governments and intergovernmental and non-governmental organizations, and requests him to continue his efforts in that regard, including considering strategies for addressing such concerns;

7. *Notes with appreciation* that an increasing number of States, United Nations agencies and regional and non-governmental organizations are making use of the Guiding Principles, encourages the further dissemination and application of the Guiding Principles, expresses its appreciation for the dissemination and promotion of the Guiding Principles at regional and other seminars on displacement, and encourages the Representative of the Secretary General

[4] See A/56/168.

to continue to initiate or support such seminars in consultation with regional organizations, intergovernmental and non-governmental organizations and other relevant institutions, and to provide support for efforts to promote capacity-building and use of the Guiding Principles;

8. *Calls upon* all Governments to continue to facilitate the activities of the Representative of the Secretary-General, in particular Governments with situations of internal displacement, encourages them to give serious consideration to inviting the Representative to visit their countries so as to enable him to study and analyse more fully the issues involved, and thanks those Governments that have already done so;

9. *Invites* Governments to give due consideration, in dialogue with the Representative of the Secretary-General, to the recommendations and suggestions addressed to them, in accordance with his mandate, and to inform him of measures taken thereon;

10. *Calls upon* Governments to provide protection and assistance, including reintegration and development assistance, to internally displaced persons, and to facilitate the efforts of relevant United Nations agencies and humanitarian organizations in these respects, including by further improving access to internally displaced persons;

11. *Notes with appreciation* the increased attention paid to the issue of internally displaced persons in the consolidated inter-agency appeals process, and encourages further efforts to improve the integration of the protection and assistance needs of internally displaced persons in consolidated appeals;

12. *Emphasizes* the central role of the Emergency Relief Coordinator for the inter-agency coordination of protection of and assistance to internally displaced persons, and in this regard urges the Senior Inter-Agency Network on Internal Displacement and all relevant United Nations humanitarian assistance, human rights and development organizations concerned to enhance further their collaboration and coordination, especially through the Inter-Agency Standing Committee, in order to promote and better carry out protection, assistance and development activities for internally displaced persons and to enhance further their accountability, as well as to provide all possible assistance and support to the Representative of the Secretary-General, and invites the Network better to inform Member States of its activities;

13. *Welcomes* the initiatives undertaken by regional organizations, such as the Organization of African Unity, the Organization of American States, the Organization for Security and Cooperation in Europe, the Council of Europe and the Economic Community of West African States, to address the protection, assistance and development needs of internally displaced persons, and encourages them and other regional organizations to strengthen their activities and their cooperation with the Representative of the Secretary-General;

14. *Notes* the establishment of the global internally displaced persons database, as advocated by the Representative of the Secretary-General, and encourages the members of the Inter-Agency Standing Committee and Governments to continue to collaborate on and support this effort, including by providing financial resources;

15. *Requests* the Secretary-General to provide his Representative, from within existing resources, with all necessary assistance to carry out his mandate effectively, and encourages the Representative to continue to seek the contribution of States, relevant organizations and institutions in order to put the work of the Representative on a more stable basis;

16. *Requests* the Representative of the Secretary-General to prepare, for consideration by the General Assembly at its fifty-eighth session, a report on the implementation of the present resolution;

17. *Decides* to continue its consideration of the question of protection of and assistance to internally displaced persons at its fifty-eighth session.

88th plenary meeting
19 December 2001

United Nations Commission on Human Rights Resolution No.2003/51 on Internally Displaced Persons, 2003*

Adoption: 23 April 2003

The Commission on Human Rights,

Deeply disturbed by the alarmingly high numbers throughout the world of persons who have been forced or obliged to flee or leave their homes or places of habitual residence and who have not crossed an internationally recognized State border, for reasons including armed conflict, violations of human rights and natural or human-made disasters,

Conscious of the human rights and humanitarian dimensions of the problem of internally displaced persons, who often do not receive adequate protection and assistance, and aware of the serious challenge this is creating for the international community and of the responsibility of States and the international community to strengthen methods and means to address better the specific protection and assistance needs of internally displaced persons,

Emphasizing the primary responsibility of national authorities to provide protection and assistance to internally displaced persons within their jurisdiction, as well as to address the root causes of their displacement in appropriate cooperation with the international community,

Noting the resolve of the international community to find durable solutions for all internally displaced persons and to strengthen international cooperation in order to help them return voluntarily to their homes in safety and with dignity or, based on their free choice, to resettle in another part of their country, and to be smoothly reintegrated into their societies,

Recalling the relevant norms of international human rights law, international humanitarian law and international refugee law, and recognizing that the protection of internally displaced persons has been strengthened by identifying, reaffirming and consolidating specific standards for their protection, in particular through the Guiding Principles on Internal Displacement (E/CN.4/1998/53/Add.2, annex),

Bearing in mind the relevant provisions of, inter alia, the United Nations Millennium Declaration (General Assembly resolution 55/2), the Vienna Declaration and Programme of Action adopted in June 1993 by the World Conference on Human Rights (A/CONF.157/23) and the Durban Declaration and Programme of Action adopted in September 2001 by the World Conference against Racism, Racial Discrimination, Xenophobia and Related Intolerance (A/CONF.189/12),

Noting that the Rome Statute of the International Criminal Court (A/CONF.183/9) defines the deportation or forcible transfer of population as a crime against humanity and the unlawful deportation or transfer of the civilian population as well as ordering the displacement of the civilian population as war crimes,

Recalling its previous relevant resolutions, in particular resolution 2002/56 of 25 April 2002 and General Assembly resolution 56/164 of 19 December 2001, and taking note of Economic and Social Council resolution 2002/32 of 26 July 2002, resolutions 2002/7 and 2002/30 of 14 and 15 August 2002 of the Sub-Commission on the Promotion and Protection of Human Rights and of the statement by the President of the Security Council of 20 December 2002 (S/PRST/2002/41),

---

* Source: U.N. Doc. E/CN.4/2003/L.11/Add.4.

1. *Takes note with appreciation* of the report of the Representative of the Secretary-General on internally displaced persons (E/CN.4/2003/86 and Add.1-6) and commends him for his efforts to promote a comprehensive strategy that focuses on the prevention of displacement and on the protection, assistance and development needs of internally displaced persons, as well as on durable solutions;

2. *Expresses concern* at the persistent problems of large numbers of internally displaced persons worldwide, in particular the risk of extreme poverty and socio-economic exclusion, their limited access to humanitarian assistance, vulnerability to human rights violations, as well as difficulties resulting from their specific situation, such as lack of food, medication or shelter and issues pertinent during their reintegration, including, in appropriate cases, the need for the restitution of or compensation for property;

3. *Expresses particular concern* at the grave problems faced by many internally displaced women and children, including violence and abuse, sexual exploitation, forced recruitment and abduction, and welcomes the commitment of the Representative of the Secretary-General to pay more systematic and in-depth attention to their special assistance, protection and development needs, as well as those of other groups with special needs among the internally displaced, such as older persons and persons with disabilities;

4. *Notes* the importance of taking the human rights and the specific protection and assistance needs of internally displaced persons into consideration, when appropriate, in peace processes and in reintegration and rehabilitation processes;

5. *Expresses its appreciation* for the catalytic role the Representative of the Secretary-General continues to play in raising the level of awareness about the plight of internally displaced persons, and for his work in developing normative and institutional frameworks for the protection and assistance of internally displaced persons, in particular the compilation and analysis of legal norms and the development of guiding principles, in undertaking country missions to engage in dialogue with Governments and other pertinent actors, as well as in conducting research and issuing reports on the causes and specific aspects of internal displacement and on particular country situations, together with proposals for preventive or remedial measures, and encourages him to continue his efforts in this regard;

6. *Welcomes* the cooperation established between the Representative of the Secretary-General and the United Nations as well as other international and regional organizations, in particular his participation in the work of the Inter-Agency Standing Committee and its subsidiary bodies, and encourages further strengthening of this collaboration in order to promote better protection, assistance and development strategies for internally displaced persons;

7. *Expresses its appreciation* of the Guiding Principles on Internal Displacement as an important tool for dealing with situations of internal displacement, welcomes the fact that an increasing number of States, United Nations agencies and regional and non-governmental organizations are applying them as a standard, and encourages all relevant actors to make use of the Guiding Principles when dealing with situations of internal displacement;

8. *Welcomes* the dissemination, promotion and application of the Guiding Principles on Internal Displacement and the fact that the Representative of the Secretary-General continues to use the Guiding Principles in his dialogues with Governments, intergovernmental and non-governmental organizations and other pertinent actors, and requests him to continue his efforts in disseminating and promoting them, inter alia through supporting and initiating their publication and translation, participation in training, and, in consultation with governments, regional organizations, intergovernmental and non-governmental organizations and other relevant institutions, the holding of national, regional and international seminars on displacement, as well as in providing support for efforts to promote capacity-building and the use of the Guiding Principles;

9. *Expresses its appreciation* to Governments and intergovernmental and non-governmental organizations which have provided assistance and protection to internally displaced persons, developed policies to address their plight and supported the work of the Representative of the Secretary-General;

10. *Calls upon* Governments to provide protection and assistance, including reintegration and development assistance, to internally displaced persons, to develop national policies aimed at addressing their plight, as well as to ensure that they benefit from public services, in particular basic social services such as health services and education, based on the principle of non-discrimination, and to facilitate the efforts of relevant United Nations agencies and humanitarian organizations in these respects, including by improving access to internally displaced persons;

11. *Encourages* all Governments, in particular Governments of countries with situations of internal displacement, to facilitate the activities of the Representative of the Secretary-General and to respond favourably to his requests for visits as well as for information, and urges Governments as well as the relevant parts of the United Nations system, also at the country level, to follow up effectively on the recommendations of the Representative of the Secretary-General and to make available information on measures taken in this regard;

12. *Stresses* the need to further strengthen inter-agency arrangements and the capacities of United Nations agencies and other relevant actors to meet the immense humanitarian challenge of internal displacement, and calls upon States to provide adequate resources for programmes to assist and protect internally displaced persons with a view to enhancing the capacities of countries with situations of internal displacement, and of the relevant intergovernmental and non-governmental organizations, to meet the needs of internally displaced persons;

13. *Emphasizes* in this regard the central role of the Emergency Relief Coordinator in inter-agency coordination for the protection and assistance of internally displaced persons, welcomes the establishment of the Unit on Internal Displacement within the Office for the Coordination of Humanitarian Affairs, and encourages them to further strengthen their collaboration with the Representative of the Secretary-General, in line with the memorandum of understanding between the Representative and the Emergency Relief Coordinator of 17 April 2002;

14. *Notes with appreciation* the activities aimed at addressing the plight of internally displaced persons undertaken by the United Nations High Commissioner for Human Rights, the United Nations High Commissioner for Refugees, the United Nations Development Programme, the United Nations Children's Fund, the World Food Programme, the World Health Organization, the International Organization for Migration, the International Labour Organization, the Food and Agriculture Organization of the United Nations, the World Bank, and by all other relevant humanitarian assistance, human rights and development agencies and organizations, including non-governmental organizations, and encourages them to further enhance their collaboration and coordination with regard to internally displaced persons, especially through the Inter-Agency Standing Committee;

15. *Encourages* the Emergency Relief Coordinator, the Representative of the Secretary-General and the Unit on Internal Displacement to further promote an effective, predictable and collaborative response among all relevant international agencies and bodies with regard to protecting and assisting internally displaced persons, at headquarters as well as in countries with situations of internal displacement, bearing in mind the role of resident or humanitarian coordinators;

16. *Notes with appreciation* the increased attention paid to internally displaced persons in the consolidated inter-agency appeals process and encourages further efforts in this regard;

17. *Acknowledges with appreciation* the work of the International Committee of the Red Cross and the other components of the International Red Cross and Red Crescent Movement in protecting and assisting internally displaced persons;

18. *Notes with appreciation* the efforts of non-governmental organizations and the increasing role of national human rights institutions in assisting internally displaced persons and in promoting and protecting their human rights;

19. *Welcomes* the initiatives undertaken by regional organizations, such as the African Union, the Organization of American States, the Organization for Security and Cooperation in Europe, the Council of Europe and the Economic Community of West African States, to address the assistance, protection and development needs of internally displaced persons and encourages them and other regional organizations to strengthen their activities and their cooperation with the Representative of the Secretary-General;

20. *Also welcomes* the attention paid by relevant special rapporteurs, working groups, experts and treaty bodies to issues of internal displacement, and calls upon them to continue to seek information on situations which have already created or could create internal displacement and to include relevant information and recommendations thereon in their reports and make them available to the Representative of the Secretary-General;

21. *Calls upon* the United Nations High Commissioner for Human Rights, in cooperation with Governments and national human rights institutions, the Representative of the Secretary-General and with other relevant parts of the United Nations system, to continue to promote the human rights of internally displaced persons, to enhance their protection on the ground and to develop projects to address their plight as part of the programme of advisory services and technical cooperation, including in the areas of human rights education, training and assistance in legislative and policy development, and to provide information thereon to the Representative for inclusion in his report to the Commission;

22. *Notes* the relevance of the global internally displaced persons database, advocated by the Representative of the Secretary-General, and encourages the members of the Inter-Agency Standing Committee and Governments to continue to collaborate on and support this effort, including by providing relevant data on situations of internal displacement and financial resources;

23. *Requests* the Secretary-General to provide his Representative, from within existing resources, with all necessary assistance to carry out his mandate effectively, and encourages the Representative of the Secretary-General to continue to seek the contribution of States, relevant organizations and institutions in order to put his work on a more stable basis;

24. *Requests* the Representative of the Secretary-General to continue to report on his activities to the General Assembly and to the Commission;

25. *Decides* to continue its consideration of the question of internal displacement at its sixtieth session.

59th meeting
23 April 2003

Principles on Housing and Property Restitution for Refugees and Displaced Persons (Pinheiro Principles), 2005*

Adoption: 28 June 2005

Preamble

Recognizing that millions of refugees and displaced persons worldwide continue to live in precarious and uncertain situations, and that all refugees and displaced persons have a right to voluntary return, in safety and dignity, to their original or former habitual homes and lands,

Underscoring that voluntary return in safety and dignity must be based on a free, informed, individual choice and that refugees and displaced persons should be provided with complete, objective, up-to-date and accurate information, including on physical, material and legal safety issues in countries or places of origin,

Reaffirming the rights of refugee and displaced women and girls, and recognizing the need to undertake positive measures to ensure that their rights to housing, land and property restitution are guaranteed,

Welcoming the many national and international institutions that have been established in recent years to ensure the restitution rights of refugees and displaced persons, as well as the many national and international laws, standards, policy statements, agreements and guidelines that have recognized and reaffirmed the right to housing, land and property restitution,

Convinced that the right to housing, land and property restitution is essential to the resolution of conflict and to post-conflict peace-building, safe and sustainable return and the establishment of the rule of law, and that careful monitoring of restitution programmes, on the part of international organizations and affected States, is indispensable to ensuring their effective implementation,

Convinced also that the implementation of successful housing, land and property restitution programmes, as a key element of restorative justice, contributes to effectively deterring future situations of displacement and building sustainable peace.

SECTION I. SCOPE AND APPLICATION

1. Scope and Application

1.1 The Principles on housing and property restitution for refugees and displaced persons articulated herein are designed to assist all relevant actors, national and international, in addressing the legal and technical issues surrounding housing, land and property restitution in situations where displacement has led to persons being arbitrarily or unlawfully deprived of their former homes, lands, properties or places of habitual residence.

1.2 The Principles on housing and property restitution for refugees and displaced persons apply equally to all refugees, internally displaced persons and to other similarly situated displaced persons who fled across national borders but who may not meet the legal definition of refugee (hereinafter "refugees and displaced persons") who were arbitrarily or unlawfully deprived of their former homes, lands, properties or places of habitual residence, regardless of the nature or circumstances by which displacement originally occurred.

* Source: U.N.Doc. E/CN.4/Sub.2/2005/17 Annex.

SECTION II. THE RIGHT TO HOUSING AND PROPERTY RESTITUTION

2. The right to housing and property restitution

2.1 All refugees and displaced persons have the right to have restored to them any housing, land and/or property of which they were arbitrarily or unlawfully deprived, or to be compensated for any housing, land and/or property that is factually impossible to restore as determined by an independent, impartial tribunal.

2.2 States shall demonstrably prioritize the right to restitution as the preferred remedy for displacement and as a key element of restorative justice. The right to restitution exists as a distinct right, and is prejudiced neither by the actual return nor non-return of refugees and displaced persons entitled to housing, land and property restitution.

SECTION III. OVERARCHING PRINCIPLES

3. The right to non-discrimination

3.1 Everyone has the right to be protected from discrimination on the basis of race, colour, sex, language, religion, political or other opinion, national or social origin, property, disability, birth or other status.

3.2 States shall ensure that de facto and de jure discrimination on the above grounds is prohibited and that all persons, including refugees and displaced persons, are considered equal before the law.

4. The right to equality between men and women

4.1 States shall ensure the equal right of men and women, and the equal right of boys and girls, to housing, land and property restitution. States shall ensure the equal right of men and women, and the equal right of boys and girls, inter alia, to voluntary return in safety and dignity, legal security of tenure, property ownership, equal access to inheritance, as well as the use, control of and access to housing, land and property.

4.2 States should ensure that housing, land and property restitution programmes, policies and practices recognize the joint ownership rights of both male and female heads of the household as an explicit component of the restitution process, and that restitution programmes, policies and practices reflect a gender-sensitive approach.

4.3 States shall ensure that housing, land and property restitution programmes, policies and practices do not disadvantage women and girls. States should adopt positive measures to ensure gender equality in this regard.

5. The right to be protected from displacement

5.1 Everyone has the right to be protected against being arbitrarily displaced from his or her home, land or place of habitual residence.

5.2 States should incorporate protections against displacement into domestic legislation, consistent with international human rights and humanitarian law and related standards, and should extend these protections to everyone within their legal jurisdiction or effective control.

5.3 States shall prohibit forced eviction, demolition of houses and destruction of agricultural areas and the arbitrary confiscation or expropriation of land as a punitive measure or as a means or method of war.

5.4 States shall take steps to ensure that no one is subjected to displacement by either State or non-State actors. States shall also ensure that individuals, corporations, and other entities within their legal jurisdiction or effective control refrain from carrying out or otherwise participating in displacement.

6. The right to privacy and respect for the home

6.1 Everyone has the right to be protected against arbitrary or unlawful interference with his or her privacy and his or her home.

6.2 States shall ensure that everyone is provided with safeguards of due process against arbitrary or unlawful interference with his or her privacy and his or her home.

7. The right to peaceful enjoyment of possessions

7.1 Everyone has the right to the peaceful enjoyment of his or her possessions.

7.2 States shall only subordinate the use and enjoyment of possessions in the public interest and subject to the conditions provided for by law and by the general principles of international law. Whenever possible, the "interest of society" should be read restrictively, so as to mean only a temporary or limited interference with the right to peaceful enjoyment of possessions.

8. The right to adequate housing

8.1 Everyone has the right to adequate housing.

8.2 States should adopt positive measures aimed at alleviating the situation of refugees and displaced persons living in inadequate housing.

9. The right to freedom of movement

9.1 Everyone has the right to freedom of movement and the right to choose his or her residence. No one shall be arbitrarily or unlawfully forced to remain within a certain territory, area or region. Similarly, no one shall be arbitrarily or unlawfully forced to leave a certain territory, area or region.

9.2 States shall ensure that freedom of movement and the right to choose one's residence are not subject to any restrictions except those which are provided by law, are necessary to protect national security, public order, public health or morals or the rights and freedoms of others, and are consistent with international human rights, refugee and humanitarian law and related standards.

SECTION IV. THE RIGHT TO VOLUNTARY RETURN IN SAFETY AND DIGNITY

10. The right to voluntary return in safety and dignity

10.1 All refugees and displaced persons have the right to return voluntarily to their former homes, lands or places of habitual residence, in safety and dignity. Voluntary return in safety and dignity must be based on a free, informed, individual choice. Refugees and displaced persons should be provided with complete, objective, up-to-date, and accurate information, including on physical, material and legal safety issues in countries or places of origin.

10.2 States shall allow refugees and displaced persons who wish to return voluntarily to their former homes, lands or places of habitual residence to do so. This right cannot be abridged under conditions of State succession, nor can it be subject to arbitrary or unlawful time limitations.

10.3 Refugees and displaced persons shall not be forced, or otherwise coerced, either directly or indirectly, to return to their former homes, lands or places of habitual residence. Refugees and displaced persons should be able to effectively pursue durable solutions to displacement other than return, if they so wish, without prejudicing their right to the restitution of their housing, land and property.

10.4 States should, when necessary, request from other States or international organizations the financial and/or technical assistance required to facilitate the effective voluntary return, in safety and dignity, of refugees and displaced persons.

SECTION V. LEGAL, POLICY, PROCEDURAL AND INSTITUTIONAL IMPLEMENTATION MECHANISMS

11. Compatibility with international human rights, refugee and humanitarian law and related standards

11.1 States should ensure that all housing, land and property restitution procedures, institutions, mechanisms and legal frameworks are fully compatible with international human rights, refugee and humanitarian law and related standards, and that the right to voluntary return in safety and dignity is recognized therein.

12. National procedures, institutions and mechanisms

12.1 States should establish and support equitable, timely, independent, transparent and non discriminatory procedures, institutions and mechanisms to assess and enforce housing, land and property restitution claims. In cases where existing procedures, institutions and mechanisms can effectively address these issues, adequate financial, human and other resources should be made available to facilitate restitution in a just and timely manner.

12.2 States should ensure that housing, land and property restitution procedures, institutions and mechanisms are age and gender sensitive, and recognize the equal rights of men and women, as well as the equal rights of boys and girls, and reflect the overarching principle of the "best interests of the child".

12.3 States should take all appropriate administrative, legislative and judicial measures to support and facilitate the housing, land and property restitution process. States should provide all relevant agencies with adequate financial, human and other resources to successfully complete their work in a just and timely manner.

12.4 States should establish guidelines that ensure the effectiveness of all relevant housing, land and property restitution procedures, institutions and mechanisms, including guidelines pertaining to institutional organization, staff training and caseloads, investigation and complaints procedures, verification of property ownership or other rights of possession, as well as decision making, enforcement and appeals mechanisms. States may integrate alternative or informal dispute resolution mechanisms into these processes, insofar as all such mechanisms act in accordance with international human rights, refugee and humanitarian law and related standards, including the right to be protected from discrimination.

12.5 Where there has been a general breakdown in the rule of law, or where States are unable to implement the procedures, institutions and mechanisms necessary to facilitate the housing, land and property restitution process in a just and timely manner, States should request the technical assistance and cooperation of relevant international agencies in order to establish provisional regimes for providing refugees and displaced persons with the procedures, institutions and mechanisms necessary to ensure effective restitution remedies.

12.6 States should include housing, land and property restitution procedures, institutions and mechanisms in peace agreements and voluntary repatriation agreements. Peace agreements should include specific undertakings by the parties to appropriately address any housing, land and property issues that require remedies under international law or threaten to undermine the peace process if left unaddressed, while demonstrably prioritizing the right to restitution as the preferred remedy in this regard.

13. Accessibility of restitution claims procedures

13.1 Everyone who has been arbitrarily or unlawfully deprived of housing, land and/or property should be able to submit a claim for restitution and/or compensation to an independent and impartial body, to have a determination made on their claim and to receive notice of such determination. States should not establish any preconditions for filing a restitution claim.

13.2 States should ensure that all aspects of the restitution claims process, including appeals procedures, are just, timely, accessible, free of charge, and are age and gender sensitive. States should adopt positive measures to ensure that women are able to participate on a fully equal basis in this process.

13.3 States should ensure that separated and unaccompanied children are able to participate and are fully represented in the restitution claims process, and that any decision in relation to the restitution claim of separated and unaccompanied children is in compliance with the overarching principle of the "best interests of the child".

13.4 States should ensure that the restitution claims process is accessible for refugees and other displaced persons regardless of their place of residence during the period of displacement, including in countries of origin, countries of asylum or countries to which they have fled. States should ensure that all affected persons are made aware of the restitution claims process, and that information about this process is made readily available, including in countries of origin, countries of asylum or countries to which they have fled.

13.5 States should seek to establish restitution claims-processing centres and offices throughout affected areas where potential claimants currently reside. In order to facilitate the greatest access to those affected, it should be possible to submit restitution claims by post or by proxy, as well as in person. States should also consider establishing mobile units in order to ensure accessibility to all potential claimants.

13.6 States should ensure that users of housing, land and/or property, including tenants, have the right to participate in the restitution claims process, including through the filing of collective restitution claims.

13.7 States should develop restitution claims forms that are simple and easy to understand and use and make them available in the main language or languages of the groups affected. Competent assistance should be made available to help persons complete and file any necessary restitution claims forms, and such assistance should be provided in a manner that is age and gender sensitive.

13.8 Where restitution claims forms cannot be sufficiently simplified owing to the complexities inherent in the claims process, States should engage qualified persons to interview potential claimants in confidence, and in a manner that is age and gender sensitive, in order to solicit the necessary information and complete the restitution claims forms on their behalf.

13.9 States should establish a clear time period for filing restitution claims. This information should be widely disseminated and should be sufficiently long to ensure that all those affected have an adequate opportunity to file a restitution claim, bearing in mind the number of potential claimants, potential difficulties of collecting information and access, the extent of displacement, the accessibility of the process for potentially disadvantaged groups and vulnerable individuals, and the political situation in the country or region of origin.

13.10 States should ensure that persons needing special assistance, including illiterate and disabled persons, are provided with such assistance in order to ensure that they are not denied access to the restitution claims process.

13.11 States should ensure that adequate legal aid is provided, if possible free of charge, to those seeking to make a restitution claim. While legal aid may be provided by either governmental or non-governmental sources (whether national or international), such legal aid should meet adequate standards of quality, non-discrimination, fairness and impartiality so as not to prejudice the restitution claims process.

13.12 States should ensure that no one is persecuted or punished for making a restitution claim.

14. Adequate consultation and participation in decision-making

14.1 States and other involved international and national actors should ensure that voluntary repatriation and housing, land and property restitution programmes are carried out with adequate consultation and participation with the affected persons, groups and communities.

14.2 States and other involved international and national actors should, in particular, ensure that women, indigenous peoples, racial and ethnic minorities, the elderly, the disabled and children are adequately represented and included in restitution decision-making processes, and have the appropriate means and information to participate effectively. The needs of vulnerable individuals including the elderly, single female heads of households, separated and unaccompanied children, and the disabled should be given particular attention.

15. Housing, land and property records and documentation

15.1 States should establish or re-establish national multipurpose cadastral or other appropriate systems for the registration of housing, land and property rights as an integral component of any restitution programme, respecting the rights of refugees and displaced persons when doing so.

15.2 States should ensure that any judicial, quasi-judicial, administrative or customary pronouncement regarding the rightful ownership of, or rights to, housing, land and/or property is accompanied by measures to ensure registration or demarcation of that housing, land and/or property as is necessary to ensure legal security of tenure. These determinations shall comply with international human rights, refugee and humanitarian law and related standards, including the right to be protected from discrimination.

15.3 States should ensure, where appropriate, that registration systems record and/or recognize the rights of possession of traditional and indigenous communities to collective lands.

15.4 States and other responsible authorities or institutions should ensure that existing registration systems are not destroyed in times of conflict or post-conflict. Measures to prevent the destruction of housing, land and property records could include protection in situ or, if necessary, short-term removal to a safe location or custody. If removed, the records should be returned as soon as possible after the end of hostilities. States and other responsible authorities may also consider establishing procedures for copying records (including in digital format), transferring them securely and recognizing the authenticity of said copies.

15.5 States and other responsible authorities or institutions should provide, at the request of a claimant or his or her proxy, copies of any documentary evidence in their possession required to make and/or support a restitution claim. Such documentary evidence should be provided free of charge, or for a minimal fee.

15.6 States and other responsible authorities or institutions conducting the registration of refugees or displaced persons should endeavour to collect information relevant to facilitating the restitution process, for example by including in the registration form questions regarding the location and status of the individual refugee's or displaced person's former home, land, property or place of habitual residence. Such information should be sought whenever information is gathered from refugees and displaced persons, including at the time of flight.

15.7 States may, in situations of mass displacement where little documentary evidence exists as to ownership or rights of possession, adopt the conclusive presumption that persons fleeing their homes during a given period marked by violence or disaster have done so for reasons related to violence or disaster and are therefore entitled to housing, land and property restitution. In such cases, administrative and judicial authorities may independently establish the facts related to undocumented restitution claims.

15.8 States shall not recognize as valid any housing, land and/or property transaction, including any transfer that was made under duress, or which was otherwise coerced or forced, either directly or indirectly, or which was carried out contrary to international human rights standards.

16. The rights of tenants and other non-owners

16.1 States should ensure that the rights of tenants, social occupancy rights holders and other legitimate occupants or users of housing, land and property are recognized within restitution programmes. To the maximum extent possible, States should ensure that such persons are able to return to and repossess and use their housing, land and property in a similar manner to those possessing formal ownership rights.

17. Secondary occupants

17.1 States should ensure that secondary occupants are protected against arbitrary or unlawful forced eviction. States shall ensure, in cases where evictions of such occupants are deemed justifiable and unavoidable for the purposes of housing, land and property restitution, that evictions are carried out in a manner that is compatible with international human rights law and standards, such that secondary occupants are afforded safeguards of due process, including an opportunity for genuine consultation, adequate and reasonable notice, and the provision of legal remedies, including opportunities for legal redress.

17.2 States should ensure that the safeguards of due process extended to secondary occupants do not prejudice the rights of legitimate owners, tenants and other rights holders to repossess the housing, land and property in question in a just and timely manner.

17.3 In cases where evictions of secondary occupants are justifiable and unavoidable, States should take positive measures to protect those who do not have the means to access any other adequate housing other than that which they are currently occupying from homelessness and other violations of their right to adequate housing. States should undertake to identify and provide alternative housing and/or land for such occupants, including on a temporary basis, as a means of facilitating the timely restitution of refugee and displaced persons' housing, land and property. Lack of such alternatives, however, should not unnecessarily delay the implementation and enforcement of decisions by relevant bodies regarding housing, land and property restitution.

17.4 In cases where housing, land and property has been sold by secondary occupants to third parties acting in good faith, States may consider establishing mechanisms to provide compensation to injured third parties. The egregiousness of the underlying displacement, however, may arguably give rise to constructive notice of the illegality of purchasing abandoned property, pre-empting the formation of bona fide property interests in such cases.

18. Legislative measures

18.1 States should ensure that the right of refugees and displaced persons to housing, land and property restitution is recognized as an essential component of the rule of law. States should ensure the right to housing, land and property restitution through all necessary legislative means, including through the adoption, amendment, reform, or repeal of relevant laws, regulations and/or practices. States should develop a legal framework for protecting the right to housing, land and property restitution which is clear, consistent and, where necessary, consolidated in a single law.

18.2 States should ensure that all relevant laws clearly delineate every person and/or affected group that is legally entitled to the restitution of their housing, land and property, most notably refugees and displaced persons. Subsidiary claimants should similarly be recognized, including resident family members at the time of displacement, spouses, domestic partners, dependents, legal heirs and others who should be entitled to claim on the same basis as primary claimants.

18.3 States should ensure that national legislation related to housing, land and property restitution is internally consistent, as well as compatible with pre-existing relevant agreements, such as peace agreements and voluntary repatriation agreements, so long as these agreements are themselves compatible with international human rights, refugee and humanitarian law and related standards.

19. Prohibition of arbitrary and discriminatory laws

19.1 States should neither adopt nor apply laws that prejudice the restitution process, in particular through arbitrary, discriminatory, or otherwise unjust abandonment laws or statutes of limitations.

19.2 States should take immediate steps to repeal unjust or arbitrary laws and laws that otherwise have a discriminatory effect on the enjoyment of the right to housing, land and property restitution, and should ensure remedies for those wrongfully harmed by the prior application of such laws.

19.3 States should ensure that all national policies related to the right to housing, land and property restitution fully guarantee the rights of women and girls to be protected from discrimination and to equality in both law and practice.

20. Enforcement of restitution decisions and judgements

20.1 States should designate specific public agencies to be entrusted with enforcing housing, land and property restitution decisions and judgements.

20.2 States should ensure, through law and other appropriate means, that local and national authorities are legally obligated to respect, implement and enforce decisions and judgements made by relevant bodies regarding housing, land and property restitution.

20.3 States should adopt specific measures to prevent the public obstruction of enforcement of housing, land and property restitution decisions and judgements. Threats or attacks against officials and agencies carrying out restitution programmes should be fully investigated and prosecuted.

20.4 States should adopt specific measures to prevent the destruction or looting of contested or abandoned housing, land and property. In order to minimize destruction and looting, States should develop procedures to inventory the contents of claimed housing, land and property within the context of housing, land and property restitution programmes.

20.5 States should implement public information campaigns aimed at informing secondary occupants and other relevant parties of their rights and of the legal consequences of non compliance with housing, land and property restitution decisions and judgements, including failing to vacate occupied housing, land and property voluntarily and damaging and/or looting of occupied housing, land and property.

21. Compensation

21.1 All refugees and displaced persons have the right to full and effective compensation as an integral component of the restitution process. Compensation may be monetary or in kind. States shall, in order to comply with the principle of restorative justice, ensure that the remedy of compensation is only used when the remedy of restitution is not factually possible, or when the injured party knowingly and voluntarily accepts compensation in lieu of restitution, or when the terms of a negotiated peace settlement provide for a combination of restitution and compensation.

21.2 States should ensure, as a rule, that restitution is only deemed factually impossible in exceptional circumstances, namely when housing, land and/or property is destroyed or when it no longer exists, as determined by an independent, impartial tribunal. Even under such circumstances the holder of the housing, land and/or property right should have the option to repair or rebuild whenever possible. In some situations, a combination of compensation and restitution may be the most appropriate remedy and form of restorative justice.

SECTION VI. THE ROLE OF THE INTERNATIONAL COMMUNITY, INCLUDING INTERNATIONAL ORGANIZATIONS

22. Responsibility of the international community

22.1 The international community should promote and protect the right to housing, land and property restitution, as well as the right to voluntary return in safety and dignity.

22.2 International financial, trade, development and other related institutions and agencies, including member or donor States that have voting rights within such bodies, should take fully into account the prohibition against unlawful or arbitrary displacement and, in particular, the prohibition under international human rights law and related standards on the practice of forced evictions.

22.3 International organizations should work with national Governments and share expertise on the development of national housing, land and property restitution policies and programmes and help ensure their compatibility with international human rights, refugee and humanitarian law and related standards. International organizations should also support the monitoring of their implementation.

22.4 International organizations, including the United Nations, should strive to ensure that peace agreements and voluntary repatriation agreements contain provisions related to housing, land and property restitution, including through the establishment of national procedures, institutions, mechanisms and legal frameworks.

22.5 International peace operations, in pursuing their overall mandate, should help to maintain a secure and stable environment wherein appropriate housing, land and property restitution policies and programmes may be successfully implemented and enforced.

22.6 International peace operations, depending on the mission context, should be requested to support the protection of the right to housing, land and property restitution, including through the enforcement of restitution decisions and judgements. Members of the Security Council should consider including this role in the mandate of peace operations.

22.7 International organizations and peace operations should avoid occupying, renting or purchasing housing, land and property over which the rights holder does not currently have access or control, and should require that their staff do the same. Similarly, international organizations and peace operations should ensure that bodies or processes under their control or supervision do not obstruct, directly or indirectly, the restitution of housing, land and property.

SECTION VII. INTERPRETATION

23. Interpretation

23.1 The Principles on housing and property restitution for refugees and displaced persons shall not be interpreted as limiting, altering or otherwise prejudicing the rights recognized under international human rights, refugee and humanitarian law and related standards, or rights consistent with these laws and standards as recognized under national law.

14. INTERNATIONAL HUMANITARIAN LAW

Geneva Convention relative to the Protection of Civilian Persons in Time of War, 1949 [excerpts]*

Adoption: 12 August 1949
Entry into force: 21 October 1950
Parties: 194 (status as of 1 April 2007)

AFGHANISTAN 26 Sep 1956, ALBANIA 27 May 1957 (*10-12, 45, 85), ALGERIA 20 Jun 1960, ANDORRA 17 Sep 1993, ANGOLA 20 Sep 1984 (*85), ANTIGUA AND BARBUDA 6 Oct 1986, ARGENTINA 18 Sep 1956, ARMENIA 7 Jun 1993, AUSTRALIA 14 Oct 1958 (*12, 45, 85), AUSTRIA 27 Aug 1953, AZERBAIJAN 1 Jun 1993, BAHAMAS 11 Jul 1975, BAHRAIN 30 Nov 1971, BANGLADESH 4 Apr 1972, BARBADOS 10 Sep 1968 (*12, 45, 85), BELARUS 3 Aug 1954, BELGIUM 3 Sep 1952, BELIZE 29 Jun 1984, BENIN 14 Dec 1961, BHUTAN 10 Jan 1991, BOLIVIA 10 Dec 1976, BOSNIA AND HERZEGOVINA 31 Dec 1992, BOTSWANA 29 Mar 1968, BRAZIL 29 Jun 1957, BRUNEI DARUSSALAM 14 Oct 1991, BULGARIA 22 Jul 1954, BURKINA FASO 7 Nov 1961, BURUNDI 27 Dec 1971, CAMBODIA 8 Dec 1958, CAMEROON 16 Sep 1963, CANADA 14 May 1965, CAPE VERDE 11 May 1984, CENTRAL AFRICAN REPUBLIC 1 Aug 1966, CHAD 5 Aug 1970, CHILE 12 Oct 1950, CHINA 28 Dec 1956 (*10-12, 45, 85), COLOMBIA 8 Nov 1961, COMOROS 21 Nov 1985, DEMOCRATIC REPUBLIC OF THE CONGO 24 Feb 1961, CONGO 4 Feb 1967, COOK ISLANDS 11 Jun 2001, COSTA RICA 15 Oct 1969, CÖTE D'IVOIRE 28 Dec 1961, CROATIA 11 May 1992, CUBA 15 Apr 1954, CYPRUS 23 May 1962, CZECH REPUBLIC 5 Feb 1993, DENMARK 27 Jun 1951, DJIBOUTI 6 Mar 1978, DOMINICA 28 Sep 1981, DOMINICAN REPUBLIC 22 Jan 1958, ECUADOR 11 Aug 1954, EGYPT 10 Nov 1952, EL SALVADOR 17 Jun 1953, EQUATORIAL GUINEA 24 Jul 1986, ERITREA 14 Aug 2000, ESTONIA 18 Jan 1993, ETHIOPIA 2 Oct 1969, FIJI 9 Aug 1971, FINLAND 22 Feb 1955, THE FORMER YUGOSLAV REPUBLIC OF MACEDONIA 1 Sep 1993 (*10-12, 45), GABON 26 Feb 1965, GAMBIA 20 Oct 1966, GEORGIA 14 Sep 1993, GERMANY 3 Sep 1954 (*4, 13), GHANA 2 Aug 1958, GREECE 5 Jun 1956, GRENADA 13 Apr 1981, GUATEMALA 14 May, GUINEA-BISSAU 21 Feb 1974 (*4, 10, 11, 13, 45), GUINEA 11 Jul 1984, GUYUNA 22 Jul 1968, HAITI 11 Apr 1957, HOLY SEE 22 Feb 1951, HONDURAS 31 Dec 1965, HUNGARY 3 Aug 1954, ICELAND 10 Aug 1965, INDIA 9 Nov 1950, INDONESIA 30 Sep 1958, IRAN (ISLAMIC REPUBLIC OF) 20 Feb 1957 (*emblem), IRAQ 14 Feb 1956, IRELAND 27 Sep 1962, ISRAEL 6 Jul 1951 (*emblem), ITALY 17 Dec 1951, JAMAICA 20 Jul 1964, JAPAN 21 Apr 1953, JORDAN 29 May 1951, KAZAKHSTAN 5 May 1992, KENYA 20 Sep 1966, KIRIBATI 5 Jan 1989, KOREA (DEMOCRATIC PEOPLE'S REPUBLIC OF) 27 Aug 1957 (*10-112, 45, 85), KOREA (REPUBLIC OF) 16 Aug 1966 (*68, 118, general), KUWAIT 2 Sep 1967, KYRGYZSTAN 18 Sep 1992, LAO PEOPLE'S DEMOCRATIC REPUBLIC 29 Oct 1956, LATVIA 24 Dec 1991, LEBANON 10 Apr 1951, LESOTHO 20 May 1968, LIBERIA 29 Mar 1954, LIBYAN ARAB JAMAHIRIYA 22 May 1956, LIECHTENSTEIN 21 Sep 1950, LITHUANIA 3 Oct 1996, LUXEMBOURG 1 Jul 1953, MADAGASCAR 18 Jul 1963, MALAWI 5 Jan 1968, MALAYSIA 24 Aug 1962, MALDIVES 18 Jun 1991, MALI 24 May 1965, MALTA 22 Aug 1968, MARSHALL ISLANDS 1 Jun 2004, MAURITANIA 30 Oct 1962, MAURITIUS 18 Aug 1970, MEXICO 29 Oct 1952, MICRONESIA 19 Sep 1995, MOLDOVA (REPUBLIC OF) 24 May 1993, MONACO 5 Jul 1950, MONGOLIA 20 Dec 1958, MONTENEGRO 2 Aug 2006, MOROCCO 26 Jul 1956,

* Source: 75 U.N.T.S. 287.

MOZAMBIQUE 14 Mar 1983, MYANMAR 25 Aug 1992, NAMIBIA 22 Aug 1991, NAURU 27 Jun 2006, NEPAL 7 Feb 1964, NETHERLANDS 3 Aug 1954, NEW ZEALAND 2 May 1959 (*45, 68, 85, general), NICARAGUA 17 Dec 1953, NIGERIA 20 Jun 1961, NIGER 21 Apr 1964, NORWAY 3 Aug 1951, OMAN 31 Jan 1974, PAKISTAN 12 Jun 1951 (*44, 68), PALAU 25 Jun 1996, PANAMA 10 Feb 1956, PAPUA NEW GUINEA 26 May 1976, PARAGUAY 23 Oct 1961, PERU 15 Feb 1956, PHILIPPINES 6 Oct 1952, POLAND 26 Nov 1954, PORTUGAL 14 Mar 1961 (*3, 10, 13, 60), QATAR 15 Oct 1975, ROMANIA 1 Jun 1954, RUSSIAN FEDERATION 10 May 1954 (*10-12, 45, 85), RWANDA 5 May 1964, SAINT KITTA AND NEVIS 14 Feb 1986, SAINT LUCIA 18 Sep 1981, SAINT VINCENT AND THE GRENADINES 1 Apr 1981, SAMOA 23 Aug 1984, SAN MARINO 29 Aug 1953, SAO TOME AND PRINCIPE 21 May 1976, SAUDI ARABIA 18 May 1963, SENEGAL 18 May 1963, SERBIA (REPUBLIC OF) 16 Oct 2001, SEYCHELLES 8 Nov 1984, SIERRA LEONE 10 Jun 1965, SINGAPORE 27 Apr 1973, SLOVAKIA 2 Apr 1993, SLOVENIA 26 Mar 1992, SOLOMON ISLANDS 6 Jul 1981, SOMALIA 12 Jul 1962, SOUTH AFRICA 31 Mar 1952, SPAIN 4 Aug 1952, SRI LANKA 28 Feb 1959, SUDAN 23 Sep 1957, SURINAME 13 Oct 1976 (*68), SWAZILAND 28 Jun 1973, SWEDEN 28 Dec 1953, SWITZERLAND 31 Mar 1950, SYRIAN ARAB REPUBLIC 2 Nov 1953, TAJIKISTAN 13 Jan 1993, TANZANIA (UNITED REPUBLIC OF) 12 Dec 1962, THAILAND 29 Dec 1954, TIMOR-LESTE 8 May 2003, TOGO 6 Jan 1962, TONGA 13 Apr 1978, TRINIDAD AND TOBAGO 24 Sep 1963, TUNISIA 4 May 1957, TURKEY 10 Feb 1954, TURKMENISTAN 10 Apr 1992, TUVALU 19 Feb 1981, UGANDA 18 May 1964, UKRAINE 3 Aug 1954 (*10-12, 45, 85), UNITED ARAB EMIRATES 10 May 1972, UNITED KINGDOM OF GREAT BRITAIN AND NORTHERN IRELAND 23 Sep 1957 (*general, territorial), UNITED STATES OF AMERICA 2 Aug 1955 (*68, general), URUGUAY 5 Mar 1969 (*87, 100, 101), UZBEKISTAN 8 Oct 1993, VANUATU 27 Oct 1982, VENEZUELA 13 Feb 1956, VIET NAM 28 Jun 1957 (*4, 10-12, 45, 85), YEMEN 16 Jul 1970, ZAMBIA 19 Oct 1966.

PART I

GENERAL PROVISIONS

Article 1

The High Contracting Parties undertake to respect and to ensure respect for the present Convention in all circumstances.

Article 2

In addition to the provisions which shall be implemented in peacetime, the present Convention shall apply to all cases of declared war or of any other armed conflict which may arise between two or more of the High Contracting Parties, even if the state of war is not recognized by one of them.

The Convention shall also apply to all cases of partial or total occupation of the territory of a High Contracting Party, even if the said occupation meets with no armed resistance.

Although one of the Powers in conflict may not be a party to the present Convention, the Powers who are parties thereto shall remain bound by it in their mutual relations. They shall furthermore be bound by the Convention in relation to the said Power, if the latter accepts and applies the provisions thereof.

Article 3

In the case of armed conflict not of an international character occurring in the territory of one of the High Contracting Parties, each Party to the conflict shall be bound to apply, as a minimum, the following provisions:

1. Persons taking no active part in the hostilities, including members of armed forces who have laid down their arms and those placed hors de combat by sickness, wounds, detention, or any other cause, shall in all circumstances be treated humanely, without any adverse distinction founded on race, colour, religion or faith, sex, birth or wealth, or any other similar criteria.

To this end, the following acts are and shall remain prohibited at any time and in any place whatsoever with respect to the above-mentioned persons:

(a) Violence to life and person, in particular murder of all kinds, mutilation, cruel treatment and torture;

(b) Taking of hostages;

(c) Outrages upon personal dignity, in particular humiliating and degrading treatment;

(d) The passing of sentences and the carrying out of executions without previous judgment pronounced by a regularly constituted court, affording all the judicial guarantees which are recognized as indispensable by civilized peoples.

2. The wounded and sick shall be collected and cared for.

An impartial humanitarian body, such as the International Committee of the Red Cross, may offer its services to the Parties to the conflict.

The Parties to the conflict should further endeavour to bring into force, by means of special agreements, all or part of the other provisions of the present Convention.

The application of the preceding provisions shall not affect the legal status of the Parties to the conflict.

Article 4

Persons protected by the Convention are those who, at a given moment and in any manner whatsoever, find themselves, in case of a conflict or occupation, in the hands of a Party to the conflict or Occupying Power of which they are not nationals.

Nationals of a State which is not bound by the Convention are not protected by it. Nationals of a neutral State who find themselves in the territory of a belligerent State, and nationals of a co-belligerent State, shall not be regarded as protected persons while the State of which they are nationals has normal diplomatic representation in the State in whose hands they are.

The provisions of Part II are, however, wider in application, as defined in Article 13.

Persons protected by the Geneva Convention for the Amelioration of the Condition of the Wounded and Sick in Armed Forces in the Field of August 12, 1949, or by the Geneva Convention for the Amelioration of the Condition of Wounded, Sick and Shipwrecked Members of Armed Forces at Sea of August 12, 1949, or by the Geneva Convention relative to the Treatment of Prisoners of War of August 12, 1949, shall not be considered as protected persons within the meaning of the present Convention.

Article 5

Where, in the territory of a Party to the conflict, the latter is satisfied that an individual protected person is definitely suspected of or engaged in activities hostile to the security of the State, such individual person shall not be entitled to claim such rights and privileges under the present Convention as would, if exercised in the favour of such individual person, be prejudicial to the security of such State.

Where in occupied territory an individual protected person is detained as a spy or saboteur, or as a person under definite suspicion of activity hostile to the security of the Occupying Power, such person shall, in those cases where absolute military security so requires, be regarded as having forfeited rights of communication under the present Convention.

In each case, such persons shall nevertheless be treated with humanity, and in case of trial, shall not be deprived of the rights of fair and regular trial prescribed by the present Convention. They shall also be granted the full rights and privileges of a protected person under the present Convention at the earliest date consistent with the security of the State or Occupying Power, as the case may be.

[...]

Article 8

Protected persons may in no circumstances renounce in part or in entirety the rights secured to them by the present Convention, and by the special agreements referred to in the foregoing Article, if such there be.

Article 9

The present Convention shall be applied with the cooperation and under the scrutiny of the Protecting Powers whose duty it is to safeguard the interests of the Parties to the conflict. For this purpose, the Protecting Powers may appoint, apart from their diplomatic or consular staff, delegates from amongst their own nationals or the nationals of other neutral Powers. The said delegates shall be subject to the approval of the Power with which they are to carry out their duties.

The Parties to the conflict shall facilitate to the greatest extent possible the task of the representatives or delegates of the Protecting Powers.

The representatives or delegates of the Protecting Powers shall not in any case exceed their mission under the present Convention. They shall, in particular, take account of the imperative necessities of security of the State wherein they carry out their duties.

Article 10

The provisions of the present Convention constitute no obstacle to the humanitarian activities which the International Committee of the Red Cross or any other impartial humanitarian organization may, subject to the consent of the Parties to the conflict concerned, undertake for the protection of civilian persons and for their relief.

Article 11

The High Contracting Parties may at any time agree to entrust to an organization which offers all guarantees of impartiality and efficacy the duties incumbent on the Protecting Powers by virtue of the present Convention.

When persons protected by the present Convention do not benefit or cease to benefit, no matter for what reason, by the activities of a Protecting Power or of an organization provided for in the first paragraph above, the Detaining Power shall request a neutral State, or such an organization, to undertake the functions performed under the present Convention by a Protecting Power designated by the Parties to a conflict.

If protection cannot be arranged accordingly, the Detaining Power shall request or shall accept, subject to the provisions of this Article, the offer of the services of a humanitarian organization, such as the International Committee of the Red Cross, to assume the humanitarian functions performed by Protecting Powers under the present Convention.

Any neutral Power, or any organization invited by the Power concerned or offering itself for these purposes, shall be required to act with a sense of responsibility towards the Party to the conflict on which persons protected by the present Convention depend, and shall be required to furnish sufficient assurances that it is in a position to undertake the appropriate functions and to discharge them impartially.

No derogation from the preceding provisions shall be made by special agreements between Powers one of which is restricted, even temporarily, in its freedom to negotiate with the other Power or its allies by reason of military events, more particularly where the whole, or a substantial part, of the territory of the said Power is occupied.

Whenever in the present Convention mention is made of a Protecting Power, such mention applies to substitute organizations in the sense of the present Article.

The provisions of this Article shall extend and be adapted to cases of nationals of a neutral State who are in occupied territory or who find themselves in the territory of a belligerent State with which the State of which they are nationals has not normal diplomatic representation.

Article 12

In cases where they deem it advisable in the interest of protected persons, particularly in cases of disagreement between the Parties to the conflict as to the application or interpretation of the provisions of the present Convention, the Protecting Powers shall lend their good offices with a view to settling the disagreement. For this purpose, each of the Protecting Powers may, either at the invitation of one Party or on its own initiative, propose to the Parties to the conflict a meeting of their representatives, and in particular of the authorities responsible for protected person, possibly on neutral territory suitably chosen. The Parties to the conflict shall be bound to give effect to the proposals made to them for this purpose. The Protecting Powers may, if necessary, propose for approval by the Parties to the conflict, a person belonging to a neutral Power or delegated by the International Committee of the Red Cross who shall be invited to take part in such a meeting.

PART II

GENERAL PROTECTION OF POPULATIONS AGAINST CERTAIN CONSEQUENCES OF WAR

Article 13

The provisions of Part II cover the whole of the populations of the countries in conflict, without any adverse distinction based, in particular, on race, nationality, religion or political opinion, and are intended to alleviate the sufferings caused by war.

[...]

Article 24

The Parties to the conflict shall take the necessary measures to ensure that children under fifteen, who are orphaned or are separated from their families as a result of the war, are not left to their own resources, and that their maintenance, the exercise of their religion and their education are facilitated in all circumstances. Their education shall, as far as possible, be entrusted to persons of a similar cultural tradition.

The Parties to the conflict shall facilitate the reception of such children in a neutral country for the duration of the conflict with the consent of the Protecting Power, if any, and under due safeguards for the observance of the principles stated in the first paragraph.

They shall, furthermore, endeavour to arrange for all children under twelve to be identified by the wearing of identity discs, or by some other means.

Article 25

All persons in the territory of a Party to the conflict, or in a territory occupied by it, shall be enabled to give news of a strictly personal nature to members of their families, wherever they may be, and to receive news from them. This correspondence shall be forwarded speedily and without undue delay.

If, as a result of circumstances, it becomes difficult or impossible to exchange family correspondence by the ordinary post, the Parties to the conflict concerned shall apply to a neutral intermediary, such as the Central Agency provided for in Article 140, and shall decide in consultation with it how to ensure the fulfilment of their obligations under the best possible conditions, in particular with the cooperation of the National Red Cross (Red Crescent, Red Lion and Sun) Societies.

If the Parties to the conflict deem it necessary to restrict family correspondence, such restrictions shall be confined to the compulsory use of standard forms containing twenty-five freely chosen words, and to the limitation of the number of these forms despatched to one each month.

Article 26

Each Party to the conflict shall facilitate enquiries made by members of families dispersed owing to the war, with the object of renewing contact with one another and of meeting, if possible. It shall encourage, in particular, the work of organizations engaged on this task provided they are acceptable to it and conform to its security regulations.

PART III

STATUS AND TREATMENT OF PROTECTED PERSONS

SECTION I

PROVISIONS COMMON TO THE TERRITORIES OF THE PARTIES TO THE CONFLICT AND TO OCCUPIED TERRITORIES

Article 27

Protected persons are entitled, in all circumstances, to respect for their persons, their honour, their family rights, their religious convictions and practices, and their manners and customs. They shall at all times be humanely treated, and shall be protected especially against all acts of violence or threats thereof and against insults and public curiosity.

Women shall be especially protected against any attack on their honour, in particular against rape, enforced prostitution, or any form of indecent assault.

Without prejudice to the provisions relating to their state of health, age and sex, all protected persons shall be treated with the same consideration by the Party to the conflict in whose power they are, without any adverse distinction based, in particular, on race, religion or political opinion.

However, the Parties to the conflict may take such measures of control and security in regard to protected persons as may be necessary as a result of the war.

Article 28

The presence of a protected person may not be used to render certain points or areas immune from military operations.

Article 29

The Party to the conflict in whose hands protected persons may be is responsible for the treatment accorded to them by its agents, irrespective of any individual responsibility which may be incurred.

Article 30

Protected persons shall have every facility for making application to the Protecting Powers, the International Committee of the Red Cross, the National Red Cross (Red Crescent, Red Lion and Sun) Society of the country where they may be, as well as to any organization that might assist them.

These several organizations shall be granted all facilities for that purpose by the authorities, within the bounds set by military or security considerations.

Apart from the visits of the delegates of the Protecting Powers and of the International Committee of the Red Cross, provided for by Article 143, the Detaining or Occupying Powers shall facilitate as much as possible visits to protected persons by the representatives of other organizations whose object is to give spiritual aid or material relief to such persons.

Article 31

No physical or moral coercion shall be exercised against protected persons, in particular to obtain information from them or from third parties.

Article 32

The High Contracting Parties specifically agree that each of them is prohibited from taking any measure of such a character as to cause the physical suffering or extermination of protected persons in their hands. This prohibition applies not only to murder, torture, corporal punishment, mutilation and medical or scientific experiments not necessitated by the medical treatment of a protected person but also to any other measures of brutality whether applied by civilian or military agents.

Article 33

No protected person may be punished for an offence he or she has not personally committed. Collective penalties and likewise all measures of intimidation or of terrorism are prohibited.

Pillage is prohibited.

Reprisals against protected persons and their property are prohibited.

Article 34

The taking of hostages is prohibited.

SECTION II

ALIENS IN THE TERRITORY OF A PARTY TO THE CONFLICT

Article 35

All protected persons who may desire to leave the territory at the outset of, or during a conflict, shall be entitled to do so, unless their departure is contrary to the national interests of the

State. The applications of such persons to leave shall be decided in accordance with regularly established procedures and the decision shall be taken as rapidly as possible. Those persons permitted to leave may provide themselves with the necessary funds for their journey and take with them a reasonable amount of their effects and articles of personal use.

If any such person is refused permission to leave the territory, he shall be entitled to have such refusal reconsidered as soon as possible by an appropriate court or administrative board designated by the Detaining Power for that purpose.

Upon request, representatives of the Protecting Power shall, unless reasons of security prevent it, or the persons concerned object, be furnished with the reasons for refusal of any request for permission to leave the territory and be given, as expeditiously as possible, the names of all persons who have been denied permission to leave.

Article 36

Departures permitted under the foregoing Article shall be carried out in satisfactory conditions as regards safety, hygiene, sanitation and food. All costs in connection therewith, from the point of exit in the territory of the Detaining Power, shall be borne by the country of destination, or, in the case of accommodation in a neutral country, by the Power whose nationals are benefited. The practical details of such movements may, if necessary, be settled by special agreements between the Powers concerned.

The foregoing shall not prejudice such special agreements as may be concluded between Parties to the conflict concerning the exchange and repatriation of their nationals in enemy hands.

Article 37

Protected persons who are confined pending proceedings or serving a sentence involving loss of liberty shall during their confinement be humanely treated.

As soon as they are released, they may ask to leave the territory in conformity with the foregoing Articles.

Article 38

With the exception of special measures authorized by the present Convention, in particular by Articles 27 and 41 thereof, the situation of protected persons shall continue to be regulated, in principle, by the provisions concerning aliens in time of peace. In any case, the following rights shall be granted to them:

1. They shall be enabled to receive the individual or collective relief that may be sent to them.

2. They shall, if their state of health so requires, receive medical attention and hospital treatment to the same extent as the nationals of the State concerned.

3. They shall be allowed to practise their religion and to receive spiritual assistance from ministers of their faith.

4. If they reside in an area particularly exposed to the dangers of war, they shall be authorized to move from that area to the same extent as the nationals of the State concerned.

5. Children under fifteen years, pregnant women and mothers of children under seven years shall benefit by any preferential treatment to the same extent as the nationals of the State concerned.

Article 39

Protected persons who, as a result of the war, have lost their gainful employment, shall be granted the opportunity to find paid employment. That opportunity shall, subject to security considerations and to the provisions of Article 40, be equal to that enjoyed by the nationals of the Power in whose territory they are.

Where a Party to the conflict applies to a protected person methods of control which result in his being unable to support himself, and especially if such a person is prevented for reasons of security from finding paid employment on reasonable conditions, the said Party shall ensure his support and that of his dependents.

Protected persons may in any case receive allowances from their home country, the Protecting Power, or the relief societies referred to in Article 30.

Article 40

Protected persons may be compelled to work only to the same extent as nationals of the Party to the conflict in whose territory they are.

If protected persons are of enemy nationality, they may only be compelled to do work which is normally necessary to ensure the feeding, sheltering, clothing, transport and health of human beings and which is not directly related to the conduct of military operations.

In the cases mentioned in the two preceding paragraphs, protected persons compelled to work shall have the benefit of the same working conditions and of the same safeguards as national workers, in particular as regards wages, hours of labour, clothing and equipment, previous training and compensation for occupational accidents and diseases.

If the above provisions are infringed, protected persons shall be allowed to exercise their right of complaint in accordance with Article 30.

Article 41

Should the Power in whose hands protected persons may be consider the measures of control mentioned in the present Convention to be inadequate, it may not have recourse to any other measure of control more severe than that of assigned residence or internment, in accordance with the provisions of Articles 42 and 43.

In applying the provisions of Article 39, second paragraph, to the cases of persons required to leave their usual places of residences by virtue of a decision placing them in assigned residence elsewhere. the Detaining Power shall be guided as closely as possible by the standards of welfare set forth in Part III, Section IV of this Convention.

Article 42

The internment or placing in assigned residence of protected persons may be ordered only if the security of the Detaining Power makes it absolutely necessary.

If any person, acting through the representatives of the Protecting Power, voluntarily demands internment, and if his situation renders this step necessary, he shall be interned by the Power in whose hands he may be.

Article 43

Any protected person who has been interned or placed in assigned residence shall be entitled to have such action reconsidered as soon as possible by an appropriate court or administrative board designated by the Detaining Power for that purpose. If the internment or placing in assigned residence is maintained, the court or administrative board shall periodically, and at least twice yearly, give consideration to his or her case, with a view to the favourable amendment of the initial decision, if circumstances permit.

Unless the protected persons concerned object, the Detaining Power shall, as rapidly as possible, give the Protecting Power the names of any protected persons who have been interned or subjected to assigned residence, or who have been released from internment or assigned residence. The decisions of the courts or boards mentioned in the first paragraph of the present Article shall also, subject to the same conditions, be notified as rapidly as possible to the Protecting Power.

Article 44

In applying the measures of control mentioned in the present Convention, the Detaining Power shall not treat as enemy aliens exclusively on the basis of their nationality de jure of an enemy State, refugees who do not, in fact, enjoy the protection of any government.

Article 45

Protected persons shall not be transferred to a Power which is not a party to the Convention.

This provision shall in no way constitute an obstacle to the repatriation of protected persons, or to their return to their country of residence after the cessation of hostilities.

Protected persons may be transferred by the Detaining Power only to a Power which is a party to the present Convention and after the Detaining Power has satisfied itself of the willingness and ability of such transferee Power to apply the present Convention. If protected persons are transferred under such circumstances, responsibility for the application of the present Convention rests on the Power accepting them, while they are in its custody. Nevertheless, if that Power fails to carry out the provisions of the present Convention in any important respect, the Power by which the protected persons were transferred shall, upon being so notified by the Protecting Power, take effective measures to correct the situation or shall request the return of the protected persons. Such request must be complied with.

In no circumstances shall a protected person be transferred to a country where he or she may have reason to fear persecution for his or her political opinions or religious beliefs.

The provisions of this Article do not constitute an obstacle to the extradition, in pursuance of extradition treaties concluded before the outbreak of hostilities, of protected persons accused of offences against ordinary criminal law.

Article 46

In so far as they have not been previously withdrawn, restrictive measures taken regarding protected persons shall be cancelled as soon as possible after the close of hostilities.

Restrictive measures affecting their property shall be cancelled, in accordance with the law of the Detaining Power, as soon as possible after the close of hostilities.

SECTION III

OCCUPIED TERRITORIES

Article 47

Protected persons who are in occupied territory shall not be deprived, in any case or in any manner whatsoever, of the benefits of the present Convention by any change introduced, as the result of the occupation of a territory, into the institutions or government of the said territory, nor by any agreement concluded between the authorities of the occupied territories and the Occupying Power, nor by any annexation by the latter of the whole or part of the occupied territory.

Article 48

Protected persons who are not nationals of the Power whose territory is occupied may avail themselves of the right to leave the territory subject to the provisions of Article 35, and decisions thereon shall be taken according to the procedure which the Occupying Power shall establish in accordance with the said Article.

Article 49

Individual or mass forcible transfers, as well as deportations of protected persons from occupied territory to the territory of the Occupying Power or to that of any other country, occupied or not, are prohibited, regardless of their motive.

Nevertheless, the Occupying Power may undertake total or partial evacuation of a given area if the security of the population or imperative military reasons do demand. Such evacuations may not involve the displacement of protected persons outside the bounds of the occupied territory except when for material reasons it is impossible to avoid such displacement. Persons thus evacuated shall be transferred back to their homes as soon as hostilities in the area in question have ceased.

The Occupying Power undertaking such transfers or evacuations shall ensure, to the greatest practicable extent, that proper accommodation is provided to receive the protected persons, that the removals are effected in satisfactory conditions of hygiene, health, safety and nutrition, and that members of the same family are not separated.

The Protecting Power shall be informed of any transfers and evacuations as soon as they have taken place.

The Occupying Power shall not detain protected persons in an area particularly exposed to the dangers of war unless the security of the population or imperative military reasons so demand.

The Occupying Power shall not deport or transfer parts of its own civilian population into the territory it occupies.

Article 50

The Occupying Power shall, with the cooperation of the national and local authorities, facilitate the proper working of all institutions devoted to the care and education of children.

The Occupying Power shall take all necessary steps to facilitate the identification of children and the registration of their parentage. It may not, in any case, change their personal status, nor enlist them in formations or organizations subordinate to it.

Should the local institutions be inadequate for the purpose, the Occupying Power shall make arrangements for the maintenance and education, if possible by persons of their own nationality, language and religion, of children who are orphaned or separated from their parents as a result of the war and who cannot be adequately cared for by a near relative or friend.

A special section of the Bureau set up in accordance with Article 136 shall be responsible for taking all necessary steps to identify children whose identity is in doubt. Particulars of their parents or other near relatives should always be recorded if available.

The Occupying Power shall not hinder the application of any preferential measures in regard to food, medical care and protection against the effects of war, which may have been adopted prior to the occupation in favour of children under fifteen years, expectant mothers, and mothers of children under seven years.

Article 51

The Occupying Power may not compel protected persons to serve in its armed or auxiliary forces. No pressure or propaganda which aims at securing voluntary enlistment is permitted.

The Occupying Power may not compel protected persons to work unless they are over eighteen years of age, and then only on work which is necessary either for the needs of the army of occupation, or for the public utility services, or for the feeding, sheltering, clothing, transportation or health of the population of the occupied country. Protected persons may not be compelled to undertake any work which would involve them in the obligation of taking part in military operations. The Occupying Power may not compel protected persons to employ forcible means to ensure the security of the installations where they are performing compulsory labour.

The work shall be carried out only in the occupied territory where the persons whose services have been requisitioned are. Every such person shall, so far as possible, be kept in his usual place of employment. Workers shall be paid a fair wage and the work shall be proportionate to their physical and intellectual capacities. The legislation in force in the occupied country concerning working conditions, and safeguards as regards, in particular, such matters as wages, hours of work, equipment, preliminary training and compensation for occupational accidents and diseases, shall be applicable to the protected persons assigned to the work referred to in this Article.

In no case shall requisition of labour lead to a mobilization of workers in an organization of a military or semi-military character.

Article 52

No contract, agreement or regulation shall impair the right of any worker, whether voluntary or not and wherever he may be, to apply to the representatives of the Protecting Power in order to request the said Power's intervention.

All measures aiming at creating unemployment or at restricting the opportunities offered to workers in an occupied territory, in order to induce them to work for the Occupying Power, are prohibited.

Article 53

Any destruction by the Occupying Power of real or personal property belonging individually or collectively to private persons, or to the State, or to other public authorities, or to social or cooperative organizations, is prohibited, except where such destruction is rendered absolutely necessary by military operations.

[...]

Article 64

The penal laws of the occupied territory shall remain in force, with the exception that they may be repealed or suspended by the Occupying Power in cases where they constitute a threat to its security or an obstacle to the application of the present Convention. Subject to the latter consideration and to the necessity for ensuring the effective administration of justice, the tribunals of the occupied territory shall continue to function in respect of all offences covered by the said laws.

The Occupying Power may, however, subject the population of the occupied territory to provisions which are essential to enable the Occupying Power to fulfil its obligations under the present Convention, to maintain the orderly government of the territory, and to ensure the security of the Occupying Power, of the members and property of the occupying forces or administration, and likewise of the establishments and lines of communication used by them.

Article 65

The penal provisions enacted by the Occupying Power shall not come into force before they have been published and brought to the knowledge of the inhabitants in their own language. The effect of these penal provisions shall not be retroactive.

Article 66

In case of a breach of the penal provisions promulgated by it by virtue of the second paragraph of Article 64, the Occupying Power may hand over the accused to its properly constituted, non-political military courts, on condition that the said courts sit in the occupied country. Courts of appeal shall preferably sit in the occupied country.

Article 67

The courts shall apply only those provisions of law which were applicable prior to the offence, and which are in accordance with general principles of law, in particular the principle that the penalty shall be proportioned to the offence. They shall take into consideration the fact that the accused is not a national of the Occupying Power.

Article 68

Protected persons who commit an offence which is solely intended to harm the Occupying Power, but which does not constitute an attempt on the life or limb of members of the occupying forces or administration, nor a grave collective danger, nor seriously damage the property of the occupying forces or administration or the installations used by them, shall be liable to internment or simple imprisonment, provided the duration of such internment or imprisonment is proportionate to the offence committed. Furthermore, internment or imprisonment shall, for such offences, be the only measure adopted for depriving protected persons of liberty. The courts provided for under Article 66 of the present Convention may at their discretion convert a sentence of imprisonment to one of internment for the same period.

The penal provisions promulgated by the Occupying Power in accordance with Articles 64 and 65 may impose the death penalty on a protected person only in cases where the person is guilty of espionage, of serious acts of sabotage against the military installations of the Occupying Power or of intentional offences which have caused the death of one or more persons, provided that such offences were punishable by death under the law of the occupied territory in force before the occupation began.

The death penalty may not be pronounced against a protected person unless the attention of the court has been particularly called to the fact that, since the accused is not a national of the Occupying Power, he is not bound to it by any duty of allegiance.

In any case, the death penalty may not be pronounced against a protected person who was under eighteen years of age at the time of the offence.

Article 69

In all cases, the duration of the period during which a protected person accused of an offence is under arrest awaiting trial or punishment shall be deducted from any period of imprisonment awarded.

Article 70

Protected persons shall not be arrested, prosecuted or convicted by the Occupying Power for acts committed or for opinions expressed before the occupation, or during a temporary interruption thereof, with the exception of breaches of the laws and customs of war.

Nationals of the Occupying Power who, before the outbreak of hostilities, have sought refuge in the territory of the occupied State, shall not be arrested, prosecuted, convicted or deported from the occupied territory, except for offences committed after the outbreak of hostilities, or for offences under common law committed before the outbreak of hostilities which, according to the law of the occupied State, would have justified extradition in time of peace.

Article 71

No sentence shall be pronounced by the competent courts of the Occupying Power except after a regular trial.

Accused persons who are prosecuted by the Occupying Power shall be promptly informed, in writing, in a language which they understand, of the particulars of the charges preferred against them, and shall be brought to trial as rapidly as possible. The Protecting Power shall be informed of all proceedings instituted by the Occupying Power against protected persons in respect of charges involving the death penalty or imprisonment for two years or more; it shall be enabled, at any time, to obtain information regarding the state of such proceedings. Furthermore, the Protecting Power shall be entitled, on request, to be furnished with all particulars of these and of any other proceedings instituted by the Occupying Power against protected persons.

The notification to the Protecting Power, as provided for in the second paragraph above, shall be sent immediately, and shall in any case reach the Protecting Power three weeks before the date of the first hearing. Unless, at the opening of the trial, evidence is submitted that the provisions of this Article are fully complied with, the trial shall not proceed. The notification shall include the following particulars:

(a) Description of the accused;

(b) Place of residence or detention;

(c) Specification of the charge or charges (with mention of the penal provisions under which it is brought);

(d) Designation of the court which will hear the case;

(e) Place and date of the first hearing.

Article 72

Accused persons shall have the right to present evidence necessary to their defence and may, in particular, call witnesses. They shall have the right to be assisted by a qualified advocate or counsel of their own choice, who shall be able to visit them freely and shall enjoy the necessary facilities for preparing the defence.

Failing a choice by the accused, the Protecting Power may provide him with an advocate or counsel. When an accused person has to meet a serious charge and the Protecting Power is not functioning, the Occupying Power, subject to the consent of the accused, shall provide an advocate or counsel.

Accused persons shall, unless they freely waive such assistance, be aided by an interpreter, both during preliminary investigation and during the hearing in court. They shall have the right at any time to object to the interpreter and to ask for his replacement.

Article 73

A convicted person shall have the right of appeal provided for by the laws applied by the court. He shall be fully informed of his right to appeal or petition and of the time limit within which he may do so.

The penal procedure provided in the present Section shall apply, as far as it is applicable, to appeals. Where the laws applied by the Court make no provision for appeals, the convicted person shall have the right to petition against the finding and sentence to the competent authority of the Occupying Power.

Article 74

Representatives of the Protecting Power shall have the right to attend the trial of any protected person, unless the hearing has, as an exceptional measure, to be held in camera in the interests of the security of the Occupying Power, which shall then notify the Protecting Power. A notification in respect of the date and place of trial shall be sent to the Protecting Power.

Any judgment involving a sentence of death, or imprisonment for two years or more, shall be communicated, with the relevant grounds, as rapidly as possible to the Protecting Power. The notification shall contain a reference to the notification made under Article 71, and in the case of sentences of imprisonment, the name of the place where the sentence is to be served. A record of judgments other than those referred to above shall be kept by the court and shall be open to inspection by representatives of the Protecting Power. Any period allowed for appeal in the case of sentences involving the death penalty, or imprisonment for two years or more, shall not run until notification of judgment has been received by the Protecting Power.

Article 75

In no case shall persons condemned to death be deprived of the right of petition for pardon or reprieve.

No death sentence shall be carried out before the expiration of a period of at least six months from the date of receipt by the Protecting Power of the notification of the final judgment confirming such death sentence, or of an order denying pardon or reprieve.

The six months period of suspension of the death sentence herein prescribed may be reduced in individual cases in circumstances of grave emergency involving an organized threat to the security of the Occupying Power or its forces, provided always that the Protecting Power is notified of such reduction and is given reasonable time and opportunity to make representations to the competent occupying authorities in respect of such death sentences.

Article 76

Protected persons accused of offences shall be detained in the occupied country, and if convicted they shall serve their sentences therein. They shall, if possible, be separated from other detainees and shall enjoy conditions of food and hygiene which will be sufficient to keep them in good health, and which will be at least equal to those obtaining in prisons in the occupied country.

They shall receive the medical attention required by their state of health.

They shall also have the right to receive any spiritual assistance which they may require.

Women shall be confined in separate quarters and shall be under the direct supervision of women.

Proper regard shall be paid to the special treatment due to minors.

Protected persons who are detained shall have the right to be visited by delegates of the Protecting Power and of the International Committee of the Red Cross, in accordance with the provisions of Article 143.

Such persons shall have the right to receive at least one relief parcel monthly.

Article 77

Protected persons who have been accused of offences or convicted by the courts in occupied territory shall be handed over at the close of occupation, with the relevant records, to the authorities of the liberated territory.

Article 78

If the Occupying Power considers it necessary, for imperative reasons of security, to take safety measures concerning protected persons, it may, at the most, subject them to assigned residence or to internment.

Decisions regarding such assigned residence or internment shall be made according to a regular procedure to be prescribed by the Occupying Power in accordance with the provisions of the present Convention. This procedure shall include the right of appeal for the parties concerned. Appeals shall be decided with the least possible delay. In the event of the decision being upheld, it shall be subject to periodical review, if possible every six months, by a competent body set up by the said Power.

Protected persons made subject to assigned residence and thus required to leave their homes shall enjoy the full benefit of Article 39 of the present Convention.

SECTION IV

REGULATIONS FOR THE TREATMENT OF INTERNEES

Chapter I

GENERAL PROVISIONS

Article 79

The Parties to the conflict shall not intern protected persons, except in accordance with the provisions of Articles 41, 42, 43, 68 and 78.

Article 80

Internees shall retain their full civil capacity and shall exercise such attendant rights as may be compatible with their status.

Article 81

Parties to the conflict who intern protected persons shall be bound to provide free of charge for their maintenance, and to grant them also the medical attention required by their state of health.

No deduction from the allowances, salaries or credits due to the internees shall be made for the repayment of these costs.

The Detaining Power shall provide for the support of those dependent on the internees, if such dependants are without adequate means of support or are unable to earn a living.

Article 82

The Detaining Power shall, as far as possible, accommodate the internees according to their nationality, language and customs. Internees who are nationals of the same country shall not be separated merely because they have different languages.

Throughout the duration of their internment, members of the same family, and in particular parents and children, shall be lodged together in the same place of internment, except when separation of a temporary nature is necessitated for reasons of employment or health or for the purposes of enforcement of the provisions of Chapter IX of the present Section. Internees may request that their children who are left at liberty without parental care shall be interned with them.

Wherever possible, interned members of the same family shall be housed in the same premises and given separate accommodation from other internees, together with facilities for leading a proper family life.

Chapter II

PLACES OF INTERNMENT

Article 83

The Detaining Power shall not set up places of internment in areas particularly exposed to the dangers of war.

The Detaining Power shall give the enemy Powers, through the intermediary of the Protecting Powers, all useful information regarding the geographical location of places of internment.

Whenever military considerations permit, internment camps shall be indicated by the letters IC, placed so as to be clearly visible in the daytime from the air. The Powers concerned may, however, agree upon any other system of marking. No place other than an internment camp shall be marked as such.

Article 84

Internees shall be accommodated and administered separately from prisoners of war and from persons deprived of liberty for any other reason.

Article 85

The Detaining Power is bound to take all necessary and possible measures to ensure that protected persons shall, from the outset of their internment, be accommodated in buildings or quarters which afford every possible safeguard as regards hygiene and health, and provide efficient protection against the rigours of the climate and the effects of the war. In no case shall permanent places of internment be situated in unhealthy areas or in districts the climate of which is injurious to the internees. In all cases where the district, in which a protected person is temporarily interned, is in an unhealthy area or has a climate which is harmful to his health, he shall be removed to a more suitable place of internment as rapidly as circumstances permit.

The premises shall be fully protected from dampness, adequately heated and lighted, in particular between dusk and lights out. The sleeping quarters shall be sufficiently spacious and well ventilated, and the internees shall have suitable bedding and sufficient blankets, account being taken of the climate, and the age, sex, and state of health of the internees.

Internees shall have for their use, day and night, sanitary conveniences which conform to the rules of hygiene and are constantly maintained in a state of cleanliness. They shall be provided with sufficient water and soap for their daily personal toilet and for washing their personal laundry; installations and facilities necessary for this purpose shall be granted to them.

Showers or baths shall also be available. The necessary time shall be set aside for washing and for cleaning.

Whenever it is necessary, as an exceptional and temporary measure, to accommodate women internees who are not members of a family unit in the same place of internment as men, the provision of separate sleeping quarters and sanitary conveniences for the use of such women internees shall be obligatory.

Article 86

The Detaining Power shall place at the disposal of interned persons, of whatever denomination, premises suitable for the holding of their religious services.

Article 87

Canteens shall be installed in every place of internment, except where other suitable facilities are available. Their purpose shall be to enable internees to make purchases, at prices not higher than local market prices, of foodstuffs and articles of everyday use, including soap and tobacco, such as would increase their personal well-being and comfort.

Profits made by canteens shall be credited to a welfare fund to be set up for each place of internment, and administered for the benefit of the internees attached to such place of internment. The Internee Committee provided for in Article 102 shall have the right to check the management of the canteen and of the said fund.

When a place of internment is closed down, the balance of the welfare fund shall be transferred to the welfare fund of a place of internment for internees of the same nationality, or, if such a place does not exist, to a central welfare fund which shall be administered for the benefit of all internees remaining in the custody of the Detaining Power. In case of a general release, the said profits shall be kept by the Detaining Power, subject to any agreement to the contrary between the Powers concerned.

Article 88

In all places of internment exposed to air raids and other hazards of war, shelters adequate in number and structure to ensure the necessary protection shall be installed. In case of alarms, the internees shall be free to enter such shelters as quickly as possible, excepting those who remain for the protection of their quarters against the aforesaid hazards. Any protective measures taken in favour of the population shall also apply to them.

All due precautions must be taken in places of internment against the danger of fire.

Chapter III

FOOD AND CLOTHING

Article 89

Daily food rations for internees shall be sufficient in quantity, quality and variety to keep internees in a good state of health and prevent the development of nutritional deficiencies. Account shall also be taken of the customary diet of the internees.

Internees shall also be given the means by which they can prepare for themselves any additional food in their possession.

Sufficient drinking water shall be supplied to internees. The use of tobacco shall be permitted.

Internees who work shall receive additional rations in proportion to the kind of labour which they perform.

Expectant and nursing mothers and children under fifteen years of age shall be given additional food, in proportion to their physiological needs.

Article 90

When taken into custody, internees shall be given all facilities to provide themselves with the necessary clothing, footwear and change of underwear, and later on, to procure further supplies if required. Should any internees not have sufficient clothing, account being taken of the climate, and be unable to procure any, it shall be provided free of charge to them by the Detaining Power.

The clothing supplied by the Detaining Power to internees and the outward markings placed on their own clothes shall not be ignominious nor expose them to ridicule.

Workers shall receive suitable working outfits, including protective clothing, whenever the nature of their work so requires.

Chapter IV

HYGIENE AND MEDICAL ATTENTION

Article 91

Every place of internment shall have an adequate infirmary, under the direction of a qualified doctor, where internees may have the attention they require, as well as an appropriate diet. Isolation wards shall be set aside for cases of contagious or mental diseases.

Maternity cases and internees suffering from serious diseases, or whose condition requires special treatment, a surgical operation or hospital care, must be admitted to any institution where adequate treatment can be given and shall receive care not inferior to that provided for the general population.

Internees shall, for preference, have the attention of medical personnel of their own nationality.

Internees may not be prevented from presenting themselves to the medical authorities for examination. The medical authorities of the Detaining Power shall, upon request, issue to every internee who has undergone treatment an official certificate showing the nature of his illness or injury, and the duration and nature of the treatment given. A duplicate of this certificate shall be forwarded to the Central Agency provided for in Article 140.

Treatment, including the provision of any apparatus necessary for the maintenance of internees in good health, particularly dentures and other artificial appliances and spectacles, shall be free of charge to the internee.

Article 92

Medical inspections of internees shall be made at least once a month. Their purpose shall be, in particular, to supervise the general state of health, nutrition and cleanliness of internees, and to detect contagious diseases, especially tuberculosis, malaria, and venereal diseases. Such inspections shall include, in particular, the checking of weight of each internee and, at least once a year, radioscopic examination.

Chapter V

RELIGIOUS, INTELLECTUAL AND PHYSICAL ACTIVITIES

Article 93

Internees shall enjoy complete latitude in the exercise of their religious duties, including attendance at the services of their faith, on condition that they comply with the disciplinary routine prescribed by the detaining authorities.

Ministers of religion who are interned shall be allowed to minister freely to the members of their community. For this purpose, the Detaining Power shall ensure their equitable allocation amongst the various places of internment in which there are internees speaking the same language and be longing to the same religion. Should such ministers be too few in number, the Detaining Power shall provide them with the necessary facilities, including means of transport, for moving from one place to another, and they shall be authorized to visit any internees who are in hospital. Ministers of religion shall be at liberty to correspond on matters concerning their ministry with the religious authorities in the country of detention and, as far as possible, with the international religious organizations of their faith. Such correspondence shall not be considered as forming a part of the quota mentioned in Article 107. It shall, however, be subject to the provisions of Article 112.

When internees do not have at their disposal the assistance of ministers of their faith, or should these latter be too few in number, the local religious authorities of the same faith may appoint, in agreement with the Detaining Power, a minister of the internees' faith or, if such a course is feasible from a denominational point of view, a minister of similar religion or a qualified layman. The latter shall enjoy the facilities granted to the ministry he has assumed. Persons so appointed shall comply with all regulations laid down by the Detaining Power in the interests of discipline and security.

Article 94

The Detaining Power shall encourage intellectual, educational and recreational pursuits, sports and games amongst internees, whilst leaving them free to take part in them or not. It shall take all practicable measures to ensure the exercise thereof, in particular by providing suitable premises.

All possible facilities shall be granted to internees to continue their studies or to take up new subjects. The education of children and young people shall be ensured; they shall be allowed to attend schools either within the place of internment or outside.

Internees shall be given opportunities for physical exercise, sports and outdoor games. For this purpose, sufficient open spaces shall be set aside in all places of internment. Special playgrounds shall be reserved for children and young people.

Article 95

The Detaining Power shall not employ internees as workers, unless they so desire. Employment which, if undertaken under compulsion by a protected person not in internment, would involve a breach of Articles 40 or 51 of the present Convention, and employment on work which is of a degrading or humiliating character are in any case prohibited.

After a working period of six weeks, internees shall be free to give up work at any moment, subject to eight days' notice.

These provisions constitute no obstacle to the right of the Detaining Power to employ interned doctors, dentists and other medical personnel in their professional capacity on behalf of their fellow internees, or to employ internees for administrative and maintenance work in places of internment and to detail such persons for work in the kitchens or for other domestic tasks, or to require such persons to undertake duties connected with the protection of internees against aerial bombardment or other war risks. No internee may, however, be required to perform tasks for which he is, in the opinion of a medical officer, physically unsuited.

The Detaining Power shall take entire responsibility for all working conditions, for medical attention, for the payment of wages, and for ensuring that all employed internees receive compensation for occupational accidents and diseases. The standards prescribed for the said working conditions and for compensation shall be in accordance with the national laws and regulations, and with the existing practice; they shall in no case be inferior to those obtaining for work of the same nature in the same district. Wages for work done shall be determined on an equitable basis by special agreements between the internees, the Detaining Power, and, if the case arises, employers other than the Detaining Power, due regard being paid to the obligation of the Detaining Power to provide for free maintenance of internees and for the medical attention which their state of health may require. Internees permanently detailed for categories of work mentioned in the third paragraph of this Article shall be paid fair wages by the Detaining Power. The working conditions and the scale of compensation for occupational accidents and diseases to internees thus detailed shall not be inferior to those applicable to work of the same nature in the same district.

Article 96

All labour detachments shall remain part of and dependent upon a place of internment. The competent authorities of the Detaining Power and the commandant of a place of internment shall be responsible for the observance in a labour detachment of the provisions of the present Convention. The commandant shall keep an up-to-date list of the labour detachments subordinate to him and shall communicate it to the delegates of the Protecting Power, of the International Committee of the Red Cross and of other humanitarian organizations who may visit the places of internment.

Chapter VI

PERSONAL PROPER AND FINANCIAL RESOURCES

Article 97

Internees shall be permitted to retain articles of personal use. Monies, cheques, bonds, etc., and valuables in their possession may not be taken from them except in accordance with established procedure. Detailed receipts shall be given therefor.

The amounts shall be paid into the account of every internee as provided for in Article 98. Such amounts may not be converted into any other currency unless legislation in force in the territory in which the owner is interned so requires or the internee gives his consent.

Articles which have above all a personal or sentimental value may not be taken away.

A woman internee shall not be searched except by a woman.

On release or repatriation, internees shall be given all articles, monies or other valuables taken from them during internment and shall receive in currency the balance of any credit to their accounts kept in accordance with Article 98, with the exception of any articles or amounts withheld by the Detaining Power by virtue of its legislation in force. If the property of an internee is so withheld, the owner shall receive a detailed receipt.

Family or identity documents in the possession of internees may not be taken away without a receipt being given. At no time shall internees be left without identity documents. If they have none, they shall be issued with special documents drawn up by the detaining authorities, which will serve as their identity papers until the end of their internment.

Internees may keep on their persons a certain amount of money, in cash or in the shape of purchase coupons, to enable them to make purchases.

Article 98

All internees shall receive regular allowances, sufficient to enable them to purchase goods and articles, such as tobacco, toilet requisites, etc. Such allowances may take the form of credits or purchase coupons.

Furthermore, internees may receive allowances from the Power to which they owe allegiance, the Protecting Powers, the organizations which may assist them, or their families, as well as the income on their property in accordance with the law of the Detaining Power. The amount of allowances granted by the Power to which they owe allegiance shall be the same for each category of internees (infirm, sick, pregnant women, etc.), but may not be allocated by that Power or distributed by the Detaining Power on the basis of discrimination between internees which are prohibited by Article 27 of the present Convention.

The Detaining Power shall open a regular account for every internee, to which shall be credited the allowances named in the present Article, the wages earned and the remittances received, together with such sums taken from him as may be available under the legislation in force in the territory in which he is interned. Internees shall be granted all facilities consistent with the legislation in force in such territory to make remittances to their families and to other dependants. They may draw from their accounts the amounts necessary for their personal expenses, within the limits fixed by the Detaining Power. They shall at all times be afforded reasonable facilities for consulting and obtaining copies of their accounts. A statement of accounts shall be furnished to the Protecting Power on request, and shall accompany the internee in case of transfer.

[...]

Protocol Additional to the Geneva Conventions of 12 August 1949, and relating to the Protection of Victims of International Armed Conflicts (Protocol I), 1977 [excerpts]*

Adoption: 8 June 1977
Entry into force: 7 December 1979
Parties: 167 (Status as of 1 April 2007)

ALBANIA 16 Jul 1993, ALGERIA 16 Aug 1989, ANGOLA 20 Sep 1984, ANTIGUA AND BARBUDA 06 Oct 1986, ARGENTINA 26 Nov 1986, ARMENIA 07 Jun 1993, AUSTRALIA 21 Jun 1991, AUSTRIA 13 Aug 1982 (*57.2, 58, 75, 85, 86), BAHAMAS 10 Apr 1980, BAHRAIN 30 Oct 1986, BANGLADESH 08 Sep 1980, BARBADOS 19 Feb 1990, BELARUS 23 Oct 1989, BELGIUM 20 May 1986, BELIZE 29 Jun 1984, BENIN 28 May 1986, BOLIVIA 08 Dec 1983, BOSNIA-HERZEGOVINA 31 Dec 1992, BOTSWANA 23 May 1979, BRAZIL 05 May 1992, BRUNEI DARUSSALAM 14 Oct 1991, BULGARIA 26 Sep 1989, BURKINA FASO 20 Oct 1987, BURUNDI 10 Jun 1993, CAMBODIA 14 Jan 1998, CAMEROON 16 Mar 1984, CANADA 20 Nov 1990 (*11, 39), CAPE VERDE 16 Mar 1995, CENTRAL AFRICAN REPUBLIC 17 Jul 1984, CHAD 17 Jan 1997, CHILE 24 Apr 1991, CHINA 14 Sep 1983 (*88.2), COLOMBIA 01 Sep 1993, COMOROS 21 Nov 1985, CONGO (DEM. REP.) 03 Jun 1982, CONGO 10 Nov 1983, COOK ISLANDS 07 May 2002, COSTA RICA 15 Dec 1983, COTE D'IVOIRE 20 Sep 1989, CROATIA 11 May 1992, CUBA 25 Nov 1982, CYPRUS 01 Jun 1979, CZECH REPUBLIC 05 Feb 1993, DENMARK 17 Jun 1982 (*75.4), DJIBOUTI 08 Apr 1991, DOMINICAN REPUBLIC 26 May 1994, DOMINICA 25 Apr 1996, ECUADOR 10 Apr 1979, EGYPT 09 Oct 1992, EL SALVADOR 23 Nov 1978, EQUATORIAL GUINEA 24 Jul 1986, ESTONIA 18 Jan 1993, ETHIOPIA 08 Apr 1994, FINLAND 07 Aug 1980, FORMER YUGOSLAV REPUBLIC OF MACEDONIA 01 Sep 1993 (*), FRANCE 11 Apr 2001, GABON 08 Apr 1980, GAMBIA 12 Jan 1989, GEORGIA 14 Sep 1993, GERMANY 14 Feb 1991, GHANA 28 Feb 1978, GREECE 31 Mar 1989, GRENADA 23 Sep 1998, GUATEMALA 19 Oct 1987, GUINEA-BISSAU 21 Oct 1986, GUINEA 11 Jul 1984, GUYANA 18 Jan 1988, HAITI 20 Dec 2006, HOLY SEE 21 Nov 1985, HONDURAS 16 Feb 1995, HUNGARY 12 Apr 1989, ICELAND 10 Apr 1987 (*75.4), IRELAND 19 May 1999 (*75.4), ITALY 27 Feb 1986, JAMAICA 29 Jul 1986, JAPAN 31 Aug 2004, JORDAN 01 May 1979, KAZAKHSTAN 05 May 1992, KENYA 23 Feb 1999, KOREA (DEM.PEOPLE'S REP.) 09 Mar 1988, KOREA (REPUBLIC OF) 15 Jan 1982, KUWAIT 17 Jan 1985, KYRGYZSTAN 18 Sep 1992, LAO PEOPLE'S DEM. REP. 18 Nov 1980, LATVIA 24 Dec 1991, LEBANON 23 Jul 1997, LESOTHO 20 May 1994, LIBERIA 30 Jun 1988, LIBYAN ARAB JAMAHIRIYA 07 Jun 1978, LIECHTENSTEIN 10 Aug 1989 (*75.4, 6), LITHUANIA 13 Jul 2000, LUXEMBOURG 29 Aug 1989, MADAGASCAR 08 May 1992, MALAWI 07 Oct 1991, MALDIVES 03 Sep 1991, MALI 08 Feb 1989, MALTA 17 Apr 1989 (*75.4), MAURITANIA 14 Mar 1980, MAURITIUS 27 Jun 2003, MEXICO 10 Mar 1983, MICRONESIA 19 Sep 1995, MOLDOVA (REPUBLIC OF) 24 May 1993, MONACO 07 Jan 2000, MONGOLIA 06 Dec 1995, MONTENEGRO (REPUBLIC OF) 02 Aug 2006, MOZAMBIQUE 14 Mar 1983, NAMIBIA 17 Jun 1994, NAURU 27 Jun 2006, NETHERLANDS 26 Jun 1987, NEW ZEALAND 08 Feb 1988, NICARAGUA 19 Jul 1999, NIGERIA 10 Oct 1988, NIGER 08 Jun 1979, NORWAY 14 Dec 1981, OMAN 29 Mar 1984, PALAU 25 Jun 1996, PANAMA 18 Sep 1995, PARAGUAY 30 Nov 1990, PERU 14 Jul 1989, POLAND 23 Oct 1991, PORTUGAL 27 May 1992, QATAR 05 Apr 1988, ROMANIA 21 Jun 1990, RUSSIAN FEDERATION 29 Sep 1989, RWANDA 19 Nov 1984, SAINT KITTS AND

* Source: 1125 U.N.T.S. 3.

NEVIS 14 Feb 1986, SAINT LUCIA 07 Oct 1982, SAINT VINCENT GRENADINES 08 Apr 1983, SAMOA 23 Aug 1984, SAN MARINO 05 Apr 1994, SAO TOME AND PRINCIPE 05 Jul 1996, SAUDI ARABIA 21 Aug 1987 (*5), SENEGAL 07 May 1985, SERBIA (REPUBLIC OF) 16 Oct 2001, SEYCHELLES 08 Nov 1984, SIERRA LEONE 21 Oct 1986, SLOVAKIA 02 Apr 1993, SLOVENIA 26 Mar 1992, SOLOMON ISLANDS 19 Sep 1988, SOUTH AFRICA 21 Nov 1995, SPAIN 21 Apr 1989, SUDAN 07 Mar 2006, SURINAME 16 Dec 1985, SWAZILAND 02 Nov 1995, SWEDEN 31 Aug 1979 (*75.4), SWITZERLAND 17 Feb 1982, SYRIAN ARAB REPUBLIC 14 Nov 1983, TAJIKISTAN 13 Jan 1993, TANZANIA (UNITED REP. OF) 15 Feb 1983, TIMOR-LESTE 12 Apr 2005, TOGO 21 Jun 1984, TONGA 20 Jan 2003, TRINIDAD AND TOBAGO 20 Jul 2001, TUNISIA 09 Aug 1979, TURKMENISTAN 10 Apr 1992, UGANDA 13 Mar 1991, UKRAINE 25 Jan 1990, UNITED ARAB EMIRATES 09 Mar 1983, UNITED KINGDOM 28 Jan 1998 (*1.4, 96.3, 28.2, 35.3, 55, 44.3, 50, 51, 57, 52, 53, 54.2, 51-55, 56, 85, 57.2, 70), URUGUAY 13 Dec 1985, UZBEKISTAN 08 Oct 1993, VANUATU 28 Feb 1985, VENEZUELA 23 Jul 1998, VIET NAM 19 Oct 1981, YEMEN 17 Apr 1990, ZAMBIA 04 May 1995, ZIMBABWE 19 Oct 1992.

Preamble

The High Contracting Parties,

Proclaiming their earnest wish to see peace prevail among peoples,

Recalling that every State has the duty, in conformity with the Charter of the United Nations, to refrain in its international relations from the threat or use of force against the sovereignty, territorial integrity or political independence of any State, or in any other manner inconsistent with the purposes of the United Nations.

Believing it necessary nevertheless to reaffirm and develop the provisions protecting the victims of armed conflicts and to supplement measures intended to reinforce their application,

Expressing their conviction that nothing in this Protocol or in the Geneva Conventions of 12 August 1949 can be construed as legitimizing or authorizing any act of aggression or any other use of force inconsistent with the Charter of the United Nations,

Reaffirming further that the provisions of the Geneva Conventions of 12 August 1949 and of this Protocol must be fully applied in all circumstances to all persons who are protected by those instruments, without any adverse distinction based on the nature or origin of the armed conflict or on the causes espoused by or attributed to the Parties to the conflicts,

Have agreed on the following:

PART I

GENERAL PROVISIONS

Article 1

General principles and scope of application

1. The High Contracting Parties undertake to respect and to ensure respect for this Protocol in all circumstances.

2. In cases not covered by this Protocol or by other international agreements, civilians and combatants remain under the protection and authority of the principles of international law derived from established custom, from the principles of humanity and from the dictates of public conscience.

3. This Protocol, which supplements the Geneva Conventions of 12 August 1949 for the protection of war victims, shall apply in the situations referred to in Article 2 common to those Conventions.

4. The situations referred to in the preceding paragraph include armed conflicts in which peoples are fighting against colonial domination and alien occupation and against racist regimes in the exercise of their right of self-determination, as enshrined in the Charter of the United Nations and the Declaration on Principles of International Law concerning Friendly Relations and Co-operation among States in accordance with the Charter of the United Nations.

[...]

PART IV

CIVILIAN POPULATION

SECTION I

GENERAL PROTECTION AGAINST EFFECTS OF HOSTILITIES

CHAPTER I

BASIC RULE AND FIELD OF APPLICATION

Article 48

Basic rule

In order to ensure respect for and protection of the civilian population and civilian objects, the Parties to the conflict shall at all times distinguish between the civilian population and combatants and between civilian objects and military objectives and accordingly shall direct their operations only against military objectives.

Article 49

Definition of attacks and scope of application

1. "Attacks" means acts of violence against the adversary, whether in offence or in defence.

2. The provisions of this Protocol with respect to attacks apply to all attacks in whatever territory conducted, including the national territory belonging to a Party to the conflict but under the control of an adverse Party.

3. The provisions of this Section apply to any land, air or sea warfare which may affect the civilian population, individual civilians or civilian objects on land. They further apply to all attacks from the sea or from the air against objectives on land but do not otherwise affect the rules of international law applicable in armed conflict at sea or in the air.

4. The provisions of this Section are additional to the rules concerning humanitarian protection contained in the Fourth Convention, particularly in Part II thereof, and in other international agreements binding upon the High Contracting Parties, as well as to other rules of international law relating to the protection of civilians and civilian objects on land, at sea or in the air against the effects of hostilities.

CHAPTER II

CIVILIANS AND CIVILIAN POPULATION

Article 50

Definition of civilians and civilian population

1. A civilian is any person who does not belong to one of the categories of persons referred to in Article 4 A (1), (2), (3) and (6) of the Third Convention and in Article 43 of this Protocol. In case of doubt whether a person is a civilian, that person shall be considered to be a civilian.

2. The civilian population comprises all persons who are civilians.

3. The presence within the civilian population of individuals who do not come within the definition of civilians does not deprive the population of its civilian character.

Article 51

Protection of the civilian population

1. The civilian population and individual civilians shall enjoy general protection against dangers arising from military operations. To give effect to this protection, the following rules, which are additional to other applicable rules of international law, shall be observed in circumstances.

2. The civilian population as such, as well as individual civilians, shall not be the object of attack. Acts or threats of violence the primary purpose of which is to spread terror among the civilian population are prohibited.

3. Civilians shall enjoy the protection afforded by this Section, unless and for such time as they take a direct part in hostilities.

4. Indiscriminate attacks are prohibited. Indiscriminate attacks are:

(a) Those which are not directed at a specific military objective;

(b) Those which employ a method or means of combat which cannot be directed at a specific military objective; or

(c) Those which employ a method or means of combat the effects of which cannot be limited as required by this Protocol; and consequently, in each such case, are of a nature to strike military objectives and civilians or civilian objects without distinction.

5. Among others, the following types of attacks are to be considered as indiscriminate:

(a) An attack by bombardment by any methods or means which treats as a single military objective a number of clearly separated and distinct military objectives located in a city, town, village or other area containing a similar concentration of civilians or civilian objects; and

(b) An attack which may be expected to cause incidental loss of civilian life, injury to civilians, damage to civilian objects, or a combination thereof, which would be excessive in relation to the concrete and direct military advantage anticipated.

6. Attacks against the civilian population or civilians by way of reprisals are prohibited.

7. The presence or movements of the civilian population or individual civilians shall not be used to render certain points or areas immune from military operations, in particular in attempts to shield military objectives from attacks or to shield, favour or impede military operations. The Parties to the conflict shall not direct the movement of the civilian population or individual civilians in order to attempt to shield military objectives from attacks or to shield military operations.

8. Any violation of these prohibitions shall not release the Parties to the conflict from their legal obligations with respect to the civilian population and civilians, including the obligation to take the precautionary measures provided for in Article 57.

CHAPTER III

CIVILIAN OBJECTS

Article 52

General protection of civilian objects

1. Civilian objects shall not be the object of attack or of reprisals. Civilian objects are all objects which are not military objectives as defined in paragraph 2.

2. Attacks shall be limited strictly to military objectives. In so far as objects are concerned, military objectives are limited to those objects which by their nature, location, purpose or use make an effective contribution to military action and whose total or partial destruction, capture or neutralization, in the circumstances ruling at the time, offers a definite military of advantage.

3. In case of doubt whether an object which is normally dedicated to civilian purposes, such as a place of worship, a house or other dwelling or a school, is being used to make an effective contribution to military action, it shall be presumed not to be so used.

Article 53

Protection of cultural objects and of places of worship

Without prejudice to the provisions of the Hague Convention for the Protection of Cultural Property in the Event of Armed Conflict of 14 May 1954, and of other relevant international instruments, it is prohibited:

(a) To commit any acts of hostility directed against the historic monuments, works of art or places of worship which constitute the cultural or spiritual heritage of peoples;

(b) To use such objects in support of the military effort;

(c) To make such objects the object of reprisals.

Article 54

Protection of objects indispensable to the survival of the civilian population

1. Starvation of civilians as a method of warfare is prohibited.

2. It is prohibited to attack, destroy, remove or render useless objects indispensable to the survival of the civilian population, such as foodstuffs, agricultural areas for the production of foodstuffs, crops, livestock, drinking water installations and supplies and irrigation works, for the specific purpose of denying them for their sustenance value to the civilian population or to the adverse Party, whatever the motive, whether in order to starve out civilians, to cause them to move away, or for any other motive.

3. The prohibitions in paragraph 2 shall not apply to such of the objects covered by it as are used by an adverse Party:

(a) As sustenance solely for the members of its armed forces; or

(b) If not as sustenance, then in direct support of military action, provided, however, that in no event shall actions against these objects be taken which may be expected to leave the civilian population with such inadequate food or water as to cause its starvation or force its movement.

4. These objects shall not be made the object of reprisals.

5. In recognition of the vital requirements of any Party to the conflict in the defence of its national territory against invasion, derogation from the prohibitions contained in paragraph 2 may be made by a Party to the conflict within such territory under its own control where required by imperative military necessity.

Article 55

Protection of the natural environment

1. Care shall be taken in warfare to protect the natural environment against widespread, long-term and severe damage. This protection includes a prohibition of the use of methods or means of warfare which are intended or may be expected to cause such damage to the natural environment and thereby to prejudice the health or survival of the population.

2. Attacks against the natural environment by way of reprisals are prohibited.

Article 56

Protection of works and installations containing dangerous forces

1. Works or installations containing dangerous forces, namely dams, dykes and nuclear electrical generating stations, shall not be made the object of attack, even where these objects are military objectives, if such attack may cause the release of dangerous forces and consequent severe losses among the civilian population. Other military objectives located at or in the vicinity of these works or installations shall not be made the object of attack if such attack may cause the release of dangerous forces from the works or installations and consequent severe losses among the civilian population.

2. The special protection against attack provided by paragraph 1 shall cease:

(a) For a dam or a dyke only if it is used for other than its normal function and in regular, significant and direct support of military operations and if such attack is the only feasible way to terminate such support;

(b) For a nuclear electrical generating station only if it provides electric power in regular, significant and direct support of military operations and if such attack is the only feasible way to terminate such support;

(c) For other military objectives located at or in the vicinity of these works or installations only if they are used in regular, significant and direct support of military operations and if such attack is the only feasible way to terminate such support.

3. In all cases, the civilian population and individual civilians shall remain entitled to all the protection accorded them by international law, including the protection of the precautionary measures provided for in Article 57. If the protection ceases and any of the works, installations or military objectives mentioned in paragraph I is attacked, all practical precautions shall be taken to avoid the release of the dangerous forces.

4. It is prohibited to make any of the works, installations or military objectives mentioned in paragraph 1 the object of reprisals.

5. The Parties to the conflict shall endeavour to avoid locating any military objectives in the vicinity of the works or installations mentioned in paragraph 1. Nevertheless, installations erected for the sole purpose of defending the protected works or installations from attack are

permissible and shall not themselves be made the object of attack, provided that they are not used in hostilities except for defensive actions necessary to respond to attacks against the protected works or installations and that their armament is limited to weapons capable only of repelling hostile action against the protected works or installations.

6. The High Contracting Parties and the Parties to the conflict are urged to conclude further agreements among themselves to provide additional protection for objects containing dangerous forces.

7. In order to facilitate the identification of the objects protected by this article, the Parties to the conflict may mark them with a special sign consisting of a group of three bright orange circles placed on the same axis, as specified in Article 16 of Annex I to this Protocol. The absence of such marking in no way relieves any Party to the conflict of its obligations under this Article.

[...]

SECTION II

RELIEF IN FAVOUR OF THE CIVILIAN POPULATION

Article 68

Field of application

The provisions of this Section apply to the civilian population as defined in this Protocol and are supplementary to Articles 23, 55, 59, 60, 61 and 62 and other relevant provisions of the Fourth Convention.

Article 69

Basic needs in occupied territories

1. In addition to the duties specified in Article 55 of the Fourth Convention concerning food and medical supplies, the Occupying Power shall, to the fullest extent of the means available to it and without any adverse distinction, also ensure the provision of clothing, bedding, means of shelter, other supplies essential to the survival of the civilian population of the occupied territory and objects necessary for religious worship.

2. Relief actions for the benefit of the civilian population of occupied territories are governed by Articles 59, 60, 61, 62, 108, 109, 110 and 111 of the Fourth Convention, and by Article 71 of this Protocol, and shall be implemented without delay.

Article 70

Relief actions

1. If the civilian population of any territory under the control of a Party to the conflict, other than occupied territory, is not adequately provided with the supplies mentioned in Article 69, relief actions which are humanitarian and impartial in character and conducted without any adverse distinction shall be undertaken, subject to the agreement of the Parties concerned in such relief actions. Offers of such relief shall not be regarded as interference in the armed conflict or as unfriendly acts. In the distribution of relief consignments, priority shall be given to those persons, such as children, expectant mothers, maternity cases and nursing mothers, who, under the Fourth Convention or under this Protocol, are to be accorded privileged treatment or special protection.

2. The Parties to the conflict and each High Contracting Party shall allow and facilitate rapid and unimpeded passage of all relief consignments, equipment and personnel provided in accordance with this Section, even if such assistance is destined for the civilian population of the adverse Party.

3. The Parties to the conflict and each High Contracting Party which allow the passage of relief consignments, equipment and personnel in accordance with paragraph 2:

(a) Shall have the right to prescribe the technical arrangements, including search, under which such passage is permitted;

(b) May make such permission conditional on the distribution of this assistance being made under the local supervision of a Protecting Power;

(c) Shall, in no way whatsoever, divert relief consignments from the purpose for which they are intended nor delay their forwarding, except in cases of urgent necessity in the interest of the civilian population concerned.

4. The Parties to the conflict shall protect relief consignments and facilitate their rapid distribution.

5. The Parties to the conflict and each High Contracting Party concerned shall encourage and facilitate effective international co-ordination of the relief actions referred to in paragraph 1.

Article 71

Personnel participating in relief actions

1. Where necessary, relief personnel may form part of the assistance provided in any relief action, in particular for the transportation and distribution of relief consignments; the participation of such personnel shall be subject to the approval of the Party in whose territory they will carry out their duties.

2. Such personnel shall be respected and protected.

3. Each Party in receipt of relief consignments shall, to the fullest extent practicable, assist the relief personnel referred to in paragraph 1 in carrying out their relief mission. Only in case of imperative military necessity may the activities of the relief personnel be limited or their movements temporarily restricted.

4. Under no circumstances may relief personnel exceed the terms of their mission under this Protocol. In particular they shall take account of the security requirements of the Party in whose territory they are carrying out their duties. The mission of any of the personnel who do not respect these conditions may be terminated.

SECTION III

TREATMENT OF PERSONS IN THE POWER OF A PARTY TO THE CONFLICT

CHAPTER I

FIELD OF APPLICATION AND PROTECTION OF PERSONS AND OBJECTS

Article 72

Field of application

The provisions of this Section are additional to the rules concerning humanitarian protection of civilians and civilian objects in the power of a Party to the conflict contained in the

Fourth Convention, particularly Parts I and m thereof, as well as to other applicable rules of international law relating to the protection of fundamental human rights during international armed conflict.

Article 73

Refugees and stateless persons

Persons who, before the beginning of hostilities, were considered as stateless persons or refugees under the relevant international instruments accepted by the Parties concerned or under the national legislation of the State of refuge or State of residence shall be protected persons within the meaning of Parts I and III of the Fourth Convention, in all circumstances and without any adverse distinction.

Article 74

Reunion of dispersed families

The High Contracting Parties and the Parties to the conflict shall facilitate in every possible way the reunion of families dispersed as a result of armed conflicts and shall encourage in particular the work of the humanitarian organizations engaged in this task in accordance with the provisions of the Conventions and of this Protocol and in conformity with their respective security regulations.

Article 75

Fundamental guarantees

1. In so far as they are affected by a situation referred to in Article 1 of this Protocol, persons who are in the power of a Party to the conflict and who do not benefit from more favourable treatment under the Conventions or under this Protocol shall be treated humanely in all circumstances and shall enjoy, as a minimum, the protection provided by this Article without any adverse distinction based upon race, colour, sex, language, religion or belief, political or other opinion, national or social origin, wealth, birth or other status, or on any other similar criteria. Each Party shall respect the person, honour, convictions and religious practices of all such persons.

2. The following acts are and shall remain prohibited at any time and in any place whatsoever, whether committed by civilian or by military agents:

(a) Violence to the life, health, or physical or mental well-being of persons, in particular:

(i) Murder;

(ii) Torture of all kinds, whether physical or mental;

(iii) Corporal punishment; and

(iv) Mutilation;

(b) Outrages upon personal dignity, in particular humiliating and degrading treatment, enforced prostitution and any form of indecent assault;

(c) The taking of hostages;

(d) Collective punishments; and

(e) Threats to commit any of the foregoing acts.

3. Any person arrested, detained or interned for actions related to the armed conflict shall be informed promptly, in a language he understands, of the reasons why these measures have been

taken. Except in cases of arrest or detention for penal offences, such persons shall be released with the minimum delay possible and in any event as soon as the circumstances justifying the arrest, detention or internment have ceased to exist.

4. No sentence may be passed and no penalty may be executed on a person found guilty of a penal offence related to the armed conflict except pursuant to a conviction pronounced by an impartial and regularly constituted court respecting the generally recognized principles of regular judicial procedure, which include the following:

(a) The procedure shall provide for an accused to be informed without delay of the particulars of the offence alleged against him and shall afford the accused before and during his trial all necessary rights and means of defence;

(b) No one shall be convicted of an offence except on the basis of individual penal responsibility;

(c) No one shall be accused or convicted of a criminal offence on account of any act or omission which did not constitute a criminal offence under the national or international law to which he was subject at the time when it was committed; nor shall a heavier penalty be imposed than that which was applicable at the time when the criminal offence was committed; if, after the commission of the offence, provision is made by law for the imposition of a lighter penalty, the offender shall benefit thereby;

(d) Anyone charged with an offence is presumed innocent until proved guilt according to law;

(e) Anyone charged with an offence shall have the right to be tried in his presence;

(f) No one shall be compelled to testify against himself or to confess guilt;

(g) Anyone charged with an offence shall have the right to examine, or have examined, the witnesses against him and to obtain the attendance and examination of witnesses on his behalf under the same conditions as witnesses against him;

(h) No one shall be prosecuted or punished by the same Party for an offence in respect of which a final judgement acquitting or convicting that person has been previously pronounced under the same law and judicial procedure;

(i) Anyone prosecuted for an offence shall have the right to have the judgement pronounced publicly; and

(j) A convicted person shall be advised on conviction of his judicial and other remedies and of the time-limits within which they may be exercised.

5. Women whose liberty has been restricted for reasons related to the armed conflict shall be held in quarters separated from men's quarters. They shall be under the immediate supervision of women. Nevertheless, in cases where families are detained or interned, they shall, whenever possible, be held in the same place and accommodated as family units.

6. Persons who are arrested, detained or interned for reasons related to the armed conflict shall enjoy the protection provided by this Article until their final release, repatriation or re-establishment, even after the end of the armed conflict.

7. In order to avoid any doubt concerning the prosecution and trial of persons accused of war crimes or crimes against humanity, the following principles shall apply:

(a) Persons who are accused of such crimes should be submitted for the purpose of prosecution and trial in accordance with the applicable rules of international law; and

(b) Any such persons who do not benefit from more favourable treatment under the Conventions or this Protocol shall be accorded the treatment provided by this Article, whether or not the crimes of which they are accused constitute grave breaches of the Conventions or of this Protocol.

8. No provision of this Article may be construed as limiting or infringing any other more favourable provision granting greater protection, under any applicable rules of international law, to persons covered by paragraph 1.

CHAPTER II

MEASURES IN FAVOUR OF WOMEN AND CHILDREN

Article 76

Protection of women

1. Women shall be the object of special respect and shall be protected in particular against rape, forced prostitution and any other form of indecent assault.

2. Pregnant women and mothers having dependent infants who are arrested, detained or interned for reasons related to the armed conflict, shall have their cases considered with the utmost priority.

3. To the maximum extent feasible, the Parties to the conflict shall endeavour to avoid the pronouncement of the death penalty on pregnant women or mothers having dependent infants, for an offence related to the armed conflict. The death penalty for such offences shall not be executed on such women.

Article 77

Protection of children

1. Children shall be the object of special respect and shall be protected against any form of indecent assault. The Parties to the conflict shall provide them with the care and aid they require, whether because of their age or for any other reason.

2. The Parties to the conflict shall take all feasible measures in order that children who have not attained the age of fifteen years do not take a direct part in hostilities and, in particular, they shall refrain from recruiting them into their armed forces. In recruiting among those persons who have attained the age of fifteen years but who have not attained the age of eighteen years, the Parties to the conflict shall endeavour to give priority to those who are oldest.

3. If, in exceptional cases, despite the provisions of paragraph 2, children who have not attained the age of fifteen years take a direct part in hostilities and fall into the power of an adverse Party, they shall continue to benefit from the special protection accorded by this Article, whether or not they are prisoners of war.

4. If arrested, detained or interned for reasons related to the armed conflict, children shall be held in quarters separate from the quarters of adults, except where families are accommodated as family units as provided in Article 75, paragraph 5.

5. The death penalty for an offence related to armed conflict shall not be executed on persons who had not attained the age of eighteen years at the time the offence was committed.

[...]

Protocol Additional to the Geneva Conventions of 12 August 1949, and relating to the Protection of Victims of Non-International Armed Conflicts (Protocol II), 1977 [excerpts]*

Adoption: 8 June 1977
Entry into force: 7 December 1978
Parties: 163 (Status as of 1 April 2007)

ALBANIA 16 Jul 1993, ALGERIA 16 Aug 1989, ANTIGUA AND BARBUDA 06 Oct 1986, ARGENTINA 26 Nov 1986, ARMENIA 07 Jun 1993, AUSTRALIA 21 Jun 1991, AUSTRIA 13 Aug 1982 (*6), BAHAMAS 10 Apr 1980, BAHRAIN 30 Oct 1986, BANGLADESH 08 Sep 1980, BARBADOS 19 Feb 1990, BELARUS 23 Oct 1989, BELGIUM 20 May 1986, BELIZE 29 Jun 1984, BENIN 28 May 1986, BOLIVIA 08 Dec 1983, BOSNIA-HERZEGOVINA 31 Dec 1992, BOTSWANA 23 May 1979, BRAZIL 05 May 1992, BRUNEI DARUSSALAM 14 Oct 1991, BULGARIA 26 Sep 1989, BURKINA FASO 20 Oct 1987, BURUNDI 10 Jun 1993, CAMBODIA 14 Jan 1998, CAMEROON 16 Mar 1984, CANADA 20 Nov 1990, CAPE VERDE 16 Mar 1995, CENTRAL AFRICAN REPUBLIC 17 Jul 1984, CHAD 17 Jan 1997, CHILE 24 Apr 1991, CHINA 14 Sep 1983, COLOMBIA 14 Aug 1995, COMOROS 21 Nov 1985, CONGO (DEM. REP.) 12 Dec 2002, CONGO 10 Nov 1983, COOK ISLANDS 07 May 2002, COSTA RICA 15 Dec 1983, CÔTE D'IVOIRE 20 Sep 1989, CROATIA 11 May 1992., CUBA 23 Dec 1999, CYPRUS 18 Mar 1996, CZECH REPUBLIC 05 Feb 1993, DENMARK 17 Jun 1982, DJIBOUTI 08 Apr 1991, DOMINICAN REPUBLIC 26 May 1994, DOMINICA 25 Apr 1996, ECUADOR 10 Apr 1979, EGYPT 09 Oct 1992, EL SALVADOR 23 Nov 1978, EQUATORIAL GUINEA 24 Jul 1986, ESTONIA 18 Jan 1993, ETHIOPIA 08 Apr 1994, FINLAND 07 Aug 1980, FORMER YUGOSLAV REPUBLIC OF MACEDONIA 01 Sep 1993, FRANCE 24 Feb 1984, GABON 08 Apr 1980, GAMBIA 12 Jan 1989, GEORGIA 14 Sep 1993, GERMANY 14 Feb 1991, GHANA 28 Feb 1978, GREECE 15 Feb 1993, GRENADA 23 Sep 1998, GUATEMALA 19 Oct 1987, GUINEA-BISSAU 21 Oct 1986, GUINEA 11 Jul 1984, GUYANA 18 Jan 1988, HAITI 20 Dec 2006, HOLY SEE 21 Nov 1985, HONDURAS 16 Feb 1995, HUNGARY 12 Apr 1989, ICELAND 10 Apr 1987, IRELAND 19 May 1999 (*6), ITALY 27 Feb 1986, JAMAICA 29 Jul 1986, JAPAN 31 Aug 2004, JORDAN 01 May 1979, KAZAKHSTAN 05 May 1992, KENYA 23 Feb 1999, KOREA (REPUBLIC OF) 15 Jan 1982, KUWAIT 17 Jan 1985, KYRGYZSTAN 18 Sep 1992, LAO PEOPLE'S DEM. REP. 18 Nov 1980, LATVIA 24 Dec 1991, LEBANON 23 Jul 1997, LESOTHO 20 May 1994, LIBERIA 30 Jun 1988, LIBYAN ARAB JAMAHIRIYA 07 Jun 1978, LIECHTENSTEIN 10 Aug 1989 (*6.2e), LITHUANIA 13 Jul 2000, LUXEMBOURG 29 Aug 1989, MADAGASCAR 08 May 1992, MALAWI 07 Oct 1991, MALDIVES 03 Sep 1991, MALI 08 Feb 1989, MALTA 17 Apr 1989 (*6.2e), MAURITANIA 14 Mar 1980, MAURITIUS 22 Mar 1982, MICRONESIA 19 Sep 1995, MOLDOVA (REPUBLIC OF) 24 May 1993, MONACO 07 Jan 2000, MONGOLIA 06 Dec 1995, MONTENEGRO (REPUBLIC OF) 02 Aug 2006, MOZAMBIQUE 12 Nov 2002, NAMIBIA 17 Jun 1994, NAURU 27 Jun 2006, NETHERLANDS 26 Jun 1987, NEW ZEALAND 08 Feb 1988, NICARAGUA 19 Jul 1999, NIGERIA 10 Oct 1988, NIGER 08 Jun 1979, NORWAY 14 Dec 1981, OMAN 29 Mar 1984, PALAU 25 Jun 1996, PANAMA 18 Sep 1995, PARAGUAY 30 Nov 1990, PERU 14 Jul 1989, PHILIPPINES 11 Dec 1986, POLAND 23 Oct 1991, PORTUGAL 27 May 1992, QATAR 05 Jan 2005, ROMANIA 21 Jun 1990, RUSSIAN FEDERATION 29 Sep 1989, RWANDA 19 Nov 1984, SAINT KITTS AND NEVIS 14 Feb 1986, SAINT LUCIA 07 Oct 1982, SAINT VINCENT GRENADINES 08 Apr

* Source: 1125 U.N.T.S. 609.

1983, SAMOA 23 Aug 1984, SAN MARINO 05 Apr 1994, SAO TOME AND PRINCIPE 05 Jul 1996, SAUDI ARABIA 28 Nov 2001, SENEGAL 07 May 1985, SERBIA (REPUBLIC OF) 16 Oct 2001, SEYCHELLES 08 Nov 1984, SIERRA LEONE 21 Oct 1986, SLOVAKIA 02 Apr 1993, SLOVENIA 26 Mar 1992, SOLOMON ISLANDS 19 Sep 1988, SOUTH AFRICA 21 Nov 1995, SPAIN 21 Apr 1989, SUDAN 13 Jul 2006, SURINAME 16 Dec 1985, SWAZILAND 02 Nov 1995, SWEDEN 31 Aug 1979, SWITZERLAND 17 Feb 1982, TAJIKISTAN 13 Jan 1993, TANZANIA (UNITED REP.OF) 15 Feb 1983, TIMOR-LESTE 12 Apr 2005, TOGO 21 Jun 1984, TONGA 20 Jan 2003, TRINIDAD AND TOBAGO 20 Jul 2001, TUNISIA 09 Aug 1979, TURKMENISTAN 10 Apr 1992, UGANDA 13 Mar 1991, UKRAINE 25 Jan 1990, UNITED ARAB EMIRATES 09 Mar 1983, UNITED KINGDOM 28 Jan 1998, URUGUAY 13 Dec 1985, UZBEKISTAN 08 Oct 1993, VANUATU 28 Feb 1985, VENEZUELA 23 Jul 1998, YEMEN 17 Apr 1990, ZAMBIA 04 May 1995, ZIMBABWE 19 Oct 1992.

Preamble

The High Contracting Parties,

Recalling that the humanitarian principles enshrined in Article 3 common to the Geneva Conventions of 12 August 1949 constitute the foundation of respect for the human person in cases of armed conflict not of an international character,

Recalling furthermore that international instruments relating to human rights offer a basic protection to the human person,

Emphasizing the need to ensure a better protection for the victims of those armed conflicts,

Recalling that, in cases not covered by the law in force, the human person remains under the protection of the principles of humanity and the dictates of the public conscience,

Have agreed on the following:

[...]

PART II

HUMANE TREATMENT

Article 4

Fundamental guarantees

1. All persons who do not take a direct part or who have ceased to take part in hostilities, whether or not their liberty has been restricted, are entitled to respect for their person, honour and convictions and religious practices. They shall in all circumstances be treated humanely, without any adverse distinction. It is prohibited to order that there shall be no survivors.

2. Without prejudice to the generality of the foregoing, the following acts against the persons referred to in paragraph I are and shall remain prohibited at any time and in any place whatsoever:

(a) Violence to the life, health and physical or mental well-being of persons, in particular murder as well as cruel treatment such as torture, mutilation or any form of corporal punishment;

(b) Collective punishments;

(c) Taking of hostages;

(d) Acts of terrorism;

(e) Outrages upon personal dignity, in particular humiliating and degrading treatment, rape, enforced prostitution and any form of indecent assault;

(f) Slavery and the slave trade in all their forms;

(g) Pillage;

(h) Threats to commit any of the foregoing acts.

3. Children shall be provided with the care and aid they require, and in particular:

(a) They shall receive an education, including religious and moral education, in keeping with the wishes of their parents, or in the absence of parents, of those responsible for their care;

(b) All appropriate steps shall be taken to facilitate the reunion of families temporarily separated;

(c) Children who have not attained the age of fifteen years shall neither be recruited in the armed forces or groups nor allowed to take part in hostilities;

(d) The special protection provided by this Article to children who have not attained the age of fifteen years shall remain applicable to them if they take a direct part in hostilities despite the provisions of sub-paragraph (c) and are captured;

(e) Measures shall be taken, if necessary, and whenever possible with the consent of their parents or persons who by law or custom are primarily responsible for their care, to remove children temporarily from the area in which hostilities are taking place to a safer area within the country and ensure that they are accompanied by persons responsible for their safety and well-being.

Article 5

Persons whose liberty has been restricted

1. In addition to the provisions of Article 4, the following provisions shall be respected as a minimum with regard to persons deprived of their liberty for reasons related to the armed conflict, whether they are interned or detained:

(a) The wounded and the sick shall be treated in accordance with Article 7;

(b) The persons referred to in this paragraph shall, to the same extent as the local civilian population, be provided with food and drinking water and be afforded safeguards as regards health and hygiene and protection against the rigours of the climate and the dangers of the armed conflict;

(c) They shall be allowed to receive individual or collective relief;

(d) They shall be allowed to practise their religion and, if requested and appropriate, to receive spiritual assistance from persons, such as chaplains, performing religious functions;

(e) They shall, if made to work, have the benefit of working conditions and safeguards similar to those enjoyed by the local civilian population.

2. Those who are responsible for the internment or detention of the persons referred to in paragraph I shall also, within the limits of their capabilities, respect the following provisions relating to such persons:

(a) Except when men and women of a family are accommodated together, women shall be held in quarters separated from those of men and shall be under the immediate supervision of women;

(b) They shall be allowed to send and receive letters and cards, the number of which may be limited by the competent authority if it deems necessary;

(c) Places of internment and detention shall not be located close to the combat zone. The persons referred to in paragraph 1 shall be evacuated when the places where they are interned or detained become particularly exposed to danger arising out of the armed conflict, if their evacuation can be carried out under adequate conditions of safety;

(d) They shall have the benefit of medical examinations;

(e) Their physical or mental health and integrity shall not be endangered by an unjustified act or omission. Accordingly, it is prohibited to subject the persons described in this Article to any medical procedure which is not indicated by the state of health of the person concerned, and which is not consistent with the generally accepted medical standards applied to free persons under similar medical circumstances.

3. Persons who are not covered by paragraph I but whose liberty has been restricted in any way whatsoever for reasons related to the armed conflict shall be treated humanely in accordance with Article 4 and with paragraphs 1 (a), (c) and (d), and 2 (b) of this Article.

4. If it is decided to release persons deprived of their liberty, necessary measures to ensure their safety shall be taken by those so deciding.

[...]

PART IV

CIVILIAN POPULATION

Article 13

Protection of the civilian population

1. The civilian population and individual civilians shall enjoy general protection against the dangers arising from military operations. To give effect to this protection, the following rules shall be observed in all circumstances.

2. The civilian population as such, as well as individual civilians, shall not be the object of attack. Acts or threats of violence the primary purpose of which is to spread terror among the civilian population are prohibited.

3. Civilians shall enjoy the protection afforded by this Part, unless and for such time as they take a direct part in hostilities.

Article 14

Protection of objects indispensable to the survival of the civilian population

Starvation of civilians as a method of combat is prohibited. It is therefore prohibited to attack, destroy, remove or render useless, for that purpose, objects indispensable to the survival of the civilian population, such as foodstuffs, agricultural areas for the production of foodstuffs, crops, livestock, drinking water installations and supplies and irrigation works.

Article 15

Protection of works and installations containing dangerous forces

Works or installations containing dangerous forces, namely dams, dykes and nuclear electrical generating stations, shall not be made the object of attack, even where these objects are military objectives, if such attack may cause the release of dangerous forces and consequent severe losses among the civilian population.

Article 16

Protection of cultural objects and of places of worship

Without prejudice to the provisions of The Hague Convention for the Protection of Cultural Property in the Event of Armed Conflict of 14 May 1954, it is prohibited to commit any acts of hostility directed against historic monuments, works of art or places of worship which constitute the cultural or spiritual heritage of peoples, and to use them in support of the military effort.

Article 17

Prohibition of forced movement of civilians

1. The displacement of the civilian population shall not be ordered for reasons related to the conflict unless the security of the civilians involved or imperative military reasons so demand. Should such displacements have to be carried out, all possible measures shall be taken in order that the civilian population may be received under satisfactory conditions of shelter, hygiene, health, safety and nutrition.

2. Civilians shall not be compelled to leave their own territory for reasons connected with the conflict.

[…]

Optional Protocol to the Convention on the Rights of the Child on the involvement of children in armed conflicts, 2000 [excerpts]*

Adoption: 25 May 2000
Entry into force: 12 February 2002
Parties: 114 (Status as of 1 April 2007)

AFGHANISTAN 24 Sep 2003 a, ANDORRA 30 Apr 2001, ARGENTINA 10 Sep 2002, ARMENIA 30 Sep 2005, AUSTRALIA 26 Sep 2006, AUSTRIA 1 Feb 2002, AZERBAIJAN 3 Jul 2002, BAHRAIN 21 Sep 2004 a, BANGLADESH 6 Sep 2000, BELARUS 25 Jan 2006 a, BELGIUM 6 May 2002, BELIZE 1 Dec 2003, BENIN 31 Jan 2005, BHUTAN signed 15 Sep 2005, BOLIVIA 22 Dec 2004 a, BOSNIA AND HERZEGOVINA 10 Oct 2003, BOTSWANA 4 Oct 2004, BRAZIL 27 Jan 2004, BULGARIA 12 Feb 2002, BURKINA FASO signed 16 Nov 2001, BURUNDI signed 13 Nov 2001, CAMBODIA 16 Jul 2004, CAMEROON signed 5 Oct 2001, CANADA 7 Jul 2000, CAPE VERDE 10 May 2002 a, CHAD 28 Aug 2002, CHILE 31 Jul 2003, CHINA signed 15 Mar 2001, COLOMBIA 25 May 2005, COSTA RICA 24 Jan 2003, CUBA 9 Feb 2007, CZECH REPUBLIC 30 Nov 2001, DEMOCRATIC REPUBLIC OF CONGO 11 Nov 2001, DENMARK 27 Aug 2002, DJIBOUTI signed 14 June 2006, DOMINICA 20 Sep 2002 a, DOMINICAN REPUBLIC signed 9 May 2002, ECUADOR 7 Jun 2004, EGYPT 6 Feb 2007 a, EL SALVADOR 18 Apr 2002, ERITREA 16 Feb 2005 a, ESTONIA signed 24 Sep 2003, FIJI signed 16 Sep 2005, FINLAND 10 Apr 2002, FRANCE 5 Feb 2003, GABON signed 8 Sept 2000, GAMBIA signed 21 Dec 2000, GERMANY 13 Dec 2004, GHANA signed 24 Sep 2003, GREECE 22 Oct 2003, GUATEMALA 9 May 2002, GUINEA-BISSAU signed 8 Sep 2000, HAITI signed 15 Aug 2002, HOLY SEE 24 Oct 2001, HONDURAS 14 Aug 2002 a, HUNGARY signed 11 Mar 2002, ICELAND 1 Oct 2001, INDIA 30 Nov 2005, INDONESIA signed 24 Sep 2001, IRELAND 18 Nov 2002, ISRAEL 18 Jul 2005, ITALY 9 May 2002, JAMAICA 9 May 2002, JAPAN 2 Aug 2004, JORDAN signed 6 Sep 2000, KAZAKHSTAN 10 Apr 2003, KENYA 28 Jan 2002, KUWAIT 16 Aug 2004 a, KYRGYZSTAN 13 Aug 2003 a, LAO PEOPLE'S DEMOCRATIC REPUBLIC 20 Sep 2006 a, LATVIA 19 Dec 2005, LEBANON signed 11 Feb 2002, LESOTHO 24 Sep 2003, LIBERIA signed 22 Sep 2004, LIBYAN ARAB JAMAHIRIYA 29 Oct 2004 a, LIECHTENSTEIN 4 Feb 2005 a, LITHUANIA 20 Feb 2003, LUXEMBOURG 4 Aug 2004, MADAGASCAR 22 Sept 2004, MALAWI signed 7 Sep 2000, MALDIVES 29 Dec 2004, MALI 16 May 2002, MALTA 9 May 2002, MAURITIUS signed 11 Nov 2001, MEXICO 15 Mar 2002, MICRONESIA (FEDERATED STATES OF) signed 8 May 2002, MONACO 13 Nov 2001, MONGOLIA 6 Oct 2004, MOROCCO 22 May 2002, MOZAMBIQUE 19 Oct 2004 a, NAMIBIA 16 Apr 2002, NAURU signed 8 Sep 2000, NEPAL 3 Jan 2007, NETHERLANDS signed 7 Sep 2000, NEW ZEALAND 12 Nov 2001, NICARAGUA 17 May 2005 a, NIGERIA signed 8 Sep 2000, NORWAY 23 Sep 2003, OMAN 17 Sep 2004 a, PAKISTAN signed 26 Sep 2001, PANAMA 8 Aug 2001, PARAGUAY 27 Sep 2002, PERU 8 May 2002, PHILIPPINES 26 Aug 2003, POLAND 7 Apr 2005, PORTUGAL 19 Aug 2003, QATAR 25 Jul 2002 a, REPUBLIC OF KOREA 24 Sep 2004, REPUBLIC OF MOLDOVA 7 Apr 2004, REPUBLIC OF SERBIA 21 Jan 2003, ROMANIA 10 Nov 2001, RUSSIAN FEDERATION signed 15 Feb 2001, RWANDA 23 Apr 2002 a, SAN MARINO signed 5 Jun 2000, SENEGAL 3 Mar 2004, SEYCHELLES signed 23 Jan 2001, SIERRA LEONE 15 May 2002, SINGAPORE signed 7 Sep 2000, SLOVAKIA 7 July 2006, SLOVENIA 23 Sep 2004, SOMALIA signed 16 Sep 2005, SOUTH AFRICA signed 8 Feb 2002, SPAIN 8 Mar 2002, SRI LANKA 8 Sep 2000, SUDAN 26 Jul

* Source: U.N.G.A. Res. 54/263.

2005, SURINAME signed 10 May 2002, SWEDEN 20 Feb 2003, SWITZERLAND 26 Jun 2002, SYRIAN ARAB REPUBLIC 17 Oct 2003 a, TAJIKISTAN 5 Aug 2002 a, THAILAND 27 Feb 2006 a, THE FORMER YUGOSLAV REPUBLIC OF MACEDONIA 12 Jan 2004, TIMOR–LESTE 2 Aug 2004 a, TOGO 28 Nov 2005, TUNISIA 2 Jan 2003, TURKEY 4 May 2004, TURKMENISTAN 29 Apr 2005 a, UGANDA 6 May 2002 a, UKRAINE 11 Jul 2005, UNITED KINGDOM OF GREAT BRITAIN AND NORTHERN IRELAND 24 Jun 2003, UNITED REPUBLIC OF TANZANIA 11 Nov 2004 a, UNITED STATES OF AMERICA 23 Dec 2002, URUGUAY 9 Sep 2003, VANUATU signed 16 Sep 2005, VENEZUELA (BOLIVERIAN REPUBLIC OF) 23 Sep 2003, VIET NAM 20 Dec 2001, YEMEN 2 Mar 2007 a.

[...]

Article 1

States Parties shall take all feasible measures to ensure that members of their armed forces who have not attained the age of 18 years do not take a direct part in hostilities.

Article 2

States Parties shall ensure that persons who have not attained the age of 18 years are not compulsorily recruited into their armed forces.

Article 3

1. States Parties shall raise in years the minimum age for the voluntary recruitment of persons into their national armed forces from that set out in article 38, paragraph 3, of the Convention on the Rights of the Child, taking account of the principles contained in that article and recognizing that under the Convention persons under the age of 18 years are entitled to special protection.

2. Each State Party shall deposit a binding declaration upon ratification of or accession to the present Protocol that sets forth the minimum age at which it will permit voluntary recruitment into its national armed forces and a description of the safeguards it has adopted to ensure that such recruitment is not forced or coerced.

3. States Parties that permit voluntary recruitment into their national armed forces under the age of 18 years shall maintain safeguards to ensure, as a minimum, that:

(a) Such recruitment is genuinely voluntary;

(b) Such recruitment is carried out with the informed consent of the person's parents or legal guardians;

(c) Such persons are fully informed of the duties involved in such military service;

(d) Such persons provide reliable proof of age prior to acceptance into national military service.

4. Each State Party may strengthen its declaration at any time by notification to that effect addressed to the Secretary-General of the United Nations, who shall inform all States Parties. Such notification shall take effect on the date on which it is received by the Secretary-General.

5. The requirement to raise the age in paragraph 1 of the present article does not apply to schools operated by or under the control of the armed forces of the States Parties, in keeping with articles 28 and 29 of the Convention on the Rights of the Child.

Article 4

1. Armed groups that are distinct from the armed forces of a State should not, under any circumstances, recruit or use in hostilities persons under the age of 18 years.

2. States Parties shall take all feasible measures to prevent such recruitment and use, including the adoption of legal measures necessary to prohibit and criminalize such practices.

3. The application of the present article shall not affect the legal status of any party to an armed conflict.

Article 5

Nothing in the present Protocol shall be construed as precluding provisions in the law of a State Party or in international instruments and international humanitarian law that are more conducive to the realization of the rights of the child.

[...]